Collins
Latin
Dictionary

HarperCollins Publishers
Westerhill Road
Bishopbriggs
Glasgow
G64 2QT
Great Britain

First Edition 1997

20 19 18 17 16 15 14

ISBN 978-0-00-722439-5

www.collins.co.uk

A catalogue record for this book is
available from the British Library

HarperCollins Publishers,
10 East 53rd Street, New York, NY 10022

COLLINS LATIN CONCISE DICTIONARY.
First US Edition 2003

ISBN 978-0-06-053690-9

www.harpercollins.com

HarperCollins books may be purchased for
educational, business, or sales promotional
use. For information, please write to:
Special Markets Department,
HarperCollins Publishers,
10 East 53rd Street, New York, NY 10022

Dictionary text typeset by
Tradespools Ltd, Somerset

Grammar text typeset by
Latimer Trend Ltd, Plymouth

Printed in Italy by Grafica Veneta S.p.A

Dictionary based on the Collins Latin Gem © 1957 by
Professor D. A. Kidd
Canterbury University

Grammar text and dictionary supplements by
Mary Wade

EDITORIAL COORDINATION
Joyce Littlejohn

LATIN CONSULTANTS
Ian Brookes
Denis Bruce
Michael D. Igoe

SERIES EDITOR
Lorna Sinclair

MANAGING EDITOR
Vivian Marr

CONTENTS

ABBREVIATIONS

adj	adjective	MED	medicine
abl	ablative	MIL	military
acc	accusative	*mod*	modern
adv	adverb	*n*	noun
AGR	agriculture	NAUT	nautical
ARCH	architecture	*neg*	negative
art	article	*nom*	nominative
ASTR	astronomy	*nt*	neuter
AUG	augury	*num*	numeral
COMM	business	*occ*	occasionally
CIRCS	circumstances	*p*	participle
compar	comparative	*pass*	passive
conj	conjunction	*perf*	perfect
cpd	compound	*perh*	perhaps
dat	dative	*pers*	person
defec	defective	PHILOS	philosophy
ECCL	ecclesiastical	*pl*	plural
esp	especially	POL	politics
excl	exclamatory	*ppa*	perfect participle active
f	feminine	*ppp*	perfect participle passive
fig	figurative	*prep*	preposition
fut	future	*pres*	present
gen	genitive	*pron*	pronoun
GEOG	geography	*prop*	properly
GRAM	grammar	PROV	proverb
impers	impersonal	*relat*	relative
imperf	imperfect	RHET	rhetoric
impv	imperative	*sg*	singular
indecl	indeclinable	*sim*	similarly
indic	indicative	*subj*	subjunctive
inf	informal	*superl*	superlative
infin	infinitive	THEAT	theatre
interj	interjection	UNIV	university
interrog	interrogative	*usu*	usually
LIT	literature	*vi*	intransitive verb
loc	locative	*voc*	vocative
m	masculine	*vt*	transitive verb
MATH	mathematics		

INTRODUCTION

Whether you are learning Latin for the first time or wish to "brush up" what you learned some time ago, this dictionary is designed to help you understand Latin and to express yourself in Latin, if you so wish.

HOW TO USE THE DICTIONARY

Entries are laid out as follows:

Headword

This is shown in **bold type**. On the Latin-English side all long vowels are shown by placing a ¯ above them. Latin nouns show the genitive singular form in bold. Latin verbs show the first person singular of the present indicative as the headword, followed by the infinitive, the first person singular of the perfect indicative and usually the past participle, all in bold type:

elegīa, -ae
elementum, -ī
ēlevō, āre
ēmātūrēscō, -ēscere, -uī

Part of Speech

Next comes the part of speech (noun, verb, adjective etc), shown in *italics*. Part of speech abbreviations used in the dictionary are shown in the abbreviations list (*p iv*). Where a word has more than one part of speech, each new part of speech is preceded by a black lozenge (♦). If a Latin headword is a preposition, the case taken by the preposition comes immediately after the part of speech, in *italics* and in brackets.

era, -ae *f*
ticklish *adj*
thunder *n* tonitrus *m* ♦ *vi* tonare, intonare.
ērgā *prep* (*with acc*) towards; against.

Meanings

Where a word or a part of speech has only one meaning, the translation comes immediately after the part of speech. However, many words have more than one meaning. Where the context is likely to show which translation is correct, variations in meaning are simply separated by a semi-colon. But usually there will also be an "indicator" in *italics* and in brackets. Some meanings relate to specific subject areas, for example religion, politics, military matters etc –

v

these indicators are in small italic capitals.

ēnsiger, -ī *adj* with his sword.
toy *n* crepundia *ntpl* ♦ *vi* ludere.
toll collector *n* exactor *m*; portitor *m*.
eō, -īre, īvī *and* **iī, itum** *vi* to go; (*MIL*) to march; (*time*) to pass; (*event*) to proceed, turn out.

Translations

Most words can be translated directly. On the English-Latin side, translations of nouns include the gender of the Latin noun in *italics*. However, sometimes a phrase is needed to show how a word is used, but in some cases a direct translation of a phrase would be meaningless: the symbol ~ in front of a translation shows that the translation is natural English, but does not mean word for word what the Latin means. Sometimes, even an approximate translation would not be very helpful (for place names, for example) – in these cases, an explanation in *italics* is given instead. In other cases, the user will need more information than simply the translation; in these cases, "indicators" are included in the translation(s), giving, for instance, the case required by a Latin verb or preposition or further details about a place or person.

thumb *n* pollex *m*; **have under one's** ~ in potestate sua habere.
elephantomacha, -ae *m fighter mounted on an elephant.*
Erymanthus, -i *m* mountain range in Arcadia (*where Hercules killed the bear*).
thwart *vt* obstare (*dat*), officere (*dat*).

Pronunciation

Since Latin pronunciation is regular, once the basic rules have been learned (*see pp viii, ix*), the dictionary does not show phonetic transcriptions against each headword, but does show all long vowels.

Other Information

The dictionary also includes:
- a basic grammar section
- information about life in Roman times:
  – how government and the army were organized – how numbers and dates were calculated and expressed – family relationships – geographical names – major Roman authors – key events in Roman history – (*important historical and mythological characters and events are listed within the body of the main text*).
- a section on Latin poetry and scansion
- a list of Latin expressions commonly used in English today

vi

LATIN ALPHABET

The Latin alphabet is the one which has been almost universally adopted by the modern languages of Europe and America. In the Classical period it had 23 letters, namely the English alphabet without letters **j**, **v** and **w**.

Letter v

The symbol **v** was the capital form of the letter **u**, but in a later age the small **v** came into use to represent the consonantal **u**, and as it is commonly so employed in modern editions of Latin authors, it has been retained as a distinct letter in this dictionary for convenience.

Letter j

The symbol **j** came to be used as the consonantal **i**, and is found in older editions of the Classics, but as it has been almost entirely discarded in modern texts, it is not used in this dictionary, and words found spelt with a **j** must therefore be looked up under **i**.

Letters w, y, z

The letter **w** may be seen in the Latinized forms of some modern names, *e.g.* **Westmonasterium**, Westminster. The letters **y** and **z** occur only in words of Greek origin.

ORTHOGRAPHY

Many Latin words which begin with a prefix can be spelled in two ways. The prefix can retain its original spelling, or it can be assimilated, changing a letter depending on the letter which follows it. Compare the following:

ad before **g**, **l**, **r** and **p**:

adpropinquare	appropinquare
adgredi	aggredi
adloquor	alloquor
adrogans	arrogans

ad is also often assimilated before **f** and **n**:

adfectus	affectus
adnexus	annexus

and **ad** is often shortened to **a** before **sc**:

adscendere	ascendere

in changes to **il** before **l**, to **im** before **m** or **p** and to **ir** before **r**.

con becomes **cor** when followed by another **r** and **col** when followed by **l**.

We have provided cross-references in the text to draw your attention to the alternative forms of words. Thus, although **arrogantia** does not appear in the Latin-English section, the cross-reference at **arr-** will point you to the entry for **adrogantia**, where the translation is given.

PRONUNCIATION

The ancient pronunciation of Latin has been established with a fair degree of certainty from the evidence of ancient authorities and inscriptions and inferences from the modern Romance languages. It is not possible, of course, to recapture the precise nuances of Classical Latin speech, but what follows is now generally accepted and generally understood as a reasonably accurate guide to the sounds of Latin as spoken by educated Romans during the two centuries from Cicero to Quintilian.

ACCENT

The Latin accent in the Classical period was a weak stress, perhaps with an element of pitch in it. It falls, as in English, on the second last syllable of the word, if that syllable is long, and on the third last syllable if the second last is short. Disyllabic words take the accent on the first syllable, unless they have already lost a final syllable, *e.g.* **illīc(e)**.

Inflected words are commonly learned with the accent wrongly placed on the last syllable, for convenience in memorizing the inflexions. But it is advisable to get the accent as well as the ending right.

The correct accent of other words can easily be found by noting carefully the quantity of the second last syllable and then accenting the word as in English, according to the rule given above. Thus **fuērunt** is accented on the second last syllable because the e is long, whereas **fuerant** is accented on the third last, because the e is short.

VOWELS

Vowels are pure and should not be diphthongized as in certain sounds of Southern English. They may be long or short. Throughout this Dictionary all vowels known or believed by the best authorities to be long are marked with a line above them; those unmarked are either known to be short or of uncertain quantity.

Short		Long	
agricola	rat	rāmus	rather
hedera	pen	avē	pay
ītaque	kin	cīvis	keen
favor	rob	ampliō	robe
nebula	full	lūna	fool

y is a Greek sound and is pronounced (both short and long) as u in French *ie* rue.

DIPHTHONGS

_ae_stas	tr_y_	
_au_diō	to_wn_	
h_ei_	pa_yee_	
m_eus_	_ay-oo_	with the accent on first sound
m_oe_cha	to_y_	
tu_i_tus	Lo_ui_s	

CONSONANTS

_b_alneae	_b_a_b_y	
ab_s_tēmius	a_ps_e	
su_bt_ractus	a_pt_	
_c_astra	_c_ar	
_ch_orda	sepul_ch_re	
inter_d_o	_d_og	
cōn_fl_ō	_f_ortune	
in_g_redior	_g_o	
_h_abeō	_h_and	(_but faintly_)
_i_aceo	_y_es	(_consonantal i = j_)
_K_alendae	oa_k_	
conge_l_ō	_l_et	
co_m_es	_m_an	(_final **m** was hardly sounded and may have simply nasalized the preceding vowel_)
pā_n_is	_n_o	
pa_ng_o	fi_n_ger	
stu_p_eō	a_p_t	
ra_ph_anus	_p_ill	
exse_qu_or	_qu_ite	
sup_r_ēmus	_br_ae	(_Scottish_)
mā_s_gnu_s_	_s_ister	(_never as in ro**s**e_)
lae_t_us	_st_op	
_th_eātrum	_t_ake	
_v_apor	_(and consonantal u)_	_w_in
de_x_tra	si_x_	(_ks, not gs_)
_z_ōna	_z_ero	

Double consonants lengthen the sound of the consonant.

Quick Reference Grammar

DECLENSIONS OF NOUNS

1st Declension

	mainly f		*m*	
SING				
Nom.	terra	crambē	Aenēās	Anchīsēs
Voc.	terra	crambē	Aenēā	Anchīsā, -ē
Acc.	terram	crambēn	Aenēam, -ān	Anchīsam, -ēn
Gen.	terrae	crambes	Aenēae	Anchīsae
Dat.	terrae	crambae	Aenēae	Anchīsae
Abl.	terra	cramba	Aenēā	Anchīsā

PLURAL		
Nom.	terrae	crambae
Voc.	terrae	crambae
Acc.	terrās	crambās
Gen.	terrārum	crambārum
Dat.	terrīs	crambīs
Abl.	terrīs	crambīs

2nd Declension

	mainly m				
SING					
Nom.	modus	Lūcius	Dēlos (f)	puer	liber
Voc.	mode	Lūcī	Dēle	puer	liber
Acc.	modum	Lūcium	Dēlon	puerum	librum
Gen.	modī	Lūcī	Dēlī	puerī	librī
Dat.	modō	Lūciō	Dēlō	puerō	librō
Abl.	modō	Lūciō	Dēlō	puerō	librō

PLURAL				
Nom.	modī		puerī	librī
Voc.	modī		puerī	librī
Acc.	modōs		puerōs	librōs
Gen.	modōrum		puerōrum	librōrum
Dat.	modīs		puerīs	librīs
Abl.	modīs		puerīs	librīs

	nt
SING	
Nom.	dōnum
Voc.	dōnum
Acc.	dōnum
Gen.	dōnī
Dat.	dōnō
Abl.	dōnō

PLURAL	
Nom.	dōna
Voc.	dōna
Acc.	dōna
Gen.	dōnōrum
Dat.	dōnīs
Abl.	dōnīs

3rd Declension

Group I: *Vowel stems, with gen pl in* -ium

	m and f		*nt*	
SING				
Nom.	clādēs	nāvis	rēte	animal
Voc.	clādēs	nāvis	rēte	animal
Acc.	clādem	nāvem, -im	rēte	animal
Gen.	clādis	nāvis	rētis	animālīs
Dat.	clādī	nāvī	rētī	animālī
Abl.	clāde	nāve, -ī	rētī	animālī
PLURAL				
Nom.	clādēs	nāvēs	rētia	animālia
Voc.	clādēs	nāvēs	rētia	animālia
Acc.	clādēs, -īs	nāvēs, -īs	rētia	animālia
Gen.	clādium	nāvium	rētium	animālium
Dat.	clādibus	nāvibus	rētibus	animālibus
Abl.	clādibus	nāvibus	rētibus	animālibus

Group II: *Consonant stems, some with gen pl in* -ium, *some in* -um *and some in either. Monosyllabic nouns ending in two consonants (e.g.* **urbs** *below) regularly have* -ium.

	m and f			*f*	*nt*
SING					
Nom.	urbs	amāns	laus	aetās	os
Voc.	urbs	amāns	laus	aetās	os
Acc.	urbem	amantem	laudem	aetātem	os
Gen.	urbis	amantis	laudis	aetātis	ossis
Dat.	urbī	amantī	laudī	aetātī	ossī
Abl.	urbe	amante	laude	aetāte	osse
PLURAL					
Nom.	urbēs	amantēs	laudēs	aetātēs	ossa
Voc.	urbēs	amantēs	laudēs	aetātēs	ossa

Acc.	urbēs	amantēs	laudēs	aetātēs	ossa
Gen.	urbium	amantium,	laudum,	aetātum,	ossium
		-um	-ium	-ium	
Dat.	urbibus	amantibus	laudibus	aetātibus	ossibus
Abl.	urbibus	amantibus	laudibus	aetātibus	ossibus

Group III: *Consonant stems, with gen pl in* **-um**

		m and f		*nt*	
SING					
Nom.	mōs	ratiō	pater	nōmen	opus
Voc.	mōs	ratiō	pater	nōmen	opus
Acc.	mōrem	ratiōnem	patrem	nōmen	opus
Gen.	mōris	ratiōnis	patris	nōminis	operis
Dat.	mōrī	ratiōnī	patrī	nōminī	operī
Abl.	mōre	ratiōne	patre	nōmine	opere
PLURAL					
Nom.	mōrēs	ratiōnēs	patrēs	nōmina	opera
Voc.	mōrēs	ratiōnēs	patrēs	nōmina	opera
Acc.	mōrēs	ratiōnēs	patrēs	nōmina	opera
Gen.	mōrum	ratiōnum	patrum	nōminum	operum
Dat.	mōribus	ratiōnibus	patribus	nōminibus	operibus
Abl.	mōribus	ratiōnibus	patribus	nōminibus	operibus

Group IV: *Greek nouns*

	m		*f*		*nt*
SING					
Nom.	āēr	hērōs	Periclēs	Naias	poēma
Voc.	āēr	hērōs	Periclē	Naias	poēma
Acc.	āera	hērōa	⎰ Periclem,	Naiada	poēma
			⎱ Periclea		
Gen.	āeris	hērōis	Periclis, -ī	Naiadis, -os	poēmatis
Dat.	āerī	hērōī	Periclī	Naiadī	poēmatī
Abl.	āere	hērōe	Periclē	Naiade	poēmate
PLURAL					
Nom.	āeres	hērōes		Naiades	poēmata
Voc.	āeres	hērōes		Naiades	poēmata
Acc.	āeras	hērōas		Naiadas	poēmata
Gen.	āerum	hērōum		Naiadum	poēmatōrum
Dat.	āeribus	hērōibus		Naiadibus	poēmatīs
Abl.	āeribus	hērōibus		Naiadibus	poēmatīs

	4th Declension		**5th Declension**	
	mainly m	*nt*	*mainly f*	
SING				
Nom.	portus	genū	diēs	rēs
Voc.	portus	genū	diēs	rēs
Acc.	portum	genū	diem	rem
Gen.	portūs	genūs	diēī	reī
Dat.	portuī	genū	diēī	reī
Abl.	portū	genū	diē	rē
PLURAL				
Nom.	portūs	genua	diēs	rēs
Voc.	portūs	genua	diēs	rēs
Acc.	portūs	genua	diēs	rēs
Gen.	portuum	genuum	diērum	rērum
Dat.	portibus, -ubus	genibus, -ubus	diēbus	rēbus
Abl.	portibus, -ubus	genibus, -ubus	diēbus	rēbus

CONJUGATIONS OF VERBS

ACTIVE

PRESENT TENSE

	First parāre prepare	Second habēre have	Third sūmere take	Fourth audīre hear

Indicative

SING				
1st pers	parō	habeō	sūmō	audiō
2nd pers	parās	habēs	sūmis	audīs
3rd pers	parat	habet	sūmit	audit
PLURAL				
1st pers	parāmus	habēmus	sūmimus	audīmus
2nd pers	parātis	habētis	sūmitis	audītīs
3rd pers	parant	habent	sūmunt	audiunt

Subjunctive

SING				
1st pers	parem	habeam	sūmam	audiam
2nd pers	parēs	habeās	sūmās	audiās
3rd pers	paret	habeat	sūmat	audiat
PLURAL				
1st pers	parēmus	habeāmus	sūmāmus	audiāmus
2nd pers	parētis	habeātis	sūmātis	audiātis
3rd pers	parent	habeant	sūmant	audiant

IMPERFECT TENSE
Indicative

SING				
1st pers	parābam	habēbam	sūmēbam	audiēbam
2nd pers	parābās	habēbās	sūmēbās	audiēbās
3rd pers	parābat	habēbat	sūmēbat	audiēbat

PLURAL				
1st pers	parābāmus	habēbāmus	sūmēbāmus	audiēbāmus
2nd pers	parābātis	habēbātis	sūmēbātis	audiēbātis
3rd pers	parābant	habēbant	sūmēbant	audiēbant

Subjunctive

SING				
1st pers	parārem	habērem	sūmerem	audīrem
2nd pers	parārēs	habērēs	sūmerēs	audīrēs
3rd pers	parāret	habēret	sūmeret	audīret

PLURAL				
1st pers	parārēmus	habērēmus	sūmerēmus	audīrēmus
2nd pers	parārētis	habērētis	sūmerētis	audīrētis
3rd pers	parārent	habērent	sūmerent	audīrent

FUTURE TENSE
Indicative

SING				
1st pers	parābō	habēbō	sūmam	audiam
2nd pers	parābis	habēbis	sūmēs	audiēs
3rd pers	parābit	habēbit	sūmet	audiet

PLURAL				
1st pers	parābimus	habēbimus	sūmēmus	audiēmus
2nd pers	parābitis	habēbitis	sūmētis	audiētis
3rd pers	parābunt	habēbunt	sūment	audient

Subjunctive

SING			
parātūrus, -a, -um			
habitūrus, -a, -um	sim	or	essem
sūmptūrus, -a, -um	sīs		essēs
audītūrus, -a, -um	sit		esset

PLURAL			
parātūrī, -ae, -a			
habitūrī, -ae, -a	simus	or	essēmus
sūmptūrī, -ae, -a	sītis		essētis
audītūrī, -ae, -a	sint		essent

PERFECT TENSE
Indicative

SING

1st pers	parāvī	habuī	sūmpsī	audīvī
2nd pers	parāvistī	habuistī	sūmpsistī	audīvistī
3rd pers	parāvit	habuit	sūmpsit	audīvit

PLURAL

1st pers	parāvimus	habuimus	sūmpsimus	audīvimus
2nd pers	parāvistis	habuistis	sūmpsistis	audīvistis
3rd pers	parāvērunt, -e	habuērunt, -e	sūmpsērunt, -e	audīvērunt, -e

Subjunctive

SING

1st pers	parāverim	habuerim	sūmpserim	audīverim
2nd pers	parāveris	habueris	sūmpseris	audīveris
3rd pers	parāverit	habuerit	sūmpserit	audīverit

PLURAL

1st pers	parāverimus	habuerimus	sūmpserimus	audīverimus
2nd pers	parāveritis	habueritis	sūmpseritis	audīveritis
3rd pers	parāverint	habuerint	sūmpserint	audīverint

PLUPERFECT TENSE
Indicative

SING

1st pers	parāveram	habueram	sūmpseram	audīveram
2nd pers	parāverās	habuerās	sūmpserās	audīverās
3rd pers	parāverat	habuerat	sūmpserat	audīverat

PLURAL

1st pers	parāverāmus	habuerāmus	sūmpserāmus	audīverāmus
2nd pers	parāverātis	habuerātis	sūmpserātis	audīverātis
3rd pers	parāverant	habuerant	sūmpserant	audīverant

Subjunctive

SING

1st pers	parāvissem	habuissem	sūmpsissem	audīvissem
2nd pers	parāvissēs	habuissēs	sūmpsissēs	audīvissēs
3rd pers	parāvisset	habuisset	sūmpsisset	audīvisset

PLURAL

1st pers	parāvissēmus	habuissēmus	sūmpsissēmus	audīvissēmus
2nd pers	parāvissētis	habuissētis	sūmpsissētis	audīvissētis
3rd pers	parāvissent	habuissent	sūmpsissent	audīvissent

FUTURE PERFECT TENSE

Indicative

SING				
1st pers	parāverō	habuerō	sūmpserō	audīverō
2nd pers	parāveris	habueris	sūmpseris	audīveris
3rd pers	parāverit	habuerit	sūmpserit	audīverit
PLURAL				
1st pers	parāverimus	habuerimus	sūmpserimus	audīverimus
2nd pers	parāveritis	habueritis	sūmpseritis	audīveritis
3rd pers	parāverint	habuerint	sūmpserint	audīverint

IMPERATIVE

Present

SING	parā	habē	sūme	audī
PLURAL	parāte	habēte	sūmite	audīte

Future

SING				
2nd pers	parātō	habētō	sūmitō	audītō
3rd pers	parātō	habētō	sūmitō	audītō
PLURAL				
2nd pers	parātōte	habētōte	sūmitōte	audītōte
3rd pers	parantō	habentō	sūmuntō	audiuntō

INFINITIVE

Present

parāre	habēre	sūmere	audīre

Perfect

parāvisse	habuisse	sūmpsisse	audīvisse

Future

parātūrus,	-a, -um, esse
habitūrus,	-a, -um, esse
sūmptūrus,	-a, -um, esse
audītūrus,	-a, -um, esse

PASSIVE

PRESENT TENSE
Indicative

SING

1st pers	paror	habeor	sūmor	audior
2nd pers	parāris	habēris	sūmeris	audīris
3rd pers	parātur	habētur	sūmitur	audītur

PLURAL

1st pers	parāmur	habēmur	sūmimur	audīmur
2nd pers	parāminī	habēminī	sūmiminī	audīminī
3rd pers	parantur	habentur	sūmuntur	audiuntur

Subjunctive

SING

1st pers	parer	habear	sūmar	audiar
2nd pers	parēris	habeāris	sūmāris	audiāris
3rd pers	parētur	habeātur	sūmātur	audiātur

PLURAL

1st pers	parēmur	habeāmur	sūmāmur	audiāmur
2nd pers	parēminī	habeāminī	sūmāminī	audiāminī
3rd pers	parentur	habeantur	sūmantur	audiantur

IMPERFECT TENSE
Indicative

SING

1st pers	parābar	habēbar	sūmēbar	audiēbar
2nd pers	parābāris	habēbāris	sūmēbāris	audiēbāris
3rd pers	parābātur	habēbātur	sūmēbātur	audiēbātur

PLURAL

1st pers	parābāmur	habēbāmur	sūmēbāmur	audiēbāmur
2nd pers	parābāmini	habēbāmini	sūmēbāminī	audiēbāminī
3rd pers	parābāntur	habēbantur	sūmēbantur	audiēbantur

Subjunctive

SING

1st pers	parārer	habērer	sūmerer	audīrer
2nd pers	parārēris	habērēris	sūmerēris	audīrēris
3rd pers	parārētur	habērētur	sūmerētur	audīrētur

1st pers	parārēmur	habērēmur	sūmerēmur	audīrēmur
2nd pers	parārēminī	habērēminī	sūmerēminī	audīrēminī
3rd pers	parārentur	habērentur	sūmerentur	audīrentur

FUTURE TENSE
Indicative

SING

1st pers	parābor	habēbor	sūmar	audiar
2nd pers	parāberis	habēberis	sūmēris	audiēris
3rd pers	parābitur	habēbitur	sūmētur	audiētur

PLURAL

1st pers	parābimur	habēbimur	sūmēmur	audiēmur
2nd pers	parābimini	habēbimini	sūmēminī	audiēminī
3rd pers	parābuntur	habēbuntur	sūmentur	audientur

PERFECT TENSE
Indicative

SING		PLURAL	
parātus, -a, -um	sum/es/est	parātī, -ae, -a	sumus/estis/sunt
habitus, -a, -um	sum/es/est	habītī, -ae, -a	sumus/estis/sunt
sūmptus, -a, -um	sum/es/est	sūmptī, -ae, -a	sumus/estis/sunt
audītus, -a, -um	sum/es/est	audītī, -ae, -a	sumus/estis/sunt

Subjunctive

SING		PLURAL	
parātus, -a, -um	sim/sīs/sit	parātī, -ae, -a	sīmus/sītis/sint
habitus, -a, -um	sim/sīs/sit	habītī, -ae, -a	sīmus/sītis/sint
sūmptus, -a, -um	sim/sīs/sit	sūmptī, -ae, -a	sīmus/sītis/sint
audītus, -a, -um	sim/sīs/sit	audītī, -ae, -a	sīmus/sītis/sint

PLUPERFECT TENSE
Indicative

SING		PLURAL	
parātus, -a, -um	eram/eras/erat	parātī, -ae, -a	eramus/eratis/erant
habitus, -a, -um	eram/eras/erat	habītī, -ae, -a	eramus/eratis/erant
sūmptus, -a, -um	eram/eras/erat	sūmptī, -ae, -a	eramus/eratis/erant
audītus, -a, -um	eram/eras/erat	audītī, -ae, -a	eramus/eratis/erant

Subjunctive

	SING		PLURAL
parātus, -a, -um	essem/essēs/esset	parātī, -ae, -a	essēmus/essētis/essent
habitus, -a, -um	essem/essēs/esset	habītī, -ae, -a	essēmus/essētis/essent
sūmptus, -a, -um	essem/essēs/esset	sūmptī, -ae, -a	essēmus/essētis/essent
audītus, -a, -um	essem/essēs/esset	audītī, -ae, -a	essēmus/essētis/essent

FUTURE PERFECT TENSE

Indicative

	SING		PLURAL
parātus, -a, -um	erō/eris/erit	parātī, -ae, -a	erimus/eritis/erunt
habitus, -a, -um	erō/eris/erit	habītī, -ae, -a	erimus/eritis/erunt
sūmptus, -a, -um	erō/eris/erit	sūmptī, -ae, -a	erimus/eritis/erunt
audītus, -a, -um	erō/eris/erit	audītī, -ae, -a	erimus/eritis/erunt

IMPERATIVE

Present

SING	parāre	habēre	sūmere	audīre
PLURAL	parāminī	habēminī	sūmiminī	audīminī

Future

SING				
2nd pers	parātor	habētor	sūmitor	audītor
3rd pers	parātor	habētor	sūmitor	audītor
PLURAL				
3rd pers	parantor	habentor	sūmuntor	audiuntor

INFINITIVE

Present

parārī	habērī	sūmī	audīrī

Perfect

parātus -a, -um, esse	habitus -a, -um, esse	sūmptus -a, -um, esse	audītus, -a, -um, esse

Future

parātum īrī	habitum īrī	sūmptum īrī	audītum īrī

VERBAL NOUNS AND ADJECTIVES

Present Participle Active

parāns	habēns	sūmēns	audiēns

Perfect Participle Passive

parātus	habitus	sūmptus	audītus

Future Participle Active

parātūrus	habitūrus	sūmptūrus	audītūrus

Gerund
(acc, gen, dat and abl)

parandum, -ī, -ō	habendum, -ī, -ō	sūmendum, -ī, -ō	audiendum, -ī, -ō

Gerundive

parandus	habendus	sūmendus	audiendus

Supines

1st	parātum	habitum	sūmptum	audītum
2nd	parātū	habitū	sūmptū	audītū

Note. *Some verbs of the 3rd conjugation have the present indicative ending in* -io; *e.g.* **capio**, *I capture.*

PRESENT TENSE

	INDICATIVE		SUBJUNCTIVE	
Active	**Passive**	**Active**	**Passive**	
capio	capior	capiam	capiar
capis	caperis	capias	capiāris
capit	capitur	capiat	capiātur
capimus	capimur	capiāmus	capiāmur
capitis	capiminī	capiātis	capiāminī
capiunt	capiuntur	capiant	capiantur

IMPERFECT TENSE

capiēbam *etc.*	capiēbar *etc.*	caperem *etc.*	caperer *etc.*

FUTURE TENSE

INFINITIVE MOOD

capiam	capiar	Present Active	capere
capiēs *etc.*	capiēris *etc.*	Present Passive	capī

PRESENT IMPERATIVE

Active		Passive	
cape	capite	capere	capiminī

PARTICIPLE   GERUND   GERUNDIVE

Pres.   capiēns   capiendum   capiendus, -a, um

In all other tenses and moods **capere** *is similar to* **sumere**.

IRREGULAR VERBS

	Esse *be*	**Posse** *be able*	**Velle** *wish*	**Ire** *go*

Present Indicative

SING				
1st Pers	sum	possum	volō	eō
2nd Pers	es	potes	vīs	īs
3rd Pers	est	potest	vult, volt	it
PLURAL				
1st Pers	sumus	possumus	volumus	īmus
2nd Pers	estis	potestis	vultis, voltis	ītis
3rd Pers	sunt	possunt	volunt	eunt

Present Subjunctive

SING				
1st Pers	sim	possim	velim	eam
2nd Pers	sīs	possīs	velīs	eās
3rd Pers	sit	possit	velit	eat
PLURAL				
1st Pers	sīmus	possīmus	velīmus	eāmus
2nd Pers	sītis	possītis	velītis	eātis
3rd Pers	sint	possint	velint	eant

Imperfect Indicative

1st Pers	eram	poteram	volēbam	ībam

Imperfect Subjunctive

1st Pers	essem	possem	vellem	īrem

Future Indicative

1st Pers	erō	poterō	volam	ībō

Future Subjunctive

1st Pers	futūrus, -a, -um sim *or* essem	—	—	itūrus, -a, -um sim *or* essem

Perfect Indicative

1st Pers	fuī	potuī	voluī	īvī, iī

Perfect Subjunctive

1st Pers	fuerim	potuerim	voluerim	īverim, ierim

Pluperfect Indicative

1st Pers	fueram	potueram	volueram	īveram, ieram

Pluperfect Subjunctive

1st Pers	fuissem	potuissem	voluissem	īvissem, iissem

Future Perfect Indicative

1st Pers	fuerō	potuerō	voluerō	īverō, ierō

Present Imperative

SING	es	—	—	ī
PLURAL	este	—	—	īte

Future Imperative

SING	estō	—	—	ītō
PLURAL	estōte	—	—	ītōte

Infinitives

PRES	esse	posse	velle	īre
PERF	fuisse	potuisse	voluisse	īvisse, iisse
FUT	futūrus, -a, -um, esse	—	—	itūrus, -a, -um, esse

Participles

PRES	—	—	—	iēns, euntis
FUT	futūrus	—	—	itūrus

Gerund and Supine

GERUND	—	—	—	eundum
SUPINE	—	—	—	itum

Latin-English

A, a

ā *prep (with abl)* from; after, since; by, in respect of; **ab epistulīs, ā manū** secretary; **ab hāc parte** on this side; **ab integrō** afresh; **ā nōbīs** on our side; **ā tergō** in the rear; **cōpiōsus ā frūmentō** rich in corn; **usque ab** ever since.

ā *interj* ah!

ab *prep see* **ā**.

abāctus *ppp of* **abigō**.

abacus, -ī *m* tray; sideboard; gaming board; panel; counting table.

abaliēnō, -āre, -āvī, -ātum *vt* to dispose of; to remove, estrange.

Abantiadēs *m* Acrisius *or* Perseus.

Abās, -antis *m a king of Argos*.

abavus, -ī *m* great-great-grandfather.

abbās, -ātis *m* abbot.

abbātia *f* abbey.

abbātissa *f* abbess.

Abdēra, -ōrum *or* **-ae** *ntpl or fs a town in Thrace*.

Abdērītānus *adj see n*.

Abdērītēs *m* Democritus *or* Protagoras.

abdicātiō, -ōnis *f* disowning, abdication.

abdicō, -āre, -āvī, -ātum *vt* to disown; to resign; **sē ~** abdicate.

abdīcō, -īcere, -īxī, -ictum *vt* (*AUG*) to be unfavourable to.

abditus *ppp of* **abdō**.

abdō, -ere, -idī, -itum *vt* to hide; to remove.

abdōmen, -inis *nt* paunch, belly; gluttony.

abdūcō, -ūcere, -ūxī, -uctum *vt* to lead away, take away; to seduce.

abductus *ppp of* **abdūcō**.

abecedārium, -iī *nt* alphabet.

abēgī *perf of* **abigō**.

abeō, -īre, -iī, -itum *vi* to go away, depart; to pass away; to be changed; to retire (*from an office*); **sīc ~** turn out like this.

abequitō, -āre, -āvī, -ātum *vi* to ride away.

aberrātiō, -ōnis *f* relief (*from trouble*).

aberrō, -āre, -āvī, -ātum *vi* to stray; to deviate; to have respite.

abfore *fut infin of* **absum**.

abfuī *perf of* **absum**.

abfutūrus *fut p of* **absum**.

abhinc *adv* since, ago.

abhorreō, -ēre, -uī *vi* to shrink from; to differ; to be inconsistent.

abiciō, -icere, -iēcī, -iectum *vt* to throw away, throw down; to abandon, degrade.

abiectus *ppp of* **abiciō** ♦ *adj* despondent; contemptible.

abiēgnus *adj* of fir.

abiēns, -euntis *pres p of* **abeō**.

abiēs, -etis *f* fir; ship.

abigō, -igere, -ēgī, -āctum *vt* to drive away.

abitus, -ūs *m* departure; exit.

abiūdicō, -āre, -āvī, -ātum *vt* to take away (*by judicial award*).

abiūnctus *ppp of* **abiungō**.

abiungō, -ungere, -ūnxī, -ūnctum *vt* to unyoke; to detach.

abiūrō, -āre, -āvī, -ātum *vt* to deny on oath.

ablātus *ppp of* **auferō**.

ablēgātiō, -ōnis *f* sending away.

ablēgō, -āre, -āvī, -ātum *vt* to send out of the way.

abligurriō, -īre, -īvī, -ītum *vt* to spend extravagantly.

ablocō, -āre, -āvī, -ātum *vt* to let (a house).

ablūdō, -dere, -sī, -sum *vi* to be unlike.

abluō, -uere, -uī, -ūtum *vt* to wash clean; to remove.

abnegō, -āre, -āvī, -ātum *vt* to refuse.

abnepōs, -ōtis *m* great-great-grandson.

abneptis *f* great-great-granddaughter.

abnoctō, -āre *vi* to stay out all night.

abnōrmis *adj* unorthodox.

abnuō, -uere, -uī, -ūtum *vt* to refuse; to deny.

aboleō, -ēre, -ēvī, -itum *vt* to abolish.

abolēscō, -ēscere, -ēvī *vi* to vanish.

abolitiō, -ōnis *f* cancelling.

abolla, -ae *f* greatcoat.

abōminātus *adj* accursed.

abōminor, -ārī, -ātus *vt* to deprecate; to detest.

Aborīginēs, -um *mpl* original inhabitants.

aborior, -īrī, -tus *vi* to miscarry.

abortiō, -ōnis *f* miscarriage.

abortīvus *adj* born prematurely.

abortus, -ūs *m* miscarriage.

abrādō, -dere, -sī, -sum *vt* to scrape off, shave.

abrāsus *ppp of* **abrādō**.

abreptus *ppp of* **abripiō**.

abripiō, -ipere, -ipuī, -eptum *vt* to drag away, carry off.

Noun declensions and verb conjugations are shown on pp xiii to xxv. The present infinitive ending of a verb shows to which conjugation it belongs: **-āre** = 1st; **-ēre** = 2nd; **-ere** = 3rd and **-īre** = 4th. Irregular verbs are shown on p xxvi

abrogātiō, -ōnis f repeal.
abrogō, -āre, -āvī, -ātum vt to annul.
abrotonum, -ī nt southernwood.
abrumpō, -umpere, -ūpī, -uptum vt to break off.
abruptus ppp of **abrumpō** ♦ adj steep; abrupt, disconnected.
abs etc see **ā**.
abscēdō, -ēdere, -essī, -essum vi to depart, withdraw; to cease.
abscīdō, -dere, -dī, -sum vt to cut off.
abscindō, -ndere, -dī, -ssum vt to tear off, cut off.
abscissus ppp of **abscindō**.
abscīsus ppp of **abscīdō** ♦ adj steep; abrupt.
abscondō, -ere, -ī and **idī, -itum** vt to conceal; to leave behind.
absēns, -entis pres p of **absum** ♦ adj absent.
absentia, -ae f absence.
absiliō, -īre, -iī and **uī** vi to spring away.
absimilis adj unlike.
absinthium, -ī and **iī** nt wormwood.
absis, -īdis f vault; (ECCL) chancel.
absistō, -istere, -titī vi to come away; to desist.
absolūtē adv fully, unrestrictedly.
absolūtiō, -ōnis f acquittal; perfection.
absolūtus ppp of **absolvō** ♦ adj complete; (RHET) unqualified.
absolvō, -vere, -vī, -ūtum vt to release, set free; (law) to acquit; to bring to completion, finish off; to pay off, discharge.
absonus adj unmusical; incongruous; ~ **ab** not in keeping with.
absorbeō, -bēre, -buī, -ptum vt to swallow up; to monopolize.
absp- etc see **asp-**.
absque prep (with abl) without, but for.
abstēmius adj temperate.
abstergeō, -gēre, -sī, -sum vt to wipe away; (fig) to banish.
absterreō, -ēre, -ui, -itum vt to scare away, deter.
abstinēns, -entis adj continent.
abstinenter adv with restraint.
abstinentia, -ae f restraint, self-control; fasting.
abstineō, -inēre, -inuī, -entum vt to withhold, keep off ♦ vi to abstain, refrain; **sē** ~ refrain.
abstitī perf of **abstistō**.
abstō, -āre vi to stand aloof.
abstractus ppp of **abstrahō**.
abstrahō, -here, -xī, -ctum vt to drag away, remove; to divert.
abstrūdō, -dere, -sī, -sum vt to conceal.
abstrūsus ppp of **abstrūdō** ♦ adj deep, abstruse; reserved.
abstulī perf of **auferō**.
absum, abesse, āfuī vi to be away, absent, distant; to keep clear of; to be different; to be missing, fail to assist; **tantum abest ut** so far from; **haud multum āfuit quīn** I was (they

were etc) within an ace of.
absūmō, -ere, -psī, -ptum vt to consume; to ruin, kill; (time) to spend.
absurdē adv out of tune; absurdly.
absurdus adj unmusical; senseless, absurd.
Absyrtus, -ī m brother of Medea.
abundāns, -antis adj overflowing; abundant; rich; abounding in.
abundanter adv copiously.
abundantia, -ae f abundance, plenty; wealth.
abundē adv abundantly, more than enough.
abundō, -āre, -āvī, -ātum vi to overflow; to abound, be rich in.
abūsiō, -ōnis f (RHET) catachresis.
abusque prep (with abl) all the way from.
abūtor, -tī, -sus vi (with abl) to use up; to misuse.
Abydēnus adj see n.
Abȳdos, Abȳdus, -ī m a town on Dardanelles.
ac etc see **atque**.
Acadēmia, -ae f Plato's Academy at Athens; Plato's philosophy; Cicero's villa.
Acadēmica ntpl Cicero's book on the Academic philosophy.
Acadēmus, -ī m an Athenian hero.
acalanthis, -dis f thistlefinch.
acanthus, -ī m bear's-breech.
Acarnānes, -um mpl the Acarnanians.
Acarnānia, -iae f a district of N.W. Greece.
Acarnānicus adj see n.
Acca Larentia, -ae, -ae f Roman goddess.
accēdō, -ēdere, -essī, -essum vi to come, go to, approach; to attack; to be added; to agree with; (duty) to take up; **ad rem pūblicam** ~ to enter politics; **prope** ~ **ad** to resemble; **~ēdit quod, hūc ~ēdit ut** moreover.
accelerō, -āre, -āvī, -ātum vt, vi to hasten.
accendō, -endere, -endī, -ēnsum vt to set on fire, light; to illuminate; (fig) to inflame, incite.
accēnseō, -ēre, -uī, -um vt to assign.
accēnsī mpl (MIL) supernumeraries.
accēnsus ppp of **accendō** and **accēnseō**.
accēnsus, -ī m officer attending a magistrate.
accentus, -ūs m accent.
accēpī perf of **accipiō**.
acceptiō, -ōnis f receiving.
acceptum nt credit side (of ledger); **in** ~ **referre** place to one's credit.
acceptus ppp of **accipiō** ♦ adj acceptable.
accersō etc see **arcessō**.
accessiō, -ōnis f coming, visiting; attack; increase, addition.
accessus, -ūs m approach, visit; flood tide; admittance, entrance.
Acciānus adj see **Accius**.
accīdō, -dere, -dī, -sum vt to fell, cut into; to eat up, impair.
accidō, -ere, -ī vi to fall (at, on); (senses) to strike; (usu misfortune) to befall, happen.
accingō, -gere, -xī, -ctum vt to gird on, arm; (fig) to make ready.
acciō, -īre, -īvī, -ītum vt to summon; to

procure.

accipiō, -ipere, -ēpī, -eptum *vt* to take, receive, accept; (*guest*) to treat; (*information*) to hear; to interpret, take as; to suffer; to approve.

accipiter, -ris *m* hawk.

accisus *ppp of* **accīdō**.

accītus *ppp of* **accīo**.

accītus, -ūs *m* summons.

Accius, -ī *m Roman tragic poet.*

acclāmātiō, -ōnis *f* shout (*of approval or disapproval*).

acclāmō, -āre, -āvī, -ātum *vi* to cry out against; to hail.

acclārō, -āre, -āvī, -ātum *vt* to make known.

acclīnātus *adj* sloping.

acclīnis *adj* leaning against; inclined.

acclīnō, -āre, -āvī, -ātum *vt* to lean against; **sē ~** incline towards.

acclīvis *adj* uphill.

acclīvitās, -ātis *f* gradient.

accola, -ae *m* neighbour.

accolō, -olere, -oluī, -ultum *vt* to live near.

accommodātē *adv* suitably.

accommodātiō, -ōnis *f* fitting together; compliance.

accommodātus *adj* suited.

accommodō, -āre, -āvī, -ātum *vt* to fit, put on; to adjust, adapt, bring to; to apply; **sē ~** devote oneself.

accommodus *adj* suitable.

accrēdō, -ere, -idī, -itum *vi* to believe.

accrēscō, -ēscere, -ēvī, -ētum *vi* to increase, be added.

accrētiō, -ōnis *f* increasing.

accubitiō, -ōnis *f* reclining (*at meals*).

accubō, -āre *vi* to lie near; to recline (*at meals*).

accumbō, -mbere, -buī, -bitum *vi* to recline at table; **in sinū ~** sit next to.

accumulātē *adv* copiously.

accumulō, -āre, -āvī, -ātum *vt* to pile up; amass; to load.

accūrātē *adv* painstakingly.

accūrātiō, -ōnis *f* exactness.

accūrātus *adj* studied.

accūrō, -āre, -āvī, -ātum *vt* to attend to.

accurrō, -rrere, -currī *and* **rrī, -rsum** *vi* to hurry to.

accursus, -ūs *m* hurrying.

accūsābilis *adj* reprehensible.

accūsātiō, -ōnis *f* accusation.

accūsātor, -ōris *m* accuser, prosecutor.

accūsātōriē *adv* like an accuser.

accūsātōrius *adj* of the accuser.

accūsō, -āre, -āvī, -ātum *vt* to accuse, prosecute; to reproach; **ambitūs ~** prosecute for bribery.

acer, -is *nt* maple.

ācer, -ris *adj* sharp; (*sensation*) keen, pungent;

(*emotion*) violent; (*mind*) shrewd; (*conduct*) eager, brave; hasty, fierce; (*circumstances*) severe.

acerbē *adv see* **acerbus**.

acerbitās, -ātis *f* bitterness; (*fig*) harshness, severity; sorrow.

acerbō, -āre, -āvī, -ātum *vt* to aggravate.

acerbus *adj* bitter, sour; harsh; (*fig*) premature; (*person*) rough, morose, violent; (*things*) troublesome, sad.

acernus *adj* of maple.

acerra, -ae *f* incense box.

acervātim *adv* in heaps.

acervō, -āre, -āvī, -ātum *vt* to pile up.

acervus, -ī *m* heap.

acēscō, -ere, acuī *vt* to turn sour.

Acestēs, -ae *m a mythical Sicilian.*

acētum, -ī *nt* vinegar; (*fig*) wit.

Achaemenēs, -is *m first Persian king; type of Oriental wealth.*

Achaeus *adj* Greek.

Achāia, -ae *f a district in W. Greece; Greece; Roman province.*

Achāicus *adj see n.*

Achātēs, -ae *m companion of Aeneas.*

Achelōius *adj see n.*

Achelōus, -ī *m river in N.W. Greece; river god.*

Acherōn, -ontis *m river in Hades.*

Acherūsius *adj see* **Acherōn**.

Achillēs, -is *m Greek epic hero.*

Achillēus *adj see n.*

Achīvus *adj* Greek.

Acidālia, -ae *f* Venus.

Acidālius *adj see n.*

acidus *adj* sour, tart; (*fig*) disagreeable.

aciēs, -ēī *f* sharp edge or point; (*eye*) sight, keen glance, pupil; (*mind*) power, apprehension; (*MIL*) line of troops, battle order, army, battle; (*fig*) debate; **prīma ~** van; **novissima ~** rearguard.

acīnacēs, -is *m* scimitar.

acinum, -ī *nt* berry, grape; fruit seed.

acinus, -ī *m* berry, grape; fruit seed.

acipēnser, -eris *m* sturgeon.

acipēnsis, -is *m* sturgeon.

aclys, -dis *f* javelin.

aconītum, -ī *nt* monkshood; poison.

acor, -ōris *m* sour taste.

acquiēscō, -ēscere, -ēvī, -ētum *vi* to rest, die; to find pleasure (in); to acquiesce.

acquīrō, -rere, -sīvī, -sītum *vt* to get in addition, acquire.

Acragās, -antis *m see* **Agrigentum**.

acrātophorum, -ī *nt* wine jar.

acrēdula, -ae *f* a bird (*unidentified*).

ācriculus *adj* peevish.

ācrimōnia, -ae *f* pungent taste; (*speech, action*) briskness, go.

Acrisiōniadēs, -ae *m* Perseus.

Acrisius, -ī *m father of Danae.*

Noun declensions and verb conjugations are shown on pp xiii to xxv. The present infinitive ending of a verb shows to which conjugation it belongs: **-āre** = 1st; **-ēre** = 2nd; **-ere** = 3rd and **-īre** = 4th. Irregular verbs are shown on p xxvi

ācriter adv see **ācer**.

ācroāma, -tis nt entertainment, entertainer.

ācroāsis, -is f public lecture.

Ācroceraunia, -ōrum ntpl a promontory in N.W. Greece.

Ācrocorinthus, -ī f fortress of Corinth.

acta, -ae f beach.

ācta, -ōrum ntpl public records, proceedings; **~ diurna, ~ pūblica** daily gazette.

Actaeus adj Athenian.

āctiō, -ōnis f action, doing; official duties, negotiations; (law) action, suit, indictment, pleading, case, trial; (RHET) delivery; (drama) plot; **~ grātiārum** expression of thanks; **~ōnem intendere, īnstituere** bring an action.

āctitō, -āre, -āvī, -ātum vt to plead, act often.

Actium, -ī and **iī** nt a town in N.W. Greece; Augustus's great victory.

Actius, -iacus adj see n.

āctivus adj of action, practical.

āctor, -ōris m driver, performer; (law) plaintiff, pleader; (COMM) agent; (RHET) orator; (drama) actor; **~ pūblicus** manager of public property; **~ summārum** cashier.

āctuāria f pinnace.

āctuāriolum, -ī m small barge.

āctuārius adj fast (ship).

āctuōsē adv actively.

āctuōsus adj very active.

āctus ppp of **agō**.

āctus, -ūs m moving, driving; right of way for cattle or vehicles; performance; (drama) playing a part, recital, act of a play.

āctūtum adv immediately.

acuī perf of **acēscō**; perf of **acuō**.

acula, -ae f small stream.

aculeātus adj prickly; (words) stinging; quibbling.

aculeus, -ī m sting, prickle barb; (fig) sting.

acūmen, -inis nt point, sting; (fig) shrewdness, ingenuity; trickery.

acuō, -uere, -uī, -ūtum vt to sharpen; to exercise; (the mind) to stimulate; to rouse (to action).

acus, -ūs f needle, pin; **acū pingere** embroider; **rem acū tangere** ≈ hit the nail on the head.

acūtē adv see **acūtus**.

acūtulus adj rather subtle.

acūtus adj sharp, pointed; (senses) keen; (sound) high-pitched; severe; intelligent.

ad prep (with acc) to, towards, against; near, at; until; (num) about; with regard to, according to; for the purpose of, for; compared with; besides; **ad Castoris** to the temple of Castor; **ad dextram** on the right; **ad hōc** besides; **ad locum** on the spot; **ad manum** at hand; **ad rem** to the point; **ad summam** in short; **ad tempus** in time; **ad ūnum omnes** all without exception; **ad urbem esse** wait outside the city gates; **ad verbum** literally; **nīl ad** nothing to do with; **usque ad** right up to.

adāctiō, -ōnis f enforcing.

adāctus ppp of **adigō**.

adāctus, -ūs m snapping (of teeth).

adaequē adv equally.

adaequō, -āre, -āvī, -ātum vt to make equal, level; to equal, match ♦ vi to be equal.

adamantēus, adamantinus adj see **adamās**.

adamās, -antis m adamant, steel; diamond.

adamō, -āre, -āvī, -ātum vt to fall in love with.

adaperiō, -īre, -uī, -tum vt to throw open.

adapertilis adj openable.

adaquō, -āre, -āvī, -ātum vt (plants, animals) to water.

adaquor vi to fetch water.

adauctus, -ūs m growing.

adaugeō, -gēre, -xī, -ctum vt to aggravate; (sacrifice) to consecrate.

adaugēscō, -ere vi to grow bigger.

adbibō, -ere, -ī vt to drink; (fig) to drink in.

adbītō, -ere vi to come near.

adc- etc see **acc-**.

addecet, -ēre vt it becomes.

addēnseō, -ēre vt to close (ranks).

addīcō, -īcere, -īxī, -ictum vi (AUG) to be favourable ♦ vt (law) to award; (auction) to knock down; (fig) to sacrifice, devote.

addictiō, -ōnis f award (at law).

addictus ppp of **addīcō** ♦ m bondsman.

addiscō, -scere, -dicī vt to learn more.

additāmentum, -ī nt increase.

additus ppp of **addō**.

addō, -ere, -idī, -itum vt to add, put to, bring to; to impart; to increase; **~ gradum** quicken pace; **~e quod** besides.

addoceō, -ēre, -uī, -tum vt to teach new.

addubitō, -āre, -āvī, -ātum vi to be in doubt ♦ vt to question.

addūcō, -ūcere, -ūxī, -uctum vt to take, bring to; to draw together, pull taut, wrinkle; (fig) to induce; (pass) to be led to believe.

adductus ppp of **addūcō** ♦ adj contracted; (fig) severe.

adedō, -edere, -ēdī, -ēsum vt to begin to eat; to eat up; to use up; to wear away.

adēmī perf of **adimō**.

ademptiō, -ōnis f taking away.

ademptus ppp of **adimō**.

adeō, -īre, -iī, -itum vt, vi to go to, approach; to address; to undertake, submit to, enter upon.

adeō adv so; (after pron) just; (after conj, adv, adj: for emphasis) indeed, very; (adding an explanation) for, in fact, thus; or rather; **~ nōn ... ut** so far from; **atque ~, sīve ~** or rather; **usque ~** so far, so long, so much.

adeps, -ipis m/f fat; corpulence.

adeptiō, -ōnis f attainment.

adeptus ppa of **adipīscor**.

adequitō, -āre, -āvī, -ātum vi to ride up (to).

adesdum come here!

adesse infin of **adsum**.

adēsus ppp of **adedō**.

adfābilis *adj* easy to talk to.

adfābilitās, -ātis *f* courtesy.

adfabrē *adv* ingeniously.

adfatim *adv* to one's satisfaction, enough, ad nauseam.

adfātur, -rī, -tus *vt* (*defec*) to speak to.

adfātus *ppa of* **adfātur**.

adfātus, -ūs *m* speaking to.

adfectātiō, -ōnis *f* aspiring; (*RHET*) affectation.

adfectātus *adj* (*RHET*) studied.

adfectiō, -ōnis *f* frame of mind, mood; disposition; goodwill; (*ASTRO*) relative position.

adfectō, -āre, -āvī, -ātum *vt* to aspire to, aim at; to try to win over; to make pretence of; **viam ~ ad** try to get to.

adfectus *ppp of* **adficiō ♦** *adj* affected with, experienced (*abl*); (*person*) disposed; (*things*) weakened; (*undertakings*) well-advanced.

adfectus, -ūs *m* disposition, mood; fondness; (*pl*) loved ones.

adferō, adferre, attulī, adlātum *and* **allātum** *vt* to bring, carry to; to bring to bear, use against; to bring news; (*explanation*) to bring forward; to contribute (*something useful*).

adficiō, -icere, -ēcī, -ectum *vt* to affect; to endow, afflict with (*abl*); **exsiliō ~** banish; **honōre ~** honour; *also used with other nouns to express the corresponding verbs.*

adfictus *ppp of* **adfingō**.

adfīgō, -gere, -xī, -xum *vt* to fasten, attach; to impress (*on the mind*).

adfingō, -ngere, -nxī, -ctum *vt* to make, form (*as part of*); to invent.

adfinis, -is *m/f* neighbour; relation (*by marriage*) ♦ *adj* neighbouring; associated with (*dat or gen*).

adfinitās, -ātis *f* relationship (*by marriage*).

adfirmātē *adv* with assurance.

adfirmātiō, -ōnis *f* declaration.

adfirmō, -āre, -āvī, -ātum *vt* to declare; to confirm.

adfixus *ppp of* **adfīgō**.

adflātus, -ūs *m* breath, exhalation; (*fig*) inspiration.

adfleō, -ēre *vi* to weep (at).

adflīctātiō, -ōnis *f* suffering.

adflīctō, -āre, -āvī, -ātum *vt* to harass, distress.

adflīctor, -ōris *m* destroyer.

adflīctus *ppp of* **adflīgō ♦** *adj* distressed, ruined; dejected; depraved.

adflīgō, -īgere, -īxī, -ictum *vt* to dash against, throw down; (*fig*) to impair, crush.

adflō, -āre, -āvī, -ātum *vt, vi* to blow on, breathe upon.

adfluēns, -entis *adj* rich (in).

adfluenter *adv* copiously.

adfluentia, -ae *f* abundance.

adfluō, -ere, -xī, -xum *vi* to flow; (*fig*) to flock in, abound in.

adfore *fut infin of* **adsum**.

adforem *imperf subj of* **adsum**.

adfuī *perf of* **adsum**.

adfulgeō, -gēre, -sī *vi* to shine on; to appear.

adfundō, -undere, -ūdī, -ūsum *vt* to pour in; to rush (troops) to.

adfūsus *adj* prostrate.

adfutūrus *fut p of* **adsum**.

adgemō, -ere *vi* to groan at.

adglomerō, -āre *vt* to add on.

adglūtinō, -āre *vt* to stick on.

adgravēscō, -ere *vi* to become worse.

adgravō, -āre, -āvī, -ātum *vt* to aggravate.

adgredior, -dī, -ssus *vt* to approach, accost; to attack; (*a task*) to undertake, take up.

adgregō, -āre, -āvī, -ātum *vt* to add, attach.

adgressiō, -ōnis *f* introductory remarks.

adgressus *ppa of* **adgredior**.

adhaereō, -rēre, -sī, -sum *vi* to stick to; (*fig*) to cling to, keep close to.

adhaerēscō, -ere *vi* to stick to *or* in; (*speech*) to falter.

adhaesiō, -ōnis *f* clinging.

adhaesus, -ūs *m* adhering.

adhibeō, -ēre, -uī, -itum *vt* to bring, put, add; to summon, consult, treat; to use, apply (*for some purpose*).

adhinniō, -īre, -īvī, -ītum *vi* to neigh to; (*fig*) to go into raptures over.

adhortātiō, -ōnis *f* exhortation.

adhortātor, -ōris *m* encourager.

adhortor, -ārī, -ātus *vt* to encourage, urge.

adhūc *adv* so far; as yet, till now; still **~ nōn** not yet.

adiaceō, -ēre, -uī *vi* to lie near, border on.

adiciō, -icere, -iēcī, -iectum *vt* to throw to; to add; to turn (mind, eyes) towards.

adiectiō, -ōnis *f* addition.

adiectus *ppp of* **adiciō**.

adiectus, -ūs *m* bringing close.

adigō, -igere, -ēgī, -āctum *vt* to drive (to); to compel; **iūs iūrandum ~** put on oath; **in verba ~** force to owe allegiance.

adimō, -imere, -ēmī, -emptum *vt* to take away (from *dat*).

adipātum *nt* pastry.

adipātus *adj* fatty; (*fig*) florid.

adipīscor, -ipīscī, -eptus *vt* to overtake; to attain, acquire.

aditus, -ūs *m* approach, access (*to a person*); entrance; (*fig*) avenue.

adiūdicō, -āre, -āvī, -ātum *vt* to award (*in arbitration*); to ascribe.

adiūmentum, -ī *nt* aid, means of support.

adiūncta *ntpl* collateral circumstances.

adiūnctiō, -ōnis *f* uniting; addition; (*RHET*) proviso; repetition.

Noun declensions and verb conjugations are shown on pp xiii to xxv. The present infinitive ending of a verb shows to which conjugation it belongs: **-āre** = 1st; **-ēre** = 2nd; **-ere** = 3rd and **-īre** = 4th. Irregular verbs are shown on p xxvi

adiūnctus *ppp of* **adiungō ♦** *adj* connected.
adiungō, -ungere, -ūnxī, -ūnctum *vt* to
yoke; to attach; (*suspicion etc*) to direct;
(*remark*) to add.
adiūrō, -āre, -āvī, -ātum *vt, vi* to swear,
swear by.
adiūtō, -āre, -āvī, -ātum *vt* to help.
adiūtor, -ōris *m* helper; (*MIL*) adjutant; (*POL*)
official; (*THEAT*) supporting cast.
adiūtrīx, -rīcis *f see* **adiūtor**.
adiūtus *ppp of* **adiuvō**.
adiuvō, -uvāre, -ūvī, -ūtum *vt* to help; to
encourage.
adj- *etc see* **adi-**.
adlābor, -bī, -psus *vi* to fall, move towards,
come to.
adlabōrō, -āre, -āvī, -ātum *vi* to work hard;
to improve by taking trouble.
adlacrimō, -āre, -āvī, -ātum *vi* to shed tears.
adlāpsus *ppa of* **adlābor**.
adlāpsus, -ūs *m* stealthy approach.
adlātrō, -āre, -āvī, -ātum *vt* to bark at; (*fig*) to
revile.
adlātus *ppp of* **adferō**.
adlaudō, -āre, -āvī, -ātum *vt* to praise
highly.
adlectō, -āre, -āvī, -ātum *vt* to entice.
adlēctus *ppp of* **adlegō**.
adlectus *ppp of* **adliciō**.
adlēgātī *mpl* deputies.
adlēgātiō, -ōnis *f* mission.
adlēgō, -āre, -āvī, -ātum *vt* to despatch,
commission; to mention.
adlegō, -egere, -ēgī, -ēctum *vt* to elect.
adlevāmentum, -ī *nt* relief.
adlevātiō, -ōnis *f* easing.
adlevō, -āre, -āvī, -ātum *vt* to lift up; to
comfort; to weaken.
adliciō, -icere, -exī, -ectum *vt* to attract.
adlīdō, -dere, -sī, -sum *vt* to dash (against);
(*fig*) to hurt.
adligō, -āre, -āvī, -ātum *vt* to tie up,
bandage; (*fig*) to bind, lay under an
obligation.
adlinō, -inere, -ēvī, -itum *vt* to smear; (*fig*) to
attach.
adlīsus *ppp of* **adlīdō**.
adlocūtiō, -ōnis *f* address; comforting
words.
adlocūtus *ppa of* **adloquor**.
adloquium, -ī *and* **iī** *nt* talk; encouragement.
adloquor, -quī, -cūtus *vt* to speak to,
address.
adlūdiō, -āre, -āvī, -ātum *vi* to play (with).
adlūdō, -dere, -sī, -sum *vi* to joke, play.
adluō, -ere, -ī *vt* to wash.
adluviēs, -ēī *f* pool left by flood water.
adluviō, -ōnis *f* alluvial land.
admātūrō, -āre, -āvī, -atum *vt* to hurry on.
admētior, -tīrī, -nsus *vt* to measure out.
adminiculor, -ārī, -ātus *vt* to prop.
adminiculum, -ī *nt* (*AGR*) stake; (*fig*) support.
administer, -rī *m* assistant.

administrātiō, -ōnis *f* services;
management.
administrātor, -ōris *m* manager.
administrō, -āre, -āvī, -ātum *vt* to manage,
govern.
admīrābilis *adj* wonderful, surprising.
admīrābilitās, -ātis *f* wonderfulness.
admīrābiliter *adv* admirably; paradoxically.
admīrātiō, -ōnis *f* wonder, surprise,
admiration.
admīror, -ārī, -ātus *vt* to wonder at, admire;
to be surprised at.
admīsceō, -scēre, -scuī, -xtum *vt* to mix in
with, add to; (*fig*) to involve; **sē ~** interfere.
admissārius, -ī *and* **iī** *m* stallion.
admissum, -ī *nt* crime.
admissus *ppp of* **admittō**.
admittō, -ittere, -īsī, -issum *vt* to let in,
admit; to set at a gallop; to allow; to commit
(a crime); **equō ~issō** charging.
admixtiō, -ōnis *f* admixture.
admixtus *ppp of* **admisceō**.
admoderātē *adv* suitably.
admoderor, -ārī, -ātus *vt* to restrain.
admodum *adv* very, quite; fully; yes; (*with
neg*) at all.
admoneō, -ēre, -uī, -itum *vt* to remind,
suggest, advise, warn.
admonitiō, -ōnis *f* reminder, suggestion,
admonition.
admonitor, -ōris *m* admonisher (*male*).
admonitrīx, -rīcis *f* admonisher (*female*).
admonitū at the suggestion, instance.
admordeō, -dēre, -sum *vt* to bite into; (*fig*) to
cheat.
admorsus *ppp of* **admordeō**.
admōtiō, -ōnis *f* applying.
admōtus *ppp of* **admoveō**.
admoveo, -ovēre, -ōvī, -ōtum *vt* to move,
bring up, apply; to lend (an ear), direct (the
mind).
admurmurātiō, -ōnis *f* murmuring.
admurmurō, -āre, -āvī, -ātum *vi* to murmur
(*of a crowd approving or disapproving*).
admutilō, -āre, -āvī, -ātum *vt* to clip close;
(*fig*) to cheat.
adnectō, -ctere, -xuī, -xum *vt* to connect, tie.
adnexus, -ūs *m* connection.
adnīsus *ppp of* **adnītor**.
adnītor, -tī, -sus *and* **-xus** *vi* to lean on; to
exert oneself.
adnīxus *ppp of* **adnītor**.
adnō, -āre *vt, vi* to swim to.
adnotō, -āre, -āvī, -ātum *vt* to comment on.
adnumerō, -āre, -āvī, -ātum *vt* to pay out; to
reckon along with.
adnuō, -uere, -uī, -ūtum *vi* to nod; to assent,
promise; to indicate.
adoleō, -olēre, -oluī, -ultum *vt* to burn; to
pile with gifts.
adolēscen- *etc see* **adulēscen-**.
adolēscō, -ēscere, -ēvī *vi* to grow up,
increase; to burn.

Adōnis, **-is** *and* **idis** *m* a beautiful youth loved by Venus.

adopertus *adj* covered.

adoptātiō, **-ōnis** *f* adopting.

adoptiō, **-ōnis** *f* adoption.

adoptīvus *adj* by adoption.

adoptō, **-āre**, **-āvī**, **-ātum** *vt* to choose; to adopt.

ador, **-ōris** *and* **oris** *nt* spelt.

adōreus *adj see* n.

adōrea *f* glory.

adorior, **-īrī**, **-tus** *vt* to accost; to attack; to set about.

adōrnō, **-āre**, **-āvī**, **-ātum** *vt* to get ready.

adōrō, **-āre**, **-āvī**, **-ātum** *vt* to entreat; to worship, revere.

adortus *ppa of* **adorior**.

adp- *etc see* **app-**.

adrādō, **-dere**, **-sī**, **-sum** *vt* to shave close.

Adrastus, **-ī** *m* a king of Argos.

adrāsus *ppp of* **adrādō**.

adrēctus *ppp of* **adrigō** ♦ *adj* steep.

adrēpō, **-ere**, **-sī**, **-tum** *vi* to creep, steal into.

adreptus *ppp of* **adripiō**.

Adria *etc see* **Hadria** *etc*.

adrīdeō, **-dēre**, **-sī**, **-sum** *vt*, *vi* to laugh, smile at; to please.

adrigō, **-igere**, **-ēxī**, **-ēctum** *vt* to raise; (*fig*) to rouse.

adripiō, **-ipere**, **-ipuī**, **-eptum** *vt* to seize; to appropriate; to take hold of; to learn quickly; (*law*) to arrest; to satirize.

adrōdō, **-dere**, **-sī**, **-sum** *vt* to gnaw, nibble at.

adrogāns, **-antis** *adj* arrogant, insolent.

adroganter *adv see* **adrogāns**.

adrogantia, **-ae** *f* arrogance, presumption, haughtiness.

adrogātiō, **-ōnis** *f* adoption.

adrogō, **-āre**, **-āvī**, **-ātum** *vt* to ask; to associate; to claim, assume; (*fig*) to award.

adsc- *etc see* **asc-**.

adsecla *etc see* **adsecula**.

adsectātiō, **-ōnis** *f* attendance.

adsectātor, **-ōris** *m* follower.

adsector, **-ārī**, **-ātus** *vt* to attend on, follow (*esp a candidate*).

adsecula, **-ae** *m* follower (*derogatory*).

adsēdī *perf of* **adsideō**; *perf of* **adsīdō**.

adsēnsiō, **-ōnis** *f* assent, applause; (PHILOS) acceptance of the evidence of the senses.

adsēnsor, **-ōris** *m* one in agreement.

adsēnsus *ppa of* **adsentior**.

adsēnsus, **-ūs** *m* assent, approval; echo; (PHILOS) acceptance of the evidence of the senses.

adsentātiō, **-ōnis** *f* flattery.

adsentātiuncula *f* trivial compliments.

adsentātor, **-ōris** *m* flatterer (*male*).

adsentātōriē *adv* ingratiatingly.

adsentātrīx, **-rīcis** *f* flatterer (*female*).

adsentiō, **-entīre**, **-ēnsī**, **-ēnsum**; **-entior**, **-entīrī**, **-ēnsus** *vi* to agree, approve.

adsentor, **-ārī**, **-ātus** *vi* to agree, flatter.

adsequor, **-quī**, **-cūtus** *vt* to overtake; to attain; to grasp (*by understanding*).

adserō, **-ere**, **-uī**, **-tum** *vt* (*law*) to declare free (*usu with* **manū**), liberate (a slave); to lay claim to, appropriate; **~ in servitūtem** claim as a slave.

adserō, **-erere**, **-ēvī**, **-itum** *vt* to plant near.

adsertiō, **-ōnis** *f* declaration of status.

adsertor, **-ōris** *m* champion.

adserviō, **-īre** *vi* to assist.

adservō, **-āre**, **-āvī**, **-ātum** *vt* to watch carefully; to keep, preserve.

adsessiō, **-ōnis** *f* sitting beside.

adsessor, **-ōris** *m* counsellor.

adsessus, **-ūs** *m* sitting beside.

adsevēranter *adv* emphatically.

adsevērātiō, **-ōnis** *f* assertion; earnestness.

adsevērō, **-āre**, **-āvī**, **-ātum** *vt* to do in earnest; to assert strongly.

adsideō, **-idēre**, **-ēdī**, **-essum** *vi* to sit by; to attend, assist; to besiege; to resemble.

adsīdō, **-īdere**, **-ēdī** *vi* to sit down.

adsiduē *adv* continually.

adsiduitās, **-ātis** *f* constant attendance; continuance, frequent recurrence.

adsiduō *adv* continually.

adsiduus *adj* constantly in attendance, busy; continual, incessant.

adsiduus, **-ī** *m* taxpayer.

adsignātiō, **-ōnis** *f* allotment (of land).

adsignō, **-āre**, **-āvī**, **-ātum** *vt* to allot (*esp land*); to assign; to impute, attribute; to consign.

adsiliō, **-ilīre**, **-iluī**, **-ultum** *vi* to leap at *or* on to.

adsimilis *adj* like.

adsimiliter *adv* similarly.

adsimulātus *adj* similar; counterfeit.

adsimulō, **-āre**, **-āvī**, **-ātum** *vt*, *vi* to compare; to pretend, imitate.

adsistō, **-istere**, **-titī** *vi* to stand (by); to defend.

adsitus *ppp of* **adserō**.

adsoleō, **-ēre** *vi* to be usual.

adsonō, **-āre** *vi* to respond.

adsp- *etc see* **asp-**.

adsternō, **-ere** *vt* to prostrate.

adstipulātor, **-ōris** *m* supporter.

adstipulor, **-ārī**, **-ātus** *vi* to agree with.

adstitī *perf of* **adsistō**; *perf of* **adstō**.

adstō, **-āre**, **-itī** *vi* to stand near, stand up; to assist.

adstrepō, **-ere** *vi* to roar.

adstrictē *adv* concisely.

adstrictus *ppp of* **adstringō** ♦ *adj* tight, narrow; concise; stingy.

Noun declensions and verb conjugations are shown on pp xiii to xxv. The present infinitive ending of a verb shows to which conjugation it belongs: **-āre** = 1st; **-ēre** = 2nd; **-ere** = 3rd and **-īre** = 4th. Irregular verbs are shown on p xxvi

adstringō, -ngere, -nxī, -ctum *vt* to draw close, tighten; to bind, oblige; to abridge.

adstruō, -ere, -xī, -ctum *vt* to build on; to add.

adstupeō, -ēre *vi* to be astonished.

adsuēfaciō, -acere, -ēcī, -actum *vt* to accustom, train.

adsuēscō, -scere, -vī, -tum *vi* to accustom, train.

adsuētūdō, -inis *f* habit.

adsuētus *ppp of* **adsuēscō** ♦ *adj* customary.

adsultō, -āre, -āvī, -ātum *vi* to jump; to attack.

adsultus, -ūs *m* attack.

adsum, -esse, -fuī *vi* to be present; to support, assist (*esp at law*); to come; to appear before (a tribunal); **animō ~** pay attention; **iam aderō** I'll be back soon.

adsūmō, -ere, -psī, -ptum *vt* to take for oneself, receive; to take also.

adsūmptiō, -ōnis *f* taking up; (*logic*) minor premise.

adsūmptīvus *adj* (*law*) which takes its defence from extraneous circumstances.

adsūmptum, -ī *nt* epithet.

adsūmptus *ppp of* **adsūmō.**

adsuō, -ere *vt* to sew on.

adsurgō, -gere, -rēxī, -rēctum *vi* to rise, stand up; to swell, increase.

adt- *etc see* **att-.**

adulātiō, -ōnis *f* (*dogs*) fawning; servility.

adulātor, -ōris *m* sycophant.

adulātōrius *adj* flattering.

adulēscēns, -entis *m/f* young man *or* woman (*usu from 15 to 30 years*).

adulēscentia, -ae *f* youth (*age 15 to 30*).

adulēscentula, -ae *f* girl.

adulēscentulus, -ī *m* quite a young man.

adulō, -āre, -āvī, -ātum; adulor, -ārī, -ātus *vt, vi* to fawn upon, flatter, kowtow.

adulter, -ī *m*, **-a, -ae** *f* adulterer, adulteress ♦ *adj* adulterous.

adulterīnus *adj* forged.

adulterium, -ī *and* **iī** *nt* adultery.

adulterō, -āre, -āvī, -ātum *vt, vi* to commit adultery; to falsify.

adultus *ppp of* **adolēscō** ♦ *adj* adult, mature.

adumbrātim *adv* in outline.

adumbrātiō, -ōnis *f* sketch; semblance.

adumbrātus *adj* false.

adumbrō, -āre, -āvī, -ātum *vt* to sketch; to represent, copy.

aduncitās, -ātis *f* curvature.

aduncus *adj* hooked, curved.

adurgeō, -ēre *vt* to pursue closely.

adūrō, -rere, -ssī, -stum *vt* to burn; to freeze; (*fig*) to fire.

adusque *prep* (*with acc*) right up to ♦ *adv* entirely.

adūstus *ppp of* **adūrō** ♦ *adj* brown.

advectīcius *adj* imported.

advectō, -āre *vt* to carry frequently.

advectus *ppp of* **advehō.**

advectus, -ūs *m* bringing.

advehō, -here, -xī, -ctum *vt* to carry, convey; (*pass*) to ride.

advēlō, -āre *vt* to crown.

advena, -ae *m/f* stranger ♦ *adj* foreign.

adveniō, -enīre, -ēnī, -entum *vi* to arrive, come.

adventīcius *adj* foreign, extraneous; unearned.

adventō, -āre, -āvī, -ātum *vi* to come nearer and nearer, advance rapidly.

adventor, -ōris *m* visitor.

adventus, -ūs *m* arrival, approach.

adversāria *ntpl* daybook.

adversārius, -ī *and* **iī** *m* opponent ♦ *adj* opposing.

adversātrīx, -īcis *f* antagonist.

adversiō, -ōnis *f* turning (the attention).

adversor, -ārī, -ātus *vi* to oppose, resist.

adversum, -ī *nt* opposite; misfortune ♦ *prep* (+ *acc*) towards, against ♦ *adv* to meet.

adversus *ppp of* **advertō** ♦ *adj* opposite, in front; hostile; **~ō flūmine** upstream; **~ae rēs** misfortune ♦ *prep* (+ *acc*) towards, against ♦ *adv* to meet.

advertō, -tere, -tī, -sum *vt* to turn, direct towards; to call attention; **animum ~** notice, perceive; (*with* ad) to attend to; (*with* in) to punish.

advesperāscit, -scere, -vit *vi* it is getting dark.

advigilō, -āre *vi* to keep watch.

advocātiō, -ōnis *f* legal assistance, counsel.

advocātus, -ī *m* supporter in a lawsuit; advocate, counsel.

advocō, -āre, -āvī, -ātum *vt* to summon; (*law*) to call in the assistance of.

advolō, -āre, -āvī, -ātum *vi* to fly to, swoop down upon.

advolvō, -vere, -vī, -ūtum *vt* to roll to; to prostrate.

advor- *etc see* **adver-.**

adytum, -ī *nt* sanctuary.

Aeacidēs, -idae *m* Achilles; Pyrrhus.

Aeacus, -ī *m* father of Peleus, and judge of the dead.

Aeaea, -ae *f* Circe's island.

Aeaeus *adj* of Circe.

aedēs, -is *f* temple; (*pl*) house.

aedicula, -ae *f* shrine; small house, room.

aedificātiō, -ōnis *f* building.

aedificātiuncula, -ae *f* little house.

aedificātor, -ōris *m* builder.

aedificium, -ī *and* **iī** *nt* building.

aedificō, -āre, -āvī, -ātum *vt* to build, construct.

aedīlicius *adj* aedile's ♦ *m* ex-aedile.

aedīlis, -is *m* aedile.

aedīlitās, -ātis *f* aedileship.

aedis, -is *see* **aedēs.**

aeditumus, aedituus, -ī *m* temple-keeper.

Aeduī, -ōrum *mpl a tribe of central Gaul.*

Aeētēs, -ae *m father of Medea.*

Aegaeus *adj* Aegean ♦ *nt* Aegean Sea.
Aegātēs, -um *fpl* islands off Sicily.
aeger, -rī *adj* ill, sick; sorrowful; weak.
Aegīna, -ae *f* a Greek island.
Aegīnēta, -ae *m* inhabitant of Aegīna.
aegis, -dis *f* shield of Jupiter or Athena, aegis.
Aegisthus, -ī *m* paramour of Clytemnestra.
aegocerōs, -ōtis *m* Capricorn.
aegrē *adv* painfully; with displeasure; with
   difficulty; hardly; ~ **ferre** be annoyed.
aegrēscō, -ere *vi* to become ill; to be
   aggravated.
aegrimōnia, -ae *f* distress of mind.
aegritūdō, -inis *f* sickness; sorrow.
aegror, -ōris *m* illness.
aegrōtātiō, -ōnis *f* illness, disease.
aegrōtō, -āre, -āvī, -ātum *vi* to be ill.
aegrōtus *adj* ill, sick.
Aegyptius *adj* see *n.*
Aegyptus, -ī *f* Egypt ♦ *m* brother of Danaus.
aelinos, -ī *m* dirge.
Aemiliānus *adj* esp Scipio, destroyer of Carthage.
Aemilius, -ī Roman family name; **Via ~ia** road in
   N. Italy.
aemulātiō, -ōnis *f* rivalry (good or bad);
   jealousy.
aemulātor, -ōris *m* zealous imitator.
aemulor, -ārī, -ātus *vt* to rival, copy; to be
   jealous.
aemulus, -ī *m* rival ♦ *adj* rivalling; jealous.
Aeneadēs, -ae *m* Trojan; Roman.
Aenēās, -ae *m* Trojan leader and hero of Virgil's
   epic.
Aenēis, -idis and **idos** *f* Aeneid.
Aenēius *adj* see *n.*
aēneus *adj* of bronze.
aenigma, -tis *nt* riddle, mystery.
aēnum, -ī *nt* bronze vessel.
aēnus *adj* of bronze.
Aeolēs, -um *mpl* the Aeolians.
Aeolia *f* Lipari Island.
Aeolidēs *m* a descendant of Aeolus.
Aeolis, -idis *f* Aeolia (N.W. of Asia Minor).
Aeolis, -idis *f* daughter of Aeolus.
Aeolius *adj* see *n.*
Aeolus, -ī *m* king of the winds.
aequābilis *adj* equal; consistent, even;
   impartial.
aequābilitās, -ātis *f* uniformity; impartiality.
aequābiliter *adv* uniformly.
aequaevus *adj* of the same age.
aequālis *adj* equal, like; of the same age,
   contemporary; uniform.
aequālitās, -ātis *f* evenness; (in politics, age)
   equality, similarity.
aequāliter *adv* evenly.
aequanimitās, -ātis *f* goodwill; calmness.
aequātiō, -ōnis *f* equal distribution.
aequē *adv* equally; just as (with **ac, atque, et,**
   quam); justly.
Aequī, -ōrum *mpl* a people of central Italy.

Aequicus, Aequiculus *adj* see *n.*
Aequimaelium, -ī and **iī** *nt* an open space in
   Rome.
aequinoctiālis *adj* see *n.*
aequinoctium, -ī and **iī** *nt* equinox.
aequiperābilis *adj* comparable.
aequiperō, -āre, -āvī, -ātum *vt* to compare;
   to equal.
aequitās, -ātis *f* uniformity; fair dealing,
   equity; calmness of mind.
aequō, -āre, -āvī, -ātum *vt* to make equal,
   level; to compare; to equal; **solō ~** raze to the
   ground.
aequor, -is *nt* a level surface, sea.
aequoreus *adj* of the sea.
aequum, -ī *nt* plain; justice.
aequus *adj* level, equal; favourable, friendly,
   fair, just; calm; **~ō animō** patiently; **~ō Marte**
   without deciding the issue; **~um est** it is
   reasonable; **ex ~ō** equally.
āēr, āeris *m* air, weather; mist.
aerāria *f* mine.
aerārium *nt* treasury.
aerārius *adj* of bronze; of money ♦ *m* a citizen
   of the lowest class at Rome; **tribūnī ~ī**
   paymasters; a wealthy middle class at Rome.
aerātus *adj* of bronze.
aereus *adj* of copper or bronze.
aerifer, -ī *adj* carrying cymbals.
aeripēs, -edis *adj* bronze-footed.
āerius *adj* of the air; lofty.
aerūgō, -inis *f* rust; (fig) envy, avarice.
aerumna, -ae *f* trouble, hardship.
aerumnōsus *adj* wretched.
aes, aeris *nt* copper, bronze; money; (pl)
   objects made of copper or bronze (esp
   statues, instruments, vessels; soldiers' pay); **~**
   aliēnum debt; **~ circumforāneum** borrowed
   money; **~ grave** Roman coin, as.
Aeschylus, -ī *m* Greek tragic poet.
Aesculāpius, -ī *m* god of medicine.
aesculētum, -ī *nt* oak forest.
aesculeus *adj* see **aesculus.**
aesculus, -ī *f* durmast oak.
Aesōn, -onis *m* father of Jason.
Aesonidēs, -ae *m* Jason.
Aesōpius *adj* see *n.*
Aesōpus, -ī *m* Greek writer of fables.
aestās, -ātis *f* summer.
aestifer, -ī *adj* heat-bringing.
aestimātiō, -ōnis *f* valuation, assessment;
   lītis ~ assessment of damages.
aestimātor, -ōris *m* valuer.
aestimō, -āre, -āvī, -ātum *vt* to value,
   estimate the value of; **māgnī ~** think highly
   of.
aestīva, -ōrum *ntpl* summer camp, campaign.
aestīvus *adj* summer.
aestuārium, -ī and **iī** *nt* tidal waters, estuary.
aestuō, -āre, -āvī, -ātum *vi* to boil, burn;

Noun declensions and verb conjugations are shown on pp xiii to xxv. The present infinitive ending of a verb shows
to which conjugation it belongs: **-āre** = 1st; **-ēre** = 2nd; **-ere** = 3rd and **-īre** = 4th. Irregular verbs are shown on p xxvi

(*movement*) to heave, toss; (*fig*) to be excited; to waver.

aestuōsus *adj* very hot; agitated.

aestus, -ūs *m* heat; surge of the sea; tide; (*fig*) passion; hesitation.

aetās, -ātis *f* age, life; time.

aetātem *adv* for life.

aetātula, -ae *f* tender age.

aeternitās, -ātis *f* eternity.

aeternō, -āre *vt* to immortalize.

aeternus *adj* eternal, immortal; lasting; in ~um for ever.

aethēr, -eris *m* sky, heaven; air.

aetherius *adj* ethereal, heavenly; of air.

Aethiops, -is *adj* Ethiopian; (*fig*) stupid.

aethra, -ae *f* sky.

Aetna, -ae *f* Etna (*in Sicily*).

Aetnaeus, Aetnēnsis *adj see n.*

Aetōlia, -iae *f* a district of N. Greece.

Aetōlus, -icus *adj see n.*

aevitās, -ātis *old form of* **aetās.**

aevum, -ī *nt* age, lifetime; eternity; in ~ for ever.

Āfer, -rī *adj* African.

āfore *fut infin of* **absum.**

Āfrānius, -ī *m* Latin comic poet.

Āfrica, -ae *f* Roman province (*now* Tunisia).

Āfricānae *fpl* panthers.

Āfricānus *adj name of two Scipios.*

Āfricus *adj* African; ♦ *m* south-west wind.

āfuī, āfutūrus *perf, fut p of* **absum.**

Agamēmnōn, -onis *m* leader of Greeks against Troy.

Agamēmnonius *adj see n.*

Aganippē, -ēs *f* a spring on Helicon.

agāsō, -ōnis *m* ostler, footman.

age, agedum come on!, well then.

agellus, -ī *m* plot of land.

Agēnōr, -oris *m* father of Europa.

Agēnoreus *adj see n.*

Agēnoridēs, -ae *m* Cadmus; Perseus.

agēns, -entis *adj* (*RHET*) effective.

ager, -rī *m* land, field; countryside; territory.

agg- *etc see* **adg-.**

agger, -is *m* rampart; mound, embankment, any built-up mass.

aggerō, -āre, -āvī, -ātum *vt* to pile up; to increase.

aggerō, -rere, -ssī, -stum *vt* to carry, bring.

aggestus, -ūs *m* accumulation.

agilis *adj* mobile; nimble, busy.

agilitās, -ātis *f* mobility.

agitābilis *adj* light.

agitātiō, -ōnis *f* movement, activity.

agitātor, -ōris *m* driver, charioteer.

agitō, -āre, -āvī, -ātum *vt* (*animals*) to drive; to move, chase, agitate; (*fig*) to excite (to action); to persecute, ridicule; to keep (*a ceremony*) ♦ *vi* to live; to deliberate.

agmen, -inis *nt* forward movement, procession, train; army on the march; ~ claudere bring up the rear; novissimum ~ rearguard; prīmum ~ van.

agna, -ae *f* ewe lamb; lamb (flesh).

agnāscor, -scī, -tus *vi* to be born after.

agnātus, -ī *m* relation (*by blood on father's side*).

agnellus, -ī *m* little lamb.

agnīnus *adj* of lamb.

agnitiō, -ōnis *f* recognition, knowledge.

agnitus *ppp of* **agnōscō.**

agnōmen, -inis *nt* an extra surname (*eg Africanus*).

agnōscō, -ōscere, -ōvī, -itum *vt* to recognize; to acknowledge, allow; to understand.

agnus, -ī *m* lamb.

agō, agere, ēgī, āctum *vt* to drive, lead; to plunder; to push forward, put forth; (*fig*) to move, rouse, persecute; to do, act, perform; (*time*) to pass, spend; (*undertakings*) to manage, wage; (*public speaking*) to plead, discuss; to negotiate, treat; (*THEAT*) to play, act the part of; ~ cum populō address the people; age come on!, well then; age age all right!; āctum est dē it is all up with; aliud ~ not attend; animam ~ expire; annum quartum ~ be three years old; causam ~ plead a cause; hōc age pay attention; id ~ ut aim at; lēge ~ go to law; nīl agis it's no use; quid agis? how are you?; rēs agitur interests are at stake; sē ~ go, come.

agrāriī *mpl* the land reform party.

agrārius *adj* of public land; lēx ~a land law.

agrestis *adj* rustic; boorish, wild, barbarous ♦ *m* countryman.

agricola, -ae *m* countryman, farmer.

Agricola, -ae *m* a Roman governor of Britain; his biography by Tacitus.

Agrigentīnus *adj see n.*

Agrigentum, -ī *nt* a town in Sicily.

agripeta, -ae *m* landgrabber.

Agrippa, -ae *m* Roman surname (*esp Augustus's minister*).

Agrippīna, -ae *f* mother of Nero; Colōnia ~a or ~ēnsis Cologne.

Agyīeus, -ēī *and* **eos** *m* Apollo.

āh *interj* ah! (*in sorrow or joy*).

aha *interj* expressing reproof *or* laughter.

ahēn- *etc see* **aēn-.**

Āiāx, -ācis *m* Ajax (*name of two Greek heroes at Troy*).

āiō *vt* (*defec*) to say, speak; ain tū?/ain vērō? really?; quid ais? I say!

āla, -ae *f* wing; armpit; (*MIL*) wing of army.

alabaster, -rī *m* perfume box.

alacer, -ris *adj* brisk, cheerful.

alacritās, -ātis *f* promptness, liveliness; joy, rapture.

alapa, -ae *f* slap on the face; a slave's freedom.

ālāriī *mpl* allied troops.

ālārius *adj* (*MIL*) on the wing.

ālātus *adj* winged.

alauda, -ae *f* lark; name of a legion of Caesar's.

alāzōn, -onis *m* braggart.

Alba Longa, -ae, -ae f a Latin town (*precursor of Rome*).
Albānus *adj* Alban; **Lacus ~, Mōns ~** *lake and mountain near Alba Longa*.
albātus *adj* dressed in white.
albeō, -ēre *vi* to be white; to dawn.
albēscō, -ere *vi* to become white; to dawn.
albicō, -āre *vi* to be white.
albidus *adj* white.
Albiōn, -ōnis f ancient name for Britain.
albitūdō, -inis f whiteness.
Albula, -ae f old name for the Tiber.
albulus *adj* whitish.
album, -ī *nt* white; records.
Albunea, -ae f a spring at Tibur; a sulphur spring near Alban Lake.
albus *adj* white, bright.
Alcaeus, -ī m Greek lyric poet.
alcēdō, -inis f kingfisher.
alcēdōnia *ntpl* halcyon days.
alcēs, -is f elk.
Alcibiadēs, -is m brilliant Athenian politician.
Alcīdēs, -ae m Hercules.
Alcinous, -ī m king of Phaeacians in the Odyssey.
ālea, -ae f gambling, dice; (*fig*) chance, hazard; **iacta ~ est** the die is cast; **in ~am dare** to risk.
āleātor, -ōris m gambler.
āleātōrius *adj* in gambling.
ālēc *etc see* **allēc**.
āleō, -ōnis m gambler.
ālēs, -itis *adj* winged; swift ♦ *m/f* bird; omen.
alēscō, -ere *vi* to grow up.
Alexander, -rī m a Greek name; Paris (*prince of Troy*); Alexander the Great (*king of Macedon*).
Alexandrēa (*later* **-īa**), **-ēae** f Alexandria in Egypt.
alga, -ae f seaweed.
algeō, -gēre, -sī *vi* to feel cold; (*fig*) to be neglected.
algēscō, -ere *vi* to catch cold.
Algidus, -ī m mountain in Latium.
algidus *adj* cold.
algor, -ōris m cold.
algū *abl sg* m with cold.
aliā *adv* in another way.
aliās *adv* at another time; at one time ... at another.
alibī *adv* elsewhere; otherwise; in one place ... in another.
alicubī *adv* somewhere.
alicunde *adv* from somewhere.
alid old form of **aliud**.
aliēnātiō, -ōnis f transfer; estrangement.
aliēnigena, -ae m foreigner.
aliēnigenus *adj* foreign; heterogeneous.
aliēnō, -āre, -āvī, -ātum *vt* to transfer (property by sale); to alienate, estrange; (*mind*) to derange.

aliēnus *adj* of another, of others; alien, strange; (*with abl or* **ab**) unsuited to, different from; hostile ♦ *m* stranger.
āliger, -ī *adj* winged.
alimentārius *adj* about food.
alimentum, -ī *nt* nourishment, food; obligation of children to parents; (*fig*) support.
alimōnium, -ī *and* **ī** *nt* nourishment.
aliō *adv* in another direction, elsewhere; one way ... another way.
aliōquī, aliōquīn *adv* otherwise, else; besides.
aliōrsum *adv* in another direction; differently.
ālipēs, -edis *adj* wing-footed; fleet.
alīptēs, -ae m sports trainer.
aliquā *adv* some way or other.
aliquam *adv:* ~ **diū** for sometime; ~ **multī** a considerable number.
aliquandō *adv* sometime, ever; sometimes; once, for once; now at last.
aliquantisper *adv* for a time.
aliquantō *adv* (*with comp*) somewhat.
aliquantulum *nt* a very little ♦ *adv* somewhat.
aliquantulus *adj* quite small.
aliquantum *adj* a good deal ♦ *adv* somewhat.
aliquantus *adj* considerable.
aliquātenus *adv* to some extent.
aliquī, -qua, -quod *adj* some, any; some other.
aliquid *adv* at all.
aliquis, -quid *pron* somebody, something; someone *or* something important.
aliquō *adv* to some place, somewhere else.
aliquot *adj* (*indecl*) some.
aliquotiēns *adv* several times.
aliter *adv* otherwise, differently; in one way ... in another.
alitus *ppp of* **alō**.
ālium, -ī *and* **ī** *nt* garlic.
aliunde *adv* from somewhere else.
alius, alia, aliud *adj* other, another; different; **alius ... alius** some ... others; **alius ex aliō** one after the other; **in alia omnia īre** oppose a measure; **nihil aliud quam** only.
all- *etc see* **adl-**.
allēc, -is *nt* fish pickle.
allex, -icis m big toe.
Allia, -ae f tributary of the Tiber (*scene of a great Roman defeat*).
Alliēnsis *adj see* **Allia**.
Allobrogēs, -um *mpl* a people of S.E. Gaul.
Allobrogicus *adj see n.*
almus *adj* nourishing; kindly.
alnus, -ī f alder.
alō, -ere, -uī, -tum *and* **-itum** *vt* to nourish, rear; to increase, promote.
Alpēs, -ium *fpl* Alps.
Alphēus, -ī m river of Olympia in S.W. Greece.
Alpīnus *adj see n.*

Noun declensions and verb conjugations are shown on pp xiii to xxv. The present infinitive ending of a verb shows to which conjugation it belongs: **-āre** = 1st; **-ēre** = 2nd; **-ere** = 3rd and **-īre** = 4th. Irregular verbs are shown on p xxvi

alsī *perf of* **algeō**.
alsius, alsus *adj* cold.
altāria, -ium *ntpl* altars, altar; altar top.
altē *adv* on high, from above; deep; from afar.
alter, -īus *adj* the one, the other (*of two*);
second, the next; fellow man; different; ~
ego, ~ **īdem** a second self; ~**um tantum** twice
as much; **ūnus et** ~ one or two.
altercātiō, -ōnis *f* dispute, debate.
altercor, -ārī, -ātus *vi* to wrangle, dispute; to
cross-examine.
alternīs *adv* alternately.
alternō, -āre, -āvī, -ātum *vt* to do by turns,
alternate.
alternus *adj* one after the other, alternate;
elegiac (verses).
alteruter, -īusutrīus *adj* one or the other.
altilis *adj* fat (*esp fowls*).
altisonus *adj* sounding on high.
altitonāns, -antis *adj* thundering on high.
altitūdō, -inis *f* height, depth; (*fig*) sublimity,
(*mind*) secrecy.
altivolāns, -antis *adj* soaring on high.
altor, -ōris *m* foster father.
altrīnsecus *adv* on the other side.
altrīx, -īcis *f* nourisher, foster mother.
altum, -ī *nt* heaven; sea (*usu out of sight of
land*); **ex ~ō repetītus** far-fetched.
altus *adj* high, deep; (*fig*) noble; profound.
ālūcinor, -ārī, -ātus *vi* to talk wildly; (*mind*) to
wander.
aluī *perf of* **alō**.
alumnus, -ī *mf* foster child; pupil.
alūta, -ae *f* soft leather; shoe, purse, face
patch.
alveārium, -ī *and* **iī** *nt* beehive.
alveolus, -ī *m* basin.
alveus, -eī *m* hollow; trough; (*ship*) hold; bath
tub; riverbed.
alvus, -ī *f* bowels; womb; stomach.
amābilis *adj* lovely, lovable.
amābilitās, -ātis *f* charm.
amābiliter *adv see* **amābilis**.
Amalthēa, -ae *f* nymph or she-goat; **cornū
~ae** horn of plenty.
Amalthēum, -ī *nt* Atticus's library.
āmandātiō *f* sending away.
āmandō, -āre, -āvī, -ātum *vt* to send away.
āmāns, -antis *adj* fond ♦ *m* lover.
amanter *adv* affectionately.
āmanuēnsis, -is *m* secretary.
amāracinum, -inī *nt* marjoram ointment.
amāracum, -i *nt*, **amāracus, -ī** *mf* sweet
marjoram.
amārē *adv see* **amārus**.
amāritiēs, -ēī *f*, **amāritūdō, -inis** *f*, **amāror,
-ōris** *m* bitterness.
amārus *adj* bitter; (*fig*) sad; ill-natured.
amāsius, -ī *and* **iī** *m* lover.
Amathūs, -ūntis *f* town in Cyprus.
Amathūsia *f* Venus.
amātiō, -ōnis *f* lovemaking.
amātor, -ōris *m* lover, paramour.

amātorculus *m* poor lover.
amatōriē *adv* amorously.
amatōrius *adj* of love, erotic.
amātrīx, -rīcis *f* mistress.
Amāzōn, -onis *f* Amazon, warrior woman.
Amāzonides *fpl* Amazons.
Amāzonius *adj see n*.
ambāctus, -ī *m* vassal.
ambāgēs, -is *f* windings; (*speech*)
circumlocution, quibbling; enigma.
ambedō, -edere, -ēdī, -ēsum *vt* to consume.
ambēsus *ppp of* **ambedō**.
ambigō, -ere *vt, vi* to wander about; to be in
doubt; to argue; to wrangle.
ambiguē *adv* doubtfully.
ambiguitās, -ātis *f* ambiguity.
ambiguus *adj* changeable, doubtful,
unreliable; ambiguous.
ambiō, -īre, -iī, -ītum *vt* to go round, encircle;
(*POL*) to canvass for votes; (*fig*) to court (for a
favour).
ambitiō, -ōnis *f* canvassing for votes;
currying favour; ambition.
ambitiōsē *adv* ostentatiously.
ambitiōsus *adj* winding; ostentatious,
ambitious.
ambitus *ppp of* **ambiō**.
ambitus, -ūs *m* circuit, circumference;
circumlocution; canvassing, bribery; **lēx de
~ū** a law against bribery.
ambō, ambae, ambō *num* both, two.
Ambracia, -ae *f* district of N.W. Greece.
Ambraciēnsis, -us *adj see n*.
ambrosia, -ae *f* food of the gods.
ambrosius *adj* divine.
ambūbāia, -ae *f* Syrian flute-girl.
ambulācrum, -ī *nt* avenue.
ambulātiō, -ōnis *f* walk, walking; walk
(*place*).
ambulātiuncula *f* short walk.
ambulō, -āre, -āvī, -ātum *vi* to walk, go; to
travel.
ambūrō, -rere, -ssī, -stum *vt* to burn up; to
make frostbitten; (*fig*) to ruin.
ambūstus *ppp of* **ambūrō**.
amellus, -ī *m* Michaelmas daisy.
āmēns, -entis *adj* mad, frantic; stupid.
āmentia, -ae *f* madness; stupidity.
āmentum, -ī *nt* strap (for throwing javelin).
ames, -itis *m* fowler's pole.
amfr- *etc see* **anfr-**.
amīca, -ae *f* friend; mistress.
amiciō, -īre, -tus *vt* to clothe, cover.
amiciter, -ē *adv see* **amīcus**.
amīcitia, -ae *f* friendship; alliance.
amictus *ppp of* **amiciō**.
amictus, -ūs *m* (manner of) dress; clothing.
amiculum, -ī *nt* cloak.
amīculus, -ī *m* dear friend.
amīcus, -ī *m* friend ♦ *adj* friendly, fond.
āmissiō, -ōnis *f* loss.
āmissus *ppp of* **āmittō**.
amita, -ae *f* aunt (*on father's side*).

āmittō, -ittere, -īsī, -issum vt to let go, lose.

Ammōn, -is m Egyptian god identified with Jupiter.

Ammōniacus adj see n.

amnicola, -ae m/f sth growing by a river.

amniculus m brook.

amnicus adj see n.

amnis, -is m river.

amō, -āre, -āvī, -ātum vt to love, like; (colloq) to be obliged to; **ita mē dī ament!** ≈ bless my soul!; **amābō** please!

amoenitās, -ātis f delightfulness (esp of scenery).

amoenus adj delightful.

āmōlior, -īrī, -ītus vt to remove.

amōmum, -ī nt cardamom.

amor, -ōris m love; (fig) strong desire; term of endearment; Cupid; (pl) love affairs.

āmōtiō, -ōnis f removal.

āmōtus ppp of **āmoveō**.

āmoveō, -ovēre, -ōvī, -ōtum vt to remove; to banish.

amphibolia, -ae f ambiguity.

Amphīōn, -onis m musician and builder of Thebes.

Amphīonius adj see n.

amphitheātrum, -ī nt amphitheatre.

Amphitrītē, -ēs f sea goddess; the sea.

Amphitryō, -ōnis m husband of Alcmena.

Amphitryōniadēs m Hercules.

amphora, -ae f a two-handled jar; liquid measure; (NAUT) measure of tonnage.

Amphrȳsius adj of Apollo.

Amphrȳsus, -ī m river in Thessaly.

ample adv see **amplūs**.

amplector, -ctī, -xus vt to embrace, encircle; (mind) to grasp; (speech) to deal with; (fig) to cherish.

amplexor, -ārī, -ātus vt to embrace, love.

amplexus ppa of **amplector**.

amplexus, -ūs m embrace, encircling.

amplificātiō, -ōnis f enlargement; (RHET) a passage elaborated for effect.

amplificē adv splendidly.

amplificō, -āre, -āvī, -ātum vt to increase, enlarge; (RHET) to enlarge upon.

ampliō, -āre, -āvī, -ātum vt to enlarge; (law) to adjourn.

ampliter adv see **amplūs**.

amplitūdō, -inis f size; (fig) distinction; (RHET) fullness.

amplius adv more (esp amount or number), further, longer; ~ **ducentī** more than 200; ~ **nōn petere** take no further legal action; ~ **prōnūntiāre** adjourn a case.

amplūs adj large, spacious; great, abundant; powerful, splendid, eminent; (sup) distinguished.

ampulla, -ae f a two-handled flask; (fig) high-flown language.

ampullārius, -ārī m flask-maker.

ampullor, -ārī vi to use high-flown language.

amputātiō, -ōnis f pruning.

amputatus adj (RHET) disconnected.

amputō, -āre, -āvī, -ātum vt to cut off, prune; (fig) to lop off.

Amūlius, -ī m king of Alba Longa, grand-uncle of Romulus.

amurca, -ae f lees of olive oil.

amussitātus adj nicely adjusted.

Amȳclae, -ārum fpl town in S. Greece.

Amȳclaeus adj see n.

amygdalum, -ī nt almond.

amystis, -dis f emptying a cup at a draught.

an conj or; perhaps; (with single question) surely not; **haud sciō** ~ I feel sure.

Anacreōn, -ontis m Greek lyric poet.

anadēma, -tis nt headband.

anagnōstēs, -ae m reader.

anapaestum, -ī nt poem in anapaests.

anapaestus adj: ~ **pēs** anapaest.

anas, -tis f duck.

anaticula f duckling.

anatīnus adj see n.

anatocismus, -ī m compound interest.

Anaxagorās, -ae m early Greek philosopher.

Anaximander, -rī m early Greek philosopher.

anceps, -ipitis adj two-headed; double; wavering, doubtful; dangerous ♦ nt danger.

Anchīsēs, -ae m father of Aeneas.

Anchīsēus adj see n.

Anchīsiadēs m Aeneas.

ancīle, -is nt oval shield (esp one said to have fallen from heaven in Numa's reign).

ancilla, -ae f servant.

ancillāris adj of a young servant.

ancillula f young servant.

ancīsus adj cut round.

ancora, -ae f anchor.

ancorārius adj see n.

ancorāle, -is nt cable.

Ancus Marcius, -ī, -ī m 4th king of Rome.

Ancȳra, -ae f Ankara (capital of Galatia).

andabata, -ae m blindfold gladiator.

Andrius adj see Andros.

androgynē, -ēs f hermaphrodite.

androgynus, -ī m hermaphrodite.

Andromachē, -ēs f wife of Hector.

Andromeda, -ae f wife of Perseus; a constellation.

Andronicus, -ī m Livius (earliest Latin poet).

Andros (-us), -ī m Aegean island.

ānellus, -ī m little ring.

anēthum, -ī nt fennel.

ānfrāctus, -ūs m bend, orbit; roundabout way; (words) digression, prolixity.

angelus, -ī m angel.

angina, -ae f quinsy.

angiportum, -ī nt alley.

angiportus, -ūs m alley.

Noun declensions and verb conjugations are shown on pp xiii to xxv. The present infinitive ending of a verb shows to which conjugation it belongs: -**āre** = 1st; -**ēre** = 2nd; -**ere** = 3rd and -**īre** = 4th. Irregular verbs are shown on p xxvi

angō, -ere _vt_ to throttle; (_fig_) to distress, torment.

angor, -ōris _m_ suffocation; (_fig_) anguish, torment.

anguicomus _adj_ with snakes for hair.

anguiculus, -ī _m_ small snake.

anguifer, -ī _adj_ snake-carrying.

anguigena, -ae _m_ one born of serpents; Theban.

anguīlla, -ae _f_ eel.

anguimanus _adj_ with a trunk.

anguipēs, -edis _adj_ serpent-footed.

anguis, -is _m/f_ snake, serpent; (_constellation_) Draco.

Anguitenēns, -entis _m_ Ophiuchus.

angulātus _adj_ angular.

angulus, -ī _m_ angle, corner; out-of-the-way place; **ad parēs ~ōs** at right angles.

angustē _adv_ close, within narrow limits; concisely.

angustiae, -ārum _fpl_ defile, strait; (_time_) shortness; (_means_) want; (_circs_) difficulty; (_mind_) narrowness; (_words_) subtleties.

angusticlāvius _adj_ wearing a narrow purple stripe.

angustō, -āre _vt_ to make narrow.

angustum, -ī _nt_ narrowness; danger.

angustus _adj_ narrow, close; (_time_) short; (_means_) scanty; (_mind_) mean; (_argument_) subtle; (_circs_) difficult.

anhēlitus, -ūs _m_ panting; breath, exhalation.

anhēlō, -āre, -āvī, -ātum _vi_ to breathe hard, pant; to exhale.

anhēlus _adj_ panting.

anicula, -ae _f_ poor old woman.

Aniēnsis, Aniēnus _adj_ of the river Anio.

Aniēnus _m_ Anio.

anīlis _adj_ of an old woman.

anīlitās, -tātis _f_ old age.

anīliter _adv_ like an old woman.

anima, -ae _f_ wind, air; breath; life; soul, mind; ghost, spirit; **~am agere, efflāre** expire; **~am comprimere** hold one's breath.

animadversiō, -ōnis _f_ observation; censure, punishment.

animadversor, -ōris _m_ observer.

animadvertō, -tere, -tī, -sum _vt_ to pay attention to, notice; to realise; to censure, punish; **~ in** punish.

animal, -ālis _nt_ animal; living creature.

animālis _adj_ of air; animate.

animāns, -antis _m/f/nt_ living creature; animal.

animātiō, -ōnis _f_ being.

animātus _adj_ disposed, in a certain frame of mind; courageous.

animō, -āre, -āvī, -ātum _vt_ to animate; to give a certain temperament to.

animōsē _adv_ boldly, eagerly.

animōsus _adj_ airy; lifelike; courageous, proud.

animula, -ae _f_ little soul.

animulus, -ī _m_ darling.

animus, -ī _m_ mind, soul; consciousness; reason, thought, opinion, imagination; heart, feelings, disposition; courage, spirit, pride, passion; will, purpose; term of endearment; **~ī** in mind, in heart; **~ī causā** for amusement; **~ō fingere** imagine; **~ō male est** I am fainting; **aequō ~ō esse** be patient, calm; **bonō ~ō esse** take courage; be well-disposed; **ex ~ō** sincerely; **ex ~ō effluere** be forgotten; **in ~ō habēre** purpose; **meō ~ō** in my opinion.

Aniō, -ēnis _m tributary of the Tiber._

Anna Perenna, -ae, -ae _f Roman popular goddess._

annālēs, -ium _mpl_ annals, chronicle.

annālis _adj_ of a year; **lēx ~** law prescribing ages for public offices.

anne _etc see_ **an**.

anniculus _adj_ a year old.

anniversārius _adj_ annual.

annōn or not.

annōna, -ae _f_ year's produce; grain; price of corn; the market.

annōsus _adj_ aged.

annōtinus _adj_ last year's.

annus, -ī _m_ year; **~ māgnus** astronomical great year; **~ solidus** a full year.

annuus _adj_ a year's; annual.

anquīrō, -rere, -sīvī, -sītum _vt_ to search for; to make inquiries; (_law_) to institute an inquiry (_dē_) _or_ prosecution (_abl or gen_).

ānsa, -ae _f_ handle; (_fig_) opportunity.

ānsātus _adj_ with a handle; (_comedy_) with arms akimbo.

ānser, -is _m_ goose.

ānserīnus _adj see_ **n**.

ante _prep_ (_with acc_) before (_in time, place, comparison_) ♦ _adv_ (_place_) in front; (_time_) before.

anteā _adv_ before, formerly.

antecapiō, -apere, -ēpī, -eptum _vt_ to take beforehand, anticipate.

antecēdō, -ēdere, -essī, -essum _vt_ to precede; to surpass.

antecellō, -ere _vi_ to excel, be superior.

anteceptus _ppp of_ **antecapiō**.

antecessiō, -ōnis _f_ preceding; antecedent cause.

antecessor, -ōris _m_ forerunner.

antecursor, -ōris _m_ forerunner, pioneer.

anteeō, -īre, -iī _vi_ to precede, surpass.

anteferō, -ferre, -tulī, -lātum _vt_ to carry before; to prefer; to anticipate.

antefīxus _adj_ attached (in front) ♦ _ntpl_ ornaments on roofs of buildings.

antegredior, -dī, -ssus _vt_ to precede.

antehabeō, -ēre _vt_ to prefer.

antehāc _adv_ formerly, previously.

antelātus _ppp of_ **anteferō**.

antelūcānus _adj_ before dawn.

antemerīdiānus _adj_ before noon.

antemittō, -ittere, -īsī, -issum _vt_ to send on in front.

antenna, -ae _f_ yardarm.

antepīlānī, -ōrum *mpl* (MIL) the front ranks.
antepōno, -ōnere, -osuī, -ositum *vt* to set before; to prefer.
antequam *conj* before.
Anterōs, -ōtis *m* avenger of slighted love.
antēs, -ium *mpl* rows.
antesignānus, -ī *m* (MIL) leader; (*pl*) defenders of the standards.
antestō, antistō, -āre, -ētī *vi* to excel, distinguish oneself.
antestor, -ārī, -ātus *vi* to call a witness.
anteveniō, -enīre, -ēnī, -entum *vt, vi* to anticipate; to surpass.
antevertō, -tere, -tī, -sum *vt* to precede; to anticipate; to prefer.
anticipātiō, -ōnis *f* foreknowledge.
anticipō, -āre, -āvī, -ātum *vt* to take before, anticipate.
anticus *adj* in front.
Antigonē, -ēs *f* daughter of Oedipus.
Antigonus, -ī *m* name of Macedonian kings.
Antiochēnsis *adj see n.*
Antiochīa, -īae *f* Antioch (*capital of Syria*).
Antiochus, -ī *m* name of kings of Syria.
antīquārius, -ī *and* **īī** *m* antiquary.
antīquē *adv* in the old style.
antīquitās, -ātis *f* antiquity, the ancients; integrity.
antīquitus *adv* long ago, from ancient times.
antīquō, -āre, -āvī, -ātum *vt* to vote against (a bill).
antīquus *adj* ancient, former, old; good old-fashioned, honest, illustrious; **antīquior** more important; **antīquissimus** most important.
antistēs, -itis *m/f* high priest, chief priestess; (*fig*) master (*in any art*).
Antisthenēs, -is *and* **ae** *m* founder of Cynic philosophy.
antistita, -ae *f* chief priestess.
antistō *etc see* **antestō.**
antitheton, -ī *nt* (RHET) antithesis.
Antōnīnus, -ī *m* name of Roman emperors (*esp Pius and Marcus Aurelius*).
Antōnius, -ī *m* Roman name (*esp the famous orator, and Mark Antony*).
antrum, -ī *nt* cave, hollow.
ānulārius, -i *m* ringmaker.
ānulātus *adj* with rings on.
ānulus, -ī *m* ring; equestrian rank.
ānus, -ī *m* rectum; ring.
anus, -ūs *f* old woman ♦ *adj* old.
ānxiē *adv see* **anxius.**
ānxietās, -ātis *f* anxiety, trouble (*of the mind*).
ānxifer, -ī *adj* disquieting.
ānxitūdō, -inis *f* anxiety.
ānxius *adj* (*mind*) troubled; disquieting.
Āones, -um *adj* Boeotian.
Āonia *f* part of Boeotia.
Āonius *adj* of Boeotia, of Helicon.

Aornos, -ī *m* lake Avernus.
apage *interj* away with!, go away!
apēliōtēs, -ae *m* east wind.
Apellēs, -is *m* Greek painter.
aper, -rī *m* boar.
aperiō, -īre, -uī, -tum *vt* to uncover, disclose, open; (*country*) to open up; (*fig*) to unfold, explain, reveal.
apertē *adv* clearly, openly.
apertum, -ī *nt* open space; **in ~ō esse** be well known; be easy.
apertus *ppp of* **aperiō** ♦ *adj* open, exposed; clear, manifest; (*person*) frank.
aperuī *perf of* **aperiō.**
apex, -icis *m* summit; crown, priest's cap; (*fig*) crown.
aphractus, -ī *f* a long open boat.
apiārius, -ī *and* **īī** *m* beekeeper.
Apīcius, -ī *m* Roman epicure.
apicula, -ae *f* little bee.
apis, -is *f* bee.
apiscor, -iscī, -tus *vt* to catch, get, attain.
apium, -ī *and* **īī** *nt* celery.
aplustre, -is *nt* decorated stern of a ship.
apoclētī, -ōrum *mpl* committee of the Aetolian League.
apodytērium, -ī *and* **īī** *nt* dressing room.
Apollināris, -ineus *adj*: **lūdī ~ināres** Roman games in July.
Apollō, -inis *m* Greek god of music, archery, prophecy, flocks and herds, and often identified with the sun.
apologus, -ī *m* narrative, fable.
apophorēta, -ōrum *ntpl* presents for guests to take home.
apoproēgmena, -ōrum *ntpl* (PHILOS) what is rejected.
apostolicus *adj see n.*
apostolus, -ī *m* (ECCL) apostle.
apothēca, -ae *f* storehouse, wine store.
apparātē *adv see* **apparātus.**
apparātiō, -ōnis *f* preparation.
apparātus *adj* ready, well-supplied, sumptuous.
apparātus, -ūs *m* preparation; equipment, munitions; pomp, ostentation.
appāreō, -ēre, -uī, -itum *vi* to come in sight, appear; to be seen, show oneself; to wait upon (*an official*); **~et** it is obvious.
appāritiō, -ōnis *f* service; domestic servants.
appāritor, -ōris *m* attendant.
apparō, -āre, -āvī, -ātum *vt* to prepare, provide.
appellātiō, -ōnis *f* accosting, appeal; title; pronunciation.
appellātor, -ōris *m* appellant.
appellitātus *adj* usually called.
appellō, -āre, -āvī, -ātum *vt* to speak to; to appeal to; (*for money*) to dun; (*law*) to sue; to call, name; to pronounce.

Noun declensions and verb conjugations are shown on pp xiii to xxv. The present infinitive ending of a verb shows to which conjugation it belongs: **-āre** = 1st; **-ēre** = 2nd; **-ere** = 3rd and **-īre** = 4th. Irregular verbs are shown on p xxvi

appellō, -ellere, -ulī, -ulsum *vt* to drive, bring (to); (*NAUT*) to bring to land.
appendicula, -ae *f* small addition.
appendix, -icis *f* supplement.
appendō, -endere, -endī, -ensum *vt* to weigh, pay.
appetēns, -entis *adj* eager; greedy.
appetenter *adv see* **appetēns.**
appetentia, -ae *f* craving.
appetītiō, -ōnis *f* grasping, craving.
appetītus *ppp of* **appetō.**
appetītus, -ūs *m* craving; natural desire (*as opposed to reason*).
appetō, -ere, -īvī, -ītum *vt* to grasp, try to get at; to attack; to desire ♦ *vi* to approach.
appingō, -ere *vt* to paint (in); (*colloq*) to write more.
Appius, -ī *m* Roman first name; **Via ~ia** *main road from Rome to Capua and Brundisium.*
applaudō, -dere, -sī, -sum *vt* to strike, clap ♦ *vi* to applaud.
applicātiō, -ōnis *f* applying (*of the mind*); **iūs ~ōnis** *the right of a patron to inherit a client's effects.*
applicātus *and* **itus** *ppp of* **applicō.**
applicō, -āre, -āvī *and* **uī, -ātum** *and* **itum** *vt* to attach, place close (to); (*NAUT*) to steer, bring to land; **sē, animum ~** devote self, attention (to).
applōrō, -āre *vt* to deplore.
appōnō, -ōnere, -osuī, -ositum *vt* to put (to, beside); (*meal*) to serve; to add, appoint; to reckon.
apporrēctus *adj* stretched nearby.
apportō, -āre, -āvī, -ātum *vt* to bring, carry (to).
apposcō, -ere *vt* to demand also.
appositē *adv* suitably.
appositus *ppp of* **appōnō** ♦ *adj* situated near; (*fig*) bordering on; suitable.
apposuī *perf of* **appōnō.**
appōtus *adj* drunk.
apprecor, -ārī, -ātus *vt* to pray to.
apprehendō, -endere, -endī, -ēnsum *vt* to take hold of; (*MIL*) to occupy; (*argument*) to bring forward.
apprīmē *adv* especially.
apprimō, -imere, -essī, -essum *vt* to press close.
approbātiō, -ōnis *f* acquiescence; proof.
approbātor, -ōris *m* approve.
approbē *adv* very well.
approbō, -āre, -āvī, -ātum *vt* to approve; to prove; to perform to someone's satisfaction.
apprōmittō, -ere *vt* to promise also.
approperō, -āre, -āvī, -ātum *vt* to hasten ♦ *vi* to hurry up.
appropinquātiō, -ōnis *f* approach.
appropinquō, -āre, -āvī, -ātum *vi* to approach.
appugnō, -āre *vt* to attack.
appulsus *ppp of* **appellō.**
appulsus, -ūs *m* landing; approach.

aprīcātiō, -ōnis *f* basking.
aprīcor, -ārī *vi* to bask.
aprīcus *adj* sunny; basking; **in ~um prōferre** bring to light.
Aprīlis *adj* April, of April.
aprūgnus *adj* of the wild boar.
aps- *etc see* **abs-.**
aptē *adv* closely; suitably, rightly.
aptō, -āre, -āvī, -ātum *vt* to fit, put on; (*fig*) to adapt; to prepare, equip.
aptus *adj* attached, joined together, fitted (with); suitable.
apud *prep* (*with acc*) 1. (*with persons*) beside, by, with, at the house of, among, in the time of; (*speaking*) in the presence of, to; (*judgment*) in the opinion of; (*influence*) with; (*faith*) in; (*authors*) in. 2. (*with places*) near, at, in; **est ~ mē** I have; **sum ~ mē** I am in my senses.
Āpūlia, -iae *f* district of S.E. Italy.
Āpūlus *adj see n.*
aput *prep see* **apud.**
aqua, -ae *f* water; **~ mihī haeret** I am in a fix; **~ intercus** dropsy; **~m adspergere** revive; **~m praebēre** entertain; **~m et terram petere** demand submission; **~ā et ignī interdīcere** outlaw.
aquae *fpl* medicinal waters, spa.
aquaeductus, -ūs *m* aqueduct; right of leading water.
aquāliculus *m* belly.
aquālis, -is *m/f* washbasin.
aquārius *adj* of water ♦ *m* water carrier, water inspector; a constellation.
aquāticus *adj* aquatic; humid.
aquātilis *adj* aquatic.
aquātiō, -ōnis *f* fetching water; watering place.
aquātor, -ōris *m* water carrier.
aquila, -ae *f* eagle; standard of a legion; (*ARCH*) gable; a constellation; **~ae senectūs** a vigorous old age.
Aquileia, -ae *f* town in N. Italy.
Aquileiēnsis *adj see n.*
aquilifer, -ī *m* chief standard-bearer.
aquilīnus *adj* eagle's.
aquilō, -ōnis *m* north wind; north.
aquilōnius *adj* northerly.
aquilus *adj* swarthy.
Aquīnās, ātis *adj see n.*
Aquīnum, -ī *nt* town in Latium.
Aquītānia, -iae *f* district of S.W. Gaul.
Aquītānus *adj see n.*
aquor, -ārī, -ātus *vi* to fetch water.
aquōsus *adj* humid, rainy.
aquula, -ae *f* little stream.
āra, -ae *f* altar; (*fig*) refuge; a constellation; **~ae et focī** hearth and home.
arabarchēs, -ae *m* customs officer in Egypt.
Arabia, -iae *f* Arabia.
Arabicē *adv* with all the perfumes of Arabia.
Arabicus, Arabicius, Arabus *adj see n.*
Arachnē, -s *f* Lydian woman changed into a spider.

arānea, -ae f spider; cobweb.

arāneola f, **-olus** m small spider.

arāneōsus adj full of spiders' webs.

arāneum, -ī nt spider's web.

arāneus, -ī m spider ♦ adj of spiders.

Arar, -is m river Saône.

Arātēus adj see **Arātus**.

arātiō, -ōnis f ploughing, farming; arable land.

arātiuncula f small plot.

arātor -ōris m ploughman, farmer; (pl) cultivators of public land.

arātrum, -ī nt plough.

Arātus, -ī m Greek astronomical poet.

Araxēs, -is m river in Armenia.

arbiter, -rī m witness; arbiter, judge, umpire; controller; ~ **bibendī** president of a drinking party.

arbitra, -ae f witness.

arbitrāriō adv with some uncertainty.

arbitrārius adj uncertain.

arbitrātus, -ūs m decision; **meō ~ū** in my judgment.

arbitrium, -ī and iī nt decision (of an arbitrator), judgment; mastery, control.

arbitror, -ārī, -ātus vt, vi to be a witness of; to testify; to think, suppose.

arbor, (arbōs), -oris f tree; ship, mast, oar; ~ **īnfēlīx** gallows.

arboreus adj of trees, like a tree.

arbustum, -ī nt plantation, orchard; (pl) trees.

arbustus adj wooded.

arbuteus adj of the strawberry tree.

arbutum, -ī nt fruit of strawberry tree.

arbutus, -ī f strawberry tree.

arca, -ae f box; moneybox, purse; coffin; prison cell; **ex ~ā absolvere** pay cash.

Arcadēs, -um mpl Arcadians.

Arcadia, -iae f district of S. Greece.

Arcadicus, -ius adj see **Arcadia**.

arcānō adv privately.

arcānum, -ī nt secret, mystery.

arcānus adj secret; able to keep secrets.

arceō, -ēre, -uī, -tum vt to enclose; to keep off, prevent.

accessitū abl sg m at the summons.

accessītus ppp of **accessō** ♦ adj far-fetched.

accessō, -ere, -īvī, -ītum vt to send for, fetch; (law) to summon, accuse; (fig) to derive.

archetypus, -ī m original.

Archilochus, -ī m Greek iambic and elegiac poet.

archimagīrus, -ī m chief cook.

Archimēdēs, -is m famous mathematician of Syracuse.

archipīrāta, -ae m pirate chief.

architectōn, -onis m master builder; master in cunning.

architector, -ārī, -ātus vt to construct; (fig) to devise.

architectūra, -ae f architecture.

architectus, -ī m architect; (fig) author.

archōn, -ontis m Athenian magistrate.

Archytās, -ae m Pythagorean philosopher of Tarentum.

arcitenēns, -entis adj holding a bow ♦ m Apollo.

Arctophylax, -cis m (constellation) Bootes.

arctos, -ī f Great Bear, Little Bear; north, north wind; night.

Arctūrus, -ī m brightest star in Boötes.

arctus etc see **artus** etc.

arcuī perf of **arceō**.

arcula, -ae f casket; (RHET) ornament.

arcuō, -āre, -āvī, -ātum vt to curve.

arcus, -ūs m bow; rainbow; arch, curve; (MATH) arc.

ardea, -ae f heron.

Ardea, -ae f town in Latium.

ardeliō, -ōnis m busybody.

ārdēns, -entis adj hot, glowing, fiery; (fig) eager, ardent.

ārdenter adv passionately.

ārdeō, -dēre, -sī, -sum vi to be on fire, burn, shine; (fig) to be fired, burn.

ārdēscō, -ere vi to catch fire, gleam; (fig) to become inflamed, wax hotter.

ārdor, -ōris m heat, brightness; (fig) ardour, passion.

arduum, -ī nt steep slope; difficulty.

arduus adj steep, high; difficult, troublesome.

ārea, -ae f vacant site, open space, playground; threshing-floor; (fig) scope (for effort).

ārefaciō, -acere, -ēcī, -actum vt to dry.

arēna etc see **harēna**.

ārēns, -entis adj arid; thirsty.

āreō, -ēre vi to be dry.

āreola, -ae f small open space.

Arēopagītēs m member of the court.

Arēopagus, -ī m Mars' Hill in Athens; a criminal court.

Arēs, -is m Greek god of war.

ārēscō, -ere vi to dry, dry up.

Arestoridēs, -ae m Argus.

aretālogus, -ī m braggart.

Arethūsa, -ae f spring near Syracuse.

Arethūsis adj Syracusan.

Argēī, -ōrum mpl sacred places in Rome; effigies thrown annually into the Tiber.

argentāria, -ae f bank, banking; silver mine.

argentārius adj of silver, of money ♦ m banker.

argentātus adj silver-plated; backed with money.

argenteus adj of silver, adorned with silver; silvery (in colour); of the silver age.

argentum, -ī nt silver, silver plate; money.

Argēus, -īvus, -olicus adj Argive; Greek.

Argīlētānus adj see n.

Argīlētum, -ī nt part of Rome (noted for

bookshops).

argilla, -ae _f_ clay.

Argō, -ūs _f_ Jason's ship.

Argolis, -olidis _f_ district about Argos.

Argonautae, -ārum _mpl_ Argonauts.

Argonauticus _adj see_ n.

Argos _nt_, **-ī, -ōrum** _mpl_ town in S.E. Greece.

Argōus _adj see_ **Argō**.

argūmentātiō, -ōnis _f_ adducing proofs.

argūmentor, -ārī, -ātus _vt, vi_ to prove, adduce as proof; to conclude.

argūmentum, -ī _nt_ evidence, proof; (_LIT_) subject matter, theme, plot (_of a play_); (_art_) subject, motif.

arguō, -uere, -uī, -ūtum _vt_ to prove, make known; to accuse, blame, denounce.

Argus, -ī _m_ monster with many eyes.

argūtē _adv_ subtly.

argūtiae, -ārum _fpl_ nimbleness, liveliness; wit, subtlety, slyness.

argūtor, -ārī, -ātus _vi_ to chatter.

argūtulus _adj_ rather subtle.

argūtus _adj_ (_sight_) clear, distinct, graceful; (_sound_) clear, melodious, noisy; (_mind_) acute, witty, sly.

argyraspis, -dis _adj_ silver-shielded.

Ariadna, -ae _f_ daughter of Minos of Crete.

Ariadnaeus _adj see_ n.

āridulus _adj_ rather dry.

āridum, -ī _nt_ dry land.

āridus _adj_ dry, withered; meagre; (_style_) flat.

ariēs, -etis _m_ ram; 1st sign of Zodiac; battering ram; beam used as a breakwater.

arietō, -āre _vt, vi_ to butt, strike hard.

Ariōn, -onis _m_ early Greek poet and musician.

Ariōnius _adj see_ n.

arista, -ae _f_ ear of corn.

Aristaeus, -ī _m_ legendary founder of beekeeping.

Aristarchus, -ī _m_ Alexandrian scholar; a severe critic.

Aristīdēs, -is _m_ Athenian statesman noted for integrity.

Aristippēus _adj see_ n.

Aristippus, -ī _m_ Greek hedonist philosopher.

aristolochia, -ae _f_ birthwort.

Aristophanēs, -is _m_ Greek comic poet.

Aristophanēus, and īus _adj see_ n.

Aristotelēs, -is _m_ Aristotle (_founder of Peripatetic school of philosophy_).

Aristotelēus, and īus _adj see_ n.

arithmētica, -ōrum _ntpl_ arithmetic.

āritūdō, -inis _f_ dryness.

Ariūsius _adj_ of Ariusia in Chios.

arma, -ōrum _ntpl_ armour, shield; arms, weapons (_of close combat only_); warfare, troops; (_fig_) defence, protection; implements, ship's gear.

armāmenta, -ōrum _ntpl_ implements, ship's gear.

armāmentārium, -ī and iī _nt_ arsenal.

armāriolum, -ī _nt_ small chest.

armārium, -ī and iī _nt_ chest, safe.

armātū _m abl_ armour; **gravī ~** with heavy-armed troops.

armātūra, -ae _f_ armour, equipment; **levis ~** light-armed troops.

armātus _adj_ armed.

Armenia, -ae _f_ Armenia.

Armeniaca, -acae _f_ apricot tree.

Armeniacum, -acī _nt_ apricot.

Armenius _adj see_ **Armenia**.

armentālis _adj_ of the herd.

armentārius, -ī and iī _m_ cattle herd.

armentum, -ī _nt_ cattle (_for ploughing_), herd (_cattle etc_).

armifer, -ī _adj_ armed.

armiger, -ī _m_ armour-bearer ♦ _adj_ armed; productive of warriors.

armilla, -ae _f_ bracelet.

armillātus _adj_ wearing a bracelet.

armipotēns, -entis _adj_ strong in battle.

armisonus _adj_ resounding with arms.

armō, -āre, -āvī, -ātum _vt_ to arm, equip; to rouse to arms (against).

armus, -ī _m_ shoulder (_esp of animals_).

Arniēnsis _adj see_ **Arnus**.

Arnus, -ī _m_ river Arno.

arō, -āre, -āvī, -ātum _vt_ to plough, cultivate; to live by farming; (_fig: sea, brow_) to furrow.

Arpīnās, -ātis _adj see_ n.

Arpīnum, -ī _nt_ town in Latium (_birthplace of Cicero_).

arquātus _adj_ jaundiced.

arr- _etc see_ **adr-**.

arrabō, -ōnis _m_ earnest money.

ars, artis _f_ skill (_in any craft_); the art (_of any profession_); science, theory; handbook; work of art; moral quality, virtue; artifice, fraud.

ārsī _perf of_ **ārdeō**.

ārsus _ppp of_ **ārdeō**.

artē _adv_ closely, soundly, briefly.

artēria, -ae _f_ windpipe; artery.

artēria, -ōrum _ntpl_ trachea.

arthrīticus _adj_ gouty.

articulātim _adv_ joint by joint; (_speech_) distinctly.

articulō, -āre, -āvī, -ātum _vt_ to articulate.

articulōsus _adj_ minutely subdivided.

articulus, -ī _m_ joint, knuckle; limb; (_words_) clause; (_time_) point, turning point; **in ipsō ~ō temporis** in the nick of time.

artifex, -icis _m_ artist, craftsman, master; (_fig_) maker, author ♦ _adj_ ingenious, artistic, artificial.

artificiōsē _adv_ skilfully.

artificiōsus _adj_ ingenious, artistic, artificial.

artificium, -ī and iī _nt_ skill, workmanship; art, craft; theory, rule of an art; ingenuity, cunning.

artō, -āre _vt_ to compress, curtail.

artolaganus, -ī _m_ kind of cake.

artopta, -ae _m_ baker; baking tin.

artus _adj_ close, narrow, tight; (_sleep_) deep; (_fig_) strict, straitened.

artus, -ūs _m_ joint; (_pl_) limbs, body; (_fig_) strength.

ārula, -ae f small altar.
arundō etc see **harundō** etc.
arvīna, -ae f grease.
arvum, -ī nt field; land, country, plain.
arvus adj ploughed.
arx, arcis f fortress, castle; height, summit; (fig) bulwark, stronghold; **arcem facere ē cloācā** make a mountain out of a molehill.
ās, assis m (weight) pound; (coin) bronze unit, of low value; (inheritance) the whole (subdivided into 12 parts); **ad assem** to the last farthing; **hērēs ex asse** sole heir.
Ascānius, -ī m son of Aeneas.
ascendō, -endere, -endī, -ēnsum vt, vi to go up, climb, embark; (fig) to rise.
ascēnsiō, -ōnis f ascent; (fig) sublimity.
ascēnsus, -ūs m ascent, rising; way up.
ascia, -ae f axe; mason's trowel.
asciō, -īre vt to admit.
ascīscō, -īscere, -īvī, -ītum vt to receive with approval; to admit (to some kind of association); to appropriate, adopt (esp customs); to arrogate to oneself.
ascītus adj acquired, alien.
Ascra, -ae f birthplace of Hesiod in Boeotia.
Ascraeus adj of Ascra; of Hesiod; of Helicon.
ascrībō, -bere, -psī, -ptum vt to add (in writing); to attribute, ascribe; to apply (an illustration); to enrol, include.
ascrīptīcius adj enrolled.
ascrīptiō, -ōnis f addition (in writing).
ascrīptīvus adj (MIL) supernumerary.
ascrīptor, -ōris m supporter.
ascrīptus ppp of **ascrībō**.
asella, -ae f young ass.
asellus, -ī m young ass.
Asia, -ae f Roman province; Asia Minor; Asia.
asīlus, -ī m gad fly.
Asis, -dis f Asia.
Āsius (Āsiānus, Āsiāticus) adj see n.
Āsōpus, -ī m river in Boeotia.
asōtus, -ī m libertine.
asparagus, -ī m asparagus.
aspargō etc see **aspergō**.
aspectābilis adj visible.
aspectō, -āre vt to look at, gaze at; to pay heed to; (places) to face.
aspectus ppp of **aspiciō**.
aspectus, -ūs m look, sight; glance, sense of sight; aspect, appearance.
aspellō, -ere vt to drive away.
asper, -ī adj rough; (taste) bitter; (sound) harsh; (weather) severe; (style) rugged; (person) violent, exasperated, unkind, austere; (animal) savage; (CIRCS) difficult.
asperē adv see adj.
aspergō, -gere, -sī, -sum vt to scatter, sprinkle; to bespatter, besprinkle; **aquam ~** revive.
aspergō, -inis f sprinkling; spray.

asperitās, -ātis f roughness, unevenness, harshness, severity; (fig) ruggedness, fierceness; trouble, difficulty.
aspernātiō, -ōnis f disdain.
aspernor, -ārī, -ātus vt to reject, disdain.
asperō, -āre, -āvī, -ātum vt to roughen, sharpen; to exasperate.
aspersiō, -ōnis f sprinkling.
aspersus ppp of **aspergō**.
aspiciō, -icere, -exī, -ectum vt to catch sight of, look at; (places) to face; (fig) to examine, consider.
aspīrātiō, -ōnis f breathing (on); evaporation; pronouncing with an aspirate.
aspīrō, -āre, -āvī, -ātum vi to breathe, blow; to favour; to aspire, attain (to) ♦ vt to blow, instil.
aspis, -dis f asp.
asportātiō, -ōnis f removal.
asportō, -āre vt to carry off.
asprēta, -ōrum ntpl rough country.
ass- etc see **ads-**.
Assaracus, -ī m Trojan ancestor of Aeneas.
asser, -is m pole, stake.
assula, -ae f splinter.
assulātim adv in splinters.
assum, -ī nt roast; (pl) sweating-bath.
assus adj roasted.
Assyria, -ae f country in W. Asia.
Assyrius adj Assyrian; oriental.
ast conj (laws) and then; (vows) then; (strong contrast) and yet.
ast- etc see **adst-**.
Astraea, -ae f goddess of Justice.
Astraeus, -ī m father of winds; **~ī frātrēs** the winds.
astrologia, -ae f astronomy.
astrologus, -ī m astronomer; astrologer.
astrum, -ī nt star, heavenly body, constellation; a great height; heaven, immortality, glory.
astu nt (indecl) city (esp Athens).
astus, -ūs m cleverness, cunning.
astūtē adv cleverly.
astūtia, -ae f slyness, cunning.
astūtus adj artful, sly.
Astyanax, -ctis m son of Hector and Andromache.
asȳlum, -ī nt sanctuary.
asymbolus adj with no contribution.
at conj (adversative) but, on the other hand; (objecting) but it may be said; (limiting) at least, but at least; (continuing) then, thereupon; (transitional) now; (with passionate appeals) but oh!, look now!; **~ enim** yes, but; **~ tamen** nevertheless.
Atābulus, -ī m sirocco.
atat interj (expressing fright, pain, surprise) oh!
atavus, -ī m great-great-great-grandfather; ancestor.

Noun declensions and verb conjugations are shown on pp xiii to xxv. The present infinitive ending of a verb shows to which conjugation it belongs: **-āre** = 1st; **-ēre** = 2nd; **-ere** = 3rd and **-īre** = 4th. Irregular verbs are shown on p xxvi

Atella, -ae *f Oscan town in Campania.*
Ātellānicus, Atellānius *adj see n.*
Atellānus *adj:* **fābula ~āna** *kind of comic show popular in Rome.*
āter, -rī *adj* black, dark; gloomy, dismal; malicious; **diēs ~rī** unlucky days.
Athamantēus *adj see* **Athamās.**
Athamantiadēs *m* Palaemon.
Athamantis *f* Helle.
Athamās, -antis *m* king of Thessaly (*who went mad*).
Athēnae, -ārum *fpl* Athens.
Athēnaeus, -iēnsis *adj see n.*
atheos, -ī *m* atheist.
athlēta, -ae *m* wrestler, athlete.
athlēticē *adv* athletically.
Athos (*dat* -ō, *acc* -ō, -on, -ōnem) *m mount Athos in Macedonia.*
Atlanticus *adj:* **mare ~anticum** Atlantic Ocean.
Atlantiadēs *m* Mercury.
Atlantis *f* lost Atlantic island; a Pleiad.
Atlās, -antis *m giant supporting the sky;* Atlas mountains.
atomus, -ī *m* atom.
atque (*before consonants* **ac**) *conj* (*connecting words*) and, and in fact; (*connecting clauses*) and moreover, and then, and so, and yet; (*in comparison*) as, than, to, from; ~ **adeō** and that too; or rather; ~ **nōn** and not rather; ~ **sī** as if; **alius** ~ different from; **contrā** ~ opposite to; **īdem** ~ same as; **plūs** ~ more than.
atquī *conj* (*adversative*) and yet, nevertheless, yes but; (*confirming*) by all means; (*minor premise*) now; ~ **sī** if now.
ātrāmentum, -ī *nt* ink; blacking.
ātrātus *adj* in mourning.
Atreus, -eī *m* son of Pelops (*king of Argos*).
Atrīdēs *m* Agamemnon; Menelaus.
ātriēnsis, -is *m* steward, major-domo.
ātriolum, -ī *nt* anteroom.
ātrium, -ī *and* **iī** *nt* hall, open central room in Roman house; forecourt of a temple; hall (*in other buildings*).
atrōcitās, -ātis *f* hideousness; (*mind*) brutality; (*PHILOS*) severity.
atrōciter *adv* savagely.
Atropos, -ī *f* one of the Fates.
atrōx, -ōcis *adj* hideous, dreadful; fierce, brutal, unyielding.
attāctus *ppp of* **attingō.**
attāctus, -ūs *m* contact.
attagēn, -is *m* heathcock.
Attalica *ntpl* garments of woven gold.
Attalicus *adj* of Attalus; of Pergamum; ornamented with gold cloth.
Attalus, -ī *m* king of Pergamum (*who bequeathed his kingdom to Rome*).
attamen *conj* nevertheless.
attat *etc see* **atat.**
attegia, -ae *f* hut.
attemperātē *adv* opportunely.
attempto *etc see* **attentō.**

attendō, -dere, -dī, -tum *vt* to direct (*the attention*); to attend to, notice.
attenē *adv* carefully.
attentiō, -ōnis *f* attentiveness.
attentō, -āre, -āvī, -ātum *vt* to test, try; (*loyalty*) to tamper with; to attack.
attentus *ppp of* **attendō ♦** *adj* attentive, intent; businesslike, careful (*esp about money*).
attentus *ppp of* **attineō.**
attenuātē *adv* simply.
attenuātus *adj* weak; (*style*) brief; refined; plain.
attenuō, -āre, -āvī, -ātum *vt* to weaken, reduce; to diminish; to humble.
atterō, -erere, -rīvī, -rītum *vt* to rub; to wear away; (*fig*) to impair, exhaust.
attestor, -ārī, -ātus *vt* to confirm.
attexō, -ere, -uī, -tum *vt* to weave on; (*fig*) to add on.
Atthis, -dis *f* Attica.
Attiānus *adj see* **Attius.**
Attica, -ae *f* district of Greece about Athens.
Atticē *adv* in the Athenian manner.
Atticissō *vi* to speak in the Athenian manner.
Atticus *adj* Attic, Athenian; (*RHET*) of a plain and direct style.
attigī *perf of* **attingō.**
attigō *see* **attingō.**
attineō, -inēre, -inuī, -entum *vt* to hold fast, detain; to guard; to reach for ♦ *vi* to concern, pertain, be of importance, avail.
attingō, -ingere, -igī, -āctum *vt* to touch; to strike, assault; to arrive at; to border on; to affect; to mention; to undertake; to concern, resemble.
Attis, -dis *m* Phrygian priest of Cybele.
Attius, -ī *m* Latin tragic poet.
attollō, -ere *vt* to lift up, erect; (*fig*) to exalt, extol.
attondeō, -ondēre, -ondī, -ōnsum *vt* to shear, prune, crop; (*fig*) to diminish; (*comedy*) to fleece.
attonitus *adj* thunderstruck, terrified, astonished; inspired.
attonō, -āre, -uī, -itum *vt* to stupefy.
attōnsus *ppp of* **attondeō.**
attorqueō, -ēre *vt* to hurl upwards.
attractus *ppp of* **attrahō.**
attrahō, -here, -xī, -ctum *vt* to drag by force, attract; (*fig*) to draw, incite.
attrectō, -āre *vt* to touch, handle; to appropriate.
attrepidō, -āre *vi* to hobble along.
attribuō, -uere, -uī, -ūtum *vt* to assign, bestow; to add; to impute, attribute; to lay as a tax.
attribūtiō, -ōnis *f* (*money*) assignment; (*GRAM*) predicate.
attribūtum, -ī *nt* (*GRAM*) predicate.
attribūtus *ppp of* **attribuō ♦** *adj* subject.
attrītus *ppp of* **atterō ♦** *adj* worn; bruised; (*fig*) impudent.
attulī *perf of* **adferō.**

au *interj* (*expressing pain, surprise*) oh!

auceps, -upis *m* fowler; (*fig*) eavesdropper; a pedantic critic.

auctārium, -ī *and* **iī** *nt* extra.

auctificus *adj* increasing.

auctiō, -ōnis *f* increase; auction sale.

auctiōnārius *adj* auction; **tabulae ~ae** catalogues.

auctiōnor, -ārī, -ātus *vi* to hold an auction.

auctitō, -āre *vt* to greatly increase.

auctō, -āre *vt* to increase.

auctor, -ōris *m/f* **1.** (*originator: of families*) progenitor; (: *of buildings*) founder; (: *of deeds*) doer. **2.** (*composer: of writings*) author, historian; (: *of knowledge*) investigator, teacher; (: *of news*) informant. **3.** (*instigator: of action*) adviser; (: *of measures*) promoter; (: *of laws*) proposer, supporter; ratifier. **4.** (*person of influence: in public life*) leader; (: *of conduct*) model; (: *of guarantees*) witness, bail; (: *of property*) seller; (: *of women and minors*) guardian; (: *of others' welfare*) champion; **mē ~ōre** at my suggestion.

auctōrāmentum, -ī *nt* contract; wages.

auctōrātus *adj* bound (*by a pledge*); hired out (*for wages*).

auctōritās, -ātis *f* **1.** source; lead, responsibility. **2.** judgment; opinion; advice, support; bidding, guidance; (*of senate*) decree; (*of people*) will. **3.** power; (*person*) influence, authority, prestige; (*things*) importance, worth; (*conduct*) example; (*knowledge*) warrant, document, authority; (*property*) right of possession.

auctumn- *etc see* **autumn-**.

auctus *ppp of* **augeō** ♦ *adj* enlarged, great.

auctus, -ūs *m* growth, increase.

aucupium, -i *and* **iī** *nt* fowling; birds caught; (*fig*) hunting (after), quibbling.

aucupō, -āre *vt* to watch for.

aucupor, -ārī, -ātus *vi* to go fowling ♦ *vt* to chase; (*fig*) to try to catch.

audācia, -ae *f* daring, courage; audacity, impudence; (*pl*) deeds of daring.

audācter, audāciter *adv see* **audāx**.

audāx, -ācis *adj* bold, daring; rash, audacious; proud.

audēns, -entis *adj* bold, brave.

audenter *adv see* **audēns**.

audentia, -ae *f* boldness, courage.

audeō, -dēre, -sus *vt, vi* to dare, venture; to be brave.

audiēns, -entis *m* hearer ♦ *adj* obedient.

audientia, -ae *f* hearing; **~m facere** gain a hearing.

audiō, -īre, -īvī *and* **iī, -ītum** *vt* to hear; to learn, be told; to be called; to listen, attend to, study under (a teacher); to examine a case; to agree with; to obey, heed; **bene/ male ~** have a good/bad reputation.

audītiō, -ōnis *f* listening; hearsay, news.

audītor, -ōris *m* hearer; pupil.

audītōrium, -i *and* **iī** *nt* lecture room, law court; audience.

audītus, -ūs *m* (sense of) hearing; a hearing; rumour.

auferō, auferre, abstulī, ablātum *vt* to take away, carry away; to mislead, lead into a digression; to take by force, steal; to win, obtain (*as the result of effort*); **aufer** away with!

Aufidus, -ō *m* river in Apulia.

aufugiō, -ugere, -ūgī *vi* to run away ♦ *vt* to flee from.

Augēās, -ae *m* king of Elis (*whose stables Hercules cleaned*).

augeō, -gēre, -xī, -ctum *vt* to increase; to enrich, bless (with); to praise, worship ♦ *vi* to increase.

augēscō, -ere *vi* to begin to grow, increase.

augmen, -inis *nt* growth.

augur, -is *m/f* augur; prophet, interpreter.

augurāle, -is *nt* part of camp where auspices were taken.

augurālis *adj* augur's.

augurātiō, -ōnis *f* soothsaying.

augurātō *adv* after taking auspices.

augurātus, -ūs *m* office of augur.

augurium, -ī *and* **iī** *nt* augury; an omen; prophecy, interpretation; presentiment.

augurius *adj* of augurs.

augurō, -āre *vt, vi* to take auguries; to consecrate by auguries; to forebode.

auguror, -ārī, -ātus *vt, vi* to take auguries; to foretell by omens; to predict, conjecture.

Augusta, -ae *f* title of the emperor's wife, mother, daughter *or* sister.

Augustālis *adj* of Augustus; **lūdī ~ēs** games in October; **praefectus ~is** governor of Egypt; **sodālēs ~ēs** priests of deified Augustus.

augustē *adv see* **augustus**.

augustus *adj* venerable, august, majestic.

Augustus, -ī *m* title given to C Octavius, first Roman emperor, and so to his successors ♦ *adj* imperial; (*month*) August, of August.

aula, -ae *f* courtyard of a Greek house; hall of a Roman house; palace, royal court; courtiers; royal power.

aula *etc see* **olla**.

aulaeum, -ī *nt* embroidered hangings, canopy, covering; (*THEAT*) curtain.

aulicī, -ōrum *mpl* courtiers.

aulicus *adj* of the court.

Aulis, -idis *and* **is** *f* port in Boeotia from which the Greeks sailed for Troy.

auloedus, -ī *m* singer accompanied by flute.

aura, -ae *f* breath of air, breeze, wind; air, upper world; vapour, odour, sound, gleam; (*fig*) winds (*of public favour*), breeze (*of prosperity*), air (*of freedom*), daylight (*of*

Noun declensions and verb conjugations are shown on pp xiii to xxv. The present infinitive ending of a verb shows to which conjugation it belongs: **-āre** = 1st; **-ēre** = 2nd; **-ere** = 3rd and **-īre** = 4th. Irregular verbs are shown on p xxvi

publicity).

aurāria, -ae *f* gold mine.

aurārius *adj* of gold.

aurātus *adj* gilt, ornamented with gold; gold.

Aurēlius, -ī *m* Roman name; **lēx ~ia** *law on the composition of juries*; **via ~ia** *main road running NW from Rome.*

aureolus *adj* gold; beautiful, splendid.

aureus *adj* gold, golden; gilded; (*fig*) beautiful splendid ♦ *m* gold coin.

aurichalcum, -ī *nt* a precious metal.

auricomus *adj* golden-leaved.

auricula, -ae *f* the external ear; ear.

aurifer, -ī *adj* gold-producing.

aurifex, -icis *m* goldsmith.

aurīga, -ae *m* charioteer, driver; groom; helmsman; a constellation.

aurigena, -ae *adj* gold-begotten.

auriger, -ī *adj* gilded.

aurīgō, -āre *vi* to compete in the chariot race.

auris, -is *f* ear; (*RHET*) judgment; (*AGR*) earthboard (*of a plough*); **ad ~em admonēre** whisper; **in utramvis ~em dormīre** sleep soundly.

aurītulus, -ī *m* "Long-Ears".

aurītus *adj* long-eared; attentive.

aurōra, -ae *f* dawn, morning; *goddess of dawn*; the East.

aurum, -ī *nt* gold; gold plate, jewellery, bit, fleece *etc*; money; lustre; the Golden Age.

auscultātiō, -ōnis *f* obedience.

auscultātor, -ōris *m* listener.

auscultō, -āre, -āvī, -ātum *vt* to listen to; to overhear ♦ *vi* (*of servants*) to wait at the door; to obey.

ausim *subj of* **audeō.**

Ausones, -um *mpl* indigenous people of central Italy.

Ausonia *f* Italy.

Ausonidae *mpl* Italians.

Ausonius, -is *adj* Italian.

auspex, -icis *m* augur, soothsayer; patron, commander; witness of a marriage contract.

auspicātō *adv* after taking auspices; at a lucky moment.

auspicātus *adj* consecrated; auspicious, lucky.

auspicium, -ī *and* **iī** *nt* augury, auspices; right of taking auspices; power, command; omen; **~ facere** give a sign.

auspicō, -āre *vi* to take the auspices.

auspicor, -ārī, -ātus *vi* to take the auspices; to make a beginning ♦ *vt* to begin, enter upon.

auster, -rī *m* south wind; south.

austērē *adv see* **austērus.**

austēritās, -ātis *f* severity.

austērus *adj* severe, serious; gloomy, irksome.

austrālis *adj* southern.

austrīnus *adj* from the south.

ausum, -ī *nt* enterprise.

ausus *ppa of* **audeō.**

aut *conj* or; either . . . or; or else *or* at least, or rather.

autem *conj* (*adversative*) but, on the other hand; (*in transitions, parentheses*) moreover, now, and; (*in dialogue*) indeed.

authepsa, -ae *f* stove.

autographus *adj* written with his own hand.

Autolycus, -ī *m* a robber.

automaton, -ī *nt* automaton.

automatus *adj* spontaneous.

Automedōn, -ontis *m* a charioteer.

autumnālis *adj* autumn, autumnal.

autumnus, -ī *m* autumn ♦ *adj* autumnal.

autumō, -āre *vt* to assert.

auxī *perf of* **augeō.**

auxilia, -iōrum *ntpl* auxiliary troops; military force.

auxiliāris *adj* helping, auxiliary; of the auxiliaries ♦ *mpl* auxiliary troops.

auxiliārius *adj* helping; auxiliary.

auxiliātor, -ōris *m* helper.

auxiliātus, -ūs *m* aid.

auxilior, -ārī, -ātus *vi* to aid, support.

auxilium, -ī *and* **iī** *nt* help, assistance.

avārē, avāriter *adv see* **avārus.**

avāritia, -ae *f* greed, selfishness.

avāritiēs, -ēī *f* avarice.

avārus *adj* greedy, covetous; eager.

avē, avēte, avētō *impv* hail!, farewell!

avehō, -here, -xī, -ctum *vt* to carry away; (*pass*) to ride away.

avellō, -ellere, -ellī *and* **ulsī (-olsī), -ulsum (-olsum)** *vt* to pull away, tear off; to take away (by force), remove.

avēna, -ae *f* oats; (*music*) reed, shepherd's pipe.

Aventīnum, -ī *nt* Aventine hill.

Aventīnus, -ī *m* Aventine hill in Rome ♦ *adj* of Aventine.

avēns, -entis *adj* eager.

aveō, -ēre *vt* to desire, long for.

Avernālis *adj* of lake Avernus.

Avernus, -ī *m* lake near Cumae (*said to be an entrance to the lower world*); the lower world ♦ *adj* birdless; of Avernus; infernal.

āverruncō, -āre *vt* to avert.

āversābilis *adj* abominable.

āversor, -ārī, -ātus *vi* to turn away ♦ *vt* to repulse, decline.

āversor, -ōris *m* embezzler.

āversum, -ī *nt* back.

āversus *ppp of* **āvertō** ♦ *adj* in the rear, behind, backwards; hostile, averse.

āvertō, -tere, -tī, -sum *vt* to turn aside, avert; to divert; to embezzle; to estrange ♦ *vi* to withdraw.

avia, -ae *f* grandmother.

avia, -ōrum *ntpl* wilderness.

aviārium, -ī *nt* aviary, haunt of birds.

aviārius *adj* of birds.

avidē *adv see* **avidus.**

aviditās, -ātis *f* eagerness, longing; avarice.

avidus *adj* eager, covetous; avaricious, greedy; hungry; vast.

avis, -is *f* bird; omen; ~ **alba** a rarity.

avītus *adj* of a grandfather; ancestral.

āvius *adj* out of the way, lonely, untrodden; wandering, astray.

āvocāmentum, -ī *nt* relaxation.

āvocātiō, -ōnis *f* diversion.

āvocō, -āre *vt* to call off; to divert, distract; to amuse.

āvolō, -āre *vi* to fly away, hurry away; to depart, vanish.

āvolsus, avulsus *ppp of* **avellō**.

avunculus, -ī *m* uncle (*on mother's side*); ~ **māgnus** great-uncle.

avus, -ī *m* grandfather; ancestor.

Axenus, -ī *m* Black Sea.

axicia, axitia, -ae *f* scissors.

āxilla -ae *f* armpit.

axis, -is *m* axle, chariot; axis, pole, sky, clime; plank.

azȳmus *adj* unleavened.

B, b

babae *interj* (*expressing wonder or joy*) oho!

Babylōn, -ōnis *f* ancient city on the Euphrates.

Babylōnia *f* the country under Babylon.

Babylōnicus, (-)ōniēnsis *adj see n.*

Babylōnius *adj* Babylonian; Chaldaean, versed in astrology.

bāca, -ae *f* berry; olive; fruit; pearl.

bācātus *adj* of pearls.

bacca *etc see* **bāca.**

baccar, -is *nt* cyclamen.

Baccha, -ae *f* Bacchante.

Bacchānal, -ālis *nt* place consecrated to Bacchus; (*pl*) festival of Bacchus.

bacchātiō, -ōnis *f* revel.

Bacchēus, -icus, -ius *adj see n.*

Bacchiadae, -ārum *mpl* kings of Corinth (founders of Syracuse).

bacchor, -ārī, -ātus *vi to celebrate the festival of Bacchus; to revel, rave; to rage.*

Bacchus, -ī *m god of wine, vegetation, poetry, and religious ecstasy; vine, wine.*

bācifer, -ī *adj* olive-bearing.

bacillum, -ī *nt* stick, lictor's staff.

Bactra, -ōrum *ntpl capital of Bactria in central Asia* (*now* Balkh).

Bactriāna *f* Bactria.

Bactriānus *and* **ius** *adj* Bactrian.

baculum, -ī *nt*, **-us, -ī** *m* stick, staff.

Baetica *f* Roman province (*now* Andalusia).

Baeticus *adj see* **Baetis.**

Baetis, -is *m* river in Spain (*now* Guadalquivir).

Bagrada, -ae *m* river in Africa (*now* Mejerdah).

Bāiae, -ārum *fpl Roman spa on Bay of Naples.*

Bāiānus *adj see n.*

bāiulō, -āre *vt* to carry (*something heavy*).

bāiulus, -ī *m* porter.

bālaena, -ae *f* whale.

balanus, -ī *f* balsam (*from an Arabian nut*); a shellfish.

balatrō, -ōnis *m* jester.

bālātus, -ūs *m* bleating.

balbus *adj* stammering.

balbūtiō, -īre *vt, vi* to stammer, speak indistinctly; (*fig*) to speak obscurely.

Baliārēs, -ium *fpl* Balearic islands.

Baliāris, Baliāricus *adj see n.*

balineum *etc see* **balneum** *etc.*

ballista, -ae *f* (MIL) catapult for shooting stones and other missiles; (*fig*) weapon.

ballistārium, -ī *and* **iī** *nt* catapult.

balneae, -ārum *fpl* bath, baths.

balneāria, -ōrum *ntpl* bathroom.

balneārius *adj* of the baths.

balneātor, -ōris *m* bath superintendent.

balneolum, -ī *nt* small bath.

balneum, -ī *nt* bath.

bālō, -āre *vi* to bleat.

balsamum, -ī *nt* balsam, balsam tree.

baltea, -ōrum *ntpl* belt (*esp swordbelt; woman's girdle; strapping*).

balteus, -ī *m* belt (*esp swordbelt; woman's girdle; strapping*).

Bandusia, -ae *f* spring near Horace's birthplace.

baptisma, -tis *nt* baptism.

baptizō, -āre (ECCL) to baptize.

barathrum, -i *nt* abyss; the lower world; (*fig*) a greedy person.

barba, -ae *f* beard.

barbarē *adv* in a foreign language, in Latin; in an uncivilized way; roughly, cruelly.

barbaria, -ae, -ēs *acc, and* **-em** *f* a foreign country (*outside Greece or Italy*); (*words*) barbarism; (*manners*) rudeness, stupidity.

barbaricus *adj* foreign, outlandish; Italian.

barbarus *adj* foreign, barbarous; (*to a Greek*) Italian; rude, uncivilized; savage, barbarous ♦ *m* foreigner, barbarian.

barbātulus *adj* with a little beard.

barbātus *adj* bearded, adult; ancient (Romans); of philosophers.

barbiger, -ī *adj* bearded.

barbitos (*acc* **-on**) *m* lyre, lute.

barbula, -ae *f* little beard.

Barcās, -ae *m* ancestor of Hannibal.

Noun declensions and verb conjugations are shown on pp xiii to xxv. The present infinitive ending of a verb shows to which conjugation it belongs: **-āre** = 1st; **-ēre** = 2nd; **-ere** = 3rd and **-īre** = 4th. Irregular verbs are shown on p xxvi

Barcīnus _adj see_ n.
bardus _adj_ dull, stupid.
bardus, -ī _m_ Gallic minstrel.
bārō, -ōnis _m_ dunce.
barrus, -ī _m_ elephant.
bascauda, -ae _f_ basket (_for the table_).
bāsiātiō, -ōnis _f_ kiss.
basilica, -ae _f_ public building used as exchange and law court.
basilicē _adv_ royally, in magnificent style.
basilicum, -ī _nt_ regal robe.
basilicus _adj_ royal, magnificent ♦ _m_ highest throw at dice.
bāsiō, -āre _vt_ to kiss.
basis, -is _f_ pedestal, base.
bāsium, -ī _and_ **iī** _nt_ kiss.
Bassareus, -eī _m_ Bacchus.
Batāvī, -ōrum _mpl_ people of Batavia (_now Holland_).
batillum, -ī _nt_ firepan.
Battiadēs, -ae _m_ Callimachus.
bātuō, -ere, -ī _vt_ to beat.
baubor, -ārī _vi_ (_of dogs_) to howl.
Baucis, -idis _f_ wife of Philemon.
beātē _adv see_ **beātus.**
beātitās, -ātis _f_ happiness.
beātitūdō, -inis _f_ happiness.
beātulus, -ī _m_ the blessed man.
beātus _adj_ happy; prosperous, well-off; rich, abundant.
Bēdriacēnsis _adj see_ n.
Bēdriācum, -ī _nt_ village in N. Italy.
Belgae, -ārum _mpl_ people of N. Gaul (_now Belgium_).
Bēlīdēs, -īdae _m_ Danaus, Aegyptus, Lynceus.
Bēlides, -um _fpl_ Danaids.
bellāria, -ōrum _ntpl_ dessert, confectionery.
bellātor, -ōris _m_ warrior, fighter ♦ _adj_ warlike.
bellātōrius _adj_ aggressive.
bellātrix, -īcis _f_ warrioress ♦ _adj_ warlike.
bellē _adv_ well, nicely; ~ **habēre** be well (in health).
Bellerophōn, -ontis _m_ slayer of Chimaera, rider of Pegasus.
Bellerophontēus _adj see_ n.
bellicōsus _adj_ warlike.
bellicus _adj_ of war, military; ~um **canere** give the signal for marching or attack.
belliger, -ī _adj_ martial.
belligerō, -āre, -āvī, -ātum _vi_ to wage war.
bellipotēns, -entis _adj_ strong in war.
bellō, -āre, -āvī, -ātum _vi_ to fight, wage war.
Bellōna, -ae _f_ goddess of war.
bellor, -ārī _vi_ to fight.
bellulus _adj_ pretty.
bellum, -ī _nt_ war, warfare; battle; ~ **gerere** wage war; ~ī in war.
bellus _adj_ pretty, handsome; pleasant, nice.
bēlua, -ae _f_ beast, monster (_esp large and fierce_); any animal; (_fig_) brute; ~ **Gaetula** India elephant.
bēluātus _adj_ embroidered with animals.

bēluōsus _adj_ full of monsters.
Bēlus, -ī _m_ Baal; an oriental king.
Bēnācus, -ī _m_ lake in N. Italy (_now_ Garda).
bene _adv_ (_compar_ **melius,** _superl_ **optimē**) well; correctly; profitably; very ♦ _interj_ bravo!, good!; ~ **dīcere** speak well; speak well of, praise; ~ **emere** buy cheap; ~ **est tibi** you are well off; ~ **facere** do well; do good to; ~ **facis** thank you; **rem ~ gerere** be successful; ~ **sē habēre** have a good time; ~ **habet** all is well, it's all right; ~ **merērī dē** do a service to; ~ **partum** honestly acquired; ~ **tē!** your health!; ~ **vēndere** sell at a high price; ~ **vīvere** live a happy life.
benedīco, -īcere, -īxī, -ictum _vt_ to speak well of, praise; (_ECCL_) to bless.
benedictiō, -ōnis _f_ (_ECCL_) blessing.
beneficentia, -ae _f_ kindness.
beneficiāriī, -ōrum _mpl_ privileged soldiers.
beneficium, -ī _and_ **iī** _nt_ benefit, favour; (_POL, MIL_) promotion; ~ō **tuō** thanks to you.
beneficus _adj_ generous, obliging.
Beneventānus _adj see_ n.
Beneventum, -ī _nt_ town in S. Italy (_now Benevento_).
benevolē _adv see_ **benevolus.**
benevolēns, -entis _adj_ kind-hearted.
benevolentia, -ae _f_ goodwill, friendliness.
benevolus _adj_ kindly, friendly; (_of servants_) devoted.
benīgnē _adv_ willingly, courteously; generously; (_colloq_) no thank you; ~ **facere** do a favour.
benīgnitās, -ātis _f_ kindness; liberality, bounty.
benīgnus _adj_ kind, friendly; favourable; liberal, lavish; fruitful, bounteous.
beō, -āre, -āvī, -ātum _vt_ to gladden, bless, enrich.
Berecyntia _f_ Cybele.
Berecyntius _adj_ of Berecyntus; of Cybele.
Berecyntus, -ī _m_ mountain in Phrygia sacred to Cybele.
Berenīcē, -ēs _f_ a queen of Egypt; **coma ~ēs** a constellation.
bēryllus, -ī _m_ beryl.
bēs, bessis _m_ two-thirds of the _as_; two-thirds.
bēstia, -ae _f_ beast; wild animal for the arena.
bēstiārius _adj_ of beasts ♦ _m_ beast fighter in the arena.
bēstiola, -ae _f_ small animal.
bēta, -ae _f_ beet.
bēta _nt indecl_ Greek letter beta.
bibī _perf of_ **bibō.**
bibliopōla, -ae _m_ bookseller.
bibliothēca, -ae, -ē, -ēs _f_ library.
bibō, -ere, -ī _vt_ to drink; to live on the banks of (a river); to drink in, absorb; (_fig_) to listen attentively, be imbued; ~ **aquas** be drowned; **Graecō mōre ~** drink to one's health.
bibulus _adj_ fond of drink, thirsty; (_things_) thirsty.
Bibulus, -ī _m_ consul with Caesar in 59 BC.

biceps, -ipitis *adj* two-headed.
biclīnium, -ī *and* **iī** *nt* dining couch for two.
bicolor, -ōris *adj* two-coloured.
bicorniger, -ī *adj* two-horned.
bicornis *adj* two-horned, two-pronged; (*rivers*) two-mouthed.
bicorpor, -is *adj* two-bodied.
bidēns, -entis *adj* with two teeth *or* prongs ♦ *m* hoe ♦ *f* sheep (*or other sacrificial animal*).
bidental, -ālis *nt* a place struck by lightning.
biduum, -ī *nt* two days.
biennium -ī *and* **iī** *nt* two years.
bifāriam *adv* in two parts, twice.
bifer, -ī *adj* flowering twice a year.
bifidus *adj* split in two.
biforis *adj* double-doored; double.
bifōrmātus, bifōrmis *adj* with two forms.
bifrōns, -ontis *adj* two-headed.
bifurcus *adj* two-pronged, forked.
bīgae, -ārum *fpl* chariot and pair.
bīgātus *adj* stamped with a chariot and pair.
biiugī, -ōrum *mpl* two horses yoked abreast; chariot with two horses.
biiugis, biiugus *adj* yoked.
bilībra, -ae *f* two pounds.
bilībris *adj* holding two pounds.
bilinguis *adj* double-tongued; bilingual; deceitful.
bīlis, -is *f* bile, gall; (*fig*) anger, displeasure; ~ **ātra, nigra** melancholy; madness.
bilīx, -īcis *adj* double-stranded.
bilūstris *adj* ten years.
bimaris *adj* between two seas.
bimarītus, -ī *m* bigamist.
bimāter, -ris *adj* having two mothers.
bimembris *adj* half man, half beast; (*pl*) Centaurs.
bimēstris *adj* of two months, two months old.
bīmulus *adj* only two years old.
bīmus *adj* two years old, for two years.
bīnī, bīnae, bīna *num* two each, two by two; a pair; (*with pl nouns having a meaning*) two.
binoctium, -ī *and* **iī** *nt* two nights.
binōminis *adj* with two names.
Biōn, -ōnis *m* satirical philosopher.
Biōnēus *adj* satirical.
bipalmis *adj* two spans long.
bipartītō *adv* in two parts, in two directions.
bipartītus *adj* divided in two.
bipatēns, -entis *adj* double-opening.
bipedālis *adj* two feet long broad *or* thick.
bipennifer, -ī *adj* wielding a battle-axe.
bipennis *adj* two-edged ♦ *f* battle-axe.
bipertītō *etc see* **bipartītō**.
bipēs, -edis *adj* two-footed ♦ *m* biped.
birēmis *adj* two-oared; with two banks of oars ♦ *f* two-oared skiff; galley with two banks of oars.
bis *adv* twice, double; ~ **ad eundem** make the same mistake twice; ~ **diē, in diē** twice a day;

~ **tantō, tantum** twice as much; ~ **terque** frequently; ~ **terve** seldom.
bissextus, -ī *m* intercalary day after 24th Feb.
Bistones, -um *mpl people of Thrace.*
Bistonis *f Thracian woman, Bacchante.*
Bistonius *adj* Thracian.
bisulcilingua, -ae *adj* fork-tongued, deceitful.
bisulcus *adj* cloven.
Bīthȳnia, -iae *f province of Asia Minor.*
Bīthȳnicus, Bīthȳnius, -us *adj see* **Bīthȳnia**.
bītō, -ere *vi* to go.
bitūmen, -inis *nt* bitumen, a kind of pitch.
bitūmineus *adj see* **bitūmen**.
bivium *nt* two ways.
bivius *adj* two-way.
blaesus *adj* lisping, indistinct.
blandē *adv see* **blandus**.
blandidicus *adj* fair-spoken.
blandiloquentia, -ae *f attractive language.*
blandiloquus, -entulus *adj* fair-spoken.
blandīmentum, -ī *nt* compliment, allurement.
blandior, -īrī, -ītus *vi* to coax, caress; to flatter, pay compliments; (*things*) to please, entice.
blanditia, -ae *f caress, flattery; charm, allurement.*
blandītim *adv* caressingly.
blandus *adj* smooth-tongued, flattering, fawning; charming, winsome.
blaterō, -āre *vi* to babble.
blatiō, -īre *vt* to babble.
blatta, -ae *f cockroach.*
blennus, -ī *m* idiot.
bliteus *adj* silly.
blitum, -ī *nt* kind of spinach.
boārius *adj* of cattle; **forum -um** *cattle market in Rome.*
Bodotria, -ae *f Firth of Forth.*
Boeōtarchēs *m chief magistrate of Boeotia.*
Boeōtia, -iae *f district of central Greece.*
Boeōtius, -us *adj see n.*
boiae, -ārum *fpl* collar.
Boiī, -ōrum *mpl people of S.E. Gaul.*
Boiohaemī, -ōrum *mpl* Bohemians.
bōlētus, -ī *m* mushroom.
bolus, -ī *m* (*dice*) throw; (*net*) cast; (*fig*) haul, piece of good luck; titbit.
bombus, -ī *m* booming, humming, buzzing.
bombȳcinus *adj* of silk.
bombȳx, -ȳcis *m* silkworm; silk.
Bona Dea, -ae, -ae *f goddess worshipped by women.*
bonitās, -ātis *f goodness; honesty, integrity; kindness, affability.*
Bonōnia, -ae *f town in N. Italy (now Bologna).*
Bonōniēnsis *adj see n.*
bonum, -ī *nt* a moral good; advantage, blessing; (*pl*) property; **cuī ~ō?** who was the

---

Noun declensions and verb conjugations are shown on pp xiii to xxv. The present infinitive ending of a verb shows to which conjugation it belongs: **-āre** = 1st; **-ēre** = 2nd; **-ere** = 3rd and **-īre** = 4th. Irregular verbs are shown on p xxvi

gainer?

bonus *adj* (*compar* **melior,** *superl* **optimus.**
good; kind; brave; loyal; beneficial; lucky
♦ *mpl* upper class party, conservatives; ~**a
aetās** prime of life; ~**ō animō** of good cheer;
well-disposed; ~**ae artēs** integrity; culture,
liberal education; ~ **a dicta** witticisms; ~**a
fidēs** good faith; ~**ī mōrēs** morality; ~**ī nummī**
genuine money; ~**a pars** large part;
conservative party; ~**ae rēs** comforts,
luxuries; prosperity; morality; ~**ā veniā** with
kind permission; ~**a verba** words of good
omen; well-chosen diction; ~**a vōx** loud voice.

boō, -āre *vi* to cry aloud.

Boōtēs, -ae *nt constellation containing Arcturus.*

Boreās, -ae *m* north wind; north.

Boreus *adj see n.*

Borysthenēs, -is *m* river Dnieper.

Borysthenidae *mpl dwellers near the Dnieper.*

Borysthenius *adj see* **Borysthenidae.**

bōs, bovis *m/f* ox, cow; kind of turbot; ~ **Lūca**
elephant; **bovī clitellās impōnere** ≈ *put a
round peg in a square hole.*

Bosporānus *adj see n.*

Bosporius *adj:* ~ **Cimmerius** *strait from Sea of
Azov to Black Sea.*

Bosporus, -ī *m strait from Black Sea to Sea of
Marmora.*

Boudicca, -ae *f British queen (falsely called
Boadicea).*

bovārius *etc see* **boārius.**

Bovillae, -ārum *fpl ancient Latin town.*

Bovillānus *adj see n.*

bovillus *adj* of oxen.

brācae, -ārum *fpl* trousers.

brācātus *adj* trousered; barbarian (*esp of
tribes beyond the Alps*).

bracchiālis *adj* of the arm.

bracchiolum, -ī *nt* dainty arm.

bracchium, -ī *and* **iī** *nt* arm, forearm;
(*shellfish*) claw; (*tree*) branch; (*sea*) arm;
(*NAUT*) yardarm; (*MIL*) outwork, mole; **levī,
mollī bracchiō** casually.

bractea *etc see* **brattea.**

brassica, -ae *f* cabbage.

brattea, -ae *f* gold leaf.

bratteola, -ae *f* very fine gold leaf.

Brennus, -ī *m Gallic chief who defeated the
Romans.*

brevī *adv* shortly, soon; briefly, in a few words.

brevia, -ium *ntpl* shoals.

breviārium, -ī *and* **iī** *nt* summary, statistical
survey, official report.

breviculus *adj* shortish.

breviloquēns, -entis *adj* brief.

brevis *adj* short, small, shallow; brief, short-
lived; concise.

brevitās, -ātis *f* shortness, smallness;
brevity, conciseness.

breviter *adv* concisely.

Brigantēs, -um *mpl British tribe in N. England.*

Briganticus *adj see n.*

Brīsēis, -idos *f captive of Achilles.*

Britannia, -iae *f* Britain; the British Isles.

Britannicus *m son of emperor Claudius.*

Britannus, (-icus) *adj see n.*

Bromius, -ī *and* **iī** *m* Bacchus.

brūma, -ae *f* winter solstice, midwinter;
winter.

brūmālis *adj* of the winter solstice; wintry; ~
flexus tropic of Capricorn.

Brundisīnus *adj see n.*

Brundisium, -ī *and* **iī** *nt* port in S.E. Italy (*now
Brindisi*).

Bruttiī, -ōrum *mpl people of the toe of Italy.*

Bruttius *adj see n.*

brūtus *adj* heavy, unwieldy; stupid, irrational.

Brūtus, -ī *m liberator of Rome from kings;
murderer of Caesar.*

bubīle, -is *nt* stall.

būbo, -ōnis *m/f* owl.

būbula, -ae *f* beef.

bubulcitor, -ārī *vi* to drive oxen.

bubulcus, -ī *m* ploughman.

būbulus *adj* of cattle.

būcaeda, -ae *m* flogged slave.

bucca, -ae *f* cheek; mouth; ranter.

buccō, -ōnis *m* babbler.

buccula, -ae *f* visor.

bucculentus *adj* fat-cheeked.

būcerus *adj* horned.

būcina, -ae *f* shepherd's horn; military
trumpet; night watch.

būcinātor, -ōris *m* trumpeter.

būcolica, -ōrum *ntpl* pastoral poetry.

būcula, -ae *f* young cow.

būfō, -ōnis *m* toad.

bulbus, -ī *m* bulb; onion.

būlē, -es *f* Greek senate.

būleuta *m* senator.

būleutērium *nt* senate house.

bulla, -ae *f* bubble; knob, stud; *gold charm
worn round the neck by children of noblemen.*

bullātus *adj* wearing the bulla; still a child.

būmastus, -ī *f* kind of vine.

būris, -is *m* plough-beam.

Burrus *old form of* **Pyrrhus.**

Busīris, -idis *m Egyptian king killed by Hercules.*

bustirapus, -ī *m* graverobber.

bustuārius *adj* at a funeral.

bustum, -ī *nt* funeral place; tomb, grave.

buxifer, -ī *adj* famed for its box trees.

buxum, -ī *nt* boxwood; flute, top, comb, tablet.

buxus, -ī *f* box tree; flute.

Byzantium, -ī *and* **iī** *nt* city on Bosporus (*later
Constantinople, now* Istanbul).

Byzantius *adj see n.*

C, c

caballīnus *adj* horse's.

caballus, -ī *m* horse.

cacātus *adj* impure.

cachinnātiō, -ōnis *f* loud laughter.

cachinnō, -āre *vi* to laugh, guffaw.

cachinnō, -ōnis *m* scoffer.

cachinnus, -ī *m* laugh, derisive laughter; (*waves*) splashing.

cacō, -āre *vi* to evacuate the bowels.

cacoēthes, -is *nt* (*fig*) itch.

cacula, -ae *m* soldier's slave.

cacūmen, -inis *nt* extremity, point, summit, treetop; (*fig*) height, limit.

cacūminō, -āre *vt* to make pointed.

Cācus, -ī *m* giant robber, son of Vulcan.

cadāver, -is *nt* corpse, carcass.

cadāverōsus *adj* ghastly.

Cadmēa, -ēae *f* fortress of Thebes.

Cadmēis, -ēidis *f* Agave; Ino; Semele.

Cadmēus, (-ēius) *adj* of Cadmus; Theban.

Cadmus, -ī *m* founder of Thebes.

cadō, -ere, cecidī, cāsum *vi* to fall; to droop, die, be killed; (ASTRO) to set; (*dice*) to be thrown; (*events*) to happen, turn out; (*money*) to be due; (*strength, speech, courage*) to diminish, cease, fail; (*wind, rage*) to subside; (*words*) to end; ~ **in** suit, agree with; come under; ~ **sub** be exposed to; **animīs** ~ be disheartened; **causā** ~ lose one's case.

cādūceātor, -ōris *m* officer with flag of truce.

cādūceus, -ī *m* herald's staff; Mercury's wand.

cādūcifer, -ī *adj* with herald's staff.

cadūcus *adj* falling, fallen; (*fig*) perishable, fleeting, vain; (*law*) without an heir ♦ *nt* property without an heir.

Cadurcī, -ōrum *mpl* Gallic tribe.

Cadurcum, -ī *nt* linen coverlet.

cadus, -ī *m* jar, flask (*esp for wine*); urn.

caecigenus *adj* born blind.

Caeciliānus *adj see n.*

Caecilius, -ī *m* Roman name (*esp early Latin comic poet*).

caecitās, -ātis *f* blindness.

caecō, -āre, -āvī, -ātum *vt* to blind; to make obscure.

Caecubum, -ī *nt* choice wine from the Ager Caecubus in S. Latium.

caecus *adj* blind; invisible, secret; dark, obscure; (*fig*) aimless, unknown, uncertain; **appāret ~ō** ≈ it's as clear as daylight; **domus ~a** a house with no windows; **~ā diē emere** buy

on credit; **~um corpus** the back.

caedēs, -is *f* murder, massacre; gore; the slain.

caedō, -ere, cecīdī, caesum *vt* to cut; to strike; to kill, cut to pieces; (*animals*) to sacrifice.

caelāmen, -inis *nt* engraved work.

caelātor, -ōris *m* engraver.

caelātūra, -ae *f* engraving in bas-relief.

caelebs, -ibis *adj* unmarried (bachelor *or* widower); (*trees*) with no vine trained on.

caeles, -itis *adj* celestial ♦ *mpl* the gods.

caelestis, -is *adj* of the sky, heavenly; divine; glorious ♦ *mpl* the gods ♦ *ntpl* the heavenly bodies.

Caeliānus *adj see n.*

caelibātus, -ūs *m* celibacy.

caelicola, -ae *m* god.

caelifer, -ī *adj* supporting the sky.

Caelius, -ī *m* Roman name; Roman hill.

caelō, -āre, -āvī, -ātum *vt* to engrave (*in relief on metals*), carve (*on wood*); (*fig*) to compose.

caelum, -ī *nt* engraver's chisel.

caelum, -ī *nt* sky, heaven; air, climate, weather; (*fig*) height of success, glory; **~um ac terrās miscēre** create chaos; **ad ~um ferre** extol; **dē ~ō dēlāpsus** a messiah; **dē ~ō servāre** watch for omens; **dē ~ō tangī** be struck by lightning; **digitō ~um attingere** ≈ be in the seventh heaven; **in ~ō esse** be overjoyed.

caementum, -ī *nt* quarrystone, rubble.

caenōsus *adj* muddy.

caenum, -ī *nt* mud, filth.

caepa, -ae *f*, **caepe, -is** *nt* onion.

Caere *nt indecl* (*gen* -itis, *abl* -ēte) *f* ancient Etruscan town.

Caeres, -itis *and* **ētis** *adj*: **~ite cērā dignī** like the disfranchised masses.

caerimōnia, -ae *f* sanctity; veneration (*for gods*); religious usage, ritual.

caeruleus, caerulus *adj* blue, dark blue, dark green, dusky ♦ *ntpl* the sea.

Caesar, -is *m* Julius (*great Roman soldier, statesman, author*); Augustus; the emperor.

Caesareus, and iānus, and īnus *adj see n.*

caesariātus *adj* bushy-haired.

caesariēs, -ēī *f* hair.

caesicius *adj* bluish.

caesim *adv* with the edge of the sword; (RHET) in short clauses.

caesius *adj* bluish grey, blue-eyed.

caespes, -itis *m* sod, turf; mass of roots.

caestus, -ūs *m* boxing glove.

caesus *ppp of* **caedō.**

caetra, -ae *f* targe.

caetrātus *adj* armed with a targe.

Caïcus, -ī *m* river in Asia Minor.

Cāiēta, -ae, -ē, -ēs *f* town in Latium.

Cāius *etc see* **Gaius.**

Noun declensions and verb conjugations are shown on pp xiii to xxv. The present infinitive ending of a verb shows to which conjugation it belongs: **-āre** = 1st; **-ēre** = 2nd; **-ere** = 3rd and **-īre** = 4th. Irregular verbs are shown on p xxvi

Calaber, -rī *adj* Calabrian.
Calabria *f S.E. peninsula of Italy.*
Calamis, -idis *m Greek sculptor.*
calamister, -rī *m,* **-rum, -rī** *nt* curling iron; (*RHET*) flourish.
calamistrātus *adj* curled; foppish.
calamitās, -ātis *f* disaster; (*MIL*) defeat; (*AGR*) damage, failure.
calamitōsē *adv see* **calamitōsus.**
calamitōsus *adj* disastrous, ruinous; blighted, unfortunate.
calamus, -ī *m* reed; stalk; pen, pipe, arrow, fishing rod.
calathiscus, -ī *m* small basket.
calathus, -ī *m* wicker basket; bowl, cup.
calātor, -ōris *m* servant.
calcāneum, -ī *nt* heel.
calcar, -āris *nt* spur.
calceāmentum, -ī *nt* shoe.
calceātus *ppp* shod.
calceolārius, -ī *and* **iī** *m* shoemaker.
calceolus, -ī *m* small shoe.
calceus, -ī *m* shoe.
Calchās, -antis *m Greek prophet at Troy.*
calcitrō, -āre *vi* to kick; (*fig*) to resist.
calcō, -āre, -āvī, -ātum *vt* to tread, trample on; (*fig*) to spurn.
calculus, -ī *m* pebble, stone; draughtsman, counting stone, reckoning, voting stone; **~um redūcere** take back a move; **~ōs subdūcere** compute; **ad ~ōs vocāre** subject to a reckoning.
caldārius *adj* with warm water.
caldus *etc see* **calidus.**
Calēdonia, -ae *f the Scottish Highlands.*
Calēdonius *adj see n.*
calefaciō, (calfacio), -facere, -fēcī, -factum *vt* to warm, heat; (*fig*) to provoke, excite.
calefactō, -āre *vt* to warm.
Calendae *see* **Kalendae.**
Calēnus *adj* of Cales ♦ *nt* wine of Cales.
caleō, -ēre *vi* to be warm, be hot, glow; (*mind*) to be inflamed; (*things*) to be pursued with enthusiasm; to be fresh.
Calēs, -ium *fpl town in Campania.*
calēscō, -ere, -uī *vi* to get hot; (*fig*) to become inflamed.
calidē *adv* promptly.
calidus *adj* warm, hot; (*fig*) fiery, eager; hasty; prompt ♦ *f* warm water ♦ *nt* warm drink.
caliendrum, -ī *nt* headdress of hair.
caliga, -ae *f* soldier's boot.
caligātus *adj* heavily shod.
cālīginōsus *adj* misty, obscure.
cālīgō, -inis *f* mist, fog; dimness, darkness; (*mind*) obtuseness; (*CIRCS*) trouble.
cālīgō, -āre *vi* to be misty, be dim; to cause dizziness.
Caligula, -ae *m emperor Gaius.*
calix, -cis *m* wine cup; cooking pot.
calleō, -ēre *vi* to be thick-skinned; (*fig*) to be unfeeling; to be wise, be skilful ♦ *vt* to know, understand.

callidē *adv see* **callidus.**
calliditās, -ātis *f* skill; cunning.
callidus *adj* skilful, clever; crafty.
Callimachus, -ī *m Greek poet of Alexandria.*
Calliopē, -ēs, *and* **ēa, -ēae** *f Muse of epic poetry.*
callis, -is *m* footpath, mountain track; pass; hill pastures.
Callistō, -ūs *f daughter of Lycaon;* (*constellation*) Great Bear.
callōsus *adj* hard-skinned; solid.
callum, -ī *nt* hard *or* thick skin; firm flesh; (*fig*) callousness.
calō, -āre, -āvī, -ātum *vt* to convoke.
cālō, -ōnis *m* soldier's servant; drudge.
calor, -ōris *m* warmth, heat; (*fig*) passion, love.
Calpē, -ēs *f* Rock of Gibraltar.
Calpurniānus *adj see n.*
Calpurnius, -ī *m Roman name.*
caltha, -ae *f* marigold.
calthula, -ae *f* yellow dress.
caluī *perf of* **calēscō.**
calumnia, -ae *f* chicanery, sharp practice; subterfuge; misrepresentation; (*law*) dishonest accusation, blackmail; being convicted of malicious prosecution; **~am iūrāre** swear that an action is brought in good faith.
calumniātor, -ōris *m* legal trickster, slanderer.
calumnior, -ārī, -ātus *vt* to misrepresent, slander; (*law*) to bring an action in bad faith; **sē ~** deprecate oneself.
calva, -ae *f* bald head.
calvitium, -ī *and* **iī** *nt* baldness.
calvor, -ārī *vt* to deceive.
calvus *adj* bald.
calx, -cis *f* heel; foot; **~ce petere, ferīre** kick; **adversus stimulum ~cēs** ≈ *kicking against the pricks.*
calx, -cis *f* pebble; lime, chalk; finishing line, end; **ad carcerēs ā ~ce revocārī** have to begin all over again.
Calydōn, -ōnis *f town in Aetolia.*
Calydōnis *adj* Calydonian.
Calydōnius *f* Deianira; **~ōnius amnis** Achelous; **~ hērōs** Meleager; **~ōnia rēgna** Daunia in S. Italy.
Calypsō, -ūs (*acc* **-ō**) *f nymph who detained Ulysses in Ogygia.*
camēlinus *adj* camel's.
camella, -ae *f* wine cup.
camēlus, -ī *m* camel.
Camēna, -ae *f* Muse; poetry.
camera, -ae *f* arched roof.
Camerīnum, -ī *nt town in Umbria.*
Camers, -tis, *and* **tīnus** *adj* of Camerinum.
Camillus, -ī *m Roman hero (who saved Rome from the Gauls).*
camīnus, -ī *m* furnace, fire; forge; **oleum addere ~ō** ≈ *add fuel to the flames.*
cammarus, -ī *m* lobster.

Campānia, -iae f district of W. Italy.
Campānicus, and **ius,** and **us** adj Campanian, Capuan.
campē, -ēs f evasion.
campester, -ris adj of the plain; of the Campus Martius ♦ nt loincloth ♦ ntpl level ground.
campus, -ī m plain; sports field; any level surface; (fig) theatre, arena (of action, debate); ~ **Martius** level ground by the Tiber (used for assemblies, sports, military drills).
Camulodūnum, -ī nt town of Trinobantes (now Colchester).
camur, -ī adj crooked.
canālis, -is m pipe, conduit, canal.
cancellī, -ōrum mpl grating, enclosure; barrier (in public places), bar of law court.
cancer, -rī m crab; (constellation) Cancer; south, tropical heat; (MED) cancer.
candefaciō, -ere vt to make dazzlingly white.
candēla, -ae f taper, tallow candle; waxed cord; ~ **am appōnere valvīs** set the house on fire.
candēlābrum, -ī nt candlestick, chandelier, lampstand.
candēns, -entis adj dazzling white; white-hot.
candeō, -ēre vi to shine, be white; to be white-hot.
candēscō, -ere vi to become white; to grow white-hot.
candidātōrius adj of a candidate.
candidātus adj dressed in white ♦ m candidate for office.
candidē adv in white; sincerely.
candidulus adj pretty white.
candidus adj white, bright; radiant, beautiful; clothed in white; (style) clear; (mind) candid, frank; (CIRCS) happy; ~**a sententia** acquittal.
candor, -ōris m whiteness, brightness, beauty; (fig) brilliance, sincerity.
cānēns, -entis adj white.
cāneō, -ēre, -uī vi to be grey, be white.
cānēscō, -ere vi to grow white; to grow old.
canīcula, -ae f bitch; Dog Star, Sirius.
canīnus adj dog's, canine; snarling, spiteful; ~ **littera** letter R.
canis, -is m/f dog, bitch; (fig) shameless or angry person; hanger-on; (dice) lowest throw; (ASTRO) Canis Major, Canis Minor; (myth) Cerberus.
canistrum, -ī nt wicker basket.
cānitiēs, -ēī f greyness; grey hair; old age.
canna, -ae f reed; pipe; gondola.
cannabis, -is f hemp.
Cannae, -ārum fpl village in Apulia (scene of great Roman defeat by Hannibal).
Cannēnsis adj see n.
canō, canere, cecinī vt, vi to sing; to play; to sing about, recite, celebrate; to prophesy; (MIL) to sound; (birds) to sing, crow.

canor, -ōris m song, tune, sound.
canōrus adj musical, melodious; singsong ♦ nt melodiousness.
Cantaber, -rī m Cantabrian.
Cantabria, -riae f district of N Spain.
Cantabricus adj see n.
cantāmen, -inis nt charm.
cantharis, -idis f beetle; Spanish fly.
cantharus, -ī m tankard.
canthērīnus adj of a horse.
canthērius, -ī and **iī** m gelding.
canticum, -ī nt aria in Latin comedy; song.
cantilēna, -ae f old song, gossip; ~**am eandem canere** keep harping on the same theme.
cantiō, -ōnis f song; charm.
cantitō, -āre, -āvī, -atum vt to sing or play often.
Cantium, -ī and **iī** nt Kent.
cantiunculae, -ārum fpl fascinating strains.
cantō, -āre, -āvī, -ātum vt, vi to sing; to play; to sing about, recite, celebrate; to proclaim, harp on; to use magic spells; to sound; to drawl.
cantor, -ōris m, **-rīx, -rīcis** f singer, musician, poet; actor.
cantus, -ūs m singing, playing, music; prophecy; magic spell.
cānus adj white, grey, hoary; old ♦ mpl grey hairs.
Canusīnus adj see n.
Canusium, -ī nt town in Apulia (famous for wool).
capācitās, -ātis f spaciousness.
capāx, -ācis adj capable of holding, spacious, roomy; capable, able, fit.
capēdō, -inis f sacrificial dish.
capēduncula f small dish.
capella, -ae f she-goat; (ASTRO) bright star in Auriga.
Capēna, -ae f old Etruscan town.
Capēnās, -us adj: **Porta** ~**a** Roman gate leading to the Via Appia.
caper, -rī m goat; odour of the armpits.
caperrō, -āre vi to wrinkle.
capessō, -ere, -īvī, -ītum vt to seize, take hold of, try to reach, make for; to take in hand, engage in; **rem pūblicam** ~ go in for politics.
capillātus adj long-haired; ancient.
capillus, -ī m hair (of head or beard); a hair.
capiō, -ere, cēpī, captum vt to take, seize; to catch, capture; (MIL) to occupy, take prisoner; (NAUT) to make, reach (a goal); (fig) to captivate, charm, cheat; (pass) to be maimed, lose the use of; to choose; (appearance) to assume; (habit) to cultivate; (duty) to undertake; (ideas) to conceive, form; (feeling) to experience; (harm) to suffer; to receive, get, inherit; to contain, hold; (fig) to bear; (mind) to grasp; **cōnsilium**

Noun declensions and verb conjugations are shown on pp xiii to xxv. The present infinitive ending of a verb shows to which conjugation it belongs: **-āre** = 1st; **-ēre** = 2nd; **-ere** = 3rd and **-īre** = 4th. Irregular verbs are shown on p xxvi

~ come to a decision; **impetum** ~ gather momentum; **initium** ~ start; **oculō capī** lose an eye; **mente captus** insane; **cupīdō eum cēpit** he felt a desire.

capis, -dis _f_ sacrificial bowl with one handle.

capistrātus _adj_ haltered.

capistrum, -ī _nt_ halter, muzzle.

capital, -ālis _nt_ capital crime.

capitālis _adj_ mortal, deadly, dangerous; (_law_) capital; important, excellent.

capitō, -ōnis _m_ bighead.

Capitōlīnus _adj_ of the Capitol; of Jupiter.

Capitōlium, -ī _nt_ Roman hill with temple of Jupiter.

capitulātim _adv_ summarily.

capitulum, -ī _nt_ small head; person, creature.

Cappadocia, -ae _f_ country of Asia Minor.

capra, -ae _f_ she-goat; odour of armpits; (_ASTRO_) Capella.

caprea, -ae _f_ roe.

Capreae, -ārum _fpl_ island of Capri.

capreolus, -ī _m_ roebuck; (_pl_) crossbeams.

Capricornus, -ī _m_ (_constellation_) Capricorn (_associated with midwinter_).

caprificus, -ī _f_ wild fig tree.

caprigenus _adj_ of goats.

caprimulgus, -ī _m_ goatherd, rustic.

caprīnus _adj_ of goats.

capripēs, -edis _adj_ goat-footed.

capsa, -ae _f_ box (_esp for papyrus rolls_).

capsō _archaic fut of_ **capiō**.

capsula, -ae _f_ small box; **dē ~ā tōtus** ≈ out of a bandbox.

Capta, -ae _f_ Minerva.

captātiō, -ōnis _f_ catching at.

captātor, -ōris _m_ one who courts; legacy hunter.

captiō, -ōnis _f_ fraud; disadvantage; (_argument_) fallacy, sophism.

captiōsē _adv see_ **captiōsus**.

captiōsus _adj_ deceptive; dangerous; captious.

captiuncula, -ae _f_ quibble.

captīvitās, -ātis _f_ captivity; capture.

captīvus _adj_ captive, captured; of captives ♦ _m/f_ prisoner of war.

captō, -āre, -āvī, -ātum _vt_ to try to catch, chase; to try to win, court, watch for; to deceive, trap.

captus _ppp of_ **capiō** ♦ _m_ prisoner.

captus, -ūs _m_ grasp, notion.

Capua, -ae _f_ chief town of Campania.

capulāris _adj_ due for a coffin.

capulus, -ī _m_ coffin; handle, hilt.

caput, -itis _nt_ head; top, extremity; (_rivers_) source; (_more rarely_) mouth; person, individual; life; civil rights; (_person_) chief, leader; (_towns_) capital; (_money_) principal; (_writing_) substance, chapter; principle, main point, the great thing; ~ **cēnae** main dish; **~itis accūsāre** charge with a capital offence; **~itis damnāre** condemn to death; **~itis dēminūtiō** loss of political rights; **~itis poena** capital punishment; **~ita cōnferre** confer in

secret; in **~ita** per head; **suprā ~ut esse** be imminent.

Cār, -is _m_ Carian.

carbaseus _adj_ linen, canvas.

carbasus, -ī _f_ (_pl_ **-a, -ōrum** _nt_) Spanish flax, fine linen; garment, sail, curtain.

carbō, -ōnis _m_ charcoal, embers.

carbōnārius, -ī and **iī** _m_ charcoal burner.

carbunculus, -ī _m_ small coal; precious stone.

carcer, -is _m_ prison; jailbird; barrier, starting place (_for races_); **ad ~ēs ā calce revocārī** have to begin all over again.

carcerārius _adj_ of a prison.

carchēsium, -ī and **iī** _nt_ drinking cup; (_NAUT_) masthead.

cardiacus, -ī _m_ dyspeptic.

cardō, -inis _m_ hinge; (_ASTRO_) pole, axis, cardinal point; (_fig_) juncture, critical moment.

carduus, -ī _m_ thistle.

cārē _adv see_ **cārus**.

cārectum, -ī _nt_ sedge.

cāreō, -ēre, -uī _vi_ (_with abl_) to be free from, not have, be without; to abstain from, be absent from; to want, miss.

cārex, -icis _f_ sedge.

Cāria, -ae _f_ district of S.W. Asia Minor.

Cāricus _adj_ Carian ♦ _f_ dried fig.

cariēs (_acc_ **-em**, _abl_ **-ē**) _f_ dry rot.

carīna, -ae _f_ keel; ship.

Carīnae, -ārum _fpl_ district of Rome.

carīnārius, -ī and **iī** _m_ dyer of yellow.

cariōsus _adj_ crumbling; (_fig_) withered.

cāris, -idis _f_ kind of crab.

cāritās, -ātis _f_ dearness, high price; esteem, affection.

carmen, -inis _nt_ song, tune; poem, poetry, verse; prophecy; (_in law, religion_) formula; moral text.

Carmentālis _adj see_ n.

Carmentis, -is, and **a, -ae** _f_ prophetess, mother of Evander.

carnārium, -ī and **iī** _nt_ fleshhook; larder.

Carneadēs, -is _m_ Greek philosopher (_founder of the New Academy_).

Carneadēus _adj see_ n.

carnifex, -icis _m_ executioner, hangman; scoundrel; murderer.

carnificīna, -ae _f_ execution; torture; **~am facere** be an executioner.

carnificō, -āre _vt_ to behead, mutilate.

carnuf- _etc see_ **carnif-**.

carō, -nis _f_ flesh.

cārō, -ere _vt_ to card.

Carpathius _adj see_ n.

Carpathus, -ī _f_ island between Crete and Rhodes.

carpatina, -ae _f_ leather shoe.

carpentum, -ī _nt_ two-wheeled coach.

carpō, -ere, -sī, -tum _vt_ to pick, pluck, gather; to tear off; to browse, graze on; (_wool_) to card; (_fig_) to enjoy, snatch; to carp at, slander; to weaken, wear down; to divide up; (*journey*) to go, travel.

carptim *adv* in parts; at different points; at different times.

carptor, -ōris *m* carver.

carptus *ppp of* **carpō.**

carrus, -ī *m* waggon.

Carthāginiēnsis *adj see n.*

Carthāgō, -inis *f* Carthage (*near Tunis*); ~ **Nova** town in Spain (*now* Cartagena).

caruncula, -ae *f* piece of flesh.

cārus *adj* dear, costly; dear, beloved.

Carystēus *adj see n.*

Carystos, -ī *f* town in Euboea (*famous for marble*).

casa, -ae *f* cottage, hut.

cascus *adj* old.

cāseolus, -ī *m* small cheese.

cāseus, -ī *m* cheese.

casia, -ae *f* cinnamon; spurge laurel.

Caspius *adj* Caspian.

Cassandra, -ae *f* Trojan princess and prophetess, doomed never to be believed.

cassēs, -ium *mpl* net, snare; spider's web.

Cassiānus *adj see n.*

cassida, -ae *f* helmet.

Cassiepēa, -ae, Cassiopē, -ēs *f* mother of Andromeda; a constellation.

cassis, -idis *f* helmet.

Cassius, -ī *m* Roman family name.

cassō, -āre *vi* to shake.

cassus *adj* empty; devoid of, without (*abl*); vain, useless; ~ **lūmine** dead; **in ~um** in vain.

Castalia, -ae *f* spring on Parnassus, (*sacred to Apollo and the Muses*).

Castalidēs, -dum *fpl* Muses.

Castalius, -s *adj see n.*

castanea, -ae *f* chestnut tree; chestnut.

castē *adv see* **castus.**

castellānus *adj* of a fortress ♦ *mpl* garrison.

castellātim *adv* in different fortresses.

castellum, -ī *nt* fortress, castle; (*fig*) defence, refuge.

castēria, -ae *f* rowers' quarters.

castīgābilis *adj* punishable.

castīgātiō, -ōnis *f* correction, reproof.

castīgātor, -ōris *m* reprover.

castīgātus *adj* small, slender.

castīgō, -āre, -āvī, -ātum *vt* to correct, punish; to reprove; to restrain.

castimōnia, -ae *f* purity, morality; chastity, abstinence.

castitās, -ātis *f* chastity.

castor, -oris *m* beaver.

Castor, -oris *m* twin brother of Pollux (*patron of sailors*); star in Gemini.

castoreum, -ī *nt* odorous secretion of the beaver.

castra, -ōrum *ntpl* camp; day's march; army life; (*fig*) party, sect; ~ **movēre** strike camp; ~ **mūnīre** construct a camp; ~ **pōnere** pitch camp; **bīna ~** two camps.

castrēnsis *adj* of the camp, military.

castrō, -āre *vt* to castrate; (*fig*) to weaken.

castrum, -ī *nt* fort.

castus *adj* clean, pure, chaste, innocent; holy, pious.

cāsū *adv* by chance.

casula, -ae *f* little cottage.

cāsus, -ūs *m* fall, downfall; event, chance, accident; misfortune, death; opportunity; (*time*) end; (*GRAM*) case.

Catadūpa, -ōrum *ntpl* Nile cataract near Syene.

catagraphus *adj* painted.

Catamītus, -ī *m* Ganymede.

cataphractēs, -ae *m* coat of mail.

cataphractus *adj* wearing mail.

cataplus, -ī *m* ship arriving.

catapulta, -ae *f* (*MIL*) catapult; (*fig*) missile.

catapultārius *adj* thrown by catapult.

cataracta, -ae *f* waterfall; sluice; drawbridge.

catasta, -ae *f* stage, scaffold.

catē *adv see* **catus.**

catēia, -ae *f* javelin.

catella, -ae *f* small chain.

catellus, -ī *m* puppy.

catēna, -ae *f* chain; fetter; (*fig*) bond, restraint; series.

catēnātus *adj* chained, fettered.

caterva, -ae *f* crowd, band; flock; (*MIL*) troop, body; (*THEAT*) company.

catervātim *adv* in companies.

cathedra, -ae *f* armchair, sedan chair; teacher's chair.

catholicus *adj* (*ECCL*) orthodox, universal.

Catilīna, -ae *m* Catiline (*conspirator suppressed by Cicero*).

Catilīnārius *adj see n.*

catillō, -āre *vt* to lick a plate.

catillus, -ī *m* small dish.

catīnus, -ī *m* dish, pot.

Catō, -ōnis *m* famous censor and author, idealised as the pattern of an ancient Roman; famous Stoic and republican leader against Caesar.

Catōniānus *adj see n.*

Catōnīnī *mpl* Cato's supporters.

catōnium, -ī *and* **iī** *nt* the lower world.

Catulliānus *adj see n.*

Catullus, -ī *m* Latin lyric poet.

catulus, -ī *m* puppy; cub, young of other animals.

catus *adj* clever, wise; sly, cunning.

Caucasius *adj see n.*

Caucasus, -ī *m* Caucasus mountains.

cauda, -ae *f* tail; ~ **am iactāre** fawn; ~ **am trahere** be made a fool of.

caudeus *adj* wooden.

caudex, -icis *m* trunk; block of wood; book, ledger; (*fig*) blockhead.

caudicālis *adj* of woodcutting.

Caudīnus *adj see n.*

Noun declensions and verb conjugations are shown on pp xiii to xxv. The present infinitive ending of a verb shows to which conjugation it belongs: **-āre** = 1st; **-ēre** = 2nd; **-ere** = 3rd and **-īre** = 4th. Irregular verbs are shown on p xxvi

Caudium, -ī _nt Samnite town._
caulae, -ārum _fpl_ opening; sheepfold.
caulis, -is _m_ stalk; cabbage.
Cauneus _adj_ Caunian.
Caunus, -ī _f town in Caria_ ♦ _fpl_ dried figs.
caupō, -ōnis _m_ shopkeeper, innkeeper.
caupōna, -ae _f_ shop, inn.
caupōnius _adj see n._
caupōnor, -ārī _vt_ to trade in.
caupōnula, -ae _f_ tavern.
Caurus, -ī _m_ north-west wind.
causa, -ae _f_ cause, reason; purpose, sake; excuse, pretext; opportunity; connection, case, position; (_law_) case, suit; (_POL_) cause, party; (_RHET_) subject matter; **~am agere, ōrāre** plead a case; **~am dēfendere** speak for the defence; **~am dīcere** defend oneself; **~ā** for the sake of; **cum ~ā** with good reason; **quā dē ~ā** for this reason; **in ~ā esse** be responsible; **per ~am** under the pretext.
causārius _adj_ (_MIL_) unfit for service.
causia, -ae _f_ Macedonian hat.
causidicus, -ī _m_ advocate.
causificor, -ārī _vi_ to make a pretext.
causor, -ārī, -ātus _vt, vi_ to pretend, make an excuse of.
caussa _etc see_ **causa.**
causula, -ae _f_ petty lawsuit; slight cause.
cautē _adv_ carefully, cautiously; with security.
cautēla, -ae _f_ caution.
cautēs, -is _f_ rock, crag.
cautim _adv_ warily.
cautiō, -ōnis _f_ caution, wariness; (_law_) security, bond, bail; **mihi ~ est** I must take care; **mea ~ est** I must see to it.
cautor, -ōris _m_ wary person; surety.
cautus _ppp of_ **caveō** ♦ _adj_ wary, provident; safe, secure.
cavaedium, -ī _and_ **iī** _nt_ inner court of a house.
cavea, -ae _f_ cage, stall, coop, hive; (_THEAT_) auditorium; theatre; **prīma ~** upper class seats; **ultima ~** lower class seats.
caveō, -ēre, cāvī, cautum _vt_ to beware of, guard against ♦ _vi_ (_with ab or abl_) to be on one's guard against; (_with dat_) to look after; (_with nē_) to take care that ... not; (_with ut_) to take good care that; (_with subj or inf_) to take care not to, do not; (_law_) to stipulate, decree; (_COMM_) to get a guarantee, give a guarantee, stand security; **cavē!** look out!
caverna, -ae _f_ hollow, cave, vault; (_NAUT_) hold.
cavilla, -ae _f_ jeering.
cavillātiō, -ōnis _f_ jeering, banter; sophistry.
cavillātor, -ōris _m_ scoffer.
cavillor, -ārī, -ātus _vt_ to scoff at ♦ _vi_ to jeer, scoff; to quibble.
cavō, -āre, -āvī, -ātum _vt_ to hollow, excavate.
cavus _adj_ hollow, concave, vaulted; (_river_) deep-channelled ♦ _nt_ cavity, hole.
Caystros, -us, -ī _m_ river in Lydia (_famous for swans_).
-ce _demonstrative particle appended to pronouns and adverbs._

Cēa, -ae _f_ Aegean island (_birthplace of Simonides_).
cecidī _perf of_ **cadō.**
cecīdī _perf of_ **caedō.**
cecinī _perf of_ **canō.**
Cecropidēs, -idae _m_ Theseus; Athenian.
Cecropis, -idis _f_ Aglauros; Procne; Philomela; Athenian, Attic.
Cecropius _adj_ Athenian ♦ _f_ Athens.
Cecrops, -is _m ancient king of Athens._
cēdō, -ere, cessī, cessum _vi_ to go, walk; to depart, withdraw, retreat; to pass away, die; (_events_) to turn out; to be changed (into); to accrue (to); to yield, be inferior (to) ♦ _vt_ to give up, concede, allow; **~ bonīs, possessiōne** make over property (to); **~ forō** go bankrupt; **~ locō** leave one's post; **~ memoriā** be forgotten.
cedo (_pl_ **cette**) _impv_ give me, bring here; tell me; let me; look at!
cedrus, -ī _f_ cedar, perfumed juniper; cedar oil.
Celaenō, -ūs _f_ a Harpy; a Pleiad.
cēlāta _ntpl_ secrets.
celeber, -ris _adj_ crowded, populous; honoured, famous; repeated.
celebrātiō, -ōnis _f_ throng; celebration.
celebrātus _adj_ full, much used; festive; famous.
celebritās, -ātis _f_ crowd; celebration; fame.
celebrō, -āre, -āvī, -ātum _vt_ to crowd, frequent; to repeat, practise; to celebrate, keep (_a festival_); to advertise, glorify.
celer, -is _adj_ quick, swift, fast; hasty.
Celerēs, -um _mpl_ royal bodyguard.
celeripēs, -edis _adj_ swift-footed.
celeritās, -ātis _f_ speed, quickness.
celeriter _adv see_ **celer.**
celerō, -āre _vt_ to quicken ♦ _vi_ to make haste.
cella, -ae _f_ granary, stall, cell; garret, hut, small room; sanctuary of a temple.
cellārius _adj_ of the storeroom ♦ _m_ steward.
cellula, -ae _f_ little room.
cēlō, -āre, -āvī, -ātum _vt_ to hide, conceal, keep secret; **id mē ~at** he keeps me in the dark about it.
celōx, -ōcis _adj_ swift ♦ _f_ fast ship, yacht.
celsus _adj_ high, lofty; (_fig_) great, eminent; haughty.
Celtae, -ārum _mpl_ Celts (_esp of central Gaul_) ♦ _nt_ the Celtic nation.
Celtibērī, -ōrum _mpl_ people of central Spain.
Celtibēria, -iae _f_ Central Spain.
Celtibēricus _adj see n._
Celticus _adj_ Celtic.
cēna, -ae _f_ dinner (_the principal Roman meal_); **inter ~am** at table.
cēnāculum, -ī _nt_ dining-room; upper room, garret.
cēnātiō _adj_ of dinner.
cēnātiō, -ōnis _f_ dining-room.
cēnātus _ppa_ having dined, after dinner ♦ _ppp_ spent in feasting.

Cenchreae, -ārum *fpl* harbour of Corinth.

cēnitō, -āre *vi* to be accustomed to dine.

cēnō, -āre, -āvī, -ātum *vi* to dine ♦ *vt* to eat, dine on.

cēnseō, -ēre, -uī, -um *vt* (*census*) to assess, rate, take a census, make a property return; (*fig*) to estimate, appreciate, celebrate; (*senate or other body*) to decree, resolve; (*member*) to express an opinion, move, vote; to advise; to judge, think, suppose, consider; **cēnsuī ~endō** for census purposes.

cēnsiō, -ōnis *f* punishment; expression of opinion.

cēnsor, -ōris *m* censor; (*fig*) severe judge, critic.

cēnsōrius *adj* of the censors, to be dealt with by the censors; (*fig*) severe; **homō ~** an ex-censor.

cēnsūra, -ae *f* censorship; criticism.

cēnsus *ppp of* **cēnseō; capite ~ī** the poorest class of Roman citizens.

cēnsus, -ūs *m* register of Roman citizens and their property, census; registered property; wealth; **~um agere, habēre** hold a census; **sine ~ū** poor.

centaurēum, -ī *nt* centaury.

Centaurēus *adj see n.*

Centaurus, -ī *m* Centaur, half man half horse.

centēnī, -um *num* a hundred each, a hundred.

centēsimus *adj* hundredth ♦ *f* hundredth part; (*interest*) 1 per cent monthly (*12 per cent per annum*).

centiceps *adj* hundred-headed.

centiēns, -ēs *adv* a hundred times.

centimanus *adj* hundred-handed.

centō, -ōnis *m* patchwork; **~ōnēs sarcīre** ≈ tell tall stories.

centum *num* a hundred.

centumgeminus *adj* hundred-fold.

centumplex *adj* hundred-fold.

centumpondium, -ī *and* **iī** *nt* a hundred pounds.

centumvirālis *adj* of the centumviri.

centumvirī, -ōrum *mpl* a bench of judges who heard special civil cases in Rome.

centunculus, -ī *m* piece of patchwork, saddlecloth.

centuria, -ae *f* (*MIL*) company; (*POL*) century (*a division of the Roman people according to property*).

centuriātim *adv* by companies, by centuries.

centuriātus *adj* divided by centuries; **comitia ~a** assembly which voted by centuries.

centuriātus, -ūs *m* division into centuries; rank of centurion.

centuriō, -āre, -āvī, -ātum *vt* (*MIL*) to assign to companies; (*POL*) to divide by centuries.

centuriō, -ōnis *m* (*MIL*) captain, centurion.

centussis, -is *m* a hundred asses.

cēnula, -ae *f* little dinner.

Ceōs, *acc* **-ō** *see* **Cea.**

Cēphēis *f* Andromeda.

Cēphēius *adj* of Cepheus.

Cēpheus *adj* Ethiopian.

Cēpheus, -eī (*acc* **-ea**) *m* king of Ethiopia (*father of Andromeda*).

Cēphīsis *adj see n.*

Cēphīsius *m* Narcissus.

Cēphīsus, -ī *m* river in central Greece.

cēpī *perf of* **capiō.**

cēra, -ae *f* wax; honey cells; writing tablet, notebook; seal; portrait of an ancestor; **prīma ~** first page.

Ceramīcus, -ī *m* Athenian cemetery.

cērārium, -ī *and* **iī** *nt* seal-duty.

cerastēs, -ae *m* a horned serpent.

cerasus, -ī *f* cherry tree; cherry.

cērātus *adj* waxed.

Ceraunia, -ōrum *nt*, **Ceraunii** *m* mountains in Epirus.

Cerbereus *adj see n.*

Cerberus, -ī *m* three-headed watchdog of Hades.

cercopithēcus, -ī *m* monkey.

cercūrus, -ī *m* Cyprian type of ship.

cerdō, -ōnis *m* tradesman.

Cereālia, -ium *ntpl* festival of Ceres.

Cereālis *adj* of Ceres; of corn, of meal.

cerebrōsus *adj* hot-headed.

cerebrum, -ī *nt* brain; understanding; quick temper.

Cerēs, -eris *f* goddess of agriculture; (*fig*) grain, bread.

cēreus *adj* waxen; wax-coloured; (*fig*) supple, easily led ♦ *m* taper.

cēriāria, -ae *f* taper maker.

cērina, -ōrum *ntpl* wax-coloured clothes.

cērintha, -ae *f* honeywort.

cernō, -ere, -crēvī, crētum *vt* to see, discern; to understand, perceive; to decide, determine; (*law*) to decide to take up (an inheritance).

cernuus *adj* face downwards.

cērōma, -atis *nt* wrestlers' ointment.

cērōmaticus *adj* smeared with wax ointment.

cerrītus *adj* crazy.

certāmen, -inis *nt* contest, match; battle, combat; (*fig*) struggle, rivalry.

certātim *adv* emulously.

certātiō, -ōnis *f* contest; debate; rivalry.

certē *adv* assuredly, of course; at least.

certō *adv* certainly, really.

certō, -āre, -āvī, -ātum *vi* to contend, compete; (*MIL*) to fight it out; (*law*) to dispute; (*with inf*) to try hard.

certus *adj* determined, fixed, definite; reliable, unerring; sure, certain; **mihi ~um est** I have made up my mind; **~um scīre, prō -ō habēre** know for certain, be sure; **~iōrem facere** inform.

cērula, -ae *f* piece of wax; **~ miniāta** red

Noun declensions and verb conjugations are shown on pp xiii to xxv. The present infinitive ending of a verb shows to which conjugation it belongs: **-āre** = 1st; **-ēre** = 2nd; **-ere** = 3rd and **-īre** = 4th. Irregular verbs are shown on p xxvi

pencil.

cērussa, -ae f white lead.

cērussātus adj painted with white lead.

cerva, -ae f hind, deer.

cervīcal, -ālis nt pillow.

cervīcula, -ae f slender neck.

cervīnus adj deer's.

cervīx, -īcis f neck; **in ~īcibus esse** be a burden (to), threaten.

cervus, -ī m stag, deer; (MIL) palisade.

cessātiō, -ōnis f delaying; inactivity, idleness.

cessātor, -ōris m idler.

cessī perf of **cēdō.**

cessiō, -ōnis f giving up.

cessō, -āre, -āvī, -ātum vi to be remiss, stop; to loiter, delay; to be idle, rest, do nothing; (land) to lie fallow; to err.

cestrosphendonē, -ēs f (MIL) engine for shooting stones.

cestus, -ī m girdle (esp of Venus).

cētārium, -ī and **iī** nt fishpond.

cētārius, -ī and **iī** m fishmonger.

cētera adv in other respects.

cēterī, -ōrum adj the rest, the others; (sg) the rest of.

cēterōquī, -n adv otherwise.

cēterum adv for the rest, otherwise; but for all that; besides.

Cethēgus, -ī m a conspirator with Catiline.

cētr- etc see **caetr-.**

cette etc see **cedo.**

cētus, -ī m (-ē ntpl) sea monster, whale.

ceu adv just as, as if.

Cēus adj see **Cēa.**

Cēyx, -ȳcis m husband of Alcyone, changed to a kingfisher.

Chalcidēnsis, (-discus) adj see n.

Chalcis, -dis f chief town of Euboea.

Chaldaeī, -aeōrum mpl Chaldeans; astrologers.

Chaldāicus adj see n.

chalybēius adj of steel.

Chalybes, -um mpl a people of Pontus (famous as ironworkers).

chalybs, -is m steel.

Chāones, -um mpl a people of Epirus.

Chāonia, -iae f Epirus.

Chāonius, -is adj see n.

Chaos (abl -ō) nt empty space, the lower world, chaos.

chara, -ae f an unidentified vegetable.

charistia, -ōrum ntpl a Roman family festival.

Charites, -um fpl the Graces.

Charōn, -ontis m Charon (ferryman of Hades).

charta, -ae f sheet of papyrus, paper; writing.

chartula, -ae f piece of paper.

Charybdis, -is f monster personifying a whirlpool in the Straits of Messina; (fig) peril.

Chattī, -ōrum mpl a people of central Germany.

Chēlae, -ārum fpl (ASTRO) the Claws (of Scorpio), Libra.

chelydrus, -ī m watersnake.

chelys (acc -yn) f tortoise; lyre.

cheragra, -ae f gout in the hands.

Cherronēsus, Chersonēsus, -ī f Gallipoli peninsula; Crimea.

chīliarchus, -ī m officer in charge of 1000 men; chancellor of Persia.

Chimaera, -ae f fire-breathing monster formed of lion, goat and serpent.

Chimaeriferus adj birthplace of Chimaera.

Chios, -ī f Aegean island (famous for wine).

Chīus adj Chian ♦ nt Chian wine; Chian cloth.

chīrographum, -ī nt handwriting; document.

Chīrōn, -ōnis m a learned Centaur (tutor of heroes).

chīronomos, -ī m/f, **chīronomōn, -untis** m mime actor.

chiūrūrgia, -ae f surgery; (fig) violent measures.

chlamydātus adj wearing a military cloak.

chlamys, -dis f Greek military cloak.

Choerilus, -ī m inferior Greek poet.

chorāgium, -i and **iī** nt producing of a chorus.

chorāgus, -ī m one who finances a chorus.

choraulēs, -ae m flute-player (accompanying a chorus).

chorda, -ae f string (of an instrument); rope.

chorēa, -ae f dance.

chorēus, -ī m trochee.

chorus, -ī m choral dance; chorus, choir of singers or dancers; band, troop.

Christiānismus, -ī m Christianity.

Christiānus adj Christian.

Christus, -ī m Christ.

Chrȳsēis, -ēidis f daughter of Chrȳsēs.

Chrȳsēs, -ae m priest of Apollo in the Iliad.

Chrȳsippēus adj see n.

Chrȳsippus, -ī m Stoic philosopher.

chrȳsolithos, -ī m/f topaz.

chrȳsos, -ī m gold.

cibārius adj food (in cpds); common ♦ ntpl rations.

cibātus, -ūs m food.

cibōrium, -ī and **iī** nt kind of drinking cup.

cibus, -ī m food, fodder, nourishment.

cicāda, -ae f cicada, cricket.

cicātrīcōsus adj scarred.

cicātrīx, -īcis f scar; (plants) mark of an incision.

ciccus, -ī m pomegranate pip.

cicer, -is nt chickpea.

Cicerō, -ōnis m great Roman orator and author.

Cicerōniānus adj see n.

cichorēum, -ī nt chicory.

Cicōnes, -um mpl people of Thrace.

cicōnia, -ae f stork.

cicur, -is adj tame.

cicūta, -ae f hemlock; pipe.

cieō, ciēre, cīvī, citum vt to move, stir, rouse; to call, invoke; (fig) to give rise to, produce; **calcem ~** make a move (in chess).

Cilicia, -ae f country in S. Asia Minor (famous for piracy).

Ciliciēnsis, (-us) adj see n.

Cilix, -cis, -ssa adj Cilician ♦ nt goats' hair garment.

Cimbrī, -ōrum mpl people of N. Germany.

Cimbricus adj see n.

cīmex, -icis m bug.

Cimmeriī, -ōrum mpl people of the Crimea; mythical race in caves near Cumae.

Cimmerius adj see n.

cinaedius adj lewd.

cinaedus, -ī m sodomite; lewd dancer.

cincinnātus adj with curled hair.

Cincinnātus, -ī m ancient Roman dictator.

cincinnus, -ī m curled hair; (fig) rhetorical ornament.

Cincius, -ī m Roman tribune; Roman historian.

cincticulus, -ī m small girdle.

cinctus ppp of **cingō**.

cinctus, -ūs m girding; ~ **Gabīnus** a ceremonial style of wearing the toga.

cinctūtus adj girded.

cinefactus adj reduced to ashes.

cinerārius, -ī and **iī** m hair curler.

cingō, -gere, -xī, -ctum vt to surround, enclose; to gird, crown; (MIL) to besiege, fortify; to cover, escort; **ferrum ~or I** put on my sword.

cingula, -ae f girth (of animals).

cingulum, -ī nt belt.

cingulus, -ī m zone.

ciniflō, -ōnis m hair curler.

cinis, -eris m ashes; (fig) ruin.

Cinna, -ae m colleague of Marius; poet friend of Catullus.

cinnamōmum, cinnamum, -ī nt cinnamon.

cinxī perf of **cingō**.

Cīnyphius adj of the Cinyps, river of N. Africa; African.

Cinyrās, -ae m father of Adonis.

Cinyrēius adj see n.

cippus, -ī m tombstone; (pl) palisade.

circā adv around, round about ♦ prep (with acc) (place) round, in the vicinity of, in; (time, number) about; with regard to.

Circaeus adj see **Circē**.

circamoerium, -ī and **iī** nt space on both sides of a wall.

Circē, -ēs and **ae** f goddess with magic powers living in Aeaea.

circēnsēs, -ium mpl the games.

circēnsis adj of the Circus.

circinō, -āre vt to circle through.

circinus, -ī m pair of compasses.

circiter adv (time, number) about ♦ prep (with acc) about, near.

circueō, circumeō, -īre, -īvī and **iī, -itum** vt, vi to go round, surround; (MIL) to encircle; to visit, go round canvassing; to deceive.

circuitiō, -ōnis f (MIL) rounds; (speech) evasiveness.

circuitus ppp of **circueō**.

circuitus, -ūs m revolution; way round, circuit; (RHET) period, periphrasis.

circulātor, -ōris m pedlar.

circulor, -ārī vi to collect in crowds.

circulus, -ī m circle; orbit; ring; social group.

circum adv round about ♦ prep (with acc) round, about; near; ~ **īnsulās mittere** send to the islands round about.

circumagō, -agere, -ēgī, -āctum vt to turn, move in a circle, wheel; (pass: time) to pass; (: mind) to be swayed.

circumarō, -āre vt to plough round.

circumcaesūra, -ae f outline.

circumcīdō, -dere, -dī, -sum vt to cut round, trim; to cut down, abridge.

circumcircā adv all round.

circumcīsus ppp of **circumcīdō** ♦ adj precipitous.

circumclūdō, -dere, -sī, -sum vt to shut in, hem in.

circumcolō, -ere vt to live round about.

circumcursō, -āre vi to run about.

circumdō, -are, -edī, -atum vt to put round; to surround, enclose.

circumdūcō, -ūcere, -ūxī, -uctum vt to lead round, draw round; to cheat; (speech) to prolong, drawl.

circumductus ppp of **circumdūcō**.

circumeō etc see **circueō**.

circumequitō, -āre vt to ride round.

circumferō, -ferre, -tulī, -lātum vt to carry round, pass round; to spread, broadcast; to purify; (pass) to revolve.

circumflectō, -ctere, -xī, -xum vt to wheel round.

circumflō, -āre vt (fig) to buffet.

circumfluō, -ere, -xī vt, vi to flow round; (fig) to overflow, abound.

circumfluus adj flowing round; surrounded (by water).

circumforāneus adj itinerant; (money) borrowed.

circumfundō, -undere, -ūdī, -ūsum vt to pour round, surround; (fig) to crowd round, overwhelm; (pass) to flow round.

circumgemō, -ere vt to growl round.

circumgestō, -āre vt to carry about.

circumgredior, -dī, -ssus vt, vi to make an encircling move, surround.

circumiaceō, -ēre vi to be adjacent.

circumiciō, -icere, -iēcī, -iectum vt to throw round, put round; to surround.

circumiecta ntpl neighbourhood.

circumiectus adj surrounding.

circumiectus, -ūs m enclosure; embrace.

circumit- etc see **circuit-**.

circumitiō, -ōnis f see **circuitiō**.

circumitus, -ūs m see **circuitus**.

circumlātus ppp of **circumferō**.

circumligō, -āre, -āvī, -ātum vt to tie to, bind

Noun declensions and verb conjugations are shown on pp xiii to xxv. The present infinitive ending of a verb shows to which conjugation it belongs: **-āre** = 1st; **-ēre** = 2nd; **-ere** = 3rd and **-īre** = 4th. Irregular verbs are shown on p xxvi

round.

circumlinō, -ere, -tum _vt_ to smear all over, bedaub.

circumluō, -ere _vt_ to wash.

circumluviō, -ōnis _f_ alluvial land.

circummittō, -ittere, -īsī, -issum _vt_ to send round.

circummoeniō (circummūniō), -īre, -īvī, -ītum _vt_ to fortify.

circummūnītiō, -ōnis _f_ investing.

circumpadānus _adj_ of the Po valley.

circumpendeō, -ēre _vi_ to hang round.

circumplaudō, -ere _vt_ to applaud on all sides.

circumplector, -ctī, -xus _vt_ to embrace, surround.

circumplicō, -āre, -āvī, -ātum _vt_ to wind round.

circumpōnō, -pōnere, -posuī, -positum _vt_ to put round.

circumpōtātiō, -ōnis _f_ passing drinks round.

circumrētiō, -īre, -īvī, -ītum _vt_ to ensnare.

circumrōdō, -rosī, -rodere _vt_ to nibble round about; (_fig_) to slander.

circumsaepiō, -īre, -sī, -tum _vt_ to fence round.

circumscindō, -ere _vt_ to strip.

circumscrībō, -bere, -psī, -ptum _vt_ to draw a line round; to mark the limits of; to restrict, circumscribe; to set aside; to defraud.

circumscrīptē _adv_ in periods.

circumscrīptiō, -ōnis _f_ circle, contour; fraud; (_RHET_) period.

circumscrīptor, -ōris _m_ defrauder.

circumscrīptus _ppp of_ **circumscrībō** ♦ _adj_ restricted; (_RHET_) periodic.

circumsecō, -āre _vt_ to cut round.

circumsedeō, -edere, -ēdī, -essum _vt_ to blockade, beset.

circumsēpiō _etc see_ **circumsaepiō**.

circumsessiō, -ōnis _f_ siege.

circumsessus _ppp of_ **circumsedeō**.

circumsīdō, -ere _vt_ to besiege.

circumsiliō, -īre _vi_ to hop about; (_fig_) to be rampant.

circumsistō, -sistere, -stetī surround.

circumsonō, -āre _vi_ to resound on all sides ♦ _vt_ to fill with sound.

circumsonus _adj_ noisy.

circumspectātrīx, -īcis _f_ spy.

circumspectiō, -ōnis _f_ caution.

circumspectō, -āre _vt, vi_ to look all round, search anxiously, be on the lookout.

circumspectus _ppp of_ **circumspiciō** ♦ _adj_ carefully considered, cautious.

circumspectus, -ūs _m_ consideration; view.

circumspiciō, -icere, -exī, -ectum _vi_ to look all round; to be careful ♦ _vt_ to survey; (_fig_) to consider, search for.

circumstantēs, -antium _mpl_ bystanders.

circumstetī _perf of_ **circumsistō**; _perf of_ **circumstō**.

circumstō, -āre, -etī _vt, vi_ to stand round; to

besiege; (_fig_) to encompass.

circumstrepō, -ere _vt_ to make a clamour round.

circumsurgēns, -entis _pres p_ rising on all sides.

circumtentus _adj_ covered tightly.

circumterō, -ere _vt_ to crowd round.

circumtextus _adj_ embroidered round the edge.

circumtonō, -āre, -uī _vt_ to thunder about.

circumvādō, -dere, -sī _vt_ to assail on all sides.

circumvagus _adj_ encircling.

circumvallō, -āre, -āvī, -ātum _vt_ to blockade, beset.

circumvectiō, -ōnis _f_ carrying about; (_sun_) revolution.

circumvector, -ārī _vi_ to travel round, cruise round; (_fig_) describe.

circumvehor, -hī, -ctus _vt, vi_ to ride round, sail round; (_fig_) to describe.

circumvēlō, -āre _vt_ to envelop.

circumveniō, -enīre, -ēnī, -entum _vt_ to surround, beset; to oppress; to cheat.

circumvertō, circumvortō, -ere _vt_ to turn round.

circumvestiō, -īre _vt_ to envelop.

circumvinciō, -īre _vt_ to lash about.

circumvīsō, -ere _vt_ to look at all round.

circumvolitō, -āre, -āvī, -ātum _vt, vi_ to fly round; to hover around.

circumvolō, -āre _vt_ to fly round.

circumvolvō, -vere _vt_ to roll round.

circus, -ī _m_ circle; the Circus Maximus (_famous Roman racecourse_); a racecourse.

Cirrha, -ae _f_ town near Delphi (_sacred to Apollo_).

Cirrhaeus _adj see n._

cirrus, -ī _m_ curl of hair; fringe.

cis _prep_ (_with acc_) on this side of; (_time_) within.

Cisalpīnus _adj_ on the Italian side of the Alps, Cisalpine.

cisium, -ī _and_ **iī** _nt_ two-wheeled carriage.

Cissēis, -dis _f_ Hecuba.

cista, -ae _f_ box, casket; ballot box.

cistella, -ae _f_ small box.

cistellātrīx, -īcis _f_ keeper of the moneybox.

cistellula, -ae _f_ little box.

cisterna, -ae _f_ reservoir.

cistophorus, -ī _m_ an Asiatic coin.

cistula, -ae _f_ little box.

citātus _adj_ quick, impetuous.

citerior (_sup_ **-imus**) _adj_ on this side, nearer.

Cithaerōn, -ōnis _m_ mountain range between Attica and Boeotia.

cithara, -ae _f_ lute.

citharista, -ae _m_, **citharistria, -ae** _f_ lute player. •

citharizō, -āre _vi_ to play the lute.

citharoedus, -ī _m_ a singer who accompanies himself on the lute.

citimus _adj_ nearest.

citō (_com_ **-ius**, _sup_ **-issimē**) _adv_ quickly, soon;

nōn ~ not easily.

citō, -āre, -āvī, -ātum *vt* to set in motion, rouse; to call (by name), appeal to, cite, mention.

citrā *adv* on this side, this way, not so far ♦ *prep* (*with acc*) on this side of, short of; (*time*) before, since; apart from; **~ quam** before.

citreus *adj* of citrus wood.

citrō *adv* hither, this way; **ultrō ~que** to and fro.

citrus, -ī *f* citrus tree; citron tree.

citus *ppp of* **cieō** ♦ *adj* quick.

cīvicus *adj* civic, civil; **corōna ~a** a civic crown for saving a citizen's life in war.

cīvīlis *adj* of citizens, civil; political, civilian; courteous, democratic; **iūs ~e** civil rights; Civil Law; code of legal procedure.

cīvīlitās, -ātis *f* politics; politeness.

cīvīliter *adv* like citizens; courteously.

cīvis, -is *m/f* citizen, fellow citizen.

cīvitās, -ātis *f* citizenship; community state; city; **~āte dōnāre** naturalize.

clādēs, -is *f* damage, disaster, ruin; defeat; (*fig*) scourge; **dare ~em** make havoc.

clam *adv* secretly; unknown ♦ *prep* (*with acc*) unknown to; **~ mē habēre** keep from me.

clāmātor, -ōris *m* bawler.

clāmitātiō, -ōnis *f* bawling.

clāmitō, -āre, -āvī, -ātum *vt, vi* to bawl, screech, cry out.

clāmō, -āre, -āvī, -ātum *vt, vi* to shout, cry out; to call upon, proclaim.

clāmor, -ōris *m* shout, cry; acclamation.

clāmōsus *adj* noisy.

clanculum *adv* secretly ♦ *prep* (*with acc*) unknown to.

clandestīnō *adv see* **clandestīnus**.

clandestīnus *adj* secret.

clangor, -ōris *m* clang, noise.

clārē *adv* brightly, loudly, clearly, with distinction.

clāreō, -ēre *vi* to be bright, be clear; to be evident; to be renowned.

clārēscō, -ere, clāruī *vi* to brighten, sound clear; to become obvious; to become famous.

clārigātiō, -ōnis *f* formal ultimatum to an enemy; fine for trespass.

clārigō, -āre *vi* to deliver a formal ultimatum.

clārisonus *adj* loud and clear.

clāritās, -ātis *f* distinctness; (*RHET*) lucidity; celebrity.

clāritūdō, -inis *f* brightness; (*fig*) distinction.

Clarius *adj* of Claros ♦ *m* Apollo.

clārō, -āre *vt* to illuminate; to explain; to make famous.

Claros, -ī *f* town in Ionia (*famous for worship of Apollo*).

clārus *adj* (*sight*) bright; (*sound*) loud; (*mind*) clear; (*person*) distinguished; **~ intonāre**

thunder from a clear sky; **vir ~issimus** a courtesy title for eminent men.

classiārius *adj* naval ♦ *mpl* marines.

classicula, -ae *f* flotilla.

classicum, -ī *nt* battle-signal; trumpet.

classicus *adj* of the first class; naval ♦ *mpl* marines.

classis, -is *f* a political class; army; fleet.

clāthrī, -ōrum *mpl* cage.

clāthrātus *adj* barred.

clātrī, -ōrum *mpl see* **clāthrī**.

claudeō, -ēre *vi* to limp; (*fig*) to be defective.

claudicātiō, -ōnis *f* limping.

claudicō, -āre *vi* to be lame; to waver, be defective.

Claudius, -ī *m* patrician family name (*esp Appius Claudius Caecus, famous censor*); the *Emperor Claudius*.

Claudius, -iānus, -iālis *adj see n*.

claudō, -dere, -sī, -sum *vt* to shut, close; to cut off, block; to conclude; to imprison, confine, blockade; **agmen ~** bring up the rear.

claudō, -ere *etc see* **claudeō**.

claudus *adj* lame, crippled; (*verse*) elegiac; (*fig*) wavering.

clausī *perf of* **claudō**.

claustra, -ōrum *ntpl* bar, bolt, lock; barrier, barricade, dam.

clausula, -ae *f* conclusion; (*RHET*) ending of a period.

clausum, -ī *nt* enclosure.

clausus *ppp of* **claudō**.

clāva, -ae *f* club, knotty branch; (*MIL*) foil.

clāvārium, -ī and iī *nt* money for buying shoe nails.

clāvātor, -ōris *m* cudgel-bearer.

clāvicula, -ae *f* vine tendril.

clāviger, -ī *m* (*Hercules*) club bearer; (*Janus*) key-bearer.

clāvis, -is *f* key.

clāvus, -ī *m* nail; tiller, rudder; purple stripe on the tunic (*broad for senators, narrow for equites*); **~um annī movēre** reckon the beginning of the year.

Cleanthēs, -is *m* Stoic philosopher.

clēmēns, -entis *adj* mild, gentle, merciful; (*weather, water*) mild, calm.

clēmenter *adv* gently, indulgently; gradually.

clēmentia, -ae *f* mildness, forbearance, mercy.

Cleopatra, -ae *f* queen of Egypt.

clepō, -ere, -sī, -tum *vt* to steal.

clepsydra, -ae *f* waterclock (*used for timing speakers*); **~am dare** give leave to speak; **~am petere** ask leave to speak.

clepta, -ae *m* thief.

cliēns, -entis *m* client, dependant; follower; vassal-state.

clienta, -ae *f* client.

Noun declensions and verb conjugations are shown on pp xiii to xxv. The present infinitive ending of a verb shows to which conjugation it belongs: **-āre** = 1st; **-ēre** = 2nd; **-ere** = 3rd and **-īre** = 4th. Irregular verbs are shown on p xxvi

clientēla, -ae *f* clientship, protection; clients.
clientulus, -ī *m* insignificant client.
clīnāmen, -inis *nt* swerve.
clīnātus *adj* inclined.
Cliō, -ūs *f* Muse of history.
clipeātus *adj* armed with a shield.
clipeus, -ī *m*, **-um, -ī** *nt* round bronze shield; disc; medallion on a metal base.
clitellae, -ārum *fpl* packsaddle, attribute of an ass.
clitellārius *adj* carrying packsaddles.
Clitumnus, -ī *m* river in Umbria.
clīvōsus *adj* hilly.
clīvus, -ī *m* slope, hill; **~ sacer** *part of the Via Sacra.*
cloāca, -ae *f* sewer, drain.
Cloācīna, -ae *f* Venus.
Clōdius, -ī *m* Roman plebeian name (*esp the tribune, enemy of Cicero*).
Cloelia, -ae *f* Roman girl hostage (*who escaped by swimming the Tiber*).
Clōthō (*acc* **-ō**) *f* one of the Fates.
clueō, -ēre, -eor, -ērī *vi* to be called, be famed.
clūnis, -is *m/f* buttock.
clūrīnus *adj* of apes.
Clūsīnus *adj see n.*
Clūsium, -ī *nt* old Etruscan town (*now* Chiusi).
Clūsius, -ī *m* Janus.
Clytaemnēstra, -ae *f* wife of Agamemnon (*whom she murdered*).
Cnidius *adj see n.*
Cnidus, -ī *f* town in Caria (*famous for worship of Venus*).
coacervātiō, -ōnis *f* accumulation.
coacervō, -āre *vt* to heap, accumulate.
coacēscō, -escere, -uī *vi* to become sour.
coāctō, -āre *vt* to force.
coāctor, -ōris *m* collector (of money).
coāctōrēs agminis rearguard.
coāctum, -ī *nt* thick coverlet.
coāctus *adj* forced.
coāctus *ppp of* **cōgō.**
coāctus, -ūs *m* compulsion.
coaedificō, -āre, -ātum *vt* to build on.
coaequō, -āre, -āvī, -ātum *vt* to make equal, bring down to the same level.
coagmentātiō, -ōnis *f* combination.
coagmentō, -āre, -āvī, -ātum *vt* to glue, join together.
coagmentum, -ī *nt* joining, joint.
coāgulum, -ī *nt* rennet.
coalēscō, -escere, -uī, -itum *vi* to grow together; (*fig*) to agree together; to flourish.
coangustō, -āre *vt* to restrict.
coarct- *etc see* **coart-.**
coarguō, -ere, -ī *vt* to convict, prove conclusively.
coartātiō, -ōnis *f* crowding together.
coartō, -āre, -āvī, -ātum *vt* to compress, abridge.
coccineus, coccinus *adj* scarlet.
coccum, -ī *nt* scarlet.

cochlea, coclea, -ae *f* snail.
cocleāre, -is *nt* spoon.
cocles, -itis *m* man blind in one eye; *surname of Horatius who defended the bridge.*
coctilis *adj* baked; of bricks.
coctus *ppp of* **coquō ♦** *adj* (*fig*) well considered.
cocus *etc see* **coquus.**
Cōcȳtius *adj see n.*
Cōcȳtus, -us, -ī *m* river in the lower world.
cōda *etc see* **cauda.**
cōdex *etc see* **caudex.**
cōdicillī, -ōrum *mpl* letter, note, petition; codicil.
Codrus, -ī *m* last king of Athens.
coēgī *perf of* **cōgō.**
coel- *etc see* **cael-.**
coemō, -emere, -ēmī, -emptum *vt* to buy up.
coemptiō, -ōnis *f* a form of Roman marriage; mock sale of an estate.
coemptiōnālis *adj* used in a mock sale; worthless.
coen- *etc see* **caen-** *or* **cēn-.**
coeō, -īre, -īvī *and* **iī, -itum** *vi* to meet, assemble; to encounter; to combine, mate; (*wounds*) to close; to agree, conspire ♦ *vt:* **~ societātem** make a compact.
coepiō, -ere, -ī, -tum *vt, vi* begin (*esp in perf tenses*); **rēs agī ~tae sunt** things began to be done; **coepisse** to have begun.
coeptō, -āre, -āvī, -ātum *vt, vi* to begin, attempt.
coeptum, -ī *nt* beginning, undertaking.
coeptus *ppp of* **coepiō.**
coeptus, -ūs *m* beginning.
coepulōnus, -ī *m* fellow-banqueter.
coerātor *etc see* **cūrātor.**
coerceō, -ēre, -uī, -itum *vt* to enclose; to confine, repress; (*fig*) to control, check, correct.
coercitiō, -ōnis *f* coercion, punishment.
coetus, coitus, -ūs *m* meeting, joining together; assembly, crowd.
cōgitātē *adv* deliberately.
cōgitātiō, -ōnis *f* thought, reflection; idea, plan; faculty of thought, imagination.
cōgitātus *adj* deliberate ♦ *ntpl* ideas.
cōgitō, -āre, -āvī, -ātum *vt, vi* to think, ponder, imagine; to feel disposed; to plan, intend.
cognātiō, -ōnis *f* relationship (by blood); kin, family; (*fig*) affinity, resemblance.
cognātus, -ī *m*, **-a, -ae** *f* relation ♦ *adj* related; (*fig*) connected, similar.
cognitiō, -ōnis *f* acquiring of knowledge, knowledge; idea, notion; (*law*) judicial inquiry; (*comedy*) recognition.
cognitor, -ōris *m* (*law*) attorney; witness of a person's identity; (*fig*) defender.
cognitus *adj* acknowledged.
cognitus *ppp of* **cognōscō.**
cognōmen, -inis *nt* surname; name.
cognōmentum, -ī *nt* surname, name.

cognōminis *adj* with the same name.

cognōminō, -āre, -āvī, -ātum *vt* to give a surname to; **verba ~āta** synonyms.

cognōscō, -ōscere, -ōvī, -itum *vt* to get to know, learn, understand; to know, recognize, identify; (*law*) to investigate; (*MIL*) to reconnoitre.

cōgō, -ere, coēgī, coāctum *vt* to collect, gather together; (*liquids*) to thicken, curdle; to contract, confine; to compel, force; to infer; **agmen ~** bring up the rear; **senātum ~** call a meeting of the senate.

cohaerentia, -ae *f* coherence.

cohaereō, -rēre, -sī, -sum *vi* to stick together, cohere; to cling to; (*fig*) to be consistent, harmonize; to agree, be consistent with.

cohaerēscō, -ere *vi* to stick together.

cohaesus *ppp of* **cohaereō.**

cohērēs, -ēdis *m/f* co-heir.

cohibeō, -ēre, -uī, -itum *vt* to hold together, encircle; to hinder, stop; (*fig*) to restrain, repress.

cohonestō, -āre *vt* to do honour to.

cohorrēscō, -ēscere, -uī *vi* to shudder all over.

cohors, -tis *f* courtyard; (*MIL*) cohort (*about 600 men*); retinue (*esp of the praetor in a province*); (*fig*) company.

cohortātiō, -ōnis *f* encouragement.

cohorticula, -ae *f* small cohort.

cohortor, -ārī, -ātus *vt* to encourage, urge.

coitiō, -ōnis *f* encounter; conspiracy.

coitus *etc see* **coetus.**

colaphus, -ī *m* blow with the fist, box.

Colchis, -idis *f* Medea's country (*at the E. end of the Black Sea*).

Colchis, -us, -icus *adj* Colchian.

cōleus *etc see* **culleus.**

cōlis *etc see* **caulis.**

collabāscō, -ere *vi* to waver also.

collabefactō, -āre *vt* to shake violently.

collabefīō, -fierī, -factus *vi* to be destroyed.

collābor, -bī, -psus *vi* to fall in ruin, collapse.

collacerātus *adj* torn to pieces.

collacrimātiō, -ōnis *f* weeping.

collactea, -ae *f* foster-sister.

collāpsus *ppa of* **collābor.**

collāre, -is *nt* neckband.

Collātia, -iae *f* ancient town near Rome ◆ *m* husband of Lucretia.

Collātīnus *adj* of Collatia.

collātiō, -ōnis *f* bringing together, combination; (*money*) contribution; (*RHET*) comparison; (*PHILOS*) analogy.

collātor, -ōris *m* contributor.

collātus *ppp of* **cōnferō.**

collaudātiō, -ōnis *f* praise.

collaudō, -āre, -āvī, -ātum *vt* to praise highly.

collaxō, -āre *vt* to make porous.

collēcta, -ae *f* money contribution.

collēctīcius *adj* hastily gathered.

collēctiō, -ōnis *f* gathering up; (*RHET*) recapitulation.

collēctus *ppp of* **colligō.**

collēctus, -ūs *m* accumulation.

collēga, -ae *m* colleague; associate.

collēgī *perf of* **colligō.**

collēgium, -ī *and* **iī** *nt* association in office; college, guild (*of magistrates, etc*).

collībertus, -ī *m* fellow freedman.

collibet, collubet, -uit *and* **itum est** *vi* it pleases.

collīdō, -dere, -sī, -sum *vt* to beat together, strike, bruise; (*fig*) to bring into conflict.

colligātiō, -ōnis *f* connection.

colligō, -āre, -āvī, -ātum *vt* to fasten, tie up; (*fig*) to combine; to restrain, check.

colligō, -igere, -ēgī, -ēctum *vt* to gather, collect; to compress, draw together; to check; (*fig*) to acquire; to think about; to infer, conclude; **animum, mentem ~** recover, rally; **sē ~** crouch; recover one's courage; **vāsa ~** (*MIL*) pack up.

Collīna Porta *gate in N.E. of Rome.*

collīneō, -āre *vt, vi* to aim straight.

collinō, -inere, -ēvī, -itum *vt* to besmear; (*fig*) to deface.

colliquefactus *adj* dissolved.

collis, -is *m* hill, slope.

collīsī *perf of* **collīdō.**

collīsus *ppp of* **collīdō.**

collitus *ppp of* **collinō.**

collocātiō, -ōnis *f* arrangement; giving in marriage.

collocō, -āre, -āvī, -ātum *vt* to place, station, arrange; to give in marriage; (*money*) to invest; (*fig*) to establish; to occupy, employ.

collocuplētō, -āre, -āvī *vt* to enrich.

collocūtiō, -ōnis *f* conversation.

colloquium, -ī *and* **iī** *nt* conversation, conference.

colloquor, -quī, -cūtus *vi* to converse, hold a conference ◆ *vt* to talk to.

collubet *etc see* **collibet.**

collūceō, -ēre *vi* to shine brightly; (*fig*) to be resplendent.

collūdō, -dere, -sī, -sum *vi* to play together *or* with; to practise collusion.

collum, -ī *nt* neck; **~ torquēre, obtorquēre, obstringere** arrest.

colluō, -uere, -uī, -ūtum *vt* to rinse, moisten.

collus *etc see* **collum.**

collūsiō, -ōnis *f* secret understanding.

collūsor, -ōris *m* playmate, fellow gambler.

collūstrō, -āre, -āvī, -ātum *vt* to light up; to survey.

colluviō, -ōnis, -ēs, -em, -ē *f* sweepings, filth; (*fig*) dregs, rabble.

collybus, -ī *m* money exchange, rate of exchange.

collȳra, -ae *f* vermicelli.

collȳricus *adj see n.*

collȳrium, -ī *and* **iī** *nt* eye lotion.

colō, -ere, -uī, cultum *vt* (AGR) to cultivate, work; (*place*) to live in; (*human affairs*) to cherish, protect, adorn; (*qualities, pursuits*) to cultivate, practise; (*gods*) to worship; (*men*) to honour, court; **vītam ~** live.

colocāsia, -ae *f*, **-a, -ōrum** *ntpl* Egyptian bean, caladium.

colōna, -ae *f* country-woman.

colōnia, -ae *f* settlement, colony; settlers.

colōnicus *adj* colonial.

colōnus, -ī *m* crofter, farmer; settler, colonist.

color (colōs), -ōris *m* colour; complexion; beauty, lustre; (*fig*) outward show; (RHET) style, tone; colourful excuse; **~ōrem mūtāre** blush, go pale; **homō nullīus ~ōris** an unknown person.

colōrātus *adj* healthily tanned.

colōrō, -āre, -āvī, -ātum *vt* to colour, tan; (*fig*) to give a colour to.

colossus, -ī *m* gigantic statue (*esp that of Apollo at Rhodes*).

colostra, colustra, -ae *f* beestings.

coluber, -rī *m* snake.

colubra, -ae *f* snake.

colubrifer, -ī *adj* snaky.

colubrīnus *adj* wily.

coluī *perf of* **colō.**

cōlum, -ī *nt* strainer.

columba, -ae *f* dove, pigeon.

columbar, -āris *nt* kind of collar.

columbārium, -ī *and* **iī** *nt* dovecote.

columbīnus *adj* pigeon's ♦ *m* little pigeon.

columbus, -ī *m* dove, cock-pigeon.

columella, -ae *f* small pillar.

columen, -inis *nt* height, summit; pillar; (*fig*) chief; prop.

columna, -ae *f* column, pillar; *a pillory in the Forum Romanum*; waterspout.

columnārium, -ī *and* **iī** *nt* pillar tax.

columnārius, -ī *m* criminal.

columnātus *adj* pillared.

colurnus *adj* made of hazel.

colus, -ī *and* **ūs** *f* (*occ m*) distaff.

cōlyphia, -ōrum *ntpl* food of athletes.

coma, -ae *f* hair (*of the head*); foliage.

comāns, -antis *adj* hairy, plumed; leafy.

cōmarchus, -ī *m* burgomaster.

comātus *adj* long-haired; leafy; **Gallia ~** Transalpine Gaul.

combibō, -ere, -ī *vt* to drink to the full, absorb.

combibō, -ōnis *m* fellow-drinker.

combūrō, -rere, -ssī, -stum *vt* to burn up; (*fig*) to ruin.

combūstus *ppp of* **combūrō.**

comedō, -ēsse, -ēdī, -ēsum *and* **-ēstum** *vt* to eat up, devour; (*fig*) to waste, squander; **sē ~**

pine away.

Cōmēnsis *adj see* **Cōmum.**

comes, -itis *m/f* companion, partner; attendant, follower; one of a magistrate's *or* emperor's retinue; (*medieval title*) count.

comēs, comēst *pres tense of* **comedō.**

comēstus, comēsus *ppp of* **comedō.**

comētēs, -ae *m* comet.

cōmicē *adv* in the manner of comedy.

cōmicus, -ī *m* comedy actor, comedy writer ♦ *adj* of comedy, comic.

cōmis *adj* courteous, friendly.

cōmissābundus *adj* carousing.

cōmissātiō, -ōnis *f* Bacchanalian revel.

cōmissātor, -ōris *m* reveller.

cōmissor, -ārī, -ātus *vi* to carouse, make merry.

cōmitās, -ātis *f* kindness, affability.

comitātus, -ūs *m* escort, retinue; company.

cōmiter *adv see* **cōmis.**

comitia, -iōrum *ntpl* assembly for the election of magistrates and other business (*esp the ~* **centuriāta**); elections.

comitiālis *adj* of the elections; **~ morbus** epilepsy.

comitiātus, -ūs *m* assembly at the elections.

comitium, -ī *and* **iī** *nt* place of assembly.

comitō, -āre, -āvī, -ātum *vt* to accompany.

comitor, -ārī, -ātus *vt, vi* to attend, follow.

commaculō, -āre, -āvī, -ātum *vt* to stain, defile.

commanipulāris, -is *m* soldier in the same company.

commeātus, -ūs *m* passage; leave, furlough; convoy (of troops *or* goods); (MIL) lines of communication, provisions, supplies.

commeditor, -ārī *vt* to practise.

commeminī, -isse *vt, vi* to remember perfectly.

commemorābilis *adj* memorable.

commemorātiō, -ōnis *f* recollection, recounting.

commemorō, -āre, -āvī, -ātum *vt* to recall, remind; to mention, relate.

commendābilis *adj* praiseworthy.

commendātīcius *adj* of recommendation *or* introduction.

commendātiō, -ōnis *f* recommendation; worth, excellence.

commendātor, -ōris *m* commender (*male*).

commendātrīx, -rīcis *f* commender (*female*).

commendātus *adj* approved, valued.

commendō, -āre, -āvī, -ātum *vt* to entrust, commit, commend (to one's care *or* charge); to recommend, set off to advantage.

commēnsus *ppa of* **commētior.**

commentāriolum, -ī *nt* short treatise.

commentārius, -ī *and* **iī** *m,* **-ium, -ī** *and* **iī** *nt* notebook; commentary, memoir; (*law*) brief.

commentātiō, -ōnis *f* studying, meditation.

commentīcius *adj* fictitious, imaginary; false.

commentor, -ārī, -ātus *vt, vi* to study, think

over, prepare carefully; to invent, compose, write.

commentor, -ōris m inventor.

commentum, -ī nt invention, fiction; contrivance.

commentus ppa of **comminīscor ♦** adj feigned, fictitious.

commeō, -āre vi to pass to and fro; to go or come often.

commercium, -ī and iī nt trade, commerce; right to trade; dealings, communication.

commercor, -ārī, -ātus vt to buy up.

commereō, -ēre, -uī, -itum; -eor, -ērī, -itus vt to deserve; to be guilty of.

commētior, -tīrī, -nsus vt to measure.

commētō, -āre vi to go often.

commictus ppp of **commingō**.

commigrō, -āre, -āvī, -ātum vi to remove, migrate.

commīlitium, -ī and iī nt service together.

commīlitō, -ōnis m fellow soldier.

comminātiō, -ōnis f threat.

commingō, -ingere, -īnxī, -īctum vt to pollute.

comminīscor, -ī, commentus vt to devise, contrive.

comminor, -ārī, -ātus vt to threaten.

comminuō, -uere, -uī, -ūtum vt to break up, smash; to diminish; to impair.

comminus adv hand to hand; near at hand.

commisceō, -scēre, -scuī, -xtum vt to mix together, join together.

commiserātiō, -ōnis f (RHET) passage intended to arouse pity.

commiserēscō, -ere vt to pity.

commiseror, -ārī vt to bewail ♦ vi (RHET) to try to excite pity.

commissiō, -ōnis f start (of a contest).

commissum, -ī nt enterprise; offence, crime; secret.

commissūra, -ae f joint, connection.

commissus ppp of **committō**.

committō, -ittere, -īsī, -issum vt to join, connect, bring together; to begin, undertake; (battle) to join, engage in; (offence) to commit, be guilty of; (punishment) to incur, forfeit; to entrust, trust; **sē urbī ~** venture into the city.

commixtus ppp of **commisceō**.

commodē adv properly, well; aptly, opportunely; pleasantly.

commoditās, -ātis f convenience, ease, fitness; advantage; (person) kindliness; (RHET) apt expression.

commodō, -āre, -āvī, -ātum vt to adjust, adapt; to give, lend, oblige with; (with dat) to oblige.

commodulē, -um adv conveniently.

commodum, -ī nt convenience; advantage, interest; pay, salary; loan; **~ō tuō** at your

leisure; **~a vītae** the good things of life.

commodum adv opportunely; just.

commodus adj proper, fit, full; suitable, easy, opportune; (person) pleasant, obliging.

commōlior, -īrī vt to set in motion.

commonefaciō, -facere, -fēcī, -factum vt to remind, recall.

commoneō, -ēre, -uī, -itum vt to remind, impress upon.

commōnstrō, -āre vt to point out.

commorātiō, -ōnis f delay, residence; (RHET) dwelling (on a topic).

commoror, -ārī, -ātus vi to sojourn, wait; (RHET) to dwell ♦ vt to detain.

commōtiō, -ōnis f excitement.

commōtiuncula f slight indisposition.

commōtus ppp of **commoveō ♦** adj excited, emotional.

commoveō, -ovēre, -ōvī, -ōtum vt to set in motion, move, dislodge, agitate; (mind) to unsettle, shake, excite, move, affect; (emotions) to stir up, provoke.

commūne, -is nt common property; state; **in ~e** for a common end; equally; in general.

commūnicātiō, -ōnis f imparting; (RHET) making the audience appear to take part in the discussion.

commūnicō, -āre, -āvī, -ātum vt to share (by giving or receiving); to impart, communicate; **cōnsilia ~ cum** make common cause with.

commūniō, -īre, -īvī and iī, -ītum vt to build (a fortification); to fortify, strengthen.

commūniō, -ōnis f sharing in common, communion.

commūnis adj common, general, universal; (person) affable, democratic; **~ia loca** public places; **~ēs locī** general topics; **~is sēnsus** popular sentiment; **aliquid ~e habēre** have something in common.

commūnitās, -ātis f fellowship; sense of fellowship; affability.

commūniter adv in common, jointly.

commūnītiō, -ōnis f preparing the way.

commurmuror, -ārī, -ātus vi to mutter to oneself.

commūtābilis adj changeable.

commūtātiō, -iōnis f change.

commūtātus, -ūs m change.

commūtō, -āre, -āvī, -ātum vt to change, exchange, interchange.

cōmō, -ere, -psī, -ptum vt to arrange, dress, adorn.

cōmoedia, -ae f comedy.

cōmoedicē adv as in comedy.

cōmoedus, -ī m comic actor.

cōmōsus adj shaggy.

compāctiō, -ōnis f joining together.

compāctus ppp of **compingō**.

compāgēs, -is, -ō, -inis f joint, structure,

Noun declensions and verb conjugations are shown on pp xiii to xxv. The present infinitive ending of a verb shows to which conjugation it belongs: **-āre** = 1st; **-ēre** = 2nd; **-ere** = 3rd and **-īre** = 4th. Irregular verbs are shown on p xxvi

framework.

compār, -aris *mf* comrade, husband, wife ♦ *adj* equal.

comparābilis *adj* comparable.

comparātē *adv* by comparison in a comparison.

comparātiō, -ōnis *f* comparison; (*ASTRO*) relative positions; agreement; preparation; procuring.

comparātīvus *adj* based on comparison.

compāreō, -ēre *vi* to be visible; to be present, be realised.

comparō, -āre, -āvī, -ātum *vt* to couple together, match; to compare; (*POL*) to agree (about respective duties); to prepare, provide; (*custom*) to establish; to procure, purchase, get.

compāscō, -ere *vt* to put (cattle) to graze in common.

compāscuus *adj* for common pasture.

compecīscor, -īscī, -tus *vi* to come to an agreement.

compectum, -tī *nt* agreement.

compediō, -īre, -ītum *vt* to fetter.

compēgī *perf of* **compingō.**

compellātiō, -ōnis *f* reprimand.

compellō, -āre, -āvī, -ātum *vt* to call, address; to reproach; (*law*) to arraign.

compellō, -ellere, -ulī, -ulsum *vt* to drive, bring together, concentrate; to impel, compel.

compendiārius *adj* short.

compendium, -ī and iī *nt* saving; abbreviating; short cut; **~ī facere** save; abridge; **~ī fierī** to be brief.

compēnsātiō, -ōnis *f* (*fig*) compromise.

compēnsō, -āre, -āvī, -ātum *vt* to balance (against), make up for.

compercō, -cere, -sī *vt*, *vi* to save; to refrain.

comperendinātiō, -iōnis *f* adjournment for two days.

comperendinātus, -ūs *m* adjournment for two days.

comperendinō, -āre *vt* to adjourn for two days.

comperiō, -īre, -ī, -tum (*occ* **-ior**) *vt* to find out, learn; **~tus** detected; found guilty; **~tum habēre** know for certain.

compēs, -edis *f* fetter, bond.

compēscō, -ere, -uī *vt* to check, suppress.

competītor, -ōris *m*, **-rīx, -rīcis** *f* rival candidate.

competō, -ere, -īvī and iī, -ītum *vi* to coincide, agree; to be capable.

compīlātiō, -ōnis *f* plundering; compilation.

compīlō, -āre, -āvī, -ātum *vt* to pillage.

compingō, -ingere, -ēgī, -āctum *vt* to put together, compose; to lock up, hide away.

compitālia, -ium and iōrum *ntpl* festival in honour of the Lares Compitales.

compitālicius *adj* of the Compitalia.

compitālis *adj* of crossroads.

compitum, -ī *nt* crossroads.

complaceō, -ēre, -uī and itus sum *vi* to please (someone else) as well, please very much.

complānō, -āre *vt* to level, raze to the ground.

complector, -ctī, -xus *vt* to embrace, clasp; to enclose; (*speech, writing*) to deal with, comprise; (*mind*) to grasp, comprehend; to honour, be fond of.

complēmentum, -ī *nt* complement.

compleō, -ēre, -ēvī, -ētum *vt* to fill up; (*MIL*) to man, make up the complement of; (*time, promise, duty*) to complete, fulfil, finish.

complētus *adj* perfect.

complexiō, -ōnis *f* combination; (*RHET*) period; (*logic*) conclusion of an argument; dilemma.

complexus, -ūs *m* embrace; (*fig*) affection, close combat; (*speech*) connection.

complicō, -āre *vt* to fold up.

complōrātiō, -iōnis *f*, **-us, -ūs** *m* loud lamentation.

complōrō, -āre, -āvī, -ātum *vt* to mourn for.

complūrēs, -ium *adj* several, very many.

complūriēns *adv* several times.

complūsculī, -ōrum *adj* quite a few.

compluvium, -ī and iī *nt* roof opening in a Roman house.

compōnō, -ōnere, -osuī, -ositum *vt* to put together, join; to compose, construct; to compare, contrast; to match, oppose; to put away, store up, stow; (*dead*) to lay out, inter; to allay, quieten, reconcile; to adjust, settle, arrange; to devise, prepare ♦ *vi* to make peace.

comportō, -āre *vt* to collect, bring in.

compos, -tis *adj* in control, in possession; sharing; **vōtī ~** having got one's wish.

compositē *adv* properly, in a polished manner.

compositiō, -ōnis *f* compounding, system; (*words*) arrangement; reconciliation; matching (of fighters).

compositor, -ōris *m* arranger.

compositūra, -ae *f* connection.

compositus *ppp of* **compōnō** ♦ *adj* orderly, regular; adapted, assumed, ready; calm, sedate; (*words*) compound; **compositō, ex compositō** as agreed.

compōtātiō, -ōnis *f* drinking party.

compotiō, -īre *vt* to put in possession (of).

compōtor, -ōris *m*, **-rīx, -rīcis** *f* fellow drinker.

comprānsor, -ōris *m* fellow guest.

comprecātiō, -ōnis *f* public supplication.

comprecor, -ārī, -ātus *vt*, *vi* to pray to; to pray for.

comprehendō (comprendō), -endere, -endī, -ēnsum *vt* to grasp, catch; to seize, arrest, catch in the act; (*words*) to comprise, recount; (*thought*) to grasp, comprehend; to hold in affection; **numerō ~** count.

comprehēnsibilis *adj* conceivable.

comprehēnsiō, -ōnis *f* grasping, seizing;

perception, idea; (*RHET*) period.

comprehēnsus, comprēnsus *ppp of*
comprehendō.

comprendō *etc see* **comprehendō.**

compressī *perf of* **comprimō.**

compressiō, -ōnis *f* embrace; (*RHET*)
compression.

compressus *ppp of* **comprimō.**

compressus, -ūs *m* compression, embrace.

comprimō, -imere, -essī, -essum *vt* to
squeeze, compress; to check, restrain; to
suppress, withhold; **animam ~** hold one's
breath; **~essīs manibus** with hands folded,
idle.

comprobātiō, -ōnis *f* approval.

comprobātor, -ōris *m* supporter.

comprobō, -āre, -āvī, -ātum *vt* to prove,
make good; to approve.

comprōmissum, -ī *nt* mutual agreement to
abide by an arbitrator's decision.

comprōmittō, -ittere, -īsī, -issum *vt* to
undertake to abide by an arbitrator's
decision.

cōmpsī *perf of* **cōmō.**

cōmptus *ppp of* **cōmō** ♦ *adj* elegant.

cōmptus, -ūs *m* coiffure; union.

compulī *perf of* **compellō.**

compulsus *ppp of* **compellō.**

compungō, -ungere, -ūnxī, -ūnctum *vt* to
prick, sting, tattoo.

computō, -āre, -āvī, -ātum *vt* to reckon,
number.

Cōmum, -ī *nt* (*also* **Novum Cōmum**) town in N.
Italy (*now* Como).

cōnāmen, -inis *nt* effort; support.

cōnāta, -ōrum *ntpl* undertaking, venture.

cōnātus, -ūs *m* effort; endeavour; inclination,
impulse.

concaedēs, -ium *fpl* barricade of felled trees.

concalefaciō, -facere, -fēcī, -factum *vt* to
warm well.

concaleō, -ēre *vi* to be hot.

concalēscō, -ēscere, -uī *vi* to become hot,
glow.

concallēscō, -ēscere, -uī *vi* to become
shrewd; to become unfeeling.

concastīgō, -āre *vt* to punish severely.

concavō, -āre *vt* to curve.

concavus *adj* hollow; vaulted, bent.

concēdō, -ēdere, -essī, -essum *vi* to
withdraw, depart; to disappear, pass away,
pass; to yield, submit, give precedence,
comply ♦ *vt* to give up, cede; to grant, allow;
to pardon, overlook.

concelebrō, -āre, -āvī, -ātum *vt* to frequent,
fill, enliven; (*study*) to pursue eagerly; to
celebrate; to make known.

concēnātiō, -ōnis *f* dining together.

concentiō, -ōnis *f* chorus.

concenturiō, -āre *vt* to marshal.

concentus, -ūs *m* chorus, concert; (*fig*)
concord, harmony.

conceptiō, -ōnis *f* conception; drawing up
legal formulae.

conceptīvus *adj* (*holidays*) movable.

conceptus *ppp of* **concipiō.**

conceptus, -ūs *m* conception.

concerpō, -ere, -sī, -tum *vt* to tear up; (*fig*) to
abuse.

concertātiō, -ōnis *f* controversy.

concertātor, -ōris *m* rival.

concertātōrius *adj* controversial.

concertō, -āre, -āvī, -ātum *vi* to fight; to
dispute.

concessiō, -ōnis *f* grant, permission; (*law*)
pleading guilty and asking indulgence.

concessō, -āre *vi* to stop, loiter.

concessus *ppp of* **concēdō.**

concessus, -ūs *m* permission.

concha, -ae *f* mussel, oyster, murex; mussel
shell, oyster shell, pearl; purple dye;
trumpet, perfume dish.

conchis, -is *f* kind of bean.

conchīta, -ae *m* catcher of shellfish.

conchȳliātus *adj* purple.

conchȳlium, -ī *and* **iī** *nt* shellfish, oyster,
murex; purple.

concidō, -ere, -ī *vi* to fall, collapse; to subside,
fail, perish.

concīdō, -dere, -dī, -sum *vt* to cut up, cut to
pieces, kill; (*fig*) to ruin, strike down; (*RHET*)
to dismember, enfeeble.

**concieō, -iēre, -īvī, -itum; conciō, -īre,
-ītum** *vt* to rouse, assemble; to stir up,
shake; (*fig*) to rouse, provoke.

conciliābulum, -ī *nt* place for public
gatherings.

conciliātiō, -ōnis *f* union; winning over
(*friends, hearers*); (*PHILOS*) inclination.

conciliātor, -ōris *m* promoter.

conciliātrix, -īcis *m*, **-īcula, -ae** *f* promoter,
matchmaker.

conciliātus, -ūs *m* combination.

conciliātus *adj* beloved; favourable.

conciliō, -āre, -āvī, -ātum *vt* to unite; to win
over, reconcile; to procure, purchase, bring
about, promote.

concilium, -ī *and* **iī** *nt* gathering, meeting;
council; (*things*) union.

concinnē *adv see* **concinnus.**

concinnitās, -ātis, -ūdō, -ūdinis *f* (*RHET*)
rhythmical style.

concinnō, -āre, -āvī, -ātum *vt* to arrange; to
bring about, produce; (*with adj*) to make.

concinnus *adj* symmetrical, beautiful; (*style*)
polished, rhythmical; (*person*) elegant,
courteous; (*things*) suited, pleasing.

concinō, -ere, -uī *vi* to sing, play, sound
together; (*fig*) to agree, harmonize ♦ *vt* to
sing about, celebrate, prophesy.

Noun declensions and verb conjugations are shown on pp xiii to xxv. The present infinitive ending of a verb shows
to which conjugation it belongs: **-āre** = 1st; **-ēre** = 2nd; **-ere** = 3rd and **-īre** = 4th. Irregular verbs are shown on p xxvi

conciō *etc see* **concieō.**

concio- *etc see* **contio-.**

concipiō, -ipere, -ēpī, -eptum *vt* to take to oneself, absorb; (*women*) to conceive; (*senses*) to perceive; (*mind*) to conceive, imagine, understand; (*feelings, acts*) to harbour, foster, commit; (*words*) to draw up, intimate formally.

concīsiō, -ōnis *f* breaking up into short clauses.

concīsus *ppp of* **concīdō ♦** *adj* broken up, concise.

concitātē *adv see* **concitātus.**

concitātiō, -ōnis *f* acceleration; (*mind*) excitement, passion; riot.

concitātor, -ōris *m* agitator.

concitātus *ppp of* **concitō ♦** *adj* fast; excited.

concitō, -āre, -āvī, -ātum *vt* to move rapidly, bestir, hurl; to urge, rouse, impel; to stir up, occasion.

concitor, -ōris *m* instigator.

concitus, concītus *ppp of* **concieō;** *ppp of* **conciō.**

conclāmātiō, -ōnis *f* great shout.

conclāmitō, -āre *vi* to keep on shouting.

conclāmō, -āre, -āvī, -ātum *vt, vi* to shout, cry out; to call to help; (*MIL*) to give the signal; (*dead*) to call by name in mourning; **vāsa ~** give the order to pack up; **~ātum est** it's all over.

conclāve, -is *nt* room.

conclūdō, -dere, -sī, -sum *vt* to shut up, enclose; to include, comprise; to end, conclude, round off (*esp with a rhythmical cadence*); (*PHILOS*) to infer, demonstrate.

conclūsē *adv* with rhythmical cadences.

conclūsiō, -ōnis *f* (*MIL*) blockade; end, conclusion; (*RHET*) period, peroration; (*logic*) conclusion.

conclūsiuncula, -ae *f* quibble.

conclūsum, -ī *nt* logical conclusion.

conclūsus *ppp of* **conclūdō.**

concoctus *ppp of* **concoquō.**

concolor, -ōris *adj* of the same colour.

concomitātus *adj* escorted.

concoquō, -quere, -xī, -ctum *vt* to boil down; to digest; (*fig*) to put up with, stomach; (*thought*) to consider well, concoct.

concordia, -ae *f* friendship, concord, union; *goddess of Concord.*

concorditer *adv* amicably.

concordō, -āre *vi* to agree, be in harmony.

concors, -dis *adj* concordant, united, harmonious.

concrēbrēscō, -ēscere, -uī *vi* to gather strength.

concrēdō, -ere, -idī, -itum *vt* to entrust.

concremō, -āre, -āvī, -ātum *vt* to burn.

concrepō, -āre, -uī, -itum *vi* to rattle, creak, clash, snap (fingers) **♦** *vt* to beat.

concrēscō, -scere, -vī, -tum *vi* to harden, curdle, congeal, clot; to grow, take shape.

concrētiō, -ōnis *f* condensing; matter.

concrētum, -ī *nt* solid matter, hard frost.

concrētus *ppa of* **concrēscō ♦** *adj* hard, thick, stiff, congealed; compounded.

concrīminor, -ārī, -ātus *vi* to bring a complaint.

concruciō, -āre *vt* to torture.

concubīna, -ae *f* (female) concubine.

concubīnātus, -ūs *m* concubinage.

concubīnus, -ī *m* (male) concubine.

concubitus, -ūs *m* reclining together (at table); sexual union.

concubius *adj:* **~iā nocte** during the first sleep **♦** *nt* the time of the first sleep.

conculcō, -āre *vt* to trample under foot, treat with contempt.

concumbō, -mbere, -buī, -bitum *vi* to lie together, lie with.

concupīscō, -īscere, -īvī, -ītum *vt* to covet, long for, aspire to.

concūrō, -āre *vt* to take care of.

concurrō, -rere, -rī, -sum *vi* to flock together, rush in; (*things*) to clash, meet; (*MIL*) to join battle, charge; (*events*) to happen at the same time, concur.

concursātiō, -ōnis *f* running together, rushing about; (*MIL*) skirmishing; (*dreams*) coherent design.

concursātor, -ōris *m* skirmisher.

concursiō, -ōnis *f* meeting, concourse; (*RHET*) repetition for emphasis.

concursō, -āre *vi* to collide; to rush about, travel about; (*MIL*) to skirmish **♦** *vt* to visit, go from place to place.

concursus, -ūs *m* concourse, gathering, collision; uproar; (*fig*) combination; (*MIL*) assault, charge.

concussī *perf of* **concutiō.**

concussus *ppp of* **concutiō.**

concussus, -ūs *m* shaking.

concutiō, -tere, -ssī, -ssum *vt* to strike, shake, shatter; (*weapons*) to hurl; (*power*) to disturb, impair; (*person*) to agitate, alarm; (*self*) to search, examine; to rouse.

condalium, -ī *and* **iī** *nt* slave's ring.

condecet, -ēre *vt impers* it becomes.

condecorō, -āre *vt* to enhance.

condemnātor, -ōris *m* accuser.

condemnō, -āre, -āvī, -ātum *vt* to condemn, sentence; to urge the conviction of; to blame, censure; **ambitūs ~** convict of bribery; **capitis ~** condemn to death; **vōtī ~ātus** obliged to fulfil a vow.

condēnsō, -āre, -eō, -ēre *vt* to compress, move close together.

condēnsus *adj* very dense, close, thick.

condiciō, -ōnis *f* arrangement, condition, terms; marriage contract, match; situation, position, circumstances; manner, mode; **eā ~ōne ut** on condition that; **sub ~ōne** conditionally; **hīs ~ōnibus** on these terms; **vītae ~** way of life.

condīcō, -īcere, -īxī, -ictum *vt, vi* to talk over, agree upon, promise; **ad cēnam ~** have a dinner engagement.

condidī *perf of* **condo.**

condignē *adv see* **condignus.**

condignus *adj* very worthy.

condīmentum, -ī *nt* spice, seasoning.

condio, -īre, -īvī, -ītum *vt* to pickle, preserve, embalm; to season; (*fig*) to give zest to, temper.

condiscipulus, -ī *m* school-fellow.

condisco, -scere, -dicī *vt* to learn thoroughly, learn by heart.

conditiō *etc see* **condicio.**

condītiō, -ōnis *f* preserving, seasoning.

conditor, -ōris *m* founder, author, composer.

conditōrium, -ī *and* **iī** *nt* coffin, urn, tomb.

condītus *adj* savoury; (*fig*) polished.

conditus *ppp of* **condo.**

condītus *ppp of* **condio.**

condo, -ere, -idī, -itum *vt* 1. (*build, found: arts*) to make, compose, write; (: *institutions*) to establish 2. (*put away for keeping, store up: fruit*) to preserve; (: *person*) to imprison; (: *dead*) to bury; (: *memory*) to lay up; (: *time*) to pass, bring to a close 3. (*put out of sight, conceal: eyes*) to close; (: *sword*) to sheathe, plunge; (: *troops*) to place in ambush.

condocefaciō, -ere *vt* to train.

condoceō, -ēre, -uī, -tum *vt* to train.

condolēscō, -ēscere, -uī *vi* to begin to ache, feel very sore.

condōnātiō, -ōnis *f* giving away.

condōnō, -āre, -āvī, -ātum *vt* to give, present, deliver up; (*debt*) to remit; (*offence*) to pardon, let off.

condormīscō, -īscere, -īvī *vi* to fall fast asleep.

condūcibilis *adj* expedient.

condūco, -ūcere, -ūxī, -uctum *vt* to bring together, assemble, connect; to hire, rent, borrow; (*public work*) to undertake, get the contract for; (*taxes*) to farm ♦ *vi* to be of use, profit.

conductī, -ōrum *mpl* hirelings, mercenaries.

conductīcius *adj* hired.

conductiō, -ōnis *f* hiring, farming.

conductor, -ōris *m* hirer, tenant; contractor.

conductum, -ī *nt* anything hired *or* rented.

conductus *ppp of* **condūco.**

conduplicō, -āre *vt* to double.

condūrō, -āre *vt* to make very hard.

condus, -ī *m* steward.

cōnectō, -ctere, -xuī, -xum *vt* to tie, fasten, link, join; (*logic*) to state a conclusion.

cōnexum, -ī *nt* logical inference.

cōnexus *ppp of* **cōnectō** ♦ *adj* connected; (*time*) following.

cōnexus, -ūs *m* combination.

cōnfābulor, -ārī, -ātus *vi* to talk (to), discuss.

cōnfarreātiō, -ōnis *f* the most solemn of Roman marriage ceremonies.

cōnfarreō, -āre, -ātum *vt* to marry by confarreatio.

cōnfātālis *adj* bound by the same destiny.

cōnfēcī *perf of* **cōnficio.**

cōnfectiō, -ōnis *f* making, completion; (*food*) chewing.

cōnfector, -ōris *m* maker, finisher; destroyer.

cōnfectus *ppp of* **cōnficio.**

cōnferciō, -cīre, -tum *vt* to stuff, cram, pack closely.

cōnferō, -ferre, -tulī, -lātum *vt* to gather together, collect; to contribute; to confer, talk over; (*MIL*) to oppose, engage in battle; to compare; (*words*) to condense; to direct, transfer; to transform (into), turn (to); to devote, bestow; to ascribe, assign, impute; (*time*) to postpone; **capita ~** put heads together, confer; **gradum ~ cum** walk beside; **sē ~** go, turn (to); **sermōnēs ~** converse; **signa ~** join battle.

cōnfertim *adv* in close order.

cōnfertus *ppp of* **cōnferciō** ♦ *adj* crowded, full; (*MIL*) in close order.

cōnfervēscō, -vēscere, -buī *vi* to boil up, grow hot.

cōnfessiō, -ōnis *f* acknowledgement, confession.

cōnfessus *ppa of* **cōnfiteor** ♦ *adj* acknowledged, certain; **in ~ō esse/in ~um venīre** be generally admitted.

cōnfestim *adv* immediately.

cōnficiō, -icere, -ēcī, -ectum *vt* to make, effect, complete, accomplish; to get together, procure; to wear out, exhaust, consume, destroy; (*COMM*) to settle; (*space*) to travel; (*time*) to pass, complete; (*PHILOS*) to be an active cause; (*logic*) to deduce; (*pass*) it follows.

cōnfictiō, -ōnis *f* fabrication.

cōnfictus *ppp of* **cōnfingo.**

cōnfīdēns, -entis *pres p of* **cōnfīdō** ♦ *adj* self-confident, bold, presumptuous.

cōnfīdenter *adv* fearlessly, insolently.

cōnfīdentia, -ae *f* confidence, self-confidence; impudence.

cōnfīdentiloquus *adj* outspoken.

cōnfīdō, -dere, -sus sum *vi* to trust, rely, be sure; **sibi ~** be confident.

cōnfīgō, -gere, -xī, -xum *vt* to fasten together; to pierce, shoot; (*fig*) to paralyse.

cōnfingō, -ingere, -inxī, -ictum *vt* to make, invent, pretend.

cōnfīnis *adj* adjoining; (*fig*) akin.

cōnfīnium, -ī *nt* common boundary; (*pl*) neighbours; (*fig*) close connection, borderland between.

cōnfiō, -fierī *occ pass of* **cōnficio.**

cōnfirmātiō, -ōnis *f* establishing; (*person*) encouragement; (*fact*) verifying; (*RHET*) adducing of proofs.

cōnfirmātor, -ōris *m* guarantor (*of money*).
cōnfirmātus *adj* resolute; proved, certain.
cōnfirmō, -āre, -āvī, -ātum *vt* to strengthen, reinforce; (*decree*) to confirm, ratify; (*mind*) to encourage; (*fact*) to corroborate, prove, assert; **sē ~** recover; take courage.
cōnfiscō, -āre *vt* to keep in a chest; to confiscate.
cōnfīsiō, -ōnis *f* assurance.
cōnfīsus *ppa of* **cōnfīdō**.
cōnfiteor, -itērī, -essus *vt, vi* to confess, acknowledge; to reveal.
cōnfīxus *ppp of* **cōnfīgō**.
cōnflagrō, -āre, -āvī, -ātum *vi* to burn, be ablaze.
cōnflīctiō, -ōnis *f* conflict.
cōnflīctō, -āre, -āvī, -ātum *vt* to strike down, contend (with); (*pass*) to fight, be harassed, be afflicted.
cōnflīctus, -ūs *m* striking together.
cōnflīgō, -gere, -xī, -ctum *vt* to dash together; (*fig*) to contrast ♦ *vi* to fight, come into conflict.
cōnflō, -āre, -āvī, -ātum *vt* to ignite; (*passion*) to inflame; to melt down; (*fig*) to produce, procure, occasion.
cōnfluēns, -entis, -entēs, -entium *m* confluence of two rivers.
cōnfluō, -ere, -xī *vi* to flow together; (*fig*) to flock together, pour in.
cōnfodiō, -odere, -ōdī, -ossum *vt* to dig; to stab.
cōnfore *fut infin of* **cōnsum**.
cōnfōrmātiō, -ōnis *f* shape, form; (*words*) arrangement; (*voice*) expression; (*mind*) idea; (*RHET*) figure.
cōnfōrmō, -āre, -āvī, -ātum *vt* to shape, fashion.
cōnfossus *ppp of* **cōnfodiō** ♦ *adj* full of holes.
cōnfrāctus *ppp of* **cōnfringō**.
cōnfragōsus *adj* broken, rough; (*fig*) hard.
cōnfrēgī *pvrf of* **cōnfringō**.
cōnfremō, -ere, -uī *vi* to murmur aloud.
cōnfricō, -āre *vt* to rub well.
cōnfringō, -ingere, -ēgī, -āctum *vt* to break in pieces, wreck; (*fig*) to ruin.
cōnfugiō, -ugere, -ūgī *vi* to flee for help (to), take refuge (with); (*fig*) to have recourse (to).
cōnfugium, -ī *and* **iī** *nt* refuge.
cōnfundō, -undere, -ūdī, -ūsum *vt* to mix, mingle, join; to mix up, confuse, throw into disorder; (*mind*) to perplex, bewilder; to diffuse, spread over.
cōnfūsē *adv* confusedly.
cōnfūsiō, -ōnis *f* combination; confusion, disorder; **ōris ~** going red in the face.
cōnfūsus *ppp of* **cōnfundō** ♦ *adj* confused, disorderly, troubled.
cōnfūtō, -āre, -āvī, -ātum *vt* to keep from boiling over; to repress; to silence, confute.
congelō, -āre, -āvī, -ātum *vt* to freeze, harden ♦ *vi* to freeze over, grow numb.

congeminō, -āre, -āvī, -ātum *vt* to double.
congemō, -ere, -uī *vi* to groan, sigh ♦ *vt* to lament.
conger, -rī *m* sea eel.
congeriēs, -ēī *f* heap, mass, accumulation.
congerō, -rere, -ssī, -stum *vt* to collect, accumulate, build; (*missiles*) to shower; (*speech*) to comprise; (*fig*) to heap (upon), ascribe.
congerō, -ōnis *m* thief.
congerrō, -ōnis *m* companion in revelry.
congestīcius *adj* piled up.
congestus *ppp of* **congerō**.
congestus, -ūs *m* accumulating; heap, mass.
congiālis *adj* holding a congius.
congiārium, -ī *and* **iī** *nt* gift of food to the people, gratuity to the army.
congius, -ī *and* **iī** *m* Roman liquid measure (*about 6 pints*).
conglaciō, -āre *vi* to freeze up.
conglīscō, -ere *vi* to blaze up.
conglobātiō, -ōnis *f* mustering.
conglobō, -āre, -āvī, -ātum *vt* to make round; to mass together.
conglomerō, -āre *vt* to roll up.
conglūtinātiō, -ōnis *f* gluing, cementing; (*fig*) combination.
conglūtinō, -āre, -āvī, -ātum *vt* to glue, cement; (*fig*) to join, weld together; to contrive.
congraecō, -āre *vt* to squander on luxury.
congrātulor, -ārī, -ātus *vi* to congratulate.
congredior, -dī, -ssus *vt, vi* to meet, accost; to contend, fight.
congregābilis *adj* gregarious.
congregātiō, -ōnis *f* union, society.
congregō, -āre, -āvī, -ātum *vt* to collect, assemble, unite.
congressiō, -ōnis *f* meeting, conference.
congressus *ppa of* **congredior**.
congressus, -ūs *m* meeting, association, union; encounter, fight.
congruēns, -entis *adj* suitable, consistent, proper; harmonious.
congruenter *adv* in conformity.
congruō, -ere, -ī *vi* to coincide; to correspond, suit; to agree, sympathize.
congruus *adj* agreeable.
conició, -icere, -iēcī, -iectum *vt* to throw together; to throw, hurl; to put, fling, drive, direct; to infer, conjecture; (*augury*) to interpret; **sē ~** rush, fly; devote oneself.
coniectiō, -ōnis *f* throwing; conjecture, interpretation.
coniectō, -āre *vt* to infer, conjecture, guess.
coniector, -ōris *m* (male) interpreter, diviner.
coniectrīx, -rīcis *f* (female) interpreter, diviner.
coniectūra, -ae *f* inference, conjecture, guess; interpretation.
coniectūrālis *adj* (*RHET*) involving a question of fact.

coniectus *ppp of* **coniciō.**

coniectus, -ūs *m* heap, mass, concourse; throwing, throw, range; (*eyes, mind*) turning, directing.

cōnifer, cōniger, -ī *adj* cone-bearing.

cōnītor, -tī, -sus *and* **-xus** *vi* to lean on; to strive, struggle on; to labour.

coniugālis *adj* of marriage, conjugal.

coniugātiō, -ōnis *f* etymological relationship.

coniugātor, -ōris *m* uniter.

coniugiālis *adj* marriage- (*in cpds*).

coniugium, -ī *and* **iī** *nt* union, marriage; husband, wife.

coniugō, -āre *vt* to form (*a friendship*); **~āta verba** words related etymologically.

coniūnctē *adv* jointly; on familiar terms; (*logic*) hypothetically.

coniūnctim *adv* together, jointly.

coniūnctiō, -ōnis *f* union, connection, association; (*minds*) sympathy, affinity; (*GRAM*) conjunction.

coniūnctum, -ī *nt* (*RHET*) connection; (*PHILOS*) inherent property (*of a body*).

coniūnctus *ppp of* **coniungō ♦** *adj* near; connected, agreeing, conforming; related, friendly, intimate.

coniungō, -ungere, -ūnxī, -ūnctum *vt* to yoke, join together, connect; (*war*) to join forces in; to unite in love, marriage, friendship; to continue without a break.

coniūnx, -ugis *m/f* consort, wife, husband, bride.

coniūrātī, -ōrum *mpl* conspirators.

coniūrātiō, -ōnis *f* conspiracy, plot; alliance.

coniūrātus *adj* (*MIL*) after taking the oath.

coniūrō, -āre, -āvī, -ātum *vi* to take an oath; to conspire, plot.

coniux *etc see* **coniūnx.**

cōnīveō, -vēre, -vī *and* **xī** *vi* to shut the eyes, blink; (*fig*) to be asleep; to connive at.

conj- *etc see* **coni-.**

conl- *etc see* **coll-.**

conm- *etc see* **comm-.**

conn- *etc see* **cōn-.**

Conōn, -is *m* Athenian commander; Greek astronomer.

cōnōpēum (-eum), -eī *nt* mosquito net.

cōnor, -ārī, -ātus *vt* to try, attempt, venture.

conp- *etc see* **comp-.**

conquassātiō, -ōnis *f* severe shaking.

conquassō, -āre, -ātum *vt* to shake, upset, shatter.

conqueror, -rī, -stus *vt, vi* to complain bitterly of, bewail.

conquestiō, -ōnis *f* complaining; (*RHET*) appeal to pity.

conquestus *ppa of* **conqueror.**

conquestus, -ūs *m* outcry.

conquiēscō, -scere, -vī, -tum *vi* to rest, take

a respite; (*fig*) to be at peace, find recreation; (*things*) to stop, be quiet.

conquīnīscō, -ere *vi* to cower, squat, stoop down.

conquīrō, -rere, -sīvī, -sītum *vt* to search for, collect.

conquīsītē *adv* carefully.

conquīsītiō, -ōnis *f* search; (*MIL*) levy.

conquīsītor, -ōris *m* recruiting officer; (*THEATRE*) claqueur.

conquīsītus *ppp of* **conquīrō ♦** *adj* select, costly.

conr- *etc see* **corr-.**

cōnsaepiō, -īre, -sī, -tum *vt* to enclose, fence round.

cōnsaeptum, -tī *nt* enclosure.

cōnsalūtātiō, -ōnis *f* mutual greeting.

cōnsalūtō, -āre, -āvī, -ātum *vt* to greet, hail.

cōnsānēscō, -ēscere, -uī *vi* to heal up.

cōnsanguineus *adj* brother, sister, kindred ♦ *mpl* relations.

cōnsanguinitās, -ātis *f* relationship.

cōnscelerātus *adj* wicked.

cōnscelerō, -āre, -āvī, -ātum *vt* to disgrace.

cōnscendō, -endere, -endī, -ēnsum *vt, vi* to climb, mount, embark.

cōnscēnsiō, -ōnis *f* embarkation.

cōnscēnsus *ppp of* **cōnscendō.**

cōnscientia, -ae *f* joint knowledge, being in the know; (sense of) consciousness; moral sense, conscience, guilty conscience.

cōnscindō, -ndere, -dī, -ssum *vt* to tear to pieces; (*fig*) to abuse.

cōnsciō, -īre *vt* to be conscious of guilt.

cōnscīscō, -scere, -vī *and* **iī, -ītum** *vt* to decide on publicly; to inflict on oneself; **mortem (sibi) ~** commit suicide.

cōnscīssus *ppp of* **cōnscindō.**

cōnscītus *ppp of* **cōnscīscō.**

cōnscius *adj* sharing knowledge, privy, in the know; aware, conscious (of); conscious of guilt ♦ *m/f* confederate, confidant.

cōnscreor, -ārī *vi* to clear the throat.

cōnscrībō, -bere, -psī, -ptum *vt* to enlist, enrol; to write, compose, draw up, prescribe.

cōnscrīptiō, -ōnis *f* document, draft.

cōnscrīptus *ppp of* **cōnscrībō; patrēs ~ī** patrician and elected plebeian members; senators.

cōnsecō, -āre, -uī, -tum *vt* to cut up.

cōnsecrātiō, -ōnis *f* consecration, deification.

cōnsecrō, -āre, -āvī, -ātum *vt* to dedicate, consecrate, deify; (*fig*) to devote; to immortalise; **caput ~** doom to death.

cōnsectārius *adj* logical, consequent ♦ *ntpl* inferences.

cōnsectātiō, -ōnis *f* pursuit.

cōnsectātrīx, -īcis *f* (*fig*) follower.

cōnsectiō, -ōnis f cutting up.

cōnsector, -ārī, -ātus vt to follow, go after, try to gain; to emulate, imitate; to pursue, chase.

cōnsecūtiō, -ōnis f (PHILOS) consequences, effect; (RHET) sequence.

cōnsēdī perf of cōnsīdō.

cōnsenēscō, -ēscere, -uī vi to grow old, grow old together; (fig) to fade, pine, decay, become obsolete.

cōnsēnsiō, -ōnis f agreement, accord; conspiracy, plot.

cōnsēnsū adv unanimously.

cōnsēnsus ppp of cōnsentiō.

cōnsēnsus, -ūs m agreement, concord; conspiracy; (PHILOS) common sensation; (fig) harmony.

cōnsentāneus adj agreeing, in keeping with; ~um est it is reasonable.

cōnsentiō, -entīre, -ēnsī, -ēnsum vi to agree, determine together; to plot, conspire; (PHILOS) to have common sensations; (fig) to harmonize, suit, be consistent (with); bellum ~ vote for war.

cōnsequēns, -entis pres p of cōnsequor ♦ adj coherent, reasonable; logical, consequent ♦ nt consequence.

cōnsequor, -quī, -cūtus vt to follow, pursue; to overtake, reach; (time) to come after; (example) to follow, copy; (effect) to result, be the consequence of; (aim) to attain, get; (mind) to grasp, learn; (events) to happen to, come to; (standard) to equal, come up to; (speech) to do justice to.

cōnserō, -erere, -ēvī, -itum vt to sow, plant; (ground) to sow with, plant with; (fig) to cover, fill.

cōnserō, -ere, -uī, -tum vt to join, string together, twine; (MIL) to join battle; manum/manūs ~ engage in close combat; ex iūre manum ~ lay claim to (in an action for possession).

cōnsertē adv connectedly.

cōnsertus ppp of cōnserō.

cōnserva, -ae f fellow slave.

cōnservātiō, -ōnis f preserving.

cōnservātor, -ōris m preserver.

cōnservitium, -ī and iī nt being fellow slaves.

cōnservō, -āre, -āvī, -ātum vt to preserve, save, keep.

cōnservus, -ī m fellow slave.

cōnsessor, -ōris m companion at table, fellow spectator; (law) assessor.

cōnsessus, -ūs m assembly; (law) court.

cōnsēvī perf of cōnserō.

cōnsīderātē adv cautiously, deliberately.

cōnsīderātiō, -ōnis f contemplation.

cōnsīderātus adj (person) circumspect; (things) well-considered.

cōnsīderō, -āre, -āvī, -ātum vt to look at, inspect; to consider, contemplate.

cōnsīdō, -īdere, -ēdī, -essum vi to sit down, take seats; (courts) to be in session; (MIL) to take up a position; (residence) to settle; (places) to subside, sink; (fig) to sink, settle down, subside.

cōnsignō, -āre, -āvī, -ātum vt to seal, sign; to attest, vouch for; to record, register.

cōnsilēscō, -ere vi to calm down.

cōnsiliārius, -ī and iī m adviser, counsellor; spokesman ♦ adj counselling.

cōnsiliātor, -ōris m counsellor.

cōnsilior, -ārī, -ātus vi to consult; (with dat) to advise.

cōnsilium, -ī and iī nt deliberation, consultation; deliberating body, council; decision, purpose; plan, measure; stratagem; advice, counsel; judgement, insight, wisdom; ~ium capere, inīre come to a decision, resolve; ~ī esse be an open question; ~iō intentionally; eō ~iō ut with the intention of; prīvātō ~iō for one's own purposes.

cōnsimilis adj just like.

cōnsipiō, -ere vi to be in one's senses.

cōnsistō, -istere, -titī vi to stand, rest, take up a position; to consist (of), depend (on); to exist, be; (fig) to stand firm, endure; (liquid) to solidify, freeze; to stop, pause, halt, come to rest; (fig) to come to a standstill, come to an end.

cōnsitiō, -ōnis f sowing, planting.

cōnsitor, -ōris m sower, planter.

cōnsitus ppp of cōnserō.

cōnsōbrīnus, -ī m, -a, -ae f cousin.

cōnsociātiō, -ōnis f society.

cōnsociō, -āre, -āvī, -ātum vt to share, associate, unite.

cōnsōlābilis adj consolable.

cōnsōlātiō, -ōnis f comfort, encouragement, consolation.

cōnsōlātor, -ōris m comforter.

cōnsōlātōrius adj of consolation.

cōnsōlor, -ārī, -ātus vt to console, comfort, reassure; (things) to relieve, mitigate.

cōnsomniō, -āre vt to dream about.

cōnsonō, -āre, -uī vi to resound; (fig) to accord.

cōnsonus adj concordant; (fig) suitable.

cōnsōpiō, -īre, -ītum vt to put to sleep.

cōnsors, -tis adj sharing in common; (things) shared in common ♦ m/f partner, colleague.

cōnsortiō, -ōnis f partnership, fellowship.

cōnsortium, -ī and iī nt society, participation.

cōnspectus ppp of cōnspiciō ♦ adj visible; conspicuous.

cōnspectus, -ūs m look, view, sight; appearing on the scene; (fig) mental picture, survey; in ~um venīre come in sight, come near.

cōnspergō, -gere, -sī, -sum vt to besprinkle; (fig) to spangle.

cōnspiciendus adj noteworthy, distinguished.

cōnspiciō, -icere, -exī, -ectum vt to observe, catch sight of; to look at (esp with admiration), contemplate; (*pass*) to attract attention, be conspicuous, be notorious; (*mind*) to see, perceive.

cōnspicor, -ārī, -ātus *vt* to observe, see, catch sight of.

cōnspicuus *adj* visible; conspicuous, distinguished.

cōnspīrātiō, -ōnis *f* concord, unanimity; plotting, conspiracy.

cōnspīrō, -āre, -āvī, -ātum *vi* to agree, unite; to plot, conspire; (*music*) to sound together.

cōnspōnsor, -ōris *m* co-guarantor.

cōnspuō, -ere *vt* to spit upon.

cōnspurcō, -āre *vt* to pollute.

cōnspūtō, -āre *vt* to spit upon (*with contempt*).

cōnstabiliō, -īre, -īvī, -itum *vt* to establish.

cōnstāns, -antis *pres p of* **cōnstō** ♦ *adj* steady, stable, constant; consistent; faithful, steadfast.

cōnstanter *adv* steadily, firmly, calmly; consistently.

cōnstantia, -ae *f* steadiness, firmness; consistency, harmony; self-possession, constancy.

cōnsternātiō, -ōnis *f* disorder, tumult; (*horses*) stampede; (*mind*) dismay, alarm.

cōnsternō, -ernere, -rāvī, -rātum *vt* to spread, cover, thatch, pave; **~rāta nāvis** decked ship.

cōnsternō, -āre, -āvī, -ātum *vt* to startle, stampede; to alarm, throw into confusion.

cōnstīpō, -āre *vt* to crowd together.

cōnstitī *perf of* **cōnsistō**.

cōnstituō, -uere, -uī, -ūtum *vt* to put, place, set down; (*MIL*) to station, post, halt; to establish, build, create; to settle, arrange, organize; to appoint, determine, fix; to resolve, decide; **bene ~ūtum corpus** a good constitution.

cōnstitūtiō, -ōnis *f* state, condition; regulation, decree; definition, point at issue.

cōnstitūtum, -ūtī *nt* agreement.

cōnstō, -āre, -itī, -ātum *vi* to stand together; to agree, correspond, tally; to stand firm, remain constant; to exist, be; to consist (of), be composed (of); (*facts*) to be established, be well-known; (*COMM*) to cost; **sibi ~** be consistent; **inter omnēs ~at** it is common knowledge; **mihi ~at** I am determined; **ratiō ~at** the account is correct.

cōnstrātum, -ī *nt* flooring, deck.

cōnstrātus *ppp of* **cōnsternō**.

cōnstringō, -ingere, -inxī, -ictum *vt* to tie up, bind, fetter; (*fig*) to restrain, restrict; (*speech*) to compress, condense.

cōnstructiō, -ōnis *f* building up; (*words*) arrangement, sequence.

cōnstruō, -ere, -xī, -ctum *vt* to heap up; to build, construct.

cōnstuprātor, -ōris *m* debaucher.

cōnstuprō, -āre *vt* to debauch, rape.

cōnsuādeō, -ēre *vi* to advise strongly.

Cōnsuālia, -ium *ntpl festival of Consus*.

cōnsuāsor, -ōris *m* earnest adviser.

cōnsūdō, -āre *vi* to sweat profusely.

cōnsuēfaciō, -facere, -fēcī, -factum *vt* to accustom.

cōnsuēscō, -scere, -vī, -tum *vt* to accustom, inure ♦ *vi* to get accustomed; to cohabit (with); (*perf tenses*) to be accustomed, be in the habit of.

cōnsuētūdō, -inis *f* custom, habit; familiarity, social intercourse; love affair; (*language*) usage, idiom; **~ine/ex ~ine** as usual; **epistulārum ~** correspondence.

cōnsuētus *ppp of* **cōnsuēscō** ♦ *adj* customary, usual.

cōnsuēvī *perf of* **cōnsuēscō**.

cōnsul, -is *m* consul; **~ dēsignātus** consul elect; **~ ōrdinārius** regular consul; **~ suffectus** *successor to a consul who has died during his term of office*; **~ iterum/tertium** consul for the second/third time; **~em creāre, dīcere, facere** elect to the consulship; **L. Domitiō App. Claudiō ~ibus** in the year 54 B.C.

cōnsulāris *adj* consular, consul's; of consular rank ♦ *m* ex-consul.

cōnsulāriter *adv* in a manner worthy of a consul.

cōnsulātus, -ūs *m* consulship; **~um petere** stand for the consulship.

cōnsulō, -ere, -uī, -tum *vi* to deliberate, take thought; (*with dat*) to look after, consult the interests of; (*with dē or in*) to take measures against, pass sentence on ♦ *vt* to consult, ask advice of; to consider; to advise (something); to decide; **bonī/optimī ~** take in good part, be satisfied with.

cōnsultātiō, -ōnis *f* deliberation; inquiry; case.

cōnsultē *adv* deliberately.

cōnsultō *adv* deliberately.

cōnsultō, -āre, -āvī, -ātum *vt, vi* to deliberate, reflect; to consult; (*with dat*) to consult the interests of.

cōnsultor, -ōris *m* counsellor; consulter, client.

cōnsultrīx, -īcis *f* protectress.

cōnsultum, -ī *nt* decree (*esp of the Senate*); consultation; response (*from an oracle*).

cōnsultus *ppp of* **cōnsulō** ♦ *adj* considered; experienced, skilled ♦ *m* lawyer; **iūris ~us** lawyer.

cōnsuluī *perf of* **cōnsulō**.

(cōnsum), futūrum, fore *vi* to be all right.

cōnsummātus *adj* perfect.

cōnsummō, -āre *vt* to sum up; to complete, perfect.

cōnsūmō, -ere, -psī, -ptum *vt* to consume,

use up, eat up; to waste, squander; to exhaust, destroy, kill; to spend, devote.

cōnsūmptiō, -ōnis f wasting.

cōnsūmptor, -ōris m destroyer.

cōnsūmptus ppp of **cōnsūmō**.

cōnsuō, -uere, -uī, -ūtum vt to sew up; (fig) to contrive.

cōnsurgō, -gere, -rēxī, -rēctum vi to rise, stand up; to be roused (to); to spring up, start.

cōnsurrēctiō, -ōnis f standing up.

Cōnsus, -ī m ancient Roman god (connected with harvest).

cōnsusurrō, -āre vi to whisper together.

cōnsūtus ppp of **cōnsuō**.

contābefaciō, -ere vt to wear out.

contābēscō, -ēscere, -uī vi to waste away.

contabulātiō, -ōnis f flooring, storey.

contabulō, -āre, -āvī, -ātum vt to board over, build in storeys.

contāctus ppp of **contingō**.

contāctus, -ūs m touch, contact; contagion, infection.

contāgēs, -is f contact, touch.

contāgiō, -ōnis f, **contāgium, -ī** and **iī** nt contact; contagion, infection; (fig) contamination, bad example.

contāminātus adj impure, vicious.

contāminō, -āre, -āvī, -ātum vt to defile; (fig) to mar, spoil.

contechnor, -ārī, -ātus vi to think out plots.

contegō, -egere, -ēxī, -ēctum vt to cover up, cover over; to protect; to hide.

contemerō, -āre vt to defile.

contemnō, -nere, -psī, -ptum vt to think light of, have no fear of, despise, defy; to disparage.

contemplātiō, -ōnis f contemplation, surveying.

contemplātor, -ōris m observer.

contemplātus, -ūs m contemplation.

contemplō, -āre, -āvī, -ātum, -or, -ārī, -ātus vt to look at, observe, contemplate.

contempsī perf of **contemnō**.

contemptim adv contemptuously, slightingly.

contemptiō, -ōnis f disregard, scorn, despising.

contemptor, -ōris m (male) despiser, defiler.

contemptrīx, -rīcis f (female) despiser, defiler.

contemptus ppp of **contemnō** ♦ adj contemptible.

contemptus, -ūs m despising, scorn; being slighted; ~uī esse be despised.

contendō, -dere, -dī, -tum vt to stretch, draw, tighten; (instrument) to tune; (effort) to strain, exert; (argument) to assert, maintain; (comparison) to compare, contrast; (course) to direct ♦ vi to exert oneself, strive; to hurry; to journey, march; to contend, compete, fight; to entreat, solicit.

contentē adv (from **contendō**) earnestly, intensely.

contentē adv (from **contineō**) closely.

contentiō, -ōnis f straining, effort; striving (after); struggle, competition, dispute; comparison, contrast, antithesis.

contentus ppp of **contendō** ♦ adj strained, tense; (fig) intent.

contentus ppp of **contineō** ♦ adj content, satisfied.

conterminus adj bordering, neighbouring.

conterō, -erere, -rīvī, -rītum vt to grind, crumble; to wear out, waste; (time) to spend, pass; (fig) to obliterate.

conterreō, -ēre, -uī, -itum vt to terrify.

contestātus adj proved.

contestor, -ārī, -ātus vt to call to witness; lītem ~ open a lawsuit by calling witnesses.

contexō, -ere, -uī, -tum vt to weave, interweave; to devise, construct; (recital) to continue.

contextē adv in a connected fashion.

contextus adj connected.

contextus, -ūs m connection, coherence.

conticēscō (-īscō), -ēscere, -uī vi to become quiet, fall silent; (fig) to cease, abate.

contigī perf of **contingō**.

contignātiō, -ōnis f floor, storey.

contignō, -āre vt to floor.

contiguus adj adjoining, near; within reach.

continēns, -entis pres p of **contineō** ♦ adj bordering, adjacent; unbroken, continuous; (time) successive, continual, uninterrupted; (person) temperate, continent ♦ nt mainland, continent; essential point (in an argument).

continenter adv (place) in a row; (time) continuously; (person) temperately.

continentia, -ae f moderation, self-control.

contineō, -inēre, -inuī, -entum vt to hold, keep together; to confine, enclose; to contain, include, comprise; (pass) to consist of, rest on; to control, check, repress.

contingō, -ingere, -igī, -āctum vt to touch, take hold of, partake of; to be near, border on; to reach, come to; to contaminate; (mind) to touch, affect, concern ♦ vi to happen, succeed.

contingō, -ere vt to moisten, smear.

continuātiō, -ōnis f unbroken, succession, series; (RHET) period.

continuī perf of **contineō**.

continuō adv immediately, without delay; (argument) necessarily.

continuō, -āre, -āvī, -ātum vt to join together, make continuous; to continue without a break; **verba ~** form a sentence.

continuus adj joined (to); continuous, successive, uninterrupted; ~ā nocte the following night; **triduum ~um** three days running.

cōntiō, -ōnis f public meeting; speech, address; rostrum; ~ōnem habēre hold a meeting; deliver an address; prō ~ōne in public.

cōntiōnābundus *adj* delivering a harangue, playing the demagogue.

cōntiōnālis *adj* suitable for a public meeting, demagogic.

cōntiōnārius *adj* fond of public meetings.

cōntiōnātor, -ōris *m* demagogue.

cōntiōnor, -ārī, -ātus *vi* to address a public meeting, harangue; to declare in public; to come to a meeting.

cōntiuncula, -ae *f* short speech.

contorqueō, -quēre, -sī, -tum *vt* to twist, turn; (*weapons*) to throw, brandish; (*words*) to deliver forcibly.

contortē *adv* intricately.

contortiō, -ōnis *f* intricacy.

contortor, -ōris *m* perverter.

contortulus *adj* somewhat complicated.

contortuplicātus *adj* very complicated.

contortus *ppp of* **contorqueō** ♦ *adj* vehement; intricate.

contrā *adv* (*place*) opposite, face to face; (*speech*) in reply; (*action*) to fight, in opposition, against someone; (*result, with* **esse**) adverse, unsuccessful; (*comparison*) the contrary, conversely, differently; (*argument*) on the contrary, on the other hand; **~ atque, quam** contrary to what, otherwise than ♦ *prep* (*with acc*) facing, opposite to; against; contrary to, in violation of.

contractiō, -ōnis *f* contracting; shortening; despondency.

contractiuncula, -ae *f* slight despondency.

contractus *ppp of* **contrahō** ♦ *adj* contracted, narrow; short; in seclusion.

contrādīcō, -dīcere, -dīxī, -dictum (*usu two words*) *vt, vi* to oppose, object; (*law*) to be counsel for the other side.

contrādictiō, -ōnis *f* objection.

contrahō, -here, -xī, -ctum *vt* to draw together, assemble; to bring about, achieve; (*comm*) to contract, make a bargain; to shorten, narrow; to limit, depress; (*blame*) to incur; (*brow*) to wrinkle; (*sail*) to shorten; (*sky*) to overcast.

contrāriē *adv* differently.

contrārius *adj* opposite, from opposite; contrary; hostile, harmful ♦ *nt* opposite, reverse; **ex ~ō** on the contrary.

contrectābiliter *adv* so as to be felt.

contrectātiō, -ōnis *f* touching.

contrectō, -āre, -āvī, -ātum *vt* to touch, handle; (*fig*) to consider.

contremīscō, -īscere, -uī *vi* to tremble all over; (*fig*) to waver ♦ *vt* to be afraid of.

contremō, -ere *vi* to quake.

contribuō, -uere, -uī, -ūtum *vt* to bring together, join, incorporate.

contristō, -āre, -āvī, -ātum *vt* to sadden, darken, cloud.

contrītus *ppp of* **conterō** ♦ *adj* trite, well-worn.

contrōversia, -ae *f* dispute, argument, debate, controversy.

contrōversiōsus *adj* much disputed.

contrōversus *adj* disputed, questionable.

contrucīdō, -āre, -āvī, -ātum *vt* to massacre.

contrūdō, -dere, -sī, -sum *vt* to crowd together.

contruncō, -āre *vt* to hack to pieces.

contrūsus *ppp of* **contrūdō.**

contubernālis, -is *m/f* tent companion; junior officer serving with a general; (*fig*) companion, mate.

contubernium, -ī *and* **iī** *nt* service in the same tent, mess; service as junior officer with a general; common tent; slaves' home.

contueor, -ērī, -itus *vt* to look at, consider, observe.

contuitus, -ūs *m* observing, view.

contulī *perf of* **cōnferō.**

contumācia, -ae *f* obstinacy, defiance.

contumāciter *adv see* **contumāx.**

contumāx, -ācis *adj* stubborn, insolent, pig-headed.

contumēlia, -ae *f* (*verbal*) insult, libel, invective; (*physical*) assault, ill-treatment.

contumēliōsē *adv* insolently.

contumēliōsus *adj* insulting, outrageous.

contumulō, -āre *vt* to bury.

contundō, -undere, -udī, -ūsum *vt* to pound, beat, bruise; (*fig*) to suppress, destroy.

contuor *etc see* **contueor.**

conturbātiō, -ōnis *f* confusion, mental disorder.

conturbātus *adj* distracted, diseased.

conturbō, -āre, -āvī, -ātum *vt* to throw into confusion; (*mind*) to derange, disquiet; (*money*) to embarrass.

contus, -ī *m* pole.

contūsus *ppp of* **contundō.**

contūtus *see* **contuitus.**

cōnūbiālis *adj* conjugal.

cōnūbium, -ī *and* **iī** *nt* marriage; **iūs ~ī** right of intermarriage.

cōnus, -ī *m* cone; (*helmet*) apex.

convador, -ārī, -ātus *vt* (*law*) to bind over.

convalēscō, -ēscere, -uī *vi* to recover, get better; (*fig*) to grow stronger, improve.

convallis, -is *f* valley with hills on all sides.

convāsō, -āre *vt* to pack up.

convectō, -āre *vt* to bring home.

convector, -ōris *m* fellow passenger.

convehō, -here, -xī, -ctum *vt* to bring in, carry.

convellō, -ellere, -ellī, -ulsum *and* **olsum** *vt* to wrench, tear away; to break up; (*fig*) to destroy, overthrow; **signa ~** decamp.

convena, -ae *adj* meeting.

convenae, -ārum *m/f* crowd of strangers, refugees.

Noun declensions and verb conjugations are shown on pp xiii to xxv. The present infinitive ending of a verb shows to which conjugation it belongs: **-āre** = 1st; **-ēre** = 2nd; **-ere** = 3rd and **-īre** = 4th. Irregular verbs are shown on p xxvi

conveniēns, -entis *pres p of* **conveniō** ♦ *adj* harmonious, consistent; fit, appropriate.

convenienter *adv* in conformity (with), consistently; aptly.

convenientia, -ae *f* conformity, harmony.

conveniō, -enīre, -ēnī, -entum *vi* to meet, assemble; (*events*) to combine, coincide; (*person*) to agree, harmonize; (*things*) to fit, suit; (*impers*) to be suitable, be proper ♦ *vt* to speak to, interview.

conventīcium, -ī *and* **iī** *nt* payment for attendance at assemblies.

conventīcius *adj* visiting regularly.

conventiculum, -ī *nt* gathering; meeting place.

conventiō, -ōnis *f* agreement.

conventum, -ī *nt* agreement.

conventus *ppp of* **conveniō**.

conventus, -ūs *m* meeting; (*law*) local assizes; (*COMM*) corporation; agreement; **~ūs agere** hold the assizes.

converrō, -rere, -rī, -sum *vt* to sweep up, brush together; (*comedy*) to give a good beating to.

conversātiō, -ōnis *f* associating (with).

conversiō, -ōnis *f* revolution, cycle; change over; (*RHET*) well-rounded period; verbal repetition at end of clauses.

conversō, -āre *vt* to turn round.

conversus *ppp of* **converrō**; *ppp of* **convertō**.

convertō, -tere, -tī, -sum *vt* to turn round, turn back; (*MIL*) to wheel; to turn, direct; to change, transform; (*writings*) to translate ♦ *vi* to return, turn, change.

convestiō, -īre, -īvī, -ītum *vt* to clothe, encompass.

convexus *adj* vaulted, rounded; hollow; sloping ♦ *nt* vault, hollow.

convīciātor, -ōris *m* slanderer.

convīcior, -ārī, -ātus *vt* to revile.

convīcium, -ī *and* **iī** *nt* loud noise, outcry; invective, abuse; reproof, protest.

convictiō, -ōnis *f* companionship.

convictor, -ōris *m* familiar friend.

convictus *ppp of* **convincō**.

convictus, -ūs *m* community life, intercourse; entertainment.

convincō, -incere, -īcī, -ictum *vt* to refute, convict, prove wrong; to prove, demonstrate.

convīsō, -ere *vt* to search, examine; to pervade.

convītium *see* **convīcium**.

convīva, -ae *m/f* guest.

convīvālis *adj* festive, convivial.

convīvātor, -ōris *m* host.

convīvium, -ī *and* **iī** *nt* banquet, entertainment; guests.

convīvor, -ārī, -ātus *vi* to feast together, carouse.

convocātiō, -ōnis *f* assembling.

convocō, -āre, -āvī, -ātum *vt* to call a meeting of, muster.

convolnerō *see* **convulnerō**.

convolō, -āre, -āvī, -ātum *vi* to flock together.

convolsus *see* **convulsus**.

convolvō, -vere, -vī, -ūtum *vt* to roll up, coil up; to intertwine.

convomō, -ere *vt* to vomit over.

convorrō *see* **converrō**.

convortō *see* **convertō**.

convulnerō, -āre *vt* to wound seriously.

convulsus *ppp of* **convellō**.

cooperiō, -īre, -uī, -tum *vt* to cover over, overwhelm.

cooptātiō, -ōnis *f* electing, nominating (of new members).

cooptō, -āre, -āvī, -ātum *vt* to elect (as a colleague).

coorior, -īrī, -tus *vi* to rise, appear; to break out, begin.

coortus, -ūs *m* originating.

cōpa, -ae *f* barmaid.

cophinus, -ī *m* basket.

cōpia, -ae *f* abundance, plenty, number; resources, wealth, prosperity; (*MIL, usu pl*) troops, force; (*words, thought*) richness, fulness, store; (*action*) opportunity, facility, means, access; **prō ~ā** according to one's resources, as good as possible considering.

cōpiolae, -ārum *fpl* small force.

cōpiōsē *adv* abundantly, fully, at great length.

cōpiōsus *adj* abounding, rich, plentiful; (*speech*) eloquent, fluent.

cōpis *adj* rich.

cōpula, -ae *f* rope, leash, grapnel; (*fig*) bond.

cōpulātiō, -ōnis *f* coupling, union.

cōpulātus *adj* connected, binding.

cōpulō, -āre, -āvī, -ātum *vt* to couple, join; (*fig*) to unite, associate.

coqua, -ae *f* cook.

coquīnō, -āre *vi* to be a cook.

coquīnus *adj* of cooking.

coquō, -quere, -xī, -ctum *vt* to cook, boil, bake; to parch, burn; (*fruit*) to ripen; (*stomach*) to digest; (*thought*) to plan, concoct; (*care*) to disquiet, disturb.

coquus (cocus), -ī *m* cook.

cor, cordis *nt* heart; (*feeling*) heart, soul; (*thought*) mind, judgement; **cordī esse** please, be agreeable.

cōram *adv* in one's presence; in person ♦ *prep* (*with abl*) in the presence of, before.

corbis, -is *m/f* basket.

corbīta, -ae *f* slow boat.

corbula, -ae *f* little basket.

corculum, -ī *nt* dear heart.

Corcȳra, -ae *f* island off W. coast of Greece (*now* Corfu).

Corcȳraeus *adj see n.*

cordātē *adv see* **cordātus**.

cordātus *adj* wise.

cordolium, -ī *and* **iī** *nt* sorrow.

Corfiniēnsis *adj see n.*

Corfinium, -ī *nt town in central Italy.*

coriandrum, -ī nt coriander.

Corinthiacus, -iēnsis, -ius adj: **~ium aes** Corinthian brass (an alloy of gold, silver and copper).

Corinthus, -ī f Corinth.

corium (corius m) **-ī** and **iī** nt hide, skin; leather, strap.

Cornēlia, -iae f mother of the Gracchi.

Cornēliānus, -ius adj: **lēgēs ~iae** Sulla's laws.

Cornēlius, -ī m famous Roman family name (esp Scipios, Gracchi, Sulla).

corneolus adj horny.

corneus adj of horn.

corneus adj of the cornel tree, of cornel wood.

cornicen, -cinis m horn-blower.

cornīcula, -ae f little crow.

corniculārius, -ī and **iī** m adjutant.

corniculum, -ī nt a horn-shaped decoration.

corniger, -ī adj horned.

cornipēs, -edis adj horn-footed.

cornīx, -īcis f crow.

cornū, -ūs, -um, -ī nt horn; anything horn-shaped; (army) wing; (bay) arm; (book) roller-end; (bow) tip; (helmet) crest-socket; (land) tongue, spit; (lyre) arm; (moon) horn; (place) side; (river) branch; (yardarm) point; anything made of horn: bow, funnel, lantern; (music) horn; (oil) cruet; anything like horn; beak, hoof, wart; (fig) strength, courage; **~ cōpiae** Amalthea's horn, symbol of plenty.

cornum, -ī nt cornelian cherry.

cornum see **cornū**.

cornus, -ī f cornelian cherry tree; javelin.

corōlla, -ae f small garland.

corōllārium, -ī and **iī** nt garland for actors; present, gratuity.

corōna, -ae f garland, crown; (ASTRO) Corona Borealis; (people) gathering, bystanders; (MIL) cordon of besiegers or defenders; **sub ~ā vēndere, vēnīre** sell, be sold as slaves.

Corōnaeus, -ēus, -ēnsis adj see **Corōnēa**.

corōnārium aurum gold collected in the provinces for a victorious general.

Corōnēa, -ēae f town in central Greece.

corōnō, -āre, -āvī, -ātum vt to put a garland on, crown; to encircle.

corporeus adj corporeal; of flesh.

corpulentus adj corpulent.

corpus, -oris nt body; substance, flesh; corpse; trunk, torso; person, individual; (fig) structure, corporation, body politic.

corpusculum, -ī nt particle; term of endearment.

corrādō, -dere, -sī, -sum vt to scrape together, procure.

corrēctiō, -ōnis f amending, improving.

corrēctor, -ōris m reformer, critic.

corrēctus ppp of **corrigō**.

corrēpō, -ere, -sī vi to creep, slink, cower.

correptē adv briefly.

correptus ppp of **corripiō**.

corrīdeō, -ēre vi to laugh aloud.

corrigia, -ae f shoelace.

corrigō, -igere, -ēxī, -ēctum vt to make straight; to put right, improve, correct.

corripiō, -ipere, -ipuī, -eptum vt to seize, carry off, get along quickly; (speech) to reprove, reproach, accuse; (passion) to seize upon, attack; (time, words) to cut short; **sē gradum, viam ~** hasten, rush.

corrōborō, -āre, -āvī, -ātum vt to make strong, invigorate.

corrōdō, -dere, -sī, -sum vt to nibble away.

corrogō, -āre vt to gather by requesting.

corrūgō, -āre vt to wrinkle.

corrumpō, -umpere, -ūpī, -uptum vt to break up, ruin, waste; to mar, adulterate, falsify; (person) to corrupt, seduce, bribe.

corruō, -ere, -ī vi to fall, collapse ♦ vt to overthrow, heap up.

corruptē adv perversely; in a lax manner.

corruptēla, -ae f corruption, bribery; seducer.

corruptiō, -ōnis f bribing, seducing; corrupt state.

corruptor, -ōris m, **-rīx, -rīcis** f corrupter, seducer.

corruptus ppp of **corrumpō** ♦ adj spoiled, corrupt, bad.

Corsus adj Corsican.

cortex, -icis m/f bark, rind; cork.

cortīna, -ae f kettle, cauldron; tripod of Apollo; (fig) vault, circle.

corulus, -ī f hazel.

Cōrus see **Caurus**.

coruscō, -āre vt to butt; to shake, brandish ♦ vi to flutter, flash, quiver.

coruscus adj tremulous, oscillating; shimmering, glittering.

corvus, -ī m raven; (MIL) grapnel.

Corybantēs, -ium mpl priests of Cybele.

Corybantius adj see n.

cōrycus, -ī m punchball.

corylētum, -ī nt hazel copse.

corylus, -ī f hazel.

corymbifer m Bacchus.

corymbus, -ī m cluster (esp of ivy berries).

coryphaeus, -ī m leader.

cōrytos, -us, -ī m quiver.

cōs f hard rock, flint; grindstone.

Cōs, Coī f Aegean island (famous for wine and weaving) ♦ nt Coan wine ♦ ntpl Coan clothes.

cosmēta, -ae m master of the wardrobe.

costa, -ae f rib; side, wall.

costum, -ī nt an aromatic plant, perfume.

cothurnātus adj buskined, tragic.

cothurnus, -ī m buskin, hunting boot; tragedy, elevated style.

cotīd see **cottīd-**.

Noun declensions and verb conjugations are shown on pp xiii to xxv. The present infinitive ending of a verb shows to which conjugation it belongs: **-āre** = 1st; **-ēre** = 2nd; **-ere** = 3rd and **-īre** = 4th. Irregular verbs are shown on p xxvi

cōtis *f see* **cōs.**

cottabus, -ī *m* game of throwing drops of wine.

cottana, -ōrum *ntpl* Syrian figs.

cottīdiānō *adv* daily.

cottīdiānus *adj* daily; everyday, ordinary.

cottīdiē *adv* every day, daily.

coturnīx, -īcis *f* quail.

Cotyttia, -ōrum *ntpl festival of Thracian goddess Cotytto.*

Cōus *adj* Coan.

covinnārius, -ī *and* **iī** *m* chariot fighter.

covinnus, -ī *m* war chariot; coach.

coxa, -ae, coxendīx, -īcis *f* hip.

coxī *perf of* **coquō.**

crābrō, -ōnis *m* hornet.

crambē-, -ēs *f* cabbage; **~ repetīta** stale repetitions.

Crantor, -oris *m Greek Academic philosopher.*

crāpula, -ae *f* intoxication, hangover.

crāpulārius *adj* for intoxication.

crās *adv* tomorrow.

crassē *adv* grossly, dimly.

Crassiānus *adj see* **Crassus.**

crassitūdō, -inis *f* thickness, density.

crassus *adj* thick, gross, dense; *(fig)* dull, stupid.

Crassus, -ī *m famous orator; wealthy politician, triumvir with Caesar and Pompey.*

crāstinum, -ī *nt* the morrow.

crāstinus *adj* of tomorrow; **diē ~ī** tomorrow.

crātēr, -is *m*, **-a, -ae** *f* bowl *(esp for mixing wine and water)*; crater; a constellation.

crātis, -is *f* wickerwork, hurdle; *(AGR)* harrow; *(MIL)* faggots for lining trenches; *(shield)* ribs; *(fig)* frame, joints.

creātiō, -ōnis *f* election.

creātor, -ōris *m*, **-rīx, -rīcis** *f* creator, father, mother.

creātus *m (with abl)* son of.

crēber, -rī *adj* dense, thick, crowded; numerous, frequent; *(fig)* prolific, abundant.

crēbrēscō, -ēscere, -uī *vi* to increase, become frequent.

crēbritās, -ātis *f* frequency.

crēbrō *adv* repeatedly.

crēdibilis *adj* credible.

crēdibiliter *adv see* **crēdibilis.**

crēditor, -ōris *m* creditor.

crēditum, -itī *nt* loan.

crēdō, -ere, -idī, -itum *vt, vi* to entrust, lend; to trust, have confidence in; to believe; to think, suppose; **~erēs** one would have thought.

crēdulitās, -ātis *f* credulity.

crēdulus *adj* credulous, trusting.

cremō, -āre, -āvī, -ātum *vt* to burn, cremate.

Cremōna, -ae *f town in N. Italy.*

Cremōnēnsis *adj see n.*

cremor, -ōris *m* juice, broth.

creō, -āre, -āvī, -ātum *vt* to create, produce, beget; to elect (to an office); to cause, occasion.

creper, -ī *adj* dark; doubtful.

crepida, -ae *f* sandal; **nē sūtor suprā ~am** ≈ *let the cobbler stick to his last.*

crepidātus *adj* wearing sandals.

crepīdō, -inis *f* pedestal, base; bank, pier, dam.

crepidula, -ae *f* small sandal.

crepitāculum, -ī *nt* rattle.

crepitō, -āre *vi* to rattle, chatter, rustle, creak.

crepitus, -ūs *m* rattling, chattering, rustling, creaking.

crepō, -āre, -uī, -itum *vi* to rattle, creak, snap (fingers) ♦ *vt* to make rattle, clap; to chatter about.

crepundia, -ōrum *ntpl* rattle, babies' toys.

crepusculum, -ī *nt* twilight, dusk; darkness.

Crēs, -ētis *m* Cretan.

crēscō, -scere, -vī, -tum *vi* to arise, appear, be born; to grow up, thrive, increase, multiply; to prosper, be promoted, rise in the world.

Crēsius *adj* Cretan.

Crēssa, -ae *f* Cretan.

Crēta, -ae *f* Crete.

crēta, -ae *f* chalk; good mark.

Crētaeus *and* **-icus** *and* **-is, -idis** *adj see n.*

crētātus *adj* chalked; dressed in white.

Crētē *see* **Crēta.**

crēteus *adj* of chalk, of clay.

crētiō, -ōnis *f* declaration of accepting an inheritance.

crētōsus *adj* chalky, clayey.

crētula, -ae *f* white clay for sealing.

crētus *ppp of* **cernō** ♦ *ppa of* **crēscō** ♦ *adj* descended, born.

Creūsa, -ae *f wife of Jason; wife of Aeneas.*

crēvī *perf of* **cernō**; *perf of* **crēscō.**

crībrum, -ī *nt* sieve.

crīmen, -inis *nt* accusation, charge, reproach; guilt, crime; cause of offence; **esse in ~ine** stand accused.

crīminātiō, -ōnis *f* complaint, slander.

crīminātor, -ōris *m* accuser.

crīminō, -āre *vt* to accuse.

crīminor, -ārī, -ātus *dep* to accuse, impeach; *(things)* to complain of, charge with.

crīminōsē *adv* accusingly, slanderously.

crīminōsus *adj* reproachful, slanderous.

crīnālis *adj* for the hair, hair- *(in cpds)* ♦ *nt* hairpin.

crīnis, -is *m* hair; *(comet)* tail.

crīnītus *adj* long-haired; crested; **stēlla ~a** comet.

crīspāns, -antis *adj* wrinkled.

crīspō, -āre *vt* to curl, swing, wave.

crīspus *adj* curled; curly-headed; wrinkled; tremulous.

crista, -ae *f* cockscomb, crest; plume.

cristātus *adj* crested, plumed.

criticus, -ī *m* critic.

croceus *adj* of saffron, yellow.

crocinus *adj* yellow ♦ *nt* saffron oil.

crōciō, -īre *vi* to croak.

crocodīlus, -ī *m* crocodile.

crocōtārius *adj* of saffron clothes.

crocōtula, -ae *f* saffron dress.

crocus, -ī *m*, **-um, -ī** *nt* saffron; yellow.

Croesus, -ī *m* king of Lydia (*famed for wealth*).

crotalistria, -ae *f* castanet dancer.

crotalum, -ī *nt* rattle, castanet.

cruciābilitās, -ātis *f* torment.

cruciāmentum, -ī *nt* torture.

cruciātus, -ūs *m* torture; instrument of torture; (*fig*) ruin, misfortune.

cruciō, -āre, -āvī, -ātum *vt* to torture; to torment.

crūdēlis *adj* hard-hearted, cruel.

crūdēlitās, -ātis *f* cruelty, severity.

crūdēliter *adv see* **crūdēlis.**

crūdēscō, -ēscere, -uī *vi* to grow violent, grow worse.

crūditās, -ātis *f* indigestion.

crūdus *adj* bleeding; (*food*) raw, undigested; (*person*) dyspeptic; (*leather*) rawhide; (*fruit*) unripe; (*age*) immature, fresh; (*voice*) hoarse; (*fig*) unfeeling, cruel, merciless.

cruentō, -āre *vt* to stain with blood, wound.

cruentus *adj* bloody, gory; bloodthirsty, cruel; blood-red.

crumēna, -ae *f* purse; money.

crumilla, -ae *f* purse.

cruor, -ōris *m* blood; bloodshed.

cruppellāriī, -ōrum *mpl* mail-clad fighters.

crūrifragius, -ī and iī *m* one whose legs have been broken.

crūs, -ūris *nt* leg, shin.

crūsta, -ae *f* hard surface, crust; stucco, embossed *or* inlaid work.

crūstulum, -ī *nt* small pastry.

crūstum, -ī *nt* pastry.

crux, -ucis *f* gallows, cross; (*fig*) torment; **abī in malam ~cem** ≈ go and be hanged!

crypta, -ae *f* underground passage, grotto.

cryptoporticus, -ūs *f* covered walk.

crystallinus *adj* of crystal ♦ *ntpl* crystal vases.

crystallum, -ī *nt*, **-us, -ī** *m* crystal.

cubiculāris, cubiculārius *adj* of the bedroom ♦ *m* valet de chambre.

cubiculum, -ī *nt* bedroom.

cubīle, -is *nt* bed, couch; (*animals*) lair, nest; (*fig*) den.

cubital, -ālis *nt* cushion.

cubitālis *adj* a cubit long.

cubitō, -āre *vi* to lie (in bed).

cubitum, -ī *nt* elbow; cubit.

cubitus, -ūs *m* lying in bed.

cubō, -āre, -uī, -itum *vi* to lie in bed; to recline at table; (*places*) to lie on a slope.

cucullus, -ī *m* hood, cowl.

cucūlus, -ī *m* cuckoo.

cucumis, -eris *m* cucumber.

cucurbita, -ae *f* gourd; cupping glass.

cucurrī *perf of* **currō.**

cūdō, -ere *vt* to beat, thresh; (*metal*) to forge; (*money*) to coin.

cūiās, -tis *pron* of what country?, of what town?

cuicuimodī (*gen of* **quisquis** *and* **modus**) of whatever kind, whatever like.

cūius *pron* (*interrog*) whose?; (*rel*) whose.

culcita, -ae *f* mattress, pillow; eyepatch.

cūleus *see* **culleus.**

culex, -icis *m/f* gnat.

culīna, -ae *f* kitchen; food.

culleus, cūleus, -ī *m* leather bag for holding liquids; a fluid measure.

culmen, -inis *nt* stalk; top, roof, summit; (*fig*) height, acme.

culmus, -ī *m* stalk, straw.

culpa, -ae *f* blame, fault; mischief; **in ~ā sum, mea ~a est** I am at fault *or* to blame.

culpātus *adj* blameworthy.

culpitō, -āre *vt* to find fault with.

culpō, -āre, -āvī, -ātum *vt* to blame, reproach.

cultē *adv* in a refined manner.

cultellus, -ī *m* small knife.

culter, -rī *m* knife, razor.

cultiō, -ōnis *f* cultivation.

cultor, -ōris *m* cultivator, planter, farmer; inhabitant; supporter, upholder; worshipper.

cultrīx, -icis *f* inhabitant; (*fig*) nurse, fosterer.

cultūra, -ae *f* cultivation, agriculture; (*mind*) care, culture; (*person*) courting.

cultus *ppp of* **colō** ♦ *adj* cultivated; (*dress*) well-dressed; (*mind*) polished, cultured ♦ *ntpl* cultivated land.

cultus, -ūs *m* cultivation, care; (*mind*) training, culture; (*dress*) style, attire; (*way of life*) refinement, civilization; (*gods*) worship; (*men*) honouring.

culullus, -ī *m* goblet.

cūlus, -ī *m* buttocks.

cum *prep* (*with abl*) with; (*denoting accompaniment, resulting circumstances, means, dealings, comparison, possession*); **~ decimō** tenfold; **~ eō quod, ut** with the proviso that; **~ prīmīs** especially; **~ magnā calamitāte cīvitātis** to the great misfortune of the community; **~ perīculō suō** at one's own peril.

cum *conj* (*time*) when, whenever, while, as, after, since; (*cause*) since, as, seeing that; (*concession*) although; (*condition*) if; (*contrast*) while, whereas; **multī annī sunt ~ in aere meō est** for many years now he has been in my debt; **aliquot sunt annī ~ vōs dēlēgī** it is now some years since I chose you; **~ māximē** just when; just then, just now; **~ prīmum** as soon as; **~ ... tum** not only ... but also; both ... and.

Noun declensions and verb conjugations are shown on pp xiii to xxv. The present infinitive ending of a verb shows to which conjugation it belongs: **-āre** = 1st; **-ēre** = 2nd; **-ere** = 3rd and **-īre** = 4th. Irregular verbs are shown on p xxvi

Cūmae, -ārum *fpl* town near Naples (*famous for its Sibyl*).

Cūmeānum, -āni *nt Cicero's Cumaean residence.*

Cūmaeus, -ānus *adj see n.*

cumba, cymba, -ae *f* boat, skiff.

cumera, -ae *f* grain chest.

cumīnum, -ī *nt* cumin.

cumque (quomque) *adv* -ever, -soever; at any time.

cumulātē *adv* fully, abundantly.

cumulātus *adj* increased; complete.

cumulō, -āre, -āvī, -ātum *vt* to heap up; to amass, increase; to fill up, overload; (*fig*) to fill, overwhelm, crown, complete.

cumulus, -ī *m* heap, mass; crowning addition, summit.

cūnābula, -ōrum *ntpl* cradle.

cūnae, -ārum *fpl* cradle.

cunctābundus *adj* hesitant, dilatory.

cunctāns, -antis *adj* dilatory, reluctant; sluggish, tough.

cunctanter *adv* slowly.

cunctātiō, -ōnis *f* delaying, hesitation.

cunctātor, -ōris *m* loiterer; one given to cautious tactics (*esp Q Fabius Maximus*).

cunctor, -ārī, -ātus *vi* to linger, delay, hesitate; to move slowly.

cūnctus *adj* the whole of; (*pl*) all together, all.

cuneātim *adv* in the form of a wedge.

cuneātus *adj* wedge-shaped.

cuneus, -ī *m* wedge; (MIL) wedge-shaped formation of troops; (THEATRE) block of seats.

cunīculus, -ī *m* rabbit; underground passage; (MIL) mine.

cunque *see* **cumque.**

cūpa, -ae *f* vat, tun.

cupidē *adv* eagerly, passionately.

Cupīdineus *adj see* **Cupīdō.**

cupiditās, -ātis *f* desire, eagerness, enthusiasm; passion, lust; avarice, greed; ambition; partisanship.

cupīdō, -inis *f* desire, eagerness; passion, lust; greed.

Cupīdō, -inis *m* Cupid (*son of Venus*).

cupidus *adj* desirous, eager; fond, loving; passionate, lustful; greedy, ambitious; partial.

cupiēns, -entis *pres p of* **cupiō ♦** *adj* eager, desirous.

cupienter *adv see* **cupiēns.**

cupiō, -ere, -īvī *and* **iī, -ītum** *vt* to wish, desire, long for; (*with dat*) to wish well.

cupītor, -ōris *m* desirer.

cupītus *ppp of* **cupiō.**

cuppēdia, -ae *f* fondness for delicacies.

cuppēdia, -ōrum *ntpl* delicacies.

cuppēdinārius, -ī *m* confectioner.

cuppēdō, -inis *f* longing, passion.

cuppes, -dis *adj* fond of delicacies.

cupressētum, -ī *nt* cypress grove.

cupresseus *adj* of cypress wood.

cupressifer, -ī *adj* cypress-bearing.

cupressus, -ī *f* cypress.

cūr *adv* why?; (*indirect*) why, the reason for.

cūra, -ae *f* care, trouble, pains (bestowed); anxiety, concern, sorrow (felt); attention (to), charge (of), concern (for); (MED) treatment, cure; (*writing*) work; (*law*) trusteeship; (*poet*) love; (*person*) mistress, guardian; **~ est** I am anxious; **~ae esse** be attended to, looked after.

cūrābilis *adj* troublesome.

cūralium, -ī *and* **iī** *nt* red coral.

cūratē *adv* carefully.

cūrātiō, -ōnis *f* charge, management; office; treatment, healing.

cūrātor, -ōris *m* manager, overseer; (*law*) guardian.

cūrātūra, -ae *f* dieting.

cūrātus *adj* cared for; earnest, anxious.

curculiō, -ōnis *m* weevil.

curculiunculus, -ī *m* little weevil.

Curēnsis *adj see n.*

Curēs, -ium *mpl* ancient Sabine town.

Cūrētēs, -um *mpl* attendants of Jupiter in Crete.

Cūrētis, -idis *adj* Cretan.

cūria, -ae *f* earliest division of the Roman people; meeting-place of a curia; senate house; senate.

cūriālis, -is *m* member of a curia.

cūriātim *adv* by curiae.

cūriātus *adj* of the curiae; **comitia ~a** earliest Roman assembly.

cūriō, -ōnis *m* president of a curia; **~ māximus** head of all the curiae.

cūriō, -ōnis *adj* emaciated.

cūriōsē *adv* carefully; inquisitively.

cūriōsitās, -ātis *f* curiosity.

cūriōsus *adj* careful, thoughtful, painstaking; inquiring, inquisitive, officious; careworn.

curis, -ītis *f* spear.

cūrō, -āre, -āvī, -ātum *vt* to take care of, attend to; to bother about; (*with gerundive*) to get something done; (*with inf*) to take the trouble; (*with ut*) to see to it that; (*public life*) to be in charge of, administer; (MED) to treat, cure; (*money*) to pay, settle up; **aliud ~ā** never mind; **corpus/cutem ~** take it easy; **prōdigia ~** avert portents.

curriculum, -ī *nt* running, race; course, lap; (*fig*) career; **~ō** at full speed.

currō, -ere, cucurrī, cursum *vi* to run; to hasten, fly ♦ *vt* to run through, traverse; **~entem incitāre** ≈ *spur a willing horse.*

currus, -ūs *m* car, chariot; triumph; team of horses; ploughwheels.

cursim *adv* quickly, at the double.

cursitō, -āre *vi* to run about, fly hither and thither.

cursō, -āre *vi* to run about.

cursor, -ōris *m* runner, racer; courier.

cursūra, -ae *f* running.

cursus, -ūs *m* running, speed; passage, journey; course, direction; (*things*) movement, flow; (*fig*) rapidity, flow, progress; **~ honōrum** succession of magistracies; ~ **rērum** course of events; **~um tenēre** keep on one's course; **~ū** at a run; **māgnō ~ū** at full speed.

curtō, -āre vt to shorten.

curtus adj short, broken off; incomplete.

curūlis adj official, curule; **aedīlis ~** patrician, aediile; **sella ~** magistrates' chair; **equī ~** horses provided for the games by the state.

curvāmen, -inis nt bend.

curvātūra, -ae f curve.

curvō, -āre, -āvī, -ātum vt to curve, bend, arch; (fig) to move.

curvus adj bent, curved, crooked; (person) aged; (fig) wrong.

cuspis, -dis f point; spear, javelin, trident, sting.

custōdēla, -ae f care, guard.

custōdia, -ae f watch, guard, care; (person) sentry, guard; (place) sentry's post, guardhouse; custody, confinement, prison; **lībera ~** confinement in one's own house.

custōdiō, -īre, -īvī and **iī, -ītum** vt to guard, defend; to hold in custody, keep watch on; to keep, preserve, observe.

custōs, -ōdis m/f guard, bodyguard, protector, protectress; jailer, warder; (MIL) sentry, spy; container.

cutīcula, -ae f skin.

cutis, -is f skin; **~em cūrāre** ≈ take it easy.

cyathissō, -āre vi to serve wine.

cyathus, -ī m wine ladle; (measure) one-twelfth of a pint.

cybaea, -ae f kind of merchant ship.

Cybēbē, Cybelē, -ēs f Phrygian mother-goddess, Magna Mater.

Cybelēius adj see n.

Cyclades, -um fpl group of Aegean islands.

cyclas, -adis f formal dress with a border.

cyclicus adj of the traditional epic stories.

Cyclōpius adj see n.

Cyclōps, -is m one-eyed giant (esp Polyphemus).

cycnēus adj of a swan, swan's.

cycnus, -ī m swan.

Cydōnius adj Cretan ♦ ntpl quinces.

cygnus see **cycnus**.

cylindrus, -ī m cylinder; roller.

Cyllēnē, -ēs and **ae** f mountain in Arcadia.

Cyllēnēus, -is, -ius adj see n.

Cyllēnius, -ī m Mercury.

cymba see **cumba**.

cymbalum, -ī nt cymbal.

cymbium, -ī and **iī** nt cup.

Cynicē adv like the Cynics.

Cynicus, -ī m a Cynic philosopher (esp Diogenes) ♦ adj Cynic.

cynocephalus, -ī m dog-headed ape.

Cynosūra, -ae f constellation of Ursa Minor.

Cynosūris, -idis adj see n.

Cynthia, -iae f Diana.

Cynthius, -ī m Apollo.

Cynthus, -ī m hill in Delos (birthplace of Apollo and Diana).

cyparissus, -ī f cypress.

Cypris, -idis f Venus.

Cyprius adj Cyprian; copper.

Cyprus, -ī f island of Cyprus (famed for its copper and the worship of Venus).

Cyrēnaeī, -aicī mpl followers of Aristippus.

Cyrēnaeus, -aicus, -ēnsis adj see n.

Cyrēnē, -ēs f, **-ae, -ārum** fpl town and province of N. Africa.

Cyrnēus adj Corsican.

Cȳrus, -ī m Persian king.

Cytaeis, -idis f Medea.

Cythēra, -ae f island S. of Greece (famed for its worship of Venus).

Cytherēa, -ēae and **-eia, -eiae** and **-eis, -ēidis** f Venus.

Cytherēus, Cythēriacus adj Cytherean; of Venus.

cytisus, -ī m/f cytisus (a kind of clover).

Cyzicēnus adj see **Cyzicum**.

Cyzicum, -ī nt, **-us, -os, -ī** f town on Sea of Marmora.

D, d

Dācī, -ōrum mpl Dacians, a people on the lower Danube.

Dācia, -iae f the country of the Dācī (now Romania).

Dācicus, -icī m gold coin of Domitian's reign.

dactylicus adj dactylic.

dactylus, -ī m dactyl.

Daedalēus adj see n.

daedalus adj artistic, skilful in creating; skilfully made, variegated.

Daedalus, -ī m mythical Athenian craftsman and inventor.

Dalmatae, -ārum mpl Dalmatians (a people on the East coast of the Adriatic).

Dalmatia, -iae f Dalmatia.

Dalmaticus adj see n.

dāma, -ae f deer; venison.

Damascēnus adj see n.

Damascus, -ī f Damascus.

damma f see **dāma**.

damnātiō, -ōnis f condemnation.

damnātōrius adj condemnatory.

damnātus adj criminal; miserable.

damnificus adj pernicious.

damnō, -āre, -āvī, -ātum *vt* to condemn, sentence; to procure the conviction of; (*heirs*) to oblige; to censure; **capitis/capite ~** condemn to death; **māiestātis, dē māiestāte ~** condemn for treason; **vōtī ~** oblige to fulfil a vow.

damnōsē *adv* ruinously.

damnōsus *adj* harmful, ruinous; spendthrift; wronged.

damnum, -ī *nt* loss, harm, damage; (*law*) fine, damages; **~ facere** suffer loss.

Danaē, -ēs *f* mother of Perseus.

Danaēius *adj see n.*

Danaī, -ōrum *and* **um** *mpl* the Greeks.

Danaidēs, -idum *fpl* daughters of Danaus.

Danaus, -ī *m* king of Argos and father of 50 daughters.

Danaus *adj* Greek.

danista, -ae *m* moneylender.

danisticus *adj* moneylending.

danō *see* **dō.**

Dānuvius, -ī *m* upper Danube.

Daphnē, -ēs *f* nymph changed into a laurel tree.

Daphnis, -idis (*acc* **-im** *and* **-in**) *m* mythical Sicilian shepherd.

dapinō, -āre *vt* to serve (food).

daps, dapis *f* religious feast; meal, banquet.

dapsilis *adj* sumptuous, abundant.

Dardania, -iae *f* Troy.

Dardanidēs, -idae *m* Trojan (*esp Aeneas*).

Dardanus, -ī *m* son of Jupiter and ancestor of Trojan kings.

Dardanus, -ius, -is, -idis *adj* Trojan.

Darēus, -ī *m* Persian king.

datārius *adj* to give away.

datātim *adv* passing from one to the other.

datiō, -ōnis *f* right to give away; (*laws*) making.

datō, -āre *vt* to be in the habit of giving.

dator, -ōris *m* giver; (*sport*) bowler.

Daulias, -adis *adj see n.*

Daulis, -dis *f* town in central Greece (*noted for the story of Procne and Philomela*).

Daunias, -iadis *f* Apulia.

Daunius *adj* Rutulian; Italian.

Daunus, -ī *m* legendary king of Apulia (*ancestor of Turnus*).

dē *prep* (*with abl: movement*) down from, from; (*origin*) from, of, out of; (*time*) immediately after, in; (*thought, talk, action*) about, concerning; (*reason*) for, because of; (*imitation*) after, in accordance with; **~ industriā** on purpose; **~ integrō** afresh; **~ nocte** during the night; **diem ~ diē** from day to day.

dea, -ae *f* goddess.

dealbō, -āre *vt* to whitewash, plaster.

deambulātiō, -ōnis *f* walk.

deambulō, -āre, -āvī, -ātum *vi* to go for a walk.

deamō, -āre, -āvī, -ātum *vt* to be in love with; to be much obliged to.

dearmātus *adj* disarmed.

deartuō, -āre, -āvī, -ātum *vt* to dismember, ruin.

deasciō, -āre *vt* to smooth with an axe; (*fig*) to cheat.

dēbacchor, -ārī, -ātus *vi* to rage furiously.

dēbellātor, -ōris *m* conqueror.

dēbellō, -āre, -āvī, -ātum *vi* to bring a war to an end ♦ *vt* to subdue; to fight out.

dēbeō, -ēre, -uī, -itum *vt* to owe; (*with inf*) to be bound, ought, should, must; to have to thank for, be indebted for; (*pass*) to be destined.

dēbilis *adj* frail, weak, crippled.

dēbilitās, -ātis *f* weakness, infirmity.

dēbilitātiō, -ōnis *f* weakening.

dēbilitō, -āre, -āvī, -ātum *vt* to cripple, disable; (*fig*) to paralyse, unnerve.

dēbitiō, -ōnis *f* owing.

dēbitor, -ōris *m* debtor.

dēbitum, -ī *nt* debt.

dēblaterō, -āre *vt* to blab.

dēcantō, -āre, -āvī, -ātum *vt* to keep on repeating ♦ *vi* to stop singing.

dēcēdō, -ēdere, -essī, -essum *vi* to withdraw, depart; to retire from a province (*after term of office*); to abate, cease, die; (*rights*) to give up, forgo; (*fig*) to go wrong, swerve (*from duty*); **dē viā ~** get out of the way.

decem *num* ten.

December, -ris *adj* of December ♦ *m* December.

decempeda, -ae *f* ten-foot rule.

decempedātor, -ōris *m* surveyor.

decemplex, -icis *adj* tenfold.

decemprīmī, -ōrum *mpl* civic chiefs of Italian towns.

decemscalmus *adj* ten-oared.

decemvirālis *adj* of the decemviri.

decemvirātus, -ūs *m* office of decemvir.

decemvirī, -ōrum *and* **um** *mpl* commission of ten men (*for public or religious duties*).

decennis *adj* ten years'.

decēns, -entis *adj* seemly, proper; comely, handsome.

decenter *adv* with propriety.

decentia, -ae *f* comeliness.

dēceptus *ppp of* **dēcipiō.**

dēcernō, -ernere, -rēvī, -rētum *vt* to decide, determine; to decree; to fight it out, decide the issue.

dēcerpō, -ere, -sī, -tum *vt* to pluck off, gather; (*fig*) to derive, enjoy.

dēcertātiō, -ōnis *f* deciding the issue.

dēcertō, -āre, -āvī, -ātum *vi* to fight it out, decide the issue.

dēcessiō, -ōnis *f* departure; retirement (from a province); deduction, disappearance.

dēcessor, -ōris *m* retiring magistrate.

dēcessus, -ūs *m* retirement (from a province); death; (*tide*) ebbing.

decet, -ēre, -uīt *vt, vi* it becomes, suits; it is

right, proper.

dēcidō, -ere, -ī vi to fall down, fall off; to die; (fig) to fail, come down.

dēcīdō, -dere, -dī, -sum vt to cut off; to settle, put an end to.

deciēns, deciēs adv ten times.

decimus, decumus adj tenth; **cum ~ō** tenfold; **~um** for the tenth time.

dēcipiō, -ipere, -ēpī, -eptum vt to ensnare; to deceive, beguile, disappoint.

dēcīsiō, -ōnis f settlement.

dēcīsus ppp of **dēcīdō**.

Decius, -ī m Roman plebeian name (esp P Decius Mus, father and son, who devoted their lives in battle).

Decius, -iānus adj see n.

dēclāmātiō, -ōnis f loud talking; rhetorical exercise on a given theme.

dēclāmātor, -ōris m apprentice in public speaking.

dēclāmātōrius adj rhetorical.

dēclāmitō, -āre vi to practise rhetoric; to bluster ♦ vt to practise pleading.

dēclāmō, -āre, -āvī, -ātum vi to practise public speaking, declaim; to bluster.

dēclārātiō, -ōnis f expression, making known.

dēclārō, -āre, -āvī, -ātum vt to make known; to proclaim, announce, reveal, express, demonstrate.

dēclīnātiō, -ōnis f swerving; avoidance; (RHET) digression; (GRAM) inflection.

dēclīnō, -āre, -āvī, -ātum vt to turn aside, deflect; (eyes) to close; to evade, shun ♦ vi to turn aside, swerve; to digress.

dēclīve nt slope, decline.

dēclīvis adj sloping, steep, downhill.

dēclīvitās, -ātis f sloping ground.

dēcocta, -ae f a cold drink.

dēcoctor, -ōris m bankrupt.

dēcoctus ppp of **dēcoquō** ♦ adj (style) ripe, elaborated.

dēcōlō, -āre vi to run out; (fig) to fail.

dēcolor, -ōris adj discoloured, faded; **~ aetās** a degenerate age.

dēcolōrātiō, -ōnis f discolouring.

dēcolōrō, -āre, -āvī, -ātum vt to discolour, deface.

dēcoquō, -quere, -xī, -ctum vt to boil down; to cook ♦ vi to go bankrupt.

decor, -ōris m comeliness, ornament, beauty.

decōrē adv becomingly, beautifully.

decorō, -āre, -āvī, -ātum vt to adorn, embellish; (fig) to distinguish, honour.

decōrum, -ī nt propriety.

decōrus adj becoming, proper; beautiful, noble; adorned.

dēcrepitus adj decrepit.

dēcrēscō, -scere, -vī, -tum vi to decrease, wane, wear away; to disappear.

dēcrētum, -ī nt decree, resolution; (PHILOS) doctrine.

dēcrētus ppp of **dēcernō**.

dēcrēvī perf of **dēcernō**; perf of **dēcrēscō**.

decuma, -ae f tithe; provincial land tax; largess.

decumāna, -ae f wife of a tithe-collector.

decumānus adj paying tithes; (MIL) of the 10th cohort or legion ♦ m collector of tithes; **~ī, ~ōrum** mpl men of the 10th legion; **porta ~a** main gate of a Roman camp.

decumātēs, -ium adj pl subject to tithes.

dēcumbō, -mbere, -buī vi to lie down; to recline at table; to fall (in fight).

decumus see **decimus**.

decuria, -ae f group of ten; panel of judges; social club.

decuriātiō, -ōnis f, **decuriātus, -ūs** m dividing into decuriae.

decuriō, -āre, -āvī, -ātum vt to divide into decuriae or groups.

decuriō, -ōnis m head of a decuria; (MIL) cavalry officer; senator of a provincial town or colony.

dēcurrō, -rrere, -currī and **rrī, -rsum** vt, vi to run down, hurry, flow, sail down; to traverse; (MIL) to parade, charge; (time) to pass through; (fig) to have recourse to.

dēcursiō, -ōnis f military manoeuvre.

dēcursus ppp of **dēcurrō**.

dēcursus, -ūs m descent, downrush; (MIL) manoeuvre, attack; (time) career.

dēcurtātus adj mutilated.

decus, -oris nt ornament, glory, beauty; honour, virtue; (pl) heroic deeds.

dēcussō, -āre vt to divide crosswise.

dēcutiō, -tere, -ssī, -ssum vt to strike down, shake off.

dēdecet, -ēre, -uit vt it is unbecoming to, is a disgrace to.

dēdecorō, -āre vt to disgrace.

dēdecōrus adj dishonourable.

dēdecus, -oris nt disgrace, shame; vice, crime.

dedī perf of **dō**.

dēdicātiō, -ōnis f consecration.

dēdicō, -āre, -āvī, -ātum vt to consecrate, dedicate; to declare (property in a census return).

dēdidī perf of **dēdō**.

dēdignor, -ārī, -ātus vt to scorn, reject.

dēdiscō, -scere, -dicī vt to unlearn, forget.

dēditīcius, -ī and **iī** m one who has capitulated.

dēditiō, -ōnis f surrender, capitulation.

dēditus ppp of **dēdō** ♦ adj addicted, devoted; **~ā operā** intentionally.

dēdō, -ere, -idī, -itum vt to give up, yield, surrender; to devote.

dēdoceō, -ēre vt to teach not to.

dēdoleō, -ēre, -uī vi to cease grieving.

Noun declensions and verb conjugations are shown on pp xiii to xxv. The present infinitive ending of a verb shows to which conjugation it belongs: **-āre** = 1st; **-ēre** = 2nd; **-ere** = 3rd and **-īre** = 4th. Irregular verbs are shown on p xxvi

dēdūcō, -ūcere, -ūxī, -uctum *vt* to bring down, lead away, deflect; (*MIL*) to lead, withdraw; (*bride*) to bring home; (*colony*) to settle; (*hair*) to comb out; (*important person*) to escort; (*law*) to evict, bring to trial; (*money*) to subtract; (*sail*) to unfurl; (*ship*) to launch; (*thread*) to spin out; (*writing*) to compose; (*fig*) to bring, reduce, divert, derive.

dēductiō, -ōnis *f* leading off; settling a colony; reduction; eviction; inference.

dēductor, -ōris *m* escort.

dēductus *ppp of* **dēdūcō** ♦ *adj* finely spun.

deerrō, -āre, -āvī, -ātum *vi* to go astray.

deesse *infin of* **dēsum.**

dēfaecō, -āre, -āvī, -ātum *vt* to clean; (*fig*) to make clear, set at ease.

dēfatīgātiō, -ōnis *f* tiring out; weariness.

dēfatīgō, -āre, -āvī, -ātum *vt* to tire out, exhaust.

dēfatīscor *etc see* **dēfetīscor.**

dēfectiō, -ōnis *f* desertion; failure, faintness; (*ASTRO*) eclipse.

dēfector, -ōris *m* deserter, rebel.

dēfectus *ppp of* **dēficiō** ♦ *adj* weak, failing.

dēfectus, -ūs *m* failure; eclipse.

dēfendō, -dere, -dī, -sum *vt* to avert, repel; to defend, protect; (*law*) to speak in defence, urge, maintain; (*THEATRE*) to play (a part); **crīmen ~** answer an accusation.

dēfēnsiō, -ōnis *f* defence, speech in defence.

dēfēnsitō, -āre *vt* to defend often.

dēfēnsō, -āre *vt* to defend.

dēfēnsor, -ōris *m* averter; defender, protector, guard.

dēferō, -ferre, -tulī, -lātum *vt* to bring down, bring, carry; to bear away; (*power, honour*) to offer, confer; (*information*) to report; (*law*) to inform against, indict; to recommend (for public services); **ad cōnsilium ~** take into consideration.

dēfervēscō, -vēscere, -vī *and* **buī** *vi* to cool down, calm down.

dēfessus *adj* tired, exhausted.

dēfetīgō *etc see* **dēfatīgō.**

dēfetīscor, -tīscī, -ssus *vi* to grow weary.

dēficiō, -icere, -ēcī, -ectum *vt, vi* to desert, forsake, fail; to be lacking, run short, cease; (*ASTRO*) to be eclipsed; **animō ~** lose heart.

dēfīgō, -gere, -xī, -xum *vt* to fix firmly; to drive in, thrust; (*eyes, mind*) to concentrate; (*fig*) to stupefy, astound; (*magic*) to bewitch.

dēfingō, -ere *vt* to make, portray.

dēfīniō, -īre, -īvī, -ītum *vt* to mark the limit of, limit; to define, prescribe; to restrict; to terminate.

dēfīnītē *adv* precisely.

dēfīnītiō, -ōnis *f* limiting, prescribing, definition.

dēfīnītīvus *adj* explanatory.

dēfīnītus *adj* precise.

dēfīō, -ierī *vi* to fail.

dēflagrātiō, -ōnis *f* conflagration.

dēflagrō, -āre, -āvī, -ātum *vi* to be burned down, perish; to cool down, abate ♦ *vt* to burn down.

dēflectō, -ctere, -xī, -xum *vt* to bend down, turn aside; (*fig*) to pervert ♦ *vi* to turn aside, deviate.

dēfleō, -ēre, -ēvī, -ētum *vt* to lament bitterly, bewail ♦ *vi* to weep bitterly.

dēflexus *ppp of* **dēflectō.**

dēflōrēscō, -ēscere, -uī *vi* to shed blooms; (*fig*) to fade.

dēfluō, -ere, -xī, -xum *vi* to flow down, float down; to fall, drop, droop; (*fig*) to come from, be derived; to flow past; (*fig*) to pass away, fail.

dēfodiō, -odere, -ōdī, -ossum *vt* to dig, dig out; to bury; (*fig*) to hide away.

dēfore *fut infin of* **dēsum.**

dēfōrmis *adj* misshapen, disfigured, ugly; shapeless; (*fig*) disgraceful, disgusting.

dēfōrmitās, -ātis *f* deformity, hideousness; baseness.

dēfōrmō, -āre, -āvī, -ātum *vt* to form, sketch; to deform, disfigure; to describe; to mar, disgrace.

dēfossus *ppp of* **dēfodiō.**

dēfraudō, -āre *vt* to cheat, defraud; **genium ~** deny oneself.

dēfrēnātus *adj* unbridled.

dēfricō, -āre, -uī, -ātum *and* **tum** *vt* to rub down; (*fig*) to satirize.

dēfringō, -ingere, -ēgī, -āctum *vt* to break off, break down.

dēfrūdō *etc see* **dēfraudō.**

dēfrutum, -ī *nt* new wine boiled down.

dēfugiō, -ugere, -ūgī *vt* to run away from, shirk ♦ *vi* to flee.

dēfuī *perf of* **dēsum.**

dēfūnctus *ppa of* **dēfungor** ♦ *adj* discharged; dead.

dēfundō, -undere, -ūdī, -ūsum *vt* to pour out.

dēfungor, -ungī, -ūnctus *vi* (*with abl*) to discharge, have done with; to die.

dēfutūrus *fut p of* **dēsum.**

dēgener, -is *adj* degenerate, unworthy, base.

dēgenerātum, -ātī *nt* degenerate character.

dēgenerō, -āre, -āvī, -ātum *vi* to degenerate, deteriorate ♦ *vt* to disgrace.

dēgerō, -ere *vt* to carry off.

dēgō, -ere, -ī *vt* (*time*) to pass, spend; (*war*) wage ♦ *vi* to live.

dēgrandinat it is hailing heavily.

dēgravō, -āre *vt* to weigh down, overpower.

dēgredior, -dī, -ssus *vi* to march down, descend, dismount.

dēgrunniō, -īre *vi* to grunt hard.

dēgustō, -āre *vt* to taste, touch; (*fig*) to try, experience.

dehinc *adv* from here; from now, henceforth; then, next.

dehīscō, -ere *vi* to gape, yawn.

dehonestāmentum, -ī *nt* disfigurement.

dehonestō, -āre *vt* to disgrace.

dehortor, -ārī, -ātus *vt* to dissuade, discourage.

Dēianīra, -ae *f* wife of Hercules.

dēiciō, -icere, -iēcī, -iectum *vt* to throw down, hurl, fell; to overthrow, kill; (*eyes*) to lower, avert; (*law*) to evict; (*MIL*) to dislodge; (*ship*) to drive off its course; (*hopes, honours*) to foil, disappoint.

dēiectiō, -ōnis *f* eviction.

dēiectus *ppp of* **dēiciō** ♦ *adj* low-lying; disheartened.

dēiectus, -ūs *m* felling; steep slope.

dēierō, -āre, -āvī, -ātum *vi* to swear solemnly.

dein *etc see* **deinde.**

deinceps *adv* successively, in order.

deinde, dein *adv* from there, next; then, thereafter; next in order.

Dēiotarus, -ī *m* king of Galatia (*defended by Cicero*).

Dēiphobus, -ī *m* son of Priam (*second husband of Helen*).

dēiungō, -ere *vt* to sever.

dēiuvō, -āre *vt* to fail to help.

dej- *etc see* **dei-.**

dēlābor, -bī, -psus *vi* to fall down, fly down, sink; (*fig*) to come down, fall into.

dēlacerō, -āre *vt* to tear to pieces.

dēlāmentor, -ārī *vt* to mourn bitterly for.

dēlāpsus *ppa of* **dēlābor.**

dēlassō, -āre *vt* to tire out.

dēlātiō, -ōnis *f* accusing, informing.

dēlātor, -ōris *m* informer, denouncer.

dēlectābilis *adj* enjoyable.

dēlectāmentum, -ī *nt* amusement.

dēlectātiō, -ōnis *f* delight.

dēlectō, -āre *vt* to charm, delight, amuse.

dēlēctus *ppp of* **dēligō.**

dēlēctus, -ūs *m* choice; *see also* **dīlēctus.**

dēlēgātiō, -ōnis *f* assignment.

dēlēgī *perf of* **dēligō.**

dēlēgō, -āre, -āvī, -ātum *vt* to assign, transfer, make over; to ascribe.

dēlēnificus *adj* charming.

dēlēnīmentum, -ī *nt* solace, allurement.

dēlēniō, -īre, -īvī, -ītum *vt* to soothe, solace; to seduce, win over.

dēlēnītor, -ōris *m* cajoler.

dēleō, -ēre, -ēvī, -ētum *vt* to destroy, annihilate; to efface, blot out.

Dēlia, -ae *f* Diana.

Dēliacus *adj* of Delos.

dēlīberābundus *adj* deliberating.

dēlīberātiō, -ōnis *f* deliberating, consideration.

dēlīberātīvus *adj* deliberative.

dēlīberātor, -ōris *m* consulter.

dēlīberātus *adj* determined.

dēlīberō, -āre, -āvī, -ātum *vt, vi* to consider, deliberate, consult; to resolve, determine; **~ārī potest** it is in doubt.

dēlībō, -āre, -āvī, -ātum *vt* to taste, sip; to pick, gather; to detract from, mar.

dēlibrō, -āre *vt* to strip the bark off.

dēlibuō, -uere, -uī, -ūtum *vt* to smear, steep.

dēlicātē *adv* luxuriously.

dēlicātus *adj* delightful; tender, soft; voluptuous, spoiled, effeminate; fastidious.

dēliciae, -ārum *fpl* delight, pleasure; whimsicalities, sport; (*person*) sweetheart, darling.

dēliciolae, -ārum *fpl* darling.

dēlicium, -ī *and* **iī** *nt* favourite.

dēlicō, -āre *vt* to explain.

dēlictum, -ī *nt* offence, wrong.

dēlicuus *adj* lacking.

dēligō, -igere, -ēgī, -ēctum *vt* to select, gather; to set aside.

dēligō, -āre, -āvī, -ātum *vt* to tie up, make fast.

dēlingō, -ere *vt* to have a lick of.

dēlīni- *etc see* **dēlēni-.**

dēlinquō, -inquere, -īquī, -ictum *vi* to fail, offend, do wrong.

dēliquēscō, -quēscere, -cuī *vi* to melt away; (*fig*) to pine away.

dēliquiō, -ōnis *f* lack.

dēlīrāmentum, -ī *nt* nonsense.

dēlīrātiō, -ōnis *f* dotage.

dēlīrō, -āre *vi* to be crazy, drivel.

dēlīrus *adj* crazy.

dēlitēscō, -ēscere, -uī *vi* to hide away, lurk; (*fig*) to skulk, take shelter under.

dēlītigō, -āre *vi* to scold.

Dēlius, -iacus *adj see n.*

Delmatae *see* **Dalmatae.**

Dēlos, -ī *f* sacred Aegean island (*birthplace of Apollo and Diana*).

Delphī, -ōrum *mpl* town in central Greece (*famous for its oracle of Apollo*); the Delphians.

Delphicus *adj see n.*

delphīnus, -ī *and* **delphīn, -is** *m* dolphin.

Deltōton, -ī *nt* (*constellation*) Triangulum.

dēlubrum, -ī *nt* sanctuary, temple.

dēluctō, -āre, -or, -ārī *vi* to wrestle.

dēlūdificō, -āre *vt* to make fun of.

dēlūdō, -dere, -sī, -sum *vt* to dupe, delude.

dēlumbis *adj* feeble.

dēlumbō, -āre *vt* to enervate.

dēmadēscō, -ēscere, -uī *vi* to be drenched.

dēmandō, -āre *vt* to entrust, commit.

dēmarchus, -ī *m* demarch (*chief of a village in Attica*).

dēmēns, -entis *adj* mad, foolish.

dēmēnsum, -ī *nt* ration.

dēmēnsus *ppa of* **dēmētior.**

dēmenter *adv see* **dēmēns.**

dēmentia, -ae *f* madness, folly.

dēmentiō, -īre *vi* to rave.

dēmereō, -ēre, -uī, -itum, -eor, -ērī *vt* to earn, deserve; to do a service to.

dēmergō, -gere, -sī, -sum *vt* to submerge, plunge, sink; (*fig*) to overwhelm.

dēmessus *ppp of* **dēmetō**.

dēmētior, -tīrī, -nsus *vt* to measure out.

dēmetō, -tere, -ssuī, -ssum *vt* to reap, harvest; to cut off.

dēmigrātiō, -ōnis *f* emigration.

dēmigrō, -āre *vi* to move, emigrate.

dēminuō, -uere, -uī, -ūtum *vt* to make smaller, lessen, detract from; **capite ~** deprive of citizenship.

dēminūtiō, -ōnis *f* decrease, lessening; (*law*) right to transfer property; **capitis ~** loss of political rights.

dēmīror, -ārī, -ātus *vt* to marvel at, wonder.

dēmissē *adv* modestly, meanly.

dēmissīcius *adj* flowing.

dēmissiō, -ōnis *f* letting down; (*fig*) dejection.

dēmissus *ppp of* **dēmittō** ♦ *adj* low-lying; drooping; humble, unassuming; dejected; (*origin*) descended.

dēmītigō, -āre *vt* to make milder.

dēmittō, -ittere, -īsī, -issum *vt* to let down, lower, sink; to send down, plunge; (*beard*) to grow; (*ship*) to bring to land; (*troops*) to move down; (*fig*) to cast down, dishearten, reduce, impress; **sē ~** stoop; descend; be disheartened.

dēmiurgus, -ī *m* chief magistrate in a Greek state.

dēmō, -ere, -psī, -ptum *vt* to take away, subtract.

Dēmocriticus, -ius, -ēus *adj see n.*

Dēmocritus, -ī *m* Greek philosopher (*author of the atomic theory*).

dēmōlior, -īrī *vt* to pull down, destroy.

dēmōlītiō, -ōnis *f* pulling down.

dēmōnstrātiō, -ōnis *f* pointing out, explanation.

dēmōnstrātīvus *adj* (*RHET*) for display.

dēmōnstrātor, -ōris *m* indicator.

dēmōnstrō, -āre, -āvī, -ātum *vt* to point out; to explain, represent, prove.

dēmorior, -ī, -tuus *vi* to die, pass away ♦ *vt* to be in love with.

dēmoror, -ārī, -ātus *vi* to wait ♦ *vt* to detain, delay.

dēmortuus *ppa of* **dēmorior**.

Dēmosthenēs, -is *m* greatest Athenian orator.

dēmoveō, -ovēre, -ōvī, -ōtum *vt* to remove, turn aside, dislodge.

dempsī *perf of* **dēmō**.

dēmptus *ppp of* **dēmō**.

dēmūgītus *adj* filled with lowing.

dēmulceō, -cēre, -sī *vt* to stroke.

dēmum *adv* (*time*) at last, not till; (*emphasis*) just, precisely; **ibi ~** just there; **modo ~** only now; **nunc ~** now at last; **post ~** not till after; **tum ~** only then.

dēmurmurō, -āre *vt* to mumble through.

dēmūtātiō, -ōnis *f* change.

dēmūtō, -āre *vt* to change, make worse ♦ *vi* to change one's mind.

dēnārius, -ī and iī *m Roman silver coin.*

dēnārrō, -āre *vt* to relate fully.

dēnāsō, -āre *vt* to take the nose off.

dēnatō, -āre *vi* to swim down.

dēnegō, -āre, -āvī, -ātum *vt* to deny, refuse, reject ♦ *vi* to say no.

dēnī, -ōrum *adj* ten each, in tens; ten; tenth.

dēnicālis *adj* for purifying after a death.

dēnique *adv* at last, finally; (*enumerating*) lastly, next; (*summing up*) in short, briefly; (*emphasis*) just, precisely.

dēnōminō, -āre *vt* to designate.

dēnōrmō, -āre *vt* to make irregular.

dēnotō, -āre, -āvī, -ātum *vt* to point out, specify; to observe.

dēns, dentis *m* tooth; ivory; prong, fluke.

dēnsē *adv* repeatedly.

dēnsō, -āre, -āvī, -ātum, dēnseō, -ēre *vt* to thicken; (*ranks*) to close.

dēnsus *adj* thick, dense, close; frequent; (*style*) concise.

dentālia, -ium *ntpl* ploughbeam.

dentātus *adj* toothed; (*paper*) polished.

dentiō, -īre *vi* to cut one's teeth; (*teeth*) to grow.

dēnūbō, -bere, -psī, -ptum *vi* to marry, marry beneath one.

dēnūdō, -āre, -āvī, -ātum *vt* to bare, strip; (*fig*) to disclose.

dēnūntiātiō, -ōnis *f* intimation, warning.

dēnūntiō, -āre, -āvī, -ātum *vt* to intimate, give notice of, declare; to threaten, warn; (*law*) to summon as witness.

dēnuō *adv* afresh, again, once more.

deonerō, -āre *vt* to unload.

deorsum, deorsus *adv* downwards.

deōsculor, -ārī *vt* to kiss warmly.

dēpacīscor *etc see* **dēpecīscor**.

dēpāctus *adj* driven in firmly.

dēpāscō, -scere, -vī, -stum, -scor, -scī *vt* to feed on, eat up; (*fig*) to devour, destroy, prune away.

dēpecīscor, -īscī, -tus *vt* to bargain for, agree about.

dēpectō, -ctere, -xum *vt* to comb; (*comedy*) to flog.

dēpectus *ppa of* **dēpecīscor**.

dēpecūlātor, -ōris *m* embezzler.

dēpecūlor, -ārī, -ātus *vt* to plunder.

dēpellō, -ellere, -ulī, -ulsum *vt* to expel, remove, cast down; (*MIL*) to dislodge; (*infants*) to wean; (*fig*) to deter, avert.

dēpendeō, -ēre *vi* to hang down, hang from; to depend on; to be derived.

dēpendō, -endere, -endī, -ēnsum *vt* to weigh, pay up.

dēperdō, -ere, -idī, -itum *vt* to lose completely, destroy, ruin.

dēpereō, -īre, -iī *vi* to perish, be completely destroyed; to be undone ♦ *vt* to be hopelessly in love with.

dēpexus *ppp of* **dēpectō**.

dēpingō, -ingere, -inxī, -ictum *vt* to paint; (*fig*) to portray, describe.

dēplangō, -gere, -xī *vt* to bewail frantically.

dēplexus *adj* grasping.

dēplōrābundus *adj* weeping bitterly.

dēplōrō, -āre, -āvī, -ātum *vi* to weep bitterly
♦ *vt* to bewail bitterly, mourn; to despair of.

dēpluit, -ere *vi* to rain down.

dēpōnō, -ōnere, -osuī, -ositum *vt* to lay down; to set aside, put away, get rid of; to wager; to deposit, entrust, commit to the care of; (*fig*) to give up.

dēpopulātiō, -ōnis *f* ravaging.

dēpopulātor, -ōris *m* marauder.

dēpopulor, -ārī, -ātus; -ō, -āre *vt* to ravage, devastate; (*fig*) to waste, destroy.

dēportō, -āre, -āvī, -ātum *vt* to carry down, carry off; to bring home (from a province); (*law*) to banish for life; (*fig*) to win.

dēposcō, -scere, -poscī *vt* to demand, require, claim.

dēpositum, -ī *nt* trust, deposit.

dēpositus *ppp of* **dēpōnō** ♦ *adj* dying, dead, despaired of.

dēprāvātē *adv* perversely.

dēprāvātiō, -ōnis *f* distorting.

dēprāvō, -āre, -āvī, -ātum *vt* to distort; (*fig*) to pervert, corrupt.

dēprecābundus *adj* imploring.

dēprecātiō, -ōnis *f* averting by prayer; imprecation, invocation; plea for indulgence.

dēprecātor, -ōris *m* intercessor.

dēprecor, -ārī, -ātus *vt* to avert (by prayer); to deprecate, intercede for.

dēprehendō, dēprendō, -endere, -endī, -ēnsum *vt* to catch, intercept; to overtake, surprise; to catch in the act, detect; (*fig*) to perceive, discover.

dēprehēnsiō, -ōnis *f* detection.

dēprehēnsus, dēprēnsus *ppp of* **dēprehendō**.

dēpressī *perf of* **dēprimō**.

dēpressus *ppp of* **dēprimō** ♦ *adj* low.

dēprimō, -imere, -essī, -essum *vt* to press down, weigh down; to dig deep; (*ship*) to sink; (*fig*) to suppress, keep down.

dēproelior, -ārī *vi* to fight it out.

dēprōmō, -ere, psī, -ptum *vt* to fetch, bring out, produce.

dēproperō, -āre *vi* to hurry up ♦ *vt* to hurry and make.

depsō, -ere *vt* to knead.

dēpudet, -ēre, -uit *v impers* not to be ashamed.

dēpūgis *adj* thin-buttocked.

dēpugnō, -āre, -āvī, -ātum *vi* to fight it out, fight hard.

dēpulī *perf of* **dēpellō**.

dēpulsiō, -ōnis *f* averting; defence.

dēpulsō, -āre *vt* to push out of the way.

dēpulsor, -ōris *m* repeller.

dēpulsus *ppp of* **dēpellō**.

dēpūrgō, -āre *vt* to clean.

dēputō, -āre *vt* to prune; to consider, reckon.

dēpȳgis *etc see* **dēpūgis**.

dēque *adv* down.

dērēctā, -ē, -ō *adv* straight.

dērēctus *ppp of* **dērigō** ♦ *adj* straight, upright, at right angles; straightforward.

dērelictiō, -ōnis *f* disregarding.

dērelinquō, -inquere, -īquī, -ictum *vt* to abandon, forsake.

dērepente *adv* suddenly.

dērēpō, -ere *vi* to creep down.

dēreptus *ppp of* **dēripiō**.

dērīdeō, -dēre, -sī, -sum *vt* to laugh at, deride.

dērīdiculum, -ī *nt* mockery, absurdity; object of derision.

dērīdiculus *adj* laughable.

dērigēscō, -ēscere, -uī *vi* to stiffen, curdle.

dērigō, -igere, -ēxī, -ēctum *vt* to turn, aim, direct; (*fig*) to regulate.

dēripiō, -ipere, -ipuī, -eptum *vt* to tear off, pull down.

dērīsor, -ōris *m* scoffer.

dērīsus *ppp of* **dērīdeō**.

dērīsus, -ūs *m* scorn, derision.

dērīvātiō, -ōnis *f* diverting.

dērīvō, -āre, -āvī, -ātum *vt* to lead off, draw off.

dērogō, -āre *vt* (*law*) to propose to amend; (*fig*) to detract from.

dērōsus *adj* gnawed away.

dēruncinō, -āre *vt* to plane off; (*comedy*) to cheat.

dēruō, -ere, -ī *vt* to demolish.

dēruptus *adj* steep ♦ *ntpl* precipice.

dēsaeviō, -īre *vi* to rage furiously; to cease raging.

dēscendō, -endere, -endī, -ēnsum *vi* to come down, go down, descend, dismount; (*MIL*) to march down; (*things*) to fall, sink, penetrate; (*fig*) to stoop (to), lower oneself.

dēscēnsiō, -ōnis *f* going down.

dēscēnsus, -ūs *m* way down.

dēscīscō, -īscere, -īvī and iī, -ītum *vi* to desert, revolt; to deviate, part company.

dēscrībō, -bere, -psī, -ptum *vt* to copy out; to draw, sketch; to describe; *see also* **dīscrībō**.

dēscrīptiō, -ōnis *f* copy; drawing, diagram; description.

dēscrīptus *ppp of* **dēscrībō**; *see also* **dīscrīptus**.

dēsecō, -āre, -uī, -tum *vt* to cut off.

dēserō, -ere, -uī, -tum *vt* to desert, abandon, forsake; (*bail*) to forfeit.

dēsertor, -ōris *m* deserter.

dēsertus *ppp of* **dēserō** ♦ *adj* desert,

Noun declensions and verb conjugations are shown on pp xiii to xxv. The present infinitive ending of a verb shows to which conjugation it belongs: **-āre** = 1st; **-ēre** = 2nd; **-ere** = 3rd and **-īre** = 4th. Irregular verbs are shown on p xxvi

uninhabited ♦ *ntpl* deserts.

dēserviō, -īre *vi* to be a slave (to), serve.

dēses, -idis *adj* idle, inactive.

dēsiccō, -āre *vt* to dry, drain.

dēsideō, -idēre, -ēdī *vi* to sit idle.

dēsīderābilis *adj* desirable.

dēsīderātiō, -ōnis *f* missing.

dēsīderium, -ī *and* **iī** *nt* longing, sense of loss; want; petition; **mē ~ tenet urbis** I miss Rome.

dēsīderō, -āre, -āvī, -ātum *vt* to feel the want of, miss; to long for, desire; (*casualties*) to lose.

dēsidia, -ae *f* idleness, apathy.

dēsidiōsē *adv* idly.

dēsidiōsus *adj* lazy, idle; relaxing.

dēsīdō, -īdere, -ēdī *vi* to sink, settle down; (*fig*) to deteriorate.

dēsignātiō, -ōnis *f* specifying; election (of magistrates).

dēsignātor *etc see* **dissignātor**.

dēsignātus *adj* elect.

dēsignō, -āre, -āvī, -ātum *vt* to trace out; to indicate, define; (POL) to elect; (*art*) to depict.

dēsiī *perf of* **dēsinō**.

dēsiliō, -īlīre, -iluī, -ultum *vi* to jump down, alight.

dēsinō, -nere, -ī *vt* to leave off, abandon ♦ *vi* to stop, desist; to end (in).

dēsipiēns, -ientis *adj* silly.

dēsipientia, -ae *f* folly.

dēsipiō, -ere *vi* to be stupid, play the fool.

dēsistō, -istere, -titī, -titum *vi* to stop, leave off, desist.

dēsitus *ppp of* **dēsinō**.

dēsōlō, -āre, -āvī, -ātum *vt* to leave desolate, abandon.

dēspectō, -āre *vt* to look down on, command a view of; to despise.

dēspectus *ppp of* **dēspiciō** ♦ *adj* contemptible.

dēspectus, -ūs *m* view, prospect.

dēspēranter *adv* despairingly.

dēspērātiō, -ōnis *f* despair.

dēspērātus *adj* despaired of, hopeless; desperate, reckless.

dēspērō, -āre, -āvī, -ātum *vt, vi* to despair, give up hope of.

dēspexī *perf of* **dēspiciō**.

dēspicātiō, -ōnis *f* contempt.

dēspicātus *adj* despised, contemptible.

dēspicātus, -ūs *m* contempt.

dēspicientia, -ae *f* contempt.

dēspiciō, -icere, -exī, -ectum *vt* to look down on; to despise ♦ *vi* to look down.

dēspoliātor, -ōris *m* robber.

dēspoliō, -āre *vt* to rob, plunder.

dēspondeō, -ondēre, -ondī *and* **opondī, -ōnsum** *vt* to pledge, promise; to betroth; to devote; to give up, despair of; **animum ~** despair.

dēspūmō, -āre *vt* to skim off.

dēspuō, -ere *vi* to spit on the ground ♦ *vt* to reject.

dēsquāmō, -āre *vt* to scale, peel.

dēstillō, -āre *vi* to drop down ♦ *vt* to distil.

dēstimulō, -āre *vt* to run through.

dēstinātiō, -ōnis *f* resolution, appointment.

dēstinātus *adj* fixed, decided.

dēstinō, -āre, -āvī, -ātum *vt* to make fast; to appoint, determine, resolve; (*archery*) to aim at; (*fig*) to intend to buy ♦ *nt* mark; intention; **~ātum est mihi** I have decided.

dēstitī *perf of* **dēsistō**.

dēstituō, -uere, -uī, -ūtum *vt* to set apart, place; to forsake, leave in the lurch.

dēstitūtiō, -ōnis *f* defaulting.

dēstitūtus *ppp of* **dēstituō**.

dēstrictus *ppp of* **dēstringō** ♦ *adj* severe.

dēstringō, -ingere, -inxī, -ictum *vt* (*leaves*) to strip; (*body*) to rub down; (*sword*) to draw; to graze, skim; (*fig*) to censure.

dēstruō, -ere, -xī, -ctum *vt* to demolish; to destroy.

dēsubitō *adv* all of a sudden.

dēsūdāscō, -ere *vi* to sweat all over.

dēsūdō, -āre *vi* to exert oneself.

dēsuēfactus *adj* unaccustomed.

dēsuētūdō, -inis *f* disuse.

dēsuētus *adj* unaccustomed, unused.

dēsultor, -ōris *m* circus rider; (*fig*) fickle lover.

dēsultūra, -ae *f* jumping down.

dēsum, deesse, -fuī *vi* to be missing, fail, fail in one's duty.

dēsūmō, -ere, -psī, -ptum *vt* to select.

dēsuper *adv* from above.

dēsurgō, -ere *vi* to rise.

dētegō, -egere, -exī, -ēctum *vt* to uncover, disclose; (*fig*) to reveal, detect.

dētendō, -endere, -ēnsum *vt* (*tent*) to strike.

dētentus *ppp of* **dētineō**.

dētergō, -gere, -sī, -sum *vt* to wipe away, clear away; to clean; to break off.

dēterior, -ōris *adj* lower; inferior, worse.

dēterius *adv* worse.

dēterminātiō, -ōnis *f* boundary, end.

dēterminō, -āre, -āvī, -ātum *vt* to bound, limit; to settle.

dēterō, -erere, -rīvī, -rītum *vt* to rub, wear away; (*style*) to polish; (*fig*) to weaken.

dēterreō, -ēre, -uī, -itum *vt* to frighten away; to deter, discourage, prevent.

dētersus *ppp of* **dētergeō**.

dētestābilis *adj* abominable.

dētestātiō, -ōnis *f* execration, curse; averting.

dētestor, -ārī, -ātus *vt* to invoke, invoke against; to curse, execrate; to avert, deprecate.

dētexō, -ere, -uī, -tum *vt* to weave, finish weaving; (*comedy*) to steal; (*fig*) to describe.

dētineō, -inēre, -inuī, -entum *vt* to hold back, detain; to keep occupied.

dētondeō, -ondēre, -ondī, -ōnsum *vt* to shear off, strip.

dētonō, -āre, -uī *vi* to cease thundering.

dētorqueō, -quēre, -sī, -tum *vt* to turn aside,

direct; to distort, misrepresent.

dētractātiō, -ōnis f declining.

dētrectātor, -ōris m disparager.

dētractiō, -ōnis f removal, departure.

dētractō etc see **dētrectō**.

dētractus ppp of **dētrahō**.

dētrahō, -here, -xī, -ctum vt to draw off, take away, pull down; to withdraw, force to leave; to detract, disparage.

dētrectō, -āre, -āvī, -ātum vt to decline, shirk; to detract from, disparage.

dētrīmentōsus adj harmful.

dētrīmentum, -ī nt loss, harm; (MIL) defeat; ~ **capere** suffer harm.

dētrītus ppp of **dēterō**.

dētrūdō, -dere, -sī, -sum vt to push down, thrust away; to dislodge, evict; to postpone; (fig) to force.

dētruncō, -āre, -āvī, -ātum vt to cut off, behead, mutilate.

dētrūsus ppp of **dētrūdō**.

dēturbō, -āre, -āvī, -ātum vt to dash down, pull down; (fig) to cast down, deprive.

Deucaliōn, -ōnis m son of Prometheus (survivor of the Flood).

Deucaliōnēus adj see **Deucaliōn**.

deūnx, -cis m eleven twelfths.

deūrō, -rere, -ssī, -stum vt to burn up; to frost.

deus, -ī (voc deus, pl dī, deos, deum, dis) m god; **dī meliōra!** Heaven forbid!; **dī tē ament!** bless you!

deūstus ppp of **deūrō**.

deūtor, -ī vi to maltreat.

dēvāstō, -āre vt to lay waste.

dēvehō, -here, -xī, -ctum vt to carry down, convey; (pass) to ride down, sail down.

dēvellō, -ellere, -ellī and **olsī, -ulsum** vt to pluck, pull out.

dēvēlō, -āre vt to unveil.

dēveneror, -ārī vt to worship; to avert by prayers.

dēveniō, -enīre, -ēnī, -entum vi to come, reach, fall into.

dēverberō, -āre, -āvī, -ātum vt to thrash soundly.

dēversor, -ārī vi to lodge, stay (as guest).

dēversor, -ōris m guest.

dēversōriolum, -ī nt small lodging.

dēversōrium, -ī and **iī** nt inn, lodging.

dēversōrius adj for lodging.

dēverticulum, -ī nt by-road, by-pass; digression; lodging place; (fig) refuge.

dēvertō, -tere, -tī, -sum vi to turn aside, put up; to have recourse to; to digress.

dēvertor, -tī, versus vi see **dēvertō**.

dēvexus adj sloping, going down, steep.

dēvinciō, -cīre, -xī, -ctum vt to tie up; (fig) to bind, lay under an obligation.

dēvincō, -incere, -īcī, -ictum vt to defeat

completely, win the day.

dēvītātiō, -ōnis f avoiding.

dēvītō, -āre vt to avoid.

dēvius adj out of the way, devious; (person) solitary, wandering off the beaten track; (fig) inconstant.

dēvocō, -āre, -āvī, -ātum vt to call down, fetch; to entice away.

dēvolō, -āre vi to fly down.

dēvolvō, -vere, -vī, -ūtum vt to roll down, fall; (wool) to spin off.

dēvorō, -āre, -āvī, -ātum vt to swallow, gulp down; to engulf, devour; (money) to squander; (tears) to repress; (trouble) to endure patiently.

dēvors-, dēvort- see **dēvers-, dēvert-**.

dēvortia, -ōrum ntpl byways.

dēvōtiō, -ōnis f devoting; (magic) spell.

dēvōtō, -āre vt to bewitch.

dēvōtus ppp of **dēvoveō** ♦ adj faithful; accursed.

dēvoveō, -ovēre, -ōvī, -ōtum vt to devote, vow, dedicate; to give up; to curse; to bewitch.

dēvulsus ppp of **dēvellō**.

dextella, -ae f little right hand.

dexter, -erī and **rī** adj right, right-hand; handy, skilful; favourable.

dexteritās, -ātis f adroitness.

dextra f right hand, right-hand side; hand; pledge of friendship.

dextrā prep (with acc) on the right of.

dextrē (compar -erius) adv adroitly.

dextrōrsum, -rsus, -vorsum adv to the right.

dī pl of **deus**.

diabathrārius, -ī and **iī** m slipper maker.

diabolus, -ī m devil.

diāconus, -ī m (ECCL) deacon.

diadēma, -tis nt royal headband, diadem.

diaeta, -ae f diet; living room.

dialectica, -ae, -ē, -ēs f dialectic, logic ♦ ntpl logical questions.

dialecticē adv dialectically.

dialecticus adj dialectical ♦ m logician.

Diālis adj of Jupiter ♦ m high priest of Jupiter.

dialogus, -ī m dialogue, conversation.

Diāna, -ae f virgin goddess of hunting (also identified with the moon and Hecate, and patroness of childbirth).

Diānius adj of Diana ♦ nt sanctuary of Diana.

diāria, -ōrum ntpl daily allowance of food or pay.

dibaphus, -ī f Roman state robe.

dica, -ae f lawsuit.

dicācitās, -ātis f raillery, repartee.

dicāculus adj pert.

dicātiō, -ōnis f declaration of citizenship.

dicāx, -ācis adj witty, smart.

dichorēus, -ī m double trochee.

diciō, -ōnis f power, sway, authority.

Noun declensions and verb conjugations are shown on pp xiii to xxv. The present infinitive ending of a verb shows to which conjugation it belongs: **-āre** = 1st; **-ēre** = 2nd; **-ere** = 3rd and **-īre** = 4th. Irregular verbs are shown on p xxvi

dicis causā for the sake of appearance.
dicō, -āre, -āvī, -ātum _vt_ to dedicate, consecrate; to deify; to devote, give over.
dīcō, -cere, -xī, dictum _vt_ to say, tell; to mention, mean, call, name; to pronounce; (_RHET_) to speak, deliver; (_law_) to plead; (_poetry_) to describe, celebrate; (_official_) to appoint; (_time, place_) to settle, fix ♦ _vi_ to speak (in public); **causam ~** plead; **iūs ~** deliver judgment; **sententiam ~** vote; **~cō** namely; **~xī** I have finished; **dictum factum** no sooner said than done.
dicrotum, -ī _nt_ bireme.
Dictaeus _adj_ Cretan.
dictamnus, -ī _f_ dittany (_a kind of wild marjoram_).
dictāta, -ōrum _ntpl_ lessons, rules.
dictātor, -ōris _m_ dictator.
dictātōrius _adj_ dictator's.
dictātūra, -ae _f_ dictatorship.
Dictē, -ēs _f_ mountain in Crete (_where Jupiter was brought up_).
dictiō, -ōnis _f_ speaking, declaring; style, expression, oratory; (_oracle_) response.
dictitō, -āre _vt_ to keep saying, assert; to plead often.
dictō, -āre, -āvī, -ātum _vt_ to say repeatedly; to dictate; to compose.
dictum, -ī _nt_ saying, word; proverb; bon mot, witticism; command.
dictus _ppp of_ **dīcō**.
Dictynna, -ae _f_ Britomartis; Diana.
Dictynnaeus _adj see n._
didicī _perf of_ **discō**.
dīdō, -ere, -idī, -itum _vt_ to distribute, broadcast.
Dīdō, -ūs _and_ **-ōnis** (_acc_ **-ō**) _f_ Queen of Carthage.
dīdūcō, -ūcere, -ūxī, -uctum _vt_ to separate, split, open up; (_MIL_) to disperse; (_fig_) to part, divide.
diēcula, -ae _f_ one little day.
diērēctus _adj_ crucified; **abī ~** go and be hanged.
diēs, -ēī _m/f_ day; set day (_usu fem_); a day's journey; (_fig_) time; **~ meus** my birthday; **~em dīcere** impeach; **~em obīre** die; **~em dē ~ē, ~em ex ~ē** from day to day; **in ~em** to a later day; for today; **in ~ēs** daily.
Diēspiter, -ris _m_ Jupiter.
diffāmō, -āre, -āvī, -ātum _vt_ to divulge; to malign.
differentia, -ae _f_ difference, diversity; species.
differitās, -ātis _f_ difference.
differō, -erre, distulī, dīlātum _vt_ to disperse; to divulge, publish; (_fig_) to distract, disquiet; (_time_) to put off, delay ♦ _vi_ to differ, be distinguished.
differtus _adj_ stuffed, crammed.
difficilis _adj_ difficult; (_person_) awkward, surly.
difficiliter _adv_ with difficulty.
difficultās, -ātis _f_ difficulty, distress, hardship; surliness.

difficulter _adv_ with difficulty.
diffīdēns, -entis _adj_ nervous.
diffīdenter _adv_ without confidence.
diffīdentia, -ae _f_ mistrust, diffidence.
diffīdō, -dere, -sus _vi_ to distrust, despair.
diffindō, -ndere, -dī, -ssum _vt_ to split, open up; (_fig_) to break off.
diffingō, -ere _vt_ to remake.
diffissus _ppp of_ **diffindō**.
diffīsus _ppa of_ **diffīdō**.
diffiteor, -ērī _vt_ to disown.
diffluēns, -entis _adj_ (_RHET_) loose.
diffluō, -ere _vi_ to flow away; to melt away; (_fig_) to wallow.
diffringō, -ere _vt_ to shatter.
diffugiō, -ugere, -ūgī _vi_ to disperse, disappear.
diffugium, -ī _and_ **iī** _nt_ dispersion.
diffunditō, -āre _vt_ to pour out, waste.
diffundō, -undere, -ūdī, -ūsum _vt_ to pour off; to spread, diffuse; to cheer, gladden.
diffūsē _adv_ expansively.
diffūsilis _adj_ diffusive.
diffūsus _ppp of_ **diffundō** ♦ _adj_ spreading; (_writing_) loose.
Dīgentia, -ae _f_ tributary of the Anio (_near Horace's villa_).
dīgerō, -rere, -ssī, -stum _vt_ to divide, distribute; to arrange, set out; to interpret.
dīgestiō, -ōnis _f_ (_RHET_) enumeration.
dīgestus _ppp of_ **dīgerō**.
digitulus, -ī _m_ little finger.
digitus, -ī _m_ finger; toe; inch; (_pl_) skill in counting; **~um porrigere, prōferre** take the slightest trouble; **~um trānsversum nōn discēdere** not swerve a finger's breadth; **attingere caelum ~ō** reach the height of happiness; **licērī ~ō** bid at an auction; **mōnstrārī ~ō** be a celebrity; **extrēmī, summī ~ī** the fingertips; **concrepāre ~īs** snap the fingers.
dīgladior, -ārī _vi_ to fight fiercely.
dignātiō, -ōnis _f_ honour, dignity.
dignē _adv see_ **dignus**.
dignitās, -ātis _f_ worth, worthiness; dignity, rank, position; political office.
dignō, -āre _vt_ to think worthy.
dignor, -ārī _vt_ to think worthy; to deign.
dignōscō, -ere _vt_ to distinguish.
dignus _adj_ worth, worthy; (_things_) fitting, proper.
dīgredior, -dī, -ssus _vi_ to separate, part; to deviate, digress.
dīgressiō, -ōnis _f_ parting; deviation; digression.
dīgressus _ppa of_ **dīgredior**.
dīgressus, -ūs _m_ parting.
dīiūdicātiō, -ōnis _f_ decision.
dīiūdicō, -āre _vt_ to decide; to discriminate.
dīiun- _etc see_ **disiun-**.
dīlābor, -bī, -psus _vi_ to dissolve, disintegrate; to flow away; (_troops_) to disperse; (_fig_) to decay, vanish.

dīlacerō, -āre *vt* to tear to pieces.
dīlāminō, -āre *vt* to split in two.
dīlaniō, -āre, -āvī, -ātum *vt* to tear to shreds.
dīlapidō, -āre *vt* to demolish.
dīlāpsus *ppa of* **dīlābor.**
dīlargior, -īrī *vt* to give away liberally.
dīlātiō, -ōnis *f* putting off, adjournment.
dīlātō, -āre, -āvī, -ātum *vt* to expand;
  (*pronunciation*) to broaden.
dīlātor, -ōris *m* procrastinator.
dīlātus *ppp of* **differō.**
dīlaudō, -āre *vt* to praise extravagantly.
dīlēctus *ppp of* **dīligō ♦** *adj* beloved.
dīlēctus, -ūs *m* selection, picking; (*MIL*) levy;
  ~**um habēre** hold a levy, recruit.
dīlēxī *perf of* **dīligō.**
dīligēns, -entis *adj* painstaking,
  conscientious, attentive (to); thrifty.
dīligenter *adv see* **dīligēns.**
dīligentia, -ae *f* carefulness, attentiveness;
  thrift.
dīligō, -igere, -ēxī, -ēctum *vt* to prize
  especially, esteem, love.
dīlōricō, -āre *vt* to tear open.
dīlūceō, -ēre *vi* to be evident.
dīlūcescit, -cēscere, -xit *vi* to dawn, begin to
  grow light.
dīlūcidē *adv see* **dīlūcidus.**
dīlūcidus *adj* clear, distinct.
dīlūculum, -ī *nt* dawn.
dīlūdium, -ī *and* **iī** *nt* interval.
dīluō, -uere, -uī, -ūtum *vt* to wash away,
  dissolve, dilute; to explain; (*fig*) to weaken,
  do away with.
dīluviēs, -iēī *f*, **-ium, -ī** *and* **iī** *nt* flood, deluge.
dīluviō, -āre *vt* to inundate.
dīmānō, -āre *vi* to spread abroad.
dīmēnsiō, -ōnis *f* measuring.
dīmēnsus *adj* measured.
dīmētior, -tīrī, -nsus *vt* to measure out.
dīmētō, -āre, -or, -ārī *vt* to mark out.
dīmicātiō, -ōnis *f* fighting, struggle.
dīmicō, -āre, -āvī, -ātum *vi* to fight, struggle,
  contend.
dīmidiātus *adj* half, halved.
dīmidius *adj* half **♦** *nt* half.
dīmissiō, -ōnis *f* sending away; discharging.
dīmissus *ppp of* **dīmittō.**
dīmittō, -ittere, -īsī, -issum *vt* to send away,
  send round; to let go, lay down; (*meeting*) to
  dismiss; (*MIL*) to disband, detach; (*fig*) to
  abandon, forsake.
dīminuō, -ere *vt* to dash to pieces.
dīmoveō, -overe, -ōvī, -ōtum *vt* to part,
  separate; to disperse; to entice away.
Dindymēnē, -ēnēs *f* Cybele.
Dindymus, -ī *m* mountain in Mysia (*sacred to
  Cybele*).
dīnōscō *see* **dīgnōscō.**
dīnumerātiō, -ōnis *f* reckoning up.

dīnumerō, -āre *vt* to count, reckon up; to pay
  out.
diōbolāris *adj* costing two obols.
dioecēsis, -is *f* district; (*ECCL*) diocese.
dioecētēs, -ae *m* treasurer.
Diogenēs, -is *m famous Cynic philosopher; a
  Stoic philosopher.*
Diomēdēs, -is *m Greek hero at the Trojan War.*
Diomēdēus *adj see n.*
Diōnaeus *adj see* **Diōnē.**
Diōnē, -ēs *and* **-a, -ae** *f mother of Venus;* Venus.
Dionȳsius, -ī *m tyrant of Syracuse.*
Dionȳsus, -ī *m* Bacchus; **-ia, -iōrum** *ntpl Greek
  festival of Bacchus.*
diōta, -ae *f* a two-handled wine jar.
diplōma, -tis *nt* letter of recommendation.
Dipylon, -ī *nt* Athenian gate.
Dircaeus *adj* Boeotian.
Dircē, -ēs *f famous spring in Boeotia.*
dīrēctus *ppp of* **dīrigō ♦** *adj* straight;
  straightforward, simple; *see also* **dērēctus.**
dīrēmī *perf of* **dirimō.**
dīremptus *ppp of* **dirimō.**
dīremptus, -ūs *m* separation.
dīreptiō, -ōnis *f* plundering.
dīreptor, -ōris *m* plunderer.
dīreptus *ppp of* **dīripiō.**
dīrēxī *perf of* **dīrigō.**
dīribeō, -ēre *vt* to sort out (*votes taken from
  ballot-boxes*).
dīribitiō, -ōnis *f* sorting.
dīribitor, -ōris *m* ballot-sorter.
dīrigō, -igere, -ēxī, -ēctum *vt* to put in line,
  arrange; *see also* **dērigō.**
dirimō, -imere, -ēmī, -emptum *vt* to part,
  divide; to interrupt, break off; to put an end
  to.
dīripiō, -ipere, -ipuī, -eptum *vt* to tear in
  pieces; to plunder, ravage; to seize; (*fig*) to
  distract.
dīritās, -ātis *f* mischief, cruelty.
**dīrumpō, disrumpō, -umpere, -ūpī,
  -uptum** *vt* to burst, break in pieces; (*fig*) to
  break off; (*pass*) to burst (with passion).
dīruō, -ere, -ī, -tum *vt* to demolish; to scatter;
  aere ~tus having one's pay stopped.
dīruptus *ppp of* **dīruō ♦** *adj* bankrupt.
dīrus *adj* ominous, fearful; (*pers*) dread,
  terrible **♦** *fpl* bad luck; the Furies **♦** *ntpl*
  terrors.
dīrutus *ppp of* **dīruō ♦** *adj* bankrupt.
dīs, dītis *adj* rich.
Dīs, Dītis *m* Pluto.
discēdō, -ēdere, -ēssī, -essum *vi* to go away,
  depart; to part, disperse; (*MIL*) to march
  away; (*result of battle*) to come off; (*POL*) to go
  over (to a different policy); to pass away,
  disappear; to leave out of consideration; **ab
  signīs** ~ break the ranks; **victor** ~ come off
  best.

disceptātiō, -ōnis *f* discussion, debate.
disceptātor, -ōris *m*, **-rīx, -rīcis** *f* arbitrator.
disceptō, -āre *vt* to debate, discuss; (*law*) to decide.
discernō, -ernere, -rēvī, -rētum *vt* to divide, separate; to distinguish between.
discerpō, -ere, -sī, -tum *vt* to tear apart, disperse; (*fig*) to revile.
discessiō, -ōnis *f* separation, departure; (*senate*) division.
discessus, -ūs *m* parting; departure; marching away.
discidium, -i *and* **iī** *nt* disintegration; separation, divorce; discord.
discīdō, -ere *vt* to cut in pieces.
discinctus *ppp of* **discingō** ♦ *adj* ungirt; negligent; dissolute.
discindō, -ndere, -dī, -ssum *vt* to tear up, cut open.
discingō, -gere, -xī, -ctum *vt* to ungird.
disciplīna, -ae *f* teaching, instruction; learning, science, school, system; training, discipline; habits.
discipulus, -ī *m*, **-a, -ae** *f* pupil, apprentice.
discissus *ppp of* **discindō**.
disclūdō, -dere, -sī, -sum *vt* to keep apart, separate out.
discō, -ere, didicī *vt* to learn, be taught, be told.
discolor, -ōris *adj* of a different colour; variegated; different.
discondūcit it is not worthwhile.
disconveniō, -īre *vi* to disagree, be inconsistent.
discordābilis *adj* disagreeing.
discordia, -ae *f* discord, disagreement.
discordiōsus *adj* seditious.
discordō, -āre *vi* to disagree, quarrel; to be unlike.
discors, -dis *adj* discordant, at variance; inconsistent.
discrepantia, -ae *f* disagreement.
discrepātiō, -ōnis *f* dispute.
discrepitō, -āre *vi* to be quite different.
discrepō, -āre, -uī *vi* to be out of tune; to disagree, differ; to be disputed.
discrētus *ppp of* **discernō**.
dīscrībō, -bere, -psī, -ptum *vt* to distribute, apportion, classify.
discrīmen, -inis *nt* interval, dividing line; distinction, difference; turning point, critical moment; crisis, danger.
discrīminō, -āre *vt* to divide.
dīscriptē *adv* in good order.
dīscriptiō, -ōnis *f* apportioning, distributing.
dīscriptus *ppp of* **dīscrībō** ♦ *adj* secluded; well-arranged.
discruciō, -āre *vt* to torture; (*fig*) to torment, trouble.
discumbō, -mbere, -buī, -bitum *vi* to recline at table; to go to bed.
discupiō, -ere *vi* to long.
discurrō, -rrere, -currī *and* **rrī, -rsum** *vi* to

run about, run different ways.
discursus, -ūs *m* running hither and thither.
discus, -ī *m* quoit.
discussus *ppp of* **discutiō**.
discutiō, -tere, -ssī, -ssum *vt* to dash to pieces, smash; to scatter; to dispel.
disertē, -im *adv* distinctly; eloquently.
disertus *adj* fluent, eloquent; explicit.
disiciō, -icere, -iēcī, -iectum *vt* to scatter, cast asunder; to break up, destroy; (*MIL*) to rout.
disiectō, -āre *vt* to toss about.
disiectus *ppp of* **disiciō**.
disiectus, -ūs *m* scattering.
disiūnctiō, -ōnis *f* separation, differing; (*logic*) statement of alternatives; (*RHET*) a sequence of short co-ordinate clauses.
disiūnctius *adv* rather in the manner of a dilemma.
disiūnctus *ppp of* **disiungō** ♦ *adj* distinct, distant, removed; (*speech*) disjointed; (*logic*) opposite.
disiungō, -ungere, -ūnxī, -ūnctum *vt* to unyoke; to separate, remove.
dispālēscō, -ere *vi* to be noised abroad.
dispandō, -āndere, -ānsum *and* **-essum** *vt* to spread out.
dispār, -aris *adj* unlike, unequal.
disparilis *adj* dissimilar.
disparō, -āre, -āvī, -ātum *vt* to segregate.
dispart- *etc see* **dispert-**.
dispectus *ppp of* **dispiciō**.
dispellō, -ellere, -ulī, -ulsum *vt* to scatter, dispel.
dispendium, -ī *and* **iī** *nt* expense, loss.
dispennō *etc see* **dispandō**.
dispēnsātiō, -ōnis *f* management, stewardship.
dispēnsātor, -ōris *m* steward, treasurer.
dispēnsō, -āre, -āvī, -ātum *vi* to weigh out, pay out; to manage, distribute; (*fig*) to regulate.
dispercutiō, -ere *vt* to dash out.
disperdō, -ere, -idī, -itum *vt* to ruin, squander.
dispereō, -īre, -iī *vi* to go to ruin, be undone.
dispergō, -gere, -sī, -sum *vt* to disperse, spread over, space out.
dispersē *adv* here and there.
dispersus *ppp of* **dispergō**.
dispertiō, -īre, -īvī, -ītum; -ior, -īrī *vt* to apportion, distribute.
dispertītiō, -ōnis *f* division.
dispessus *ppp of* **dispandō**.
dispiciō, -icere, -exī, -ectum *vt* to see clearly, see through; to distinguish, discern; (*fig*) to consider.
displiceō, -ēre *vi* (*with dat*) to displease; **sibi ~** be in a bad humour.
displōdō, -dere, -sum *vt* to burst with a crash.
dispōnō, -ōnere, -osuī, -ositum *vt* to set out, arrange; (*MIL*) to station.

dispositē *adv* methodically.
dispositiō, -ōnis *f* arrangement.
dispositūra, -ae *f* arrangement.
dispositus *ppp of* **dispōnō ♦** *adj* orderly.
dispositus, -ūs *m* arranging.
dispudet, -ēre, -uit *v impers* to be very ashamed.
dispulsus *ppp of* **dispellō.**
disputātiō, -ōnis *f* argument.
disputātor, -ōris *m* debater.
disputō, -āre, -āvī, -ātum *vt* to calculate; to examine, discuss.
disquīrō, -ere *vt* to investigate.
disquīsitiō, -ōnis *f* inquiry.
disrumpō *etc see* **dīrumpō.**
dissaepiō, -īre, -sī, -tum *vt* to fence off, separate off.
dissaeptum, -ī *nt* partition.
dissāvior, -ārī *vt* to kiss passionately.
dissēdī *perf of* **dissideō.**
dissēminō, -āre *vt* to sow, broadcast.
dissēnsiō, -ōnis *f* disagreement, conflict.
dissēnsus, -ūs *m* dissension.
dissentāneus *adj* contrary.
dissentiō, -entīre, -ēnsī, -ēnsum *vi* to disagree, differ; to be unlike, be inconsistent.
dissēp- *etc see* **dissaep-.**
disserēnō, -āre *vi* to clear up.
disserō, -erere, -ēvī, -itum *vt* to sow, plant at intervals.
disserō, -ere, -uī, -tum *vt* to set out in order, arrange; to examine, discuss.
disserpō, -ere *vi* to spread imperceptibly.
dissertō, -āre *vt* to discuss, dispute.
dissideō, -idēre, -ēdī, -essum *vi* to be distant; to disagree, quarrel; to differ, be unlike, be uneven.
dissignātiō, -ōnis *f* arrangement.
dissignātor, -ōris *m* master of ceremonies; undertaker.
dissignō, -āre *vt* to arrange, regulate; *see also* **dēsignō.**
dissiliō, -īre, -uī *vi* to fly apart, break up.
dissimilis *adj* unlike, different.
dissimiliter *adv* differently.
dissimilitūdō, -inis *f* unlikeness.
dissimulanter *adv* secretly.
dissimulantia, -ae *f* dissembling.
dissimulātiō, -ōnis *f* disguising, dissembling; Socratic irony.
dissimulātor, -ōris *m* dissembler.
dissimulō, -āre, -āvī, -ātum *vt* to dissemble, conceal, pretend that ... not, ignore.
dissipābilis *adj* diffusible.
dissipātiō, -ōnis *f* scattering, dispersing.
dissipō, dissupō, -āre, -āvī, -ātum *vt* to scatter, disperse; to spread, broadcast; to squander, destroy; (*MIL*) to put to flight.
dissitus *ppp of* **disserō.**

dissociābilis *adj* disuniting; incompatible.
dissociātiō, -ōnis *f* separation.
dissociō, -āre, -āvī, -ātum *vt* to disunite, estrange.
dissolūbilis *adj* dissoluble.
dissolūtē *adv* loosely, negligently.
dissolūtiō, -ōnis *f* breaking up, destruction; looseness; (*law*) refutation; (*person*) weakness.
dissolūtum, -ī *nt* asyndeton.
dissolūtus *ppp of* **dissolvō ♦** *adj* loose; lax, careless; licentious.
dissolvō, -vere, -vī, -ūtum *vt* to unloose, dissolve; to destroy, abolish; to refute; to pay up, discharge (debt); to free, release.
dissonus *adj* discordant, jarring, disagreeing, different.
dissors, -tis *adj* not shared.
dissuādeō, -dēre, -sī, -sum *vt* to advise against, oppose.
dissuāsiō, -ōnis *f* advising against.
dissuāsor, -ōris *m* opposer.
dissultō, -āre *vi* to fly asunder.
dissuō, -ere *vt* to undo, open up.
dissupō *etc see* **dissipō.**
distaedet, -ēre *v impers* to weary, disgust.
distantia, -ae *f* diversity.
distendō (-nō), -dere, -dī, -tum *vt* to stretch out, swell.
distentus *ppp of* **distendō ♦** *adj* full **♦** *ppp of* **distineō ♦** *adj* busy.
disterminō, -āre *vt* to divide, limit.
distichon, -ī *nt* couplet.
distinctē *adv* distinctly, lucidly.
distinctiō, -ōnis *f* differentiating, difference; (*GRAM*) punctuation; (*RHET*) distinction between words.
distinctus *ppp of* **distinguō ♦** *adj* separate, distinct; ornamented, set off; lucid.
distinctus, -ūs *m* difference.
distineō, -inēre, -inuī, -entum *vt* to keep apart, divide; to distract; to detain, occupy; to prevent.
distinguō, -guere, -xī, -ctum *vt* to divide, distinguish, discriminate; to punctuate; to adorn, set off.
distō, -āre *vi* to be apart, be distant; to be different.
distorqueō, -quēre, -sī, -tum *vt* to twist, distort.
distortiō, -ōnis *f* contortion.
distortus *ppp of* **distorqueō ♦** *adj* deformed.
distractiō, -ōnis *f* parting, variance.
distractus *ppp of* **distrahō ♦** *adj* separate.
distrahō, -here, -xī, -ctum *vt* to tear apart, separate, estrange; to sell piecemeal, retail; (*mind*) to distract, perplex; **aciem ~** break up a formation; **contrōversiās ~** end a dispute; **vōcēs ~** leave a hiatus.
distribuō, -uere, -uī, -ūtum *vt* to distribute,

Noun declensions and verb conjugations are shown on pp xiii to xxv. The present infinitive ending of a verb shows to which conjugation it belongs: **-āre** = 1st; **-ēre** = 2nd; **-ere** = 3rd and **-īre** = 4th. Irregular verbs are shown on p xxvi

divide.

distribūtē *adv* methodically.

distribūtiō, -ōnis *f* distribution, division.

districtus *ppp of* **distringō ♦** *adj* busy, occupied; perplexed; severe.

distringō, -ngere, -nxī, -ctum *vt* to draw apart; to engage, distract; (*MIL*) to create a diversion against.

distruncō, -āre *vt* to cut in two.

distulī *perf of* **differō**.

disturbō, -āre, -āvī, -ātum *vt* to throw into confusion; to demolish; to frustrate, ruin.

dītēscō, -ere *vi* to grow rich.

dīthyrambicus *adj* dithyrambic.

dīthyrambus, -ī *m* dithyramb.

dītiae, -ārum *fpl* wealth.

dītiō *etc see* **diciō**.

dītō, -āre *vt* to enrich.

diū (*comp* **diūtius**, *sup* **diūtissimē**) *adv* long, a long time; long ago; by day.

diurnum, -ī *nt* day-book; **ācta ~a** Roman daily gazette.

diurnus *adj* daily, for a day; by day, day- (*in cpds*).

dīus *adj* divine, noble.

diūtinē *adv* long.

diūtinus *adj* long, lasting.

diūtissimē, -ius *etc see* **diū**.

diūturnitās, -ātis *f* long time, long duration.

diūturnus *adj* long, lasting.

dīva, -ae *f* goddess.

dīvāricō, -āre *vt* to spread.

dīvellō, -ellere, -ellī, -ulsum *vt* to tear apart, tear in pieces; (*fig*) to tear away, separate, estrange.

dīvendō, -ere, -itum *vt* to sell in lots.

dīverberō, -āre *vt* to divide, cleave.

dīverbium, -ī *and* **iī** *nt* (*comedy*) passage in dialogue.

dīversē *adv* in different directions, variously.

dīversitās, -ātis *f* contradiction, disagreement, difference.

dīversus, dīvorsus *ppp of* **dīvertō ♦** *adj* in different directions, apart; different; remote; opposite, conflicting; hostile **♦** *mpl* individuals.

dīvertō, -tere, -tī, -sum *vi* to turn away; differ.

dīves, -itis *adj* rich.

dīvexō, -āre *vt* to pillage.

dīvidia, -ae *f* worry, concern.

dīvidō, -idere, -īsī, -īsum *vt* to divide, break open; to distribute, apportion; to separate, keep apart; to distinguish; (*jewel*) to set off; **sententiam ~** *take the vote separately on the parts of a motion*.

dīviduus *adj* divisible; divided.

dīvīnātiō, -ōnis *f* foreseeing the future, divination; (*law*) inquiry to select the most suitable prosecutor.

dīvīnē *adv* by divine influence; prophetically; admirably.

dīvīnitās, -ātis *f* divinity; divination; divine

quality.

dīvīnitus *adv* from heaven, by divine influence; excellently.

dīvīnō, -āre, -āvī, -ātum *vt* to foresee, prophesy.

dīvīnus *adj* divine, of the gods; prophetic; superhuman, excellent **♦** *m* soothsayer **♦** *nt* sacrifice; oath; **rēs ~a** religious service, sacrifice; **~a hūmānaque** all things in heaven and earth; **~ī crēdere** believe on oath.

dīvīsī *perf of* **dīvidō**.

dīvīsiō, -ōnis *f* division; distribution.

dīvīsor, -ōris *m* distributor; bribery agent.

dīvīsus *ppp of* **dīvidō ♦** *adj* separate.

dīvīsus, -ūs *m* division.

dīvitiae, -ārum *fpl* wealth; (*fig*) richness.

dīvor- *etc see* **dīver-**.

dīvortium, -ī *and* **iī** *nt* separation; divorce (by consent); road fork, watershed.

dīvulgātus *adj* widespread.

dīvulgō, -āre, -āvī, -ātum *vt* to publish, make public.

dīvulsus *ppp of* **dīvellō**.

dīvum, -ī *nt* sky; **sub ~ō** in the open air.

dīvus *adj* divine; deified **♦** *m* god.

dīxī *perf of* **dīcō**.

dō, dare, dedī, datum *vt* to give; to permit, grant; to put, bring, cause, make; to give up, devote; to tell; to impute; **fābulam ~** produce a play; **in fugam ~** put to flight; **litterās ~** post a letter; **manūs ~** surrender; **nōmen ~** enlist; **operam ~** take pains, do one's best; **poenās ~** pay the penalty; **vēla ~** set sail; **verba ~** cheat.

doceō, -ēre, -uī, -tum *vt* to teach; to inform, tell; **fābulam ~** produce a play.

dochmius, -ī *and* **iī** *m* dochmiac foot.

docilis *adj* easily trained, docile.

docilitās, -ātis *f* aptness for being taught.

doctē *adv* skilfully, cleverly.

doctor, -ōris *m* teacher, instructor.

doctrīna, -ae *f* instruction, education, learning; science.

doctus *ppp of* **doceō ♦** *adj* learned, skilled; cunning, clever.

documentum, -ī *nt* lesson, example, proof.

Dōdōna, -ae *f* town in Epirus (*famous for its oracle of Jupiter*).

Dōdōnaeus, -is, -idis *adj see* **Dōdōna**.

dōdrāns, -antis *m* three-fourths.

dogma, -tis *nt* philosophical doctrine.

dolābra, -ae *f* pickaxe.

dolēns, -entis *pres p of* **doleō ♦** *adj* painful.

dolenter *adv* sorrowfully.

doleō, -ēre, -uī, -itum *vt, vi* to be in pain, be sore; to grieve, lament, be sorry (for); to pain; **cuī ~et meminit** ≈ *once bitten, twice shy*.

dōliāris *adj* tubby.

dōliolum, -ī *nt* small cask.

dōlium, -ī *and* **iī** *nt* large wine jar.

dolō, -āre, -āvī, -ātum *vt* to hew, shape with an axe.

dolō, -ōnis *m* pike; sting; fore-topsail.

Dolopes, -um *mpl* people of Thessaly.
Dolopia, -iae *f* the country of the people of Thessaly.
dolor, -ōris *m* pain, pang; sorrow, trouble; indignation, resentment; (*RHET*) pathos.
dolōsē *adv see* **dolōsus**.
dolōsus *adj* deceitful, crafty.
dolus, -ī *m* deceit, guile, trick; ~ **malus** wilful fraud.
domābilis *adj* tameable.
domesticus *adj* domestic, household; personal, private; of one's own country, internal ♦ *mpl* members of a household; **bellum** ~ civil war.
domī *adv* at home.
domicilium, -ī *and* **iī** *nt* dwelling.
domina, -ae *f* mistress, lady of the house; wife, mistress; (*fig*) lady.
domināns, -antis *pres p of* **dominor** ♦ *adj* (*words*) literal ♦ *m* tyrant.
dominātiō, -ōnis *f* mastery, tyranny.
dominātor, -ōris *m* lord.
dominātrīx, -rīcis *f* queen.
dominātus, -ūs *m* mastery, sovereignty.
dominicus *adj* (*ECCL*) the Lord's.
dominium, -ī *and* **iī** *nt* absolute ownership; feast.
dominor, -ārī, -ātus *vi* to rule, be master; (*fig*) to lord it.
dominus, -ī *m* master, lord; owner; host; despot; (*ECCL*) the Lord.
Domitiānus *adj m* Roman Emperor.
Domitius, -ī *m* Roman plebeian name (*esp with surname Ahenobarbus*).
domitō, -āre *vt* to break in.
domitor, -ōris *m*, **-rīx, -rīcis** *f* tamer; conqueror.
domitus *ppp of* **domō**.
domitus, -ūs *m* taming.
domō, -āre, -uī, -itum *vt* to tame, break in; to conquer.
domus, -ūs *and* **ī** *f* house (*esp in town*); home, native place; family; (*PHILOS*) sect; ~**ī** at home; in peace; ~**ī habēre** have of one's own, have plenty of; ~**um** home(wards); ~**ō** from home.
dōnābilis *adj* deserving a present.
dōnārium, -ī *and* **iī** *nt* offering; altar, temple.
dōnātiō, -ōnis *f* presenting.
dōnātīvum, -ī *nt* largess, gratuity.
dōnec (dōnicum, dōnique) *conj* until; while, as long as.
dōnō, -āre, -āvī, -ātum *vt* to present, bestow; to remit, condone (*for another's sake*); (*fig*) to sacrifice.
dōnum, -ī *nt* gift; offering.
dorcas, -dis *f* gazelle.
Dōrēs, -um *mpl* Dorians (*mostly the Greeks of the Peloponnese*).
Dōricus *adj* Dorian; Greek.
Dōris, -dis *f* a sea nymph; the sea.

dormiō, -īre, -īvī, -ītum *vi* to sleep, be asleep.
dormītātor, -ōris *m* dreamer.
dormītō, -āre *vi* to be drowsy, nod.
dorsum, -ī *nt* back; mountain ridge.
dōs, dōtis *f* dowry; (*fig*) gift, talent.
Dossēnus, -ī *m* hunchback, clown.
dōtālis *adj* dowry (*in cpds*), dotal.
dōtātus *adj* richly endowed.
dōtō, -āre *vt* to endow.
drachma (drachuma), -ae *f* a Greek silver coin.
dracō, -ōnis *m* serpent, dragon; (*ASTRO*) Draco.
dracōnigena, -ae *adj* sprung from dragon's teeth.
drāpeta, -ae *m* runaway slave.
Drepanum, -ī, -a, -ōrum *nt* town in W. Sicily.
dromas, -dis *m* dromedary.
dromos, -ī *m* racecourse at Sparta.
Druidēs, -um, -ae, -ārum *mpl* Druids.
Drūsiānus *adj see* **Drūsus**.
Drūsus, -ī *m* Roman surname (*esp famous commander in Germany under Augustus*).
Dryades, -um *fpl* woodnymphs, Dryads.
Dryopes, -um *mpl* a people of Epirus.
dubiē *adv* doubtfully.
dubitābilis *adj* doubtful.
dubitanter *adv* doubtingly, hesitatingly.
dubitātiō, -ōnis *f* wavering, uncertainty, doubting; hesitancy, irresolution; (*RHET*) misgiving.
dubitō, -āre, -āvī, -ātum *vt, vi* to waver, be in doubt, wonder, doubt; to hesitate, stop to think.
dubium *nt* doubt.
dubius *adj* wavering, uncertain; doubtful, indecisive; precarious; irresolute ♦ *nt* doubt; **in ~um vocāre** call in question; **in ~um venīre** be called in question; **sine ~ō, haud ~ē** undoubtedly.
ducēnī, -ōrum *adj* 200 each.
ducentēsima, -ae *f* one-half per cent.
ducentī, -ōrum *num* two hundred.
ducentiēs, -iēns *adv* 200 times.
dūcō, -cere, -xī, ductum *vt* to lead, guide, bring, take; to draw, draw out; to reckon, consider; (*MIL*) to lead, march, command; (*breath*) to inhale; (*ceremony*) to conduct; (*changed aspect*) to take on, receive; (*dance*) to perform; (*drink*) to quaff; (*metal*) to shape, beat out; (*mind*) to attract, induce, deceive; (*oars*) to pull; (*origin*) to derive, trace; (*time*) to prolong, put off, pass; (*udders*) to milk; (*wool*) to spin; (*a work*) to construct, compose, make; (*COMM*) to calculate; **īlia** ~ become broken-winded; **in numerō hostium** ~ regard as an enemy; **ōs** ~ make faces; **parvī** ~ think little of; **ratiōnem** ~ have regard for; **uxōrem** ~ marry.
ductim *adv* in streams.
ductitō, -āre *vt* to lead on, deceive; to marry.

Noun declensions and verb conjugations are shown on pp xiii to xxv. The present infinitive ending of a verb shows to which conjugation it belongs: **-āre** = 1st; **-ēre** = 2nd; **-ere** = 3rd and **-īre** = 4th. Irregular verbs are shown on p xxvi

ductō, -āre *vt* to lead, draw; to take home; to cheat.

ductor, -ōris *m* leader, commander; guide, pilot.

ductus *ppp of* **dūcō**.

ductus, -ūs *m* drawing, drawing off; form; command, generalship.

dūdum *adv* a little while ago, just now; for long; **haud** ~ not long ago; **iam** ~ **adsum** I have been here a long time; **quam** ~ how long.

duellum *etc see* **bellum**.

Duillius, -ī *m* consul who defeated the Carthaginians at sea.

duim *pres subj of* **dō**.

dulce, -iter *adv see* **dulcis**.

dulcēdō, -inis *f* sweetness; pleasantness, charm.

dulcēscō, -ere *vi* to become sweet.

dulciculus *adj* rather sweet.

dulcifer, -ī *adj* sweet.

dulcis *adj* sweet; pleasant, lovely; kind, dear.

dulcitūdō, -inis *f* sweetness.

dūlicē *adv* like a slave.

Dūlichium, -ī *nt* island in the Ionian Sea near Ithaca.

Dūlichius *adj* of Dulichium; of Ulysses.

dum *conj* while, as long as; provided that, if only; until ♦ *adv* (*enclitic*) now, a moment; (*with neg*) yet.

dūmētum, -ī *nt* thicket, thornbushes.

dummodo *conj* provided that.

dūmōsus *adj* thorny.

dumtaxat *adv* at least; only, merely.

dūmus, -ī *m* thornbush.

duo, duae, duo *num* two.

duodeciēns, -ēs *adv* twelve times.

duodecim *num* twelve.

duodecimus *adj* twelfth.

duodēnī, -ōrum *adj* twelve each, in dozens.

duodēquadrāgēsimus *adj* thirty-eighth.

duodēquadrāgintā *num* thirty-eight.

duodēquīnquāgēsimus *adj* forty-eighth.

duodētrīciēns *adv* twenty-eight times.

duodētrīgintā *num* twenty-eight.

duodēvīcēnī *adj* eighteen each.

duodēvīgintī *num* eighteen.

duoetvīcēsimānī, -ānōrum *mpl* soldiers of the 22nd legion.

duoetvīcēsimus *adj* twenty-second.

duovirī, duumvirī, -ōrum *mpl* a board of two men; colonial magistrates; ~ **nāvālēs** naval commissioners (for supply and repair); ~ **sacrōrum** keepers of the Sibylline Books.

duplex, -icis *adj* double, twofold; both; (*person*) false.

duplicārius, -ī *and* **iī** *m* soldier receiving double pay.

dupliciter *adv* doubly, on two accounts.

duplicō, -āre, -āvī, -ātum *vt* to double, increase; to bend.

duplus *adj* double, twice as much ♦ *nt* double ♦ *f* double the price.

dupondius, -ī *and* **iī** *m* coin worth two asses.

dūrābilis *adj* lasting.

dūrāmen, -inis *nt* hardness.

dūrateus *adj* wooden.

dūrē, -iter *adv* stiffly; hardily; harshly, roughly.

dūrēscō, -ēscere, -uī *vi* to harden.

dūritās, -ātis *f* harshness.

dūritia, -ae, -ēs, -em *f* hardness; hardiness; severity; want of feeling.

dūrō, -āre, -āvī, -ātum *vt* to harden, stiffen; to make hardy, inure; (*mind*) to dull ♦ *vi* to harden; to be patient, endure; to hold out, last; (*mind*) to be steeled.

dūruī *perf of* **dūrēscō**.

dūrus *adj* hard, harsh, rough; hardy, tough; rude, uncultured; (*character*) severe, unfeeling, impudent, miserly; (*CIRCS*) hard, cruel.

duumvirī *etc see* **duovirī**.

dux, ducis *m* leader, guide; chief, head; (*MIL*) commander, general.

dūxī *perf of* **dūcō**.

Dymantis, -antidis *f* Hecuba.

Dymās, -antis *m* father of Hecuba.

dynamis, -is *f* plenty.

dynastēs, -ae *m* ruler, prince.

Dyrrhachīnus *adj see n*.

Dyrrhachium (Dyrrachium), -ī *nt* Adriatic port (*now* Durazzo).

E, e

ē *prep see* **ex**.

ea *f pron* she, it ♦ *adj see* **is**.

eā *adv* there, that way.

eādem *adv* the same way; at the same time.

eadem *f adj see* **idem**.

eāīdem, eapse *f of* **ipse**.

eapse *f of* **ipse**.

eātenus *adv* so far.

ebenus *etc see* **hebenus**.

ēbibō, -ere, -ī *vt* to drink up, drain; to squander; to absorb.

ēblandior, -īrī *vt* to coax out, obtain by flattery; ~**ītus** obtained by flattery.

Eborācum, -ī *nt* York.

ēbrietās, ātis *f* drunkenness.

ēbriolus *adj* tipsy.

ēbriōsitās, -ātis *f* addiction to drink.

ēbriōsus *adj* drunkard; (*berry*) juicy.

ēbrius *adj* drunk; full; (*fig*) intoxicated.

ēbulliō, -īre *vi* to bubble up ♦ *vt* to brag about.

ebulus, -ī *m*, **-um, -ī** *nt* danewort, dwarf elder.

ebur, -is *nt* ivory; ivory work.

Eburācum, -ī nt York.
eburātus adj inlaid with ivory.
eburneolus adj of ivory.
eburneus, eburnus adj of ivory; ivory-white.
ēcastor interj by Castor!
ecce adv look!, here is!, there is!; lo and
    behold!; ~**a**, ~**am**, ~**illam**, ~**istam** here she is!;
    ~**um**, ~**illum** here he is!; ~**ōs**, ~**ās** here they
    are!
eccerē interj there now!
eccheuma, -tis nt pouring out.
ecclēsia, -ae f a Greek assembly; (ECCL)
    congregation, church.
eccum etc see **ecce**.
ecdicus, -ī m civic lawyer.
ecf- see **eff-**.
echidna, -ae f viper; ~ **Lernaea** hydra.
echīnus, -ī m sea-urchin; hedgehog; a rinsing
    bowl.
Echīōn, -onis m Theban hero.
Echīonidēs m Pentheus.
Echīonius adj Theban.
Ēchō, -us f wood nymph; echo.
ecloga, -ae f selection; eclogue.
ecquandō adv ever.
ecquī, -ae, -od adj interrog any.
ecquid, -ī adv whether.
ecquis, -id pron interrog anyone, anything.
ecquō adv anywhere.
eculeus, -ī m foal; rack.
edācitās, -ātis f gluttony.
edāx, -ācis adj gluttonous; (fig) devouring,
    carking.
ēdentō, -āre vt to knock the teeth out of.
ēdentulus adj toothless; old.
edepol interj by Pollux, indeed.
ēdī perf of **edō**.
ēdīcō, -īcere, -īxī, -ictum vt to declare; to
    decree, publish an edict.
ēdictiō, -ōnis f decree.
ēdictō, -āre vt to proclaim.
ēdictum, -ī nt proclamation, edict (esp a
    praetor's).
ēdidī perf of **ēdō**.
ēdiscō, -ere, ēdidicī vt to learn well, learn by
    heart.
ēdisserō, -ere, -uī, -tum vt to explain in
    detail.
ēdissertō, -āre vt to explain fully.
ēditīcius adj chosen by the plaintiff.
ēditiō, -ōnis f publishing, edition; statement;
    (law) designation of a suit.
ēditus ppp of **ēdō** ♦ adj high; descended ♦ nt
    height; order.
edō, edere and **ēsse, ēdī, ēsum** vt to eat; (fig)
    to devour.
ēdō, -ere, -idī, -itum vt to put forth,
    discharge; to emit; to give birth to, produce;
    (speech) to declare, relate, utter; (action) to
    cause, perform; (book) to publish; (POL) to

promulgate; **lūdōs** ~ put on a show; **tribūs** ~
    nominate tribes of jurors.
ēdoceō, -ere, -uī, -ctum vt to instruct
    clearly, teach thoroughly.
ēdomō, -āre, -uī, -itum vt to conquer,
    overcome.
Ēdōnus adj Thracian.
ēdormiō, -īre vi to have a good sleep ♦ vt to
    sleep off.
ēdormīscō, -ere vt to sleep off.
ēducātiō, -ōnis f bringing up, rearing.
ēducātor, -ōris m foster father, tutor.
ēducātrix, -īcis f nurse.
ēducō, -āre, -āvī, -ātum vt to bring up, rear,
    train; to produce.
ēdūcō, -ūcere, -ūxī, -uctum vt to draw out,
    bring away; to raise up, erect; (law) to
    summon; (MIL) to lead out, march out; (ship)
    to put to sea; (young) to hatch, rear, train.
edūlis adj edible.
ēdūrō, -āre vi to last out.
ēdūrus adj very hard.
effarciō etc see **efferciō**.
effātus ppa of **effor** ♦ adj solemnly pronounced,
    declared ♦ nt axiom; (pl) predictions.
effectiō, -ōnis f performing; efficient cause.
effector, -ōris m, **-rīx, -rīcis** f producer,
    author.
effectus ppp of **efficiō**.
effectus, -ūs m completion, performance;
    effect.
effēminātē adv see **effēminātus**.
effēminātus adj effeminate.
effēminō, -āre, -āvī, -ātum vt to make a
    woman of; to enervate.
efferātus adj savage.
efferciō, -cīre, -tum vt to cram full.
efferitās, -ātis f wildness.
efferō, -āre, -āvī, -ātum vt to make wild; (fig)
    to exasperate.
efferō (ecferō), -re, extulī, ēlātum vt to
    bring out, carry out; to lift up, raise; (dead)
    to carry to the grave; (emotion) to transport;
    (honour) to exalt; (news) to spread abroad;
    (soil) to produce; (trouble) to endure to the
    end; **sē** ~ rise; be conceited.
effertus ppp of **efferciō** ♦ adj full, bulging.
efferus adj savage.
effervēscō, -vēscere, -buī vi to boil over; (fig)
    to rage.
effervō, -ere vi to boil up.
effētus adj exhausted.
efficācitās, -ātis f power.
efficāciter adv effectually.
efficāx, -ācis adj capable, effective.
efficiēns, -entis pres p of **efficiō** ♦ adj effective,
    efficient.
efficienter adv efficiently.
efficientia, -ae f power, efficacy.
efficiō, -icere, -ēcī, -ectum vt to make,

Noun declensions and verb conjugations are shown on pp xiii to xxv. The present infinitive ending of a verb shows
to which conjugation it belongs: **-āre** = 1st; **-ēre** = 2nd; **-ere** = 3rd and **-īre** = 4th. Irregular verbs are shown on p xxvi

accomplish; to cause, bring about; (*numbers*) to amount to; (*soil*) to yield; (*theory*) to make out, try to prove.

effictus *ppp of* **effingō**.

effigiēs, -ēī, -a, -ae *f* likeness, copy; ghost; portrait, statue; (*fig*) image, ideal.

effingō, -ngere, -nxī, -ctum *vt* to form, fashion; to portray, represent; to wipe clean; to fondle.

efflāgitātiō, -ōnis *f* urgent demand.

efflāgitātus, -ūs *m* urgent request.

efflāgitō, -āre *vt* to demand urgently.

efflīctim *adv* desperately.

efflīctō, -āre *vt* to strike dead.

effligō, -gere, -xī, -ctum *vt* to exterminate.

efflō, -āre, -āvī, -ātum *vt* to breathe out, blow out ♦ *vi* to billow out; **animam ~** expire.

efflōrēscō, -ēscere, -uī *vi* to blossom forth.

effluō, -ere, -xī *vi* to run out, issue, emanate; (*fig*) to pass away, vanish; (*rumour*) to get known; **ex animō ~** become forgotten.

effluvium, -ī *and* **iī** *nt* outlet.

effodiō, -odere, -ōdī, -ossum *vt* to dig up; (*eyes*) to gouge out; (*house*) to ransack.

effor, -ārī, -ātus *vt* to speak, utter; (*augury*) to ordain; (*logic*) to state a proposition.

effossus *ppp of* **effodiō**.

effrēnātē *adv see* **effrēnātus**.

effrēnātiō, -ōnis *f* impetuousness.

effrēnātus *adj* unbridled, violent, unruly.

effrēnus *adj* unbridled.

effringō, -ingere, -ēgī, -āctum *vt* to break open, smash.

effugiō, -ugere, -ūgī *vi* to run away, escape ♦ *vt* to flee from, escape; to escape the notice of.

effugium, -ī *and* **iī** *nt* flight, escape; means of escape.

effulgeō, -gēre, -sī *vi* to shine out, blaze.

effultus *adj* supported.

effundō, -undere, -ūdī, -ūsum *vt* to pour forth, pour out; (*crops*) to produce in abundance; (*missiles*) to shoot; (*rider*) to throw; (*speech*) to give vent to; (*effort*) to waste; (*money*) to squander; (*reins*) to let go; **sē ~, ~undī** rush out; indulge (in).

effūsē *adv* far and wide; lavishly, extravagantly.

effūsiō, -ōnis *f* pouring out, rushing out; profusion, extravagance; exuberance.

effūsus *ppp of* **effundō** ♦ *adj* vast, extensive; loose, straggling; lavish, extravagant.

effūtiō, -īre *vt* to blab, chatter.

ēgelidus *adj* mild, cool.

egēns, -entis *pres p of* **egeō** ♦ *adj* needy.

egēnus *adj* destitute.

egeō, -ēre, -uī *vi* to be in want; (*with abl or gen*) to need, want.

Ēgeria, -ae *f* nymph who taught Numa.

ēgerō, -rere, -ssī, -stum *vt* to carry out; to discharge, emit.

egestās, -ātis *f* want, poverty.

ēgestus *ppp of* **ēgerō**.

ēgī *perf of* **agō**.

ego *pron* I; **~met** I (*emphatic*).

ēgredior, -dī, -ssus *vi* to go out, come out; to go up, climb; (*MIL*) to march out; (*NAUT*) to disembark, put to sea; (*speech*) to digress ♦ *vt* to go beyond, quit; (*fig*) to overstep, surpass.

ēgregiē *adv* uncommonly well, singularly.

ēgregius *adj* outstanding, surpassing; distinguished, illustrious.

ēgressus *ppa of* **ēgredior**.

ēgressus, -ūs *m* departure; way out; digression; (*NAUT*) landing; (*river*) mouth.

eguī *perf of* **egeō**.

ēgurgitō, -āre *vt* to lavish.

ehem *interj* (*expressing surprise*) ha!, so!

ēheu *interj* (*expressing pain*) alas!

eho *interj* (*expressing rebuke*) look here!

eī *dat of* **is**.

ei *interj* (*expressing alarm*) oh!

eia *interj* (*expressing delight, playful remonstrance, encouragement*) aha!, come now!, come on!

ēiaculor, -ārī *vt* to shoot out.

ēiciō, -icere, -iēcī, -iectum *vt* to throw out, drive out, put out; (*joint*) to dislocate; (*mind*) to banish; (*NAUT*) to bring to land, run aground, wreck; (*rider*) to throw; (*speech*) to utter; (*THEAT*) to hiss off; **sē ~** rush out, break out.

ēiectāmenta, -ōrum *ntpl* refuse.

ēiectiō, -ōnis *f* banishment.

ēiectō, -āre *vt* to throw up.

ēiectus *ppp of* **ēiciō** ♦ *adj* shipwrecked.

ēiectus, -ūs *m* emitting.

ēierō, ēiūrō, -āre *vt* to abjure, reject on oath, forswear; (*office*) to resign; **bonam cōpiam ~** declare oneself bankrupt.

ēiulātiō, -ōnis *f*, **ēiulātus, -ūs** *m* wailing.

ēiulō, -āre *vi* to wail, lament.

ēius *pron* his, her, its; **~modī** such.

ej- *etc see* **ei-**.

ēlābor, -bī, -psus *vi* to glide away, slip off; to escape, get off; to pass away.

ēlabōrātus *adj* studied.

ēlabōrō, -āre, -āvī, -ātum *vi* to exert oneself, take great pains ♦ *vt* to work out, elaborate.

ēlāmentābilis *adj* very mournful.

ēlanguēscō, -ēscere, -ī *vi* to grow faint; to relax.

ēlāpsus *ppa of* **ēlābor**.

ēlātē *adv* proudly.

ēlātiō, -ōnis *f* ecstasy, exaltation.

ēlātrō, -āre *vt* to bark out.

ēlātus *ppp of* **efferō** ♦ *adj* high; exalted.

ēlavō, -avāre, -āvī, -autum *and* **-ōtum** *vt* to wash clean; (*comedy*) to rob.

Ēlea, -ae *f* town in S. Italy (*birthplace of Parmenides*).

Ēleātēs, -āticus *adj see n.*

ēlecebra, -ae *f* snare.

ēlēctē *adv* choicely.

ēlēctilis *adj* choice.

ēlectiō, -ōnis f choice, option.
ēlectō, -āre vt to coax out.
ēlectō, -āre vt to select.
Electra, -ae f a Pleiad (daughter of Atlas; sister of Orestes).
ēlectrum, -ī nt amber; an alloy of gold and silver.
ēlēctus ppp of **ēligō** ♦ adj select, choice.
ēlēctus, -ūs m choice.
ēlegāns, -antis adj tasteful, refined, elegant; fastidious; (things) fine, choice.
ēleganter adv with good taste.
ēlegantia, -ae f taste, finesse, elegance; fastidiousness.
ēlēgī perf of **ēligō**.
elegī, -ōrum mpl elegiac verses.
elegīa, -ae f elegy.
Eleleides, -eidum fpl Bacchantes.
Eleleus, -eī m Bacchus.
elementum, -ī nt element; (pl) first principles, rudiments; beginnings; letters (of alphabet).
elenchus, -ī m a pear-shaped pearl.
elephantomacha, -ae m fighter mounted on an elephant.
elephantus, -ī, elephās, -antis m elephant; ivory.
Ēleus, -ius, -ias adj Elean; Olympian.
Eleusīn, -is f Eleusis (Attic town famous for its mysteries of Demeter).
Eleusīus adj see **Eleusīn**.
eleutheria, -ae f liberty.
ēlevō, -āre vt to lift, raise; to alleviate; to make light of, lessen, disparage.
ēliciō, -ere, -uī, -itum vt to lure out, draw out; (god) to call down; (spirit) to conjure up; (fig) to elicit, draw.
ēlīdō, -dere, -sī, -sum vt to dash out, squeeze out; to drive out; to crush, destroy.
ēligō, -igere, -ēgī, -ēctum vt to pick, pluck out; to choose.
ēlīminō, -āre vt to carry outside.
ēlīmō, -āre vt to file; (fig) to perfect.
ēlinguis adj speechless; not eloquent.
ēlinguō, -āre vt to tear the tongue out of.
Ēlis, -idis f district and town in W. Peloponnese (famous for Olympia).
Elissa, -ae f Dido.
ēlīsus ppp of **ēlīdō**.
ēlixus adj boiled.
elleborōsus adj quite mad.
elleborus, -ī m, **-um, -ī** nt hellebore.
ellum, ellam there he (she) is!
ēlocō, -āre vt to lease, farm out.
ēlocūtiō, -ōnis f delivery, style.
ēlocūtus ppa of **ēloquor**.
ēlogium, -ī and **iī** nt short saying; inscription; (will) clause.
ēloquēns, -entis adj eloquent.
ēloquenter adv see adj.

ēloquentia, -ae f eloquence.
ēloquium, -ī and **iī** nt eloquence.
ēloquor, -quī, -cūtus vt, vi to speak out, speak eloquently.
ēlūceō, -cēre, -xī vi to shine out, glitter.
ēluctor, -ārī, -ātus vi to struggle, force a way out ♦ vt to struggle out of, surmount.
ēlūcubrō, -āre, -or, -ārī, -ātus vt to compose by lamplight.
ēlūdificor, -ārī, -ātus vt to cheat, play up.
ēlūdō, -dere, -sī, -sum vt to parry, ward off, foil; to win off at play; to outplay, outmanoeuvre; to cheat, make fun of ♦ vi to finish one's sport.
ēlūgeō, -gēre, -xī vt to mourn for.
ēlumbis adj feeble.
ēluō, -uere, -uī, -ūtum vt to wash clean; (money) to squander; (fig) to wash away, get rid of.
ēlūsus ppp of **ēlūdō**.
ēlūtus ppp of **ēluō** ♦ adj insipid.
ēluviēs, -em -ē f discharge; overflowing.
ēluviō, -ōnis f deluge.
Elysium, -ī nt Elysium.
Elysius adj Elysian.
em interj there you are!
ēmancipātiō, -ōnis f giving a son his independence; conveyance of property.
ēmancipō, -āre vt to declare independent; to transfer, give up, sell.
ēmānō, -āre, -āvī, -ātum vi to flow out; to spring (from); (news) to leak out, become known.
Ēmathia, -ae f district of Macedonia; Macedonia, Thessaly.
Ēmathius adj Macedonian, Pharsalian; **~des, ~dum** fpl Muses.
ēmātūrēscō, -ēscere, -uī vi to soften.
emāx, -ācis adj fond of buying.
emblēma, -tis nt inlaid work, mosaic.
embolium, -ī and **iī** nt interlude.
ēmendābilis adj corrigible.
ēmendātē adv see **ēmendātor**.
ēmendātiō, -ōnis f correction.
ēmendātor, -ōris m, **-rīx, -rīcis** f corrector.
ēmendātus adj faultless.
ēmendō, -āre, -āvī, -ātum vt to correct, improve.
ēmēnsus ppa of **ēmētior** ♦ adj traversed.
ēmentior, -īrī, -ītus vi to tell lies ♦ vt to pretend, fabricate; **~ītus** pretended.
ēmercor, -ārī vt to purchase.
ēmereō, -ēre, -uī, -itum, -eor, -ērī vt to earn fully, deserve; to lay under an obligation; to complete one's term of service.
ēmergō, -gere, -sī, -sum vt to raise out; (fig) to extricate ♦ vi to rise, come up, emerge; (fig) to get clear, extricate oneself; (impers) it becomes evident.
ēmeritus ppa of **ēmereor** ♦ adj superannuated,

Noun declensions and verb conjugations are shown on pp xiii to xxv. The present infinitive ending of a verb shows to which conjugation it belongs: **-āre** = 1st; **-ēre** = 2nd; **-ere** = 3rd and **-īre** = 4th. Irregular verbs are shown on p xxvi

worn-out ♦ *m* veteran.

ēmersus *ppp of* **ēmergō.**

emetica, -ae *f* emetic.

ēmētior, -tīrī, -nsus *vt* to measure out; to traverse, pass over; (*time*) to live through; (*fig*) to impart.

ēmetō, -ere *vt* to harvest.

ēmī *perf of* **emō.**

ēmicō, -āre, -uī, -ātum *vi* to dart out, dash out, flash out; (*fig*) to shine.

ēmigrō, -āre, -āvī, -ātum *vi* to remove, depart.

ēminēns, -entis *pres p of* **ēmineō** ♦ *adj* high, projecting; (*fig*) distinguished, eminent.

ēminentia, -ae *f* prominence; (*painting*) light.

ēmineō, -ēre, -uī *vi* to stand out, project; to be prominent, be conspicuous, distinguish oneself.

ēminor, -ārī *vi* to threaten.

ēminus *adv* at *or* from a distance.

ēmīror, -ārī *vt* to marvel at.

ēmissārium, -ī *and* **iī** *nt* outlet.

ēmissārius, -ī *and* **iī** *m* scout.

ēmissīcius *adj* prying.

ēmissiō, -ōnis *f* letting go, discharge.

ēmissus *ppp of* **ēmittō.**

ēmissus, -ūs *m* emission.

ēmittō, -ittere, -īsī, -issum *vt* to send out, let out; to let go, let slip; (*missile*) to discharge; (*person*) to release, free; (*sound*) to utter; (*writing*) to publish.

emō, -ere, ēmī, emptum *vt* to buy, procure; to win over; **bene ~** buy cheap; **male ~** buy dear; **in diem ~** buy on credit.

ēmoderor, -ārī *vt* to give expression to.

ēmodulor, -ārī *vt* to sing through.

ēmōlior, -īrī *vt* to accomplish.

ēmolliō, -īre, -iī, -ītum *vt* to soften; to mollify; to enervate.

ēmolumentum, -ī *nt* profit, advantage.

ēmoneō, -ēre *vt* to strongly advise.

ēmorior, -ī, -tuus *vi* to die; (*fig*) to pass away.

ēmortuālis *adj* of death.

ēmoveō, -ovēre, -ōvī, -ōtum *vt* to remove, drive away.

Empedoclēs, -is *m* Sicilian philosopher.

Empedoclēus *adj see n.*

empīricus, -ī *m* empirical doctor.

emporium, -ī *and* **iī** *nt* market, market town.

emptiō, -ōnis *f* buying; a purchase.

emptitō, -āre *vt* to often buy.

emptor, -ōris *m* purchaser.

emptus *ppp of* **emō.**

ēmulgeō, -ēre *vt* to drain.

ēmunctus *ppp of* **ēmungō** ♦ *adj* discriminating.

ēmungō, -gere, -xī, -ctum *vt* to blow the nose of; (*comedy*) to cheat.

ēmūniō, -īre, -īvī, -ītum *vt* to strengthen, secure; to build up; to make roads through.

ēn *interj* (*drawing attention*) look!, see!; (*excited question*) really, indeed; (*command*) come now!

ēnārrābilis *adj* describable.

ēnārrō, -āre, -āvī, -ātum *vt* to describe in detail.

ēnāscor, -scī, -tus *vi* to sprout, grow.

ēnatō, -āre *vi* to swim ashore; (*fig*) to escape.

ēnātus *ppa of* **ēnāscor.**

ēnāvigō, -āre *vi* to sail clear, clear ♦ *vt* to sail over.

Enceladus, -ī *m* giant under Etna.

Endymiōn, -ōnis *m* a beautiful youth loved by the Moon, and doomed to lasting sleep.

ēnecō, -āre, -uī *and* **-āvī, -tum** *and* **ātum** *vt* to kill; to wear out; to torment.

ēnervātus *adj* limp.

ēnervis *adj* enfeebled.

ēnervō, -āre, -āvī, -ātum *vt* to weaken, unman.

ēnicō *etc see* **ēnecō.**

enim *conj* (*affirming*) yes, truly, in fact; (*explaining*) for, for instance, of course; **at ~** but it will be objected; **quid ~** well?; **sed ~** but actually.

enimvērō *conj* certainly, yes indeed.

Enīpeus, -eī *m* river in Thessaly.

ēnīsus *ppa of* **ēnītor.**

ēniteō, -ēre, -uī *vi* to shine, brighten up; (*fig*) to be brilliant, distinguish oneself.

ēnitēscō, -ēscere, -uī *vi* to shine, be brilliant.

ēnītor, -tī, -sus *and* **xus** *vi* to struggle up, climb; to strive, make a great effort ♦ *vt* to give birth to; to climb.

ēnīxē *adv* earnestly.

ēnīxus *ppa of* **ēnītor** ♦ *adj* strenuous.

Enniānus *adj see n.*

Ennius, -ī *m* greatest of the early Latin poets.

Ennosigaeus, -ī *m* Earthshaker, Neptune.

ēnō, -āre, -āvī *vi* to swim out, swim ashore; to fly away.

ēnōdātē *adv* lucidly.

ēnōdātiō, -ōnis *f* unravelling.

ēnōdis *adj* free from knots; plain.

ēnōdō, -āre, -āvī, -ātum *vt* to elucidate.

ēnōrmis *adj* irregular; immense.

ēnōtēscō, -ēscere, -uī *vi* to get known.

ēnotō, -āre *vt* to make a note of.

ēnsiculus, -ī *m* little sword.

ēnsiger, -ī *adj* with his sword.

ēnsis, -is *m* sword.

enthymēma, -tis *nt* argument.

ēnūbō, -bere, -psī *vi* to marry out of one's station; to marry and go away.

ēnucleātē *adv* plainly.

ēnucleātus *adj* (*style*) straightforward; (*votes*) honest.

ēnucleō, -āre *vt* to elucidate.

ēnumerātiō, -ōnis *f* enumeration; (*RHET*) recapitulation.

ēnumerō, -āre *vt* to count up; to pay out; to relate.

ēnūntiātiō, -ōnis *f* proposition.

ēnūntiātum, -ī *nt* proposition.

ēnūntiō, -āre *vt* to disclose, report; to

express; to pronounce.

ēnūptiō, -ōnis f marrying out of one's station.

ēnūtriō, -īre vt to feed, bring up.

eō, īre, īvī and **iī, itum** vi to go; (*MIL*) to march; (*time*) to pass; (*event*) to proceed, turn out; **in alia omnia ~** vote against a bill; **in sententiam ~** support a motion; **sīc eat** so may he fare!; **ī** (*mocking*) go on!

eō adv (*place*) thither, there; (*purpose*) with a view to; (*degree*) so far, to such a pitch; (*time*) so long; (*cause*) on that account, for the reason; (*with compar*) **eō** besides; **accēdit eō** besides; **rēs erat eō locī** such was the state of affairs; **eō magis** all the more.

eōdem adv to the same place, purpose or person; **~ locī** in the same place.

Ēōs f dawn ♦ m morning star; Oriental.

Ēous adj at dawn, eastern.

Epamīnōndās, -ae m Theban general.

epāstus adj eaten up.

ephēbus, -ī m youth (*18 to 20*).

ephēmeris, -idis f diary.

Ephesius adj see n.

Ephesus, -ī f Ionian town in Asia Minor.

ephippiātus adj riding a saddled horse.

ephippium, -ī and **iī** nt saddle.

ephorus, -ī m a Spartan magistrate, ephor.

Ephyra, -ae, -ē, -ēs f Corinth.

Ephyrēius adj see **Ephyra**.

Epicharmus, -ī m Greek philosopher and comic poet.

epichysis, -is f kind of jug.

epicōpus adj rowing.

Epicūrēus, -īus adj epic.

Epicūrus, -ī m famous Greek philosopher.

Epidaurius adj see n.

Epidaurus, -ī f town in E. Peloponnese.

epidīcticus adj (*RHET*) for display.

epigramma, -tis nt inscription; epigram.

epilogus, -ī m peroration.

epimēnia, -ōrum ntpl a month's rations.

Epimēthis, -dis f Pyrrha (*daughter of Epimetheus*).

epirēdium, -ī and **iī** nt trace.

Ēpīrōtēs, -ōtae m native of Epirus.

Ēpīrōticus, -ēnsis adj see n.

Ēpīrus, -os, -ī f district of N.W. Greece.

episcopus, -ī m bishop.

epistolium, -ī and **iī** nt short note.

epistula, -ae f letter; **ab ~īs** secretary.

epitaphium, -ī and **iī** nt funeral oration.

epithēca, -ae f addition.

epitoma, -ae, -ē, -ēs f abridgement.

epityrum, -ī nt olive salad.

epops, -is m hoopoe.

epos (*pl -ē*) nt epic.

ēpōtō, -āre, -āvī, -um vt to drink up, drain; to waste in drink; to absorb.

epulae, -ārum fpl dishes; feast, banquet.

epulāris adj at a banquet.

epulō, -ōnis m guest at a feast; priest in charge of religious banquets.

epulor, -ārī, -ātus vi to be at a feast ♦ vt to feast on.

epulum, -ī nt banquet.

equa, -ae f mare.

eques, -itis m horseman, trooper; (*pl*) cavalry; knight, member of the equestrian order.

equester, -ris adj equestrian; cavalry- (*in cpds*).

equidem adv (*affirming*) indeed, of course, for my part; (*concessive*) to be sure.

equīnus adj horse's.

equīria, -ōrum ntpl horseraces.

equitātus, -ūs m cavalry.

equitō, -āre vi to ride.

equuleus etc see **eculeus**.

equulus, -ī m colt.

equus, -ī m horse; (*ASTRO*) Pegasus; **~ bipēs** seahorse; **~ō merēre** serve in the cavalry; **~īs virīsque** with might and main.

era, -ae f mistress (of the house); (*goddess*) Lady.

ērādīcō, -āre vt to root out, destroy.

ērādō, -dere, -sī, -sum vt to erase, obliterate.

Eratō f Muse of lyric poetry.

Eratosthenēs, -is m famous Alexandrian geographer.

Erebēus adj see n.

Erebus, -ī m god of darkness; the lower world.

Erechtheus, -eī m legendary king of Athens.

Erechthēus adj see n.

Erechthīdae mpl Athenians.

Erechthis, -idis f Orithyia; Procris.

ērēctus ppp of **ērigō** ♦ adj upright, lofty; noble, haughty; alert, tense; resolute.

ērēpō, -ere, -sī vi to creep out, clamber up ♦ vt to crawl over, climb.

ēreptiō, -ōnis f seizure, robbery.

ēreptor, -ōris m robber.

ēreptus ppp of **ēripiō**.

ergā prep (*with acc*) towards; against.

ergastulum, -ī nt prison (*esp for slaves*); (*pl*) convicts.

ergō adv therefore, consequently; (*questions, commands*) then, so; (*resuming*) well then; (*with gen*) for the sake of, because of.

Erichthonius, -ī m a king of Troy; a king of Athens ♦ adj Trojan; Athenian.

ēricius, -ī and **iī** m hedgehog; (*MIL*) beam with iron spikes.

Ēridanus, -ī m mythical name of river Po.

erifuga, -ae m runaway slave.

ērigō, -igere, -ēxī, -ēctum vt to make upright, raise up, erect; to excite; to encourage.

Ērigonē, -ēs f (*constellation*) Virgo.

Ērigonēius adj see n.

Noun declensions and verb conjugations are shown on pp xiii to xxv. The present infinitive ending of a verb shows to which conjugation it belongs: **-āre** = 1st; **-ēre** = 2nd; **-ere** = 3rd and **-īre** = 4th. Irregular verbs are shown on p xxvi

erīlis *adj* the master's, the mistress's.

Erīnȳs, -yos *f* Fury; (*fig*) curse, frenzy.

Eriphȳla, -ae *f* mother of Alcmaeon (*who killed her*).

ēripiō, -ipere, -ipuī, -eptum *vt* to tear away, pull away, take by force; to rob; to rescue; **sē ~ escape**.

ērogātiō, -ōnis *f* paying out.

ērogitō, -āre *vt* to enquire.

ērogō, -āre, -āvī, -ātum *vt* to pay out, expend; to bequeath.

errābundus *adj* wandering.

errāticus *adj* roving, shifting.

errātiō, -ōnis *f* wandering, roving.

errātum, -ī *nt* mistake, error.

errātus, -ūs *m* wandering.

errō, -āre, -āvī, -ātum *vi* to wander, stray, lose one's way; to waver; to make a mistake, err ♦ *vt* to traverse; **stēllae ~antēs** planets.

errō, -ōnis *m* vagabond.

error, -ōris *m* wandering; meander, maze; uncertainty; error, mistake, delusion; deception.

ērubēscō, -ēscere, -uī *vi* to blush; to feel ashamed ♦ *vt* to blush for, be ashamed of; to respect.

ērūca, -ae *f* colewort.

ēructō, -āre *vt* to belch, vomit; to talk drunkenly about; to throw up.

ērudiō, -īre, -iī, -ītum *vt* to educate, instruct.

ērudītē *adv* learnedly.

ērudītiō, -ōnis *f* education, instruction; learning, knowledge.

ērudītulus *adj* somewhat skilled.

ērudītus *ppp of* **ērudiō** ♦ *adj* learned, educated, accomplished.

ērumpō, -umpere, -ūpī, -uptum *vt* to break open; to make break out ♦ *vi* to burst out, break through; to end (in).

ēruō, -ere, -ī, -tum *vt* to uproot, tear out; to demolish, destroy; to elicit, draw out; to rescue.

ēruptiō, -ōnis *f* eruption; (*MIL*) sally.

ēruptus *ppp of* **ērumpō**.

erus, -ī *m* master (of the house); owner.

ērutus *ppp of* **ēruō**.

ervum, -ī *nt* vetch.

Erycīnus *adj* of Eryx; of Venus; Sicilian ♦ *f* Venus.

Erymanthius, -is *adj see n.*

Erymanthus *and* **-ī** *m* mountain range in Arcadia, (*where Hercules killed the bear*).

Eryx, -cis *m* town and mountain in the extreme W. of Sicily.

esca, -ae *f* food, tit-bits; bait.

escārius *adj* of food; of bait ♦ *ntpl* dishes.

ēscendō, -endere, -endī, -ēnsum *vi* to climb up, go up ♦ *vt* to mount.

ēscēnsiō, -ōnis *f* raid (from the coast); disembarkation.

esculentus *adj* edible, tasty.

Esquiliae, -iārum *fpl* Esquiline hill in Rome.

Esquilīnus *adj* Esquiline ♦ *f* Esquiline gate.

essedārius, -ī *and* **iī** *m* chariot fighter.

essedum, -ī *nt* war chariot.

essitō, -āre *vt* to usually eat.

ēst *pres of* **edō**.

ēstrīx, -īcis *f* glutton.

ēsuriālis *adj* of hunger.

ēsuriō, -īre, -ītum *vi* to be hungry ♦ *vt* to hunger for.

ēsuritiō, -ōnis *f* hunger.

ēsus *ppp of* **edō**.

et *conj* and; (*repeated*) both … and; (*adding emphasis*) in fact, yes; (*comparing*) as, than ♦ *adv* also, too; even.

etenim *conj* (*adding an explanation*) and as a matter of fact, in fact.

etēsiae, -ārum *fpl* Etesian winds.

etēsius *adj see n.*

ēthologus, -ī *m* mimic.

etiam *adv* also, besides; (*emphatic*) even, actually; (*affirming*) yes, certainly; (*indignant*) really!; (*time*) still, as yet; again; **~ atque ~** again and again; **~ cavēs!** do be careful!; **nihil ~** nothing at all.

etiamdum *adv* still, as yet.

etiamnum, etiamnunc *adv* still, till now, till then; besides.

etiamsī *conj* even if, although.

etiamtum, etiamtunc *adv* till then, still.

Etrūria, -ae *f* district of Italy north of Rome.

Etruscus *adj* Etruscan.

etsī *conj* even if, though; and yet.

etymologia, -ae *f* etymology.

eu *interj* well done!, bravo!

Euan *m* Bacchus.

Euander *and* **rus, -rī** *m* Evander (*ancient king on the site of Rome*).

Euandrius *adj see n.*

euax *interj* hurrah!

Euboea, -oeae *f* Greek island.

Euboicus *adj* Euboean.

euge, eugepae *interj* bravo!, cheers!

Euhan *m* Bacchus.

euhāns, -antis *adj* shouting the Bacchic cry.

Euhias *f* Bacchante.

Euhius, -ī *m* Bacchus.

euhoe *interj* ecstatic cry of Bacchic revellers.

Euius, -ī *m* Bacchus.

Eumenides, -um *fpl* Furies.

eunūchus, -ī *m* eunuch.

Euphrātēs, -is *m* river Euphrates.

Eupolis, -dis *m* Athenian comic poet.

Eurīpidēs, -is *m* Athenian tragic poet.

Eurīpidēus *adj see n.*

Eurīpus, -ī *m* strait between Euboea and mainland; a channel, conduit.

Eurōpa, -ae *and* **ē, -ēs** *f* mythical princess of Tyre (*who was carried by a bull to Crete*); continent of Europe.

Eurōpaeus *adj see n.*

Eurōtās, -ae *m* river of Sparta.

Eurōus *adj* eastern.

Eurus, -ī *m* east wind; south-east wind.

Eurydicē, -ēs *f* wife of Orpheus.

Eurystheus, -eī m king of Mycenae (who imposed the labours on Hercules).

euschēmē adv gracefully.

Euterpē, -ēs f Muse of music.

Euxīnus m the Black (Sea).

ēvādō, -dere, -sī, -sum vi to come out; to climb up; to escape; to turn out, result, come true ♦ vt to pass, mount; to escape from.

ēvagor, -ārī, -ātus vi (MIL) to manoeuvre; (fig) to spread ♦ vt to stray beyond.

ēvalēscō, -ēscere, -uī vi to grow, increase; to be able; to come into vogue.

Ēvander etc see **Euander**.

ēvānēscō, -ēscere, -uī vi to vanish, die away, lose effect.

ēvangelium, -ī and iī nt (ECCL) Gospel.

ēvānidus adj vanishing.

ēvāsī perf of **ēvādō**.

ēvastō, -āre vt to devastate.

ēvehō, -here, -xī, -ctum vt to carry out; to raise up, exalt; to spread abroad; (pass) to ride, sail, move out.

ēvellō, -ellere, -ellī, -ulsum vt to tear out, pull out; to eradicate.

ēveniō, -enīre, -ēnī, -entum vi to come out; to turn out, result; to come to pass, happen, befall.

ēventum, -ī nt result, issue; occurrence, event; fortune, experience.

ēventus, -ūs m result, issue; success; fortune, fate.

ēverberō, -āre vt to beat violently.

ēverriculum, -ī nt dragnet.

ēverrō, -rere, -rī, -sum vt to sweep out, clean out.

ēversiō, -ōnis f overthrow, destruction.

ēversor, -ōris m destroyer.

ēversus ppp of **ēverrō**; ppp of **ēvertō**.

ēvertō, -tere, -tī, -sum vt to turn out, eject; to turn up, overturn; to overthrow, ruin, destroy.

ēvestīgātus adj tracked down.

ēvictus ppp of **ēvincō**.

ēvidēns, -entis adj visible, plain, evident.

ēvidenter adv see **ēvidēns**.

ēvidentia, -ae f distinctness.

ēvigilō, -āre, -āvī, -ātum vi to be wide awake ♦ vt to compose carefully.

ēvīlēscō, -ere vi to become worthless.

ēvinciō, -cīre, -xī, -ctum vt to garland, crown.

ēvincō, -incere, -īcī, -ictum vt to overcome, conquer; to prevail over; to prove.

ēvirō, -āre vt to castrate.

ēviscerō, -āre vt to disembowel, tear to pieces.

ēvītābilis adj avoidable.

ēvītō, -āre, -āvī, -ātum vt to avoid, clear.

ēvocātī, -ōrum mpl veteran volunteers.

ēvocātor, -ōris m enlister.

ēvocō, -āre, -āvī, -ātum vt to call out, summon; to challenge; to call up; to call forth, evoke.

ēvolō, -āre, -āvī, -ātum vi to fly out, fly away; to rush out; (fig) to rise, soar.

ēvolūtiō, -ōnis f unrolling (a book).

ēvolvō, -vere, -vī, -ūtum vt to roll out, roll along; to unroll, unfold; (book) to open, read; (fig) to disclose, unravel, disentangle.

ēvomō, -ere, -uī, -itum vt to vomit up, disgorge.

ēvulgō, -āre, -āvī, -ātum vt to divulge, make public.

ēvulsiō, -ōnis f pulling out.

ēvulsus ppp of **ēvellō**.

ex, ē prep (with abl) (place) out of, from, down from; (person) from; (time) after, immediately after, since; (change) from being; (source, material) of; (cause) by reason of, through; (conformity) in accordance with; **ex itinere** on the march; **ex parte** in part; **ex quō** since; **ex rē, ex ūsū** for the good of; **ē rē pūblicā** constitutionally; **ex sententiā** to one's liking; **aliud ex aliō** one thing after another; **ūnus ex** one of.

exacerbō, -āre vt to exasperate.

exāctiō, -ōnis f expulsion; supervision; tax; (debts) calling in.

exāctor, -ōris m expeller; superintendent; tax collector.

exāctus ppp of **exigō** ♦ adj precise, exact.

exacuō, -uere, -uī, -ūtum vt to sharpen; (fig) to quicken, inflame.

exadversum, -us adv, prep (with acc) right opposite.

exaedificātiō, -ōnis f construction.

exaedificō, -āre vt to build up; to finish the building of.

exaequātiō, -ōnis f levelling.

exaequō, -āre, -āvī, -ātum vt to level out; to compensate; to put on an equal footing; to equal.

exaestuō, -āre vi to boil up.

exaggerātiō, -ōnis f exaltation.

exaggerō, -āre, -āvī, -ātum vt to pile up; (fig) to heighten, enhance.

exagitātor, -ōris m critic.

exagitō, -āre, -āvī, -ātum vt to disturb, harass; to scold, censure; to excite, incite.

exagōga, -ae f export.

exalbēscō, -ēscere, -uī vi to turn quite pale.

exāmen, -inis nt swarm, crowd; tongue of a balance; examining.

examinō, -āre, -āvī, -ātum vt to weigh; to consider, test.

examussim adv exactly, perfectly.

exanclō, -āre vt to drain; to endure to the end.

exanimālis adj dead; deadly.

exanimātiō, -ōnis f panic.

exanimis adj lifeless, breathless; terrified.

Noun declensions and verb conjugations are shown on pp xiii to xxv. The present infinitive ending of a verb shows to which conjugation it belongs: **-āre** = 1st; **-ēre** = 2nd; **-ere** = 3rd and **-īre** = 4th. Irregular verbs are shown on p xxvi

exanimō, -āre, -āvī, -ātum *vt* to wind; to kill; to terrify, agitate; (*pass*) to be out of breath.

exanimus *see* **exanimis.**

exārdēscō, -dēscere, -sī, -sum *vi* to catch fire, blaze up; (*fig*) to be inflamed, break out.

exārēscō, -ēscere, -uī *vi* to dry, dry up.

exarmō, -āre *vt* to disarm.

exarō, -āre, -āvi, -ātum *vt* to plough up; to cultivate, produce; (*brow*) to furrow; (*writing*) to pen.

exārsī *perf of* **exārdēscō.**

exasciātus *adj* hewn out.

exasperō, -āre, -āvī, -ātum *vt* to roughen; (*fig*) to provoke.

exauctōrō, -āre, -āvī, -ātum *vt* (MIL) to discharge, release; to cashier.

exaudiō, -īre, -īvī, -ītum *vt* to hear clearly; to listen to; to obey.

exaugeō, -ēre *vt* to increase.

exaugurātiō, -ōnis *f* desecrating.

exaugurō, -āre *vt* to desecrate.

exauspicō, -āre *vi* to take an omen.

exbibō *etc see* **ēbibō.**

excaecō, -āre *vt* to blind; (*river*) to block up.

excandēscentia, -ae *f* growing anger.

excandēscō, -ēscere, -uī *vi* to burn, be inflamed.

excantō, -āre *vt* to charm out, spirit away.

excarnificō, -āre *vt* to tear to pieces.

excavō, -āre *vt* to hollow out.

excēdō, -ēdere, -essī, -essum *vi* to go out, go away; to die, disappear; to advance, proceed (to); to digress ♦ *vt* to leave; to overstep, exceed.

excellēns, -entis *pres p of* **excellō** ♦ *adj* outstanding, excellent.

excellenter *adv see* **excellēns.**

excellentia, -ae *f* superiority, excellence.

excellō, -ere *vi* to be eminent, excel.

excelsē *adv* loftily.

excelsitās, -ātis *f* loftiness.

excelsum, -ī *nt* height.

excelsus *adj* high, elevated; eminent, illustrious.

exceptiō, -ōnis *f* exception, restriction; (*law*) objection.

exceptō, -āre *vt* to catch, take out.

exceptus *ppp of* **excipiō.**

excernō, -ernere, -rēvī, -rētum *vt* to sift out, separate.

excerpō, -ere, -sī, -tum *vt* to take out; to select, copy out extracts; to leave out, omit.

excessus, -ūs *m* departure, death.

excetra, -ae *f* snake.

excidiō, -ōnis *f* destruction.

excidium, -ī *and* **iī** *nt* overthrow, destruction.

excidō, -ere, -ī *vi* to fall out, fall; (*speech*) to slip out, escape; (*memory*) to get forgotten, escape; (*person*) to fail, lose; (*things*) to disappear, be lost.

excīdō, -dere, -dī, -sum *vt* to cut off, hew out, fell; to raze; (*fig*) to banish.

excieō *vt see* **exciō.**

exciō, -īre, -īvī *and* **iī, -itum** *and* **ītum** *vt* to call out, rouse, summon; to occasion, produce; to excite.

excipiō, -ipere, -ēpī, -eptum *vt* to take out, remove; to exempt, make an exception of, mention specifically; to take up, catch, intercept, overhear; to receive, welcome, entertain; to come next to, follow after, succeed.

excīsiō, -ōnis *f* destroying.

excīsus *ppp of* **excīdō.**

excitātus *adj* loud, strong.

excitō, -āre, -āvī, -ātum *vt* to rouse, wake up, summon; to raise, build; to call on (to stand up); (*fig*) to encourage, revive, excite.

excitus, excītus *ppp of* **exciō.**

exclāmātiō, -ōnis *f* exclamation.

exclāmō, -āre, -āvī, -ātum *vi* to cry out, shout ♦ *vt* to exclaim, call.

exclūdō, -dere, -sī, -sum *vt* to shut out, exclude; to shut off, keep off; (*egg*) to hatch out; (*eye*) to knock out; (*fig*) to prevent, except.

exclūsiō, -ōnis *f* shutting out.

exclūsus *ppp of* **exclūdō.**

excoctus *ppp of* **excoquō.**

excōgitātiō, -ōnis *f* thinking out, devising.

excōgitō, -āre, -āvī, -ātum *vt* to think out, contrive.

excolō, -olere, -oluī, -ultum *vt* to work carefully; to perfect, refine.

excoquō, -quere, -xī, -ctum *vt* to boil away; to remove with heat, make with heat; to dry up.

excors, -dis *adj* senseless, stupid.

excrēmentum, -ī *nt* excretion.

excreō *etc see* **exscreō.**

excrēscō, -scere, -vī, -tum *vi* to grow, rise up.

excrētus *ppp of* **excernō.**

excruciō, -āre, -āvī, -ātum *vt* to torture, torment.

excubiae, -ārum *fpl* keeping guard, watch; sentry.

excubitor, -ōris *m* sentry.

excubō, -āre, -uī, -itum *vi* to sleep out of doors; to keep watch; (*fig*) to be on the alert.

excūdō, -dere, -dī, -sum *vt* to strike out, hammer out; (*egg*) to hatch; (*fig*) to make, compose.

exculcō, -āre *vt* to beat, tramp down.

excultus *ppp of* **excolō.**

excurrō, -rrere, -currī *and* **rrī, -rsum** *vi* to run out, hurry out; to make an excursion; (MIL) to make a sortie; (*place*) to extend, project; (*fig*) to expand.

excursiō, -ōnis *f* raid, sortie; (*gesture*) stepping forward; (*fig*) outset.

excursor, -ōris *m* scout.

excursus, -ūs *m* excursion, raid, charge.

excūsābilis *adj* excusable.

excūsātē *adv* excusably.

excūsātiō, -ōnis *f* excuse, plea.

excūsō, -āre, -āvī, -ātum vt to excuse; to apologize for; to plead as an excuse.

excussus ppp of **excutiō**.

excūsus ppp of **excūdō**.

excutiō, -tere, -ssī, -ssum vt to shake out, shake off; to knock out, drive out, cast off; (fig) to discard, banish; to examine, inspect.

exdorsuō, -āre vt to fillet.

exec- etc see **exsec-**.

exedō, -ēsse, -ēdī, -ēsum vt to eat up; to wear away, destroy; (feelings) to prey on.

exedra, -ae f hall, lecture room.

exedrium, -ī and **iī** nt sitting room.

exēmī perf of **eximō**.

exemplar, -āris nt copy; likeness; model, ideal.

exemplārēs mpl copies.

exemplum, -ī nt copy; example, sample, precedent, pattern; purport, nature; warning, object lesson; ~ **dare** set an example; **~ī causā, gratiā** for instance.

exemptus ppp of **eximō**.

exenterō, -āre vt (comedy) to empty, clean out; to torture.

exeō, -īre, -iī, -itum vi to go out, leave; to come out, issue; (MIL) to march out; (time) to expire; to spring up, rise ♦ vt to pass beyond; to avoid; **~ ex potestāte** lose control.

exeq- etc see **exseq-**.

exerceō, -ēre, -uī, -itum vt to keep busy, supervise; (ground) to work, cultivate; (MIL) to drill, exercise; (mind) to engage, employ; (occupation) to practise, follow, carry on; (trouble) to worry, harass; **sē ~** practise, exercise.

exercitātiō, -ōnis f practice, exercise, experience.

exercitātus adj practised, trained, versed; troubled.

exercitium, -ī and **iī** nt exercising.

exercitō, -āre vt to exercise.

exercitor, -ōris m trainer.

exercitus ppp of **exerceō** ♦ adj disciplined; troubled; troublesome.

exercitus, -ūs m army (esp the infantry); assembly; troop, flock; exercise.

exerō etc see **exserō**.

exēsor, -ōris m corroder.

exēsus ppp of **exedō**.

exhālātiō, -ōnis f vapour.

exhālō, -āre vt to exhale, breathe out ♦ vi to steam; to expire.

exhauriō, -rīre, -sī, -stum vt to drain off; to empty; to take away, remove; (fig) to exhaust, finish; (trouble) to undergo, endure to the end.

exhērēdō, -āre vt to disinherit.

exhērēs, -ēdis adj disinherited.

exhibeō, -ēre, -uī, -itum vt to hold out, produce (in public); to display, show; to cause, occasion.

exhilarātus adj delighted.

exhorrēscō, -ēscere, -uī vi to be terrified ♦ vt to be terrified at.

exhortātiō, -ōnis f encouragement.

exhortor -ārī, -ātus vt to encourage.

exigō, -igere, -ēgī, -āctum vt to drive out, thrust; (payment) to exact, enforce; to demand, claim; (goods) to dispose of; (time) to pass, complete; (work) to finish; (news) to ascertain; to test, examine, consider.

exiguē adv briefly, slightly, hardly.

exiguitās, -ātis f smallness, meagreness.

exiguus adj small, short, meagre ♦ nt a little bit.

exiliō etc see **exsiliō**.

exīlis adj thin, small, meagre; poor; (style) flat, insipid.

exīlitās, -ātis f thinness, meagreness.

exīliter adv feebly.

exilium etc see **exsilium**.

exim see **exinde**.

eximiē adv exceptionally.

eximius adj exempt; select; distinguished, exceptional.

eximō, -imere, -ēmī, -emptum vt to take out, remove; to release, free; to exempt; (time) to waste; (fig) to banish.

exin see **exinde**.

exināniō, -īre, -iī, -ītum vt to empty; to pillage.

exinde adv (place) from there, next; (time) then, thereafter, next; (measure) accordingly.

exīstimātiō, -ōnis f opinion, judgment; reputation, character; (money) credit.

exīstimātor, -ōris m judge, critic.

exīstimō, -āre, -āvī, -ātum vt to value, estimate, judge, think, consider.

existō etc see **exsistō**.

exīstumō vt see **exīstimō**.

exitiābilis adj deadly, fatal.

exitiālis adj deadly.

exitiōsus adj pernicious, fatal.

exitium, -ī and **iī** nt destruction, ruin.

exitus, -ūs m departure; way out, outlet; conclusion, end; death; outcome, result.

exlēx, -ēgis adj above the law, lawless.

exoculō, -āre vt to knock the eyes out of.

exodium, -ī and **iī** nt afterpiece.

exolēscō, -scere, -vī, -tum vi to decay, become obsolete.

exolētus adj full-grown.

exonerō, -āre, -āvī, -ātum vt to unload, discharge; (fig) to relieve, exonerate.

exoptātus adj welcome.

exoptō, -āre, -āvī, -ātum vt to long for, desire.

exōrābilis adj sympathetic.

exōrātor, -ōris m successful pleader.

Noun declensions and verb conjugations are shown on pp xiii to xxv. The present infinitive ending of a verb shows to which conjugation it belongs: **-āre** = 1st; **-ēre** = 2nd; **-ere** = 3rd and **-īre** = 4th. Irregular verbs are shown on p xxvi

exōrdior, -dīrī, -sus vt to lay the warp; to begin.

exōrdium, -ī and **iī** nt beginning; (RHET) introductory section.

exorior, -īrī, -tus vi to spring up, come out, rise; to arise, appear, start.

exōrnātiō, -ōnis f embellishment.

exōrnātor, -ōris m embellisher.

exōrnō, -āre, -āvī, -ātum vt to equip, fit out; to embellish, adorn.

exōrō, -āre, -āvī, -ātum vt to prevail upon, persuade; to obtain, win by entreaty.

exōrsus ppa of **exōrdior** ♦ adj begun ♦ ntpl preamble.

exōrsus, -ūs m beginning.

exortus ppa of **exorior**.

exortus, -ūs m rising; east.

exos, -ossis adj boneless.

exōsculor, -ārī, -ātus vt to kiss fondly.

exossō, -āre vt to bone.

exōstra, -ae f stage mechanism; (fig) public.

exōsus adj detesting.

exōticus adj foreign.

expallēscō, -ēscere, -uī vi to turn pale, be afraid.

expalpō, -āre vt to coax out.

expandō, -ere vt to unfold.

expatrō, -āre vt to squander.

expavēscō, -ere, expāvī vi to be terrified ♦ vt to dread.

expect- etc see **exspect-**.

expediō, -īre, -īvī and **iī, -ītum** vt to free, extricate, disentangle; to prepare, clear (for action); to put right, settle; to explain, relate; (impers) it is useful, expedient.

expedītē adv readily, freely.

expedītiō, -ōnis f (MIL) expedition, enterprise.

expedītus ppp of **expediō** ♦ adj light-armed; ready, prompt; at hand ♦ m light-armed soldier; **in ~ō esse, habēre** be, have in readiness.

expellō, -ellere, -ulī, -ulsum vt to drive away, eject, expel; to remove, repudiate.

expendō, -endere, -endī, -ēnsum vt to weigh out; to pay out; (penalty) to suffer; (mind) to ponder, consider, judge.

expēnsum, -ī nt payment, expenditure.

expergēfaciō, -facere, -fēcī, -factum vt to rouse, excite.

expergīscor, -gīscī, -rēctus vi to wake up; to bestir oneself.

expergō, -ere, -ī, -itum vt to awaken.

experiēns, -entis pres p of **experior** ♦ adj enterprising.

experientia, -ae f experiment; endeavour; experience, practice.

experīmentum, -ī nt proof, test; experience.

experior, -īrī, -tus vt to test, make trial of; to attempt, experience; (law) to go to law; (perf tenses) to know from experience.

experrēctus ppa of **expergīscor**.

expers, -tis adj having no part in, not sharing; free from, without.

expertus ppa of **experior** ♦ adj proved, tried; experienced.

expetessō, -ere vt to desire.

expetō, -ere, -īvī and **iī, -ītum** vt to aim at, tend towards; to desire, covet; to attack; to demand, require ♦ vi to befall, happen.

expiātiō, -ōnis f atonement.

expictus ppp of **expingō**.

expīlātiō, -ōnis f pillaging.

expīlātor, -ōris m plunderer.

expīlō, -āre, -āvī, -ātum vt to rob, plunder.

expingō, -ingere, -inxī, -ictum vt to portray.

expiō, -āre, -āvī, -ātum vt to purify; to atone for, make amends for; to avert (evil).

expīrō etc see **exspīrō**.

expiscor, -ārī, -ātus vt to try to find out, ferret out.

explānātē adv see **explānātus**.

explānātiō, -ōnis f explanation.

explānātor, -ōris m interpreter.

explānātus adj distinct.

explānō, -āre, -āvī, -ātum vt to state clearly, explain; to pronounce clearly.

explaudō etc see **explōdō**.

explēmentum, -ī nt filling.

expleō, -ēre, -ēvī, -ētum vt to fill up; to complete; (desire) to satisfy, appease; (duty) to perform, discharge; (loss) to make good; (time) to fulfil, complete.

explētiō, -ōnis f satisfying.

explētus ppp of **expleō** ♦ adj complete.

explicātē adv plainly.

explicātiō, -ōnis f uncoiling; expounding, analyzing.

explicātor, -ōris m, **-rīx, -rīcis** f expounder.

explicātus adj spread out; plain, clear.

explicātus, -ūs m explanation.

explicitus adj easy.

explicō, -āre, -āvī and **uī, -ātum** and **itum** vt to unfold, undo, spread out; (book) to open; (MIL) to deploy, extend; (difficulty) to put in order, settle; (speech) to develop, explain; to set free.

explōdō, -dere, -sī, -sum vt to hiss off, drive away; (fig) to reject.

explōrātē adv with certainty.

explōrātiō, -ōnis f spying.

explōrātor, -ōris m spy, scout.

explōrātus adj certain, sure.

explōrō, -āre, -āvī, -ātum vt to investigate, reconnoitre; to ascertain; to put to the test.

explōsī perf of **explōdō**.

explōsiō, -ōnis f driving off (the stage).

explōsus ppp of **explōdō**.

expoliō, -īre, -īvī, -ītum vt to smooth off, polish; (fig) to refine, embellish.

expolītiō, -ōnis f smoothing off; polish, finish.

expōnō, -ōnere, -osuī, -ositum vt to set out, put out; (child) to expose; (NAUT) to disembark; (money) to offer; (fig) to set forth, expose, display; (speech) to explain, expound.

exporrigō, -igere, -ēxī, -ēctum *vt* to extend, smooth out.

exportātiō, -ōnis *f* exporting.

exportō, -āre, -āvī, -ātum *vt* to carry out, export.

exposcō, -ere, expoposcī *vt* to implore, pray for; to demand.

expositīcius *adj* foundling.

expositiō, -ōnis *f* narration, explanation.

expositus *ppp of* **expōnō** ♦ *adj* open, affable; vulgar.

expostulātiō, -ōnis *f* complaint

expostulō, -āre, -āvī, -ātum *vt* to demand urgently; to complain of, expostulate.

expōtus *ppp of* **ēpōtō**.

expressus *ppp of* **exprimō** ♦ *adj* distinct, prominent.

exprimō, -imere, -essī, -essum *vt* to squeeze out, force out; to press up; (*fig*) to extort, wrest; (*art*) to mould, model; (*words*) to imitate, portray, translate, pronounce.

exprobrātiō, -ōnis *f* reproach.

exprobrō, -āre, -āvī, -ātum *vt* to reproach, cast up.

exprōmō, -ere, -psī, -ptum *vt* to bring out, fetch out; (*acts*) to exhibit, practise; (*feelings*) to give vent to; (*speech*) to disclose, state.

expugnābilis *adj* capable of being taken by storm.

expugnācior, -ōris *adj* more effective.

expugnātiō, -ōnis *f* storming, assault.

expugnātor, -ōris *m* stormer.

expugnō, -āre, -āvī, -ātum *vt* to storm, reduce; to conquer; (*fig*) to overcome, extort.

expulī *perf of* **expellō**.

expulsiō, -ōnis *f* expulsion.

expulsor, -ōris *m* expeller.

expulsus *ppp of* **expellō**.

expultrīx, -īcis *f* expeller.

expungō, -ungere, -ūnxī, -ūnctum *vt* to prick out, cancel.

expūrgātiō, -ōnis *f* excuse.

expūrgō, -āre *vt* to purify; to justify.

exputō, -āre *vt* to consider, comprehend.

exquīrō, -rere, -sīvī, -sītum *vt* to search out, investigate; to inquire; to devise.

exquīsītē *adv* with particular care.

exquīsītus *ppp of* **exquīrō** ♦ *adj* well thought out, choice.

exsaeviō, -īre *vi* to cease raging.

exsanguis *adj* bloodless, pale; feeble.

exsarciō, -cīre, -tum *vt* to repair.

exsatiō, -āre *vt* to satiate, satisfy.

exsaturābilis *adj* appeasable.

exsaturō, -āre *vt* to satiate.

exsce- *etc see* **esce-**.

exscindō, -ndere, -dī, -ssum *vt* to extirpate.

exscreō, -āre *vt* to cough up.

exscrībō, -bere, -psī, -ptum *vt* to copy out; to note down.

exsculpō, -ere, -sī, -tum *vt* to carve out; to erase; (*fig*) to extort.

exsecō, -āre, -uī, -tum *vt* to cut out; to castrate.

exsecrābilis *adj* cursing, deadly.

exsecrātiō, -ōnis *f* curse; solemn oath.

exsecrātus *adj* accursed.

exsecror, -ārī, -ātus *vt* to curse; to take an oath.

exsectiō, -ōnis *f* cutting out.

exsecūtiō, -ōnis *f* management; discussion.

exsecūtus *ppa of* **exsequor**.

exsequiae, -ārum *fpl* funeral, funeral rites.

exsequiālis *adj* funeral.

exsequor, -quī, -cūtus *vt* to follow, pursue; to follow to the grave; (*duty*) to carry out, accomplish; (*speech*) to describe, relate; (*suffering*) to undergo; (*wrong*) to avenge, punish.

exserciō *vt see* **exsarciō**.

exserō, -ere, -uī, -tum *vt* to put out, stretch out; to reveal.

exsertō, -āre *vt* to stretch out repeatedly.

exsertus *ppp of* **exserō** ♦ *adj* protruding.

exsībilō, -āre *vt* to hiss off.

exsiccātus *adj* (*style*) uninteresting.

exsiccō, -āre, -āvī, -ātum *vt* to dry up; to drain.

exsicō *etc see* **exsecō**.

exsignō, -āre *vt* to write down in detail.

exsiliō, -īre, -uī *vi* to jump up, spring out; to start.

exsilium, -ī *and* **iī** *nt* banishment, exile; retreat.

exsistō, -istere, -titī, -titum *vi* to emerge, appear; to arise, spring (from); to be, exist.

exsolvō, -vere, -vī, -ūtum *vt* to undo, loosen, open; to release, free; to get rid of, throw off; (*debt, promise*) to discharge, fulfil, pay up; (*words*) to explain.

exsomnis *adj* sleepless, watchful.

exsorbeō, -ēre, -uī *vt* to suck, drain; to devour, endure.

exsors, -tis *adj* chosen, special; free from.

exspargō *etc see* **exspergō**.

exspatior, -ārī, -ātus *vi* to go off the course.

exspectābilis *adj* to be expected.

exspectātiō, -ōnis *f* waiting, expectation.

exspectātus *adj* looked for, welcome.

exspectō, -āre, -āvī, -ātum *vt* to wait for, till; to see; to expect; to hope for, dread; to require.

exspergō, -gere, -sum *vt* to scatter; to diffuse.

exspēs *adj* despairing.

exspīrātiō, -ōnis *f* exhalation.

exspīrō, -āre, -āvī, -ātum *vt* to breathe out, exhale; to emit ♦ *vi* to rush out; to expire,

Noun declensions and verb conjugations are shown on pp xiii to xxv. The present infinitive ending of a verb shows to which conjugation it belongs: -āre = 1st; -ēre = 2nd; -ere = 3rd and -īre = 4th. Irregular verbs are shown on p xxvi

come to an end.

exsplendēscō, -ere *vi* to shine.

exspoliō, -āre *vt* to pillage.

exspuō, -uere, -uī, -ūtum *vt* to spit out, eject; (*fig*) to banish.

exsternō, -āre *vt* to terrify.

exstillō, -āre *vi* to drip.

exstimulātor, -ōris *m* instigator.

exstimulō, -āre *vt* to goad on; to excite.

exstīnctiō, -ōnis *f* annihilation.

exstīnctor, -ōris *m* extinguisher; destroyer.

exstinguō, -guere, -xī, -ctum *vt* to put out, extinguish; to kill, destroy, abolish.

exstirpō, -āre *vt* to root out, eradicate.

exstitī *perf of* **exsistō.**

exstō, -āre *vi* to stand out, project; to be conspicuous, be visible; to be extant, exist, be.

exstrūctiō, -ōnis *f* erection.

exstruō, -ere, -xī, -ctum *vt* to heap up; to build up, construct.

exsūdō, -āre *vi* to come out in sweat ♦ *vt* (*fig*) to toil through.

exsūgō, -gere, -xī, -ctum *vt* to suck out.

exsul, -is *m/f* exile.

exsulō, -āre, -āvī, -ātum *vi* to be an exile.

exsultātiō, -ōnis *f* great rejoicing.

exsultim *adv* friskily.

exsultō, -āre, -āvī, -ātum *vi* to jump up, prance; (*fig*) to exult, run riot, boast; (*speech*) to range at will.

exsuperābilis *adj* superable.

exsuperantia, -ae *f* superiority.

exsuperō, -āre, -āvī, -ātum *vi* to mount up; to gain the upper hand, excel ♦ *vt* to go over; to surpass; to overpower.

exsurdō, -āre *vt* to deafen; (*fig*) to dull.

exsurgō, -gere, -rēxī, -rēctum *vi* to rise, stand up; to recover.

exsuscitō, -āre *vt* to wake up; (*fire*) to fan; (*mind*) to excite.

exta, -ōrum *ntpl* internal organs.

extābēscō, -ēscere, -uī *vi* to waste away; to vanish.

extāris *adj* sacrificial.

extemplō *adv* immediately, on the spur of the moment; **quom ~** as soon as.

extemporālis *adj* extempore.

extempulō *see* **extemplō.**

extendō, -dere, -dī, -tum *and* **extēnsum** *vt* to stretch out, spread, extend; to enlarge, increase; (*time*) to prolong; **sē ~** exert oneself; **īre per ~tum fūnem** walk the tightrope.

extēnsus *ppp of* **extendō.**

extentō, -āre *vt* to strain, exert.

extentus *ppp of* **extendō** ♦ *adj* broad.

extenuātiō, -ōnis *f* (RHET) diminution.

extenuō, -āre, -āvī, -ātum *vt* to thin out, rarefy; to diminish, weaken.

exter *adj* from outside; foreign.

exterebrō, -āre *vt* to bore out; to extort.

extergeō, -gēre, -sī, -sum *vt* to wipe off, clean; to plunder.

exterior, -ōris *adj* outer, exterior.

exterius *adv* on the outside.

exterminō, -āre *vt* to drive out, banish; (*fig*) to put aside.

externus *adj* outward, external; foreign, strange.

exterō, -erere, -rīvī, -rītum *vt* to rub out, wear away.

exterreō, -ēre, -uī, -itum *vt* to frighten.

extersus *ppp of* **extergeō.**

exterus *see* **exter.**

extexō, -ere *vt* to unweave; (*fig*) to cheat.

extimēscō, -ēscere, -uī *vi* to be very frightened ♦ *vt* to be very afraid of.

extimus *adj* outermost, farthest.

extin- *etc see* **exstin-.**

extispex, -icis *m* diviner.

extollō, -ere *vt* to lift up, raise; (*fig*) to exalt, beautify; (*time*) to defer.

extorqueō, -quēre, -sī, -tum *vt* to wrench out, wrest; to dislocate; (*fig*) to obtain by force, extort.

extorris *adj* banished, in exile.

extortor, -ōris *m* extorter.

extortus *ppp of* **extorqueō.**

extrā *adv* outside; **~ quam** except that, unless ♦ *prep* (*with acc*) outside, beyond; free from; except.

extrahō, -here, -xī, -ctum *vt* to draw out, pull out; to extricate, rescue; to remove; (*time*) to prolong, waste.

extrāneus, -ī *m* stranger ♦ *adj* external, foreign.

extraōrdinārius *adj* special, unusual.

extrārius *adj* external; unrelated ♦ *m* stranger.

extrēmitās, -ātis *f* extremity, end.

extrēmum, -ī *nt* end; **ad ~** at last.

extrēmum *adv* for the last time.

extrēmus *adj* outermost, extreme; last; utmost, greatest, meanest.

extrīcō, -āre, -āvī, -ātum *vt* to disentangle, extricate; to clear up.

extrīnsecus *adv* from outside, from abroad; on the outside.

extrītus *ppp of* **exterō.**

extrūdō, -dere, -sī, -sum *vt* to drive out; to keep out; (*sale*) to push.

extulī *perf of* **efferō.**

extumeō, -ēre *vi* to swell up.

extundō, -undere, -udī, -ūsum *vt* to beat out, hammer out; (*comedy*) to extort; (*fig*) to form, compose.

exturbō, -āre, -āvī, -ātum *vt* to drive out, throw out, knock out; (*wife*) to put away; (*fig*) to banish, disturb.

exūberō, -āre *vi* to abound.

exul *etc see* **exsul.**

exulcerō, -āre, -āvī, -ātum *vt* to aggravate.

exululō, -āre *vi* to howl wildly ♦ *vt* to invoke with cries.

exūnctus *ppp of* **exungō.**

exundō, -āre *vi* to overflow; to be washed up.

exungō, -ere *vt* to anoint liberally.

exuō, -uere, -uī, -ūtum *vt* to draw out, put off; to lay aside; to strip.

exūrō, -rere, -ssī, -stum *vt* to burn up; to dry up; to burn out; (*fig*) to inflame.

exūstiō, -ōnis *f* conflagration.

exūtus *ppp of* **exuō.**

exuviae, -ārum *fpl* clothing, arms; hide; spoils.

F, f

faba, -ae *f* bean.

fabālis *adj* bean- (*in cpds*).

fābella, -ae *f* short story, fable; play.

faber, -rī *m* craftsman (*in metal, stone, wood*), tradesman, smith; (*MIL*) artisan; ~ **ferrārius** blacksmith; ~ **tignārius** carpenter ♦ *adj* skilful.

Fabius, -ī *m* Roman family name (*esp Q F Maximus Cunctator, dictator against Hannibal*).

Fabius, -iānus *adj see n.*

fabrē *adv* skilfully.

fabrēfaciō, -facere, -fēcī, -factum *vt* to make, build, forge.

fabrica, -ae *f* art, trade; work of art; workshop; (*comedy*) trick.

fabricātiō, -ōnis *f* structure.

fabricātor, -ōris *m* artificer.

Fabricius, -ī *m* Roman family name (*esp C F Luscinus, incorruptible commander against Pyrrhus*).

Fabricius, -iānus *adj see n.*

fabricō, -āre; -or, -ārī, -ātus *vt* to make, build, forge.

fabrīlis *adj* artificer's ♦ *ntpl* tools.

fābula, -ae *f* story; common talk; play, drama; fable; ~ae! nonsense!; **lupus in ~ā** ≈ *talk of the devil!*

fābulor, -ārī, -ātus *vi* to talk, converse ♦ *vt* to say, invent.

fābulōsus *adj* legendary.

facessō, -ere, -īvī, -ītum *vt* to perform, carry out; to cause (trouble) ♦ *vi* to go away, retire.

facetē *adv* humorously; brilliantly.

facētiae, -ārum *fpl* wit, clever talk, humour.

facētus *adj* witty, humorous; fine, genteel, elegant.

faciēs, -ēī *f* form, shape; face, looks; appearance, aspect, character.

facile *adv* easily; unquestionably; readily; pleasantly.

facilis *adj* easy; well-suited; ready, quick; (*person*) good-natured, approachable; (*fortune*) prosperous.

facilitās, -ātis *f* ease, readiness; (*speech*) fluency; (*person*) good nature, affability.

facinorōsus *adj* criminal.

facinus, -oris *nt* deed, action; crime.

faciō, -ere, fēcī, factum (*imp* **fac,** *pass* **fīō**) *vt* to make, create, compose, cause; to do, perform; (*profession*) to practise; (*property*) to put under; (*value*) to regard, think of; (*words*) to represent, pretend, suppose ♦ *vi* to do, act; (*religion*) to offer sacrifice; (*with* **ad** *or dat*) to be of use; **cōpiam ~** afford an opportunity; **damnum ~** suffer loss; **metum ~** excite fear; **proelium ~** join battle; **rem ~** make money; **verba ~** talk; **māgnī ~** think highly of; **quid tibi faciam?** how am I to answer you?; **quid tē faciam?** what am I to do with you?; **fac sciam** let me know; **fac potuisse** suppose one could have.

factiō, -ōnis *f* making, doing; group, party, faction (*esp in politics and chariot racing*).

factiōsus *adj* factious, oligarchical.

factitō, -āre, -āvī, -ātum *vt* to keep making or doing; to practise; to declare (to be).

factor, -ōris *m* (*sport*) batsman.

factum, -ī *nt* deed, exploit.

factus *ppp of* **faciō.**

facula, -ae *f* little torch.

facultās, -ātis *f* means, opportunity; ability; abundance, supply, resources.

fācundē *adv see* **fācundus.**

fācundia, -ae *f* eloquence.

fācundus *adj* fluent, eloquent.

faeceus *adj* impure.

faecula, -ae *f* wine lees.

faenebris *adj* of usury.

faenerātiō, -ōnis *f* usury.

faenerātō *adv* with interest.

faenerātor, -ōris *m* moneylender.

faenerō, -āre; -or, -ārī, -ātus *vt* to lend at interest; to ruin with usury; (*fig*) to trade in.

faenīlia, -um *ntpl* hayloft.

faenum, -ī *nt* hay; ~ **habet in cornū** he is dangerous.

faenus, -oris *nt* interest; capital lent at interest; (*fig*) profit, advantage.

faenusculum, -ī *nt* a little interest.

Faesulae, -ārum *fpl* town in Etruria (*now Fiesole*).

Faesulānus *adj see n.*

faex, faecis *f* sediment, lees; brine (*of pickles*); (*fig*) dregs.

fāgineus, fāginus *adj* of beech.

fāgus, -ī *f* beech.

fala, -ae *f* siege tower, used in assaults; (*Circus*) pillar.

falārica, -ae *f* a missile, firebrand.
falcārius, -ī *and* **iī** *m* sicklemaker.
falcātus *adj* scythed; sickle-shaped.
falcifer, -ī *adj* scythe-carrying.
Falernus *adj* Falernian (*of a district in N. Campania famous for its wine*) ♦ *nt* Falernian wine.
Faliscī, -ōrum *mpl* a people of S.E. Etruria (*with chief town Falerii*).
Faliscus *adj see n.*
fallācia, -ae *f* trick, deception.
fallāciter *adv see* **fallāx.**
fallāx, -ācis *adj* deceitful, deceptive.
fallō, -lere, fefellī, -sum *vt* to deceive, cheat, beguile; to disappoint, fail, betray; (*promise*) to break; to escape the notice of, be unknown to; (*pass*) to be mistaken; **mē ~lit** I am mistaken; I do not know.
falsē *adv* wrongly, by mistake; fraudulently.
falsidicus *adj* lying.
falsificus *adj* deceiving.
falsiiūrius *adj* perjurious.
falsiloquus *adj* lying.
falsiparēns, -entis *adj* with a pretended father.
falsō *adv see* **falsē.**
falsus *ppp of* **fallō** ♦ *adj* false, mistaken; deceitful; forged, falsified; sham, fictitious ♦ *nt* falsehood, error.
falx, falcis *f* sickle, scythe; pruning hook; (*MIL*) siege hook.
fāma, -ae *f* talk, rumour, tradition; public opinion; reputation, fame; infamy.
famēlicus *adj* hungry.
famēs, -is *f* hunger; famine; (*fig*) greed; (*RHET*) poverty of expression.
fāmigerātiō, -ōnis *f* rumour.
fāmigerātor, -ōris *m* telltale.
familia, -ae *f* domestics, slaves of a household; family property, estate; family, house; school, sect; **pater ~ās** master of a household; **~am dūcere** be head of a sect, company *etc.*
familiāris *adj* domestic, household, family; intimate, friendly; (*entrails*) relating to the sacrificer ♦ *m* servant; friend.
familiāritās, -ātis *f* intimacy, friendship.
familiāriter *adv* on friendly terms.
fāmōsus *adj* celebrated; infamous; slanderous.
famula, -ae *f* maidservant, handmaid.
famulāris *adj* of servants.
famulātus, -ūs *m* slavery.
famulor, -ārī *vi* to serve.
famulus, -ī *m* servant, attendant ♦ *adj* serviceable.
fānāticus *adj* inspired; frantic, frenzied.
fandī *gerund of* **for.**
fandum, -ī *nt* right.
fānum, -ī *nt* sanctuary temple.
fār, farris *nt* spelt; corn; meal.
farciō, -cīre, -sī, -tum *vt* to stuff, fill full.
farīna, -ae *f* meal, flour.

farrāgō, -inis *f* mash, hotch-potch; medley.
farrātus *adj* of corn; filled with corn.
farsī *perf of* **farciō.**
fartem, -im *f acc* filling; mincemeat.
fartor, -ōris *m* fattener, poulterer.
fartus *ppp of* **farciō.**
fās *nt* divine law; right; **~ est** it is lawful, possible.
fascia, -ae *f* band, bandage; streak of cloud.
fasciculus, -ī *m* bundle, packet.
fascinō, -āre *vt* to bewitch, (*esp with the evil eye*).
fascinum, -ī *nt*, **-us, -ī** *m* charm.
fasciola, -ae *f* small bandage.
fascis, -is *m* bundle, faggot; soldier's pack, burden; (*pl*) rods and axe carried before the highest magistrates; high office (*esp the consulship*).
fassus *ppa of* **fateor.**
fāstī, -ōrum *mpl* register of days for legal and public business; calendar; registers of magistrates and other public records.
fastīdiō, -īre, -iī, -ītum *vt* to loathe, dislike, despise ♦ *vi* to feel squeamish, be disgusted; to be disdainful.
fastīdiōsē *adv* squeamishly; disdainfully.
fastīdiōsus *adj* squeamish, disgusted; fastidious, nice; disagreeable.
fastīdium, -ī *and* **iī** *nt* squeamishness, distaste; disgust, aversion; disdain, pride.
fastīgātē *adv* in a sloping position.
fastīgātus *adj* sloping up *or* down.
fastīgium, -ī *and* **iī** *nt* gable, pediment; slope; height, depth; top, summit; (*fig*) highest degree, acme, dignity; (*speech*) main headings.
fāstus *adj* lawful for public business.
fastus, -ūs *m* disdain, pride.
Fāta *ntpl* the Fates.
fātālis *adj* fateful, destined; fatal, deadly.
fātāliter *adv* by fate.
fateor, -tērī, -ssus *vt* to confess, acknowledge; to reveal, bear witness to.
fāticanus, -inus *adj* prophetic.
fātidicus *adj* prophetic ♦ *m* prophet.
fātifer, -ī *adj* deadly.
fatīgātiō, -ōnis *f* weariness.
fatīgō, -āre, -āvī, -ātum *vt* to tire, exhaust; to worry, importune; to wear down, torment.
fātiloqua, -ae *f* prophetess.
fatīscō, -ere, -or, -ī *vi* to crack, split; (*fig*) to become exhausted.
fatuitās, -ātis *f* silliness.
fātum, -ī *nt* divine word, oracle; fate, destiny; divine will; misfortune, doom, death; **~ō obīre** die a natural death.
fātur, fātus *3rd pers, ppa of* **for.**
fatuus *adj* silly; unwieldy ♦ *m* fool.
faucēs, -ium *fpl* throat; pass, narrow channel, chasm; (*fig*) jaws.
Faunus, -ī *m* father of Latinus (*god of forests and herdsmen, identified with Pan*); (*pl*) woodland spirits, Fauns.

faustē *adv see* **faustus.**

faustitās, -ātis *f* good fortune, fertility.

faustus *adj* auspicious, lucky.

fautor, -ōris *m* supporter, patron.

fautrīx, -īcis *f* protectress.

favea, -ae *f* pet slave.

faveō, -ēre, fāvī, fautum *vi* (*with dat*) to favour, befriend, support; **~ linguīs** keep silence.

favilla, -ae *f* embers, ashes; (*fig*) spark.

favitor *etc see* **fautor.**

Favōnius, -ī *m* west wind, zephyr.

favor, -ōris *m* favour, support; applause.

favōrābilis *adj* in favour; pleasing.

favus, -ī *m* honeycomb.

fax, facis *f* torch, wedding torch, funeral torch; marriage, death; (*ASTRO*) meteor; (*fig*) flame, fire, instigator; guide; **facem praeferre** act as guide.

faxim, faxō *old subj and fut of* **faciō.**

febrīcula, -ae *f* slight fever.

febris, -is *f* fever.

Februārius, -ī *m* February ♦ *adj* of February.

februum, -ī *nt* purification; **Februa** *pl festival of purification in February.*

fēcī *perf of* **faciō.**

fēcunditās, -ātis *f* fertility; (*style*) exuberance.

fēcundō, -āre *vt* to fertilise.

fēcundus *adj* fertile, fruitful; fertilising; (*fig*) abundant, rich, prolific.

fefellī *perf of* **fallō.**

fel, fellis *nt* gall bladder, bile; poison; (*fig*) animosity.

fēlēs, -is *f* cat.

fēlīcitās, -ātis *f* happiness, good luck.

fēlīciter *adv* abundantly; favourably; happily.

fēlīx, -īcis *adj* fruitful; auspicious, favourable; fortunate, successful.

fēmella, -ae *f* girl.

fēmina, -ae *f* female, woman.

fēmineus *adj* woman's, of women; unmanly.

femur, -oris *and* **inis** *nt* thigh.

fēn- *etc see* **faen-.**

fenestra, -ae *f* window; (*fig*) loophole.

fera, -ae *f* wild beast.

ferācius *adv* more fruitfully.

fērālis *adj* funereal; of the Feralia; deadly ♦ *ntpl festival of the dead in February.*

ferāx, -ācis *adj* fruitful, productive.

ferbuī *perf of* **ferveō.**

ferculum, -ī *nt* litter, barrow; dish, course.

ferē *adv* almost, nearly, about; quite; just; usually, generally, as a rule; (*with neg*) hardly; **nihil ~** hardly anything.

ferentārius, -ī *and* **iī** *m* a light-armed soldier.

Feretrius, -ī *m* an epithet of Jupiter.

feretrum, -ī *nt* bier.

fēriae, -ārum *fpl* festival, holidays; (*fig*) peace, rest.

fēriātus *adj* on holiday, idle.

ferīnus *adj* of wild beasts ♦ *f* game.

feriō, -īre *vt* to strike, hit; to kill, sacrifice; (*comedy*) to cheat; **foedus ~** conclude a treaty.

feritās, -ātis *f* wildness, savagery.

fermē *see* **ferē.**

fermentum, -ī *nt* yeast; beer; (*fig*) passion, vexation.

ferō, ferre, tulī, lātum *vt* to carry, bring, bear; to bring forth, produce; to move, stir, raise; to carry off, sweep away, plunder; (*pass*) to rush, hurry, fly, flow, drift; (*road*) to lead; (*trouble*) to endure, suffer, sustain; (*feelings*) to exhibit, show; (*speech*) to talk about, give out, celebrate; (*bookkeeping*) to enter; (*CIRCS*) to allow, require; **sē ~** rush, move; profess to be, boast; **condiciōnem, lēgem ~** propose terms, a law; **iūdicem ~** sue; **sententiam, suffrāgium ~** vote; **signa ~** march; attack; **aegrē, graviter ~** be annoyed at; **laudibus ~** extol; **in oculīs ~** be very fond of; **prae sē ~** show, declare; **fertur, ferunt** it is said, they say; **ut mea fert opīniō** in my opinion.

ferōcia, -ae *f* courage; spirit; pride, presumption.

ferōcitās, -ātis *f* high spirits, aggressiveness; presumption.

ferōciter *adv* bravely; insolently.

Fērōnia, -ae *f* old Italian goddess.

ferōx, -ōcis *adj* warlike, spirited, daring; proud, insolent.

ferrāmentum, -ī *nt* tool, implement.

ferrārius *adj* of iron; **faber ~** blacksmith ♦ *f* iron-mine, iron-works.

ferrātus *adj* ironclad, ironshod ♦ *mpl* men in armour.

ferreus *adj* of iron, iron; (*fig*) hard, cruel; strong, unyielding.

ferrūgineus *adj* rust-coloured, dark.

ferrūgō, -inis *f* rust; dark colour; gloom.

ferrum, -ī *nt* iron; sword; any iron implement; force of arms; **~ et ignis** devastation.

fertilis *adj* fertile, productive; fertilising.

fertilitās, -ātis *f* fertility.

ferula, -ae *f* fennel; staff, rod.

ferus *adj* wild; uncivilised, cruel ♦ *m* beast.

fervēfaciō, -ere, -tum *vt* to boil.

fervēns, -entis *pres p of* **ferveō** ♦ *adj* hot; raging; (*fig*) impetuous, furious.

ferventer *adv* hotly.

ferveō, -vēre, -buī *vi* to boil, burn; (*fig*) to rage, bustle, be agitated.

fervēscō, -ere *vi* to boil up, grow hot.

fervidus *adj* hot, raging; (*fig*) fiery, violent.

fervō, -vere, -vī *vi see* **ferveō.**

fervor, -ōris *m* seething; heat; (*fig*) ardour, passion.

Fescennīnus *adj* Fescennine (*a kind of ribald*

song, perhaps from Fescennium in Etruria).
fessus *adj* tired, worn out.
festīnanter *adv* hastily.
festīnātiō, -ōnis *f* haste, hurry.
festīnō, -āre *vi* to hurry, be quick ♦ *vt* to hasten, accelerate.
festīnus *adj* hasty, quick.
fēstīvē *adv* gaily; humorously.
fēstīvitās, -ātis *f* gaiety, merriment; humour, fun.
fēstīvus *adj* gay, jolly; delightful; (*speech*) humorous.
festūca, -ae *f* rod (*with which slaves were manumitted*).
fēstus *adj* festal, on holiday ♦ *nt* holiday; feast.
fētiālis, -is *m* priest who carried out the ritual in making war and peace.
fētūra, -ae *f* breeding; brood.
fētus *adj* pregnant; newly delivered; (*fig*) productive, full of.
fētus, -ūs *m* breeding, bearing, producing; brood, young; fruit, produce; (*fig*) production.
fiber, -rī *m* beaver.
fibra, -ae *f* fibre; section of lung *or* liver; entrails.
fībula, -ae *f* clasp, brooch; clamp.
fīcēdula, -ae *f* fig pecker.
fictē *adv* falsely.
fictilis *adj* clay, earthen ♦ *nt* jar; clay figure.
fictor, -ōris *m* sculptor; maker, inventor.
fictrīx, -īcis *f* maker.
fictūra, -ae *f* shaping, invention.
fictus *ppp of* **fingō** ♦ *adj* false, fictitious ♦ *nt* falsehood.
fīculnus *adj* of the fig tree.
fīcus, -ī *and* **ūs** *f* fig tree; fig.
fidēlē *adv* faithfully, surely, firmly.
fidēlia, -ae *f* pot, pail; **dē eādem ~ā duōs parietēs dealbāre** ≈ *kill two birds with one stone.*
fidēlis *adj* faithful, loyal; trustworthy, sure.
fidēlitās, -ātis *f* faithfulness, loyalty.
fidēliter *adv* faithfully, surely, firmly.
Fīdēnae, -ārum *fpl* ancient Latin town.
Fīdēnās, -ātis *adj see n.*
fīdēns, -entis *pres p of* **fīdō** ♦ *adj* bold, resolute.
fīdenter *adv see* **fidens.**
fīdentia, -ae *f* self-confidence.
fidēs, -eī *f* trust, faith, belief; trustworthiness, honour, loyalty, truth; promise, assurance, word; guarantee, safe-conduct, protection; (*COMM*) credit; (*law*) good faith; **~ mala** dishonesty; **rēs ~que** entire resources; **~em facere** convince; **~em servāre ergā** keep faith with; **dī vostram ~em!** for Heaven's sake!; **ex fidē bonā** in good faith.
fidēs, -is *f* (*usu pl*) stringed instrument, lyre, lute; (*ASTRO*) Lyra.
fidī *perf of* **findō.**
fidicen, -inis *m* musician; lyric poet.
fidicina, -ae *f* music girl.
fidicula, -ae *f* small lute.

Fidius, -ī *m* an epithet of Jupiter.
fīdō, -dere, -sus *vi* (*with dat or abl*) to trust, rely on.
fīdūcia, -ae *f* confidence, assurance; self-confidence; (*law*) trust, security.
fīdūciārius *adj* to be held in trust.
fīdus *adj* trusty, reliable; sure, safe.
fīgō, -gere, -xī, -xum *vt* to fix, fasten, attach; to drive in, pierce; (*speech*) to taunt.
figulāris *adj* a potter's.
figulus, -ī *m* potter; builder.
figūra, -ae *f* shape, form; nature, kind; phantom; (*RHET*) figure of speech.
figūrō, -āre *vt* to form, shape.
fīlātim *adv* thread by thread.
fīlia, -ae *f* daughter.
fīlicātus *adj* with fern patterns.
fīliola, -ae *f* little daughter.
fīliolus, -ī *m* little son.
fīlius, -ī *and* **iī** *m* son; **terrae ~** a nobody.
filix, -cis *f* fern.
fīlum, -ī *nt* thread; band of wool, fillet; string, shred, wick; contour, shape; (*speech*) texture, quality.
fimbriae, -ārum *fpl* fringe, end.
fimus, -ī *m* dung; dirt.
findō, -ndere, -dī, -ssum *vt* to split, divide; to burst.
fingō, -ere, finxī, fictum *vt* to form, shape, make; to mould, model; to dress, arrange; to train; (*mind, speech*) to imagine, suppose, represent, sketch; to invent, fabricate; **vultum ~** compose the features.
fīniō, -īre, -īvī, -ītum *vt* to bound, limit; to restrain; to prescribe, define, determine; to end, finish, complete ♦ *vi* to finish, die.
fīnis, -is *m* (*occ f*) boundary, border; (*pl*) territory; bound, limit; end; death; highest point, summit; aim, purpose; **~ bonōrum** the chief good; **quem ad ~em?** how long?; **~e genūs** up to the knee.
fīnītē *adv* within limits.
fīnītimus *adj* neighbouring, adjoining; akin, like ♦ *mpl* neighbours.
fīnītor, -ōris *m* surveyor.
fīnitumus *adj see* **fīnitimus.**
fīnītus *ppp of* **fīniō** ♦ *adj* (*RHET*) well-rounded.
finxī *perf of* **fingō.**
fīō, fierī, factus *vi* to become, arise; to be made, be done; to happen; **quī fit ut?** how is it that?; **ut fit** as usually happens; **quid mē fīet?** what will become of me?
firmāmen, -inis *nt* support.
firmāmentum, -ī *nt* support, strengthening; (*fig*) mainstay.
firmātor, -ōris *m* establisher.
firmē *adv* powerfully, steadily.
firmitās, -ātis *f* firmness, strength; steadfastness, stamina.
firmiter *adv see* **firmē.**
firmitūdō, -inis *f* strength, stability.
firmō, -āre, -āvī, -ātum *vt* to strengthen, support, fortify; (*mind*) to encourage,

steady; (*fact*) to confirm, prove, assert.

firmus *adj* strong, stable, firm; (*fig*) powerful, constant, sure, true.

fiscella, -ae *f* wicker basket.

fiscina, -ae *f* wicker basket.

fiscus, -ī *m* purse, moneybox; public exchequer; imperial treasury, the emperor's privy purse.

fissilis *adj* easy to split.

fissiō, -ōnis *f* dividing.

fissum, -ī *nt* slit, fissure.

fissus *ppp of* **findō**.

fistūca, -ae *f* rammer.

fistula, -ae *f* pipe, tube; panpipes; (*MED*) ulcer.

fistulātor, -ōris *m* panpipe player.

fīsus *ppa of* **fīdō**.

fixī *perf of* **fīgō**.

fīxus *ppp of* **fīgō** ♦ *adj* fixed, fast, permanent.

flābellifera, -ae *f* fanbearer.

flābellum, -ī *nt* fan.

flābilis *adj* airy.

flābra, -ōrum *ntpl* blasts, gusts; wind.

flacceō, -ēre *vi* to flag, lose heart.

flaccēscō, -ere *vi* to flag, droop.

flaccidus *adj* flabby, feeble.

flaccus *adj* flap-eared.

Flaccus, -ī *m* surname of Horace.

flagellō, -āre *vt* to whip, lash.

flagellum, -ī *nt* whip, lash; strap, thong; (*vine*) shoot; (*polyp*) arm; (*feelings*) sting.

flāgitātiō, -ōnis *f* demand.

flāgitātor, -ōris *m* demander, dun.

flāgitiōsē *adv* infamously.

flāgitiōsus *adj* disgraceful, profligate.

flāgitium, -ī *and* **iī** *nt* offence, disgrace, shame; scoundrel.

flāgitō, -āre, -āvī, -ātum *vt* to demand, importune, dun; (*law*) to summon.

flagrāns, -antis *pres p of* **flagrō** ♦ *adj* hot, blazing; brilliant; passionate.

flagranter *adv* passionately.

flagrantia, -ae *f* blazing; (*fig*) shame.

flagrō, -āre *vi* to blaze, burn, be on fire; (*feelings*) to be excited, be inflamed; (*ill-will*) to be the victim of.

flagrum, -ī *nt* whip, lash.

flāmen, -inis *m* priest of a particular deity.

flāmen, -inis *nt* blast, gale, wind.

flāminica, -ae *f* wife of a priest.

Flāminīnus, -ī *m* Roman surname (*esp the conqueror of Philip V of Macedon*).

flāminium, -ī *and* **iī** *nt* priesthood.

Flāminius, -ī *m* Roman family name (*esp the consul defeated by Hannibal*).

Flāminius, -iānus *adj*: **Via ~ia** road from Rome N.E. to Ariminum.

flamma, -ae *f* flame, fire; torch, star; fiery colour; (*fig*) passion; danger, disaster.

flammeolum, -ī *nt* bridal veil.

flammēscō, -ere *vi* to become fiery.

flammeus *adj* fiery, blazing; flame-coloured ♦ *nt* bridal veil.

flammifer, -ī *adj* fiery.

flammō, -āre, -āvī, -ātum *vi* to blaze ♦ *vt* to set on fire, burn; (*fig*) to inflame, incense.

flammula, -ae *f* little flame.

flātus, -ūs *m* blowing, breath; breeze; (*fig*) arrogance.

flāvēns, -entis *adj* yellow, golden.

flāvēscō, -ere *vi* to turn yellow.

Flāviānus *adj see n.*

Flāvius, -ī *m* Roman family name (*esp the emperors Vespasian, Titus and Domitian*).

flāvus *adj* yellow, golden.

flēbilis *adj* lamentable; tearful, mournful.

flēbiliter *adv see* **flēbilis**.

flectō, -ctere, -xī, -xum *vt* to bend, turn; to turn aside, wheel; (*promontory*) to round; (*mind*) to direct, persuade, dissuade ♦ *vi* to turn, march.

fleō, -ēre, -ēvī, -ētum *vi* to weep, cry ♦ *vt* to lament, mourn for.

flētus, -ūs *m* weeping, tears.

flexanimus *adj* moving.

flexī *perf of* **flectō**.

flexibilis *adj* pliant, flexible; fickle.

flexilis *adj* pliant.

flexiloquus *adj* ambiguous.

flexiō, -ōnis *f* bending, winding, (*voice*) modulation.

flexipēs, -edis *adj* twining.

flexuōsus *adj* tortuous.

flexūra, -ae *f* bending.

flexus *ppp of* **flectō** ♦ *adj* winding.

flexus, -ūs *m* winding, bending; change.

flīctus, -ūs *m* collision.

flō, -āre, -āvī, -ātum *vt, vi* to blow; (*money*) to coin.

floccus, -ī *m* bit of wool; triviality; **~ī nōn faciō** ≈ *I don't care a straw for.*

Flōra, -ae *f* goddess of flowers.

Flōrālis *adj see n.*

flōrēns, -entis *pres p of* **flōreō** ♦ *adj* in bloom; bright; prosperous, flourishing.

flōreō, -ēre, -uī *vi* to blossom, flower; (*age*) to be in one's prime; (*wine*) to froth; (*fig*) to flourish, prosper; (*places*) to be gay with.

flōrēscō, -ere *vi* to begin to flower; to grow prosperous.

flōreus *adj* of flowers, flowery.

flōridulus *adj* pretty, little.

flōridus *adj* of flowers, flowery; fresh, pretty; (*style*) florid, ornate.

flōrifer, -ī *adj* flowery.

flōrilegus *adj* flower-sipping.

flōrus *adj* beautiful.

flōs, -ōris *m* flower, blossom; (*wine*) bouquet; (*age*) prime, heyday; (*youth*) downy beard, youthful innocence; (*fig*) crown, glory; (*speech*) ornament.

Noun declensions and verb conjugations are shown on pp xiii to xxv. The present infinitive ending of a verb shows to which conjugation it belongs: **-āre** = 1st; **-ēre** = 2nd; **-ere** = 3rd and **-īre** = 4th. Irregular verbs are shown on p xxvi

flōsculus, -ī *m* little flower; (*fig*) pride, ornament.

flūctifragus *adj* surging.

flūctuātiō, -ōnis *f* wavering.

flūctuō, -āre *vi* to toss, wave; (*fig*) to rage, swell, waver.

flūctuōsus *adj* stormy.

flūctus, -ūs *m* wave; flowing, flood; (*fig*) disturbance; **~ūs** (*pl*) **in simpulō** ≈ *a storm in a teacup.*

fluēns, -entis *pres p of* **fluō** ♦ *adj* lax, loose, enervated; (*speech*) fluent.

fluenta, -ōrum *ntpl* stream, flood.

fluenter *adv* in a flowing manner.

fluentisonus *adj* wave-echoing.

fluidus *adj* flowing, fluid; lax, soft; relaxing.

fluitō, -āre *vi* to flow, float about; to wave, flap, move unsteadily; (*fig*) to waver.

flūmen, -inis *nt* stream, river; (*fig*) flood, flow, fluency; **adversō ~ine** upstream; **secundō ~ine** downstream.

flūmineus *adj* river- (*in cpds*).

fluō, -ere, -xī, -xum *vi* to flow; to overflow, drip; (*fig*) to fall in, fall away, vanish; (*speech*) to run evenly; (*CIRCS*) to proceed, tend.

flūtō *etc see* **fluitō**.

fluviālis *adj* river- (*in cpds*).

fluviātilis *adj* river- (*in cpds*).

flūvidus *etc see* **fluidus**.

fluvius, -ī *and* **iī** *m* river, stream.

fluxi *perf of* **fluō**.

fluxus *adj* flowing, loose, leaky; (*person*) lax, dissolute; (*thing*) frail, fleeting, unreliable.

fōcāle, -is *nt* scarf.

foculus, -ī *m* stove, fire.

focus, -ī *m* hearth, fireplace; pyre, altar; (*fig*) home.

fodicō, -āre *vt* to nudge, jog.

fodiō, -ere, fōdī, fossum *vt* to dig; to prick, stab; (*fig*) to goad.

foedē *adv see* **foedus**.

foederātus *adj* confederated.

foedifragus *adj* perfidious.

foeditās, -ātis *f* foulness, hideousness.

foedō, -āre, -āvī, -ātum *vt* to mar, disfigure; to disgrace, sully.

foedus *adj* foul, hideous, revolting; vile, disgraceful.

foedus, -eris *nt* treaty, league; agreement, compact; law.

foen- *etc see* **faen-**.

foeteō, -ēre *vi* to stink.

foetidus *adj* stinking.

foetor, -ōris *m* stench.

foetu- *etc see* **fētu-**.

foliātum, -ī *nt* nard oil.

folium, -ī *and* **iī** *nt* leaf.

folliculus, -ī *m* small bag; eggshell.

follis, -is *m* bellows; punchball; purse.

fōmentum, -ī *nt* poultice, bandage; (*fig*) alleviation.

fōmes, -itis *m* tinder, kindling.

fōns, fontis *m* spring, source; water; (*fig*) origin, fountainhead.

fontānus *adj* spring- (*in cpds*).

fonticulus, -ī *m* little spring.

for, fārī, fātus *vt, vi* to speak, utter.

forābilis *adj* penetrable.

forāmen, -inis *nt* hole, opening.

forās *adv* out, outside.

forceps, -ipis *m/f* tongs, forceps.

forda, -ae *f* cow in calf.

fore, forem *fut infin, imperf subj of* **sum**.

forēnsis *adj* public, forensic; of the marketplace.

foris, -is *f* (*usu pl*) door; (*fig*) opening, entrance.

forīs *adv* out of doors, outside, abroad; from outside, from abroad; **~ cēnāre** dine out.

fōrma, -ae *f* form, shape, appearance; mould, stamp, last; (*person*) beauty; (*fig*) idea, nature, kind.

fōrmāmentum, -ī *nt* shape.

fōrmātūra, -ae *f* shaping.

Formiae, -ārum *fpl* town in S. Latium.

Formiānus *adj* of Formiae ♦ *nt* villa at Formiae.

formīca, -ae *f* ant.

formīcinus *adj* crawling.

formīdābilis *adj* terrifying.

formīdō, -āre, -āvī, -ātum *vt, vi* to fear, be terrified.

formīdō, -inis *f* terror, awe, horror; scarecrow.

formīdolōsē *adv see* **formīdolōsus**.

formīdolōsus *adj* fearful, terrifying; afraid.

fōrmō, -āre, -āvī, -ātum *vt* to shape, fashion, form.

fōrmōsitās, -ātis *f* beauty.

fōrmōsus *adj* beautiful, handsome.

fōrmula, -ae *f* rule, regulation; (*law*) procedure, formula; (*PHILOS*) principle.

fornācula, -ae *f* small oven.

fornāx, -ācis *f* furnace, oven, kiln.

fornicātus *adj* arched.

fornix, -icis *m* arch, vault; brothel.

forō, -āre *vt* to pierce.

Foroiūliēnsis *adj see* **Forum Iuli**.

fors, fortis *f* chance, luck ♦ *adv* perchance; **~te** by chance, as it happened; perhaps; **nē ~te** in case; **sī ~te** if perhaps; in the hope that.

forsan, forsit, forsitan *adv* perhaps.

fortasse, -is *adv* perhaps, possibly; (*irony*) very likely.

forticulus *adj* quite brave.

fortis *adj* strong, sturdy; brave, manly, resolute.

fortiter *adv* vigorously; bravely.

fortitūdō, -inis *f* courage, resolution; strength.

fortuītō *adv* by chance.

fortuītus *adj* casual, accidental.

fortūna, -ae *f* chance, luck, fortune; good luck, success; misfortune; circumstances, lot; (*pl*) possessions; **~ae fīlius** Fortune's

favourite; **~am habēre** be successful.
fortūnātē *adv see* **fortūnātus.**
fortūnātus *adj* happy, lucky; well off, rich, blessed.
fortūnō, -āre *vt* to bless, prosper.
forulī, -ōrum *mpl* bookcase.
forum, -ī *nt* public place, market; market town; *Roman Forum between the Palatine and Capitol*; public affairs, law courts, business; **~ boārium** cattle market; **~ olitōrium** vegetable market; **~ piscātorium** fish market; **~ agere** hold an assize; **~ attingere** enter public life; **cēdere ~ō** go bankrupt; **utī ~ō** take advantage of a situation.
Forum Iūli colony in S. Gaul (*now* Fréjus).
forus, -ī *m* gangway; block of seats; (*bees*) cell frame.
fossa, -ae *f* ditch, trench.
fossiō, -ōnis *f* digging.
fossor, -ōris *m* digger.
fossus *ppp of* **fodiō.**
fōtus *ppp of* **foveō.**
fovea, -ae *f* pit, pitfall.
foveō, -ēre, fōvī, fōtum *vt* to warm, keep warm; (*MED*) to foment; to fondle, keep; (*fig*) to cherish, love, foster, pamper, encourage; **castra ~** remain in camp.
frāctus *ppp of* **frangō** ♦ *adj* weak, faint.
frāga, -ōrum *ntpl* strawberries.
fragilis *adj* brittle, fragile; frail, fleeting.
fragilitās, -ātis *f* frailness.
fragmen, -inis *nt* (*pl*) fragments, ruins, wreck.
fragmentum, -ī *nt* fragment, remnant.
fragor, -ōris *m* crash, din; disintegration.
fragōsus *adj* crashing, roaring, breakable; rough.
frāgrāns, -antis *adj* fragrant.
framea, -ae *f* German spear.
frangō, -angere, -ēgī, -āctum *vt* to break, shatter, wreck; to crush, grind; (*fig*) to break down, weaken, humble; (*emotion*) to touch, move; **cervīcem ~** strangle.
frāter, -ris *m* brother; cousin; (*fig*) friend, ally.
frāterculus, -ī *m* brother.
frāternē *adv* like a brother.
frāternitās, -ātis *f* brotherhood.
frāternus *adj* brotherly, a brother's, fraternal.
frātricīda, -ae *m* fratricide.
fraudātiō, -ōnis *f* deceit, fraud.
fraudātor, -ōris *m* swindler.
fraudō, -āre, -āvī, -ātum *vt* to cheat, defraud; to steal, cancel.
fraudulentus *adj* deceitful, fraudulent.
fraus, -audis *f* deceit, fraud; delusion, error; offence, wrong; injury, damage; **lēgī ~dem facere** evade the law; **in ~dem incidere** be disappointed; **sine ~de** without harm.
fraxineus, fraxinus *adj* of ash.
fraxinus, -ī *f* ash tree; ashen spear.

Fregellae, -ārum *fpl* town in S. Latium.
Fregellānus *adj see* n.
frēgī *perf of* **frangō.**
fremebundus *adj* roaring.
fremitus, -ūs *m* roaring, snorting, noise.
fremō, -ere, -uī, -itum *vi* to roar, snort, grumble ♦ *vt* to shout for, complain.
fremor, -ōris *m* murmuring.
frendō, -ere *vi* to gnash the teeth.
frēnō, -āre, -āvī, -ātum *vt* to bridle; (*fig*) to curb, restrain.
frēnum, -ī *nt* (*pl* **-a, -ōrum** *nt*, **-ī, -ōrum** *m*) bridle, bit; (*fig*) curb, check; **~ōs dare** give vent to; **~um mordēre** ≈ *take the bit between one's teeth.*
frequēns, -entis *adj* crowded, numerous, populous; regular, repeated, frequent; **~ senatus** a crowded meeting of the senate.
frequentātiō, -ōnis *f* accumulation.
frequenter *adv* in large numbers; repeatedly, often.
frequentia, -ae *f* full attendance, throng, crowd.
frequentō, -āre, -āvī, -ātum *vt* to crowd, populate; to visit repeatedly, frequent; to repeat; (*festival*) to celebrate, keep.
fretēnsis *adj* of the Straits of Messina.
fretum, -ī *nt* strait; sea; (*fig*) violence; **~ Siciliēnse** Straits of Messina.
fretus, -ūs *m* strait.
frētus *adj* relying, confident.
fricō, -āre, -uī, -tum *vt* to rub, rub down.
frīctus *ppp of* **frīgō.**
frīgefactō, -āre *vt* to cool.
frīgeō, -ēre *vi* to be cold; (*fig*) to be lifeless, flag; to be coldly received, fall flat.
frīgerāns *adj* cooling.
frīgescō, -ere *vi* to grow cold; to become inactive.
frīgida, -ae *f* cold water.
frīgidē *adv* feebly.
frīgidulus *adj* rather cold, faint.
frīgidus *adj* cold, cool; chilling; (*fig*) dull, torpid; (*words*) flat, uninteresting.
frīgō, -gere, -xī, -ctum *vt* to roast, fry.
frīgus, -oris *nt* cold; cold weather, winter; death; (*fig*) dullness, inactivity; coldness, indifference.
friguttiō, -īre *vi* to stammer.
friō, -āre *vt* to crumble.
fritillus, -ī *m* dice box.
frīvolus *adj* empty, paltry.
frīxī *perf of* **frīgō.**
frondātor, -ōris *m* vinedresser, pruner.
frondeō, -ēre *vi* to be in leaf.
frondēscō, -ere *vi* to become leafy, shoot.
frondeus *adj* leafy.
frondifer, -ī *adj* leafy.
frondōsus *adj* leafy.
frōns, -ondis *f* leaf, foliage; garland of leaves.

Noun declensions and verb conjugations are shown on pp xiii to xxv. The present infinitive ending of a verb shows to which conjugation it belongs: **-āre** = 1st; **-ēre** = 2nd; **-ere** = 3rd and **-īre** = 4th. Irregular verbs are shown on p xxvi

frōns, -ontis _f_ forehead, brow; front, facade; (_fig_) look, appearance, exterior; **~ontem contrahere** frown; **ā ~onte** in front; **in ~onte** in breadth.

frontālia, -um _ntpl_ frontlet.

frontō, -ōnis _m_ a broad-browed man.

frūctuārius _adj_ productive; paid for out of produce.

fructuōsus _adj_ productive; profitable.

frūctus _ppa of_ **fruor.**

frūctus, -ūs _m_ enjoyment; revenue, income; produce, fruit; (_fig_) consequence, reward; **~uī esse** be an asset (to); **~um percipere** reap the fruits (of).

frūgālis _adj_ thrifty, worthy.

frūgālitās, -ātis _f_ thriftiness, restraint.

frūgāliter _adv_ temperately.

frūgēs _etc see_ **frūx.**

frūgī _adj_ (_indecl_) frugal, temperate, honest; useful.

frūgifer, -ī _adj_ fruitful, fertile.

frūgiferēns, -entis _adj_ fruitful.

frūgilegus _adj_ food-gatherering.

frūgiparus _adj_ fruitful.

frūmentārius _adj_ of corn, corn- (_in cpds_) ♦ _m_ corn dealer; **lēx ~a** law about the distribution of corn; **rēs ~a** commissariat.

frūmentātiō, -ōnis _f_ foraging.

frūmentātor, -ōris _m_ corn merchant, forager.

frūmentor, -ārī, -ātus _vi_ to go foraging.

frūmentum, -ī _nt_ corn, grain, (_pl_) crops.

frūnīscor, -ī _vt_ to enjoy.

fruor, -uī, -ūctus _vt, vi_ (_usu with abl_) to enjoy, enjoy the company of; (_law_) to have the use and enjoyment of.

frūstillātim _adv_ in little bits.

frūstrā _adv_ in vain, for nothing; groundlessly; in error; **~ esse** be deceived; **~ habēre** foil.

frūstrāmen, -inis _nt_ deception.

frūstrātiō, -ōnis _f_ deception, frustration.

frūstrō, -āre; -or, -ārī, -ātus _vt_ to deceive, trick.

frūstulentus _adj_ full of crumbs.

frūstum, -ī _nt_ bit, scrap.

frutex, -icis _m_ bush, shrub; (_comedy_) blockhead.

fruticētum, -ī _nt_ thicket.

fruticor, -ārī _vi_ to sprout.

fruticōsus _adj_ bushy.

frūx, -ūgis _f_, **-ūgēs, -ūgum** fruits of the earth, produce; (_fig_) reward, success; virtue; **sē ad ~ūgem bonam recipere** reform.

fuam _old pres subj of_ **sum.**

fūcātus _adj_ counterfeit, artificial.

fūcō, -āre, -āvī, -ātum _vt_ to paint, dye (_esp red_).

fūcōsus _adj_ spurious.

fūcus, -ī _m_ red dye, rouge; bee glue; (_fig_) deceit, pretence.

fūcus, -ī _m_ drone.

fūdī _perf of_ **fundō.**

fuga, -ae _f_ flight, rout; banishment; speed,

swift passing; refuge; (_fig_) avoidance, escape; **~am facere, in ~am dare** put to flight.

fugācius _adv_ more timidly.

fugāx, -ācis _adj_ timorous, shy, fugitive; swift, transient; (_with gen_) avoiding.

fūgī _perf of_ **fugiō.**

fugiēns, -entis _pres p of_ **fugiō** ♦ _adj_ fleeting, dying; averse (to).

fugiō, -ere, fūgī, -itum _vi_ to flee, run away, escape; to go into exile; (_fig_) to vanish, pass swiftly ♦ _vt_ to flee from, escape from; to shun, avoid; (_fig_) to escape, escape notice of; **~e quaerere** do not ask; **mē ~it** I do not notice _or_ know.

fugitīvus, -ī _m_ runaway slave, truant, deserter ♦ _adj_ fugitive.

fugitō, -āre _vt_ to flee from, shun.

fugō, -āre, -āvī, -ātum _vt_ to put to flight; to banish; to rebuff.

fulcīmen, -inis _nt_ support.

fulciō, -cīre, -sī, -tum _vt_ to prop, support; to strengthen, secure; (_fig_) to sustain, bolster up.

fulcrum, -ī _nt_ bedpost; couch.

fulgeō, -gēre, -sī _vi_ to flash, lighten; to shine; (_fig_) to be illustrious.

fulgidus _adj_ flashing.

fulgō _etc see_ **fulgeō.**

fulgor, -ōris _m_ lightning; flash, brightness; (_fig_) splendour.

fulgur, -is _nt_ lightning; thunderbolt; splendour.

fulgurālis _adj_ on lightning as an omen.

fulgurātor, -ōris _m_ interpreter of lightning.

fulgurītus _adj_ struck by lightning.

fulgurō, -āre _vi_ to lighten.

fulica, -ae _f_ coot.

fūlīgō, -inis _f_ soot; black paint.

fulix, -cis _f see_ **fulica.**

fullō, -ōnis _m_ fuller.

fullōnius _adj_ fuller's.

fulmen, -inis _nt_ thunderbolt; (_fig_) disaster.

fulmenta, -ae _f_ heel of a shoe.

fulmineus _adj_ of lightning; (_fig_) deadly.

fulminō, -āre _vi_ to lighten; (_fig_) to threaten.

fulsī _perf of_ **fulciō;** _perf of_ **fulgeō.**

fultūra, -ae _f_ support.

fultus _ppp of_ **fulciō.**

Fulvia, -iae _f_ wife of M. Antony.

Fulvius, -ī _m_ Roman family name.

fulvus _adj_ yellow, tawny, dun.

fūmeus _adj_ smoking.

fūmidus _adj_ smoky, smoking.

fūmifer, -ī _adj_ smoking.

fūmificō, -āre _vi_ to burn incense.

fūmificus _adj_ steaming.

fūmō, -āre _vi_ to smoke, steam.

fūmōsus _adj_ smoky, smoked.

fūmus, -ī _m_ smoke, steam.

fūnāle, -is _nt_ cord; wax torch; chandelier.

fūnambulus, -ī _m_ tightrope walker.

fūnctiō, -ōnis _f_ performance.

fūnctus _ppa of_ **fungor.**

fūnda, -ae f sling; dragnet.

fundāmen, -inis nt foundation.

fundāmentum, -ī nt foundation; **~a agere, iacere** lay the foundations.

Fundānus adj see **Fundī.**

fundātor, -ōris m founder.

Fundī, -ōrum mpl coast town in Latium.

funditō, -āre vt to sling.

funditor, -ōris m slinger.

funditus adv utterly, completely; at the bottom.

fundō, -āre, -āvī, -ātum vt to found; to secure; (fig) to establish, make secure.

fundō, -ere, fūdī, fūsum vt to pour, shed, spill; (metal) to cast; (solids) to hurl, scatter, shower; (MIL) to rout; (crops) to produce in abundance; (speech) to utter; (fig) to spread, extend.

fundus, -ī m bottom; farm, estate; (law) authorizer.

fūnebris adj funeral- (in cpds); murderous.

fūnerātus adj killed.

fūnereus adj funeral- (in cpds); fatal.

fūnestō, -āre vt to pollute with murder, desecrate.

fūnestus adj deadly, fatal; sorrowful, in mourning.

fungīnus adj of a mushroom.

fungor, -gi, fūnctus vt, vi (usu with abl) to perform, discharge, do; to be acted on.

fungus, -ī m mushroom, fungus; (candle) clot on the wick.

fūniculus, -ī m cord.

fūnis, -is m rope, rigging; **~em dūcere** be the master.

fūnus, -eris nt funeral; death; corpse; ruin, destruction.

fūr, fūris m thief; slave.

fūrācissimē adv most thievishly.

fūrāx, -ācis adj thieving.

furca, -ae f fork; fork-shaped pole; pillory.

furcifer, -ī m gallows rogue.

furcilla, -ae f little fork.

furcillō, -āre vt to prop up.

furcula, -ae f forked prop; **~ae Caudīnae** Pass of Caudium.

furenter adv furiously.

furfur, -is m bran; scurf.

Furia, -ae f Fury, avenging spirit; madness, frenzy, rage.

furiālis adj of the Furies; frantic, fearful; infuriating.

furiāliter adv madly.

furibundus adj mad, frenzied.

furiō, -āre, -āvī, -ātum vt to madden.

furiōsē adv in a frenzy.

furiōsus adj mad, frantic.

furnus, -ī m oven.

furō, -ere vi to rave, rage, be mad, be crazy.

fūror, -ārī, -ātus vt to steal; to pillage; to impersonate.

furor, -ōris m madness, frenzy, passion.

fūrtificus adj thievish.

fūrtim adv by stealth, secretly.

fūrtīvē adv secretly.

fūrtīvus adj stolen; secret, furtive.

fūrtō adv secretly.

fūrtum, -ī nt theft, robbery; (pl) stolen goods; (fig) trick, intrigue.

fūrunculus, -ī m pilferer.

furvus adj black, dark.

fuscina, -ae f trident.

fuscō, -āre vt to blacken.

fuscus adj dark, swarthy; (voice) husky, muffled.

fūsē adv diffusely.

fūsilis adj molten, softened.

fūsiō, -ōnis f outpouring.

fūstis, -is m stick, club, cudgel; (MIL) beating to death.

fūstuārium, -ī and iī nt beating to death.

fūsus ppp of **fundō** ♦ adj broad, diffuse; copious.

fūsus, -ī m spindle.

futtile adv in vain.

futtilis adj brittle; worthless.

futtilitās, -ātis f futility.

futūrum, -ī nt future.

futūrus fut p of **sum** ♦ adj future, coming.

G, g

Gabiī, -iōrum mpl ancient town in Latium.

Gabinius, -ī m Roman family name (esp Aulus, tribune 67 B.C.).

Gabinius, -iānus adj: **lēx ~ia** law giving Pompey command against the pirates.

Gabīnus adj see **Gabiī.**

Gādēs, -ium fpl town in Spain (now Cadiz).

Gāditānus adj see n.

gaesum, -ī nt Gallic javelin.

Gaetūlī, -ōrum mpl African people N of Sahara.

Gaetūlus, -icus adj Gaetulian; African.

Gāius, -ī m Roman praenomen (esp emperor Caligula).

Gāius, -ia m/f (wedding ceremony) bridegroom, bride.

Galatae, -ārum mpl Galatians of Asia Minor.

Galatia, -iae f Galatia.

Galba, -ae m Roman surname (esp emperor 68–9).

galbaneus adj of galbanum, a Syrian plant.

Noun declensions and verb conjugations are shown on pp xiii to xxv. The present infinitive ending of a verb shows to which conjugation it belongs: **-āre** = 1st; **-ēre** = 2nd; **-ere** = 3rd and **-īre** = 4th. Irregular verbs are shown on p xxvi

galbinus *adj* greenish-yellow ♦ *ntpl* pale green clothes.
galea, -ae *f* helmet.
galeātus *adj* helmeted.
galērītus *adj* rustic.
galērum, -ī *nt*, **-us, -ī** *m* leather hood, cap; wig.
galla, -ae *f* oak apple.
Gallī, -ōrum *mpl* Gauls (people of what is now France and N. Italy).
Gallia, -iae *f* Gaul.
Gallicānus *adj* of Italian Gaul.
Gallicus *adj* Gallic ♦ *f* a Gallic shoe.
gallīna, -ae *f* hen; **~ae albae fīlius** fortune's favourite.
gallīnāceus *adj* of poultry.
gallīnārius, -ī *and* **iī** *m* poultry farmer.
Gallograecī, -ōrum *mpl* Galatians.
Gallograecia, -iae *f* Galatia.
gallus, -ī *m* cock.
Gallus, -ī *m* Gaul; Roman surname (esp the lyric poet; priest of Cybele).
ganēa, -ae *f* low eating house.
ganeō, -ōnis *m* profligate.
ganeum, -ī *nt* low eating house.
Gangaridae, -ārum *mpl* a people on the Ganges.
Gangēs, -is *m* river Ganges.
Gangēticus *adj* see n.
ganniō, -īre *vi* to yelp; (fig) to grumble.
gannītus, -ūs *m* yelping.
Ganymēdēs, -is *m* Ganymede, (cup bearer in Olympus).
Garamantes, -um *mpl* N. African tribe.
Garamantis, -idis *adj* see n.
Gargānus, -ī *m* mountain in E. Italy.
garriō, -īre *vi* to chatter.
garrulitās, -ātis *f* chattering.
garrulus *adj* talkative, babbling.
garum, -ī *nt* fish sauce.
Garumna, -ae *f* river Garonne.
gaudeō, -ēre, gāvīsus *vt, vi* to rejoice, be pleased, delight (in); **in sē, in sinū ~** be secretly pleased.
gaudium, -ī *and* **iī** *nt* joy, delight, enjoyment.
gaulus, -ī *m* bucket.
gausape, -is *nt*, **-a, -ōrum** *pl* a woollen cloth, frieze.
gāvīsus *ppa of* **gaudeō**.
gāza, -ae *f* treasure, riches.
gelidē *adv* feebly.
gelidus *adj* cold, frosty; stiff, numb; chilling ♦ *f* cold water.
gelō, -āre *vt* to freeze.
Gelōnī, -ōrum *mpl* Scythian tribe (now Ukraine).
gelū, -ūs *nt* frost, cold; chill.
gemebundus *adj* groaning.
gemellipara, -ae *f* mother of twins.
gemellus *adj* twin, double; alike ♦ *m* twin.
geminātiō, -ōnis *f* doubling.
geminō, -āre, -āvī, -ātum *vt* to double, bring together; to repeat ♦ *vi* to be double.

geminus *adj* twin, double, both; similar ♦ *mpl* twins (esp Castor and Pollux).
gemitus, -ūs *m* groan, sigh; moaning sound.
gemma, -ae *f* bud, precious stone, jewel; jewelled cup, signet.
gemmātus *adj* bejewelled.
gemmeus *adj* jewelled; sparkling.
gemmifer, -ī *adj* gem-producing.
gemmō, -āre *vi* to bud, sprout; to sparkle.
gemō, -ere, -uī, -itum *vi* to sigh, groan, moan ♦ *vt* to bewail.
Gemōniae, -ārum *fpl* steps in Rome on which bodies of criminals were thrown.
genae, -ārum *fpl* cheeks; eyes, eye sockets.
geneālogus, -ī *m* genealogist.
gener, -ī *m* son-in-law.
generālis *adj* of the species; universal.
generāliter *adv* generally.
generāscō, -ere *vi* to be produced.
generātim *adv* by species, in classes; in general.
generātor, -ōris *m* producer.
generō, -āre, -āvī, -ātum *vt* to breed, procreate.
generōsus *adj* high-born, noble; well-stocked; generous, chivalrous; (things) noble, honourable.
genesis, -is *f* birth; horoscope.
genethliacon, -ī *nt* birthday poem.
genetīvus *adj* native, inborn.
genetrix, -īcis *f* mother.
geniālis *adj* nuptial; joyful, genial.
geniāliter *adv* merrily.
geniculātus *adj* jointed.
genista, -ae *f* broom.
genitābilis *adj* productive.
genitālis *adj* fruitful, generative; of birth.
genitāliter *adv* fruitfully.
genitor, -ōris *m* father, creator.
genitus *ppp of* **gignō**.
genius, -ī *and* **iī** *m* guardian spirit; enjoyment, inclination; talent; **~iō indulgēre** enjoy oneself.
gēns, gentis *f* clan, family, stock, race; tribe, people, nation; descendant; (pl) foreign peoples; **minimē gentium** by no means; **ubi gentium** where in the world.
genticus *adj* national.
gentīlicius *adj* family.
gentīlis *adj* family, hereditary; national ♦ *m* kinsman.
gentīlitās, -ātis *f* clan relationship.
genū, -ūs *nt* knee.
genuālia, -um *ntpl* garters.
genuī *perf of* **gignō**.
genuīnus *adj* natural.
genuīnus *adj* of the cheek ♦ *mpl* back teeth.
genus, -eris *nt* birth, descent, noble birth, descendant, race; kind, class, species, respect, way; (logic) genus, general term; **id ~** of that kind; **in omnī ~ere** in all respects.
geōgraphia, -ae *f* geography.
geōmetrēs, -ae *m* geometer.

geōmetria, -ae f geometry.

geōmetricus adj geometrical ♦ ntpl geometry.

germānē adv sincerely.

Germānī, -ōrum mpl Germans.

Germānia, -iae f Germany.

Germānicus adj, m cognomen of Nero Claudius Drusus and his son.

germānitās, -ātis f brotherhood, sisterhood; relation of sister colonies.

germānus adj of the same parents, full (brother, sister); genuine, true ♦ m full brother ♦ f full sister.

germen, -inis nt bud, shoot; embryo; (fig) germ.

gerō, -rere, -ssī, -stum vt to carry, wear; to bring; (plants) to bear, produce; (feelings) to entertain, show; (activity) to conduct, manage, administer, wage; (time) spend; **mōrem** ~ comply, humour; **persōnam** ~ play a part; **sē** ~ behave; **sē medium** ~ be neutral; **prae sē** ~ exhibit; **rēs ~stae** exploits.

gerō, -ōnis nt carrier.

gerrae, -ārum fpl trifles, nonsense.

gerrō, -ōnis m idler.

gerulus, -ī m carrier.

Gēryōn, -onis m mythical three-bodied king killed by Hercules.

gessī perf of **gerō**.

gestāmen, -inis nt arms, ornaments, burden; litter, carriage.

gestiō, -ōnis f performance.

gestiō, -īre vi to jump for joy, be excited; to be very eager.

gestitō, -āre vt to always wear or carry.

gestō, -āre vt to carry about, usually wear; to fondle; to blab; (pass) to go for a ride, drive, sail.

gestor, -ōris m telltale.

gestus ppp of **gerō**.

gestus, -ūs m posture, gesture; gesticulation.

Getae, -ārum mpl Thracian tribe on the lower Danube.

Geticus adj Getan, Thracian.

gibbus, -ī m hump.

Gigantes, -um mpl Giants, sons of Earth.

Gigantēus adj see n.

gignō, -ere, genuī, genitum vt to beget, bear, produce; to cause.

gilvus adj pale yellow, dun.

gingīva, -ae f gum.

glaber, -rī adj smooth, bald ♦ m favourite slave.

glaciālis adj icy.

glaciēs, -ēī f ice.

glaciō, -āre vt to freeze.

gladiātor, -ōris m gladiator; (pl) gladiatorial show.

gladiātōrius adj of gladiators ♦ nt gladiators' pay.

gladiātūra, -ae f gladiator's profession.

gladius, -ī and **iī** m sword; (fig) murder, death; **~ium stringere** draw the sword; **suō sibi ~iō iugulāre** ≈ beat at his own game.

glaeba, -ae f sod, clod of earth; soil; lump.

glaebula, -ae f small lump; small holding.

glaesum etc see **glēsum**.

glandifer, -ī adj acorn-bearing.

glandium, -ī and **iī** nt glandule (in meat).

glāns, -andis f acorn, nut; bullet.

glārea, -ae f gravel.

glāreōsus adj gravelly.

glaucūma, -ae f cataract; **~am ob oculōs obicere** ≈ throw dust in the eyes of.

glaucus adj bluish grey.

glēba etc see **glaeba**.

glēsum, -ī nt amber.

glīs, -īris m dormouse.

glīscō, -ere vi to grow, swell, blaze up.

globōsus adj spherical.

globus, -ī m ball, sphere; (MIL) troop; mass, crowd, cluster.

glōmerāmen, -inis nt bell.

glomerō, -āre, -āvī, -ātum vt to form into a ball, gather, accumulate.

glomus, -eris nt ball of thread, clue.

glōria, -ae f glory, fame; ambition, pride, boasting; (pl) glorious deeds.

glōriātiō, -ōnis f boasting.

glōriola, -ae f a little glory.

glōrior, -ārī, -ātus vt, vi to boast, pride oneself.

glōriōsē adv see **glōriōsus**.

glōriōsus adj famous, glorious; boastful.

glūten, -inis nt glue.

glūtinātor, -ōris m bookbinder.

gluttiō, -īre vt to gulp down.

gnāruris, gnārus adj knowing, expert; known.

gnātus see **nātus**.

gnāvus see **nāvus**.

Gnōsius and **iacus** and **ias** adj of Cnossos, Cretan.

Gnōsis, -idis f Ariadne.

Gnōsus, -ī f Cnossos (ancient capital of Crete) ♦ f Ariadne.

gōbiō, -ōnis, gōbius, -ī and **iī** m gudgeon.

Gorgiās, -ae m Sicilian sophist and teacher of rhetoric.

Gorgō, -ōnis f mythical monster capable of turning men to stone, Medusa.

Gorgoneus adj: **equus** ~ Pegasus; **lacus** ~ Hippocrene.

Gortȳna, -ae f Cretan town.

Gortȳnius, -iacus adj Gortynian, Cretan.

gōrȳtos, -ī m quiver.

grabātus, -ī m camp bed, low couch.

Gracchānus adj see n.

Gracchus, -ī m Roman surname (esp the famous tribunes Tiberius and Gaius).

gracilis adj slender, slight, meagre, poor;

Noun declensions and verb conjugations are shown on pp xiii to xxv. The present infinitive ending of a verb shows to which conjugation it belongs: **-āre** = 1st; **-ēre** = 2nd; **-ere** = 3rd and **-īre** = 4th. Irregular verbs are shown on p xxvi

(*style*) plain.

gracilitās, -ātis *f* slimness, leanness; (*style*) simplicity.

grāculus, -ī *m* jackdaw.

gradātim *adv* step by step, gradually.

gradātiō, -ōnis *f* (*RHET*) climax.

gradior, -adī, -essus *vi* to step, walk.

Grādīvus, -ī *m* Mars.

gradus, -ūs *m* step, pace; stage, step towards; firm stand, position, standing; (*pl*) stair, steps; (*hair*) braid; (*MATH*) degree; (*fig*) degree, rank; **citātō, plēnō ~ū** at the double; **suspēnsō ~ū** on tiptoe; **dē ~ū deicī** be disconcerted.

Graecē *adv* in Greek.

Graecia, -iae *f* Greece; **Māgna ~** S. Italy.

graecissō, -āre *vi* to ape the Greeks.

graecor, -ārī *vi* to live like Greeks.

Graeculus *adj* (*contemptuous*) Greek.

Graecus *adj* Greek.

Grāiugena, -ae *m* Greek.

Grāius *adj* Greek.

grallātor, -ōris *m* stiltwalker.

grāmen, -inis *nt* grass; herb.

grāmineus *adj* grassy; of cane.

grammaticus *adj* literary, grammatical ♦ *m* teacher of literature and language ♦ *f/ntpl* grammar, literature, philology.

grānāria, -ōrum *ntpl* granary.

grandaevus *adj* aged, very old.

grandēscō, -ere *vi* to grow.

grandiculus *adj* quite big.

grandifer, -ī *adj* productive.

grandiloquus, -ī *m* grand speaker; boaster.

grandinat, -āre *vi* it hails.

grandis *adj* large, great, tall; old; strong; (*style*) grand, sublime; **~ nātū** old.

granditās, -ātis *f* grandeur.

grandō, -inis *f* hail.

grānifer, -ī *adj* grain-carrying.

grānum, -ī *nt* seed, grain.

graphicē *adv* nicely.

graphicus *adj* fine, masterly.

graphium, -ī and iī *nt* stilus, pen.

grassātor, -ōris *m* vagabond; robber, footpad.

grassor, -ārī, -ātus *vi* to walk about, prowl, loiter; (*action*) to proceed; (*fig*) to attack, rage against.

grātē *adv* with pleasure; gratefully.

grātēs *fpl* thanks.

grātia, -ae *f* charm, grace; favour, influence, regard, friendship; kindness, service; gratitude, thanks; **~am facere** excuse; **~am referre** return a favour; **in ~am redīre cum** be reconciled to; **~ās agere** thank; **~ās habēre** feel grateful; **~ā** (*with gen*) for the sake of; **eā ~ā** on that account; **~īs** for nothing.

Grātiae, -ārum *fpl* the three Graces.

grātificātiō, -ōnis *f* obligingness.

grātificor, -ārī *vi* to do a favour, oblige ♦ *vt* to make a present of.

gratiīs, grātīs *adv* for nothing.

grātiōsus *adj* in favour, popular; obliging.

grātor, -ārī, -ātus *vi* to rejoice, congratulate.

grātuītō *adv* for nothing.

grātuītus *adj* free, gratuitous.

grātulābundus *adj* congratulating.

grātulātiō, -ōnis *f* rejoicing; congratulation; public thanksgiving.

grātulor, -ārī, -ātus *vt, vi* to congratulate; to give thanks.

grātus *adj* pleasing, welcome, dear; grateful, thankful; (*acts*) deserving thanks; **~um facere** do a favour.

gravātē *adv* reluctantly, grudgingly.

gravātim *adv* unwillingly.

gravēdinōsus *adj* liable to colds.

gravēdō, -inis *f* cold in the head.

graveolēns, -entis *adj* strong-smelling.

gravēscō, -ere *vi* to become heavy; to grow worse.

graviditās, -ātis *f* pregnancy.

gravidō, -āre *vt* to impregnate.

gravidus *adj* pregnant; loaded, full.

gravis *adj* heavy; loaded, pregnant; (*smell*) strong, offensive; (*sound*) deep, bass; (*body*) sick; (*food*) indigestible; (*fig*) oppressive, painful, severe; important, influential, dignified.

gravitās, -ātis *f* weight, severity, sickness; importance, dignity, seriousness; **annōnae ~** high price of corn.

graviter *adv* heavily; strongly, deeply; severely, seriously, violently; gravely, with dignity; **~ ferre** be vexed at.

gravō, -āre *vt* to load, weigh down; to oppress, aggravate.

gravor, -ārī *vt, vi* to feel annoyed, object to, disdain.

gregālis *adj* of the herd, common ♦ *m* comrade.

gregārius *adj* common; (*MIL*) private.

gregātim *adv* in crowds.

gremium, -ī *nt* bosom, lap.

gressus *ppa of* **gradior.**

gressus, -ūs *m* step; course.

grex, -egis *m* flock, herd; company, troop.

grunniō, -īre *vi* to grunt.

grunnītus, -ūs *m* grunting.

grūs, -uis *f* crane.

grȳps, -ȳpis *m* griffin.

gubernāclum (gubernāculum), -ī *nt* rudder, tiller; helm, government.

gubernātiō, -ōnis *f* steering, management.

gubernātor, -ōris *m* steersman, pilot, governor.

gubernātrīx, -īcis *f* directress.

gubernō, -āre, -āvī, -ātum *vt* to steer, pilot; to manage, govern.

gula, -ae *f* gullet, throat; gluttony, palate.

gulōsus *adj* dainty.

gurges, -itis *m* abyss, deep water, flood; (*person*) spendthrift.

gurguliō, -ōnis *f* gullet, windpipe.

gurgustium, -ī and iī *nt* hovel, shack.

gustātus, -ūs m sense of taste; flavour.
gustō, -āre, -āvī, -ātum vt to taste; to have a snack; (fig) to enjoy, overhear; **prīmīs labrīs ~** have a superficial knowledge of.
gustus, -ūs m tasting; preliminary dish.
gutta, -ae f drop; spot, speck.
guttātim adv drop by drop.
guttur, -is nt throat, gluttony.
gūtus, -ī m flask.
Gyās, -ae m giant with a hundred arms.
Gȳgaeus adj see n.
Gȳgēs, -is and **ae** m king of Lydia (famed for his magic ring).
gymnasiarchus, -ī m master of a gymnasium.
gymnasium, -ī and **iī** nt sports ground, school.
gymnasticus adj gymnastic.
gymnicus adj gymnastic.
gynaecēum, -ēī and **ium, -ī** nt women's quarters.
gypsātus adj coated with plaster.
gypsum, -ī nt plaster of Paris; a plaster figure.
gȳrus, -ī m circle, coil, ring; course.

H, h

ha interj (expressing joy or laughter) hurrah!, ha ha!
habēna, -ae f strap; (pl) reins; (fig) control; **~ās dare, immittere** allow to run freely.
habeō, -ēre, -uī, -itum vt to have, hold; to keep, contain, possess; (fact) to know; (with infin) to be in a position to; (person) to treat, regard, consider; (action) to make, hold, carry out ♦ vi to have possessions; **ōrātiōnem ~** make a speech; **in animō ~** intend; **prō certō ~** be sure; **sē ~** find oneself, be; **sibi, sēcum ~** keep to oneself; (fight) **~et a** hit!; **bene ~et** it is well; **sīc ~et** so it is; **sīc ~ētō** be sure of this.
habilis adj manageable, handy; suitable, nimble, expert.
habilitās, -ātis f aptitude.
habitābilis adj habitable.
habitātiō, -ōnis f dwelling, house.
habitātor, -ōris m tenant, inhabitant.
habitō, -āre, -āvī, -ātum vt to inhabit ♦ vi to live, dwell; to remain, be always (in).
habitūdō, -inis f condition.
habitus ppp of **habeō** ♦ adj stout; in a humour.
habitus, -ūs m condition, appearance; dress;

character, quality; disposition, feeling.
hāc adv this way.
hāctenus adv thus far, so far; till now.
Hadria, -ae f town in N. Italy; Adriatic Sea.
Hadriānus, -ānī m emperor Hadrian.
Hadriāticus and **acus** adj of emperor Hadrian.
haedilia, -ae f little kid.
haedinus adj kid's.
haedulus, -ī m little kid.
haedus, -ī m kid; (ASTRO, usu pl) the Kids (a cluster in Auriga).
Haemonia, -ae f Thessaly.
Haemonius adj Thessalian.
Haemus, -ī m mountain range in Thrace.
haereō, -rēre, -sī, -sum vi to cling, stick, be attached; (nearness) to stay close, hang on; (continuance) to linger, remain (at); (stoppage) to stick fast, come to a standstill, be at a loss.
haerēscō, -ere vi to adhere.
haeresis, -is f sect.
haesī perf of **haereō**.
haesitantia, -ae f stammering.
haesitātiō, -ōnis f stammering; indecision.
haesitō, -āre vi to get stuck; to stammer; to hesitate, be uncertain.
hahae, hahahae see **ha**.
hālitus, -ūs m breath, vapour.
hallex, -icis m big toe.
hallūc- see **ālūc-**.
hālō, -āre vi to be fragrant ♦ vt to exhale.
hāluc etc see **ālūc**.
halyaeetos, -ī m osprey.
hama, -ae f water bucket.
Hamādryas, -adis f woodnymph.
hāmātilis adj with hooks.
hāmātus adj hooked.
Hamilcar, -is m father of Hannibal.
hāmus, -ī m hook; talons.
Hannibal, -is m famous Carthaginian general in 2nd Punic War.
hara, -ae f stye, pen.
harēna, -ae f sand; desert, seashore; arena (in the amphitheatre).
harēnōsus adj sandy.
hariola, -ae f, **hariolus, -ī** m soothsayer.
hariolor, -ārī vi to prophesy; to talk nonsense.
harmonia, -ae f concord, melody; (fig) harmony.
harpagō, -āre vt to steal.
harpagō, -ōnis m grappling hook; (person) robber.
harpē, -ēs f scimitar.
Harpȳiae, -ārum fpl Harpies (mythical monsters, half woman, half bird).
harundifer, -ī adj reed-crowned.
harundineus adj reedy.
harundinōsus adj abounding in reeds.
harundō, -inis f reed, cane; fishing rod; shaft, arrow; (fowling) limed twig; (music) pipe,

flute; (*toy*) hobbyhorse; (*weaving*) comb; (*writing*) pen.

haruspex, -icis *m* diviner (*from entrails*); prophet.

haruspica, -ae *f* soothsayer.

haruspicīnus *adj* of divination by entrails ♦ *f* art of such divination.

haruspicium, -ī *and* **iī** *nt* divination.

Hasdrubal, -is *m* brother of Hannibal.

hasta, -ae *f* spear, pike; sign of an auction sale; **sub ~ā vēndere** put up for auction.

hastātus *adj* armed with a spear ♦ *mpl* first line of Roman army in battle; **prīmus ~** 1st company of hastati.

hastīle, -is *nt* shaft, spear, javelin; vine prop.

hau, haud *adv* not, not at all.

hauddum *adv* not yet.

haudquāquam *adv* not at all, not by any means.

hauriō, -rīre, -sī, -stum *vt* to draw, draw off, derive; to drain, empty, exhaust; to take in, drink, swallow, devour.

haustus *ppp of* **hauriō**.

haustus, -ūs *m* drawing (water); drinking; drink, draught.

haut *etc see* **haud**.

hebdomas, -dis *f* week.

Hēbē, -ēs *f* goddess of youth (*cup bearer to the gods*).

hebenus, -ī *f* ebony.

hebeō, -ēre *vi* to be blunt, dull, sluggish.

hebes, -tis *adj* blunt, dull, sluggish; obtuse, stupid.

hebēscō, -ere *vi* to grow dim *or* dull.

hebetō, -āre *vt* to blunt, dull, dim.

Hebrus, -ī *m* Thracian river (*now* Maritza).

Hecatē, -ēs *f* goddess of magic (*and often identified with Diana*).

Hecatēius, -eis *adj see n.*

hecatombē, -ēs *f* hecatomb.

Hector, -is *m* son of Priam (*chief warrior of the Trojans against the Greeks*).

Hectoreus *adj* of Hector; Trojan.

Hecuba, -ae *and* **ē, -ēs** *f* wife of Priam.

hedera, -ae *f* ivy.

hederiger, -ī *adj* wearing ivy.

hederōsus *adj* covered with ivy.

hēdychrum, -ī *nt* a cosmetic perfume.

hei, heia *etc see* **ei, eia**.

Helena, -ae *and* **ē, -ēs** *f* Helen (*wife of Menelaus, abducted by Paris*).

Helenus, -ī *m* son of Priam (*with prophetic powers*).

Hēliades, -um *fpl* daughters of the Sun (*changed to poplars or alders, and their tears to amber*).

Helicē, -ēs *f* the Great Bear.

Helicōn, -ōnis *m* mountain in Greece sacred to Apollo and the Muses.

Helicōniades, -um *fpl* the Muses.

Helicōnius *adj see* **Helicōn**.

Hellas, -dis *f* Greece.

Hellē, -ēs *f* mythical Greek princess (*carried by the golden-fleeced ram, and drowned in the Hellespont*).

Hellēspontius, -iacus *adj see n.*

Hellēspontus, -ī *m* Hellespont (*now* Dardanelles).

helluō, -ōnis *m* glutton.

helluor, -ārī *vi* to be a glutton.

helvella, -ae *f* a savoury herb.

Helvētiī, -ōrum *mpl* people of E. Gaul (*now* Switzerland).

Helvētius, -cus *adj see n.*

hem *interj* (*expressing surprise*) eh?, well well!

hēmerodromus, -ī *m* express courier.

hēmicillus, -ī *m* mule.

hēmicyclium, -ī *and* **iī** *nt* semicircle with seats.

hēmina, -ae *f* half a pint.

hendecasyllabī, -ōrum *mpl* hendecasyllabics, verses of eleven syllables.

heptēris, -is *f* ship with seven banks of oars.

hera *etc see* **era**.

Hēra, -ae *f* Greek goddess identified with Juno.

Hēraclītus, -ī *m* early Greek philosopher.

Hēraea, -aeōrum *ntpl* festival of Hera.

herba, -ae *f* blade, young plant; grass, herb, weed.

herbēscō, -ere *vi* to grow into blades.

herbeus *adj* grass-green.

herbidus *adj* grassy.

herbifer, -ī *adj* grassy.

herbōsus *adj* grassy, made of turf; made of herbs.

herbula, -ae *f* little herb.

hercīscō, -ere *vt* to divide an inheritance.

hercle *interj* by Hercules!

herctum, -ī *nt* inheritance.

Hercule *interj* by Hercules!

Herculēs, -is *and* **ī** *m* mythical Greek hero, later deified.

Herculeus *adj:* **arbor ~** poplar; **urbs ~** Herculaneum.

here *etc see* **herī**.

hērēditārius *adj* inherited; about an inheritance.

hērēditās, -ātis *f* inheritance; **~ sine sacrīs** a gift without awkward obligations.

hērēdium, -ī *and* **iī** *nt* inherited estate.

hērēs, -ēdis *m/f* heir, heiress; (*fig*) master, successor.

herī *adv* yesterday.

herīlis *etc see* **erilis**.

Hermēs, -ae *m* Greek god identified with Mercury; Hermes pillar.

Hernicī, -ōrum *mpl* people of central Italy.

Hernicus *adj see n.*

Hērodotus, -ī *m* first Greek historian.

hērōicus *adj* heroic, epic.

hērōīna, -ae *f* demigoddess.

hērōis, -dis *f* demigoddess.

hērōs, -is *m* demigod, hero.

hērōus *adj* heroic, epic.

herus *etc see* **erus**.

Hēsiodēus, -ius *adj see n.*
Hēsiodus, -ī *m* Hesiod (*Greek didactic poet*).
Hesperia, -iae *f* Italy; Spain.
Hesperides, -idum *fpl keepers of a garden in the far West.*
Hesperius, -is *adj* western.
Hesperus, -ī *m* evening star.
hesternus *adj* of yesterday.
heu *interj* (*expressing dismay or pain*) oh!, alas!
heus *interj* (*calling attention*) ho!, hallo!
hexameter, -rī *m* hexameter verse.
hexēris, -is *f* ship with six banks of oars.
hiātus, -ūs *m* opening, abyss; open mouth, gaping; (*GRAM*) hiatus.
Hibēres, -um *mpl* Spaniards.
Hibēria, -iae *f* Spain.
hīberna, -ōrum *ntpl* winter quarters.
hībernācula, -ōrum *ntpl* winter tents.
Hibernia, -ae *f* Ireland.
hībernō, -āre *vi* to winter, remain in winter quarters.
hībernus *adj* winter, wintry.
Hibērus, -icus *adj* Spanish.
Hibērus, -ī *m* river Ebro.
hibīscum, -ī *nt* marsh mallow.
hibrida, hybrida, -ae *m/f* mongrel, half-breed.
hīc, haec, hōc *pron, adj* this; he, she, it; my, the latter, the present; **hīc homō** I; **hōc magis** the more; **hōc est** that is.
hīc *adv* here; herein; (*time*) at this point.
hīce, haece, hōce *emphatic forms of* **hīc, haec, hōc.**
hīcine, haecine, hōcine *emphatic forms of* **hīc, haec, hōc.**
hiemālis *adj* winter, stormy.
hiemō, -āre *vi* to pass the winter; to be wintry, stormy.
hiems, (hiemps), -is *f* winter; stormy weather, cold.
Hierōnymus, -ī *m* Jerome.
Hierosolyma, -ōrum *ntpl* Jerusalem.
Hierosolymārius *adj see n.*
hietō, -āre *vi* to yawn.
hilare *adv see* **hilaris.**
hilaris *adj* cheerful, merry.
hilaritās, -ātis *f* cheerfulness.
hilaritūdō, -inis *f* merriment.
hilarō, -āre *vt* to cheer, gladden.
hilarulus *adj* a gay little thing.
hilarus *etc see* **hilaris.**
hīllae, -ārum *fpl* smoked sausage.
Hīlōtae, -ārum *mpl* Helots (*of Sparta*).
hīlum, -ī *nt* something, a whit.
hinc *adv* from here, hence; on this side; from this source, for this reason; (*time*) henceforth.
hinniō, -īre *vi* to neigh.
hinnītus, -ūs *m* neighing.
hinnuleus, -ī *m* fawn.

hiō, -āre *vi* to be open, gape, yawn; (*speech*) to be disconnected, leave a hiatus ♦ *vt* to sing.
hippagōgī, -ōrum *fpl* cavalry transports.
hippocentaurus, -ī *m* centaur.
hippodromos, -ī *m* racecourse.
Hippolytus, -ī *m* son of Theseus (*slandered by stepmother Phaedra*).
hippomanes, -is *nt* mare's fluid; membrane on foal's forehead.
Hippōnactēus *adj* of Hipponax ♦ *m* iambic verse used by Hipponax.
Hippōnax, -ctis *m* Greek satirist.
hippotoxotae, -ārum *mpl* mounted archers.
hīra, -ae *f* the empty gut.
hircīnus *adj* of a goat.
hircōsus *adj* goatish.
hircus, -ī *m* he-goat; goatish smell.
hirnea, -ae *f* jug.
hirq- *etc see* **hirc-.**
hirsūtus *adj* shaggy, bristly; uncouth.
hirtus *adj* hairy, shaggy; rude.
hirūdō, -inis *f* leech.
hirundinīnus *adj* swallows'.
hirundō, -inis *f* swallow.
hīscō, -ere *vi* to gape; to open the mouth ♦ *vt* to utter.
Hispānia, -iae *f* Spain.
Hispāniēnsis, -us *adj* Spanish.
hispidus *adj* hairy, rough.
Hister, -rī *m* lower Danube.
historia, -ae *f* history, inquiry; story.
historicus *adj* historical ♦ *m* historian.
histricus *adj* of the stage.
histriō, -ōnis *m* actor.
histriōnālis *adj* of an actor.
histriōnia, -ae *f* acting.
hiulcē *adv* with hiatus.
hiulcō, -āre *vt* to split open.
hiulcus *adj* gaping, open; (*speech*) with hiatus.
hodiē *adv* today; nowadays, now; up to the present.
hodiernus *adj* today's.
holitor, -ōris *m* market gardener.
holitōrius *adj* for market gardeners.
holus, -eris *nt* vegetables.
holusculum, -ī *nt* small cabbage.
Homēricus *adj see n.*
Homērus, -ī *m* Greek epic poet, Homer.
homicīda, -ae *m* killer, murderer.
homicīdium, -ī and ī ī *nt* murder.
homō, -inis *m/f* human being, man; (*pl*) people, the world; (*derogatory*) fellow, creature; **inter ~inēs esse** be alive; see the world.
homullus, -ī, homunciō, -ōnis, homunculus, -ī *m* little man, poor creature, mortal.
honestās, -ātis *f* good character, honourable reputation; sense of honour, integrity;

Noun declensions and verb conjugations are shown on pp xiii to xxv. The present infinitive ending of a verb shows to which conjugation it belongs: **-āre** = 1st; **-ēre** = 2nd; **-ere** = 3rd and **-īre** = 4th. Irregular verbs are shown on p xxvi

(*things*) beauty.

honestē *adv* decently, virtuously.

honestō, -āre *vt* to honour, dignify, embellish.

honestus *adj* honoured, respectable; honourable, virtuous; (*appearance*) handsome ♦ *m* gentleman ♦ *nt* virtue, good; beauty.

honor, -ōris *m* honour, esteem; public office, position, preferment; award, tribute, offering; ornament, beauty; ~**ōris causā** out of respect; for the sake of; ~**ōrem praefārī** apologize for a remark.

honōrābilis *adj* a mark of respect.

honōrārius *adj* done out of respect, honorary.

honōrātē *adv* honourably.

honōrātus *adj* esteemed, distinguished; in high office; complimentary.

honōrificē *adv* in complimentary terms.

honōrificus *adj* complimentary.

honōrō, -āre, -āvī, -ātum *vt* to do honour to, embellish.

honōrus *adj* complimentary.

honōs *etc see* **honor.**

hōra, -ae *f* hour; time, season; (*pl*) clock; **in ~ās** hourly; **in ~am vīvere** ≈ *live from hand to mouth.*

hōraeum, -ī *nt* pickle.

Horātius, -ī *m* Roman family name (*esp the defender of Rome against Porsenna*); *the lyric poet Horace.*

Horātius *adj see n.*

hordeum, -ī *nt* barley.

horia, -ae *f* fishing smack.

hōrnō *adv* this year.

hōrnōtinus *adj* this year's.

hōrnus *adj* this year's.

hōrologium, -ī *and* **iī** *nt* clock.

horrendus *adj* fearful, terrible; awesome.

horrēns, -entis *pres p of* **horreō** ♦ *adj* bristling, shaggy.

horreō, -ēre, -uī *vi* to stand stiff, bristle; to shiver, shudder, tremble ♦ *vt* to dread; to be afraid, be amazed.

horrēscō, -ere *vi* to stand on end, become rough; to begin to quake; to start, be terrified ♦ *vt* to dread.

horreum, -ī *nt* barn, granary, store.

horribilis *adj* terrifying; amazing.

horridē *adv see* **horridus.**

horridulus *adj* protruding a little; unkempt; (*fig*) uncouth.

horridus *adj* bristling, shaggy, rough, rugged; shivering; (*manners*) rude, uncouth; frightening.

horrifer, -ī *adj* chilling; terrifying.

horrificē *adv* in awesome manner.

horrificō, -āre *vt* to ruffle; to terrify.

horrificus *adj* terrifying.

horrisonus *adj* dread-sounding.

horror, -ōris *m* bristling; shivering, ague; terror, fright, awe, a terror.

hōrsum *adv* this way.

hortāmen, -inis *nt* encouragement.

hortāmentum, -ī *nt* encouragement.

hortātiō, -ōnis *f* harangue, encouragement.

hortātor, -ōris *m* encourager.

hortātus, -ūs *m* encouragement.

Hortēnsius, -ī *m* Roman family name (*esp an orator in Cicero's time*).

hortor, -ārī, -ātus *vt* to urge, encourage, exhort, harangue.

hortulus, -ī *m* little garden.

hortus, -ī *m* garden; (*pl*) park.

hospes, -itis *m*, **hospita, -ae** *f* host, hostess; guest, friend; stranger, foreigner ♦ *adj* strange.

hospitālis *adj* host's, guest's; hospitable.

hospitālitās, -ātis *f* hospitality.

hospitāliter *adv* hospitably.

hospitium, -ī *and* **iī** *nt* hospitality, friendship; lodging, inn.

hostia, -ae *f* victim, sacrifice.

hostiātus *adj* provided with victims.

hosticus *adj* hostile; strange ♦ *nt* enemy territory.

hostīlis *adj* of the enemy, hostile.

hostīliter *adv* in hostile manner.

hostīmentum, -ī *nt* recompense.

hostiō, -īre *vt* to requite.

hostis, -is *m/f* enemy.

hūc *adv* hither, here; to this, to such a pitch; ~ **illūc** hither and thither.

hui *interj* (*expressing surprise*) ho!, my word!

hūiusmodī *such.*

hūmānē, -iter *adv* humanly; gently, politely.

hūmānitās, -ātis *f* human nature, mankind; humanity, kindness, courtesy; culture, refinement.

hūmānitus *adv* in accordance with human nature; kindly.

hūmānus *adj* human, humane, kind, courteous; cultured, refined, well-educated; ~**ō māior** superhuman.

humātiō, -ōnis *f* burying.

hūme-, hūmi- *see* **ūme-, ūmi-.**

humilis *adj* low, low-lying, shallow; (*condition*) lowly, humble, poor; (*language*) commonplace; (*mind*) mean, base.

humilitās, -ātis *f* low position, smallness, shallowness; lowliness, insignificance; meanness, baseness.

humiliter *adv* meanly, humbly.

humō, -āre, -āvī, -ātum *vt* to bury.

humus, -ī *f* earth, ground; land; ~**ī** on the ground.

hyacinthinus *adj* of the hyacinthus.

hyacinthus, -ī *m* iris, lily.

Hyades, -um *fpl* Hyads (*a group of stars in Taurus*).

hyaena, -ae *f* hyena.

hyalus, -ī *m* glass.

Hybla, -ae *f* mountain in Sicily (*famous for bees*).

Hyblaeus *adj see n.*

hybrida *etc see* **hibrida.**

Hydaspēs, -is *m* tributary of river Indus (*now* Jelum).

Hȳdra, -ae *f* hydra (*a mythical dragon with seven heads*).

hydraulus, -ī *m* water organ.

hydria, -ae *f* ewer.

Hydrochous, -ī *m* Aquarius.

hydrōpicus *adj* suffering from dropsy.

hydrōps, -is *m* dropsy.

hydrus, -ī *m* serpent.

Hylās, -ae *m* a youth loved by Hercules.

Hymēn, -enis, Hymenaeus, -ī *m* god of marriage; wedding song; wedding.

Hymettius *adj see n.*

Hymettus, -ī *m* mountain near Athens (*famous for honey and marble*).

Hypanis, -is *m* river of Sarmatia (*now* Bug).

Hyperboreī, -ōrum *mpl* fabulous people in the far North.

Hyperboreus *adj see n.*

Hyperīōn, -onis *m* father of the Sun; the Sun.

hypodidasculus, -ī *m* assistant teacher.

hypomnēma, -tis *nt* memorandum.

Hyrcānī, -ōrum *mpl* people on the Caspian Sea.

Hyrcānus *adj* Hyrcanian.

I, i

Iacchus, -ī *m* Bacchus; wine.

iaceō, -ēre, -uī *vi* to lie; to be ill, lie dead; (*places*) to be situated, be flat *or* low-lying, be in ruins; (*dress*) to hang loose; (*fig*) to be inactive, be downhearted; (*things*) to be dormant, neglected, despised.

iaciō, -ere, iēcī, iactum *vt* to throw; to lay, build; (*seed*) to sow; (*speech*) to cast, let fall, mention.

iactāns, -antis *pres p of* **iactō** ♦ *adj* boastful.

iactanter *adv* ostentatiously.

iactantia, -ae *f* boasting, ostentation.

iactātiō, -ōnis *f* tossing, gesticulation; boasting, ostentation; ~ **populāris** publicity.

iactātus, -ūs *m* waving.

iactitō, -āre *vt* to mention, bandy.

iactō, -āre, -āvī, -ātum *vt* to throw, scatter; to shake, toss about; (*mind*) to disquiet; (*ideas*) to consider, discuss, mention; (*speech*) to boast of; **sē ~** waver, fluctuate; to behave ostentatiously, be officious.

iactūra, -ae *f* throwing overboard; loss, sacrifice.

iactus *ppp of* **iaciō**.

iactus, -ūs *m* throwing, throw; **intrā tēlī iactum** within spear's range.

iacuī *perf of* **iaceō**.

iaculābilis *adj* missile.

iaculātor, -ōris *m* thrower, shooter; light-armed soldier.

iaculātrīx, -īcis *f* huntress.

iaculor, -ārī, -ātus *vt* to throw, hurl, shoot; to throw the javelin; to shoot at, hit; (*fig*) to aim at, attack.

iaculum, -ī *nt* javelin; fishing net.

iāien- *etc see* **iēn-**.

iam *adv* (*past*) already, by then; (*present*) now, already; (*future*) directly, very soon; (*emphasis*) indeed, precisely; (*inference*) therefore, then surely; (*transition*) moreover, next; **iam dūdum** for a long time, long ago; immediately; **iam iam** right now, any moment now; **non ~** no longer; **iam ... iam** at one time ... at another; **iam nunc** just now; **iam prīdem** long ago, for a long time; **iam tum** even at that time; **sī iam** supposing for the purpose of argument.

iambēus *adj* iambic.

iambus, -ī *m* iambic foot; iambic poetry.

lānālis *adj see* **lānus**.

lāniculum, -ī *nt* Roman hill across the Tiber.

iānitor, -ōris *m* doorkeeper, porter.

iānua, -ae *f* door; entrance; (*fig*) key.

lānuārius *adj* of January ♦ *m* January.

lānus, -ī *m* god of gateways and beginnings; archway, arcade.

lapetīonidēs, -ae *m* Atlas.

lapetus, -ī *m* a Titan (*father of Atlas and Prometheus*).

lāpyx, -gis *adj* Iapygian; Apulian ♦ *m* west-north-west wind from Apulia.

lāsōn, -onis *m* Jason (*leader of Argonauts, husband of Medea*).

lāsonius *adj see n.*

iaspis, -dis *f* jasper.

Ībēr- *etc see* **Hībēr-**.

ibi *adv* there; then; in this, at it.

ibīdem *adv* in the same place; at that very moment.

Ibis, -is *and* **idis** *f* ibis.

Īcarium, -ī *nt* Icarian Sea.

Īcarius *adj see n.*

Īcarus, -ī *m* son of Daedalus (*drowned in the Aegean*).

īcō, -ere, -ī, ictum *vt* to strike; **foedus ~** make a treaty.

ictericus *adj* jaundiced.

ictis, -dis *f* weasel.

ictus *ppp of* **īcō**.

ictus, -ūs *m* stroke, blow; wound; (*metre*) beat.

Īda, -ae, -ē, -ēs *f* mountain in Crete; mountain near Troy.

Īdaeus *adj* Cretan; Trojan.

idcircō *adv* for that reason; for the purpose.

Noun declensions and verb conjugations are shown on pp xiii to xxv. The present infinitive ending of a verb shows to which conjugation it belongs: **-āre** = 1st; **-ēre** = 2nd; **-ere** = 3rd and **-īre** = 4th. Irregular verbs are shown on p xxvi

īdem, eadem, idem *pron* the same; also, likewise.

identidem *adv* repeatedly, again and again.

ideō *adv* therefore, for this reason, that is why.

idiōta, -ae *m* ignorant person, layman.

īdōlon, -ī *nt* apparition.

idōneē *adv see* **idōneus.**

idōneus *adj* fit, proper, suitable, sufficient.

Īdūs, -uum *fpl* Ides (*the 15th March, May, July, October, the 13th of other months*).

iēcī *perf of* **iaciō.**

iecur, -oris *and* **inoris** *nt* liver; (*fig*) passion.

iecusculum, -ī *nt* small liver.

iēiūniōsus *adj* hungry.

iēiūnitās, -ātis *f* fasting; (*fig*) meagreness.

iēiūnium, -ī *and* **iī** *nt* fast; hunger; leanness.

iēiūnus *adj* fasting, hungry; (*things*) barren, poor, meagre; (*style*) feeble.

iēntāculum, -ī *nt* breakfast.

igitur *adv* therefore, then, so.

ignārus *adj* ignorant, unaware; unknown.

ignāvē, -iter *adv* without energy.

ignāvia, -ae *f* idleness, laziness; cowardice.

ignāvus *adj* idle, lazy, listless; cowardly; relaxing.

ignēscō, -ere *vi* to take fire, burn.

igneus *adj* burning, fiery.

igniculus, -ī *m* spark; (*fig*) fire, vehemence.

ignifer, -ī *adj* fiery.

ignigena, -ae *m* the fireborn (Bacchus).

ignipēs, -edis *adj* fiery-footed.

ignipotēns, -entis *adj* fire-working (Vulcan).

ignis, -is *m* fire, a fire; firebrand, lightning; brightness, redness; (*fig*) passion, love.

ignōbilis *adj* unknown, obscure; low-born.

ignōbilitās, -ātis *f* obscurity; low birth.

ignōminia, -ae *f* dishonour, disgrace.

ignōminiōsus *adj* (*person*) degraded, disgraced; (*things*) shameful.

ignōrābilis *adj* unknown.

ignōrantia, -ae *f* ignorance.

ignōrātiō, -ōnis *f* ignorance.

ignōrō, -āre, -āvī, -ātum *vt* to not know, be unacquainted with; to disregard.

ignōscō, -scere, -vī, -tum *vt, vi* to forgive, pardon.

ignōtus *adj* unknown; low-born; ignorant.

īlex, -icis *f* holm oak.

īlia, -um *ntpl* groin; entrails; ~ **dūcere** become broken-winded.

Īlia, -ae *f* mother of Romulus and Remus.

Īliadēs, -adae *m* son of Ilia; Trojan.

Īlias, -dis *f* the Iliad; a Trojan woman.

īlicet *adv* it's all over, let us go; immediately.

īlicō *adv* on the spot; instantly.

īlignus *adj* of holm oak.

Īlīthyia, -ae *f* Greek goddess of childbirth.

Īlium, -on, -ī *nt*, **-os, -ī** *f* Troy.

Īlius, -acus *adj* Trojan.

illā *adv* that way.

illābefactus *adj* unbroken.

illābor, -bī, -psus *vi* to flow into, fall down.

illabōrō, -āre *vi* to work (at).

illāc *adv* that way.

illacessītus *adj* unprovoked.

illacrimābilis *adj* unwept; inexorable.

illacrimō, -āre; -or, -ārī *vi* to weep over, lament; to weep.

illaesus *adj* unhurt.

illaetābilis *adj* cheerless.

illāpsus *ppa of* **illābor.**

illaqueō, -āre *vt* to ensnare.

illātus *ppp of* **īnferō.**

illaudātus *adj* wicked.

ille, -a, -ud *pron and adj* that, that one; he, she, it; the famous; the former, the other; **ex ~ō** since then.

illecebra, -ae *f* attraction, lure, bait, decoy bird.

illecebrōsus *adj* seductive.

illectus *ppp of* **illiciō.**

illēctus *adj* unread.

illepidē *adv see* **illepidus.**

illepidus *adj* inelegant, churlish.

illex, -icis *m/f* lure.

illēx, -ēgis *adj* lawless.

illexī *perf of* **illiciō.**

illībātus *adj* unimpaired.

illīberālis *adj* ungenerous, mean, disobliging.

illīberālitās, -ātis *f* meanness.

illīberāliter *adv see* **illīberālis.**

illic, -aec, -ūc *pron* he, she, it; that.

illīc *adv* there, yonder; in that matter.

illiciō, -icere, -exī, -ectum *vt* to seduce, decoy, mislead.

illicitātor, -ōris *m* sham bidder (at an auction).

illicitus *adj* unlawful.

illīdō, -dere, -sī, -sum *vt* to strike, dash against.

illigō, -āre, -āvī, -ātum *vt* to fasten on, attach; to connect; to impede, encumber, oblige.

illim *adv* from there.

illīmis *adj* clear.

illinc *adv* from there; on that side.

illinō, -inere, -ēvī, -itum *vt* to smear over, cover, bedaub.

illiquefactus *adj* melted.

illīsī *perf of* **illīdō.**

illīsus *ppp of* **illīdō.**

illitterātus *adj* uneducated, uncultured.

illitus *ppp of* **illinō.**

illō *adv* (to) there; to that end.

illōtus *adj* dirty.

illūc *adv* (to) there; to that; to him/her.

illūceō, -ēre *vi* to blaze.

illūcēscō, -cēscere, -xī *vi* to become light, dawn.

illūdō, -dere, -sī, -sum *vt, vi* to play, amuse oneself; to abuse; to jeer at, ridicule.

illūmināte *adv* luminously.

illūminō, -āre, -āvī, -ātum *vt* to light up; to enlighten; to embellish.

illūsiō, -ōnis *f* irony.

illūstris *adj* bright, clear; distinct, manifest;

distinguished, illustrious.

illūstrō, -āre, -āvī, -ātum *vt* to illuminate; to make clear, explain; to make famous.

illūsus *ppp of* **illūdō.**

illuviēs, -ēī *f* dirt, filth; floods.

Illyria, -ae *f*, **-cum, -cī** *nt* Illyria.

Illyricus, -us *adj see* **Illyricum.**

Illyriī, -ōrum *mpl people E. of the Adriatic.*

Ilva, -ae *f* Italian island (*now* Elba).

imāginārius *adj* fancied.

imāginātiō, -ōnis *f* fancy.

imāginor, -ārī, *vt* to picture to oneself.

imāgō, -inis *f* likeness, picture, statue; portrait of ancestor; apparition, ghost; echo, mental picture, idea; (*fig*) semblance, mere shadow; (*RHET*) comparison.

imbēcillē *adv* faintly.

imbēcillitās, -ātis *f* weakness, helplessness.

imbēcillus *adj* weak, frail; helpless.

imbellis *adj* non-combatant; peaceful; cowardly.

imber, -ris *m* rain, heavy shower; water; (*fig*) stream, shower.

imberbis, imberbus *adj* beardless.

imbibō, -ere, -ī *vt* (*mind*) to conceive; to resolve.

imbrex, -icis *f* tile.

imbricus *adj* rainy.

imbrifer, -ī *adj* rainy.

imbuō, -uere, -uī, -ūtum *vt* to wet, steep, dip; (*fig*) to taint, fill; to inspire, accustom, train; to begin, be the first to explore.

imitābilis *adj* imitable.

imitāmen, -inis *nt* imitation; likeness.

imitāmenta, -ōrum *ntpl* pretence.

imitātiō, -ōnis *f* imitation.

imitātor,-ōris *m*, **-rīx,-rīcis** *f* imitator.

imitātus *adj* copied.

imitor, -ārī, -ātus *vt* to copy, portray; to imitate, act like.

immadēscō, -ēscere, -uī *vi* to become wet.

immāne *adv* savagely.

immānis *adj* enormous, vast; monstrous, savage, frightful.

immānitās, -ātis *f* vastness; savageness, barbarism.

immānsuētus *adj* wild.

immātūritās, -ātis *f* over-eagerness.

immātūrus *adj* untimely.

immedicābilis *adj* incurable.

immemor, -is *adj* unmindful, forgetful, negligent.

immemorābilis *adj* indescribable, not worth mentioning.

immemorātus *adj* hitherto untold.

immēnsitās, -ātis *f* immensity.

immēnsum, -ī *nt* infinity, vast extent ♦ *adv* exceedingly.

immēnsus *adj* immeasurable, vast, unending.

immerēns, -entis *adj* undeserving.

immergō, -gere, -sī, -sum *vt* to plunge, immerse.

immeritō *adv* unjustly.

immeritus *adj* undeserving, innocent; undeserved.

immersābilis *adj* never foundering.

immersus *ppp of* **immergō.**

immētātus *adj* unmeasured.

immigrō, -āre, -āvī, -ātum *vi* to move (into).

immineō, -ēre, -uī *vi* to overhang, project; to be near, adjoin, impend; to threaten, be a menace to; to long for, grasp at.

imminuō, -uere, -uī, -ūtum *vt* to lessen, shorten; to impair; to encroach on, ruin.

imminūtiō, -ōnis *f* mutilation; (*RHET*) understatement.

immisceō, -scēre, -scuī, -xtum *vt* to intermingle, blend; **sē ~** join, meddle with.

immiserābilis *adj* unpitied.

immisericorditer *adv* unmercifully.

immisericors, -dis *adj* pitiless.

immissiō, -ōnis *f* letting grow.

immissus *ppp of* **immittō.**

immītis *adj* unripe; severe, inexorable.

immittō, -ittere, -īsī, -issum *vt* to let in, put in; to graft on; to let go, let loose, let grow; to launch, throw; to incite, set on.

immīxtus *ppp of* **immisceō.**

immo *adv* (correcting preceding words) no, yes; on the contrary, or rather; **~ sī** ah, if only.

immōbilis *adj* motionless; immovable.

immoderātē *adv* extravagantly.

immoderātiō, -ōnis *f* excess.

immoderātus *adj* limitless; excessive, unbridled.

immodestē *adv* extravagantly.

immodestia, -ae *f* license.

immodestus *adj* immoderate.

immodicē *adv see* **immodicus.**

immodicus *adj* excessive, extravagant, unruly.

immodulātus *adj* unrhythmical.

immolātiō, -ōnis *f* sacrifice.

immolātor, -ōris *m* sacrificer.

immōlītus *adj* erected.

immolō, -āre, -āvī, -ātum *vt* to sacrifice; to slay.

immorior, -ī, -tuus *vi* to die upon; to waste away.

immorsus *adj* bitten; (*fig*) stimulated.

immortālis *adj* immortal, everlasting.

immortālitās, -ātis *f* immortality; lasting fame.

immortāliter *adv* infinitely.

immōtus *adj* motionless, unmoved, immovable.

immūgiō, -īre, -iī *vi* to roar (in).

immulgeō, -ēre *vt* to milk.

immundus *adj* unclean, dirty.

immūniō, -īre, -īvī *vt* to strengthen.

Noun declensions and verb conjugations are shown on pp xiii to xxv. The present infinitive ending of a verb shows to which conjugation it belongs: **-āre** = 1st; **-ēre** = 2nd; **-ere** = 3rd and **-īre** = 4th. Irregular verbs are shown on p xxvi

immūnis _adj_ with no public obligations, untaxed, free from office; exempt, free (from).

immūnitās, -ātis _f_ exemption, immunity, privilege.

immūnītus _adj_ undefended; (_roads_) unmetalled.

immurmurō, -āre _vi_ to murmur (at).

immūtābilis _adj_ unalterable.

immūtābilitās, -ātis _f_ immutability.

immūtātiō, -ōnis _f_ exchange; (_RHET_) metonymy.

immūtātus _adj_ unchanged.

immūtō, -āre, -āvī, -ātum _vt_ to change; (_words_) to substitute by metonymy.

impācātus _adj_ aggressive.

impāctus _ppp of_ **impingō**.

impār, -aris _adj_ unequal, uneven, unlike; no match for, inferior; (_metre_) elegiac.

imparātus _adj_ unprepared, unprovided.

impariter _adv_ unequally.

impāstus _adj_ hungry.

impatiēns, -entis _adj_ unable to endure, impatient.

impatienter _adv_ intolerably.

impatientia, -ae _f_ want of endurance.

impavidē _adv see_ **impavidus**.

impavidus _adj_ fearless, undaunted.

impedīmentum, -ī _nt_ hindrance, obstacle; (_pl_) baggage, luggage, supply train.

impediō, -īre, -īvī _and_ **iī, -ītum** _vt_ to hinder, entangle; to encircle; (_fig_) to embarrass, obstruct, prevent.

impedītiō, -ōnis _f_ obstruction.

impedītus _adj_ (_MIL_) hampered with baggage, in difficulties; (_place_) difficult, impassable; (_mind_) busy, obsessed.

impēgī _perf of_ **impingō**.

impellō, -ellere, -ulī, -ulsum _vt_ to strike, drive; to set in motion, impel, shoot; to incite, urge on; (_fig_) to overthrow, ruin.

impendeō, -ēre _vi_ to overhang; to be imminent, threaten.

impendiō _adv_ very much.

impendium, -ī _and_ **iī** _nt_ expense, outlay; interest on a loan.

impendō, -endere, -endī, -ēnsum _vt_ to weigh out, pay out, spend; (_fig_) to devote.

impenetrābilis _adj_ impenetrable.

impēnsa, -ae _f_ expense, outlay.

impēnsē _adv_ very much; earnestly.

impēnsus _ppp of_ **impendō** ♦ _adj_ (_cost_) high, dear; (_fig_) great, earnest.

imperātor, -ōris _m_ commander-in-chief, general; emperor; chief, master.

imperātōrius _adj_ of a general; imperial.

imperātum, -ī _nt_ order.

imperceptus _adj_ unknown.

impercussus _adj_ noiseless.

imperditus _adj_ not slain.

imperfectus _adj_ unfinished, imperfect.

imperfossus _adj_ not stabbed.

imperiōsus _adj_ powerful, imperial; tyrannical.

imperītē _adv_ awkwardly.

imperītia, -ae _f_ inexperience.

imperītō, -āre _vt, vi_ to rule, command.

imperītus _adj_ inexperienced, ignorant.

imperium, -ī _and_ **iī** _nt_ command, order; mastery, sovereignty, power; military command, supreme authority; empire; (_pl_) those in command, the authorities.

impermissus _adj_ unlawful.

imperō, -āre, -āvī, -ātum _vt, vi_ to order, command; to requisition, demand; to rule, govern, control; to be emperor.

imperterritus _adj_ undaunted.

impertiō, -īre, -īvī _and_ **iī, -ītum** _vt_ to share, communicate, impart.

imperturbātus _adj_ unruffled.

impervius _adj_ impassable.

impetibilis _adj_ intolerable.

impetis (_gen_), **-e** (_abl_) _m_ force; extent.

impetrābilis _adj_ attainable; successful.

impetrātiō, -ōnis _f_ favour.

impetriō, -īre _vt_ to succeed with the auspices.

impetrō, -āre, -āvī, -ātum _vt_ to achieve; to obtain, secure (_a request_).

impetus, -ūs _m_ attack, onset; charge; rapid motion, rush; (_mind_) impulse, passion.

impexus _adj_ unkempt.

impiē _adv_ wickedly.

impietās, -ātis _f_ impiety, disloyalty, unfilial conduct.

impiger, -rī _adj_ active, energetic.

impigrē _adv see adj_.

impigritās, -ātis _f_ energy.

impingō, -ingere, -ēgī, -āctum _vt_ to dash, force against; to force upon; (_fig_) to bring against, drive.

impiō, -āre _vt_ to make sinful.

impius _adj_ (_to gods_) impious; (_to parents_) undutiful; (_to country_) disloyal; wicked, unscrupulous.

implācābilis _adj_ implacable.

implācābiliter _adv see adj_.

implācātus _adj_ unappeased.

implacidus _adj_ savage.

impleō, -ēre, -ēvī, -ētum _vt_ to fill; to satisfy; (_time, number_) to make up, complete; (_duty_) to discharge, fulfil.

implexus _adj_ entwined; involved.

implicātiō, -ōnis _f_ entanglement.

implicātus _adj_ complicated, confused.

implicitē _adv_ intricately.

implicō, -āre, -āvī _and_ **uī, -ātum** _and_ **itum** _vt_ to entwine, enfold, clasp; (_fig_) to entangle, involve; to connect closely, join.

implōrātiō, -ōnis _f_ beseeching.

implōrō, -āre, -āvī, -ātum _vt_ to invoke, entreat, appeal to.

implūmis _adj_ unfledged.

impluō, -ere _vi_ to rain upon.

impluvium, -ī _and_ **iī** _nt_ roof-opening of the Roman atrium; rain basin in the atrium.

impolītē _adv_ without ornament.

impolītus–inānitās

impolītus *adj* unpolished, inelegant.

impollūtus *adj* unstained.

impōnō, -ōnere, -osuī, -ositum *vt* to put in, lay on, place; to embark; (*fig*) to impose, inflict, assign; to put in charge; (*tax*) to impose; (*with dat*) to impose upon, cheat.

importō, -āre, -āvī, -ātum *vt* to bring in, import; (*fig*) to bring upon, introduce.

importūnē *adv see adj.*

importūnitās, -ātis *f* insolence, ill nature.

importūnus *adj* unsuitable; troublesome; ill-natured, uncivil, bullying.

importuōsus *adj* without a harbour.

impos, -tis *adj* not master (of).

impositus, impostus *ppp of* **impōnō.**

impotēns, -entis *adj* powerless, weak; with no control over; headstrong, violent.

impotenter *adv* weakly; violently.

impotentia, -ae *f* poverty; want of self-control, violence.

impraesentiārum *adv* at present.

imprānsus *adj* fasting, without breakfast.

imprecor, -ārī *vt* to invoke.

impressiō, -ōnis *f* (*MIL*) thrust, raid; (*mind*) impression; (*speech*) emphasis; (*rhythm*) beat.

impressus *ppp of* **imprimō.**

imprīmīs *adv* especially.

imprimō, -imere, -essī, -essum *vt* to press upon, impress, imprint, stamp.

improbātiō, -ōnis *f* blame.

improbē *adv* badly, wrongly; persistently.

improbitās, -ātis *f* badness, dishonesty.

improbō, -āre, -āvī, -ātum *vt* to disapprove, condemn, reject.

improbulus *adj* a little presumptuous.

improbus *adj* bad, inferior (in quality); wicked, perverse, cruel; unruly, persistent, rebellious.

imprōcērus *adj* undersized.

imprōdictus *adj* not postponed.

imprōmptus *adj* unready, slow.

improperātus *adj* lingering.

improsper, -ī *adj* unsuccessful.

improsperē *adv* unfortunately.

imprōvidē *adv see adj.*

imprōvidus *adj* unforeseeing, thoughtless.

imprōvīsus *adj* unexpected; ~ō, de ~ō, ex ~ō unexpectedly.

imprūdēns, -entis *adj* unforeseeing, not expecting; ignorant, unaware.

imprūdenter *adv* thoughtlessly, unawares.

imprūdentia, -ae *f* thoughtlessness; ignorance; aimlessness.

impūbēs, -eris *and* **is** *adj* youthful; chaste.

impudēns, -entis *adj* shameless, impudent.

impudenter *adv see adj.*

impudentia, -ae *f* impudence.

impudīcitia, -ae *f* lewdness.

impudīcus *adj* shameless; immodest.

impugnātiō, -ōnis *f* assault.

impugnō, -āre, -āvī, -ātum *vt* to attack; (*fig*) to oppose, impugn.

impulī *perf of* **impellō.**

impulsiō, -ōnis *f* pressure; (*mind*) impulse.

impulsor, -ōris *m* instigator.

impulsus *ppp of* **impellō.**

impulsus, -ūs *m* push, pressure, impulse; (*fig*) instigation.

impūne *adv* safely, with impunity.

impūnitās, -ātis *f* impunity.

impūnītē *adv* with impunity.

impūnītus *adj* unpunished.

impūrātus *adj* vile.

impūrē *adv see adj.*

impūritās, -ātis *f* uncleanness.

impūrus *adj* unclean; infamous, vile.

imputātus *adj* unpruned.

imputō, -āre, -āvī, -ātum *vt* to put to one's account; to ascribe, credit, impute.

īmulus *adj* little tip of.

īmus *adj* lowest, deepest, bottom of; last.

in *prep* (*with abl*) in, on, at; among; in the case of; (*time*) during; (*with acc*) into, on to, to, towards; against; (*time*) for, till; (*purpose*) for; ~ armīs under arms; ~ equō on horseback; ~ eō esse ut be in the position of; be on the point of; ~ hōrās hourly; ~ modum in the manner of; ~ rem of use; ~ universum in general.

inaccessus *adj* unapproachable.

inacēscō, -ere *vi* to turn sour.

Īnachidēs, -idae *m* Perseus; Epaphus.

Īnachis, -idis *f* Io.

Īnachius *adj* of Inachus, Argive, Greek.

Īnachus, -ī *m* first king of Argos.

inadsuētus *adj* unaccustomed.

inadūstus *adj* unsinged.

inaedificō, -āre, -āvī, -ātum *vt* to build on, erect; to wall up, block up.

inaequābilis *adj* uneven.

inaequālis *adj* uneven; unequal; capricious.

inaequāliter *adv see adj.*

inaequātus *adj* unequal.

inaequō, -āre *vt* to level up.

inaestimābilis *adj* incalculable; invaluable; valueless.

inaestuō, -āre *vi* to rage in.

inamābilis *adj* hateful.

inamārēscō, -ere *vi* to become bitter.

inambitiōsus *adj* unambitious.

inambulātiō, -ōnis *f* walking about.

inambulō, -āre *vi* to walk up and down.

inamoenus *adj* disagreeable.

inanimus *adj* lifeless, inanimate.

ināniō, -īre *vt* to make empty.

inānis *adj* empty, void; poor, unsubstantial; useless, worthless, vain, idle ♦ *nt* (*PHILOS*) space; (*fig*) vanity.

inānitās, -ātis *f* empty space; inanity.

ināniter *adv* idly, vainly.
inarātus *adj* fallow.
inārdēscō, -dēscere, -sī *vi* to be kindled, flare up.
inass- *etc see* **inads-**.
inattenuātus *adj* undiminished.
inaudāx, -ācis *adj* timorous.
inaudiō, -īre *vt* to hear of, learn.
inaudītus *adj* unheard of, unusual; without a hearing.
inaugurātō *adv* after taking the auspices.
inaugurō, -āre *vi* to take auspices ♦ *vt* to consecrate, inaugurate.
inaurēs, -ium *fpl* earrings.
inaurō, -āre, -āvi, -ātum *vt* to gild; (*fig*) to enrich.
inauspicātō *adv* without taking the auspices.
inauspicātus *adj* done without auspices.
inausus *adj* unattempted.
incaeduus *adj* uncut.
incalēscō, -ēscere, -uī *vi* to grow hot; (*fig*) to warm, glow.
incalfaciō, -ere *vt* to heat.
incallidē *adv* unskilfully.
incallidus *adj* stupid, simple.
incandēscō, -ēscere, -uī *vi* to become hot; to turn white.
incānēscō, -ēscere, -uī *vi* to grow grey.
incantātus *adj* enchanted.
incānus *adj* grey.
incassum *adv* in vain.
incastigātus *adj* unrebuked.
incautē *adv* negligently.
incautus *adj* careless, heedless; unforeseen, unguarded.
incēdō, -ēdere, -ēssī, -ēssum *vi* to walk, parade, march; (*MIL*) to advance; (*feelings*) to come upon.
incelebrātus *adj* not made known.
incēnātus *adj* supperless.
incendiārius, -ī and ii *m* incendiary.
incendium, -ī and ii *nt* fire, conflagration; heat; (*fig*) fire, vehemence, passion.
incendō, -ere, -ī, incēnsum *vt* to set fire to, burn; to light, brighten; (*fig*) to inflame, rouse, incense.
incēnsiō, -ōnis *f* burning.
incēnsus *ppp of* **incendō**.
incēnsus *adj* not registered.
incēpī *perf of* **incipiō**.
inceptiō, -ōnis *f* undertaking.
inceptō, -āre *vt* to begin, attempt.
inceptor, -ōris *m* originator.
inceptum, -ī *nt* beginning, undertaking, attempt.
inceptus *ppp of* **incipiō**.
incērō, -āre *vt* to cover with wax.
incertō *adv* not for certain.
incertus *adj* uncertain, doubtful, unsteady ♦ *nt* uncertainty.
incēssō, -ere, -īvī *vt* to attack; (*fig*) to assail.
incēssus, -ūs *m* gait, pace, tramp; invasion; approach.

incestē *adv see adj.*
incestō, -āre *vt* to pollute, dishonour.
incestus *adj* sinful; unchaste, incestuous ♦ *nt* incest.
incestus, -ūs *m* incest.
incho- *etc see* **incoh-**.
incidō, -idere, -idī, -āsum *vi* to fall upon, fall into; to meet, fall in with, come across; to befall, occur, happen; **in mentem** ~ occur to one.
incīdō, -dere, -dī, -sum *vt* to cut open; to cut up; to engrave, inscribe; to interrupt, cut short.
incīle, -is *nt* ditch.
incīlō, -āre *vt* to rebuke.
incingō, -gere, -xī, -ctum *vt* to gird, wreathe; to surround.
incinō, -ere *vt* to sing, play.
incipiō, -ipere, -ēpī, -eptum *vt, vi* to begin.
incipissō, -ere *vt* to begin.
incīsē *adv* in short clauses.
incīsim *adv* in short clauses.
incīsiō, -ōnis *f* clause.
incīsum, -ī *nt* clause.
incīsus *ppp of* **incīdō**.
incitāmentum, -ī *nt* incentive.
incitātē *adv* impetuously.
incitātiō, -ōnis *f* inciting; rapidity.
incitātus *ppp of* **incitō** ♦ *adj* swift, rapid; **equō ~ō** at a gallop.
incitō, -āre, -āvī, -ātum *vt* to urge on, rush; to rouse, encourage, excite; to inspire; to increase; **sē ~** rush; **currentem ~** ≈ *spur a willing horse*.
incitus *adj* swift.
incitus *adj* immovable; **ad ~ās, ~a redigere** bring to a standstill.
inclāmō, -āre *vt, vi* to call out, cry out to; to scold, abuse.
inclārēscō, -ēscere, -uī *vi* to become famous.
inclēmēns, -entis *adj* severe.
inclēmenter *adv* harshly.
inclēmentia, -ae *f* severity.
inclīnātiō, -ōnis *f* leaning, slope; (*fig*) tendency, inclination, bias; (*CIRCS*) change; (*voice*) modulation.
inclīnātus *adj* inclined, prone; falling; (*voice*) deep.
inclīnō, -āre, -āvī, -ātum *vt* to bend, turn; to turn back; (*fig*) to incline, direct, transfer; to change ♦ *vi* to bend, sink; (*MIL*) to give way; (*fig*) to change, deteriorate; to incline, tend, turn in favour.
inclitus *etc see* **inclutus**.
inclūdō, -dere, -sī, -sum *vt* to shut in, keep in, enclose; to obstruct, block; (*fig*) to include; (*time*) to close, end.
inclūsiō, -ōnis *f* imprisonment.
inclūsus *ppp of* **inclūdō**.
inclutus *adj* famous, glorious.
incoctus *ppp of* **incoquō**.
incoctus *adj* uncooked, raw.
incōgitābilis *adj* thoughtless.

incōgitāns, -antis *adj* thoughtless.

incōgitantia, -ae *f* thoughtlessness.

incōgitō, -āre *vt* to contrive.

incognitus *adj* unknown, unrecognised; (*law*) untried.

incohātus *adj* unfinished.

incohō, -āre, -āvī, -ātum *vt* to begin, start.

incola, -ae *f* inhabitant, resident.

incolō, -ere, -uī *vt* to live in, inhabit ♦ *vi* to live, reside.

incolumis *adj* safe and sound, unharmed.

incolumitās, -ātis *f* safety.

incomitātus *adj* unaccompanied.

incommendātus *adj* unprotected.

incommodē *adv* inconveniently, unfortunately.

incommoditās, -ātis *f* inconvenience, disadvantage.

incommodō, -āre *vi* to be inconvenient, annoy.

incommodum, -ī *nt* inconvenience, disadvantage, misfortune.

incommodus *adj* inconvenient, troublesome.

incommūtābilis *adj* unchangeable.

incompertus *adj* unknown.

incompositē *adv see adj.*

incompositus *adj* in disorder, irregular.

incōmptus *adj* undressed, inelegant.

inconcēssus *adj* forbidden.

inconciliō, -āre *vt* to win over (by guile); to trick, inveigle, embarrass.

inconcinnus *adj* inartistic, awkward.

inconcussus *adj* unshaken, stable.

inconditē *adv* confusedly.

inconditus *adj* undisciplined, not organised; (*language*) artless.

incōnsīderātē *adv see adj.*

incōnsīderātus *adj* thoughtless, ill-advised.

incōnsōlābilis *adj* incurable.

incōnstāns, -antis *adj* fickle, inconsistent.

incōnstanter *adv* inconsistently.

incōnstantia, -ae *f* fickleness, inconsistency.

incōnsultē *adv* indiscreetly.

incōnsultū without consulting.

incōnsultus *adj* indiscreet, ill-advised; unanswered; not consulted.

incōnsūmptus *adj* unconsumed.

incontāminātus *adj* untainted.

incontentus *adj* untuned.

incontinēns, -entis *adj* intemperate.

incontinenter *adv* without self-control.

incontinentia, -ae *f* lack of self-control.

inconveniēns, -entis *adj* ill-matched.

incoquō, -quere, -xī, -ctum *vt* to boil; to dye.

incorrēctus *adj* unrevised.

incorruptē *adv* justly.

incorruptus *adj* unspoiled; uncorrupted, genuine.

incrēbrēscō, incrēbēscō, -ēscere, -uī *vi* to increase, grow, spread.

incrēdibilis *adj* incredible, extraordinary.

incrēdibiliter *adv see adj.*

incrēdulus *adj* incredulous.

incrēmentum, -ī *nt* growth, increase; addition; offspring.

increpitō, -āre *vt* to rebuke; to challenge.

increpō, -āre, -uī, -itum *vi* to make a noise, sound; (*news*) to be noised abroad ♦ *vt* to cause to make a noise; to exclaim against, rebuke.

incrēscō, -scere, -vī *vi* to grow in, increase.

incrētus *adj* sifted in.

incruentātus *adj* unstained with blood.

incruentus *adj* bloodless, without bloodshed.

incrūstō, -āre *vt* to encrust.

incubō, -āre, -uī, -itum *vi* to lie in or on; (*fig*) to brood over.

incubuī *perf of* **incubō**; *perf of* **incumbō**.

inculcō, -āre, -āvī, -ātum *vt* to force in; to force upon, impress on.

inculpātus *adj* blameless.

incultē *adv* uncouthly.

incultus *adj* uncultivated; (*fig*) neglected, uneducated, rude.

incultus, -ūs *m* neglect, squalor.

incumbō, -mbere, -buī, -bitum *vi* to lean, recline on; to fall upon, throw oneself upon; to oppress, lie heavily upon; (*fig*) to devote attention to, take pains with; to incline.

incūnābula, -ōrum *ntpl* swaddling clothes; (*fig*) cradle, infancy, birthplace, origin.

incūrātus *adj* neglected.

incūria, -ae *f* negligence.

incūriōsē *adv* carelessly.

incūriōsus *adj* careless, indifferent.

incurrō, -rrere, -rrī *and* **curri, -rsum** *vi* to run into, rush, attack; to invade; to meet with, get involved in; (*events*) to occur, coincide.

incursiō, -ōnis *f* attack; invasion, raid; collision.

incursō, -āre *vt, vi* to run into, assault; to frequently invade; (*fig*) to meet, strike.

incursus, -ūs *m* assault, striking; (*mind*) impulse.

incurvō, -āre *vt* to bend, crook.

incurvus *adj* bent, crooked.

incūs, -ūdis *f* anvil.

incūsātiō, -ōnis *f* blaming.

incūsō, -āre, -āvī, -ātum *vt* to find fault with, accuse.

incussī *perf of* **incutiō**.

incussus *ppp of* **incutiō**.

incussus, -ūs *m* shock.

incustōdītus *adj* unguarded, unconcealed.

incūsus *adj* forged.

incutiō, -tere, -ssī, -ssum *vt* to strike, dash against; to throw; (*fig*) to strike into, inspire with.

indāgātiō, -ōnis *f* search.

indāgātor, -ōris *m* explorer.

Noun declensions and verb conjugations are shown on pp xiii to xxv. The present infinitive ending of a verb shows to which conjugation it belongs: **-āre** = 1st; **-ēre** = 2nd; **-ere** = 3rd and **-īre** = 4th. Irregular verbs are shown on p xxvi

indāgātrīx, -rīcis *f* female explorer.
indāgō, -āre *vt* to track down; (*fig*) to trace, investigate.
indāgō, -inis *f* (*hunt*) drive, encirclement.
indaudiō *etc see* **inaudiō**.
inde *adv* from there, from that, from them; on that side; from then, ever since; after that, then.
indēbitus *adj* not due.
indēclīnātus *adj* constant.
indecor, -is *adj* dishonourable, a disgrace.
indecōrē *adv* indecently.
indecorō, -āre *vt* to disgrace.
indecōrus *adj* unbecoming, unsightly.
indēfēnsus *adj* undefended.
indēfessus *adj* unwearied, tireless.
indēflētus *adj* unwept.
indēiectus *adj* undemolished.
indēlēbilis *adj* imperishable.
indēlībātus *adj* unimpaired.
indemnātus *adj* unconvicted.
indēplōrātus *adj* unlamented.
indēprēnsus *adj* undetected.
indeptus *ppa of* **indipīscor**.
indēsertus *adj* unforsaken.
indēstrictus *adj* unscathed.
indētōnsus *adj* unshorn.
indēvītātus *adj* unerring.
index, -icis *m* forefinger; witness, informer; (*book, art*) title, inscription; (*stone*) touchstone; (*fig*) indication, pointer, sign.
India, -iae *f* India.
indicātiō, -ōnis *f* value.
indīcente mē without my telling.
indicium, -ī *and* **iī** *nt* information, evidence; reward for information; indication, sign, proof; **~ profitērī, offerre** ≈ *turn King's evidence*; **~ postulāre, dare** ask, grant permission to give evidence.
indicō, -āre, -āvī, -ātum *vt* to point out; to disclose, betray; to give information, give evidence; to put a price on.
indīcō, -īcere, -īxī, -ictum *vt* to declare, proclaim, appoint.
indictus *ppp of* **indīcō**.
indictus *adj* not said, unsung; **causā ~ā** without a hearing.
Indicus *adj see n.*
indidem *adv* from the same place *or* thing.
indidī *perf of* **indō**.
indifferēns, -entis *adj* neither good nor bad.
indigena, -ae *m* native ♦ *adj* native.
indigēns, -entis *adj* needy.
indigentia, -ae *f* need; craving.
indigeō, -ēre, -uī *vi* (*with abl*) to need, want, require; to crave.
indiges, -etis *m* national deity.
indigestus *adj* confused.
indignābundus *adj* enraged.
indignāns, -antis *adj* indignant.
indignātiō, -ōnis *f* indignation.
indignē *adv* unworthily; indignantly.
indignitās, -ātis *f* unworthiness, enormity;

insulting treatment; indignation.
indignor, -ārī, -ātus *vt* to be displeased with, be angry at.
indignus *adj* unworthy, undeserving; shameful, severe; undeserved.
indigus *adj* in want.
indīligēns, -entis *adj* careless.
indīligenter *adv see adj.*
indīligentia, -ae *f* carelessness.
indipīscor, -ī, indeptus *vt* to obtain, get, reach.
indīreptus *adj* unplundered.
indiscrētus *adj* closely connected, indiscriminate, indistinguishable.
indisertē *adv* without eloquence.
indisertus *adj* not eloquent.
indispositus *adj* disorderly.
indissolūbilis *adj* imperishable.
indistinctus *adj* confused, obscure.
inditus *ppp of* **indō**.
indīviduus *adj* indivisible; inseparable ♦ *nt* atom.
indō, -ere, -idī, -itum *vt* to put in *or* on; to introduce; to impart, impose.
indocilis *adj* difficult to teach, hard to learn; untaught.
indoctē *adv* unskilfully.
indoctus *adj* untrained, illiterate, ignorant.
indolentia, -ae *f* freedom from pain.
indolēs, -is *f* nature, character, talents.
indolēscō, -ēscere, -uī *vi* to feel sorry.
indomitus *adj* untamed, wild; ungovernable.
indormiō, -īre *vi* to sleep on; to be careless.
indōtātus *adj* with no dowry; unhonoured; (*fig*) unadorned.
indubitō, -āre *vi* to begin to doubt.
indubius *adj* undoubted.
indūcō, -ūcere, -ūxī, -uctum *vt* to bring in, lead on; to introduce; to overlay, cover over; (*fig*) to move, persuade, seduce; (*bookkeeping*) to enter; (*dress*) to put on; (*public show*) to exhibit; (*writing*) to erase; **animum, in animum ~** determine, imagine.
inductiō, -ōnis *f* leading, bringing on; (*mind*) purpose, intention; (*logic*) induction.
inductus *ppp of* **indūcō**.
indugredior *etc see* **ingredior**.
induī *perf of* **induō**.
indulgēns, -entis *pres p of* **indulgeō** ♦ *adj* indulgent, kind.
indulgenter *adv* indulgently.
indulgentia, -ae *f* indulgence, gentleness.
indulgeō, -gēre, -sī *vi* (*with dat*) to be kind to, indulge, give way to; to indulge in ♦ *vt* to concede; **sibi ~** take liberties.
induō, -uere, -uī, -ūtum *vt* (*dress*) to put on; (*fig*) to assume, entangle.
indup- *etc see* **imp-**.
indūrēscō, -ēscere, -uī *vi* to harden.
indūrō, -āre *vt* to harden.
Indus, -ī *m* Indian; Ethiopian; mahout.
Indus *adj see n.*
industria, -ae *f* diligence; **dē, ex ~ā** on

purpose.

industrie *adv see* **industrius**.

industrius *adj* diligent, painstaking.

indutiae, -arum *fpl* truce, armistice.

indutus *ppp of* **induo**.

indutus, -us *m* wearing.

induviae, -arum *fpl* clothes.

induxi *perf of* **induco**.

inebrio, -are *vt* to intoxicate; (*fig*) to saturate.

inedia, -ae *f* starvation.

ineditus *adj* unpublished.

inelegans, -antis *adj* tasteless.

ineleganter *adv* without taste.

ineluctabilis *adj* inescapable.

inemorior, -i *vi* to die in.

inemptus *adj* unpurchased.

inenarrabilis *adj* indescribable.

inenodabilis *adj* inexplicable.

ineo, -ire, -ivi *and* **ii, -itum** *vi* to go in, come in; to begin ♦ *vt* to enter; to begin, enter upon, form, undertake; **consilium** ~ form a plan; **gratiam** ~ win favour; **numerum** ~ enumerate; **rationem** ~ calculate, consider, contrive; **suffragium** ~ vote; **viam** ~ find out a way.

inepte *adv see adj*.

ineptia, -ae *f* stupidity; (*pl*) nonsense.

ineptio, -ire *vi* to play the fool.

ineptus *adj* unsuitable; silly, tactless, absurd.

inermis, inermus *adj* unarmed, defenceless; harmless.

inerrans, -antis *adj* fixed.

inerro, -are *vi* to wander about in.

iners, -tis *adj* unskilful; inactive, indolent, timid; insipid.

inertia, -ae *f* lack of skill; idleness, laziness.

ineruditus *adj* uneducated.

inesco, -are *vt* to entice, deceive.

inevectus *adj* mounted.

inevitabilis *adj* inescapable.

inexcitus *adj* peaceful.

inexcusabilis *adj* with no excuse.

inexercitatus *adj* untrained.

inexhaustus *adj* unexhausted.

inexorabilis *adj* inexorable; (*things*) severe.

inexperrectus *adj* unawakened.

inexpertus *adj* inexperienced; untried.

inexpiabilis *adj* inexpiable; implacable.

inexplebilis *adj* insatiable.

inexpletus *adj* incessant.

inexplicabilis *adj* inexplicable; impracticable, unending.

inexplorato *adv* without making a reconnaissance.

inexploratus *adj* unreconnoitred.

inexpugnabilis *adj* impregnable, safe.

inexspectatus *adj* unexpected.

inexstinctus *adj* unextinguished; insatiable, imperishable.

inexsuperabilis *adj* insurmountable.

inextricabilis *adj* inextricable.

infabre *adv* unskilfully.

infabricatus *adj* unfashioned.

infacetus *adj* not witty, crude.

infacundus *adj* ineloquent.

infamia, -ae *f* disgrace, scandal.

infamis *adj* infamous, disreputable.

infamo, -are, -avi, -atum *vt* to disgrace, bring into disrepute.

infandus *adj* unspeakable, atrocious.

infans, -antis *adj* mute, speechless; young, infant; tongue-tied; childish ♦ *m/f* infant, child.

infantia, -ae *f* inability to speak; infancy; lack of eloquence.

infatuo, -are *vt* to make a fool of.

infaustus *adj* unlucky.

infector, -oris *m* dyer.

infectus *ppp of* **inficio**.

infectus *adj* undone, unfinished; **re ~a** without achieving one's purpose.

infecunditas, -atis *f* infertility.

infecundus *adj* unfruitful.

infelicitas, -atis *f* misfortune.

infeliciter *adv see adj*.

infelico, -are *vt* to make unhappy.

infelix, -icis *adj* unfruitful; unhappy, unlucky.

infense *adv* aggressively.

infenso, -are *vt* to make dangerous, make hostile.

infensus *adj* hostile, dangerous.

infercio, -ire *vt* to cram in.

inferiae, -arum *fpl* offerings to the dead.

inferior, -oris *compar of* **inferus**.

inferius *compar of* **infra**.

inferne *adv* below.

infernus *adj* beneath; of the lower world, infernal ♦ *mpl* the shades ♦ *ntpl* the lower world.

infero, -re, intuli, illatum *vt* to carry in, bring to, put on; to move forward; (*fig*) to introduce, cause; (*book-keeping*) to enter; (*logic*) to infer; **bellum** ~ make war (on); **pedem** ~ advance; **se** ~ repair, rush, strut about; **signa** ~ attack, charge.

inferus (*compar* ~**ior**, *superl* **infimus**) *adj* lower, below ♦ *mpl* the dead, the lower world ♦ *compar* lower; later; inferior ♦ *superl* lowest, bottom of; meanest, humblest.

infervesco, -vescere, -bui *vi* to boil.

infeste *adv* aggressively.

infesto, -are *vt* to attack.

infestus *adj* unsafe; dangerous, aggressive.

inficet- *see* **infacet-**.

inficio, -icere, -eci, -ectum *vt* to dip, dye, discolour; to taint, infect; (*fig*) to instruct, corrupt, poison.

infidelis *adj* faithless.

infidelitas, -atis *f* disloyalty.

infideliter *adv* treacherously.

infīdus *adj* unsafe, treacherous.
infīgō, -gere, -xī, -xum *vt* to thrust, drive in; (*fig*) to impress, imprint.
infimus *superl of* **inferus**.
infindō, -ere *vt* to cut into, plough.
infinitās, -ātis *f* boundless extent, infinity.
infinitē *adv* without end.
infinitiō, -ōnis *f* infinity.
infinitus *adj* boundless, endless, infinite; indefinite.
infirmātiō, -ōnis *f* invalidating, refuting.
infirmē *adv* feebly.
infirmitās, -ātis *f* weakness; infirmity, sickness.
infirmō, -āre *vt* to weaken; to invalidate, refute.
infirmus *adj* weak, indisposed; weak-minded; (*things*) trivial.
infit *vi* (*defec*) begins.
infitiālis *adj* negative.
infitiās eō deny.
infitiātiō, -ōnis *f* denial.
infitiātor, -ōris *m* denier (of a debt).
infitior, -ārī, -ātus *vt* to deny, repudiate.
infixus *ppp of* **infīgō**.
inflammātiō, -ōnis *f* (*fig*) exciting.
inflammō, -āre, -āvī, -ātum *vt* to set on fire, light; (*fig*) to inflame, rouse.
inflātē *adv* pompously.
inflātiō, -ōnis *f* flatulence.
inflātus, -ūs *m* blow; inspiration ♦ *adj* blown up, swollen; (*fig*) puffed up, conceited; (*style*) turgid.
inflectō, -ctere, -xī, -xum *vt* to bend, curve; to change; (*voice*) to modulate; (*fig*) to affect, move.
inflētus *adj* unwept.
inflexiō, -ōnis *f* bending.
inflexus *ppp of* **inflectō**.
infligō, -gere, -xī, -ctum *vt* to dash against, strike; to inflict.
inflō, -āre, -āvī, -ātum *vt* to blow, inflate; (*fig*) to inspire, puff up.
influō, -ere, -xī, -xum *vi* to flow in; (*fig*) to stream, pour in.
infodiō, -odere, -ōdī, -ossum *vt* to dig in, bury.
informātiō, -ōnis *f* sketch, idea.
informis *adj* shapeless; hideous.
informō, -āre, -āvī, -ātum *vt* to shape, fashion; to sketch; to educate.
infortūnātus *adj* unfortunate.
infortūnium, -ī *and* **iī** *nt* misfortune.
infossus *ppp of* **infodiō**.
infrā (*compar* **inferius**) *adv* underneath, below ♦ *compar* lower down ♦ *prep* (*with acc*) below, beneath, under; later than.
infrāctiō, -ōnis *f* weakening.
infrāctus *ppp of* **infringō**.
infragilis *adj* strong.
infremō, -ere, -uī *vi* to growl.
infrēnātus *ppp of* **infrēnō**.
infrēnātus *adj* without a bridle.

infrendō, -ere *vi* to gnash.
infrēnis, -us *adj* unbridled.
infrēnō, -āre, -āvī, -ātum *vt* to put a bridle on, harness; (*fig*) to curb.
infrequēns, -entis *adj* not crowded, infrequent; badly attended.
infrequentia, -ae *f* small number; emptiness.
infringō, -ingere, -ēgī, -āctum *vt* to break, bruise; (*fig*) to weaken, break down, exhaust.
infrōns, -ondis *adj* leafless.
infūcātus *adj* showy.
infula, -ae *f* woollen band, fillet, badge of honour.
infumus *etc see* **infimus**.
infundō, -undere, -ūdī, -ūsum *vt* to pour in *or* on; to serve; (*fig*) to spread.
infuscō, -āre *vt* to darken; to spoil, tarnish.
infūsus *ppp of* **infundō**.
ingeminō, -āre *vt* to redouble ♦ *vi* to be redoubled.
ingemīscō, -īscere, -uī *vi* to groan, sigh ♦ *vt* to sigh over.
ingemō, -ere, -uī *vt, vi* to sigh for, mourn.
ingenerō, -āre, -āvī, -ātum *vt* to engender, produce, create.
ingeniātus *adj* with a natural talent.
ingeniōsē *adv* cleverly.
ingeniōsus *adj* talented, clever; (*things*) naturally suited.
ingenitus *ppp of* **ingignō** ♦ *adj* inborn, natural.
ingenium, -ī *and* **iī** *nt* nature; (*disposition*) bent, character; (*intellect*) ability, talent, genius; (*person*) genius.
ingēns, -entis *adj* huge, mighty, great.
ingenuē *adv* liberally, frankly.
ingenuitās, -ātis *f* noble birth, noble character.
ingenuus *adj* native, innate; free-born; noble, frank; delicate.
ingerō, -rere, -ssī, -stum *vt* to carry in; to heap on; to throw, hurl; (*fig*) to press, obtrude.
ingignō, -ignere, -enuī, -enitum *vt* to engender, implant.
inglōrius *adj* inglorious.
ingluviēs, -ēī *f* maw; gluttony.
ingrātē *adv* unwillingly; ungratefully.
ingrātiīs, ingrātis *adv* against one's will.
ingrātus *adj* disagreeable, unwelcome; ungrateful, thankless.
ingravēscō, -ere *vi* to grow heavy, become worse, increase.
ingravō, -āre *vt* to weigh heavily on; to aggravate.
ingredior, -dī, -ssus *vt, vi* to go in, enter; to walk, march; to enter upon, engage in; to commence, begin to speak.
ingressiō, -ōnis *f* entrance; beginning; pace.
ingressus, -ūs *m* entrance; (*MIL*) inroad; beginning; walking, gait.
ingruō, -ere, -ī *vi* to fall upon, assail.
inguen, -inis *nt* groin.
ingurgitō, -āre *vt* to pour in; **sē ~** gorge

oneself; (*fig*) to be absorbed in.

ingustātus *adj* untasted.

inhabilis *adj* unwieldy, awkward; unfit.

inhabitābilis *adj* uninhabitable.

inhabitō, -āre *vt* to inhabit.

inhaereō, -rēre, -sī, -sum *vi* to stick in, cling to; to adhere, be closely connected with; to be always in.

inhaerēscō, -ere *vi* to take hold, cling fast.

inhālō, -āre *vt* to breathe on.

inhibeō, -ēre, -uī, -itum *vt* to check, restrain, use, practise; ~ **rēmīs/nāvem** back water.

inhibitiō, -ōnis *f* backing water.

inhiō, -āre *vi* to gape ♦ *vt* to gape at, covet.

inhonestē *adv see adj.*

inhonestō, -āre *vt* to dishonour.

inhonestus *adj* dishonourable, inglorious; ugly.

inhonōrātus *adj* unhonoured; unrewarded.

inhonōrus *adj* defaced.

inhorreō, -ēre, -uī *vt* to stand erect, bristle.

inhorrēscō, -ēscere, -uī *vi* to bristle up; to shiver, shudder, tremble.

inhospitālis *adj* inhospitable.

inhospitālitās, -ātis *f* inhospitality.

inhospitus *adj* inhospitable.

inhūmānē *adv* savagely; uncivilly.

inhūmānitās, -ātis *f* barbarity; discourtesy, churlishness, meanness.

inhūmāniter *adv* = **inhūmānē.**

inhūmānus *adj* savage, brutal; ill-bred, uncivil, uncultured.

inhumātus *adj* unburied.

inibi *adv* there, therein; about to happen.

iniciō, -icere, -iēcī, -iectum *vt* to throw into, put on; (*fig*) to inspire, cause; (*speech*) to hint, mention; **manum ~** take possession.

iniectus, -ūs *m* putting in, throwing over.

inimīcē *adv* hostilely.

inimīcitia, -ae *f* enmity.

inimīcō, -āre *vt* to make enemies.

inimīcus *adj* unfriendly, hostile; injurious ♦ *m/f* enemy; ~**issimus** greatest enemy.

inīquē *adv* unequally, unjustly.

inīquitās, -ātis *f* unevenness; difficulty; injustice, unfair demands.

inīquus *adj* unequal, uneven; adverse, unfavourable, injurious; unfair, unjust; excessive; impatient, discontented ♦ *m* enemy.

initiō, -āre *vt* to initiate.

initium, -ī *and* **iī** *nt* beginning; (*pl*) elements, first principles; holy rites, mysteries.

initus *ppp of* **ineō.**

initus, -ūs *m* approach; beginning.

iniūcundē *adv see adj.*

iniūcunditās, -ātis *f* unpleasantness.

iniūcundus *adj* unpleasant.

iniungō, -ungere, -ūnxī, -ūnctum *vt* to join, attach; (*fig*) to impose, inflict.

iniūrātus *adj* unsworn.

iniūria, -ae *f* wrong, injury, injustice; insult, outrage; severity, revenge; unjust possession; ~**ā** unjustly.

iniūriōsē *adv* wrongfully.

iniūriōsus *adj* unjust, wrongful; harmful.

iniūrius *adj* wrong, unjust.

iniūssū without orders (from).

iniūssus *adj* unbidden.

iniūstē *adv see adj.*

iniūstitia, -ae *f* injustice, severity.

iniūstus *adj* unjust, wrong; excessive, severe.

inl- *etc see* **ill-.**

inm- *etc see* **imm-.**

innābilis *adj* that none may swim.

innāscor, -scī, -tus *vi* to be born in, grow up in.

innatō, -āre *vt* to swim in, float on; to swim, flow into.

innātus *ppa of* **innāscor** ♦ *adj* innate, natural.

innāvigābilis *adj* unnavigable.

innectō, -ctere, -xuī, -xum *vt* to tie, fasten together, entwine; (*fig*) to connect; to contrive.

innītor, -tī, -xus *and* **sus** *vi* to rest, lean on; to depend.

innō, -āre *vi* to swim in, float on, sail on.

innocēns, -entis *adj* harmless; innocent; upright, unselfish.

innocenter *adv* blamelessly.

innocentia, -ae *f* innocence; integrity, unselfishness.

innocuē *adv* innocently.

innocuus *adj* harmless; innocent; unharmed.

innōtēscō, -ēscere, -uī *vi* to become known.

innovō, -āre *vt* to renew; **sē ~** return.

innoxius *adj* harmless, safe; innocent; unharmed.

innuba, -ae *adj* unmarried.

innūbilus *adj* cloudless.

innūbō, -bere, -psī *vi* to marry into.

innumerābilis, -ātis *adj* countless.

innumerābilitās, -ātis *f* countless number.

innumerābiliter *adv* innumerably.

innumerālis *adj* numberless.

innumerus *adj* countless.

innuō, -ere, -ī *vi* to give a nod.

innūpta, -ae *adj* unmarried.

Īnō, -ūs *f* daughter of Cadmus.

inoblītus *adj* unforgetful.

inobrutus *adj* not overwhelmed.

inobservābilis *adj* unnoticed.

inobservātus *adj* unobserved.

inoffēnsus *adj* without hindrance, uninterrupted.

inofficiōsus *adj* irresponsible; disobliging.

inolēns, -entis *adj* odourless.

inolēscō, -scere, -vī *vi* to grow in.

inōminātus *adj* inauspicious.

inopia, -ae *f* want, scarcity, poverty,

Noun declensions and verb conjugations are shown on pp xiii to xxv. The present infinitive ending of a verb shows to which conjugation it belongs: **-āre** = 1st; **-ēre** = 2nd; **-ere** = 3rd and **-īre** = 4th. Irregular verbs are shown on p xxvi

helplessness.
inopīnāns, -antis *adj* unaware.
inopīnātō *adv* unexpectedly.
inopīnātus *adj* unexpected; off one's guard.
inopīnus *adj* unexpected.
inopiōsus *adj* in want.
inops, -is *adj* destitute, poor, in need (of);
helpless, weak; (*speech*) poor in ideas.
inōrātus *adj* unpleaded.
inōrdinātus *adj* disordered, irregular.
inōrnātus *adj* unadorned, plain; uncelebrated.
īnous *adj see n.*
inp- *etc see* **imp-**.
inquam *vt* (*defec*) to say; (*emphatic*) I repeat,
maintain.
inquiēs, -ētis *adj* restless.
inquiētō, -āre *vt* to unsettle, make difficult.
inquiētus *adj* restless, unsettled.
inquilīnus, -ī *m* inhabitant, tenant.
inquinātē *adv* filthily.
inquinātus *adj* filthy, impure.
inquinō, -āre, -āvī, -ātum *vt* to defile, stain,
contaminate.
inquīrō, -rere, -sīvī, -sītum *vt* to search for,
inquire into; (*law*) to collect evidence.
inquīsītiō, -ōnis *f* searching, inquiry; (*law*)
inquisition.
inquīsītor, -ōris *m* searcher, spy;
investigator.
inquīsītus *ppp of* **inquīrō**.
inquīsītus *adj* not investigated.
inr- *etc see* **irr-**.
īnsalūtātus *adj* ungreeted.
īnsānābilis *adj* incurable.
īnsānē *adv* madly.
īnsānia, -ae *f* madness; folly, mania, poetic
rapture.
īnsāniō, -īre, -īvī, -ītum *vi* to be mad, rave; to
rage; to be inspired.
īnsānitās, -ātis *f* unhealthiness.
īnsānum *adv* (*slang*) frightfully.
īnsānus *adj* mad; frantic, furious; outrageous.
īnsatiābilis *adj* insatiable; never cloying.
īnsatiābiliter *adv see adj.*
īnsatietās, -ātis *f* insatiateness.
īnsaturābilis *adj* insatiable.
īnsaturābiliter *adv see adj.*
īnscendō, -endere, -endī, -ēnsum *vt, vi* to
climb up, mount, embark.
īnscēnsiō, -ōnis *f* going on board.
īnscēnsus *ppp of* **īnscendō**.
īnsciēns, -entis *adj* unaware; stupid.
īnscienter *adv* ignorantly.
īnscientia, -ae *f* ignorance, inexperience;
neglect.
īnscītē *adv* clumsily.
īnscītia, -ae *f* ignorance, stupidity,
inattention.
īnscītus *adj* ignorant, stupid.
īnscius *adj* unaware, ignorant.
īnscrībō, -bere, -psī, -ptum *vt* to write on,
inscribe; to ascribe, assign; (*book*) to entitle;
(*for sale*) to advertise.

īnscrīptiō, -ōnis *f* inscribing, title.
īnscrīptus *ppp of* **īnscrībō**.
īnsculpō, -ere, -sī, -tum *vt* to carve in,
engrave on.
īnsectātiō, -ōnis *f* hot pursuit; (*words*)
abusing, persecution.
īnsectātor, -ōris *m* persecutor.
īnsector, -ārī, -ātus; -ō, -āre *vt* to pursue,
attack, criticise.
īnsectus *adj* notched.
īnsēdābiliter *adv* incessantly.
īnsēdī *perf of* **īnsīdō**.
īnsenēscō, -ēscere, -uī *vi* to grow old in.
īnsēnsilis *adj* imperceptible.
īnsepultus *adj* unburied.
īnsequēns, -entis *pres p of* **īnsequor** ♦ *adj* the
following.
īnsequor, -quī, -cūtus *vt* to follow, pursue
hotly; to proceed; (*time*) to come after, come
next; (*fig*) to attack, persecute.
īnserō, -erere, -ēvī, -itum *vt* to graft; (*fig*) to
implant.
īnserō, -ere, -uī, -tum *vt* to let in, insert; to
introduce, mingle, involve.
īnsertō, -āre *vt* to put in.
īnsertus *ppp of* **īnserō**.
īnserviō, -īre, -iī, -ītum *vt, vi* to be a slave (to);
to be devoted, submissive (to).
īnsessus *ppp of* **īnsīdō**.
īnsībilō, -āre *vi* to whistle in.
īnsideō, -ēre *vi* to sit on *or* in; to remain fixed
♦ *vt* to hold, occupy.
īnsidiae, -ārum *fpl* ambush; (*fig*) trap,
trickery.
īnsidiātor, -ōris *nt* soldier in ambush; (*fig*)
waylayer, plotter.
īnsidior, -ārī, -ātus *vi* to lie in ambush; (*with
dat*) to lie in wait for, plot against.
īnsidiōsē *adv* insidiously.
īnsidiōsus *adj* artful, treacherous.
īnsīdō, -idere, -ēdī, -essum *vi* to settle on;
(*fig*) to become fixed, rooted in ♦ *vt* to
occupy.
īnsigne, -is *nt* distinguishing mark, badge,
decoration; (*pl*) insignia, honours; (*speech*)
purple passages.
īnsigniō, -īre *vt* to distinguish.
īnsignis *adj* distinguished, conspicuous.
īnsignītē *adv* remarkably.
īnsigniter *adv* markedly.
īnsilia, -um *ntpl* treadle (of a loom).
īnsiliō, -īre, -uī *vi* to jump into *or* onto.
īnsimulātiō, -ōnis *f* accusation.
īnsimulō, -āre, -āvī, -ātum *vt* to charge,
accuse, allege (*esp falsely*).
īnsincērus *adj* adulterated.
īnsinuātiō, -ōnis *f* ingratiating.
īnsinuō, -āre, -āvī, -ātum *vt* to bring in,
introduce stealthily ♦ *vi* to creep in, worm
one's way in, penetrate; **sē ~** ingratiate
oneself; to make one's way into.
īnsipiēns, -entis *adj* senseless, foolish.
īnsipienter *adv* foolishly.

īnsipientia, -ae f folly.

īnsistō, -istere, -titī vi to stand on, step on; to stand firm, halt, pause; to tread on the heels, press on, pursue; to enter upon, apply oneself to, begin; to persist, continue.

īnsitiō, -ōnis f grafting; grafting time.

īnsitīvus adj grafted; (fig) spurious.

īnsitor, -ōris m grafter.

īnsitus ppp of īnserō ♦ adj innate; incorporated.

īnsociābilis adj incompatible.

īnsōlābiliter adv unconsolably.

īnsolēns, -entis adj unusual, unaccustomed; excessive, extravagant, insolent.

īnsolenter adv unusually; immoderately, insolently.

īnsolentia, -ae f inexperience, novelty, strangeness; excess, insolence.

īnsolēscō, -ere vi to become insolent, elated.

īnsolidus adj soft.

īnsolitus adj unaccustomed, unusual.

īnsomnia, -ae f sleeplessness.

īnsomnis adj sleepless.

īnsomnium, -ī and iī nt dream.

īnsonō, -āre, -uī vi to resound, sound; to make a noise.

īnsōns, -ontis adj innocent; harmless.

īnsōpītus adj sleepless.

īnspectō, -āre vt to look at.

īnspectus ppp of īnspiciō.

īnsperāns, -antis adj not expecting.

īnsperātus adj unexpected; ~ō, ex ~ō unexpectedly.

īnspergō, -gere, -sī, -sum vt to sprinkle on.

īnspiciō, -icere, -exī, -ectum vt to look into; to examine, inspect; (MIL) to review; (mind) to consider, get to know.

īnspīcō, -āre vt to sharpen.

īnspīrō, -āre, -āvī, -ātum vt, vi to blow on, breathe into.

īnspoliātus adj unpillaged.

īnspūtō, -āre vt to spit on.

īnstābilis adj unsteady, not firm; (fig) inconstant.

īnstāns, -antis pres p of īnstō ♦ adj present; urgent, threatening.

īnstanter adv vehemently.

īnstantia, -ae f presence; vehemence.

īnstar nt (indecl) likeness, appearance; as good as, worth.

īnstaurātiō, -ōnis f renewal.

īnstaurātīvus adj renewed.

īnstaurō, -āre, -āvī, -ātum vt to renew, restore; to celebrate; to requite.

īnsternō, -ernere, -rāvī, -rātum vt to spread over, cover.

īnstīgātor, -ōris m instigator.

īnstīgātrīx, -rīcis f female instigator.

īnstīgō, -āre vt to goad, incite, instigate.

īnstillō, -āre vt to drop on, instil.

īnstimulātor, -ōris m instigator.

īnstimulō, -āre vt to urge on.

īnstinctor, -ōris m instigator.

īnstinctus adj incited, inspired.

īnstinctus, -ūs m impulse, inspiration.

īnstipulor, -ārī, -ātus vi to bargain for.

īnstita, -ae f flounce of a lady's tunic.

īnstitī perf of īnsistō.

īnstitiō, -ōnis f stopping.

īnstitor, -ōris m pedlar.

īnstituō, -uere, -uī, -ūtum vt to set, implant; to set up, establish, build, appoint; to marshal, arrange, organize; to teach, educate; to undertake, resolve on.

īnstitūtiō, -ōnis f custom; arrangement; education; (pl) principles of education.

īnstitūtum, -ī nt way of life, tradition, law; stipulation, agreement; purpose; (pl) principles.

īnstō, -āre, -itī vi to stand on or in; to be close, be hard on the heels of, pursue; (events) to approach, impend; (fig) to press on, work hard at; (speech) to insist, urge.

īnstrātus ppp of īnsternō.

īnstrēnuus adj languid, slow.

īnstrepō, -ere vi to creak.

īnstructiō, -ōnis f building; setting out.

īnstructius adv in better style.

īnstructor, -ōris m preparer.

īnstructus ppp of īnstruō ♦ adj provided, equipped; prepared, versed.

īnstructus, -ūs m equipment.

īnstrūmentum, -ī nt tool, instrument; equipment, furniture, stock; (fig) means, provision; dress, embellishment.

īnstruō, -ere, -xī, -ctum vt to erect, build up; (MIL) to marshal, array; to equip, provide, prepare; (fig) to teach, train.

īnsuāsum, -ī nt a dark colour.

īnsuāvis adj disagreeable.

īnsūdō, -āre vi to perspire on.

īnsuēfactus adj accustomed.

īnsuēscō, -scere, -vī, -tum vt to train, accustom ♦ vi to become accustomed.

īnsuētus ppp of īnsuēscō.

īnsuētus adj unaccustomed, unused; unusual.

īnsula, -ae f island; block of houses.

īnsulānus, -ī m islander.

īnsulsē adv see adj.

īnsulsitās, -ātis f lack of taste, absurdity.

īnsulsus adj tasteless, absurd, dull.

īnsultō, -āre, vt, vi to jump on, leap in; (fig) to exult, taunt, insult.

īnsultūra, -ae f jumping on.

īnsum, inesse, īnfuī vi to be in or on; to belong to.

īnsūmō, -ere, -psī, -ptum vt to spend, devote.

īnsuō, -uere, -uī, -ūtum vt to sew in, sew up in.

Noun declensions and verb conjugations are shown on pp xiii to xxv. The present infinitive ending of a verb shows to which conjugation it belongs: -āre = 1st; -ēre = 2nd; -ere = 3rd and -īre = 4th. Irregular verbs are shown on p xxvi

īnsuper *adv* above, on top; besides, over and above; (*prep with abl*) besides.

īnsuperābilis *adj* unconquerable, impassable.

īnsurgō, -gere, -rēxī, -rēctum *vi* to stand up, rise to; to rise, grow, swell; to rise against.

īnsusurrō, -āre *vt, vi* to whisper.

īnsūtus *ppp of* **īnsuō**.

intābēscō, -ēscere, -uī *vi* to melt away, waste away.

intāctilis *adj* intangible.

intāctus *adj* untouched, intact; untried; undefiled, chaste.

intāminātus *adj* unsullied.

intēctus *ppp of* **integō**.

intēctus *adj* uncovered, unclad; frank.

integellus *adj* fairly whole *or* pure.

integer, -rī *adj* whole, complete, unimpaired, intact; sound, fresh, new; (*mind*) unbiassed, free; (*character*) virtuous, pure, upright; (*decision*) undecided, open; **in ~rum restituere** restore to a former state; **ab, dē, ex ~rō** afresh; **~rum est mihi** I am at liberty (to).

integō, -egere, -ēxī, -ēctum *vt* to cover over; to protect.

integrāscō, -ere *vi* to begin all over again.

integrātiō, -ōnis *f* renewing.

integrē *adv* entirely; honestly; correctly.

integritās, -ātis *f* completeness, soundness; integrity, honesty; (*language*) correctness.

integrō, -āre *vt* to renew, replenish, repair; (*mind*) to refresh.

integumentum, -ī *nt* cover, covering, shelter.

intellēctus *ppp of* **intellegō**.

intellēctus, -ūs *m* understanding; (*word*) meaning.

intellegēns, -entis *pres p of* **intellegō** ♦ *adj* intelligent, a connoisseur.

intellegenter *adv* intelligently.

intellegentia, -ae *f* discernment, understanding; taste.

intellegō, -egere, -ēxī, -ēctum *vt* to understand, perceive, realize; to be a connoisseur.

intemerātus *adj* pure, undefiled.

intemperāns, -antis *adj* immoderate, extravagant; incontinent.

intemperanter *adv* extravagantly.

intemperantia, -ae *f* excess, extravagance; arrogance.

intemperātē *adv* dissolutely.

intemperātus *adj* excessive.

intemperiae, -ārum *fpl* inclemency; madness.

intemperiēs, -ēī *f* inclemency, storm; (*fig*) fury.

intempestīvē *adv* inopportunely.

intempestīvus *adj* unseasonable, untimely.

intempestus *adj* (*night*) the dead of; unhealthy.

intemptātus *adj* untried.

intendō, -dere, -dī, -tum *vt* to stretch out, strain, spread; (*weapon*) to aim; (*tent*) to pitch; (*attention, course*) to direct, turn; (*fact*) to increase, exaggerate; (*speech*) to maintain; (*trouble*) to threaten ♦ *vi* to make for, intend; **animō ~** purpose; **sē ~** exert oneself.

intentē *adv* strictly.

intentiō, -ōnis *f* straining, tension; (*mind*) exertion, attention; (*law*) accusation.

intentō, -āre *vt* to stretch out, aim; (*fig*) to threaten with, attack.

intentus *ppp of* **intendō** ♦ *adj* taut; attentive, intent; strict; (*speech*) vigorous.

intentus, -ūs *m* stretching out.

intepeō, -ēre *vi* to be warm.

intepēscō, -ēscere, -uī *vi* to be warmed.

inter *prep* (*with acc*) between, among, during, in the course of; in spite of; **~ haec** meanwhile; **~ manūs** within reach; **~ nōs** confidentially; **~ sē** mutually, one another; **~ sīcāriōs** in the murder court; **~ viam** on the way.

interāmenta, -ōrum *ntpl* ship's timbers.

interaptus *adj* joined together.

interārēscō, -ere *vi* to wither away.

interbibō, -ere *vi* to drink up.

interbītō, -ere *vi* to fall through.

intercalāris *adj* intercalary.

intercalārius *adj* intercalary.

intercalō, -āre *vt* to intercalate.

intercapēdō, -inis *f* interruption, respite.

intercēdō, -ēdere, -ēssī, -ēssum *vi* to come between, intervene; to occur; to become surety; to interfere, obstruct; (*tribune*) to protest, veto.

interceptiō, -ōnis *f* taking away.

interceptor, -ōris *m* embezzler.

interceptus *ppp of* **intercipiō**.

intercēssiō, -ōnis *f* (*law*) becoming surety; (*tribune*) veto.

intercēssor, -ōris *m* mediator, surety; interposer of the veto; obstructor.

intercīdō, -ere, -ī *vi* to fall short; to happen in the meantime; to get lost, become obsolete, be forgotten.

intercīdō, -dere, -dī, -sum *vt* to cut through, sever.

intercinō, -ere *vt* to sing between.

intercipiō, -ipere, -ēpi, -eptum *vt* to intercept; to embezzle, steal; to cut off, obstruct.

intercīsē *adv* piecemeal.

intercīsus *ppp of* **intercīdō**.

interclūdō, -dere, -sī, -sum *vt* to cut off, block, shut off, prevent; **animam ~** suffocate.

interclūsiō, -ōnis *f* stoppage.

interclūsus *ppp of* **interclūdō**.

intercolumnium, -ī *and* **iī** *nt* space between two pillars.

intercurrō, -ere *vi* to mingle with; to intercede; to hurry in the meantime.

intercursō, -āre *vi* to crisscross; to attack

between the lines.

intercursus, -ūs *m* intervention.

intercus, -tis *adj*: **aqua ~** dropsy.

interdīcō, -īcere, -īxī, -ictum *vt, vi* to forbid, interdict; (*praetor*) to make a provisional order; **aquā et ignī ~** banish.

interdictiō, -ōnis *f* prohibiting, banishment.

interdictum, -ī *nt* prohibition; provisional order (by a praetor).

interdiū *adv* by day.

interdō, -are *vt* to make at intervals; to distribute; **nōn ~uim** I wouldn't care.

interductus, -ūs *m* punctuation.

interdum *adv* now and then, occasionally.

intereā *adv* meanwhile, in the meantime; nevertheless.

interēmī *perf of* **interimō**.

interemptus *ppp of* **interimō**.

intereō, -īre, -iī, -itum *vi* to be lost, perish, die.

interequitō, -āre *vt, vi* to ride between.

interesse *infin of* **intersum**.

interfātiō, -ōnis *f* interruption.

interfātur, -ārī, -ātus *vi* to interrupt.

interfectiō, -ōnis *f* killing.

interfector, -ōris *m* murderer.

interfectrīx, -rīcis *f* murderess.

interfectus *ppp of* **interficiō**.

interficiō, -icere, -ēcī, -ectum *vt* to kill, destroy.

interfiō, -ierī *vi* to pass away.

interfluō, -ere, -xī *vt, vi* to flow between.

interfodiō, -ere *vt* to pierce.

interfugiō, -ere *vi* to flee among.

interfuī *perf of* **intersum**.

interfulgeō, -ēre *vi* to shine amongst.

interfūsus *ppp* lying between; marked here and there.

interiaceō, -ēre *vi* to lie between.

interibi *adv* in the meantime.

intericiō, -icere, -iēcī, -iectum *vt* to put amongst or between, interpose, mingle; **annō ~iectō** after a year.

interiectus, -ūs *m* coming in between; interval.

interiī *perf of* **intereō**.

interim *adv* meanwhile, in the meantime; sometimes; all the same.

interimō, -imere, -ēmī, -emptum *vt* to abolish, destroy, kill.

interior, -ōris *adj* inner, interior; nearer, on the near side; secret, private; more intimate, more profound.

interitiō, -ōnis *f* ruin.

interitus, -ūs *m* destruction, ruin, death.

interiūnctus *adj* joined together.

interius *adv* inwardly; too short.

interlābor, -ī *vi* to glide between.

interlegō, -ere *vt* to pick here and there.

interlinō, -inere, -ēvī, -itum *vt* to smear in

parts; to erase here and there.

interloquor, -quī, -cūtus *vi* to interrupt.

interlūceō, -cēre, -xī *vi* to shine through, be clearly seen.

interlūnia, -ōrum *ntpl* new moon.

interluō, -ere *vt* to wash, flow between.

intermēnstruus *adj* of the new moon ♦ *nt* new moon.

interminātus *ppa of* **interminor** ♦ *adj* forbidden.

interminātus *adj* endless.

interminor, -ārī, -ātus *vi* to threaten; to forbid threateningly.

intermisceō, -scēre, -scuī, -xtum *vt* to mix, intermingle.

intermissiō, -ōnis *f* interruption.

intermittō, -ittere, -īsī, -issum *vt* to break off; to interrupt; to omit, neglect; to allow to elapse ♦ *vi* to cease, pause.

intermixtus *ppp of* **intermisceō**.

intermorior, -ī, -tuus *vi* to die suddenly.

intermortuus *adj* falling unconscious.

intermundia, -ōrum *ntpl* space between worlds.

intermūrālis *adj* between two walls.

internātus *adj* growing among.

internecīnus *adj* murderous, of extermination.

interneciō, -ōnis *f* massacre, extermination.

internecīvus *adj* = **internecīnus**.

internectō, -ere *vt* to enclasp.

internōdia, -ōrum *ntpl* space between joints.

internōscō, -scere, -vī, -tum *vt* to distinguish between.

internūntia, -iae *f* messenger, mediator, go-between.

internūntiō, -āre *vi* to exchange messages.

internūntius, -ī and iī *m* messenger, mediator, go-between.

internus *adj* internal, civil ♦ *ntpl* domestic affairs.

interō, -erere, -rīvī, -rītum *vt* to rub in; (*fig*) to concoct.

interpellātiō, -ōnis *f* interruption.

interpellātor, -ōris *m* interrupter.

interpellō, -āre, -āvī, -ātum *vt* to interrupt; to disturb, obstruct.

interpolis *adj* made up.

interpolō, -āre *vt* to renovate, do up; (*writing*) to falsify.

interpōnō, -ōnere, -osuī, -ositum *vt* to put between *or* amongst, insert; (*time*) to allow to elapse; (*person*) to introduce, admit; (*pretext etc*) to put forward, interpose; **fidem ~** pledge one's word; **sē ~** interfere, become involved.

interpositiō, -ōnis *f* introduction.

interpositus *ppp of* **interpōnō**.

interpositus, -ūs *m* obstruction.

interpres, -tis *m/f* agent, negotiator;

Noun declensions and verb conjugations are shown on pp xiii to xxv. The present infinitive ending of a verb shows to which conjugation it belongs: **-āre** = 1st; **-ēre** = 2nd; **-ere** = 3rd and **-īre** = 4th. Irregular verbs are shown on p xxvi

interpreter, explainer, translator.
interpretātiō, -ōnis *f* interpretation, exposition, meaning.
interpretātus *adj* translated.
interpretor, -ārī, -ātus *vt* to interpret, explain, translate, understand.
interprimō, -imere, -essī, -essum *vt* to squeeze.
interpūnctiō, -ōnis *f* punctuation.
interpūnctus *adj* well-divided ♦ *ntpl* punctuation.
interquiēscō, -scere, -vī *vi* to rest awhile.
interrēgnum, -ī *nt* regency, interregnum; interval between consuls.
interrēx, -ēgis *m* regent; deputy consul.
interritus *adj* undaunted, unafraid.
interrogātiō, -ōnis *f* question; (*law*) cross-examination; (*logic*) syllogism.
interrogātiuncula, -ae *f* short argument.
interrogō, -āre, -āvī, -ātum *vt* to ask, put a question; (*law*) to cross-examine, bring to trial.
interrumpō, -umpere, -ūpī, -uptum *vt* to break up, sever; (*fig*) to break off, interrupt.
interruptē *adv* interruptedly.
intersaepiō, -īre, -sī, -tum *vt* to shut off, close.
interscindō, -ndere, -dī, -ssum *vt* to cut off, break down.
interserō, -erere, -ēvī, -itum *vt* to plant at intervals.
interserō, -ere, -uī, -tum *vt* to interpose.
intersitus *ppp of* **interserō.**
interspīrātiō, -ōnis *f* pause for breath.
interstinguō, -guere, -ctum *vt* to mark, spot; to extinguish.
interstringō, -ere *vt* to strangle.
intersum, -esse, -fuī *vi* to be between; to be amongst, be present at; (*time*) to elapse; **~est** there is a difference; it is of importance, it concerns, it matters; **meā ~est** it is important for me.
intertextus *adj* interwoven.
intertrahō, -here, -xī *vt* to take away.
intertrīmentum, -ī *nt* wastage; loss, damage.
interturbātiō, -ōnis *f* confusion.
intervallum, -ī *nt* space, distance, interval; (*time*) pause, interval, respite; difference.
intervellō, -ere *vt* to pluck out; to tear apart.
interveniō, -enīre, -ēnī, -entum *vi* to come on the scene, intervene; to interfere (with), interrupt; to happen, occur.
interventor, -ōris *m* intruder.
interventus, -ūs *m* appearance, intervention; occurrence.
intervertō, -tere, -tī, -sum *vt* to embezzle; to rob, cheat.
intervīsō, -ere, -ī, -um *vt* to have a look at, look and see; to visit occasionally.
intervolitō, -āre *vi* to fly about, amongst.
intervomō, -ere *vt* to throw up (amongst).
intervortō *vt see* **intervertō.**
intestābilis *adj* infamous, wicked.

intestātō *adv* without making a will.
intestātus *adj* intestate; not convicted by witnesses.
intestīnus *adj* internal ♦ *nt and ntpl* intestines, entrails.
intexō, -ere, -uī, -tum *vt* to inweave, embroider, interlace.
intibum, -ī *nt* endive.
intimē *adv* most intimately, cordially.
intimus *adj* innermost; deepest; secret; intimate ♦ *m* most intimate friend.
intingō (intinguō), -gere, -xī, -ctum *vt* to dip in.
intolerābilis *adj* unbearable; irresistible.
intolerandus *adj* intolerable.
intolerāns, -antis *adj* impatient; unbearable.
intoleranter *adv* excessively.
intolerantia, -ae *f* insolence.
intonō, -āre, -uī, -ātum *vi* to thunder, thunder out.
intōnsus *adj* unshorn, unshaven; long-haired, bearded; uncouth.
intorqueō, -quēre, -sī, -tum *vt* to twist, wrap round; to hurl at.
intortus *ppp of* **intorqueō** ♦ *adj* twisted, curled; confused.
intrā *adv* inside, within ♦ *prep* (*with acc*) inside, within; (*time*) within, during; (*amount*) less than, within the limits of.
intrābilis *adj* navigable.
intractābilis *adj* formidable.
intractātus *adj* not broken in; unattempted.
intremīscō, -īscere, -uī *vi* to begin to shake.
intremō, -ere *vi* to tremble.
intrepidē *adv see adj.*
intrepidus *adj* calm, brave; undisturbed.
intrīcō, -āre *vt* to entangle.
intrīnsecus *adv* on the inside.
intrītus *adj* not worn out.
intrīvī *perf of* **interō.**
intrō *adv* inside, in.
intrō, -āre, -āvī, -ātum *vt, vi* to go in, enter; to penetrate.
intrōdūcō, -ūcere, -ūxī, -uctum *vt* to bring in, introduce, escort in; to institute.
intrōductiō, -ōnis *f* bringing in.
introeō, -īre, -iī, -itum *vi* to go into, enter.
intrōferō, -ferre, -tulī, -lātum *vt* to carry inside.
intrōgredior, -dī, -ssus *vi* to step inside.
introitus, -ūs *m* entrance; beginning.
intrōlātus *ppp of* **intrōferō.**
intrōmittō, -ittere, -īsī, -issus *vt* to let in, admit.
intrōrsum, intrōrsus *adv* inwards, inside.
intrōrumpō, -ere *vi* to break into.
intrōspectō, -āre *vt* to look in at.
intrōspiciō, -icere, -exī, -ectum *vt* to look inside; to look at, examine.
intubum *etc see* **intibum.**
intueor, -ērī, -itus *vt* to look at, watch; to contemplate, consider; to admire.
intumēscō, -ēscere, -uī *vi* to begin to swell,

rise; to increase; to become angry.

intumulātus *adj* unburied.

intuor *etc see* **intueor**.

inturbidus *adj* undisturbed; quiet.

intus *adv* inside, within, in; from within.

intūtus *adj* unsafe; unguarded.

inula, -ae *f* elecampane.

inultus *adj* unavenged; unpunished.

inumbrō, -āre *vt* to shade; to cover.

inundō, -āre, -āvī, -ātum *vt, vi* to overflow, flood.

inunguō, -unguere, -ūnxī, -ūnctum *vt* to anoint.

inurbānē *adv see adj.*

inurbānus *adj* rustic, unmannerly, unpolished.

inurgeō, -ēre *vi* to push, butt.

inūrō, -rere, -ssī, -stum *vt* to brand; (*fig*) to brand, inflict.

inūsitātē *adv* strangely.

inūsitātus *adj* unusual, extraordinary.

inūstus *ppp of* **inūrō**.

inūtilis *adj* useless; harmful.

inūtilitās, -ātis *f* uselessness, harmfulness.

inūtiliter *adv* unprofitably.

invādō, -dere, -sī, -sum *vt, vi* to get in, make one's way in; to enter upon; to fall upon, attack, invade; to seize, take possession of.

invalēscō, -ēscere, -uī *vi* to grow stronger.

invalidus *adj* weak; inadequate.

invāsī *perf of* **invādō**.

invectiō, -ōnis *f* importing; invective.

invectus *ppp of* **inveho**.

invehō, -here, -xī, -ctum *vt* to carry in, bring in; **sē ~** attack.

invehor, -hī, -ctus *vi* to ride, drive, sail in or into, enter; to attack; to inveigh against.

invēndibilis *adj* unsaleable.

inveniō, -enīre, -ēnī, -entum *vt* to find, come upon; to find out, discover; to invent, contrive; to win, get.

inventiō, -ōnis *f* invention; (*RHET*) compiling the subject-matter.

inventor, -ōris *m* inventor, discoverer.

inventrīx, -rīcis *f* inventor, discoverer.

inventus *ppp of* **inveniō** ♦ *nt* invention, discovery.

invenustus *adj* unattractive; unlucky in love.

inverēcundus *adj* immodest, shameless.

invergō, -ere *vt* to pour upon.

inversiō, -ōnis *f* transposition; irony.

inversus *ppp of* **invertō** ♦ *adj* upside down, inside out; perverted.

invertō, -tere, -tī, -sum *vt* to turn over, invert; to change, pervert.

invesperāscit, -ere *vi* it is dusk.

investīgātiō, -ōnis *f* search.

investīgātor, -ōris *m* investigator.

investīgō, -āre, -āvī, -ātum *vt* to follow the trail of; (*fig*) to track down, find out.

inveterāscō, -scere, -vī *vi* to grow old (in); to become established, fixed, inveterate; to grow obsolete.

inveterātiō, -ōnis *f* chronic illness.

inveterātus *adj* of long standing, inveterate.

invexī *perf of* **invehō**.

invicem *adv* in turns, alternately; mutually, each other.

invictus *adj* unbeaten; unconquerable.

invidentia, -ae *f* envy.

invideō, -idēre, -īdī, -īsum *vt, vi* to cast an evil eye on; (*with dat*) to envy, grudge; to begrudge.

invidia, -ae *f* envy, jealousy, ill-will; unpopularity.

invidiōsē *adv* spitefully.

invidiōsus *adj* envious, spiteful; enviable; invidious, hateful.

invidus *adj* envious, jealous, hostile.

invigilō, -āre *vi* to be awake over; to watch over, be intent on.

inviolābilis *adj* invulnerable; inviolable.

inviolātē *adv* inviolately.

inviolātus *adj* unhurt; inviolable.

invīsitātus *adj* unseen, unknown, strange.

invīsō, -ere, -ī, -um *vt* to go and see, visit, have a look at; to inspect.

invīsus *adj* hateful, detested; hostile.

invīsus *adj* unseen.

invītāmentum, -ī *nt* attraction, inducement.

invītātiō, -ōnis *f* invitation; entertainment.

invītātus, -ūs *m* invitation.

invītē *adv* unwillingly.

invītō, -āre, -āvī, -ātum *vt* to invite; to treat, entertain; to summon; to attract, induce.

invītus *adj* against one's will, reluctant.

invius *adj* trackless, impassable; inaccessible.

invocātus *ppp of* **invocō**.

invocātus *adj* unbidden, uninvited.

invocō, -āre, -āvī, -ātum *vt* to call upon, invoke; to appeal to; to call.

involātus, -ūs *m* flight.

involitō, -āre *vi* to play upon.

involō, -āre *vi* to fly at, pounce on, attack.

involūcre, -is *nt* napkin.

involūcrum, -ī *nt* covering, case.

involūtus *ppp of* **involvō** ♦ *adj* complicated.

involvō, -vere, -vī, -ūtum *vt* to roll on; to wrap up, envelop, entangle.

involvolus, -ī *m* caterpillar.

invulnerātus *adj* unwounded.

iō *interj* (*joy*) hurrah!; (*pain*) oh!; (*calling*) ho there!

Iōannēs, -is *m* John.

iocātiō, -ōnis *f* joke.

iocor, -ārī, -ātus *vt, vi* to joke, jest.

iocōsē *adv* jestingly.

iocōsus *adj* humorous, playful.

ioculāris *adj* laughable, funny ♦ *ntpl* jokes.

ioculārius *adj* ludicrous.

Noun declensions and verb conjugations are shown on pp xiii to xxv. The present infinitive ending of a verb shows to which conjugation it belongs: **-āre** = 1st; **-ēre** = 2nd; **-ere** = 3rd and **-īre** = 4th. Irregular verbs are shown on p **xxvi**

ioculātor, -ōris m jester.
ioculor, -ārī vi to joke.
ioculus, -ī m a bit of fun.
iocus, -ī m (pl -**a, -ōrum** nt) joke, jest; **extrā ~um** joking apart; **per ~um** for fun.
Iōnes, -um mpl Ionians.
Iōnia, -iae f Ionia, coastal district of Asia Minor.
Iōnium, -ī nt Ionian Sea, W. of Greece.
Iōnius, -icus adj Ionian.
iōta nt (indecl) Greek letter I.
Iovis gen of **Iuppiter**.
Iphianasse, -ae f Iphigenia.
Iphigenīa, -ae f daughter of Agamemnon (who sacrificed her at Aulis to Diana).
ipse, -a, -um, -īus prep self, himself etc; in person, for one's own part, of one's own accord, by oneself; just, precisely, very; the master, the host.
ipsissimus his very own self; **nunc ~um** right now.
īra, -ae f anger, rage; object of indignation.
īrācundē adv angrily.
īrācundia, -ae f irascibility, quick temper; rage, resentment.
īrācundus adj irascible, choleric; resentful.
īrāscor, -ī vi to be angry, get furious.
īrātē adv see adj.
īrātus adj angry, furious.
īre infin of **eō**.
Īris, -dis (acc -**m**) f messenger of the gods; the rainbow.
īrōnīa, -ae f irony.
irrāsus adj unshaven.
irraucēscō, -cēscere, -sī vi to become hoarse.
irredivīvus adj irreparable.
irreligātus adj not tied.
irreligiōsē adv see adj.
irreligiōsus adj impious.
irremeābilis adj from which there is no returning.
irreparābilis adj irretrievable.
irrepertus adj undiscovered.
irrēpō, -ere, -sī vi to steal into, insinuate oneself into.
irreprehēnsus adj blameless.
irrequiētus adj restless.
irresectus adj unpared.
irresolūtus adj not slackened.
irrētiō, -īre, -iī, -ītum vt to ensnare, entangle.
irretortus adj not turned back.
irreverentia, -ae f disrespect.
irrevocābilis adj irrevocable; implacable.
irrevocātus adj without an encore.
irrīdeō, -dēre, -sī, -sum vi to laugh, joke ♦ vt to laugh at, ridicule.
irrīdiculē adv unwittily.
irrīdiculum, -ī nt laughing stock.
irrigātiō, -ōnis f irrigation.
irrigō, -āre, -āvī, -ātum vt to water, irrigate; to inundate; (fig) to shed over, flood, refresh.
irriguus adj well-watered, swampy; refreshing.
irrīsiō, -ōnis f ridicule, mockery.

irrīsor, -ōris m scoffer.
irrīsus ppp of **irrīdeō**.
irrīsus, -ūs m derision.
irrītābilis adj excitable.
irrītāmen, -inis nt excitement, provocation.
irrītātiō, -ōnis f incitement, irritation.
irrītō, -āre, -āvī, -ātum vt to provoke, incite, enrage.
irritus adj invalid, null and void; useless, vain, ineffective; (person) unsuccessful; **ad ~um cadere** come to nothing.
irrogātiō, -ōnis f imposing.
irrogō, -āre vt to propose (a measure) against; to impose.
irrōrō, -āre vt to bedew.
irrumpō, -umpere, -ūpī, -uptum vt, vi to rush in, break in; to intrude, invade.
irruō, -ere, -ī vi to force a way in, rush in, attack; (speech) to make a blunder.
irruptiō, -ōnis f invasion, raid.
irruptus ppp of **irrumpō**.
irruptus adj unbroken.
is, ea, id pron he, she, it; this, that, the; such; **nōn is sum quī** I am not the man to; **id** (with vi) for this reason; **id quod** what; **ad id** hitherto; for the purpose; besides; **in eō est** it has come to this; one is on the point of; it depends on this.
Ismara, -ōrum ntpl, -**us, -ī** m Mt Ismarus in Thrace.
Ismarius adj Thracian.
Īsocratēs, -is m Athenian orator and teacher of rhetoric.
istāc adv that way.
iste, -a, -ud, -īus pron that of yours; (law) your client, the plaintiff, the defendant; (contemptuous) the fellow; that, such.
Isthmius adj, ntpl the Isthmian Games.
Isthmus (-os), -ī m Isthmus of Corinth.
istic, -aec, -uc and **oc** pron that of yours, that.
istīc adv there; in this, on this occasion.
istinc adv from there; of that.
istīusmodī such, of that kind.
istō, istōc adv to you, there, yonder.
istōrsum adv in that direction.
istūc adv (to) there, to that.
ita adv thus, so; as follows; yes; accordingly; **itane?** really?; **nōn ita** not so very; **ita ut** just as; **ita ... ut so**, to such an extent that; on condition that; only in so far as; **ita ... ut nōn** without; **ut ... ita** just as ... so; although ... nevertheless.
Italī, -ōrum mpl Italians.
Italia, -iae f Italy.
Italicus, -is, -us adj Italian.
itaque conj and so, therefore, accordingly.
item adv likewise, also.
iter, -ineris nt way, journey, march; a day's journey or march; route, road, passage; (fig) way, course; **~ mihi est** I have to go to; **~ dare** grant a right of way; **~ facere** to journey, march, travel; **ex, in ~inere** on the way, on the march; **māgnīs ~ineribus** by forced

marches.

iterātiō, -ōnis f repetition.

iterō, -āre, -āvī, -ātum vt to repeat, renew; to plough again.

iterum adv again, a second time; ~ atque ~ repeatedly.

Ithaca, -ae, -ē, -ēs f island W. of Greece (home of Ulysses).

Ithacēnsis, -us adj Ithacan.

Ithacus, -ī m Ulysses.

itidem adv in the same way, similarly.

itiō, -ōnis f going.

itō, -āre vi to go.

itus, -ūs m going, movement, departure.

iuba, -ae f mane; crest.

Iuba, -ae m king of Numidia (supporter of Pompey).

iubar, -is nt brightness, light.

iubātus adj crested.

iubeō, -bēre, -ssī, -ssum vt to order, command, tell; (greeting) to bid; (MED) to prescribe; (POL) to decree, ratify, appoint.

iūcundē adv agreeably.

iūcunditās, -ātis f delight, enjoyment.

iūcundus adj delightful, pleasing.

Iūdaea, -ae f Judaea, Palestine.

Iūdaeus, -ī m Jew.

Iūdaeus, Iūdaicus adj Jewish.

iūdex, -icis m judge; (pl) panel of jurors; (fig) critic.

iūdicātiō, -ōnis f judicial inquiry; opinion.

iūdicātum, -ī nt judgment, precedent.

iūdicātus, -ūs m office of judge.

iūdiciālis adj judicial, forensic.

iūdiciārius adj judiciary.

iūdicium, -ī and **iī** nt trial; court of justice; sentence; judgment, opinion; discernment, taste, tact; **in ~ vocāre, ~ō arcessere** sue, summon.

iūdicō, -āre, -āvī, -ātum vt to judge, examine, sentence, condemn; to form an opinion of, decide; to declare.

iugālis adj yoked together; nuptial.

iugātiō, -ōnis f training (of a vine).

iūgerum, -ī nt a land measure (240 x 120 feet).

iūgis adj perpetual, never-failing.

iūglāns, -andis f walnut tree.

iugō, -āre, -āvī, -ātum vt to couple, marry.

iugōsus adj hilly.

Iugulae, -ārum fpl Orion's Belt.

iugulō, -āre, -āvī, -ātum vt to cut the throat of, kill, murder.

iugulus, -ī m, **-um, -ī** nt throat.

iugum, -ī nt (animals) yoke, collar; pair, team; (MIL) yoke of subjugation; (mountain) ridge, height, summit; (ASTRO) Libra; (loom) crossbeam; (ship) thwart; (fig) yoke, bond.

Iugurtha, -ae m king of Numidia (rebel against Rome).

Iugurthīnus adj see n.

Iūlēus adj of Iulus; of Caesar; of July.

Iūlius, -ī m Roman family name (esp Caesar); (month) July.

Iūlius, -iānus adj see n.

Iūlus, -ī m son of Aeneas, Ascanius.

iūmentum, -ī nt beast of burden, packhorse.

iunceus adj of rushes; slender.

iuncōsus adj rushy.

iūnctiō, -ōnis f union.

iūnctūra, -ae f joint; combination; relationship.

iūnctus ppp of **iungō ♦** adj connected, attached.

iuncus, -ī m rush.

iungō, -gere, iūnxī, iūnctum vt to join together, unite; to yoke, harness; to mate; (river) to span, bridge; (fig) to bring together, connect, associate; (agreement) to make; (words) to compound.

iūnior, -ōris adj younger.

iūniperus, -ī f juniper.

Iūnius, -ī m Roman family name; (month) June.

Iūnius adj of June.

Iūnō, -ōnis f Roman goddess wife of Jupiter, patroness of women and marriage.

Iūnōnālis adj see n.

Iūnōnicola, -ae m worshipper of Juno.

Iūnōnigena, -ae m Vulcan.

Iūnōnius adj = **Iūnōnālis**.

Iuppiter, Iovis m Jupiter (king of the gods, god of sky and weather); ~ **Stygius** Pluto; **sub Iove** in the open air.

iūrātor, -ōris m sworn judge.

iūrecōnsultus etc see **iūriscōnsultus**.

iūreiūrō, -āre vi to swear.

iūreperītus etc see **iūrisperītus**.

iūrgium, -ī and **iī** nt quarrel, brawl.

iūrgō, -āre vi to quarrel, squabble ♦ vt to scold.

iūridiciālis adj of law, juridical.

iūriscōnsultus, -ī m lawyer.

iūrisdictiō, -ōnis f administration of justice; authority.

iūrisperītus adj versed in the law.

iūrō, -āre, -āvī, -ātum vi, vt to swear, take an oath; to conspire; **in nōmen ~** swear allegiance to; **in verba ~** take a prescribed form of oath; **~ātus** having sworn, under oath.

iūs, iūris nt broth, soup.

iūs, iūris nt law, right, justice; law court; jurisdiction, authority; ~ **gentium** international law; ~ **pūblicum** constitutional law; **summum ~** the strict letter of the law; ~ **dīcere** administer justice; **suī iūris** independent; **iūre** rightly, justly.

iūsiūrandum, iūrisiūrandī nt oath.

iussī perf of **iubeō**.

iussū abl m by order.

iussus ppp of **iubeō ♦** nt order, command, prescription.

Noun declensions and verb conjugations are shown on pp xiii to xxv. The present infinitive ending of a verb shows to which conjugation it belongs: -**āre** = 1st; -**ēre** = 2nd; -**ere** = 3rd and -**īre** = 4th. Irregular verbs are shown on p xxvi

iūstē *adv* duly, rightly.
iūstificus *adj* just dealing.
iūstitia, -ae *f* justice, uprightness, fairness.
iūstitium, -ī *and* **iī** *nt* cessation of legal business.
iūstus *adj* just, fair; lawful, right; regular, proper ♦ *nt* right ♦ *ntpl* rights; formalities, obsequies.
iūtus *ppp of* **iuvō**.
iuvenālis *adj* youthful ♦ *ntpl* youthful games.
Iuvenālis, -is *m* Juvenal (*Roman satirist*).
iuvenāliter *adv* vigorously, impetuously.
iuvenca, -ae *f* heifer; girl.
iuvencus, -ī *m* bullock; young man ♦ *adj* young.
iuvenēscō, -ēscere, -uī *vi* to grow up; to grow young again.
iuvenīlis *adj* youthful.
iuvenīliter *adv see* adj.
iuvenis *adj* young ♦ *m/f* young man *or* woman (*20-45 years*), man, warrior.
iuvenor, -ārī *vi* to behave indiscreetly.
iuventa, -ae *f* youth.
iuventās, -ātis *f* youth.
iuventūs, -ūtis *f* youth, manhood; men, soldiers.
iuvō, -āre, iūvī, iūtum *vt* to help, be of use to; to please, delight; **~at mē** I am glad.
iuxtā *adv* near by, close; alike, just the same ♦ *prep* (*with acc*) close to, hard by; next to; very like, next door to; **~ ac, cum, quam** just the same as.
iuxtim *adv* near; equally.
īvī *perf of* **eō**.
Ixīōn, -onis *m* Lapith king (*bound to a revolving wheel in Tartarus*).
Ixīoneus *adj see* n.
Ixīonidae, -ārum *mpl* Centaurs.
Ixīonidēs, -ae *m* Pirithous.

J, j

J *see* **I**.

K, k

Kalendae, -ārum *fpl* Kalends, first day of each month.
Karthāgō *see* **Carthāgō**.

L, l

labāscō, -ere *vi* to totter, waver.
lābēcula, -ae *f* aspersion.
labefaciō, -facere, -fēcī, -factum (*pass -fīō, -fierī*) *vt* to shake; (*fig*) to weaken, ruin.
labefactō, -āre, -āvī, -ātum *vt* to shake; (*fig*) to weaken, destroy.
labellum, -ī *nt* lip.
lābellum, -ī *nt* small basin.
Laberius, -ī *m* Roman family name (*esp a writer of mimes*).
lābēs, -is *f* sinking, fall; ruin, destruction.
lābēs, -is *f* spot, blemish; disgrace, stigma; (*person*) blot.
labia, -iae *f* lip.
Labiēnus, -ī *m* Roman surname (*esp Caesar's officer who went over to Pompey*).
labiōsus *adj* large-lipped.
labium, -ī *and* **iī** *nt* lip.
labō, -āre *vi* to totter, be unsteady, give way; to waver, hesitate, collapse.
lābor, -bī, -psus *vi* to slide, glide; to sink, fall; to slip away, pass away; (*fig*) to fade, decline, perish; to be disappointed, make a mistake.
labor (-ōs), -ōris *m* effort, exertion, labour; work, task; hardship, suffering, distress; (*ASTRO*) eclipse.
labōrifer, -ī *adj* sore afflicted.
labōriōsē *adv* laboriously, with difficulty.
labōriōsus *adj* troublesome, difficult; industrious.
labōrō, -āre, -āvī, -ātum *vi* to work, toil, take pains; to suffer, be troubled (with), be in distress; to be anxious, worried ♦ *vt* to work out, make, produce.
labōs *etc see* **labor**.
labrum, -ī *nt* lip; edge, rim; **primīs ~īs gustāre** acquire a smattering of.
lābrum, -ī *nt* tub, vat; bath.
lābrusca, -ae *f* wild vine.
lābruscum, -ī *nt* wild grape.

labyrinthēus *adj* labyrinthine.
labyrinthus, -ī *m* labyrinth, maze (*esp that of Cnossos in Crete*).
lac, lactis *nt* milk.
Lacaena, -ae *f* Spartan woman ♦ *adj* Spartan.
Lacedaemōn (-ō), -onis (*acc* **-ona**) *f* Sparta.
Lacedaemonius *adj* Spartan.
lacer, -ī *adj* torn, mangled, lacerated; tearing.
lacerātiō, -ōnis *f* tearing.
lacerna, -ae *f* cloak (*worn in cold weather*).
lacernātus *adj* cloaked.
lacerō, -āre, -āvī, -ātum *vt* to tear, lacerate, mangle; (*ship*) to wreck; (*speech*) to slander, abuse; (*feeling*) to torture, distress; (*goods, time*) to waste, destroy.
lacerta, -ae *f* lizard; a seafish.
lacertōsus *adj* brawny.
lacertus, -ī *m* upper arm, arm; (*pl*) brawn, muscle.
lacertus, -ī *m* lizard; a sea fish.
lacessō, -ere, -īvī *and* **iī, -ītum** *vt* to strike, provoke, challenge; (*fig*) to incite, exasperate.
Lachesis, -is *f* one of the Fates.
lacinia, -ae *f* flap, corner (*of dress*).
Lacīnium, -ī *nt* promontory in S. Italy, with a temple of Juno.
Lacīnius *adj see n.*
Lacō (-ōn), -ōnis *m* Spartan; Spartan dog.
Lacōnicus *adj* Spartan ♦ *nt* sweating bath.
lacrima, -ae *f* tear; (*plant*) gumdrop.
lacrimābilis *adj* mournful.
lacrimābundus *adj* bursting into tears.
lacrimō, -āre, -āvī, -ātum *vt, vi* to weep, weep for.
lacrimōsus *adj* tearful; lamentable.
lacrimula, -ae *f* tear, crocodile tear.
lacrum- *etc see* **lacrim-**.
lactāns, -antis *adj* giving milk; sucking.
lactātiō, -ōnis *f* allurement.
lactēns, -entis *adj* sucking; milky, juicy.
lacteolus *adj* milk-white.
lactēs, -ium *fpl* guts, small intestines.
lactēscō, -ere *vi* to turn to milk.
lacteus *adj* milky, milk-white.
lactō, -āre *vt* to dupe, wheedle.
lactūca, -ae *f* lettuce.
lacūna, -ae *f* hole, pit; pool, pond; (*fig*) deficiency.
lacūnar, -āris *nt* panel ceiling.
lacūnō, -āre *vt* to panel.
lacūnōsus *adj* sunken.
lacus, -ūs *m* vat, tank; lake; reservoir, cistern.
laedō, -dere, -sī, -sum *vt* to hurt, strike, wound; (*fig*) to offend, annoy, break.
Laelius, -ī *m* Roman family name (*esp the friend of Scipio*).
laena, -ae *f* a lined cloak.
Lāērtēs, -ae *m* father of Ulysses.
Lāērtiadēs *m* Ulysses.

Lāērtius *adj see n.*
laesī *perf of* **laedō**.
laesiō, -ōnis *f* attack.
Laestrygonēs, -um *mpl* fabulous cannibals of Campania, founders of Formiae.
Laestrygonius *adj see n.*
laesus *ppp of* **laedō**.
laetābilis *adj* joyful.
laetē *adv* gladly.
laetificō, -āre *vt* to gladden.
laetificus *adj* glad, joyful.
laetitia, -ae *f* joy, delight, exuberance.
laetor, -ārī, -ātus *vi* to rejoice, be glad.
laetus *adj* glad, cheerful; delighting (in); pleasing, welcome; (*growth*) fertile, rich; (*style*) exuberant.
laevē *adv* awkwardly.
laevus *adj* left; stupid; ill-omened, unfortunate; (*augury*) lucky, favourable ♦ *f* left hand.
laganum, -ī *nt* a kind of oilcake.
lagēos, -ī *f* a Greek vine.
lagoena, -ae *f* flagon.
lagōis, -idis *f* a kind of grouse.
lagōna, -ae *f* flagon.
Lāiadēs, -ae *m* Oedipus.
Lāius, -ī *m* father of Oedipus.
lallō, -āre *vi* to sing a lullaby.
lāma, -ae *f* bog.
lamberō, -āre *vt* to tear to pieces.
lambō, -ere, -ī *vt* to lick, touch; (*river*) to wash.
lāmenta, -ōrum *ntpl* lamentation.
lāmentābilis *adj* mournful, sorrowful.
lāmentārius *adj* sorrowful.
lāmentātiō, -ōnis *f* weeping, lamentation.
lāmentor, -ārī, -ātus *vi* to weep, lament ♦ *vt* to weep for, bewail.
lamia, -ae *f* witch.
lāmina (lammina, lāmna), -ae *f* plate, leaf (*of metal, wood*); blade; coin.
lampas, -dis *f* torch; brightness, day.
Lamus, -ī *m* Laestrygonian king.
lāna, -ae *f* wool.
lānārius, -ī *and* **iī** *m* wool-worker.
lānātus *adj* woolly.
lancea, -ae *f* spear, lance.
lancinō, -āre, *vt* to tear up; to squander.
lāneus *adj* woollen.
languefaciō, -ere *vt* to make weary.
langueō, -ēre *vi* to be weary, be weak, droop; to be idle, dull.
languēscō, -ēscere, -uī *vi* to grow faint, droop.
languidē *adv see adj.*
languidulus *adj* languid.
languidus *adj* faint, languid, sluggish; listless, feeble.
languor, -ōris *m* faintness, fatigue, weakness; dullness, apathy.
laniātus, -ūs *m* mangling; (*mind*) anguish.

Noun declensions and verb conjugations are shown on pp xiii to xxv. The present infinitive ending of a verb shows to which conjugation it belongs: -**āre** = 1st; -**ēre** = 2nd; -**ere** = 3rd and -**īre** = 4th. Irregular verbs are shown on p xxvi

laniēna, -ae f butcher's shop.
lānificium, -ī and **iī** nt wool-working.
lānificus adj wool-working.
lāniger, -ī adj fleecy ♦ m/f ram, sheep.
laniō, -āre, -āvī, -ātum vt to tear to pieces, mangle.
lanista, -ae m trainer of gladiators, fencing master; (fig) agitator.
lānitium, -ī and **iī** nt woolgrowing.
lanius, -ī and **iī** m butcher.
lanterna, -ae f lamp.
lanternārius, -ī and **iī** m guide.
lānūgō, -inis f down, woolliness.
Lānuvīnus adj see n.
Lānuvium, -ī nt Latin town on the Appian Way.
lānx, lancis f dish, platter; (balance) scale.
Lāomedōn, -ontis m king of Troy (father of Priam).
Lāomedontēus adj and **ontiadēs, -ae** m son of Lāomedōn; (pl) Trojans.
Lāomedontius adj Trojan.
lapathum, -ī nt, **-us, -ī** f sorrel.
lapicīda, -ae m stonecutter.
lapicīdīnae, -ārum fpl quarries.
lapidārius adj stone- (in cpds).
lapidātiō, -ōnis f throwing of stones.
lapidātor, -ōris m stone thrower.
lapideus adj of stones, stone- (in cpds).
lapidō, -āre vt to stone ♦ vi to rain stones.
lapidōsus adj stony; hard as stone.
lapillus, -ī m stone, pebble; precious stone, mosaic piece.
lapis, -dis m stone; milestone, boundary stone, tombstone; precious stone; marble; auctioneer's stand; (abuse) blockhead; **bis ad eundem (offendere)** ≈ make the same mistake twice; **Juppiter ~** the Jupiter stone.
Lapithae, -ārum and **-um** mpl Lapiths (mythical people of Thessaly).
Lapithaeus, -ēius adj see n.
lappa, -ae f goosegrass.
lāpsiō, -ōnis f tendency.
lāpsō, -āre vi to slip, stumble.
lāpsus ppa of **lābor**.
lāpsus, -ūs m fall, slide, course, flight; error, failure.
laqueāria, -ium ntpl panelled ceiling.
laqueātus adj panelled, with a panelled ceiling.
laqueus, -ī m noose, snare, halter; (fig) trap.
Lār, Laris m tutelary deity, household god; hearth, home.
lārdum etc see **lāridum**.
largē adv plentifully, generously, very much.
largificus adj bountiful.
largifluus adj copious.
largiloquus adj talkative.
largior, -īrī, -ītus vt to give freely, lavish; to bestow, confer ♦ vi to give largesses.
largitās, -ātis f liberality, abundance.
largiter adv = **large**.
largītiō, -ōnis f giving freely, distributing; bribery.

largītor, -ōris m liberal giver, dispenser; spendthrift; briber.
largus adj copious, ample; liberal, bountiful.
lāridum, -ī nt bacon fat.
Lārissa (Lārīsa), -ae f town in Thessaly.
Lārissaeus, -ēnsis adj see n.
Lārius, -ī m lake Como.
larix, -cis f larch.
larva, -ae f ghost; mask.
larvātus adj bewitched.
lasanum, -ī nt pot.
lasārpīcifer, -ī adj producing asafoetida.
lascīvia, -ae f playfulness; impudence, lewdness.
lascīviō, -īre vi to frolic, frisk; to run wild, be irresponsible.
lascīvus adj playful, frisky; impudent, lustful.
laserpīcium, -ī and **iī** nt silphium.
lassitūdō, -inis f fatigue, heaviness.
lassō, -āre, vt to tire, fatigue.
lassulus adj rather weary.
lassus adj tired, exhausted.
lātē adv widely, extensively; **longē ~que** far and wide, everywhere.
latebra, -ae f hiding place, retreat; (fig) loophole, pretext.
latebricola, -ae adj low-living.
latebrōsē adv in hiding.
latebrōsus adj secret, full of coverts; porous.
latēns, -entis pres p of **lateō** ♦ adj hidden, secret.
latenter adv in secret.
lateō, -ēre, -uī vi to lie hid, lurk, skulk; to be in safety, live a retired life; to be unknown, escape notice.
later, -is m brick, tile; **~em lavāre** ≈ waste one's time.
laterāmen, -inis nt earthenware.
laterculus, -ī m small brick, tile; kind of cake.
latericius adj of bricks ♦ nt brickwork.
lāterna etc see **lanterna**.
latēscō, -ere vi to hide oneself.
latex, -icis m water; any other liquid.
Latiar, -iaris nt festival of Jupiter Latiaris.
Latiaris adj Latin.
latibulum, -ī nt hiding place, den, lair.
lāticlāvius adj with a broad purple stripe ♦ m senator, patrician.
lātifundium, -ī and **iī** nt large estate.
Latīnē adv in Latin, into Latin; **~ loquī** speak Latin, speak plainly, speak correctly; **~ reddere** translate into Latin.
Latīnitās, -ātis f good Latin, Latinity; Latin rights.
Latīnus adj Latin ♦ m legendary king of the Laurentians.
lātiō, -ōnis f bringing; proposing.
latitō, -āre vi to hide away, lurk, keep out of the way.
lātitūdō, -inis f breadth, width; size; broad pronunciation.
Latium, -ī nt district of Italy including Rome; Latin rights.

Latius = Latiaris, Latinus.
Lātōis, -idis f Diana.
Lātōis , -ius adj see n.
lātom- etc see **lautum-**.
Lātōna, -ae f mother of Apollo and Diana.
Lātōnigenae, -ārum pl Apollo and Diana.
Lātōnius adj, f Diana.
lātor, -ōris m proposer.
Lātōus adj of Latona ♦ m Apollo.
lātrātor, -ōris m barker.
lātrātus, -ūs m barking.
lātrō, -āre vi to bark; to rant, roar ♦ vt to bark at; to clamour for.
latrō, -ōnis m mercenary soldier; bandit, brigand; (*chess*) man.
latrōcinium, -ī and **iī** nt highway robbery, piracy.
latrōcinor, -ārī, -ātus vi to serve as a mercenary; to be a brigand or pirate.
latrunculus, -ī m brigand; (*chess*) man.
lātumiae etc see **lautumiae**.
lātus ppp of **ferō**.
lātus adj broad, wide; extensive; (*pronunciation*) broad; (*style*) diffuse.
latus, -eris nt side, flank; lungs; body; ~ dare expose oneself; ~ **tegere** walk beside; ~eris dolor pleurisy; ab ~ere on the flank.
latusculum, -ī nt little side.
laudābilis adj praiseworthy.
laudābiliter adv laudably.
laudātiō, -ōnis f commendation, eulogy; panegyric, testimonial.
laudātor, -ōris m, **-rīx, -rīcis** f praiser, eulogizer; speaker of a funeral oration.
laudātus adj excellent.
laudō, -āre, -āvī, -ātum vt to praise, commend, approve; to pronounce a funeral oration over; to quote, name.
laurea, -ae f bay tree; crown of bay; triumph.
laureātus adj crowned with bay; (*despatches*) victorious.
Laurentēs, -um mpl Laurentians (*people of ancient Latium*).
Laurentius adj see n.
laureola, -ae f triumph.
laureus adj of bay.
lauricomus adj bay-covered.
lauriger, -ī adj crowned with bay.
laurus, -ī f bay tree; bay crown; victory, triumph.
laus, laudis f praise, approval; glory, fame; praiseworthy act, merit, worth.
lautē adv elegantly, splendidly; excellently.
lautia, -ōrum ntpl State banquet.
lautitia, -ae f luxury.
lautumiae, -ārum fpl stone quarry; prison.
lautus ppp of **lavō** ♦ adj neat, elegant, sumptuous; fine, grand, distinguished.
lavābrum, -ī nt bath.
lavātiō, -ōnis f washing, bath; bathing gear.

Lāvīnium, -ī nt town of ancient Latium.
Lāvīnius adj see n.
lavō, -āre, lāvī, lautum (lavātum and **lōtum)** vt to wash, bathe; to wet, soak, wash away.
laxāmentum, -ī nt respite, relaxation.
laxē adv loosely, freely.
laxitās, -ātis f roominess.
laxō, -āre, -āvī, -ātum vt to extend, open out; to undo; to slacken; (*fig*) to release, relieve; to relax, abate ♦ vi (*price*) to fall off.
laxus adj wide, loose, roomy; (*time*) deferred; (*fig*) free, easy.
lea, -ae f lioness.
leaena, -ae f lioness.
Lēander, -rī m Hero's lover (*who swam the Hellespont*).
lebēs, -ētis m basin, pan, cauldron.
lectīca, -ae f litter, sedan chair.
lectīcārius, -ī and **iī** m litter-bearer.
lectīcula, -ae f small litter; bier.
lēctiō, -ōnis f selecting; reading, calling the roll.
lectisterniātor, -ōris m arranger of couches.
lectisternium, -ī and **iī** nt religious feast.
lēctitō, -āre vt to read frequently.
lēctiuncula, -ae f light reading.
lēctor, -ōris m reader.
lectulus, -ī m couch, bed.
lectus, -ī m couch, bed; bier.
lēctus ppp of **legō** ♦ adj picked; choice, excellent.
Lēda, -ae and **ē, -ēs** f mother of Castor, Pollux, Helen and Clytemnestra.
Lēdaeus adj see n.
lēgātiō, -ōnis f mission, embassy; members of a mission; (MIL) staff appointment, command of a legion; **lībera** ~ free commission (to visit provinces); **vōtīva** ~ free commission for paying a vow in a province.
lēgātor, -ōris m testator.
lēgātum, -ī nt legacy, bequest.
lēgātus, -ī m delegate, ambassador; deputy, lieutenant; commander (of a legion).
lēgifer, -ī adj law-giving.
legiō, -ōnis f legion (*up to 6000 men*); (*pl*) troops, army.
legiōnārius adj legionary.
lēgirupa, -ae; -iō, -iōnis m lawbreaker.
lēgitimē adv lawfully, properly.
lēgitimus adj lawful, legal; right, proper.
legiuncula, -ae f small legion.
lēgō, -āre, -āvī, -ātum vt to send, charge, commission; to appoint as deputy or lieutenant; (*will*) to leave, bequeath.
legō, -ere, lēgī, lēctum vt to gather, pick; to choose, select; (*sail*) to furl; (*places*) to traverse, pass, coast along; (*view*) to scan; (*writing*) to read, recite; **senātum** ~ call the

---

Noun declensions and verb conjugations are shown on pp xiii to xxv. The present infinitive ending of a verb shows to which conjugation it belongs: **-āre** = 1st; **-ēre** = 2nd; **-ere** = 3rd and **-īre** = 4th. Irregular verbs are shown on p xxvi

roll of the senate.

lēgulēius, -ī and **iī** m pettifogging lawyer.

legūmen, -inis nt pulse, bean.

lembus, -ī m pinnace, cutter.

Lemnias f Lemnian woman.

Lemnicola, -ae m Vulcan.

lēmniscātus adj beribboned.

lēmniscus, -ī m ribbon (hanging from a victor's crown).

Lēmnius adj see n.

Lēmnos (-us), -ī f Aegean island, abode of Vulcan.

Lemurēs, -um mpl ghosts.

lēna, -ae f procuress; seductress.

Lēnaeus adj Bacchic ♦ m Bacchus.

lēnīmen, -inis nt solace, comfort.

lēnīmentum, -ī nt sop.

lēniō, -īre, -īvī and **iī, -ītum** vt to soften, soothe, heal, calm.

lēnis adj soft, smooth, mild, gentle, calm.

lēnitās, -ātis f softness, smoothness, mildness, tenderness.

lēniter adv softly, gently; moderately, half-heartedly.

lēnitūdō, -inis f smoothness, mildness.

lēnō, -ōnis m pander, brothel keeper; go-between.

lēnōcinium, -ī and **iī** nt pandering; allurement; meretricious ornament.

lēnōcinor, -ārī, -ātus vi to pay court to; to promote.

lēnōnius adj pander's.

lēns, lentis f lentil.

lentē adv slowly; calmly, coolly.

lentēscō, -ere vi to become sticky, soften; to relax.

lentīscifer, -ī adj bearing mastic trees.

lentīscus, -ī f mastic tree.

lentitūdō, -inis f slowness, dullness, apathy.

lentō, -āre vt to bend.

lentulus adj rather slow.

lentus adj sticky, sluggish; pliant; slow, lasting, lingering; (person) calm, at ease, indifferent.

lēnunculus, -ī m skiff.

leō, -ōnis m lion.

Leōnidās, -ae m Spartan king who fell at Thermopylae.

leōnīnus adj lion's.

Leontīnī, -ōrum mpl town in Sicily.

Leontīnus adj see n.

lepas, -dis f limpet.

lepidē adv neatly, charmingly; (reply) very well, splendidly.

lepidus adj pleasant, charming, neat, witty.

lepōs (lepor), -ōris m pleasantness, charm; wit.

lepus, -oris m hare.

lepusculus, -ī m young hare.

Lerna, -ae and **ē, -ēs** f marsh near Argos (where Hercules killed the Hydra).

Lernaeus adj Lernaean.

Lesbias, -iadis f Lesbian woman.

Lesbis, Lesbius adj see n.

Lesbos (-us), -ī f Aegean island (home of Alcaeus and Sappho).

Lesbous f Lesbian woman.

lētālis adj deadly.

Lēthaeus adj of Lethe; infernal; soporific.

lēthargicus, -ī m lethargic person.

lēthargus, -ī m drowsiness.

Lēthē, -ēs f river in the lower world, which caused forgetfulness.

lētifer, -ī adj fatal.

lētō, -āre vt to kill.

lētum, -ī nt death; destruction.

Leucadius adj see n.

Leucas, -dis and **dia, -diae** f island off W. Greece.

Leucothea, -ae, -ē, -ēs f Ino (a sea goddess).

Leuctra, -ōrum ntpl battlefield in Boeotia.

Leuctricus adj see n.

levāmen, -inis nt alleviation, comfort.

levāmentum, -ī nt mitigation, consolation.

levātiō, -ōnis f relief; diminishing.

lēvī perf of **linō**.

leviculus adj rather vain.

levidēnsis adj slight.

levipēs, -edis adj light-footed.

levis adj (weight) light; (MIL) light-armed; (fig) easy, gentle; (importance) slight, trivial; (motion) nimble, fleet; (character) fickle, unreliable.

lēvis adj smooth; (youth) beardless, delicate.

levisomnus adj light-sleeping.

levitās, -ātis f lightness; nimbleness; fickleness, frivolity.

lēvitās, -ātis f smoothness; fluency.

leviter adv lightly; slightly; easily.

levō, -āre vt to lighten, ease; (fig) to alleviate, lessen; to comfort, relieve; to impair; (danger) to avert; **sē ~** rise.

lēvō, -āre vt to smooth, polish.

lēvor, -ōris m smoothness.

lēx, lēgis f law, statute; bill; rule, principle; contract, condition; **lēgem ferre** propose a bill; **lēgem perferre** carry a motion; **lēge agere** proceed according to law; **sine lēge** out of control.

lībāmen, -inis nt offering, libation.

lībāmentum, -ī nt offering, libation.

lībātiō, -ōnis f libation.

lībella, -ae f small coin, as; level; **ad ~am** exactly; **ex ~ā** sole heir.

libellus, -ī m small book; notebook, diary, letter; notice, programme, handbill; petition, complaint; lampoon.

libēns, -entis adj willing, glad.

libenter adv willingly, with pleasure.

liber, -rī m inner bark (of a tree); book; register.

Līber, -ī m Italian god of fertility (identified with Bacchus).

līber, -ī adj free, open, unrestricted, undisturbed; (with abl) free from; (speech) frank; (POL) free, not slave, democratic.

Lībera, -ae *f* Proserpine; Ariadne.
Līberālia, -ālium *ntpl festival of Liber in March.*
līberālis *adj* of freedom, of free citizens, gentlemanly, honourable; generous, liberal; handsome.
līberālitās, -ātis *f* courtesy, kindness; generosity; bounty.
līberāliter *adv* courteously, nobly; generously.
līberātiō, -ōnis *f* delivery, freeing; (*law*) acquittal.
līberātor, -ōris *m* liberator, deliverer.
līberē *adv* freely, frankly, boldly.
līberī, -ōrum *mpl* children.
līberō, -āre, -āvī, -ātum *vt* to free, set free, release; to exempt; (*law*) to acquit; (*slave*) to give freedom to; **fidem ~** keep one's promise; **nōmina ~** cancel debts.
līberta, -ae *f* freedwoman.
lībertās, -ātis *f* freedom, liberty; status of a freeman; (*POL*) independence; freedom of speech, outspokenness.
lībertīnus *adj* of a freedman, freed ♦ *m* freedman ♦ *f* freedwoman.
lībertus, -ī *m* freedman.
libet (lubet), -ēre, -uit *and* **itum est** *vi* (*impers*) it pleases; **mihi ~** I like; **ut ~** as you please.
libīdinōsē *adv* wilfully.
libīdinōsus *adj* wilful, arbitrary, extravagant; sensual, lustful.
libīdō (lubīdō), -inis *f* desire, passion; wilfulness, caprice; lust.
libita, -ōrum *ntpl* pleasure, fancy.
Libitīna, -ae *f* goddess of burials.
lībō, -āre, -āvī, -ātum *vt* to taste, sip, touch; to pour (*a libation*), offer; to extract, take out; to impair.
lībra, -ae *f* pound; balance, pair of scales; **ad ~am** of equal size.
lībrāmentum, -ī *nt* level surface, weight (*to give balance or movement*); (*water*) fall.
lībrāria, -ae *f* head spinner.
lībrāriolus, -ī *m* copyist.
lībrārium, -ī *and* **iī** *nt* bookcase.
lībrārius *adj* of books ♦ *m* copyist.
lībrātus *adj* level; powerful.
lībrīlis *adj* weighing a pound.
lībritor, -ōris *m* slinger.
lībrō, -āre, -āvī, -ātum *vt* to poise, hold balanced; to swing, hurl.
lībum, -ī *nt* cake.
Liburna, -ae *f* a fast galley, frigate.
Liburnī, -ōrum *mpl* people of Illyria.
Liburnus *adj* Liburnian.
Libya, -ae, -ē, -ēs *f* Africa.
Libycus *adj* African.
Libyes, -um *mpl* Libyans, people in N. Africa.
Libyssus, Libystinus, Libystis *adj* = **Libycus**.
licēns, -entis *adj* free, bold, unrestricted.
licenter *adv* freely, lawlessly.

licentia, -ae *f* freedom, license; lawlessness, licentiousness.
liceō, -ēre, -uī *vi* to be for sale, value at.
liceor, -ērī, -itus *vt, vi* to bid (at an auction), bid for.
licet, -ēre, -uit *and* **itum est** *vi* (*impers*) it is permitted, it is lawful; (*reply*) all right ♦ *conj* although; **mihi ~** I may.
Licinius, -ī *m* Roman family name (*esp with surname Crassus*).
Licinius *adj see n.*
licitātiō, -ōnis *f* bidding (*at a sale*).
licitor, -ārī, *vi* to make a bid.
licitus *adj* lawful.
līcium, -ī *and* **iī** *nt* thread.
līctor, -ōris *m* lictor (*an attendant with fasces preceding a magistrate*).
licuī *perf of* **liceō**; *perf of* **liquēscō**.
liēn, -ēnis *m* spleen.
ligāmen, -inis *nt* band, bandage.
ligāmentum, -ī *nt* bandage.
Liger, -is *m* river Loire.
lignārius, -ī *and* **iī** *m* carpenter.
lignātiō, -ōnis *f* fetching wood.
lignātor, -ōris *m* woodcutter.
ligneolus *adj* wooden.
ligneus *adj* wooden.
lignor, -ārī *vi* to fetch wood.
lignum, -ī *nt* wood, firewood, timber; **in silvam ~a ferre** ≈ carry coals to Newcastle.
ligō, -āre, -āvī, -ātum *vt* to tie up, bandage; (*fig*) to unite.
ligō, -ōnis *m* mattock, hoe.
ligula, -ae *f* shoestrap.
Ligur, -ris *m/f* Ligurian.
Liguria, -riae *f* district of N.W. Italy.
ligūriō (ligurriō), -īre *vt* to lick; to eat daintily; (*fig*) to feast on, lust after.
ligūrītiō, -ōnis *f* daintiness.
Ligus, -ris *m/f* Ligurian.
Ligusticus, -stīnus *adj see n.*
ligustrum, -ī *nt* privet.
līlium, -ī *and* **iī** *nt* lily; (*MIL*) spiked pit.
līma, -ae *f* file; (*fig*) revision.
līmātius *adv* more elegantly.
līmātulus *adj* refined.
līmāx, -ācis *f* slug, snail.
limbus, -ī *m* fringe, hem.
līmen, -inis *nt* threshold, lintel; doorway; entrance; house, home; (*fig*) beginning.
līmes, -itis *m* path between fields, boundary; path, track, way; frontier, boundary line.
līmō, -āre, -āvī, -ātum *vt* to file; (*fig*) to polish, refine; to file down, investigate carefully; to take away from.
līmōsus *adj* muddy.
limpidus *adj* clear, limpid.
līmus *adj* sidelong, askance.
līmus, -ī *m* mud, slime, dirt.
līmus, -ī *m* ceremonial apron.

Noun declensions and verb conjugations are shown on pp xiii to xxv. The present infinitive ending of a verb shows to which conjugation it belongs: **-āre** = 1st; **-ēre** = 2nd; **-ere** = 3rd and **-īre** = 4th. Irregular verbs are shown on **p xxvi**

līnea, -ae *f* line, string; plumbline; boundary; **ad ~am, rectā ~ā** vertically; **extrēmā ~ā amāre** love at a distance.

līneāmentum, -ī *nt* line; feature; outline.

līneus *adj* flaxen, linen.

lingō, -ere *vt* to lick.

lingua, -ae *f* tongue; speech, language; tongue of land; **~ Latīna** Latin.

lingula, -ae *f* tongue of land.

līniger, -ī *adj* linen-clad.

linō, -ere, lēvī, litum *vt* to daub, smear; to overlay; (*writing*) to rub out; (*fig*) to befoul.

linquō, -ere, līquī *vt* to leave, quit; to give up, let alone; (*pass*) to faint, swoon; **~itur ut** it remains to.

linteātus *adj* canvas.

linteō, -ōnis *m* linen weaver.

linter, -ris *f* boat; trough.

linteum, -ī *nt* linen cloth, canvas; sail.

linteus *adj* linen.

lintriculus, -ī *m* small boat.

līnum, -ī *nt* flax; linen; thread, line, rope; net.

Lipara, -ae, -ē, -ēs *f* island N. of Sicily (*now* Lipari).

Liparaeus, -ēnsis *adj see n.*

lippiō, -īre *vi* to have sore eyes.

lippitūdō, -inis *f* inflammation of the eyes.

lippus *adj* blear-eyed, with sore eyes; (*fig*) blind.

liquefaciō, -facere, -fēcī, -factum (*pass* -fīō) *vt* to melt, dissolve; to decompose; (*fig*) to enervate.

liquēns, -entis *adj* fluid, clear.

liquēscō, -ere, licuī *vi* to melt; to clear; (*fig*) to grow soft, waste away.

liquet, -ēre, licuit *vi* (*impers*) it is clear, it is evident; **nōn ~** not proven.

līquī *perf of* **linquō**.

liquidō *adv* clearly.

liquidus *adj* fluid, liquid, flowing; clear, transparent, pure; (*mind*) calm, serene ♦ *nt* liquid water.

liquō, -āre *vt* to melt; to strain.

līquor, -ī *vi* to flow; (*fig*) to waste away.

liquor, -ōris *m* fluidity; liquid, the sea.

Līris, -is *m* river between Latium and Campania.

līs, lītis *f* quarrel, dispute; lawsuit; matter in dispute; **lītem aestimāre** assess damages.

litātiō, -ōnis *f* favourable sacrifice.

lītera *etc see* **littera**.

lītigātor, -ōris *m* litigant.

lītigiōsus *adj* quarrelsome, contentious; disputed.

lītigium, -ī *and* **iī** *nt* quarrel.

lītigō, -āre *vi* to quarrel; to go to law.

litō, -āre, -āvī, -ātum *vi* to offer an acceptable sacrifice, obtain favourable omens; (*with dat*) to propitiate ♦ *vt* to offer successfully.

lītorālis *adj* of the shore.

lītoreus *adj* of the shore.

littera, -ae *f* letter (of the alphabet).

litterae, -ārum *fpl* writing; letter, dispatch; document, ordinance; literature; learning; scholarship; **~ās discere** learn to read and write; **homō trium ~ārum** thief (*of fur*); **sine ~īs** uncultured.

litterārius *adj* of reading and writing.

litterātē *adv* in clear letters; literally.

litterātor, -ōris *m* grammarian.

litterātūra, -ae *f* writing, alphabet.

litterātus *adj* with letters on it, branded; educated, learned.

litterula, -ae *f* small letter; short note; (*pl*) studies.

litūra, -ae *f* correction, erasure, blot.

litus *ppp of* **linō**.

lītus, -oris *nt* shore, beach, coast; bank; **~ arāre** labour in vain.

lituus, -ī *m* augur's staff; trumpet; (*fig*) starter.

līvēns, -entis *pres p of* **līveō** ♦ *adj* bluish, black and blue.

līveō, -ēre *vi* to be black and blue; to envy.

līvēscō, -ere *vi* to turn black and blue.

Līviānus *adj* = **Līvius**.

līvidulus *adj* a little jealous.

līvidus *adj* bluish, black and blue; envious, malicious.

Līvius, -ī Roman family name (*esp the first Latin poet*); *the famous historian,* Livy.

Līvius *adj see n.*

līvor, -ōris *m* bluish colour; envy, malice.

lixa, -ae *m* sutler, camp-follower.

locātiō, -ōnis *f* leasing; lease, contract.

locātōrius *adj* concerned with leases.

locitō, -āre *vt* to let frequently.

locō, -āre, -āvī, -ātum *vt* to place, put; to give in marriage; to let, lease, hire out; to contract for; (*money*) to invest.

loculus, -ī *m* little place; (*pl*) satchel, purse.

locuplēs, -ētis *adj* rich, opulent; reliable, responsible.

locuplētō, -āre *vt* to enrich.

locus, -ī *m* (*pl* -ī *and* -a *nt*) place, site, locality, region; (*MIL*) post; (*theatre*) seat; (*book*) passage; (*speech*) topic, subject, argument; (*fig*) room, occasion; situation, state; rank, position; **~ī** individual spots; **~a regiones,** ground; **~ī commūnēs** general arguments; **~ō** (*with gen*) instead of; **in ~ō** opportunely; **eō ~ī** in the position; **intereā ~ī** meanwhile.

lōcusta, -ae *f* locust.

locūtiō, -ōnis *f* speech; pronunciation.

locūtus *ppa of* **loquor**.

lōdīx, -īcis *f* blanket.

logica, -ōrum *ntpl* logic.

logos (-us), -ī *m* word; idle talk; witticism.

lōlīg- *etc see* **lollīg-**.

lolium, -ī *and* **iī** *nt* darnel.

lollīgō, -inis *f* cuttlefish.

lōmentum, -ī *nt* face cream.

Londinium, -ī *nt* London.

longaevus *adj* aged.

longē *adv* far, far off; (*time*) long; (*compar*) by far, very much; **~ esse** be far away, of no

avail; ~ **latēque** everywhere.
longinquitās, -ātis f length; distance; duration.
longinquus adj distant, remote; foreign, strange; lasting, wearisome; (hope) long deferred.
longitūdō, -inis f length; duration; **in ~inem** lengthwise.
longiusculus adj rather long.
longulē adv rather far.
longulus adj rather long.
longurius, -ī and **iī** m long pole.
longus adj long; vast; (time) long, protracted, tedious; (hope) far-reaching; ~**a nāvis** warship; ~**um est** it would be tedious; **nē** ~**um faciam** ≈ to cut a long story short.
loquācitās, -ātis f talkativeness.
loquāciter adv see adj.
loquāculus adj somewhat talkative.
loquāx, -ācis adj talkative, chattering.
loquella, -ae f language, words.
loquor, -quī, cūtus vt, vi to speak, talk, say; to talk about, mention; (fig) to indicate; **rēs** ~**quitur ipsa** the facts speak for themselves.
lōrārius, -ī and **iī** m flogger.
lōrātus adj strapped.
lōreus adj of leather strips.
lōrīca, -ae f breastplate; parapet.
lōrīcātus adj mailed.
lōripēs, -edis adj bandylegged.
lōrum, -ī nt strap; whip, lash; leather charm; (pl) reins.
lōtos (-us), -ī f lotus.
lōtus ppp of **lavō**.
lubēns see **libēns**.
lubentia, -ae f pleasure.
lubet, lubīdō see **libet, libīdō**.
lūbricō, -āre vt to make slippery.
lūbricus adj slippery, slimy; gliding, fleeting; (fig) dangerous, hazardous.
Lūca bōs f elephant.
Lūcānia, -iae f district of S. Italy.
Lūcanica f kind of sausage.
Lūcanus adj Lucanian ♦ m the epic poet Lucan.
lūcar, -āris nt forest tax.
lucellum, -ī nt small gain.
lūceō, -cēre, -xī vi to shine, be light; (impers) to dawn, be daylight; (fig) to shine, be clear; **meridiē nōn ~cēre** ≈ (argue) that black is white.
Lūcerēs, -um mpl a Roman patrician tribe.
Lūceria, -iae f town in Apulia.
Lūcerīnus adj see n.
lucerna, -ae f lamp; (fig) ≈ midnight oil.
lūcēscō, -ere vi to begin to shine, get light, dawn.
lūcidē adv clearly.
lūcidus adj bright, clear; (fig) lucid.
lūcifer, -ī adj light-bringing ♦ m morning star, Venus; day.
lūcifugus adj shunning the light.

Lūcīlius, -ī m Roman family name (esp the first Latin satirist).
Lūcīna, -ae f goddess of childbirth.
lūcīscō etc see **lūcēscō**.
Lucmō (Lucumō), -ōnis m Etruscan prince or priest.
Lucrētia, -iae f wife of Collatinus, ravished by Tarquin.
Lucrētius, -ī m Roman family name (esp the philosophic poet).
lucrifuga, -ae m non-profiteer.
Lucrīnēnsis adj see n.
Lucrīnus, -ī m lake near Baiae (famous for oysters).
lucror, -ārī, -ātus vt to gain, win, acquire.
lucrōsus adj profitable.
lucrum, -ī nt profit, gain; greed; wealth; ~**ī facere** gain, get the credit of; ~**ō esse** be of advantage; **in ~īs pōnere** count as gain.
luctāmen, -inis nt struggle, exertion.
luctātiō, -ōnis f wrestling; fight, contest.
luctātor, -ōris m wrestler.
lūctificus adj baleful.
lūctisonus adj mournful.
luctor, -ārī, -ātus vi to wrestle; to struggle, fight.
lūctuōsus adj sorrowful, lamentable.
lūctus, -ūs m mourning, lamentation; mourning (dress).
lūcubrātiō, -ōnis f work by lamplight, nocturnal study.
lūcubrō, -āre, -āvī, -ātum vi to work by night ♦ vt to compose by night.
lūculentē adv splendidly, right.
lūculenter adv very well.
lūculentus adj bright; (fig) brilliant, excellent, rich, fine.
Lūcullus, -ī m Roman surname (esp the conqueror of Mithridates).
lūcus, -ī m grove; wood.
lūdia, -ae f woman gladiator.
lūdibrium, -ī and **iī** nt mockery, derision; laughing stock; sport, play; ~**iō habēre** make fun of.
lūdibundus adj playful; safely, easily.
lūdicer, -rī adj playful; theatrical.
lūdicum, -ī nt public show, play; sport.
lūdificātiō, -ōnis f ridicule; tricking.
lūdificātor, -ōris m mocker.
lūdificō, -āre, -or, -ārī, -ātus vt to make a fool of, ridicule; to delude, thwart.
lūdiō, -ōnis m actor.
lūdius, -ī and **iī** m actor; gladiator.
lūdō, -dere, -sī, -sum vi to play; to sport, frolic; to dally, make love ♦ vt to play at; to amuse oneself with; to mimic, imitate; to ridicule, mock; to delude.
lūdus, -ī m game, sport, play; (pl) public spectacle, games; school; (fig) child's play; fun, jest; (love) dalliance; ~**um dare** humour;

~ōs facere put on a public show; make fun of.
luella, -ae f atonement.
luēs, -is f plague, pest; misfortune.
Lugdūnēnsis adj see n.
Lugdūnum, -ī nt town in E. Gaul (now Lyons).
lūgeō, -gēre, -xī vt, vi to mourn; to be in mourning.
lūgubris adj mourning; disastrous; (sound) plaintive ♦ ntpl mourning dress.
lumbī, -ōrum mpl loins.
lumbrīcus, -ī m worm.
lūmen, -inis nt light; lamp, torch; day; eye; life; (fig) ornament, glory; clarity.
lūmināre, -is nt window.
lūminōsus adj brilliant.
lūna, -ae f moon; month; crescent.
lūnāris adj of the moon.
lūnātus adj crescent-shaped.
lūnō, -āre vt to bend into a crescent.
luō, -ere, -ī vt to pay; to atone for; to avert by expiation.
lupa, -ae f she-wolf; prostitute.
lupānar, -āris nt brothel.
lupātus adj toothed ♦ m and ntpl curb.
Lupercal, -ālis nt a grotto sacred to Pan.
Lupercālia, -ālium ntpl festival of Pan in February.
Lupercus, -ī m Pan; priest of Pan.
lupīnum, -ī nt lupin; sham money, counters.
lupīnus adj wolf's.
lupīnus, -ī m lupin; sham money, counters.
lupus, -ī m wolf; (fish) pike; toothed bit; grapnel; ~ **in fābulā** ≈ talk of the devil.
lūridus adj pale yellow, ghastly pallid.
lūror, -ōris m yellowness.
lūscinia, -ae f nightingale.
luscitiōsus adj purblind.
luscus adj one-eyed.
lūsiō, -ōnis f play.
Lūsitānia, -iae f part of W. Spain (including what is now Portugal).
Lūsitānus adj see n.
lūsitō, -āre vi to play.
lūsor, -ōris m player; humorous writer.
lūstrālis adj lustral, propitiatory; quinquennial.
lūstrātiō, -ōnis f purification; roving.
lūstrō, -āre, -āvī, -ātum vt to purify; (motion) to go round, encircle, traverse; (MIL) to review; (eyes) to scan, survey; (mind) to consider; (light) to illuminate.
lūstror, -ārī vi to frequent brothels.
lūstrum, -ī nt den, lair; (pl) wild country; (fig) brothels; debauchery.
lūstrum, -ī nt purificatory sacrifice; (time) five years.
lūsus ppp of **lūdō**.
lūsus, -ūs m play, game, sport; dalliance.
lūteolus adj yellow.
Lutetia, -ae f town in N. Gaul (now Paris).
lūteus adj yellow, orange.
luteus adj of clay; muddy, dirty, (fig) vile.
lutitō, -āre vt to throw mud at.

lutulentus adj muddy, filthy; (fig) foul.
lūtum, -ī nt dyer's weed; yellow.
lutum, -ī nt mud, mire; clay.
lūx, lūcis f light; daylight; day; life; (fig) public view; glory, encouragement, enlightenment; **lūce** in the daytime; **prīmā lūce** at daybreak; **lūce carentēs** the dead.
lūxī perf of **lūceō**; perf of **lūgeō**.
luxor, -ārī vi to live riotously.
luxuria, -ae, -ēs, -ēī f rankness, profusion; extravagance, luxury.
luxuriō, -āre, -or, -ārī vi to grow to excess, be luxuriant; (fig) to be exuberant, run riot.
luxuriōsē adv voluptuously.
luxuriōsus adj luxuriant; excessive, extravagant; voluptuous.
luxus, -ūs m excess, debauchery, pomp.
Lyaeus, -ī m Bacchus; wine.
Lycaeus, -ī m mountain in Arcadia (sacred to Pan).
Lycāōn, -onis m father of Callisto, the Great Bear.
Lycāonius adj see n.
Lycēum (Lycīum), -ī nt Aristotle's school at Athens.
lychnūchus, -ī m lampstand.
lychnus, -ī m lamp.
Lycia, -ae f country in S.W. Asia Minor.
Lycius adj Lycian.
Lyctius adj Cretan.
Lycurgus, -ī m Thracian king killed by Bacchus; Spartan lawgiver; Athenian orator.
Lȳdia, -iae f country of Asia Minor.
Lȳdius adj Lydian; Etruscan.
Lȳdus, -ī m Lydian.
lympha, -ae f water.
lymphāticus adj crazy, frantic.
lymphātus adj distracted.
Lynceus, -eī m keen-sighted Argonaut.
lynx, lyncis m/f lynx.
lyra, -ae f lyre; lyric poetry.
lyricus adj of the lyre, lyrical.
Lysiās, -ae m Athenian orator.

M, m

Macedō, -onis m Macedonian.
Macedonia f Macedonia.
Macedonicus, -onius adj see n.
macellum, -ī nt market.
maceō, -ēre vi to be lean.
macer, -rī adj lean, meagre; poor.
māceria, -ae f wall.
mācerō, -āre vt to soften; (body) to enervate; (mind) to distress.

macēscō–male

macēscō, -ere vi to grow thin.
machaera, -ae f sword.
machaerophorus, -ī m soldier armed with a sword.
Machāon, -onis m legendary Greek surgeon.
Machāonius adj see n.
māchina, -ae f machine, engine; (fig) scheme, trick.
māchināmentum, -ī nt engine.
māchinātiō, -ōnis f mechanism, machine; (fig) contrivance.
māchinātor, -ōris m engineer; (fig) contriver.
māchinor, -ārī, -ātus vt to devise, contrive; (fig) to plot, scheme.
maciēs, -ēī f leanness, meagreness; poorness.
macilentus adj thin.
macrēscō, -ere vi to grow thin.
macritūdō, -inis f leanness.
macrocollum, -ī nt large size of paper.
mactābilis adj deadly.
mactātus, -ūs m sacrifice.
macte blessed; well done!
mactō, -āre, -āvī, -ātum vt to sacrifice; to punish, kill.
mactō, -āre vt to glorify.
macula, -ae f spot, stain; (net) mesh; (fig) blemish, fault.
maculō, -āre, -āvī, -ātum vt to stain, defile.
maculōsus adj dappled, mottled; stained, polluted.
madefaciō, -facere, -fēcī, -factum (pass -fīō, -fierī) vt to wet, soak.
madeō, -ēre vi to be wet, be drenched; to be boiled soft; (comedy) to be drunk; (fig) to be steeped in.
madēscō, -ere vi to get wet, become moist.
madidus adj wet, soaked; sodden; drunk.
madulsa, -ae m drunkard.
Maeander (-ros), -rī m a winding river of Asia Minor; winding, wandering.
Maecēnās, -ātis m friend of Augustus, patron of poets.
maena, -ae f sprat.
Maenala, -ōrum ntpl mountain range in Arcadia.
Maenalis, -ius adj of Maenalus; Arcadian.
Maenalus (-os), -ī m Maenala.
Maenas, -dis f Bacchante.
Maeniānum nt balcony.
Maenius, -ī m Roman family name; ~ia columna whipping post in the Forum.
Maeonia, -ae f Lydia.
Maeonidēs, -dae m Homer.
Maeonius, -s adj Lydian; Homeric; Etruscan.
Maeōticus, -us adj Scythian, Maeotic.
Maeōtis, -dis f Sea of Azov.
maereō, -ēre vi to mourn, be sad.
maeror, -ōris m mourning, sorrow, sadness.
maestiter adv see adj.
maestitia, -ae f sadness, melancholy.
maestus adj sad, sorrowful; gloomy;

mourning.
māgālia, -um ntpl huts.
mage etc see **magis**.
magicus adj magical.
magis (mage) adv more; eō ~ the more, all the more.
magister, -rī m master, chief, director; (school) teacher; (fig) instigator; ~ equitum chief of cavalry, second in command to a dictator; ~ mōrum censor; ~ sacrōrum chief priest.
magisterium, -ī and **iī** nt presidency, tutorship.
magistra, -ae f mistress, instructress.
magistrātus, -ūs m magistracy, office; magistrate, official.
magnanimitās, -ātis f greatness.
māgnanimus adj great, brave.
Magnēs, -ētis m Magnesian; magnet.
Magnēsia f district of Thessaly.
Magnēsius, -essus, -ētis adj see n.
magnidicus adj boastful.
magnificē adv grandly; pompously.
magnificentia, -ae f greatness, grandeur; pomposity.
magnificō, -āre vt to esteem highly.
magnificus (compar **-entior** superl **-entissimus**) adj great, grand, splendid; pompous.
magniloquentia, -ae f elevated language; pomposity.
magniloquus adj boastful.
magnitūdō, -inis f greatness, size, large amount; dignity.
magnopere adv greatly, very much.
magnus (compar **māior** superl **māximus**) adj great, large, big, tall; (voice) loud; (age) advanced; (value) high, dear; (fig) grand, noble, important; **avunculus** ~ great-uncle; **~a loquī** boast; **~ī aestimāre** think highly of; **~ī esse** be highly esteemed; **~ō stāre** cost dear; **~ō opere** very much.
magus, -ī m wise man; magician ♦ adj magic.
Māia, -ae f mother of Mercury.
māiestās, -ātis f greatness, dignity, majesty; treason; **~ātem laedere, minuere** offend against the sovereignty of; **lēx ~ātis** law against treason.
māior, -ōris compar of **māgnus**; ~ **nātū** older, elder.
māiōrēs, -ōrum mpl ancestors; **in ~us crēdere/ferre** exaggerate.
Māius, -ī m May ♦ adj of May.
māiusculus adj somewhat greater; a little older.
māla, -ae f cheek, jaw.
malacia, -ae f dead calm.
malacus adj soft.
male (compar **pēius,** superl **pessimē**) adv badly, wrongly, unfortunately; not; (with words having bad sense) very much; **~ est animō** I

Noun declensions and verb conjugations are shown on pp xiii to xxv. The present infinitive ending of a verb shows to which conjugation it belongs: **-āre** = 1st; **-ēre** = 2nd; **-ere** = 3rd and **-īre** = 4th. Irregular verbs are shown on p xxvi

feel ill; **~ sānus** insane; **~ dīcere** abuse, curse;
~ facere harm.
maledicē _adv_ abusively.
maledictiō, -ōnis _f_ abuse.
maledictum, -ī _nt_ curse.
maledicus _adj_ scurrilous.
malefactum, -ī _nt_ wrong.
maleficē _adv see adj._
maleficium, -ī _and_ **iī** _nt_ misdeed, wrong,
mischief.
maleficus _adj_ wicked ♦ _m_ criminal.
malesuādus _adj_ seductive.
malevolēns, -entis _adj_ spiteful.
malevolentia, -ae _f_ ill-will.
malevolus _adj_ ill-disposed, malicious.
mālifer, -ī _adj_ apple-growing.
malignē _adv_ spitefully; grudgingly.
malignitās, -ātis _f_ malice; stinginess.
malignus _adj_ unkind, ill-natured, spiteful;
stingy; (_soil_) unfruitful; (_fig_) small, scanty.
malitia, -ae _f_ badness, malice; roguishness.
malitiōsē _adv see adj._
malitiōsus _adj_ wicked, crafty.
maliv- _etc see_ **malev-**.
mālle _infin of_ **mālō**.
malleolus, -ī _m_ hammer; (_MIL_) fire-brand.
malleus, -ī _m_ hammer, mallet, maul.
mālō, -le, -uī _vt_ to prefer; would rather.
malobathrum, -ī _nt_ an oriental perfume.
māluī _perf of_ **mālō**.
mālum, -ī _nt_ apple, fruit.
malum, -ī _nt_ evil, wrong, harm, misfortune;
(_interj_) mischief.
mālus, -ī _f_ apple tree.
mālus, -ī _m_ mast, pole.
malus (_compar_ **pēior** _superl_ **pessimus**) _adj_ bad,
evil, harmful; unlucky; ugly; **ī in ~am rem** go
to hell!
malva, -ae _f_ mallow.
Māmers, -tis _m_ Mars.
Māmertīnī, -ōrum _mpl mercenary troops who
occupied Messana._
mamma, -ae _f_ breast; teat.
mammilla, -ae _f_ breast.
mānābilis _adj_ penetrating.
manceps, -ipis _m_ purchaser; contractor.
mancipium, -ī _and_ **iī** _nt_ formal purchase;
property; slave.
mancipō, -āre _vt_ to sell, deliver up.
mancup- _etc see_ **mancip-**.
mancus _adj_ crippled.
mandātum, -ī _nt_ commission, command;
(_law_) contract.
mandātus, -ūs _m_ command.
mandō, -āre, -āvī, -ātum _vt_ to entrust,
commit; to commission, command.
mandō, -ere, -ī, mānsum _vt_ to chew, eat,
devour.
mandra, -ae _f_ drove of cattle.
mandūcus, -ī _m_ masked figure of a glutton.
māne _nt_ (_indecl_) morning ♦ _adv_ in the morning,
early.
maneō, -ēre, mānsī, mānsum _vi_ to remain;

to stay, stop; to last, abide, continue ♦ _vt_ to
wait for, await; **in condiciōne ~** abide by an
agreement.
Mānēs, -ium _mpl_ ghosts, shades of the dead;
the lower world; bodily remains.
mangō, -ōnis _m_ dealer.
manicae, -ārum _fpl_ sleeves, gloves;
handcuffs.
manicātus _adj_ with long sleeves.
manicula, -ae _f_ little hand.
manifestō, -āre _vt_ to disclose.
manifestō _adv_ clearly, evidently.
manifestus _adj_ clear, obvious; convicted,
caught.
manipl- _etc see_ **manipul-**.
manipulāris _adj_ of a company ♦ _m_ private (in
the ranks); fellow soldier.
manipulātim _adv_ by companies.
manipulus, -ī _m_ bundle (_esp of hay_); (_MIL_)
company.
Manlius, -iānus _adj see n._
Manlius, -ī _m_ Roman family name (_esp the
saviour of the Capitol from the Gauls_); a severe
disciplinarian.
mannus, -ī _m_ Gallic horse.
mānō, -āre, -āvī, -ātum _vi_ to flow, drip,
stream; (_fig_) to spread, emanate.
mānsī _perf of_ **maneō**.
mānsiō, -ōnis _f_ remaining, stay.
mānsitō, -āre _vi_ to stay on.
mānsuēfaciō, -facere, -fēcī, -factum (_pass
-fīō, -fierī_) _vt_ to tame.
mānsuēscō, -scere, -vī, -tum _vt_ to tame ♦ _vi_
to grow tame, grow mild.
mānsuētē _adv see adj._
mānsuētūdō, -inis _f_ tameness; gentleness.
mānsuētus _ppp of_ **mānsuēscō** ♦ _adj_ tame;
mild, gentle.
mānsus _ppp of_ **mandō**; _ppp of_ **maneō**.
mantēle, -is _nt_ napkin, towel.
mantēlum, -ī _nt_ cloak.
mantica, -ae _f_ knapsack.
manticinor, -ārī, -ātus _vi_ to be a prophet.
mantō, -āre _vi_ to remain, wait.
Mantua, -ae _f_ birthplace of Vergil in N. Italy.
manuālis _adj_ for the hand.
manubiae, -ārum _fpl_ money from sale of booty.
manūbrium, -ī _and_ **iī** _nt_ handle, haft.
manuleātus _adj_ with long sleeves.
manūmissiō, -ōnis _f_ emancipation (of a
slave).
manūmittō, -ittere, -īsī, -issum _vt_ to
emancipate, make free.
manupretium, -ī _and_ **iī** _nt_ pay, wages, reward.
manus, -ūs _f_ hand; corps, band, company;
(_elephant_) trunk; (_art_) touch; (_work_)
handiwork, handwriting; (_war_) force, valour,
hand to hand fighting; (_fig_) power; **~ extrēma**
finishing touch; **~ ferrea** grappling iron; **~um
dare** give up, yield; **~ū** artificially; **~ū mittere**
emancipate; **ad ~um** at hand; **in ~ū** obvious;
subject; **in ~ūs venīre** come to hand; **in ~ibus**
well known; at hand; **in ~ibus habēre** be

engaged on; fondle; **per ~ūs** forcibly; **per ~ūs trādere** hand down.

mapālia, -um *ntpl* huts.

mappa, -ae *f* napkin, cloth.

Marathōn, -ōnis *f* Attic village famous for Persian defeat.

Marathōnius *adj see n.*

Marcellia, -iōrum *ntpl* festival of the Marcelli.

Marcellus, -ī *m* Roman surname (*esp the captor of Syracuse*).

marceō, -ēre *vi* to droop, be faint.

marcēscō, -ere *vi* to waste away, grow feeble.

Marciānus *adj see n.*

marcidus *adj* withered; enervated.

Marcius, -ī *m* Roman family name (*esp Ancus, fourth king*).

Marcius *adj see n.*

mare, -is *nt* sea; **~ nostrum** Mediterranean; **~ inferum** Tyrrhenian Sea; **~ superum** Adriatic.

Mareōticus *adj* Mareotic; Egyptian.

margarīta, -ae *f* pearl.

marginō, -āre *vt* to put a border *or* kerb on.

margō, -inis *m/f* edge, border, boundary; **~ cēnae** side dishes.

Mariānus *adj see n.*

Marīca, -ae *f* nymph of Minturnae.

marīnus *adj* of the sea.

marītālis *adj* marriage- (*in cpds*).

maritimus *adj* of the sea, maritime, coastal ♦ *ntpl* coastal area.

marītō, -āre *vt* to marry.

marītus, -i *m* husband ♦ *adj* nuptial.

Marius, -ī *m* Roman family name (*esp the victor over Jugurtha and the Teutons*).

Marius *adj see n.*

marmor, -is *nt* marble; statue, tablet; sea.

marmoreus *adj* of marble; like marble.

Marō, -ōnis *m* surname of Vergil.

marra, -ae *f* kind of hoe.

Mars, Martis *m* god of war, father of Romulus; war, conflict; planet Mars; **aequō Marte** on equal terms; **suō Marte** by one's own exertions.

Marsī, -ōrum *mpl* people of central Italy, famous as fighters.

Marsicus, -us *adj* Marsian.

marsuppium, -ī *and* **iī** *nt* purse.

Mārtiālis *adj* of Mars.

Mārticola, -ae *m* worshipper of Mars.

Mārtigena, -ae *m* son of Mars.

Mārtius *adj* of Mars; of March; warlike.

mās, maris *m* male, man ♦ *adj* male; manly.

māsculus *adj* male, masculine; manly.

Masinissa, -ae *m* king of Numidia.

massa, -ae *f* lump, mass.

Massicum, -ī *nt* Massic wine.

Massicus, -ī *m* mountain in Campania, famous for vines.

Massilia, -ae *f* Greek colony in Gaul (*now Marseilles*).

Massiliēnsis *adj see n.*

mastīgia, -ae *nt* scoundrel.

mastrūca, -ae *f* sheepskin.

mastrūcātus *adj* wearing sheepskin.

matara, -ae *and* **is, -is** *f* Celtic javelin.

matelliō, -ōnis *m* pot.

māter, -ris *f* mother; **Māgna ~** Cybele.

mātercula, -ae *f* poor mother.

māteria, -ae; -ēs, -ēi *f* matter, substance; wood, timber; (*fig*) subject matter, theme; occasion, opportunity; (*person*) ability, character.

māteriārius, -ī *and* **iī** *m* timber merchant.

māteriātus *adj* timbered.

māteriēs *etc see* **māteria.**

māterior, -ārī *vi* to fetch wood.

māternus *adj* mother's.

mātertera, -ae *f* aunt (maternal).

mathēmaticus, -ī *m* mathematician; astrologer.

mātricīda, -ae *m* matricide.

mātricīdium, -ī *and* **iī** *nt* a mother's murder.

mātrimōnium, -ī *and* **iī** *nt* marriage.

mātrimus *adj* whose mother is still alive.

mātrōna, -ae *f* married woman, matron, lady.

mātrōnālis *adj* a married woman's.

matula, -ae *f* pot.

mātūrē *adv* at the right time; early, promptly.

mātūrēscō, -ēscere, -uī *vi* to ripen.

mātūritās, -ātis *f* ripeness; (*fig*) maturity, perfection, height.

mātūrō, -āre, -āvī, -ātum *vt* to bring to maturity; to hasten, be too hasty with ♦ *vi* to make haste.

mātūrus *adj* ripe, mature; timely, seasonable; early.

Mātūta, -ae *f* goddess of dawn.

mātūtīnus *adj* morning, early.

Mauritānia, -ae *f* Mauretania (*now Morocco*).

Maurus, -ī *m* Moor ♦ *adj* Moorish, African.

Maurūsius *adj see n.*

Māvors, -tis *m* Mars.

Māvortius *adj see n.*

maxilla, -ae *f* jaw.

maximē *adv* most, very much, especially; precisely, just; certainly, yes; **cum ~** just as; **quam ~** as much as possible.

maximitās, -ātis *f* great size.

maximus *superl of* **magnus.**

māxum- *etc see* **māxim-.**

māzonomus, -ī *m* dish.

meāpte my own.

meātus, -ūs *m* movement, course.

mēcastor *interj* by Castor!

mēcum with me.

meddix tuticus *m* senior Oscan magistrate.

Mēdēa, -ae *f* Colchian wife of Jason, expert in magic.

Noun declensions and verb conjugations are shown on pp xiii to xxv. The present infinitive ending of a verb shows to which conjugation it belongs: **-āre** = 1st; **-ēre** = 2nd; **-ere** = 3rd and **-īre** = 4th. Irregular verbs are shown on p xxvi

Mēdēis *adj* magical.
medentēs, -entum *mpl* doctors.
medeor, -ērī *vi* (*with dat*) to heal, remedy.
mediastīnus, -ī *m* drudge.
mēdica, -ae *f* lucern (*kind of clover*).
medicābilis *adj* curable.
medicāmen, -inis *nt* drug, medicine;
   cosmetic; (*fig*) remedy.
medicāmentum, -ī *nt* drug, medicine; potion,
   poison; (*fig*) relief; embellishment.
medicātus, -ūs *m* charm.
medicīna, -ae *f* medicine; cure; (*fig*) remedy,
   relief.
medicō, -āre, -āvī, -ātum *vt* to cure; to steep,
   dye.
medicor, -ārī *vt, vi* to cure.
medicus *adj* healing ♦ *m* doctor.
medietās, -ātis *f* mean.
medimnum, -ī *nt*, **-us, -ī** *m* bushel.
mediocris *adj* middling, moderate, average.
mediocritās, -ātis *f* mean, moderation;
   mediocrity.
mediocriter *adv* moderately, not particularly;
   calmly.
Mediolānēnsis *adj see n.*
Mediolānum, -ī *nt* town in N. Italy (*now*
   Milan).
meditāmentum, -ī *nt* preparation, drill.
meditātiō, -ōnis *f* thinking about;
   preparation, practice.
meditātus *adj* studied.
mediterrāneus *adj* inland.
meditor, -ārī, -ātus *vt, vi* to think over,
   contemplate, reflect; to practise, study.
medius *adj* middle, the middle of;
   intermediate; intervening; middling,
   moderate; neutral ♦ *nt* middle; public ♦ *m*
   mediator; ~**um complectī** clasp round the
   waist; ~**um sē gerere** be neutral; ~**ō** midway;
   ~**ō temporis** meanwhile; **in** ~**um** for the
   common good; **in** ~**um prōferre** publish; **dē**
   ~**ō tollere** do away with; **ē** ~**ō abīre** die,
   disappear; **in** ~**ō esse** be public; **in** ~**ō positus**
   open to all; **in** ~**ō relinquere** leave undecided.
medius fidius *interj* by Heaven!
medix *etc see* **meddix.**
medulla, -ae *f* marrow, pith.
medullitus *adv* from the heart.
medullula, -ae *f* marrow.
Mēdus, -ī *m* Mede, Persian.
Mēdus *adj see n.*
Medūsa, -ae *f* Gorgon, whose look turned
   everything to stone.
Medūsaeus *adj*: ~ **equus** Pegasus.
Megalēnsia (Megalēsia), -um *ntpl* festival of
   Cybele in April.
Megara, -ae *f*, **-ōrum** *ntpl* town in Greece near
   the Isthmus.
Megarēus and **icus** *adj* Megarean.
megistānes, -um *mpl* grandees.
mehercle, mehercule, mehercules *interj* by
   Hercules!
mēiō, -ere *vi* to make water.

mel, mellis *nt* honey.
melancholicus *adj* melancholy.
melē *pl* melos.
Meleager (-ros), -rī *m* prince of Calydon.
melicus *adj* musical; lyrical.
melilōtos, -ī *f* kind of clover.
melimēla, -ōrum *ntpl* honey apples.
Mēlīnum, -ī *nt* Melian white.
melior, -ōris *adj* better.
melisphyllum, -ī *nt* balm.
Melita, -ae *f* Malta.
Melitēnsis *adj* Maltese.
melius *nt* melior ♦ *adv* better.
meliusculē *adv* fairly well.
meliusculus *adj* rather better.
mellifer, -ī *adj* honey-making.
mellītus *adj* honeyed; sweet.
melos, -ī *nt* tune, song.
Melpomenē, -ēs *f* Muse of tragedy.
membrāna, -ae *f* skin, membrane, slough;
   parchment.
membrānula, -ae *f* piece of parchment.
membrātim *adv* limb by limb; piecemeal; in
   short sentences.
membrum, -ī *nt* limb, member; part, division;
   clause.
mēmet *emphatic form of* **mē.**
meminī, -isse *vi* (*with gen*) to remember,
   think of; to mention.
Memnōn, -onis *m* Ethiopian king, killed at Troy.
Memnonius *adj see n.*
memor, -is *adj* mindful, remembering; in
   memory (of).
memorābilis *adj* memorable, remarkable.
memorandus *adj* noteworthy.
memorātus, -ūs *m* mention.
memorātus *adj* famed.
memoria, -ae *f* memory, remembrance; time,
   lifetime; history; **haec** ~ our day; ~**ae**
   prōdere hand down to posterity; **post**
   hominum ~**am** since the beginning of
   history.
memoriola, -ae *f* weak memory.
memoriter *adv* from memory; accurately.
memorō, -āre, -āvī, -ātum *vt* to mention,
   say, speak.
Memphis, -is and **idos** *f* town in middle Egypt.
Memphītēs and **ītis** and **īticus** *adj* of
   Memphis; Egyptian.
Menander (-ros), -rī *m* Greek writer of comedy.
Menandrēus *adj see n.*
menda, -ae *f* fault.
mendācium, -ī and **iī** *nt* lie.
mendāciunculum, -ī *nt* fib.
mendāx, -ācis *adj* lying; deceptive, unreal ♦
   m liar.
mendīcitās, -ātis *f* beggary.
mendīcō, -āre; -or, -ārī, *vi* to beg, go begging.
mendīcus *adj* beggarly, poor ♦ *m* beggar.
mendōsē *adv see adj.*
mendōsus *adj* faulty; wrong, mistaken.
mendum, -ī *nt* fault, blunder.
Menelāēus *adj see n.*

Menelāus, -ī *m brother of Agamemnon, husband of Helen.*

Menoetiadēs, -ae *m* Patroclus.

mēns, mentis *f* mind, understanding; feelings, heart; idea, plan, purpose; courage; **venit in mentem** it occurs; **mente captus** insane; **eā mente ut** with the intention of.

mēnsa, -ae *f* table; meal, course; counter, bank; **secunda ~** dessert.

mēnsārius, -ī *and* **iī** *m* banker.

mēnsiō, -ōnis *f* (*metre*) quantity.

mēnsis, -is *m* month.

mēnsor, -ōris *m* measurer, surveyor.

mēnstruālis *adj* for a month.

mēnstruus *adj* monthly; for a month ♦ *nt* a month's provisions.

mēnsula, -ae *f* little table.

mēnsūra, -ae *f* measure, measurement; standard, standing; amount, size, capacity.

mēnsus *ppa of* **mētior.**

menta, -ae *f* mint.

Menteus *adj see n.*

mentiēns, -ientis *m* fallacy.

mentiō, -ōnis *f* mention, hint.

mentior, -īrī, -ītus *vi* to lie, deceive ♦ *vt* to say falsely; to feign, imitate.

mentītus *adj* lying, false.

Mentor, -is *m* artist in metalwork; ornamental cup.

mentum, -ī *nt* chin.

meō, -āre *vi* to go, pass.

mephītis, -is *f* noxious vapour, malaria.

merācus *adj* pure.

mercābilis *adj* buyable.

mercātor, -ōris *m* merchant, dealer.

mercātūra, -ae *f* commerce; purchase; goods.

mercātus, -ūs *m* trade, traffic; market, fair.

mercēdula, -ae *f* poor wages, small rent.

mercēnārius *adj* hired, mercenary ♦ *m* servant.

mercēs, -ēdis *f* pay, wages, fee; bribe; rent; (*fig*) reward, retribution, cost.

mercimōnium, -ī *and* **iī** *nt* wares, goods.

mercor, -ārī, -ātus *vt* to trade in, purchase.

Mercurius, -ī *m messenger of the gods, god of trade, thieves, speech and the lyre;* **stēlla ~ī** *planet Mercury.*

Mercuriālis *adj see n.*

merda, -ae *f* dung.

merenda, -ae *f* lunch.

mereō, -ēre, -uī; -eor, -ērī, -itus *vt, vi* to deserve; to earn, win, acquire; (*MIL*) to serve; **bene ~ dē** do a service to, serve well; **~ equō** serve in the cavalry.

meretrīcius *adj* a harlot's.

meretrīcula, -ae *f* pretty harlot.

meretrīx, -īcis *f* harlot.

mergae, -ārum *fpl* pitchfork.

merges, -itis *f* sheaf.

mergō, -gere, -sī, -sum *vt* to dip, immerse, sink; (*fig*) to bury, plunge, drown.

mergus, -ī *m* (*bird*) diver.

merīdiānus *adj* midday; southerly.

merīdiātiō, -ōnis *f* siesta.

merīdiēs, -ēī *f* midday, noon; south.

merīdiō, -āre, *vi* to take a siesta.

meritō, -āre *vt* to learn.

meritō *adv* deservedly.

meritōrius *adj* money-earning ♦ *ntpl* lodgings.

meritum, -ī *nt* service, kindness, merit; blame.

meritus *ppp of* **mereō** ♦ *adj* deserved, just.

merops, -is *f* bee-eater.

mersī *perf of* **mergō.**

mersō, -āre *vt* to immerse, plunge; to overwhelm.

mersus *ppp of* **mergō.**

merula, -ae *f* blackbird.

merum, -ī *nt* wine.

merus *adj* pure, undiluted; bare, mere.

merx, mercis *f* goods, wares.

Messalla, -ae *m* Roman surname (*esp ~ Corvīnus Augustan orator, soldier and literary patron*).

Messallīna, -īnae *f wife of emperor Claudius; wife of Nero.*

Messāna, -ae *f* Sicilian town (*now* Messina).

messis, -is *f* harvest.

messor, -ōris *m* reaper.

messōrius *adj* a reaper's.

messuī *perf of* **metō.**

messus *ppp of* **metō.**

mēta, -ae *f* pillar at each end of the Circus course; turning point, winning post; (*fig*) goal, end, limit.

metallum, -ī *nt* mine, quarry; metal.

mētātor, -ōris *m* surveyor.

Metaurus, -ī *m river in Umbria, famous for the defeat of Hasdrubal.*

Metellus, -ī *m Roman surname (esp the commander against Jugurtha).*

Mēthymna, -ae *f town in Lesbos.*

Mēthymnaeus *adj see n.*

mētior, -tīrī, -nsus *vt* to measure, measure out; to traverse; (*fig*) to estimate, judge.

metō, -tere, -ssuī, -ssum *vt* to reap, gather; to mow, cut down.

mētor, -ārī, -ātus *vt* to measure off, lay out.

metrēta, -ae *f* liquid measure (*about 9 gallons*).

metuculōsus *adj* frightful.

metuō, -uere, -uī, -ūtum *vt* to fear, be apprehensive.

metus, -ūs *m* fear, alarm, anxiety.

meus *adj* my, mine.

mī *dat of* **ego;** *voc and mpl of* **meus.**

mīca, -ae *f* crumb, grain.

micō, -āre, -uī *vi* to quiver, flicker, beat, flash, sparkle.

Midās, -ae *m Phrygian king whose touch turned*

Noun declensions and verb conjugations are shown on pp xiii to xxv. The present infinitive ending of a verb shows to which conjugation it belongs: **-āre** = 1st; **-ēre** = 2nd; **-ere** = 3rd and **-īre** = 4th. Irregular verbs are shown on p xxvi

everything to gold.

migrātiō, -ōnis _f_ removal, change.

migrō, -āre, -āvī, -ātum _vi_ to remove, change, pass away ♦ _vt_ to transport, transgress.

mīles, -itis _m_ soldier, infantryman; army troops.

Mīlēsius _adj see n._

Mīlētus, -tī _f_ town in Asia Minor.

mīlia, -um _ntpl_ thousands; ~ **passuum** miles.

mīliārium (milliārium), -ī _and_ **iī** _nt_ milestone.

mīlitāris _adj_ military, a soldier's.

mīlitāriter _adv_ in a soldierly fashion.

mīlitia, -ae _f_ military service, war; the army; ~**ae** on service; **domī ~aeque** at home and abroad.

mīlitō, -āre _vi_ to serve, be a soldier.

milium, -ī _and_ **iī** _nt_ millet.

mīlle, (_pl_ ~ia) _num_ a thousand; ~ **passūs** a mile.

mīllensimus, -ēsimus _adj_ thousandth.

mīllia _etc see_ **mīlia.**

mīlliārium _etc see_ **mīliārium.**

mīlliēns, -ēs _adv_ a thousand times.

Milō, -ōnis _m_ tribune who killed Clodius and was defended by Cicero.

Milōniānus _adj see n._

Miltiadēs, -is _m_ Athenian general, victor at Marathon.

mīluīnus _adj_ resembling a kite; rapacious.

mīluus (mīlvus), -ī _m_ kite; gurnard.

mīma, -ae _f_ actress.

Mimallonis, -dis _f_ Bacchante.

mīmicē _adv see adj._

mīmicus _adj_ farcical.

Mimnermus, -ī _m_ Greek elegiac poet.

mīmula, -ae _f_ actress.

mīmus, -ī _m_ actor; mime, farce.

mina, -ae _f_ Greek silver coin.

mināciter _adv see adj._

minae, -ārum _fpl_ threats; (_wall_) pinnacles.

minanter _adv_ threateningly.

minātiō, -ōnis _f_ threat.

mināx, -ācis _adj_ threatening; projecting.

Minerva, -ae _f_ goddess of wisdom and arts, esp weaving; (_fig_) talent, genius; working in wool; **sūs ~am** ≈ "teach your grandmother!"

miniānus _adj_ red-leaded.

miniātulus _adj_ painted red.

minimē _adv_ least, very little; (_reply_) no, not at all.

minimus _adj_ least, smallest, very small; youngest.

miniō, -āre, -āvī, -ātum _vt_ to colour red.

minister, -rī _m_, **~ra, ~rae** _f_ attendant, servant; helper, agent, tool.

ministerium, -ī _and_ **iī** _nt_ service, office, duty; retinue.

ministrātor, -ōris _m_, **~rīx, ~rīcis** _f_ assistant, handmaid.

ministrō, -āre _vt_ to serve, supply; to manage.

minitābundus _adj_ threatening.

minitor, -ārī, -ō, -āre _vt, vi_ to threaten.

minium, -ī _and_ **iī** _nt_ vermilion, red lead.

Mīnōis, -idis _f_ Ariadne.

Mīnōius, -us _adj see n._

minor, -ārī, -ātus _vt, vi_ to threaten; to project.

minor, -ōris _adj_ smaller, less, inferior; younger; (_pl_) descendants.

Mīnōs, -is _m_ king of Crete, judge in the lower world.

Mīnōtaurus, -ī _m_ monster of the Cretan labyrinth, half bull, half man.

Minturnae, -ārum _fpl_ town in S. Latium.

Minturnēnsis _adj see n._

minum- _etc see_ **minim-.**

minuō, -uere, -uī, -ūtum _vt_ to make smaller, lessen; to chop up; to reduce, weaken ♦ _vi_ (_tide_) to ebb.

minus _nt_ minor ♦ _adv_ less; not, not at all; **quō ~** (_prevent_) from.

minusculus _adj_ smallish.

minūtal, -ālis _nt_ mince.

minūtātim _adv_ bit by bit.

minūtē _adv_ in a petty manner.

minūtus _ppp of_ **minuō** ♦ _adj_ small; paltry.

mīrābilis _adj_ wonderful, extraordinary.

mīrābiliter _adv see adj._

mīrābundus _adj_ astonished.

mīrāculum, -ī _nt_ marvel, wonder; amazement.

mīrandus _adj_ wonderful.

mīrātiō, -ōnis _f_ wonder.

mīrātor, -ōris _m_ admirer.

mīrātrīx, -īcis _adj_ admiring.

mīrē _adv see adj._

mīrificē _adv see adj._

mīrificus _adj_ wonderful.

mirmillō _see_ **murmillō.**

mīror, -ārī, -ātus _vt_ to wonder at, be surprised at, admire ♦ _vi_ to wonder, be surprised.

mīrus _adj_ wonderful, strange; ~**um quam, quantum** extraordinarily.

miscellānea, -ōrum _ntpl_ (_food_) hotchpotch.

misceō, -scēre, -scuī, -xtum _vt_ to mix, mingle, blend; to join, combine; to confuse, embroil.

misellus _adj_ poor little.

Mīsēnēnsis _adj see n._

Mīsēnum, -ī _nt_ promontory and harbour near Naples.

miser, -ī _adj_ wretched, poor, pitiful, sorry.

miserābilis _adj_ pitiable, sad, plaintive.

miserābiliter _adv see adj._

miserandus _adj_ deplorable.

miserātiō, -ōnis _f_ pity, compassion, pathos.

miserē _adv see adj._

misereō, -ēre, -uī, -eor, -ērī, -itus _vt, vi_ (_with gen_) to pity, sympathize with; ~**et mē** I pity, I am sorry.

miserēscō, -ere _vi_ to feel pity.

miseria, -ae _f_ misery, trouble, distress.

misericordia, -ae _f_ pity, sympathy, mercy.

misericors, -dis _adj_ sympathetic, merciful.

miseriter _adv_ sadly.

miseror, -ārī, -ātus _vt_ to deplore; to pity.

mīsī *perf of* **mittō**.

missa, -ae *f* (*ECCL*) mass.

missilis *adj* missile.

missiō, -ōnis *f* sending; release; (*MIL*) discharge; (*gladiators*) quarter; (*events*) end; **sine ~ōne** to the death.

missitō, -āre *vt* to send repeatedly.

missus *ppp of* **mittō**.

missus, -ūs *m* sending; throwing; ~ **sagittae** bowshot.

mitella, -ae *f* turban.

mītēscō, -ere *vi* to ripen; to grow mild.

Mithridātēs, -is *m* king of Pontus, defeated by Pompey.

Mithridātēus, -icus *adj see n.*

mītigātiō, -ōnis *f* soothing.

mītigō, -āre, -āvī, -ātum *vt* to ripen, soften; to calm, pacify.

mītis *adj* ripe, mellow; soft, mild; gentle.

mitra, -ae *f* turban.

mittō, -ere, mīsī, missum *vt* to send, dispatch; to throw, hurl; to let go, dismiss; to emit, utter; (*news*) to send word; (*gift*) to bestow; (*event*) to end; (*speech*) to omit, stop; **sanguinem ~** bleed; **ad cēnam ~** invite to dinner; **missum facere** forgo.

mītulus, -ī *m* mussel.

mixtim *adv* promiscuously.

mixtūra, -ae *f* mingling.

Mnēmosynē, -ēs *f* mother of the Muses.

mnēmosynon, -ī *nt* souvenir.

mōbilis *adj* movable; nimble, fleet; excitable, fickle.

mōbilitās, -ātis *f* agility, rapidity; fickleness.

mōbiliter *adv* rapidly.

mōbilitō, -āre *vt* to make rapid.

moderābilis *adj* moderate.

moderāmen, -inis *nt* control; government.

moderanter *adv* with control.

moderātē *adv* with restraint.

moderātim *adv* gradually.

moderātiō, -ōnis *f* control, government; moderation; rules.

moderātor, -ōris *m* controller, governor.

moderātrīx, -īcis *f* mistress, controller.

moderātus *adj* restrained, orderly.

moderor, -ārī, -ātus *vt, vi* (*with dat*) to restrain, check; (*with acc*) to manage, govern, guide.

modestē *adv* with moderation; humbly.

modestia, -ae *f* temperate behaviour, discipline; humility.

modestus *adj* sober, restrained; well-behaved, disciplined; modest, unassuming.

modiālis *adj* holding a peck.

modicē *adv* moderately; slightly.

modicus *adj* moderate; middling, small, mean.

modificātus *adj* measured.

modius, -ī *and* **iī** *m* corn measure, peck.

modo *adv* only; at all, in any way; (*with imp*) just; (*time*) just now, a moment ago, in a moment ♦ *conj* if only; **nōn ~** not only; **non ~ ... sed** not only ... but also ...; ~ **nōn** all but, almost; ~ ... ~ sometimes ... sometimes; ~ ... **tum** at first ... then.

modulātē *adv* melodiously.

modulātor, -ōris *m* musician.

modulātus *adj* played, measured.

modulor, -ārī, - ātus *vt* to modulate, play, sing.

modulus, -ī *m* measure.

modus, -ī *m* measure; size; metre; music; way, method; limit, end; **ēius ~ī** such; ~**ō, in, ~um** like.

moecha, -ae *f* adulteress.

moechor, -ārī *vi* to commit adultery.

moechus, -ī *m* adulterer.

moenera *etc see* **mūnus**.

moenia, -um *ntpl* defences, walls; town, stronghold.

moeniō *etc see* **mūniō**.

Moesī, -ōrum *mpl* people on lower Danube (*now* Bulgaria).

mola, -ae *f* millstone, mill; grains of spelt.

molāris, -is *m* millstone; (*tooth*) molar.

mōlēs, -is *f* mass, bulk, pile; dam, pier, massive structure; (*fig*) greatness, weight, effort, trouble.

molestē *adv see adj.*

molestia, -ae *f* trouble, annoyance, worry; (*style*) affectation.

molestus *adj* irksome, annoying; (*style*) laboured.

mōlīmen, -inis *nt* exertion, labour; importance.

mōlimentum, -ī *nt* great effort.

mōlior, -īrī, -ītus *vt* to labour at, work, build; to wield, move, heave; to undertake, devise, occasion ♦ *vi* to exert oneself, struggle.

mōlītiō, -ōnis *f* laborious work.

mōlītor, -ōris *m* builder.

mollēscō, -ere *vi* to soften, become effeminate.

molliculus *adj* tender.

molliō, -īre, -īvī, -ītum *vt* to soften, make supple; to mitigate, make easier; to demoralize.

mollis *adj* soft, supple; tender, gentle; (*character*) sensitive, weak, unmanly; (*poetry*) amatory; (*opinion*) changeable; (*slope*) easy.

molliter *adv* softly, gently; calmly; voluptuously.

mollitia, -ae, -ēs, -ēī *f* softness, suppleness; tenderness, weakness, effeminacy.

mollitūdō, -inis *f* softness; susceptibility.

molō, -ere *vt* to grind.

Molossī, -ōrum *mpl* Molossians, people in Epirus.

Molossicus, -us *adj see n.*

Molossis, -idis *f* country of the Molossians.

Noun declensions and verb conjugations are shown on pp xiii to xxv. The present infinitive ending of a verb shows to which conjugation it belongs: **-āre** = 1st; **-ēre** = 2nd; **-ere** = 3rd and **-īre** = 4th. Irregular verbs are shown on p xxvi

Molossus, -ī *m* Molossian hound.
mōly, -os *nt* a magic herb.
mōmen, -inis *nt* movement, momentum.
mōmentum, -ī *nt* movement; change; (*time*) short space, moment; (*fig*) cause, influence, importance; **nullīus ~ī** unimportant.
momordī *perf of* **mordeō.**
Mona, -ae *f* Isle of Man; Anglesey.
monachus, -ī *m* monk.
monēdula, -ae *f* jackdaw.
moneō, -ēre, -uī, -itum *vt* to remind, advise, warn; to instruct, foretell.
monēris, -is *f* galley with one bank of oars.
monērula *etc see* **monēdula.**
monēta, -ae *f* mint; money; stamp.
monīle, -is *nt* necklace, collar.
monim- *etc see* **monum-.**
monitiō, -ōnis *f* admonishing.
monitor, -ōris *m* admonisher; prompter; teacher.
monitum, -ī *nt* warning; prophecy.
monitus, -ūs *m* admonition; warning.
monogrammus *adj* shadowy.
monopodium, -ī *and* **iī** *nt* table with one leg.
mōns, montis *m* mountain.
mōnstrātor, -ōris *m* shower, inventor.
mōnstrātus *adj* distinguished.
mōnstrē *adv see adj.*
mōnstrō, -āre, -āvī, -ātum *vt* to point out, show; to inform, instruct; to appoint; to denounce.
mōnstrum, -ī *nt* portent, marvel; monster.
mōnstruōsus *adj* unnatural.
montānus *adj* mountainous; mountain- (*in cpds*), highland.
monticola, -ae *m* highlander.
montivagus *adj* mountain-roving.
montuōsus, montōsus *adj* mountainous.
monumentum, -ī *nt* memorial, monument; record.
Mopsopius *adj* Athenian.
mora, -ae *f* delay, pause; hindrance; space of time, sojourn; **~am facere** put off.
mora, -ae *f* division of the Spartan army.
mōrālis *adj* moral.
morātor, -ōris *m* delayer.
mōrātus *adj* mannered, of a nature; (*writing*) in character.
morbidus *adj* unwholesome.
morbus, -ī *m* illness, disease; distress.
mordāciter *adv see adj.*
mordāx, -ācis *adj* biting, sharp, pungent; (*fig*) snarling, carking.
mordeō, -dēre, momordī, -sum *vt* to bite; to bite into, grip; (*cold*) to nip; (*words*) to sting, hurt, mortify.
mordicus *adv* with a bite; (*fig*) doggedly.
mōres *pl of* **mōs.**
morētum, -ī *nt* salad.
moribundus *adj* dying, mortal; deadly.
mōrigeror, -ārī, -ātus *vi* (*with dat*) to gratify, humour.
mōrigerus *adj* obliging, obedient.

morior, -ī, -tuus *vi* to die; to decay, fade.
moritūrus *fut p of* **morior.**
mōrologus *adj* foolish.
moror, -ārī, -ātus *vi* to delay, stay, loiter ♦ *vt* to detain, retard; to entertain; (*with neg*) to heed, object; **nihil, nīl ~** have no objection to; to not care for; to withdraw a charge against.
mōrōsē *adv see adj.*
mōrōsitās, -ātis *f* peevishness.
mōrōsus *adj* peevish, difficult.
Morpheus, -eos *m* god of dreams.
mors, mortis *f* death; corpse; **mortem sibi cōnscīscere** commit suicide; **mortis poena** capital punishment.
morsiuncula, -ae *f* little kiss.
morsus, -ūs *m* bite; grip; (*fig*) sting, vexation.
mortālis *adj* mortal; transient; man-made ♦ *m* human being.
mortālitās, -ātis *f* mortality, death.
mortārium, -ī *and* **iī** *nt* mortar.
mortifer, -ī *adj* fatal.
mortuus *ppa of* **morior** ♦ *adj* dead ♦ *m* dead man.
mōrum, -ī *nt* blackberry, mulberry.
mōrus, -ī *f* black mulberry tree.
mōrus *adj* foolish ♦ *m* fool.
mōs, mōris *m* nature, manner; humour, mood; custom, practice, law; (*pl*) behaviour, character, morals; **~ māiōrum** national tradition; **mōrem gerere** oblige, humour; **mōre, in mōrem** like.
Mosa, -ae *m* river Meuse.
Mōsēs, -is *m* Moses.
mōtiō, -ōnis *f* motion.
mōtō, -āre *vt* to keep moving.
mōtus *ppp of* **moveō.**
mōtus, -ūs *m* movement; dance, gesture; (*mind*) impulse, emotion; (*POL*) rising, rebellion; **terrae ~** earthquake.
movēns, -entis *pres p of* **moveō** ♦ *adj* movable ♦ *ntpl* motives.
moveō, -ēre, mōvī, mōtum *vt* to move, set in motion; to disturb; to change; to dislodge, expel; to occasion, begin; (*opinion*) to shake; (*mind*) to affect, influence, provoke ♦ *vi* to move; **castra ~** strike camp; **sē ~** budge; to dance.
mox *adv* presently, soon, later on; next.
Mōysēs *see* **Mōsēs.**
mūcidus *adj* snivelling; mouldy.
Mūcius, -ī *m* Roman family name (*esp Scaevola, who burned his right hand before Porsena*).
mūcrō, -ōnis *m* point, edge; sword.
mūcus, -ī *m* mucus.
mūgilis, -is *m* mullet.
muginor, -ārī *vi* to hesitate.
mūgiō, -īre *vi* to bellow, groan.
mūgītus, -ūs *m* lowing, roaring.
mūla, -ae *f* she-mule.
mulceō, -cēre, -sī, -sum *vt* to stroke, caress;

to soothe, alleviate, delight.

Mulciber, -is *and* **ī** *m* Vulcan.

mulcō, -āre, -āvī, -ātum *vt* to beat, ill-treat, damage.

mulctra, -ae *f*, **-ārium, -ārī,** *and* **āriī, -um, -ī** *nt* milkpail.

mulgeō, -ēre, mulsī *vt* to milk.

muliebris *adj* woman's, feminine; effeminate.

muliebriter *adv* like a woman; effeminately.

mulier, -is *f* woman; wife.

mulierārius *adj* woman's.

muliercula, -ae *f* girl.

mulierōsitās, -ātis *f* fondness for women.

mulierōsus *adj* fond of women.

mūlīnus *adj* mulish.

mūliō, -ōnis *m* mule driver.

mūliōnius *adj* mule driver's.

mullus, -ī *m* red mullet.

mulsī *perf of* **mulceō**; *perf of* **mulgeō**.

mulsus *ppp of* **mulceō**.

mulsus *adj* honeyed, sweet ♦ *nt* honey-wine, mead.

multa, -ae *f* penalty, fine; loss.

multangulus *adj* many-angled.

multāticius *adj* fine- (*in cpds*).

multātiō, -ōnis *f* fining.

multēsimus *adj* very small.

multicavus *adj* many-holed.

multīcia, -ōrum *ntpl* transparent garments.

multifāriam *adv* in many places.

multifidus *adj* divided into many parts.

multifōrmis *adj* of many forms.

multiforus *adj* many-holed.

multigeneris, -us *adj* of many kinds.

multiiugis, -us *adj* yoked together; complex.

multiloquium, -ī *and* **iī** *nt* talkativeness.

multiloquus *adj* talkative.

multimodīs *adv* variously.

multiplex, -icis *adj* with many folds, tortuous; many-sided, manifold, various; (*comparison*) far greater; (*character*) fickle, sly.

multiplicō, -āre, -āvī, -ātum *vt* to multiply, enlarge.

multipotēns, -entis *adj* very powerful.

multitūdō, -inis *f* great number, multitude, crowd.

multivolus *adj* longing for much.

multō *adv* much, far, by far; (*time*) long.

multō, -āre, -āvī, -ātum *vt* to punish, fine.

multum *adv* much, very, frequently.

multus (*compar* **plūs** *superl* **plūrimus**) *adj* much, many; (*speech*) lengthy, tedious; (*time*) late; **~ā nocte** late at night; **nē ~a ≈** *to cut a long story short*.

mūlus, -ī *m* mule.

Mulvius *adj* Mulvian (*a Tiber bridge above Rome*).

mundānus, -ī *m* world citizen.

munditia, -ae, -ēs, -ēī *f* cleanness; neatness, elegance.

mundus *adj* clean, neat, elegant; **in ~ō esse** be in readiness.

mundus, -ī *m* toilet gear; universe, world, heavens; mankind.

mūnerigerulus, -ī *m* bringer of presents.

mūnerō, -āre, -or, -ārī *vt* to present, reward.

mūnia, -ōrum *ntpl* official duties.

mūniceps, -ipis *m/f* citizen (*of a municipium*), fellow-citizen.

mūnicipālis *adj* provincial.

mūnicipium, -ī *and* **iī** *nt* provincial town, burgh.

mūnificē *adv see adj.*

mūnificentia, -ae *f* liberality.

mūnificō, -āre *vt* to treat generously.

mūnificus *adj* liberal.

mūnīmen, -inis *nt* defence.

mūnīmentum, -ī *nt* defencework, protection.

mūniō, -īre, -iī, -ītum *vt* to fortify, secure, strengthen; (*road*) to build; (*fig*) to protect.

mūnis *adj* ready to oblige.

mūnītiō, -ōnis *f* building; fortification; (*river*) bridging.

mūnītō, -āre *vt* (*road*) to open up.

mūnītor, -ōris *m* sapper, builder.

mūnus, -eris *nt* service, duty; gift; public show; entertainment; tax; (*funeral*) tribute; (*book*) work.

mūnusculum, -ī *nt* small present.

mūraena, -ae *f* a fish.

mūrālis *adj* wall- (*in cpds*), mural, for fighting from *or* attacking walls.

mūrex, -icis *m* purple-fish; purple dye, purple; jagged rock.

muria, -ae *f* brine.

murmillō, -ōnis *m* kind of gladiator.

murmur, -is *nt* murmur, hum, rumbling, roaring.

murmurillum, -ī *nt* low murmur.

murmurō, -āre *vi* to murmur, rumble; to grumble.

murra, -ae *f* myrrh.

murreus *adj* perfumed; made of the stone called murra.

murrina, -ae *f* myrrh wine.

murrina, -ōrum *ntpl* murrine vases.

murt- *etc see* **myrt-**.

mūrus, -ī *m* wall; dam; defence.

mūs, mūris *m/f* mouse, rat.

Mūsa, -ae *f* goddess inspiring an art; poem; (*pl*) studies.

mūsaeus *adj* poetic, musical.

musca, -ae *f* fly.

mūscipula, -ae *f*, **-um, -ī** *nt* mousetrap.

mūscōsus *adj* mossy.

mūsculus, -ī *m* mouse; muscle; (*MIL*) shed.

mūscus, -ī *m* moss.

mūsicē *adv* very pleasantly.

mūsicus *adj* of music, of poetry ♦ *m* musician ♦ *f* music, culture ♦ *ntpl* music.

Noun declensions and verb conjugations are shown on pp xiii to xxv. The present infinitive ending of a verb shows to which conjugation it belongs: **-āre** = 1st; **-ēre** = 2nd; **-ere** = 3rd and **-īre** = 4th. Irregular verbs are shown on p xxvi

mussitō, -āre *vi* to say nothing; to mutter ♦ *vt* to bear in silence.

mussō, -āre *vt, vi* to say nothing, brood over; to mutter, murmur.

mustāceum, -ī *nt*, **-us, -ī** *m* wedding cake.

mūstēla, -ae *f* weasel.

mustum, -ī *nt* unfermented wine, must; vintage.

mūtābilis *adj* changeable, fickle.

mūtābilitās, -ātis *f* fickleness.

mūtātiō, -ōnis *f* change, alteration; exchange.

mutilō, -āre, -āvī, -ātum *vt* to cut off, maim; to diminish.

mutilus *adj* maimed.

Mutina, -ae *f* town in N. Italy (now Modena).

Mutinēnsis *adj see n.*

mūtiō *etc see* **muttiō.**

mūtō, -āre, -āvī, -ātum *vt* to shift; to change, alter; to exchange, barter ♦ *vi* to change; ~āta verba figurative language.

muttiō, -īre *vi* to mutter, mumble.

mūtuātiō, -ōnis *f* borrowing.

mūtuē *adv* mutually, in turns.

mūtuitō, -āre *vt* to try to borrow.

mūtuō *adv* = **mūtuē.**

mūtuor, -ārī, -ātus *vt* to borrow.

mūtus *adj* dumb, mute; silent, still.

mūtuum, -ī *nt* loan.

mūtuus *adj* borrowed, lent; mutual, reciprocal; **~um dare** lend; **~um sūmere** borrow; **~um facere** return like for like.

Mycēnae, -ārum *fpl* Agamemnon's capital in S. Greece.

Mycēnaeus, -ēnsis *adj*, **-is, -idis** *f* Iphigenia.

Mygdonius *adj* Phrygian.

myoparō, -ōnis *m* pirate galley.

myrīca, -ae *f* tamarisk.

Myrmidones, -um *mpl* followers of Achilles.

Myrōn, -ōnis *m* famous Greek sculptor.

myropōla, -ae *m* perfumer.

myropōlium, -ī *and* **iī** *nt* perfumer's shop.

myrothēcium, -ī *and* **iī** *nt* perfume-box.

myrrh- *etc see* **murr-.**

myrtētum, -ī *nt* myrtlegrove.

myrteus *adj* myrtle- (in cpds).

Myrtoum mare Sea N.W. of Crete.

myrtum, -ī *nt* myrtle-berry.

myrtus, -ī *and* **ūs** *f* myrtle.

Mȳsia, -iae *f* country of Asia Minor.

Mȳsius, -us *adj see n.*

mysta, -ae *m* priest of mysteries.

mystagōgus, -ī *m* initiator.

mystērium, -ī *and* **iī** *nt* secret religion, mystery; secret.

mysticus *adj* mystic.

Mytilēnae, -ārum *fpl*; **-ē, -es** *f* capital of Lesbos.

Mytilēnaeus *adj see n.*

Mytilēnēnsis *adj see n.*

N, n

nablium, -ī *and* **iī** *nt* kind of harp.

nactus *ppa of* **nancīscor.**

nae *etc see* **nē.**

naenia *etc see* **nēnia.**

Naeviānus *adj see n.*

Naevius, -ī *m* early Latin poet.

naevus, -ī *m* mole (on the body).

Nāias, -adis *and* **s, -dis** *f* water nymph, Naiad.

Nāicus *adj see n.*

nam *conj* (explaining) for; (illustrating) for example; (transitional) now; (interrog) but; (enclitic) an emphatic particle.

namque *conj* for, for indeed, for example.

nancīscor, -ī, nactus *and* **nanctus** *vt* to obtain, get; to come upon, find.

nānus, -ī *m* dwarf.

Napaeae, -ārum *fpl* dell nymphs.

nāpus, -ī *m* turnip.

Narbō, -ōnis *m* town in S. Gaul.

Narbōnēnsis *adj see n.*

narcissus, -ī *m* narcissus.

nardus, -ī *f*, **-um, -ī** *nt* nard, nard oil.

nāris, -is *f* nostril; (pl) nose; (fig) sagacity, scorn.

nārrābilis *adj* to be told.

nārrātiō, -ōnis *f* narrative.

nārrātor, -ōris *m* storyteller, historian.

nārrātus, -ūs *m* narrative.

nārrō, -āre, -āvī, -ātum *vt* to tell, relate, say; **male ~** bring bad news.

narthēcium, -ī *and* **iī** *nt* medicine chest.

nāscor, -scī, -tus *vi* to be born; to originate, grow, be produced.

Nāsō, -ōnis *m* surname of Ovid.

nassa, -ae *f* wicker basket for catching fish; (fig) snare.

nasturtium, -ī *and* **iī** *nt* cress.

nāsus, -ī *m* nose.

nāsūtē *adv* sarcastically.

nāsūtus *adj* big-nosed; satirical.

nāta, -ae *f* daughter.

nātālicius *adj* of one's birthday, natal ♦ *f* birthday party.

nātālis *adj* of birth, natal ♦ *m* birthday ♦ *mpl* birth, origin.

nātātiō, -ōnis *f* swimming.

natātor, -ōris *m* swimmer.

nātiō, -ōnis *f* tribe, race; breed, class.

natis, -is *f* (usu pl) buttocks.

nātīvus *adj* created; inborn, native, natural.

natō, -āre *vi* to swim, float; to flow, overflow; (eyes) to swim, fail; (fig) to waver.

nātrix, -īcis *f* watersnake.

nātū *abl m* by birth, in age; **grandis ~, māgnō ~** quite old; **māior ~** older; **māximus ~** oldest.

nātūra, -ae f birth; nature, quality, character; natural order of things; the physical world; (*physics*) element; **rērum ~** Nature.

nātūrālis adj by birth; by nature, natural.

nātūrāliter adv by nature.

nātus ppa of **nāscor** ♦ m son ♦ adj born, made (for); old, of age; **prō, ē rē nātā** under the circumstances, as things are; **annōs vīgintī ~** 20 years old.

nauarchus, -ī m captain.

naucī: nōn esse, facere, habēre to be worthless, consider worthless.

nauclēricus adj skipper's.

nauclērus, -ī m skipper.

naufragium, -ī and **iī** nt shipwreck, wreck; **~ facere** be shipwrecked.

naufragus adj shipwrecked, wrecked; (*sea*) dangerous to shipping ♦ m shipwrecked man; (*fig*) ruined man.

naulum, -ī nt fare.

naumachia, -ae f mock sea fight.

nausea, -ae f seasickness.

nauseō, -āre vi to be sick; (*fig*) to disgust.

nauseola, -ae f squeamishness.

nauta, (nāvita), -ae m sailor, mariner.

nauticus adj nautical, sailors' ♦ mpl seamen.

nāvālis adj naval, of ships ♦ nt and ntpl dockyard; rigging.

nāvicula, -ae f boat.

nāviculāria, -ae f shipping business.

nāviculārius, -ī and **iī** m ship-owner.

nāvifragus adj dangerous.

nāvigābilis adj navigable.

nāvigātiō, -ōnis f voyage.

nāviger, -ī adj ship-carrying.

nāvigium, -ī and **iī** nt vessel, ship.

nāvigō, -āre, -āvī, -ātum vi to sail, put to sea ♦ vt to sail across, navigate.

nāvis, -is f ship; **~ longa** warship; **~ mercātōria** merchantman; **~ onerāria** transport; **~ praetōria** flagship; **~em dēdūcere** launch; **~em solvere** set sail; **~em statuere** heave to; **~em subdūcere** beach; **~ibus atque quadrīgīs** with might and main.

nāvita etc see **nauta**.

nāvitās, -ātis f energy.

nāviter adv energetically; absolutely.

nāvō, -āre vt to perform energetically; **operam ~** be energetic; to come to the assistance (of).

nāvus adj energetic.

Naxos, -ī f Aegean island (*famous for wines and the story of Ariadne*).

nē interj truly, indeed.

nē adv not ♦ conj that not, lest; (*fear*) that; (*purpose*) so that ... not, to avoid, to prevent.

-ne enclitic (*introducing a question*).

Neāpolis, -is f Naples.

Neāpolītānus adj see n.

nebula, -ae f mist, vapour, cloud.

nebulō, -ōnis m idler, good-for-nothing.

nebulōsus adj misty, cloudy.

nec etc see **neque**.

necdum adv and not yet.

necessāriē, -ō adv of necessity, unavoidably.

necessārius adj necessary, inevitable; indispensable; (*kin*) related ♦ m/f relative ♦ ntpl necessities.

necesse adj (*indecl*) necessary, inevitable; needful.

necessitās, -ātis f necessity, compulsion; requirement, want; relationship, connection.

necessitūdō, -inis f necessity, need, want; connection; friendship (*pl*) relatives.

necessum etc see **necesse**.

necne adv or not.

necnōn adv also, besides.

necō, -āre, -āvī, -ātum vt to kill, murder.

necopīnāns, -antis adj unaware.

necopīnātō adv see adj.

necopīnātus adj unexpected.

necopīnus adj unexpected; unsuspecting.

nectar, -is nt nectar (*the drink of the gods*).

nectareus adj of nectar.

nectō, -ctere, -xī and **xuī, -xum** vt to tie, fasten, connect; to weave; (*fig*) to bind, enslave (*esp for debt*); to contrive, frame.

nēcubi conj so that nowhere.

nēcunde conj so that from nowhere.

nēdum adv much less, much more.

nefandus adj abominable, impious.

nefāriē adv see adj.

nefārius adj heinous, criminal.

nefās nt (*indecl*) wickedness, sin, wrong ♦ interj horror!, shame!

nefāstus adj wicked; unlucky; (*days*) closed to public business.

negātiō, -ōnis f denial.

negitō, -āre vt to deny, refuse.

neglēctiō, -ōnis f neglect.

neglēctus ppp of **neglegō**.

neglēctus, -ūs m neglecting.

neglegēns, -entis pres p of **neglegō** ♦ adj careless, indifferent.

neglegenter adv carelessly.

neglegentia, -ae f carelessness, neglect, coldness.

neglegō, -egere, -ēxī, -ēctum vt to neglect, not care for; to slight, disregard; to overlook.

negō, -āre, -āvī, -ātum vt, vi to say no; to say not, deny; to refuse, decline.

negōtiālis adj business- (*in cpds*).

negōtiāns, -antis m businessman.

negōtiātiō, -ōnis f banking business.

negōtiātor, -ōris m businessman, banker.

negōtiolum, -ī nt trivial matter.

negōtior, -ārī, -ātus vi to do business, trade.

negōtiōsus adj busy.

negōtium, -ī *and* **iī** *nt* business, work; trouble; matter, thing; **quid est ~i?** what is the matter?

Nēlēius *adj see n.*

Nēleus, -eī *m* father of Nestor.

Nēlēus *adj see n.*

Nemea, -ae *f* town in S. Greece, where Hercules killed the lion.

Nemea, -ōrum *ntpl* Nemean Games.

Nemeaeus *adj* Nemean.

nēmō, -inis *m/f* no one, nobody ♦ *adj* no; **~ nōn** everybody; **nōn ~** many; **~ ūnus** not a soul.

nemorālis *adj* sylvan.

nemorēnsis *adj* of the grove.

nemoricultrīx, -īcis *f* forest dweller.

nemorivagus *adj* forest-roving.

nemorōsus *adj* well-wooded; leafy.

nempe *adv* (*confirming*) surely, of course, certainly; (*in questions*) do you mean?

nemus, -ōris *nt* wood, grove.

nēnia, -ae *f* dirge; incantation; song, nursery rhyme.

neō, nēre, nēvī, nētum *vt* to spin; to weave.

Neoptolemus, -ī *m* Pyrrhus (*son of Achilles*).

nepa, -ae *f* scorpion.

nepōs, -ōtis *m* grandson; descendant; spendthrift.

nepōtīnus, -ī *m* little grandson.

neptis, -is *f* granddaughter.

Neptūnius *adj*: **~ hērōs** Theseus.

Neptūnus, -ī *m* Neptune (*god of the sea*); sea.

nēquam *adj* (*indecl*) worthless, bad.

nēquāquam *adv* not at all, by no means.

neque, nec *adv* not ♦ *conj* and not, but not; neither, nor; **~ ... et** not only not ... but also.

nequeō, -īre, -īvī, -ītum *vi* to be unable, cannot.

nēquīquam *adv* fruitlessly, for nothing; without good reason.

nēquior, nēquissimus *compar, superl of* **nēquam.**

nēquiter *adv* worthlessly, wrongly.

nēquitia, -ae, -ēs *f* worthlessness, badness.

Nērēis, -ēidis *f* Nereid, sea nymph.

Nērēius *adj see n.*

Nēreus, -eī *m* a sea god; the sea.

Nēritius *adj* of Neritos; Ithacan.

Nēritos, -ī *m* island near Ithaca.

Nerō, -ōnis *m* Roman surname (*esp the emperor*).

Nerōniānus *adj see n.*

nervōsē *adv* vigorously.

nervōsus *adj* sinewy, vigorous.

nervulī, -ōrum *mpl* energy.

nervus, -ī *m* sinew; string; fetter, prison; (*shield*) leather; (*pl*) strength, vigour, energy.

nesciō, -īre, -īvī *and* **iī, -ītum** *vt* to not know, be ignorant of; to be unable; **~ quis, quid** somebody, something; **~ an** probably.

nescius *adj* ignorant, unaware; unable; unknown.

Nestor, -oris *m* Greek leader at Troy (*famous for his great age and wisdom*).

neu *etc see* **nēve.**

neuter, -rī *adj* neither; neuter.

neutiquam *adv* by no means, certainly not.

neutrō *adv* neither way.

nēve, neu *conj* and not; neither, nor.

nēvī *perf of* **neō.**

nex, necis *f* murder, death.

nexilis *adj* tied together.

nexum, -ī *nt* personal enslavement.

nexus *ppp of* **nectō.**

nexus, -ūs *m* entwining, grip; (*law*) bond, obligation, (*esp enslavement for debt*).

nī *adv* not ♦ *conj* if not, unless; that not; **quid nī?** why not?

nīcētērium, -ī *and* **iī** *nt* prize.

nictō, -āre *vi* to wink.

nīdāmentum, -ī *nt* nest.

nīdor, -ōris *m* steam, smell.

nīdulus, -ī *m* little nest.

nīdus, -ī *m* nest; (*pl*) nestlings; (*fig*) home.

niger, -rī *adj* black, dark; dismal, ill-omened; (*character*) bad.

nigrāns, -antis *adj* black, dusky.

nigrēscō, -ere *vi* to blacken, grow dark.

nigrō, -āre *vi* to be black.

nigror, -ōris *m* blackness.

nihil, nīl *nt* (*indecl*) nothing ♦ *adv* not; **~ ad nōs** it has nothing to do with us; **~ est** it's no use; **~ est quod** there is no reason why; **~ nisi** nothing but, only; **~ nōn** everything; **nōn ~** something.

nihilum, -ī *nt* nothing; **~ī esse** be worthless; **~ō minus** none the less.

nīl, nīlum *see* **nihil, nihilum.**

Nīliacus *adj* of the Nile; Egyptian.

Nīlus, -ī *m* Nile; conduit.

nimbifer, -ī *adj* stormy.

nimbōsus *adj* stormy.

nimbus, -ī *m* cloud, rain, storm.

nimiō *adv* much, far.

nīmīrum *adv* certainly, of course.

nimis *adv* too much, very much; **nōn ~** not very.

nimium *adv* too, too much; very, very much.

nimius *adj* too great, excessive; very great ♦ *nt* excess.

ningit, ninguit, -ere *vi* it snows.

ninguēs, -ium *fpl* snow.

Nioba, -ae, -ē, -ēs *f* daughter of Tantalus (*changed to a weeping rock*).

Niobēus *adj see n.*

Nīreus, -eī *and* **eos** *m* handsomest of the Greeks at Troy.

Nīsaeus, -ēius *adj see n.*

Nīsēis, -edis *f* Scylla.

nisi *conj* if not, unless; except, but.

nīsus *ppa of* **nītor.**

nīsus, -ūs *m* pressure, effort; striving, soaring.

Nīsus, -ī *m* father of Scylla.

nītēdula, -ae *f* dormouse.

nitēns, -entis *pres p of* **niteō** ♦ *adj* bright;

brilliant, beautiful.

niteō, -ēre vi to shine, gleam; to be sleek, be greasy; to thrive, look beautiful.

nitēscō, -ere, nituī vi to brighten, shine, glow.

nitidiusculē adv rather more finely.

nitidiusculus adj a little shinier.

nitidē adv magnificently.

nitidus adj bright, shining; sleek; blooming; smart, spruce; (speech) refined.

nitor, -ōris m brightness, sheen; sleekness, beauty; neatness, elegance.

nītor, -tī, -sus and **xus** vi to rest on, lean on; to press, stand firmly; to press forward, climb; to exert oneself, strive, labour; to depend on.

nitrum, -ī nt soda.

nivālis adj snowy.

niveus adj of snow, snowy, snow-white.

nivōsus adj snowy.

nix, nivis f snow.

nīxor, -ārī vi to rest on; to struggle.

nīxus ppp of **nītor**.

nīxus, -ūs m pressure; labour.

nō, nāre, nāvī vi to swim, float; to sail, fly.

nōbilis adj known, noted, famous, notorious; noble, high-born; excellent.

nōbilitās, -ātis f fame; noble birth; the nobility; excellence.

nōbilitō, -āre, -āvī, -ātum vt to make famous or notorious.

nocēns, -entis pres p of **noceō** ♦ adj harmful; criminal, guilty.

noceō, -ēre, -uī, -itum vi (with dat) to harm, hurt.

nocīvus adj injurious.

noctifer, -ī m evening star.

noctilūca, -ae f moon.

noctivagus adj night-wandering.

noctū adv by night.

noctua, -ae f owl.

noctuābundus adj travelling by night.

nocturnus adj night- (in cpds), nocturnal.

nōdō, -āre, -āvī, -ātum vt to knot, tie.

nōdōsus adj knotty.

nōdus, -ī m knot; knob; girdle; (fig) bond, difficulty.

nōlō, -le, -uī vt, vi to not wish, be unwilling, refuse; ~ī, ~īte do not.

Nomas, -dis m/f nomad; Numidian.

nōmen, -inis nt name; title; (COMM) demand, debt; (GRAM) noun; (fig) reputation, fame; account, pretext; ~ dare profitērī enlist; ~ dēferre accuse; ~ina facere enter the items of a debt.

nōmenclātor, -ōris m slave who told his master the names of people.

nōminātim adv by name, one by one.

nōminātiō, -ōnis f nomination.

nōminitō, -āre vt to usually name.

nōminō, -āre, -āvī, -ātum vt to name, call; to mention; to make famous; to nominate; to accuse, denounce.

nomisma, -tis nt coin.

nōn adv not; no.

Nōnae, -ārum fpl Nones (7th day of March, May, July, October, 5th of other months).

nōnāgēsimus adj ninetieth.

nōnāgiēns, -ēs adv ninety times.

nōnāgintā num ninety.

nōnānus adj of the ninth legion.

nōndum adv not yet.

nōngentī, -ōrum num nine hundred.

nonna, -ae f nun.

nōnne adv do not?, is not? etc.; (indirect) whether not.

nōnnullus adj some.

nōnnunquam adv sometimes.

nōnus adj ninth ♦ f ninth hour.

nōnusdecimus adj nineteenth.

Nōricum, -ī nt country between the Danube and the Alps.

Nōricus adj see n.

nōrma, -ae f rule.

nōs pron we, us; I, me.

nōscitō, -āre vt to know, recognise; to observe, examine.

nōscō, -scere, -vī, -tum vt to get to know, learn; to examine; to recognise, allow; (perf) to know.

nōsmet pron (emphatic) see **nōs**.

noster, -rī adj our, ours; for us; my; (with names) my dear, good old ♦ m our friend ♦ mpl our side, our troops; ~rī, ~rum of us.

nostrās, -ātis adj of our country, native.

nota, -ae f mark, sign, note; (writing) note, letter; (pl) memoranda, shorthand, secret writing; (books) critical mark, punctuation; (wine, etc) brand, quality; (gesture) sign; (fig) sign, token; (censor's) black mark; (fig) stigma, disgrace.

notābilis adj remarkable; notorious.

notābiliter adv perceptibly.

notārius, -ī and **iī** m shorthand writer; secretary.

notātiō, -ōnis f marking; choice; observation; (censor) stigmatizing; (words) etymology.

nōtēscō, -ere, nōtuī vi to become known.

nothus adj bastard; counterfeit.

nōtiō, -ōnis f (law) cognisance, investigation; (PHILOS) idea.

nōtitia, -ae, -ēs, -ēī f fame; acquaintance; (PHILOS) idea, preconception.

notō, -āre, -āvī, -ātum vt to mark, write; to denote; to observe; to brand, stigmatize.

nōtuī perf of **nōtēscō**.

nōtus ppp of **nōscō** ♦ adj known, familiar; notorious ♦ mpl acquaintances.

Notus (-os), -ī m south wind.

novācula, -ae f razor.

Noun declensions and verb conjugations are shown on pp xiii to xxv. The present infinitive ending of a verb shows to which conjugation it belongs: -āre = 1st; -ēre = 2nd; -ere = 3rd and -īre = 4th. Irregular verbs are shown on p xxvi

novālis, -is f, **-e, -is** nt fallow land; field; crops.
novātrix, -īcis f renewer.
nově adv unusually.
novellus adj young, fresh, new.
novem num nine.
November, -ris adj of November ♦ m November.
novendecim num nineteen.
novendiālis adj nine days'; on the ninth day.
novēnī, -ōrum adj in nines; nine.
Novēnsilēs, -ium mpl new gods.
noverca, -ae f stepmother.
novercālis adj stepmother's.
nōvī perf of **nōscō**.
novīcius adj new.
noviēns, -ēs adv nine times.
novissimē adv lately; last of all.
novissimus adj latest, last, rear.
novitās, -ātis f newness, novelty; strangeness.
novō, -āre, -āvī, -ātum vt to renew, refresh; to change; (words) to coin; **rēs ~** effect a revolution.
novus adj new, young, fresh, recent; strange, unusual; inexperienced; **~ homō** upstart, first of his family to hold curule office; **~ae rēs** revolution; **~ae tabulae** cancellation of debts; **quid ~ī** what news?
nox, noctis f night; darkness, obscurity; **nocte, noctū** by night; **dē nocte** during the night.
noxa, -ae f hurt, harm; offence, guilt; punishment.
noxia, -ae f harm, damage; guilt, fault.
noxius adj harmful; guilty.
nūbēcula, -ae f cloudy look.
nūbēs, -is f cloud; (fig) gloom; veil.
nūbifer, -ī adj cloud-capped; cloudy.
nūbigena, -ae m cloudborn, Centaur.
nūbilis adj marriageable.
nūbilus adj cloudy; gloomy, sad ♦ ntpl clouds.
nūbō, -bere, -psī, -ptum vi (women) to be married.
nucleus, -ī m nut, kernel.
nūdius day since, days ago; **~ tertius** the day before yesterday.
nūdō, -āre, -āvī, -ātum vt to bare, strip, expose; (MIL) to leave exposed; to plunder; (fig) to disclose, betray.
nūdus adj naked, bare; exposed, defenceless; wearing only a tunic; (fig) destitute, poor; mere; unembellished, undisguised; **vestīmenta dētrahere ~ō** ≈ draw blood from a stone.
nūgae, -ārum fpl nonsense, trifles; (person) waster.
nūgātor, -ōris m silly creature, liar.
nūgātōrius adj futile.
nūgāx, -ācis adj frivolous.
nūgor, -ārī, -ātus vi to talk nonsense; to cheat.
nullus, -īus (dat -ī) adj no, none; not, not at all; non-existent, of no account ♦ m/f nobody.

num interrog particle surely not? (indirect) whether, if.
Numa, -ae m second king of Rome.
nūmen, -inis nt nod, will; divine will, power; divinity, god.
numerābilis adj easy to count.
numerātus adj in cash ♦ nt ready money.
numerō, -āre, -āvī, -ātum vt to count, number; (money) to pay out; (fig) to reckon, consider as.
numerō adv just now, quickly, too soon.
numerōsē adv rhythmically.
numerōsus adj populous; rhythmical.
numerus, -ī m number; many, numbers; (MIL) troop; (fig) a cipher; (pl) mathematics; rank, category, regard; rhythm, metre, verse; **in ~ō esse, habērī** be reckoned as; **nullō ~ō** of no account.
Numida adj see n.
Numidae, -ārum mpl Numidians (people of N. Africa).
Numidia, -iae f the country of the Numidians.
Numidicus adj see n.
Numitor, -ōris m king of Alba (grandfather of Romulus).
nummārius adj money- (in cpds), financial; mercenary.
nummātus adj moneyed.
nummulī, -ōrum mpl some money, cash.
nummus, -ī m coin, money, cash; (Roman coin) sestertius; (Greek coin) two-drachma piece.
numnam, numne see num.
numquam adv never; **~ nōn** always; **nōn ~** sometimes.
numquid (question) do you? does he? etc; (indirect) whether.
nunc adv now; at present, nowadays; but as it is; **~ ... ~** at one time ... at another.
nuncupātiō, -ōnis f pronouncing.
nuncupō, -āre, -āvī, -ātum vt to call, name; to pronounce formally.
nūndinae, -ārum fpl market day; market; trade.
nūndinātiō, -ōnis f trading.
nūndinor, -ārī vi to trade, traffic; to flock together ♦ vt to buy.
nūndinum, -ī nt market time; **trīnum ~** 17 days.
nunq- etc see **numq-**.
nūntiātiō, -ōnis f announcing.
nūntiō, -āre, -āvī, -ātum vt to announce, report, tell.
nūntius adj informative, speaking ♦ m messenger; message, news; injunction; notice of divorce ♦ nt message.
nūper adv recently, lately.
nūpsī perf of **nūbō**.
nūpta, -ae f bride, wife.
nūptiae, -ārum fpl wedding, marriage.
nūptiālis adj wedding- (in cpds), nuptial.
nurus, -ūs f daughter-in-law; young woman.
nūsquam adv nowhere; in nothing, for nothing.

nūtō, -āre *vi* to nod; to sway, totter, falter.
nūtrīcius, -ī *m* tutor.
nūtrīcō, -āre, -or, -ārī *vt* to nourish, sustain.
nūtrīcula, -ae *f* nurse.
nūtrīmen, -inis *nt* nourishment.
nūtrīmentum, -ī *nt* nourishment, support.
nūtriō, -īre, -īvī, -ītum *vt* to suckle, nourish, rear, nurse.
nūtrīx, -īcis *f* nurse, foster mother.
nūtus, -ūs *m* nod; will, command; (*physics*) gravity.
nux, nucis *f* nut; nut tree, almond tree.
Nyctēis, -idis *f* Antiopa.
nympha, -ae, -ē, -ēs *f* bride; nymph; water.
Nysa, -ae *f* birthplace of Bacchus.
Nysaeus, -ēis, -ius *adj see n.*

O, o

ō *interj* (*expressing joy, surprise, pain, etc*) oh!; (*with voc*) O!
ob *prep* (*with acc*) in front of; for, on account of, for the sake of; **quam ~ rem** accordingly.
obaerātus *adj* in debt ♦ *m* debtor.
obambulō, -āre *vi* to walk past, prowl about.
obarmō, -āre *vt* to arm (against).
obarō, -āre *vt* to plough up.
obc- *etc see* **occ-**.
obdō, -ere, -idī, -itum *vt* to shut; to expose.
obdormīscō, -īscere, -īvī *vi* to fall asleep ♦ *vt* to sleep off.
obdūcō, -ūcere, -ūxī, -uctum *vt* to draw over, cover; to bring up; (*drink*) to swallow; (*time*) to pass.
obductō, -āre *vt* to bring as a rival.
obductus *ppp of* **obdūcō**.
obdūrēscō, -ēscere, -uī *vi* to harden; to become obdurate.
obdūrō, -āre *vi* to persist, stand firm.
obdutiō, -ōnis *f* veiling.
obeō, -īre, -īvī, *and* **iī, -itum** *vi* to go to, meet; to die; (*ASTRO*) to set ♦ *vt* to visit, travel over; to survey, go over; to envelop; (*duty*) to engage in, perform; (*time*) to meet; **diem ~ die**; (*law*) to appear on the appointed day.
obequitō, -āre *vi* to ride up to.
oberrō, -āre *vi* to ramble about; to make a mistake.
obēsus *adj* fat, plump; coarse.
ōbex, -icis *m/f* bolt, bar, barrier.
obf- *etc see* **off-**.
obg- *etc see* **ogg-**.

obhaerēscō, -rēscere, -sī *vi* to stick fast.
obiaceō, -ēre *vi* to lie over against.
obiciō, -icere, -iēcī, -iectum *vt* to throw to, set before; (*defence*) to put up, throw against; (*fig*) to expose, give up; (*speech*) to taunt, reproach.
obiectātiō, -ōnis *f* reproach.
obiectō, -āre *vt* to throw against; to expose, sacrifice; to reproach; (*hint*) to let on.
obiectus *ppp of* **obiciō** ♦ *adj* opposite, in front of; exposed ♦ *ntpl* accusations.
obiectus, -ūs *m* putting in the way, interposing.
obīrātus *adj* angered.
obiter *adv* on the way; incidentally.
obitus *ppp of* **obeō**.
obitus, -ūs *m* death, ruin; (*ASTRO*) setting; visit.
obiūrgātiō, -ōnis *f* reprimand.
obiūrgātor, -ōris *m* reprover.
obiūrgātōrius *adj* reproachful.
obiūrgitō, -āre *vt* to keep on reproaching.
obiūrgō, -āre, -āvī, -ātum *vt* to scold, rebuke; to deter by reproof.
oblanguēscō, -ēscere, -uī *vi* to become feeble.
oblātrātrīx, -īcis *f* nagging woman.
oblātus *ppp of* **offerō**.
oblectāmentum, -ī *nt* amusement.
oblectātiō, -ōnis *f* delight.
oblectō, -āre, -āvī, -ātum *vt* to delight, amuse, entertain; to detain; (*time*) to spend pleasantly; **sē ~** enjoy oneself.
oblīdō, -dere, -sī, -sum *vt* to crush, strangle.
obligātiō, -ōnis *f* pledge.
obligō, -āre, -āvī, -ātum *vt* to tie up, bandage; to put under an obligation, embarrass; (*law*) to render liable, make guilty; to mortgage.
oblīmō, -āre *vt* to cover with mud.
oblinō, -inere, -ēvī, -itum *vt* to smear over; to defile; (*fig*) to overload.
oblīquē *adv* sideways; indirectly.
oblīquō, -āre *vt* to turn aside, veer.
oblīquus *adj* slanting, downhill; from the side, sideways; (*look*) askance, envious; (*speech*) indirect.
oblīsus *ppp of* **oblīdō**.
oblītēscō, -ere *vi* to hide away.
oblitterō, -āre, -āvī, -ātum *vt* to erase, cancel; (*fig*) to consign to oblivion.
oblitus *ppp of* **oblinō**.
oblītus *ppa of* **oblīvīscor**.
oblīviō, -ōnis *f* oblivion, forgetfulness.
oblīviōsus *adj* forgetful.
oblīvīscor, -vīscī, -tus *vt, vi* to forget.
oblīvium, -ī *and* **iī** *nt* forgetfulness, oblivion.
oblocūtor, -ōris *m* contradicter.
oblongus *adj* oblong.
obloquor, -quī, -cūtus *vi* to contradict, interrupt; to abuse; (*music*) to accompany.

Noun declensions and verb conjugations are shown on pp xiii to xxv. The present infinitive ending of a verb shows to which conjugation it belongs: **-āre** = 1st; **-ēre** = 2nd; **-ere** = 3rd and **-īre** = 4th. Irregular verbs are shown on p xxvi

obluctor, -ārī *vi* to struggle against.
obmōlior, -īrī *vt* to throw up (*as a defence*).
obmurmurō, -āre *vi* to roar in answer.
obmūtēscō, -ēscere, -uī *vi* to become silent; to cease.
obnātus *adj* growing on.
obnītor, -tī, -xus *vi* to push against, struggle; to stand firm, resist.
obnīxē *adv* resolutely.
obnīxus *ppa of* **obnītor** ♦ *adj* steadfast.
obnoxiē *adv* slavishly.
obnoxiōsus *adj* submissive.
obnoxius *adj* liable, addicted; culpable; submissive, slavish; under obligation, indebted; exposed (to danger).
obnūbō, -bere, -psī, -ptum *vt* to veil, cover.
obnūntiātiō, -ōnis *f* announcement of an adverse omen.
obnūntiō, -āre *vt* to announce an adverse omen.
oboediēns, -entis *pres p of* **oboediō** ♦ *adj* obedient.
oboedienter *adv* readily.
oboedientia, -ae *f* obedience.
oboediō, -īre *vi* to listen; to obey, be subject to.
oboleō, -ēre, -uī *vt* to smell of.
oborior, -īrī, -tus *vi* to arise, spring up.
obp- *etc see* **opp-**.
obrēpō, -ere, -sī, -tum *vt, vi* to creep up to, steal upon, surprise; to cheat.
obrētiō, -īre *vt* to entangle.
obrigēscō, -ēscere, -uī *vi* to stiffen.
obrogō, -āre, -āvī, -ātum *vt* to invalidate (*by making a new law*).
obruō, -ere, -ī, -tum *vt* to cover over, bury, sink; to overwhelm, overpower ♦ *vi* to fall to ruin.
obrussa, -ae *f* test, touchstone.
obrutus *ppp of* **obruō**.
obsaepiō, -īre, -sī, -tum *vt* to block, close.
obsaturō, -āre *vt* to sate, glut.
obscaen- *etc see* **obscen-**.
obscēnē *adv* indecently.
obscēnitās, -ātis *f* indecency.
obscēnus *adj* filthy; indecent; ominous.
obscūrātiō, -ōnis *f* darkening, disappearance.
obscūrē *adv* secretly.
obscūritās, -ātis *f* darkness; (*fig*) uncertainty; (*rank*) lowliness.
obscūrō, -āre, -āvī, -ātum *vt* to darken; to conceal, suppress; (*speech*) to obscure; (*pass*) to become obsolete.
obscūrus *adj* dark, shady, hidden; (*fig*) obscure, indistinct; unknown, ignoble; (*character*) reserved.
obsecrātiō, -ōnis *f* entreaty; public prayer.
obsecrō, -āre *vt* to implore, appeal to.
obsecundō, -āre *vi* to comply with, back up.
obsēdī *perf of* **obsideō**.
obsēp- *etc see* **obsaep-**.
obsequēns, -entis *pres p of* **obsequor** ♦ *adj*
compliant; (*gods*) gracious.
obsequenter *adv* compliantly.
obsequentia, -ae *f* complaisance.
obsequiōsus *adj* complaisant.
obsequium, -ī *and* **iī** *nt* compliance, indulgence; obedience, allegiance.
obsequor, -quī, -cūtus *vi* to comply with, yield to, indulge.
obserō, -āre *vt* to bar, close.
obserō, -erere, -ēvī, -itum *vt* to sow, plant; to cover thickly.
observāns, -antis *pres p of* **observō** ♦ *adj* attentive, respectful.
observantia, -ae *f* respect.
observātiō, -ōnis *f* watching; caution.
observitō, -āre *vt* to observe carefully.
observō, -āre, -āvī, -ātum *vt* to watch, watch for; to guard; (*laws*) to keep, comply with; (*person*) to pay respect to.
obses, -idis *m/f* hostage; guarantee.
obsessiō, -ōnis *f* blockade.
obsessor, -ōris *m* frequenter; besieger.
obsessus *ppp of* **obsideō**.
obsideō, -idēre, -ēdī, -essum *vt* to sit at, frequent; (MIL) to blockade, besiege; to block, fill, take up; to guard, watch for ♦ *vi* to sit.
obsidiō, -ōnis *f* siege, blockade; (*fig*) imminent danger.
obsidium, -ī *and* **iī** *nt* siege, blockade; hostageship.
obsīdō, -ere *vt* to besiege, occupy.
obsignātor, -ōris *m* sealer; witness.
obsignō, -āre, -āvī, -ātum *vt* to seal up; to sign and seal; (*fig*) to stamp.
obsistō, -istere, -titī, -titum *vi* to put oneself in the way, resist.
obsitus *ppp of* **obserō**.
obsolefīō, -fierī *vi* to wear out, become degraded.
obsolēscō, -scere, -vī, -tum *vi* to wear out, become out of date.
obsolētius *adv* more shabbily.
obsolētus *ppa of* **obsolēscō** ♦ *adj* worn out, shabby; obsolete; (*fig*) ordinary, mean.
obsōnātor, -ōris *m* caterer.
obsōnātus, -ūs *m* marketing.
obsōnium, -ī *and* **iī** *nt* food eaten with bread, (*usu fish*).
obsōnō, -āre, -or, -ārī *vi* to cater, buy provisions; to provide a meal.
obsonō, -āre *vi* to interrupt.
obsorbeō, -ēre *vt* to swallow, bolt.
obstantia, -ium *ntpl* obstructions.
obstetrīx, -īcis *f* midwife.
obstinātiō, -ōnis *f* determination, stubbornness.
obstinātē *adv* firmly, obstinately.
obstinātus *adj* firm, resolute; stubborn.
obstinō, -āre *vi* to be determined, persist.
obstipēscō *etc see* **obstupēscō**.
obstīpus *adj* bent, bowed, drawn back.
obstitī *perf of* **obstō**; *perf of* **obstō**.
obstō, -āre, -itī *vi* to stand in the way; to

obstruct, prevent.

obstrepō, -ere, -uī, -itum *vi* to make a noise; to shout against, cry down, molest ♦ *vt* to drown (in noise); to fill with noise.

obstrictus *ppp of* **obstringō**.

obstringō, -ingere, -inxī, -ictum *vt* to bind up, tie round; (*fig*) to confine, hamper; to lay under an obligation.

obstructiō, -ōnis *f* barrier.

obstructus *ppp of* **obstruō**.

obstrūdō (obtrūdō), -dere, -sī, -sum *vt* to force on to; to gulp down.

obstruō, -ere, -xī, -ctum *vt* to build up against, block; to shut, hinder.

obstupefaciō, -facere, -fēcī, -factum (*pass* **-fīō, -fierī**) *vt* to astound, paralyse.

obstupēscō, -ēscere, -uī *vi* to be astounded, paralysed.

obstupidus *adj* stupefied.

obsum, -esse, -fuī *vi* to be against, harm.

obsuō, -uere, -uī, -ūtum *vt* to sew on, sew up.

obsurdēscō, -ēscere, -uī *vi* to grow deaf; to turn a deaf ear.

obsūtus *ppp of* **obsuō**.

obtegō, -egere, -ēxī, -ēctum *vt* to cover over; to conceal.

obtemperātiō, -ōnis *f* obedience.

obtemperō, -āre, -āvī, -ātum *vi* (*with dat*) to comply with, obey.

obtendō, -dere, -dī, -tum *vt* to spread over, stretch over against; to conceal; to make a pretext of.

obtentus *ppp of* **obtendō**; *ppp of* **obtineō**.

obtentus, -ūs *m* screen; pretext.

obterō, -erere, -rīvī, -rītum *vt* to trample on, crush; to disparage.

obtestātiō, -ōnis *f* adjuring; supplication.

obtestor, -ārī, -ātus *vt* to call to witness; to entreat.

obtexō, -ere, -uī *vt* to overspread.

obticeō, -ēre *vi* to be silent.

obticēscō, -ēscere, -uī *vi* to be struck dumb.

obtigī *perf of* **obtingō**.

obtigō *see* **obtegō**.

obtineō, -inēre, -inuī, -entum *vt* to hold, possess; to maintain; to gain, obtain ♦ *vi* to prevail, continue.

obtingō, -ngere, -gī *vi* to fall to one's lot; to happen.

obtorpēscō, -ēscere, -uī *vi* to become numb, lose feeling.

obtorqueō, -quēre, -sī, -tum *vt* to twist about, wrench.

obtrectātiō, -ōnis *f* disparagement.

obtrectātor, -ōris *m* disparager.

obtrectō, -āre *vt, vi* to detract, disparage.

obtrītus *ppp of* **obterō**.

obtrūdō *etc see* **obstrūdō**.

obtruncō, -āre *vt* to cut down, slaughter.

obtueor, -ērī, -or, -ī *vt* to gaze at, see clearly.

obtulī *perf of* **offerō**.

obtundō, -undere, -udī, -ūsum *and* **-ūnsum** *vt* to beat, thump; to blunt; (*speech*) to deafen, annoy.

obturbō, -āre *vt* to throw into confusion; to bother, distract.

obturgēscō, -ere *vi* to swell up.

obtūrō, -āre *vt* to stop up, close.

obtūsus, obtūnsus *ppp of* **obtundō** ♦ *adj* blunt; (*fig*) dulled, blurred, unfeeling.

obtūtus, -ūs *m* gaze.

obumbrō, -āre *vt* to shade, darken; (*fig*) to cloak, screen.

obuncus *adj* hooked.

obūstus *adj* burnt, hardened in fire.

obvallātus *adj* fortified.

obveniō, -enīre, -ēnī, -entum *vi* to come up; to fall to; to occur.

obversor, -ārī *vi* to move about before; (*visions*) to hover.

obversus *ppp of* **obvertō** ♦ *adj* turned towards ♦ *mpl* enemy.

obvertō, -tere, -tī, -sum *vt* to direct towards, turn against.

obviam *adv* to meet, against; ~ **ire** to go to meet.

obvius *adj* in the way, to meet; opposite, against; at hand, accessible; exposed.

obvolvō, -vere, -vī, -ūtum *vt* to wrap up, muffle up; (*fig*) to cloak.

occaecō, -āre, -āvī, -ātum *vt* to blind, obscure, conceal; to benumb.

occallēscō, -ēscere, -uī *vi* to grow a thick skin; to become hardened.

occanō, -ere *vi* to sound the attack.

occāsiō, -ōnis *f* opportunity, convenient time; (*MIL*) surprise.

occāsiuncula, -ae *f* opportunity.

occāsus, -ūs *m* setting; west; downfall, ruin.

occātiō, -ōnis *f* harrowing.

occātor, -ōris *m* harrower.

occēdō, -ere *vi* to go up to.

occentō, -āre *vt, vi* to serenade; to sing a lampoon.

occēpī *perf of* **occipiō**.

occepsō *archaic fut of* **occipiō**.

occeptō, -āre *vt* to begin.

occidēns, -entis *pres p of* **occidō** ♦ *m* west.

occīdiō, -ōnis *f* massacre; **~ōne occīdere** annihilate.

occīdō, -dere, -dī, -sum *vt* to fell; to cut down, kill; to pester.

occidō, -idere, -idī, -āsum *vi* to fall; to set; to die, perish, be ruined.

occiduus *adj* setting; western; failing.

occinō, -ere, -uī *vi* to sing inauspiciously.

occipiō, -ipere, -ēpī, -eptum *vt, vi* to begin.

occipitium, -ī *and* **iī** *nt* back of the head.

occīsiō, -ōnis *f* massacre.

occīsor, -ōris *m* killer.

occīsus *ppp of* **occīdō.**
occlāmitō, -āre *vi* to bawl.
occlūdō, -dere, -sī, -sum *vt* to shut up; to stop.
occō, -āre *vt* to harrow.
occubō, -āre *vi* to lie.
occulcō, -āre *vt* to trample down.
occulō, -ere, -uī, -tum *vt* to cover over, hide.
occultātiō, -ōnis *f* concealment.
occultātor, -ōris *m* hider.
occultē *adv* secretly.
occultō, -āre, -āvī, -ātum *vt* to conceal, secrete.
occultus *ppp of* **occulō** ♦ *adj* hidden, secret; (*person*) reserved, secretive ♦ *nt* secret, hiding.
occumbō, -mbere, -buī, -bitum *vi* to fall, die.
occupātiō, -ōnis *f* taking possession; business; engagement.
occupātus *adj* occupied, busy.
occupō, -āre, -āvī, -ātum *vt* to take possession of, seize; to occupy, take up; to surprise, anticipate; (*money*) to lend, invest.
occurrō, -rere, -rī, -sum *vi* to run up to, meet; to attack; to fall in with; to hurry to; (*fig*) to obviate, counteract; (*words*) to object; (*thought*) to occur, suggest itself.
occursātiō, -ōnis *f* fussy welcome.
occursō, -āre *vi* to run to meet, meet; to oppose; (*thought*) to occur.
occursus, -ūs *m* meeting.
Ōceanītis, -ītidis *f daughter of Ocean.*
Ōceanus, -ī *m* Ocean, a stream encircling the earth; the Atlantic.
ocellus, -ī *m* eye; darling, gem.
ōcior, -ōris *adj* quicker, swifter.
ōcius *adv* more quickly; sooner, rather; quickly.
ocrea, -ae *f* greave.
ocreātus *adj* greaved.
Octāviānus *adj* of Octavius ♦ *m* Octavian (*a surname of Augustus*).
Octāvius, -ī *m* Roman family name (*esp the emperor Augustus; his father*).
octāvum *adv* for the eighth time.
octāvus *adj* eighth ♦ *f* eighth hour.
octāvusdecimus *adj* eighteenth.
octiēns, -ēs *adv* eight times.
octingentēsimus *adj* eight hundredth.
octingentī, -ōrum *num* eight hundred.
octipēs, -edis *adj* eight-footed.
octō *num* eight.
Octōber, -ris *adj* of October ♦ *m* October.
octōgēnī, -ōrum *adj* eighty each.
octōgēsimus *adj* eightieth.
octōgiēns, -ēs *adv* eighty times.
octōgintā *num* eighty.
octōiugis *adj* eight together.
octōnī, -ōrum *adj* eight at a time, eight each.
octōphoros *adj* (*litter*) carried by eight bearers.
octuplicātus *adj* multiplied by eight.

octuplus *adj* eightfold.
octussis, -is *m* eight asses.
oculātus *adj* with eyes; visible; ~ā diē vēndere sell for cash.
oculus, -ī *m* eye; sight; (*plant*) bud; (*fig*) darling, jewel; ~ōs adicere ad glance at, covet; ante ~ōs pōnere imagine; ex ~īs out of sight; esse in ~īs be in view; be a favourite.
ōdī, -isse *vt* to hate, dislike.
odiōsē *adv see adj.*
odiōsus *adj* odious, unpleasant.
odium, -ī and iī *nt* hatred, dislike, displeasure; insolence; ~iō esse be hateful, be disliked.
odor (-ōs), -ōris *m* smell, perfume, stench; (*fig*) inkling, suggestion.
odōrātiō, -ōnis *f* smelling.
odōrātus *adj* fragrant, perfumed.
odōrātus, -ūs *m* sense of smell; smelling.
odōrifer, -ī *adj* fragrant; perfume-producing.
odōrō, -āre *vt* to perfume.
odōror, -ārī, -ātus *vt* to smell, smell out; (*fig*) to search out; to aspire to; to get a smattering of.
odōrus *adj* fragrant; keen-scented.
odōs *etc see* **odor.**
Odrysius *adj* Thracian.
Odyssēa, -ae *f* Odyssey.
Oeagrius *adj* Thracian.
Oebalia, -iae *f* Tarentum.
Oebalidēs, -idae *m* Castor, Pollux.
Oebalis, -idis *f* Helen.
Oebalius *adj* Spartan.
Oebalus, -ī *m* king of Sparta.
Oedipūs, -odis and ī *m* king of Thebes; solver of riddles.
oenophorum, -ī *nt* wine basket.
Oenopia, -ae *f* Aegina.
Oenotria, -ae *f* S.E. Italy.
Oenotrius *adj* Italian.
oestrus, -ī *m* gadfly; (*fig*) frenzy.
Oeta, -ae, -ē, -ēs *f* mountain range in Thessaly, associated with Hercules.
Oetaeus *adj see n.*
ofella, -ae *f* morsel.
offa, -ae *f* pellet, lump; swelling.
offectus *ppp of* **officiō.**
offendō, -endere, -endī, -ēnsum *vt* to hit; to hit on, come upon; to offend, blunder; to take offence; to fail, come to grief.
offēnsa, -ae *f* displeasure, enmity; offence, injury.
offēnsiō, -ōnis *f* stumbling; stumbling block; misfortune, indisposition; offence, displeasure.
offēnsiuncula, -ae *f* slight displeasure; slight check.
offēnsō, -āre *vt, vi* to dash against.
offēnsus *ppp of* **offendō** ♦ *adj* offensive; displeased ♦ *nt* offence.
offēnsus, -ūs *m* shock; offence.
offerō, -re, obtulī, oblātum *vt* to present, show; to bring forward, offer; to expose; to cause, inflict; sē ~ encounter.

offerumenta, -ae *f* present.
officīna, -ae *f* workshop factory.
officiō, -icere, -ēcī, -ectum *vt* to obstruct; to interfere with; to hurt, prejudice.
officiōsē *adv* courteously.
officiōsus *adj* obliging; dutiful.
officium, -ī *and* **iī** *nt* service, attention; ceremonial; duty, sense of duty; official duty, function.
offigō, -ere *vt* to fasten, drive in.
offirmātus *adj* determined.
offirmō, -āre *vt, vi* to persevere in.
offlectō, -ere *vt* to turn about.
offrēnātus *adj* checked.
offūcia, -ae *f (cosmetic)* paint; *(fig)* trick.
offulgeō, -gēre, -sī *vi* to shine on.
offundō, -undere, -ūdī, -ūsum *vt* to pour out to; to pour over; to spread; to cover, fill.
offūsus *ppp of* **offundō**.
ogganniō, -īre *vi* to growl at.
oggerō, -ere *vt* to bring, give.
Ogygius *adj* Theban.
oh *interj (expressing surprise, joy, grief)* oh!
ohē *interj (expressing surfeit)* stop!, enough!
oi *interj (expressing complaint, weeping)* oh!, oh dear!
oiei *interj (lamenting)* oh dear!
Oīleus, -eī *m* father of the less famous Ajax.
olea, -ae *f* olive; olive tree.
oleāginus *adj* of the olive tree.
oleārius *adj* oil- *(in cpds)* ♦ *m* oil seller.
oleaster, -rī *m* wild olive.
olēns, -entis *pres p of* **oleō** ♦ *adj* fragrant; stinking, musty.
oleō, -ēre, -uī *vt, vi* to smell, smell of; *(fig)* to betray.
oleum, -ī *nt* olive oil, oil; wrestling school; **~ et operam perdere** waste time and trouble.
olfaciō, -facere, -fēcī, -factum *vt* to smell, scent.
olfactō, -āre *vt* to smell at.
olidus *adj* smelling, rank.
ōlim *adv* once, once upon a time; at the time, at times; for a good while; one day (in the future).
olit- *etc see* **holit-**.
olīva, -ae *f* olive, olive tree; olive branch, olive staff.
olīvētum, -ī *nt* olive grove.
olīvifer, -ī *adj* olive-bearing.
olīvum, -ī *nt* oil; wrestling school; perfume.
olla, -ae *f* pot, jar.
olle, ollus *etc see* **ille**.
olor, -ōris *m* swan.
olōrīnus *adj* swan's.
olus *etc see* **holus**.
Olympia, -ae *f* site of the Greek games in Elis.
Olympia, -ōrum *ntpl* Olympic Games.
Olympiacus *adj* = **Olympicus**.
Olympias, -adis *f* Olympiad, period of four years.

Olympicus, -us *adj* Olympic.
Olympionīcēs, -ae *m* Olympic winner.
Olympus, -ī *m* mountain in N. Greece, abode of the gods; heaven.
omāsum, -ī *nt* tripe; paunch.
ōmen, -inis *nt* omen, sign; solemnity.
ōmentum, -ī *nt* bowels.
ōminor, -ārī, -ātus *vt* to forebode, prophesy.
ōmissus *ppp of* **ōmittō** ♦ *adj* remiss.
ōmittō, -ittere, -īsī, -issum *vt* to let go; to leave off, give up; to disregard, overlook; *(speech)* to pass over, omit.
omnifer, -ī *adj* all-sustaining.
omnigenus *adj* of all kinds.
omnimodīs *adv* wholly.
omnīnō *adv* entirely, altogether, at all; in general; *(concession)* to be sure, yes; *(number)* in all, just; **~ nōn** not at all.
omniparēns, -entis *adj* mother of all.
omnipotēns, -entis *adj* almighty.
omnis *adj* all, every, any; every kind of; the whole of ♦ *nt* the universe ♦ *mpl* everybody ♦ *ntpl* everything.
omnituēns, -entis *adj* all-seeing.
omnivagus *adj* roving everywhere.
omnivolus *adj* willing everything.
onager, -rī *m* wild ass.
onerārius *adj (beast)* of burden; *(ship)* transport.
onerō, -āre, -āvī, -ātum *vt* to load, burden; *(fig)* to overload, oppress; to aggravate.
onerōsus *adj* heavy, burdensome, irksome.
onus, -eris *nt* load, burden, cargo; *(fig)* charge, difficulty.
onustus *adj* loaded, burdened; *(fig)* filled.
onyx, -chis *m/f* onyx; onyx box.
opācitās, -ātis *f* shade.
opācō, -āre *vt* to shade.
opācus *adj* shady; dark.
ope *abl of* **ops**.
opella, -ae *f* light work, small service.
opera, -ae *f* exertion, work; service; care, attention; leisure, time; *(person)* workman, hired rough; **~am dare** pay attention; do one's best; **~ae pretium** worth while; **~ā meā** thanks to me.
operārius *adj* working ♦ *m* workman.
operculum, -ī *nt* cover, lid.
operīmentum, -ī *nt* covering.
operiō, -īre, -uī, -tum *vt* to cover; to close; *(fig)* to overwhelm, conceal.
operor, -ārī, -ātus *vi* to work, take pains, be occupied.
operōsē *adv* painstakingly.
operōsus *adj* active, industrious; laborious, elaborate.
opertus *ppp of* **operiō** ♦ *adj* covered, hidden ♦ *nt* secret.
opēs *pl of* **ops**.

Noun declensions and verb conjugations are shown on pp xiii to xxv. The present infinitive ending of a verb shows to which conjugation it belongs: **-āre** = 1st; **-ēre** = 2nd; **-ere** = 3rd and **-īre** = 4th. Irregular verbs are shown on p xxvi

opicus *adj* barbarous, boorish.
opifer, -ī *adj* helping.
opifex, -icis *m/f* maker; craftsman, artisan.
ōpiliō, -ōnis *m* shepherd.
opīmitās, -ātis *f* abundance.
opīmus *adj* rich, fruitful, fat; copious,
sumptuous; (*style*) overloaded; **spolia ~a**
spoils of an enemy commander killed by a
Roman general.
opīnābilis *adj* conjectural.
opīnātiō, -ōnis *f* conjecture.
opīnātor, -ōris *m* conjecturer.
opīnātus, -ūs *m* supposition.
opīniō, -ōnis *f* opinion, conjecture, belief;
reputation, esteem; rumour; **contrā, praeter
~ōnem** contrary to expectation.
opīniōsus *adj* dogmatic.
opīnor, -ārī, -ātus *vi* to think, suppose,
imagine ♦ *adj* imagined.
opiparē *adv see adj*.
opiparus *adj* rich, sumptuous.
opitulor, -ārī, -ātus *vi* (*with dat*) to help.
oportet, -ēre, -uit *vt* (*impers*) ought, should.
oppēdō, -ere *vi* to insult.
opperior, -īrī, -tus *vt, vi* to wait, wait for.
oppetō, -ere, -īvī, -ītum *vt* to encounter; to
die.
oppidānus *adj* provincial ♦ *mpl* townsfolk.
oppidō *adv* quite, completely, exactly.
oppidulum, -ī *nt* small town.
oppidum, -ī *nt* town.
oppignerō, -āre *vt* to pledge.
oppilō, -āre *vt* to stop up.
oppleō, -ēre, -ēvī, -ētum *vt* to fill, choke up.
oppōnō, -ōnere, -osuī, -ositum *vt* to put
against, set before; to expose; to present;
(*argument*) to adduce, reply, oppose;
(*property*) to pledge, mortgage.
opportūnitās, -ātis *f* suitableness,
advantage; good opportunity.
opportūnē *adv* opportunely.
opportūnus *adj* suitable, opportune; useful;
exposed.
oppositiō, -ōnis *f* opposing.
oppositus *ppp of* **oppōnō** ♦ *adj* against,
opposite.
oppositus, -ūs *m* opposing.
oppsuī *perf of* **oppōnō**.
oppressiō, -ōnis *f* violence; seizure;
overthrow.
oppressus *ppp of* **opprimō**.
oppressus, -ūs *m* pressure.
opprimō, -imere, -essī, -essum *vt* to press
down, crush; to press together, close; to
suppress, overwhelm, overthrow; to
surprise, seize.
opprobrium, -ī and iī *nt* reproach, disgrace,
scandal.
opprobrō, -āre *vt* to taunt.
oppugnātiō, -ōnis *f* attack, assault.
oppugnātor, -ōris *m* assailant.
oppugnō, -āre, -āvī, -ātum *vt* to attack,
assault.

ops, -opis *f* power, strength; help.
Ops goddess of plenty.
ops- *etc see* **obs-**.
optābilis *adj* desirable.
optātiō, -ōnis *f* wish.
optātus *adj* longed for ♦ *nt* wish; **~ātō**
according to one's wish.
optimās, -ātis *adj* aristocratic ♦ *mpl* the
nobility.
optimē *adv* best, very well; just in time.
optimus *adj* best, very good; excellent; **~ō iūre**
deservedly.
optiō, -ōnis *f* choice ♦ *m* assistant.
optīvus *adj* chosen.
optō, -āre, -āvī, -ātum *vt* to choose; to wish
for.
optum- *etc see* **optim-**.
opulēns, -entis *adj* rich.
opulentia, -ae *f* wealth; power.
opulentō, -āre *vt* to enrich.
opulentē, -er *adv* sumptuously.
opulentus *adj* rich, sumptuous, powerful.
opum *fpl* resources, wealth.
opus, -eris *nt* work, workmanship; (*art*) work,
building, book; (*MIL*) siege work; (*colloq*)
business; (*with* **esse**) need; **virō ~ est** a man is
needed; **māgnō ~ere** much, greatly.
opusculum, -ī *nt* little work.
ōra, -ae *f* edge, boundary; coast; country,
region; (*NAUT*) hawser.
ōrāculum, -ī *nt* oracle, prophecy.
ōrātē *adv see adj*.
ōrātiō, -ōnis *f* speech, language; a speech,
oration; eloquence; prose; emperor's
message; **~ōnem habēre** deliver a speech.
ōrātiuncula, -ae *f* short speech.
ōrātor, -ōris *m* speaker, spokesman, orator.
ōrātōrius *adj* oratorical.
ōrātrīx, -īcis *f* suppliant.
ōrātus, -ūs *m* request.
orbātor, -ōris *m* bereaver.
orbiculātus *adj* round.
orbis, -is *m* circle, ring, disc, orbit; world;
(*movement*) cycle, rotation; (*style*) rounding
off; **~ lacteus** Milky Way; **~ signifer** Zodiac; **~
fortūnae** wheel of Fortune; **~ terrārum** the
earth, world; **in ~em cōnsistere** form a
circle; **in ~em īre** go the rounds.
orbita, -ae *f* rut, track, path.
orbitās, -ātis *f* childlessness, orphanhood,
widowhood.
orbitōsus *adj* full of ruts.
orbō, -āre, -āvī, -ātum *vt* to bereave, orphan,
make childless.
orbus *adj* bereaved, orphan, childless;
destitute.
orca, -ae *f* vat.
orchas, -dis *f* kind of olive.
orchēstra, -ae *f* senatorial seats (in the
theatre).
Orcus, -ī *m* Pluto; the lower world; death.
ōrdinārius *adj* regular.
ōrdinātim *adv* in order, properly.

ōrdinātiō, -ōnis f orderly arrangement.

ōrdinātus adj appointed.

ōrdinō, -āre, -āvī, -ātum vt to arrange, regulate, set in order.

ōrdior, -dīrī, -sus vt, vi to begin, undertake.

ōrdō, -inis m line, row, series; order, regularity, arrangement; (MIL) rank, line, company, (pl) captains; (building) course, layer; (seats) row; (POL) class, order, station; **ex ~ine** in order, in one's turn; one after the other; **extrā ~inem** irregularly, unusually.

Orēas, -dis f mountain nymph.

Orestēs, -is and **ae** m son of Agamemnon, whom he avenged by killing his mother.

Orestēus adj see n.

orexis, -is f appetite.

organum, -ī nt instrument, organ.

orgia, -ōrum ntpl Bacchic revels; orgies.

orichalcum, -ī nt copper ore, brass.

ōricilla, -ae f lobe.

oriēns, -entis pres p of **orior** ♦ m morning; east.

orīgō, -inis f beginning, source; ancestry, descent; founder.

Orīōn, -onis and **ōnis** m mythical hunter and constellation.

orior, -īrī, -tus vi to rise; to spring, descend.

oriundus adj descended, sprung.

ōrnāmentum, -ī nt equipment, dress; ornament, decoration; distinction, pride of.

ōrnātē adv elegantly.

ōrnātus ppp of **ōrnō** ♦ adj equipped, furnished; embellished, excellent.

ōrnātus, -ūs m preparation; dress; equipment; embellishment.

ōrnō, -āre, -āvī, -ātum vt to fit out, equip, dress, prepare; to adorn, embellish, honour.

ornus, -ī f manna ash.

ōrō, -āre, -āvī, -ātum vt to speak, plead; to beg, entreat; to pray.

Orontēs, -is and **ī** m river of Syria.

Orontēus adj Syrian.

Orpheus, -eī and **eos** (acc **-ea**) m legendary Thracian singer, who went down to Hades for Eurydice.

Orphēus, -icus adj see n.

ōrsus ppa of **ōrdior** ♦ ntpl beginning; utterance.

ōrsus, -ūs m beginning.

ortus ppa of **orior** ♦ adj born, descended.

ortus, -ūs m rising; east; origin, source.

Ortygia, -ae and **ē, -ēs** f Delos.

Ortygius adj see n.

oryx, -gis m gazelle.

oryza, -ae f rice.

os, ossis nt bone; (fig) very soul.

ōs, -ōris nt mouth; face; entrance, opening; effrontery; **ūnō ōre** unanimously; **in ōre esse** be talked about; **quō ōre redībō** how shall I have the face to go back?

oscen, -inis m bird of omen.

ōscillum, -ī nt little mask.

ōscitāns, -antis pres p of **ōscitō** ♦ adj listless, drowsy.

ōscitanter adv half-heartedly.

ōscitō, -āre; -or, -ārī vi to yawn, be drowsy.

ōsculātiō, -ōnis f kissing.

ōsculor, -ārī, -ātus vt to kiss; to make a fuss of.

ōsculum, -ī nt sweet mouth; kiss.

Oscus adj Oscan.

Osīris, -is and **idis** m Egyptian god, husband of Isis.

Ossa, -ae f mountain in Thessaly.

osseus adj bony.

ossifraga, -ae f osprey.

ostendō, -dere, -dī, -tum vt to hold out, show, display; to expose; to disclose, reveal; (speech) to say, make known.

ostentātiō, -ōnis f display; showing off, ostentation; pretence.

ostentātor, -ōris m displayer, boaster.

ostentō, -āre vt to hold out, proffer, exhibit; to show off, boast of; to make known, indicate.

ostentum, -ī nt portent.

ostentus ppp of **ostendō**.

ostentus, -ūs m display, appearance; proof.

Ōstia, -ae f, **-ōrum** ntpl port at the Tiber mouth.

ōstiārium, -ī and **iī** nt door tax.

ōstiātim adv from door to door.

Ōstiēnsis adj see n.

ōstium, -ī and **iī** nt door; entrance, mouth.

ostrea, -ae f oyster.

ostreōsus adj rich in oysters.

ostreum, -ī nt oyster.

ostrifer, -ī adj oyster-producing.

ostrīnus adj purple.

ostrum, -ī nt purple; purple dress or coverings.

ōsus, ōsūrus ppa and fut p of **ōdī**.

Othō, -ōnis m author of a law giving theatre seats to Equites; Roman emperor after Galba.

Othōniānus adj see n.

ōtiolum, -ī nt bit of leisure.

ōtior, -ārī vi to have a holiday, be idle.

ōtiōsē adv leisurely; quietly; fearlessly.

ōtiōsus adj at leisure, free; out of public affairs; neutral, indifferent; quiet, unexcited; (things) free, idle ♦ m private citizen, civilian.

ōtium, -ī and **iī** nt leisure, time (for), idleness, retirement; peace, quiet.

ovātiō, -ōnis f minor triumph.

ovīle, -is nt sheep fold, goat fold.

ovillus adj of sheep.

ovis, -is f sheep.

ovō, -āre vi to rejoice; to celebrate a minor triumph.

ōvum, -ī nt egg.

Noun declensions and verb conjugations are shown on pp xiii to xxv. The present infinitive ending of a verb shows to which conjugation it belongs: **-āre** = 1st; **-ēre** = 2nd; **-ere** = 3rd and **-īre** = 4th. Irregular verbs are shown on p xxvi

P, p

pābulātiō, -ōnis *f* foraging.
pābulātor, -ōris *m* forager.
pābulor, -ārī *vi* to forage.
pābulum, -ī *nt* food, fodder.
pācālis *adj* of peace.
pācātus *adj* peaceful, tranquil ♦ *nt* friendly country.
Pachȳnum, -ī *nt* S.E. point of Sicily (*now* Cape Passaro).
pācifer, -ī *adj* peace-bringing.
pācificātiō, -ōnis *f* peacemaking.
pācificātor, -ōris *m* peacemaker.
pācificātōrius *adj* peacemaking.
pācificō, -āre *vi* to make a peace ♦ *vt* to appease.
pācificus *adj* peacemaking.
pacīscor, -īscī, -tus *vi* to make a bargain, agree ♦ *vt* to stipulate for; to barter.
pācō, -āre, -āvī, -ātum *vt* to pacify, subdue.
pactiō, -ōnis *f* bargain, agreement, contract; collusion; (*words*) formula.
Pactōlus, -ī *m* river of Lydia (*famous for its gold*).
pactor, -ōris *m* negotiator.
pactum, -ī *nt* agreement, contract.
pactus *ppa of* **pacīscor** ♦ *adj* agreed, settled; betrothed.
Pācuvius, -ī *m* Latin tragic poet.
Padus, -ī *m* river Po.
paeān, -ānis *m* healer, epithet of Apollo; hymn of praise, shout of joy; (*metre*) paeon.
paedagōgus, -ī *m* slave who took children to school.
paedor, -ōris *m* filth.
paelex, -icis *f* mistress, concubine.
paelicātus, -ūs *m* concubinage.
Paelignī, -ōrum *mpl* people of central Italy.
Paelignus *adj see n.*
paene *adv* almost, nearly.
paenīnsula, -ae *f* peninsula.
paenitendus *adj* regrettable.
paenitentia, -ae *f* repentance.
paenitet, -ēre, -uit *vt, vi* (*impers*) to repent, regret, be sorry; to be dissatisfied; **an ~et** is it not enough?
paenula, -ae *f* travelling cloak.
paenulātus *adj* wearing a cloak.
paeōn, -ōnis *m* metrical foot of one long and three short syllables.
paeōnius *adj* healing.
Paestānus *adj see n.*
Paestum, -ī *nt* town in S. Italy.
paetulus *adj* with a slight cast in the eye.
paetus *adj* with a cast in the eye.
pāgānus *adj* rural ♦ *m* villager, yokel.

pāgātim *adv* in every village.
pāgella, -ae *f* small page.
pāgina, -ae *f* (*book*) page, leaf.
pāginula, -ae *f* small page.
pāgus, -ī *m* village, country district; canton.
pāla, -ae *f* spade; (*ring*) bezel.
palaestra, -ae *f* wrestling school, gymnasium; exercise, wrestling; (*RHET*) exercise, training.
palaestricē *adv* in gymnastic fashion.
palaestricus *adj* of the wrestling school.
palaestrīta, -ae *m* head of a wrestling school.
palam *adv* openly, publicly, well-known ♦ *prep* (*with abl*) in the presence of.
Palātīnus *adj* Palatine; imperial.
Palātium, -ī *nt* Palatine Hill in Rome; palace.
palātum, -ī *nt* palate; taste, judgment.
palea, -ae *f* chaff.
paleāria, -ium *ntpl* dewlap.
Palēs, -is *f* goddess of shepherds.
Palīlis *adj* of Pales ♦ *ntpl festival of Pales.*
palimpsēstus, -ī *m* palimpsest.
Palinūrus, -ī *m* pilot of Aeneas; promontory in S. Italy.
paliūrus, -ī *m* Christ's thorn.
palla, -ae *f* woman's robe; tragic costume.
Palladium, -dī *nt* image of Pallas.
Palladius *adj* of Pallas.
Pallantēus *adj see n.*
Pallas, -dis *and* **dos** *f* Athene, Minerva; oil; olive tree.
Pallās, -antis *m* ancestor or son of Evander.
pallēns, -entis *pres p of* **palleō** ♦ *adj* pale; greenish.
palleō, -ēre, -uī *vi* to be pale or yellow; to fade; to be anxious.
pallēscō, -escere, -uī *vi* to turn pale, turn yellow.
palliātus *adj* wearing a Greek cloak.
pallidulus *adj* palish.
pallidus *adj* pale, pallid, greenish; in love.
palliolum, -ī *nt* small cloak, cape, hood.
pallium, -ī *and* **iī** *nt* coverlet; Greek cloak.
pallor, -ōris *m* paleness, fading; fear.
palma, -ae *f* (*hand*) palm, hand; (*oar*) blade; (*tree*) palm, date; branch; (*fig*) prize, victory, glory.
palmāris *adj* excellent.
palmārius *adj* prizewinning.
palmātus *adj* palm-embroidered.
palmes, -itis *m* pruned shoot, branch.
palmētum, -ī *nt* palm grove.
palmifer, -ī *adj* palm-bearing.
palmōsus *adj* palm-clad.
palmula, -ae *f* oar blade.
pālor, -ārī, -ātus *vi* to wander about, straggle.
palpātiō, -ōnis *f* flatteries.
palpātor, -ōris *m* flatterer.
palpebra, -ae *f* eyelid.
palpitō, -āre *vi* to throb, writhe.
palpō, -āre; -or, -ārī *vt* to stroke; to coax, flatter.
palpus, -ī *m* coaxing.

paludāmentum-parō

paludāmentum, -ī nt military cloak.
paludātus adj in a general's cloak.
paludōsus adj marshy.
palumbēs, -is m/f wood pigeon.
pālus, -ī m stake, pale.
palūs, -ūdis f marsh, pool, lake.
palūster, -ris adj marshy.
pampineus adj of vineshoots.
pampinus, -ī m vineshoot.
Pān, -ānos (acc -āna) m Greek god of shepherds, hills and woods, esp associated with Arcadia.
panacēa, -ae f a herb supposed to cure all diseases.
Panaetius, -ī m Stoic philosopher.
Panchāaeus adj see n.
Panchāaius adj see n.
Panchāia, -iae f part of Arabia.
panchrēstus adj good for everything.
pancratium, -ī and **iī** nt all-in boxing and wrestling match.
pandiculor, -āre vi to stretch oneself.
Pandīōn, -onis m king of Athens, father of Procne and Philomela.
Pandīonius adj see n.
pandō, -ere, -ī, pānsum and **passum** vt to spread out, stretch, extend; to open; (fig) to disclose, explain.
pandus adj curved, bent.
pangō, -ere, panxī and **pepigī, pāctum** vt to drive in, fasten; to make, compose; to agree, settle.
pānicula, -ae f tuft.
pānicum, -ī nt Italian millet.
pānis, -is m bread, loaf.
Pāniscus, -ī m little Pan.
panniculus, -ī m rag.
Pannonia, -ae f country on the middle Danube.
Pannonius adj see n.
pannōsus adj ragged.
pannus, -ī m piece of cloth, rag, patch.
Panormus, -ī f town in Sicily (now Palermo).
pānsa adj splayfoot.
pānsus ppp of **pandō**.
panthēra, -ae f panther.
Panthoidēs, -ae m Euphorbus.
Panthūs, -ī m priest of Apollo at Troy.
panticēs, -um mpl bowels; sausages.
panxī perf of **pangō**.
papae interj (expressing wonder) ooh!
pāpas, -ae m tutor.
papāver, -is nt poppy.
papāvereus adj see n.
Paphius adj see n.
Paphos, -ī f town in Cyprus, sacred to Venus.
pāpiliō, -ōnis m butterfly.
papilla, -ae f teat, nipple; breast.
pappus, -ī m woolly seed.
papula, -ae f pimple.
papӯrifer, -ī adj papyrus-bearing.
papӯrum, -ī nt papyrus; paper.

papӯrus, -ī m/f papyrus; paper.
pār, paris adj equal, like; a match for; proper, right ♦ m peer, partner, companion ♦ nt pair;
pār parī respondēre return like for like;
parēs cum paribus facillimē congregantur ≈ birds of a feather flock together; **lūdere pār impār** play at evens and odds.
parābilis adj easy to get.
parasīta, -ae f woman parasite.
parasītaster, -rī m sorry parasite.
parasīticus adj of a parasite.
parasītus, -ī m parasite, sponger.
parātē adv with preparation; carefully; promptly.
parātiō, -ōnis f trying to get.
paratragoedō, -āre vi to talk theatrically.
parātus ppp of **parō** ♦ adj ready; equipped; experienced.
parātus, -ūs m preparation, equipment.
Parca, -ae f Fate.
parcē adv frugally; moderately.
parcō, -cere, pepercī, -sum vt, vi (with dat) to spare, economize; to refrain from, forgo; (with inf) to forbear, stop.
parcus adj sparing, thrifty; niggardly, scanty; chary.
pardus, -ī m panther.
pārēns, -entis pres p of **pāreō** ♦ adj obedient ♦ mpl subjects.
parēns, -entis m/f parent, father, mother; ancestor; founder.
parentālis adj parental ♦ ntpl festival in honour of dead ancestors and relatives.
parentō, -āre vi to sacrifice in honour of dead parents or relatives; to avenge (with the death of another).
pāreō, -ēre, -uī, -itum vi to be visible, be evident; (with dat) to obey, submit to, comply with; ~et it is proved.
pariēs, -etis m wall.
parietinae, -ārum fpl ruins.
Parīlia, -ium ntpl festival of Pales.
parīlis adj equal.
pariō, -ere, peperī, -tum vt to give birth to; to produce, create, cause; to procure.
Paris, -idis m son of Priam (abductor of Helen).
pariter adv equally, alike; at the same time, together.
paritō, -āre vt to get ready.
Parius adj see **Paros**.
parma, -ae f shield, buckler.
parmātus adj armed with a buckler.
parmula, -ae f little shield.
Parnāsis, -idis adj Parnassian.
Parnāsius adj = **Parnāsis**.
Parnāsus, -ī m mount Parnassus in central Greece, sacred to the Muses.
parō, -āre, -āvī, -ātum vt to prepare, get ready, provide; to intend, set about; to procure, get, buy; to arrange.

Noun declensions and verb conjugations are shown on pp xiii to xxv. The present infinitive ending of a verb shows to which conjugation it belongs: **-āre** = 1st; **-ēre** = 2nd; **-ere** = 3rd and **-īre** = 4th. Irregular verbs are shown on **p xxvi**

parocha, -ae _f_ provision of necessaries (_to officials travelling_).

parochus, -ī _m_ purveyor; host.

paropsis, -dis _f_ dish.

Paros, -ī _f_ Aegean island (_famous for white marble_).

parra, -ae _f_ owl.

Parrhasis, -idis, -ius _adj_ Arcadian.

parricīda, -ae _m_ parricide, assassin; traitor.

parricīdium, -ī _and_ **iī** parricide, murder; high treason.

pars, -tis _f_ part, share, fraction; party, side; direction; respect, degree; (_with pl verb_) some; (_pl_) stage part, role; duty, function; **māgna ~** the majority; **māgnam ~tem** largely; **in eam ~tem** in that direction, on that side, in that sense; **nullā ~te** not at all; **omnī ~te** entirely; **ex ~te** partly; **ex alterā ~te** on the other hand; **ex māgnā ~te** to a large extent; **prō ~te** to the best of one's ability; **~tēs agere** play a part; **duae ~tēs** two-thirds; **trēs ~tēs** three-fourths; **multīs ~ibus** a great deal.

parsimōnia, -ae _f_ thrift, frugality.

parthenicē, -ēs _f_ a plant.

Parthenopē, -ēs _f_ old name of Naples.

Parthenopēius _adj see n._

Parthī, -ōrum _mpl_ Parthians (_Rome's great enemy in the East_).

Parthicus, -us _adj see n._

particeps, -ipis _adj_ sharing, partaking ♦ _m_ partner.

participō, -āre _vt_ to share, impart, inform.

particula, -ae _f_ particle.

partim _adv_ partly, in part; mostly; some ... others.

partiō, -īre, -īvī, -ītum; -ior, -īrī _vt_ to share, distribute, divide.

partītē _adv_ methodically.

partītiō, -ōnis _f_ distribution, division.

parturiō, -īre _vi_ to be in labour; (_fig_) to be anxious ♦ _vt_ to teem with, be ready to produce; (_mind_) to brood over.

partus _ppp of_ **pariō** ♦ _ntpl_ possessions.

partus, -ūs _m_ birth; young.

parum _adv_ too little, not enough; not very, scarcely.

parumper _adv_ for a little while.

parvitās, -ātis _f_ smallness.

parvulus, parvolus _adj_ very small, slight; quite young ♦ _m_ child.

parvus (_comp_ **minor** _superl_ **minimus**) _adj_ small, little, slight; (_time_) short; (_age_) young; **~ī esse** be of little value.

Pascha, -ae _f_ Easter.

pāscō, -scere, -vī, -stum _vt_ to feed, put to graze; to keep, foster; (_fig_) to feast, cherish ♦ _vi_ to graze, browse.

pāscuus _adj_ for pasture ♦ _nt_ pasture.

Pāsiphaē, -ēs _f_ wife of Minos (_mother of the Minotaur_).

passer, -is _m_ sparrow; (_fish_) plaice; **~ marīnus** ostrich.

passerculus, -ī _m_ little sparrow.

passim _adv_ here and there, at random; indiscriminately.

passum, -ī _nt_ raisin wine.

passus _ppp of_ **pandō** ♦ _adj_ spread out, dishevelled; dried.

passus _ppa of_ **patior**.

passus, -ūs _m_ step, pace; footstep; **mille ~ūs** mile; **mīlia ~uum** miles.

pastillus, -ī _m_ lozenge.

pāstor, -ōris _m_ shepherd.

pāstōrālis _adj_ shepherd's, pastoral.

pāstōricius, pāstōrius _adj_ shepherd's.

pāstus _ppp of_ **pāscō**.

pāstus, -ūs _m_ pasture, food.

Patara, -ae _f_ town in Lycia (_with oracle of Apollo_).

Pataraeus _and_ **eus** _adj see n._

Patavīnus _adj see n._

Patavium, -ī _nt_ birthplace of Livy (_now Padua_).

patefaciō, -facere, -fēcī, -factum (_pass_ **-fīō, -fierī**) _vt_ to open, open up; to disclose.

patefactiō, -ōnis _f_ disclosing.

patefīō _etc see_ **patefaciō**.

patella, -ae _f_ small dish, plate.

patēns, -entis _pres p of_ **pateō** ♦ _adj_ open, accessible, exposed; broad; evident.

patenter _adv_ clearly.

pateō, -ēre, -uī _vi_ to be open, accessible, exposed; to extend; to be evident, known.

pater, -ris _m_ father; (_pl_) forefathers; senators.

patera, -ae _f_ dish, saucer, bowl.

paterfamiliās, patrisfamiliās _m_ master of the house.

paternus _adj_ father's, paternal; native.

patēscō, -ere _vi_ to open out; to extend; to become evident.

patibilis _adj_ endurable; sensitive.

patibulātus _adj_ pilloried.

patibulum, -ī _nt_ fork-shaped yoke, pillory.

patiēns, -entis _pres p of_ **patior** ♦ _adj_ able to endure; patient; unyielding.

patienter _adv_ patiently.

patientia, -ae _f_ endurance, stamina; forbearance; submissiveness.

patina, -ae _f_ dish, pan.

patior, -tī, -ssus _vt_ to suffer, experience; to submit to; to allow, put up with; **facile ~** be well pleased with; **aegrē ~** be displeased with.

Patrae, -ārum _fpl_ Greek seaport (_now_ Patras).

patrātor, -ōris _m_ doer.

patrātus _adj_: **pater ~** officiating priest.

Patrēnsis _adj see n._

patria, -ae _f_ native land, native town, home.

patricius _adj_ patrician ♦ _m_ aristocrat.

patrimōnium, -ī _and_ **iī** _nt_ inheritance, patrimony.

patrimus _adj_ having a father living.

patrissō, -āre _vi_ to take after one's father.

patrītus _adj_ of one's father.

patrius _adj_ father's; hereditary, native.

patrō, -āre, -āvī, -ātum *vt* to achieve, execute, complete.

patrōcinium, -ī *and* **iī** *nt* patronage, advocacy, defence.

patrōcinor, -ārī *vi* (*with dat*) to defend, support.

patrōna, -ae *f* patron goddess; protectress, safeguard.

patrōnus, -ī *m* patron, protector; (*law*) advocate, counsel.

patruēlis *adj* cousin's ♦ *m* cousin.

patruus, -ī *m* (paternal) uncle ♦ *adj* uncle's.

patulus *adj* open; spreading, broad.

paucitās, -ātis *f* small number, scarcity.

pauculus *adj* very few.

paucus *adj* few, little ♦ *mpl* a few, the select few ♦ *ntpl* a few words.

paulātim *adv* little by little, gradually.

paulisper *adv* for a little while.

Paullus, -ī *m* = **Paulus**.

paulō *adv* a little, somewhat.

paululus *adj* very little ♦ *nt* a little bit.

paulum *adv* = **paulō**.

paulus *adj* little.

Paulus, -ī *m* Roman surname (*esp victor of Pydna*).

pauper, -is *adj* poor; meagre ♦ *mpl* the poor.

pauperculus *adj* poor.

pauperiēs, -ēī *f* poverty.

pauperō, -āre *vt* to impoverish; to rob.

paupertās, -ātis *f* poverty, moderate means.

pausa, -ae *f* stop, end.

pauxillātim *adv* bit by bit.

pauxillulus *adj* very little.

pauxillus *adj* little.

pavefactus *adj* frightened.

paveō, -ēre, pāvī *vi* to be terrified, quake ♦ *vt* to dread, be scared of.

pavēscō, -ere *vt, vi* to become alarmed (at).

pāvī *perf of* **pāscō**.

pavidē *adv* in a panic.

pavidus *adj* quaking, terrified.

pavīmentātus *adj* paved.

pavīmentum, -ī *nt* pavement, floor.

paviō, -īre *vt* to strike.

pavitō, -āre *vi* to be very frightened; to shiver.

pāvō, -ōnis *m* peacock.

pavor, -ōris *m* terror, panic.

pāx, pācis *f* peace; (*gods*) grace; (*mind*) serenity ♦ *interj* enough!; **pāce tuā** by your leave.

peccātum, -ī *nt* mistake, fault, sin.

peccō, -āre, -āvī, -ātum *vi* to make a mistake, go wrong, offend.

pecorōsus *adj* rich in cattle.

pecten, -inis *m* comb; (*fish*) scallop; (*loom*) reed; (*lyre*) plectrum.

pectō, -ctere, -xī, -xum *vt* to comb.

pectus, -oris *nt* breast; heart, feeling; mind;

thought.

pecū *nt* flock of sheep; (*pl*) pastures.

pecuārius *adj* of cattle ♦ *m* cattle breeder ♦ *ntpl* herds.

pecūlātor, -ōris *m* embezzler.

pecūlātus, -ūs *m* embezzlement.

pecūliāris *adj* one's own; special.

pecūliātus *adj* provided with money.

pecūliōsus *adj* with private property.

pecūlium, -ī *and* **iī** *nt* small savings, private property.

pecūnia, -ae *f* property; money.

pecūniārius *adj* of money.

pecūniōsus *adj* moneyed, well-off.

pecus, -oris *nt* cattle, herd, flock; animal.

pecus, -udis *f* sheep, head of cattle, beast.

pedālis *adj* a foot long.

pedārius *adj* (*senator*) without full rights.

pedes, -itis *m* foot soldier, infantry ♦ *adj* on foot.

pedester, -ris *adj* on foot, pedestrian; infantry- (*in cpds*); on land; (*writing*) in prose, prosaic.

pedetemptim *adv* step by step, cautiously.

pedica, -ae *f* fetter, snare.

pedis, -is *m* louse.

pedisequa, -ae *f* handmaid.

pedisequus, -ī *m* attendant, lackey.

peditātus, -ūs *m* infantry.

pedum, -ī *nt* crook.

Pēgaseus *and* **is, -idis** *adj* Pegasean.

Pēgasus, -ī *m* mythical winged horse (*associated with the Muses*).

pēgma, -tis *nt* bookcase; stage elevator.

pēierō, -āre *vi* to perjure oneself.

pēior, -ōris *compar of* **malus**.

pēius *adv* worse.

pelagius *adj* of the sea.

pelagus, -ī (*pl* **-ē**) *nt* sea, open sea.

pelamys, -dis *f* young tunny fish.

Pelasgī, -ōrum *mpl* Greeks.

Pelasgias *and* **is** *and* **us** *adj* Grecian.

Pēleus, -eī *and* **eos** (*acc* **-ea**) *m* king of Thessaly (*father of Achilles*).

Peliās, -ae *m* uncle of Jason.

Pēlias *and* **iacus** *and* **ius** *adj see* **Pēlion**.

Pēlīdēs, -īdae *m* Achilles; Neoptolemus.

Pēlion, -ī *nt* mountain in Thessaly.

Pella, -ae, -ē, -ēs *f* town of Macedonia (*birthplace of Alexander*).

pellācia, -ae *f* attraction.

Pellaeus *adj* of Pella; Alexandrian; Egyptian.

pellāx, -ācis *adj* seductive.

pellēctiō, -ōnis *f* reading through.

pellectus *ppp of* **pelliciō**.

pellegō *etc see* **perlegō**.

pelliciō, -icere, -exī, -ectum *vt* to entice, inveigle.

pellicula, -ae *f* skin, fleece.

pelliō, -ōnis *m* furrier.

pellis, -is _f_ skin, hide; leather, felt; tent.
pellītus _adj_ wearing skins, with leather coats.
pellō, -ere, pepulī, pulsum _vt_ to push, knock,
drive; to drive off, rout, expel; (_lyre_) to play;
(_mind_) to touch, affect; (_feeling_) to banish.
pellūc- _etc see_ **perlūc-**.
Pelopēis _and_ **ēius** _and_ **ēus** _adj see n._
Pelopidae, -idārum _mpl_ house of Pelops.
Pelopōias _adj see n._
Peloponnēsiacus, -ius _adj see n._
Peloponnēsus, -ī _f_ Peloponnese, S. Greece.
Pelops, -is _m_ son of Tantalus (_grandfather of
Agamemnon_).
pelōris, -idis _f_ a large mussel.
pelta, -ae _f_ light shield.
peltastae, -ārum _mpl_ peltasts.
peltātus _adj_ armed with the pelta.
Pēlūsiacus _adj see n._
Pēlūsium, -ī _nt_ Eygptian town at the E. mouth of
the Nile.
Pēlūsius _adj see n._
pelvis, -is _f_ basin.
penārius _adj_ provision- (_in cpds_).
Penātēs, -ium _mpl_ spirits of the larder,
household gods; home.
penātiger, -ī _adj_ carrying his home gods.
pendeō, -ēre, pependī _vi_ to hang; to
overhang, hover; to hang down, be flabby;
(_fig_) to depend; to gaze, listen attentively;
(_mind_) to be in suspense, be undecided.
pendō, -ere, pependī, pēnsum _vt_ to weigh;
to pay; (_fig_) to ponder, value ♦ _vi_ to weigh.
pendulus _adj_ hanging; in doubt.
Pēnēēis _and_ **ēius** _and_ **ēus** _adj see n._
Pēnelopē, ēs _and_ **a, -ae** _f_ wife of Ulysses
(_famed for her constancy_).
Pēnelopēus _adj see n._
penes _prep_ (_with acc_) in the power or
possession of; in the house of, with.
penetrābilis _adj_ penetrable; piercing.
penetrālis _adj_ penetrating; inner, inmost ♦
ntpl inner room, interior, sanctuary; remote
parts.
penetrō, -āre, -āvī, -ātum _vt, vi_ to put into,
penetrate, enter.
Pēnēus, -ī _m_ chief river of Thessaly.
pēnicillus, -ī _m_ painter's brush, pencil.
pēniculus, -ī _m_ brush; sponge.
pēnis, -is _m_ penis.
penite _adj_ inwardly.
penitus _adv_ inside, deep within; deeply, from
the depths; utterly, thoroughly.
penna, pinna, -ae _f_ feather, wing; flight.
pennātus _adj_ winged.
penniger, -ī _adj_ feathered.
pennipotēns, -entis _adj_ winged.
pennula, -ae _f_ little wing.
pēnsilis _adj_ hanging, pendent.
pēnsiō, -ōnis _f_ payment, instalment.
pēnsitō, -āre _vt_ to pay; to consider.
pēnsō, -āre, -āvī, -ātum _vt_ to weight out; to
compensate, repay; to consider, judge.
pēnsum, -ī _nt_ spinner's work; task, duty;

weight, value; **~ī esse** be of importance; **~ī
habēre** care at all about.
pēnsus _ppp of_ **pendō**.
pentēris, -is _f_ quinquereme.
Pentheus, -eī _and_ **eos** _m_ king of Thebes (_killed
by Bacchantes_).
pēnūria, -ae _f_ want, need.
penus, -ūs _and_ **ī** _m/f_, **-um, -ī, -us, -oris**
_nt_ provisions, store of food.
pependī _perf of_ **pendeō**; _perf of_ **pendō**.
pepercī _perf of_ **parcō**.
peperī _perf of_ **pariō**.
pepigī _perf of_ **pangō**.
peplum, -ī _nt_, **-us, -ī** _m_ state robe of Athena.
pepulī _perf of_ **pellō**.
per _prep_ (_with acc: space_) through, all over;
(: _time_) throughout, during; (: _means_) by, by
means of; (: _cause_) by reason of, for the sake
of; **~ īram** in anger; **~ manūs** from hand to
hand; **~ mē** as far as I am concerned; **~ vim**
forcibly; **~ ego tē deōs ōrō** in Heaven's name
I beg you.
pēra, -ae _f_ bag.
perabsurdus _adj_ very absurd.
peraccommodātus _adj_ very convenient.
perācer, -ris _adj_ very sharp.
peracerbus _adj_ very sour.
peracēscō, -ēscere, -uī _vi_ to get vexed.
perāctiō, -ōnis _f_ last act.
perāctus _ppp of_ **peragō**.
peracūtē _adv_ very acutely.
peracūtus _adj_ very sharp, very clear.
peradulēscēns, -entis _adj_ very young.
peraequē _adv_ quite equally, uniformly.
peragitātus _adj_ harried.
peragō, -agere, -ēgī, -āctum _vt_ to carry
through, complete; to pass through, pierce;
to disturb; (_law_) to prosecute to a conviction;
(_words_) to go over, describe.
peragrātiō, -ōnis _f_ travelling.
peragrō, -āre, -āvī, -ātum _vt_ to travel
through, traverse.
peramāns, -antis _adj_ very fond.
peramānter _adv_ devotedly.
perambulō, -āre _vt_ to walk through, traverse.
peramoenus _adj_ very pleasant.
peramplus _adj_ very large.
perangustē _adv see adj._
perangustus _adj_ very narrow.
perantiquus _adj_ very old.
perappositus _adj_ very suitable.
perarduus _adj_ very difficult.
perargūtus _adj_ very witty.
perarō, -āre _vt_ to furrow; to write (on wax).
perattentē _adv see adj._
perattentus _adj_ very attentive.
peraudiendus _adj_ to be heard to the end.
perbacchor, -ārī _vt_ to carouse through.
perbeātus _adj_ very happy.
perbellē _adv_ very nicely.
perbene _adv_ very well.
perbenevolus _adj_ very friendly.
perbenignē _adv_ very kindly.

perbibō, -ere, -ī *vt* to drink up, imbibe.
perbītō, -ere *vi* to perish.
perblandus *adj* very charming.
perbonus *adj* very good.
perbrevis *adj* very short.
perbreviter *adv* very briefly.
perca, -ae *f* perch.
percalefactus *adj* quite hot.
percalēscō, -ēscere, -uī *vi* to become quite hot.
percallēscō, -ēscere, -uī *vi* to become quite hardened ♦ *vt* to become thoroughly versed in.
percārus *adj* very dear.
percautus *adj* very cautious.
percelebrō, -āre *vt* to talk much of.
perceler, -is *adj* very quick.
perceleriter *adv see adj.*
percellō, -ellere, -ulī, -ulsum *vt* to knock down, upset; to strike; (*fig*) to ruin, overthrow; to discourage, unnerve.
percēnseō, -ēre, -uī *vt* to count over; (*place*) to travel through; (*fig*) to review.
perceptiō, -ōnis *f* harvesting; understanding, idea.
perceptus *ppp of* **percipiō.**
percieō, -iēre, -iō, -īre *vt* to rouse, excite.
percipiō, -ipere, -ēpī, -eptum *vt* to take, get hold of; to gather in; (*senses*) to feel; (*mind*) to learn, grasp, understand.
percitus *ppp of* **percieō** ♦ *adj* roused, excited; excitable.
percoctus *ppp of* **percoquō.**
percolō, -āre *vt* to filter through.
percolō, -olere, -oluī, -ultum *vt* to embellish; to honour.
percōmis *adj* very friendly.
percommodē *adv* very conveniently.
percommodus *adj* very suitable.
percontātiō, -ōnis *f* asking questions.
percontātor, -ōris *m* inquisitive person.
percontor, -ārī, -ātus *vt* to question, inquire.
percontumāx, -ācis *adj* very obstinate.
percoquō, -quere, -xī, -ctum *vt* to cook thoroughly, heat, scorch, ripen.
percrēbēscō, percrēbrēscō, -ēscere, -uī *vi* to be spread abroad.
percrepō, -āre, -uī *vi* to resound.
perculī *perf of* **percellō.**
perculsus *ppp of* **percellō.**
percultus *ppp of* **percolō.**
percunct- *etc see* **percont-.**
percupidus *adj* very fond.
percupiō, -ere *vi* to wish very much.
percūriōsus *adj* very inquisitive.
percūrō, -āre *vt* to heal completely.
percurrō, -rrere, -currī *and* **rrī, -rsum** *vt* to run through, hurry over; (*fig*) to run over, look over ♦ *vi* to run along; to pass.
percursātiō, -ōnis *f* travelling through.

percursiō, -ōnis *f* running over.
percursō, -āre *vi* to rove about.
percursus *ppp of* **percurrō.**
percussiō, -ōnis *f* beating; (*fingers*) snapping; (*music*) time.
percussor, -ōris *m* assassin.
percussus *ppp of* **percutiō.**
percussus, -ūs *m* striking.
percutiō, -tere, -ssī, -ssum *vt* to strike, beat; to strike through, kill; (*feeling*) to shock, impress, move; (*colloq*) to trick.
perdēlīrus *adj* quite crazy.
perdidī *perf of* **perdō.**
perdifficilis *adj* very difficult.
perdifficiliter *adv* with great difficulty.
perdignus *adj* most worthy.
perdīligēns, -entis *adj* very diligent.
perdīligenter *adv see adj.*
perdiscō, -scere, -dicī *vt* to learn by heart.
perdisertē *adv* very eloquently.
perditē *adv* desperately; recklessly.
perditor, -ōris *m* destroyer.
perditus *ppp of* **perdō** ♦ *adj* desperate, ruined; abandoned, profligate.
perdiū *adv* for a very long time.
perdiūturnus *adj* protracted.
perdīves, -itis *adj* very rich.
perdīx, -īcis *m/f* partridge.
perdō, -ere, -idī, -itum *vt* to destroy, ruin; to squander, waste; to lose; **dī tē ~uint** curse you!
perdoceō, -ēre, -uī, -tum *vt* to teach thoroughly.
perdolēscō, -ēscere, -uī *vi* to take it to heart.
perdomō, -āre, -uī, -itum *vt* to subjugate, tame completely.
perdormīscō, -ere *vi* to sleep on.
perdūcō, -ūcere, -ūxī, -uctum *vt* to bring, guide to; to induce, seduce; to spread over; to prolong, continue.
perductō, -āre *vt* to guide.
perductor, -ōris *m* guide; pander.
perductus *ppp of* **perdūcō.**
perduelliō, -ōnis *f* treason.
perduellis, -is *m* enemy.
perduint *archaic subj of* **perdō.**
perdūrō, -āre *vi* to endure, hold out.
peredō, -edere, -ēdī, -ēsum *vt* to consume, devour.
peregrē *adv* away from home, abroad; from abroad.
peregrīnābundus *adj* travelling.
peregrīnātiō, -ōnis *f* living abroad, travel.
peregrīnātor, -ōris *m* traveller.
peregrīnitās, -ātis *f* foreign manners.
peregrīnor, -ārī, -ātus *vi* to be abroad, travel; to be a stranger.
peregrīnus *adj* foreign, strange ♦ *m* foreigner, alien.
perēlegāns, -antis *adj* very polished.

Noun declensions and verb conjugations are shown on pp xiii to xxv. The present infinitive ending of a verb shows to which conjugation it belongs: **-āre** = 1st; **-ēre** = 2nd; **-ere** = 3rd and **-īre** = 4th. Irregular verbs are shown on p xxvi

perēleganter _adv_ in a very polished manner.
perēloquēns, -entis _adj_ very eloquent.
perēmī _perf of_ **perimō**.
peremnia, -ium _ntpl_ auspices taken on crossing a river.
peremptus _ppp of_ **perimō**.
perendiē _adv_ the day after tomorrow.
perendinus _adj_ (the day) after tomorrow.
perennis _adj_ perpetual, unfailing.
perennitās, -ātis _f_ continuance.
perennō, -āre _vi_ to last a long time.
pereō, -īre, -īī, -itum _vi_ to be lost, pass away, perish, die; (_fig_) to be wasted, be in love, be undone.
perequitō, -āre _vt, vi_ to ride up and down.
pererrō, -āre, -āvī, -ātum _vt_ to roam over, cover.
pererudītus _adj_ very learned.
perēsus _ppp of_ **peredō**.
perexcelsus _adj_ very high.
perexiguē _adv_ very meagrely.
perexiguus _adj_ very small, very short.
perfacētē _adv_ very wittily.
perfacētus _adj_ very witty.
perfacile _adv_ very easily.
perfacilis _adj_ very easy; very courteous.
perfamiliāris _adj_ very intimate ♦ _m_ very close friend.
perfectē _adv_ fully.
perfectiō, -ōnis _f_ completion, perfection.
perfector, -ōris _m_ perfecter.
perfectus _ppp of_ **perficiō** ♦ _adj_ complete, perfect.
perferō, -ferre, -tulī, -lātum _vt_ to carry through, bring, convey; to bear, endure, put up with; (_work_) to finish, bring to completion; (_law_) to get passed; (_message_) to bring news.
perficiō, -icere, -ēcī, -ectum _vt_ to carry out, finish, complete; to perfect; to cause, make.
perficus _adj_ perfecting.
perfidēlis _adj_ very loyal.
perfidia, -ae _f_ treachery, dishonesty.
perfidiōsē _adv see adj._
perfidiōsus _adj_ treacherous, dishonest.
perfidus _adj_ treacherous, faithless.
perfīgō, -gere, -xī, -xum _vt_ to pierce.
perflābilis _adj_ that can be blown through.
perflāgitiōsus _adj_ very wicked.
perflō, -āre _vt_ to blow through, blow over.
perfluctuō, -āre _vt_ to flood through.
perfluō, -ere, -xī _vi_ to run out, leak.
perfodiō, -odere, -ōdī, -ossum _vt_ to dig through, excavate, pierce.
perforō, -āre, -āvī, -ātum _vt_ to bore through, pierce.
perfortiter _adv_ very bravely.
perfossor, -ōris _m_: ~ **parietum** burglar.
perfossus _ppp of_ **perfodiō**.
perfrāctus _ppp of_ **perfringō**.
perfrēgī _perf of_ **perfringō**.
perfremō, -ere _vi_ to snort along.
perfrequēns, -entis _adj_ much frequented.
perfricō, -āre, -uī, -tum _and_ **ātum** _vt_ to rub all

over; **ōs** ~ put on a bold face.
perfrīgefaciō, -ere _vt_ to make shudder.
perfrīgēscō, -gēscere, -xī _vi_ to catch a bad cold.
perfrīgidus _adj_ very cold.
perfringō, -ingere, -ēgī, -āctum _vt_ to break through, fracture, wreck; (_fig_) to violate; to affect powerfully.
perfrīxī _perf of_ **perfrīgēscō**.
perfrūctus _ppa of_ **perfruor**.
perfruor, -uī, -ūctus _vi_ (_with abl_) to enjoy to the full; to fulfil.
perfuga, -ae _m_ deserter.
perfugiō, -ugere, -ūgī _vi_ to flee for refuge, desert to.
perfugium, -ī _and_ **iī** _nt_ refuge, shelter.
perfūnctiō, -ōnis _f_ performing.
perfūnctus _ppa of_ **perfungor**.
perfundō, -undere, -ūdī, -ūsum _vt_ to pour over, drench, besprinkle; to dye; (_fig_) to flood, fill.
perfungor, -gī, perfūnctus _vi_ (_with abl_) to perform, discharge; to undergo.
perfurō, -ere _vi_ to rage furiously.
perfūsus _ppp of_ **perfundō**.
Pergama, -ōrum _ntpl_ Troy.
Pergamēnus _adj see n._
Pergameus _adj_ Trojan.
Pergamum, -ī _nt_ town in Mysia (_famous for its library_).
pergaudeō, -ēre _vi_ to be very glad.
pergō, -gere, -rēxī, -rēctum _vi_ to proceed, go on, continue ♦ _vt_ to go on with, continue.
pergraecor, -ārī _vi_ to have a good time.
pergrandis _adj_ very large; very old.
pergraphicus _adj_ very artful.
pergrātus _adj_ very pleasant.
pergravis _adj_ very weighty.
pergraviter _adv_ very seriously.
pergula, -ae _f_ balcony; school; brothel.
perhibeō, -ēre, -uī, -itum _vt_ to assert, call, cite.
perhīlum _adv_ very little.
perhonōrificē _adv_ very respectfully.
perhonōrificus _adj_ very complimentary.
perhorrēscō, -ēscere, -uī _vi_ to shiver, tremble violently ♦ _vt_ to have a horror of.
perhorridus _adj_ quite horrible.
perhūmāniter _adv see adj._
perhūmānus _adj_ very polite.
Periclēs, -is _and_ **ī** _m_ famous Athenian statesman and orator.
perīclitātiō, -ōnis _f_ experiment.
perīclitor, -ārī, -ātus _vt_ to test, try; to risk, endanger ♦ _vi_ to attempt, venture; to run a risk, be in danger.
perīculōsē _adv see adj._
perīculōsus _adj_ dangerous, hazardous.
perīculum (perīclum), -ī _nt_ danger, risk; trial, attempt; (_law_) lawsuit, writ.
peridōneus _adj_ very suitable.
periī _perf of_ **pereō**.
perillūstris _adj_ very notable; highly honoured.

perimbēcillus *adj* very weak.
perimō, -imere, -ēmī, -emptum *vt* to destroy, prevent, kill.
perincommodē *adv see adj.*
perincommodus *adj* very inconvenient.
perinde *adv* just as, exactly as.
perindulgēns, -entis *adj* very tender.
perinfirmus *adj* very feeble.
peringeniōsus *adj* very clever.
periniquus *adj* very unfair; very discontented.
perinsignis *adj* very conspicuous.
perinvītus *adj* very unwilling.
periodus, -ī *f* sentence, period.
Peripatēticī, -ōrum *mpl* Peripatetics (*followers of Aristotle*).
peripetasmata, -um *ntpl* curtains.
perirātus *adj* very angry.
periscelis, -dis *f* anklet.
peristrōma, -atis *nt* coverlet.
peristylum, -ī *nt* colonnade, peristyle.
perītē *adv* expertly.
perītia, -ae *f* practical knowledge, skill.
perītus *adj* experienced, skilled, expert.
periūcundē *adv see adj.*
periūcundus *adj* very enjoyable.
periūrium, -ī and iī *nt* perjury.
periūrō *see* **pēierō.**
periūrus *adj* perjured, lying.
perlābor, -bī, -psus *vi* to glide along or through, move on.
perlaetus *adj* very glad.
perlāpsus *ppa of* **perlābor.**
perlātē *adv* very extensively.
perlateō, -ēre *vi* to lie quite hidden.
perlātus *ppp of* **perferō.**
perlegō, -egere, -ēgī, -ēctum *vt* to survey; to read through.
perlevis *adj* very slight.
perleviter *adv see adj.*
perlibēns, -entis *adj* very willing.
perlibenter *adv see adj.*
perlīberālis *adj* very genteel.
perlīberāliter *adv* very liberally.
perlibet, -ēre *vi* (*impers*) (I) should very much like.
perliciō *etc see* **pellaciō.**
perlitō, -āre, -āvī, -ātum *vi* to sacrifice with auspicious results.
perlongē *adv* very far.
perlongus *adj* very long, very tedious.
perlub- *etc see* **perlib-.**
perlūceō, -cēre, -xī *vi* to shine through, be transparent; (*fig*) to be quite intelligible.
perlūcidulus *adj* transparent.
perlūcidus *adj* transparent; very bright.
perlūctuōsus *adj* very mournful.
perluō, -ere *vt* to wash thoroughly; (*pass*) to bathe.
perlūstrō, -āre *vt* to traverse; (*fig*) to survey.

permāgnus *adj* very big, very great.
permānanter *adv* by flowing through.
permānāscō, -ere *vi* to penetrate.
permaneō, -anēre, -ānsī, -ānsum *vi* to last, persist, endure to the end.
permānō, -āre, -āvī, -ātum *vi* to flow or ooze through, penetrate.
permānsiō, -ōnis *f* continuing, persisting.
permarīnus *adj* of seafaring.
permātūrēscō, -ēscere, -uī *vi* to ripen fully.
permediocris *adj* very moderate.
permēnsus *ppa of* **permētior.**
permeō, -āre *vt, vi* to pass through, penetrate.
permētior, -tīrī, -nsus *vt* to measure out; to traverse.
permīrus *adj* very wonderful.
permisceō, -scēre, -scuī, -xtum *vt* to mingle, intermingle; to throw into confusion.
permissiō, -ōnis *f* unconditional surrender; permission.
permissus *ppp of* **permittō.**
permissus, -ūs *m* leave, permission.
permitiālis *adj* destructive.
permitiēs, -ēī *f* ruin.
permittō, -ittere, -īsī, -issum *vt* to let go, let pass; to hurl; to give up, entrust, concede; to allow, permit.
permixtē *adv see adj.*
permixtiō, -ōnis *f* mixture; disturbance.
permixtus *ppp of* **permisceō** ♦ *adj* promiscuous, disordered.
permodestus *adj* very moderate.
permolestē *adv* with much annoyance.
permolestus *adj* very troublesome.
permōtiō, -ōnis *f* excitement; emotion.
permōtus *ppp of* **permoveō.**
permoveō, -ovēre, -ōvī, -ōtum *vt* to stir violently; (*fig*) to influence, induce; to excite, move deeply.
permulceō, -cēre, -sī, -sum *vt* to stroke, caress; (*fig*) to charm, flatter; to soothe, appease.
permulsus *ppp of* **permulceō.**
permultus *adj* very much, very many.
permūniō, -īre, -īvī, -ītum *vt* to finish fortifying; to fortify strongly.
permūtātiō, -ōnis *f* change, exchange.
permūtō, -āre, -āvī, -ātum *vt* to change completely; to exchange; (*money*) to remit by bill of exchange.
perna, -ae *f* ham.
pernecessārius *adj* very necessary; very closely related.
pernecesse *adj* indispensable.
pernegō, -āre *vi* to deny flatly.
perniciābilis *adj* ruinous.
perniciēs, -ēī *f* destruction, ruin, death.
perniciōsē *adv see adj.*
perniciōsus *adj* ruinous.

Noun declensions and verb conjugations are shown on pp xiii to xxv. The present infinitive ending of a verb shows to which conjugation it belongs: **-āre** = 1st; **-ēre** = 2nd; **-ere** = 3rd and **-īre** = 4th. Irregular verbs are shown on p xxvi

pernīcitās, -ātis f agility, swiftness.
pernīciter adv nimbly.
pernimius adj much too much.
pernīx, -īcis adj nimble, agile, swift.
pernōbilis adj very famous.
pernoctō, -āre vi to stay all night.
pernōscō, -scere, -vī, -tum vt to examine thoroughly; to become fully acquainted with, know thoroughly.
pernōtēscō, -ēscere, -uī vi to become generally known.
pernōtus ppp of **pernōscō**.
pernox, -octis adj all night long.
pernumerō, -āre vt to count up.
pērō, -ōnis m rawhide boot.
perobscūrus adj very obscure.
perodiōsus adj very troublesome.
perofficiōsē adv very attentively.
peroleō, -ēre vi to give off a strong smell.
peropportūnē adv very opportunely.
peropportūnus adj very timely.
peroptātō adv very much to one's wish.
peropus est it is most essential.
perōrātiō, -ōnis f peroration.
perōrnātus adj very ornate.
perōrnō, -āre vt to give great distinction to.
perōrō, -āre, -āvī, -ātum vt to plead at length; (speech) to bring to a close; to conclude.
perōsus adj detesting.
perpācō, -āre vt to quieten completely.
perparcē adv very stingily.
perparvulus adj very tiny.
perparvus adj very small.
perpāstus adj well fed.
perpauculus adj very very few.
perpaucus adj very little, very few.
perpaulum, -ī nt a very little.
perpauper, -is adj very poor.
perpauxillum, -ī nt a very little.
perpellō, -ellere, -ulī, -ulsum vt to urge, force, influence.
perpendiculum, -ī nt plumbline; **ad ~** perpendicularly.
perpendō, -endere, -endī, -ēnsum vt to weigh carefully, judge.
perperam adv wrongly, falsely.
perpes, -etis adj continuous.
perpessiō, -ōnis f suffering, enduring.
perpessus ppa of **perpetior**.
perpetior, -tī, -ssus vt to endure patiently, allow.
perpetrō, -āre, -āvī, -ātum vt to perform, carry out.
perpetuitās, -ātis f continuity, uninterrupted duration.
perpetuō adv without interruption, forever, utterly.
perpetuō, -āre vt to perpetuate, preserve.
perpetuus adj continuous, entire; universal; **in ~um** forever.
perplaceō, -ēre vi to please greatly.
perplexē adv obscurely.

perplexor, -ārī vi to cause confusion.
perplexus adj confused, intricate, obscure.
perplicātus adj interlaced.
perpluō, -ere vi to let the rain through, leak.
perpoliō, -īre, -īvī, -ītum vt to polish thoroughly.
perpolītus adj finished, refined.
perpopulor, -ārī, -ātus vt to ravage completely.
perpōtātiō, -ōnis f drinking bout.
perpōtō, -āre vi to drink continuously ♦ vt to drink off.
perprimō, -ere vt to lie on.
perpugnāx, -ācis adj very pugnacious.
perpulcher, -rī adj very beautiful.
perpulī perf of **perpellō**.
perpūrgō, -āre, -āvī, -ātum vt to make quite clean; to explain.
perpusillus adj very little.
perquam adv very, extremely.
perquīrō, -rere, -sīvī, -sītum vt to search for, inquire after; to examine carefully.
perquīsītius adv more accurately.
perrārō adv very seldom.
perrārus adj very uncommon.
perreconditus adj very abstruse.
perrēpō, -ere vt to crawl over.
perrēptō, -āre, -āvī, -ātum vt, vi to creep about or through.
perrēxī perf of **pergō**.
perrīdiculē adv see adj.
perrīdiculus adj very laughable.
perrogātiō, -ōnis f passing (of a law).
perrogō, -āre vt to ask one after another.
perrumpō, -umpere, -ūpī, -uptum vt, vi to break through, force a way through; (fig) to break down.
perruptus ppp of **perrumpō**.
Persae, -ārum mpl Persians.
persaepe adv very often.
persalsē adv see adj.
persalsus adj very witty.
persalūtātiō, -ōnis f greeting everyone in turn.
persalūtō, -āre vt to greet in turn.
persanctē adv most solemnly.
persapiēns, -entis adj very wise.
persapienter adv see adj.
perscienter adv very discreetly.
perscindō, -ndere, -dī, -ssum vt to tear apart.
perscītus adj very smart.
perscrībō, -bere, -psī, -ptum vt to write in full; to describe, report; (record) to enter; (money) to make over in writing.
perscrīptiō, -ōnis f entry; assignment.
perscrīptor, -ōris m writer.
perscrīptus ppp of **perscrībō**.
perscrūtor, -ārī, -ātus vt to search, examine thoroughly.
persecō, -āre, -uī, -tum vt to dissect; to do away with.
persector, -ārī vt to investigate.

persecūtiō, -ōnis *f (law)* prosecution.
persecūtus *ppa of* **persequor.**
persedeō, -edere, -ēdī, -essum *vi* to remain sitting.
persegnis *adj* very slow.
Persēius *adj see* **Persēus.**
persentiō, -entīre, -ēnsī *vt* to see clearly; to feel deeply.
persentīscō, -ere *vi* to begin to see; to begin to feel.
Persephonē, -ēs *f* Proserpine.
persequor, -quī, -cūtus *vt* to follow all the way; to pursue, chase, hunt after; to overtake; *(pattern)* to be a follower of, copy; *(enemy)* to proceed against, take revenge on; *(action)* to perform, carry out; *(words)* to write down, describe.
Persēs, -ae *m* last king of Macedonia.
Persēs, -ae *m* Persian.
Perseus, -eī *and* **eos** *(acc* **-ea)** *m* son of Danaë *(killer of Medusa, rescuer of Andromeda).*
Persēus *adj see n.*
persevērāns, -antis *pres p of* **persevērō ♦** *adj* persistent.
persevēranter *adv see adj.*
persevērantia, -ae *f* persistence.
persevērō, -āre, -āvī, -ātum *vi* to persist **♦** *vt* to persist in.
persevērus *adj* very strict.
Persicus *adj* Persian; of Perses.
Persicum *nt* peach.
persīdō, -īdere, -ēdī, -essum *vi* to sink down into.
persignō, -āre *vt* to record.
persimilis *adj* very like.
persimplex, -icis *adj* very simple.
Persis, -idis *f* Persia.
persistō, -istere, -titī *vi* to persist.
persōlus *adj* one and only.
persolūtus *ppp of* **persolvō.**
persolvō, -vere, -vī, -ūtum *vt* to pay, pay up; to explain.
persōna, -ae *f* mask; character, part; person, personality.
persōnātus *adj* masked; in an assumed character.
personō, -āre, -uī, -itum *vi* to resound, ring (with); to play **♦** *vt* to make resound; to cry aloud.
perspectē *adv* intelligently.
perspectō, -āre *vt* to have a look through.
perspectus *ppp of* **perspiciō ♦** *adj* well-known.
perspeculor, -ārī *vt* to reconnoitre.
perspergō, -gere, -sī, -sum *vt* to besprinkle.
perspicāx, -ācis *adj* sharp, shrewd.
perspicientia, -ae *f* full understanding.
perspiciō, -icere, -exī, -ectum *vt* to see through; to examine, observe.
perspicuē *adv* clearly.
perspicuitās, -ātis *f* clarity.

perspicuus *adj* transparent; clear, evident.
persternō, -ernere, -rāvī, -rātum *vt* to pave all over.
perstimulō, -āre *vt* to rouse violently.
perstitī *perf of* **persistō;** *perf of* **perstō.**
perstō, -āre, -itī, -ātum *vi* to stand fast; to last; to continue, persist.
perstrātus *ppp of* **persternō.**
perstrepō, -ere *vi* to make a lot of noise.
perstrictus *ppp of* **perstringō.**
perstringō, -ingere, -inxī, -ictum *vt* to graze, touch lightly; *(words)* to touch on, belittle, censure; *(senses)* to dull, deaden.
perstudiōsē *adv* very eagerly.
perstudiōsus *adj* very fond.
persuādeō, -dēre, -sī, -sum *vi (with dat)* to convince, persuade; **~sum habeō, mihi ~sum est** I am convinced.
persuāsiō, -ōnis *f* convincing.
persuāsus, -ūs *m* persuasion.
persubtīlis *adj* very fine.
persultō, -āre *vt, vi* to prance about, frisk over.
pertaedet, -dēre, -sum est *vt (impers)* to be weary of, be sick of.
pertegō, -egere, -ēxī, -ēctum *vt* to cover over.
pertemptō, -āre *vt* to test carefully; to consider well; to pervade, seize.
pertendō, -ere, -ī *vi* to push on, persist **♦** *vt* to go on with.
pertenuis *adj* very small, very slight.
perterebrō, -āre *vt* to bore through.
pertergeō, -gēre, -sī, -sum *vt* to wipe over; to touch lightly.
perterrefaciō, -ere *vt* to scare thoroughly.
perterreō, -ēre, -uī, -itum *vt* to frighten thoroughly.
perterricrepus *adj* with a terrifying crash.
perterritus *adj* terrified.
pertexō, -ere, -uī, -tum *vt* to accomplish.
pertica, -ae *f* pole, staff.
pertimefactus *adj* very frightened.
pertimēscō, -ēscere, -uī *vt, vi* to be very alarmed, be very afraid of.
pertinācia, -ae *f* perseverance, stubbornness.
pertināciter *adv see adj.*
pertināx, -ācis *adj* very tenacious; unyielding, stubborn.
pertineō, -ēre, -uī *vi* to extend, reach; to tend, lead to, concern; to apply, pertain, belong; **quod ~et ad** as far as concerns.
pertingō, -ere *vi* to extend.
pertolerō, -āre *vt* to endure to the end.
pertorqueō, -ēre *vt* to distort.
pertractātē *adv* in a hackneyed fashion.
pertractātiō, -ōnis *f* handling.
pertractō, -āre *vt* to handle, feel all over; *(fig)* to treat, study.
pertractus *ppp of* **pertrahō.**

Noun declensions and verb conjugations are shown on pp xiii to xxv. The present infinitive ending of a verb shows to which conjugation it belongs: **-āre** = 1st; **-ēre** = 2nd; **-ere** = 3rd and **-īre** = 4th. Irregular verbs are shown on p xxvi

pertrahō, -here, -xī, -ctum *vt* to drag across, take forcibly; to entice.

pertrect- *etc see* **pertract-**.

pertristis *adj* very sad, very morose.

pertulī *perf of* **perferō**.

pertumultuōsē *adv* very excitedly.

pertundō, -undere, -udī, -ūsum *vt* to perforate.

perturbātē *adv* in confusion.

perturbātiō, -ōnis *f* confusion, disturbance; emotion.

perturbātrīx, -īcis *f* disturber.

perturbātus *ppp of* **perturbō** ♦ *adj* troubled; alarmed.

perturbō, -āre, -āvī, -ātum *vt* to throw into disorder, upset, alarm.

perturpis *adj* scandalous.

pertūsus *ppp of* **pertundō** ♦ *adj* in holes, leaky.

perungō, -ungere, -ūnxī, -ūnctum *vt* to smear all over.

perurbānus *adj* very refined; over-fine.

perūrō, -rere, -ssī, -stum *vt* to burn up, scorch; to inflame, chafe; to freeze, nip.

Perusia, -iae *f* Etruscan town (*now* Perugia).

Perusīnus *adj see n*.

perūstus *ppp of* **perūrō**.

perūtilis *adj* very useful.

pervādō, -dere, -sī, -sum *vt, vi* to pass through, spread through; to penetrate, reach.

pervagātus *adj* widespread, well-known; general.

pervagor, -ārī, -ātus *vi* to range, rove about; to extend, spread ♦ *vt* to pervade.

pervagus *adj* roving.

pervariē *adv* very diversely.

pervastō, -āre, -āvī, -ātum *vt* to devastate.

pervāsus *ppp of* **pervādō**.

pervectus *ppp of* **pervehō**.

pervehō, -here, -xī, -ctum *vt* to carry, convey, bring through; (*pass*) to ride, drive, sail through; to attain.

pervellō, -ere, -ī *vt* to pull, twitch, pinch; to stimulate; to disparage.

perveniō, -enīre, -ēnī, -entum *vi* to come to, arrive, reach; to attain to.

pervēnor, -ārī *vi* to chase through.

perversē *adv* perversely.

perversitās, -ātis *f* perverseness.

perversus (pervorsus) *ppp of* **pervertō** ♦ *adj* awry, squint; wrong, perverse.

pervertō, -tere, -tī, -sum *vt* to overturn, upset; to overthrow, undo; (*speech*) to confute.

pervesperī *adv* very late.

pervestīgātiō, -ōnis *f* thorough search.

pervestīgō, -āre, -āvī, -ātum *vt* to track down; to investigate.

pervetus, -eris *adj* very old.

pervetustus *adj* antiquated.

pervicācia, -ae *f* obstinacy; firmness.

pervicāciter *adv see adj*.

pervicāx, -ācis *adj* obstinate, wilful; dogged.

pervictus *ppp of* **pervincō**.

pervideō, -idēre, -īdī, -īsum *vt* to look over, survey; to consider; to discern.

pervigeō, -ēre, -uī *vi* to continue to flourish.

pervigil, -is *adj* awake, watchful.

pervigilātiō, -ōnis *f* vigil.

pervigilium, -ī *and* **iī** *nt* vigil.

pervigilō, -āre, -āvī, -ātum *vt, vi* to stay awake all night, keep vigil.

pervīlis *adj* very cheap.

pervincō, -incere, -īcī, -ictum *vt, vi* to conquer completely; to outdo, surpass; to prevail upon, effect; (*argument*) to carry a point, maintain, prove.

pervīvō, -ere *vi* to survive.

pervius *adj* passable, accessible.

pervolgō *etc see* **pervulgō**.

pervolitō, -āre *vt, vi* to fly about.

pervolō, -āre, -āvī, -ātum *vt, vi* to fly through *or* over, fly to.

pervolō, -elle, -oluī *vi* to wish very much.

pervolūtō, -āre *vt* (*books*) to read through.

pervolvō, -vere, -vī, -ūtum *vt* to tumble about; (*book*) to read through; (*pass*) to be very busy (with).

pervor- *etc see* **perver-**.

pervulgātus *adj* very common.

pervulgō, -āre, -āvī, -ātum *vt* to make public, impart; to haunt.

pēs, pedis *m* foot; (*length*) foot; (*verse*) foot, metre; (*sailrope*) sheet; **pedem cōnferre** come to close quarters; **pedem referre** go back; **ante pedēs** self-evident; **pedibus** on foot, by land; **pedibus īre in sententiam** take sides; **pedibus aequīs** (*NAUT*) with the wind right aft; **servus ā pedibus** footman.

pessimē *superl of* **male**.

pessimus *superl of* **malus**.

pessulus, -ī *m* bolt.

pessum *adv* to the ground, to the bottom; **~ dare** put an end to, ruin, destroy; **~ īre** sink, perish.

pestifer, -ī *adj* pestilential; baleful, destructive.

pestilēns, -entis *adj* unhealthy; destructive.

pestilentia, -ae *f* plague, pest; unhealthiness.

pestilitās, -ātis *f* plague.

pestis, -is *f* plague, pest; ruin, destruction.

petasātus *adj* wearing the petasus.

petasunculus, -ī *m* small leg of pork.

petasus, -ī *m* broadbrimmed hat.

petessō, -ere *vt* to be eager for.

petītiō, -ōnis *f* thrust, attack; request, application; (*office*) candidature, standing for; (*law*) civil suit, right of claim.

petītor, -ōris *m* candidate; plaintiff.

petītūriō, -īre *vt* to long to be a candidate.

petītus *ppp of* **petō**.

petītus, -ūs *m* falling to.

petō, -ere, -īvī *and* **iī, -ītum** *vt* to aim at, attack; (*place*) to make for, go to; to seek, look for, demand, ask; to go and fetch; (*law*) to sue; (*love*) to court; (*office*) to stand for.

petorritum, -ī nt carriage.

petrō, -ōnis m yokel.

Petrōnius, -ī m arbiter of fashion under Nero.

petulāns, -antis adj pert, impudent, lascivious.

petulanter adv see adj.

petulantia, -ae f pertness, impudence.

petulcus adj butting.

pexus ppp of pectō.

Phaeāccius and cus, -x adj Phaeacian.

Phaeāces, -cum mpl fabulous islanders in the Odyssey.

Phaedra, -ae f stepmother of Hippolytus.

Phaedrus, -ī m pupil of Socrates; writer of Latin fables.

Phaethōn, -ontis m son of the Sun (killed while driving his father's chariot).

Phaethonteus adj see n.

Phaethontiades, -um fpl sisters of Phaethon.

phalangae, -ārum fpl wooden rollers.

phalangītae, -ārum mpl soldiers of a phalanx.

phalanx, -gis f phalanx; troops, battle order.

Phalaris, -dis m tyrant of Agrigentum.

phalerae, -ārum fpl medallions, badges; (horse) trappings.

phalerātus adj wearing medallions; ornamented.

Phalēreus, -icus adj see n.

Phalērum, -ī nt harbour of Athens.

pharetra, -ae f quiver.

pharetrātus adj wearing a quiver.

Pharius adj see n.

pharmaceutria, -ae f sorceress.

pharmacopōla, -ae m quack doctor.

Pharsālicus, -ius adj see n.

Pharsālus (-os), -ī f town in Thessaly (where Caesar defeated Pompey).

Pharus (-os), -ī f island off Alexandria with a famous lighthouse; lighthouse.

phasēlus, -ī m/f French beans; (boat) pinnace.

Phāsiacus adj Colchian.

Phāsiānus, -āna m/f pheasant.

Phāsis, -dis and dos m river of Colchis.

Phāsis adj see n.

phasma, -tis nt ghost.

Pherae, -ārum fpl town in Thessaly (home of Admetus).

Pheraeus adj see n.

phiala, -ae f saucer.

Phīdiacus adj see n.

Phīdiās, -ae m famous Athenian sculptor.

philēma, -tis nt kiss.

Philippī, -ōrum mpl town in Macedonia (where Brutus and Cassius were defeated).

Philippēus adj see n.

Philippicae fpl Cicero's speeches against Antony.

Philippicus adj see n.

Philippus, -ī m king of Macedonia; gold coin.

philitia, (phīditia), -ōrum ntpl public meals at Sparta.

Philō (-ōn), -ōnis m Academic philosopher (teacher of Cicero).

Philoctētēs, -ae m Greek archer who gave Hercules poisoned arrows.

philologia, -ae f study of literature.

philologus adj scholarly, literary.

Philomēla, -ae f sister of Procne; nightingale.

philosophē adv see adj.

philosophia, -ae f philosophy.

philosophor, -ārī, -ātus vi to philosophize.

philosophus, -ī m philosopher ♦ adj philosophical.

philtrum, -ī nt love potion.

philyra, -ae f inner bark of the lime tree.

phīmus, -ī m dice box.

Phlegethōn, -ontis m a river of Hades.

Phlegethontis adj see n.

Phlīāsius adj see n.

Phlīūs, -ūntis f town in Peloponnese.

phōca, -ae f seal.

Phōcaicus adj see n.

Phōcēus adj see n.

Phōcis, -idis f country of central Greece.

Phōcius adj see n.

Phoebas, -adis f prophetess.

Phoebē, -ēs f Diana, the moon.

Phoebēius, -ēus adj see n.

Phoebigena, -ae m son of Phoebus, Aesculapius.

Phoebus, -ī m Apollo; the sun.

Phoenīcē, -cēs f Phoenicia.

Phoenīces, -cum mpl Phoenicians.

phoenīcopterus, -ī m flamingo.

Phoenīssus adj Phoenician ♦ f Dido.

Phoenīx, -īcis m friend of Achilles.

phoenīx, -īcis m phoenix.

Phorcis, -idos = Phorcýnis.

Phorcus, -ī m son of Neptune (father of Medusa).

Phorcýnis, -ýnidos f Medusa.

Phraātēs, -ae m king of Parthia.

phrenēsis, -is f delirium.

phrenēticus adj mad, delirious.

Phrixēus adj see n.

Phrixus, -ī m Helle's brother (who took the ram with the golden fleece to Colchis).

Phryges, -um mpl Phrygians; Trojans.

Phrygia, -iae f Phrygia (country of Asia Minor); Troy.

Phrygius adj Phrygian, Trojan.

Phthia, -ae f home of Achilles in Thessaly.

Phthīōta, -ōtēs, -ōtae m native of Phthia.

phthisis f consumption.

Phthīus adj see n.

phy interj bah!

phylaca, -ae f prison.

phylarchus, -ī m chieftain.

physica, -ae and ē, -ēs f physics.

physicē adv scientifically.

Noun declensions and verb conjugations are shown on pp xiii to xxv. The present infinitive ending of a verb shows to which conjugation it belongs: -āre = 1st; -ēre = 2nd; -ere = 3rd and -īre = 4th. Irregular verbs are shown on p xxvi

physicus *adj* of physics, natural ♦ *m* natural philosopher ♦ *ntpl* physics.
physiognōmōn, -onis *m* physiognomist.
physiologia, -ae *f* natural philosophy, science.
piābilis *adj* expiable.
piāculāris *adj* atoning ♦ *ntpl* sin offerings.
piāculum, -ī *nt* sin offering; victim; atonement, punishment; sin, guilt.
piāmen, -inis *nt* atonement.
pīca, -ae *f* magpie.
picāria, -ae *f* pitch hut.
picea, -ae *f* pine.
Picēns, -entis *adj* = **Picēnus**.
Picēnum, -ēnī *nt* Picenum.
Picēnus *adj* of Picenum in E. Italy.
piceus *adj* pitch black; of pitch.
pictor, -ōris *m* painter.
pictūra, -ae *f* painting; picture.
pictūrātus *adj* painted; embroidered.
pictus *ppp of* **pingō** ♦ *adj* coloured, tattooed; (*style*) ornate; (*fear*) unreal.
pīcus, -ī *m* woodpecker.
piē *adv* religiously, dutifully.
Pīeris, -dis *f* Muse.
Pīerius *adj* of the Muses, poetic.
pietās, -ātis *f* sense of duty (*to gods, family, country*), piety, filial affection, love, patriotism.
piger, -rī *adj* reluctant, slack, slow; numbing, dull.
piget, -ēre, -uit *vt* (*impers*) to be annoyed, dislike; to regret, repent.
pigmentārius, -ī and iī *m* dealer in paints.
pigmentum, -ī *nt* paint, cosmetic; (*style*) colouring.
pignerātor, -ōris *m* mortgagee.
pignerō, -āre *vt* to pawn, mortgage.
pigneror, -ārī, -ātus *vt* to claim, accept.
pignus, -oris and eris *nt* pledge, pawn, security; wager, stake; (*fig*) assurance, token; (*pl*) children, dear ones.
pigritia, -ae, -ēs, -ēī *f* sluggishness, indolence.
pigrō, -āre, -or, -ārī *vi* to be slow, be slack.
pīla, -ae *f* mortar.
pīla, -ae *f* pillar; pier.
pila, -ae *f* ball, ball game.
pīlānus, -ī *m* soldier of the third line.
pīlātus *adj* armed with javelins.
pīlentum, -ī *nt* carriage.
pilleātus *adj* wearing the felt cap.
pilleolus, -ī *m* skullcap.
pilleum, -ī *nt*, **pilleus, -ī** *m* felt cap presented to freed slaves; (*fig*) liberty.
pilōsus *adj* hairy.
pīlum, -ī *nt* javelin.
pīlus, -ī *m* division of triarii; **prīmus ~** chief centurion.
pilus, -ī *m* hair; a whit.
Pimplēa, -ae and is, -idis *f* Muse.
Pimplēus *adj* of the Muses.
Pindaricus *adj see n.*

Pindarus, -ī *m* Pindar (*Greek lyric poet*).
Pindus, -ī *m* mountain range in Thessaly.
pīnētum, -ī *nt* pine wood.
pīneus *adj* pine- (*in cpds*).
pingō, -ere, pinxī, pictum *vt* to paint, embroider; to colour; (*fig*) to embellish, decorate.
pinguēscō, -ere *vi* to grow fat, become fertile.
pinguis *adj* fat, rich, fertile; (*mind*) gross, dull; (*ease*) comfortable, calm; (*weather*) thick ♦ *nt* grease.
pīnifer, -ī, pīniger, -ī *adj* pine-clad.
pinna, -ae *f* feather; wing, arrow; battlement; (*fish*) fin.
pinnātus *adj* feathered, winged.
pinniger, -ī *adj* winged; finny.
pinnipēs, -edis *adj* wing-footed.
pinnirapus, -ī *m* plume-snatcher.
pinnula, -ae *f* little wing.
pīnotērēs, -ae *m* hermit crab.
pīnsō, -ere *vt* to beat, pound.
pīnus, -ūs and ī *f* stone pine, Scots fir; ship, torch, wreath.
pinxī *perf of* **pingō**.
piō, -āre *vt* to propitiate, worship; to atone for, avert; to avenge.
piper, -is *nt* pepper.
pīpilō, -āre *vi* to chirp.
Pīraea, -ōrum *ntpl* Piraeus (*port of Athens*).
Pīraeeus and us, -ī *m* main port of Athens.
Pīraeus *adj see n.*
pīrāta, -ae *m* pirate.
pīrāticus *adj* pirate ♦ *f* piracy.
Pīrēnē, -ēs *f* spring in Corinth.
Pīrēnis, -idis *adj see n.*
Pīrithous, -ī *m* king of the Lapiths.
pirum, -ī *nt* pear.
pirus, -ī *f* pear tree.
Pīsa, -ae *f* Greek town near the Olympic Games site.
Pīsae, -ārum *fpl* town in Etruria (*now Pisa*).
Pīsaeus *adj see n.*
Pīsānus *adj see n.*
piscārius *adj* fish- (*in cpds*), fishing- (*in cpds*).
piscātor, -ōris *m* fisherman.
piscātōrius *adj* fishing- (*in cpds*).
piscātus, -ūs *m* fishing; fish; catch, haul.
pisciculus, -ī *m* little fish.
piscīna, -ae *f* fishpond; swimming pool.
piscīnārius, -ī and iī *m* person keen on fish ponds.
piscis -is *m* fish; (*ASTRO*) Pisces.
piscor, -ārī, -ātus *vi* to fish.
piscōsus *adj* full of fish.
pisculentus *adj* full of fish.
Pīsistratidae, -idārum *mpl* sons of Pisistratus.
Pīsistratus, -ī *m* tyrant of Athens.
pistillum, -ī *nt* pestle.
pistor, -ōris *m* miller; baker.
pistrilla, -ae *f* little mortar.
pīstrīnum, -ī *nt* mill, bakery; drudgery.
pistris, -is and īx, -īcis *f* sea monster, whale;

swift ship.

pithēcium, -ī and **iī** nt little ape.

pītuīta, -ae f phlegm; catarrh, cold in the head.

pītuītōsus adj phlegmatic.

pius adj dutiful, conscientious; godly, holy; filial, affectionate; patriotic; good, upright ♦ mpl the blessed dead.

pix, picis f pitch.

plācābilis adj easily appeased.

plācābilitās, -ātis f readiness to condone.

plācāmen, -inis, plācāmentum, -ī nt peace-offering.

plācātē adv calmly.

plācātiō, -ōnis f propitiating.

plācātus ppp of **plācō** ♦ adj calm, quiet, reconciled.

placenta, -ae f cake.

Placentia, -iae f town in N. Italy (now Piacenza).

Placentīnus adj see n.

placeō, -ēre, -uī, -itum vi (with dat) to please, satisfy; **~et** it seems good, it is agreed, resolved; **mihi ~eō** I am pleased with myself.

placidē adv peacefully, gently.

placidus adj calm, quiet, gentle.

placitum, -ī nt principle, belief.

placitus ppa of **placeō** ♦ adj pleasing; agreed on.

plācō, -āre, -āvī, -ātum vt to calm, appease, reconcile.

plāga, -ae f blow, stroke, wound.

plaga, -ae f region, zone.

plaga, -ae f hunting net, snare, trap.

plagiārius, -ī and **iī** m plunderer, kidnapper.

plāgigerulus adj much flogged.

plāgōsus adj fond of punishing.

plagula, -ae f curtain.

planctus, -ūs m beating the breast, lamentation.

plānē adv plainly, clearly; completely, quite; certainly.

plangō, -gere, -xī, -ctum vt, vi to beat noisily; to beat in grief; to lament loudly, bewail.

plangor, -ōris m beating; loud lamentation.

plānipēs, -edis m ballet dancer.

plānitās, -ātis f perspicuity.

plānitiēs, -ēī, (-a, -ae) f level ground, plain.

planta, -ae f shoot, slip; sole, foot.

plantāria, -ium ntpl slips, young trees.

plānus adj level, flat; plain, clear ♦ nt level ground; **dē ~ō** easily.

planus, -ī m impostor.

platalea, -ae f spoonbill.

platea, -ae f street.

Platō, -ōnis m Plato (founder of the Academic school of philosophy).

Platōnicus adj see n.

plaudō, -dere, -sī, -sum vt to clap, beat, stamp ♦ vi to clap, applaud; to approve, be pleased with.

plausibilis adj praiseworthy.

plausor, -ōris m applauder.

plaustrum, -ī nt waggon, cart; (ASTRO) Great Bear; **~ percellere** upset the applecart.

plausus ppp of **plaudō**.

plausus, -ūs m flapping; clapping, applause.

Plautīnus adj see n.

Plautus, -ī m early Latin comic poet.

plēbēcula, -ae f rabble.

plēbēius adj plebeian; common, low.

plēbicola, -ae m friend of the people.

plēbiscītum, -ī nt decree of the people.

plēbs (plēbēs), -is f common people, plebeians; lower classes, masses.

plectō, -ere vt to punish.

plēctrum, -ī nt plectrum; lyre, lyric poetry.

Plēias, -dis f Pleiad; (pl) the Seven Sisters.

plēnē adv fully, entirely.

plēnus adj full, filled; (fig) sated; (age) mature; (amount) complete; (body) stout, plump; (female) pregnant; (matter) solid; (style) copious; (voice) loud; **ad ~um** abundantly.

plērumque adv generally, mostly.

plērusque adj a large part, most; (pl) the majority, the most; very many.

plexus adj plaited, interwoven.

Plīas see **Plēias**.

plicātrīx, -īcis f clothes folder.

plicō, -āre, -āvī and **uī, -ātum** and **itum** vt to fold, coil.

Plīnius, -ī m Roman family name (esp Pliny the Elder, who died in the eruption of Vesuvius); Pliny the Younger, writer of letters.

plōrātus, -ūs m wailing.

plōrō, -āre, -āvī, -ātum vi to wail, lament ♦ vt to weep for, bewail.

plōstellum, -ī nt cart.

ploxenum, -ī nt cart box.

pluit, -ere, -it vi (impers) it is raining.

plūma, -ae f soft feather, down.

plumbeus adj of lead; (fig) heavy, dull, worthless.

plumbum, -ī nt lead; bullet, pipe, ruler; **~ album** tin.

plūmeus adj down, downy.

plūmipēs, -edis adj feather-footed.

plūmōsus adj feathered.

plūrimus superl of **multus**.

plūs, -ūris compar of **multus** ♦ adv more.

plūsculus adj a little more.

pluteus, -ī m shelter, penthouse; parapet; couch; bookcase.

Plūtō, -ōnis m king of the lower world.

Plūtōnius adj see n.

pluvia, -ae f rain.

pluviālis adj rainy.

pluvius adj rainy, rain- (in cpds).

pōcillum, -ī nt small cup.

pōculum, -ī nt cup; drink, potion.

Noun declensions and verb conjugations are shown on pp xiii to xxv. The present infinitive ending of a verb shows to which conjugation it belongs: **-āre** = 1st; **-ēre** = 2nd; **-ere** = 3rd and **-īre** = 4th. Irregular verbs are shown on p xxvi

podagra, -ae *f* gout.
podagrōsus *adj* gouty.
podium, -ī *and* **iī** *nt* balcony.
poēma, -tis *nt* poem.
poena, -ae *f* penalty, punishment; **poenas dare** to be punished.
Poenī, -ōrum *mpl* Carthaginians.
Poenus, Pūnicus *adj* Punic.
poēsis, -is *f* poetry, poem.
poēta, -ae *m* poet.
poēticē *adv* poetically.
poēticus *adj* poetic ♦ *f* poetry.
poētria, -ae *f* poetess.
pol *interj* by Pollux!, truly.
polenta, -ae *f* pearl barley.
poliō, -īre, -īvī, -ītum *vt* to polish; to improve, put in good order.
polītē *adv* elegantly.
polītīa, -ae *f* Plato's Republic.
politicus *adj* political.
polītus *adj* polished, refined, cultured.
pollen, -inis *nt* fine flour, meal.
pollēns, -entis *pres p of* **polleō** ♦ *adj* powerful, strong.
pollentia, -ae *f* power.
polleō, -ēre *vi* to be strong, be powerful.
pollex, -icis *m* thumb.
polliceor, -ērī, -itus *vt* to promise, offer.
pollicitātiō, -ōnis *f* promise.
pollicitor, -ārī, -ātus *vt* to promise.
pollicitum, -ī *nt* promise.
Polliō, -ōnis *m* Roman surname (*esp C. Asinius, soldier, statesman and literary patron under Augustus*).
pollis, -inis *m/f see* **pollen.**
pollūcibiliter *adv* sumptuously.
pollūctus *adj* offered up ♦ *nt* offering.
polluō, -uere, -uī, -ūtum *vt* to defile, pollute, dishonour.
Pollūx, -ūcis *m* twin brother of Castor (*famous as a boxer*).
polus, -ī *m* pole, North pole; sky.
Polyhymnia, -ae *f* a Muse.
Polyphēmus, -ī *m* one-eyed Cyclops.
pōlypus, -ī *m* polypus.
pōmārium, -ī *and* **iī** *nt* orchard.
pōmārius, -ī *and* **iī** *m* fruiterer.
pōmerīdiānus *adj* afternoon.
pōmērium, -ī *and* **iī** *nt* free space round the city boundary.
pōmifer, -ī *adj* fruitful.
pōmoerium *see* **pōmērium.**
pōmōsus *adj* full of fruit.
pompa, -ae *f* procession; retinue, train; ostentation.
Pompeiānus *adj see n.*
Pompeiī, -ōrum *mpl Campanian town buried by an eruption of Vesuvius.*
Pompeius, -ī *m* Roman family name (*esp Pompey the Great*).
Pompeius, -ānus *adj see n.*
Pompilius, -ī *m* Numa (*second king of Rome*).
Pompilius *adj see n.*

Pomptīnus *adj* Pomptine (*name of marshy district in S. Latium*).
pōmum, -ī *nt* fruit; fruit tree.
pōmus, -ī *f* fruit tree.
ponderō, -āre *vt* to weigh; to consider, reflect on.
ponderōsus *adj* heavy, weighty.
pondō *adv* in weight; pounds.
pondus, -eris *nt* weight; mass, burden; (*fig*) importance, authority; (*character*) firmness; (*pl*) balance.
pōne *adv* behind.
pōnō, -ere, posuī, positum *vt* to put, place, lay, set; to lay down, lay aside; (*fig*) to regard, reckon; (*art*) to make, build; (*camp*) to pitch; (*corpse*) to lay out, bury; (*example*) to take; (*food*) to serve; (*hair*) to arrange; (*hope*) to base, stake; (*hypothesis*) to suppose, assume; (*institution*) to lay down, ordain; (*money*) to invest; (*sea*) to calm; (*theme*) to propose; (*time*) to spend, devote; (*tree*) to plant; (*wager*) to put down ♦ *vi* (*wind*) to abate.
pōns, pontis *m* bridge; drawbridge; (*ship*) gangway, deck.
ponticulus, -ī *m* small bridge.
Ponticus *see* **Pontus.**
pontifex, -icis *m* high priest, pontiff.
pontificālis *adj* pontifical.
pontificātus, -ūs *m* high priesthood.
pontificius *adj* pontiff's.
pontō, -ōnis *m* ferryboat.
pontus, -ī *m* sea.
Pontus, -ī *m* Black Sea; *kingdom of Mithridates in Asia Minor.*
popa, -ae *m* minor priest.
popanum, -ī *nt* sacrificial cake.
popellus, -ī *m* mob.
popīna, -ae *f* eating house, restaurant.
popīnō, -ōnis *m* glutton.
popl- *etc see* **pūbl-.**
poples, -itis *m* knee.
poposcī *perf of* **poscō.**
poppysma, -tis *nt* clicking of the tongue.
populābilis *adj* destroyable.
populābundus *adj* ravaging.
populāris *adj* of, from, for the people; popular, democratic; native ♦ *m* fellow countryman ♦ *mpl* the people's party, the democrats.
populāritās, -ātis *f* courting popular favour.
populāriter *adv* vulgarly; democratically.
populātiō, -ōnis *f* plundering; plunder.
populātor, -ōris *m* ravager.
pōpuleus *adj* poplar- (*in cpds*).
pōpulifer, -ī *adj* rich in poplars.
populor, -ārī, -ātus; -ō, -āre *vt* to ravage, plunder; to destroy, ruin.
populus, -ī *m* people, nation; populace, the public; large crowds; district.
pōpulus, -ī *f* poplar tree.
porca, -ae *f* sow.
porcella, -ae *f*, **-us, -ī** *m* little pig.

porcīna, -ae f pork.
porcīnārius, -ī and **iī** m pork seller.
Porcius, -ī m family name of Cato.
Porcius adj see n.
porculus, -ī m porker.
porcus, -ī m pig, hog.
porgō etc see **porrigō**.
Porphyriōn, -ōnis m a Giant.
porrēctiō, -ōnis f extending.
porrēctus ppp of **porrigō** ♦ adj long, protracted; dead.
porrēxī perf of **porrigō**.
porriciō, -ere vt to make an offering of; **inter caesa et porrēcta** ≈ at the eleventh hour.
porrigō, -igere, -ēxī, -ēctum vt to stretch, spread out, extend; to offer, hold out.
porrigō, -inis f scurf, dandruff.
porrō adv forward, a long way off; (time) in future, long ago; (sequence) next, moreover, in turn.
porrum, -ī nt leek.
Porsena, Porsenna, Porsinna, -ae f king of Clusium in Etruria.
porta, -ae f gate; entrance, outlet.
portātiō, -ōnis f carrying.
portendō, -dere, -dī, -tum vt to denote, predict.
portentificus adj marvellous.
portentōsus adj unnatural.
portentum, -ī nt omen, unnatural happening; monstrosity, monster; (story) marvel.
porthmeus, -eī and **eos** m ferryman.
porticula, -ae f small gallery.
porticus, -ūs m portico, colonnade; (MIL) gallery; (PHILOS) Stoicism.
portiō, -ōnis f share, instalment; **prō ~ōne** proportionally.
portitor, -ōris m customs officer.
portitor, -ōris m ferryman.
portō, -āre, -āvī, -ātum vt to carry, convey, bring.
portōrium, -ī and **iī** nt customs duty, tax.
portula, -ae f small gate.
portuōsus adj well-off for harbours.
portus, -ūs m harbour, port; (fig) safety, haven.
pōsca, -ae f a vinegar drink.
poscō, -ere, poposcī vt to ask, require, demand; to call on.
Posīdōnius, -ī m Stoic philosopher (teacher of Cicero).
positiō, -ōnis f position, climate.
positor, -ōris m builder.
positūra, -ae f position; formation.
positus ppp of **pōnō** ♦ adj situated.
posse infin of **possum**.
possēdī perf of **possideō**; perf of **possīdō**.
possessiō, -ōnis f seizing; occupation; possession, property.
possessiuncula, -ae f small estate.

possessor, -ōris m occupier, possessor.
possessus ppp of **possideō** and **possīdō**.
possideō, -idēre, -ēdī, -essum vt to hold, occupy; to have, possess.
possīdō, -īdere, -ēdī, -essum vt to take possession of.
possum, -sse, -tuī vi to be able, can; to have power, avail.
post adv (place) behind; (time) after; (sequence) next ♦ prep (with acc) behind; after, since; **paulō ~** soon after; **~ urbem conditam** since the foundation of the city.
posteā adv afterwards, thereafter; next, then; **~ quam** conj after.
posterior, -ōris adj later, next; inferior, less important.
posterius adv later.
posterus adj next, following ♦ mpl posterity.
postferō, -re vt to put after, sacrifice.
postgenitī, -ōrum mpl later generations.
posthabeō, -ēre, -uī, -itum vt to put after, neglect.
posthāc adv hereafter, in future.
postibi adv then, after that.
postīculum, -ī nt small back building.
postīcus adj back- (in cpds), hind- (in cpds) ♦ nt back door.
postideā adv after that.
postillā adv afterwards.
postis, -is m doorpost, door.
postlīminium, -ī and **iī** nt right of recovery.
postmerīdiānus adj in the afternoon.
postmodo, postmodum adv shortly, presently.
postpōnō, -ōnere, -osuī, -ositum vt to put after, disregard.
postputō, -āre vt to consider less important.
postquam conj after, when.
postrēmō adv finally.
postrēmus adj last, rear; lowest, worst.
postrīdiē adv next day, the day after.
postscaenium, -ī and **iī** nt behind the scenes.
postscrībō, -ere vt to write after.
postulātiō, -ōnis f demand, claim; complaint.
postulātum, -ī nt demand, claim.
postulātus, -ūs m claim.
postulō, -āre, -āvī, -ātum vt to demand, claim; (law) to summon, prosecute; to apply for a writ (to prosecute).
postumus adj last, last-born.
postus etc see **positus**.
posuī perf of **pōnō**.
pōtātiō, -ōnis f drinking.
pōtātor, -ōris m toper.
pote etc see **potis**.
potēns, -entis adj able, capable; powerful, strong, potent; master of, ruling over; successful in carrying out.
potentātus, -ūs m political power.

Noun declensions and verb conjugations are shown on pp xiii to xxv. The present infinitive ending of a verb shows to which conjugation it belongs: **-āre** = 1st; **-ēre** = 2nd; **-ere** = 3rd and **-īre** = 4th. Irregular verbs are shown on p xxvi

potenter _adv_ powerfully; competently.

potentia, -ae _f_ power, force, efficacy; tyranny.

potērium, -ī _and_ **iī** _nt_ goblet.

potesse _archaic infin of_ **possum.**

potestās, -ātis _f_ power, ability; control, sovereignty, authority; opportunity, permission; (_person_) magistrate; (_things_) property; **~ātem suī facere** allow access to oneself.

potin can (you)?, is it possible?

pōtiō, -ōnis _f_ drink, draught, philtre.

potiō, -īre _vt_ to put into the power of.

potior, -īrī, -ītus _vi_ (_with gen and abl_) to take possession of, get hold of, acquire; to be master of.

potior, -ōris _adj_ better, preferable.

potis _adj_ (_indecl_) able; possible.

potissimum _adv_ especially.

potissimus _adj_ chief, most important.

pōtitō, -āre _vt_ to drink much.

potius _adv_ rather, more.

pōtō, -āre, -āvī, -ātum _and_ **um** _vt_ to drink.

pōtor, -ōris _m_ drinker.

pōtrix, -īcis _f_ woman tippler.

potuī _perf of_ **possum.**

pōtulenta, -ōrum _ntpl_ drinks.

pōtus _ppp of_ **pōtō** ♦ _adj_ drunk.

pōtus, -ūs _m_ drink.

prae _adv_ in front, before; in comparison ♦ _prep_ (_with abl_) in front of; compared with; (_cause_) because of, for; **~ sē** openly; **~ sē ferre** display; **~ manū** to hand.

praeacūtus _adj_ pointed.

praealtus _adj_ very high, very deep.

praebeō, -ēre, -uī, -itum _vt_ to hold out, proffer; to give, supply; to show, represent; **sē ~** behave, prove.

praebibō, -ere, -ī _vt_ to toast.

praebitor, -ōris _m_ purveyor.

praecalidus _adj_ very hot.

praecānus _adj_ prematurely grey.

praecautus _ppp of_ **praecaveō.**

praecaveō, -avēre, -āvī, -autum _vt_ to guard against ♦ _vi_ to beware, take precautions.

praecēdō, -dere, -ssī, -ssum _vt_ to go before; to surpass ♦ _vi_ to lead the way; to excel.

praecellō, -ere _vi_ to excel, be distinguished ♦ _vt_ to surpass.

praecelsus _adj_ very high.

praecentiō, -ōnis _f_ prelude.

praecentō, -āre _vi_ to sing an incantation for.

praeceps, -ipitis _adj_ head first, headlong; going down, precipitous; rapid, violent, hasty; inclined (to); dangerous ♦ _nt_ edge of an abyss, precipice; danger ♦ _adv_ headlong; into danger.

praeceptiō, -ōnis _f_ previous notion; precept.

praeceptor, -ōris _m_ teacher.

praeceptrīx, -rīcis _f_ teacher.

praeceptum, -ī _nt_ maxim, precept; order.

praeceptus _ppp of_ **praecipiō.**

praecerpō, -ere, -sī, -tum _vt_ to gather prematurely; to forestall.

praecīdō, -dere, -dī, -sum _vt_ to cut off, damage; (_fig_) to cut short, put an end to.

praecinctus _ppp of_ **praecingō.**

praecingō, -ingere, -inxī, -inctum _vt_ to gird in front; to surround.

praecinō, -inere, -inuī, -entum _vt_ to play before; to chant a spell ♦ _vt_ to predict.

praecipiō, -ipere, -ēpī, -ēptum _vt_ to take beforehand, get in advance; to anticipate; to teach, admonish, order.

praecipitanter _adv_ at full speed.

praecipitem _acc of_ **praeceps.**

praecipitō, -āre, -āvī, -ātum _vt_ to throw down, throw away, hasten; (_fig_) to remove, carry away, ruin ♦ _vi_ to rush headlong, fall; to be hasty.

praecipuē _adv_ especially, chiefly.

praecipuus _adj_ special; principal, outstanding.

praecīsē _adv_ briefly, absolutely.

praecīsus _ppp of_ **praecīdō** ♦ _adj_ steep.

praeclārē _adv_ very clearly; excellently.

praeclārus _adj_ very bright; beautiful, splendid; distinguished, noble.

praeclūdō, -dere, -sī, -sum _vt_ to close, shut against; to close to, impede.

praecō, -ōnis _m_ crier, herald; auctioneer.

praecōgitō, -āre _vt_ to premeditate.

praecognitus _adj_ foreseen.

praecolō, -olere, -oluī, -ultum _vt_ to cultivate early.

praecompositus _adj_ studied.

praecōnium, -ī _and_ **iī** _nt_ office of a crier; advertisement; commendation.

praecōnius _adj_ of a public crier.

praecōnsūmō, -ere, -ptum _vt_ to use up beforehand.

praecontrectō, -āre _vt_ to consider beforehand.

praecordia, -ōrum _ntpl_ midriff; stomach; breast, heart; mind.

praecorrumpō, -umpere, -ūpī, -uptum _vt_ to bribe beforehand.

praecox, -cis _adj_ early, premature.

praecultus _ppp of_ **praecolō.**

praecurrentia, -ium _ntpl_ antecedents.

praecurrō, -rrere, -currī _and_ **rrī, -rsum** _vi_ to hurry on before, precede; to excel ♦ _vt_ to anticipate; to surpass.

praecursiō, -ōnis _f_ previous occurrence; (_RHET_) preparation.

praecursor, -ōris _m_ advance guard; scout.

praecutiō, -ere _vt_ to brandish before.

praeda, -ae _f_ booty, plunder; (_animal_) prey; (_fig_) gain.

praedābundus _adj_ plundering.

praedamnō, -āre _vt_ to condemn beforehand.

praedātiō, -ōnis _f_ plundering.

praedātor, -ōris _m_ plunderer.

praedātōrius _adj_ marauding.

praedēlassō, -āre _vt_ to weaken beforehand.

praedēstinō, -āre _vt_ to predetermine.

praediātor, -ōris *m* buyer of landed estates.
praediātōrius *adj* relating to the sale of estates.
praedicābilis *adj* laudatory.
praedicātiō, -ōnis *f* proclamation; commendation.
praedicātor, -ōris *m* eulogist.
praedicō, -āre, -āvī, -ātum *vt* to proclaim, make public; to declare; to praise, boast.
praedīcō, -īcere, -īxī, -ictum *vt* to mention beforehand, prearrange; to foretell; to warn, command.
praedictiō, -ōnis *f* foretelling.
praedictum, -ī *nt* prediction; command; prearrangement.
praedictus *ppp of* **praedīcō**.
praediolum, -ī *nt* small estate.
praediscō, -ere *vt* to learn beforehand.
praedispositus *adj* arranged beforehand.
praeditus *adj* endowed, provided.
praedium, -ī *and* **iī** *nt* estate.
praedīves, -itis *adj* very rich.
praedō, -ōnis *m* robber, pirate.
praedor, -ārī, -ātus *vt, vi* to plunder, rob; (*fig*) to profit.
praedūcō, -ūcere, -ūxī, -uctum *vt* to draw in front.
praedulcis *adj* very sweet.
praedūrus *adj* very hard, very tough.
praeēmineō, -ēre *vt* to surpass.
praeeō, -īre, -īvī *and* **iī, -itum** *vi* to lead the way, go first; (*formula*) to dictate, recite first ♦ *vt* to precede, outstrip.
praeesse *infin of* **praesum**.
praefātiō, -ōnis *f* formula; preface.
praefātus *ppa of* **praefor**.
praefectūra, -ae *f* superintendence; governorship; *Italian town governed by Roman edicts*, prefecture; district, province.
praefectus *ppp of* **praeficiō** ♦ *m* overseer, director, governor, commander; ~ **classis** admiral; ~ **legiōnis** colonel; ~ **urbis** *or* **urbī** city prefect (of Rome).
praeferō, -ferre, -tulī, -lātum *vt* to carry in front, hold out; to prefer; to show, display; to anticipate; (*pass*) to hurry past, outflank.
praeferōx, -ōcis *adj* very impetuous, very insolent.
praefervidus *adj* very hot.
praefestīnō, -āre *vi* to be too hasty; to hurry past.
praefica, -ae *f* hired mourner.
praeficiō, -icere, -ēcī, -ectum *vt* to put in charge, give command over.
praefīdēns, -entis *adj* over-confident.
praefīgō, -gere, -xī, -xum *vt* to fasten in front, set up before; to tip, point; to transfix.
praefīniō, -īre, -īvī *and* **iī, -ītum** *vt* to determine, prescribe.
praefiscinē, -ī *adv* without offence.

praeflōrō, -āre *vt* to tarnish.
praefluō, -ere *vt, vi* to flow past.
praefocō, -āre *vt* to choke.
praefodiō, -odere, -ōdī *vt* to dig in front of; to bury beforehand.
praefor, -ārī, -ātus *vt, vi* to say in advance, preface; to pray beforehand; to predict.
praefrāctē *adv* resolutely.
praefrāctus *ppp of* **praefringō** ♦ *adj* abrupt; stern.
praefrīgidus *adj* very cold.
praefringō, -ingere, -ēgī, -āctum *vt* to break off, shiver.
praefuī *perf of* **praesum**.
praefulciō, -cīre, -sī, -tum *vt* to prop up; to use as a prop.
praefulgeō, -ulgēre, -ulsī *vt* to shine conspicuously; to outshine.
praegelidus *adj* very cold.
praegestiō, -īre *vi* to be very eager.
praegnāns, -antis *adj* pregnant; full.
praegracilis *adj* very slim.
praegrandis *adj* very large, very great.
praegravis *adj* very heavy; very wearisome.
praegravō, -āre *vt* to weigh down; to eclipse.
praegredior, -dī, -ssus *vt, vi* to go before; to go past; to surpass.
praegressiō, -ōnis *f* precession, precedence.
praegustātor, -ōris *m* taster.
praegustō, -āre *vt* to taste beforehand.
praehibeō, -ēre *vt* to offer, give.
praeiaceō, -ēre *vt* to lie in front of.
praeiūdicium, -ī *and* **iī** *nt* precedent, example; prejudgment.
praeiūdicō, -āre, -āvī, -ātum *vt* to prejudge, decide beforehand.
praeiuvō, -āre *vt* to give previous assistance to.
praelabor, -bī, -psus *vt, vi* to move past, move along.
praelambō, -ere *vt* to lick first.
praelātus *ppp of* **praeferō**.
praelegō, -ere *vt* to coast along.
praeligō, -āre *vt* to bind, tie up.
praelongus *adj* very long, very tall.
praeloquor, -quī, -cūtus *vi* to speak first.
praelūceō, -cēre, -xī *vi* to light, shine; to outshine.
praelūstris *adj* very magnificent.
praemandāta *ntpl* warrant of arrest.
praemandō, -āre, -āvī, -ātum *vt* to bespeak.
praemātūrē *adv* too soon.
praemātūrus *adj* too early, premature.
praemedicātus *adj* protected by charms.
praemeditātiō, -ōnis *f* thinking over the future.
praemeditātus *adj* premeditated.
praemeditor, -ārī, -ātus *vt* to think over, practise.
praemetuenter *adv* anxiously.

Noun declensions and verb conjugations are shown on pp xiii to xxv. The present infinitive ending of a verb shows to which conjugation it belongs: **-āre** = 1st; **-ēre** = 2nd; **-ere** = 3rd and **-īre** = 4th. Irregular verbs are shown on p xxvi

praemetuō, -ere *vi* to be anxious ♦ *vt* to fear the future.

praemissus *ppp of* **praemittō**.

praemittō, -ittere, -īsī, -issum *vt* to send in advance.

praemium, -ī *and* **iī** *nt* prize, reward.

praemolestia, -ae *f* apprehension.

praemōlior, -īrī *vt* to prepare thoroughly.

praemoneō, -ēre, -uī, -itum *vt* to forewarn, foreshadow.

praemonitus, -ūs *m* premonition.

praemōnstrātor, -ōris *m* guide.

praemōnstrō, -āre *vt* to guide; to predict.

praemordeō, -ēre *vt* to bite off; to pilfer.

praemorior, -ī, -tuus *vi* to die too soon.

praemūniō, -īre, -īvī, -ītum *vt* to fortify, strengthen, secure.

praemūnītiō, -ōnis *f* (*RHET*) preparation.

praenārrō, -āre *vt* to tell beforehand.

praenatō, -āre *vt* to flow past.

Praeneste, -is *nt/f* Latin town (*now* Palestrina).

Praenestīnus *adj see* n.

praeniteō, -ēre, -uī *vi* to seem more attractive.

praenōmen, -inis *nt* first name.

praenōscō, -ere *vt* to foreknow.

praenōtiō, -ōnis *f* preconceived idea.

praenūbilus *adj* very gloomy.

praenūntia, -iae *f* harbinger.

praenūntiō, -āre *vt* to foretell.

praenūntius, -ī *and* **iī** *m* harbinger.

praeoccupō, -āre, -āvī, -ātum *vt* to take first, anticipate.

praeolit mihi I get a hint of.

praeoptō, -āre, -āvī, -ātum *vt* to choose rather, prefer.

praepandō, -ere *vt* to spread out; to expound.

praeparātiō, -ōnis *f* preparation.

praeparō, -āre, -āvī, -ātum *vt* to prepare, prepare for; **ex ~ātō** by arrangement.

praepediō, -īre, -īvī, -ītum *vt* to shackle, tether; to hamper.

praependeō, -ēre *vi* to hang down in front.

praepes, -etis *adj* swift, winged; of good omen ♦ *f* bird.

praepilātus *adj* tipped with a ball.

praepinguis *adj* very rich.

praepolleō, -ēre *vi* to be very powerful, be superior.

praeponderō, -āre *vt* to outweigh.

praepōnō, -ōnere, -osuī, -ositum *vt* to put first, place in front; to put in charge, appoint commander; to prefer.

praeportō, -āre *vt* to carry before.

praepositiō, -ōnis *f* preference; (*GRAM*) preposition.

praepositus *ppp of* **praepōnō** ♦ *m* overseer, commander.

praepossum, -sse, -tuī *vi* to gain the upper hand.

praeposterē *adv* the wrong way round.

praeposterus *adj* inverted, perverted; absurd.

praepotēns, -entis *adj* very powerful.

praeproperanter *adv* too hastily.

praeproperē *adv* too hastily.

praeproperus *adj* overhasty, rash.

praepūtium, -ī *and* **iī** *nt* foreskin.

praequam *adv* compared with.

praequestus *adj* complaining beforehand.

praeradiō, -āre *vt* to outshine.

praerapidus *adj* very swift.

praereptus *ppp of* **praeripiō**.

praerigēscō, -ēscere, -uī *vi* to become very stiff.

praeripiō, -ipere, -ipuī, -eptum *vt* to take before, forestall; to carry off prematurely; to frustrate.

praerōdō, -dere, -sum *vt* to bite the end of, nibble off.

praerogātīva, -ae *f* tribe or century with the first vote, the first vote; previous election; omen, sure token.

praerogātīvus *adj* voting first.

praerōsus *ppp of* **praerōdō**.

praerumpō, -umpere, -ūpī, -uptum *vt* to break off.

praeruptus *ppp of* **praerumpō** ♦ *adj* steep, abrupt; headstrong.

praes, -aedis *m* surety; property of a surety.

praesaep- *etc see* **praesēp-**.

praesāgiō, -īre *vt* to have a presentiment of, forebode.

praesāgītiō, -ōnis *f* foreboding.

praesāgium, -ī *and* **iī** *nt* presentiment; prediction.

praesāgus *adj* foreboding, prophetic.

praesciō, -īre, -iī *vt* to know before.

praescīscō, -ere *vt* to find out beforehand.

praescius *adj* foreknowing.

praescrībō, -bere, -psī, -ptum *vt* to write first; to direct, command; to dictate, describe; to put forward as a pretext.

praescrīptiō, -ōnis *f* preface, heading; order, rule; pretext.

praescrīptum, -ī *nt* order, rule.

praescrīptus *ppp of* **praescrībō**.

praesecō, -āre, -uī, -tum *and* **-ātum** *vt* to cut off, pare.

praesēns, -entis *adj* present, in person; (*things*) immediate, ready, prompt; (*mind*) resolute; (*gods*) propitious ♦ *ntpl* present state of affairs; **in ~ēns** for the present; **~in rē ~entī** on the spot.

praesēnsiō, -ōnis *f* foreboding; preconception.

praesēnsus *ppp of* **praesentiō**.

praesentārius *adj* instant, ready.

praesentia, -ae *f* presence; effectiveness.

praesentiō, -entīre, -ēnsī, -ēnsum *vt* to presage, have a foreboding of.

praesēpe, -is *nt*, **-ēs, -is** *f* stable, fold, pen; hovel; hive.

praesēpiō, -īre, -sī, -tum *vt* to barricade.

praesēpis *f* = **praesēpe**.

praesertim *adv* especially.

praeserviō, -īre *vi* to serve as a slave.

praeses, -idis *m* guardian, protector; chief, ruler.

praesideō, -idēre, -ēdī *vi* to guard, defend; to preside over, direct.

praesidiārius *adj* garrison-.

praesidium, -ī *and* **iī** *nt* defence, protection; support, assistance; guard, garrison, convoy; defended position, entrenchment.

praesignificō, -āre *vt* to foreshadow.

praesignis *adj* conspicuous.

praesonō, -āre, -uī *vi* to sound before.

praespargō, -ere *vt* to strew before.

praestābilis *adj* outstanding; preferable.

praestāns, -antis *pres p of* **praestō** ♦ *adj* outstanding, pre-eminent.

praestantia, -ae *f* pre-eminence.

praestes, -itis *adj* presiding, guardian.

praestīgiae, -ārum *fpl* illusion, sleight of hand.

praestīgiātor, -ōris *m*, **-rīx, -rīcis** *f* conjurer, cheat.

praestinō, -āre *vt* to buy.

praestitī *perf of* **praestō**.

praestituō, -uere, -uī, -ūtum *vt* to prearrange, prescribe.

praestitus *ppp of* **praestō**.

praestō *adv* at hand, ready.

praestō, -āre, -itī, -itum *and* **ātum** *vi* to be outstanding, be superior; (*impers*) it is better ♦ *vt* to excel; to be responsible for, answer for; (*duty*) to discharge, perform; (*quality*) to show, prove; (*things*) to give, offer, provide; **sē ~** behave, prove.

praestōlor, -ārī, -ātus *vt, vi* to wait for, expect.

praestrictus *ppp of* **praestringō**.

praestringō, -ingere, -inxī, -ictum *vt* to squeeze; to blunt, dull; (*eyes*) to dazzle.

praestruō, -ere, -xī, -ctum *vt* to block up; to build beforehand.

praesul, -is *mlf* public dancer.

praesultātor, -ōris *m* public dancer.

praesultō, -āre *vi* to dance before.

praesum, -esse, -fuī *vi* (*with dat*) to be at the head of, be in command of; to take the lead; to protect.

praesūmō, -ere, -psī, -ptum *vt* to take first; to anticipate; to take for granted.

praesūtus *adj* sewn over at the point.

praetemptō, -āre *vt* to feel for, grope for; to test in advance.

praetendō, -dere, -dī, -tum *vt* to hold out, put before, spread in front of; to give as an excuse, allege.

praetentō *etc see* **praetemptō**.

praetentus *ppp of* **praetendō** ♦ *adj* lying over against.

praetepeō, -ēre, -uī *vi* to glow before.

praeter *adv* beyond; excepting ♦ *prep* (*with acc*) past, along; except, besides; beyond, more than, in addition to, contrary to.

praeteragō, -ere *vt* to drive past.

praeterbitō, -ere *vt, vi* to pass by.

praeterdūcō, -ere *vt* to lead past.

praetereā *adv* besides; moreover; henceforth.

praetereō, -īre, -iī, -itum *vi* to go past ♦ *vt* to pass, overtake; to escape, escape the notice of; to omit, leave out, forget, neglect; to reject, exclude; to surpass; to transgress.

praeterequitāns, -antis *adj* riding past.

praeterfluō, -ere *vt, vi* to flow past.

praetergredior, -dī, -ssus *vt* to pass, march past; to surpass.

praeterhāc *adv* further, more.

praeteritus *ppp of* **praetereō** ♦ *adj* past, gone by ♦ *ntpl* the past.

praeterlābor, -bī, -psus *vt* to flow past, move past ♦ *vi* to slip away.

praeterlātus *adj* driving, flying past.

praetermeō, -āre *vi* to pass by.

praetermissiō, -ōnis *f* omission, passing over.

praetermittō, -ittere, -īsī, -issum *vt* to let pass; to omit, neglect; to make no mention of; to overlook.

praeterquam *adv* except, besides.

praetervectiō, -ōnis *f* passing by.

praetervehor, -hī, -ctus *vt, vi* to ride past, sail past; to march past; to pass by, pass over.

praetervolō, -āre *vt, vi* to fly past; to escape.

praetexō, -ere, -uī, -tum *vt* to border, fringe; to adorn; to pretend, disguise.

praetextātus *adj* wearing the toga praetexta, under age.

praetextus *ppp of* **praetexō** ♦ *adj* wearing the toga praetexta ♦ *f* toga with a purple border; Roman tragedy ♦ *nt* pretext.

praetextus, -ūs *m* splendour; pretence.

praetimeō, -ēre *vi* to be afraid in advance.

praetinctus *adj* dipped beforehand.

praetor, -ōris *m* chief magistrate, commander; praetor; propraetor, governor.

praetōriānus *adj* of the emperor's bodyguard.

praetōrium, -ī *and* **iī** *nt* general's tent, camp headquarters; governor's residence; council of war; palace, grand building; emperor's bodyguard.

praetōrius *adj* praetor's, praetorian; of a propraetor; of the emperor's bodyguard ♦ *m* ex-praetor; **~ia cohors** bodyguard of general *or* emperor; **porta ~ia** camp gate facing the enemy.

praetorqueō, -ēre *vt* to strangle first.

praetrepidāns, -antis *adj* very impatient.

praetruncō, -āre *vt* to cut off.

praetulī *perf of* **praeferō**.

praetūra, -ae *f* praetorship.

Noun declensions and verb conjugations are shown on pp xiii to xxv. The present infinitive ending of a verb shows to which conjugation it belongs: **-āre** = 1st; **-ēre** = 2nd; **-ere** = 3rd and **-īre** = 4th. Irregular verbs are shown on p xxvi

praeumbrāns, -antis *adj* obscuring.
praeūstus *adj* hardened at the point; frostbitten.
praeut *adv* compared with.
praevaleō, -ēre, -uī *vi* to be very powerful, have most influence, prevail.
praevalidus *adj* very strong, very powerful; too strong.
praevāricātiō, -ōnis *f* collusion.
praevāricātor, -ōris *m* advocate guilty of collusion.
praevāricor, -ārī, -ātus *vi* (*with dat*) to favour by collusion.
praevehor, -hī, -ctus *vi* to ride, fly in front, flow past.
praeveniō, -enīre, -ēnī, -entum *vt, vi* to come before; to anticipate, prevent.
praeverrō, -ere *vt* to sweep before.
praevertō, -ere, -ī, -or, -ī *vt* to put first, prefer; to turn to first, attend first to; to oustrip; to anticipate, frustrate, prepossess.
praevideō, -idēre, -īdī, -īsum *vt* to foresee.
praevitiō, -āre *vt* to taint beforehand.
praevius *adj* leading the way.
praevolō, -āre *vi* to fly in front.
pragmaticus *adj* of affairs ♦ *m* legal expert.
prandeō, -ēre, -ī *vi* to take lunch ♦ *vt* to eat.
prandium, -ī *and* **iī** *nt* lunch.
prānsor, -ōris *m* guest at lunch.
prānsus *adj* having lunched, fed.
prasinus *adj* green.
prātēnsis *adj* meadow.
prātulum, -ī *nt* small meadow.
prātum, -ī *nt* meadow; grass.
prāvē *adv* wrongly, badly.
prāvitās, -ātis *f* irregularity; perverseness, depravity.
prāvus *adj* crooked, deformed; perverse, bad, wicked.
Prāxitelēs, -is *m famous Greek sculptor.*
Prāxitelius *adj see n.*
precāriō *adv* by request.
precārius *adj* obtained by entreaty.
precātiō, -ōnis *f* prayer.
precātor, -ōris *m* intercessor.
preces *pl of* **prex.**
preciae, -ārum *fpl* kind of vine.
precor, -ārī, -ātus *vt, vi* to pray, beg, entreat; to wish (well), curse.
prehendō, -endere, -endī, -ēnsum *vt* to take hold of, catch; to seize, detain; to surprise; (*eye*) to take in; (*mind*) to grasp.
prehēnsō *etc see* **prēnsō.**
prehēnsus *ppp of* **prehendō.**
prēlum, -ī *nt* wine press, oil press.
premō, -mere, -ssī, -ssum *vt* to press, squeeze, press together, compress; (*eyes*) to close; (*reins*) to tighten; (*trees*) to prune; to press upon, lie, sit, stand on, cover, conceal, surpass; to press hard on, follow closely; (*coast*) to hug; to press down, lower, burden; (*fig*) to overcome, rule; (*words*) to disparage; to press in, sink, stamp, plant; to press back,

repress, check, stop.
prendō *etc see* **prehendō.**
prēnsātiō, -ōnis *f* canvassing.
prēnsō (prehēnsō), -āre, -āvī, -ātum *vt* to clutch at, take hold of, buttonhole.
prēnsus *ppp of* **prehendō.**
presbyter, -ī *m* (*ECCL*) elder.
pressē *adv* concisely, accurately, simply.
pressī *perf of* **premō.**
pressiō, -ōnis *f* fulcrum.
pressō, -āre *vt* to press.
pressus *ppp of* **premō** ♦ *adj* (*style*) concise, compressed; (*pace*) slow; (*voice*) subdued.
pressus, -ūs *m* pressure.
prēstēr, -ēris *m* waterspout.
pretiōsē *adv* expensively.
pretiōsus *adj* valuable, expensive; extravagant.
pretium, -ī *and* **iī** *nt* price, value; worth; money, fee, reward; **māgnī -ī, in -iō** valuable; **operae ~** worth while.
prex, -ecis *f* request, entreaty; prayer; good wish; curse.
Priamēis, -ēidis *f* Cassandra.
Priamēius *adj see* **Priamus.**
Priamidēs, -idae *m* son of Priam.
Priamus, -ī *m* king of Troy.
Priāpus, -ī *m* god of fertility and of gardens.
prīdem *adv* long ago, long.
prīdiē *adv* the day before.
prīmaevus *adj* youthful.
prīmānī, -ōrum *mpl* soldiers of the 1st legion.
prīmārius *adj* principal, first-rate.
prīmigenus *adj* original.
prīmipīlāris, -is *m* chief centurion.
prīmipīlus, -ī *m* chief centurion.
prīmitiae, -ārum *fpl* first fruits.
prīmitus *adv* originally.
prīmō *adv* at first; firstly.
prīmōrdium, -ī *and* **iī** *nt* beginning; **~ia rērum** atoms.
prīmōris *adj* first, foremost, tip of; principal ♦ *mpl* nobles; (*MIL*) front line.
prīmulum *adv* first.
prīmulus *adj* very first.
prīmum *adv* first, to begin with, in the first place; for the first time; **cum, ubi, ut ~** as soon as; **quam ~** as soon as possible; **~ dum** in the first place.
prīmus *adj* first, foremost, tip of; earliest; principal, most eminent; **~ veniō** I am the first to come; **prima lux** dawn, daylight; **~ō mēnse** at the beginning of the month; **~īs digitīs** with the fingertips; **~ās agere** play the leading part; **~ās dare** give first place to; **in ~īs** in the front line; especially.
prīnceps, -ipis *adj* first, in front, chief, most eminent ♦ *m* leader, chief; first citizen, emperor; (*MIL*) company, captain, captaincy ♦ *pl* (*MIL*) the second line.
prīncipālis *adj* original; chief; the emperor's.
prīncipātus, -ūs *m* first place; post of commander-in-chief; emperorship.

prīncipiālis *adj* from the beginning.

prīncipium, -ī *and* **iī** *nt* beginning, origin; first to vote ♦ *pl* first principles; (*MIL*) front line; camp headquarters.

prior, -ōris (*nt* **-us**) *adj* former, previous, first; better, preferable ♦ *mpl* forefathers.

prīscē *adv* strictly.

prīscus *adj* former, ancient, old-fashioned.

prīstinus *adj* former, original; of yesterday.

prius *adv* previously, before; in former times; **~ quam** before, sooner than.

prīvātim *adv* individually, privately; at home.

prīvātiō, -ōnis *f* removal.

prīvātus *adj* individual, private; not in public office ♦ *m* private citizen.

Prīvernās, -ātis *adj see n.*

Prīvernum, -ī *nt* old Latin town.

prīvīgna, -ae *f* stepdaughter.

prīvīgnus, -ī *m* stepson; *pl* stepchildren.

prīvilēgium, -ī *and* **iī** *nt* law in favour of *or* against an individual.

prīvō, -āre, -āvī, -ātum *vt* to deprive, rob; to free.

prīvus *adj* single, one each; own, private.

prō *adv* (*with* **ut** *and* **quam**) in proportion (as) ♦ *prep* (*with abl*) in front of, on the front of; for, on behalf of, instead of, in return for; as, as good as; according to, in proportion to, by virtue of; **~ eō ac** just as; **~ eō quod** just because; **~ eō quantum, ut** in proportion as.

prō *interj* (*expressing wonder or sorrow*) O!, alas!

proāgorus, -ī *m* chief magistrate (*in Sicilian towns*).

proavītus *adj* ancestral.

proavus, -ī *m* great-grandfather, ancestor.

probābilis *adj* laudable; credible, probable.

probābilitās, -ātis *f* credibility.

probābiliter *adv* credibly.

probātiō, -ōnis *f* approval; testing.

probātor, -ōris *m* approver.

probātus *adj* tried, excellent; acceptable.

probē *adv* well, properly; thoroughly, well done!

probitās, -ātis *f* goodness, honesty.

probō, -āre, -āvī, -ātum *vt* to approve, approve of; to appraise; to recommend; to prove, show.

probrōsus *adj* abusive; disgraceful.

probrum, -ī *nt* abuse, reproach; disgrace; infamy, unchastity.

probus *adj* good, excellent; honest, upright.

procācitās, -ātis *f* impudence.

procāciter *adv* insolently.

procāx, -ācis *adj* bold, forward, insolent.

prōcēdō, -ēdere, -essī, -essum *vi* to go forward, advance; to go out, come forth; (*time*) to go on, continue; (*fig*) to make progress, get on; (*events*) to turn out, succeed.

procella, -ae *f* hurricane, storm; (*MIL*) charge.

procellōsus *adj* stormy.

procer, -is *m* chief, noble, prince.

prōcēritās, -ātis *f* height; length.

prōcērus *adj* tall; long.

prōcessiō, -ōnis *f* advance.

prōcessus, -ūs *m* advance, progress.

prōcidō, -ere, -ī *vi* to fall forwards, fall down.

prōcinctus, -ūs *m* readiness (for action).

prōclāmātor, -ōris *m* bawler.

prōclāmō, -āre *vi* to cry out.

prōclīnātus *adj* tottering.

prōclīnō, -āre *vt* to bend.

prōclīvē *adv* downwards; easily.

prōclīvis, -us *adj* downhill, steep; (*mind*) prone, willing; (*act*) easy; **in ~ī** easy.

prōclīvitās, -ātis *f* descent; tendency.

prōclīvus *etc see* **prōclīvis.**

Procnē, -ēs *f* wife of Tereus (*changed to a swallow*); swallow.

prōcōnsul, -is *m* proconsul, governor.

prōcōnsulāris *adj* proconsular.

prōcōnsulātus, -ūs *m* proconsulship.

prōcrāstinātiō, -ōnis *f* procrastination.

prōcrāstinō, -āre *vt* to put off from day to day.

prōcreātiō, -ōnis *f* begetting.

prōcreātor, -ōris *m* creator, parent.

prōcreātrix, -īcis *f* mother.

prōcreō, -āre *vt* to beget, produce.

prōcrēscō, -ere *vi* to be produced, grow up.

Procrūstēs, -ae *m* Attic highwayman (*who tortured victims on a bed*).

prōcubō, -āre *vi* to lie on the ground.

prōcūdō, -dere, -dī, -sum *vt* to forge; to produce.

procul *adv* at a distance, far, from afar.

prōculcō, -āre *vt* to trample down.

prōcumbō, -mbere, -buī, -bitum *vi* to fall forwards, bend over; to sink down, be broken down.

prōcūrātiō, -ōnis *f* management; (*religion*) expiation.

prōcūrātor, -ōris *m* administrator, financial agent; (*province*) governor.

prōcūrātrix, -īcis *f* governess.

prōcūrō, -āre, -āvī, -ātum *vt* to take care of, manage; to expiate ♦ *vi* to be a procurator.

prōcurrō, -rrere, -currī *and* **rrī, -rsum** *vi* to rush forward; to jut out.

prōcursātiō, -ōnis *f* charge.

prōcursātor, -ōris *m* skirmisher.

prōcursō, -āre *vi* to make a sally.

prōcursus, -ūs *m* charge.

prōcurvus *adj* curving forwards.

procus, -ī *m* nobleman.

procus, -ī *m* wooer, suitor.

Procyōn, -ōnis *m* Lesser Dog Star.

prōdeambulō, -āre *vi* to go out for a walk.

prōdeō, -īre, -iī, -itum *vi* to come out, come forward, appear; to go ahead, advance; to

---

Noun declensions and verb conjugations are shown on pp xiii to xxv. The present infinitive ending of a verb shows to which conjugation it belongs: **-āre** = 1st; **-ēre** = 2nd; **-ere** = 3rd and **-īre** = 4th. Irregular verbs are shown on p xxvi

project.
prŏdesse *infin of* **prōsum**.
prŏdīcō, -īcere, -īxī, -ictum *vt* to appoint, adjourn.
prŏdictātor, -ōris *m* vice-dictator.
prŏdigē *adv* extravagantly.
prŏdigentia, -ae *f* profusion.
prŏdigiāliter *adv* unnaturally.
prōdigiōsus *adj* unnatural, marvellous.
prōdigium, -ī *and* **iī** *nt* portent; unnatural deed; monster.
prōdigō, -igere, -ēgī, -āctum *vt* to squander.
prōdigus *adj* wasteful; lavish, generous.
prōditiō, -ōnis *f* betrayal.
prōditor, -ōris *m* traitor.
prōditus *ppp of* **prōdō**.
prōdō, -ere, -idī, -itum *vt* to bring forth, produce; to make known, publish; to betray, give up; (*tradition*) to hand down.
prōdoceō, -ēre *vt* to preach.
prodromus, -ī *m* forerunner.
prōdūcō, -ūcere, -ūxī, -uctum *vt* to bring forward, bring out; to conduct; to drag in front; to draw out, extend; (*acting*) to perform; (*child*) to beget, bring up; (*fact*) to bring to light; (*innovation*) to introduce; (*rank*) to promote; (*slave*) to put up for sale; (*time*) to prolong, protract, put off; (*tree*) to cultivate; (*vowel*) to lengthen.
prōductē *adv* long.
prōductiō, -ōnis *f* lengthening.
prōductō, -āre *vt* to spin out.
prōductus *ppp of* **prōdūcō** ♦ *adj* lengthened, long.
proēgmenon, -ī *nt* a preferred thing.
proeliātor, -ōris *m* fighter.
proelior, -ārī, -ātus *vi* to fight, join battle.
proelium, -ī *and* **iī** *nt* battle, conflict.
profānō, -āre *vt* to desecrate.
profānus *adj* unholy, common; impious; ill-omened.
profātus *ppa of* **profor**.
profectiō, -ōnis *f* departure; source.
profectō *adv* really, certainly.
profectus *ppa of* **proficīscor**.
profectus *ppp of* **prōficiō**.
profectus, -ūs *m* growth, progress, profit.
prōferō, -ferre, -tulī, -lātum *vt* to bring forward, forth or out; to extend, enlarge; (*time*) to prolong, defer; (*instance*) to mention, quote; (*knowledge*) to publish, reveal; **pedem ~** proceed; **signa ~** advance.
professiō, -ōnis *f* declaration; public register; profession.
professor, -ōris *m* teacher.
professōrius *adj* authoritative.
professus *ppa of* **profiteor**.
profēstus *adj* not holiday, working.
prōficiō, -icere, -ēcī, -ectum *vi* to make progress, profit; to be of use.
proficīscor, -icīscī, -ectus *vi* to set out, start; to originate, proceed.
profiteor, -itērī, -essus *vt* to declare,

profess; to make an official return of; to promise, volunteer.
prōflīgātor, -ōris *m* spendthrift.
prōflīgātus *adj* dissolute.
prōflīgō, -āre, -āvī, -ātum *vt* to dash to the ground; to destroy, overthrow; to bring almost to an end; to degrade.
prōflō, -āre *vt* to breathe out.
prōfluēns, -entis *pres p of* **prōfluō** ♦ *adj* flowing; fluent ♦ *f* running water.
prōfluenter *adv* easily.
prōfluentia, -ae *f* fluency.
prōfluō, -ere, -xī *vi* to flow on, flow out; (*fig*) to proceed.
prōfluvium, -ī *and* **iī** *nt* flowing.
profor, -ārī, -ātus *vi* to speak, give utterance.
profugiō, -ugere, -ūgī *vi* to flee, escape; to take refuge (with) ♦ *vt* to flee from.
profugus *adj* fugitive; exiled; nomadic.
prōfui *perf of* **prōsum**.
profundō, -undere, -ūdī, -ūsum *vt* to pour out, shed; to bring forth, produce; to prostrate; to squander; **sē ~** burst forth, rush out.
profundus *adj* deep, vast, high; infernal; (*fig*) profound, immoderate ♦ *nt* depths, abyss.
profūsē *adv* in disorder, extravagantly.
profūsus *ppp of* **profundō** ♦ *adj* lavish; excessive.
prōgener, -ī *m* grandson-in-law.
prōgenerō, -āre *vt* to beget.
prōgeniēs, -ēī *f* descent; offspring, descendants.
prōgenitor, -ōris *m* ancestor.
prōgignō, -ignere, -enuī, -enitum *vt* to beget, produce.
prōgnātus *adj* born, descended ♦ *m* son, descendant.
Prognē *see* **Procnē**.
prōgnōstica, -ōrum *ntpl* weather signs.
prōgredior, -dī, -ssus *vi* to go forward, advance; to go out.
prōgressiō, -ōnis *f* advancing, increase; (*RHET*) climax.
prōgressus *ppa of* **prōgredior**.
prōgressus, -ūs *m* advance, progress; (*events*) march.
prōh *see* **prō** *interj*.
prohibeō, -ēre, -uī, -itum *vt* to hinder, prevent; to keep away, protect; to forbid.
prohibitiō, -ōnis *f* forbidding.
prōiciō, -icere, -iēcī, -iectum *vt* to throw down, fling forwards; to banish; (*building*) to make project; (*fig*) to discard, renounce; to forsake; (*words*) to blurt out; (*time*) to defer; **sē ~** rush forward, run into danger; to fall prostrate.
prōiectiō, -ōnis *f* forward stretch.
prōiectus *ppp of* **prōiciō** ♦ *adj* projecting, prominent; abject, useless; downcast; addicted (to).
prōiectus, -ūs *m* jutting out.
proinde, proin *adv* consequently, therefore;

just (as).

prōlābor, -bī, -psus *vi* to slide, move forward; to fall down; (*fig*) to go on, come to; to slip out; to fail, fall, sink into ruin.

prōlāpsiō, -ōnis *f* falling.

prōlāpsus *ppa of* **prōlābor**.

prōlātiō, -ōnis *f* extension; postponement; adducing.

prōlātō, -āre *vt* to extend; to postpone.

prōlātus *ppp of* **prōferō**.

prōlectō, -āre *vt* to entice.

prōlēs, -is *f* offspring; child; descendants, race.

prōlētārius, -ī *and* **iī** *m* citizen of the lowest class.

prōliciō, -cere, -xī *vt* to entice.

prōlixē *adv* fully, copiously, willingly.

prōlixus *adj* long, wide, spreading; (*person*) obliging; (*CIRCS*) favourable.

prōlogus, -ī *m* prologue.

prōloquor, -quī, -cūtus *vt* to speak out.

prōlubium, -ī *and* **iī** *nt* inclination.

prōlūdō, -dere, -sī, -sum *vi* to practise.

prōluō, -uere, -uī, -ūtum *vt* to wash out, wash away.

prōlūsiō, -ōnis *f* prelude.

prōluviēs, -ēī *f* flood; excrement.

prōmereō, -ēre, -uī; prōmereor, -ērī, -itus *vt* to deserve, earn.

prōmeritum, -ī *nt* desert, merit, guilt.

Promētheus, -eī *and* **eos** *m* demigod who stole fire from the gods.

Promēthēus *adj see n.*

prōminēns, -entis *pres p of* **prōmineō** ♦ *adj* projecting ♦ *nt* headland, spur.

prōmineō, -ēre, -uī *vi* to jut out, overhang; to extend.

prōmiscam, -ē, -uē *adv* indiscriminately.

prōmiscuus (prōmiscus) *adj* indiscriminate, in common; ordinary; open to all.

prōmīsī *perf of* **prōmittō**.

prōmissiō, -ōnis *f* promise.

prōmissor, -ōris *m* promiser.

prōmissum, -ī *nt* promise.

prōmissus *ppp of* **prōmittō** ♦ *adj* long.

prōmittō, -ittere, -īsī, -issum *vt* to let grow; to promise, give promise of.

prōmō, -ere, -psī, -ptum *vt* to bring out, produce; to disclose.

prōmont- *etc see* **prōmunt-**.

prōmōtus *ppp of* **prōmoveō** ♦ *ntpl* preferable things.

prōmoveō, -ovēre, -ōvī, -ōtum *vt* to move forward, advance; to enlarge; to postpone; to disclose.

prōmpsī *perf of* **prōmō**.

prōmptē *adv* readily; easily.

prōmptō, -āre *vt* to distribute.

prōmptū *abl m*: **in ~** at hand, in readiness; obvious, in evidence; easy.

prōmptus *ppp of* **prōmō** ♦ *adj* at hand, ready; prompt, resolute; easy.

prōmulgātiō, -ōnis *f* promulgating.

prōmulgō, -āre, -āvī, -ātum *vt* to make public, publish.

prōmulsis, -idis *f* hors d'oeuvre.

prōmunturium, -ī *and* **iī** *nt* headland, promontory, ridge.

prōmus, -ī *m* cellarer, butler.

prōmūtuus *adj* as a loan in advance.

prōnepōs, -ōtis *m* great-grandson.

pronoea, -ae *f* providence.

prōnōmen, -inis *nt* pronoun.

prōnuba, -ae *f* matron attending a bride.

prōnūntiātiō, -ōnis *f* declaration; (*RHET*) delivery; (*logic*) proposition.

prōnūntiātor, -ōris *m* narrator.

prōnūntiātum, -ātī *nt* proposition.

prōnūntiō, -āre, -āvī, -ātum *vt* to declare publicly, announce; to recite, deliver; to narrate; to nominate.

prōnurus, -ūs *f* granddaughter-in-law.

prōnus *adj* leaning forward; headlong, downwards; sloping, sinking; (*fig*) inclined, disposed, favourable; easy.

prooemium, -ī *and* **iī** *nt* prelude, preface.

propāgātiō, -ōnis *f* propagating; extension.

propāgātor, -ōris *m* enlarger.

propāgō, -āre, -āvī, -ātum *vt* to propagate; to extend; to prolong.

propāgō, -inis *f* (*plant*) layer, slip; (*men*) offspring, posterity.

prōpalam *adv* openly, known.

prōpatulum, -ī *nt* open space.

prōpatulus *adj* open.

prope *adv* (*comp* **propius,** *superl* **proximē**) near; nearly ♦ *prep* (*with acc*) near, not far from.

propediem *adv* very soon.

prōpellō, -ellere, -ulī, -ulsum *vt* to drive, push forward, impel; to drive away, keep off.

propemodum, -o *adv* almost.

prōpendeō, -endēre, -endī, -ēnsum *vi* to hang down; to preponderate; to be disposed (to).

prōpēnsē *adv* willingly.

prōpēnsiō, -ōnis *f* inclination.

prōpēnsus *adj* inclining; inclined, well-disposed; important.

properanter *adv* hastily, quickly.

properantia, -ae *f* haste.

properātiō, -ōnis *f* haste.

properātō *adv* quickly.

properātus *adj* speedy.

properē *adv* quickly.

properipēs, -edis *adj* swiftfooted.

properō, -āre, -āvī, -ātum *vt* to hasten, do with haste ♦ *vi* to make haste, hurry.

Propertius, -ī *m* Latin elegiac poet.

properus *adj* quick, hurrying.

Noun declensions and verb conjugations are shown on pp xiii to xxv. The present infinitive ending of a verb shows to which conjugation it belongs: **-āre** = 1st; **-ēre** = 2nd; **-ere** = 3rd and **-īre** = 4th. Irregular verbs are shown on p xxvi

prōpexus *adj* combed forward.
propīnō, -āre *vt* to drink as a toast; to pass on (a cup).
propinquitās, -ātis *f* nearness; relationship, friendship.
propinquō, -āre *vi* to approach ♦ *vt* to hasten.
propinquus *adj* near, neighbouring; related ♦ *m/f* relation ♦ *nt* neighbourhood.
propior, -ōris *adj* nearer; more closely related, more like; (*time*) more recent.
propitiō, -āre *vt* to appease.
propitius *adj* favourable, gracious.
propius *adv* nearer, more closely.
prōpōla, -ae *f* retailer.
prōpolluō, -ere *vt* to defile further.
prōpōnō, -ōnere, -osuī, -ositum *vt* to set forth, display; to publish, declare; to propose, resolve; to imagine; to expose; (*logic*) to state the first premise; **ante oculōs ~** picture to oneself.
Propontiacus *adj see n.*
Propontis, -idis *and* **idos** *f* Sea of Marmora.
prōporrō *adv* furthermore; utterly.
prōportiō, -ōnis *f* symmetry, analogy.
prōpositiō, -ōnis *f* purpose; theme; (*logic*) first premise.
prōpositum, -ī *nt* plan, purpose; theme; (*logic*) first premise.
prōpositus *ppp of* **prōpōnō**.
prōpraetor, -ōris *m* propraetor, governor; vice-praetor.
propriē *adv* properly, strictly; particularly.
proprietās, -ātis *f* peculiarity, property.
proprītim *adv* properly.
proprius *adj* one's own, peculiar; personal, characteristic; permanent; (*words*) literal, regular.
propter *adv* near by ♦ *prep* (*with acc*) near, beside; on account of; by means of.
proptereā *adv* therefore.
prōpudium, -ī *and* **iī** *nt* shameful act; villain.
prōpugnāculum, -ī *nt* bulwark, tower; defence.
prōpugnātiō, -ōnis *f* defence.
prōpugnātor, -ōris *m* defender, champion.
prōpugnō, -āre *vi* to make a sortie; to fight in defence.
prōpulsātiō, -ōnis *f* repulse.
prōpulsō, -āre, -āvī, -ātum *vt* to repel, avert.
prōpulsus *ppp of* **prōpellō**.
Propylaea, -ōrum *ntpl* gateway to the Acropolis of Athens.
prō quaestōre *m* proquaestor.
prōquam *conj* according as.
prōra, -ae *f* prow, bows; ship.
prōrēpō, -ere, -sī, -tum *vi* to crawl out.
prōrēta -ae *m* man at the prow.
prōreus, -eī *m* man at the prow.
prōripiō, -ipere, -ipuī, -eptum *vt* to drag out; to hurry away; **sē ~** rush out, run away.
prōrogātiō, -ōnis *f* extension; deferring.
prōrogō, -āre, -āvī, -ātum *vt* to extend, prolong, continue; to defer.

prōrsum *adv* forwards; absolutely.
prōrsus *adv* forwards; absolutely; in short.
prōrumpō, -umpere, -ūpī, -uptum *vt* to fling out; (*pass*) to rush forth ♦ *vi* to break out, burst forth.
prōruō, -ere, -ī, -tum *vt* to throw down, demolish ♦ *vi* to rush forth.
prōruptus *ppp of* **prōrumpō**.
prōsāpia, -ae *f* lineage.
proscaenium, -ī *and* **iī** *nt* stage.
proscindō, -ndere, -dī, -ssum *vt* to plough up; (*fig*) to revile.
prōscrībō, -bere, -psī, -ptum *vt* to publish in writing; to advertise; to confiscate; to proscribe, outlaw.
prōscrīptiō, -ōnis *f* advertisement; proscription.
prōscrīpturiō, -īre *vi* to want to have a proscription.
prōscrīptus *ppp of* **prōscrībō** ♦ *m* outlaw.
prōsecō, -āre, -uī, -tum *vt* to cut off (for sacrifice).
prōsēminō, -āre *vt* to scatter; to propagate.
prōsentiō, -entīre, -ēnsī *vt* to see beforehand.
prōsequor, -quī, -cūtus *vt* to attend, escort; to pursue, attack; to honour (with); (*words*) to proceed with, continue.
Proserpina, -ae *f* Proserpine (*daughter of Ceres and wife of Pluto*).
proseucha, -ae *f* place of prayer.
prōsiliō, -īre, -uī *vi* to jump up, spring forward; to burst out, spurt.
prōsocer, -ī *m* wife's grandfather.
prōspectō, -āre *vt* to look out at, view; to look forward to, await; (*place*) to look towards.
prōspectus *ppp of* **prōspiciō**.
prōspectus, -ūs *m* sight, view, prospect; gaze.
prōspeculor, -ārī *vi* to look out, reconnoitre ♦ *vt* to watch for.
prosper, prosperus *adj* favourable, successful.
prosperē *adv see adj.*
prosperitās, -ātis *f* good fortune.
prosperō, -āre *vt* to make successful, prosper.
prosperus *etc see* **prosper**.
prōspicientia, -ae *f* foresight.
prōspiciō, -icere, -exī, -ectum *vi* to look out, watch; to see to, take precautions ♦ *vt* to descry, watch for; to foresee; to provide; (*place*) to command a view of.
prōsternō, -ernere, -rāvī, -rātum *vt* to throw in front, prostrate; to overthrow, ruin; **sē ~** fall prostrate; to demean oneself.
prōstibulum, -ī *nt* prostitute.
prōstituō, -uere, -uī, -ūtum *vt* to put up for sale, prostitute.
prōstō, -āre, -itī *vi* to project; to be on sale; to prostitute oneself.
prōstrātus *ppp of* **prōsternō**.
prōsubigō, -ere *vt* to dig up.

prōsum, -desse, -fuī *vi* (*with dat*) to be useful to, benefit.

Prōtagorās, -ae *m* Greek sophist (*native of Abdera*).

prōtēctus *ppp of* **prōtegō**.

prōtegō, -egere, -ēxī, -ēctum *vt* to cover over, put a projecting roof on; (*fig*) to shield, protect.

prōtēlō, -āre *vt* to drive off.

prōtēlum, -ī *nt* team of oxen; (*fig*) succession.

prōtendō, -dere, -dī, -tum *vt* to stretch out, extend.

prōtentus *ppp of* **prōtendō**.

prōterō, -erere, -rīvī, -rītum *vt* to trample down, crush; to overthrow.

prōterreō, -ēre, -uī, -itum *vt* to scare away.

protervē *adv* insolently; boldly.

protervitās, -ātis *f* forwardness, insolence.

protervus *adj* forward, insolent, violent.

Prōtesilāeus *adj see n*.

Prōtesilāus, -ī *m* first Greek killed at Troy.

Prōteus, -eī *and* **eos** *m* seagod with power to assume many forms.

prothȳmē *adv* gladly.

prōtinam *adv* immediately.

prōtinus *adv* forward, onward; continuously; right away, forthwith.

prōtollō, -ere *vt* to stretch out; to put off.

prōtractus *ppp of* **prōtrahō**.

prōtrahō, -here, -xī, -ctum *vt* to draw on (to); to drag out; to bring to light, reveal.

prōtrītus *ppp of* **prōterō**.

prōtrūdō, -dere, -sī, -sum *vt* to thrust forward, push out; to postpone.

prōtulī *perf of* **prōferō**.

prōturbō, -āre, -āvī, -ātum *vt* to drive off; to overthrow.

prout *conj* according as.

prōvectus *ppp of* **prōvehō** ♦ *adj* advanced.

prōvehō, -here, -xī, -ctum *vt* to carry along, transport; to promote, advance, bring to; (*speech*) to prolong; (*pass*) to drive, ride, sail on.

prōveniō, -enīre, -ēnī, -entum *vi* to come out, appear; to arise, grow; to go on, prosper, succeed.

prōventus, -ūs *m* increase; result, success.

prōverbium, -ī *and* **iī** *nt* saying, proverb.

prōvidēns, -entis *pres p of* **prōvideō** ♦ *adj* prudent.

prōvidenter *adv* with foresight.

prōvidentia, -ae *f* foresight, forethought.

prōvideō, -idēre, -īdī, -īsum *vi* to see ahead; to take care, make provision ♦ *vt* to foresee; to look after, provide for; to obviate.

prōvidus *adj* foreseeing, cautious, prudent; provident.

prōvincia, -ae *f* sphere of action, duty, province.

prōvinciālis *adj* provincial ♦ *mpl* provincials.

prōvīsiō, -ōnis *f* foresight; precaution.

prōvīsō *adv* with forethought.

prōvīsō, -ere *vi* to go and see.

prōvīsor, -ōris *m* foreseer; provider.

prōvīsus *ppp of* **prōvideō**.

prōvīsus, -ūs *m* looking forward; foreseeing; providing providence.

prōvīvō, -vere, -xī *vi* to live on.

prōvocātiō, -ōnis *f* challenge; appeal.

prōvocātor, -ōris *m* kind of gladiator.

prōvocō, -āre, -āvī, -ātum *vt* to challenge, call out; to provoke; to bring about ♦ *vi* to appeal.

prōvolō, -āre *vi* to fly out, rush out.

prōvolvō, -vere, -vī, -ūtum *vt* to roll forward, tumble over; (*pass*) to fall down, humble oneself, be ruined; **sē ~** wallow.

prōvomō, -ere *vt* to belch forth.

proximē *adv* next, nearest; (*time*) just before or after; (*with acc*) next to, very close to, very like.

proximitās, -ātis *f* nearness; near relationship; similarity.

proximus *adj* nearest, next; (*time*) previous, last, following, next; most akin, most like ♦ *m* next of kin ♦ *nt* next door.

proxum *etc see* **proxim-**.

prūdēns, -entis *adj* foreseeing, aware; wise, prudent, circumspect; skilled, versed (in).

prūdenter *adv* prudently; skilfully.

prūdentia, -ae *f* prudence, discretion; knowledge.

pruīna, -ae *f* hoar frost.

pruīnōsus *adj* frosty.

prūna, -ae *f* live coal.

prūnitius *adj* of plum tree wood.

prūnum, -ī *nt* plum.

prūnus, -ī *f* plum tree.

prūriō, -īre *vi* to itch.

prytanēum, -ī *nt* Greek town hall.

prytanis, -is *m* Greek chief magistrate.

psallō, -ere *vi* to play the lyre *or* lute.

psaltērium, -ī *and* **iī** *nt* kind of lute.

psaltria, -ae *f* girl musician.

psecas, -adis *f* slave who perfumed the lady's hair.

psēphisma, -tis *nt* decree of the people.

Pseudocatō, -ōnis *m* sham Cato.

pseudomenos, -ī *m* sophistical argument.

pseudothyrum, -ī *nt* back door.

psithius *adj* psithian (*kind of Greek vine*).

psittacus, -ī *m* parrot.

psychomantēum (-īum), -ī *nt* place of necromancy.

-pte *enclitic* (*to pronouns*) self, own.

ptisanārium, -ī *and* **iī** *nt* gruel.

Ptolemaeēus, -us *adj see n*.

Ptolemaeus, -ī *m* Ptolemy (*name of Egyptian kings*).

pūbēns, -entis *adj* full-grown; (*plant*) juicy.

Noun declensions and verb conjugations are shown on pp xiii to xxv. The present infinitive ending of a verb shows to which conjugation it belongs: -āre = 1st; -ēre = 2nd; -ere = 3rd and -īre = 4th. Irregular verbs are shown on p xxvi

pūbertās, -ātis f manhood; signs of puberty.
pūbēs (pūber), -eris adj grown up, adult; (plant) downy.
pūbēs, -is f hair at age of puberty; groin; youth, men, people.
pūbēscō, -ēscere, -uī vi to grow to manhood, become mature; to become clothed.
pūblicānus adj of public revenue ♦ m tax farmer.
pūblicātiō, -ōnis f confiscation.
pūblicē adv by or for the State, at the public expense; all together.
pūblicitus adv at the public expense; in public.
pūblicō, -āre, -āvī, -ātum vt to confiscate; to make public.
Pūblicola, -ae m P. Valerius (an early Roman consul).
pūblicum, -ī nt State revenue; State territory; public.
pūblicus adj of the State, public, common ♦ m public official; **~a causa** criminal trial; **rēs ~a** the State; **dē ~ō** at the public expense; **in ~ō** in public.
Publius, -ī m Roman first name.
pudendus adj shameful.
pudēns, -entis adj bashful, modest.
pudenter adv modestly.
pudet, -ēre, -uit and **itum est** vt (impers) to shame, be ashamed.
pudibundus adj modest.
pudīcē adv see adj.
pudīcitia, -ae f modesty, chastity.
pudīcus adj modest, chaste.
pudor, -ōris m shame, modesty, sense of honour; disgrace.
puella, -ae f girl; sweetheart, young wife.
puellāris adj girlish, youthful.
puellula, -ae f little girl.
puellus, -ī m little boy.
puer, -ī m boy, child; son; slave.
puerīlis adj boyish, child's; childish, trivial.
puerīliter adv like a child; childishly.
pueritia, -ae f childhood, youth.
puerperium, -ī and **iī** nt childbirth.
puerperus adj to help childbirth ♦ f woman in labour.
puertia etc see **pueritia**.
puerulus, -ī m little boy, slave.
pugil, -is m boxer.
pugilātiō, -iōnis f, **-us, -ūs** m boxing.
pugillāris adj that can be held in the hand ♦ mpl, ntpl writing tablets.
pugillātōrius adj: **follis ~** punchball.
pugiō, -ōnis m dirk, dagger.
pugiunculus, -ī m small dagger.
pugna, -ae f fight, battle.
pugnācitās, -ātis f fondness for a fight.
pugnāciter adv aggressively.
pugnāculum, -ī nt fortress.
pugnātor, -ōris m fighter.
pugnāx, -ācis adj fond of a fight, aggressive; obstinate.

pugneus adj with the fist.
pugnō, -āre, -āvī, -ātum vi to fight; to disagree; to struggle; **sēcum ~** be inconsistent; **~ātum est** the battle was fought.
pugnus, -ī m fist.
pulchellus adj pretty little.
pulcher, -rī adj beautiful, handsome; fine, glorious.
pulchrē adv excellently; well done!
pulchritūdō, -inis f beauty, excellence.
pūlēium, pūlegium, -ī and **iī** nt pennyroyal.
pūlex, -icis m flea.
pullārius, -ī and **iī** m keeper of the sacred chickens.
pullātus adj dressed in black.
pullulō, -āre vi to sprout.
pullus, -ī m young (of animals), chicken.
pullus adj dark-grey; mournful ♦ nt dark grey clothes.
pulmentārium, -ārī and **-āriī, -um, -ī** nt relish; food.
pulmō, -ōnis m lung.
pulmōneus adj of the lungs.
pulpa, -ae f fleshy part.
pulpāmentum, -ī nt tit-bits.
pulpitum, -ī nt platform, stage.
puls, pultis f porridge.
pulsātiō, -ōnis f beating.
pulsō, -āre, -āvī, -ātum vt to batter, knock, strike.
pulsus ppp of **pellō**.
pulsus, -ūs m push, beat, blow; impulse.
pultiphagus, -ī m porridge eater.
pultō, -āre vt to beat, knock at.
pulvereus adj of dust, dusty, fine as dust; raising dust.
pulverulentus adj dusty; laborious.
pulvillus, -ī m small cushion.
pulvīnar, -āris nt sacred couch; seat of honour.
pulvīnus, -ī m cushion, pillow.
pulvis, -eris m dust, powder; arena; effort.
pulvisculus, -ī m fine dust.
pūmex, -icis m pumice stone; stone, rock.
pūmiceus adj of soft stone.
pūmicō, -āre vt to smooth with pumice stone.
pūmiliō, -ōnis m/f dwarf, pygmy.
pūnctim adv with the point.
pūnctum, -ī nt point, dot; vote; (time) moment; (speech) short section.
pūnctus ppp of **pungō**.
pungō, -ere, pupugī, pūnctum vt to prick, sting, pierce; (fig) to vex.
Pūnicānus adj in the Carthaginian style.
Pūnicē adv in Punic.
pūniceus adj reddish, purple.
Pūnicum, -ī nt pomegranate.
Pūnicus adj Punic, Carthaginian; purple-red.
pūniō (poeniō), -īre, -ior, -īrī vt to punish; to avenge.
pūnītor, -ōris m avenger.
pūpa, -ae f doll.

pūpilla–quadrantārius

pūpilla, -ae f ward; (eye) pupil.
pūpillāris adj of a ward, of an orphan.
pūpillus, -ī m orphan, ward.
puppis, -is f after part of a ship, stern; ship.
pupugī perf of **pungō**.
pūpula, -ae f (eye) pupil.
pūpulus, -ī m little boy.
pūrē adv cleanly, brightly; plainly, simply, purely, chastely.
pūrgāmen, -inis nt sweepings, dirt; means of expiation.
pūrgāmentum, -ī nt refuse, dirt.
pūrgātiō, -ōnis f purging; justification.
pūrgō, -āre, -āvī, -ātum vt to cleanse, purge, clear away; to exculpate, justify; to purify.
pūriter adv cleanly, purely.
purpura, -ae f purple-fish, purple; purple cloth; finery, royalty.
purpurātus adj wearing purple ♦ m courtier.
purpureus adj red, purple, black; wearing purple; bright, radiant.
purpurissum, -ī nt kind of rouge.
pūrus adj clear, unadulterated, free from obstruction or admixture; pure, clean; plain, unadorned; (moral) pure, chaste ♦ nt clear sky.
pūs, pūris nt pus; (fig) malice.
pusillus adj very little; petty, paltry.
pūsiō, -ōnis m little boy.
pūstula, -ae f pimple, blister.
putāmen, -inis nt peeling, shell, husk.
putātiō, -ōnis f pruning.
putātor, -ōris m pruner.
puteal, -ālis nt low wall round a well or sacred place.
puteālis adj well- (in cpds).
pūteō, -ēre vi to stink.
Puteolānus adj see n.
Puteolī, -ōrum mpl town on the Campanian coast.
puter, putris, -ris adj rotten, decaying; crumbling, flabby.
putēscō, -ēscere, -uī vi to become rotten.
puteus, -ī m well; pit.
pūtidē adv see **pūtidus**.
pūtidiusculus adj somewhat nauseating.
pūtidus adj rotten, stinking; (speech) affected, nauseating.
putō, -āre, -āvī, -ātum vt to think, suppose; to think over; to reckon, count; (money) to settle; (tree) to prune.
pūtor, -ōris m stench.
putrefaciō, -facere, -fēcī, -factum vt to make rotten; to make crumble.
putrēscō, -ere vi to rot, moulder.
putridus adj rotten, decayed; withered.
putris etc see **puter**.
putus adj perfectly pure.
putus, -ī m boy.
pycta, -ēs, -ae m boxer.

Pydna, -ae f town in Macedonia.
Pydnaeus adj see n.
pȳga, -ae f buttocks.
Pygmaeus adj Pygmy.
Pyladēs, -ae and **is** m friend of Orestes.
Pyladēus adj see n.
Pylae, -ārum fpl Thermopylae.
Pylaicus adj see n.
Pylius adj see n.
Pylos, -ī f Pylus (Peloponnesian town, home of Nestor).
pyra, -ae f funeral pyre.
Pȳramaeus adj see **Pȳramus**.
pȳramis, -idis f pyramid.
Pȳramus, -ī m lover of Thisbe.
Pȳrēnē, -ēs f Pyrenees.
pyrethrum, -ī nt Spanish camomile.
Pyrgēnsis adj see **Pyrgī**.
Pyrgī, -ōrum mpl ancient town in Etruria.
pyrōpus, -ī m bronze.
Pyrrha, -ae and **ē, -ēs** f wife of Deucalion.
Pyrrhaeus adj see n.
Pyrrhō, -ōnis m Greek philosopher (founder of the Sceptics).
Pyrrhōnēus adj see n.
Pyrrhus, -ī m son of Achilles; king of Epirus, enemy of Rome.
Pȳthagorās, -ae m Greek philosopher who founded a school in S. Italy.
Pȳthagorēus, -icus adj Pythagorean.
Pȳthius, -icus adj Pythian, Delphic ♦ m Apollo ♦ f priestess of Apollo ♦ ntpl Pythian Games.
Pȳthō, -ūs f Delphi.
Pȳthōn, -ōnis m serpent killed by Apollo.
pȳtisma, -tis nt what is spit out.
pȳtissō, -āre vi to spit out wine.
pyxis, -dis f small box, toilet box.

quā adv where, which way; whereby; as far as; partly ... partly.
quācumque adv wherever; anyhow.
quādam: ~ **tenus** adv only so far.
quadra, -ae f square; morsel; table.
quadrāgēnī, -ōrum adj forty each.
quadrāgēsimus adj fortieth ♦ f 2 ½ per cent tax.
quadrāgiēns, -ēs adv forty times.
quadrāgintā num forty.
quadrāns, -antis m quarter; (coin) quarter as.
quadrantārius adj of a quarter.

quadrātum, -ī nt square; (ASTRO) quadrature.
quadrātus ppp of **quadrō ♦** adj square; **~ō agmine** in battle order.
quadriduum, -ī nt four days.
quadriennium, -ī and **iī** nt four years.
quadrifāriam adv in four parts.
quadrifidus adj split in four.
quadrīgae, -ārum fpl team of four; chariot.
quadrīgārius, -ī and **iī** m chariot racer.
quadrīgātus adj stamped with a chariot.
quadrīgulae, -ārum fpl little four horse team.
quadriiugī, -ōrum mpl team of four.
quadriiugis, -us adj of a team of four.
quadrilībris adj weighing four pounds.
quadrīmulus adj four years old.
quadrīmus adj four years old.
quadringēnārius adj of four hundred each.
quadringēnī, -ōrum adj four hundred each.
quadringentēsimus adj four-hundredth.
quadringentī, -ōrum num four hundred.
quadringentiēns, -ēs adv four hundred times.
quadripertītus adj fourfold.
quadrirēmis, -is f quadrireme.
quadrivium, -ī and **iī** nt crossroads.
quadrō, -āre vt to make square; to complete ♦ vi to square, fit, agree.
quadrum, -ī nt square.
quadrupedāns, -antis adj galloping.
quadrupēs, -edis adj four-footed, on all fours ♦ m/f quadruped.
quadruplātor, -ōris m informer, twister.
quadruplex, -icis adj four-fold.
quadruplum, -ī nt four times as much.
quaeritō, -āre vt to search diligently for; to earn (a living); to keep on asking.
quaerō, -rere, -sīvī and **siī, -sītum** vt to look for, search for; to seek, try to get; to acquire, earn; (plan) to think out, work out; (question) to ask, make inquiries; (law) to investigate; (with infin) to try, wish; **quid ~ris?** in short; **sī ~ris/~rimus** to tell the truth.
quaesītiō, -ōnis f inquisition.
quaesītor, -ōris m investigator, judge.
quaesītus ppp of **quaerō ♦** adj special; far-fetched ♦ nt question ♦ ntpl gains.
quaesīvī perf of **quaerō**.
quaesō, -ere vt to ask, beg.
quaesticulus, -ī m slight profit.
quaestiō, -ōnis f seeking, questioning; investigation, research; criminal trial; court; **servum in ~ōnem ferre** take a slave for questioning by torture; **~ōnēs perpetuae** standing courts.
quaestiuncula, -ae f trifling question.
quaestor, -ōris m quaestor, treasury official.
quaestōrius adj of a quaestor ♦ m ex-quaestor ♦ nt quaestor's tent or residence.
quaestuōsus adj lucrative, productive; money-making; wealthy.
quaestūra, -ae f quaestorship; public money.
quaestus, -ūs m profit, advantage; money-making, occupation; **~uī habēre** make money

out of; **~um facere** make a living.
quālibet adv anywhere; anyhow.
quālis adj (interrog) what kind of?; (relat) such as, even as.
quāliscumque adj of whatever kind; any, whatever.
quāliscunque adj = **quāliscumque**.
quālitās, -ātis f quality, nature.
quāliter adv just as.
quālubet adv anywhere; anyhow.
quālus, -ī m wicker basket.
quam adv (interrog, excl) how?, how much?; (comparison) as, than; (with superl) as ... as possible; (emphatic) very; **dīmidium ~ quod** half of what; **quīntō diē ~** four days after.
quamdiū adv how long?; as long as.
quamlibet, quamlubet adv as much as you like, however.
quamobrem adv (interrog) why?; (relat) why ♦ conj therefore.
quamquam conj although; and yet.
quamvīs adv however, ever so ♦ conj however much, although.
quānam adv what way.
quandō adv (interrog) when?; (relat) when; (with sī, nē, num) ever ♦ conj when; since.
quandōcumque, quandocunque adv whenever, as often as; some day.
quandōque adv whenever; some day ♦ conj seeing that.
quandō quidem conj seeing that, since.
quanquam etc see **quamquam**.
quantillus adj how little, how much.
quantopere adv how much; (after **tantopere**) as.
quantulus adj how little, how small.
quantuluscumque adj however small, however trifling.
quantum adv how much; as much as; **~cumque** as much as ever; **~libet** however much; **~vīs** as much as you like; although.
quantus adj how great; so great as, such as; **~ī** how dear, how highly; **~ō** (with compar) how much; the; **in ~um** as far as.
quantuscumque adj however great, whatever size.
quantuslibet adj as great as you like.
quantus quantus adj however great.
quantusvīs adj however great.
quāpropter adv why; and therefore.
quāquā adv whatever way.
quārē adv how, why; whereby; and therefore.
quartadecumānī, -ōrum mpl men of the fourteenth legion.
quartānus adj every four days ♦ f quartan fever ♦ mpl men of the fourth legion.
quartārius, -ī and **iī** m quarter pint.
quartus adj fourth; **quartum/quartō** for the fourth time.
quartusdecimus adj fourteenth.
quasi adv as if; as it were; (numbers) about.
quasillus, -ī m, **-um, -ī** nt wool basket.
quassātiō, -ōnis f shaking.

quassō, -āre, -āvī, -ātum *vt* to shake, toss; to shatter, damage.

quassus *ppp of* **quatiō** ♦ *adj* broken.

quatefaciō, -facere, -fēcī *vt* to shake, give a jolt to.

quātenus *adv* (*interrog*) how far?; how long?; (*relat*) as far as; in so far as, since.

quater *adv* four times; ~ **deciēs** fourteen times.

quaternī, -ōrum *adj* four each, in fours.

quatiō, -tere, -ssum *vt* to shake, disturb, brandish; to strike, shatter; (*fig*) to agitate, harass.

quattuor *num* four.

quattuordecim *num* fourteen.

quattuorvirātus, -ūs *m* membership of quattuorvirī.

quattuorvirī, -ōrum *mpl* board of four officials.

-que *conj* and; both ... and; (*after neg*) but.

quemadmodum *adv* (*interrog*) how?; (*relat*) just as.

queō, -īre, -īvī *and* **iī, -itum** *vi* to be able, can.

quercētum, -ī *nt* oak forest.

querceus *adj* of oak.

quercus, -ūs *f* oak; garland of oak leaves; acorn.

querēla, querella, -ae *f* complaint; plaintive sound.

queribundus *adj* complaining.

querimōnia, -ae *f* complaint; elegy.

queritor, -ārī *vi* to complain much.

quernus *adj* oak- (*in cpds*).

queror, -rī, -stus *vt, vi* to complain, lament; (*birds*) to sing.

querquetulānus *adj* of oakwoods.

querulus *adj* complaining; plaintive, warbling.

questus *ppa of* **queror**.

questus, -ūs *m* complaint, lament.

quī, quae, quod *pron* (*interrog*) what?, which?; (*relat*) who, which, that; what; and this, he, etc.; (*with* **sī, nisi, nē, num**) any.

quī *adv* (*interrog*) how?; (*relat*) with which, whereby; (*indef*) somehow; (*excl*) indeed.

quia *conj* because; ~**nam** why?

quicquam *nt see* **quisquam**.

quicque *nt see* **quisque**.

quicquid *nt see* **quisquis**.

quīcum with whom, with which.

quīcumque, quīcunque *pron* whoever, whatever, all that; every possible.

quid *nt see* **quis** ♦ *adv* why?

quīdam, quaedam, quoddam *pron* a certain, a sort of, a ....

quiddam *nt* something.

quidem *adv* (*emphatic*) in fact; (*qualifying*) at any rate; (*conceding*) it is true; (*alluding*) for instance; **nē ... ~** not even.

quidlibet *nt* anything.

quidnam *nt see* **quisnam**.

quidnī *adv* why not?

quidpiam *nt* = **quispiam**.

quidquam *nt* = **quisquam**.

quidquid *nt* = **quisquis**.

quiēs, -ētis *f* rest, peace, quiet; sleep, dream, death; neutrality; lair.

quiēscō, -scere, -vī, -tum *vi* to rest, keep quiet; to be at peace, keep neutral; to sleep; (*with acc and infin*) to stand by and see; (*with infin*) to cease.

quiētē *adv* peacefully, quietly.

quiētus *ppa of* **quiēscō** ♦ *adj* at rest; peaceful, neutral; calm, quiet, asleep.

quīlibet, quaelibet, quodlibet *pron* any, anyone at all.

quīn *adv* (*interrog*) why not?; (*correcting*) indeed, rather ♦ *conj* who not; but that, but, without; (*preventing*) from; (*doubting*) that.

quīnam, quaenam, quodnam *pron* which?, what?

Quīnct- *etc see* **Quīnt-**.

quīncunx, -uncis *m* five-twelfths; number five on a dice; **in ~uncem dispositī** arranged in oblique lines.

quīndeciēns, -ēs *adv* fifteen times.

quīndecim *num* fifteen; ~ **prīmī** fifteen chief magistrates.

quīndecimvirālis *adj* of the council of fifteen.

quīndecimvirī, -ōrum *mpl* council of fifteen.

quīngēnī, -ōrum *adj* five hundred each.

quīngentēsimus *adj* five-hundredth.

quīngentī, -ōrum *num* five hundred.

quīngentiēns, -ēs *adv* five hundred times.

quīnī, -ōrum *adj* five each; five; ~ **dēnī** fifteen each; ~ **vīcēnī** twenty-five each.

quīnquāgēnī, -ōrum *adj* fifty each.

quīnquāgēsimus *adj* fiftieth ♦ *f* 2 per cent tax.

quīnquāgintā *num* fifty.

Quīnquātria, -iōrum *and* **ium** *ntpl* festival of Minerva.

Quīnquātrūs, -uum *fpl* festival of Minerva.

quīnque *num* five.

quīnquennālis *adj* quinquennial; lasting five years.

quīnquennis *adj* five years old; quinquennial.

quīnquennium, -ī *and* **iī** *nt* five years.

quīnquepartītus *adj* fivefold.

quīnqueprīmī, -ōrum *mpl* five leading men.

quīnquerēmis *adj* five-banked ♦ *f* quinquereme.

quīnquevirātus, -ūs *m* membership of the board of five.

quīnquevirī, -ōrum *mpl* board of five.

quīnquiēns, -ēs *adv* five times.

quīnquiplicō, -āre *vt* to multiply by five.

quīntadecimānī, -ōrum *mpl* men of the fifteenth legion.

quīntānus *adj* of the fifth ♦ *f* street in a camp

Noun declensions and verb conjugations are shown on pp xiii to xxv. The present infinitive ending of a verb shows to which conjugation it belongs: **-āre** = 1st; **-ēre** = 2nd; **-ere** = 3rd and **-īre** = 4th. Irregular verbs are shown on p xxvi

between the 5th and 6th maniples ♦ *mpl* men of the fifth legion.

Quīntiliānus, -ī *m* Quintilian (*famous teacher of rhetoric in Rome*).

Quīntīlis *adj* of July.

quīntum, -ō *adv* for the fifth time.

Quīntus, -ī *m* Roman first name.

quīntus *adj* fifth.

quīntusdecimus *adj* fifteenth.

quippe *adv* (*affirming*) certainly, of course ♦ *conj* (*explaining*) for in fact, because, since; ~ **quī** since I, he *etc.*

quippiam *etc see* **quispiam**.

quippinī *adv* certainly.

Quirīnālis *adj* of Romulus; Quirinal (hill).

Quirīnus, -ī *m* Romulus ♦ *adj* of Romulus.

Quirīs, -ītis *m* inhabitant of *Cures*; Roman citizen; citizen.

quirītātiō, -ōnis *f* shriek.

Quirītēs *pl* inhabitants of *Cures*; Roman citizens.

quirītō, -āre *vi* to cry out, wail.

quis, quid *pron* who?, what?; (*indef*) anyone, anything.

quīs *poetic form of* **quibus**.

quisnam, quaenam, quidnam *pron* who?, what?

quispiam, quaepiam, quodpiam *and* **quidpiam** *pron* some, some one, something.

quisquam, quaequam, quicquam *and* **quidquam** *pron* any, anyone, anything; **nec ~** and no one.

quisque, quaeque, quodque *pron* each, every, every one; **quidque, quicque** everything; **decimus ~** every tenth; **optimus ~** all the best; **prīmus ~** the first possible.

quisquiliae, -ārum *fpl* refuse, rubbish.

quisquis, quaequae, quodquod, quidquid *and* **quicquid** *pron* whoever, whatever, all.

quīvīs, quaevīs, quodvīs, quidvīs *pron* any you please, anyone, anything.

quīvīscumque, quaevīscumque, quodvīscumque *pron* any whatsoever.

quō *adv* (*interrog*) where?; whither?; for what purpose?, what for?; (*relat*) where, to which (place), to whom; (*with compar*) the (more); (*with sī*) anywhere ♦ *conj* (*with subj*) in order that; **nōn ~** not that.

quoad *adv* how far?; how long? ♦ *conj* as far as, as long as; until.

quōcircā *conj* therefore.

quōcumque *adv* whithersoever.

quod *conj* as for, in that, that; because; why; **~ sī** but if.

quōdam modo *adv* in a way.

quoi, quōius *old forms of* **cui, cūius**.

quōlibet *adv* anywhere, in any direction.

quom *etc see* **cum** *conj*.

quōminus *conj* that not; (*preventing*) from.

quōmodo *adv* (*interrog*) how?; (*relat*) just as; **~cumque** howsoever; **~nam** how?

quōnam *adv* where, where to?

quondam *adv* once, formerly; sometimes;

(*fut*) one day.

quoniam *conj* since, seeing that.

quōpiam *adv* anywhere.

quōquam *adv* anywhere.

quoque *adv* also, too.

quōquō *adv* to whatever place, wherever.

quōquō modo *adv* howsoever.

quōquō versus, -um *adv* in every direction.

quōrsus, quōrsum *adv* where to?, in what direction?; what for?, to what end?

quot *adj* how many; as many as, every.

quotannīs *adv* every year.

quotcumque *adj* however many.

quotēnī, -ōrum *adj* how many.

quotīd- *etc see* **cottīd-**.

quotiēns, -ēs *adv* how often?; (*relat*) as often as.

quotiēnscumque *adv* however often.

quotquot *adj* however many.

quotumus *adj* which number?, what date?.

quotus *adj* what number, how many; **~ quisque** how few; **~a hōra** what time.

quotuscumque *adj* whatever number, however big.

quōusque *adv* how long, till when; how far.

quōvīs *adv* anywhere.

quum *etc see* **cum** *conj*.

R, r

rabidē *adv* furiously.

rabidus *adj* raving, mad; impetuous.

rabiēs, -em, -ē *f* madness, rage, fury.

rabiō, -ere *vi* to rave.

rabiōsē *adv* wildly.

rabiōsulus *adj* somewhat rabid.

rabiōsus *adj* furious, mad.

rabula, -ae *m* wrangling lawyer.

racēmifer, -ī *adj* clustered.

racēmus, -ī *m* stalk of a cluster; bunch of grapes; grape.

radiātus *adj* radiant.

rādīcitus *adv* by the roots; utterly.

rādīcula, -ae *f* small root.

radiō, -āre *vt* to irradiate ♦ *vi* to radiate, shine.

radius, -ī *and* **iī** *m* stick, rod; (*light*) beam, ray; (*loom*) shuttle; (*MATH*) rod for drawing figures, radius of a circle; (*plant*) long olive; (*wheel*) spoke.

rādīx, -īcis *f* root; radish; (*hill*) foot; (*fig*) foundation, origin.

rādō, -dere, -sī, -sum *vt* to scrape, shave, scratch; to erase; to touch in passing, graze, pass along.

raeda, -ae *f* four-wheeled carriage.

raedārius, -ī *and* **iī** *m* driver.

Raetī, -ōrum *mpl* Alpine people between Italy and Germany.

Raetia, -iae *f* country of the Raetī.

Raeticus *and* **ius** *and* **us** *adj see n.*

rāmālia, -ium *ntpl* twigs, brushwood.

rāmentum, -ī *nt* shavings, chips.

rāmeus *adj* of branches.

rāmex, -icis *m* rupture, blood vessels of the lungs.

Ramnēnsēs, Ramnēs, -ium *mpl* one of the original Roman tribes; a century of equites.

rāmōsus *adj* branching.

rāmulus, -ī *m* twig, sprig.

rāmus, -ī *m* branch, bough.

rāna, -ae *f* frog; frogfish.

rancēns, -entis *adj* putrid.

rancidulus *adj* rancid.

rancidus *adj* rank, rancid; disgusting.

rānunculus, -ī *m* tadpole.

rapācida, -ae *m* son of a thief.

rapācitās, -ātis *f* greed.

rapāx, -ācis *adj* greedy, grasping, ravenous.

raphanus, -ī *m* radish.

rapidē *adv* swiftly, hurriedly.

rapiditās, -ātis *f* rapidity.

rapidus *adj* tearing, devouring; swift, rapid; hasty, impetuous.

rapīna, -ae *f* pillage, robbery; booty, prey.

rapiō, -ere, -uī, -tum *vt* to tear, snatch, carry off; to seize, plunder; to hurry, seize quickly.

raptim *adv* hastily, violently.

raptiō, -ōnis *f* abduction.

raptō, -āre, -āvī, -ātum *vt* to seize and carry off, drag away, move quickly; to plunder, lay waste; (*passion*) to agitate.

raptor, -ōris *m* plunderer, robber, ravisher.

raptus *ppp of* **rapiō** ♦ *nt* plunder.

raptus, -ūs *m* carrying off, abduction; plundering.

rāpulum, -ī *nt* small turnip.

rāpum, -ī *nt* turnip.

rārēfaciō, -facere, -fēcī, -factum (*pass* -fīō, -fierī) *vt* to rarefy.

rārēscō, -ere *vi* to become rarefied, grow thin; to open out.

rāritās, -ātis *f* porousness, open texture; thinness, fewness.

rārō, -ē *adv* seldom.

rārus *adj* porous, open in texture; thin, scanty; scattered, straggling, here and there; (*MIL*) in open order; few, infrequent; uncommon, rare.

rāsī *perf of* **rādō**.

rāsilis *adj* smooth, polished.

rāstrum, -ī *nt* hoe, mattock.

rāsus *ppp of* **rādō**.

ratiō, -ōnis *f* 1. (*reckoning of*) account, calculation; list, register; affair, business.

2. (*relation*) respect, consideration; procedure, method, system, way, kind. 3. (*reason*) reasoning, thought; cause, motive; science, knowledge, philosophy; ~ atque ūsus theory and practice; ~ est it is reasonable; Stōicōrum ~ Stoicism; ~ōnem dūcere, inīre calculate; ~ōnem habēre take account of, have to do with, consider; ~ōnem reddere give an account of; cum ~ōne reasonably; meae ~ōnēs my interests; ā ~ōnibus accountant.

ratiōcinātiō, -ōnis *f* reasoning; syllogism.

ratiōcinātīvus *adj* syllogistic.

ratiōcinātor, -ōris *m* accountant.

ratiōcinor, -ārī, -ātus *vt, vi* to calculate; to consider; to argue, infer.

ratiōnālis *adj* rational; syllogistic.

ratis, -is *f* raft; boat.

ratiuncula, -ae *f* small calculation; slight reason; petty syllogism.

ratus *ppa of* **reor** ♦ *adj* fixed, settled, sure; valid; prō ~ā (parte) proportionally; ~um dūcere, facere, habēre ratify.

raucisonus *adj* hoarse.

raucus *adj* hoarse; harsh, strident.

raudus, -eris *nt* copper coin.

raudusculum, -ī *nt* bit of money.

Ravenna, -ae *f* port in N.E. Italy.

Ravennās, -ātis *adj see n.*

rāvis, -im *f* hoarseness.

rāvus *adj* grey, tawny.

rea, -ae *f* defendant, culprit.

rēapse *adv* in fact, actually.

Reāte, -is *nt* ancient Sabine town.

Reātīnus *adj see n.*

rebellātiō, -ōnis *f* revolt.

rebellātrīx, -īcis *f* rebellious.

rebelliō, -ōnis *f* revolt.

rebellis *adj* rebellious ♦ *mpl* rebels.

rebellium, -ī *and* **iī** *nt* revolt.

rebellō, -āre *vi* to revolt.

rebītō, -ere *vi* to return.

reboō, -āre *vi* to re-echo ♦ *vt* to make resound.

recalcitrō, -āre *vi* to kick back.

recaleō, -ēre *vi* to be warm again.

recalēscō, -ere *vi* to grow warm again.

recalfaciō, -facere, -fēcī *vt* to warm again.

recalvus *adj* bald in front.

recandēscō, -ēscere, -uī *vi* to whiten (*in response to*); to glow.

recantō, -āre, -āvī, -ātum *vt* to recant; to charm away.

reccidī *perf of* **recidō**.

recēdō, -ēdere, -essī, -essum *vi* to move back, withdraw, depart; (*place*) to recede; (*head*) to be severed.

recellō, -ere *vi* to spring back.

recēns, -entis *adj* fresh, young, recent; (*writer*) modern; (*with ab*) immediately after ♦ *adv* newly, just.

Noun declensions and verb conjugations are shown on pp xiii to xxv. The present infinitive ending of a verb shows to which conjugation it belongs: **-āre** = 1st; **-ēre** = 2nd; **-ere** = 3rd and **-īre** = 4th. Irregular verbs are shown on p xxvi

recēnseō, -ēre, -uī, -um vt to count; to review.
recēnsiō, -ōnis f revision.
recēnsus ppp of **recēnseō**.
recēpī perf of **recipiō**.
receptāculum, -ī nt receptacle, reservoir; refuge, shelter.
receptō, -āre vt to take back; to admit, harbour; to tug hard at.
receptor, -ōris m (male) receiver, shelterer.
receptrīx, -īcis f (female) receiver, shelterer.
receptum, -ī nt obligation.
receptus ppp of **recipiō**.
receptus, -ūs m withdrawal; retreat; return; refuge; ~uī canere sound the retreat.
recessī perf of **recēdō**.
recessim adv backwards.
recessus, -ūs m retreat, departure; recess, secluded spot; (tide) ebb.
recidīvus adj resurrected; recurring.
recidō, -idere, -cidī, -āsum vi to fall back; to recoil, relapse; (fig) to fall, descend.
recīdō, -dere, -dī, -sum vt to cut back, cut off.
recingō, -gere, -ctum vt to ungird, loose.
recinō, -ere vt, vi to re-echo, repeat; to sound a warning.
reciper- etc see **recuper-**.
recipiō, -ipere, -ēpī, -eptum vt to take back, retake; to get back, regain, rescue; to accept, admit; (MIL) to occupy; (duty) to undertake; (promise) to pledge, guarantee; sē ~ withdraw, retreat; nōmen ~ receive notice of a prosecution.
reciprocō, -āre vt to move to and fro; (ship) to bring round to another tack; (proposition) to reverse ♦ vi (tide) to rise and fall.
reciprocus adj ebbing.
recīsus ppp of **recīdō**.
recitātiō, -ōnis f reading aloud, recital.
recitātor, -ōris m reader, reciter.
recitō, -āre, -āvī, -ātum vt to read out, recite.
reclāmātiō, -ōnis f outcry (of disapproval).
reclāmitō, -āre vi to cry out against.
reclāmō, -āre vi to cry out, protest; to reverberate.
reclīnis adj leaning back.
reclīnō, -āre, -āvī, -ātum vt to lean back.
reclūdō, -dere, -sī, -sum vt to open up; to disclose.
reclūsus ppp of **reclūdō**.
recoctus ppp of **recoquō**.
recōgitō, -āre vi to think over, reflect.
recognitiō, -ōnis f review.
recognōscō, -ōscere, -ōvī, -itum vt to recollect; to examine, review.
recolligō, -igere, -ēgī, -ēctum vt to gather up; (fig) to recover, reconcile.
recolō, -olere, -oluī, -ultum vt to recultivate; to resume; to reflect on, contemplate; to revisit.
recomminīscor, -ī vi to recollect.

recompositus adj rearranged.
reconciliātiō, -ōnis f restoration, reconciliation.
reconciliō, -āre, -āvī, -ātum vt to win back again, restore, reconcile.
reconcinnō, -āre vt to repair.
reconditus ppp of **recondō** ♦ adj hidden, secluded; abstruse, profound; (disposition) reserved.
recondō, -ere, -idī, -itum vt to store away, stow; to hide away, bury.
reconflō, -āre vt to rekindle.
recoquō, -quere, -xī, -ctum vt to cook again, boil again; to forge again, recast; (fig) to rejuvenate.
recordātiō, -ōnis f recollection.
recordor, -ārī, -ātus vt, vi to recall, remember; to ponder over.
recreō, -āre, -āvī, -ātum vt to remake, reproduce; to revive, refresh.
recrepō, -āre vt, vi to ring, re-echo.
recrēscō, -scere, -vī vi to grow again.
recrūdēscō, -ēscere, -uī vi (wound) to open again; (war) to break out again.
rēctā adv straight forward, right on.
rēctē adv straight; correctly, properly, well; quite; (inf) good, all right, no thank you.
rēctiō, -ōnis f government.
rēctor, -ōris m guide, driver, helmsman; governor, master.
rēctum, -ī nt right, virtue.
rēctus ppp of **regō** ♦ adj straight; upright, steep; right, correct, proper; (moral) good, virtuous.
recubō, -āre vi to lie, recline.
recultus ppp of **recolō**.
recumbō, -mbere, -buī vi to lie down, recline; to fall, sink down.
recuperātiō, -ōnis f recovery.
recuperātor, -ōris m recapturer; (pl) board of justices who tried civil cases requiring a quick decision, esp cases involving foreigners.
recuperātōrius adj of the recuperatores.
recuperō, -āre, -āvī, -ātum vt to get back, recover, recapture.
recūrō, -āre vt to restore.
recurrō, -ere, -ī vi to run back; to return, recur; to revert.
recursō, -āre vi to keep coming back, keep recurring.
recursus, -ūs m return, retreat.
recurvō, -āre vt to bend back, curve.
recurvus adj bent, curved.
recūsātiō, -ōnis f refusal, declining; (law) objection, counterplea.
recūsō, -āre, -āvī, -ātum vt to refuse, decline, be reluctant; (law) to object, plead in defence.
recussus adj reverberating.
redāctus ppp of **redigō**.
redambulō, -āre vi to come back.
redamō, -āre vt to love in return.
redārdēscō, -ere vi to blaze up again.

redarguō, -ere, -ī *vt* to refute, contradict.
redauspicō, -āre *vi* to take auspices for going back.
redditus *ppp of* **reddō**.
reddō, -ere, -idī, -itum *vt* to give back, return, restore; to give in, response, repay; to give up, deliver, pay; (*copy*) to represent, reproduce; (*speech*) to report, repeat, recite, reply; to translate; (*with adj*) to make; **iūdicium** ~ fix the date for a trial; **iūs** ~ administer justice.
redēgī *perf of* **redigō**.
redēmī *perf of* **redimō**.
redemptiō, -ōnis *f* ransoming; bribing; (*revenue*) farming.
redemptō, -āre *vt* to ransom.
redemptor, -ōris *m* contractor.
redemptūra, -ae *f* contracting.
redemptus *ppp of* **redimō**.
redeō, -īre, -iī, -itum *vi* to go back, come back, return; (*speech*) to revert; (*money*) to come in; (*CIRCS*) to be reduced to, come to.
redhālō, -āre *vt* to exhale.
redhibeō, -ēre *vt* to take back.
redigō, -igere, -ēgī, -āctum *vt* to drive back, bring back; (*money*) to collect, raise; (*to a condition*) to reduce, bring; (*number*) to reduce; **ad irritum** ~ make useless.
rediī *perf of* **redeō**.
redimīculum, -ī *nt* band.
redimiō, -īre, -iī, -ītum *vt* to bind, crown, encircle.
redimō, -imere, -ēmī, -emptum *vt* to buy back; to ransom, redeem; to release, rescue; (*good*) to procure; (*evil*) to avert; (*fault*) to make amends for; (*COMM*) to undertake by contract, hire.
redintegrō, -āre, -āvī, -ātum *vt* to restore, renew, refresh.
redipīscor, -ī *vt* to get back.
reditiō, -ōnis *f* returning.
reditus, -ūs *m* return, returning; (*money*) revenue.
redivīvus *adj* renovated.
redoleō, -ēre, -uī *vi* to give out a smell ♦ *vt* to smell of, smack of.
redomitus *adj* broken in again.
redōnō, -āre *vt* to restore; to give up.
redūcō, -ūcere, -ūxī, -uctum *vt* to draw back; to lead back, bring back; to escort home; to marry again; (*troops*) to withdraw; (*fig*) to restore; (*to a condition*) to make into.
reductiō, -ōnis *f* restoration.
reductor, -ōris *m* man who brings back.
reductus *ppp of* **redūcō** ♦ *adj* secluded, aloof.
reduncus *adj* curved back.
redundantia, -ae *f* extravagance.
redundō, -āre, -āvī, -ātum *vi* to overflow; to abound, be in excess; (*fig*) to stream.
reduvia, -ae *f* hangnail.

redux, -cis *adj* (*gods*) who brings back; (*men*) brought back, returned.
refectus *ppp of* **reficiō**.
refellō, -ere, -ī *vt* to disprove, rebut.
referciō, -cīre, -sī, -tum *vt* to stuff, cram, choke full.
referiō, -īre *vt* to hit back; to reflect.
referō, -ferre, -ttulī, -lātum *vt* to bring back, carry back; to give back, pay back, repay; to repeat, renew; (*authority*) to refer to, trace back to; (*blame, credit*) to ascribe; (*likeness*) to reproduce, resemble; (*memory*) to recall; (*news*) to report, mention; (*opinion*) to reckon amongst; (*record*) to enter; (*senate*) to lay before, move; (*speech*) to reply, say in answer; **grātiam** ~ be grateful, requite; **pedem, gradum** ~ return; retreat; **ratiōnēs** ~ present an account; **sē** ~ return.
rēfert, -ferre, -tulit *vi* (*impers*) it is of importance, it matters, it concerns; **meā** ~ it matters to me.
refertus *ppp of* **referciō** ♦ *adj* crammed, full.
referveō, -ēre *vi* to boil over.
refervēscō, -ere *vi* to bubble up.
reficiō, -icere, -ēcī, -ectum *vt* to repair, restore; (*body, mind*) to refresh, revive; (*money*) to get back, get in return; (*POL*) to re-elect.
refīgō, -gere, -xī, -xum *vt* to unfasten, take down; (*fig*) to annul.
refingō, -ere *vt* to remake.
refixus *ppp of* **refīgō**.
reflāgitō, -āre *vt* to demand back.
reflātus, -ūs *m* contrary wind.
reflectō, -ctere, -xī, -xum *vt* to bend back, turn back; (*fig*) to bring back ♦ *vi* to give way.
reflexus *ppp of* **reflectō**.
reflō, -āre, -āvī, -ātum *vi* to blow contrary ♦ *vt* to breathe out again.
refluō, -ere *vi* to flow back, overflow.
refluus *adj* ebbing.
reformīdō, -āre *vt* to dread; to shun in fear.
reformō, -āre *vt* to reshape.
refōtus *ppp of* **refoveō**.
refoveō, -ovēre, -ōvī, -ōtum *vt* to refresh, revive.
refrāctāriolus *adj* rather stubborn.
refrāctus *ppp of* **refringō**.
refrāgor, -ārī, -ātus *vi* (*with dat*) to oppose, thwart.
refrēgī *perf of* **refringō**.
refrēnō, -āre *vt* to curb, restrain.
refricō, -āre, -uī, -ātum *vt* to scratch open; to reopen, renew ♦ *vi* to break out again.
refrīgerātiō, -ōnis *f* coolness.
refrīgerō, -āre, -āvī, -ātum *vi* to cool, cool off; (*fig*) to flag.
refrīgēscō, -gēscere, -xī *vi* to grow cold; (*fig*) to flag, grow stale.

Noun declensions and verb conjugations are shown on pp xiii to xxv. The present infinitive ending of a verb shows to which conjugation it belongs: **-āre** = 1st; **-ēre** = 2nd; **-ere** = 3rd and **-īre** = 4th. Irregular verbs are shown on p xxvi

refringō, -ingere, -ēgī, -āctum *vt* to break open; to break off; (*fig*) to break, check.
refrīxī *perf of* **refrīgēscō**.
refugiō, -ugere, -ūgī *vi* to run back, flee, shrink ♦ *vt* to run away from, shun.
refugium, -ī *and* **iī** *nt* refuge.
refugus *adj* fugitive, receding.
refulgeō, -gēre, -sī *vi* to flash back, reflect light.
refundō, -undere, -ūdī, -ūsum *vt* to pour back, pour out; (*pass*) to overflow.
refūsus *ppp of* **refundō**.
refūtātiō, -ōnis *f* refutation.
refūtātus, -ūs *m* refutation.
refūtō, -āre, -āvī, -ātum *vt* to check, repress; to refute, disprove.
rēgālis *adj* king's, royal, regal.
rēgāliter *adv* magnificently; tyrannically.
regerō, -rere, -ssī, -stum *vt* to carry back, throw back.
rēgia, -ae *f* palace; court; (*camp*) royal tent; (*town*) capital.
rēgiē *adv* regally; imperiously.
rēgificus *adj* magnificent.
regignō, -ere *vt* to reproduce.
Rēgillānus *and* **ēnsis** *adj see* **Rēgillus**.
Rēgillus, -ī *m* Sabine town; lake in Latium (*scene of a Roman victory over the Latins*).
regimen, -inis *nt* guiding, steering; rudder; rule, command, government; ruler.
rēgīna, -ae *f* queen, noblewoman.
Rēgīnus *adj see* **Rēgium**.
regiō, -ōnis *f* direction, line; boundary line; quarter, region; district, ward, territory; (*fig*) sphere, province; ē ~ōne in a straight line; (*with gen*) exactly opposite.
regiōnātim *adv* by districts.
Rēgium, -ī *and* **iī** *nt* town in extreme S. of Italy, (*now* Reggio).
rēgius *adj* king's, kingly, royal, princely, magnificent.
reglūtinō, -āre *vt* to unstick.
rēgnātor, -ōris *m* ruler.
rēgnātrīx, -īcis *adj* imperial.
rēgnō, -āre, -āvī, -ātum *vi* to be king, rule, reign; to be supreme, lord it; (*things*) to prevail, predominate ♦ *vt* to rule over.
rēgnum, -ī *nt* kingship, monarchy; sovereignty, supremacy; despotism; kingdom; domain.
regō, -ere, rēxī, rēctum *vt* to keep straight, guide, steer; to manage, direct; to control, rule, govern; ~ fīnēs (*law*) mark out the limits.
regredior, -dī, -ssus *vi* to go back, come back, return; (*MIL*) to retire.
regressus *ppa of* **regredior**.
regressus, -ūs *m* return; retreat.
rēgula, -ae *f* rule, ruler; stick, board; (*fig*) rule, pattern, standard.
rēgulus, -ī *m* petty king, chieftain; prince.
Rēgulus, -ī *m* Roman consul taken prisoner by the Carthaginians.

regustō, -āre *vt* to taste again.
rēiciō, -icere, -iēcī, -iectum *vt* to throw back, throw over the shoulder, throw off; to drive back, repel; to cast off, reject; to reject with contempt, scorn; (*jurymen*) to challenge, refuse; (*matter for discussion*) to refer; (*time*) to postpone; sē ~ fling oneself.
rēiectāneus *adj* to be rejected.
rēiectiō, -ōnis *f* rejection; (*law*) challenging.
rēiectō, -āre *vt* to throw back.
rēiectus *ppp of* **rēiciō**.
relābor, -bī, -psus *vi* to glide back, sink back, fall back.
relanguēscō, -ēscere, -ī *vi* to faint; to weaken.
relātiō, -ōnis *f* (*law*) retorting; (*pl*) magistrate's report; (*RHET*) repetition.
relātor, -ōris *m* proposer of a motion.
relātus *ppp of* **referō**.
relātus, -ūs *m* official report; recital.
relaxātiō, -ōnis *f* easing.
relaxō, -āre, -āvī, -ātum *vt* to loosen, open out; (*fig*) to release, ease, relax, cheer.
relēctus *ppp of* **relegō**.
relēgātiō, -ōnis *f* banishment.
relēgō, -āre, -āvī, -ātum *vt* to send away, send out of the way; to banish; (*fig*) to reject; to refer, ascribe.
relegō, -egere, -ēgī, -ēctum *vt* to gather up; (*place*) to traverse, sail over again; (*speech*) to go over again, reread.
relentēscō, -ere *vi* to slacken off.
relēvī *perf of* **relinō**.
relevō, -āre, -āvī, -ātum *vt* to lift up; to lighten; (*fig*) to relieve, ease, comfort.
relictiō, -ōnis *f* abandoning.
relictus *ppp of* **relinquō**.
relicuus *etc see* **reliquus**.
religātiō, -ōnis *f* tying up.
religiō, -ōnis *f* religious scruple, reverence, awe; religion; superstition; scruples, conscientiousness; holiness, sanctity (*in anything*); object of veneration, sacred place; religious ceremony, observance.
religiōsē *adv* devoutly; scrupulously, conscientiously.
religiōsus *adj* devout, religious; superstitious; involving religious difficulty; scrupulous, conscientious; (*objects*) holy, sacred.
religō, -āre, -āvī, -ātum *vt* to tie up, fasten behind; (*ship*) to make fast, moor; (*fig*) to bind.
relinō, -inere, -ēvī *vt* to unseal.
relinquō, -inquere, -īquī, -ictum *vt* to leave, leave behind; to bequeath; to abandon, forsake; (*argument*) to allow; (*pass*) to remain.
rēliquiae, -ārum *fpl* leavings, remainder, relics.
reliquus *adj* remaining, left; (*time*) subsequent, future; (*debt*) outstanding ♦ *nt* remainder, rest; arrears ♦ *mpl* the rest; ~um est it remains, the next point is; ~ī facere

leave behind, leave over, omit; **in ~um** for the future.
rell- *etc see* **rel-**.
relūceō, -cēre, -xī *vi* to blaze.
relūcēscō, -cēscere, -xī *vi* to become bright again.
reluctor, -ārī, -ātus *vi* to struggle against, resist.
remaneō, -anēre, -ānsī *vi* to remain behind; to remain, continue, endure.
remānō, -āre *vi* to flow back.
remānsiō, -ōnis *f* remaining behind.
remedium, -ī *and* **iī** *nt* cure, remedy, medicine.
remēnsus *ppa of* **remētior**.
remeō, -āre *vi* to come back, go back, return.
remētior, -tīrī, -nsus *vt* to measure again; to go back over.
rēmex, -igis *m* rower, oarsman.
Rēmī, -ōrum *mpl* people of Gaul (*in region of what is now* Rheims).
rēmigātiō, -ōnis *f* rowing.
rēmigium, -ī *and* **iī** *nt* rowing; oars; oarsmen.
rēmigō, -āre *vi* to row.
remigrō, -āre *vi* to move back, return (home).
reminīscor, -ī *vt, vi* (*usu with gen*) to remember, call to mind.
remisceō, -scēre, -xtum *vt* to mix up, mingle.
remissē *adv* mildly, gently.
remissiō, -ōnis *f* release; (*tension*) slackening, relaxing; (*payment*) remission; (*mind*) slackness, mildness, relaxation; (*illness*) abating.
remissus *ppp of* **remittō** ♦ *adj* slack; negligent; mild, indulgent, cheerful.
remittō, -ittere, -īsī, -issum *vt* to let go back, send back, release; to slacken, loosen, relax; to emit, produce; (*mind*) to relax, relieve; (*notion*) to discard, give up; (*offence, penalty*) to let off, remit; (*right*) to resign, sacrifice; (*sound*) to give back ♦ *vi* to abate.
remixtus *ppp of* **remisceō**.
remōlior, -īrī, -ītus *vt* to heave back.
remollēscō, -ere *vi* to become soft again, be softened.
remolliō, -īre *vt* to weaken.
remora, -ae *f* hindrance.
remorāmina, -um *ntpl* hindrances.
remordeō, -dēre, -sum *vt* (*fig*) to worry, torment.
remoror, -ārī, -ātus *vi* to linger, stay behind ♦ *vt* to hinder, delay, defer.
remorsus *ppp of* **remordeō**.
remōtē *adv* far.
remōtiō, -ōnis *f* removing.
remōtus *ppp of* **removeō** ♦ *adj* distant, remote; secluded; (*fig*) far removed, free from.
removeō, -ovēre, -ōvī, -ōtum *vt* to move back, withdraw, set aside; to subtract.

remūgiō, -īre *vi* to bellow in answer, re-echo.
remulceō, -cēre, -sī *vt* to stroke; (*tail*) to droop.
remulcum, -ī *nt* towrope.
remūnerātiō, -ōnis *f* recompense, reward.
remūneror, -ārī, -ātus *vt* to repay, reward.
remurmurō, -āre *vi* to murmur in answer.
rēmus, -ī *m* oar.
Remus, -ī *m* brother of Romulus.
rēnārrō, -āre *vt* to tell over again.
rēnāscor -scī, -tus *vi* to be born again; to grow, spring up again.
rēnātus *ppa of* **rēnāscor**.
rēnāvigō, -āre *vi* to sail back.
reneō, -ēre *vt* to unspin, undo.
rēnēs, -um *mpl* kidneys.
renīdeō, -ēre *vi* to shine back, be bright; to be cheerful, smile, laugh.
renīdēscō, -ere *vi* to reflect the gleam of.
renītor, -ī *vi* to struggle, resist.
renō, -āre *vi* to swim back.
rēnō, -ōnis *m* fur.
renōdō, -āre *vt* to tie back in a knot.
renovāmen, -inis *nt* new condition.
renovātiō, -ōnis *f* renewal; compound interest.
renovō, -āre, -āvī, -ātum *vt* to renew, restore; to repair, revive, refresh; (*speech*) to repeat; **faenus ~** take compound interest.
renumerō, -āre *vt* to pay back.
renūntiātiō, -ōnis *f* report, announcement.
renūntiō, -āre, -āvī, -ātum *vt* to report, bring back word; to announce, make an official statement; (*election*) to declare elected, return; (*duty*) to refuse, call off, renounce.
renūntius, -ī *and* **iī** *m* reporter.
renuō, -ere, -ī *vt, vi* to deny, decline, refuse.
renūtō, -āre *vi* to refuse firmly.
reor, rērī, ratus *vi* to think, suppose.
repāgula, -ōrum *ntpl* (*door*) bolts, bars.
repandus *adj* curving back, turned up.
reparābilis *adj* retrievable.
reparcō, -ere *vi* to be sparing with, refrain.
reparō, -āre, -āvī, -ātum *vt* to retrieve, recover; to restore, repair; to purchase; (*mind, body*) to refresh; (*troops*) to recruit.
repastinātiō, -ōnis *f* digging up again.
repellō, -ellere, -pulī, -ulsum *vt* to push back, drive back, repulse; to remove, reject.
rependō, -endere, -endī, -ēnsum *vt* to return by weight; to pay, repay; to requite, compensate.
repēns, -entis *adj* sudden; new.
repēnsus *ppp of* **rependō**.
repentē *adv* suddenly.
repentīnō *adv* suddenly.
repentīnus *adj* sudden, hasty; upstart.
repercō *etc see* **reparcō**.
repercussus *ppp of* **repercutiō**.
repercussus, -ūs *m* reflection, echo.

Noun declensions and verb conjugations are shown on pp xiii to xxv. The present infinitive ending of a verb shows to which conjugation it belongs: -**āre** = 1st; -**ēre** = 2nd; -**ere** = 3rd and -**īre** = 4th. Irregular verbs are shown on p xxvi

repercutiō, -tere, -ssī, -ssum *vt* to make rebound, reflect, echo.

reperiō, -īre, repperī, -tum *vt* to find, find out; to get, procure; to discover, ascertain; to devise, invent.

repertor, -ōris *m* discoverer, inventor, author.

repertus *ppp of* **reperiō** ♦ *ntpl* discoveries.

repetītiō, -ōnis *f* repetition; (*RHET*) anaphora.

repetītor, -ōris *m* reclaimer.

repetītus *ppp of* **repetō** ♦ *adj*: **altē/longē ~** far-fetched.

repetō, -ere, -īvī *and* **iī, -ītum** *vt* to go back to, revisit; to fetch back, take back; (*MIL*) to attack again; (*action, speech*) to resume, repeat; (*memory*) to recall, think over; (*origin*) to trace, derive; (*right*) to claim, demand back; **rēs ~** demand satisfaction; reclaim one's property; **pecūniae ~undae** extortion.

repetundae, -ārum *fpl* extortion (*by a provincial governor*).

repexus *adj* combed.

repleō, -ēre, -ēvī, -ētum *vt* to fill up, refill; to replenish, make good, complete; to satiate, fill to overflowing.

replētus *adj* full.

replicātiō, -ōnis *f* rolling up.

replicō, -āre *vt* to roll back, unroll, unfold.

rēpō, -ere, -sī, -tum *vi* to creep, crawl.

repōnō, -ōnere, -osuī, -ositum *vt* to put back, replace, restore; to bend back; to put (in the proper place); (*performance*) to repeat; (*something received*) to repay; (*store*) to lay up, put away; (*task*) to lay aside, put down; (*hope*) to place, rest; (*with* **prō**) substitute; **in numerō, in numerum ~** count, reckon among.

reportō, -āre, -āvī, -ātum *vt* to bring back, carry back; (*prize*) to win, carry off; (*words*) to report.

reposcō, -ere *vt* to demand back; to claim, require.

repositus *ppp of* **repōnō** ♦ *adj* remote.

repostor, -ōris *m* restorer.

repostus *etc see* **repositus**.

repōtia, -ōrum *ntpl* second drinking.

repperī *perf of* **reperiō**.

reppulī *perf of* **repellō**.

repraesentātiō, -ōnis *f* vivid presentation; (*COMM*) cash payment.

repraesentō, -āre, -āvī, -ātum *vt* to exhibit, reproduce; to do at once, hasten; (*COMM*) to pay cash.

reprehendō, -endere, -endī, -ēnsum *vt* to hold back, catch, restrain; to hold fast, retain; to blame, rebuke, censure; to refute.

reprehēnsiō, -ōnis *f* check; blame, reprimand, refutation.

reprehēnsō, -āre *vt* to keep holding back.

reprehēnsor, -ōris *m* censurer, critic, reviser.

reprehēnsus *ppp of* **reprehendō**.

reprendō *etc see* **reprehendō**.

repressor, -ōris *m* restrainer.

repressus *ppp of* **reprimō**.

reprimō, -imere, -essī, -essum *vt* to keep back, force back; to check, restrain, suppress.

reprōmissiō, -ōnis *f* counterpromise.

reprōmittō, -ittere, -īsī, -issum *vt* to promise in return, engage oneself.

rēptō, -āre *vi* to creep about, crawl along.

repudiātiō, -ōnis *f* rejection.

repudiō, -āre, -āvī, -ātum *vt* to reject, refuse, scorn; (*wife*) to divorce.

repudium, -ī *and* **iī** *nt* divorce; repudiation.

repuerāscō, -ere *vi* to become a child again; to behave like a child.

repugnanter *adv* reluctantly.

repugnantia, -ium *ntpl* contradictions.

repugnō, -āre, -āvī, -ātum *vi* to oppose, resist; to disagree, be inconsistent.

repulsa, -ae *f* refusal, denial, repulse; (*election*) rebuff.

repulsō, -āre *vi* to throb, reverberate.

repulsus *ppp of* **repellō**.

repulsus, -ūs *m* (*light*) reflection; (*sound*) echoing.

repungō, -ere *vt* to prod again.

repūrgō, -āre, -āvī, -ātum *vt* to clear again, cleanse again; to purge away.

reputātiō, -ōnis *f* pondering over.

reputō, -āre, -āvī, -ātum *vt* to count back; to think over, consider.

requiēs, -ētis *f* rest, relaxation, repose.

requiēscō, -scere, -vī, -tum *vi* to rest, find rest; to cease ♦ *vt* to stay.

requiētus *adj* rested, refreshed.

requīritō, -āre *vt* to keep asking after.

requīrō, -rere, -sīvī *and* **siī, -sītum** *vt* to search for, look for; to ask, inquire after; (*with* **ex** *or* **ab**) to question; to need, want, call for; to miss, look in vain for.

requīsītus *ppp of* **requīrō**.

rēs, reī *f* thing, object; circumstance, case, matter, affair; business, transaction; fact, truth, reality; possessions, wealth, money; advantage, interest; (*law*) case; (*MIL*) campaign, operations; (*POL*) politics, power, the State; (*writing*) subject matter, story, history; **~ mihi est tēcum** I have to do with you; **~ dīvīna** sacrifice; **~ mīlitāris** war; **~ pūblica** public affairs, politics, the State, republic; **~ rūstica** agriculture; **rem facere** get rich; **rem gerere** wage war, fight; **ad rem** to the point, to the purpose; **in rem** usefully; **ob rem** to the purpose; **ob eam rem** therefore; **ī in malam rem** go to the devil!; **contrā rem pūblicam** unconstitutionally; **ē rē pūblicā** constitutionally; **rē vērā** in fact, actually; **eā rē** for that reason; **tuā rē, ex tuā rē** to your advantage; **ab rē** unhelpfully; **ē rē (nātā)** as things are; **prō rē** according to circumstances; **rēs adversae** failure, adversity; **rēs dubiae** danger; **rēs gestae**

achievements, career; **rēs novae** revolution; **rēs prosperae, secundae** success, prosperity; **rērum māximus** greatest in the world; **rērum scrīptor** historian.

resacrō *etc see* **resecrō**.

resaeviō, -īre *vi* to rage again.

resalūtō, -āre *vt* to greet in return.

resānēscō, -ēscere, -uī *vi* to heal up again.

resarciō, -cīre, -tum *vt* to patch up, repair.

rescindō, -ndere, -dī, -ssum *vt* to cut back, cut open, break down; to open up; (*law, agreement*) to repeal, annul.

rescīscō, -īscere, -īvī *and* **iī, -ītum** *vt* to find out, learn.

rescissus *ppp of* **rescindō**.

rescrībō, -bere, -psī, -ptum *vt* to write back, reply; to rewrite, revise; (*emperors*) to give a decision; (MIL) to transfer, re-enlist; (*money*) to place to one's credit, pay back.

rescrīptus *ppp of* **rescrībō** ♦ *nt* imperial rescript.

resecō, -āre, -uī, -tum *vt* to cut back, cut short; to curtail; **ad vīvum ~** cut to the quick.

resecrō, -āre *vt* to pray again; to free from a curse.

resectus *ppp of* **resecō**.

resecūtus *ppa of* **resequor**.

resēdī *perf of* **resideō**; *perf of* **resīdō**.

resēminō, -āre *vt* to reproduce.

resequor, -quī, -cūtus *vt* to answer.

reserō, -āre, -āvī, -ātum *vt* to unbar, unlock; to disclose.

reservō, -āre, -āvī, -ātum *vt* to keep back, reserve; to preserve, save.

reses, -idis *adj* remaining; inactive; idle; calm.

resideō, -idēre, -ēdī *vi* to remain behind; to be idle, be listless; (*fig*) to remain, rest.

resīdō, -idere, -ēdī *vi* to sit down, sink down, settle; to subside; (*fig*) to abate, calm down.

residuus *adj* remaining, left over; (*money*) outstanding.

resignō, -āre *vt* to unseal, open; (*fig*) to reveal; (COMM) to cancel, pay back.

resiliō, -īre, -uī *vi* to spring back; to recoil, rebound, shrink.

resīmus *adj* turned up.

rēsīna, -ae *f* resin.

rēsīnātus *adj* smeared with resin.

resipiō, -ere *vt* to savour of, smack of.

resipīscō, -īscere, -iī *and* **uī** *vi* to come to one's senses.

resistō, -istere, -titī *vi* to stand still, stop, halt; to resist, oppose; to rise again.

resolūtus *ppp of* **resolvō**.

resolvō, -vere, -vī, -ūtum *vt* to unfasten, loosen, open, release; to melt, dissolve; to relax; (*debt*) to pay up; (*difficulty*) to banish, dispel; (*tax*) to abolish; (*words*) to explain.

resonābilis *adj* answering.

resonō, -āre *vi* to resound, re-echo ♦ *vt* to echo the sound of; to make resound.

resonus *adj* echoing.

resorbeō, -ēre *vt* to suck back, swallow again.

respectō, -āre *vi* to look back; to gaze about, watch ♦ *vt* to look back at, look for; to have regard for.

respectus *ppp of* **respiciō**.

respectus, -ūs *m* looking back; refuge; respect, regard.

respergō, -gere, -sī, -sum *vt* to besprinkle, splash.

respersiō, -ōnis *f* sprinkling.

respersus *ppp of* **respergō**.

respiciō, -icere, -exī, -ectum *vt* to look back at, see behind; (*help*) to look to; (*care*) to have regard for, consider, respect ♦ *vi* to look back, look.

respīrāmen, -inis *nt* windpipe.

respīrātiō, -ōnis *f* breathing; exhalation; taking breath, pause.

respīrātus, -ūs *m* inhaling.

respīrō, -āre, -āvī, -ātum *vt, vi* to breathe, blow back; to breathe again, revive; (*things*) to abate.

resplendeō, -ēre *vi* to flash back, shine brightly.

respondeō, -ondēre, -ondī, -ōnsum *vt* to answer, reply; (*lawyer, priest, oracle*) to advise, give a response; (*law court*) to appear; (*pledge*) to promise in return; (*things*) to correspond, agree, match; **pār parī ~** return like for like, give tit for tat.

respōnsiō, -ōnis *f* answering; refutation.

respōnsitō, -āre *vi* to give advice.

respōnsō, -āre *vt, vi* to answer back; to defy.

respōnsor, -ōris *m* answerer.

respōnsum, -ī *nt* answer, reply; response, opinion, oracle.

rēspūblica, reīpūblicae *f* public affairs, politics, the State, republic.

respuō, -ere, -ī *vt* to spit out, eject; to reject, refuse.

restagnō, -āre *vi* to overflow; to be flooded.

restaurō, -āre *vt* to repair, rebuild.

resticula, -ae *f* rope, cord.

restinctiō, -ōnis *f* quenching.

restinctus *ppp of* **restinguō**.

restinguō, -guere, -xī, -ctum *vt* to extinguish, quench; (*fig*) to destroy.

restiō, -ōnis *m* rope maker.

restipulātiō, -ōnis *f* counterobligation.

restipulor, -ārī *vt* to stipulate in return.

restis, -is *f* rope.

restitī *perf of* **resistō**; *perf of* **restō**.

restitō, -āre *vi* to stay behind, hesitate.

restituō, -uere, -uī, -ūtum *vt* to replace, restore; to rebuild, renew; to give back, return; (*to a condition*) to reinstate; (*decision*) to quash, reverse; (*character*) to reform.

restitūtiō, -ōnis _f_ restoration; reinstating.
restitūtor, -ōris _m_ restorer.
restitūtus _ppp of_ **restituō.**
restō, -āre, -itī _vi_ to stand firm; to resist; to remain, be left; to be in store (for); **quod ~at** for the future.
restrictē _adv_ sparingly; strictly.
restrictus _ppp of_ **restringō** ♦ _adj_ tight, short; niggardly; severe.
restringō, -ngere, -nxī, -ctum _vt_ to draw back tightly, bind fast; (_teeth_) to bare; (_fig_) to check.
resultō, -āre _vi_ to rebound; to re-echo.
resūmō, -ere, -psī, -ptum _vt_ to take up again, get back, resume.
resupīnō, -āre _vt_ to turn back, throw on one's back.
resupīnus _adj_ lying back, face upwards.
resurgō, -gere, -rēxī, -rēctum _vi_ to rise again, revive.
resuscitō, -āre _vt_ to revive.
retardātiō, -ōnis _f_ hindering.
retardō, -āre, -āvī, -ātum _vt_ to retard, detain, check.
rēte, -is _nt_ net; (_fig_) snare.
retēctus _ppp of_ **retegō.**
retegō, -egere, -ēxī, -ēctum _vt_ to uncover, open; to reveal.
retemptō, -āre _vt_ to try again.
retendō, -endere, -endī, -entum _and_ **ēnsum** _vt_ to slacken, relax.
retēnsus _ppp of_ **retendō.**
retentiō, -ōnis _f_ holding back.
retentō _etc see_ **retemptō.**
retentō, -āre _vt_ to keep back, hold fast.
retentus _ppp of_ **retendō;** _ppp of_ **retineō.**
retēxī _perf of_ **retegō.**
retexō, -ere, -uī, -tum _vt_ to unravel; (_fig_) to break up, cancel; to renew.
rētiārius, -ī _and_ **iī** _m_ net-fighter.
reticentia, -ae _f_ saying nothing; pause.
reticeō, -ēre, -uī _vi_ to be silent, say nothing ♦ _vt_ to keep secret.
rēticulum, -ī _nt_ small net, hairnet; network bag.
retināculum, -ī _nt_ tether, hawser.
retinēns, -entis _pres p of_ **retineō** ♦ _adj_ tenacious, observant.
retinentia, -ae _f_ memory.
retineō, -inēre, -inuī, -entum _vt_ to hold back, detain, restrain; to keep, retain, preserve.
retinniō, -īre _vi_ to ring.
retonō, -āre _vi_ to thunder in answer.
retorqueō, -quēre, -sī, -tum _vt_ to turn back, twist.
retorridus _adj_ dried up, wizened.
retortus _ppp of_ **retorqueō.**
retractātiō, -ōnis _f_ hesitation.
retractō, -āre, -āvī, -ātum _vt_ to rehandle, take up again; to reconsider, revise; to withdraw ♦ _vi_ to draw back, hesitate.
retractus _ppp of_ **retrahō** ♦ _adj_ remote.

retrahō, -here, -xī, -ctum _vt_ to draw back, drag back; to withdraw, remove.
retrectō _etc see_ **retractō.**
retribuō, -uere, -uī, -ūtum _vt_ to restore, repay.
retrō _adv_ back, backwards, behind; (_time_) back, past.
retrōrsum _adv_ backwards, behind; in reverse order.
retrūdō, -dere, -sum _vt_ to push back; to withdraw.
rettulī _perf of_ **referō.**
retundō, -undere, -udī _and_ **tudī, -ūsum** _and_ **ūnsum** _vt_ to blunt; (_fig_) to check, weaken.
retūnsus, retūsus _ppp of_ **retundō** ♦ _adj_ blunt, dull.
reus, -ī _m_ the accused, defendant; guarantor, debtor, one responsible; culprit, criminal; **vōtī ~** one who has had a prayer granted.
revalēscō, -ēscere, -uī _vi_ to recover.
revehō, -here, -xī, -ctum _vt_ to carry back, bring back; (_pass_) to ride, drive, sail back.
revellō, -ellere, -ellī, -ulsum (olsum) _vt_ to pull out, tear off; to remove.
revēlō, -āre _vt_ to unveil, uncover.
reveniō, -enīre, -ēnī, -entum _vi_ to come back, return.
rēvērā _adv_ in fact, actually.
reverendus _adj_ venerable, awe-inspiring.
reverēns, -entis _pres p of_ **revereor** ♦ _adj_ respectful, reverent.
reverenter _adv_ respectfully.
reverentia, -ae _f_ respect, reverence, awe.
revereor, -ērī, -itus _vt_ to stand in awe of; to respect, revere.
reversiō (revorsiō), -ōnis _f_ turning back; recurrence.
reversus _ppa of_ **revertor.**
revertō, -ere, -ī; revertor, -tī, -sus _vi_ to turn back, return; to revert.
revexī _perf of_ **revehō.**
revictus _ppp of_ **revincō.**
revinciō, -cīre, -xī, -ctum _vt_ to tie back, bind fast.
revincō, -incere, -īcī, -ictum _vt_ to conquer, repress; (_words_) to refute, convict.
revinctus _ppp of_ **revinciō.**
revirēscō, -ēscere, -uī _vi_ to grow green again; to be rejuvenated; to grow strong again, flourish again.
revīsō, -ere _vt, vi_ to come back to, revisit.
revīvēscō, -vīscō, -vīscere, -xī _vi_ to come to life again, revive.
revocābilis _adj_ revocable.
revocāmen, -inis _nt_ recall.
revocātiō, -ōnis _f_ recalling; (_word_) withdrawing.
revocō, -āre, -āvī, -ātum _vt_ to call back, recall; (_action_) to revoke; (_former state_) to recover, regain; (_growth_) to check; (_guest_) to invite in return; (_judgment_) to apply, refer; (_law_) to summon again; (_performer_) to encore; (_troops_) to withdraw.

revolō, -āre *vi* to fly back.

revolsus *etc see* **revulsus**.

revolūbilis *adj* that may be rolled back.

revolūtus *ppp of* **revolvō**.

revolvō, -vere, -vī, -ūtum *vt* to roll back, unroll, unwind; (*speech*) to relate, repeat; (*thought*) to think over; (*writing*) to read over; (*pass*) to revolve, return, come round.

revomō, -ere, -uī *vt* to disgorge.

revor- *etc see* **rever-**.

revulsus *ppp of* **revellō**.

rēx, rēgis *m* king; tyrant, despot; leader; patron, rich man.

rēxī *perf of* **regō**.

Rhadamanthus, -ī *m judge in the lower world.*

Rhaetī *etc see* **Raetī**.

Rhamnūs, -ūntis *f town in Attica* (*famous for its statue of Nemesis*).

Rhamnūsis, -ūsidis *f* Nemesis.

Rhamnūsius *adj see* n.

rhapsōdia, -ae *f a book of Homer.*

Rhea, -ae *f* Cybele.

Rhea Silvia, -ae, -ae *f mother of Romulus and Remus.*

Rhēgium *etc see* **Rēgium**.

Rhēnānus *adj* Rhenish.

rhēnō *etc see* **rēnō**.

Rhēnus, -ī *m* Rhine.

Rhēsus, -ī *m* Thracian king (*killed at Troy*).

rhētor, -oris *m* teacher of rhetoric; orator.

rhētorica, -ae *and* **ē, -ēs** *f* art of oratory, rhetoric.

rhētoricē *adv* rhetorically, in an oratorical manner.

rhētoricī, -ōrum *mpl* teachers of rhetoric.

rhētoricus *adj* rhetorical, on rhetoric.

rhīnocerōs, -ōtis *m* rhinoceros.

rhō *nt* (*indecl*) Greek letter rho.

Rhodanus, -ī *m* Rhone.

Rhodius *adj see* **Rhodopē**.

Rhodopē, -ēs *f mountain range in Thrace.*

Rhodopēius *adj* Thracian.

Rhodos (Rhodus), -ī *f* island of Rhodes.

Rhoetēum, -ī *nt promontory on the Dardanelles* (*near Troy*).

Rhoetēus *adj* Trojan.

rhombus, -ī *m* magician's circle; (*fish*) turbot.

rhomphaea, -ae *f long barbarian javelin.*

rhythmicus, -ī *m* teacher of prose rhythm.

rhythmos (-us), -ī *m* rhythm, symmetry.

rīca, -ae *f* sacrificial veil.

ricinium, -ī *and* **iī** *nt small cloak with hood.*

rictum, -ī *nt,* **-us, -ūs** *m* open mouth, gaping jaws.

rīdeō, -dēre, -sī, -sum *vi* to laugh, smile ♦ *vt* to laugh at, smile at; to ridicule

rīdibundus *adj* laughing.

rīdiculāria, -ium *ntpl* jokes.

rīdiculē *adv* jokingly; absurdly.

rīdiculus *adj* amusing, funny; ridiculous, silly

♦ *m* jester ♦ *nt* joke.

rigēns, -entis *pres p of* **rigeō** ♦ *adj* stiff, rigid, frozen.

rigeō, -ēre *vi* to be stiff.

rigēscō, -ēscere, -uī *vi* to stiffen, harden; to bristle.

rigidē *adv* rigorously.

rigidus *adj* stiff, rigid, hard; (*fig*) hardy, strict, inflexible.

rigō, -āre *vt* to water, moisten, bedew; to convey (water).

rigor, -ōris *m* stiffness, hardness; numbness, cold; strictness, severity.

riguī *perf of* **rigēscō**.

riguus *adj* irrigating; watered.

rīma, -ae *f* crack, chink.

rīmor, -ārī, -ātus *vt* to tear open; to search for, probe, examine; to find out.

rīmōsus *adj* cracked, leaky.

ringor, -ī *vi* to snarl.

rīpa, -ae *f* river bank; shore.

Rīphaeī, -ōrum *mpl mountain range in N. Scythia.*

Rīphaeus *adj see* **Rīphaeī**.

rīpula, -ae *f* riverbank.

riscus, -ī *m* trunk, chest.

rīsī *perf of* **rīdeō**.

rīsor, -ōris *m* scoffer.

rīsus, -ūs *m* laughter, laugh; laughing stock.

rīte *adv* with the proper formality *or* ritual; duly, properly, rightly; in the usual manner; fortunately.

rītus, -ūs *m* ritual, ceremony; custom, usage; ~ū after the manner of.

rīvālis, -is *m* rival in love.

rīvālitās, -ātis *f* rivalry in love.

rīvulus, -ī *m* brook.

rīvus, -ī *m* stream, brook; **ē ~ō flūmina māgna facere** ≈ *make a mountain of a molehill.*

rixa, -ae *f* quarrel, brawl, fight.

rixor, -ārī, -ātus *vi* to quarrel, brawl, squabble.

rōbīginōsus *adj* rusty.

rōbīgō, -inis *f* rust; blight, mould, mildew.

rōboreus *adj* of oak.

rōborō, -āre *vt* to strengthen, invigorate.

rōbur, -oris *nt* oak; hard wood; prison, dungeon (*at Rome*); (*fig*) strength, hardness, vigour; best part, élite, flower.

rōbustus *adj* of oak; strong, hard; robust, mature.

rōdō, -dere, -sī, -sum *vt* to gnaw; (*rust*) to corrode; (*words*) to slander.

rogālis *adj* of a pyre.

rogātiō, -ōnis *f* proposal, motion, bill; request; (*RHET*) question.

rogātiuncula, -ae *f* unimportant bill; question.

rogātor, -ōris *m* proposer; polling clerk.

rogātus, -ūs *m* request.

Noun declensions and verb conjugations are shown on pp xiii to xxv. The present infinitive ending of a verb shows to which conjugation it belongs: **-āre** = 1st; **-ēre** = 2nd; **-ere** = 3rd and **-īre** = 4th. Irregular verbs are shown on p xxvi

rogitō, -āre _vt_ to ask for, inquire eagerly.
rogō, -āre, -āvī, -ātum _vt_ to ask, ask for; (_bill_) to propose, move; (_candidate_) to put up for election; **lēgem ~, populum ~** introduce a bill; **magistrātum populum ~** nominate for election to an office; **milites sacrāmentō ~** administer the oath to the troops; **mālō emere quam rogāre** I'd rather buy it than borrow it.
rogus, -ī _m_ funeral pyre.
Rōma, -ae _f_ Rome.
Rōmānus _adj_ Roman.
Rōmuleus, -us _adj_ of Romulus; Roman.
Rōmulidae, -idārum _mpl_ the Romans.
Rōmulus, -ī _m founder and first king of Rome._
rōrāriī, -ōrum _mpl_ skirmishers.
rōridus _adj_ dewy.
rōrifer, -ī _adj_ dew-bringing.
rōrō, -āre _vi_ to distil dew; to drip, trickle ♦ _vt_ to bedew, wet.
rōs, rōris _m_ dew; moisture, water; (_plant_) rosemary; **~ marīnus** rosemary.
rosa, -ae _f_ rose; rose bush.
rosāria, -ōrum _ntpl_ rose garden.
rōscidus _adj_ dewy; wet.
Roscius, -ī _m_ L. **~ Othō** _tribune in 67 BC, whose law reserved theatre seats for the equites;_ Q. **~ Gallus** _famous actor defended by Cicero;_ Sex. **~** _of Ameria, defended by Cicero._
Roscius, -iānus _adj see n._
rosētum, -ī _nt_ rosebed.
roseus _adj_ rosy; of roses.
rōsī _perf of_ **rōdō.**
rōstrātus _adj_ beaked, curved; **columna ~a** _a column commemorating a naval victory._
rōstrum, -ī _nt_ (_bird_) beak, bill; (_animal_) snout, muzzle; (_ship_) beak, end of prow; (_pl_) orators' platform in the Forum.
rōsus _ppp of_ **rōdō.**
rota, -ae _f_ wheel; potter's wheel, torture wheel; car, disc.
rotō, -āre, -āvī, -ātum _vt_ to turn, whirl, roll; (_pass_) to revolve.
rotundē _adv_ elegantly.
rotundō, -āre _vt_ to round off.
rotundus _adj_ round, circular, spherical; (_style_) well-turned, smooth.
rubefaciō, -facere, -fēcī, -factum _vt_ to redden.
rubēns, -entis _pres p of_ **rubeō** ♦ _adj_ red; blushing.
rubeō, -ēre _vi_ to be red; to blush.
ruber, -rī _adj_ red; **mare ~rum** Red Sea; Persian Gulf; **ōceanus ~** Indian Ocean; **Saxa ~ra** _stone quarries between Rome and Veii._
rubēscō, -ēscere, -uī _vi_ to redden, blush.
rubēta, -ae _f_ toad.
rubēta, -ōrum _ntpl_ bramble bushes.
rubeus _adj_ of bramble.
Rubicō, -ōnis _m stream marking the frontier between Italy and Gaul._
rubicundulus _adj_ reddish.
rubicundus _adj_ red, ruddy.

rūbīg- _etc see_ **rōbīg-.**
rubor, -ōris _m_ redness; blush; bashfulness; shame.
rubrīca, -ae _f_ red earth, red ochre.
rubuī _perf of_ **rubēscō.**
rubus, -ī _m_ bramble bush; bramble, blackberry.
ructō, -āre; -or, -ārī _vt, vi_ to belch.
ructus, -us _m_ belching.
rudēns, -entis _pres p of_ **rudō** ♦ _m_ rope; (_pl_) rigging.
Rudiae, -iārum _fpl_ town in S. Italy (_birthplace of Ennius_).
rudiārius, -ī _and_ **iī** _m_ retired gladiator.
rudīmentum, -ī _nt_ first attempt, beginning.
Rudīnus _adj see_ **Rudiae.**
rudis _adj_ unwrought, unworked, raw; coarse, rough, badly-made; (_age_) new, young; (_person_) uncultured, unskilled, clumsy; ignorant (of), inexperienced (in).
rudis, -is _f_ stick, rod; foil (_for fighting practice_); (_fig_) discharge.
rudō, -ere, -īvī, -ītum _vi_ to roar, bellow, bray; to creak.
rūdus, -eris _nt_ rubble, rubbish; piece of copper.
rūdus, -eris _nt_ copper coin.
Rūfulī, -ōrum _mpl_ military tribunes (_chosen by the general_).
rūfulus _adj_ red-headed.
rūfus _adj_ red, red-haired.
rūga, -ae _f_ wrinkle, crease.
rūgō, -āre _vi_ to become creased.
rūgōsus _adj_ wrinkled, shrivelled, corrugated.
ruī _perf of_ **ruō.**
ruīna, -ae _f_ fall, downfall; collapse, falling in; debris, ruins; destruction, disaster, ruin (_fig_).
ruīnōsus _adj_ collapsing; ruined.
rumex, -icis _f_ sorrel.
rūmificō, -āre _vt_ to report.
Rūmīna, -ae _f goddess of nursing mothers;_ **fīcus ~ālis** the fig tree of Romulus and Remus (_under which the she-wolf suckled them_).
rūminātiō, -ōnis _f_ chewing the cud; (_fig_) ruminating.
rūminō, -āre _vt, vi_ to chew the cud.
rūmor, -ōris _m_ noise, cheering; rumour, hearsay; public opinion; reputation.
rumpia _etc see_ **rhomphaea.**
rumpō, -ere, rūpī, ruptum _vt_ to break, burst, tear; to break down, burst through; (_activity_) to interrupt; (_agreement_) to violate, annul; (_delay_) to put an end to; (_voice_) to give vent to; (_way_) to force through.
rūmusculī, -ōrum _mpl_ gossip.
rūna, -ae _f_ dart.
runcō, -āre _vt_ to weed.
ruō, -ere, -ī, -tum _vi_ to fall down, tumble; to rush, run, hurry; to come to ruin ♦ _vt_ to dash down, hurl to the ground; to throw up, turn up.
rūpēs, -is _f_ rock, cliff.

rūpī *perf of* **rumpō.**
ruptor, -ōris *m* violator.
ruptus *ppp of* **rumpō.**
rūricola, -ae *adj* rural, country- (*in cpds*).
rūrigena, -ae *m* countryman.
rūrsus, rūrsum (rūsum) *adv* back, backwards; on the contrary, in return; again.
rūs, rūris *nt* the country, countryside; estate, farm; **rūs** to the country; **rūrī** in the country; **rūre** from the country.
ruscum, -ī *nt* butcher's-broom.
russus *adj* red.
rūsticānus *adj* country- (*in cpds*), rustic.
rūsticātiō, -ōnis *f* country life.
rūsticē *adv* in a countrified manner, awkwardly.
rūsticitās, -ātis *f* country manners, rusticity.
rūsticor, -ārī *vi* to live in the country.
rūsticulus, -ī *m* yokel.
rūsticus *adj* country- (*in cpds*), rural; simple, rough, clownish ♦ *m* countryman.
rūsum *see* **rūrsus.**
rūta, -ae *f* (*herb*) rue; (*fig*) unpleasantness.
ruta caesa *ntpl* minerals and timber on an estate.
rutilō, -āre *vt* to colour red ♦ *vi* to glow red.
rutilus *adj* red, auburn.
rutrum, -ī *nt* spade, shovel, trowel.
rūtula, -ae *f* little piece of rue.
Rutulī, -ōrum *mpl* ancient Latin people.
Rutulus *adj* Rutulian.
Rutupiae, -iārum *fpl* seaport in Kent (*now* Richborough).
Rutupīnus *adj see n.*
rutus *ppp of* **ruō.**

S, s

Saba, -ae *f* town in Arabia Felix.
Sabaeus *adj see n.*
Sabāzia, -iōrum *ntpl* festival of Bacchus.
Sabāzius, -ī *m* Bacchus.
sabbata, -ōrum *ntpl* Sabbath, Jewish holiday.
Sabellus, -ī *m* Sabine, Samnite.
Sabellus, -icus *adj see n.*
Sabīnī, -ōrum *mpl* Sabines (*a people of central Italy*).
Sabīnus *adj* Sabine ♦ *f* Sabine woman ♦ *nt* Sabine estate; Sabine wine; **herba ~a** savin (*a kind of juniper*).
Sabrīna, -ae *f* river Severn.

saburra, -ae *f* sand, ballast.
Sacae, -ārum *mpl* tribe of Scythians.
saccipērium, -ī *and* **iī** *nt* purse-pocket.
saccō, -āre *vt* to strain, filter.
sacculus, -ī *m* little bag, purse.
saccus, -ī *m* bag, purse, wallet.
sacellum, -ī *nt* chapel.
sacer, -rī *adj* sacred, holy; devoted for sacrifice, forfeited; accursed, criminal, infamous; **Mōns ~** hill to which the Roman plebs seceded; **Via ~ra** street from the Forum to the Capitol.
sacerdōs, -ōtis *m/f* priest, priestess.
sacerdōtium, -ī *and* **iī** *nt* priesthood.
sacrāmentum, -ī *nt* deposit made by parties to a lawsuit; civil lawsuit, dispute; (*MIL*) oath of allegiance, engagement.
sacrārium, -ī *and* **iī** *nt* shrine, chapel.
sacrātus *adj* holy, hallowed; **~āta lēx** a law whose violation was punished by devotion to the infernal gods.
sacricola, -ae *m/f* sacrificing priest or priestess.
sacrifer, -ī *adj* carrying holy things.
sacrificālis *adj* sacrificial.
sacrificātiō, -ōnis *f* sacrificing.
sacrificium, -ī *and* **iī** *nt* sacrifice.
sacrificō, -āre *vt, vi* to sacrifice.
sacrificulus, -ī *m* sacrificing priest; **rēx ~** high priest.
sacrificus *adj* sacrificial.
sacrilēgium, -ī *and* **iī** *nt* sacrilege.
sacrilegus *adj* sacrilegious; profane, wicked ♦ *m* templerobber.
sacrō, -āre, -āvī, -ātum *vt* to consecrate; to doom, curse; to devote, dedicate; to make inviolable; (*poetry*) to immortalize.
sacrōsanctus *adj* inviolable, sacrosanct.
sacruficō *etc see* **sacrificō.**
sacrum, -ī *nt* holy thing, sacred vessel; shrine; offering, victim; rite; (*pl*) sacrifice, worship, religion; **~ra facere** sacrifice; **inter ~rum saxumque** ≈ with one's back to the wall; **hērēditās sine ~rīs** a gift with no awkward obligations.
saeclum *etc see* **saeculum.**
saeculāris *adj* centenary; (*ECCL*) secular, pagan.
saeculum, -ī *nt* generation, lifetime, age; the age, the times; century; **in ~a** (*ECCL*) for ever.
saepe *adv* often, frequently.
saepe numerō *adv* very often.
saepēs, -is *f* hedge, fence.
saepīmentum, -ī *nt* enclosure.
saepiō, -īre, -sī, -tum *vt* to hedge round, fence in, enclose; (*fig*) to shelter, protect.
saeptus *ppp of* **saepiō** ♦ *nt* fence, wall; stake, pale; (*sheep*) fold; (*Rome*) voting area in the Campus Martius.
saeta, -ae *f* hair, bristle.

Noun declensions and verb conjugations are shown on pp xiii to xxv. The present infinitive ending of a verb shows to which conjugation it belongs: **-āre** = 1st; **-ēre** = 2nd; **-ere** = 3rd and **-īre** = 4th. Irregular verbs are shown on **p xxvi**

saetiger, -ī *adj* bristly.

saetōsus *adj* bristly, hairy.

saevē, -iter *adv* fiercely, cruelly.

saevidicus *adj* furious.

saeviō, -īre, -iī, -ītum *vi* to rage, rave.

saevitia, -ae *f* rage; ferocity, cruelty.

saevus *adj* raging, fierce; cruel, barbarous.

sāga, -ae *f* fortune teller.

sagācitās, -ātis *f* (*dogs*) keen scent; (*mind*) shrewdness.

sagāciter *adv* keenly; shrewdly.

sagātus *adj* wearing a soldier's cloak.

sagāx, -ācis *adj* (*senses*) keen, keen-scented; (*mind*) quick, shrewd.

sagīna, -ae *f* stuffing, fattening; food, rich food; fatted animal.

sagīnō, -are *vt* to cram, fatten; to feed, feast.

sāgiō, -īre *vi* to perceive keenly.

sagitta, -ae *f* arrow.

sagittārius, -ī and iī *m* archer.

sagittifer, -ī *adj* armed with arrows.

sagmen, -inis *nt* tuft of sacred herbs (*used as a mark of inviolability*).

sagulum, -ī *nt* short military cloak.

sagum, -ī *nt* military cloak; woollen mantle.

Saguntīnus *adj see* **Saguntum.**

Saguntum, -ī *nt,* **-us (os), -ī** *f town in E. Spain.*

sāgus *adj* prophetic.

sāl, salis *m* salt; brine, sea; (*fig*) shrewdness, wit, humour, witticism; good taste.

salacō, -ōnis *m* swaggerer.

Salamīnius *adj see* **Salamīs.**

Salamīs, -īnis *f Greek island near Athens; town in Cyprus.*

salapūtium, -ī and iī *nt* manikin.

salārius *adj* salt- (*in cpds*) ♦ *nt* allowance, salary.

salāx, -ācis *adj* lustful, salacious.

salebra, -ae *f* roughness, rut.

Saliāris *adj* of the Salii; sumptuous.

salictum, -ī *nt* willow plantation.

salientēs, -ium *fpl* springs.

salignus *adj* of willow.

Saliī, -ōrum *mpl priests of Mars.*

salillum, -ī *nt* little saltcellar.

salīnae, -ārum *fpl* saltworks.

salīnum, -ī *nt* saltcellar.

saliō, -īre, -uī, -tum *vi* to leap, spring; to throb.

saliunca, -ae *f* Celtic nard.

salīva, -ae *f* saliva, spittle; taste.

salix, -icis *f* willow.

Sallustiānus *adj see* **Sallustius.**

Sallustius, -ī *m* Sallust (*Roman historian*); *his wealthy grand-nephew.*

Salmōneus, -eos *m* son of Aeolus (*punished in Tartarus for imitating lightning*).

Salmōnis, -idis *f his daughter Tyro.*

salsāmentum, -ī *nt* brine, pickle; salted fish.

salsē *adv* wittily.

salsus *adj* salted; salt, briny; (*fig*) witty.

saltātiō, -ōnis *f* dancing, dance.

saltātor, -ōris *m* dancer.

saltātōrius *adj* dancing- (*in cpds*).

saltātrīx, -īcis *f* dancer.

saltātus, -ūs *m* dance.

saltem *adv* at least, at all events; **nōn ~** not even.

saltō, -āre *vt, vi* to dance.

saltuōsus *adj* wooded.

saltus, -ūs *m* leap, bound.

saltus, -ūs *m* woodland pasture, glade; pass, ravine.

salūber *adj see* **salūbris.**

salūbris *adj* health-giving, wholesome; healthy, sound.

salūbritās, -ātis *f* healthiness; health.

salūbriter *adv* wholesomely; beneficially.

saluī *perf of* **saliō.**

salum, -ī *nt* sea, high sea.

salūs, -ūtis *f* health; welfare, life; safety; good wish, greeting; **~ūtem dīcere** greet; bid farewell.

salūtāris *adj* wholesome, healthy; beneficial; **~ littera** letter A (*for* **absolvō** = *acquittal*).

salūtāriter *adv* beneficially.

salūtātiō, -ōnis *f* greeting; formal morning visit, levee.

salūtātor, -ōris *m* morning caller; male courtier.

salūtātrīx, -rīcis *f* morning caller; female courtier.

salūtifer, -ī *adj* health-giving.

salūtigerulus *adj* carrying greetings.

salūtō, -āre, -āvī, -ātum *vt* to greet, salute, wish well; to call on, pay respects to.

salvē *adv* well, in good health; all right.

salvē *impv of* **salveō.**

salveō, -ēre *vi* to be well, be in good health; **~ē, ~ētō, ~ēte** hail!, good day!, goodbye!; **~ēre iubeō** I bid good day.

salvus, salvos *adj* safe, alive, intact, well; without violating; all right; **~ sīs** good day to you!; **~ā rēs est** all is well; **~ā lēge** without breaking the law.

Samaous *adj see* **Samē.**

Samarobrīva, -ae *f* Belgian town (*now Amiens*).

sambūca, -ae *f* harp.

sambūcistria, -ae *f* harpist.

Samē, -ēs *f old name of the Greek island Cephallenia.*

Samius *adj* Samian ♦ *ntpl* Samian pottery.

Samnīs, -ītis *adj* Samnite.

Samnium, -ī and iī *nt district of central Italy.*

Samos (-us), -ī *f Aegean island off Asia Minor (famous for its pottery and as the birthplace of Pythagoras).*

Samothrācēs, -um *mpl* Samothracians.

Samothrācia, -iae *and* **a, -ae** *f* Samothrace (*island in the N. Aegean*).

Samothrācius *adj see* **n.**

sānābilis *adj* curable.

sānātiō, -ōnis *f* healing.

sanciō, -cīre, -xī, -ctum *vt* to make sacred or inviolable; to ordain, ratify; to enact a punishment against.

sanctimōnia, -ae f sanctity; chastity.

sanctiō, -ōnis f decree, penalty for violating a law.

sanctitās, -ātis f sacredness; integrity, chastity.

sanctitūdō, -inis f sacredness.

sanctō adv solemnly, religiously.

sanctor, -ōris m enacter.

sanctus ppp of **sanciō** ♦ adj sacred, inviolable; holy, venerable; pious, virtuous, chaste.

sandaligerula, -ae f sandalbearer.

sandalium, -ī and **iī** nt sandal, slipper.

sandapila, -ae f common bier.

sandȳx, -ȳcis f scarlet.

sānē adv sensibly; (intensive) very, doubtless; (ironical) to be sure, of course; (concessive) of course, indeed; (in answer) certainly, surely; (with impv) then, if you please; ~ **quam** very much; **haud** ~ not so very, not quite.

sanguen etc see **sanguis**.

sanguināns, -antis adj bloodthirsty.

sanguinārius adj bloodthirsty.

sanguineus adj bloody, of blood; blood-red.

sanguinolentus adj bloody; blood-red; sanguinary.

sanguis, -inis m blood, bloodshed; descent, family; offspring; (fig) strength, life; ~**inem dare** shed one's blood; ~**inem mittere** let blood.

saniēs, -em, -ē f diseased blood, matter; venom.

sānitās, -ātis f (body) health, sound condition; (mind) sound sense, sanity; (style) correctness, purity.

sanna, -ae f grimace, mocking.

sanniō, -ōnis m clown.

sānō, -āre, -āvī, -ātum vt to cure, heal; (fig) to remedy, relieve.

Sanquālis avis f osprey.

sānus adj (body) sound, healthy; (mind) sane, sensible; (style) correct; **male** ~ mad, inspired; **sānun es?** are you in your senses?

sanxī perf of **sanciō**.

sapa, -ae f new wine.

sapiēns, -entis pres p of **sapiō** ♦ adj wise, discreet ♦ m wise man, philosopher; man of taste.

sapienter adv wisely, sensibly.

sapientia, -ae f wisdom, discernment; philosophy; knowledge.

sapiō, -ere, -īvī and **uī** vi to have a flavour or taste; to have sense, be wise ♦ vt to taste of, smell of, smack of; to understand.

sapor, -ōris m taste, flavour; (food) delicacy; (fig) taste, refinement.

Sapphicus adj see **Sapphō**.

Sapphō, -ūs f famous Greek lyric poetess, native of Lesbos.

sarcina, -ae f bundle, burden; (MIL) pack.

sarcinārius adj baggage- (in cpds).

sarcinātor, -ōris m patcher.

sarcinula, -ae f little pack.

sarciō, -cīre, -sī, -tum vt to patch, mend, repair.

sarcophagus, -ī m sepulchre.

sarculum, -ī nt light hoe.

Sardēs (-is), -ium fpl Sardis (capital of Lydia).

Sardiānus adj see **Sardēs**.

Sardinia, -iniae f island of Sardinia.

sardonyx, -chis f sardonyx.

Sardus, -ōus, -iniēnsis adj see **Sardinia**.

sariō, -īre, -īvī and **uī** vt to hoe, weed.

sarīsa, -ae f Macedonian lance.

sarīsophorus, -ī m Macedonian lancer.

Sarmatae, -ārum mpl Sarmatians (a people of S.E. Russia).

Sarmaticus, -is adj see **Sarmatae**.

sarmentum, -ī nt twigs, brushwood.

Sarpēdōn, -onis m king of Lycia.

Sarra, -ae f Tyre.

sarrācum, -ī nt cart.

Sarrānus adj Tyrian.

sarriō etc see **sariō**.

sarsī perf of **sarciō**.

sartāgō, -inis f frying pan.

sartor, -ōris m hoer, weeder.

sartus ppp of **sarciō**.

sat etc see **satis**.

satagō, -ere vi to have one's hands full, be in trouble; to bustle about, fuss.

satelles, -itis m/f attendant, follower; assistant, accomplice.

satiās, -ātis f sufficiency; satiety.

satietās, -ātis f sufficiency; satiety.

satin, satine see **satisne**.

satiō, -āre, -āvī, -ātum vt to satisfy, appease; to fill, saturate; to glut, cloy, disgust.

satiō, -ōnis f sowing, planting; (pl) fields.

satis, sat adj enough, sufficient ♦ adv enough, sufficiently; tolerably, fairly, quite; ~ **accipiō** take sufficient bail; ~ **agō, agitō** have one's hands full, be harassed; ~ **dō** offer sufficient bail; ~ **faciō** satisfy; give satisfaction, make amends; (creditor) pay.

satisdatiō, -ōnis f giving security.

satisdō see **satis**.

satisfaciō see **satis**.

satisfactiō, -ōnis f amends, apology.

satisne adv quite, really.

satius compar of **satis**; better, preferable.

sator, -ōris m sower, planter; father; promoter.

satrapēs, -is m satrap (Persian governor).

satur, -ī adj filled, sated; (fig) rich.

satura, -ae f mixed dish; medley; (poem) satire; **per ~am** confusingly.

saturēia, -ōrum ntpl (plant) savory.

saturitās, -ātis f repletion; fulness, plenty.

Saturnālia, -ium and **iōrum** ntpl festival of

Noun declensions and verb conjugations are shown on pp xiii to xxv. The present infinitive ending of a verb shows to which conjugation it belongs: **-āre** = 1st; **-ēre** = 2nd; **-ere** = 3rd and **-īre** = 4th. Irregular verbs are shown on p xxvi

Saturn in December.

Saturnia, -iae f Juno.

Saturnīnus, -ī m revolutionary tribune in 103 and 100 B.C.

Saturnius adj see n.

Saturnus, -ī m Saturn (god of sowing, ruler of the Golden Age); the planet Saturn.

saturō, -āre, -āvī, -ātum vt to fill, glut, satisfy; to disgust.

satus ppp of **serō** ♦ m son ♦ f daughter ♦ ntpl crops.

satus, -ūs m sowing, planting; begetting.

satyriscus, -ī m little satyr.

satyrus, -ī m satyr.

sauciātiō, -ōnis f wounding.

sauciō, -āre vt to wound, hurt.

saucius adj wounded, hurt; ill, stricken.

Sauromatae etc see **Sarmatae**.

sāviātiō, -ōnis f kissing.

sāviolum, -ī nt sweet kiss.

sāvior, -ārī vt to kiss.

sāvium, -ī and **iī** nt kiss.

saxātilis adj rock- (in cpds).

saxētum, -ī nt rocky place.

saxeus adj of rock, rocky.

saxificus adj petrifying.

saxōsus adj rocky, stony.

saxulum, -ī nt small rock.

saxum, -ī nt rock, boulder; the Tarpeian Rock.

scaber, -rī adj rough, scurfy; mangy, itchy.

scabiēs, -em, -ē f roughness, scurf; mange, itch.

scabillum, -ī nt stool; a castanet played with the foot.

scabō, -ere, scābī vt to scratch.

Scaea porta, -ae, -ae f the west gate of Troy.

scaena, -ae f stage, stage setting; (fig) limelight, public life; outward appearance, pretext.

scaenālis adj theatrical.

scaenicus adj stage- (in cpds), theatrical ♦ m actor.

Scaevola, -ae m early Roman who burned his hand off before Porsenna; famous jurist of Cicero's day.

scaevus adj on the left; perverse ♦ f omen.

scālae, -ārum fpl steps, ladder, stairs.

scalmus, -ī m tholepin.

scalpellum, -ī nt scalpel, lancet.

scalpō, -ere, -sī, -tum vt to carve, engrave; to scratch.

scalprum, -ī nt knife, penknife; chisel.

scalpurriō, -īre vi to scratch.

Scamander, -rī m river of Troy (also called Xanthus).

scammōnea, -ae f (plant) scammony.

scamnum, -ī nt bench, stool; throne.

scandō, -ere vt, vi to climb, mount.

scapha, -ae f boat, skiff.

scaphium, -ī and **iī** nt a boat-shaped cup.

scapulae, -ārum fpl shoulder blades; shoulders.

scāpus, -ī m shaft; (loom) yarnbeam.

scarus, -ī m (fish) scar.

scatebra, -ae f gushing water.

scateō, -ēre; -ō, -ere vi to bubble up, gush out; (fig) to abound, swarm.

scatūrīginēs, -um fpl springs.

scatūriō, -īre vi to gush out; (fig) to be full of.

scaurus adj large-ankled.

scelerātē adv wickedly.

scelerātus adj desecrated; wicked, infamous, accursed; pernicious.

scelerō, -āre vt to desecrate.

scelerōsus adj vicious, accursed.

scelestē adv wickedly.

scelestus adj wicked, villainous, accursed; unlucky.

scelus, -eris nt wickedness, crime, sin; (person) scoundrel; (event) calamity.

scēn- etc see **scaen-**.

scēptrifer, -ī adj sceptered.

scēptrum, -ī nt staff, sceptre; kingship, power.

scēptūchus, -ī m sceptre-bearer.

scheda etc see **scida**.

schēma, -ae f form, figure, style.

Schoenēis, -eidis f Atalanta.

Schoenēius adj see **Schoenēis**.

Schoeneus, -eī m father of Atalanta.

schoenobatēs, -ae m rope dancer.

schola, -ae f learned discussion, dissertation; school; sect, followers.

scholasticus adj of a school ♦ m rhetorician.

scida, -ae f sheet of paper.

sciēns, -entis pres p of **sciō** ♦ adj knowing, purposely; versed in, acquainted with.

scienter adv expertly.

scientia, -ae f knowledge, skill.

scīlicet adv evidently, of course; (concessive) no doubt; (ironical) I suppose, of course.

scilla etc see **squilla**.

scindō, -ndere, -dī, -ssum vt to cut open, tear apart, split, break down; to divide, part.

scintilla, -ae f spark.

scintillō, -āre vi to sparkle.

scintillula, -ae f little spark.

sciō, -īre, -īvī, -ītum vt to know; to have skill in; (with infin) to know how to; **quod ~iam** as far as I know; **~ītō** you may be sure.

Scīpiadēs, -ae m Scipio.

scīpiō, -ōnis m staff.

Scipiō, -ōnis m famous Roman family name (esp the conqueror of Hannibal Africanus); Aemilianus (destroyer of Carthage and patron of literature).

scirpeus adj rush (in cpds) ♦ f wickerwork frame.

scirpiculus, -ī m rush basket.

scirpus, -ī m bulrush.

scīscitor, -ārī, -ātus; -ō, -āre vt to inquire; to question.

scīscō, -scere, -vī, -tum vt to inquire, learn; (POL) to approve, decree, appoint.

scissus *ppp of* **scindō ♦** *adj* split; (*voice*) harsh.

scītāmenta, -ōrum *ntpl* dainties.

scītē *adv* cleverly, tastefully.

scītor, -ārī, -ātus *vt, vi* to inquire; to consult.

scītulus *adj* neat, smart.

scītum, -ī *nt* decree, statute.

scītus *ppp of* **sciō;** *ppp of* **scīscō ♦** *adj* clever, shrewd, skilled; (*words*) sensible, witty; (*appearance*) fine, smart.

scītus, -ūs *m* decree.

sciūrus, -ī *m* squirrel.

scīvī *perf of* **sciō;** *perf of* **scīscō.**

scobis, -is *f* sawdust, filings.

scomber, -rī *m* mackerel.

scōpae, -ārum *fpl* broom.

Scopās, -ae *m famous Greek sculptor.*

scopulōsus *adj* rocky.

scopulus, -ī *m* rock, crag, promontory; (*fig*) danger.

scorpiō, -ōnis, -us *and* **os, -ī** *m* scorpion; (*MIL*) a kind of catapult.

scortātor, -ōris *m* fornicator.

scorteus *adj* of leather.

scortor, -ārī *vi* to associate with harlots.

scortum, -ī *nt* harlot, prostitute.

screātor, -ōris *m* one who clears his throat noisily.

screātus, -ūs *m* clearing the throat.

scrība, -ae *m* clerk, writer.

scrībō, -bere, -psī, -ptum *vt* to write, draw; to write down, describe; (*document*) to draw up; (*law*) to designate; (*MIL*) to enlist.

scrīnium, -ī *and* **iī** *nt* book box, lettercase.

scrīptiō, -ōnis *f* writing; composition; text.

scrīptitō, -āre, -āvī, -ātum *vt* to write regularly, compose.

scrīptor, -ōris *m* writer, author; secretary; **rērum ~** historian.

scrīptula, -ōrum *ntpl* lines of a squared board.

scrīptum, -ī *nt* writing, book, work; (*law*) ordinance; **duōdecim ~a** Twelve Lines (*a game played on a squared board*).

scrīptūra, -ae *f* writing; composition; document; (*POL*) tax on public pastures; (*will*) provision.

scrīptus *ppp of* **scrībō.**

scrīptus, -ūs *m* clerkship.

scrīpulum, -ī *nt* small weight, scruple.

scrobis, -is *f* ditch, trench; grave.

scrōfa, -ae *f* breeding sow.

scrōfipāscus, -ī *m* pig breeder.

scrūpeus *adj* stony, rough.

scrūpōsus *adj* rocky, jagged.

scrūpulōsus *adj* stony, rough; (*fig*) precise.

scrūpulum *etc see* **scrīpulum.**

scrūpulus, -ī *m* small sharp stone; (*fig*) uneasiness, doubt, scruple.

scrūpus, -ī *m* sharp stone; (*fig*) uneasiness.

scrūta, -ōrum *ntpl* trash.

scrūtor, -ārī, -ātus *vt* to search, probe into, examine; to find out.

sculpō, -ere, -sī, -tum *vt* to carve, engrave.

sculpōneae, -ārum *fpl* clogs.

sculptilis *adj* carved.

sculptor, -ōris *m* sculptor.

sculptus *ppp of* **sculpō.**

scurra, -ae *m* jester; dandy.

scurrīlis *adj* jeering.

scurrīlitās, -ātis *f* scurrility.

scurror, -ārī *vi* to play the fool.

scūtāle, -is *nt* sling strap.

scūtātus *adj* carrying a shield.

scutella, -ae *f* bowl.

scutica, -ae *f* whip.

scutra, -ae *f* flat dish.

scutula, -ae *f* small dish.

scutula *f* wooden roller; secret letter.

scutulāta, -ae *f* a checked garment.

scūtulum, -ī *nt* small shield.

scūtum, -ī *nt* shield.

Scylla, -ae *f* dangerous rock *or* sea monster (*in the Straits of Messina*).

Scyllaeus *adj see* **Scylla.**

scymnus, -ī *m* cub.

scyphus, -ī *m* wine cup.

Scyrius, -ias *adj see* **Scyros.**

Scyros *and* **us, -ī** *f* Aegean island near Euboea.

scytala *see* **scutula.**

Scytha *and* **ēs, -ae** *m* Scythian.

Scythia, -iae *f* Scythia (*country N.E. of the Black Sea*).

Scythicus *adj* Scythian.

Scythis, -idis *f* Scythian woman.

sē *pron* himself, herself, itself, themselves; one another; **apud ~** at home; in his senses; **inter ~** mutually.

sēbum, -ī *nt* tallow, suet, grease.

sēcēdō, -ēdere, -essī, -essum *vi* to withdraw, retire; to revolt, secede.

sēcernō, -ernere, -rēvī, -rētum *vt* to separate, set apart; to dissociate; to distinguish.

sēcessiō, -ōnis *f* withdrawal; secession.

sēcessus, -ūs *m* retirement, solitude; retreat, recess.

sēclūdō, -dere, -sī, -sum *vt* to shut off, seclude; to separate, remove.

sēclūsus *ppp of* **sēclūdō ♦** *adj* remote.

secō, -āre, -uī, -tum *vt* to cut; to injure; to divide; (*MED*) to operate on; (*motion*) to pass through; (*dispute*) to decide.

sēcrētiō, -ōnis *f* separation.

sēcrētō *adv* apart, in private, in secret.

sēcrētum, -ī *nt* privacy, secrecy; retreat, remote place; secret, mystery.

sēcrētus *ppp of* **sēcernō ♦** *adj* separate; solitary, remote; secret, private.

secta, -ae *f* path; method, way of life; (*POL*) party; (*PHILOS*) school.

Noun declensions and verb conjugations are shown on pp xiii to xxv. The present infinitive ending of a verb shows to which conjugation it belongs: **-āre** = 1st; **-ēre** = 2nd; **-ere** = 3rd and **-īre** = 4th. Irregular verbs are shown on p xxvi

sectārius *adj* leading.

sectātor, -ōris *m* follower, adherent.

sectilis *adj* cut; for cutting.

sectiō, -ōnis *f* auctioning of confiscated goods.

sector, -ōris *m* cutter; buyer at a public sale.

sector, -ārī, -ātus *vt* to follow regularly, attend; to chase, hunt.

sectūra, -ae *f* digging.

sectus *ppp of* **secō.**

sēcubitus, -ūs *m* lying alone.

sēcubō, -āre, -uī *vi* to sleep by oneself; to live alone.

secuī *perf of* **secō.**

sēcul- *etc see* **saecul-.**

sēcum with himself *etc.*

secundānī, -ōrum *mpl* men of the second legion.

secundārius *adj* second-rate.

secundō *adv* secondly.

secundō, -āre *vt* to favour, make prosper.

secundum *prep* (*place*) behind, along; (*time*) after; (*rank*) next to; (*agreement*) according to, in favour of ♦ *adv* behind.

secundus *adj* following, next, second; inferior; favourable, propitious, fortunate ♦ *fpl* (*play*) subsidiary part; (*fig*) second fiddle ♦ *ntpl* success, good fortune; ~**ō flūmine** downstream; **rēs ~ae** prosperity, success.

secūricula, -ae *f* little axe.

secūrifer, -ī *adj* armed with an axe.

secūriger, -ī *adj* armed with an axe.

secūris, -is *f* axe; (*fig*) death blow; (*POL*) authority, supreme power.

sēcūritās, -ātis *f* freedom from anxiety, composure; negligence; safety, feeling of security.

sēcūrus *adj* untroubled, unconcerned; carefree, cheerful; careless.

secus *nt* (*indecl*) sex.

secus *adv* otherwise, differently; badly; **nōn ~** even so.

secūtor, -ōris *m* pursuer.

sed *conj* but; but also, but in fact.

sēdātē *adv* calmly.

sēdātiō, -ōnis *f* calming.

sēdātus *ppp of* **sēdō** ♦ *adj* calm, quiet, composed.

sēdecim *num* sixteen.

sēdēcula, -ae *f* low stool.

sedentārius *adj* sitting.

sedeō, -ēre, sēdī, sessum *vi* to sit; (*army*) to be encamped, blockade; (*magistrates*) to be in session; (*clothes*) to suit, fit; (*places*) to be low-lying; (*heavy things*) to settle, subside; (*weapons*) to stick fast; (*inactivity*) to be idle; (*thought*) to be firmly resolved.

sēdēs, -is *f* seat, chair; abode, home; site, ground, foundation.

sēdī *perf of* **sedeō.**

sedīle, -is *nt* seat, chair.

sēditiō, -ōnis *f* insurrection, mutiny.

sēditiōsē *adv* seditiously.

sēditiōsus *adj* mutinous, factious; quarrelsome; troubled.

sēdō, -āre, -āvī, -ātum *vt* to calm, allay, lull.

sēdūcō, -ūcere, -ūxī, -uctum *vt* to take away, withdraw; to divide.

sēductiō, -ōnis *f* taking sides.

sēductus *ppp of* **sēdūcō** ♦ *adj* remote.

sēdulitās, -ātis *f* earnestness, assiduity; officiousness.

sēdulō *adv* busily, diligently; purposely.

sēdulus *adj* busy, diligent, assiduous; officious.

seges, -itis *f* cornfield; crop.

Segesta, -ae *f* town in N.W. Sicily.

Segestānus *adj see* **Segesta.**

segmentātus *adj* flounced.

segmentum, -ī *nt* brocade.

segne, -iter *adv* slowly, lazily.

segnipēs, -edis *adj* slow of foot.

segnis *adj* slow, sluggish, lazy.

segnitia, -ae *and* **ēs, -em, -ē** *f* slowness, sluggishness, sloth.

sēgregō, -āre, -āvī, -ātum *vt* to separate, put apart; to dissociate.

sēiugātus *adj* separated.

sēiugis, -is *m* chariot and six.

sēiūnctim *adv* separately.

sēiūnctiō, -ōnis *f* separation.

sēiūnctus *ppp of* **sēiungō.**

sēiungō, -gere, sēiūnxī, sēiūnctum *vt* to separate, part.

sēlēctiō, -ōnis *f* choice.

sēlēctus *ppp of* **sēligō.**

Seleucus, -ī *m* king of Syria.

sēlībra, -ae *f* half pound.

sēligō, -igere, -ēgī, -ēctum *vt* to choose, select.

sella, -ae *f* seat, chair, stool, sedan chair; ~ **curūlis** *chair of office for higher magistrates.*

sellisternia, -ōrum *ntpl* sacred banquets to goddesses.

sellula, -ae *f* stool; sedan chair.

sellulārius, -ī *and* **ī ī** *m* mechanic.

sēmanimus *etc see* **sēmianimis.**

semel *adv* once; once for all; first; ever; ~ **atque iterum** again and again; ~ **aut iterum** once or twice.

Semelē, -ēs *f* mother of Bacchus.

Semelēius *adj see* **Semelē.**

sēmen, -inis *nt* seed; (*plant*) seedling, slip; (*men*) race, child; (*physics*) particle; (*fig*) origin, instigator.

sēmentifer, -ī *adj* fruitful.

sēmentis, -is *f* sowing, planting; young corn.

sēmentīvus *adj* of seed time.

sēmermis *etc see* **sēmiermis.**

sēmēstris *adj* half-yearly, for six months.

sēmēsus *adj* half-eaten.

sēmet *pron* self, selves.

sēmiadapertus *adj* half-open.

sēmianimis, -us *adj* half-dead.

sēmiapertus *adj* half-open.

sēmibōs, -ovis *adj* half-ox.

sēmicaper, -rī *adj* half-goat.
sēmicremātus, sēmicremus *adj* half-burned.
sēmicubitālis *adj* half a cubit long.
sēmideus *adj* half-divine ♦ *m* demigod.
sēmidoctus *adj* half-taught.
sēmiermis, -us *adj* half-armed.
sēmiēsus *adj* half-eaten.
sēmifactus *adj* half-finished.
sēmifer, -ī *adj* half-beast; half-savage.
sēmigermānus *adj* half-German.
sēmigravis *adj* half-overcome.
sēmigrō, -āre *vi* to go away.
sēmihiāns, -antis *adj* half-opened.
sēmihomō, -inis *m* half-man, half-human.
sēmihōra, -ae *f* half an hour.
sēmilacer, -ī *adj* half-mangled.
sēmilautus *adj* half-washed.
sēmilīber, -ī *adj* half-free.
sēmilixa, -ae *m* not much better than a camp follower.
sēmimarīnus *adj* half in the sea.
sēmimās, -āris *m* hermaphrodite ♦ *adj* castrated.
sēmimortuus *adj* half-dead.
sēminārium, -ī and iī *nt* nursery, seed plot.
sēminātor, -ōris *m* originator.
sēminecis *adj* half-dead.
sēminium, -ī and iī *nt* procreation; breed.
sēminō, -āre *vt* to sow; to produce; to beget.
sēminūdus *adj* half-naked; almost unarmed.
sēmipāgānus *adj* half-rustic.
sēmiplēnus *adj* half-full, half-manned.
sēmiputātus *adj* half-pruned.
Semiramis, -is and idis *f* queen of Assyria.
Semiramius *adj see n.*
sēmirāsus *adj* half-shaven.
sēmireductus *adj* half turned back.
sēmirefectus *adj* half-repaired.
sēmirutus *adj* half-demolished, half in ruins.
sēmis, -issis *m* (*coin*) half an as; (*interest*) ½ per cent per month (*i.e. 6 per cent per annum*); (*area*) half an acre.
sēmisepultus *adj* half-buried.
sēmisomnus *adj* half-asleep.
sēmisupīnus *adj* half lying back.
sēmita, -ae *f* path, way.
sēmitālis *adj* of byways.
sēmitārius *adj* frequenting byways.
sēmiūst- *etc see* **sēmūst-**.
sēmivir, -ī *adj* half-man; emasculated; unmanly.
sēmivīvus *adj* half-dead.
sēmodius, -ī and iī *m* half a peck.
sēmōtus *ppp of* **sēmoveō** ♦ *adj* remote; distinct.
sēmoveō, -ovēre, -ōvī, -ōtum *vt* to put aside, separate.
semper *adv* always, ever, every time.
sempiternus *adj* everlasting, lifelong.

Semprōnius, -ī *m* Roman family name (*esp the Gracchi*).
Semprōnius, -iānus *adj see n.*
sēmūncia, -ae *f* half an ounce; a twenty-fourth.
sēmūnciārius *adj* (*interest*) at the rate of one twenty-fourth.
sēmūstulātus *adj* half-burned.
sēmūstus *adj* half-burned.
senāculum, -ī *nt* open air meeting place (*of the Senate*).
sēnāriolus, -ī *m* little trimeter.
sēnārius, -ī and iī *m* (iambic) trimeter.
senātor, -ōris *m* senator.
senātōrius *adj* senatorial, in the Senate.
senātus, -ūs *m* Senate; meeting of the Senate.
senātūscōnsultum, -ī *nt* decree of the Senate.
Seneca, -ae *m* Stoic philosopher, tutor of Nero.
senecta, -ae *f* old age.
senecta *adj* old, aged.
senectūs, -ūtis *f* old age; old men.
seneō, -ēre *vi* to be old.
senēscō, -ēscere, -uī *vi* to grow old; (*fig*) to weaken, wane, pine away.
senex, -is (*compar* **-ior**) *adj* old (*over 45*) ♦ *m/f* old man, old woman.
sēnī, -ōrum *adj* six each, in sixes; six; ~ **dēnī** sixteen each.
senīlis *adj* of an old person, senile.
sēniō, -ōnis *m* number six on a dice.
senior *compar of* **senex**.
senium, -ī and iī *nt* weakness of age, decline; affliction; peevishness.
Senonēs, -um *mpl* tribe of S. Gaul.
sēnsī *perf of* **sentiō**.
sēnsifer, -ī *adj* sensory.
sēnsilis *adj* having sensation.
sēnsim *adv* tentatively, gradually.
sēnsus *ppp of* **sentiō** ♦ *ntpl* thoughts.
sēnsus, -ūs *m* (*body*) feeling, sensation, sense; (*intellect*) understanding, judgment, thought; (*emotion*) sentiment, attitude, frame of mind; (*language*) meaning, purport, sentence; **commūnis** ~ universal human feelings, human sympathy, social instinct.
sententia, -ae *f* opinion, judgment; purpose, will; (*law*) verdict, sentence; (POL) vote, decision; (*language*) meaning, sentence, maxim, epigram; **meā ~ā** in my opinion; **dē meā ~ā** in accordance with my wishes; **ex meā ~ā** to my liking; **ex animī meī ~ā** to the best of my knowledge and belief; **in ~am pedibus īre** support a motion.
sententiola, -ae *f* phrase.
sententiōsē *adv* pointedly.
sententiōsus *adj* pithy.
senticētum, -ī *nt* thornbrake.
sentīna, -ae *f* bilge water; (*fig*) dregs, scum.
sentiō, -īre, -sēnsī, -sēnsum *vt* (*senses*) to

Noun declensions and verb conjugations are shown on pp xiii to xxv. The present infinitive ending of a verb shows to which conjugation it belongs: **-āre** = 1st; **-ēre** = 2nd; **-ere** = 3rd and **-īre** = 4th. Irregular verbs are shown on p xxvi

feel, see, perceive; (*CIRCS*) to experience, undergo; (*mind*) to observe, understand; (*opinion*) to think, judge; (*law*) to vote, decide.

sentis, -is *m* thorn, brier.

sentīscō, -ere *vt* to begin to perceive.

sentus *adj* thorny; untidy.

senuī *perf of* **senēscō**.

seorsum, seorsus *adv* apart, differently.

sēparābilis *adj* separable.

sēparātim *adv* apart, separately.

sēparātiō, -ōnis *f* separation, severing.

sēparātius *adv* less closely.

sēparātus *adj* separate, different.

sēparō, -āre, -āvī, -ātum *vt* to part, separate, divide; to distinguish.

sepeliō, -elīre, -elīvī *and* **eliī, -ultum** *vt* to bury; (*fig*) to overwhelm, overcome.

sēpia, -ae *f* cuttlefish.

Sēplasia, -ae *f* street in Capua where perfumes were sold.

sēpōnō, -ōnere, -osuī, -ositum *vt* to put aside, pick out; to reserve; to banish; to appropriate; to separate.

sēpositus *ppp of* **sēpōnō** ♦ *adj* remote; distinct, choice.

sēpse *pron* oneself.

septem *num* seven.

September, -ris *m* September ♦ *adj of* September.

septemdecim *etc see* **septendecim**.

septemfluus *adj* with seven streams.

septemgeminus *adj* sevenfold.

septemplex, -icis *adj* sevenfold.

septemtriō *etc see* **septentriōnēs**.

septemvirālis *adj* of the septemviri ♦ *mpl* the septemviri.

septemvirātus, -ūs *m* office of septemvir.

septemvirī, -ōrum *mpl* board of seven officials.

septēnārius, -ī *and* **iī** *m* verse of seven feet.

septendecim *num* seventeen.

septēnī, -ōrum *adj* seven each, in sevens.

septentriō, -ōnis *m*, **-ōnēs, -ōnum** *mpl* Great Bear, Little Bear; north; north wind.

septentriōnālis *adj* northern ♦ *ntpl* northern regions.

septiēns, -ēs *adv* seven times.

septimānī, -ōrum *mpl* men of the seventh legion.

septimum *adv* for the seventh time; ~ **decimus** seventeenth.

septimus *adj* seventh.

septingentēsimus *adj* seven hundredth.

septingentī, -ōrum *adj* seven hundred.

septuāgēsimus *adj* seventieth.

septuāgintā *adj* seventy.

septuennis *adj* seven years old.

septumus *adj see* **septimus**.

septūnx, -ūncis *m* seven ounces, seven-twelfths.

sepulcrālis *adj* funeral.

sepulcrētum, -ī *nt* cemetery.

sepulcrum, -ī *nt* grave, tomb.

sepultūra, -ae *f* burial, funeral.

sepultus *ppp of* **sepeliō**.

Sequāna, -ae *f* river Seine.

Sequānī, -ōrum *mpl* people of N. Gaul.

sequāx, -ācis *adj* pursuing, following.

sequens, -entis *pres p of* **sequor** ♦ *adj* following, next.

sequester, -rī *and* **ris** *m* trustee; agent, mediator.

sequestrum, -rī *nt* deposit.

sēquius *compar of* **secus**; otherwise; **nihilō ~** nonetheless.

sequor, -quī, -cūtus *vt, vi* to follow; to accompany, go with; (*time*) to come after, come next, ensue; (*enemy*) to pursue; (*objective*) to make for, aim at; (*pulling*) to come away easily; (*share, gift*) to go to, come to; (*words*) to come naturally.

sera, -ae *f* door bolt, bar.

Serāpēum, -ēī *nt* temple of Serapis.

Serāpis, -is *and* **idis** *m* chief Egyptian god.

serēnitās, -ātis *f* fair weather.

serēnō, -āre *vt* to clear up, brighten up.

serēnus *adj* fair, clear; (*wind*) fair-weather; (*fig*) cheerful, happy ♦ *nt* clear sky, fair weather.

Sēres, -um *mpl* Chinese.

serēscō, -ere *vi* to dry off.

sēria, -ae *f* tall jar.

sērica, -ōrum *ntpl* silks.

Sēricus *adj* Chinese; silk.

seriēs, -em, -ē *f* row, sequence, succession.

sēriō *adv* in earnest, seriously.

sēriola, -ae *f* small jar.

Serīphius *adj see* **Serīphus**.

Serīphus (-os), -ī *f* Aegean island.

sērius *adj* earnest, serious.

sērius *compar of* **sērō**.

sermō, -ōnis *m* conversation, talk; learned discussion, discourse; common talk, rumour; language, style; every day language, prose; (*pl*) Satires (of Horace).

sermōcinor, -ārī *vi* to converse.

sermunculus, -ī *m* gossip, rumour.

serō, -ere, sēvī, -satum *vt* to sow, plant; (*fig*) to produce, sow the seeds of.

serō, -ere, -tum *vt* to sew, join, wreathe; (*fig*) to compose, devise, engage in.

sērō (*compar* **-ius**) *adv* late; too late.

serpēns, -entis *m/f* snake, serpent; (*constellation*) Draco.

serpentigena, -ae *m* offspring of a serpent.

serpentipēs, -edis *adj* serpent-footed.

serperastra, -ōrum *ntpl* splints.

serpō, -ere, -sī, -tum *vi* to creep, crawl; (*fig*) to spread slowly.

serpyllum, -ī *nt* wild thyme.

serra, -ae *f* saw.

serrācum *etc see* **sarrācum**.

serrātus *adj* serrated, notched.

serrula, -ae *f* small saw.

Sertōriānus *adj see* **Sertōrius**.

Sertōrius, -ī *m commander under Marius, who held out against Sulla in Spain.*

sertus *ppp of* **serō ♦** *ntpl* garlands.

serum, -ī *nt* whey, serum.

sērum, -ī *nt* late hour.

sērus *adj* late; too late; **~ā nocte** late at night.

serva, -ae *f* maidservant, slave.

servābilis *adj* that cannot be saved.

servātor, -ōris *m* deliverer; watcher.

servātrīx, -īcis *f* deliverer.

servīlis *adj* of slaves, servile.

servīliter *adv* slavishly.

Servīlius, -ī *m Roman family name of many consuls.*

Servīlius, -ānus *adj see n.*

serviō, -īre, -īvī *and* **iī, -ītum** *vi* to be a slave; (*with dat*) to serve, be of use to, be good for; (*property*) to be mortgaged.

servitium, -ī *and* **iī** *nt* slavery, servitude; slaves.

servitūdō, -inis *f* slavery.

servitūs, -ūtis *f* slavery, service; slaves; (*property*) liability.

Servius, -ī *m sixth king of Rome; famous jurist of Cicero's day.*

servō, -āre, -āvī, -ātum *vt* to save, rescue; to keep, preserve, retain; to store, reserve; to watch, observe, guard; (*place*) to remain in.

servolus, -ī *m* young slave.

servos, -ī *m see* **servus**.

servula, -ae *f* servant girl.

servulus, -ī *m* young slave.

servus, -ī *m* slave, servant **♦** *adj* slavish, serving; (*property*) liable to a burden.

sescēnāris *adj* a year and a half old.

sescēnī, -ōrum *adj* six hundred each.

sescentēsimus *adj* six hundredth.

sescentī, -ōrum *num* six hundred; an indefinitely large number.

sescentiēns, -ēs *adv* six hundred times.

sēsē *etc see* **sē**.

seselis, -is *f* (*plant*) seseli.

sesqui *adv* one and a half times.

sesquialter, -ī *adj* one and a half.

sesquimodius, -ī *and* **iī** *m* a peck and a half.

sesquioctāvus *adj* of nine to eight.

sesquiopus, -eris *nt* a day and a half's work.

sesquipedālis *adj* a foot and a half.

sesquipēs, -edis *m* a foot and a half.

sesquiplāga, -ae *f* a blow and a half.

sesquiplex, -icis *adj* one and a half times.

sesquitertius *adj* of four to three.

sessilis *adj* for sitting on.

sessiō, -ōnis *f* sitting; seat; session; loitering.

sessitō, -āre, -āvī *vi* to sit regularly.

sessiuncula, -ae *f* small meeting.

sessor, -ōris *m* spectator; resident.

sēstertium, -ī *nt* 1000 sesterces; **dēna ~ia** 10,000 sesterces; **centēna mīlia ~ium** 100,000 sesterces; **deciēns ~ium** 1,000,000 sesterces.

sēstertius, -ī *and* **iī** *m* sesterce, a silver coin.

Sestius, -ī *m tribune defended by Cicero.*

Sestius, -iānus *adj* of a Sestius.

Sestos (-us), -ī *f* town on Dardanelles (*home of Hero*).

Sestus *adj see* **Sestos**.

sēt- *etc see* **saet-**.

Sētia, -iae *f* town in S. Latium (*famous for wine*).

Sētiaīnus *adj see* **Sētia**.

sētius *compar of* **secus**.

seu *etc see* **sīve**.

sevērē *adv* sternly, severely.

sevēritās, -ātis *f* strictness, austerity.

sevērus *adj* strict, stern; severe, austere; grim, terrible.

sēvī *perf of* **serō**.

sēvocō, -āre *vt* to call aside; to withdraw, remove.

sēvum *etc see* **sēbum**.

sex *num* six.

sexāgēnārius *adj* sixty years old.

sexāgēnī, -ōrum *adj* sixty each.

sexāgēsimus *adj* sixtieth.

sexāgiēns, -ēs *adv* sixty times.

sexāgintā *num* sixty.

sexangulus *adj* hexagonal.

sexcēn- *etc see* **sescēn-**.

sexcēnārius *adj* of six hundred.

sexennis *adj* six years old, after six years.

sexennium, -ī *and* **iī** *nt* six years.

sexiēns, -ēs *adv* six times.

sexprīmī, -ōrum *mpl* a provincial town, council.

sextadecimānī, -ōrum *mpl* men of the sixteenth legion.

sextāns, -antis *m* a sixth; (*coin, weight*) a sixth of an as.

sextārius, -ī *and* **iī** *m* pint.

Sextīlis, -is *m* August **♦** *adj* of August.

sextula, -ae *f* a sixth of an ounce.

sextum *adv* for the sixth time.

sextus *adj* sixth; **~ decimus** sixteenth.

sexus, -ūs *m* sex.

sī *conj* if; if only; to see if; **sī forte** in the hope that; **sī iam** assuming for the moment; **sī minus** if not; **sī quandō** whenever; **sī quidem** if indeed; since; **sī quis** if anyone, whoever; **mīrum sī** surprising that; **quod sī** and if, but if.

sībila, -ōrum *ntpl* whistle, hissing.

sībilō, -āre *vi* to hiss, whistle **♦** *vt* to hiss at.

sībilus, -ī *m* whistle, hissing.

sībilus *adj* hissing.

Sibulla, Sibylla, -ae *f* prophetess, Sibyl.

Sibyllīnus *adj see* **Sibylla**.

sīc *adv* so, thus, this way, as follows; as one is, as things are; on this condition; yes.

sīca, -ae *f* dagger.

Sicānī, -ōrum *mpl* ancient people of Italy

(later of Sicily).

Sicānia, -iae f Sicily.

Sicānus, -ius adj Sicanian, Sicilian.

sīcārius, -ī and **iī** m assassin, murderer.

siccē adv (speech) firmly.

siccitās, -ātis f dryness, drought; (body) firmness; (style) dullness.

siccō, -āre, -āvī, -ātum vt to dry; to drain, exhaust; (sore) to heal up.

siccoculus adj dry-eyed.

siccus adj dry; thirsty, sober; (body) firm, healthy; (argument) solid, sound; (style) flat, dull ♦ nt dry land.

Sicilia, -ae f Sicily.

sicilicula, -ae f little sickle.

Siciliēnsis, -s, -dis adj Sicilian.

sīcine is this how?

sīcubi adv if anywhere, wheresoever.

Siculus adj Sicilian.

sīcunde adv if from anywhere.

sīcut, sīcutī adv just as, as in fact; (comparison) like, as; (example) as for instance; (with subj) as if.

Sicyōn, -ōnis f town in N. Peloponnese.

Sicyōnius adj see **Sicyōn.**

sīdereus adj starry; (fig) radiant.

Sidicīnī, -ōrum mpl people of Campania.

Sidicīnus adj see n.

sīdō, -ere, -ī vi to sit down, settle; to sink, subside; to stick fast.

Sīdōn, -ōnis f famous Phoenician town.

Sīdōnis, -ōnidis adj Phoenician ♦ f Europa; Dido.

Sīdōnius adj Sidonian, Phoenician.

sīdus, -eris nt constellation; heavenly body, star; season, climate, weather; destiny; (pl) sky; (fig) fame, glory.

siem archaic subj of **sum.**

Sigambrī etc see **Sugambrī.**

Sīgēum, -ī nt promontory near Troy.

Sīgēus, -ius adj Sigean.

sigilla, -ōrum ntpl little figures; seal.

sigillātus adj decorated with little figures.

signātor, -ōris m witness (to a document).

signifer, -ī adj with constellations; ~ orbis Zodiac ♦ m (MIL) standard-bearer.

significanter adv pointedly, tellingly.

significātiō, -ōnis f indication, signal, token; sign of approval; (RHET) emphasis; (word) meaning.

significō, -āre, -āvī, -ātum vt to indicate, show; to betoken, portend; (word) to mean.

signō, -āre, -āvī, -ātum vt to mark, stamp, print; (document) to seal; (money) to coin, mint; (fig) to impress, designate, note.

signum, -ī nt mark, sign, token; (MIL) standard; signal, password; (art) design, statue; (document) seal; (ASTRO) constellation; ~a cōnferre join battle; ~a cōnstituere halt; ~a convertere wheel about; ~a ferre move camp; attack; ~a inferre attack; ~a prōferre advance; ~a sequī march in order; ab ~īs discēdere leave the ranks; sub ~īs īre march

in order.

Sīla, -ae f forest in extreme S. Italy

sīlānus, -ī m fountain, jet of water.

silēns, -entis pres p of **sileō** ♦ adj still, silent ♦ mpl the dead.

silentium, -ī and **iī** nt stillness, silence; (fig) standstill, inaction.

Sīlēnus, -ī m old and drunken companion of Bacchus.

sileō, -ēre, -uī vi to be still, be silent; to cease ♦ vt to say nothing about.

siler, -is nt willow.

silēscō, -ere vi to calm down, fall silent.

silex, -icis m flint, hard stone; rock.

silicernium, -ī and **iī** nt funeral feast.

silīgō, -inis f winter wheat; fine flour.

siliqua, -ae f pod, husk; (pl) pulse.

sillybus, -ī m label bearing a book's title.

Silurēs, -um mpl British tribe in S. Wales.

silūrus, -ī m sheatfish.

sīlus adj snub-nosed.

silva, -ae f wood, forest; plantation, shrubbery; (plant) flowering stem; (LIT) material.

Silvānus, -ī m god of uncultivated land.

silvēscō, -ere vi to run to wood.

silvestris adj wooded, forest- (in cpds); wild; pastoral.

silvicola, -ae m/f sylvan.

silvicultrīx, -īcis adj living in the woods.

silvifragus adj tree-breaking.

silvōsus adj woody.

sīmia, -ae f ape.

simile, -is nt comparison, parallel.

similis adj like, similar; ~ atque like what; vērī ~ probable.

similiter adv similarly.

similitūdō, -inis f likeness, resemblance; imitation; analogy; monotony; (RHET) simile.

sīmiolus, -ī m monkey.

simītū adv at the same time, together.

sīmius, -ī and **iī** m ape.

Simoīs, -entis m river of Troy.

Simōnidēs, -is m Greek lyric poet of Ceos (famous for dirges).

Simōnidēus adj see n.

simplex, -icis adj single, simple; natural, straightforward; (character) frank, sincere.

simplicitās, -ātis f singleness; frankness, innocence.

simpliciter adv simply, naturally; frankly.

simplum, -ī nt simple sum.

simpulum, -ī nt small ladle; **excitāre flūctūs in ~ō** ≈ raise a storm in a teacup.

simpuvium, -ī and **iī** nt libation bowl.

simul adv at the same time, together, at once; likewise, also; both ... and; ~ ac atque, ut as soon as ♦ conj as soon as.

simulācrum, -ī nt likeness, image, portrait, statue; phantom, ghost; (writing) symbol; (fig) semblance, shadow.

simulāmen, -inis nt copy.

simulāns, -antis pres p of **simulō** ♦ adj

imitative.

simulāte *adv* deceitfully.

simulātiō, -ōnis *f* pretence, shamming, hypocrisy.

simulātor, -ōris *m* imitator; pretender, hypocrite.

simulatque *conj* as soon as.

simulō, -āre, -āvī, -ātum *vt* to imitate, represent; to impersonate; to pretend, counterfeit.

simultās, -ātis *f* feud, quarrel.

sīmulus *adj* snub-nosed.

sīmus *adj* snub-nosed.

sīn *conj* but if; ~ **aliter, minus** but if not.

sināpi, -is *nt*, **-is, -is** *f* mustard.

sincērē *adv* honestly.

sincēritās, -ātis *f* integrity.

sincērus *adj* clean, whole, genuine; (*fig*) pure, sound, honest.

sincipitāmentum, -ī *nt* half a head.

sinciput, -itis *nt* half a head; brain.

sine *prep* (*with abl*) without, -less (*in cpds*).

singillātim *adv* singly, one by one.

singulāris *adj* one at a time, single, sole; unique, extraordinary.

singulāriter *adv* separately; extremely.

singulārius *adj* single.

singulī, -ōrum *adj* one each, single, one.

singultim *adv* in sobs.

singultō, -āre *vi* to sob, gasp, gurgle ♦ *vt* to gasp out.

singultus, -ūs *m* sob, gasp, death rattle.

singulus *etc see* **singulī**.

sinister, -rī *adj* left; (*fig*) perverse, unfavourable; (*Roman auspices*) lucky; (*Greek auspices*) unlucky.

sinistra, -rae *f* left hand, left-hand side.

sinistrē *adv* badly.

sinistrōrsus, -um *adv* to the left.

sinō, -ere, sīvī, situm *vt* to let, allow; to let be; **nē dī sīrint** God forbid!

Sinōpē, -ēs *f* Greek colony on the Black Sea.

Sinōpēnsis, -eus *adj see* **Sinōpē**.

Sinuessa, -ae *f* town on the borders of Latium and Campania.

Sinuessānus *adj see* **Sinuessa**.

sīnum *etc see* **sīnus**.

sinuō, -āre, -āvī, -ātum *vt* to wind, curve.

sinuōsus *adj* winding, curved.

sinus, -ūs *m* curve, fold; (*fishing*) net; (*GEOG*) bay, gulf, valley; (*hair*) curl; (*ship*) sail; (*toga*) fold, pocket, purse; (*person*) bosom; (*fig*) protection, love, heart, hiding place; **in -ū gaudēre** be secretly glad.

sīnus, -ī *m* large cup.

sīparium, -ī *and* **iī** *nt* act curtain.

sīphō, -ōnis *m* siphon; fire engine.

sīquandō *adv* if ever.

sīquī, sīquis *pron* if any, if anyone, whoever.

sīquidem *adv* if in fact ♦ *conj* since.

sirempse *adj* the same.

Sīrēn, -ēnis *f* Siren.

sīris, sīrit *perf subj of* **sinō**.

Sīrius, -ī *m* Dog Star ♦ *adj* of Sirius.

sirpe, -is *nt* silphium.

sīrus, -ī *m* corn pit.

sīs (*for* **sī vīs**) *adv* please.

sistō, -ere, stitī, statum *vt* to place, set, plant; (*law*) to produce in court; (*monument*) to set up; (*movement*) to stop, arrest, check ♦ *vi* to stand, rest; (*law*) to appear in court; (*movement*) to stand still, stop, stand firm; **sē** ~ appear, present oneself; **tūtum** ~ see safe; **vadimōnium** ~ duly appear in court; **~ī nōn potest** the situation is desperate.

sistrum, -ī *nt* Egyptian rattle, cymbal.

sisymbrium, -ī *and* **iī** *nt* fragrant herb, perhaps mint.

Sīsyphius *adj*, **-idēs, -idae** *m* Ulysses.

Sīsyphus, -ī *m* criminal condemned in Hades to roll a rock repeatedly up a hill.

sitella, -ae *f* lottery urn.

Sīthonis, -idis *adj* Thracian.

Sīthonius *adj* Thracian.

sitīculōsus *adj* thirsty, dry.

sitiēns, -entis *pres p of* **sitiō** ♦ *adj* thirsty, dry; parching; (*fig*) eager.

sitienter *adv* eagerly.

sitiō, -īre *vi* to be thirsty; to be parched ♦ *vt* to thirst for, covet.

sitis, -is *f* thirst; drought.

sittybus *etc see* **sillybus**.

situla, -ae *f* bucket.

situs *ppp of* **sinō** ♦ *adj* situated, lying; founded; (*fig*) dependent.

situs, -ūs *m* situation, site; structure; neglect, squalor, mould; (*mind*) dullness.

sīve *conj* or if; or; whether ... or.

sīvī *perf of* **sinō**.

smaragdus, -ī *m/f* emerald.

smīlax, -acis *f* bindweed.

Smintheus, -eī *m* Apollo.

Smyrna, -ae *f* Ionian town in Asia Minor.

Smyrnaeus *adj see* **Smyrna**.

sobol- *etc see* **subol-**.

sōbriē *adv* temperately; sensibly.

sōbrīna, -ae *f* cousin (*on the mother's side*).

sōbrīnus, -ī *m* cousin (*on the mother's side*).

sōbrius *adj* sober; temperate, moderate; (*mind*) sane, sensible.

soccus, -ī *m* slipper (*esp the sock worn by actors in comedy*); comedy.

socer, -ī *m* father-in-law.

sociābilis *adj* compatible.

sociālis *adj* of allies, confederate; conjugal.

sociāliter *adv* sociably.

sociennus, -ī *m* friend.

societās, -ātis *f* fellowship, association; alliance.

sociō, -āre, -āvī, -ātum *vt* to unite, associate,

Noun declensions and verb conjugations are shown on pp xiii to xxv. The present infinitive ending of a verb shows to which conjugation it belongs: -**āre** = 1st; -**ēre** = 2nd; -**ere** = 3rd and -**īre** = 4th. Irregular verbs are shown on p xxvi

share.

sociofraudus, -ī m deceiver of friends.

socius adj associated, allied ♦ m friend, companion; partner, ally.

sōcordia, -ae f indolence, apathy; folly.

sōcordius adv more carelessly, lazily.

sōcors, -dis adj lazy, apathetic; stupid.

Sōcratēs, -is m famous Athenian philosopher.

Sōcraticus adj of Socrates, Socratic ♦ mpl the followers of Socrates.

socrus, -ūs f mother-in-law.

sodālicium, -ī and **iī** nt fellowship; secret society.

sodālicius adj of fellowship.

sodālis, -is m/f companion, friend; member of a society, accomplice.

sodālitās, -ātis f companionship, friendship; society, club; secret society.

sodālitius etc see **sodālicius.**

sodēs adv please.

sōl, sōlis m sun; sunlight, sun's heat; (poetry) day; (myth) Sun god; ~ oriēns, ~is ortus east; ~ occidēns, ~is occāsus west.

sōlāciolum, -ī nt a grain of comfort.

sōlācium, -ī and **iī** nt comfort, consolation, relief.

sōlāmen, -inis nt solace, relief.

sōlāris adj of the sun.

sōlārium, -ī and **iī** nt sundial; clock; balcony, terrace.

sōlātium etc see **sōlācium.**

sōlātor, -ōris m consoler.

soldūriī, -ōrum mpl retainers.

soldus etc see **solidus.**

solea, -ae f sandal, shoe; fetter; (fish) sole.

soleārius, -ī and **iī** m sandal makeŕ.

soleātus adj wearing sandals.

soleō, -ēre, -itus vi to be accustomed, be in the habit, usually do; **ut ~ as usual.**

solidē adv for certain.

soliditās, -ātis f solidity.

solidō, -āre vt to make firm, strengthen.

solidus adj solid, firm, dense; whole, complete; (fig) sound, genuine, substantial ♦ nt solid matter, firm ground.

sōliferreum, -ī nt an all-iron javelin.

sōlistimus adj (AUG) most favourable.

sōlitārius adj solitary, lonely.

sōlitūdō, -inis f solitariness, loneliness; destitution; (place) desert.

solitus ppa of **soleō** ♦ adj usual, customary ♦ nt custom; **plūs ~ō** more than usual.

solium, -ī and **iī** nt seat, throne; tub; (fig) rule.

sōlivagus adj going by oneself; single.

sollemne, -is nt religious rite, festival; usage, practice.

sollemnis adj annual, regular; religious, solemn; usual, ordinary.

sollemniter adv solemnly.

sollers, -tis adj skilled, clever, expert; ingenious.

sollerter adv cleverly.

sollertia, -ae f skill, ingenuity.

sollicitātiō, -ōnis f inciting.

sollicitō, -āre, -āvī, -ātum vt to stir up, disturb; to trouble, distress, molest; to rouse, urge, incite, tempt, tamper with.

sollicitūdō, -inis f uneasiness, anxiety.

sollicitus adj agitated, disturbed; (mind) troubled, worried, alarmed; (things) anxious, careful; (cause) disquieting.

solliferreum etc see **sōliferreum.**

sollistimus etc see **sōlistimus.**

soloecismus, -ī m grammatical mistake.

Solōn, -ōnis m famous Athenian lawgiver.

sōlor, -ārī, -ātus vt to comfort, console; to relieve, ease.

sōlstitiālis adj of the summer solstice; midsummer.

sōlstitium, -ī and **iī** nt summer solstice; midsummer, summer heat.

solum, -ī nt ground, floor, bottom; soil, land, country; (foot) sole; (fig) basis; **~ō aequāre** raze to the ground.

sōlum adv only, merely.

sōlus (gen **-īus,** dat **-ī**) see **vicis;** adj only, alone; lonely, forsaken; (place) lonely, deserted.

solūtē adv loosely, freely, carelessly, weakly, fluently.

solūtiō, -ōnis f loosening; payment.

solūtus ppp of **solvō** ♦ adj loose, free; (from distraction) at ease, at leisure, merry; (from obligation) exempt; (from restraint) free, independent, unprejudiced; (moral) lax, weak, insolent; (language) prose, unrhythmical; (speaker) fluent; **ōrātiō ~a, verba ~a** prose.

solvō, -vere, -vī, -ūtum vt to loosen, undo; to free, release, acquit, exempt; to dissolve, break up, separate; to relax, slacken, weaken; to cancel, remove, destroy; to solve, explain; to pay, fulfil; (argument) to refute; (discipline) to undermine; (feelings) to get rid of; (hair) to let down; (letter) to open; (sail) to unfurl; (siege) to raise; (troops) to dismiss ♦ vi to set sail; to pay; **nāvem ~** set sail; **poenās ~** be punished; **praesēns ~** pay cash; **rem ~** pay; **sacrāmentō ~** discharge; **~vendō esse** be solvent.

Solyma, -ōrum ntpl Jerusalem.

Solymus adj of the Jews.

somniculōsē adv sleepily.

somniculōsus adj sleepy.

somnifer, -ī adj soporific; fatal.

somniō, -āre vt to dream, dream about; to talk nonsense.

somnium, -ī and **iī** nt dream; nonsense, fancy.

somnus, -ī m sleep; sloth.

sonābilis adj noisy.

sonipēs, -edis m steed.

sonitus, -ūs m sound, noise.

sonivius adj noisy.

sonō, -āre, -uī, -itum vi to sound, make a noise ♦ vt to utter, speak, celebrate; to sound like.

sonor, -ōris m sound, noise.

sonōrus *adj* noisy, loud.

sōns, sontis *adj* guilty.

sonticus *adj* critical; important.

sonus, -ī *m* sound, noise; (*fig*) tone.

sophistēs, -ae *m* sophist.

Sophoclēs, -is *m* famous Greek tragic poet.

Sophoclēus *adj* of Sophocles, Sophoclean.

sophus *adj* wise.

sōpiō, -īre, -īvī, -ītum *vt* to put to sleep; (*fig*) to calm, lull.

sopor, -ōris *m* sleep; apathy.

sopōrifer, -ī *adj* soporific, drowsy.

sopōrō, -āre *vt* to lull to sleep; to make soporific.

sopōrus *adj* drowsy.

Sōracte, -is *nt* mountain in S. Etruria.

sorbeō, -ēre, -uī *vt* to suck, swallow; (*fig*) to endure.

sorbillō, -āre *vt* to sip.

sorbitiō, -ōnis *f* drink, broth.

sorbum, -ī *nt* service berry.

sorbus, -ī *f* service tree.

sordeō, -ēre *vi* to be dirty, be sordid; to seem shabby; to be of no account.

sordēs, -is *f* dirt, squalor, shabbiness; mourning; meanness; vulgarity; (*people*) rabble.

sordēscō, -ere *vi* to become dirty.

sordidātus *adj* shabbily dressed, in mourning.

sordidē *adv* meanly, vulgarly.

sordidulus *adj* soiled, shabby.

sordidus *adj* dirty, squalid, shabby; in mourning; poor, mean; base, vile.

sōrex, -icis *m* shrewmouse.

sōricīnus *adj* of the shrewmouse.

sōrītēs, -ae *m* chain syllogism.

soror, -ōris *f* sister.

sorōricīda, -ae *m* murderer of a sister.

sorōrius *adj* of a sister.

sors, sortis *f* lot; allotted duty; oracle, prophecy; fate, fortune; (*money*) capital, principal.

sōrsum *etc see* **seōrsum**.

sortilegus *adj* prophetic ♦ *m* soothsayer.

sortior, -īrī, -ītus *vi* to draw *or* cast lots ♦ *vt* to draw lots for, allot, obtain by lot; to distribute, share; to choose; to receive.

sortītiō, -ōnis *f* drawing lots, choosing by lot.

sortītus *ppa of* **sortior** ♦ *adj* assigned, allotted; ~ō by lot.

sortītus, -ūs *m* drawing lots.

Sosius, -ī *m* Roman family name (*esp two brothers Sosii, famous booksellers in Rome*).

sōspes, -itis *adj* safe and sound, unhurt; favourable, lucky.

sōspita, -ae *f* saviour.

sōspitālis *adj* beneficial.

sōspitō, -āre *vt* to preserve, prosper.

sōtēr, -ēris *m* saviour.

spādīx, -īcis *adj* chestnut-brown.

spadō, -ōnis *m* eunuch.

spargō, -gere, -sī, -sum *vt* to throw, scatter, sprinkle; to strew, spot, moisten; to disperse, spread abroad.

sparsus *ppp of* **spargō** ♦ *adj* freckled.

Sparta, -ae, -ē, -ēs *f* famous Greek city.

Spartacus, -ī *m* gladiator who led a revolt against Rome.

Spartānus, -icus *adj* Spartan.

Spartiātēs, -iātae *m* Spartan.

spartum, -ī *nt* Spanish broom.

sparulus, -ī *m* bream.

sparus, -ī *m* hunting spear.

spatha, -ae *f* broadsword.

spatior, -ārī, -ātus *vi* to walk; to spread.

spatiōsē *adv* greatly; after a time.

spatiōsus *adj* roomy, ample, large; (*time*) prolonged.

spatium, -ī *and* **iī** *nt* space, room, extent; (*between points*) distance; (*open space*) square, walk, promenade; (*race*) lap, track, course; (*time*) period, interval; (*opportunity*) time, leisure; (*metre*) quantity.

speciēs, -ēī *f* seeing, sight; appearance, form, outline; (*thing seen*) sight; (*mind*) idea; (*in sleep*) vision, apparition; (*fair show*) beauty, splendour; (*false show*) pretence, pretext; (*classification*) species; **in ~em** for the sake of appearances; like; **per ~em** under the pretence; **sub ~ē** under the cloak.

specillum, -ī *nt* probe.

specimen, -inis *nt* sign, evidence, proof; pattern, ideal.

speciōsē *adv* handsomely.

speciōsus *adj* showy, beautiful; specious, plausible.

spectābilis *adj* visible; notable, remarkable.

spectāclum, spectāculum, -ī *nt* sight, spectacle; public show, play; theatre, seats.

spectāmen, -inis *nt* proof.

spectātiō, -ōnis *f* looking; testing.

spectātor, -ōris *m* onlooker, observer, spectator; critic.

spectātrix, -īcis *f* observer.

spectātus *ppp of* **spectō** ♦ *adj* tried, proved; worthy, excellent.

spectiō, -ōnis *f* the right to take auspices.

spectō, -āre, -āvī, -ātum *vt* to look at, observe, watch; (*place*) to face; (*aim*) to look to, bear in mind, contemplate, tend towards; (*judging*) to examine, test.

spectrum, -ī *nt* spectre.

specula, -ae *f* watchtower, lookout; height.

spēcula, -ae *f* slight hope.

speculābundus *adj* on the lookout.

speculāris *adj* transparent ♦ *ntpl* window.

speculātor, -ōris *m* explorer, investigator; (*MIL*) spy, scout.

speculātōrius *adj* for spying, scouting ♦ *f* spy

Noun declensions and verb conjugations are shown on pp xiii to xxv. The present infinitive ending of a verb shows to which conjugation it belongs: **-āre** = 1st; **-ēre** = 2nd; **-ere** = 3rd and **-īre** = 4th. Irregular verbs are shown on p xxvi

boat.

speculātrīx, -īcis _f_ watcher.

speculor, -ārī, -ātus _vt_ to spy out, watch for, observe.

speculum, -ī _nt_ mirror.

specus, -ūs _m, nt_ cave; hollow, chasm.

spēlaeum, -ī _nt_ cave, den.

spēlunca, -ae _f_ cave, den.

spērābilis _adj_ to be hoped for.

spērāta, -ātae _f_ bride.

Sperchēis, -idis _adj see_ **Sperchēus.**

Sperchēus (-os), -ī _m river in Thessaly._

spernō, -ere, sprēvī, sprētum _vt_ to remove, reject, scorn.

spērō, -āre, -āvī, -ātum _vt_ to hope, hope for, expect; to trust; to look forward to.

spēs, speī _f_ hope, expectation; **praeter spem** unexpectedly; **spē dēiectus** disappointed.

Speusippus, -ī _m successor of Plato in the Academy._

sphaera, -ae _f_ ball, globe, sphere.

Sphinx, -ingis _f fabulous monster near Thebes._

spīca, -ae _f_ (_grain_) ear; (_plant_) tuft; (ASTRO) brightest star in Virgo.

spīceus _adj_ of ears of corn.

spīculum, -ī _nt_ point, sting; dart, arrow.

spīna, -ae _f_ thorn; prickle; fish bone; spine, back; (_pl_) difficulties, subtleties.

spīnētum, -ī _nt_ thorn hedge.

spīneus _adj_ of thorns.

spīnifer, -ī _adj_ prickly.

spīnōsus _adj_ thorny, prickly; (_style_) difficult.

spintēr, -ēris _nt_ elastic bracelet.

spīnus, -ī _f_ blackthorn, sloe.

spīra, -ae _f_ coil; twisted band.

spīrābilis _adj_ breathable, life-giving.

spīrāculum, -ī _nt_ vent.

spīrāmentum, -ī _nt_ vent, pore; breathing space.

spīritus, -ūs _m_ breath, breathing; breeze, air; inspiration; character, spirit, courage, arrogance.

spīrō, -āre, -āvī, -ātum _vi_ to breathe, blow; to be alive; to be inspired ♦ _vt_ to emit, exhale; (_fig_) to breathe, express.

spissātus _adj_ condensed.

spissē _adv_ closely; slowly.

spissēscō, -ere _vi_ to thicken.

spissus _adj_ thick, compact, crowded; slow; (_fig_) difficult.

splendeō, -ēre _vi_ to be bright, shine; to be illustrious.

splendēscō, -ere _vi_ to become bright.

splendidē _adv_ brilliantly, magnificently, nobly.

splendidus _adj_ bright, brilliant, glittering; (_sound_) clear; (_dress, house_) magnificent; (_person_) illustrious; (_appearance_) showy.

splendor, -ōris _m_ brightness, lustre; magnificence; clearness; nobility.

spoliātiō, -ōnis _f_ plundering.

spoliātor, -ōris _m_ robber.

spoliātrīx, -īcis _f_ robber.

spoliō, -āre, -āvī, -ātum _vt_ to strip; to rob, plunder.

spolium, -ī _and_ **iī** _nt_ (_beast_) skin; (_enemy_) spoils, booty.

sponda, -ae _f_ bed frame; bed, couch.

spondālium, -ī _and_ **iī** _nt_ hymn accompanied by the flute.

spondeō, -ēre, spopondī, spōnsum _vt_ to promise, pledge, vow; (_law_) to go bail for; (_marriage_) to betroth.

spondēus, -ī _m_ spondee.

spongia, -ae _f_ sponge; coat of mail.

spōnsa, -ae _f_ fiancée, bride.

spōnsālia, -ium _ntpl_ engagement.

spōnsiō, -ōnis _f_ promise, guarantee; (_law_) agreement that the loser in a suit pays the winner a sum; bet.

spōnsor, -ōris _m_ guarantor, surety.

spōnsus _ppp of_ **spondeō** ♦ _m_ fiancé, bridegroom ♦ _nt_ agreement, covenant.

spōnsus, -ūs _m_ contract, surety.

sponte _f_ (_abl_) voluntarily, of one's own accord; unaided, by oneself; spontaneously.

spopondī _perf of_ **spondeō**.

sportella, -ae _f_ fruit basket.

sportula, -ae _f_ small basket; gift to clients, dole.

sprētiō, -ōnis _f_ contempt.

sprētor, -ōris _m_ despiser.

sprētus _ppp of_ **spernō**.

sprēvī _perf of_ **spernō**.

spūma, -ae _f_ foam, froth.

spūmēscō, -ere _vi_ to become frothy.

spūmeus _adj_ foaming, frothy.

spūmifer, -ī _adj_ foaming.

spūmiger, -ī _adj_ foaming.

spūmō, -āre _vi_ to foam, froth.

spūmōsus _adj_ foaming.

spuō, -uere, -uī, -ūtum _vi_ to spit ♦ _vt_ to spit out.

spurcē _adv_ obscenely.

spurcidicus _adj_ obscene.

spurcificus _adj_ obscene.

spurcitia, -ae _and_ **ēs, -ēī** _f_ filth, smut.

spurcō, -āre _vt_ to befoul.

spurcus _adj_ filthy, nasty, foul.

spūtātilicus _adj_ despicable.

spūtātor, -ōris _m_ spitter.

spūtō, -āre _vt_ to spit out.

spūtum, -ī _nt_ spit, spittle.

squāleō, -ēre, -uī _vi_ to be rough, stiff, clotted; to be parched; to be neglected, squalid, filthy; to be in mourning.

squālidē _adv_ rudely.

squālidus _adj_ rough, scaly; neglected, squalid, filthy; (_speech_) unpolished.

squālor, -ōris _m_ roughness; filth, squalor.

squāma, -ae _f_ scale; scale armour.

squāmeus _adj_ scaly.

squāmifer, -ī _adj_ scaly.

squāmiger, -ī _adj_ scaly ♦ _mpl_ fishes.

squāmōsus _adj_ scaly.

squilla, -ae _f_ prawn, shrimp.

st–stīpendium

st *interj* sh!

stabilīmentum, -ī *nt* support.

stabiliō, -īre *vt* to make stable; to establish.

stabilis *adj* firm, steady; (*fig*) steadfast, unfailing.

stabilitās, -ātis *f* firmness, steadiness, reliability.

stabulō, -āre *vt* to house, stable ♦ *vi* to have a stall.

stabulum, -ī *nt* stall, stable, steading; lodging, cottage; brothel.

stacta, -ae *f* myrrh oil.

stadium, -ī *and* **iī** *nt* stade, furlong; racetrack.

Stagīra, -ōrum *ntpl* town in Macedonia (*birthplace of Aristotle*).

Stagīrītēs, -ītae *m* Aristotle.

stagnō, -āre *vi* to form pools; to be inundated ♦ *vt* to flood.

stagnum, -ī *nt* standing water, pool, swamp; waters.

stāmen, -inis *nt* warp; thread; (*instrument*) string; (*priest*) fillet.

stāmineus *adj* full of threads.

stata *adj*: **Stata māter** Vesta.

statārius *adj* standing, stationary, steady; calm ♦ *f* refined comedy ♦ *mpl* actors in this comedy.

statēra, -ae *f* scales.

statim *adv* steadily; at once, immediately; **~ ut** as soon as.

statiō, -ōnis *f* standing still; station, post, residence; (*pl*) sentries; (*NAUT*) anchorage.

Statius, -ī *m* Caecilius (*early writer of comedy*); Papinius (*epic and lyric poet of the Silver Age*).

statīvus *adj* stationary ♦ *ntpl* standing camp.

stator, -ōris *m* attendant, orderly.

Stator, -ōris *m* the Stayer (*epithet of Jupiter*).

statua, -ae *f* statue.

statūmen, -inis *nt* (*ship*) rib.

statuō, -uere, -uī, -ūtum *vt* to set up, place; to bring to a stop; to establish, constitute; to determine, appoint; to decide, settle; to decree, prescribe; (*with infin*) to resolve, propose; (*with acc and infin*) to judge, consider, conclude; (*army*) to draw up; (*monument*) to erect; (*price*) to fix; (*sentence*) to pass; (*tent*) to pitch; (*town*) to build; **condiciōnem ~** dictate (to); **fīnem ~** put an end (to); **iūs ~** lay down a principle; **modum ~** impose restrictions; **apud animum ~** make up one's mind; **dē sē ~** commit suicide; **gravius ~ in** deal severely with.

statūra, -ae *f* height, stature.

status *ppp of* **sistō** ♦ *adj* appointed, due.

status, -ūs *m* posture, attitude; position; (*social*) standing, status, circumstances; (*POL*) situation, state, form of government; (*nature*) condition; **reī pūblicae ~** the political situation; constitution; **dē ~ū movēre** dislodge.

statūtus *ppp of* **statuō**.

stega, -ae *f* deck.

stēliō *see* **stēlliō**.

stēlla, -ae *f* star; **~ errāns** planet.

stēllāns, -antis *adj* starry.

stēllātus *adj* starred; set in the sky.

stēllifer, -ī *adj* starry.

stēlliger, -ī *adj* starry.

stēlliō, -ōnis *m* newt.

stemma, -tis *nt* pedigree.

stercoreus *adj* filthy.

stercorō, -āre *vt* to manure.

stercus, -oris *nt* dung.

sterilis *adj* barren, sterile; bare, empty; unprofitable, fruitless.

sterilitās, -ātis *f* barrenness.

sternāx, -ācis *adj* bucking.

sternō, -ere, strāvī, strātum *vt* to spread, cover, strew; to smooth, level; to stretch out, extend; to throw to the ground, prostrate; to overthrow; (*bed*) to make; (*horse*) to saddle; (*road*) to pave.

sternūmentum, -ī *nt* sneezing.

sternuō, -ere, -ī *vt, vi* to sneeze.

Steropē, -ēs *f* a Pleiad.

sterquilīnium, -ī *and* **iī, (-um, -ī)** *nt* dung heap.

stertō, -ere, -uī *vi* to snore.

Stēsichorus, -ī *m* Greek lyric poet.

stetī *perf of* **stō**.

Sthenelēius *and* **eis** *and* **ēidis** *adj see n.*

Sthenelus, -ī *m* father of Eurystheus; father of Cycnus.

stigma, -tis *nt* brand.

stigmatiās, -ae *m* branded slave.

stilla, -ae *f* drop.

stillicidium, -ī *and* **iī** *nt* dripping water, rainwater from the eaves.

stillō, -āre, -āvī, -ātum *vi* to drip, trickle ♦ *vt* to let fall in drops, distil.

stilus, -ī *m* stake; pen; (*fig*) writing, composition, style; **~um vertere** erase.

stimulātiō, -ōnis *f* incentive.

stimulātrīx, -īcis *f* provocative woman.

stimuleus *adj* smarting.

stimulō, -āre, -āvī, -ātum *vt* to goad; to trouble, torment; to rouse, spur on, excite.

stimulus, -ī *m* goad; (*MIL*) stake; (*pain*) sting, pang; (*incentive*) spur, stimulus.

stinguō, -ere *vt* to extinguish.

stīpātiō, -ōnis *f* crowd, retinue.

stīpātor, -ōris *m* attendant; (*pl*) retinue, bodyguard.

stīpendiārius *adj* tributary, liable to a money tax; (*MIL*) receiving pay ♦ *mpl* tributary peoples.

stīpendium, -ī *and* **iī** *nt* tax tribute; soldier's pay; military service, campaign; **~ merēre, merērī** serve; **~ ēmerērī** complete one's period of service.

Noun declensions and verb conjugations are shown on pp xiii to xxv. The present infinitive ending of a verb shows to which conjugation it belongs: **-āre** = 1st; **-ēre** = 2nd; **-ere** = 3rd and **-īre** = 4th. Irregular verbs are shown on p xxvi

stīpes, -itis *m* log, trunk; tree; (*insult*) blockhead.

stīpō, -āre, -āvī, -ātum *vt* to press, pack together; to cram, stuff full; to crowd round, accompany in a body.

stips, stipis *f* donation, contribution.

stipula, -ae *f* stalk, blade, stubble; reed.

stipulātiō, -ōnis *f* promise, bargain.

stipulātiuncula, -ae *f* slight stipulation.

stipulātus *adj* promised.

stipulor, -ārī *vt, vi* to demand a formal promise, bargain, stipulate.

stīria, -ae *f* icicle.

stirpēs *etc see* **stirps**.

stirpitus *adj* thoroughly.

stirps, -is *f* lower trunk and roots, stock; plant, shoot; family, lineage, progeny; origin; **ab ~e** utterly.

stīva, -ae *f* plough handle.

stlattārius *adj* seaborne.

stō, stāre, stetī, statum *vi* to stand; to remain in position, stand firm; to be conspicuous; (*fig*) to persist, continue; (*battle*) to go on; (*hair*) to stand on end; (*NAUT*) to ride at anchor; (*play*) to be successful; (*price*) to cost; (*with* **ab, cum, prō**) to be on the side of, support; (*with* **in**) to rest, depend on; (*with* **per**) to be the fault of; **stat sententia** one's mind is made up; **per Āfrānium stetit quōminus dīmicārētur** thanks to Afranius there was no battle.

Stōicē *adv* like a Stoic.

Stōicus *adj* Stoic ♦ *m* Stoic philosopher ♦ *ntpl* Stoicism.

stola, -ae *f* long robe (*esp worn by matrons*).

stolidē *adv* stupidly.

stolidus *adj* dull, stupid.

stomachor, -ārī, -ātus *vi* to be vexed, be annoyed.

stomachōsē *adv see adj*.

stomachōsus *adj* angry, irritable.

stomachus, -ī *m* gullet; stomach; taste, liking; dislike, irritation, chagrin.

stōrea (storia), -ae *f* rush mat, rope mat.

strabō, -ōnis *m* squinter.

strāgēs, -is *f* heap, confused mass; havoc, massacre.

strāgulus *adj* covering ♦ *nt* bedspread, rug.

strāmen, -inis *nt* straw, litter.

strāmentum, -ī *nt* straw, thatch; straw bed; covering, rug.

strāmineus *adj* straw-thatched.

strangulō, -āre, -āvī, -ātum *vt* to throttle, choke.

strangūria, -ae *f* difficult discharge of urine.

stratēgēma, -tis *nt* a piece of generalship, stratagem.

stratēgus, -ī *m* commander, president.

stratiōticus *adj* military.

strātum, -ī *nt* coverlet, blanket; bed, couch; horsecloth, saddle; pavement.

strātus *ppp of* **sternō** ♦ *adj* prostrate.

strāvī *perf of* **sternō**.

strēnuē *adv* energetically, quickly.

strēnuitās, -ātis *f* energy, briskness.

strēnuus *adj* brisk, energetic, busy; restless.

strepitō, -āre *vi* to make a noise, rattle, rustle.

strepitus, -ūs *m* din, clatter, crashing, rumbling; sound.

strepō, -ere, -uī *vi* to make a noise, clang, roar, rumble, rustle *etc* ♦ *vt* to bawl out.

strīāta, -ae *f* scallop.

strictim *adv* superficially, cursorily.

strictūra, -ae *f* mass of metal.

strictus *ppp of* **stringō** ♦ *adj* close, tight.

strīdeō, -ēre, -ī; -ō, -ere, -ī *vi* to creak, hiss, shriek, whistle.

strīdor, -ōris *m* creaking, hissing, grating.

strīdulus *adj* creaking, hissing, whistling.

strigilis *f* scraper, strigil.

strigō, -āre *vi* to stop, jib.

strigōsus *adj* thin, scraggy; (*style*) insipid.

stringō, -ngere, -nxī, -ctum *vt* to draw together, draw tight; to touch, graze; to cut off, prune, trim; (*sword*) to draw; (*mind*) to affect, pain.

stringor, -ōris *m* twinge.

strix, -igis *f* screech owl.

stropha, -ae *f* trick.

Strophades, -um *fpl islands off S Greece*.

strophiārius, -ī *and* **iī** *m* maker of breastbands.

strophium, -ī *and* **iī** *nt* breastband; headband.

structor, -ōris *m* mason, carpenter; (*at table*) server, carver.

structūra, -ae *f* construction, structure; works.

structus *ppp of* **struō**.

struēs, -is *f* heap, pile.

struix, -icis *f* heap, pile.

strūma, -ae *f* tumour.

strūmōsus *adj* scrofulous.

struō, -ere, -xī, -ctum *vt* to pile up; to build, erect; to arrange in order; to make, prepare; to cause, contrive, plot.

strūtheus *adj* sparrow- (*in cpds*).

strūthiocamēlus, -ī *m* ostrich.

Strymōn, -onis *m* river between Macedonia and Thrace (*now* Struma).

Strymonius *adj* Strymonian, Thracian.

studeō, -ēre, -uī *vi* (*usu with dat*) to be keen, be diligent, apply oneself to; to study; (*person*) to be a supporter of.

studiōsē *adv* eagerly, diligently.

studiōsus *adj* (*usu with gen*) keen on, fond of, partial to; studious ♦ *m* student.

studium, -ī *and* **iī** *nt* enthusiasm, application, inclination; fondness, affection; party spirit, partisanship; study, literary work.

stultē *adv* foolishly.

stultiloquentia, -ae *f* foolish talk.

stultiloquium, -ī *and* **iī** *nt* foolish talk.

stultitia, -ae *f* folly, silliness.

stultividus *adj* simple-sighted.

stultus *adj* foolish, silly ♦ *m* fool.

stupefaciō, -facere, -fēcī, -factum (*pass* -fīō, -fierī) *vt* to stun, astound.

stupeō, -ēre, -uī *vi* to be stunned, be astonished; to be brought to a standstill ♦ *vt* to marvel at.

stupēscō, -ere *vi* to become amazed.

stūpeus *etc see* **stuppeus.**

stupiditās, -ātis *f* senselessness.

stupidus *adj* senseless, astounded; dull, stupid.

stupor, -ōris *m* numbness, bewilderment; dullness, stupidity.

stuppa, -ae *f* tow.

stuppeus *adj* of tow.

stuprō, -āre, -āvī, -ātum *vt* to defile; to ravish.

stuprum, -ī *nt* debauchery, unchastity.

sturnus, -ī *m* starling.

Stygius *adj* of the lower world, Stygian.

stylus *etc see* **stilus.**

Stymphalicus, (-ius, -is) *adj* Stymphalian.

Stymphalum, -ī *nt*, **Stymphalus, -ī** *m* district of Arcadia (*famous for birds of prey killed by Hercules*).

Styx, -ygis *and* **ygos** *f* river of Hades.

Styxius *adj see* **n.**

suādēla, -ae *f* persuasion.

suādeō, -dēre, -sī, -sum *vi* (*with dat*) to advise, urge, recommend.

suāsiō, -ōnis *f* speaking in favour (of a proposal); persuasive type of oratory.

suāsor, -ōris *m* adviser; advocate.

suāsus *ppp of* **suādeō.**

suāsus, -ūs *m* advice.

suāveolēns, -entis *adj* fragrant.

suāviātiō *etc see* **sāviātiō.**

suāvidicus *adj* charming.

suāviloquēns, -entis *adj* charming.

suāviloquentia, -ae *f* charm of speech.

suāvior *etc see* **sāvior.**

suāvis *adj* sweet, pleasant, delightful.

suāvitās, -ātis *f* sweetness, pleasantness, charm.

suāviter *adv see* **suāvis.**

suāvium *etc see* **sāvium.**

sub *prep* **1.** *with abl* (*place*) under, beneath; (*hills, walls*) at the foot of, close to; (*time*) during, at; (*order*) next to; (*rule*) under, in the reign of. **2.** *with acc* (*place*) under, along under; (*hills, walls*) up to, to; (*time*) up to, just before, just after; ~ **ictum venīre** come within range; ~ **manum** to hand.

subabsurdē *adv see* **adj.**

subabsurdus *adj* somewhat absurd.

subaccūsō, -āre *vt* to find some fault with.

subāctiō, -ōnis *f* working (the soil).

subāctus *ppp of* **subigō.**

subadroganter *adv* a little conceitedly.

subagrestis *adj* rather boorish.

subalāris *adj* carried under the arms.

subamārus *adj* rather bitter.

subaquilus *adj* brownish.

subauscultō, -āre *vt, vi* to listen secretly, eavesdrop.

subbasilicānus, -ī *m* lounger.

subblandior, -īrī *vi* (*with dat*) to flirt with.

subc- *etc see* **succ-.**

subdidī *perf of* **subdō.**

subdifficilis *adj* rather difficult.

subdiffīdō, -ere *vi* to be a little doubtful.

subditīcius *adj* sham.

subditīvus *adj* sham.

subditus *ppp of* **subdō** ♦ *adj* spurious.

subdō, -ere, -idī, -itum *vt* to put under, plunge into; to subdue; to substitute, forge.

subdoceō, -ēre *vt* to teach as an assistant.

subdolē *adv* slily.

subdolus *adj* sly, crafty, underhand.

subdubitō, -āre *vi* to be a little undecided.

subdūcō, -ūcere, -ūxī, -uctum *vt* to pull up, raise; to withdraw, remove; to take away secretly, steal; (*account*) to balance; (*ship*) to haul up, beach; **sē** ~ steal away, disappear.

subductiō, -ōnis *f* (*ship*) hauling up; (*thought*) reckoning.

subductus *ppp of* **subdūcō.**

subedō, -esse, -ēdī *vt* to wear away underneath.

subēgī *perf of* **subigō.**

subeō, -īre, -iī, -itum *vi* to go under, go in; to come up to, climb, advance; to come immediately after; to come to the assistance; to come as a substitute, succeed; to come secretly, steal in; to come to mind, suggest itself ♦ *vt* to enter, plunge into; to climb; to approach, attack; to take the place of; to steal into; to submit to, undergo, suffer; (*mind*) to occur to.

sūber, -is *nt* cork tree; cork.

subesse *infin of* **subsum.**

subf- *etc see* **suff-.**

subg- *etc see* **sugg-.**

subhorridus *adj* somewhat uncouth.

subiaceō, -ēre, -uī *vi* to lie under, be close (to); to be connected (with).

subiciō, -icere, -iēcī, -iectum *vt* to put under, bring under; to bring up, throw up; to bring near; to submit, subject, expose; to subordinate, deal with under; to append, add on, answer; to adduce, suggest; to substitute; to forge; to suborn; **sē** ~ grow up.

subiectē *adv* submissively.

subiectiō, -ōnis *f* laying under; forging.

subiectō, -āre *vt* to lay under, put to; to throw up.

subiector, -ōris *m* forger.

subiectus *ppp of* **subiciō** ♦ *adj* neighbouring, bordering; subject, exposed.

subigitātiō, -ōnis *f* lewdness.

subigitō, -āre *vt* to behave improperly to.

Noun declensions and verb conjugations are shown on pp xiii to xxv. The present infinitive ending of a verb shows to which conjugation it belongs: **-āre** = 1st; **-ēre** = 2nd; **-ere** = 3rd and **-īre** = 4th. Irregular verbs are shown on p xxvi

subigō, -igere, -ēgī, -āctum vt to bring up to; to impel, compel; to subdue, conquer; (animal) to tame, break in; (blade) to sharpen; (boat) to row, propel; (cooking) to knead; (earth) to turn up, dig; (mind) to train.

subiī perf of **subeō**.

subimpudēns, -entis adj rather impertinent.

subinānis adj rather empty.

subinde adv immediately after; repeatedly.

subīnsūlsus adj rather insipid.

subinvideō, -ēre vi to be a little envious of.

subinvīsus adj somewhat odious.

subinvītō, -āre vt to invite vaguely.

subīrāscor, -scī, -tus vi to be rather angry.

subīrātus adj rather angry.

subitārius adj sudden, emergency (in cpds).

subitō adv suddenly.

subitus ppp of **subeō** ♦ adj sudden, unexpected; (man) rash; (troops) hastily raised ♦ nt surprise, emergency.

subiūnctus ppp of **subiungō**.

subiungō, -ungere, -ūnxī, -ūnctum vt to harness; to add, affix; to subordinate, subdue.

sublābor, -bī, -psus vi to sink down; to glide away.

sublāpsus ppa of **sublābor**.

sublātē adv loftily.

sublātiō, -ōnis f elevation.

sublātus ppp of **tollō** ♦ adj elated.

sublectō, -āre vt to coax.

sublēctus ppp of **sublegō**.

sublegō, -egere, -ēgī, -ēctum vt to gather up; to substitute; (child) to kidnap; (talk) to overhear.

sublestus adj slight.

sublevātiō, -ōnis f alleviation.

sublevō, -āre, -āvī, -ātum vt to lift up, hold up; to support, encourage; to lighten, alleviate.

sublica, -ae f pile, palisade.

sublicius adj on piles.

subligāculum, -ī, subligar, -āris nt loincloth.

subligō, -āre vt to fasten on.

sublīmē adv aloft, in the air.

sublīmis adj high, raised high, lifted up; (character) eminent, aspiring; (language) lofty, elevated.

sublīmitās, -ātis f loftiness.

sublīmus etc see **sublīmis**.

sublingiō, -ōnis m scullion.

sublinō, -inere, -ēvī, -itum vt: **ōs ~** to fool, bamboozle.

sublitus ppp of **sublinō**.

sublūceō, -ēre vi to glimmer.

sublūō, -ere vt (river) to flow past the foot of.

sublūstris adj faintly luminous.

sublūtus ppp of **sublūō**.

subm- etc see **summ-**.

subnātus adj growing up underneath.

subnectō, -ctere, -xuī, -xum vt to tie under, fasten on.

subnegō, -āre vt to half refuse.

subnexus ppp of **subnectō**.

subniger, -rī adj darkish.

subnīxus and **sus** adj supported, resting (on); relying (on).

subnuba, -ae f rival.

subnūbilus adj overcast.

subō, -āre vi to be in heat.

subobscēnus adj rather indecent.

subobscūrus adj somewhat obscure.

subodiōsus adj rather odious.

suboffendō, -ere vi to give some offence.

subolēs, -is f offspring, children.

subolēscō, -ere vi to grow up.

subolet, -ēre vi (impers) there is a faint scent; **~ mihi** I detect, have an inkling.

suborior, -īrī vi to spring up in succession.

subōrnō, -āre, -āvī, -ātum vt to fit out, equip; to instigate secretly, suborn.

subortus, -ūs m rising up repeatedly.

subp- etc see **supp-**.

subrancidus adj slightly tainted.

subraucus adj rather hoarse.

subrēctus ppp of **subrigō**.

subrēmigō, -āre vi to paddle under (water).

subrēpō, -ere, -sī, -tum vi to creep along, steal up to.

subreptus ppp of **subripiō**.

subrīdeō, -dēre, -sī vi to smile.

subrīdiculē adv rather funnily.

subrigō, -igere, -ēxī, -ēctum vt to lift, raise.

subringor, -ī vi to make a wry face, be rather vexed.

subripiō, -ipere, -ipuī and **upuī, -eptum** vt to take away secretly, steal.

subrogō, -āre vt to propose as successor.

subrōstrānī, -ōrum mpl idlers.

subrubeō, -ēre vi to blush slightly.

subrūfus adj ginger-haired.

subruō, -ere, -ī, -tum vt to undermine, demolish.

subrūsticus adj rather countrified.

subrutus ppp of **subruō**.

subscrībō, -bere, -psī, -ptum vt to write underneath; (document) to sign, subscribe; (censor) to set down; (law) to add to an indictment, prosecute; (fig) to record; (with dat) to assent to, approve.

subscrīptiō, -ōnis f inscription underneath; signature; (censor) noting down; (law) subscription (to an indictment); register.

subscrīptor, -ōris m subscriber (to an indictment).

subscrīptus ppp of **subscrībō**.

subsecīvus etc see **subsicīvus**.

subsecō, -āre, -uī, -ctum vt to cut off, clip.

subsēdī perf of **subsīdō**.

subsellium, -ī and **iī** nt bench, seat; (law) the bench, the court.

subsentiō, -entīre, -ēnsī vt to have an inkling of.

subsequor, -quī, -cūtus vt, vi to follow closely; to support; to imitate.

subserviō, -īre vi to be a slave; (fig) to comply

(with).

subsicīvus *adj* left over; (*time*) spare; (*work*) overtime.

subsidiārius *adj* in reserve ♦ *mpl* reserves.

subsidium, -ī *and* **iī** *nt* reserve ranks, reserve troops; relief, aid, assistance.

subsīdō, -īdere, -ēdī, -essum *vi* to sit down, crouch, squat; to sink down, settle, subside; (*ambush*) to lie in wait; (*residence*) to stay, settle ♦ *vt* to lie in wait for.

subsignānus *adj* special reserve (troops).

subsignō, -āre *vt* to register; to guarantee.

subsiliō, -īre, -uī *vi* to leap up.

subsistō, -istere, -titī *vi* to stand still, make a stand; to stop, halt; to remain, continue, hold out; (*with dat*) to resist ♦ *vt* to withstand.

subsortior, -īrī, -ītus *vt* to choose as a substitute by lot.

subsortītiō, -ōnis *f* choosing of substitutes by lot.

substantia, -ae *f* means, wealth.

substernō, -ernere, -rāvī, -rātum *vt* to scatter under, spread under; (*fig*) to put at one's service.

substitī *perf of* **subsistō**.

substituō, -uere, -uī, -ūtum *vt* to put next; to substitute; (*idea*) to present, imagine.

substitūtus *ppp of* **substituō**.

substō, -āre *vi* to hold out.

substrātus *ppp of* **substernō**.

substrictus *ppp of* **substringō** ♦ *adj* narrow, tight.

substringō, -ngere, -nxī, -ctum *vt* to bind up; to draw close; to check.

substructiō, -ōnis *f* foundation.

substruō, -ere, -xī, -ctum *vt* to lay, pave.

subsultō, -āre *vi* to jump up.

subsum, -esse *vi* to be underneath; to be close to, be at hand; (*fig*) to underlie, be latent in.

subsūtus *adj* fringed at the bottom.

subtēmen, -inis *nt* woof; thread.

subter *adv* below, underneath ♦ *prep* (*with acc and abl*) beneath; close up to.

subterdūcō, -cere, -xī *vt* to withdraw secretly.

subterfugiō, -ugere, -ūgī *vt* to escape from, evade.

subterlābor, -ī *vt, vi* to flow past under; to slip away.

subterrāneus *adj* underground.

subtexō, -ere, -uī, -tum *vt* to weave in; to veil, obscure.

subtīlis *adj* slender, fine; (*senses*) delicate, nice; (*judgment*) discriminating, precise; (*style*) plain, direct.

subtīlitās, -ātis *f* fineness; (*judgment*) acuteness, exactness; (*style*) plainness, directness.

subtīliter *adv* finely; accurately; simply.

subtimeō, -ēre *vt* to be a little afraid of.

subtractus *ppp of* **subtrahō**.

subtrahō, -here, -xī, -ctum *vt* to draw away from underneath; to take away secretly; to withdraw, remove.

subtristis *adj* rather sad.

subturpiculus *adj* a little bit mean.

subturpis *adj* rather mean.

subtus *adv* below, underneath.

subtūsus *adj* slightly bruised.

subūcula, -ae *f* shirt, vest.

sūbula, -ae *f* awl.

subulcus, -ī *m* swineherd.

Subūra, -ae *f* a disreputable quarter of Rome.

Subūrānus *adj see* **Subūra**.

suburbānitās, -ātis *f* nearness to Rome.

suburbānus *adj* near Rome ♦ *nt* villa near Rome ♦ *mpl* inhabitants of the towns near Rome.

suburbium, -ī *and* **iī** *nt* suburb.

suburgeō, -ēre *vt* to drive close (to).

subvectiō, -ōnis *f* transport.

subvectō, -āre *vt* to carry up regularly.

subvectus *ppp of* **subvehō**.

subvectus, -ūs *m* transport.

subvehō, -here, -xī, -ctum *vt* to carry up, transport upstream.

subveniō, -enīre, -ēnī, -entum *vi* (*with dat*) to come to the assistance of, relieve, reinforce.

subventō, -āre *vi* (*with dat*) to come quickly to help.

subvereor, -ērī *vi* to be a little afraid.

subversor, -ōris *m* subverter.

subversus *ppp of* **subvertō**.

subvertō, -tere, -tī, -sum *vt* to turn upside down, upset; to overthrow, subvert.

subvexī *perf of* **subvehō**.

subvexus *adj* sloping upwards.

subvolō, -āre *vi* to fly upwards.

subvolvō, -ere *vt* to roll uphill.

subvortō *etc see* **subvertō**.

succavus *adj* hollow underneath.

succēdō, -ēdere, -essī, -essum *vt, vi* (*with dat*) to go under, pass into, take on; (*with dat, acc,* **in**) to go up, climb; (*with dat, acc, ad,* **sub**) to march on, advance to; (*with dat,* **in**) to come to take the place of, relieve; (*with dat,* **in, ad**) to follow after, succeed, succeed to; (*result*) to turn out, be successful.

succendō, -endere, -endī, -ēnsum *vt* to set fire to, kindle; (*fig*) to fire, inflame.

succēnseō *etc see* **suscēnseō**.

succēnsus *ppp of* **succendō**.

succenturiātus *adj* in reserve.

succenturiō, -ōnis *m* under-centurion.

successī *perf of* **succēdō**.

successiō, -ōnis *f* succession.

successor, -ōris *m* successor.

successus *ppp of* **succēdō**.

successus, -ūs *m* advance uphill; result, success.

succīdia, -ae *f* leg *or* side of meat, flitch.

succīdō, -dere, -dī, -sum *vt* to cut off, mow down.

succidō, -ere, -ī *vi* to sink, give way.

succiduus *adj* sinking, failing.

succinctus *ppp of* **succingō**.

succingō, -gere, -xī, -ctum *vt* to gird up, tuck up; to equip, arm.

succingulum, -ī *nt* girdle.

succinō, -ere *vi* to chime in.

succīsus *ppp of* **succīdō**.

succlāmātiō, -ōnis *f* shouting, barracking.

succlāmō, -āre, -āvī, -ātum *vt* to shout after, interrupt with shouting.

succontumēliōsē *adv* somewhat insolently.

succrēscō, -ere *vi* to grow up (from *or* to).

succrispus *adj* rather curly.

succumbō, -mbere, -buī, -bitum *vi* to fall, sink under; to submit, surrender.

succurrō, -rere, -rī, -sum *vi* to come quickly up; to run to the help of, succour; (*idea*) to occur.

succus *etc see* **sūcus**.

succussus, -ūs *m* shaking.

succustōs, -ōdis *m* assistant keeper.

succutiō, -tere, -ssī, -ssum *vt* to toss up.

sūcidus *adj* juicy, fresh, plump.

sūcinum, -ī *nt* amber.

sūctus *ppp of* **sūgō**.

sucula, -ae *f* winch, windlass.

sucula, -ae *f* piglet; (*pl*) the Hyads.

sūcus, -ī *m* juice, sap; medicine, potion; taste, flavour; (*fig*) strength, vigour, life.

sūdārium, -ī *and* **iī** *nt* handkerchief.

sūdātōrius *adj* for sweating ♦ *nt* sweating bath.

sudis, -is *f* stake, pile, pike, spike.

sūdō, -āre, -āvī, -ātum *vi* to sweat, perspire; to be drenched with; to work hard ♦ *vt* to exude.

sūdor, -ōris *m* sweat, perspiration; moisture; hard work, exertion.

sudus *adj* cloudless, clear ♦ *nt* fine weather.

sueō, -ēre *vi* to be accustomed.

suēscō, -scere, -vī, -tum *vi* to be accustomed ♦ *vt* to accustom.

Suessa, -ae *f* town in Latium.

Suessiōnēs, -um *mpl* people of Gaul (*now* Soissons).

suētus *ppp of* **suēscō** ♦ *adj* accustomed; usual.

Suēvī, -ōrum *mpl* people of N.E. Germany.

sūfes, -etis *m* chief magistrate of Carthage.

suffarcinātus *adj* stuffed full.

suffectus *ppp of* **sufficiō** ♦ *adj* (*consul*) appointed to fill a vacancy during the regular term of office.

sufferō, -re *vt* to support, undergo, endure.

suffes *etc see* **sūfes**.

sufficiō, -icere, -ēcī, -ectum *vt* to dye, tinge; to supply, provide; to appoint in place (of another), substitute ♦ *vi* to be adequate,

suffice.

suffīgō, -gere, -xī, -xum *vt* to fasten underneath, nail on.

suffimen, -inis, suffimentum, -ī *nt* incense.

suffiō, -īre *vt* to fumigate, perfume.

suffixus *ppp of* **suffīgō**.

sufflāmen, -inis *nt* brake.

sufflō, -āre *vt* to blow up; to puff up.

suffocō, -āre *vt* to choke, stifle.

suffodiō, -odere, -ōdī, -ossum *vt* to stab; to dig under, undermine.

suffossus *ppp of* **suffodiō**.

suffrāgātiō, -ōnis *f* voting for, support.

suffrāgātor, -ōris *m* voter, supporter.

suffrāgātōrius *adj* supporting a candidate.

suffrāgium, -ī *and* **iī** *nt* vote, ballot; right of suffrage; (*fig*) judgment, approval; **~ ferre** vote.

suffrāgor, -ārī, -ātus *vi* to vote for; to support, favour.

suffringō, -ere *vt* to break.

suffugiō, -ugere, -ūgī *vt* to run for shelter ♦ *vt* to elude.

suffugium, -ī *and* **iī** *nt* shelter, refuge.

suffulciō, -cīre, -sī, -tum *vt* to prop up, support.

suffundō, -undere, -ūdī, -ūsum *vt* to pour in; to suffuse, fill; to tinge, colour, blush; to overspread.

suffūror, -ārī *vi* to filch.

suffuscus *adj* darkish.

suffūsus *ppp of* **suffundō**.

Sugambrī, -ōrum *mpl* people of N.W. Germany.

suggerō, -rere, -ssī, -stum *vt* to bring up to, supply; to add on, put next.

suggestum, -ī *nt* platform.

suggestus *ppp of* **suggerō**.

suggestus, -ūs *m* platform, stage.

suggrandis *adj* rather large.

suggredior, -dī, -ssus *vi* to come up close, approach ♦ *vt* to attack.

sūgillātiō, -ōnis *f* affronting.

sūgillātus *adj* bruised; insulted.

sūgō, -gere, -xī, -ctum *vt* to suck.

suī *gen of* **sē**.

suī *perf of* **suō**.

suillus *adj* of pigs.

sulcō, -āre *vt* to furrow, plough.

sulcus, -ī *m* furrow; trench; track.

sulfur *etc see* **sulpur**.

Sulla, -ae *m* famous Roman dictator.

Sullānus *adj see n.*

sullāturiō, -īre *vi* to hanker after being a Sulla.

Sulmō, -ōnis *m* town in E. Italy (*birthplace of Ovid*).

Sulmōnēnsis *adj see n.*

sultis *adv* please.

sum, esse, fuī *vi* to be, exist; **~ ab** belong to; **~ ad** be designed for; **~ ex** consist of; **est, sunt** there is, are; **est mihi I have; mihi tēcum nīl est** I have nothing to do with you; **est quod** something; there is a reason for; **est ubi**

sometimes; **est ut** it is possible that; **est** (*with gen*) to belong to, to be the duty of, be characteristic of; (*with infin*) it is possible, it is permissible; **sunt quī** some; **fuit Ilium** Troy is no more.

sūmen, -inis *nt* udder, teat; sow.

summa, -ae *f* main part, chief point, main issue; gist, summary; sum, amount, the whole; supreme power; **~ rērum** the general interest, the whole responsibility; **~ summārum** the universe; **ad ~am** in short, in fact; in conclusion; **in ~ā** in all; after all.

Summānus, -ī *m* god of nocturnal thunderbolts.

summās, -ātis *adj* high-born, eminent.

summātim *adv* cursorily, summarily.

summātus, -ūs *m* sovereignty.

summē *adv* in the highest degree, extremely.

summergō, -gere, -sī, -sum *vt* to plunge under, sink.

summersus *ppp of* **summergō**.

sumministrō, -āre, -āvī, -ātum *vt* to provide, furnish.

summissē *adv* softly; humbly, modestly.

summissiō, -ōnis *f* lowering.

summissus *ppp of* **summittō** ♦ *adj* low; (*voice*) low, calm; (*character*) mean, grovelling, submissive, humble.

summittō, -ittere, -īsī, -issum *vt* (*growth*) to send up, raise, rear; to despatch, supply; to let down, lower, reduce, moderate; to supersede; to send secretly; **animum ~** submit; **sē ~** condescend.

summolestē *adv* with some annoyance.

summolestus *adj* a little annoying.

summoneō, -ēre, -uī *vt* to drop a hint to.

summorōsus *adj* rather peevish.

summōtor, -ōris *m* clearer.

summōtus *ppp of* **summoveō**.

summoveō, -ovēre, -ōvī, -ōtum *vt* to move away, drive off; to clear away (to make room); to withdraw, remove, banish; (*fig*) to dispel.

summum, -ī *nt* top, surface.

summum *adv* at the most.

summus *adj* highest, the top of, the surface of; last, the end of; (*fig*) utmost, greatest, most important; (*person*) distinguished, excellent ♦ *m* head of the table.

summūtō, -āre *vt* to substitute.

sūmō, -ere, -psī, -ptum *vt* to take, take up; to assume, arrogate; (*action*) to undertake; (*argument*) to assume, take for granted; (*dress*) to put on; (*punishment*) to exact; (*for a purpose*) to use, spend.

sūmptiō, -ōnis *f* assumption.

sūmptuārius *adj* sumptuary.

sūmptuōsē *adv see adj*.

sūmptuōsus *adj* expensive, lavish, extravagant.

sūmptus *ppp of* **sūmō**.

sūmptus, -ūs *m* expense, cost.

Sūnium, -ī and iī *nt* S.E. promontory of Attica.

suō, suere, suī, sūtum *vt* to sew, stitch, join together.

suōmet, suōpte *emphatic abl of* **suus**.

suovetaurīlia, -ium *ntpl* sacrifice of a pig, sheep and bull.

supellex, -ectilis *f* furniture, goods, outfit.

super *etc adj see* **superus**.

super *adv* above, on the top; besides, moreover; left, remaining ♦ *prep* (*with abl*) upon, above; concerning; besides; (*time*) at; (*with acc*) over, above, on; beyond; besides, over and above.

superā *etc see* **suprā**.

superābilis *adj* surmountable, conquerable.

superaddō, -ere, -itum *vt* to add over and above.

superāns, -antis *pres p of* **superō** ♦ *adj* predominant.

superātor, -ōris *m* conqueror.

superbē *adv* arrogantly, despotically.

superbia, -ae *f* arrogance, insolence, tyranny; pride, lofty spirit.

superbiloquentia, -ae *f* arrogant speech.

superbiō, -īre *vi* to be arrogant, take a pride in; to be superb.

superbus *adj* arrogant, insolent, overbearing; fastidious; superb, magnificent.

supercilium, -ī and iī *nt* eyebrow; (*hill*) brow, ridge; (*fig*) arrogance.

superēmineō, -ēre *vt* to overtop.

superesse *infin of* **supersum**.

superficiēs, -ēī *f* surface; (*law*) a building (*esp on another's land*).

superfiō, -ierī *vi* to be left over.

superfīxus *adj* fixed on top.

superfluō, -ere *vi* to overflow.

superfuī *perf of* **supersum**.

superfundō, -undere, -ūdī, -ūsum *vt, vi* to pour over, shower; (*pass*) to overflow, spread out.

superfūsus *ppp of* **superfundō**.

supergredior, -dī, -ssus *vt* to surpass.

superiaciō, -iacere, -iēcī, -iectum and iactum *vt* to throw over, overspread; to overtop; (*fig*) to exaggerate.

superiectus *ppp of* **superiaciō**.

superimmineō, -ēre *vt* to overhang.

superimpendēns, -entis *adj* overhanging.

superimpōnō, -ōnere, -osuī, -ositum *vt* to place on top.

superimpositus *ppp of* **superimpōnō**.

superincidēns, -entis *adj* falling from above.

superincubāns, -antis *adj* lying upon.

superincumbō, -ere *vi* to fling oneself down upon.

superingerō, -ere *vt* to pour down.

superiniciō, -icere, -iēcī, -iectum *vt* to throw upon, put on top.

Noun declensions and verb conjugations are shown on pp xiii to xxv. The present infinitive ending of a verb shows to which conjugation it belongs: **-āre** = 1st; **-ēre** = 2nd; **-ere** = 3rd and **-īre** = 4th. Irregular verbs are shown on p xxvi

superiniectus *ppp of* **superinicō**.
superīnsternō, -ere *vt* to lay over.
superior, -ōris *adj* higher, upper; (*time, order*) preceding, previous, former; (*age*) older; (*battle*) victorious, stronger; (*quality*) superior, greater.
superlātiō, -ōnis *f* exaggeration.
superlātus *adj* exaggerated.
supernē *adv* at the top, from above.
supernus *adj* upper; celestial.
superō, -āre, -āvī, -ātum *vi* to rise above, overtop; to have the upper hand; to be in excess, be abundant; to be left over, survive ♦ *vt* to pass over, surmount, go beyond; to surpass, outdo; (*MIL*) to overcome, conquer; (*NAUT*) to sail past, double.
superobruō, -ere *vt* to overwhelm.
superpendēns, -entis *adj* overhanging.
superpōnō, -ōnere, -osuī, -ositum *vt* to place upon; to put in charge of.
superpositus *ppp of* **superpōnō**.
superscandō, -ere *vt* to climb over.
supersedeō, -edēre, -ēdī, -essum *vi* to forbear, desist from.
superstes, -itis *adj* standing over; surviving.
superstitiō, -ōnis *f* awful fear, superstition.
superstitiōsē *adv* superstitiously; scrupulously.
superstitiōsus *adj* superstitious; prophetic.
superstō, -āre *vt, vi* to stand over, stand on.
superstrātus *adj* spread over.
superstruō, -ere, -xī, -ctum *vt* to build on top.
supersum, -esse, -fuī *vi* to be left, remain; to survive; to be in abundance, be sufficient; to be in excess.
supertegō, -ere *vt* to cover over.
superurgēns, -entis *adj* pressing from above.
superus (*compar* -ior, *superl* **suprēmus**, **summus**) *adj* upper, above ♦ *mpl* the gods above; the living ♦ *ntpl* the heavenly bodies; higher places; **mare ~um** Adriatic Sea.
supervacāneus *adj* extra, superfluous.
supervacuus *adj* superfluous, pointless.
supervādō, -ere *vt* to climb over, surmount.
supervehor, -hī, -ctus *vt* to ride past, sail past.
superveniō, -enīre, -ēnī, -entum *vt* to overtake, come on top of ♦ *vi* to come on the scene, arrive unexpectedly.
superventus, -ūs *m* arrival.
supervolitō, -āre *vt* to fly over.
supervolō, -āre *vt, vi* to fly over.
supīnō, -āre, -āvī, -ātum *vt* to upturn, lay on its back.
supīnus *adj* lying back, face up; sloping, on a slope; backwards; (*mind*) indolent, careless.
suppāctus *ppp of* **suppingō**.
suppaenitet, -ēre *vt impers* to be a little sorry.
suppalpor, -ārī *vi* to coax gently.
suppār, -aris *adj* nearly equal.
supparasītor, -ārī *vi* to flatter gently.

supparus, -ī *m*, **supparum, -ī** *nt* woman's linen garment; topsail.
suppeditātiō, -ōnis *f* abundance.
suppeditō, -āre, -āvī, -ātum *vi* to be at hand, be in full supply, be sufficient; to be rich in ♦ *vt* to supply, furnish.
suppēdō, -ere *vi* to break wind quietly.
suppetiae, -ārum *fpl* assistance.
suppetior, -ārī, -ātus *vi* to come to the assistance of.
suppetō, -ere, -īvī, and ī, -ītum *vi* to be available, be in store; to be equal to, suffice for.
suppīlō, -āre *vt* to steal.
suppingō, -ingere, -āctum *vt* to fasten underneath.
supplantō, -āre *vt* to trip up.
supplēmentum, -ī *nt* full complement; reinforcements.
suppleō, -ēre *vt* to fill up, make good, make up to the full complement.
supplex, -icis *adj* suppliant, in entreaty.
supplicātiō, -ōnis *f* day of prayer, public thanksgiving.
suppliciter *adv* in supplication.
supplicium, -ī and iī *nt* prayer, entreaty; sacrifice; punishment, execution, suffering; **~iō afficere** execute.
supplicō, -āre, -āvī, -ātum *vi* (*with dat*) to entreat, pray to, worship.
supplōdō, -dere, -sī *vt* to stamp.
supplōsiō, -ōnis *f* stamping.
suppōnō, -ōnere, -osuī, -ositum *vt* to put under, apply; to subject; to add on; to substitute, falsify.
supportō, -āre *vt* to bring up, transport.
supposītīcius *adj* spurious.
suppositiō, -ōnis *f* substitution.
suppositus *ppp of* **suppōnō**.
supposuī *perf of* **suppōnō**.
suppressiō, -ōnis *f* embezzlement.
suppressus *ppp of* **supprimō** ♦ *adj* (*voice*) low.
supprimō, -imere, -essī, -essum *vt* to sink; to restrain, detain, put a stop to; to keep secret, suppress.
supprōmus, -ī *m* underbutler.
suppudet, -ēre *vt* (*impers*) to be a little ashamed.
suppūrō, -āre *vi* to fester.
suppus *adj* head downwards.
supputō, -āre *vt* to count up.
suprā *adv* above, up on top; (*time*) earlier, previously; (*amount*) more; **~ quam** beyond what ♦ *prep* (*with acc*) over, above; beyond; (*time*) before; (*amount*) more than, over.
suprāscandō, -ere *vt* to surmount.
suprēmum *adv* for the last time.
suprēmus *adj* highest; last, latest; greatest, supreme ♦ *ntpl* moment of death; funeral rites; testament.
sūra, -ae *f* calf (of the leg).
sūrculus, -ī *m* twig, shoot; graft, slip.
surdaster, -rī *adj* rather deaf.

surditās, -ātis f deafness.

surdus adj deaf; silent.

surēna, -ae m grand vizier (of the Parthians).

surgō, -ere, surrēxī, surrēctum vi to rise, get up, stand up; to arise, spring up, grow.

surpere etc = surripere etc.

surr- etc see subr-.

surrēxī perf of surgō.

surruptīcius adj stolen.

surrupuī perf of subripiō.

sūrsum, sūrsus adv upwards, up, high up; ~ deōrsum up and down.

sūs, suis m/f pig, boar, hog, sow.

Sūsa, -ōrum ntpl ancient Persian capital.

suscēnseō, -ēre, -uī vi to be angry, be irritated.

susceptiō, -ōnis f undertaking.

susceptus ppp of suscipiō.

suscipiō, -ipere, -ēpī, -eptum vt to take up, undertake; to receive, catch; (child) to acknowledge; to beget; to take under one's protection.

suscitō, -āre, -āvī, -ātum vt to lift, raise; to stir, rouse, awaken; to encourage, excite.

suspectō, -āre vt, vi to look up at, watch; to suspect, mistrust.

suspectus ppp of suspiciō ♦ adj suspected, suspicious.

suspectus, -ūs m looking up; esteem.

suspendium, -ī and iī nt hanging.

suspendō, -endere, -endī, -ēnsum vt to hang, hang up; (death) to hang; (building) to support; (mind) to keep in suspense; (movement) to check, interrupt; (pass) to depend.

suspēnsus ppp of suspendō ♦ adj raised, hanging, poised; with a light touch; (fig) in suspense, uncertain, anxious; dependent; ~ō gradū on tiptoe.

suspicāx, -ācis adj suspicious.

suspiciō, -icere, -exī, -ectum vt to look up at, look up to; to admire, respect; to mistrust.

suspiciō, -ōnis f mistrust, suspicion.

suspīciōsē adv suspiciously.

suspīciōsus adj suspicious.

suspicor, -ārī, -ātus vt to suspect; to surmise, suppose.

suspīrātus, -ūs m sigh.

suspīritus, -ūs m deep breath, difficult breathing; sigh.

suspīrium, -ī and iī nt deep breath, sigh.

suspīrō, -āre, -āvī, -ātum vi to sigh ♦ vt to sigh for; to exclaim with a sigh.

susque dēque adv up and down.

sustentāculum, -ī nt prop.

sustentātiō, -ōnis f forbearance.

sustentō, -āre, -āvī, -ātum vt to hold up, support; (fig) to uphold, uplift; (food, means) to sustain, support; (enemy) to check, hold; (trouble) to suffer; (event) to hold back, postpone.

sustineō, -inēre, -inuī, -entum vt to hold up, support; to check, control; (fig) to uphold, maintain; (food, means) to sustain, support; (trouble) to bear, suffer, withstand; (event) to put off.

sustollō, -ere vt to lift up, raise; to destroy.

sustulī perf of tollō.

susurrātor, -ōris m whisperer.

susurrō, -āre vt, vi to murmur, buzz, whisper.

susurrus, -ūs m murmuring, whispering.

susurrus adj whispering.

sūtēla, -ae f trick.

sūtilis adj sewn.

sūtor, -ōris m shoemaker; ~ nē suprā crepidam ≈ let the cobbler stick to his last.

sūtōrius adj shoemaker's; ex-cobbler.

sūtrīnus adj shoemaker's.

sūtūra, -ae f seam.

sūtus ppp of suō.

suus adj his, her, its, their; one's own, proper, due, right ♦ mpl one's own troops, friends, followers etc ♦ nt one's own property.

Sybaris, -is f town in S. Italy (noted for its debauchery).

Sybarīta, -ītae m Sybarite.

Sychaeus, -ī m husband of Dido.

sȳcophanta, -ae m slanderer, cheat, sycophant.

sȳcophantia, -ae f deceit.

sȳcophantiōsē adv deceitfully.

sȳcophantor, -ārī, vi to cheat.

Syēnē, -ēs f town in S. Egypt (now Assuan).

syllaba, -ae f syllable.

syllabātim adv syllable by syllable.

symbola, -ae f contribution.

symbolus, -ī m token, symbol.

symphōnia, -ae f concord, harmony.

symphōniacus adj choir (in cpds).

Symplēgades, -um fpl clashing rocks in the Black Sea.

synedrus, -ī m senator (in Macedonia).

Synephēbī, -ōrum mpl Youths Together (comedy by Caecilius).

syngrapha, -ae f promissory note.

syngraphus, -ī m written contract; passport, pass.

Synnada, -ōrum ntpl town in Phrygia (famous for marble).

Synnadēnsis adj see n.

synodūs, -ontis m bream.

synthesis, -is f dinner service; suit of clothes; dressinggown.

Syphāx, -ācis m king of Numidia.

Syrācūsae, -ārum fpl Syracuse.

Syrācūsānus, Syrācūsānius, Syrācosius adj Syracusan.

Syria, -iae f country at the E. end of the Mediterranean.

Syrius, -us and iacus, -iscus adj Syrian.

Noun declensions and verb conjugations are shown on pp xiii to xxv. The present infinitive ending of a verb shows to which conjugation it belongs: -āre = 1st; -ēre = 2nd; -ere = 3rd and -īre = 4th. Irregular verbs are shown on p xxvi

syrma, -ae *f* robe with a train; (*fig*) tragedy.
Syrtis, -is *f* Gulf of Sidra in N. Africa; sandbank.

T, t

tabella, -ae *f* small board, sill; writing tablet, voting tablet, votive tablet; picture; (*pl*) writing, records, dispatches.
tabellārius *adj* about voting ♦ *m* courier.
tābeō, -ēre *vi* to waste away; to be wet.
taberna, -ae *f* cottage; shop; inn; (*circus*) stalls.
tabernāculum, -ī *nt* tent; ~ **capere** choose a site (for auspices).
tabernāriī, -ōrum *mpl* shopkeepers.
tābēs, -is *f* wasting away, decaying, melting; putrefaction; plague, disease.
tābēscō, -ēscere, -uī *vi* to waste away, melt, decay; (*fig*) to pine, languish.
tābidulus *adj* consuming.
tābidus *adj* melting, decaying; pining; corrupting, infectious.
tābificus *adj* melting, wasting.
tabula, -ae *f* board, plank; writing tablet; votive tablet; map; picture; auction; (*pl*) account books, records, lists, will; ~ **Sullae** Sulla's proscriptions; **XII ~ae** Twelve Tables of Roman laws; **~ae novae** cancellation of debts.
tabulārium, -ī *and* **iī** *nt* archives.
tabulātiō, -ōnis *f* flooring, storey.
tabulātum, -ī *nt* flooring, storey; (*trees*) layer, row.
tābum, -ī *nt* decaying matter; disease, plague.
taceō, -ēre, -uī, -itum *vi* to be silent, say nothing; to be still, be hushed ♦ *vt* to say nothing about, not speak of.
tacitē *adv* silently; secretly.
taciturnitās, -ātis *f* silence, taciturnity.
taciturnus *adj* silent, quiet.
tacitus *ppp of* **taceō** ♦ *adj* silent, mute, quiet; secret, unmentioned; tacit, implied; **per ~um** quietly.
Tacitus, -ī *m* famous Roman historian.
tāctilis *adj* tangible.
tāctiō, -ōnis *f* touching; sense of touch.
tāctus *ppp of* **tangō**.
tāctus, -ūs *m* touch, handling, sense of touch; influence.
taeda, -ae *f* pitch pine, pinewood; torch; plank; (*fig*) wedding.
taedet, -ēre, -uit *and* **taesum est** *vt* (*impers*) to be weary (of), loathe.
taedifer, -ī *adj* torch-bearing.
taedium, -ī *and* **iī** *nt* weariness, loathing.

Taenaridēs, -idae *m* Spartan (*esp Hyacinthus*).
Taenarius, -is *adj* of Taenarus; Spartan.
Taenarum (-on), -ī *nt*, **Taenarus (-os), -ī** *m/f* town and promontory in S. Greece (*now* Matapan); the lower world.
taenia, -ae *f* hairband, ribbon.
taesum est *perf of* **taedet**.
taeter, -rī *adj* foul, hideous, repulsive.
taetrē *adv* hideously.
taetricus *see* **tetricus**.
tagāx, -ācis *adj* light-fingered.
Tagus, -ī *m* river of Lusitania (*now* Tagus).
tālāris *adj* reaching to the ankles ♦ *ntpl* winged sandals; a garment reaching to the ankles.
tālārius *adj* of dice.
Talāsius, -ī *and* **iī** *m* god of weddings; wedding cry.
tālea, -ae *f* rod, stake.
talentum, -ī *nt* talent, *a Greek weight about 25.4kg*; a large sum of money (*esp the Attic talent of 60 minae*).
tāliō, -ōnis *f* retaliation in kind.
tālis *adj* such; the following.
talpa, -ae *f* mole.
tālus, -ī *m* ankle; heel; (*pl*) knuckle bones, oblong dice.
tam *adv* so, so much, so very.
tamdiū *adv* so long, as long.
tamen *adv* however, nevertheless, all the same.
Tāmesis, -is *and* **a, -ae** *m* Thames.
tametsī *conj* although.
tamquam *adv* as, just as, just like ♦ *conj* as if.
Tanagra, -ae *f* town in Boeotia.
Tanais, -is *m* river in Sarmatia (*now* Don).
Tanaquil, -ilis *f* wife of the elder Tarquin.
tandem *adv* at last, at length, finally; (*question*) just.
tangō, -ere, tetigī, tāctum *vt* to touch, handle; (*food*) to taste; (*with force*) to hit, strike; (*with liquid*) to sprinkle; (*mind*) to affect, move; (*place*) to reach; to border on; (*task*) to take in hand; (*by trick*) to take in, fool; (*in words*) to touch on, mention; **dē caelō tāctus** struck by lightning.
tanquam *see* **tamquam**.
Tantaleus *adj*, **-idēs, -idae** *m* Pelops, Atreus, Thyestes *or* Agamemnon.
Tantalis, -idis *f* Niobe *or* Hermione.
Tantalus, -ī *m* father of Pelops (*condemned to hunger and thirst in Tartarus, or to the threat of an overhanging rock*).
tantillus *adj* so little, so small.
tantisper *adv* so long, just for a moment.
tantopere *adv* so much.
tantulus *adj* so little, so small.
tantum *adv* so much, so, as; only, merely; ~ **modo** only; ~ **nōn** all but, almost; ~ **quod** only just.
tantummodo *adv* only.
tantundem *adv* just as much, just so much.
tantus *adj* so great; so little ♦ *nt* so much; so little; **~ī esse** be worth so much, be so dear,

be so important; **~ō** so much, so far; (*with compar*) so much the; **~ō opere** so much; **in ~um** to such an extent; **tria ~a** three times as much.

tantusdem *adj* just so great.

tapēta, -ae *m*, **-ia, -ium** *ntpl* carpet, tapestry, hangings.

Taprobanē, -ēs *f* Ceylon.

tardē *adv* slowly, tardily.

tardēscō, -ere *vi* to become slow, falter.

tardipēs, -edis *adj* limping.

tarditās, -ātis *f* slowness, tardiness; (*mind*) dullness.

tardiusculus *adj* rather slow.

tardō, -āre, -āvī, -ātum *vt* to retard, impede ♦ *vi* to delay, go slow.

tardus *adj* slow, tardy, late; (*mind*) dull; (*speech*) deliberate.

Tarentīnus *adj* Tarentine.

Tarentum, -ī *nt* town in S. Italy (*now* Taranto).

tarmes, -itis *m* woodworm.

Tarpēius *adj* Tarpeian; **mōns ~** *the Tarpeian Rock on the Capitoline Hill from which criminals were thrown*.

tarpezīta, -ae *m* banker.

Tarquiniēnsis *adj* of Tarquinii.

Tarquiniī, -iōrum *mpl* ancient town in Etruria.

Tarquinius *adj* of Tarquin.

Tarquinius, -ī *m* Tarquin (*esp Priscus, the fifth king of Rome, and Superbus, the last king*).

Tarracīna, -ae *f*, **-ae, -ārum** *fpl* town in Latium.

Tarracō, -ōnis *f* town in Spain (*now* Tarragona).

Tarracōnēnsis *adj see n.*

Tarsēnsis *adj see n.*

Tarsus, -ī *f* capital of Cilicia.

Tartareus *adj* infernal.

Tartarus (-os), -ī *m*, **-a, -ōrum** *ntpl* Tartarus, the lower world (*esp the part reserved for criminals*).

tat *interj* hallo there!

Tatius, -ī *m* Sabine king (*who ruled jointly with Romulus*).

Tatius *adj see n.*

Taum, -ī *nt* Firth of Tay.

taureus *adj* bull's ♦ *f* whip of bull's hide.

Taurī, -ōrum *mpl* Thracians of the Crimea.

Tauricus *adj see n.*

tauriformis *adj* bull-shaped.

Taurīnī, -ōrum *mpl* people of N. Italy (*now* Turin).

taurīnus *adj* bull's.

Tauromenītānus *adj see n.*

Tauromenium, -ī and iī *nt* town in E. Sicily.

taurus, -ī *m* bull.

Taurus, -ī *m* mountain range in S.E. Asia Minor.

taxātiō, -ōnis *f* valuing.

taxeus *adj* of yews.

taxillus, -ī *m* small dice.

taxō, -āre *vt* to value, estimate.

taxus, -ī *f* yew.

Tāygeta, -ōrum *ntpl*, **Tāygetus, -ī** *m* mountain range in S. Greece.

Tāygetē, -ēs *f* a Pleiad.

tē *acc and abl of* **tū**.

-te *suffix for* **tū**.

Teānēnsis *adj see n.*

Teānum, -ī *nt* town in Apulia; town in Campania.

techina, -ae *f* trick.

Tecmessa, -ae *f* wife of Ajax.

tēctor, -ōris *m* plasterer.

tēctōriolum, -ī *nt* a little plaster.

tēctōrium, -ī and iī *nt* plaster, stucco.

tēctōrius *adj* of a plasterer.

tēctum, -ī *nt* roof, ceiling, canopy; house, dwelling, shelter.

tēctus *ppp of* **tegō** ♦ *adj* hidden; secret, reserved, close.

tēcum with you.

Tegea, -ae *f* town in Arcadia.

Tegeaeus *adj* Arcadian ♦ *m* the god Pan ♦ *f* Atalanta.

Tegeātae, -ātārum *mpl* Tegeans.

teges, -etis *f* mat.

tegillum, -ī *nt* hood, cowl.

tegimen, -inis *nt* covering.

tegimentum, -ī *nt* covering.

tegm- *etc see* **tegim-**.

tegō, -ere, -texī, -tēctum *vt* to cover; to hide, conceal; to protect, defend; to bury; **latus ~** walk by the side of.

tēgula, -ae *f* tile; (*pl*) tiled roof.

tegum- *etc see* **tegim**.

Tēius *adj* of Teos.

tēla, -ae *f* web; warp; yarnbeam, loom; (*fig*) plan.

Telamōn, -ōnis *m* father of Ajax.

Tēlegonus, -ī *m* son of Ulysses and Circe.

Tēlemachus, -ī *m* son of Ulysses and Penelope.

Tēlephus, -ī *m* king of Mysia (*wounded by Achilles' spear*).

tellūs, -ūris *f* the earth; earth, ground; land, country.

tēlum, -ī *nt* weapon, missile; javelin, sword; (*fig*) shaft, dart.

temerārius *adj* accidental; rash, thoughtless.

temerē *adv* by chance, at random; rashly, thoughtlessly; **nōn ~** not for nothing; not easily; hardly ever.

temeritās, -ātis *f* chance; rashness, thoughtlessness.

temerō, -āre, -āvī, -ātum *vt* to desecrate, disgrace.

tēmētum, -ī *nt* wine, alcohol.

temnō, -ere *vt* to slight, despise.

tēmō, -ōnis *m* beam (of plough or carriage); cart; (ASTRO) the Plough.

Tempē *ntpl* famous valley in Thessaly.

temperāmentum, -ī *nt* moderation,

Noun declensions and verb conjugations are shown on pp xiii to xxv. The present infinitive ending of a verb shows to which conjugation it belongs: **-āre** = 1st; **-ēre** = 2nd; **-ere** = 3rd and **-īre** = 4th. Irregular verbs are shown on p xxvi

compromise.

temperāns, -antis *pres p of* **temperō** ♦ *adj* moderate, temperate.

temperanter *adv* with moderation.

temperantia, -ae *f* moderation, self-control.

temperātē *adv* with moderation.

temperātiō, -ōnis *f* proper mixture, composition, constitution; organizing power.

temperātor, -ōris *m* organizer.

temperātus *ppp of* **temperō** ♦ *adj* moderate, sober.

temperī *adv* in time, at the right time.

temperiēs, -ēī *f* due proportion; temperature, mildness.

temperō, -āre, -āvī, -ātum *vt* to mix in due proportion, blend, temper; to regulate, moderate, tune; to govern, rule ♦ *vi* to be moderate, forbear, abstain; (*with dat*) to spare, be lenient to.

tempestās, -ātis *f* time, season, period; weather; storm; (*fig*) storm, shower.

tempestīvē *adv* at the right time, appropriately.

tempestīvitās, -ātis *f* seasonableness.

tempestīvus *adj* timely, seasonable, appropriate; ripe, mature; early.

templum, -ī *nt* space marked off for taking auspices; open space, region, quarter; sanctuary; temple.

temporārius *adj* for the time, temporary.

temptābundus *adj* making repeated attempts.

temptāmentum, -ī *nt* trial, attempt, proof.

temptāmina, -um *ntpl* attempts, essays.

temptātiō, -ōnis *f* trial, proof; attack.

temptātor, -ōris *m* assailant.

temptō, -āre, -āvī, -ātum *vt* to feel, test by touching; to make an attempt on, attack; to try, essay, attempt; to try to influence, tamper with, tempt, incite; **vēnās ~** feel the pulse.

tempus, -oris *nt* time; right time, opportunity; danger, emergency, circumstance; (*head*) temple; (*verse*) unit of metre; (*verb*) tense; **~ore** at the right time, in time; **ad ~us** at the right time; for the moment; **ante ~us** too soon; **ex ~ore** on the spur of the moment; to suit the circumstances; **in ~ore** in time; **in ~us** temporarily; **per ~us** just in time; **prō ~ore** to suit the occasion.

tēmulentus *adj* intoxicated.

tenācitās, -ātis *f* firm grip; stinginess.

tenāciter *adv* tightly, firmly.

tenāx, -ācis *adj* gripping, tenacious; sticky; (*fig*) firm, persistent; stubborn; stingy.

tendicula, -ae *f* little snare.

tendō, -ere, tetendī, tentum *and* **tēnsum** *vt* to stretch, spread; to strain; (*arrow*) to aim, shoot; (*bow*) to bend; (*course*) to direct; (*lyre*) to tune; (*tent*) to pitch; (*time*) to prolong; (*trap*) to lay ♦ *vi* to encamp; to go, proceed; to

aim, tend; (*with infin*) to endeavour, exert oneself.

tenebrae, -ārum *fpl* darkness, night; unconsciousness, death, blindness; (*place*) dungeon, haunt, the lower world; (*fig*) ignorance, obscurity.

tenebricōsus *adj* gloomy.

tenebrōsus *adj* dark, gloomy.

Tenedius *adj see n.*

Tenedos (-us), -ī *f Aegean island near Troy.*

tenellulus *adj* dainty little.

teneō, -ēre, -uī *vt* to hold, keep; to possess, occupy, be master of; to attain, acquire; (*argument*) to maintain, insist; (*category*) to comprise; (*goal*) to make for; (*interest*) to fascinate; (*law*) to bind, be binding on; (*mind*) to grasp, understand, remember; (*movement*) to hold back, restrain ♦ *vi* to hold on, last, persist; (*rumour*) to prevail; **cursum ~** keep on one's course; **sē ~** remain; to refrain.

tener, -ī *adj* tender, delicate; young, weak; effeminate; (*poet*) erotic.

tenerāscō, -ere *vi* to grow weak.

tenerē *adv* softly.

teneritās, -ātis *f* weakness.

tenor, -ōris *m* steady course; **ūnō ~ōre** without a break, uniformly.

tēnsa, -ae *f carriage bearing the images of the gods in procession.*

tēnsus *ppp of* **tendō** ♦ *adj* strained.

tentā- *etc see* **temptā-**.

tentīgō, -inis *f* lust.

tentō *etc see* **temptō**.

tentōrium, -ī *and* **iī** *nt* tent.

tentus *ppp of* **tendō**.

tenuiculus *adj* paltry.

tenuis *adj* thin, fine; small, shallow; (*air*) rarefied; (*water*) clear; (*condition*) poor, mean, insignificant; (*style*) refined, direct, precise.

tenuitās, -ātis *f* thinness, fineness; poverty, insignificance; (*style*) precision.

tenuiter *adv* thinly; poorly; with precision; superficially.

tenuō, -āre, -āvī, -ātum *vt* to make thin, attenuate, rarefy; to lessen, reduce.

tenus *prep* (*with gen or abl*) as far as, up to, down to; **verbō ~** in name, nominally.

Teos, -ī *f* town on coast of Asia Minor (*birthplace of Anacreon*).

tepefaciō, -facere, -fēcī, -factum *vt* to warm.

tepeō, -ēre *vi* to be warm, be lukewarm; (*fig*) to be in love.

tepēscō, -ēscere, -uī *vi* to grow warm; to become lukewarm, cool off.

tepidus *adj* warm, lukewarm.

tepor, -ōris *m* warmth; coolness.

ter *adv* three times, thrice.

terdeciēns *and* **ēs** *adv* thirteen times.

terebinthus, -ī *f* turpentine tree.

terebra, -ae *f* gimlet.

terebrō, -āre *vt* to bore.
terēdō, -inis *f* grub.
Terentia, -iae *f* Cicero's wife.
Terentius, -ī *m* Roman family name (*esp the comic poet Terence*).
Terentius, -iānus *adj see n.*
teres, -etis *adj* rounded (*esp cylindrical*), smooth, shapely; (*fig*) polished, elegant.
Tēreus, -eī *and* **eos** *m* king of Thrace (*husband of Procne, father of Itys*).
tergeminus *adj* threefold, triple.
tergeō, -gēre, -sī, -sum *vt* to wipe off, scour, clean; to rub up, burnish.
tergīnum, -ī *nt* rawhide.
tergiversātiō, -ōnis *f* refusal, subterfuge.
tergiversor, -ārī, -ātus *vi* to hedge, boggle, be evasive.
tergō *etc see* **tergeō.**
tergum, -ī *nt* back; rear; (*land*) ridge; (*water*) surface; (*meat*) chine; (*skin*) hide, leather, anything made of leather; **~a vertere** take to flight; **ā ~ō** behind, in the rear.
tergus, -oris *see* **tergum.**
termes, -itis *m* branch.
Terminālia, -ium *ntpl* Festival of the god of Boundaries.
terminātiō, -ōnis *f* decision; (*words*) clausula.
terminō, -āre, -āvī, -ātum *vt* to set bounds to, limit; to define, determine; to end.
terminus, -ī *m* boundary line, limit, bound; god of boundaries.
ternī, -ōrum *adj* three each; three.
terō, -ere, -trīvī, trītum *vt* to rub, crush, grind; to smooth, sharpen; to wear away, use up; (*road*) to frequent; (*time*) to waste; (*word*) to make commonplace.
Terpsichorē, -ēs *f* Muse of dancing.
terra, -ae *f* dry land, earth, ground, soil; land, country; **orbis ~ārum** the world; **ubi ~ārum** where in the world.
terrēnus *adj* of earth; terrestrial, land- (*in cpds*) ♦ *nt* land.
terreō, -ēre, -uī, -itum *vt* to frighten, terrify; to scare away; to deter.
terrestris *adj* earthly, on earth, land- (*in cpds*).
terribilis *adj* terrifying, dreadful.
terricula, -ōrum *ntpl* scare, bogy.
terrificō, -āre *vt* to terrify.
terrificus *adj* alarming, formidable.
terrigena, -ae *m* earth-born.
terriloquus *adj* alarming.
territō, -āre *vt* to frighten, intimidate.
territōrium, -ī *and* **iī** *nt* territory.
territus *adj* terrified.
terror, -ōris *m* fright, alarm, terror; a terror.
tersī *perf of* **tergeō.**
tersus *ppp of* **tergeō** ♦ *adj* clean; neat, terse.
tertiadecimānī, -ōrum *mpl* men of the thirteenth legion.
tertiānus *adj* recurring every second day ♦ *f a*

fever ♦ *mpl* men of the third legion.
tertiō *adv* for the third time; thirdly.
tertium *adv* for the third time.
tertius *adj* third; **~ decimus (decumus)** thirteenth.
terūncius, -ī *and* **iī** *m* quarter-as; a fourth; (*fig*) farthing.
tesqua (tesca), -ōrum *ntpl* waste ground, desert.
tessella, -ae *f* cube of mosaic stone.
tessera, -ae *f* cube, dice; (*MIL*) password; token (*for mutual recognition of friends*); ticket (*for doles*).
tesserārius, -ī *and* **iī** *m* officer of the watch.
testa, -ae *f* brick, tile; (*earthenware*) pot, jug, sherd; (*fish*) shell, shellfish.
testāmentārius *adj* testamentary ♦ *m* forger of wills.
testāmentum, -ī *nt* will, testament.
testātiō, -ōnis *f* calling to witness.
testātus *ppa of* **testor** ♦ *adj* public.
testiculus, -ī *m* testicle.
testificātiō, -ōnis *f* giving evidence, evidence.
testificor, -ārī, -ātus *vt* to give evidence, vouch for; to make public, bring to light; to call to witness.
testimōnium, -ī *and* **iī** *nt* evidence, testimony; proof.
testis, -is *m/f* witness; eyewitness.
testis, -is *m* testicle.
testor, -ārī, -ātus *vt* to give evidence, testify; to prove, vouch for; to call to witness, appeal to ♦ *vi* to make a will.
testū (*abl -ū*) *nt* earthenware lid, pot.
testūdineus *adj* of tortoiseshell, tortoise- (*in cpds*).
testūdō, -inis *f* tortoise; tortoiseshell; lyre, lute; (*MIL*) shelter for besiegers, covering of shields; (*building*) vault.
testum, -ī *nt* earthenware lid, pot.
tēte *emphatic acc of* **tū.**
tetendī *perf of* **tendō.**
tēter *etc see* **taeter.**
Tēthys, -os *f* sea goddess; the sea.
tetigī *perf of* **tangō.**
tetrachmum, tetradrachmum, -ī *nt* four drachmas.
tetraō, -ōnis *m* blackcock, grouse *or* capercailzie.
tetrarchēs, -ae *m* tetrarch, ruler.
tetrarchia, -ae *f* tetrarchy.
tetricus *adj* gloomy, sour.
tetulī *archaic perf of* **ferō.**
Teucer, -rī *m* son of Telamon of Salamis; son-in-law of Dardanus.
Teucrī, -rōrum *mpl* Trojans.
Teucria, -riae *f* Troy.
Teutonī, -ōrum *and* **es, -um** *mpl* Teutons (*a German people*).

Noun declensions and verb conjugations are shown on pp xiii to xxv. The present infinitive ending of a verb shows to which conjugation it belongs: **-āre** = 1st; **-ēre** = 2nd; **-ere** = 3rd and **-īre** = 4th. Irregular verbs are shown on p xxvi

Teutonicus *adj* Teutonic, German.

tēxī *perf of* **tegō**.

texō, -ere, -uī, -tum *vt* to weave; to plait; to build, make; (*fig*) to compose, contrive.

textilis *adj* woven ♦ *nt* fabric.

textor, -ōris *m* weaver.

textrīnum, -ī *nt* weaving; shipyard.

textūra, -ae *f* web, fabric.

textus *ppp of* **texō** ♦ *nt* web, fabric.

textus, -ūs *m* texture.

texuī *perf of* **texō**.

Thāis, -idis *f an Athenian courtesan*.

thalamus, -ī *m* room, bedroom; marriage bed; marriage.

thalassicus *adj* sea-green.

thalassinus *adj* sea-green.

Thalēs, -is *and* **ētis** *m* early Greek philosopher (*one of the seven wise men*).

Thalia, -ae *f Muse of comedy*.

thallus, -ī *m* green bough.

Thamyrās, -ae *m blinded Thracian poet*.

Thapsitānus *adj see* **Thapsus**.

Thapsus (-os), -ī *f* town in N. Africa (*scene of Caesar's victory*).

Thasius *adj see* **Thasus**.

Thasus (-os), -ī *f Greek island in N. Aegean*.

Thaumantias, -dis *f* Iris.

theātrālis *adj* of the theatre, in the theatre.

theātrum, -ī *nt* theatre; audience; (*fig*) theatre, stage.

Thēbae, -ārum *fpl* Thebes (*capital of Boeotia*); town in Upper Egypt.

Thēbais, -aidis *f* Theban woman; *epic poem by Statius*.

Thēbānus *adj* Theban.

thēca, -ae *f* case, envelope.

Themis, -dis *f goddess of justice*.

Themistoclēs, -ī *and* **is** *m famous Athenian statesman*.

Themistocleus *adj see* **Themistoclēs**.

thēnsaurārius *adj* of treasure.

thēnsaurus *see* **thēsaurus**.

theologus, -ī *m* theologian.

Theophrastus, -ī *m* Greek philosopher (*successor to Aristotle*).

Theopompēus, -īnus *adj see* n.

Theopompus, -ī *m* Greek historian.

thermae, -ārum *fpl* warm baths.

Thermōdōn, -ontis *m* river of Pontus (*where the Amazons lived*).

Thermōdontēus, -ontiacus *adj* Amazonian.

thermopōlium *nt* restaurant serving warm drinks.

thermopotō, -āre *vt* to refresh with warm drinks.

Thermopylae, -ārum *fpl famous Greek pass defended by Leonidas*.

thēsaurus, -ī *m* treasure, store; storehouse, treasury.

Thēseus, -eī *and* **eos** *m* Greek hero (*king of Athens*).

Thēsēus, -ēius *adj*, **-īdēs, -īdae** *m* Hippolytus; (*pl*) Athenians.

Thespiae, -ārum *fpl Boeotian town near Helicon*.

Thespiēnsis *and* **as, -adis** *adj* Thespian.

Thespis, -is *m traditional founder of Greek tragedy*.

Thessalia, -iae *f* Thessaly (*district of N. Greece*).

Thessalicus, -us *and* **is, -idis** *adj* Thessalian.

Thetis, -idis *and* **idos** *f* sea nymph (*mother of Achilles*); the sea.

thiasus, -ī *m* Bacchic dance.

Thoantēus *adj see* n.

Thoās, -antis *m* king of Crimea (*killed by Orestes*); king of Lemnos (*father of Hypsipyle*).

tholus, -ī *m* rotunda.

thōrāx, -ācis *m* breastplate.

Thrāca, -ae, (-ē, -ēs), (-ia, -iae) *f* Thrace.

Thracius, (Thrēicius) *adj* Thracian.

Thrasea, -ae *m Stoic philosopher under Nero*.

Thrasymachus, -ī *m Greek sophist*.

Thrāx, -ācis *m* Thracian; *kind of gladiator*.

Thrēssa, -ae, (Thrēissa, -ae) *f* Thracian woman.

Thrēx, -ēcis *m kind of gladiator*.

Thūcydidēs, -is *m famous Greek historian*.

Thūcydidius *adj* Thucydidean.

Thūlē, -ēs *f* island in the extreme N. (*perhaps Shetland*).

thunnus *see* **thynnus**.

thūr, -is *nt* = **tūs, tūris**.

Thūriī, -iōrum *mpl* town in S. Italy.

Thūrīnus *adj see* n.

thūs *see* **tūs**.

thȳa (thȳia), -ae *f* citrus tree.

Thybris, -is *and* **idis** *m* river Tiber.

Thyestēs, -ae *m* brother of Atreus (*whose son's flesh he served up to him to eat*).

Thyestēus *adj*, **-iadēs, -iadae** *m* Aegisthus.

Thyias (Thȳas), -adis *f* Bacchante.

Thȳlē *see* **Thūlē**.

thymbra, -ae *f* savory.

thymum, -ī *nt* garden thyme.

Thȳnia, -iae *f* Bithynia.

thynnus, -ī *m* tunnyfish.

Thȳnus, (-iacus), (-ias) *adj* Bithynian.

Thyōneus, -eī *m* Bacchus.

thyrsus, -ī *m* Bacchic wand.

tiāra, -ae *f*, **-ās, -ae** *m* turban.

Tiberiānus *adj see* n.

Tiberīnus, -inis *adj*, **-īnus, -īnī** *m* Tiber.

Tiberis (Tibris), -is *m* river Tiber.

Tiberius, -ī *m* Roman praenomen (*esp the second emperor*).

tibi *dat of* **tū**.

tībia, -ae *f* shinbone; pipe, flute.

tībīcen, -inis *m* flute player; pillar.

tībīcina, -ae *f* flute player.

tībīcinium, -ī *and* **iī** *nt* flute playing.

Tibullus, -ī *m* Latin elegiac poet.

Tībur, -is *nt* town on the river Anio (*now Tivoli*).

Tīburs, -tis, (-tīnus), (-nus) *adj* Tiburtine.

Tīcīnus, -ī *m* tributary of the river Po.

Tigellīnus, -ī m favourite of Nero.
tigillum, -ī nt small log, small beam.
tignārius adj working in wood; **faber ~** carpenter.
tignum, -ī nt timber, trunk, log.
Tigrānēs, -is m king of Armenia.
tigris, -is and **idis** f tiger.
tīlia, -ae f lime tree.
Tīmaeus, -ī m Sicilian historian; Pythagorean philosopher; a dialogue of Plato.
timefactus adj frightened.
timeō, -ēre, -uī vt, vi to fear, be afraid.
timidē adv timidly.
timiditās, -ātis f timidity, cowardice.
timidus adj timid, cowardly.
timor, -ōris m fear, alarm; a terror.
tinctilis adj dipped in.
tinctus ppp of **tingō.**
tinea, -ae f moth, bookworm.
tingō, -gere, -xī, -ctum vt to dip, soak; to dye, colour; (fig) to imbue.
tinnīmentum, -ī nt ringing noise.
tinniō, -īre vt, vi to ring, tinkle.
tinnītus, -ūs m ringing, jingle.
tinnulus adj ringing, jingling.
tintinnābulum, -ī nt bell.
tintinō, -āre vi to ring.
tīnus, -ī m a shrub, laurustinus.
tinxī perf of **tingō.**
Tīphys, -os m helmsman of the Argo.
tippula, -ae f water spider.
Tīresiās, -ae m blind soothsayer of Thebes.
Tīridātēs, -ae m king of Armenia.
tīrō, -ōnis m recruit, beginner.
Tīrō, -ōnis m Cicero's freedman secretary.
tīrōcinium, -ī and **iī** nt first campaign; recruits; (fig) first attempt, inexperience.
Tīrōniānus adj see **Tīrō.**
tīrunculus, -ī m young beginner.
Tīryns, -this f ancient town in S.E. Greece (home of Hercules).
Tīrynthius adj of Tiryns, of Hercules ♦ m Hercules.
tis archaic gen of **tū.**
Tīsiphonē, -ēs f a Fury.
Tīsiphonēus adj guilty.
Tītān, -ānis, (-ānus, -ānī) m Titan (an ancient race of gods); the sun.
Tītānius, (-āniacus), (-ānis) adj see n.
Tīthōnius adj see n.
Tīthōnus, -ī m consort of Aurora (granted immortality without youth).
tītillātiō, -ōnis f tickling.
tītillō, -āre vt to tickle.
titubanter adv falteringly.
titubātiō, -ōnis f staggering.
titubō, -āre vi to stagger, totter; to stammer; to waver, falter.
titulus, -ī m inscription, label, notice; title of honour; fame; pretext.

Tityos, -ī m giant punished in Tartarus.
Tmōlus, -ī m mountain in Lydia.
toculiō, -ōnis m usurer.
tōfus, -ī m tufa.
toga, -ae f toga (dress of the Roman citizen); (fig) peace; **~ candida** dress of election candidates; **~ picta** ceremonial dress of a victor in triumph; **~ praetexta** purple-edged toga of magistrates and children; **~ pūra, virīlis** plain toga of manhood.
togātus adj wearing the toga ♦ m Roman citizen; client ♦ f drama on a Roman theme.
togula, -ae f small toga.
tolerābilis adj bearable, tolerable; patient.
tolerābiliter adv patiently.
tolerāns, -antis pres p of **tolerō** ♦ adj patient.
toleranter adv patiently.
tolerantia, -ae f endurance.
tolerātiō, -ōnis f enduring.
tolerātus adj tolerable.
tolerō, -āre, -āvī, -ātum vt to bear, endure; to support, sustain.
tollēnō, -ōnis m crane, derrick, lift.
tollō, -ere, sustulī, sublātum vt to lift, raise; to take away, remove; to do away with, abolish, destroy; (anchor) to weigh; (child) to acknowledge, bring up; (mind) to elevate, excite, cheer; (passenger) to take on board; **signa ~** decamp.
Tolōsa, -ae f Toulouse.
Tolōsānus adj see **Tolōsa.**
tolūtim adv at a trot.
tomāculum, -ī nt sausage.
tōmentum, -ī nt stuffing, padding.
Tomis, -is f town on the Black Sea (to which Ovid was exiled).
Tomītānus adj see **Tomis.**
Tonāns, -antis m Thunderer (epithet of Jupiter).
tondeō, -ēre, totondī, tōnsum vt to shear, clip, shave; to crop, reap, mow; to graze, browse on; (fig) to fleece, rob.
tonitrālis adj thunderous.
tonitrus, -ūs m, **-ua, -uōrum** ntpl thunder.
tonō, -āre, -uī vi to thunder ♦ vt to thunder out.
tōnsa, -ae f oar.
tōnsillae, -ārum fpl tonsils.
tōnsor, -ōris m barber.
tōnsōrius adj for shaving.
tōnstrīcula, -ae f barber girl.
tōnstrīna, -ae f barber's shop.
tōnstrīx, -īcis f woman barber.
tōnsūra, -ae f shearing, clipping.
tōnsus ppp of **tondeō.**
tōnsus, -ūs m coiffure.
tōphus see **tōfus.**
topiārius adj of ornamental gardening ♦ m topiarist ♦ f topiary.
topicē, -ēs f the art of finding topics.

Noun declensions and verb conjugations are shown on pp xiii to xxv. The present infinitive ending of a verb shows to which conjugation it belongs: **-āre** = 1st; **-ēre** = 2nd; **-ere** = 3rd and **-īre** = 4th. Irregular verbs are shown on p xxvi

toral, -ālis *nt* valance.
torcular, -āris *and* **um, -ī** *nt* press.
toreuma, -tis *nt* embossed work, relief.
tormentum, -ī *nt* windlass, torsion catapult, artillery; shot; rack, torture; (*fig*) torment, anguish.
tormina, -um *ntpl* colic.
torminōsus *adj* subject to colic.
tornō, -āre, -āvī, -ātum *vt* to turn (in a lathe), round off.
tornus, -ī *m* lathe.
torōsus *adj* muscular.
torpēdō, -inis *f* numbness, lethargy; (*fish*) electric ray.
torpeō, -ēre *vi* to be stiff, be numb; to be stupefied.
torpēscō, -ēscere, -uī *vi* to grow stiff, numb, listless.
torpidus *adj* benumbed.
torpor, -ōris *m* numbness, torpor, listlessness.
torquātus *adj* wearing a neckchain.
Torquātus, -ī *m* surname of Manlius.
torqueō, -quēre, -sī, -tum *vt* to turn, twist, bend, wind; (*missile*) to whirl, hurl, brandish; (*body*) to rack, torture; (*mind*) to torment.
torquēs *and* **is, -is** *m/f* neckchain, necklace, collar.
torrēns, -entis *pres p of* **torreō** ♦ *adj* scorching, hot; rushing, rapid ♦ *m* torrent.
torreō, -ēre, -uī, tostum *vt* to parch, scorch, roast.
torrēscō, -ere *vi* to become parched.
torridus *adj* parched, dried up; frostbitten.
torris, -is *m* brand, firebrand.
torsī *perf of* **torqueō**.
tortē *adv* awry.
tortilis *adj* twisted, winding.
tortor, -ārī *vi* to writhe.
tortor, -ōris *m* torturer, executioner.
tortuōsus *adj* winding; (*fig*) complicated.
tortus *ppp of* **torqueō** ♦ *adj* crooked; complicated.
tortus, -ūs *m* twisting, writhing.
torulus, -ī *m* tuft (of hair).
torus, -ī *m* knot, bulge; muscle, brawn; couch, bed; (*earth*) bank, mound; (*language*) ornament.
torvitās, -ātis *f* wildness, grimness.
torvus *adj* wild, grim, fierce.
tostus *ppp of* **torreō**.
tot *adj* (*indecl*) so many, as many.
totidem *adj* (*indecl*) just as many, the same number of.
totiēns, totiēs *adv* so often, as often.
totondī *perf of* **tondeō**.
tōtus (*gen* -**īus**, *dat* -**ī**) *adj* entire, the whole, all; entirely, completely taken up with; **ex ~ō** totally; **in ~ō** on the whole.
toxicum, -ī *nt* poison.
trabālis *adj* for beams; **clāvus ~** large nail.
trabea, -ae *f* ceremonial robe.
trabeātus *adj* wearing a ceremonial robe.

trabs, -abis *f* beam, timber; tree; ship; roof.
Trāchīn, -inis *f* town in Thessaly (*where Hercules cremated himself*).
Trāchīnius *adj see* **Trāchīn**.
tractābilis *adj* manageable, tractable.
tractātiō, -ōnis *f* handling, treatment.
tractātus, -ūs *m* handling.
tractim *adv* slowly, little by little.
tractō, -āre, -āvī, -ātum *vt* to maul; to handle, deal with, manage; (*activity*) to conduct, perform; (*person*) to treat; (*subject*) to discuss, consider.
tractus *ppp of* **trahō** ♦ *adj* fluent.
tractus, -ūs *m* dragging, pulling, drawing; train, track; (*place*) extent, region, district; (*movement*) course; (*time*) lapse; (*word*) drawling.
trādidī *perf of* **trādō**.
trāditiō, -ōnis *f* surrender; handing down.
trāditor, -ōris *m* traitor.
trāditus *ppp of* **trādō**.
trādō, -ere, -idī, -itum *vt* to hand over, deliver, surrender; to commit, entrust; to betray; to bequeath, hand down; (*narrative*) to relate, record; (*teaching*) to propound; **sē ~** surrender, devote oneself.
trādūcō (trānsdūcō), -ūcere, -ūxī, -uctum *vt* to bring across, lead over, transport across; to transfer; to parade, make an exhibition of (in public); (*time*) to pass, spend.
trāductiō, -ōnis *f* transference; (*time*) passage; (*word*) metonymy.
trāductor, -ōris *m* transferrer.
trāductus *ppp of* **trādūcō**.
trādux, -ucis *m* vine layer.
tragicē *adv* dramatically.
tragicocōmoedia, -ae *f* tragicomedy.
tragicus *adj* of tragedy, tragic; in the tragic manner, lofty; terrible, tragic ♦ *m* writer of tragedy.
tragoedia, -ae *f* tragedy; (*fig*) bombast.
tragoedus, -ī *m* tragic actor.
trāgula, -ae *f* kind of javelin.
trahea, -ae *f* sledge.
trahō, -here, -xi, -ctum *vt* to draw, drag, pull, take with one; to pull out, lengthen; to draw together, contract; to carry off, plunder; (*liquid*) to drink, draw; (*money*) to squander; (*wool*) to spin; (*fig*) to attract; (*appearance*) to take on; (*consequence*) to derive, get; (*praise, blame*) to ascribe, refer; (*thought*) to ponder; (*time*) to spin out.
trāiciō, -icere, -iēcī, -iectum *vt* to throw across, shoot across; (*troops*) to get across, transport; (*with weapon*) to pierce, stab; (*river, etc*) to cross; (*fig*) to transfer ♦ *vi* to cross.
trāiectiō, -ōnis *f* crossing, passage; (*fig*) transferring; (*RHET*) exaggeration; (*words*) transposition.
trāiectus *ppp of* **trāiciō**.
trāiectus, -ūs *m* crossing, passage.

trālāt- *etc see* **trānslāt-**.

Trallēs, -ium *fpl* town in Lydia.

Tralliānus *adj see n*.

trālūceō *etc see* **trānslūceō**.

trāma, -ae *f* woof, web.

trāmes, -itis *m* footpath, path.

trāmittō *etc see* **trānsmittō**.

trānatō *etc see* **trānsnatō**.

trānō, -āre, -āvī, -ātum *vt, vi* to swim across; (*air*) to fly through.

tranquillē *adv* quietly.

tranquillitās, -ātis *f* quietness, calm; (*fig*) peace, quiet.

tranquillō, -āre *vt* to calm.

tranquillus *adj* quiet, calm ♦ *nt* calm sea.

trāns *prep* (*with acc*) across, over, beyond.

trānsabeō, -īre, -iī *vt* to pierce.

trānsāctor, -ōris *m* manager.

trānsāctus *ppp of* **trānsigō**.

trānsadigō, -ere *vt* to drive through, pierce.

Trānsalpīnus *adj* Transalpine.

trānscendō (trānsscendō), -endere, -endī, -ēnsum *vt, vi* to pass over, surmount; to overstep, surpass, transgress.

trānscrībō (trānsscrībō), -bere, -psī, -ptum *vt* to copy out; (*fig*) to make over, transfer.

trānscurrō, -rere, -rī, -sum *vt, vi* to run across, run past, traverse.

trānscursus, -ūs *m* running through; (*speech*) cursory remark.

trānsd- *etc see* **trād-**.

trānsēgī *perf of* **trānsigō**.

trānsenna, -ae *f* net, snare; trellis, latticework.

trānseō, -īre, -iī, -itum *vt, vi* to pass over, cross over; to pass along *or* through; to pass by; to outstrip, surpass, overstep; (*change*) to turn into; (*speech*) to mention briefly, leave out, pass on; (*time*) to pass, pass away.

trānsferō, -ferre, -tulī, -lātum *vt* to bring across, transport, transfer; (*change*) to transform; (*language*) to translate; (*RHET*) to use figuratively; (*time*) to postpone; (*writing*) to copy.

trānsfīgō, -gere, -xī, -xum *vt* to pierce; to thrust through.

trānsfīxus *ppp of* **trānsfīgō**.

trānsfodiō, -odere, -ōdī, -ossum *vt* to run through, stab.

trānsfōrmis *adj* changed in shape.

trānsfōrmō, -āre *vt* to change in shape.

trānsfossus *ppp of* **trānsfodiō**.

trānsfuga, -ae *m/f* deserter.

trānsfugiō, -ugere, -ūgī *vi* to desert, come over.

trānsfugium, -ī *and* **iī** *nt* desertion.

trānsfundō, -undere, -ūdī, -ūsum *vt* to decant, transfuse.

trānsfūsiō, -ōnis *f* transmigration.

trānsfūsus *ppp of* **trānsfundō**.

trānsgredior, -dī, -ssus *vt, vi* to step across, cross over, cross; to pass on; to exceed.

trānsgressiō, -ōnis *f* passage; (*words*) transposition.

trānsgressus *ppa of* **trānsgredior**.

trānsgressus, -ūs *m* crossing.

trānsiciō *etc see* **trāiciō**.

trānsigō, -igere, -ēgī, -āctum *vt* to carry through, complete, finish; (*difference*) to settle; (*time*) to pass, spend; (*with* **cum**) to put an end to; (*with weapon*) to stab.

trānsiī *perf of* **trānseō**.

trānsiliō, trānssiliō, -īre, -uī *vi* to jump across ♦ *vt* to leap over; (*fig*) to skip, disregard; to exceed.

trānsitiō, -ōnis *f* passage; desertion; (*disease*) infection.

trānsitō, -āre *vi* to pass through.

trānsitus *ppp of* **trānseō**.

trānsitus, -ūs *m* passing over, passage; desertion; passing by; transition.

trānslātīcius, trālātīcius *adj* traditional, customary, common.

trānslātiō, trālātiō, -ōnis *f* transporting, transferring; (*language*) metaphor.

trānslātīvus *adj* transferable.

trānslātor, -ōris *m* transferrer.

trānslātus *ppp of* **trānsferō**.

trānslegō, -ere *vt* to read through.

trānslūceō, -ēre *vi* to be reflected; to shine through.

trānsmarīnus *adj* overseas.

trānsmeō, -āre *vi* to cross.

trānsmigrō, -āre *vi* to emigrate.

trānsmissiō, -ōnis *f* crossing.

trānsmissus *ppp of* **trānsmittō**.

trānsmissus, -ūs *m* crossing.

trānsmittō, -ittere, -īsī, -issum *vt* to send across, put across; to let pass through; to transfer, entrust, devote; to give up, pass over; (*place*) to cross over, go through, pass ♦ *vi* to cross.

trānsmontānus *adj* beyond the mountains.

trānsmoveō, -ovēre, -ōvī, -ōtum *vt* to move, transfer.

trānsmūtō, -āre *vt* to shift.

trānsnatō, trānatō, -āre *vi* to swim across ♦ *vt* to swim.

trānsnō *etc see* **trānō**.

Trānspadānus *adj* north of the Po.

trānspectus, -ūs *m* view.

trānspiciō, -ere *vt* to look through.

trānspōnō, -ōnere, -osuī, -ositum *vt* to transfer.

trānsportō, -āre *vt* to carry across, transport, remove.

trānspositus *ppp of* **trānspōnō**.

Trānsrhēnānus *adj* east of the Rhine.

trānss- *etc see* **trāns-**.

Noun declensions and verb conjugations are shown on pp xiii to xxv. The present infinitive ending of a verb shows to which conjugation it belongs: **-āre** = 1st; **-ēre** = 2nd; **-ere** = 3rd and **-īre** = 4th. Irregular verbs are shown on p xxvi

Trānstiberīnus *adj* across the Tiber.
trānstineō, -ēre *vi* to get through.
trānstrum, -ī *nt* thwart.
trānstulī *perf of* **trānsferō**.
trānsultō, -āre *vi* to jump across.
trānsūtus *adj* pierced.
trānsvectiō, -ōnis *f* crossing.
trānsvectus *ppp of* **trānsvehō**.
trānsvehō, -here, -xī, -ctum *vt* to carry across, transport.
trānsvehor, -hī, -ctus *vi* to cross, pass over; (*parade*) to ride past; (*time*) to elapse.
trānsverberō, -āre *vt* to pierce through, wound.
trānsversus (trāversus) *adj* lying across, crosswise, transverse; **digitum ~um** a finger's breadth; **dē ~ō** unexpectedly; **ex ~ō** sideways.
trānsvolitō, -āre *vt* to fly through.
trānsvolō, -āre *vt, vi* to fly across, fly through; to move rapidly across; to fly past, disregard.
trānsvorsus *etc see* **trānsversus**.
trapētus, -ī *m* olive mill, oil mill.
trapezīta *etc see* **tarpezīta**.
Trapezūs, -ūntis *f* Black Sea town (*now* Trebizond).
Trasumennus (Trasimēnus), -ī *m* lake in Etruria (*where Hannibal defeated the Romans*).
trāv- *see* **trānsv-**.
trāvectiō *etc see* **trānsvectiō**.
traxī *perf of* **trahō**.
trecēnī, -ōrum *adj* three hundred each.
trecentēsimus *adj* three-hundredth.
trecentī, -ōrum *num* three hundred.
trecentiēns, -ēs *adv* three hundred times.
trechedīpna, -ōrum *ntpl* dinner shoes (of parasites).
tredecim *num* thirteen.
tremebundus *adj* trembling.
tremefaciō, -facere, -fēcī, -factum *vt* to shake.
tremendus *adj* formidable, terrible.
tremēscō (tremīscō), -ere *vi* to begin to shake ♦ *vt* to be afraid of.
tremō, -ere, -uī *vi* to tremble, quake, quiver ♦ *vt* to tremble at, dread.
tremor, -ōris *m* shaking, quiver, tremor; earthquake.
tremulus *adj* trembling, shivering.
trepidanter *adv* with agitation.
trepidātiō, -ōnis *f* agitation, alarm, consternation.
trepidē *adv* hastily, in confusion.
trepidō, -āre, -āvī, -ātum *vi* to be agitated, bustle about, hurry; to be alarmed; to flicker, quiver ♦ *vt* to start at.
trepidus *adj* restless, anxious, alarmed; alarming, perilous.
trēs, trium *num* three.
trēssis, -is *m* three asses.
trēsvirī, triumvirōrum *mpl* three commissioners, triumvirs.

Trēverī, -ōrum *mpl* people of E. Gaul (*about what is now* Trèves).
Trēvericus *adj see n.*
triangulum, -ī *nt* triangle.
triangulus *adj* triangular.
triāriī, -ōrum *mpl* the third line (*in Roman battle order*), the reserves.
tribuārius *adj* of the tribes.
tribūlis, -is *m* fellow tribesman.
tribulum, -ī *nt* threshing sledge.
tribulus, -ī *m* star thistle.
tribūnal, -ālis *nt* platform; judgment seat; camp platform, cenotaph.
tribūnātus, -ūs *m* tribuneship, rank of tribune.
tribūnicius *adj* of a tribune ♦ *m* ex-tribune.
tribūnus, -ī *m* tribune; **~ plēbis** tribune of the people, a magistrate who defended the rights of the plebeians; **~ mīlitum** *or* **mīlitāris** military tribune, an officer under the legatus; **~ī aerāriī** paymasters.
tribuō, -uere, -uī, -ūtum *vt* to assign, allot; to give, bestow, pay; to concede, allow; to ascribe, attribute; (*subject*) to divide; (*time*) to devote.
tribus, -ūs *m* tribe.
tribūtārius *adj*: **~ae tabellae** letters of credit.
tribūtim *adv* by tribes.
tribūtiō, -ōnis *f* distribution.
tribūtum, -ī *nt* contribution, tribute, tax.
tribūtus *ppp of* **tribuō**.
tribūtus *adj* arranged by tribes.
trīcae, -ārum *fpl* nonsense; tricks, vexations.
trīcēnī, -ōrum *adj* thirty each, in thirties.
triceps, -ipitis *adj* three-headed.
trīcēsimus *adj* thirtieth.
trichila, -ae *f* arbour, summerhouse.
trīciēns, -ēs *adv* thirty times.
trīclīnium, -ī and iī *nt* dining couch; dining room.
trīcō, -ōnis *m* mischief-maker.
trīcor, -ārī *vi* to make mischief, play tricks.
tricorpor, -is *adj* three-bodied.
tricuspis, -idis *adj* three-pointed.
tridēns, -entis *adj* three-pronged ♦ *m* trident.
tridentifer, -ī *adj* trident-wielding.
tridentiger, -ī *adj* trident-wielding.
triduum, -ī *nt* three days.
triennia, -ium *ntpl* a triennial festival.
triennium, -ī and iī *nt* three years.
triēns, -entis *m* a third; (*coin*) a third of an as; (*measure*) a third of a pint.
trientābulum, -ī *nt* land given by the State as a third of a debt.
trientius *adj* sold for a third.
triērarchus, -ī *m* captain of a trireme.
triēris, -is *f* trireme.
triētēricus *adj* triennial ♦ *ntpl* festival of Bacchus.
triētēris, -idis *f* three years; a triennial festival.
trifāriam *adv* in three parts, in three places.
trifaux, -aucis *adj* three-throated.

trifidus *adj* three-forked.
trifōrmis *adj* triple.
trifūr, -ūris *m* archthief.
trifurcifer, -ī *m* hardened criminal.
trigeminus *adj* threefold, triple ♦ *mpl* triplets.
trigintā *num* thirty.
trigōn, -ōnis *m* a ball game.
trilībris *adj* three-pound.
trilinguis *adj* three-tongued.
trilīx, -icis *adj* three-ply, three-stranded.
trimēstris *adj* of three months.
trimetrus, -ī *m* trimeter.
trīmus *adj* three years old.
Trīnacria, -iae *f* Sicily.
Trīnacrius, -is, -idis *adj* Sicilian.
trīnī, -ōrum *adj* three each, in threes; triple.
Trinobantēs, -um *mpl* British tribe in East Anglia.
trinōdis *adj* three-knotted.
triōbolus, -ī *m* half-a-drachma.
Triōnēs, -um *mpl* the Plough; the Little Bear.
tripartītō *adv* in *or* into three parts.
tripartītus, tripertītus *adj* divided into three parts.
tripectorus *adj* three-bodied.
tripedālis *adj* three-foot.
tripert- *etc see* **tripart-**.
tripēs, -edis *adj* three-legged.
triplex, -icis *adj* triple, threefold ♦ *nt* three times as much ♦ *mpl* three-leaved writing tablet.
triplus *adj* triple.
Triptolemus, -ī *m* inventor of agriculture, judge in Hades.
tripudiō, -āre *vi* to dance.
tripudium, -ī *and* **iī** *nt* ceremonial dance, dance; a favourable omen (*when the sacred chickens ate greedily*).
tripūs, -odis *f* tripod; the Delphic oracle.
triquetrus *adj* triangular; Sicilian.
trirēmis *adj* with three banks of oars ♦ *f* trireme.
trīs *etc see* **trēs**.
triscurria, -ōrum *ntpl* sheer fooling.
tristē *adv* sadly; severely.
trīstī = **trīvistī**.
tristiculus *adj* rather sad.
tristificus *adj* ominous.
tristimōnia, -ae *f* sadness.
tristis *adj* sad, glum, melancholy; gloomy, sombre, dismal; (*taste*) bitter; (*smell*) offensive; (*temper*) severe, sullen, ill-humoured.
tristitia, -ae *f* sadness, sorrow, melancholy; moroseness, severity.
tristitiēs, -ēī *f* sorrow.
trisulcus *adj* three-forked.
tritavus, -ī *m* great-great-great-grandfather.
trīticeus *adj* of wheat, wheaten.
trīticum, -ī *nt* wheat.

Trītōn, -ōnis *m* sea god (*son of Neptune*); African lake (*where Minerva was born*).
Trītōnius, -ōniacus, -ōnis *adj* of Lake Triton, of Minerva ♦ *f* Minerva.
trītūra, -ae *f* threshing.
trītus *ppp of* **terō** ♦ *adj* well-worn; (*judgment*) expert; (*language*) commonplace, trite.
trītus, -ūs *m* rubbing, friction.
triumphālis *adj* triumphal ♦ *ntpl* insignia of a triumph.
triumphō, -āre, -āvī, -ātum *vi* to celebrate a triumph; to triumph, exult ♦ *vt* to triumph over, win by conquest.
triumphus, -ī *m* triumphal procession, victory parade; triumph, victory.
triumvir, -ī *m* commissioner, triumvir; mayor (*of a provincial town*).
triumvirālis *adj* triumviral.
triumvirātus, -ūs *m* office of triumvir, triumvirate.
triumvirī, -ōrum *mpl* three commissioners, triumvirs.
trivenēfica, -ae *f* old witch.
trivī *perf of* **terō**.
Trivia, -ae *f* Diana.
triviālis *adj* common, popular.
trivium, -ī *and* **iī** *nt* crossroads; public street.
trivius *adj* of the crossroads.
Trōas, -adis *f* the district of Troy, Troad; Trojan woman ♦ *adj* Trojan.
trochaeus, -ī *m* trochee; tribrach.
trochlea, -ae *f* block and tackle.
trochus, -ī *m* hoop.
Trōglodytae, -ārum *mpl* cave dwellers of Ethiopia.
Trōia, -ae *f* Troy.
Trōilus, -ī *m* son of Priam.
Trōiugena, -ae *m/f* Trojan; Roman.
Trōius *and* **ānus** *and* **cus** *adj* Trojan.
tropaeum, -ī *nt* victory memorial, trophy; victory; memorial, token.
Trōs, -ōis *m* king of Phrygia; Trojan.
trucīdātiō, -ōnis *f* butchery.
trucīdō, -āre, -āvī, -ātum *vt* to slaughter, massacre.
truculentē *adv see* **truculentus**.
truculentia, -ae *f* ferocity, inclemency.
truculentus *adj* ferocious, grim, wild.
trudis, -is *f* pike.
trūdō, -dere, -sī, -sum *vt* to push, thrust, drive; (*buds*) to put forth.
trulla, -ae *f* ladle, scoop; washbasin.
truncō, -āre, -āvī, -ātum *vt* to lop off, maim, mutilate.
truncus, -ī *m* (*tree*) trunk, bole; (*human*) trunk, body; (*abuse*) blockhead ♦ *adj* maimed, broken, stripped (of); defective.
trūsī *perf of* **trūdō**.
trūsitō, -āre *vt* to keep pushing.
trūsus *ppp of* **trūdō**.

Noun declensions and verb conjugations are shown on pp xiii to xxv. The present infinitive ending of a verb shows to which conjugation it belongs: **-āre** = 1st; **-ēre** = 2nd; **-ere** = 3rd and **-īre** = 4th. Irregular verbs are shown on p xxvi

trutina, -ae *f* balance, scales.
trux, -ucis *adj* savage, grim, wild.
trȳgōnus, -ī *m* stingray.
tū *pron* you, thou.
tuātim *adv* in your usual fashion.
tuba, -ae *f* trumpet, war trumpet.
tūber, -is *nt* swelling, lump; (*food*) truffle.
tuber, -is *f* kind of apple tree.
tubicen, -inis *m* trumpeter.
tubilūstria, -ōrum *ntpl* festival of trumpets.
tuburcinor, -ārī *vi* to gobble up, guzzle.
tubus, -ī *m* pipe.
tuditō, -āre *vt* to strike repeatedly.
tueor, -ērī, -itus *and* **tūtus** *vt* to see, watch, look; to guard, protect, keep.
tugurium, -ī *and* **iī** *nt* hut, cottage.
tuitiō, -ōnis *f* defence.
tuitus *ppa of* **tueor**.
tulī *perf of* **ferō**.
Tulliānum, -ī *nt State dungeon of Rome.*
Tulliānus *adj see* **Tullius**.
Tulliola, -ae *f* little Tullia (*Cicero's daughter*).
Tullius, -ī *and* **iī** *m* Roman family name (*esp the sixth king*); *the orator Cicero.*
Tullus, -ī *m* third king of Rome.
tum *adv* (*time*) then, at that time; (*sequence*) then, next ♦ *conj* moreover, besides; ~ ... ~ at one time ... at another; ~ ... **cum** at the time when, whenever; **cum** ... ~ not only ... but; ~ **dēmum** only then; ~ **ipsum** even then; ~ **māximē** just then; ~ **vērō** then more than ever.
tumefaciō, -facere, -fēcī, -factum *vt* to make swell; (*fig*) to puff up.
tumeō, -ēre *vi* to swell, be swollen; (*emotion*) to be excited; (*pride*) to be puffed up; (*language*) to be turgid.
tumēscō, -ēscere, -uī *vi* to begin to swell, swell up.
tumidus *adj* swollen, swelling; (*emotion*) excited, enraged; (*pride*) puffed up; (*language*) bombastic.
tumor, -ōris *m* swelling, bulge; hillock; (*fig*) commotion, excitement.
tumulō, -āre *vt* to bury.
tumulōsus *adj* hilly.
tumultuārius *adj* hasty; (*troops*) emergency.
tumultuātiō, -ōnis *f* commotion.
tumultuō, -āre; -or, -ārī *vi* to make a commotion, be in an uproar.
tumultuōsē *adv see* **tumultuōsus**.
tumultuōsus *adj* uproarious, excited, turbulent.
tumultus, -ūs *m* commotion, uproar, disturbance; (MIL) rising, revolt, civil war; (*weather*) storm; (*mind*) disorder.
tumulus, -ī *m* mound, hill; burial mound, barrow.
tunc *adv* (*time*) then, at that time; (*sequence*) then, next; ~ **dēmum** only then; ~ **quoque** then too; even so.
tundō, -ere, tutudī, tūnsum *and* **tūsum** *vt* to beat, thump, hammer; (*grain*) to pound;

(*speech*) to din, importune.
Tūnēs, -ētis *m* Tunis.
tunica, -ae *f* tunic; (*fig*) skin, husk.
tunicātus *adj* wearing a tunic.
tunicula, -ae *f* little tunic.
tūnsus *ppp of* **tundō**.
tuor *etc see* **tueor**.
turba, -ae *f* disorder, riot, disturbance; brawl, quarrel; crowd, mob, troop, number.
turbāmenta, -ōrum *ntpl* propaganda.
turbātē *adv* in confusion.
turbātiō, -ōnis *f* confusion.
turbātor, -ōris *m* agitator.
turbātus *ppp of* **turbō** ♦ *adj* troubled, disorderly.
turbellae, -ārum *fpl* stir, row.
turben *etc see* **turbō**.
turbidē *adv* in disorder.
turbidus *adj* confused, wild, boisterous; (*water*) troubled, muddy; (*fig*) disorderly, troubled, alarmed, dangerous.
turbineus *adj* conical.
turbō, -āre, -āvī, -ātum *vt* to disturb, throw into confusion; (*water*) to trouble, make muddy.
turbō, -inis *m* whirl, spiral, rotation; reel, whorl, spindle; (*toy*) top; (*wind*) tornado, whirlwind; (*fig*) storm.
turbulentē *and* **er** *adv* wildly.
turbulentus *adj* agitated, confused, boisterous, stormy; troublemaking, seditious.
turdus, -ī *m* thrush.
tūreus *adj* of incense.
turgeō, -gēre, -sī *vi* to swell, be swollen; (*speech*) to be bombastic.
turgēscō, -ere *vi* to swell up, begin to swell; (*fig*) to become enraged.
turgidulus *adj* poor swollen.
turgidus *adj* swollen, distended; bombastic.
tūribulum, -ī *nt* censer.
tūricremus *adj* incense-burning.
tūrifer, -ī *adj* incense-producing.
tūrilegus *adj* incense-gathering.
turma, -ae *f* troop, squadron (*of cavalry*); crowd.
turmālis *adj* of a troop; equestrian.
turmātim *adv* troop by troop.
Turnus, -ī *m* Rutulian king (*chief opponent of Aeneas*).
turpiculus *adj* ugly little; slightly indecent.
turpificātus *adj* debased.
turpilucricupidus *adj* fond of filthy lucre.
turpis *adj* ugly, deformed, unsightly; base, disgraceful ♦ *nt* disgrace.
turpiter *adv* repulsively; shamefully.
turpitūdō, -inis *f* deformity; disgrace, infamy.
turpō, -āre *vt* to disfigure, soil.
turriger, -ī *adj* turreted.
turris, -is *f* tower, turret; siege tower; (*elephant*) howdah; (*fig*) mansion.
turrītus *adj* turreted; castellated; towering.

U, u

tursī *perf of* **turgeō.**
turtur, -is *m* turtledove.
tūs, tūris *nt* incense, frankincense.
Tusculānēnsis *adj* at Tusculum.
Tusculānum, -ānī *nt* villa at Tusculum (*esp Cicero's*).
Tusculānus *adj* Tusculan.
tūsculum, -ī *nt* a little incense.
Tusculum, -ī *nt Latin town near Rome.*
Tusculus *adj* Tusculan.
Tuscus *adj* Etruscan.
tussiō, -īre *vi* to cough, have a cough.
tussis, -is *f* cough.
tūsus *ppp of* **tundō.**
tūtāmen, -inis *nt* defence.
tūtāmentum, -ī *nt* protection.
tūte *emphatic form of* **tū.**
tūtē *adv* safely, in safety.
tūtēla, -ae *f* keeping, charge, protection; (*of minors*) guardianship, wardship; (*person*) watcher, guardian; ward, charge.
tūtemet *emphatic form of* **tū.**
tūtor, -ārī, -ātus, -ō, -āre *vt* to watch, guard, protect; to guard against.
tūtor, -ōris *m* protector; (*law*) guardian.
tutudī *perf of* **tundō.**
tūtus *ppp of* **tueō** ♦ *adj* safe, secure; cautious ♦ *nt* safety.
tuus *adj* your, yours, thy, thine; your own, your proper; of you.
Tȳdeus, -eī *and* **eos** *m father of Diomede.*
Tȳdīdēs, -īdae *m* Diomede.
tympanotrība, -ae *m* timbrel player.
tympanum (typanum), -ī *nt* drum, timbrel (*esp of the priests of Cybele*); (*mechanism*) wheel.
Tyndareus, -eī *m* king of Sparta (*husband of Leda*).
Tyndaridae, -idārum *mpl* Castor and Pollux.
Tyndaris, -idis *f* Helen; Clytemnestra.
Typhōeus, -eos *m* giant under Etna.
Typhōius, -is *adj see n.*
typus, -ī *m* figure.
tyrannicē *adv see* **tyrannicus.**
tyrannicīda, -ae *m* tyrannicide.
tyrannicus *adj* tyrannical.
tyrannis, -idis *f* despotism, tyranny.
tyrannoctonus, -ī *m* tyrannicide.
tyrannus, -ī *m* ruler, king; despot, tyrant.
Tyrās, -ae *m* river Dniester.
Tyrius *adj* Tyrian, Phoenician, Carthaginian; purple.
tyrotarīchos, -ī *m* dish of salt fish and cheese.
Tyrrhēnia, -iae *f* Etruria.
Tyrrhēnus *adj* Etruscan, Tyrrhenian.
Tyrtaeus, -ī *m* Spartan war poet.
Tyrus (-os), -ī *f* Tyre (*famous Phoenician seaport*).

ūber, -is *nt* breast, teat; (*fig*) richness.
ūber, -is *adj* fertile, plentiful, rich (in); (*language*) full, copious.
ūberius (*superl* **-rime**) *compar adj* more fully, more copiously.
ūbertās, -ātis *f* richness, plenty, fertility.
ūbertim *adv* copiously.
ubī *adv* (*interrog*) where; (*relat*) where, in which, with whom; when
ubicumque *adv* wherever; everywhere.
Ubiī, -ōrum *mpl* German tribe on the lower Rhine.
ubīnam *adv* where (in fact)?
ubīquāque *adv* everywhere.
ubīque *adv* everywhere, anywhere.
ubiubī *adv* wherever.
ubivīs *adv* anywhere.
ūdus *adj* wet, damp.
ulcerō, -āre *vt* to make sore, wound.
ulcerōsus *adj* full of sores; wounded.
ulcīscor, -ī, ultus *vt* to take vengeance on, punish; to take vengeance for, avenge.
ulcus, -eris *nt* sore, ulcer; ~ **tangere** touch on a delicate subject.
ūlīgō, -inis *f* moisture, marshiness.
Ulixēs, -is *m* Ulysses, Odysseus (*king of Ithaca, hero of Homer's Odyssey*).
ullus (*gen* **-īus**, *dat* **-ī**) *adj* any.
ulmeus *adj* of elm.
ulmus, -ī *f* elm; (*pl*) elm rods.
ulna, -ae *f* elbow; arm; (*measure*) ell.
ulterior, -ōris *compar adj* farther, beyond, more remote.
ulterius *compar of* **ultrā.**
ultimus *superl adj* farthest, most remote, the end of; (*time*) earliest, latest, last; (*degree*) extreme, greatest, lowest ♦ *ntpl* the end; ~**um** for the last time; **ad** ~**um** finally.
ultiō, -ōnis *f* vengeance, revenge.
ultor, -ōris *m* avenger, punisher.
ultrā *adv* beyond, farther, besides ♦ *prep* (*with acc*) beyond, on the far side of; (*time*) past; (*degree*) over and above.
ultrīx, -īcis *adj* avenging.
ultrō *adv* on the other side, away; besides; of one's own accord, unasked, voluntarily.
ultrō tribūta *ntpl* State expenditure for public works.
ultus *ppa of* **ulcīscor.**
ulula, -ae *f* screech owl.
ululātus, -ūs *m* wailing, shrieking, yells, whoops.

Noun declensions and verb conjugations are shown on pp xiii to xxv. The present infinitive ending of a verb shows to which conjugation it belongs: **-āre** = 1st; **-ēre** = 2nd; **-ere** = 3rd and **-īre** = 4th. Irregular verbs are shown on p xxvi

ululō, -āre, -āvī, -ātum *vi* to shriek, yell, howl
♦ *vt* to cry out to.
ulva, -ae *f* sedge.
umbella, -ae *f* parasol.
Umber, -rī *adj* Umbrian ♦ *m* Umbrian dog.
umbilīcus, -ī *m* navel; (*fig*) centre; (*book*)
roller end; (*sea*) cockle *or* pebble.
umbō, -ōnis *m* boss (*of a shield*); shield; elbow.
umbra, -ae *f* shadow, shade; (*dead*) ghost;
(*diner*) uninvited guest; (*fish*) grayling;
(*painting*) shade; (*place*) shelter, school,
study; (*unreality*) semblance, mere shadow.
umbrāculum, -ī *nt* arbour; school; parasol.
umbrāticola, -ae *m* lounger.
umbrāticus *adj* fond of idling; in retirement.
umbrātilis *adj* in retirement, private,
academic.
Umbria, -riae *f* Umbria (*district of central Italy*).
umbrifer, -ī *adj* shady.
umbrō, -āre *vt* to shade.
umbrōsus *adj* shady.
ūmectō, -āre *vt* to wet, water.
ūmectus *adj* damp, wet.
ūmeō, -ēre *vi* to be damp, be wet.
umerus, -ī *m* upper arm, shoulder.
ūmēscō, -ere *vi* to become damp, get wet.
ūmidē *adv* with damp.
ūmidulus *adj* dampish.
ūmidus *adj* wet, damp, dank, moist.
ūmor, -ōris *m* liquid, fluid, moisture.
umquam, unquam *adv* ever, at any time.
ūnā *adv* together.
ūnanimāns, -antis *adj* in full agreement.
ūnanimitās, -ātis *f* concord.
ūnanimus *adj* of one accord, harmonious.
ūncia, -ae *f* a twelfth; (*weight*) ounce; (*length*)
inch.
ūnciārius *adj* of a twelfth; (*interest*) 8⅓ per
cent.
ūnciātim *adv* little by little.
uncīnātus *adj* barbed.
ūnciola, -ae *f* a mere twelfth.
ūnctiō, -ōnis *f* anointing.
ūnctitō, -āre *vt* to anoint regularly.
ūnctiusculus *adj* rather too unctuous.
ūnctor, -ōris *m* anointer.
ūnctūra, -ae *f* anointing (of the dead).
ūnctus *ppp of* **ungō** ♦ *adj* oiled; greasy,
resinous; (*fig*) rich, sumptuous ♦ *nt*
sumptuous dinner.
uncus, -ī *m* hook, grappling-iron.
uncus *adj* hooked, crooked, barbed.
unda, -ae *f* wave, water; (*fig*) stream, surge.
unde *adv* from where, whence; from whom,
from which; ~ **petitur** the defendant; ~ **unde**
from wherever; somehow or other.
ūndeciēns *and* **ēs** *adv* eleven times.
ūndecim *num* eleven.
ūndecimus *adj* eleventh.
undecumque *adv* from wherever.
ūndēnī, -ōrum *adj* eleven each, eleven.
ūndēnōnāgintā *num* eighty-nine.
ūndeoctōgintā *num* seventy-nine.

ūndēquadrāgintā *num* thirty-nine.
ūndēquīnquāgēsimus *adj* forty-ninth.
ūndēquīnquāgintā *num* forty-nine.
ūndēsexāgintā *num* fifty-nine.
ūndētrīcēsimus *adj* twenty-ninth.
ūndēvīcēsimānī, -ōrum *mpl* men of the
nineteenth legion.
ūndēvīcēsimus *adj* nineteenth.
ūndēvīgintī *num* nineteen.
undique *adv* from every side, on all sides,
everywhere; completely.
undisonus *adj* sea-roaring.
undō, -āre *vi* to surge; (*fig*) to roll, undulate.
undōsus *adj* billowy.
ūnetvīcēsimānī, -ōrum *mpl* men of the twenty-
first legion.
ūnetvīcēsimus *adj* twenty-first.
ungō (unguō), -gere, ūnxī, ūnctum *vt* to
anoint, smear, grease.
unguen, -inis *nt* fat, grease, ointment.
unguentārius, -ī *and* **iī** *m* perfumer.
unguentātus *adj* perfumed.
unguentum, -ī *nt* ointment, perfume.
unguiculus, -ī *m* fingernail.
unguis, -is *m* nail (*of finger or toe*); claw, talon,
hoof; **ad ~em** with perfect finish;
trānsversum ~em a hair's breadth; **dē tenerō
~ī** from earliest childhood.
ungula, -ae *f* hoof, talon, claw.
unguō *etc see* **ungō**.
ūnicē *adv* solely, extraordinarily.
ūnicolor, -ōris *adj* all one colour.
ūnicus *adj* one and only, sole; unparalleled,
unique.
ūnifōrmis *adj* simple.
ūnigena, -ae *adj* only-begotten; of the same
parentage.
ūnimanus *adj* with only one hand.
ūniō, -ōnis *m* a single large pearl.
ūniter *adv* together in one.
ūniversālis *adj* general.
ūniversē *adv* in general.
ūniversitās, -ātis *f* the whole; the universe.
ūniversus *adj* all taken together, entire,
general ♦ *mpl* the community as a whole ♦ *nt*
the universe; **in ~um** in general.
unquam *etc see* **umquam**.
ūnus *num* one ♦ *adj* sole, single, only; one and
the same; the outstanding one; an
individual; ~ **et alter** one or two; ~ **quisque**
every single one; **nēmō ~** not a single one; **ad
~um** to a man.
ūnxī *perf of* **ungō**.
ūpiliō, -ōnis *m* shepherd.
upupa, -ae *f* hoopoe; crowbar.
Ūrania, -ae *and* **ē, -ēs** *f* Muse of astronomy.
urbānē *adv* politely; wittily, elegantly.
urbānitās, -ātis *f* city life; refinement,
politeness; wit.
urbānus *adj* town (*in cpds*), city (*in cpds*);
refined, polite; witty, humorous;
impertinent ♦ *m* townsman.
urbicapus, -ī *m* taker of cities.

urbs, urbis *f* city; Rome.
urceolus, -ī *m* jug.
urceus, -ī *m* pitcher, ewer.
ūrēdō, -inis *f* blight.
urgeō, -gēre, -sī *vt, vi* to force on, push forward; to press hard on, pursue closely; to crowd, hem in; to burden, oppress; (*argument*) to press, urge; (*work, etc*) to urge on, ply hard, follow up.
ūrīna, -ae *f* urine.
ūrīnātor, -ōris *m* diver.
urna, -ae *f* water jar, urn; voting urn, lottery urn, cinerary urn, money jar.
urnula, -ae *f* small urn.
ūrō, -ere, ūssī, ūstum *vt* to burn; to scorch, parch; (*cold*) to nip; (*MED*) to cauterize; (*rubbing*) to chafe, hurt; (*passion*) to fire, inflame; (*vexation*) to annoy, oppress.
ursa, -ae *f* she-bear, bear; (*ASTRO*) Great Bear, Lesser Bear.
ursī *perf of* **urgeō**.
ursīnus *adj* bear's.
ursus, -ī *m* bear.
urtīca, -ae *f* nettle.
ūrus, -ī *m* wild ox.
Usipetēs, -etum, (-iī, -iōrum) *mpl* German tribe on the Rhine.
ūsitātē *adv* in the usual manner.
ūsitātus *adj* usual, familiar.
uspiam *adv* anywhere, somewhere.
usquam *adv* anywhere; in any way, at all.
usque *adv* all the way (to, from), right on, right up to; (*time*) all the time, as long as, continuously; (*degree*) even, as much as; ~ **quāque** everywhere; every moment, on every occasion.
ūssī *perf of* **ūrō**.
ūstor, -ōris *m* cremator.
ūstulō, -āre *vt* to burn.
ūstus *ppp of* **ūrō**.
ūsūcapiō, -apere, -ēpī, -aptum *vt* to acquire ownership of, take over.
ūsūcapiō, -ōnis *f* ownership by use *or* possession.
ūsūra, -ae *f* use, enjoyment; interest, usury.
ūsūrārius *adj* for use and enjoyment; paying interest.
ūsurpātiō, -ōnis *f* making use (of).
ūsurpō, -āre, -āvī, -ātum *vt* to make use of, employ, exercise; (*law*) to take possession of, enter upon; (*senses*) to perceive, make contact with; (*word*) to call by, speak of.
ūsus *ppa of* **ūtor**.
ūsus, -ūs *m* use, enjoyment, practice; experience, skill; usage, custom; intercourse, familiarity; usefulness, benefit, advantage; need, necessity; ~ **est, venit** there is need (of); ~**uī esse, ex** ~**ū esse** be of use, be of service; ~**ū venīre** happen; ~ **et frūctus** use and enjoyment, usufruct.

ut, utī *adv* how; (*relat*) as; (*explaining*) considering how, according as; (*place*) where; ~ **in ōrātōre** for an orator ♦ *conj* 1. *with indic*: (*manner*) as; (*concessive*) while, though; (*time*) when, as soon as. 2. *with subj*: (*expressing the idea of a verb*) that, to; (*purpose*) so that, to; (*causal*) seeing that; (*concessive*) granted that, although; (*result*) that, so that; (*fear*) that not; ~ ... **ita** while ... nevertheless; ~ **nōn** without; ~ **quī** seeing that I, he, *etc*; ~ **quisque māximē** the more.
utcumque (utcunque) *adv* however; whenever; one way or another.
ūtēnsilis *adj* of use ♦ *ntpl* necessaries.
ūter, -ris *m* bag, skin, bottle.
uter (*gen* -**rīus**, *dat* -**rī**), -**ra**, -**rum** *pron* which (of two), the one that; one or the other.
utercumque, utracumque, utrumcumque *pron* whichever (of two).
uterlibet, utralibet, utrumlibet *pron* whichever (of the two) you please, either one.
uterque, utraque, utrumque *pron* each (of two), either, both.
uterum, -ī *nt*, **uterus, -ī** *m* womb; child; belly.
utervīs, utravīs, utrumvīs *pron* whichever (of two) you please; either.
ūtī *infin of* **ūtor**.
utī *etc see* **ut**.
ūtibilis *adj* useful, serviceable.
Utica, -ae *f* town near Carthage (*where Cato committed suicide*).
Uticēnsis *adj see n*.
ūtilis *adj* useful, expedient, profitable; fit (for).
ūtilitās, -ātis *f* usefulness, expediency, advantage.
ūtiliter *adv* usefully, advantageously.
utinam *adv* I wish!, would that!, if only!
utique *adv* at least, by all means, especially.
ūtor, ūtī, ūsus *vi* (*with abl*) to use, employ; to possess, enjoy; to practise, experience; (*person*) to be on intimate terms with, find; **ūtendum rogāre** borrow.
utpote *adv* inasmuch as, as being.
ūtrārius, -ī *and* **iī** *m* watercarrier.
ūtriculārius, -ī *and* **iī** *m* bagpiper.
utrimque (utrinque) *adv* on both sides, on either side.
utrō *adv* in which direction.
utrobīque *see* **utrubīque**.
utrōque *adv* in both directions, both ways.
utrubī *adv* on which side.
utrubīque *adv* on both sides, on either side.
utrum *adv* whether.
utut *adv* however.
ūva, -ae *f* grape, bunch of grapes; vine; cluster.
ūvēscō, -ere *vi* to become wet.
ūvidulus *adj* moist.
ūvidus *adj* wet, damp; drunken.

Noun declensions and verb conjugations are shown on pp xiii to xxv. The present infinitive ending of a verb shows to which conjugation it belongs: -**āre** = 1st; -**ēre** = 2nd; -**ere** = 3rd and -**īre** = 4th. Irregular verbs are shown on p xxvi

uxor, -ōris *f* wife.
uxorcula, -ae *f* little wife.
uxōrius *adj* of a wife; fond of his wife.

V, v

vacāns, -antis *pres p of* **vacō** ♦ *adj* unoccupied; (*woman*) single.
vacātiō, -ōnis *f* freedom, exemption; exemption from military service; payment for exemption from service.
vacca, -ae *f* cow.
vaccīnium, -ī *and* **iī** *nt* hyacinth.
vaccula, -ae *f* heifer.
vacēfiō, -ierī *vi* to become empty.
vacillō, -āre *vi* to stagger, totter; to waver, be unreliable.
vacīvē *adv* at leisure.
vacīvitās, -ātis *f* want.
vacīvus *adj* empty, free.
vacō, -āre, -āvī, -ātum *vi* to be empty, vacant, unoccupied; to be free, aloof (from); to have time for, devote one's time to; **~at** there is time.
vacuātus *adj* empty.
vacuēfaciō, -facere, -fēcī, -factum *vt* to empty, clear.
vacuitās, -ātis *f* freedom, exemption; vacancy.
vacuus *adj* empty, void, wanting; vacant; free (from); clear; disengaged, at leisure; (*value*) worthless; (*woman*) single ♦ *nt* void, space.
vadimōnium, -ī *and* **iī** *nt* bail, security; **~ sistere** appear in court; **~ dēserere** default.
vādō, -ere *vi* to go, go on, make one's way.
vador, -ārī, -ātus *vt* to bind over by bail.
vadōsus *adj* shallow.
vadum, -ī *nt* shoal, shallow, ford; water, sea; bottom.
vae *interj* woe!, alas!
vafer, -rī *adj* crafty, subtle.
vafrē *adv* artfully.
vagē *adv* far afield.
vāgina, -ae *f* sheath, scabbard; (*grain*) husk.
vāgiō, -īre *vi* to cry.
vāgītus, -ūs *m* crying, bleating.
vagor, -ārī, -ātus *vi* to wander, rove, go far afield; (*fig*) to spread.
vāgor, -ōris *m* cry.
vagus *adj* wandering, unsettled; (*fig*) fickle, wavering, vague.
vah *interj* (*expressing surprise, joy, anger*) oh!, ah!
valdē *adv* greatly, intensely; very.
valē, valēte *interj* goodbye, farewell.

valēns, -entis *pres p of* **valeō** ♦ *adj* strong, powerful, vigorous; well, healthy.
valenter *adv* strongly.
valentulus *adj* strong.
valeō, -ēre, -uī, -itum *vi* to be strong; to be able, have the power (to); to be well, fit, healthy; (*fig*) to be powerful, effective, valid; (*force*) to prevail; (*money*) to be worth; (*word*) to mean; **~ apud** have influence over, carry weight with; **~ēre iubeō** say goodbye to; **~ē dīcō** say goodbye; **~eās** away with you!
valēscō, -ere *vi* to grow strong, thrive.
valētūdinārium, -ī *and* **iī** *nt* hospital.
valētūdō, -inis *f* state of health, health; illness.
valgus *adj* bow-legged.
validē *adv* powerfully, very.
validus *adj* strong, powerful, able; sound, healthy; effective.
vallāris *adj* (*decoration*) for scaling a rampart.
vallēs, vallis, -is *f* valley.
vallō, -āre, -āvī, -ātum *vt* to palisade, entrench, fortify.
vallum, -ī *nt* rampart, palisade, entrenchment.
vallus, -ī *m* stake; palisade, rampart; (*comb*) tooth.
valvae, -ārum *fpl* folding door.
vānēscō, -ere *vi* to disappear, pass away.
vānidicus, -ī *m* liar.
vāniloquentia, -ae *f* idle talk.
vāniloquus *adj* untruthful; boastful.
vānitās, -ātis *f* emptiness; falsehood, worthlessness, fickleness; vanity.
vānitūdō, -inis *f* falsehood.
vannus, -ī *f* winnowing fan.
vānus *adj* empty; idle, useless, groundless; false, untruthful, unreliable; conceited.
vapidus *adj* spoilt, corrupt.
vapor, -ōris *m* steam, vapour; heat.
vapōrārium, -ī *and* **iī** *nt* steam pipe.
vapōrō, -āre *vt* to steam, fumigate, heat ♦ *vi* to burn.
vappa, -ae *f* wine that has gone flat; (*person*) good-for-nothing.
vāpulō, -āre *vi* to be flogged, beaten; to be defeated.
variantia, -ae *f* diversity.
variātiō, -ōnis *f* difference.
vāricō, -āre *vi* to straddle.
vāricōsus *adj* varicose.
vāricus *adj* with feet wide apart.
variē *adv* diversely, with varying success.
varietās, -ātis *f* difference, diversity.
variō, -āre, -āvī, -ātum *vt* to diversify, variegate; to make different, change, vary ♦ *vi* to change colour; to differ, vary.
varius *adj* coloured, spotted, variegated; diverse, changeable, various; (*ability*) versatile; (*character*) fickle.
Varius, -ī *m* epic poet (*friend of Vergil and Horace*).
varix, -icis *f* varicose vein.

Waterstones

Unit 69
Eastgate Shopping Centre
Inverness
IV2 3PR
01463 233500

SALE TRANSACTION

COLLINS LATIN DICTI	£12.99
9780007224395	
NHM JURASSIC EGGS	£9.99
5055394004351	
Balance to pay	£22.98
Cash	£25.00
CHANGE	£2.02

WATERSTONES REWARDS POINTS
WATERSTONES REWARDS POINTS WOULD HAVE
EARNED YOU 68 POINTS TODAY
ON ITEMS WORTH £22.98
Apply now at thewaterstonescard.com

VAT Reg No. GB 108 2770 24

STORE	TILL	OP NO.	TRANS.	DATE	TIME
0680	1	753281	302837	28/03/2016	16 28

999020680001302837 4

Waterstones

Refunds & exchanges

Varrō, -ōnis m consul defeated at Cannae; antiquarian writer of Cicero's day.
Varrōniānus adj see **Varrō.**
vārus adj knock-kneed; crooked; contrary.
vas, vadis m surety, bail.
vās, vāsis (pl **vāsa, -ōrum**) nt vessel, dish; utensil, implement; (MIL) baggage.
vāsārium, -ī and **iī** nt furnishing allowance (of a governor).
vāsculārius, -ī and **iī** m metalworker.
vāsculum, -ī nt small dish.
vastātiō, -ōnis f ravaging.
vastātor, -ōris m ravager.
vastē adv (size) enormously; (speech) coarsely.
vastificus adj ravaging.
vastitās, -ātis f desolation, desert; devastation, destruction.
vastitiēs, -ēī f ruin.
vastō, -āre, -āvī, -ātum vt to make desolate, denude; to lay waste, ravage.
vastus adj empty, desolate, uncultivated; ravaged, devastated; (appearance) uncouth, rude; (size) enormous, vast.
vāsum etc see **vās.**
vātēs, -is m/f prophet, prophetess; poet, bard.
Vāticānus adj Vatican (hill on right bank of Tiber).
vāticinātiō, -ōnis f prophesying, prediction.
vāticinātor, -ōris m prophet.
vāticinor, -ārī, -ātus vt, vi to prophesy; to celebrate in verse; to rave, rant.
vāticinus adj prophetic.
-ve conj or; either ... or.
vēcordia, -ae f senselessness; insanity.
vēcors, -dis adj senseless, foolish, mad.
vectīgal, -ālis nt tax; honorarium (to a magistrate); income.
vectiō, -ōnis f transport.
vectis, -is m lever, crowbar; (door) bolt, bar.
Vectis, -is f Isle of Wight.
vectō, -āre vt to carry; (pass) to ride.
vector, -ōris m carrier; passenger, rider.
vectōrius adj transport (in cpds).
vectūra, -ae f transport; (payment) carriage, fare.
vectus ppp of **vehō.**
Vediovis, -is = **Vēiovis.**
vegetus adj lively, sprightly.
vēgrandis adj small.
vehemēns, -entis adj impetuous, violent; powerful, strong.
vehementer adv violently, eagerly; powerfully, very much.
vehementia, -ae f vehemence.
vehiculum, -ī nt carriage, cart; (sea) vessel.
vehō, -here, -xī, -ctum vt to carry, convey; (pass) to ride, sail, drive.
Vēiēns, -entis, (-entānus), (-us) adj see **Vēiī.**
Vēiī, -ōrum mpl ancient town in S. Etruria.
Vēiovis, -is m ancient Roman god (anti-Jupiter).

vel conj or, or perhaps; or rather; or else; either ... or ♦ adv even, if you like; perhaps; for instance; ~ **māximus** the very greatest.
Vēlābrum, -ī nt low ground between Capitol and Palatine hills.
vēlāmen, -inis nt covering, garment.
vēlāmentum, -ī nt curtain; (pl) draped olive branches carried by suppliants.
vēlārium, -ī and **iī** nt awning.
vēlātī, -ōrum mpl supernumerary troops.
vēles, -itis m light-armed soldier, skirmisher.
vēlifer, -ī adj carrying sail.
vēlificātiō, -ōnis f sailing.
vēlificō, -āre vi to sail ♦ vt to sail through.
vēlificor, -ārī vi to sail; (with dat) to make an effort to obtain.
Velīnus, -ī m a Sabine lake.
vēlitāris adj of the light-armed troops.
vēlitātiō, -ōnis f skirmishing.
vēlitēs pl of **vēles.**
vēlitor, -ārī vi to skirmish.
vēlivolus adj sail-winged.
velle infin of **volō.**
vellicō, -āre vt to pinch, pluck, twitch; (speech) to taunt, disparage.
vellō, -ere, vellī and **vulsī, vulsum** vt to pluck, pull, pick; to pluck out, tear up.
vellus, -eris nt fleece, pelt; wool; fleecy clouds.
vēlō, -āre, -āvī, -ātum vt to cover up, clothe, veil; (fig) to conceal.
vēlōcitās, -ātis f speed, rapidity.
vēlōciter adv rapidly.
vēlōx, -ōcis adj fast, quick, rapid.
vēlum, -ī nt sail; curtain, awning; rēmīs ~īsque with might and main; ~a dare set sail.
velut, velutī adv as, just as; for instance; just as if.
vēmēns etc see **vehemēns.**
vēna, -ae f vein, artery; vein of metal; water course; (fig) innermost nature of feelings, talent, strength; ~ās temptāre feel the pulse; ~ās tenēre have one's finger on the pulse (of).
vēnābulum, -ī nt hunting spear.
Venāfrānus adj see n.
Venāfrum, -ī nt Samnite town famous for olive oil.
vēnālicius adj for sale ♦ m slave dealer.
vēnālis adj for sale; bribable ♦ m slave offered for sale.
vēnāticus adj hunting (in cpds).
vēnātiō, -ōnis f hunting; a hunt; public show of fighting wild beasts; game.
vēnātor, -ōris m hunter.
vēnātōrius adj hunter's.
vēnātrix, -īcis f huntress.
vēnātūra, -ae f hunting.
vēnātus, -ūs m hunting.
vēndibilis adj saleable; (fig) popular.

Noun declensions and verb conjugations are shown on pp xiii to xxv. The present infinitive ending of a verb shows to which conjugation it belongs: **-āre** = 1st; **-ēre** = 2nd; **-ere** = 3rd and **-īre** = 4th. Irregular verbs are shown on p xxvi

vēnditātiō, -ōnis *f* showing off, advertising.

vēnditātor, -ōris *m* braggart.

vēnditiō, -ōnis *f* sale.

vēnditō, -āre *vt* to try to sell; to praise up, advertise; **sē ~ ingratiate oneself (with).

vēnditor, -ōris *m* seller.

vēndō (*pass* **vēneō**), **-ere, -idī, -itum** *vt* to sell; to betray; to praise up.

venēficium, -ī *and* **iī** *nt* poisoning; sorcery.

venēficus *adj* poisonous; magic ♦ *m* sorcerer ♦ *f* sorceress.

venēnātus *adj* poisonous; magic.

venēnifer, -ī *adj* poisonous.

venēnō, -āre *vt* to poison.

venēnum, -ī *nt* drug, potion; dye; poison; magic charm; (*fig*) mischief; charm.

vēneō, -īre, -iī, -itum *vi* to be sold.

venerābilis *adj* honoured, venerable.

venerābundus *adj* reverent.

venerātiō, -ōnis *f* respect, reverence.

venerātor, -ōris *m* reverencer.

Venereus, Venerius *adj* of Venus ♦ *m* highest throw at dice.

veneror, -ārī, -ātus *vt* to worship, revere, pray to; to honour, respect; to ask for, entreat.

Venetia, -iae *f* district of the Veneti.

Veneticus *adj see n.*

Venetus *adj* Venetian; (*colour*) blue.

vēnī *perf of* **veniō.**

venia, -ae *f* indulgence, favour, kindness; permission, leave; pardon, forgiveness; **bonā tuā ~ā** by your leave; **bonā ~ā audīre** give a fair hearing.

vēnī ī *perf of* **vēneō.**

veniō, -īre, vēnī, ventum *vi* to come; (*fig*) to fall into, incur, go as far as; **in amīcitiam ~** make friends (with); **in spem ~** entertain hopes.

vēnor, -ārī, -ātus *vt, vi* to hunt, chase.

venter, -ris *m* stomach, belly; womb, unborn child.

ventilātor, -ōris *m* juggler.

ventilō, -āre *vt* to fan, wave, agitate.

ventiō, -ōnis *f* coming.

ventitō, -āre *vi* to keep coming, come regularly.

ventōsus *adj* windy; like the wind; fickle; conceited.

ventriculus, -ī *m* belly; (*heart*) ventricle.

ventriōsus *adj* pot-bellied.

ventulus, -ī *m* breeze.

ventus, -ī *m* wind.

vēnūcula, -ae *f* kind of grape.

vēnum, vēnō for sale.

vēnumdō (vēnundō), -āre, -edī, -atum *vt* to sell, put up for sale.

venus, -eris *f* charm, beauty; love, mating.

Venus, -eris *f* goddess of love; planet Venus; highest throw at dice.

Venusia, -iae *f* town in Apulia (*birthplace of Horace*).

Venusīnus *adj see* **Venusia.**

venustās, -ātis *f* charm, beauty.

venustē *adv* charmingly.

venustulus *adj* charming little.

venustus *adj* charming, attractive, beautiful.

vēpallidus *adj* very pale.

veprēcula, -ae *f* little brier bush.

veprēs, -is *m* thornbush, bramblebush.

vēr, vēris *nt* spring; **~ sacrum** offerings of firstlings.

vērātrum, -ī *nt* hellebore.

vērāx, -ācis *adj* truthful.

verbēna, -ae *f* vervain; (*pl*) *sacred boughs carried by heralds or priests.*

verber, -is *nt* lash, scourge; (*missile*) strap; (*pl*) flogging, strokes.

verberābilis *adj* deserving a flogging.

verberātiō, -ōnis *f* punishment.

verbereus *adj* deserving a flogging.

verberō, -āre, -āvī, -ātum *vt* to flog, beat, lash.

verberō, -ōnis *m* scoundrel.

verbōsē *adv* verbosely.

verbōsus *adj* wordy.

verbum, -ī *nt* word; saying, expression; (*GRAM*) verb; (*pl*) language, talk; **~ ē (dē, prō) ~ō** literally; **ad ~um** word for word; **~ī causa (grātiā)** for instance; **~ō** orally; briefly; **~a dare** cheat, fool; **~a facere** talk; **meīs ~īs** in my name.

vērē *adv* really, truly, correctly.

verēcundē *adv see adj.*

verēcundia, -ae *f* modesty, shyness; reverence, dread; shame.

verēcundor, -ārī *vi* to be bashful, feel shy.

verēcundus *adj* modest, shy, bashful.

verendus *adj* venerable.

vereor, -ērī, -itus *vt, vi* to fear, be afraid; to revere, respect.

verētrum, -ī *nt* the private parts.

Vergiliae, -ārum *fpl* the Pleiads.

Vergilius, -ī *m* Vergil, Virgil (*famous epic poet*).

vergō, -ere *vt* to turn, incline ♦ *vi* to turn, incline, decline; (*place*) to face.

vēridicus *adj* truthful.

vērī similis *adj* probable.

vērī similitūdō, -inis *f* probability.

vēritās, -ātis *f* truth, truthfulness; reality, real life; (*character*) integrity; (*language*) etymology.

veritus *ppa of* **vereor.**

vermiculātus *adj* inlaid with wavy lines, mosaic.

vermiculus, -ī *m* grub.

vermina, -um *ntpl* stomach pains.

vermis, -is *m* worm.

verna, -ae *f* slave born in his master's home.

vernāculus *adj* of home-born slaves; native.

vernīlis *adj* slavish; (*remark*) smart.

vernīliter *adv* slavishly.

vērnō, -āre *vi* to bloom, be spring-like; to be young.

vernula, -ae *f* young home-born slave; native.

vērnus *adj* of spring.
vērō *adv* in fact, assuredly; (*confirming*) certainly, yes; (*climax*) indeed; (*adversative*) but in fact; minimē ~ certainly not.
Vērōna, -ae *f* town in N. Italy (*birthplace of Catullus*).
Vērōnēnsis *adj see* Vērōna.
verpus, -ī *m* circumcised man.
verrēs, -is *m* boar.
Verrēs, -is *m* praetor prosecuted by Cicero.
verrīnus *adj* boar's, pork (*in cpds*).
Verrius *and* īnus *adj see n.*
verrō, -rere, -rī, -sum *vt* to sweep, scour; to sweep away, carry off.
verrūca, -ae *f* wart; (*fig*) slight blemish.
verrūcōsus *adj* warty.
verruncō, -āre *vi* to turn out successfully.
versābundus *adj* rotating.
versātilis *adj* revolving; versatile.
versicolor, -ōris *adj* of changing *or* various colours.
versiculus, -ī *m* short line; (*pl*) unpretentious verses.
versificātor, -ōris *m* versifier.
versipellis *adj* of changed appearance; crafty ♦ *m* werewolf.
versō, -āre, -āvī, -ātum *vt* to keep turning, wind, twist; (*fig*) to upset, disturb, ruin; (*mind*) to ponder, consider.
versor, -ārī, -ātus *vi* to live, be, be situated; to be engaged (in), be busy (with).
versum *adv* turned, in the direction.
versūra, -ae *f* borrowing to pay a debt; loan.
versus *ppp of* vertō ♦ *adv* turned, in the direction.
versus, -ūs *m* line, row; verse; (*dance*) step.
versūtē *adv* craftily.
versūtiae, -ārum *fpl* tricks.
versūtiloquus *adj* sly.
versūtus *adj* clever; crafty, deceitful.
vertex, -icis *m* whirlpool, eddy; whirlwind; crown of the head, head; top, summit; (*sky*) pole.
verticōsus *adj* eddying, swirling.
vertīgō, -inis *f* turning round; dizziness.
vertō, -tere, -tī, -sum *vt* to turn; to turn over, invert; to turn round; to turn into, change, exchange; (*cause*) to ascribe, impute; (*language*) to translate; (*war*) to overthrow, destroy; (*pass*) to be (in), be engaged (in) ♦ *vi* to turn; to change; to turn out; in fugam ~ put to flight; terga ~ flee; solum ~ emigrate; vitiō ~ blame; annō ~tente in the course of a year.
Vertumnus, -ī *m* god of seasons.
verū, -ūs *nt* spit; javelin.
vērum *adv* truly, yes; but actually; but, yet; ~ tamen nevertheless.
vērum, -ī *nt* truth, reality; right; ~ī similis probable.
vērus *adj* true, real, actual; truthful; right,

reasonable.
verūtum, -ī *nt* javelin.
verūtus *adj* armed with the javelin.
vervēx, -ēcis *m* wether.
vēsānia, -ae *f* madness.
vēsāniēns, -entis *adj* raging.
vēsānus *adj* mad, insane; furious, raging.
vēscor, -ī *vi* (*with abl*) to feed, eat; to enjoy.
vēscus *adj* little, feeble; corroding.
vēsīca, -ae *f* bladder; purse; football.
vēsīcula, -ae *f* small bladder, blister.
vespa, -ae *f* wasp.
Vespasiānus, -ī *m* Roman emperor.
vesper, -is *and* ī *m* evening; supper; evening star; west; ~e, ~ī in the evening.
vespera, -ae *f* evening.
vesperāscō, -ere *vi* to become evening, get late.
vespertīliō, -ōnis *m* bat.
vespertīnus *adj* evening (*in cpds*), in the evening; western.
vesperūgō, -inis *f* evening star.
Vesta, -ae *f* Roman goddess of the hearth.
Vestālis *adj* Vestal ♦ *f* virgin priestess of Vesta.
vester, -rī *adj* your, yours.
vestibulum, -ī *nt* forecourt, entrance.
vestīgium, -ī *and* iī *nt* footstep, footprint, track; (*fig*) trace, sign, vestige; (*time*) moment, instant; ē ~iō instantly.
vestīgō, -āre, -āvī, -ātum *vt* to track, trace, search for, discover.
vestīmentum, -ī *nt* clothes.
vestiō, -īre, -iī, -ītum *vt* to clothe, dress; to cover, adorn.
vestipica, -ae *f* wardrobe woman.
vestis, -is *f* clothes, dress; coverlet, tapestry, blanket; (*snake*) slough; ~em mūtāre change one's clothes; go into mourning.
vestispica *etc see* vestipica.
vestītus, -ūs *m* clothes, dress; covering; mūtāre ~um go into mourning; redīre ad suum ~um come out of mourning.
Vesuvius, -ī *m* the volcano Vesuvius.
veterānus *adj* veteran.
veterāscō, -scere, -vī *vi* to grow old.
veterātor, -ōris *m* expert, old hand; sly fox.
veterātōriē *adv see* veterātōrius.
veterātōrius *adj* crafty.
veterīnus *adj* of burden ♦ *f and* ntpl beasts of burden.
veternōsus *adj* lethargic, drowsy.
veternus, -ī *m* lethargy, drowsiness.
vetitus *ppp of* vetō ♦ *nt* prohibition.
vetō, -āre, -uī, -itum *vt* to forbid, prohibit, oppose; (*tribune*) to protest.
vetulus *adj* little old, poor old.
vetus, -eris *adj* old, former ♦ *mpl* the ancients ♦ *fpl* the old shops (*in the Forum*) ♦ *ntpl* antiquity, tradition.
vetustās, -ātis *f* age, long standing; antiquity;

great age, future age.

vetustus *adj* old, ancient; old-fashioned.

vexāmen, -inis *nt* shaking.

vexātiō, -ōnis *f* shaking; trouble, distress.

vexātor, -ōris *m* troubler, opponent.

vexī *perf of* **vehō.**

vexillārius, -ī *and* **iī** *m* standard-bearer, ensign; (*pl*) special reserve of veterans.

vexillum, -ī *nt* standard, flag; company, troop; ~ **prōpōnere** hoist the signal for battle.

vexō, -āre, -āvī, -ātum *vt* to shake, toss, trouble, distress, injure, attack.

via, -ae *f* road, street, way; journey, march; passage; (*fig*) way, method, fashion; the right way; ~ **ā** properly; **inter ~ās** on the way.

viālis *adj* of the highways.

viārius *adj* for the upkeep of roads.

viāticātus *adj* provided with travelling money.

viāticus *adj* for a journey ♦ *nt* travelling allowance; (*MIL*) prizemoney, savings.

viātor, -ōris *m* traveller; (*law*) summoner.

vībix, -īcis *f* weal.

vibrō, -āre, -āvī, -ātum *vt* to wave, shake, brandish, hurl, launch ♦ *vi* to shake, quiver, vibrate; to shimmer, sparkle.

vīburnum, -ī *nt* wayfaring-tree *or* guelder rose.

vīcānus *adj* village (*in cpds*) ♦ *mpl* villagers.

Vica Pota, -ae, -ae *f* goddess of victory.

vicārius *adj* substituted ♦ *m* substitute, proxy; underslave.

vīcātim *adv* from street to street; in villages.

vice (*with gen*) on account of; like.

vicem in turn; (*with gen*) instead of; on account of; like; **tuam ~** on your account.

vīcēnārius *adj* of twenty.

vīcēnī, -ōrum *adj* twenty each, in twenties.

vicēs *pl of* **vicis.**

vīcēsimānī, -ōrum *mpl* men of the twentieth legion.

vīcēsimārius *adj* derived from the 5 per cent tax.

vīcēsimus *adj* twentieth ♦ *f* a 5 per cent tax.

vīcī *perf of* **vincō.**

vicia, -ae *f* vetch.

vīciēns *and* **ēs** *adv* twenty times.

vīcīnālis *adj* neighbouring.

vīcīnia, -ae *f* neighbourhood, nearness.

vīcīnitās, -ātis *f* neighbourhood, nearness.

vīcīnus *adj* neighbouring, nearby; similar, kindred ♦ *m/f* neighbour ♦ *nt* neighbourhood.

vicis *gen* (*acc* **-em**, *abl* **-e**) *f* interchange, alternation, succession; recompense; retaliation; fortune, changing conditions; duty, function, place; **in ~em** in turn, mutually.

vicissim *adv* in turn, again.

vicissitūdō, -inis *f* interchange, alternation.

victima, -ae *f* victim, sacrifice.

victimārius, -ī *and* **iī** *m* assistant at sacrifices.

victitō, -āre *vi* to live, subsist.

victor, -ōris *m* conqueror, victor, winner ♦ *adj*

victorious.

victōria, -ae *f* victory.

victōriātus, -ūs *m* silver coin stamped with Victory.

Victōriola, -ae *f* little statue of Victory.

victrīx, -īcis *f* conqueror ♦ *adj* victorious.

victus *ppp of* **vincō.**

victus, -ūs *m* sustenance, livelihood; way of life.

vīculus, -ī *m* hamlet.

vīcus, -ī *m* (*city*) quarter, street; (*country*) village, estate.

vidēlicet *adv* clearly, evidently; (*ironical*) of course; (*explaining*) namely.

video, -ēre, vīdī, vīsum *vt* to see, look at; (*mind*) to observe, be aware, know; to consider, think over; to see to, look out for; to live to see; (*pass*) to seem, appear; to seem right, be thought proper; **mē ~ē** rely on me; **vīderit** let him see to it; **mihi ~eor esse** I think I am; **sī (tibi) vidētur** if you like.

viduāta *adj* widowed.

viduitās, -ātis *f* bereavement, want; widowhood.

vīdulus, -ī *m* trunk, box.

viduō, -āre *vt* to bereave.

viduus *adj* bereft, bereaved; unmarried; (*with abl*) without ♦ *f* widow; spinster.

Vienna, -ae *f* town in Gaul on the Rhone.

viētus *adj* shrivelled.

vigeō, -ēre, -uī *vi* to thrive, flourish.

vigēscō, -ere *vi* to begin to flourish, become lively.

vigēsimus *etc see* **vīcēsimus.**

vigil, -is *adj* awake, watching, alert ♦ *m* watchman, sentinel; (*pl*) the watch, police.

vigilāns, -antis *pres p of* **vigilō** ♦ *adj* watchful.

vigilanter *adv* vigilantly.

vigilantia, -ae *f* wakefulness; vigilance.

vigilāx, -ācis *adj* watchful.

vigilia, -ae *f* lying awake, sleeplessness; keeping watch, guard; a watch; the watch, sentries; vigil; vigilance.

vigilō, -āre, -āvī, -ātum *vi* to remain awake; to keep watch; to be vigilant ♦ *vt* to spend awake, make while awake at night.

vīgintī *num* twenty.

vīgintīvirātus, -ūs *m* membership of a board of twenty.

vīgintīvirī, -ōrum *mpl* a board *or* commission of twenty men.

vigor, -ōris *m* energy, vigour.

vīlica, -ae *f* wife of a steward.

vīlicō, -āre *vi* to be an overseer.

vīlicus, -ī *m* overseer, manager of an estate, steward.

vīlis *adj* cheap; worthless, poor, mean, common.

vīlitās, -ātis *f* cheapness, low price; worthlessness.

vīliter *adv* cheaply.

vīlla, -ae *f* country house, villa.

vīllic- *etc see* **vīlic-.**

villōsus adj hairy, shaggy.
vīllula, -ae f small villa.
vīllum, -ī nt a drop of wine.
villus, -ī m hair, fleece; (cloth) nap.
vīmen, -inis nt osier; basket.
vīmentum, -ī nt osier.
Vīminālis adj Viminal (hill of Rome).
vīmineus adj of osiers, wicker.
vīnāceus adj grape (in cpds).
Vīnālia, -ium ntpl Wine festival.
vīnārius adj of wine, wine (in cpds) ♦ m vintner
  ♦ nt wine flask.
vincibilis adj easily won.
vinciō, -īre, -xī, -ctum vt to bind, fetter; to
  encircle; (fig) to confine, restrain, envelop,
  attach.
vinclum nt see **vinculum**.
vincō, -ere, vīcī, victum vt to conquer,
  defeat, subdue; to win, prevail, be
  successful; (fig) to surpass, excel; (argument)
  to convince, refute, prove conclusively;
  (life) to outlive.
vinctus ppp of **vinciō**.
vinculum, -ī nt bond, fetter, chain; (pl) prison.
vīndēmia, -ae f vintage grape harvest.
vīndēmiātor, -ōris m vintager.
vīndēmiola, -ae f small vintage.
Vīndēmitor, -ōris m the Vintager (a star in
  Virgo).
vindex, -icis m champion, protector;
  liberator; avenger ♦ adj avenging.
vindicātiō, -ōnis f punishment of offences.
vindiciae, -ārum fpl legal claim; ~ās ab
  lībertāte in servitūtem dare condemn a free
  person to slavery.
vindicō, -āre, -āvī, -ātum vt to lay claim to;
  to claim, appropriate; to liberate, protect,
  champion; to avenge, punish; **in lībertātem ~**
  emancipate.
vindicta, -ae f rod used in manumitting a
  slave; defence, deliverance; revenge,
  punishment.
vīnea, -ae f vineyard; vine; (MIL) penthouse
  (for besiegers).
vīnētum, -ī nt vineyard.
vīnitor, -ōris m vine-dresser.
vinnulus adj delightful.
vīnolentia, -ae f wine drinking.
vīnolentus adj drunk.
vīnōsus adj fond of wine, drunken.
vīnum, -ī nt wine.
vinxī perf of **vinciō**.
viola, -ae f violet; stock.
violābilis adj vulnerable.
violāceus adj violet.
violārium, -ī and **iī** nt violet bed.
violārius, -ī and **iī** m dyer of violet.
violātiō, -ōnis f desecration.
violātor, -ōris m violator, desecrator.
violēns, -entis adj raging, vehement.

violenter adv violently, furiously.
violentia, -ae f violence, impetuosity.
violentus adj violent, impetuous, boisterous.
violō, -āre, -āvī, -ātum vt to do violence to,
  outrage, violate; (agreement) to break.
vīpera, -ae f viper, adder, snake.
vīpereus adj snake's, serpent's.
vīperīnus adj snake's, serpent's.
vir, virī m man; grown man; brave man, hero;
  husband; (MIL) footsoldier.
virāgō, -inis f heroine, warrior maid.
virecta, -ōrum ntpl grassy sward.
vireō, -ēre, -uī vi to be green; (fig) to be fresh,
  flourish.
virēs pl of **vīs**.
virēscō, -ere vi to grow green.
virga, -ae f twig; graft; rod, staff, walking
  stick, wand; (colour) stripe.
virgātor, -ōris m flogger.
virgātus adj made of osiers; striped.
virgētum, -ī nt thicket of osiers.
virgeus adj of brushwood.
virgidēmia, -ae f crop of flogging.
virginālis adj maidenly, of maids.
virginārius adj of maids.
virgineus adj maidenly, virgin, of virgins.
virginitās, -ātis f maidenhood.
virgō, -inis f maid, virgin; young woman, girl;
  constellation Virgo; a Roman aqueduct.
virgula, -ae f wand.
virgulta, -ōrum ntpl thicket, shrubbery;
  cuttings, slips.
virguncula, -ae f little girl.
viridāns, -antis adj green.
viridārium, -ī and **iī** nt plantation, garden.
viridis adj green; fresh, young, youthful ♦ ntpl
  greenery.
viriditās, -ātis f verdure, greenness;
  freshness.
viridor, -ārī vi to become green.
virīlis adj male, masculine; man's, adult;
  manly, brave, bold; ~ **pars** one's individual
  part or duty; **prō ~ī parte, portiōne** to the best
  of one's ability.
virīlitās, -ātis f manhood.
virīliter adv manfully.
virītim adv individually, separately.
virōsus adj slimy; rank.
virtūs, -ūtis f manhood, full powers; strength,
  courage, ability, worth; (MIL) valour,
  prowess, heroism; (moral) virtue; (things)
  excellence, worth.
vīrus, -ī nt slime; poison; offensive smell; salt
  taste.
vīs (acc **vim**, abl **vī**, pl **vīrēs**) f power, force,
  strength; violence, assault; quantity,
  amount; (mind) energy, vigour; (word)
  meaning, import; (pl) strength; (MIL) troops;
  per vim forcibly; **dē vī damnārī** be convicted

Noun declensions and verb conjugations are shown on pp xiii to xxv. The present infinitive ending of a verb shows
to which conjugation it belongs: **-āre** = 1st; **-ēre** = 2nd; **-ere** = 3rd and **-īre** = 4th. Irregular verbs are shown on p xxvi

of assault; **prō vīribus** with all one's might.

vīs *2nd pers of* **volō**.

viscātus *adj* limed.

viscerātiō, -ōnis *f* public distribution of meat.

viscō, -āre *vt* to make sticky.

viscum, -ī *nt* mistletoe; bird lime.

viscus, -eris (*usu pl* **-era, -erum**) *nt* internal organs; flesh; womb, child; (*fig*) heart, bowels.

vīsendus *adj* worth seeing.

vīsiō, -ōnis *f* apparition; idea.

vīsitō, -āre *vt* to see often; to visit.

vīsō, -ere, -ī, -um *vt* to look at, survey; to see to; to go and see, visit.

Visurgis, -is *m* river Weser.

vīsus *ppp of* **video** ♦ *nt* vision.

vīsus, -ūs *m* sight, the faculty of seeing; a sight, vision.

vīta, -ae *f* life, livelihood; way of life; career, biography.

vītābilis *adj* undesirable.

vītābundus *adj* avoiding, taking evasive action.

vītālis *adj* of life, vital ♦ *nt* subsistence ♦ *ntpl* vitals.

vītāliter *adv* with life.

vītātiō, -ōnis *f* avoidance.

Vitellius, -ī *m* Roman emperor in AD 69.

Vitellius, -iānus *adj see n.*

vitellus, -ī *m* little calf; (*egg*) yolk.

vīteus *adj* of the vine.

vīticula, -ae *f* little vine.

vītigenus *adj* produced from the vine.

vitilēna, -ae *f* procuress.

vitiō, -āre, -āvī, -ātum *vt* to spoil, corrupt, violate; to falsify.

vitiōsē *adv* badly, defectively.

vitiōsitās, -ātis *f* vice.

vitiōsus *adj* faulty, corrupt; wicked, depraved; ~ **cōnsul** *a consul whose election had a religious flaw in it.*

vītis, -is *f* vine; vine branch; centurion's staff, centurionship.

vītisator, -ōris *m* vine planter.

vitium, -ī *and* **iī** *nt* fault, flaw, defect; (*moral*) failing, offence, vice; (*religion*) flaw in the auspices.

vītō, -āre, -āvī, -ātum *vt* to avoid, evade, shun.

vītor, -ōris *m* basket maker, cooper.

vitreus *adj* of glass; glassy ♦ *ntpl* glassware.

vītricus, -ī *m* stepfather.

vitrum, -ī *nt* glass; woad.

vitta, -ae *f* headband, sacrificial fillet.

vittātus *adj* wearing a fillet.

vitula, -ae *f* (*of cow*) calf.

vitulīnus *adj* of veal ♦ *f* veal.

vītulor, -ārī *vi* to hold a celebration.

vitulus, -ī *m* calf; foal; ~ **marīnus** seal.

vituperābilis *adj* blameworthy.

vituperātiō, -ōnis *f* blame, censure; scandalous conduct.

vituperātor, -ōris *m* critic.

vituperō, -āre *vt* to find fault with, disparage; (*omen*) to spoil.

vīvārium, -ī *and* **iī** *nt* fishpond, game preserve.

vīvātus *adj* animated.

vīvāx, -ācis *adj* long-lived; lasting; (*sulphur*) inflammable.

vīvēscō, -ere *vi* to grow, become active.

vīvidus *adj* full of life; (*art*) true to life, vivid; (*mind*) lively.

vīvirādīx, -īcis *f* a rooted cutting, layer.

vīvīscō *etc see* **vīvēscō**.

vīvō, -vere, -xī, -ctum *vi* to live, be alive; to enjoy life; (*fame*) to last, be remembered; (*with abl*) to live on; ~**ve** farewell!; ~**xērunt** they are dead.

vīvus *adj* alive, living; (*light*) burning; (*rock*) natural; (*water*) running; ~**ō videntīque** before his very eyes; **mē ~ō** as long as I live, in my lifetime; **ad ~um resecāre** cut to the quick; **dē ~ō dētrahere** take out of capital.

vix *adv* with difficulty, hardly, scarcely.

vixdum *adv* hardly, as yet.

vīxī *perf of* **vīvō**.

vocābulum, -ī *nt* name, designation; (*GRAM*) noun.

vōcālis *adj* speaking, singing, tuneful ♦ *f* vowel.

vocāmen, -inis *nt* name.

vocātiō, -ōnis *f* invitation; (*law*) summons.

vocātus, -ūs *m* summons, call.

vōciferātiō, -ōnis *f* loud cry, outcry.

vōciferor, -ārī *vt* to cry out loud, shout.

vocitō, -āre, -āvī, -ātum *vt* to usually call; to shout.

vocīvus *etc see* **vacīvus**.

vocō, -āre, -āvī, -ātum *vt* to call, summon; to call, name; (*gods*) to call upon; (*guest*) to invite; (*MIL*) to challenge; (*fig*) to bring (*into some condition or plight*); ~ **dē** name after; ~**in dubium** ~ call in question; **in iūdicium** ~ call to account.

vōcula, -ae *f* weak voice; soft tone; gossip.

volaema *ntpl* kind of large pear.

Volaterrae, -ārum *fpl* old Etruscan town (*now* Volterra).

Volaterrānus *adj see n.*

volāticus *adj* winged; fleeting, inconstant.

volātilis *adj* winged; swift; fleeting.

volātus, -ūs *m* flight.

Volcānius *adj see n.*

Volcānus, -ī *m* Vulcan (*god of fire*); fire.

volēns, -entis *pres p of* **volō** ♦ *adj* willing, glad, favourable; **mihi ~entī est** it is acceptable to me.

volg- *etc see* **vulg-**.

volitō, -āre *vi* to fly about, flutter; to hurry, move quickly; (*fig*) to hover, soar; to get excited.

voln- *etc see* **vuln-**.

volō, -āre, -āvī, -ātum *vi* to fly; to speed.

volō, velle, voluī *vt* to wish, want; to be

willing; to will, purpose, determine; (*opinion*) to hold, maintain; (*word, action*) to mean; ~ **dīcere** I mean; **bene** ~ like; **male** ~ dislike; **ōrātum tē** ~ I beg you; **paucīs tē** ~ a word with you!; **numquid vīs?** (*before leaving*) is there anything else?; **quid sibi vult?** what does he mean?; what is he driving at?; **velim faciās** please do it; **vellem fēcissē** I wish you had done it.

volōnēs, -um *mpl* volunteers.

volpēs *etc see* **vulpēs.**

Volscī, -ōrum *mpl* people in S. Latium.

Volscus *adj* Volscian.

volsella, -ae *f* tweezers.

volsus *ppp of* **vellō.**

volt, voltis *older forms of* **vult, vultis.**

Voltumna, -ae *f patron goddess of Etruria.*

voltus *etc see* **vultus.**

volūbilis *adj* spinning, revolving; (*fortune*) fickle; (*speech*) fluent.

volūbilitās, -ātis *f* whirling motion; roundness; fluency; inconstancy.

volūbiliter *adv* fluently.

volucer, -ris *adj* winged; flying, swift; fleeting.

volucris, -is *f* bird; insect.

volūmen, -inis *nt* roll, book; coil, eddy, fold.

voluntārius *adj* voluntary ♦ *mpl* volunteers.

voluntās, -ātis *f* will, wish, inclination; attitude, goodwill; last will, testament; **suā ~āte** of one's own accord; **ad ~ātem** with the consent (of).

volup *adv* agreeably, to one's satisfaction.

voluptābilis *adj* agreeable.

voluptās, -ātis *f* pleasure, enjoyment; (*pl*) entertainments, sports.

voluptuārius *adj* pleasureable, agreeable; voluptuous.

volūtābrum, -ī *nt* wallowing place.

volūtātiō, -ōnis *f* wallowing.

volūtō, -āre *vt* to roll about, turn over; (*mind*) to occupy, engross; (*thought*) to ponder, think over; (*pass*) to wallow, flounder.

volūtus *ppp of* **volvō.**

volva, -ae *f* womb; (*dish*) sow's womb.

volvō, -vere, -vī, -ūtum *vt* to roll, turn round; to roll along; (*air*) to breathe; (*book*) to open; (*circle*) to form; (*thought*) to ponder, reflect on; (*time*) to roll on; (*trouble*) to undergo; (*pass*) to roll, revolve ♦ *vi* to revolve, elapse.

vōmer, -eris *m* ploughshare.

vomica, -ae *f* sore, ulcer, abscess, boil.

vōmis *etc see* **vōmer.**

vomitiō, -ōnis *f* vomiting.

vomitus, -ūs *m* vomiting, vomit.

vomō, -ere, -uī, -itum *vt* to vomit, throw up; to emit, discharge.

vorāgō, -inis *f* abyss, chasm, depth.

vorāx, -ācis *adj* greedy, ravenous; consuming.

vorō, -āre, -āvī, -ātum *vt* to swallow, devour; (*sea*) to swallow up; (*reading*) to devour.

vors-, vort- *etc see* **vers-, vert-** *etc.*

vōs *pron* you.

Vosegus, -ī *m* Vosges mountains.

voster *etc see* **vester.**

vōtīvus *adj* votive, promised in a vow.

votō *etc see* **vetō.**

vōtum, -ī *nt* vow, prayer; votive offering; wish, longing; **~ī damnārī** have one's prayer granted.

vōtus *ppp of* **voveō.**

voveō, -ēre, vōvī, vōtum *vt* to vow, promise solemnly; to dedicate; to wish.

vōx, vōcis *f* voice; sound, cry, call; word, saying, expression; accent; **ūnā vōce** unanimously.

Vulcānus *see* **Volcānus.**

vulgāris *adj* common, general.

vulgāriter *adv* in the common fashion.

vulgātor, -ōris *m* betrayer.

vulgātus *adj* common; generally known; notorious.

vulgivagus *adj* roving; inconstant.

vulgō *adv* publicly, commonly, usually, everywhere.

vulgō, -āre, -āvī, -ātum *vt* to make common, spread; to publish, divulge, broadcast; to prostitute; to level down.

vulgus, -ī *nt* (*occ m*) the mass of the people, the public; crowd, herd; rabble, populace.

vulnerātiō, -ōnis *f* wounding, injury.

vulnerō, -āre, -āvī, -ātum *vt* to wound, hurt; to damage.

vulnificus *adj* wounding, dangerous.

vulnus, -eris *nt* wound, injury; (*things*) damage, hole; (*fig*) blow, misfortune, pain.

vulpēcula, -ae *f* little fox.

vulpēs, -is *f* fox; (*fig*) cunning.

vulsī *perf of* **vellō.**

vulsus *ppp of* **vellō.**

vulticulus, -ī *m* a mere look (from).

vultum *etc see* **vultus.**

vultuōsus *adj* affected.

vultur, -is *m* vulture.

vulturius, -ī *and* **iī** *m* vulture, bird of prey; (*dice*) an unlucky throw.

Vulturnus, -ī *m* river in Campania.

vultus, -ūs *m* look, expression (*esp* in the eyes); face; (*things*) appearance.

vulva *etc see* **volva.**

Noun declensions and verb conjugations are shown on pp xiii to xxv. The present infinitive ending of a verb shows to which conjugation it belongs: -**āre** = 1st; -**ēre** = 2nd; -**ere** = 3rd and -**īre** = 4th. Irregular verbs are shown on p xxvi

X, x

Xanthippē, -ēs *f wife of Socrates.*
Xanthus, -ī *m river of Troy (identified with Scamander); river of Lycia.*
xenium, -ī *and* **iī** *nt present.*

Xenocratēs, -is *m disciple of Plato.*
Xenophanēs, -is *m early Greek philosopher.*
Xenophōn, -ontis *m famous Greek historian.*
Xenophontēus *adj see n.*
xērampelinae, -ārum *fpl* dark-coloured clothes.
Xerxēs, -is *m Persian king defeated at Salamis.*
xiphiās, -ae *m* swordfish.
xystum, -ī *nt,* **xystus, -ī** *m* open colonnade, walk, avenue.

Z, z

Zacynthius *adj see n.*
Zacynthus (-os), -ī *f* island off W. Greece (*now* Zante).
Zama, -ae *f* town in Numidia (*where Scipio defeated Hannibal*).
Zamēnsis *adj see n.*
zāmia, -ae *f* harm.
Zanclaeus *and* **ēius** *adj see n.*
Zanclē, -ēs *f old name of Messana.*
zēlotypus *adj* jealous.

Zēnō *and* **ōn, -ōnis** *m founder of Stoicism; a philosopher of Elea; an Epicurean teacher of Cicero.*
Zephyrītis, -idis *f* Arsinoe (*queen of Egypt*).
Zephyrus, -ī *m* west wind, zephyr; wind.
Zēthus, -ī *m brother of Amphion.*
Zeuxis, -is *and* **idis** *m famous Greek painter.*
zmaragdus *etc see* **smaragdus.**
Zmyrna *etc see* **Smyrna.**
zōdiacus, -ī *m* zodiac.
zōna, -ae *f* belt, girdle; (*GEOG*) zone; (*ASTRO*) Orion's Belt.
zōnārius *adj* of belts; **sector** ~ cutpurse ♦ *m* belt maker.
zōnula, -ae *f* little belt.
zōthēca, -ae *f* private room.
zōthēcula, -ae *f* cubicle.

ROMAN LIFE AND CULTURE

KEY EVENTS IN ROMAN HISTORY

B.C.

753	Foundation of Rome. Romulus became first king.
600-510	Rome ruled by Etruscan kings.
510	Expulsion of Tarquin and republic established.
507	Consecration of Temple of Jupiter on Capitol.
451	Code of Twelve Tables laid basis of Roman law.
390	Gauls sacked Rome.
367	Lex Liciniae Sextiae; plebeians allowed to be consul.
354	Treaty with Samnites.
343-341	First Samnite war; Romans occupied northern Campania.
340-338	Latin War; separate treaties made with Latins.
327-304	Second Samnite war; Rome increased influence in southern Italy.
321	Samnites defeated Romans at Caudine Forks; truce.
312	Appian Way, first Roman road, built.
298-290	Third Samnite war; Rome now all-powerful in southern Italy.
287	Hortensian Law; People's Assembly became a law-making body.
282-272	Wars with Tarentum and King Pyrrhus of Epirus.
270	Whole peninsula under Roman power.
264-241	First Punic war; Rome defended Greek cities in Sicily.
260	Fleet built; first naval victory at Mylae against Carthaginians.
241	Roman victory over Carthage secured Sicily, source of corn supply.
226	River Ebro treaty; Carthage should not cross into northern Spain.
218-201	Second Punic war against Hannibal.
216	Rome defeated at Battle of Cannae.
214-205	First Macedonian war with Philip V.
202	Scipio defeated Hannibal at Zama.
201	Peace concluded with Carthage; Rome now controlled the western Mediterranean.
200-196	Second Macedonian war; freedom of Greece proclaimed.
172-168	Third Macedonian war; Perseus crushed at Pydna.
148	Macedonia became a Roman province.
146	Carthage destroyed; Corinth destroyed.
133	Tiberius Gracchus became tribune; his assassination caused class conflict.
123-122	Gaius Gracchus carried out political/economic reforms.
121	Gaius was killed.
111-105	Marius and Sulla conducted war against Jugurtha of Numidia.
91-89	Social war between Rome and allies.
89-85	War with Mithridates VI of Pontus.
83-82	Civil war between Sulla and Marius; Sulla captured Rome.
81-79	Sulla, dictator, restored constitution, introduced reforms.
78	Death of Sulla.

77-72	Pompey fought Sertorius in Spain.
73-71	Spartacus' slave revolt.
70	Pompey and Crassus joint consuls; tribunes restored.
67	End of war against Mithridates; pirates controlled by Pompey.
63	Cicero suppressed Catiline's conspiracy.
60	First Triumvirate (Caesar, Pompey, Crassus) was formed.
58-51	Caesar conquered Gaul.
53	Battle of Carrhae; Rome defeated by Parthians; Crassus killed.
49	Caesar crossed Rubicon; civil war with Pompey began.
48	Pompey defeated by Caesar at Pharsalus; Caesar became dictator.
44	Caesar assassinated; Antony sought revenge against conspirators.
43	Second Triumvirate (Antony, Octavian, Lepidus).
42	Battle of Philippi; Triumvirate defeated Brutus and Cassius.
41-40	Antony and Octavian divided territory.
33-32	Rupture between Antony and Octavian.
31	Battle of Actium; Octavian defeated Antony and Cleopatra at sea.
27	Octavian returned powers to Senate; received name Augustus.
18	Julian laws promoted morality, condemned adultery, regulated divorce.
12	Augustus became Pontifex Maximus, head of state religion.
2	Augustus became 'pater patriae', father of his country; apex of his power.

A.D.

4	Tiberius adopted as Augustus' heir.
6	Annexation of Judaea.
9	Varus' three legions destroyed in Germany.
14	Death of Augustus.
14-37	Tiberius emperor; efficient administrator but unpopular.
14-16	Germanicus' successful campaign in Germany.
19	Germanicus died mysteriously; funeral at Antioch.
21-22	Sefanus organized Praetorian Guard.
26-31	Sefanus powerful in Rome; executed in 31.
37-41	Caligula emperor; cruel and tyrannical, was murdered by a tribune.
41-54	Claudius emperor; conquered Britain; showed political judgement.
57-68	Nero emperor; great fire (64); Christians persecuted.
68-69	Year of four emperors - Galba, Otho, Vitellius, Vespasian.
69-79	Vespasian began Flavian dynasty. Colosseum built.
70	Titus, Vespasian's son, captured Jerusalem, destroyed the Temple.
79-81	Titus emperor. Vesuvius erupted (79), Pompeii destroyed.
81-96	Domitian emperor. Border built in Germany; period ended in terror.
96-98	Nerva emperor after Domitian's assassination.
98-117	Trajan emperor - conqueror of Dacia and Parthian empire.
117-138	Hadrian, cultured traveller, soldier and administrator of empire.
122	Hadrian's Wall built between Solway and Tyne.
138-161	Antoninus Pius emperor; orderly, peaceful rule.
141-143	Antonine's Wall built between Forth and Clyde.
161-180	Marcus Aurelius emperor; Commodus, his son, shared power (177-180).

162	War with Parthia.
175-180	War against Germans on the Danube.
180-192	Commodus emperor.
193-211	Septimius Severus became emperor after crisis; died in Britain. Authorized special benefits for army.
211-217	Deterioration under criminal rule of Caracalla.
212	All free men of the empire became citizens.
284-305	Diocletian and Maximian co-emperors, empire divided into 12 dioceses. Prices imposed throughout empire.
303	Christians persecuted by Diocletian.
312	Constantine's victory at Milvian Bridge gave him Rome.
313	Edict of Milan ended persecution of Christians.
324	Constantine became sole emperor.
325	Council of Nicaea made Christianity religion of the empire.
330	Constantine made Byzantium seat of government; renamed it Constantinople.
337	Constantine died a Christian, trying to reorganize the empire.
379-395	Emperor Theodosius kept empire formally intact.
410	Alaric and Goths captured and destroyed Rome.

GOVERNMENT AND ADMINISTRATION

Republic

There was no written constitution. The Republic evolved from the struggle between the Senate and the People - Senatus Populusque Romanus - SPQR.

The Senate (Senatus)
This was the governing body, largely in the hands of the nobles (nobiles) or patricians (patricii).

- it prepared proposals to bring before the people
- it passed decrees (senatus consulta)
- it dealt with emergencies
- it controlled finances and building contracts
- it appointed magistrates to provinces
- it directed foreign relations
- it supervised state religion

The People (Populus)
The resolutions of the people, plebiscita, could have the force of law, but the Senate was allowed greater control. There were four assemblies:

- comitia curiata   formal duties
- comitia centuriata   elected magistrates
- comitia tributa   elected lesser magistrates
- concilium plebis   passed plebiscita

The Knights (Equites)
A third element, or class, emerged (originally from Rome's cavalry) to engage in trade and finance. These businessmen acquired more political influence and became wealthy. By the time of Cicero, they could enter the Senate. Cicero tried to reconcile the three classes, **senatores**, **equites** and **plebs** by his **concordia ordinum** (harmony of the classes).

Magistrates (Magistratus)
A magistrate was an official elected annually by the people. Offices were held in a strict order - **cursus honorum**. After ten years' military service, a young man could begin on the lowest rung of the ladder as follows:

Age	Office	Number	Duties
28	**Quaestor**	(8)	• administered finance maintained public records
30	**Aedile**	(4)	• maintained roads, water supply organized games and festivals
33(39)	**Praetor**	(6)	• civil judge could introduce laws

39(43)	**Consul**	(2)	• commanded army
			  conducted elections
			  presided over Senate
			  carried out its decrees

Other magistrates:

Tribune (10)
(tribunus plebis)

- defended plebs' rights
  had right of veto

Censor (2)

- conducted census (every 5 years)
  conducted purification
  revised roll of senators

Dictator (1)

- ruled in crisis (maximum of 6 months)
  conducted military and domestic
  matters

Imperium (supreme power) was held by consuls and praetors and dictators.
Potestas (power to enforce laws) was held by all magistrates.
Lictores (lictors _or_ officials) carried **fasces** (bundles of rods) in front of
consuls, praetors and dictators as a sign of their authority.

ORGANIZATION OF THE ARMY

Empire

At the time of Augustus there were 28 **legions** (later 25), each legion consisting of approximately 5000 infantrymen, trained for close combat. It was organized as follows:

Legio	Legion	5000 men
10 Cohortes	Cohorts	500 men
6 Centuriae	Centuries	80/100 men

Officers	
Legatus	legionary commander
6 **Tribuni Militum**	tribunes
60 **Centuriones**	centurions (from ranks), in charge of centuries

Recruitment	Citizens
Length of service	20/25 years
Duties	Offensive in important battles, repelling invasion *etc*
Pay	250/300 denarii per day
On retirement	Land or cash bounty

Additional **auxiliary forces** were recruited to help the legions. Particularly necessary were cavalry, drawn from all parts of the Empire, slingers, bowmen, etc. Infantrymen were often recruited locally and formed cohorts of about 500 men.

Auxilia	Auxiliaries	
Ala	Cavalry unit	500 men approx.
16 Turmae	turmae	32 men
Cohors	Infantry unit	500 men

Officers	
Decurio	Decurion (cavalry officer)

Recruitment	Non-citizens
Length of service	25 years
Duties	Frontier skirmishes, occupation, assisting legions

| **Pay** | 100 denarii per day |
| **On retirement** | Citizenship for self/family |

The **Praetorian Guard** was the Emperor's special bodyguard. Three cohorts were based in Rome, six more in nearby towns.

| **Praetorium** | Praetorian Guard | 4500 men |
| **9 Cohortes** | cohorts | 500 men |

Officers		
2 Praefecti Praetorio	praetorian prefects	
Recruitment	Citizens (Italy)	
Length of service	16 years	
Duties	Preserving emperor's power and safety	
Pay	1000 denarii per day	
On retirement	5000 denarii	

FAMILY TREE

tritavus *m* tritavia
(great-great-great-great-grandfather) (great-great-great-great-great-grandmother)

atavus *m* atavia
(great-great-great-grandfather) (great-great-great-great-grandmother)

abavus *m* abavia
(great-great-grandfather) (great-great-grandmother)

proavus *m* proavia
(great-grandfather) (great-grandmother)

avus *m* avia
(grandfather) (grandmother)

noverca *m* pater *m* māter *m* vitricus
(stepmother) (father) (mother) (stepfather)

Left branch (paternal):

patruus māximus (great-great-granduncle)

patruus māior (great-granduncle)

patruus māgnus (granduncle)

patruus (uncle)

amita māxima (great-great-grandaunt)

amita māior (great-grandaunt)

amita māgna (grandaunt)

amita (aunt)

Right branch (maternal):

mātertera māxima (great-great-grandaunt)

mātertera māior (great-grandaunt)

mātertera māgna (grandaunt)

mātertera (aunt)

avunculus māximus (great-great-granduncle)

avunculus māior (great-granduncle)

avunculus māgnus (granduncle)

avunculus (uncle)

In-laws:

prōsocer *m* prōsocrus
(grandfather-in-law) (grandmother-in-law)

socer *m* socrus
(father-in-law) (mother-in-law)

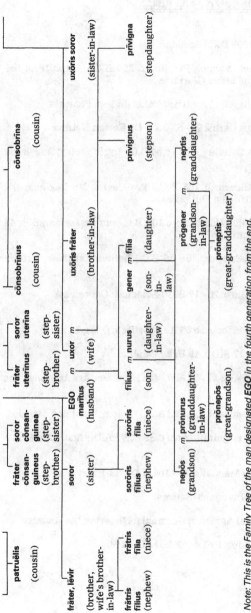

Note: This is the Family Tree of the man designated *EGO* in the fourth generation from the end.

MAJOR WRITERS

ENNIUS (Quintus Ennius: b 239 B.C.) **Annales**.

PLAUTUS (Titus Maccus *or* Maccius Plautus: b 254 B.C.) **Amphitruo**; the **Aulularia**; the **Menaechmi** and **Miles Gloriosus**.

TERENCE (Publius Terentius Afer) **Andria; Mother-in-law; Phormio**.

LUCRETIUS (Titus Lucretius Carus: 94 - 55 B.C.) **De Rerum Natura**.

CATULLUS (Gaius Valerius Catullus: c.84 - c.54 B.C.) Lyric poetry; **Ave atque vale**.

CICERO (Marcus Tullius Cicero: b 106 B.C.) **Pro Caelio; De Legibus;** the **Tusculan Disputations; De Officiis; Philippics**.

JULIUS CAESAR (Gaius Iulius Caesar: b c.102 B.C. and assassinated in 44 B.C.) **Bellum Gallicum; Bellum Civile**.

SALLUST (Gaius Sallustius Crispus: 86 - 35 B.C.) **Bellum Catilinae; Bellum Iugurthinum**.

VIRGIL (Publius Vergilius Maro: 70 - 19 B.C.) **Eclogues; Georgics;** the **Aeneid**.

HORACE (Quintus Horatius Flaccus: b 65 A.D.) **Satires; Odes; Epistles**.

LIVY (Titus Livius: 59 B.C. - 17 A.D.) **Ab Urbe Condita**.

OVID (Publius Ovidius Naso: 43 B.C. - 17 A.D.) the **Heroides, Ars Amatoria;** the **Metamorphoses; Tristia**.

SENECA (Lucius Annaeus Seneca: 4 B.C. - 65 A.D.) **Dialogi; Epistolae Morales**.

QUINTILIAN (Marcus Fabius Quintilianus: c.35 - c.95 A.D.) **Institutio Oratorio**.

MARTIAL (Marcus Valerius Martialis: 40 - 104 A.D.) the **Epigrams**.

JUVENAL (Decimus Iunius Iuvenalis) **Satires**.

TACITUS (Cornelius Tacitus) **Agricola; Germania; Histories;** the **Annals**.

PLINY (Gaius Plinius Secundus: b 61 *or* 62 A.D.) **Letters**.

GEOGRAPHICAL NAMES

The following list of geographical names and their adjectives includes both ancient and medieval Latin forms. The former are printed in Roman type, the latter in Italics. Medieval place names tend to have a variety of Latin forms, but only one has been selected in each case; occasionally both the ancient and the medieval forms have been given. Modern names which have a ready-made Latin form (e.g. America) have been omitted, and many names not included in this selection can be easily Latinized on the analogy of those which do appear.

Aachen	Aquīsgrānum nt	adj Aquīsgrānēnsis
Aberdeen	Aberdōnia f	adj Aberdōnēnsis
Abergavenny	Gobannium nt	
Aberystwith	Aberistyvium nt	
Adige, River	Athesis m	
Adriatic	Mare superum nt	adj Hadriāticus
Aegean	Mare Aegaeum nt	adj Aegaeus
Afghanistan	Ariāna f	adj Ariānus
Africa	Libya f,	adj Libycus,
	Africa f	Africānus
Agrigento	Agrigentum nt	adj Agrigentīnus
Aisne, River	Axona m	
Aix-en-Provence	Aquae Sextiae fpl	adj Aquēnsis
Aix-la-Chapelle	Aquīsgrānum nt	adj Aquisgrānēnsis
Aix-Les-Bains	Aquae Grātiānae fpl	
Ajaccio	Adiacium nt	adj Adiacēnsis
Aldborough	Isurium (nt)	
	Brigantum	
Alexandria	Alexandrēa,	
	Alexandrīa f	adj Alexandrīnus
Algiers	Algerium nt	adj Algerīnus
Alps	Alpēs fpl	adj Alpīnus
Alsace	Alsatia f	
Amalfi	Amalphis f	adj Amalphītānus
Ambleside	Galava f	
Amiens	Ambiānum nt	adj Ambiānēnsis
Amsterdam	Amstelodamum nt	adj Amstelodamēnsis
Ancaster	Causennae fpl	
Angers	Andegāvum nt	adj Andegāvēnsis
Anglesey	Mona f	
Aniene, River	Aniō m	adj Aniēnus
Anjou	Andegāvēnsis ager m	
Ankara	Ancyra f	adj Ancyrānus
Antibes	Antipolis f	adj Antipolītānus
Antioch	Antiochīa f	adj Antiochēnus
Antwerp	Antwerpium nt	adj Antwerpiēnsis
Anzio	Antium nt	adj Antiās, Antiānus
Aosta	Augusta Praetōria f	
Apennines	Mōns Apennīnus m	

Aragon	Aragōnia f	
Archangel	Archangelopolis f	
Ardennes	Arduenna f	
Arezzo	Ārētium nt	adj Ārētīnus
Argenteuil	Argentōlium nt	
Argyll	Argadia f	
Arles	Arelās f	adj Arelātēnsis
Armagh	Armācha f	adj Armāchānus
Arno, River	Arnus m	adj Arniēnsis
Arras	Atrebatēs mpl	adj Atrebatēnsis
Artois	Atrebatēs mpl	
Assisi	Assīsium nt	adj Assīsiēnsis
Athens	Athēnae fpl	adj Athēniēnsis
Atlantic	Mare Atlanticum nt	
Augsburg	Augusta (f) Vindelicōrum	adj Augustānus
Autun	Augustodūnum nt	adj Augustodūnēnsis
Auvergne	Arvernī mpl	adj Arvernus
Aventine	Aventīnus m	
Avignon	Aveniō f	adj Aveniōnēnsis
Avon, River	Auvona m	
Babylon	Babylōn f	adj Babylōnius
Baden-Baden	Aquae Aurēliae fpl	
Balearic Islands	Baliārēs Insulae fpl	adj Baliāricus
Balkh	Bactra ntpl	adj Bactriānus
Baltic	Balticum Mare nt	
Bangor	Bangertium nt	adj Bangertiēnsis
Barcelona	Barcinō f	adj Barcinōnēnsis
Bari	Bārium nt	adj Bārēnsis
Basle	Basilēa f	adj Basilēēnsis
Basques	Vasconēs mpl	adj Vasconicus
Bath	Aquae (fpl) Sulis	
Bayeux	Augustodūrum nt	
Bayreuth	Barūthum nt	
Beauvais	Bellovacī mpl	adj Bellovacēnsis
Beirut	Bērȳtus f	adj Bērȳtius
Belgium	Belgae mpl	adj Belgicus
Bergen	Bergae fpl	
Berlin	Berolīnum nt	adj Berolīnēnsis
Berne	Vērona f	
Berwick	Barvicum nt	
Besançon	Vesontiō m	adj Bisuntīnus
Black Sea	Pontus (Euxīnus) m	adj Ponticus
Bobbio	Bobbium nt	adj Bobbiēnsis
Bohemia	Boiohaemī mpl	
Bologna	Bonōnia f	adj Bonōniēnsis
Bonn	Bonna f	
Bordeaux	Burdigala f	adj Burdigalēnsis
Boulogne	Bonōnia f	adj Bononiēnsis
Bourges	Avāricum nt	adj Avāricēnsis
Brabant	Brabantia f	
Braganza	Brigantia f	adj Brigantiēnsis

Brancaster	Branodūnum *nt*	
Brandenburg	Brandenburgia *f*	*adj* Brandenburgēnsis
Bremen	Brēma *f*	*adj* Brēmēnsis
Breslau	Bratislavia *f*	*adj* Bratislaviēnsis
Brindisi	Brundisium *nt*	*adj* Brundisīnus
Bristol	Bristolium *nt*	*adj* Bristoliēnsis
Britain	Britannia *f*	*adj* Britannicus
Brittany	Armoricae *fpl*	
Bruges	Brugae *fpl*	*adj* Brugēnsis
Brunswick	Brunsvīcum *nt*	*adj* Brunsvīcēnsis
Brussels	Bruxellae *fpl*	*adj* Bruxellēnsis
Bucharest	Bucarestum *nt*	*adj* Bucarestiēnsis
Burgos	Burgī *mpl*	*adj* Burgitānus
Burgundy	Burgundiōnēs *mpl*	
Cadiz	Gādēs *fpl*	*adj* Gāditānus
Caen	Cadomum *nt*	*adj* Cadomēnsis
Caerleon	Isca *f*	
Caermarthen	Maridūnum *nt*	
Caernarvon	Segontium *nt*	
Caerwent	Venta (*f*) Silurum	
Cagliari	Caralis *f*	*adj* Caralītānus
Cairo	Cairus *f*	
Calais	Calētum *nt*	*adj* Calētanus
Cambrai	Camerācum *nt*	*adj* Camerācēnsis
Cambridge	Cantabrigia *f*	*adj* Cantabrigiēnsis
Campagna	Campānia *f*	*adj* Campānus
Cannes	Canoē *f*	
Canterbury	Durovernum *nt*,	*adj* Cantuāriēnsis
	Cantuāria *f*	
Capri	Capreae *fpl*	*adj* Capreēnsis
Cardigan	Ceretica *f*	
Carlisle	Luguvallium *nt*	
Cartagena	Carthāgō Nova *f*	
Carthage	Carthāgō *f*	*adj* Carthāginiēnsis
Caspian Sea	Mare Caspium *nt*	
Cevennes	Gebenna *f*	*adj* Gebennicus
Ceylon	Tāprobanē *f*	
Champagne	Campānia *f*	*adj* Campānicus
Chartres	Carnūtēs *mpl*	*adj* Carnōtēnus
Chelmsford	Caesaromagus *m*	
Cherbourg	Caesaris burgus *m*	
Chester	Deva *f*	
Chichester	Rēgnum *nt*	
China	Sēres *mpl*	*adj* Sēricus
Cirencester	Corinium (*nt*)	
	Dobunōrum	
Clairvaux	Clāra Vallis *f*	*adj* Clāravallēnsis
Clermont	Nemossus *f*	
Cluny	Clīniacum *nt*	*adj* Clīniacēnsis
Clyde, *River*	Clōta *f*	
Colchester	Camulodūnum *nt*	
Cologne	Colōnia Agrippīna *f*	*adj* Colōniēnsis

Como, *Lake*	Lārius *m*	*adj* Lārius
Constance, *Lake*	Lacus Brigantīnus *m*	
Copenhagen	Hafnia *f*	
Corbridge	Corstopitum *nt*	
Cordoba	Corduba *f*	*adj* Cordubēnsis
Corfu	Corcȳra *f*	*adj* Corcȳraeus
Corinth	Corinthus *f*	*adj* Corinthius
Cork	Corcagia *f*	*adj* Corcagiēnsis
Cornwall	Cornubia *f*	
Cracow	Cracovia *f*	*adj* Cracoviēnsis
Crete	Crēta *f*	*adj* Crētēnsis, Crēticus
Cumberland	Cumbria *f*	
Cyprus	Cyprus *f*	*adj* Cyprius
Cyrene	Cȳrēnae *fpl*	*adj* Cȳrēnaicus
Damascus	Damascus *f*	*adj* Damascēnus
Danube, *River*	*(lower)* Ister *m*,	
	(upper) Dānuvius *m*	
Dardanelles	Hellēspontus *m*	*adj* Hellēspontius
Dee, *River*	Deva *f*	
Denmark	Dānia *f*	*adj* Dānicus
Derby	Derventiō *m*	
Devon	Devōnia *f*	
Dijon	Diviō *f*	*adj* Diviōnēnsis
Dneiper, *River*	Borysthenēs *m*	
Dneister, *River*	Danaster *m*	
Don, *River* (Russian)	Tanais *m*	
Doncaster	Dānum *nt*	
Dorchester	Durnovāria *f*	
Douro, *River*	Durius *m*	
Dover	Dubrī *mpl*	
Dover, *Straits of*	Fretum Gallicum *nt*	
Dresden	Dresda *f*	*adj* Dresdēnsis
Dublin	Dublīnum *nt*	*adj* Dublīnēnsis
Dumbarton	Britannodūnum *nt*	
Dundee	Taodūnum *nt*	
Dunstable	Durocobrīvae *fpl*	
Durham	Dunelmum *nt*	*adj* Dunelmēnsis
Ebro, *River*	Hibērus *m*	
Eden, *River*	Itūna *f*	
Edinburgh	Edinburgum *nt*	*adj* Edinburgēnsis
Egypt	Aegyptus *f*	*adj* Aegyptius
Elba	Ilva *f*	
Elbe, *River*	Albis *m*	
England	Anglia *f*	*adj* Anglicus
Etna	Aetna *f*	*adj* Aetnaeus
Europe	Eurōpa	*adj* Eurōpaeus
Exeter	Isca *(f)* Dumnoniōrum	
Fiesole	Faesulae *fpl*	*adj* Faesulānus
Flanders	Menapiī *mpl*	
Florence	Flōrentia *f*	*adj* Flōrentīnus
Fontainebleau	Bellofontānum *nt*	
Forth, *River*	Bodotria *f*	

France	Gallia *f*	*adj* Gallicus
Frankfurt	*Francofurtum nt*	
Frejus	Forum (*nt*) Iūliī	*adj* Foroiūliēnsis
Friesland	Frīsiī *mpl*	*adj* Frīsius
Gallipoli	*Callipolis f*	*adj* Callipolitānus
Galloway	*Gallovidia f*	
Ganges	Gangēs *m*	*adj* Gangēticus
Garda, Lake	Bēnācus *m*	
Garonne, River	Garumna *f*	
Gaul	Gallia *f*	*adj* Gallicus
Gdansk	*Gedānum m*	
Geneva	Genāva *f*	*adj* Genāvēnsis
Geneva, Lake	Lemannus lacus *m*	
Genoa	Genua *f*	*adj* Genuēnsis
Germany	Germānia *f*	*adj* Germānicus
Ghent	*Gandavum nt*	*adj* Gandavēnsis
Gibraltar	Calpē *f*	*adj* Calpētānus
Gibraltar, Straits of	Fretum Gāditānum *nt*	
Glasgow	*Glasgua f*	*adj* Glasguēnsis
Gloucester	Glēvum *nt*	
Gothenburg	*Gothoburgum nt*	
Graz	*Graecium nt*	
Greece	Graecia *f*	*adj* Graecus
Greenwich	*Grenovīcum nt*	
Grenoble	Grātiānopolis *f*	
Groningen	*Groninga f*	
Guadalquivir, River	Baetis *m*	
Guadiana, River	Anas *m*	
Guernsey	*Sarnia f*	
Hague, The	Haga (*f*) Comitis	
Halle	*Halla f*	*adj* Hallēnsis
Hamadān	Ecbatana *ntpl*	
Hamburg	*Hamburgum nt*	*adj* Hamburgēnsis
Hanover	*Hannovera f*	
Harwich	*Harvīcum nt*	
Havre	Grātiae Portus *m*	
Hebrides	Ebūdae Insulae *fpl*	
Hexham	Axelodūnum *nt*	
Holland	Batāvī *mpl*	*adj* Batāvus
Ibiza	Ebusus *f*	*adj* Ebusitānus
Ilkley	Olicāna *f*	
Inn, River	Aenus *m*	
Ipswich	*Gippevīcum nt*	
Ireland	Hibernia *f*	*adj* Hibernicus
Isar, River	Isara *f*	
Istanbul	Bӯzantium *nt*	*adj* Bӯzantīnus
Italy	Italia *f*	*adj* Italicus
Jersey	Caesarea *f*	
Jerusalem	Hierosolyma *ntpl*	*adj* Hierosolymītānus
Jutland	Chersonnēsus Cimbrica *f*	
Karlsbad	*Aquae Carolīnae fpl*	

Kent	Cantium *nt*	
Kiel	*Chilonium nt*	
Koblenz	Cōnfluentēs *mpl*	
Lancaster	*Lancastria f*	
Lanchester	Longovicium *nt*	
Land's End	Bolerium Prōmunturium *nt*	
Lausanne	Lausōnium *nt*	*adj* Lausōniēnsis
Lebanon	Libanus *m*	
Leeds	*Ledesia f*	
Leicester	Ratae (*fpl*) Coritānōrum	
Leiden	Lugdūnum (*nt*) Batāvōrum	
Leipsig	*Lipsia f*	*adj* Lipsiēnsis
Lērida	Ilerda *f*	*adj* Ilerdēnsis
Lichfield	*Etocētum nt*	
Limoges	Augustorītum *nt*	
Lincoln	Lindum *nt*	
Lisbon	Olisīpō *m*	*adj* Olisīpōnēnsis
Lizard Point	Damnonium Prōmunturium *nt*	
Loire, *River*	Liger *m*	*adj* Ligericus
Lombardy	*Langobardia f*	
London	Londinium *nt*	*adj* Londiniēnsis
Lorraine	*Lōthāringia f*	
Lucerne	*Lūceria f*	*adj* Lūcernēnsis
Lund	Londinium (*nt*) Gothōrum	
Lyons	Lugdūnum *nt*	*adj* Lugdūnēnsis
Madrid	*Matrītum nt*	*adj* Matrītēnsis
Maggiore, *Lake*	Verbannus *m*	
Main, *River*	Moenus *m*	
Mainz	Mogontiacum *nt*	
Majorca	Baliāris Māior *f*	
Malta	Melita *f*	
Man, *Isle of*	Monapia *f*	
Manchester	Mancunium *nt*	
Marmara, *Sea of*	Propontis *f*	
Marne, *River*	*Māterna f*	
Marseilles	Massilia *f*	*adj* Massiliēnsis
Matapan	Taenarum *nt*	*adj* Taenarius
Mediterranean	Mare internum *nt*	
Melun	Melodūnum *nt*	
Mērida	Ēmerita *f*	*adj* Ēmeritēnsis
Messina	Messāna *f*	*adj* Messānius
Metz	Dīvodūrum *nt*	
Meuse, *River*	Mosa *f*	
Milan	Mediōlānum *nt*	*adj* Mediōlānēnsis
Minorca	Baliāris Minor *f*	
Modena	Mutina *f*	*adj* Mutinēnsis
Mons	Montēs *mpl*	
Monte Cassino	Casīnum *nt*	*adj* Casīnās
Moray	*Moravia f*	

Morocco	Maurētānia f	adj Maurus
Moscow	Moscovia f	
Moselle, *River*	Mosella f	
Munich	Monacum nt	adj Monacēnsis
Nantes	Namnētēs mpl	
Naples	Neāpolis f	adj Neāpolitānus
Neckar, *River*	Nīcer m	
Newcastle	Pōns (m) Aeliī, Novum Castrum nt	adj Novocastrēnsis
Nice	Nīcaea f	adj Nicaeēnsis
Nile, *River*	Nīlus m	adj Nīlōticus
Nîmes	Nemausus f	adj Nemausēnsis
Norway	Norvēgia f	adj Norvēgiānus
Norwich	Nordovīcum nt	
Oder, *River*	Viadrus m	
Oporto	Portus Calēnsis m	
Orange	Arausiō f	
Orkneys	Orcades fpl	
Orléans	Aurēliānum nt	adj Aurēliānēnsis
Oudenarde	Aldenarda f	
Oxford	Oxonia f	adj Oxoniēnsis
Padua	Patavium nt	adj Patavīnus
Palermo	Panormus m	adj Panormitānus
Paris	Lutetia f, Parīsiī mpl	adj Parīsiēnsis
Patras	Patrae fpl	adj Patrēnsis
Persian Gulf	Mare Rubrum nt	
Piacenza	Placentia f	adj Placentīnus
Po, *River*	Padus	adj Padānus
Poitiers	Limōnum nt	
Poland	Polōnia f	
Portsmouth	Māgnus Portus m	
Portugal	Lūsitānia f	
Pozzuoli	Puteolī mpl	adj Puteolānus
Prague	Prāga f	adj Prāgēnsis
Provence	Prōvincia f	
Pyrenees	Pȳrēnaeī montēs mpl	
Red Sea	Sinus Arābicus m	
Rheims	Dūrocortorum nt	
Rhine, *River*	Rhēnus m	adj Rhēnānus
Rhodes	Rhodos f	adj Rhodius
Rhône, *River*	Rhodanus m	
Richborough	Rutupiae fpl	adj Rutupīnus
Rimini	Arīminum	adj Arīminēnsis
Rochester	Dūrobrīvae fpl	
Rome	Rōma f	adj Rōmānus
Rotterdam	Roterodamum nt	adj Roterodamēnsis
Rouen	Rothomagus f	adj Rothomagēnsis
Saar, *River*	Sangona f	
Salisbury	Sarisberia f	
Salzburg	Iuvāvum nt	adj Salisburgēnsis
Saône, *River*	Arar m	

Savoy	*Sabaudia f*	
Scheldt, *River*	Scaldis *m*	
Schleswig	*Slesvīcum nt*	
Scilly Isles	Cassiterides *fpl*	
Scotland	Calēdonia *f*	*adj* Calēdonius
Seine, *River*	Sēquana *f*	
Severn, *River*	Sabrīna *f*	
Seville	Hīspalis *f*	*adj* Hispalēnsis
Shrewsbury	*Salōpia f*	
Sicily	Sicilia *f*	*adj* Siculus
Sidra, *Gulf of*	Syrtis (māior) *f*	
Silchester	Callēva *(f)* Atrebatum	
Soissons	Augusta *(f)* Suessiōnum	
Solway Firth	Itūna *(f)* aestuārium	
Somme, *River*	Samara *f*	
Spain	Hispānia *f*	*adj* Hispānus
St. Albans	Verulamium *nt*	
St. Andrews	*Andreopolis f*	
St. Bernard	*(Great)* Mōns Pennīnus *m*, *(Little)* Alpis Grāia *f*	
St. Gallen	*Sangallēnse coenobium nt*	*adj Sangallēnsis*
St. Gotthard	Alpēs summae *fpl*	
St. Moritz	Agaunum *nt*	*adj* Agaunēnsis
Strasbourg	Argentorātus *f*	*adj* Argentorātēnsis
Swabia	Suēvia *f*	*adj* Suēvicus
Sweden	*Suēcia f*	*adj Suēcicus*
Switzerland	Helvētia *f*	*adj* Helvēticus
Syracuse	Syrācūsae *fpl*	*adj* Syrācūsānus
Tangier	Tingī *f*	*adj* Tingitānus
Taranto	Tarentum *nt*	*adj* Tarentīnus
Tarragona	Tarracō *f*	*adj* Tarracōnēnsis
Tay, *River*	*Taus m*	
Thames, *River*	Tamesis *m*	
Thebes	Thēbae *fpl*	*adj* Thēbānus
Tiber, *River*	Tiberis *m*	*adj* Tiberīnus
Tivoli	Tībur *nt*	*adj* Tīburtīnus
Toledo	Tolētum *nt*	*adj* Tolētānus
Toulon	*Tolōna f*	*adj Tolōnēnsis*
Toulouse	Tolōsa *f*	*adj* Tolōsānus
Tours	Caesarodūnum *nt*	
Trèves, Trier	Augusta *(f)* Treverōrum	
Trieste	Tergeste *nt*	*adj* Tergestīnus
Tripoli	Tripolis *f*	*adj* Tripolitānus
Tunis	Tūnēs *f*	*adj* Tūnētānus
Turin	Augusta *(f)* Taurīnōrum	*adj* Taurīnus
Tuscany	Etrūria *f*	*adj* Etrūscus
Tyrrhenian Sea	Mare īnferum *nt*	
Utrecht	*Ultrāiectum nt*	*adj Ultrāiectēnsis*
Vardar, *River*	Axius *m*	
Venice	Venetī *mpl, Venetiae fpl*	*adj* Venetus
Verdun	*Virodūnum nt*	*adj Virodūnēnsis*

Versailles	*Versāliae fpl*	*adj Versāliēnsis*
Vichy	Aquae (*fpl*) Sōlis	
Vienna	*Vindobona f*	*adj Vindobenēnsis*
Vosges	Vosegus *m*	
Wales	*Cambria f*	
Wallsend	Segedūnum *nt*	
Warsaw	*Varsavia f*	*adj Varsaviēnsis*
Wash, *The*	Metaris (*m*) aestuārium	
Wear, *River*	Vedra *f*	
Weser, *River*	Visurgis *m*	
Westminster	*Westmonastērium nt*	*adj Westmonastēriēnsis*
Wiesbaden	Mattiacum *nt*	*adj* Mattiacus
Wight, *Isle of*	Vectis *f*	
Winchester	Venta (*f*) Belgārum	
Worcester	Vigornia *f*	
Worms	*Vormatia f*	
Wroxeter	Viroconium *nt*	
York	Eburācum *nt*	*adj* Eburācēnsis
Zuider Zee	Flēvō *m*	
Zurich	*Turicum nt*	*adj* Tigurīnus

NUMERALS

	Cardinal		Ordinal	
1	ūnus	I	prīmus	1st
2	duo	II	secundus, alter	2nd
3	trēs	III	tertius	3rd
4	quattuor	IV	quārtus	4th
5	quīnque	V	quīntus	5th
6	sex	VI	sextus	6th
7	septem	VII	septimus	7th
8	octō	VIII	octāvus	8th
9	novem	IX	nōnus	9th
10	decem	X	decimus	10th
11	undecim	XI	undecimus	11th
12	duodecim	XII	duodecimus	12th
13	tredecim	XIII	tertius decimus	13th
14	quattuordecim	XIV	quārtus decimus	14th
15	quīndecim	XV	quīntus decimus	15th
16	sēdecim	XVI	sextus decimus	16th
17	septendecim	XVII	septimus decimus	17th
18	duodēvīgintī	XVIII	duodēvīcēsimus	18th
19	ūndēvīgintī	XIX	ūndēvīcēsimus	19th
20	vīgintī	XX	vīcēsimus	20th
21	vīgintī ūnus	XXI	vīcēsimus prīmus	21st
28	duodētrīgintā	XXVIII	duodētrīcēsimus	28th
29	ūndētrīgintā	XXIX	ūndētrīcēsimus	29th
30	trīgintā	XXX	trīcēsimus	30th
40	quadrāgintā	XL	quadrāgēsimus	40th
50	quīnquāgintā	L	quīnquāgēsimus	50th
60	sexāgintā	LX	sexāgēsimus	60th
70	septuāgintā	LXX	septuāgēsimus	70th
80	octōgintā	LXXX	octōgēsimus	80th
90	nōnāgintā	XC	nōnāgēsimus	90th
100	centum	C	centēsimus	100th
101	centum et ūnus	CI	centēsimus prīmus	101st
122	centum vīgintī duo	CXXII	centēsimus vīcēsimus alter	122nd
200	ducentī	CC	ducentēsimus	200th
300	trecentī	CCC	trecentēsimus	300th
400	quadringentī	CCCC	quadringentēsimus	400th
500	quīngentī	D	quīngentēsimus	500th
600	sēscentī	DC	sēscentēsimus	600th
700	septingentī	DCC	septingentēsimus	700th
800	octingentī	DCCC	octingentēsimus	800th
900	nōngentī	DCCCC	nōngentēsimus	900th
1000	mīlle	M	mīllēsimus	1000th
1001	mīlle et ūnus	MI	mīllēsimus prīmus	1001st
1102	mīlle centum duo	MCII	mīllēsimus centēsimus alter	1102nd
3000	tria mīlia	MMM	ter mīllēsimus	3000th
5000	quīnque mīlia	IↃↃ	quīnquiēs mīllēsimus	5000th
10,000	decem mīlia	CCIↃↃ	deciēs mīllēsimus	10,000th
100,000	centum mīlia	CCCIↃↃↃ	centiēs mīllēsimus	100,000th
1,000,000	deciēs centēna mīlia	CCCCIↃↃↃↃ	deciēs centiēs mīllēsimus	1,000,000th

NUMERALS

	Distributive		Adverb	
1	singulī	I	semel	1st
2	bīnī	II	bis	2nd
3	ternī (trīnī)	III	ter	3rd
4	quaternī	IV	quater	4th
5	quīnī	V	quīnquiēs	5th
6	sēnī	VI	sexiēs	6th
7	septēnī	VII	septiēs	7th
8	octōnī	VIII	octiēs	8th
9	novēnī	IX	noviēs	9th
10	dēnī	X	deciēs	10th
11	undēnī	XI	undeciēs	11th
12	duodēnī	XII	duodeciēs	12th
13	ternī dēnī	XIII	ter deciēs	13th
14	quaternī dēnī	XIV	quattuordeciēs	14th
15	quīnī dēnī	XV	quīndeciēs	15th
16	sēnī dēnī	XVI	sēdeciēs	16th
17	septēnī dēnī	XVII	septiēs deciēs	17th
18	duodēvīcēnī	XVIII	duodēvīciēs	18th
19	ūndēvīcēnī	XIX	ūndēvīciēs	19th
20	vīcēnī	XX	vīciēs	20th
21	vīcēnī singulī	XXI	semel et vīciēs	21st
28	duodētrīcēnī	XXVIII	duodētrīciēs	28th
29	ūndētrīcēnī	XXIX	ūndētrīciēs	29th
30	trīcēnī	XXX	trīciēs	30th
40	quadrāgēnī	XL	quadrāgiēs	40th
50	quīnquāgēnī	L	quīnquāgiēs	50th
60	sexāgēnī	LX	sexāgiēs	60th
70	septuāgēnī	LXX	septuāgiēs	70th
80	octōgēnī	LXXX	octōgiēs	80th
90	nōnagēnī	XC	nōnāgiēs	90th
100	centēnī	C	centiēs	100th
101	centēnī singulī	CI	semel et centiēs	101st
122	centēnī vīcēnī bīnī	CXXII	centiēs vīciēs bis	122nd
200	ducēnī	CC	ducentiēs	200th
300	trecēnī	CCC	trecentiēs	300th
400	quadringēnī	CCCC	quadringentiēs	400th
500	quīngēnī	D	quīngentiēs	500th
600	sexcēnī	DC	sexcentiēs	600th
700	septingēnī	DCC	septingentiēs	700th
800	octingēnī	DCCC	octingentiēs	800th
900	nōngēnī	DCCCC	nōngentiēs	900th
1000	singula mīlia	M	mīlliēs	1000th
1001	singula mīlia singulī	MI	semel et mīlliēs	1001st
1102	singula mīlia centēnī bīnī	MCII	mīlliēs centiēs bis	1102nd
3000	trīna mīlia	MMM	ter mīlliēs	3000th
5000	quīna mīlia	IƆƆ	quīnquiēs mīlliēs	5000th
10,000	dēna mīlia	CCIƆƆ	deciēs mīlliēs	10,000th
100,000	centēna mīlia	CCCIƆƆƆ	centiēs mīlliēs	100,000th
1,000,000	deciēs centēna mīlia	CCCCIƆƆƆƆ	mīlliēs mīlliēs	1,000,000th

DATES

MONTHS

Three days of the month have special names:

Kalendae the 1st.

Nōnae the 5th of most months, but the 7th of March, May, July and October.

> "In March, July, October, May,
> The Nones are on the 7th day."

Idūs the 13th of most months, but the 15th of March, May, July and October.

If the date is one of these three days, it is expressed in the ablative, with the adjective of the month in agreement, *e.g.*

1st January, **Kalendīs Iānuāriīs**, usually abbreviated **Kal. Ian.**

The day immediately before any of these three is expressed by **prīdiē** with the accusative, *e.g.*

4th February, **prīdiē Nōnās Februāriās**, usually abbreviated **prid. Non. Feb.**

All other dates are expressed as so many days before the next named day, and in reckoning the interval both the date and the named day are counted, *e.g.* the 11th is the 5th day before the 15th.

The formula is all in the accusative, begining with the words **ante diem**, *e.g.* 11th March, **ante diem quīntum Idūs Martiās**, usually abbreviated **a.d. V Id. Mar.**

The following selection of dates for April and May should be a sufficient guide to the dates of any month in the year:—

APRIL		MAY
Kal. Apr.	1	Kal. Mai.
a.d IV Non. Apr.	2	a.d. VI Non. Mai.
a.d. III Non. Apr.	3	a.d. V Non. Mai.
prid. Non. Apr.	4	a.d. IV Non. Mai.
Non. Apr.	5	a.d. III Non. Mai.
a.d. VIII Id. Apr.	6	prid. Non. Mai.
a.d. VII Id. Apr.	7	Non. Mai.
a.d. VI Id. Apr.	8	a.d. VIII Id. Mai.
a.d. V Id. Apr.	9	a.d. VII Id. Mai.
a.d. IV Id. Apr.	10	a.d. VI Id. Mai.
a.d. III Id. Apr.	11	a.d. V Id. Mai.
prid. Id. Apr.	12	a.d. IV Id. Mai.
Id. Apr.	13	a.d. III Id. Mai.
a.d. XVIII Kal. Mai.	14	prid. Id. Mai.
a.d. XVII Kal. Mai.	15	Id. Mai.
a.d. XVI Kal. Mai.	16	a.d. XVII Kal. Iun.

a.d. XV Kal. Mai.	17	a.d. XVI Kal. Iun.
a.d. XII Kal. Mai.	20	a.d. XIII Kal. Iun.
a.d. VII Kal. Mai.	25	a.d. VIII Kal. Iun.
prid. Kal. Mai.	30	a.d. III Kal. Iun.
—	31	prid. Kal. Iun.

YEARS

A year is denoted either by giving the names of the consuls or by reckoning the number of years from the traditional date of the foundation of Rome, 753 B.C. (A date B.C. should be subtracted from 754, a date A.D. should be added to 753.)

E.g. "In the year 218 B.C.," *either* P. Cornelio Scipione Ti. Sempronio Longo coss. *or* a. u. c. DXXXVI.

MEASURES

Length

12 ūnciae = 1 pēs
5 pedēs = 1 passus
125 passūs = 1 stadium
8 stadia = mīlle passūs

The Roman mile was about 1.48 km.

Area

100 pedēs quadrātī = 1 scrīpulum
144 scrīpula = 1 āctus quadrātus
2 āctūs quadrātī = 1 iugerum
2 iugera = 1 hērēdium
100 hērēdia = 1 centuria

The **iugerum** was about 2529.28 square metres.

Capacity

	4 cochleāria	= 1 cyathus
	12 cyathī	= 1 sextārius
(liquid)	6 sextāriī	= 1 congius
	8 congiī	= 1 amphora
	20 amphorae	= 1 culleus
(dry)	8 sextāriī	= 1 sēmodius
	2 sēmodiī	= 1 modius

The **sextārius** was about half a litre, the **modius** about 9 litres.

Weight

4 scrīpula = 1 sextula
6 sextulae = 1 ūncia
12 ūnciae = 1 lībra

The Roman lb. was about 326 gr, and the **ūncia** was therefore about 27 gr. The twelfths of the **lībra** have the following names, which are also used to denote fractions generally, *e.g.* **hērēs ex triente**, heir to a third of an estate.

¹⁄₁₂ ūncia	⁵⁄₁₂ quīncūnx	¾ dōdrāns
⅙ sextāns	½ sēmis	⅚ dextāns
¼ quadrāns	⁷⁄₁₂ septūnx	¹¹⁄₁₂ deūnx
⅓ triēns	⅔ bēs	

MONEY

Roman

2½	assēs	= 1 sēstertius (*or* nummus)
4	sēstertii	= 1 dēnārius
25	dēnāriī	= 1 aureus

The sesterce is represented by a symbol for 2½, properly **II S(ēmis)**, usually standardized in the form HS. The *ntpl* **sēstertia** with the distributive numeral denotes thousands of sesterces, and the numeral adverb with the *gen pl* **sēstertium** (understanding **centēna milia**) means hundred thousands, *e.g.*

10,000	sesterces	= dēna sēstertia	= HS X̄
1,000,000	"	= deciēs sēstertium	= HS IX̄I

Greek

100 drachumae	= 1 mina
60 minae	= 1 talentum

LATIN VERSE

QUANTITY

Both vowels and syllables in Latin may be described as long or short. A long vowel or syllable is one on which the voice dwells for a longer time than on a short one, in much the same way as a minim is long compared with a crotchet in musical notation.

A syllable is long if the vowel in it is either long in itself or followed by two or more consonants. The letter **x** counts as a double consonant, the letter **h** not at all, and the following pairs of consonants occurring in the same word after a short vowel do not necessarily make the syllable long:

br, cr, dr, fr, gr, pr, tr; fl, gl, pl.

A syllable is short if its vowel is a short one and not followed by two or more consonants (except for the groups noted in the preceding paragraph).

Examples: In **dūcō** both the vowels are long ("by nature") and therefore the two syllables are long.

In **deus** both the vowels are short, neither is followed by more than one consonant, and therefore the two syllables are short; but if a word beginning with a consonant follows, then the syllable **-us** will become long.

In **adsunt** both the vowels are short, but they are both followed by two consonants, and the two syllables are therefore "long by position".

This long or short characteristic of Latin vowels and syllables is called "quantity." To determine the quantities of vowels no general rules can be given, and some of them are now not known for certain. The vowel quantities of words will have to be learned when the words are learned, or else looked up when the need arises. In final syllables, however, there is a certain regularity to be found, and the following table shows the commonest of these:

ENDING

	Long	Short
-a	*1st decl abl sing* *1st conj impv sing* *numerals and most adverbs*	*1st decl nom and voc sing* *all nom and acc ntpl* **ita, quia**
-e	*5th decl abl sing* *2nd conj impv sing* *most adverbs* *Greek nouns*	*all other noun and verb endings* **bene, male** *enclitics*

-i	*all endings, except*	**quasi, nisi:** *and sometimes* **mihi, tibi, sibi, ibi, ubi**
-o	*all endings, except*	*sometimes iambic words, esp* **cito, duo, ego, homo, modo, puto, rogo, scio**
-u	*all endings*	
-as	*all endings, except*	*Greek nouns*
-es	*all endings, except*	*3rd decl nom sing with short* **-e-** *in stem* **es** (be) *and compounds* **penes**
-is	*1st and 2nd decl dat and abl pl* *3rd decl acc pl* *4th conj 2nd pers sing* **vīs, sīs, velīs**	*all others*
-os	*all endings, except*	*2nd decl nom sing* **os** (bone) **compos, impos**
-us	*3rd decl nom sing with long* **-u-** *in stem* *4th decl gen sing and nom and acc pl*	*all others*

METRES

Latin Verse is a pattern of long and short syllables, grouped together in "feet" or in lyric lines.

FEET

The commonest Feet employed in Latin metres are:

Anapaest	(short—short—long)	⌣ ⌣ —
Dactyl	(long—short—short)	— ⌣ ⌣
Iambus	(short—long)	⌣ —
Proceleusmatic	(short—short—short—short)	⌣ ⌣ ⌣ ⌣
Spondee	(long—long)	— —
Tribrach	(short—short—short)	⌣ ⌣ ⌣
Trochee	(long—short)	— ⌣

CAESURA AND DIAERESIS

The longer lines usually have a regular break near the middle, occurring either in the middle of a foot (**Caesura**) or at the end of a foot (**Diaeresis**). This break need not imply a pause in the sense of the words, but merely the end of a word, provided that it does not go too closely with the word following, as in the case of a preposition before a noun. See examples on pages 4–9 where the caesura is marked †, and the diaeresis //.

ELISION

A vowel or a vowel followed by **m** at the end of a word ("open vowel") is regularly elided before a vowel at the beginning of the next word in the same line. In reciting, the elided syllable should not be dropped entirely, but slurred into the following vowel. An open vowel at the end of a line does not elide before a vowel at the beginning of the next line.

FINAL SYLLABLES

Where the metre requires the final syllable in a line to be long, this syllable may in fact be a short one. This position in the line is commonly called a **syllaba anceps**, and marked down as being either long or short. It is perhaps better to regard this syllable, when the vowel is short, as long by position, since metrical length is a matter of duration, and the end of a line calls naturally for a slight pause in reading, even if the sense runs on to the next line. In the metrical schemes which follow, a long final syllable should be understood in this sense: it may in itself be a short one.

Latin metres fall into three fairly distinct categories, associated with three different genres of verse: 1. *Dactylic*
2. *Iambic and Trochaic*
3. *Lyric*

DACTYLIC VERSE

The Dactylic metres are the **Hexameter** and the **Pentameter**. The Hexameter is the medium of epic, didactic and pastoral poetry, of satires and epistles, and other examples of occasional verse. In conjunction with the Pentameter it forms the **Elegiac Couplet**, the metre most commonly used for love poetry, occasional pieces, and the epigram.

Dactylic Hexameter

The first four feet may be either **dactyls** or **spondees**, the 5th is regularly a dactyl, the 6th always a spondee. In Virgil and later poets the last word is either disyllabic or trisyllabic. A **Caesura** normally occurs in either the 3rd or the 4th foot, and pastoral poetry often has the "Bucolic Diaeresis" at the end of the 4th foot. In Virgilian and later usage there is a tendency for words and feet to overlap in the first four feet and to coincide in the last two. Similarly in the first part of the line the metrical ictus and the normal accent of the spoken word tend to fall on different syllables, whereas they regularly coincide in the last two feet.

Example:

Clāss(em) āp|teñt tăcĭ|tĭ⁺ sŏcĭ|ōsqu(e) ād | lītŏră| tōrquēnt

(*Virgil, Aen.* 4, 289)

Occasional lines will be found in the poets, which deliberately violate the above rules for the sake of obtaining some special effect,

pēr cō|nūbĭă| nōstrā,⁺ pĕr| īncēp|tōs hўmĕ|nāeōs

(*Aen.* 4, 316)

The above echoes Greek hexameter, where the final word is Greek and has four syllables, and the caesura comes between the two short syllables of the dactyl in the 3rd foot:

cūm sŏcĭ|īs nā|tōquĕ⁺ pĕ|nātĭbŭs| ēt māg|nīs dīs

(*Aen.* 3, 12)

Note the solemn, archaic touch, suggesting a line of Ennius, where the 5th foot is a spondee, and the last word is monosyllabic.

pāŕtŭrĭ|ent̄ mōn|tēs,† nā|scētūr| rĭdĭcŭ|lŭs mūs

(Hor, A. P. 139)

The monosyllabic ending, above, creates a comic effect.

Dactylic Pentameter

This line has two equal parts of 2½ feet each. The two feet in the first part may be either **dactyls** or **spondees**, those in the second part are always dactylic. The two half-feet are long (though the final syllable may be a short one), and there is always a diaeresis between the two parts of the line. In Ovid and later poets the last word in the line is regularly disyllabic.

Example:

Aēnē|ān ănĭ|mō // nōxqŭe dĭ|ēsqŭe rĕ|fērt

(Ovid, Her. 7, 26)

SCANSION

The following procedure may assist beginners to scan a normal hexameter or pentameter correctly:—

1. Mark off elisions.
2. Mark the first syllable long, and (Hexameter) the last five dactyl and spondee, or (Pentameter) the last seven syllables, two dactyls and a long syllable.
3. Mark all diphthongs long.
4. Mark all syllables that are long by position, omitting any doubtful cases.
5. Mark any other syllables known to be long.
6. Mark any syllables known to be short.
7. Fill in the few (if any) remaining syllables, and identify the principal caesura.
8. Read the line aloud.

IAMBIC AND TROCHAIC VERSE

The Iambic and Trochaic metres occur mainly in dramatic verse, but some are found elsewhere, as in the lyrics of Catullus and Horace. The principal Iambic metres are the **Senarius**, the **Septenarius**, and the **Octonarius**; the principal Trochaic metres are the Septenarius and Octonarius.

Iambic Senarius

Basically this line consists of six iambic feet, but in practice such a line is very rare.

Example:

Phăsēl|lŭs ĭl|lĕ quĕm| vĭ dē|tĭs, hōs|pĭ tēs

(*Cat.* 4, 1)

In drama the last foot is always iambic, and the 5th regularly a spondee. The **spondee** is also very common in the first four feet, the **dactyl** and the **tribrach** are frequent, occasionally the **anapaest** is found, and, more rarely, the **proceleusmatic**. There is usually a **caesura** in either the third or the fourth foot.

Example:

Ĭn hāc| hă bĭ tās|sĕ plă tē|ā dĭc|tūmst Chrȳ|sĭdēm

(*Ter, And.* 796)

Iambic Septenarius

This line consists of seven and a half feet, basically iambic, but allowing the same variations as in the Senarius. The 4th foot is regularly an Iambus, and is usually followed by a diaeresis: this is an aid to identifying the line.

Example:

N(am) ĭdcĭr|c(o) āccēr|sōr nūp|tĭ ās| quōd m(i) ād|pără|rī sēn|sĭt

(*Ter, And.* 690)

Iambic Octonarius

This line has eight iambic feet, with the same variations as in the other iambic lines. The 4th and 8th feet are regularly iambic, and a diaeresis follows the 4th foot.

Example:

Cūrā|bĭ tūr.| sēd pă tĕr| ă dēst.| că vĕt(e) ēs|sĕ trĭs|tēm sēn|tĭ ăt

(*Ter, And.* 403)

Trochaic Septenarius

Apart from drama, this line is common in popular verses, and comes into its own in later Latin poetry. It consists of seven and a half **trochees**, but in practice only the seventh foot is regularly trochaic, while the others may be **spondee, dactyl, tribrach,** or (more rarely) **anapaest**. There is usually a **diaeresis** after the 4th foot.

Example:

Crās ă|mēt quī| nūnqu(am) ă|māvĭt,| quĭqu(e) ă| māvĭt| crās ă|mēt

(*Pervigilium Veneris*)

Trochaic Octonarius

This is a line of eight trochees, allowing the same variations as above. There is a diaeresis after the 4th foot.

Example:

Prōin tū| sōllĭ cĭ|tūdĭn|(em) īstām| fālsām| quāe t(e) ēx|crŭcĭăt| mīttās

(*Ter, Heaut.* 177)

LYRIC VERSE

In most lyric metres the line is not to be subdivided into feet, but is itself the unit of scansion, and has a fixed number of syllables. The commonest, which are those used by Catullus and Horace, are the **Hendecasyllabic**, the **Asclepiads**, the **Glyconic** and the **Pherecratic**, which occur either singly or in combinations to form either couplets or stanzas of four lines. Beside these groupings there are the **Alcaic** and **Sapphic** stanzas. Elisions occur much more rarely than in the other metres.

Hendecasyllabic

This is Catullus's favourite line. It consists of eleven syllables in the following pattern:

‒ ‒ ‒ ˘˘ ‒ ˘ ‒ ˘ ‒ ‒

Either the first or the second syllable may occasionally be short, and there is usually a caesura after the 5th syllable.

Example:

Vīvāmūs, mĕă Lēsbĭ(a), ātqu(e) ămēmūs

(*Cat.* 5, 1)

Asclepiads

There are two Asclepiad lines, of which the **Lesser** is by far the commoner. It has twelve syllables, in the following pattern with a caesura after the 6th syllable:

$$- - - \smile \smile - - \smile \smile - \smile -$$

Māecēnās, ătăvīs† ēdĭtĕ rēgĭbūs

(Hor, Od. I, 1, 1)

The **Greater Asclepiad** is formed by adding a **choriambus** $- \smile \smile -$ after the 6th syllable with a **diaeresis** both before and after it.

Example:

Nūllām, Vārĕ, săcrā vītĕ prĭūs sēvĕrĭs ārbŏrēm

(Hor. Od. I, 18, 1)

Glyconic

The **Glyconic** occurs by itself in Catullus, but more usually it is found in combination with the **Lesser Asclepiad** or the **Pherecratic**. It consists of eight syllables ($- - - \smile \smile - \smile -$), so that it is like a Lesser Asclepiad minus the **choriambus**. It has no regular caesura.

Example:

Dōnēc grātŭs ĕrām tĭbī

(Hor. Od. III, 9, 1)

Pherecratic

The **Pherecratic** is a Glyconic minus the second last (short) syllable. It is found only in combination with other lines.

Example:

Sūspēndīssĕ pŏtēntī

(Hor, Od. I, 5, 11)

Alcaic Stanza

The **Alcaic stanza** has four lines, of which the first two have the same pattern
⏑ ‒ ⏑ ‒ ‒ ⏑ ⏑ ‒ ⏑ ‒. In these there is a regular **caesura** after the 5th syllable. The
third line is ⏑ ‒ ⏑ ‒ ‒ ‒ ⏑ ‒ ‒ and the 4th ‒ ⏑ ⏑ ‒ ⏑ ⏑ ‒ ⏑ ‒ ‒. Neither of the last two
lines has a regular break in it.

Example:

Nūnc ēst bǐbēndūm,[†] nūnc pědě lǐběrō
pūlsāndā tēllūs,[†] nūnc Sǎlǐārǐbūs
ōrnārě pūlvīnār děōrūm
tēmpǔs ěrāt dǎpǐbūs, sǒdālēs.

(Hor, Od. I. 37, 1-4)

Sapphic Stanza

The **Sapphic stanza** also has four lines, of which the first three are the same:
‒ ⏑ ‒ ⏑ ‒ ⏑ ⏑ ‒ ⏑ ‒ ‒. As in the Alcaic there is a **caesura** after the 5th syllable. The
last line is a short **Adonic** ‒ ⏑ ⏑ ‒ ‒

Example:

Īntěgēr vītae[†] scělěrīsquě pūrūs
nōn ěgēt Māurīs[†] iǎcǔlīs něqu(e) ārcū
nēc věnēnātīs[†] grǎvǐdā sǎgǐttīs,
Fūscě, phǎrētrā.

(Hor, Od. I. 22, 1-4)

LATIN PHRASES USED IN ENGLISH

What follows is a list of some of the Latin phrases used in English today.

ab initio	from the beginning.
ab ovo	(lit: from the egg) from the beginning.
absit omen	(lit: may the (evil) omen be absent) may the presentiment not become real or take place.
ab urbe condita	(used in dates) from the foundation of the city (*i.e. from the foundation of Rome in 753 B.C.*).
A.D.	abbr for **anno Domini**.
ad hoc	(lit: for this) for a particular purpose only: **an ad hoc committee; an ad hoc decision.**
ad hominem	(lit: according to the person) **1** directed against a person rather than against his or her arguments. **2** based on or appealing to emotion rather than reason.
ad infinitum	without end; endlessly; to infinity.
ad interim	for the meantime; for the present: **ad interim measures.**
ad-lib	(abbr for **ad libitum**) ♦ *adj* improvised; impromptu ♦ *adv* without restraint; freely; as one pleases ♦ *vb* to improvise and deliver without preparation.
ad libitum	(lit: according to pleasure) as one pleases.
ad majorem Dei gloriam	for the greater glory of God (*the Jesuit motto*).
ad nauseam	(lit: to (the point of) nausea) to a disgusting extent.
ad rem	(lit: to the matter) to the point; without digression: **to reply ad rem; an ad rem discussion.**
advocatus diaboli	devil's advocate.
ad valorem	(lit: according to value) in proportion to the estimated value of the goods taxed.
aet.	(abbr for **aetatis**) at the age of.
Agnus Dei	Lamb of God.
alma mater	(lit: nurturing mother) one's former university, college or school.
alter ego	(lit: other self) **1** a second self. **2** a very close and intimate friend.
a.m.	abbr for **ante meridiem**.
AMDG	abbr for **ad majorem Dei gloriam**.
amor patriae	love of one's country; patriotism.
an.	(abbr for **anno**) in the year.
anno Domini	in the year of our Lord.
anno urbis conditae	in the year of the foundation of the city (*i.e. of Rome in 753 B.C., used in dates*)
anno regni	in the year of the reign (of).

annus mirabilis	(lit: wonderful year) a year of wonders.
antebellum	(lit: before the war) of or during the period before a war, especially the American Civil War.
ante meridiem	before noon.
ante-mortem	before death (*esp in legal or medical contexts*).
a.p.	(abbr for **ante prandium**) before a meal (*in prescriptions*).
apparatus criticus	(lit: critical apparatus) textual notes (*list of variant readings, etc., relating to a document, especially in a scholarly edition of a text*).
aq.	abbr for **aqua**.
aqua vitae	(lit: water of life) brandy.
a.r.	abbr for **anno regni**.
arbiter elegantiae *or* **elegantiarum**	judge in a matter of taste.
arcus senilis	(lit: senile bow) opaque circle around the cornea of th eye (*often seen in elderly people*).
argumentum ad hominem	(lit: argument according to the person: Logic) **1** fallacious argument that attacks not an opponent's beliefs but his motives or character. **2** argument that shows an opponent's statement to be inconsistent wit his other beliefs.
ars longa vita brevis	art is long, life is short.
AUC	abbr for: **1 ab urbe condita. 2 anno urbis conditae.**
aut vincere aut mori	death or victory.
aurora australis	the southern lights.
aurora borealis	the northern lights.
ave	**1** hail! **2** farewell!
ave atque vale	hail and farewell!
Ave Maria	Hail Mary.
beatae memoriae	of blessed memory.
Beata Virgo	the Blessed Virgin.
Beata Virgo Maria	the Blessed Virgin Mary.
b.i.d	(abbr for **bis in die**) twice a day (*in prescriptions*).
bis dat, qui cito dat	the person who gives promptly gives twice.
BV	abbr for **Beata Virgo**.
c, ca	abbr for **circa**.
camera obscura	(lit: dark chamber) camera obscura.
carpe diem	(lit: seize the day) enjoy the pleasures of the moment, without concern for the future.
casus belli	(lit: occasion of war) **1** an event or act used to justify a war. **2** the immediate cause of a quarrel.
caveat emptor	let the buyer beware.
cetera desunt	the rest is missing.

ceteris paribus	other things being equal.
circa	around.
Codex Juris Canonici	(lit: book of canon law) the official code of canon law (*in the Roman Catholic Church*).
cogito, ergo sum	I think, therefore I am (*the basis of Descartes' philosophy*).
compos mentis	of sound mind; sane.
coram populo	in the presence of the people; openly.
corpus delicti	(lit: the body of the crime: LAW) the body of facts that constitute an offence.
Corpus Juris Canonici	(lit: body of canon law) the official compilation of canon law (*in the Roman Catholic Church*).
Corpus Juris Civilis	(lit: body of civil law) the body of Roman or civil law.
corrigenda	things to be corrected.
corpus vile	(lit: worthless body) person or thing fit only to be the object of an experiment.
culpa	1 (*LAW*) an act of neglect. 2 (*gen*) a fault; sin; guilt.
cum grano salis	with a grain of salt; not too literally.
cum laude	(*chiefly US*) with praise (*the lowest of three designations for above-average achievement in examinations*).
curriculum vitae	(lit: the course of one's life) curriculum vitae.
de facto	*adv* in fact ♦ *adj* existing in fact.
de gustibus non est disputandum	there is no arguing about tastes.
de jure	according to law; by right; legally.
de mortuis nil nisi bonum	say nothing but good of the dead.
de novo	anew.
Deo gratias	thanks be to God.
Deo Optimo Maximo	to God, the best, the Greatest.
Deo volente	God willing.
de profundis	out of the depths of misery or dejection.
deus ex machina	(lit: the god from the machine) 1 (*in ancient Greek and Roman drama*) a god introduced into a play to resolve the plot. 2 any unlikely or artificial device serving this purpose.
Dies Irae	(lit: the day of wrath) 1 a famous Latin hymn of the 13th century, describing the Last Judgment. It is used in the Mass for the dead. 2 a musical setting of this hymn, usually part of a setting of the Requiem.
disjecta membra	the scattered remains.
DOM	abbr for **Deo Optimo Maximo**.
dramatis personae	(lit: the persons of the drama) the list of characters in a drama.

Ecce Homo	behold the man (*the words of Pontius Pilate to Christ's accusers* [*John 19:5*]).
editio princeps	(lit: the first edition) the first printed edition of a work
e.g., eg	abbr for **exempli gratia**.
emeritus	retired from office.
e pluribus unum	one out of many (*motto of USA*).
ER	1 (abbr for **Elizabeth Regina**) Queen Elizabeth; 2 (abbr for **Eduardus Rex**) King Edward.
errare est humanum	to err is human.
erratum (*pl* **errata**)	error.
et seq.	(abbr for **et sequens**) and the following.
et seqq.	(abbr for **et sequentia**) and those that follow.
ex	(lit: out of, from) 1 (*FINANCE*) not participating in; excluding; without: **ex bonus; ex dividend; ex rights**. 2 (*COMMERCE*) without charge to the buyer until removed from: **ex quay; ex ship; ex works**.
ex cathedra	(lit: from the chair) 1 with authority. 2 defined by the pope as infallibly true, to be accepted by all Roman Catholics.
exeat	(lit: let him or her go out) formal leave of absence.
exempli gratia	for example.
exeunt	they go out (*used as a stage direction*).
exeunt omnes	they all go out (*used as a stage direction*).
exit	he or she goes out (*used as a stage direction*).
ex libris	(lit: from the books (of)) from the collection or library of.
ex officio	by right of position or office.
ex parte	(*LAW*) on behalf of one side or party only (*of an application in a judicial proceeding*): **an ex parte injunction**.
ex post facto	having retrospective effect: **an ex post facto law**.
ex silentio	(lit: from silence) based on a lack of evidence to the contrary (*of a theory, assumption etc*).
extempore	(lit: instantaneously) without planning or preparation; impromptu.
ex voto	*adv, adj* in accordance with a vow ♦ *n* offering made in fulfilment of a vow.
facile princeps	(lit: easily first) an obvious leader.
fecit (*abbr* **fec**)	(he or she) made it (*used formerly on works of art next to the artist's name*).
felo de se	suicide.
festina lente	more haste, less speed.
fiat lux	let there be light.
Fidei Defensor	defender of the faith.

...dus Achates	(lit: faithful Achates) faithful friend or companion (*the name of the faithful companion of Aeneas in Virgil's Aeneid*).
...oruit	(he or she) flourished (*used to indicate the period when a historical figure, whose birth and death dates are unknown, was most active*).
...ns et origo	the source and origin.
...enius loci	(lit: genius of the place) 1 the guardian spirit of a place. 2 the special atmosphere of a particular place.
...loria in Excelsis Deo	(lit: glory to God in the highest) 1 the Greater Doxology, beginning in Latin with these words. 2 a musical setting of this.
...loria Patri	(lit: glory to the father) 1 the Lesser Doxology, beginning in Latin with these words. 2 a musical setting of this.
...inc illae lacrimae	hence those tears.
...J	(abbr for **hic jacet**) here lies (*on gravestones*).
...JS	(abbr for **hic jacet sepultus**) here lies buried (*on gravestones*).
...orrible dictu	horrible to relate.
...id.	abbr for **ibidem**.
...idem	in the same place (*in annotations, bibliographies, etc., when referring to a book, article, chapter, or page previously cited*).
...d est	that is (to say); in other words.
...dem	the same (*used to refer to an article, chapter, etc., previously cited*).
...e.	abbr for **id est**.
...gn.	abbr for **ignotus**.
...gnoratio elenchi	(lit: an ignorance of proof: *Logic*) 1 a purported refutation of a proposition that does not in fact prove it false but merely establishes a related but strictly irrelevant proposition. 2 the fallacy of arguing in this way.
...gnotum per ignotius	(lit: the unknown by means of the more unknown) an explanation that is obscurer than the thing to be explained.
...gnotus	unknown.
...gnis fatuus	will o' the wisp.
...mp.	1 (abbr for **Imperator**) Emperor; 2 (abbr for **Imperatrix**) Empress.
...n absentia	in one's absence; in the absence of: **he was condemned in absentia.**
...n aeternum	forever; eternally.
...n articulo mortis	at the point of death.

in camera	(lit: in the chamber) in private.
in extenso	at full length.
in extremis	(lit: in the furthest reaches) **1** in extremity; in dire straits. **2** at the point of death.
infra	below.
infra dig	(abbr for **infra dignitatem**) beneath one's dignity.
in loco parentis	in place of a parent (*said of a person acting in a parental capacity*).
in medias res	(lit: into the midst of things) in or into the middle of events or a narrative.
in memoriam	in memory of; as a memorial to (*used in obituaries, epitaphs etc*).
in perpetuum	for ever.
in personam	(lit: against the person) directed against a specific person or persons (*LAW: of a judicial act*).
in propria persona	in person; personally.
in rem	(lit: against the matter) directed against property rather than against specific person (*LAW: of a judicial act*).
in rerum natura	in the nature of things.
INRI	(lit: Jesus of Nazareth, King of the Jews) abbr for **Iesu Nazarenus Rex Iudaeorum** (*the inscription placed over Christ's head during the Crucifixion*).
in situ	(lit: in position) in the natural, original, or appropriate position.
inter alia	among other things.
inter alios	among other people.
inter vivos	(*LAW*) between living people: **an inter vivos gift**.
in toto	totally; entirely; completely.
in utero	within the womb.
in vacuo	in a vacuum.
in vino veritas	in wine there is truth.
in vitro	(lit: in glass) made to occur outside the body of the organism in an artificial environment (*of biological processes or reactions*): **in vitro fertilization**.
in vivo	(lit: in a living (thing)) occurring or carried out in the living organism (*of biological processes or experiments*).
ipse dixit	(lit: he himself said it) an arbitrary and unsupported assertion.
ipsissima verba	the very words.
ipso facto	by the fact itself.
i.q.	(lit: the same as) abbr for **idem quod**.
lapsus linguae	a slip of the tongue.
lc	(abbr for **(in) loco citato**) in the place cited.

ex loci	the law of the place.
ex non scripta	the unwritten law; common law.
ex scripta	the written law; statute law.
ex talionis	the law of revenge or retaliation.
loc. cit.	(abbr for **(in) loco citato**) in the place cited (*in textual annotation*).
magna cum laude	(chiefly US) with great praise (*the second of three designations for above-average achievement in examinations*).
magnum opus	a great work of art or literature (*especially the greatest single work of an artist*).
mala fide	undertaken in bad faith.
mare clausum	(lit: closed sea: LAW) a sea coming under the jurisdiction of one nation and closed to all others.
mare liberum	(lit: free sea: LAW) a sea open to navigation by shipping of all nations.
mare nostrum	(lit: our sea) the Mediterranean.
mater	mother (*often used facetiously*).
mater dolorosa	(lit: sorrowful mother) the Virgin Mary sorrowing for the dead Christ (*especially as depicted in art*).
materfamilias	(lit: mother of family) the mother of a family or the female head of a family.
materia medica	(lit: medical matter) **1** the branch of medical science concerned with the study of drugs used in the treatment of disease. **2** the drugs used in the treatment of disease.
mea culpa	(lit: my fault) an acknowledgement of guilt.
memento mori	(lit: remember you must die) an object, such as a skull, intended to remind people of the inevitability of death.
mens sana in corpore sano	a healthy mind in a healthy body.
mens rea	(lit: guilty mind: LAW) a criminal intention or knowledge that an act is wrong.
miles gloriosus	a braggart soldier (*especially as a stock figure in comedy*).
mirabile dictu	wonderful to relate.
mittimus	(lit: we send) a warrant of commitment to prison or a command to a jailer directing him to hold someone in prison.
modus operandi	procedure; method of operating; manner of working.
modus ponens	(lit: mood that affirms) the principle that whenever a conditional statement and its antecedent are given to be true its consequent may be validly inferred.

modus tollens	(lit: mood that denies) the principle that whenever a conditional statement and the negation of its consequent are given to be true, the negation of its antecedent may be validly inferred.
modus vivendi	(lit: way of living) a working arrangement between conflicting interests; practical compromise.
motu proprio	(lit: of his own accord) an administrative papal bull.
multum in parvo	much in a small space.
mutatis mutandis	with the necessary changes.
NB, N.B., nb, n.b.	(abbr for **nota bene**) note well.
nem. con.	(abbr for **nemine contradicente**) no-one contradicting; unanimously.
nemo me impune lacessit	no-one provokes me with impunity.
ne plus ultra	(lit: not more beyond) the extreme or perfect point or state.
nihil	nil; nothing.
nihil obstat	there is no obstacle.
nil desperandum	(lit: nothing to be despaired of) never despair.
nisi prius	(lit: unless previously) 1 *in England* (a) a direction that a case be brought up to Westminster for trial before a single judge and jury. (b) the writ giving this direction 2 *in the US* a court where civil actions are tried by a single judge sitting with a jury as distinguished from an appellate court.
nolens volens	whether willing or unwilling.
noli me tangere	(lit: do not touch me) a warning against interfering with or against touching a person or thing.
nolle prosequi	(lit: do not pursue) an entry made on the court record when the plaintiff in a civil suit or prosecutor in a criminal prosecution undertakes not to continue the action or prosecution.
nolo contendere	(lit: I do not wish to contend) a plea made by a defendant to a criminal charge having the same effect in those proceedings as a plea of guilty but not precluding him from denying the charge in a subsequent action.
non compos mentis	(lit: not in control of one's mind) mentally incapable of managing one's own affairs; of unsound mind; insane.
non prosequitur	(lit: he does not proceed) a judgment in favour of a defendant when the plaintiff failed to take the necessary steps in an action within the time allowed.
non sequitur	(lit: it does not follow) 1 (*gen*) a statement having little or no relevance to what preceded it. 2 (*Logic*) a conclusion that does not follow from the premises.
nulli secundus	second to none.

numen	(lit: divine power) **1** (*especially in ancient Roman religion*) a deity or spirit presiding over a thing or place. **2** a guiding principle, force, or spirit.
Nunc Dimittis	(lit: now let depart) **1** the Canticle of Simeon (*Luke 2:29-32*). **2** a musical setting of this.
ob.	**1** abbr for **obiit**. **2** (abbr for **obiter**) incidentally; in passing.
obiit	he or she died (*on gravestones*).
obiter dictum	(lit: something said in passing) **1** (*LAW*) an observation by a judge on some point of law not directly in issue in the case before him and thus neither requiring his decision nor serving as a precedent, but nevertheless of persuasive authority. **2** any comment, remark, or observation made in passing.
obscurum per obscurius	(lit: the obscure by means of the more obscure) an explanation that is obscurer than the thing to be explained.
omnium-gatherum	(*often facetious*) a miscellaneous collection; assortment.
onus probandi	(*LAW*) the burden of proof.
op. cit.	(abbr of **opere citato**) in the work cited.
opus anglicanum	(lit: English work) fine embroidery (*especially of church vestments*).
ora pro nobis	pray for us.
O tempora! O mores!	oh the times! oh the customs!
p.a.	abbr of **per annum**.
pace	by leave of; with due deference to (*used to acknowledge politely someone who disagrees with the speaker or writer*).
pari passu	with equal speed or progress; equably (*often used to refer to the right of creditors to receive assets from the same source without one taking precedence*).
passim	here and there; throughout (*used to indicate that what is referred to occurs frequently in the work cited*).
paterfamilias	(lit: father of the family) **1** the male head of a household. **2** the head of a household having authority over its members.
pax vobiscum	peace be with you.
peccavi	(lit: I have sinned) a confession of guilt.
peculium	(lit: property) property that a father or master allowed his child or slave to hold as his own.
per annum	every year; year by year.
per ardua ad astra	through difficulties to the stars (*motto of the RAF*).
per capita	(lit: according to heads) of or for each person.
per contra	on the contrary.

per diem	(lit: for the day) **1** every day; by the day. **2** an allowance for daily expenses, usually those incurred while working.
per mensem	every month; by the month.
per pro	(abbr for **per procurationem**) by delegation to; through the agency of (*used when signing documents on behalf of someone else*).
persona grata	an acceptable person (*especially a diplomat acceptable to the government of the country to which he is sent*).
persona non grata	unacceptable or unwelcome person.
petitio principii	(lit: an assumption at the beginning: *Logic*) a form of fallacious reasoning in which the conclusion has been assumed in the premises; begging the question.
pia mater	(lit: pious mother) the innermost of the three membranes that cover the brain and spinal cord.
pinxit	(he or she) painted this (*used formerly on works of art next to the artist's name*).
p.m., P.M., pm, PM	abbr. for **1** post meridiem **2** postmortem.
post-bellum	(lit: after war) of or during the period after a war, especially the American Civil War.
post hoc	(lit: after this: *Logic*) the fallacy of assuming that temporal succession is evidence of causal relation.
post hoc, ergo propter hoc	after this, therefore because of this (*a fallacy of reasoning*).
post meridiem	after noon.
postmortem	(lit: after death) *n* **1** dissection and examination of a dead body to determine the cause of death. **2** analysis or study of a recently completed event ♦ *adj* occurring after death.
pp	abbr for **1** per pro. **2** post prandium after a meal (*in prescriptions*).
PPS	(lit: after postscript; abbr for **post postscriptum**) additional postscript.
pr	(abbr for: **per rectum**) through the rectum (*in prescriptions*).
prima facie	at a first view.
primum mobile	(lit: first moving (thing)) prime mover.
primus inter pares	first among equals.
prn	(abbr for **pro re nata**) as the situation demands, as needed (*in prescriptions*).
pro forma	(lit: for form's sake) **1** prescribing a set form or procedure. **2** performed in a set manner.
pro patria	for one's country.
pro rata	in proportion.
pro tempore	for the time being.
proxime accessit	(lit: he or she came next) the runner-up.

q.e.	(abbr for **quod est**) which is.
QED	abbr for **quod erat demonstrandum**.
QEF	abbr for **quod erat faciendum**.
quid pro quo	(lit: something for something) **1** a reciprocal exchange. **2** something given in compensation, especially an advantage or object given in exchange for another.
quis custodiet ipsos custodes?	who will guard the guards?
q.l.	(abbr for **quantum libet**) as much as you please (*in prescriptions*).
qm	(abbr for **quaque mane**) every morning (*in prescriptions*).
qn	(abbr for **quaque nocte**) every night (*in prescriptions*).
quod erat demonstrandum	which was to be proved.
quod erat faciendum	which was to be done.
quot homines, tot sententiæ	there are as many opinions as there are people.
quo vadis?	whither goest thou?
qqv	(abbr for **quae vide**) which (*words, items etc*) see (*denoting a cross reference to more than one item*).
qs	(abbr for **quantum sufficit**) as much as will suffice (*in prescriptions*).
qv	(abbr for **quod vide**) which (word, item etc) see (*denoting a cross reference*).
rara avis	(lit: rare bird) an unusual, uncommon or exceptional person or thing.
reductio ad absurdum	(lit: reduction to the absurd) **1** a method of disproving a proposition by showing that its inevitable consequences would be absurd. **2** a method of indirectly proving a proposition by assuming its negation to be true and showing that this leads to an absurdity. **3** application of a principle or a proposed principle to an instance in which it is absurd.
requiescat	(lit: may he or she rest) a prayer for the repose of the souls of the dead.
requiescat in pace	may he or she rest in peace.
res gestae	(lit: things done) **1** things done or accomplished; achievements. **2** (*LAW*) incidental facts and circumstances that are admissible in evidence because they introduce or explain the matter in issue.
res ipsa loquitur	(*LAW*) the thing or matter speaks for itself.
res judicata	(*LAW*) a matter already adjudicated upon that cannot be raised again.
res publica	(lit: the public thing) the state, republic, or commonwealth.

resurgam	I shall rise again.
RI	1 (abbr for **Regina et Imperatrix**) Queen and Empress. 2 (abbr for **Rex et Imperator**) King and Emperor.
rigor mortis	(lit: rigidity of death) the stiffness of joints and muscular rigidity of a dead body.
RIP	abbr for **requiescat** or **requiescant in pace**.
risus sardonicus	(lit: sardonic laugh) fixed contraction of the facial muscles resulting in a peculiar distorted grin, caused especially by tetanus.
sanctum sanctorum	(lit: holy of holies) 1 (_Bible_) the holy of holies. 2 (_often facetious_) an especially private place.
sartor resartus	the tailor patched.
schola cantorum	(lit: school of singers) a choir or choir school maintained by a church.
scire facias	(lit: cause (him) to know) 1 (_LAW, rare_) a judicial writ founded upon some record, such as a judgement, letters patent, etc., requiring the person against whom it is brought to show cause why the record should not be enforced or annulled. 2 a proceeding begun by the issue of such a writ.
semper fidelis	always faithful.
semper idem	always the same.
seq.	(abbr for **sequens**) the following (one).
seqq.	(abbr for **sequentia**) the following (ones).
seriatim	in order.
sic	thus (_often used to call attention to some quoted mistake_).
sic itur ad astra	such is the way to the stars.
sic transit gloria mundi	so passes the glory of the world.
si monumentum requiris, circumspice	if you seek (his) monument, look around you (_inscription on the architect Sir Christopher Wren's tomb in St Paul's Cathedral_).
sine die	without a day.
sine prole	(_LAW_) without issue.
sine qua non	(lit: without which not) an indispensable condition or requirement.
sl	(abbr for **sine loco**) without place (_of publication_).
sp	abbr for **sine prole**.
spiritus asper	rough breathing.
spiritus lenis	smooth breathing.
SPQR	(abbr for **Senatus Populusque Romanus**) the Senate and People of Rome.
sq.	(abbr for **sequens**) the following (one).
sqq.	(abbr for **sequentia**) the following (ones).

Stabat Mater	(lit: the mother was standing) 1 a Latin hymn, probably of the 13th century, commemorating the sorrows of the Virgin Mary at the crucifixion and used in the Mass and various other services. 2 a musical setting of this hymn.
status quo	(lit: the state in which) the existing state of affairs.
stet	let it stand.
sub judice	before a court of law or a judge; under judicial consideration.
sub rosa	(lit: under the rose) secretly.
sub voce	under the word.
sui generis	(lit: of its own kind) unique.
sui juris	(lit: of one's own right) (*LAW*) of full age and not under disability; legally competent to manage one's own affairs; independent.
summa cum laude	(*chiefly U.S.*) with the utmost praise (*the highest of three designations for above-average achievement in examinations. In Britain it is sometimes used to designate a first-class honours degree*).
summum bonum	the principle of goodness in which all moral values are included or from which they are derived; highest or supreme good.
suo jure	(*chiefly LAW*) in one's own right.
suo loco	(*chiefly LAW*) in a person or thing's own or rightful place.
supra	above.
sursum corda	lift up your hearts (to God).
SV	abbr for **sub voce**.
tabula rasa	(lit: a scraped tablet) 1 the mind in its uninformed original state. 2 an opportunity for a fresh start; clean slate.
taedium vitae	(lit: weariness of life) the feeling that life is boring and dull.
Te Deum	(lit: Thee, God) 1 an ancient Latin hymn in rhythmic prose, sung or recited at matins in the Roman Catholic Church and in English translation at morning prayer in the Church of England and used by both churches as an expression of thanksgiving on special occasions. 2 a musical setting of this hymn. 3 a service of thanksgiving in which the recital of this hymn forms a central part.
te igitur	(lit: Thee, therefore: *Roman Catholic Church*) the first prayer of the canon of the Mass.
tempore	in the time of.
tempus fugit	time flies.
terminus ad quem	(lit: the end to which) the aim or terminal point.
terminus a quo	(lit: the end from which) the starting point; beginning.

terra firma	the solid earth; firm ground.
terra incognita	an unexplored or unknown land, region or area for study.
tertium quid	a third something.
t.i.d.	(abbr for **ter in die**) three times a day (*in prescriptions*)
tu quoque	you likewise (*a retort made by a person accused of a crime implying that the accuser is also guilty of the same crime*).
uberrima fides	utmost good faith.
ubique	everywhere.
ubi supra	where (mentioned or cited) above.
ultima Thule	(lit: the most distant Thule) **1** the utmost boundary or limit. **2** a remote goal or aim.
ultra vires	beyond one's powers.
una voce	with one voice.
urbi et orbi	(*Roman Catholic Church*) to the city and the world (*a phrase qualifying the solemn papal blessing*).
ut dict.	(abbr for **ut dictum**) as directed.
ut infra	as below.
ut supra	as above.
v.	abbr for **1 verso**. **2 versus**. **3 vide**.
vade in pace	go in peace.
vade mecum	(lit: go with me) a handbook or other aid carried on the person for immediate use when needed.
væ victis	woe to the conquered!
vale	farewell!
veni, vidi, vici	I came, I saw, I conquered.
venire facias	(lit: you must make come: *LAW*) a writ directing a sheriff to summon suitable persons to form a jury.
verbatim et litteratim	word for word and letter for letter.
verb. sap.	(abbr for **verbum sapienti sat est**) a word is enough to the wise.
verso	**1** the back of a sheet of printed paper. **2** the side of a coin opposite to the obverse; reverse.
versus	**1** against; in opposition to. **2** as opposed to; in contrast with.
via	by way of.
via media	a middle course.
vice	in the place of; instead of; as a substitute for.
vice versa	the other way round.
vide	see.
videlicet	namely; to wit.

vi et armis	(lit: by force and arms) a kind of trespass accompanied by force and violence.
VIR	(abbr for **Victoria Imperatrix Regina**) Victoria, Empress and Queen.
virginibus puerisque	for maidens and youths.
vis inertiæ	the power of inertia.
viva voce	(lit: with living voice) *adv, adj* by word of mouth ♦ *n* an oral examination.
viz.	abbr for **videlicet**.
vl	(abbr for **varia lecto**) variant reading.
vollente Deo	God willing.
vox populi	the voice of the people; popular or public opinion.
vox populi, vox Dei	the voice of the people is the voice of God.
VR	(abbr for **Victoria Regina**) Queen Queen Victoria.
VRI	(abbr for **Victoria Regina et Imperatrix**) Victoria, Queen and Empress.

English-Latin

A, a

a, an *art* not translated; (*a certain*) quīdam; **twice a day** bis in diē; **four acres a man** quaterna in singulōs iūgera.

aback *adv*: **taken ~** dēprehēnsus.

abaft *adv* in puppī ♦ *prep* post, pōne.

abandon *vt* relinquere; (*wilfully*) dērelinquere, dēserere; (*to danger*) ōbicere; (*to pleasure*) dēdere; (*plan*) abicere; **~ hope** spem abicere.

abandoned *adj* perditus.

abase *vt* dēprimere; **~ oneself** sē prōsternere.

abash *vt* perturbāre; rubōrem incutere (*dat*).

abate *vt* minuere, imminuere; (*a portion*) remittere ♦ *vi* (*fever*) dēcēdere; (*passion*) dēfervēscere; (*price*) laxāre; (*storm*) cadere.

abatement *n* remissiō *f*, dēminūtiō *f*.

abbess *n* abbātissa *f*.

abbey *n* abbātia *f*.

abbot *n* abbās *m*.

abbreviate *vt* imminuere.

abbreviation *n* (*writing*) nota *f*.

abdicate *vt* sē abdicāre (*abl*).

abdication *n* abdicātiō *f*.

abduct *vt* abripere.

abduction *n* raptus *m*.

aberration *n* error *m*.

abet *vt* adiuvāre, adesse (*dat*), favēre (*dat*).

abettor *n* adiūtor *m*, minister *m*, fautor *m*, socius *m*.

abeyance *n*: **in ~** intermissus; **be in ~** iacēre.

abhor *vt* ōdisse, invīsum habēre.

abhorrence *n* odium *nt*.

abhorrent *adj*: **~ to** aliēnus ab.

abide *vi* (*dwell*) habitāre; (*tarry*) commorārī; (*last*) dūrāre; **~ by** *vt fus* stāre (*abl*), perstāre in (*abl*).

abiding *adj* perpetuus, diūturnus.

ability *n* (*to do*) facultās *f*, potestās *f*; (*physical*) vīrēs *fpl*; (*mental*) ingenium *nt*; **to the best of my ~** prō meā parte, prō virīlī parte.

abject *adj* abiectus, contemptus; (*downcast*) dēmissus.

abjectly *adv* humiliter, dēmissē.

abjure *vt* ēiūrāre.

ablative *n* ablātīvus *m*.

ablaze *adj* flāgrāns, ardēns.

able *adj* perītus, doctus; **be ~** posse, valēre.

able-bodied *adj* rōbustus.

ablution *n* lavātiō *f*.

ably *adv* perītē, doctē.

abnegation *n* abstinentia *f*.

abnormal *adj* inūsitātus; (*excess*) immodicus.

abnormally *adv* inūsitātē, praeter mōrem.

aboard *adv* in nāvī; **go ~** nāvem cōnscendere; **put ~** impōnere.

abode *n* domicilium *nt*, sēdes *f*.

abolish *vt* tollere, ē mediō tollere, abolēre; (*law*) abrogāre.

abolition *n* dissolūtiō *f*, (*law*) abrogātiō *f*.

abominable *adj* dētestābilis, nefārius.

abominably *adv* nefāriē, foedē.

abominate *vt* dētestārī.

abomination *n* odium *nt*; (*thing*) nefas *nt*.

aboriginal *adj* prīscus.

aborigines *n* aborīginēs *mpl*.

abortion *n* abortus *m*.

abortive *adj* abortīvus; (*fig*) inritus; **be ~** ad inritum redigī.

abound *vi* abundāre, superesse; **~ in** abundāre (*abl*), adfluere (*abl*).

abounding *adj* abundāns, adfluēns; cōpiōsus ab.

about *adv* (*place*) *usu expressed by cpd verbs*; (*number*) circiter, ferē, fermē ♦ *prep* (*place*) circā, circum (*acc*); (*number*) circā, ad (*acc*); (*time*) sub (*acc*); (*concerning*) dē (*abl*); **~ to die** moritūrus; **I am ~ to go** in eō est ut eam.

above *adv* suprā; **from ~** dēsuper; **over and ~** īnsuper ♦ *prep* suprā (*acc*); (*motion*) super (*acc*); (*rest*) super (*abl*); **be ~** (*conduct*) indignārī.

abreast *adv* (*ships*) aequātīs prōrīs; **walk ~ of** latus tegere (*dat*).

abridge *vt* contrahere, compendī facere.

abridgement *n* epitomē *f*.

abroad *adv* peregrē; (*out of doors*) forīs; **be ~** peregrīnārī; **from ~** peregrē.

abrogate *vt* dissolvere; (*law*) abrogāre.

abrupt *adj* subitus, repentīnus; (*speech*) concīsus.

abscess *n* vomica *f*.

abscond *vi* aufugere.

absence *n* absentia *f*; **in my ~** mē absente; **leave of ~** commeātus *m*.

absent *adj* absēns; **be ~** abesse; **~ oneself** *vi* deesse, nōn adesse.

absent-minded *adj* immemor, parum attentus.

absolute *adj* absolūtus, perfectus; (*not limited*) īnfīnītus; (*not relative*) simplex; **~ power** rēgnum *nt*, dominātus *m*; **~ ruler** rēx.

absolutely *adv* absolūtē, omnīnō.

absolution *n* venia *f*.

absolve vt absolvere, exsolvere; (from punishment) condōnāre.

absorb vt bibere, absorbēre; (fig) distringere; **I am ~ed in** tōtus sum in (abl).

absorbent adj bibulus.

abstain vi abstinēre, sē abstinēre; (from violence) temperāre.

abstemious adj sobrius.

abstinence n abstinentia f, continentia f.

abstinent adj abstinēns, sobrius.

abstract adj mente perceptus, cōgitātiōne comprehēnsus ♦ n epitomē f ♦ vt abstrahere, dēmere.

abstraction n (idea) nōtiō f; (inattention) animus parum attentus.

abstruse adj reconditus, obscūrus, abstrūsus.

absurd adj ineptus, absurdus.

absurdity n ineptiae fpl, insulsitās f.

absurdly adv ineptē, absurdē.

abundance n cōpia f, abundantia f; **there is ~ of** abundē est (gen).

abundant adj cōpiōsus, abundāns, largus; **be ~** abundāre.

abundantly adv abundē, abundanter, adfātim.

abuse vt abūtī (abl); (words) maledīcere (dat) ♦ n probra ntpl, maledicta ntpl, convīcium nt, contumēlia f.

abusive adj maledicus, contumēliōsus.

abut vi adiacēre, ~ting on cōnfīnis (dat), fīnitimus (dat).

abysmal adj profundus.

abyss n profundum nt, vorāgō f; (water) gurges m; (fig) barathrum nt.

academic adj scholasticus; (style) umbrātilis; (sect) Acadēmicus.

academy n schola f; (Plato's) Acadēmīa f.

accede vi adsentīrī; ~ **to** accipere.

accelerate vt, vi adcelerāre, festīnāre; (process) mātūrāre.

accent n vōx f; (intonation) sonus m; (mark) apex m ♦ vt (syllable) acuere; (word) sonum admovēre (dat).

accentuate vt exprimere.

accept vt accipere.

acceptable adj acceptus, grātus, probābilis; **be ~** placēre.

acceptation n significātiō f.

access n aditus m; (addition) accessiō f; (illness) impetus m.

accessary n socius m, particeps m.

accessible adj (person) adfābilis, facilis; **be ~** (place) patēre; (person) facilem sē praebēre.

accession n (addition) accessiō f; (king's) initium rēgnī.

accident n cāsus m, calamitās f.

accidental adj fortuītus.

accidentally adv cāsū, fortuītō.

acclaim vt adclāmāre.

acclamation n clāmor m, studium nt.

acclimatize vt aliēnō caelō adsuēfacere.

accommodate vt accommodāre, aptāre; (lodging) hospitium parāre (dat); ~ **oneself to** mōrigerārī (dat).

accommodating adj facilis.

accommodation n hospitium nt.

accompany vt comitārī; (courtesy) prōsequī; (to Forum) dēdūcere; (music) concinere (dat).

accomplice n socius m, particeps m, cōnscius m.

accomplish vt efficere, perficere, patrāre.

accomplished adj doctus, perītus.

accomplishment n effectus m, perfectiō f, fīnis m; ~s pl artēs fpl.

accord vi inter sē congruere, cōnsentīre ♦ vt dare, praebēre, praestāre ♦ n cōnsēnsus m, concordia f; (music) concentus m; **of one's own ~** suā sponte, ultrō; **with one ~** unā vōce.

accordance n: **in ~ with** ex, ē (abl), secundum (acc).

according adv: ~ **to** ex, ē (abl), secundum (acc); (proportion) prō (abl); ~ **as** prōut.

accordingly adv itaque, igitur, ergō.

accost vt appellāre, adloquī, compellāre.

account n ratiō f; (story) nārrātiō f, expositiō f; **on ~ of** ob (acc); propter (acc), causā (gen); **be of no ~** (person) nihilī aestimārī, nēquam esse; **on that ~** idcircō ideō; **on your ~** tuā grātiā, tuō nōmine; **give an ~** ratiōnem reddere; **present an ~** ratiōnem referre; **take ~ of** ratiōnem habēre (gen); **put down to my ~** mihī expēnsum ferre; **the ~s balance** ratiō cōnstat/convenit.

account vi: ~ **for** ratiōnēs reddere, adferre (cūr); **that ~s for it** haec causa est; (PROV) hinc illae lacrimae.

accountant n ā ratiōnibus, ratiōcinātor m.

accountable adj reus; **I am ~ for** mihi ratiō reddenda est (gen).

account book n tabulae fpl; cōdex acceptī et expēnsī.

accoutred adj īnstructus, ōrnātus.

accoutrements n ōrnāmenta ntpl, arma ntpl.

accredited adj pūblicā auctōritāte missus.

accretion n accessiō f.

accrue vi (addition) cēdere; (advantage) redundāre.

accumulate vt cumulāre, congerere, coacervāre ♦ vi crēscere, cumulārī.

accumulation n cumulus m, acervus m.

accuracy n cūra f; (writing) subtīlitās f.

accurate adj (work) exāctus, subtīlis; (worker) dīligēns.

accurately adv subtīliter, ad amussim, dīligenter.

accursed adj sacer; (fig) exsecrātus, scelestus.

accusation n (act) accūsātiō f; (charge) crīmen nt; (unfair) īnsimulātiō f; (false) calumnia f; **bring an ~ against** accūsāre; (to a magistrate) nōmen dēferre (gen).

accusative n (case) accūsātīvus m.

accuse vt accūsāre, crīminārī, reum facere; (falsely) īnsimulāre; **the ~d** reus; (said by prosecutor) iste.

accuser n accūsātor m; (civil suit) petītor m; (informer) dēlātor m.

accustom *vt* adsuĕfacere; **~ oneself** adsuēscere, consuēscere.
accustomed *adj* adsuētus; **be ~** solēre; **become ~** adsuēscere, consuēscere.
ace *n* ūniō *f*; **I was within an ~ of going** minimum āfuit quin īrem.
acerbity *n* acerbitās *f*.
ache *n* dolor *m* ♦ *vi* dolēre.
achieve *vt* cōnficere, patrāre; (*win*) cōnsequī, adsequī.
achievement *n* factum *nt*, rēs gesta.
acid *adj* acidus.
acknowledge *vt* (*fact*) agnōscere; (*fault*) fatērī, cōnfitērī; (*child*) tollere; (*service*) grātias agere prō (*abl*); **I have to ~ your letter of 1st March** accēpī litterās tuās Kal. Mart. datās.
acknowledgement *n* cōnfessiō *f*; grātia *f*.
acme *n* fastīgium *nt*, flōs *m*.
aconite *n* aconītum *nt*.
acorn *n* glāns *f*.
acoustics *n* rēs audītōria *f*.
acquaint *vt* certiōrem facere, docēre; **~ oneself with** cognōscere; **~ed with** gnārus (*gen*), perītus (*gen*).
acquaintance *n* (*with fact*) cognitiō *f*, scientia *f*; (*with person*) familiāritās *f*, ūsus *m*; (*person*) nōtus *m*, familiāris *m*.
acquiesce *vi* (*assent*) adquiēscere; (*submit*) aequō animō patī.
acquiescence *n*: **with your ~** tē nōn adversante, pāce tuā.
acquire *vt* adquīrere, adipīscī, cōnsequī; nancīscī.
acquirements *n* artēs *fpl*.
acquisition *n* (*act*) comparātiō *f*, quaestus *m*; (*thing*) quaesītum *nt*.
acquisitive *adj* quaestuōsus.
acquit *vt* absolvere; **~ oneself** sē praestāre, officiō fungī.
acquittal *n* absolūtiō *f*.
acre *n* iūgerum *nt*.
acrid *adj* asper, ācer.
acrimonious *adj* acerbus, truculentus.
acrimony *n* acerbitās *f*.
acrobat *n* fūnambulus *m*.
acropolis *n* arx *f*.
across *adv* trānsversus ♦ *prep* trāns (*acc*).
act *n* factum *nt*, facinus *nt*; (*play*) āctus *m*; (*POL*) āctum *nt*, senātūs cōnsultum *nt*, dēcrētum *nt*; **I was in the ~ of saying** in eō erat ut dīcerem; **caught in the ~** dēprehēnsus ♦ *vi* facere, agere; (*conduct*) sē gerere; (*stage*) histriōnem esse, partēs agere; (*pretence*) simulāre ♦ *vt*: **~ a part** partēs agere, persōnam sustinēre; **~ the part of** agere; **~ as** esse, munere fungī (*gen*); **~ upon** (*instructions*) exsequī.
action *n* (*doing*) āctiō *f*; (*deed*) factum *nt*, facinus *nt*; (*legal*) āctiō *f*, līs *f*; (*MIL*) proelium *nt*; (*of play*) āctiō *f*; (*of speaker*) gestus *m*; **bring an ~ against** lītem intendere, āctiōnem īnstituere (*dat*); **be in ~** agere, rem gerere;

(*MIL*) pugnāre, in aciē dīmicāre; **man of ~** vir strēnuus.
active *adj* impiger, strēnuus, sēdulus, nāvus.
actively *adv* impigrē, strēnuē, nāviter.
activity *n* (*motion*) mōtus *m*; (*energy*) industria *f*, sēdulitās *f*.
actor *n* histriō *m*; (*in comedy*) cōmoedus *m*; (*in tragedy*) tragoedus *m*.
actress *n* mīma *f*.
actual *adj* vērus, ipse.
actually *adv* rē vērā.
actuate *vt* movēre, incitāre.
acumen *n* acūmen *nt*, ingenī aciēs, argūtiae *fpl*.
acute *adj* acūtus, ācer; (*pain*) ācer; (*speech*) argūtus, subtīlis.
acutely *adv* acūtē, ācriter, argūtē.
acuteness *n* (*mind*) acūmen *nt*, aciēs *f*, subtīlitas *f*.
adage *n* prōverbium *nt*.
adamant *n* adamās *m* ♦ *adj* obstinātus.
adamantine *adj* adamantinus.
adapt *vt* accommodāre.
adaptable *adj* flexibilis, facile accommodandus.
adaptation *n* accommodātiō *f*.
add *vt* addere, adicere, adiungere; **be ~ed** accēdere.
adder *n* vīpera *f*.
addicted *adj* dēditus.
addition *n* adiūnctiō *f*, accessiō *f*; additāmentum *nt*, incrēmentum *nt*; **in ~** īnsuper, praetereā; **in ~ to** praeter (*acc*).
additional *adj* novus, adiūnctus.
addled *adj* (*egg*) inritus; (*brain*) inānis.
address *vt* compellāre, alloquī; (*crowd*) cōntiōnem habēre apud (*acc*); (*letter*) īnscrībere; **~ oneself** (*to action*) accingī ♦ *n* adloquium *nt*; (*public*) cōntiō *f*, ōratiō *f*; (*letter*) īnscrīptiō *f*.
adduce *vt* (*argument*) adferre; (*witness*) prōdūcere.
adept *adj* perītus.
adequate *adj* idōneus, dignus, pār; **be ~** sufficere.
adequately *adv* satis, ut pār est.
adhere *vi* haerēre, adhaerēre; **~ to** inhaerēre (*dat*), inhaerēscere in (*abl*); (*agreement*) manēre, stāre in (*abl*).
adherent *n* adsectātor *m*; (*of party*) fautor *m*; (*of person*) clīēns *m*.
adhesive *adj* tenax.
adieu *interj* valē, valēte; **bid ~ to** valēre iubēre.
adjacent *adj* fīnitimus, vīcīnus; **be ~ to** adiacēre (*dat*).
adjoin *vi* adiacēre (*dat*).
adjoining *adj* fīnitimus, adiūnctus; proximus.
adjourn *vt* (*short time*) differre; (*longer time*) prōferre; (*case*) ampliāre ♦ *vi* rem differre, prōferre.
adjournment *n* dīlātiō *f*, prōlātiō *f*.
adjudge *vt* addīcere, adiūdicāre.
adjudicate *vi* dēcernere.

adjudicator n arbiter m.
adjunct n appendix f, accessiō f.
adjure vt obtestārī, obsecrāre.
adjust vt (_adapt_) accommodāre; (_put in order_)
  compōnere.
adjutant n (_MIL_) optiō m; (_civil_) adiūtor m.
administer vt administrāre, gerere; (_justice_)
  reddere; (_oath to_) iūreiūrandō adigere;
  (_medicine_) dare, adhibēre.
administration n administrātiō f.
administrator n administrātor m, prōcūrātor
  m.
admirable adj admīrābilis, ēgregius.
admirably adv ēgregiē.
admiral n praefectus classis; ~'s **ship** nāvis
  praetōria.
admiralty n praefectī classium.
admiration n admīrātiō f, laus f.
admire vt admīrārī; mirārī.
admirer n laudātor m; amātor m.
admissible adj aequus.
admission n (_entrance_) aditus m; (_of guilt etc_)
  cōnfessiō f.
admit vt (_let in_) admittere, recipere, accipere;
  (_to membership_) adscīscere; (_argument_)
  concēdere; (_fault_) fatērī; ~ **of** patī, recipere.
admittedly adv sānē.
admonish vt admonēre, commonēre, hortārī.
admonition n admonitiō f.
ado n negōtium nt; **make much ~ about nothing**
  fluctūs in simpulō excitāre; **without more ~**
  prōtinus, sine morā.
adolescence n prīma adulēscentia f.
adolescent adj adulēscēns ♦ n adulēscentulus m.
adopt vt (_person_) adoptāre; (_custom_)
  adscīscere; ~ **a plan** consilium capere.
adoption n (_person_) adoptiō f; (_custom_)
  adsūmptiō f; **by ~** adoptīvus.
adoptive adj adoptīvus.
adorable adj amābilis, venustus.
adorably adv venustē.
adoration n (_of gods_) cultus m; (_of kings_)
  venerātiō f; (_love_) amor m.
adore vt (_worship_) venerārī; (_love_) adamāre.
adorn vt ōrnāre, exōrnāre, decorāre.
adornment n ōrnāmentum nt, decus nt;
  ōrnātus m.
adrift adj fluctuāns; **be ~** fluctuāre.
adroit adj sollers, callidus.
adroitly adv callidē, scītē.
adroitness n sollertia f, calliditās f.
adulation n adūlātiō f, adsentātiō f.
adulatory adj blandus.
adult adj adultus.
adulterate vt corrumpere, adulterāre.
adulterer n adulter m.
adulteress n adultera f.
adulterous adj incestus.
adultery n adulterium nt; **commit ~**
  adulterāre.
adults npl pūberēs mpl.
adumbrate vt adumbrāre.
advance vt prōmovēre; (_a cause_) fovēre;

(_money_) crēdere; (_opinion_) dīcere; (_to
  honours_) prōvehere; (_time_) mātūrāre ♦ vi
  prōcēdere, prōgredī, adventāre; (_MIL_) signa
  prōferre, pedem īnferre; (_progress_)
  prōficere; (_walk_) incēdere; ~ **to the attack**
  signa īnferre ♦ n prōgressus m, prōcessus m;
  (_attack_) impetus m; (_money_) mūtuae
  pecūniae; **in ~** mātūrius; **fix in ~** praefīnīre;
  get in ~ praecipere.
advanced adj prōvectus; **well ~** (_task_)
  adfectus.
advancement n (_POL_) honōs m.
advantage n (_benefit_) commodum nt, bonum
  nt, ūsus m; (_of place or time_) opportūnitās f;
  (_profit_) fructus m; (_superiority_) praestantia f; **it
  is an ~** bono est; **be of ~ to** prōdesse (_dat_),
  ūsuī esse (_dat_); **to your ~** in rem tuam; **it is to
  your ~** tibi expedit, tuā interest; **take ~ of**
  (_CIRCS_) ūtī; (_person_) dēcipere, fallere; **have an
  ~ over** praestāre (_dat_); **be seen to ~** māximē
  placēre.
advantageous adj ūtilis, opportūnus.
advantageously adv ūtiliter, opportūnē.
advent n adventus m.
adventitious adj fortuītus.
adventure n (_exploit_) facinus memorābile nt;
  (_hazard_) perīculum nt.
adventurer n vir audāx m; (_social_) parasītus m.
adventurous adj audāx.
adversary n adversārius m, hostis m.
adverse adj adversus, contrārius, inimīcus.
adversely adv contrāriē, inimīcē, male.
adversity n rēs adversae fpl, calamitās f.
advert vi: ~ **to** attingere.
advertise vt prōscrībere; vēnditāre.
advertisement n prōscrīptiō f, libellus m.
advice n cōnsilium nt; (_POL_) auctōritās f; (_legal_)
  respōnsum nt; **ask ~ of** cōnsulere; **on the ~ of**
  Sulla auctōre Sullā.
advisable adj ūtilis, operae pretium.
advise vt monēre, suādēre (_dat_), cēnsēre (_dat_);
  ~ **against** dissuādēre.
advisedly adv cōnsultō.
adviser n auctor m, suāsor m.
advocacy n patrōcinium nt.
advocate n patrōnus m, causidicus m;
  (_supporter_) auctor m; **be an ~** causam dīcere
  ♦ vt suādēre, cēnsēre.
adze n ascia f.
aedile n aedīlis m.
aedile's adj aedīlicius.
aedileship n aedīlitās f.
aegis n aegis f; (_fig_) praesidium nt.
Aeneid n Aenēis f.
aerial adj āerius.
aesthetic adj pulchritūdinis amāns,
  artificiōsus.
afar adv procul; **from ~** procul.
affability n cōmitās f, facilitās f, bonitās f.
affable adj cōmis, facilis, commodus.
affably adv cōmiter.
affair n negōtium nt, rēs f.
affect vt afficere, movēre, commovēre;

(*concern*) attingere; (*pretence*) simulāre.
affectation *n* simulātiō *f*; (*RHET*) adfectātiō *f*; (*in diction*) īnsolentia *f*; quaesīta *ntpl*.
affected *adj* (*style*) molestus, pūtidus.
affectedly *adv* pūtidē.
affecting *adj* miserābilis.
affection *n* amor *m*, cāritās *f*, studium *nt*; (*family*) pietās *f*.
affectionate *adj* amāns, pius.
affectionately *adv* amanter, piē.
affiance *vt* spondēre.
affidavit *n* testimōnium *nt*.
affinity *n* affīnitās *f*, cognātiō *f*.
affirm *vt* adfirmāre, adsevērāre.
affirmation *n* adfirmātiō *f*.
affirmative *adj*: **I reply in the ~** āiō.
affix *vt* adfīgere, adiungere.
afflict *vt* adflīctāre, angere, vexāre; affligere.
affliction *n* miseria *f*, dolor *m*, rēs adversae *fpl*.
affluence *n* cōpia *f*, opēs *fpl*.
affluent *adj* dīves, opulentus, locuplēs.
afford *vt* praebēre, dare; **I cannot ~** rēs mihi nōn suppetit ad.
affray *n* rixa *f*, pugna *f*.
affright *vt* terrēre ♦ *n* terror *m*, pavor *m*.
affront *vt* offendere, contumēliam dīcere (*dat*) ♦ *n* iniūria *f*, contumēlia *f*.
afield *adv* forīs; **far ~** peregrē.
afloat *adj* natāns; **be ~** natāre.
afoot *adv* pedibus; **be ~** gerī.
aforesaid *adj* suprā dictus.
afraid *adj* timidus; **be ~ of** timēre, metuere; verērī.
afresh *adv* dēnuō, dē integrō.
Africa *n* Africa *f*.
aft *adv* in puppī, puppim versus.
after *adj* posterior ♦ *adv* post (*acc*), posteā; **the day ~** postrīdiē ♦ *conj* postquam; **the day ~** postrīdiē quam ♦ *prep* post (*acc*); (*in rank*) secundum (*acc*); (*in imitation*) ad (*acc*), dē (*abl*); **~ all** tamen, dēnique; **~ reading the book** librō lēctō; **one thing ~ another** aliud ex aliō; **immediately ~** statim ab.
aftermath *n* ēventus *m*.
afternoon *n*: **in the ~** post merīdiem ♦ *adj* postmerīdiānus.
afterthought *n* posterior cōgitātiō *f*.
afterwards *adv* post, posteā, deinde.
again *adv* rūrsus, iterum; **~ and ~** etiam atque etiam, identidem; **once ~** dēnuō; (*new point in a speech*) quid?
against *prep* contrā (*acc*), adversus (*acc*), in (*acc*); **~ the stream** adversō flūmine; **~ one's will** invitus.
agape *adj* hiāns.
age *n* (*life*) aetās *f*; (*epoch*) aetās *f*, saeculum *nt*; **old ~** senectūs *f*; **he is of ~** suī iūris est; **he is eight years of ~** octō annōs nātus est, nōnum annum agit; **of the same ~** aequālis.
aged *adj* senex, aetāte prōvectus; (*things*) antīquus.
agency *n* opera *f*; **through the ~ of** per (*acc*).
agent *n* āctor *m*, prōcūrātor *m*; (*in crime*)

minister *m*.
aggrandize *vt* augēre, amplificāre.
aggrandizement *n* amplificātiō *f*.
aggravate *vt* (*wound*) exulcerāre; (*distress*) augēre; **become ~d** ingravēscere.
aggravating *adj* molestus.
aggregate *n* summa *f*.
aggression *n* incursiō *f*, iniūria *f*.
aggressive *adj* ferōx.
aggressiveness *n* ferōcitās *f*.
aggressor *n* oppugnātor *m*.
aggrieved *adj* īrātus; **be ~** indignārī.
aghast *adj* attonitus, stupefactus; **stand ~** obstupēscere.
agile *adj* pernix, vēlōx.
agility *n* pernīcitās *f*.
agitate *vt* agitāre; (*mind*) commovēre, perturbāre.
agitation *n* commōtiō *f*, perturbātiō *f*, trepidātiō *f*; (*POL*) tumultus *m*.
agitator *n* turbātor *m*, concitātor *m*.
aglow *adj* fervidus ♦ *adv*: **be ~** fervēre.
ago *adv* abhinc (*acc*); **three days ~** abhinc trēs diēs; **long ~** antīquitus, iamprīdem, iamdūdum; **a short time ~** dūdum.
agog *adj* sollicitus, ērēctus.
agonize *vt* cruciāre, torquēre.
agonizing *adj* horribilis.
agony *n* cruciātus *m*, dolor *m*.
agrarian *adj* agrārius; **~ party** agrāriī *mpl*.
agree *vi* (*together*) cōnsentīre, congruere; (*with*) adsentīrī (*dat*), sentīre cum; (*bargain*) pacīscī; (*facts*) cōnstāre, convenīre; (*food*) facilem esse ad concoquendum; **~ upon** cōnstituere, compōnere; **it is agreed** constat (inter omnes).
agreeable *adj* grātus, commodus, acceptus.
agreeableness *n* dulcēdō *f*, iūcunditās *f*.
agreeably *adv* iūcundē.
agreement *n* (*together*) cōnsēnsus *m*, concordia *f*; (*with*) adsēnsus *m*; (*pact*) pactiō *f*, conventum *nt*, foedus *nt*; **according to ~** compāctō, ex compositō; **be in ~** cōnsentīre, congruere.
agricultural *adj* rūsticus, agrestis.
agriculture *n* rēs rūstica *f*, agrī cultūra *f*.
aground *adv*: **be ~** sīdere; **run ~** in lītus ēicī, offendere.
ague *n* horror *m*, febris *f*.
ahead *adv* ante; **go ~** anteīre, praeīre; **go-~** *adj* impiger; **ships in line ~** agmen nāvium.
aid *vt* adiuvāre, succurrere (*dat*), subvenīre (*dat*) ♦ *n* auxilium *nt*, subsidium *nt*.
aide-de-camp *n* optiō *m*.
ail *vt* dolēre ♦ *vi* aegrōtāre, labōrāre, languēre.
ailing *adj* aeger, īnfirmus.
ailment *n* morbus *m*, valētūdō *f*.
aim *vt* intendere; **~ at** petere; (*fig*) adfectāre, spectāre, sequī; (*with verb*) id agere ut ♦ *n* fīnis *m*, prōpositum *nt*.
aimless *adj* inānis, vānus.
aimlessly *adv* sine ratiōne.
aimlessness *n* vānitās *f*.

air n āēr m; (*breeze*) aura f; (*look*) vultus m,
speciēs f; (*tune*) modus m; **in the open** ~ sub
dīvō; ~**s** fastus m; **give oneself** ~**s** sē iactāre.
airily adv hilarē.
airy adj (*of air*) āerius; (*light*) tenuis; (*place*)
apertus; (*manner*) hilaris.
aisle n āla f.
ajar adj sēmiapertus.
akin adj cōnsanguineus, cognātus.
alacrity n alacritās f.
alarm n terror m, formīdō f, trepidātiō f;
(*sound*) clāmor m; **sound an** ~ ad arma
conclāmāre; **give the** ~ increpāre; **be in a**
state of ~ trepidāre ♦ vt terrēre, perterrēre,
perturbāre.
alarming adj formīdolōsus.
alas interj heu.
albeit conj etsī, etiamsī.
alcove n zōthēca f.
alder n alnus f.
alderman n decuriō m.
ale n cervīsia f.
alehouse n caupōna f, taberna f.
alert adj prōmptus, alacer, vegetus.
alertness n alacritās f.
alien adj externus; ~ **to** abhorrēns ab ♦ n
peregrīnus m.
alienate vt aliēnāre, abaliēnāre, āvertere,
āvocāre.
alienation n aliēnātiō f.
alight vi (*from horse*) dēscendere, dēsilīre;
(*bird*) īnsīdere.
alight adj: **be** ~ ārdēre; **set** ~ accendere.
alike adj pār, similis ♦ adv aequē, pariter.
alive adj vīvus; **be** ~ vīvere.
all adj omnis; (*together*) ūniversus, cūnctus;
(*whole*) tōtus; ~ **but** paene; ~ **for** studiōsus
(*gen*); ~ **in** cōnfectus; ~ **of** tōtus; ~ **over with**
āctum dē (*abl*); ~ **the best men** optimus
quisque; ~ **the more** eō plūs, tantō plūs; **at** ~
ullō modō, quid; **it is** ~ **up with** actum est de
(*abl*); **not at** ~ haudquāquam ♦ n fortūnae fpl.
allay vt sēdāre, mītigāre, lēnīre.
allegation n adfirmātiō f; (*charge*) īnsimulātiō
f.
allege vt adfirmāre, praetendere; (*in excuse*)
excūsāre.
allegiance n fidēs f; **owe** ~ **to** in fidē esse (*gen*);
swear ~ **to** in verba iūrāre (*gen*).
allegory n allēgoria f, immūtāta ōrātiō f.
alleviate vt mītigāre, adlevāre, sublevāre.
alleviation n levātiō f, levāmentum nt.
alley n (*garden*) xystus m; (*town*) angiportus m.
alliance n societās f, foedus nt.
allied adj foederātus, socius; (*friends*)
coniūnctus.
alligator n crocodīlus m.
allocate vt adsignāre, impertīre.
allot vt adsignāre, distribuere; **be** ~**ted**
obtingere.
allotment n (*land*) adsignātiō f.
allow vt sinere, permittere (*dat*), concēdere
(*dat*), patī; (*admit*) fatērī, concēdere;

(*approve*) comprobāre; **it is** ~**ed** licet (*dat* +
infin); ~ **for** vt fus ratiōnem habēre (*gen*).
allowance n venia f, indulgentia f; (*pay*)
stīpendium nt; (*food*) cibāria ntpl; (*for travel*)
viāticum nt; **make** ~ **for** indulgēre (*dat*),
ignōscere (*dat*), excusāre.
alloy n admixtum nt.
all right adj rēctē; **it is** ~ bene est.
allude vi: ~ **to** dēsignāre, attingere,
significāre.
allure vt adlicere, pellicere.
allurement n blanditia f, blandīmentum nt,
illecebra f.
alluring adj blandus.
alluringly adv blandē.
allusion n mentiō f, indicium nt.
alluvial adj: ~ **land** adluviō f.
ally n socius m ♦ vt sociāre, coniungere.
almanac n fāstī mpl.
almighty adj omnipotēns.
almond n (*nut*) amygdalum nt; (*tree*) amygdala
f.
almost adv paene, ferē, fermē, propemodum.
alms n stipem (*no nom*) f.
aloe n aloē f.
aloft adj sublīmis ♦ adv sublīmē.
alone adj sōlus, sōlitārius, ūnus ♦ adv sōlum.
along prep secundum (*acc*), praeter (*acc*) ♦ adv
porrō; **all** ~ iamdūdum, ab initiō; ~ **with** unā
cum (*abl*).
alongside adv: **bring** ~ adpellere; **come** ~ ad
crepīdinem accēdere.
aloof adv procul; **stand** ~ sē removēre ♦ adj
sēmōtus.
aloofness n sōlitūdō f, sēcessus m.
aloud adv clārē, māgnā vōce.
alphabet n elementa ntpl.
Alps n Alpēs fpl.
already adv iam.
also adv etiam, et, quoque; īdem.
altar n āra f.
alter vt mūtāre, commūtāre; (*order*) invertere.
alteration n mūtātiō f, commūtātiō f.
altercation n altercātiō f, iūrgium nt.
alternate adj alternus ♦ vt variāre.
alternately adv invicem.
alternation n vicem (*no nom*) f, vicissitūdō f.
alternative adj alter, alius ♦ n optiō f.
although conj quamquam (*indic*), etsī/etiamsī
(+ *cond clause*); quamvīs (+ *subj*).
altitude n altitūdō f.
altogether adv omnīnō; (*emphasis*) plānē,
prōrsus.
altruism n beneficentia f.
alum n alūmen nt.
always adv semper.
amalgamate vt miscēre, coniungere.
amalgamation n coniūnctiō f, temperātiō f.
amanuensis n librārius m.
amass vt cumulāre, coacervāre.
amateur n idiōta m.
amatory adj amātōrius.
amaze vt obstupefacere; attonāre; **be** ~**d**

obstupēscere.
amazement n stupor m; **in ~** attonitus,
    stupefactus.
ambassador n lēgātus m.
amber n sūcinum nt.
ambidextrous adj utrīusque manūs compos.
ambiguity n ambiguitās f; (RHET) amphibolia f.
ambiguous adj ambiguus, anceps, dubius.
ambiguously adv ambiguē.
ambition n glōria f, laudis studium.
ambitious adj glōriae cupidus, laudis avidus.
amble vi ambulāre.
ambrosia n ambrosia f.
ambrosial adj ambrosius.
ambuscade n īnsidiae fpl.
ambush n īnsidiae fpl ♦ vt īnsidiārī (dat).
ameliorate vt corrigere, meliōrem reddere.
amelioration n prōfectus m.
amenable adj facilis, docilis.
amend vt corrigere, ēmendāre.
amendment n ēmendātiō f.
amends n (apology) satisfactiō f; **make ~ for**
    expiāre; **make ~ to** satisfacere (dat).
amenity n (scenery) amoenitās f; (comfort)
    commodum nt.
amethyst n amethystus f.
amiability n benignitās f, suāvitās f.
amiable adj benignus, suāvis.
amiably adv benignē, suāviter.
amicable adj amīcus, cōmis.
amicably adv amīcē, cōmiter.
amid, amidst prep inter (acc).
amiss adv perperam, secus, incommodē; **take**
    ~ aegrē ferre.
amity n amīcitia f.
ammunition n tēla ntpl.
amnesty n venia f.
among, amongst prep inter (acc), apud (acc).
amorous adj amātōrius, amāns.
amorously adv cum amōre.
amount vi: **~ to** efficere; (fig) esse ♦ n summa
    f.
amours n amōrēs mpl.
amphibious adj anceps.
amphitheatre n amphitheātrum nt.
ample adj amplus, satis.
amplification n amplificātiō f.
amplify vt amplificāre.
amplitude n amplitūdō f, cōpia f.
amputate vt secāre, amputāre.
amuck adv: **run ~** bacchārī.
amulet n amulētum nt.
amuse vt dēlectāre, oblectāre.
amusement n oblectāmentum nt, dēlectātiō f;
    for ~ animī causā.
amusing adj rīdiculus, facētus.
an indef art see **a**.
anaemic adj exsanguis.
analogous adj similis.
analogy n prōportiō f, comparātiō f.
analyse vt excutere, perscrūtārī.
analysis n explicātiō f.
anapaest n anapaestus m.

anarchical adj sēditiōsus.
anarchy n reī pūblicae perturbātiō, lēgēs
    nullae fpl, licentia f.
anathema n exsecrātiō f; (object) pestis f.
ancestor n proavus m; **~s** pl māiōrēs mpl.
ancestral adj patrius.
ancestry n genus nt, orīgō f.
anchor n ancora f; **lie at ~** in ancorīs stāre;
    weigh ~ ancoram tollere ♦ vi ancoram
    iacere.
anchorage n statiō f.
ancient adj antīquus, prīscus, vetustus; **~**
    history, ~ world antīquitās f; **from/in ~ times**
    antīquitus; **the ~s** veterēs.
and conj et, atque, ac, -que; **~ . . . not** nec,
    neque; **~ so** itaque.
anecdote n fābella f.
anent prep dē (abl).
anew adv dēnuō, ab integrō.
angel n angelus m.
angelic adj angelicus; (fig) dīvīnus, eximius.
anger n īra f ♦ vt inrītāre.
angle n angulus m ♦ vi hāmō piscārī.
angler n piscātor m.
Anglesey n Mona f.
angrily adv īrātē.
angry adj īrātus; **be ~** īrāscī (dat).
anguish n cruciātus m, dolor m; (mind) angor
    m.
angular adj angulātus.
animal n animal nt; (domestic) pecus f; (wild)
    fera f.
animate vt animāre.
animated adj excitātus, vegetus.
animation n ārdor m, alacritās f.
animosity n invidia f, inimīcitia f.
ankle n tālus m.
annalist n annālium scrīptor.
annals n annālēs mpl.
annex vt addere.
annexation n adiectiō f.
annihilate vt dēlēre, exstinguere, perimere.
annihilation n exstinctiō f, interneciō f.
anniversary n diēs anniversārius; (public)
    sollemne nt.
annotate vt adnotāre.
annotation n adnotātiō f.
announce vt nūntiāre; (officially) dēnūntiāre,
    prōnūntiāre; (election result) renūntiāre.
announcement n (official) dēnūntiātiō f;
    (news) nūntius m.
announcer n nūntius m.
annoy vt inrītāre, vexāre; **be ~ed with** aegrē
    ferre.
annoyance n molestia f, vexātiō f; (felt) dolor
    m.
annoying adj molestus.
annual adj annuus, anniversārius.
annually adv quotannīs.
annuity n annua ntpl.
annul vt abrogāre, dissolvere, tollere.
annulment n abrogātiō f.
anoint vt ungere, illinere.

anomalous _adj_ novus.
anomaly _n_ novitās _f._
anon _adv_ mox.
anonymous _adj_ incertī auctōris.
anonymously _adv_ sine nōmine.
another _adj_ alius; (_second_) alter; **of** ~ aliēnus; **one after** ~ alius ex aliō; **one** ~ inter sē, alius alium; **in** ~ **place** alibī; **to** ~ **place** aliō; **in** ~ **way** aliter; **at** ~ **time** aliās.
answer _vt_ respondēre (_dat_); (_by letter_) rescrībere (_dat_); (_agree_) respondēre, congruere; ~ **a charge** crīmen dēfendere; ~ **for** _vt fus_ (_surety_) praestāre; (_account_) ratiōnem referre; (_substitute_) īnstar esse (_gen_) ♦ _n_ respōnsum _nt_; (_to a charge_) dēfēnsiō _f_; ~ **to the name of** vocārī; **give an** ~ respondēre.
answerable _adj_ reus; **I am** ~ **for** ... ratiō mihī reddenda est ... (_gen_).
ant _n_ formīca _f._
antagonism _n_ simultās _f_, inimīcitia _f._
antagonist _n_ adversārius _m_, hostis _m._
antarctic _adj_ antarcticus.
antecedent _adj_ antecēdēns, prior.
antediluvian _adj_ prīscus, horridus, Deucaliōnēus.
antelope _n_ dorcas _f._
anterior _adj_ prior.
anteroom _n_ vestibulum _nt._
anthology _n_ excerpta _ntpl_; **make an** ~ excerpere.
anthropology _n_ rēs hūmānae _fpl._
anticipate _vt_ (_expect_) exspectāre; (_forestall_) antevenīre, occupāre, (_in thought_) animō praecipere.
anticipation _n_ exspectātiō _f_, spēs _f_; praesūmptiō _f._
antics _n_ gestus _m_, ineptiae _fpl._
anticyclo..e _n_ serēnitās _f._
antidote _n_ remedium _nt_, medicāmen _nt._
antipathy _n_ fastīdium _nt_, odium _nt_; (_things_) repugnantia _f._
antiphonal _adj_ alternus.
antiphony _n_ alterna _ntpl._
antipodes _n_ contrāria pars terrae.
antiquarian _adj_ historicus.
antiquary _n_ antīquārius _m._
antiquated _adj_ prīscus, obsolētus.
antique _adj_ antīquus, prīscus.
antiquity _n_ antīquitās _f_, vetustās _f_, veterēs _mpl._
antithesis _n_ contentiō _f_, contrārium _nt._
antlers _n_ cornua _ntpl._
anvil _n_ incūs _f._
anxiety _n_ sollicitūdō _f_, metus _m_, cūra _f_; anxietās _f._
anxious _adj_ sollicitus, anxius; avidus; cupidus.
any _adj_ ullus; (_interrog_) ecquī; (_after_ **sī, nisī, num, nē**) quī; (_indef_) quīvīs, quīlibet; **hardly** ~ nullus ferē; ~ **further** longius; ~ **longer** (_of time_) diutius.
anybody _pron_ aliquis; (_indef_) quīvīs, quīlibet;

(_after_ **sī, nisī, num, nē**) quis; (_interrog_) ecquis, numquis; (_after neg_) quisquam; **hardly** ~ nēmō ferē.
anyhow _adv_ ullō modō, quōquō modō.
anyone _pron see_ **anybody**.
anything _pron_ aliquid; quidvīs, quidlibet; (_interrog_) ecquid, numquid; (_after neg_) quicquam; (_after_ **sī, nisī, num, nē**) quid; **hardly** ~ nihil ferē.
anywhere _adv_ usquam, ubīvīs.
apace _adv_ citō, celeriter.
apart _adv_ seōrsum, sēparātim ♦ _adj_ dīversus; **be six feet** ~ sex pedēs distāre; **set** ~ sēpōnere; **stand** ~ distāre; **joking** ~ remōtō iocō; ~ **from** praeter (_acc_).
apartment _n_ cubiculum _nt_, conclāve _nt._
apathetic _adj_ lentus, languidus, ignāvus.
apathy _n_ lentitūdō _f_, languor _m_, ignāvia _f._
ape _n_ sīmia _f_ ♦ _vt_ imitārī.
aperture _n_ hiātus _m_, forāmen _nt_, rīma _f._
apex _n_ fastīgium _nt._
aphorism _n_ sententia _f._
apiary _n_ alveārium _nt._
apiece _adv_ in singulōs; **two** ~ bīnī.
aplomb _n_ cōnfīdentia _f._
apocryphal _adj_ commentīcius.
apologetic _adj_ cōnfitēns, veniam petēns.
apologize _vi_ veniam petere, sē excūsāre.
apology _n_ excūsātiō _f._
apoplectic _adj_ apoplēcticus.
apoplexy _n_ apoplēxis _f._
apostle _n_ apostolus _m._
apothecary _n_ medicāmentārius _m._
appal _vt_ perterrēre, cōnsternere.
appalling _adj_ dīrus.
apparatus _n_ īnstrūmenta _ntpl_, ōrnāmenta _ntpl._
apparel _n_ vestis _f_, vestīmenta _ntpl._
apparent _adj_ manifestus, apertus, ēvidēns.
apparently _adv_ speciē, ut vidētur.
apparition _n_ vīsum _nt_, speciēs _f._
appeal _vi_ (_to magistrate_) appellāre; (_to people_) prōvocāre ad; (_to gods_) invocāre, testārī; (_to senses_) placēre (_dat_) ♦ _n_ appellātiō _f_, prōvocātiō _f_, testātiō _f._
appear _vi_ (_in sight_) appārēre; (_in court_) sistī; (_in public_) prōdīre; (_at a place_) adesse, advenīre; (_seem_) vidērī.
appearance _n_ (_coming_) adventus _m_; (_look_) aspectus _m_, faciēs _f_; (_semblance_) speciēs _f_; (_thing_) vīsum _nt_; **for the sake of ~s in** speciem; (_formula_) dicis causā; **make one's** ~ prōcēdere, prōdīre.
appeasable _adj_ plācābilis.
appease _vt_ plācāre, lēnīre, mītigāre, sēdāre.
appeasement _n_ plācātiō _f_; (_of enemy_) pācificātiō _f._
appellant _n_ appellātor _m._
appellation _n_ nōmen _nt._
append _vt_ adiungere, subicere.
appendage _n_ appendix _f_, adiūnctum _nt._
appertain _vi_ pertinēre.
appetite _n_ adpetītus _m_; (_for food_) fāmēs _f._
applaud _vt_ plaudere; (_fig_) laudāre.

applause n plausus m; (fig) adsēnsiō f, adprobātiō f.

apple n pōmum nt; mālum nt; **~ tree** mālus f; **~ of my eye** ocellus meus; **upset the ~ cart** plaustrum percellere.

appliance n māchina f, īnstrūmentum nt.

applicable adj aptus, commodus; **be ~** pertinēre.

applicant n petītor m.

application n (work) industria f; (mental) intentiō f; (asking) petītiō f; (MED) fōmentum nt.

apply vt adhibēre, admovēre; (use) ūtī (abl); **~ oneself to** sē adplicāre, incumbere in (acc) ♦ vi pertinēre; (to a person) adīre (acc); (for office) petere.

appoint vt (magistrate) creāre, facere, cōnstituere; (commander) praeficere; (guardian, heir) īnstituere; (time) dīcere, statuere; (for a purpose) dēstināre; (to office) creāre.

appointment n cōnstitūtum nt; (duty) mandātum nt; (office) magistrātus m; **have an ~ with** cōnstitūtum habēre cum; **keep an ~** ad cōnstitūtum venīre.

apportion vt dispertīre, dīvīdere; (land) adsignāre.

apposite adj aptus, appositus.

appraisal n aestimātiō f.

appraise vt aestimāre.

appreciable adj haud exiguus.

appreciate vt aestimāre.

appreciation n aestimātiō f.

apprehend vt (person) comprehendere; (idea) intellegere, mente comprehendere; (fear) metuere, timēre.

apprehension n comprehēnsiō f; metus m, formīdō f.

apprehensive adj anxius, sollicitus; **be ~ of** metuere.

apprentice n discipulus m, tīrō m.

apprenticeship n tīrōcinium nt.

apprise vt docēre, certiōrem facere.

approach vt appropinquāre ad (acc), accēdere ad; (person) adīre ♦ vi (time) adpropinquāre; (season) appetere ♦ n (act) accessus m, aditus m; (time) adpropinquātiō f; (way) aditus m; **make ~es to** adīre ad, ambīre, petere.

approachable adj (place) patēns; (person) facilis.

approbation n adprobātiō f, adsēnsiō f.

appropriate adj aptus, idōneus, proprius ♦ vt adscīscere, adsūmere.

appropriately adv aptē, commodē.

approval n adprobātiō f, adsēnsus m, favor m.

approve vt, vi adprobāre, comprobāre, adsentīrī (dat); (law) scīscere.

approved adj probātus, spectātus.

approximate adj propinquus ♦ vi: **~ to** accēdere ad.

approximately adv prope, propemodum; (number) ad (acc).

appurtenances n īnstrūmenta ntpl, apparātus

m.

apricot n armēniacum nt; **~ tree** n armēniaca f.

April n mēnsis Aprīlis m; **of ~** Aprīlis.

apron n operīmentum nt.

apropos of prep quod attinet ad.

apse n apsis f.

apt adj aptus, idōneus; (pupil) docilis, prōmptus; **~ to** prōnus, prōclīvis ad; **be ~ to** solēre.

aptitude n ingenium nt, facultās f.

aptly adv aptē.

aquarium n piscīna f.

aquatic adj aquātilis.

aqueduct n aquae ductus m.

aquiline adj (nose) aduncus.

arable land n arvum nt.

arbiter n arbiter m.

arbitrarily adv ad libīdinem, licenter.

arbitrary adj libīdinōsus (act); (ruler) superbus.

arbitrate vi dīiūdicāre, disceptāre.

arbitration n arbitrium nt, dīiūdicātiō f.

arbitrator n arbiter m, disceptātor m.

arbour n umbrāculum nt.

arbutus n arbutus f.

arc n arcus m.

arcade n porticus f.

arch n fornix m, arcus m ♦ vt arcuāre ♦ adj lascīvus, vafer.

archaeologist n antīquitātis investīgātor m.

archaeology n antīquitātis investīgātiō f.

archaic adj prīscus.

archaism n verbum obsolētum nt.

archbishop n archiepiscopus m.

arched adj fornicātus.

archer n sagittārius m.

archery n sagittāriōrum ars f.

architect n architectus m.

architecture n architectūra f.

architrave n epistylium nt.

archives n tabulae (pūblicae) fpl.

arctic adj arcticus, septentriōnālis ♦ n septentriōnēs mpl.

ardent adj ārdēns, fervidus, vehemēns.

ardently adv ārdenter, ācriter, vehementer.

ardour n ārdor m, fervor m.

arduous adj difficilis, arduus.

area n regiō f; (MATH) superficiēs f.

arena n harēna f.

argonaut n argonauta m.

argosy n onerāria f.

argue vi (discuss) disserere, disceptāre; (dispute) ambigere; disputāre; (reason) argūmentārī ♦ vt (prove) arguere.

argument n (discussion) contrōversia f, disputātiō f; (reason) ratiō f; (proof, theme) argūmentum nt.

argumentation n argūmentātiō f.

argumentative adj lītigiōsus.

aria n canticum nt.

arid adj āridus, siccus.

aright adv rectē, vērē.

arise vi orīrī, coorīrī, exsistere; **~ from** nāscī ex, proficīscī ab.

aristocracy *n* optimātēs *mpl*, nōbilēs *mpl*; (*govt*) optimātium dominātus *m*.
aristocrat *n* optimās *m*.
aristocratic *adj* patricius, generōsus.
arithmetic *n* numerī *mpl*, arithmētica *ntpl*.
ark *n* arca *f*.
arm *n* bracchium *nt*; (*upper*) lacertus *m*; (*sea*) sinus *m*; (*weapon*) tēlum *nt* ♦ *vt* armāre ♦ *vi* arma capere.
armament *n* bellī apparātus *m*; cōpiae *fpl*.
armed *adj* (*men*) armātus; **light-~ troops** levis armātūra *f*, vēlitēs *mpl*.
armistice *n* indutiae *fpl*.
armlet *n* armilla *f*.
armour *n* arma *ntpl*; (*kind of*) armātūra *f*.
armourer *n* (armōrum) faber *m*.
armoury *n* armāmentārium *nt*.
armpit *n* āla *f*.
arms *npl* (*MIL*) arma *ntpl*; **by force of ~** vī et armīs; **under ~** in armīs.
army *n* exercitus *m*; (*in battle*) aciēs *f*; (*on march*) agmen *nt*.
aroma *n* odor *m*.
aromatic *adj* frāgrāns.
around *adv* circum (*acc*), circā (*acc*) ♦ *prep* circum (*acc*).
arouse *vt* suscitāre, ērigere, excitāre.
arraign *vt* accūsāre.
arrange *vt* (*in order*) compōnere, ōrdināre, dīgerere, dispōnere; (*agree*) pacīscī; **~ a truce** indūtias compōnere.
arrangement *n* ōrdō *m*, collocātiō *f*, dispositiō *f*; pactum *nt*, cōnstitūtum *nt*.
arrant *adj* summus.
array *n* vestis *f*, habitus *m*; (*MIL*) aciēs *f* ♦ *vt* vestīre, exōrnāre; (*MIL*) īnstruere.
arrears *n* residuae pecūniae *fpl*, reliqua *ntpl*.
arrest *vt* comprehendere, adripere; (*attention*) in sē convertere; (*movement*) morārī, tardāre ♦ *n* comprehēnsiō *f*.
arrival *n* adventus *m*.
arrive *vi* advenīre (ad + *acc*), pervenīre (ad + *acc*).
arrogance *n* superbia *f*, adrogantia *f*, fastus *m*.
arrogant *adj* superbus, adrogāns.
arrogantly *adv* superbē, adroganter.
arrogate *vt* adrogāre.
arrow *n* sagitta *f*.
arsenal *n* armāmentārium *nt*.
arson *n* incēnsiōnis crīmen *nt*.
art *n* ars *f*, artificium *nt*; **fine ~s** ingenuae artēs.
artery *n* artēria *f*.
artful *adj* callidus, vafer, astūtus.
artfully *adv* callidē, astūtē.
artfulness *n* astūtia *f*, dolus *m*.
artichoke *n* cinara *f*.
article *n* rēs *f*, merx *f*; (*clause*) caput *nt*; (*term*) condiciō *f*.
articulate *adj* explānātus, distinctus ♦ *vi* explānāre, exprimere.
articulately *adv* explānātē, clārē.
articulation *n* prōnūntiātiō *f*.
artifice *n* ars *f*, artificium *nt*, dolus *m*.

artificer *n* artifex *m*, opifex *m*, faber *m*.
artificial *adj* (*work*) artificiōsus; (*appearance*) fūcātus.
artificially *adv* arte, manū.
artillery *n* tormenta *ntpl*.
artisan *n* faber *m*, opifex *m*.
artist *n* artifex *m*; pictor *m*.
artistic *adj* artificiōsus, ēlegāns.
artistically *adv* artificiōsē, ēleganter.
artless *adj* (*work*) inconditus; (*person*) simplex.
artlessly *adv* inconditē; simpliciter, sine dolō.
artlessness *n* simplicitās *f*.
as *adv* (*before adj, adv*) tam; (*after* **aequus, īdem, similis**) ac, atque; (*correlative*) quam, quālis, quantus ♦ *conj* (*compar*) ut (+ *indic*), sīcut, velut, quemadmodum; (*cause*) cum (+ *indic*), quōniam, quippe quī; (*time*) dum, ut ♦ *relat pron* quī, quae, quod (+ *subj*); **~ being** utpote; **~ follows** ita; **~ for** quod attinet ad; **~ if** quasī, tamquam sī, velut; (= *while*) usu expressed by *pres part*; **~ it were** ut ita dīcam; **~ yet** adhūc; **~ soon ~** simul ac/atque (+ *perf indic*); **~ … as possible** quam (+ *superl*).
as *n* (*coin*) as *m*.
ascend *vt, vi* ascendere.
ascendancy *n* praestantia *f*, auctōritās *f*.
ascendant *adj* surgēns, potēns; **be in the ~** praestāre.
ascent *n* ascēnsus *m*; (*slope*) clīvus *m*.
ascertain *vt* comperīre, cognōscere.
ascetic *adj* nimis abstinēns, austērus.
asceticism *n* dūritia *f*.
ascribe *vt* adscrībere, attribuere, adsignāre.
ash *n* (*tree*) fraxinus *f* ♦ *adj* fraxineus.
ashamed *adj*: **I am ~** pudet mē; **~ of** pudet (+ *acc of person*, + *gen of thing*).
ashen *adj* pallidus.
ashes *n* cinis *m*.
ashore *adv* (*motion*) in lītus; (*rest*) in lītore; **go ~** ēgredī.
Asia *n* Asia *f*.
aside *adv* sēparatim, sē- (*in cpd*).
ask *vt* (*question*) rogāre, quaerere; (*request*) petere, poscere; (*beg, entreat*) orāre; **~ for** *vt fus* petere; rogāre; scīscitārī; percontārī.
askance *adv* oblīquē; **look ~ at** līmīs oculīs aspicere, invidēre (*dat*).
askew *adv* prāvē.
aslant *adv* oblīquē.
asleep *adj* sōpītus; **be ~** dormīre; **fall ~** obdormīre, somnum inīre.
asp *n* aspis *f*.
asparagus *n* asparagus *m*.
aspect *n* (*place*) aspectus *m*; (*person*) vultus *m*; (*CIRCS*) status *m*; **have a southern ~** ad merīdiem spectāre; **there is another ~ to the matter** aliter sē rēs habet.
aspen *n* pōpulus *f*.
asperity *n* acerbitās *f*.
asperse *vt* maledīcere (*dat*), calumniārī.
aspersion *n* calumnia *f*; **cast ~s on** calumniārī, īnfāmiā aspergere.
asphalt *n* bitūmen *nt*.

asphyxia *n* strangulātiō *f*.
asphyxiate *vt* strangulāre.
aspirant *n* petītor *m*.
aspirate *n* (*GRAM*) aspīrātiō *f*.
aspiration *n* spēs *f*; (*POL*) ambitiō *f*.
aspire *vi*: ~ **to** adfectāre, petere, spērāre.
ass *n* asinus *m*, asellus *m*; (*fig*) stultus.
assail *vt* oppugnāre, adorīrī, aggredī.
assailable *adj* expugnābilis.
assailant *n* oppugnātor *m*.
assassin *n* sīcārius *m*, percussor *m*.
assassinate *vt* interficere, occīdere, iugulāre.
assassination *n* caedēs *f*, parricidium *nt*.
assault *vt* oppugnāre, adorīrī, aggredī;
(*speech*) invehī in (*acc*) ♦ *n* impetus *m*,
oppugnātiō *f*; (*personal*) vīs *f*.
assay *vt* (*metal*) spectāre; temptāre, cōnārī.
assemble *vt* convocāre, congregāre, cōgere ♦
vi convenīre, congregārī.
assembly *n* coetus *m*, conventus *m*; (*plebs*)
concilium *nt*; (*Roman people*) comitia *ntpl*;
(*troops*) cōntiō *f*; (*things*) congeriēs *f*.
assent *vi* adsentīrī, adnuere ♦ *n* adsēnsus *m*.
assert *vt* adfirmāre, adsevērāre, dīcere.
assertion *n* adfirmātiō *f*, adsevērātiō *f*, dictum
nt, sententia *f*.
assess *vt* cēnsēre, aestimāre; ~ **damages**
lītem aestimāre.
assessment *n* cēnsus *m*, aestimātiō *f*.
assessor *n* cēnsor *m*; (*assistant*) cōnsessor *m*.
assets *n* bona *ntpl*.
assiduity *n* dīligentia *f*, sēdulitās *f*, industria *f*.
assiduous *adj* dīligēns, sēdulus, industrius.
assign *vt* tribuere, attribuere; (*land*)
adsignāre; (*in writing*) perscrībere; (*task*)
dēlēgāre; (*reason*) adferre.
assignation *n* cōnstitūtum *nt*.
assignment *n* adsignātiō *f*, perscrīptiō *f*; (*task*)
mūnus *nt*, pēnsum *nt*.
assimilate *vt* aequāre; (*food*) concoquere;
(*knowledge*) concipere.
assist *vt* adiuvāre, succurrere (*dat*), adesse
(*dat*).
assistance *n* auxilium *nt*, opem (*no nom*) *f*;
come to the ~ of subvenīre (*dat*); **be of ~ to**
auxiliō esse (*dat*).
assistant *n* adiūtor *m*, minister *m*.
assize *n* conventus *m*; **hold ~s** conventūs
agere.
associate *vt* cōnsociāre, coniungere ♦ *vi* rem
inter sē cōnsociāre; ~ **with** familiāriter ūtī
(*abl*) ♦ *n* socius *m*, sodālis *m*.
association *n* societās *f*; (*club*) sodālitās *f*.
assort *vt* dīgerere, dispōnere ♦ *vi* congruere.
assortment *n* (*of goods*) variae mercēs *fpl*.
assuage *vt* lēnīre, mītigāre, sēdāre.
assume *vt* (*for oneself*) adsūmere, adrogāre;
(*hypothesis*) pōnere; (*office*) inīre.
assumption *n* (*hypothesis*) sūmptiō *f*, positum
nt.
assurance *n* (*given*) fidēs *f*, pignus *nt*; (*felt*)
fīdūcia *f*; (*boldness*) cōnfīdentia *f*.
assure *vt* cōnfirmāre, prōmittere (*dat*).

assured *adj* (*person*) fīdēns; (*fact*) explōrātus,
certus.
assuredly *adv* certō, certē, profectō, sānē.
astern *adv* ā puppī; (*movement*) retrō; ~ **of**
post.
asthma *n* anhēlitus *m*.
astonish *vt* obstupefacere; attonāre.
astonished *adj* attonitus, stupefactus; **be ~ed**
at admīrārī.
astonishing *adj* mīrificus, mīrus.
astonishment *n* stupor *m*, admīrātiō *f*.
astound *vt* obstupefacere.
astray *adj* vagus; **go ~** errāre, aberrāre,
deerrāre.
astride *adj* vāricus.
astrologer *n* Chaldaeus *m*, mathēmaticus *m*.
astrology *n* Chaldaeōrum dīvīnātiō *f*.
astronomer *n* astrologus *m*.
astronomy *n* astrologia *f*.
astute *adj* callidus, vafer.
astuteness *n* calliditās *f*.
asunder *adv* sēparātim, dis- (*in cpd*).
asylum *n* asÿlum *nt*.
at *prep* in (*abl*), ad (*acc*); (*time*) *usu expressed by*
abl; (*towns, small islands*) *loc*; ~ **the house of**
apud (*acc*); ~ **all events** saltem; *see also* **dawn,**
hand, house *etc*.
atheism *n* deōs esse negāre.
atheist *n* atheos *m*; **be an ~** deōs esse negāre.
Athenian *adj* Atheniensis.
Athens *n* Athenae *fpl*; **at/from ~** Athenis; **to ~**
Athenas.
athirst *adj* sitiens; (*fig*) avidus.
athlete *n* athlēta *m*.
athletic *adj* rōbustus, lacertōsus.
athletics *n* athlētica *ntpl*.
athwart *prep* trāns (*acc*).
atlas *n* orbis terrārum dēscrīptiō *f*.
atmosphere *n* āēr *m*.
atom *n* atomus *f*, corpus indīviduum *nt*.
atone *vi*: ~ **for** expiāre.
atonement *n* expiātiō *f*, piāculum *nt*.
atrocious *adj* immānis, nefārius, scelestus.
atrociously *adv* nefāriē, scelestē.
atrociousness *n* immānitās *f*.
atrocity *n* nefas *nt*, scelus *nt*, flāgitium *nt*.
atrophy *vi* marcēscere.
attach *vt* adiungere, adfīgere, illigāre; (*word*)
subicere; ~**ed to** amāns (*gen*).
attachment *n* vinculum *nt*; amor *m*, studium
nt.
attack *vt* oppugnāre, adorīrī, aggredī;
impetum facere in (*acc*); (*speech*) īnsequī,
invehī in (*acc*); (*disease*) ingruere in (*acc*) ♦ *n*
impetus *m*, oppugnātiō *f*, incursus *m*.
attacker *n* oppugnātor *m*.
attain *vt* adsequī, adipīscī, cōnsequī; ~ **to**
pervenīre ad.
attainable *adj* impetrābilis, in prōmptū.
attainder *n*: **bill of ~** prīvilēgium *nt*.
attainment *n* adeptiō *f*.
attainments *npl* doctrīna *f*, ērudītiō *f*.
attaint *vt* māiestātis condemnāre.

attempt *vt* cōnārī, temptāre; (*with effort*) mōlīrī ♦ *n* cōnātus *m*, inceptum *nt*; (*risk*) perīculum *nt*; **first ~s** rudīmenta *ntpl*.

attend *vt* (*meeting*) adesse (*dat*), interesse (*dat*); (*person*) prōsequī, comitārī; (*master*) appārēre (*dat*); (*invalid*) cūrāre ♦ *vi* animum advertere, animum attendere; **~ to** (*task*) adcūrāre; **~ upon** prōsequī, adsectārī; **~ the lectures of** audīre; **not ~** aliud agere; **~ first to** praevertere (*dat*); **well ~ed** frequēns; **thinly ~ed** īnfrequēns.

attendance *n* (*courtesy*) adsectātiō *f*; (*MED*) cūrātiō *f*; (*service*) apparitiō *f*; **constant ~** adsiduitās *f*; **full ~** frequentia *f*; **poor ~** īnfrequentia *f*; **dance ~ on** haerēre (*dat*).

attendant *n* famulus *m*, minister *m*; (*on candidate*) sectātor *m*; (*on nobleman*) adsectātor *m*; (*on magistrate*) apparitor *m*.

attention *n* animadversiō *f*, animī attentiō *f*; (*to work*) cūra *f*; (*respect*) observantia *f*; **attract ~** digitō mōnstrārī; **call ~ to** indicāre; **pay ~ to** animadvertere, observāre; ratiōnem habēre (*gen*); **~ !** hōc age!

attentive *adj* intentus; (*to work*) dīligēns.

attentively *adv* intentē, dīligenter.

attenuate *vt* attenuāre.

attest *vt* cōnfirmāre, testārī.

attestation *n* testificātiō *f*.

attestor *n* testis *m*.

attic *n* cēnāculum *nt*.

attire *vt* vestīre ♦ *n* vestis *f*, habitus *m*.

attitude *n* (*body*) gestus *m*, status *m*, habitus *m*; (*mind*) ratiō *f*.

attorney *n* āctor *m*; advocātus *m*.

attract *vt* trahere, attrahere, adlicere.

attraction *n* vīs attrahendī; illecebra *f*, invītāmentum *nt*.

attractive *adj* suāvis, venustus, lepidus.

attractively *adv* suāviter, venustē, lepidē.

attractiveness *n* venustās *f*, lepōs *m*.

attribute *vt* tribuere, attribuere, adsignāre ♦ *n* proprium *nt*.

attrition *n* attrītus *m*.

attune *vt* modulārī.

auburn *adj* flāvus.

auction *n* auctiō *f*; (*public*) hasta *f*; **hold an ~** auctiōnem facere; **sell by ~** sub hastā vēndere.

auctioneer *n* praecō *m*.

audacious *adj* audāx; protervus.

audaciously *adv* audācter, protervē.

audacity *n* audācia *f*, temeritās *f*.

audible *adj*: **be ~** exaudīrī posse.

audibly *adv* clārā vōce.

audience *n* audītōrēs *mpl*; (*interview*) aditus *m*; **give an ~ to** admittere.

audit *vt* īnspicere ♦ *n* ratiōnum īnspectiō *f*.

auditorium *n* cavea *f*.

auditory *adj* audītōrius.

auger *n* terebra *f*.

augment *vt* augēre, adaugēre ♦ *vi* crēscere, augērī.

augmentation *n* incrēmentum *nt*.

augur *n* augur *m*; **~'s staff** lituus *m* ♦ *vi* augurārī; (*fig*) portendere.

augural *adj* augurālis.

augurship *n* augurātus *m*.

augury *n* augurium *nt*, auspicium *nt*; ōmen *nt*; **take ~ies** augurārī; **after taking ~ies** augurātō.

august *adj* augustus.

August *n* mēnsis Augustus, Sextīlis; **of ~** Sextīlis.

aunt *n* (*paternal*) amita *f*; (*maternal*) mātertera *f*.

auspices *n* auspicium *nt*; **take ~** auspicārī; **after taking ~** auspicātō; **without taking ~** inauspicātō.

auspicious *adj* faustus, fēlīx.

auspiciously *adv* fēlīciter, prosperē.

austere *adj* austērus, sevērus, dūrus.

austerely *adv* sevērē.

austerity *n* sevēritās *f*, dūritia *f*.

authentic *adj* vērus, certus.

authenticate *vt* recognōscere.

authenticity *n* auctōritās *f*, fidēs *f*.

author *n* auctor *m*, inventor *m*; scrīptor *m*.

authoress *n* auctor *f*.

authoritative *adj* fīdus; imperiōsus.

authority *n* auctōritās *f*, potestās *f*, iūs *nt*; (*MIL*) imperium *nt*; (*LIT*) auctor *m*, scrīptor *m*; **enforce ~** iūs suum exsequī; **have great ~** multum pollēre; **on Caesar's ~** auctōre Caesare; **an ~ on** perītus (*gen*).

authorize *vt* potestātem facere (*dat*), mandāre; (*law*) sancīre.

autobiography *n* dē vītā suā scrīptus liber *m*.

autocracy *n* imperium singulāre *nt*, tyrannis *f*.

autocrat *n* tyrannus *m*, dominus *m*.

autocratic *adj* imperiōsus.

autograph *n* manus *f*, chīrographum *nt*.

automatic *adj* necessārius.

automatically *adv* necessāriō.

autonomous *adj* līber.

autonomy *n* lībertās *f*.

Autumn *n* auctumnus *m*.

autumnal *adj* auctumnālis.

auxiliaries *npl* auxilia *ntpl*, auxiliāriī *mpl*.

auxiliary *adj* auxiliāris ♦ *n* adiūtor *m*; **~ forces** auxilia *ntpl*; novae cōpiae *fpl*.

avail *vi* valēre ♦ *vt* prōdesse (*dat*); **~ oneself of** ūtī (*abl*) ♦ *n* ūsus *m*; **of no ~** frustrā.

available *adj* ad manum, in prōmptū.

avalanche *n* montis ruīna *f*.

avarice *n* avāritia *f*, cupīditās *f*.

avaricious *adj* avārus, cupidus.

avariciously *adv* avārē.

avenge *vt* ulcīscī (+ *abl*), vindicāre.

avenger *n* ultor *m*, vindex *m*.

avenue *n* xystus *m*; (*fig*) aditus *m*, iānua *f*.

aver *vt* adfirmāre, adsevērāre.

average *n* medium *nt*; **on the ~** ferē.

averse *adj* āversus (ab); **be ~ to** abhorrēre ab.

aversion *n* odium *nt*, fastīdium *nt*.

avert *vt* arcēre, dēpellere; (*by prayer*) dēprecārī.

aviary n aviārium nt.
avid adj avidus.
avidity n aviditās f.
avidly adv avidē.
avoid vt vītāre, fugere, dēclīnāre; (battle) dētrectāre.
avoidance n fuga f, dēclīnātiō f.
avow vt fatērī, cōnfitērī.
avowal n cōnfessiō f.
avowed adj apertus.
avowedly adv apertē, palam.
await vt exspectāre; (future) manēre.
awake vt suscitāre, exsuscitāre ♦ vi expergīscī ♦ adj vigil.
awaken vt exsuscitāre.
award vt tribuere; (law) adiūdicāre ♦ n (decision) arbitrium nt, iūdicium nt; (thing) praemium nt.
aware adj gnārus ♦ adj conscius (gen); **be ~** scīre; **become ~ of** percipere.
away adv ā-, ab- (in cpd); **be ~** abesse ab (abl); **far ~** procul, longē; **make ~ with** dē mediō tollere.
awe n formīdō f, reverentia f, rēligiō f; **stand in ~ of** verērī; (gods) venerārī.
awe-struck adj stupidus.
awful adj terribilis, formīdolōsus, dīrus.
awfully adv formīdolōsē.
awhile adv aliquamdiū, aliquantisper, parumper.
awkward adj incallidus, inconcinnus; (to handle) inhabilis; (fig) molestus.
awkwardly adv incallidē, imperītē.
awkwardness n imperītia f, īnscītia f.
awl n sūbula f.
awning n vēlum nt.
awry adj prāvus, dissidēns.
axe n secūris f.
axiom n prōnūntiātum nt, sententia f.
axiomatic adj ēvidēns, manifestus.
axis n axis m.
axle n axis m.
aye adv semper; **for ~** in aeternum.
azure adj caeruleus.

B, b

baa vi bālāre ♦ n bālātus m.
babble vi garrīre, blaterāre.
babbler n garrulus m.
babbling adj garrulus.
babe n īnfāns m/f.
babel n dissonae vōcēs fpl.
baboon n sīmia f.
baby n īnfāns m/f.
Bacchanalian adj Bacchicus.
Bacchante n Baccha f.

bachelor n caelebs m; (degree) baccalaureus m.
back n tergum nt; (animal) dorsum nt; (head) occipitium nt; **at one's ~** ā tergō; **behind one's ~** (fig) clam (acc); **put one's ~ up** stomachum movēre (dat); **turn one's ~ on** sē āvertere ab ♦ adj āversus, postīcus ♦ adv retrō, retrōrsum, re- (in cpds) ♦ vt obsecundāre (dat), adesse (dat); **~ water** inhibēre rēmīs, inhibēre nāvem ♦ vi: **~ out of** dētrectāre, dēfugere.
backbite vt obtrectāre (dat), maledīcere (dat).
backbone n spīna f.
backdoor n postīcum nt.
backer n fautor m.
background n recessus m, umbra f.
backing n fidēs f, favor m.
backslide vi dēscīscere.
backward adj āversus; (slow) tardus; (late) sērus.
backwardness n tardītās f, pigritia f.
backwards adv retrō, retrōrsum.
bacon n lārdum nt.
bad adj malus, prāvus, improbus, turpis; **go ~** corrumpī; **be ~ for** obesse (dat), nocēre (dat).
badge n īnsigne nt, īnfula f.
badger n mēles f ♦ vt sollicitāre
badly adv male, prāvē, improbē, turpiter.
badness n prāvitās f, nēquitia f, improbitās f.
baffle vt ēlūdere, fallere, frustrārī.
bag n saccus m, folliculus m; **hand~** mantica f.
bagatelle n nūgae fpl, floccus m.
baggage n impedīmenta ntpl, vāsa ntpl, sarcinae fpl; **~ train** impedīmenta ntpl; **without ~** expedītus.
bail n vadimōnium nt; (person) vas m; **become ~ for** spondēre prō (abl); **accept ~ for** vadārī; **keep one's ~** vadimōnium obīre ♦ vt spondēre prō (abl).
bailiff n (POL) apparitor m; (private) vīlicus m.
bait n esca f, illecebra f ♦ vt lacessere.
bake vt coquere, torrēre.
bakehouse n pistrīna f.
baker n pistor m.
bakery n pistrīna f.
balance n (scales) lībra f, trutina f; (equilibrium) lībrāmentum nt; (money) reliqua ntpl ♦ vt lībrāre; (fig) compēnsāre; **the account ~s** ratiō cōnstat.
balance sheet n ratiō acceptī et expēnsī.
balcony n podium nt, Maeniānum nt.
bald adj calvus; (style) āridus, iēiūnus.
baldness n calvitium nt; (style) iēiūnitās f.
bale n fascis m; **~ out** vt exhaurīre.
baleful adj fūnestus, perniciōsus, tristis.
balk n tignum nt ♦ vt frustrārī, dēcipere.
ball n globus m; (play) pila f; (wool) glomus nt; (dance) saltātiō f.
ballad n carmen nt.
ballast n saburra f.
ballet n saltātiō f.
ballot n suffrāgium nt.
ballot box n urna f.
balm n unguentum nt; (fig) sōlātium nt.
balmy adj lēnis, suāvis.

balsam–battle

balsam n balsamum nt.
balustrade n cancellī mpl.
bamboozle vt cōnfundere.
ban vt interdīcere (dat), vetāre ♦ n interdictum nt.
banal adj trītus.
banana n ariēna f; (tree) pāla f.
band n vinculum nt, redimīculum nt; (head) īnfula f; (men) caterva f, manus f, grex f ♦ vi: ~ **together** cōnsociārī.
bandage n fascia f, īnfula f ♦ vt obligāre, adligāre.
bandbox n: out of a ~ (fig) dē capsulā.
bandeau n redimīculum nt.
bandit n latrō m.
bandy vt iactāre; ~ **words** altercārī ♦ adj vārus.
bane n venēnum nt, pestis f, perniciēs f.
baneful adj perniciōsus, pestifer.
bang vt pulsāre ♦ n fragor m.
bangle n armilla f.
banish vt pellere, expellere, ēicere; (law) aquā et ignī interdīcere (dat); (temporarily) relēgāre; (feeling) abstergēre.
banishment n (act) aquae et ignis interdictiō f; relēgātiō f; (state) exsilium nt, fuga f.
bank n (earth) agger m; (river) rīpa f; (money) argentāria f.
banker n argentārius m; (public) mēnsārius m.
bankrupt adj: be ~ solvendō nōn esse; **declare oneself** ~ bonam cōpiam ēiūrāre; **go** ~ dēcoquere ♦ n dēcoctor m.
banner n vexillum nt.
banquet n cēna f, epulae fpl; convīvium nt; (religious) daps f ♦ vi epulārī.
banter n cavillātiō f ♦ vi cavillārī.
baptism n baptisma nt.
baptize vt baptizāre.
bar n (door) sera f; (gate) claustrum nt; (metal) later m; (wood) asser m; (lever) vectis m; (obstacle) impedīmentum nt; (law-court) cancellī mpl; (barristers) advocātī mpl; (profession) forum nt; **of the** ~ forēnsis; **practise at the** ~ causās agere.
bar vt (door) obserāre; (way) obstāre (dat), interclūdere, prohibēre; (exception) excipere, exclūdere.
barb n aculeus m, dēns m, hāmus m.
barbarian n barbarus m ♦ adj barbarus.
barbarism n barbaria f.
barbarity n saevitia f, ferōcia f, immānitās f, inhūmānitās f.
barbarous adj barbarus, saevus, immānis, inhūmānus.
barbarously adv barbarē, inhūmānē.
barbed adj hāmātus.
barber n tōnsor m; ~'s **shop** tōnstrīna f.
bard n vātēs m/f; (Gallic) bardus m.
bare adj nūdus; (mere) merus; **lay** ~ nūdāre, aperīre, dētegere ♦ vt nūdāre.
barefaced adj impudēns.
barefoot adj nūdis pedibus.
bare-headed adj capite aperto.
barely adv vix.

bargain n pactum nt, foedus nt; **make a** ~ pacīscī; **make a bad** ~ male emere; **into the** ~ grātiīs ♦ vi pacīscī.
barge n linter f.
bark n cortex m; (dog) lātrātus m; (ship) nāvis f, ratis f ♦ vi lātrāre.
barking n latratus m.
barley n hordeum nt; **of** ~ hordeāceus.
barn n horreum nt.
barrack vt obstrepere (dat).
barracks n castra ntpl.
barrel n cūpa f; ligneum vās nt.
barren adj sterilis.
barrenness n sterilitās f.
barricade n claustrum nt, mūnīmentum nt ♦ vt obsaepīre, obstruere; ~ **off** intersaepīre.
barrier n impedīmentum nt; (racecourse) carcer nt.
barrister n advocātus m, patrōnus m, causidicus m.
barrow n ferculum nt; (mound) tumulus m.
barter vt mūtāre ♦ vi mercēs mūtāre ♦ n mūtātiō f, commercium nt.
base adj turpis, vīlis; (birth) humilis, ignōbilis; (coin) adulterīnus.
base n fundāmentum nt; (statue) basis f; (hill) rādīcēs fpl; (MIL) castra ntpl.
baseless adj falsus, inānis.
basely adv turpiter.
basement n basis f; (storey) īmum tabulātum nt.
baseness n turpitūdō f.
bashful adj pudīcus, verēcundus.
bashfulness n pudor m, verēcundia f.
basic adj prīmus.
basin n alveolus m, pelvis f; **wash**~ aquālis m.
basis n fundāmentum nt.
bask vi aprīcārī.
basket n corbis f, fiscus m; (for bread) canistrum nt; (for wool) quasillum nt.
basking n aprīcātiō f.
bas-relief n toreuma nt.
bass adj (voice) gravis.
bastard adj nothus.
bastion n prōpugnāculum nt.
bat n vespertīliō m; (games) clāva f.
batch n numerus m.
Bath n Aquae Sulis fpl.
bath n balneum nt; (utensil) lābrum nt, lavātiō f; **Turkish** ~ Lacōnicum nt; **cold** ~ frīgidārium nt; **hot** ~ calidārium nt; ~ **superintendent** balneātor m ♦ vt lavāre.
bathe vt lavāre ♦ vi lavārī, perluī.
bathroom n balneāria ntpl.
baths n (public ~) balneae fpl.
batman n cālō m.
baton n virga f, scīpiō m.
battalion n cohors f.
batter vt quassāre, pulsāre, verberāre.
battering ram n ariēs m.
battery n (assault) vīs f.
battle n pugna f, proelium nt, certāmen nt; **a** ~ **was fought** pugnatum est; **pitched** ~ iūstum

proelium; **line of** ~ aciēs *f*; **drawn** ~ anceps
proelium ♦ *vi* pugnāre, contendere; ~ **order**
aciēs *f*.
battle-axe *n* bipennis *f*.
battlefield, battle-line *n* aciēs *f*.
battlement *n* pinna *f*.
bawl *vt* vōciferārī, clāmitāre.
bay *n* (*sea*) sinus *m*; (*tree*) laurus *f*, laurea *f*; **of** ~
laureus; **at** ~ interclūsus ♦ *adj* (*colour*) spādīx
♦ *vi* (*dog*) lātrāre.
be *vi* esse; (*CIRCS*) versārī; (*condition*) sē habēre;
~ **at** adesse (*dat*); ~ **amongst** interesse (*dat*); ~
in inesse (*dat*); **consul-to-** ~ cōnsul
dēsignātus; **how are you?** quid agis?; **so** ~ **it**
estō; *see also* **absent, here** *etc.*
beach *n* lītus *nt*, acta *f* ♦ *vt* (*ship*) subdūcere.
beacon *n* ignis *m*.
bead *n* pilula *f*.
beadle *n* apparitor *m*.
beak *n* rōstrum *nt*.
beaked *adj* rōstrātus.
beaker *n* cantharus *m*, scyphus *m*.
beam *n* (*wood*) trabs *f*, tignum *nt*; (*balance*)
iugum *nt*; (*light*) radius *m*; (*ship*) latus *nt*; **on**
the ~ ā latere ♦ *vi* fulgēre; (*person*) adrīdēre.
beaming *adj* hilaris.
bean *n* faba *f*.
bear *n* ursus *m*, ursa *f*; **Great B**~ septentriōnēs
mpl, Arctos *f*; **Little B**~ septentriō minor *m*,
Cynosūra *f*; ~**'s** ursīnus ♦ *vt* (*carry*) ferre,
portāre; (*endure*) ferre, tolerāre, patī;
(*produce*) ferre, fundere; (*child*) parere; ~
down upon appropinquāre; ~ **off** ferre; ~ **out**
vt arguere; ~ **up** *vi*: ~ **up under** obsistere (*dat*),
sustinēre; ~ **upon** innītī (*dat*); (*refer*)
pertinēre ad; ~ **with** *vt fus* indulgēre (*dat*); ~
oneself sē gerere; **I cannot** ~ **to** addūcī nōn
possum ut.
bearable *adj* tolerābilis.
beard *n* barba *f* ♦ *vt* ultrō lacessere.
bearded *adj* barbātus.
beardless *adj* imberbis.
bearer *n* bāiulus *m*; (*letter*) tabellārius *m*; (*litter*)
lectīcārius *m*; (*news*) nūntius *m*.
bearing *n* (*person*) gestus *m*, vultus *m*;
(*direction*) regiō *f*; **have no** ~ **on** nihil
pertinēre ad; **I have lost my** ~**s** ubi sim
nesciō.
beast *n* bestia *f*; (*large*) bēlua *f*; (*wild*) fera *f*;
(*domestic*) pecus *f*.
beastliness *n* foed>itās *f*, stuprum *nt*.
beastly *adj* foedus.
beast of burden *n* iūmentum *nt*.
beat *n* ictus *m*; (*heart*) palpitātiō *f*; (*music*)
percussiō *f*; (*oars, pulse*) pulsus *m*.
beat *vt* ferīre, percutere, pulsāre; (*the body in*
grief) plangere; (*punish*) caedere; (*whip*)
verberāre; (*conquer*) vincere, superāre ♦ *vi*
palpitāre, micāre; ~ **back** repellere; ~ **in**
perfringere; ~ **out** excutere; (*metal*)
extundere; ~ **a retreat** receptui canere; ~
about the bush circuitiōne ūtī; **be** ~**en**
vāpulāre; **dead** ~ cōnfectus.

beating *n* verbera *ntpl*; (*defeat*) clādēs *f*;
(*time*) percussiō *f*; **get a** ~ vāpulāre.
beatitude *n* beātitūdō *f*, fēlīcitās *f*.
beau *n* nitidus homō *m*; (*lover*) amāns *m*.
beauteous *adj* pulcher, fōrmōsus.
beautiful *adj* pulcher, fōrmōsus; (*looks*)
decōrus; (*scenery*) amoenus.
beautifully *adv* pulchrē.
beautify *vt* exōrnāre, decorāre.
beauty *n* fōrma *f*, pulchritūdō *f*, amoenitās *f*.
beaver *n* castor *m*, fiber *m*; (*helmet*) buccula *f*.
becalmed *adj* ventō dēstitūtus.
because *conj* quod, quia, quōniam (+ *indic*),
quippe quī; ~ **of** propter (*acc*).
beck *n* nūtus *m*.
beckon *vt* innuere, vocāre.
become *vi* fierī; **what will** ~ **of me?** quid me
fīet? ♦ *vt* decēre, convenīre in (*acc*).
becoming *adj* decēns, decōrus.
becomingly *adv* decōrē, convenienter.
bed *n* cubīle *nt*, lectus *m*, lectulus *m*; **go to** ~
cubitum īre; **make a** ~ lectum sternere; **be**
~**ridden** lectō tenērī; **camp** ~ grabātus *m*;
flower~ pulvīnus *m*; **marriage** ~ lectus
geniālis *m*; **river**~ alveus *m*.
bedaub *vt* illinere, oblinere.
bedclothes *n* strāgula *ntpl*.
bedding *n* strāgula *ntpl*.
bedeck *vt* ōrnāre, exōrnāre.
bedew *vt* inrōrāre.
bedim *vt* obscūrāre.
bedpost *n* fulcrum *nt*.
bedraggled *adj* sordidus, madidus.
bedroom *n* cubiculum *nt*.
bedstead *n* sponda *f*.
bee *n* apis *f*; **queen** ~ rēx *m*.
beech *n* fāgus *f* ♦ *adj* fāginus.
beef *n* būbula *f*.
beehive *n* alvus *f*.
beekeeper *n* apiārius *m*.
beer *n* cervīsia *f*, fermentum *nt*.
beet *n* bēta *f*.
beetle *n* (*insect*) scarabaeus *m*; (*implement*)
fistūca *f*.
beetling *adj* imminēns, mināx.
befall *vi, vt* accidere, ēvenīre (*dat*); (*good*)
contingere (*dat*).
befit *vt* decēre, convenīre in (*acc*).
before *adv* ante, anteā, antehāc ♦ *prep* ante
(*acc*); (*place*) prō (*abl*); (*presence*) apud (*acc*),
cōram (*abl*) ♦ *conj* antequam, priusquam.
beforehand *adv* ante, anteā; prae (*in cpd*).
befoul *vt* inquināre, foedāre.
befriend *vt* favēre (*dat*), adiuvāre; (*in trouble*)
adesse (*dat*).
beg *vt* ōrāre, obsecrāre, precārī, poscere ab,
petere ab; ~ **for** petere ♦ *vi* mendīcāre.
beget *vt* gignere, prōcreāre, generāre.
begetter *n* generātor *m*, creātor *m*.
beggar *m* mendīcus *m*.
beggarly *adj* mendīcus, indigēns.
beggary *n* mendīcitās *f*, indigentia *f*.
begin *vi, vt* incipere, coepisse; (*speech*)

exōrdīrī; (*plan*) īnstituere, incohāre; (*time*)
inīre; ~ **with** incipere ab.

beginning *n* initium *nt*, prīncipium *nt*,
exōrdium *nt*, inceptiō *f*; (*learning*) rudīmenta
ntpl, elementa *ntpl*; (*origin*) orīgō *f*, fōns *m*; **at**
the ~ of spring ineunte vēre.

begone *interj* apage, tē āmovē.

begotten *adj* genitus, nātus.

begrudge *vt* invidēre (*dat*).

beguile *vt* dēcipere, fallere.

behalf *n*: **on ~ of** prō (*abl*); **on my ~** meō
nōmine.

behave *vi* sē gerere, sē praebēre (*with adj*);
well ~d bene mōrātus.

behaviour *n* mōrēs *mpl*.

behead *vt* dētruncāre, secūrī percutere.

behest *n* iūssum *nt*.

behind *adv* pōne, post, ā tergō ♦ *prep* post (*acc*),
pōne (*acc*).

behindhand *adv* sērō; **be ~** parum prōficere.

behold *vt* aspicere, cōnspicere, intuērī ♦ *interj*
ecce, ēn.

beholden *adj* obnoxius, obstrictus, obligātus.

behoof *n* ūsus *m*.

behove *vt* oportēre.

being *n* (*life*) animātiō *f*; (*nature*) nātūra *f*;
(*person*) homō *m/f*.

bejewelled *adj* gemmeus, gemmātus.

belabour *vt* verberāre, caedere.

belated *adj* sērus.

belch *vi* ructāre, ēructāre.

beldam *n* anus *f*.

beleaguer *vt* obsidēre, circumsedēre.

belie *vt* abhorrēre ab, repugnāre.

belief *n* fidēs *f*, opīniō *f*; (*opinion*) sententia *f*; **to**
the best of my ~ ex animī meī sententiā; **past**
~ incrēdibilis.

believe *vt, vi* (*thing*) crēdere; (*person*) crēdere
(*dat*); (*suppose*) crēdere, putāre, arbitrārī,
opīnārī; **~ in gods** deōs esse crēdere; **make ~**
simulāre.

believer *n* deōrum cultor *m*; Christiānus *m*.

belike *adv* fortasse.

belittle *vt* obtrectāre.

bell *n* tintinnābulum *nt*; (*public*) campāna *f*.

belle *n* fōrmōsa *f*, pulchra *f*.

belles-lettres *n* litterae *fpl*.

bellicose *adj* ferōx.

belligerent *adj* bellī particeps.

bellow *vi* rūdere, mūgīre ♦ *n* mūgītus *m*.

bellows *n* follis *m*.

belly *n* abdōmen *nt*, venter *m*; (*sail*) sinus *m* ♦ *vi*
tumēre.

belong *vi* esse (*gen*), proprium esse (*gen*),
inesse (*dat*); (*concern*) attinēre, pertinēre.

belongings *n* bona *ntpl*.

beloved *adj* cārus, dīlectus, grātus.

below *adv* īnfrā, subter ♦ *adj* īnferus ♦ *prep*
īnfrā (*acc*), sub (*abl, acc*).

belt *n* zōna *f*; (*sword*) balteus *m*.

bemoan *vt* dēplōrāre, lāmentārī.

bemused *adj* stupefactus, stupidus.

bench *n* subsellium *nt*; (*rowing*) trānstrum *nt*;

(*law*) iūdicēs *mpl*; **seat on the ~** iūdicātus *m*.

bend *vt* flectere, curvāre, inclīnāre; (*bow*)
intendere; (*course*) tendere, flectere; (*mind*)
intendere ♦ *vi* sē īnflectere; (*person*) sē
dēmittere; **~ back** reflectere; **~ down** *vi*
dēflectere; **be** sē dēmittere ♦ *n* flexus *m*,
ānfrāctus *m*.

beneath *adv* subter ♦ *prep* sub (*acc or abl*).

benediction *n* bonae precēs *fpl*.

benedictory *adj* faustus.

benefaction *n* beneficium *nt*, dōnum *nt*.

benefactor *n* patrōnus *m*; **be a ~** bene merērī
(dē).

beneficence *n* beneficentia *f*, līberālitās *f*.

beneficent *adj* beneficus.

beneficial *adj* ūtilis, salūbris.

benefit *n* beneficium *nt*; (*derived*) fructus *m*;
have the ~ of fruī (*abl*) ♦ *vt* prōdesse (*dat*),
usuī esse (*dat*).

benevolence *n* benevolentia *f*, benignitās *f*.

benevolent *adj* benevolus, benignus.

benevolently *adv* benevolē, benignē.

benighted *adj* nocte oppressus; (*fig*) ignārus,
indoctus.

benign *adj* benignus, cōmis.

bent *n* (*mind*) inclīnātiō *f*, ingenium *nt* ♦ *adj*
curvus, flexus; (*mind*) attentus; **be ~ on**
studēre (*dat*).

benumb *vt* stupefacere.

benumbed *adj* stupefactus, torpidus; **be ~**
torpēre.

bequeath *vt* lēgāre.

bequest *n* lēgātum *nt*.

bereave *vt* orbāre, prīvāre.

bereavement *n* damnum *nt*.

bereft *adj* orbus, orbātus, prīvātus.

berry *n* bāca *f*.

berth *n* statiō *f*; **give a wide ~ to** dēvītāre.

beryl *n* bēryllus *m*.

beseech *vt* implōrāre, ōrāre, obsecrāre.

beset *vt* obsidēre, circumsedēre.

beside *prep* ad (*acc*), apud (*acc*); (*close*) iuxtā
(*acc*); **~ the point** nihil ad rem; **be ~ oneself**
nōn esse apud sē.

besides *adv* praetereā, accēdit quod; (*in*
addition) īnsuper ♦ *prep* praeter (*acc*).

besiege *vt* obsidēre, circumsedēre.

besieger *n* obsessor *m*.

besmear *vt* illinere.

besmirch *vt* maculāre.

besom *n* scōpae *fpl*.

besotted *adj* stupidus.

bespatter *vt* aspergere.

bespeak *vt* (*order*) imperāre; (*denote*)
significāre.

besprinkle *vt* aspergere.

best *adj* optimus; **the ~ part** māior pars ♦ *n* flōs
m, rōbur *nt*; **do one's ~** prō virīlī parte agere;
do one's ~ to operam dare ut; **have the ~ of it**
vincere; **make the ~ of (a situation)** aequō
animō accipere; **to the ~ of one's ability** prō
virīlī parte; **to the ~ of my knowledge** quod
sciam ♦ *adv* optimē.

bestial *adj* foedus.
bestir *vt* movēre; ~ **oneself** expergīscī.
bestow *vt* dōnāre, tribuere, dare, cōnferre.
bestride *vt* (*horse*) sedēre in (*abl*).
bet *n* pignus *nt* ♦ *vt* oppōnere ♦ *vi* pignore contendere.
betake *vt* cōnferre, recipere; ~ **o.s.** sē cōnferre.
bethink *vt*: ~ **oneself** sē colligere; ~ **oneself of** respicere.
betide *vi* accidere, ēvenīre.
betoken *vt* significāre; (*foretell*) portendere.
betray *vt* prōdere, trādere; (*feelings*) arguere; **without ~ing one's trust** salvā fidē.
betrayal *n* prōditiō *f*.
betrayer *n* prōditor *m*; (*informer*) index *m*.
betroth *vt* spondēre, dēspondēre.
betrothal *n* spōnsālia *ntpl*.
better *adj* melior; **it is ~ to** praestat (*infin*); **get the ~ of** vincere, superāre; **I am ~** (*in health*) melius est mihī; **I had ~ go** praestat īre; **get ~** convalēscere; **think ~ of** sententiam mūtāre dē ♦ *adv* melius ♦ *vt* corrigere; ~ **oneself** prōficere.
betterment *n* prōfectus *m*.
between *prep* inter (*acc*).
beverage *n* pōtiō *f*.
bevy *n* manus *f*, grex *f*.
bewail *vt* dēflēre, lāmentārī, dēplōrāre.
beware *vt* cavēre.
bewilder *vt* cōnfundere, perturbāre.
bewildered *adj* attonitus.
bewilderment *n* perturbātiō *f*, admīrātiō *f*.
bewitch *vt* fascināre; (*fig*) dēlēnīre.
beyond *adv* ultrā, suprā ♦ *prep* ultrā (*acc*), extrā (*acc*); (*motion*) trāns (*acc*); (*amount*) ultrā, suprā (*acc*); **go/pass ~** excēdere, ēgredī.
bezel *n* pāla *f*.
bias *n* inclīnātiō *f*; (*party*) favor *m* ♦ *vt* inclīnāre.
biassed *adj* prōpēnsior.
bibber *n* pōtor *m*, pōtātor *m*.
Bible *n* litterae sacrae *fpl*.
bibulous *adj* bibulus.
bicephalous *adj* biceps.
bicker *vi* altercārī, iūrgāre.
bid *vt* iubēre; (*guest*) vocāre, invītāre ♦ *vi* (*at auction*) licērī; ~ **for** licērī; ~ **good day** salvēre iubēre; **he ~s fair to make progress** spēs est eum prōfecturum esse.
biddable *adj* docilis.
bidding *n* iussum *nt*; (*auction*) licitātiō *f*.
bide *vt* manēre, opperīrī.
biennial *adj* biennālis.
bier *n* ferculum *nt*.
bifurcate *vi* sē scindere.
bifurcation *n* (*road*) trivium *nt*.
big *adj* māgnus, grandis, amplus; (*with child*) gravida; **very ~** permāgnus; **talk ~** glōriārī.
bight *n* sinus *m*.
bigness *n* māgnitūdō *f*, amplitūdō *f*.
bigot *n* nimis obstinātus fautor *m*.

bigoted *adj* contumāx.
bigotry *n* contumācia *f*, nimia obstinātiō *f*.
bile *n* bīlis *f*, fel *nt*.
bilgewater *n* sentīna *f*.
bilk *vt* fraudāre.
bill *n* (*bird*) rōstrum *nt*; (*implement*) falx *f*; (*law*) rogātiō *f*, lēx *f*; (*money*) syngrapha *f*; (*notice*) libellus *m*, titulus *m*; **introduce a ~** populum rogāre, lēgem ferre; **carry a ~** lēgem perferre.
billet *n* hospitium *nt* ♦ *vt* in hospitia dīvidere.
billhook *n* falx *f*.
billow *n* fluctus *m*.
billowy *adj* undōsus.
billy goat *n* caper *m*.
bin *n* lacus *m*.
bind *vt* adligāre, dēligāre, vincīre; (*by oath*) adigere; (*by obligation*) obligāre, obstringere; (*wound*) obligāre; ~ **fast** dēvincīre; ~ **together** conligāre; ~ **over** *vt* vadārī.
binding *n* compāgēs *f* ♦ *adj* (*law*) ratus; **it is ~ on** oportet.
bindweed *n* convolvulus *m*.
biographer *n* vītae nārrātor *m*.
biography *n* vīta *f*.
bipartite *adj* bipartītus.
biped *n* bipēs *m*.
birch *n* bētula *f*; (*flogging*) virgae ulmeae *fpl*.
bird *n* avis *f*; ~**s of a feather** parēs cum paribus facillimē congregantur; **kill two ~s with one stone** ūnō saltū duōs aprōs capere, dē eādem fidēliā duōs parietēs dealbāre; ~**'s-eye view of** dēspectus in (*acc*).
birdcatcher *n* auceps *m*.
birdlime *n* viscum *nt*.
birth *n* (*act*) partus *m*; (*origin*) genus *nt*; **low ~** ignōbilitās *f*; **high ~** nōbilitās *f*; **by ~** nātū, ortū.
birthday *n* nātālis *m*.
birthday party *n* nātālicia *ntpl*.
birthplace *n* locus nātālis *m*; (*fig*) incūnābula *ntpl*.
birthright *n* patrimōnium *nt*.
bisect *vt* dīvidere.
bishop *n* epīscopus *m*.
bison *n* ūrus *m*.
bit *n* pars *f*; (*food*) frustum *nt*; (*broken off*) fragmentum *nt*; (*horse*) frēnum *nt*; ~ **by ~** minūtātim; **a ~** *adv* aliquantulum; **a ~ sad** tristior.
bitch *n* canis *f*.
bite *vt* mordēre; (*frost*) ūrere ♦ *n* morsus *m*; **with a ~** mordicus.
biting *adj* mordāx.
bitter *adj* (*taste*) acerbus, amārus; (*words*) asper.
bitterly *adv* acerbē, asperē.
bittern *n* būtiō *m*, ardea *f*.
bitterness *n* acerbitās *f*.
bitumen *n* bitūmen *nt*.
bivouac *n* excubiae *fpl* ♦ *vi* excubāre.
bizarre *adj* īnsolēns.

blab *vt, vi* garrīre, effūtīre.
black *adj* (*dull*) āter; (*glossy*) niger; (*dirt*)
sordidus; (*eye*) līvidus; (*looks*) trux; ~ **and**
blue līvidus; ♦ *n* ātrum *nt*, nigrum *nt*; **dressed**
in ~ ātrātus; (*in mourning*) sordidātus.
blackberry *n* mōrum *nt*.
blackbird *n* merula *f*.
blacken *vt* nigrāre, nigrum reddere;
(*character*) īnfāmāre, obtrectāre (*dat*).
blackguard *n* scelestus, scelerātus *m*.
blacking *n* ātrāmentum *nt*.
blacklist *n* prōscrīptiō *f*.
black magic *n* magicae artēs *fpl*.
blackmail *n* minae *fpl* ♦ *vt* minīs cōgere.
black mark *n* nota *f*.
blacksmith *n* faber *m*.
bladder *n* vēsīca *f*.
blade *n* (*grass*) herba *f*; (*oar*) palma *f*; (*sword*)
lāmina *f*.
blame *vt* reprehendere, culpāre; **I am to** ~
reus sum ♦ *n* reprehēnsiō *f*, culpa *f*.
blameless *adj* innocēns.
blamelessly *adv* innocenter.
blamelessness *n* innocentia *f*, integritās *f*.
blameworthy *adj* accūsābilis, nocēns.
blanch *vi* exalbēscere, pallēscere.
bland *adj* mītis, lēnis.
blandishment *n* blanditiae *fpl*.
blank *adj* vacuus, pūrus; (*look*) stolidus.
blanket *n* lōdīx *f*; **wet** ~ nimium sevērus.
blare *vi* canere, strīdere ♦ *n* clangor *m*, strīdor
m.
blarney *n* lēnōcinium *nt*.
blaspheme *vi* maledīcere.
blasphemous *adj* maledicus, impius.
blasphemy *n* maledicta *ntpl*, impietās *f*.
blast *n* flātus *m*, īnflātus *m* ♦ *vt* disicere,
discutere; (*crops*) rōbīgine adficere.
blatant *adj* raucus.
blaze *n* flamma *f*, ignis *m*, fulgor *m* ♦ *vi*
flāgrāre, ārdēre, fulgēre; ~ **up** exārdēscere
♦ *vt*: ~ **abroad** pervulgāre.
blazon *vt* promulgāre.
bleach *vt* candidum reddere.
bleak *adj* dēsertus, tristis, inamoenus.
bleary-eyed *adj* lippus.
bleat *vi* bālāre ♦ *n* bālātus *m*.
bleed *vi* sanguinem fundere ♦ *vt* sanguinem
mittere (*dat*); **my heart** ~**s** animus mihī dolet.
bleeding *adj* crūdus, sanguineus ♦ *n* sanguinis
missiō *f*.
blemish *n* macula *f*, vitium *nt* ♦ *vt* maculāre,
foedāre.
blend *vt* miscēre, immiscēre, admiscēre ♦ *n*
coniūnctiō *f*.
bless *vt* beāre; laudāre; (*ECCL*) benedīcere; ~
with augēre (*abl*); ~ **my soul!** ita mē dī ament!
blessed *adj* beātus, fortūnātus; (*emperors*)
dīvus.
blessing *n* (*thing*) commodum *nt*, bonum *nt*;
(*ECCL*) benedictiō *f*.
blight *n* rōbīgō *f*, ūrēdō *f* ♦ *vt* rōbīgine adficere;
(*fig*) nocēre (*dat*).

blind *adj* caecus; (*in one eye*) luscus; (*fig*)
ignārus, stultus; (*alley*) nōn pervius; (*forces*)
necessārius; **turn a** ~ **eye to** cōnīvēre in (*abl*)
♦ *vt* excaecāre, caecāre; (*fig*) occaecāre;
(*with light*) praestringere.
blindfold *adj* capite obvolūtō.
blindly *adv* temerē.
blindness *n* caecitās *f*; (*fig*) temeritās *f*,
īnsipientia *f*.
blink *vi* nictāre.
bliss *n* fēlīcitās *f*, laetitia *f*.
blissful *adj* fēlīx, beātus, laetus.
blissfully *adv* fēlīciter, beātē.
blister *n* pustula *f*.
blithe *adj* hilaris, laetus.
blithely *adv* hilare, laetē.
blizzard *n* hiems *f*.
bloated *adj* tumidus, turgidus.
blob *n* gutta *f*, particula *f*.
block *n* (*wood*) stīpes *m*, caudex *m*; (*stone*)
massa *f*; (*houses*) īnsula *f*; ~ **letter** quadrāta
littera; **stumbling** ~ offēnsiō *f*.
block *vt* claudere, obstruere, interclūdere; ~
the way obstāre.
blockade *n* obsidiō *f*; **raise a** ~ obsidiōnem
solvere ♦ *vt* obsidēre, interclūdere.
blockhead *n* caudex *m*, bārō *m*, truncus *m*.
blockhouse *n* castellum *nt*.
blond *adj* flāvus.
blood *n* sanguis *m*; (*shed*) cruor *m*; (*murder*)
caedēs *f*; (*kin*) genus *nt*; **let** ~ sanguinem
mittere; **staunch** ~ sanguinem supprimere;
bad ~ simultās *f*; **in cold** ~ cōnsultō; **own flesh**
and ~ cōnsanguineus.
bloodless *adj* exsanguis; (*victory*) incruentus.
bloodshed *n* caedēs *f*.
bloodshot *adj* sanguineus.
bloodstained *adj* cruentus.
bloodsucker *n* hirūdō *f*.
bloodthirsty *adj* sanguinārius.
blood vessel *n* vēna *f*.
bloody *adj* cruentus.
bloom *n* flōs *m*; **in** ~ flōrēns ♦ *vi* flōrēre,
flōrēscere, vigēre.
blossom *n* flōs *m* ♦ *vi* efflōrēscere, flōrēre.
blot *n* macula *f*; (*erasure*) litūra *f* ♦ *vt* maculāre;
~ **out** dēlēre, oblitterāre.
blotch *n* macula *f*.
blotched *adj* maculōsus.
blow *vt, vi* (*wind*) flāre; (*breath*) adflāre,
anhēlāre; (*instrument*) canere; (*flower*)
efflōrēscere; (*nose*) ēmungere; ~ **out** *vi*
exstinguere; ~ **over** *vi* (*storm*) cadere; (*fig*)
abīre; ~ **up** *vt* īnflāre; (*destroy*) discutere,
disturbāre ♦ *n* ictus *m*; (*on the cheek*) alapa *f*;
(*fig*) plāga *f*; (*misfortune*) calamitās *f*; **aim a** ~
at petere; **come to** ~**s** ad manūs venīre.
blowy *adj* ventōsus.
bludgeon *n* fustis *m*.
blue *adj* caeruleus; **black and** ~ līvidus; **true** ~
fīdissimus; ~ **blood** nōbilitās *f*.
bluff *n* rūpēs *f*, prōmunturium *nt* ♦ *adj*

inurbānus ♦ *vt* fallere, dēcipere, verba dare (*dat*), impōnere (*dat*).

blunder *vi* errāre, offendere ♦ *n* error *m*, errātum *nt*; (*in writing*) mendum *nt*.

blunt *adj* hebes; (*manners*) horridus, rūsticus, inurbānus; **be ~** hebēre ♦ *vt* hebetāre, obtundere, retundere.

bluntly *adv* līberius, plānē et apertē.

blur *n* macula *f* ♦ *vt* obscūrāre.

blurt *vt*: **~ out** ēmittere.

blush *vi* rubēre, ērubēscere ♦ *n* rubor *m*.

bluster *vi* dēclāmitāre, lātrāre.

boa *n* boa *f*.

Boadicea *n* Boudicca *f*.

boar *n* verrēs *m*; (*wild*) aper *m*.

board *n* tabula *f*; (*table*) mēnsa *f*; (*food*) vīctus *m*; (*committee*) concilium *nt*; (*judicial*) quaestiō *f*; (*of ten men*) decemvirī *mpl*; (*gaming*) abacus *m*, alveus *m*; **on ~** in nāvī; **go on ~** in nāvem cōnscendere; **go by the ~** intercidere, perīre; **above ~** sine fraude ♦ *vt* (*building*) contabulāre; (*ship*) cōnscendere; (*person*) vīctum praebēre (*dat*) ♦ *vi*: **~ with** dēvertere ad.

boarder *n* hospes *m*.

boast *vi* glōriārī, sē iactāre; **~ of** glōriārī dē (*abl*) ♦ *n* glōria *f*, glōriātiō *f*, iactātiō *f*.

boastful *adj* glōriōsus.

boastfully *adv* glōriōsē.

boasting *n* glōriātiō *f* ♦ *adj* glōriōsus.

boat *n* linter *f*, scapha *f*, cymba *f*; (*ship*) nāvis *f*; **be in the same ~** (*fig*) in eādem nāvī esse.

boatman *n* nauta *m*.

boatswain *n* hortātor *m*.

bobbin *n* fūsus *m*.

bode *vt* portendere, praesāgīre.

bodiless *adj* sine corpore.

bodily *adj* corporeus.

bodkin *n* acus *f*.

body *n* corpus *nt*; (*dead*) cadāver *nt*; (*small*) corpusculum *nt*; (*person*) homō *m/f*; (*of people*) globus *m*, numerus *m*; (*of troops*) manus *f*, caterva *f*; (*of cavalry*) turma *f*; (*of officials*) collēgium *nt*; (*heavenly*) astrum *nt*; **in a ~** ūniversī, frequentēs.

bodyguard *n* custōs *m*, stīpātōrēs *mpl*; (*emperor's*) praetōriānī *mpl*.

bog *n* palūs *f*.

bogey *n* mōnstrum *nt*.

boggle *vi* tergiversārī, haesitāre.

boggy *adj* palūster.

bogus *adj* falsus, fictus.

Bohemian *adj* līberior, solūtior, libīdinōsus.

boil *vt* coquere; (*liquid*) fervefacere; **~ down** dēcoquere ♦ *vi* fervēre, effervēscere; (*sea*) exaestuāre; (*passion*) exārdēscere, aestuāre; **~ over** effervēscere ♦ *n* (*MED*) fūrunculus *m*.

boiler *n* cortīna *f*.

boiling *adj* (*hot*) fervēns.

boisterous *adj* (*person*) turbulentus, vehemēns; (*sea*) turbidus, agitātus; (*weather*) procellōsus, violentus.

boisterously *adv* turbidē, turbulentē.

boisterousness *n* tumultus *m*, violentia *f*.

bold *adj* audāx, fortis, intrepidus; (*impudent*) impudēns, protervus; (*language*) līber; (*headland*) prōminēns; **make ~** audēre.

boldly *adv* audācter, fortiter, intrepidē; impudenter.

boldness *n* audācia *f*, cōnfīdentia *f*; impudentia *f*, petulantia *f*; (*speech*) lībertās *f*.

bolster *n* pulvīnus *m* ♦ *vt*: **~ up** sustinēre, cōnfirmāre.

bolt *n* (*door*) claustrum *nt*, pessulus *m*, sera *f*; (*missile*) tēlum *nt*, sagitta *f*; (*lightning*) fulmen *nt*; **make a ~ for it** prōripere, aufugere; **a ~ from the blue** rēs subita, rēs inopīnāta ♦ *vi* (*door*) obserāre, obdere.

bombard *vt* tormentīs verberāre; (*fig*) lacessere.

bombast *n* ampullae *fpl*.

bombastic *adj* tumidus, īnflātus; **be ~** ampullārī.

bond *n* vinculum *nt*, catēna *f*, compes *f*; (*of union*) cōpula *f*, iugum *nt*, nōdus *m*; (*document*) syngrapha *f*; (*agreement*) foedus *nt* ♦ *adj* servus, addictus.

bondage *n* servitūs *f*, famulātus *m*.

bone *n* os *nt*; (*fish*) spīna *f* ♦ *vt* exossāre.

boneless *adj* exos.

bonfire *n* ignis festus *m*.

bonhomie *n* festīvitās *f*.

bon mot *n* dictum *nt*, sententia *f*.

bonny *adj* pulcher, bellus.

bony *adj* osseus.

boo *vt* explōdere.

book *n* liber *m*; (*small*) libellus *m*; (*scroll*) volūmen *nt*; (*modern form*) cōdex *m*; **~s** (*COMM*) rationēs *fpl*, tabulae *fpl*; **bring to ~** in iūdicium vocāre.

bookbinder *n* glūtinātor *m*.

bookcase *n* librārium *nt*, pēgma *nt*.

bookish *adj* litterārum studiōsus.

book-keeper *n* āctuārius *m*.

bookseller *n* librārius *m*, bibliopōla *m*.

bookshop *n* bibliothēca *f*, librāria taberna *f*.

bookworm *n* tinea *f*.

boom *n* (*spar*) longurius *m*; (*harbour*) ōbex *m/f* ♦ *vi* resonāre.

boon *n* bonum *nt*, beneficium *nt*, dōnum *nt* ♦ *adj* festīvus; **~ companion** sodālis *m*, compōtor *m*.

boor *n* agrestis *m*, rūsticus *m*.

boorish *adj* agrestis, rūsticus, inurbānus.

boorishly *adv* rūsticē.

boost *vt* efferre; (*wares*) vēnditāre.

boot *n* calceus *m*; (*MIL*) caliga *f*; (*rustic*) pērō *m*; (*tragic*) cothurnus *m* ♦ *vi* prōdesse; **to ~** īnsuper, praetereā.

booted *adj* calceātus, caligātus.

booth *n* taberna *f*.

bootless *adj* inūtilis, vānus.

bootlessly *adv* frustrā.

booty *n* praeda *f*, spolia *ntpl*.

border *n* ōra *f*, margō *f*; (*country*) fīnis *m*; (*dress*) limbus *m* ♦ *vt* praetexere, margināre;

fīnīre ♦ *vi*: ~ **on** adiacēre (*dat*), imminēre (*dat*), attingere; (*fig*) fīnitimum esse (*dat*).
bordering *adj* fīnitimus.
bore *vt* perforāre, perterebrāre; (*person*) obtundere, fatīgāre; ~ **out** exterebrāre ♦ *n* terebra *f*; (*hole*) forāmen *nt*; (*person*) homō importūnus *m*, ineptus *m*.
boredom *n* lassitūdō *f*.
borer *n* terebra *f*.
born *adj* nātus; **be** ~ nāscī.
borough *n* mūnicipium *nt*.
borrow *vt* mūtuārī.
borrowed *adj* mūtuus; (*fig*) aliēnus.
borrowing *n* mūtuātiō *f*; (*to pay a debt*) versūra *f*.
bosky *adj* nemorōsus.
bosom *n* sinus *m*; (*fig*) gremium *nt*; ~ **friend** familiāris *m/f*, sodālis *m*; **be a** ~ **friend of** ab latere esse (*gen*).
boss *n* bulla *f*; (*shield*) umbō *m*.
botanist *n* herbārius *m*.
botany *n* herbāria *f*.
botch *vt* male sarcīre, male gerere.
both *pron* ambō, uterque (*gen* **utriusque**, *each of two*) ♦ *adv*: ~ ... **and** et ... et, cum ... tum.
bother *n* negōtium *nt* ♦ *vt* vexāre, molestus esse (*dat*) ♦ *vi* operam dare.
bothersome *adj* molestus.
bottle *n* lagoena *f*, amphora *f* ♦ *vt* (*wine*) diffundere.
bottom *n* fundus *m*; (*ground*) solum *nt*; (*ship*) carīna *f*; **the** ~ **of** īmus; **be at the** ~ **of** (*cause*) auctōrem esse; **go to the** ~ pessum īre, perīre; **send to the** ~ pessum dare; **from the** ~ funditus, ab īnfimō.
bottomless *adj* profundus, fundō carēns.
bottommost *adj* īnfimus.
bough *n* rāmus *m*.
boulder *n* saxum *nt*.
boulevard *n* platea *f*.
bounce *vi* salīre, resultāre.
bound *n* fīnis *m*, modus *m*, terminus *m*; (*leap*) saltus *m*; **set** ~**s to** modum facere (*dat*) ♦ *vt* fīnīre, dēfīnīre, termināre ♦ *vi* salīre, saltāre ♦ *adj* adligātus, obligātus, obstrictus; **be** ~ **to** (*duty*) dēbēre; **it is** ~ **to happen** necesse est ēveniat; **be** ~ **for** tendere in (*acc*); **be storm**~ tempestāte tenērī.
boundaries *npl* fīnēs *mpl*.
boundary *n* fīnis *m*; (*of fields*) terminus *m*; (*fortified*) līmes *m*; ~ **stone** terminus *m*.
boundless *adj* immēnsus, īnfīnītus.
boundlessness *n* īnfīnitās *f*, immēnsum *nt*.
bounteous *adj see* **bountiful**.
bounteously *adv* largē, līberāliter, cōpiōsē.
bountiful *adj* largus, līberālis, benignus.
bounty *n* largitās *f*, līberālitās *f*; (*store*) cōpia *f*.
bouquet *n* corollārium *nt*; (*of wine*) flōs *m*.
bourn *n* fīnis *m*.
bout *n* certāmen *nt*; (*drinking*) cōmissātiō *f*.
bovine *adj* būbulus; (*fig*) stolidus.
bow *n* arcus *m*; (*ship*) prōra *f*; (*courtesy*) salūtātiō *f*; **have two strings to one's** ~

duplicī spē ūtī; **rain**~ arcus *m* ♦ *vi* flectere, inclīnāre ♦ *vi* caput dēmittere.
bowels *n* alvus *f*; (*fig*) viscera *ntpl*.
bower *n* umbrāculum *nt*, trichila *f*.
bowl *n* (*cooking*) catīnus *m*; (*drinking*) calix *m*; (*mixing wine*) crātēra *f*; (*ball*) pila *f* ♦ *vt* volvere; ~ **over** prōruere.
bow-legged *adj* valgus.
bowler *n* (*game*) dator *m*.
bowstring *n* nervus *m*.
box *n* arca *f*, capsa *f*; (*for clothes*) cista *f*; (*for medicine*) pyxis *f*; (*for perfume*) alabaster *m*; (*tree*) buxus *f*; (*wood*) buxum *nt*; (*blow on ears*) alapa *f* ♦ *vt* inclūdere; ~ **the ears of** alapam dūcere (*dat*), colaphōs īnfringere (*dat*) ♦ *vi* (*fight*) pugnīs certāre.
boxer *n* pugil *m*.
boxing *n* pugilātiō *f*.
boxing glove *n* caestus *m*.
boy *n* puer *m*; **become a** ~ **again** repuerāscere.
boycott *vt* repudiāre.
boyhood *n* pueritia *f*; **from** ~ ā puerō.
boyish *adj* puerīlis.
boyishly *adv* puerīliter.
brace *n* (*building*) fībula *f*; (*strap*) fascia *f*; (*pair*) pār *nt* ♦ *vt* adligāre; (*strengthen*) firmāre.
bracelet *n* armilla *f*.
bracing *adj* (*air*) salūbris.
bracken *n* filix *f*.
bracket *n* uncus *m*.
brackish *adj* amārus.
bradawl *n* terebra *f*.
brag *vi* glōriārī, sē iactāre.
braggart *n* glōriōsus *m*.
braid *vt* nectere.
brain *n* cerebrum *nt*; ingenium *nt*.
brainless *adj* sōcors, stultus.
brainy *adj* ingeniōsus.
brake *n* (*wood*) dūmētum *nt*; (*on wheel*) sufflāmen *nt*.
bramble *n* rubus *m*.
bran *n* furfur *m*.
branch *n* rāmus *m*; (*kind*) genus *nt* ♦ *vi*: ~ **out** rāmōs porrigere.
branching *adj* rāmōsus.
brand *n* (*fire*) torris *m*, fax *f*; (*mark*) nota *f*; (*sword*) ēnsis *m*; (*variety*) genus *nt* ♦ *vt* (*mark*) inūrere; (*stigma*) notāre; ~ **new** recēns.
brandish *vt* vibrāre.
brass *n* orichalcum *nt*.
bravado *n* ferōcitās *f*; **out of** ~ per speciem ferōcitātis.
brave *adj* fortis, ācer ♦ *vt* adīre, patī.
bravely *adv* fortiter, ācriter.
bravery *n* fortitūdō *f*, virtūs *f*.
bravo *interj* bene, euge, macte.
brawl *n* rixa *f*, iūrgium *nt* ♦ *vi* rixārī.
brawn *n* lacertī *mpl*.
brawny *adj* lacertōsus, rōbūstus.
bray *vi* rūdere.
brazen *adj* aēneus; (*fig*) impudēns.
brazier *n* foculus *m*.
breach *n* (*in wall*) ruīna *f*; (*of friendship*)

dissēnsiō *f* ♦ *vt* perfringere; ~ **of trust** mala fidēs; **commit a ~ of promise** prōmissīs nōn stāre.
breach of the peace *n* iūrgium *nt*, tumultus *m*.
bread *n* pānis *m*.
breadth *n* lātitūdō *f*; **in** ~ in lātitūdinem (*acc*).
break *vt* frangere, perfringere; ~ **down** *vt* īnfringere, dīruere; ~ **in** *vt* (*animal*) domāre; ~ **into pieces** dīrumpere; ~ **off** *vt* abrumpere, dēfringere; (*action*) dīrimere; ~ **open** effringere, solvere; ~ **through** *vt fus* interrumpere; ~ **up** *vt* dissolvere, interrumpere; ~ **one's word** fidem fallere, violāre; **without ~ing the law** salvīs lēgibus ♦ *vi* rumpī, frangī; (*day*) illūcēscere; (*strength*) dēficere; ~ **off** *vi* dēsinere; ~ **into** intrāre; ~ **out** *vi* ērumpere; (*sore*) recrūdēscere; (*trouble*) exārdēscere; ~ **up** *vi* dīlābī, dissolvī; (*meeting*) dīmittī; ~ **through** *vi* inrumpere; ~ **with** dissidēre ab ♦ *n* intermissiō *f*, intervallum *nt*.
breakable *adj* fragilis.
breakage *n* frāctum *nt*.
breakdown *n* (*activity*) mora *f*; (*health*) dēbilitās *f*.
breaker *n* fluctus *m*.
breakfast *n* ientāculum *nt*, prandium *nt* ♦ *vi* ientāre, prandēre.
breakwater *n* mōlēs *f*.
bream *n* sparulus *m*.
breast *n* pectus *nt*; (*woman's*) mamma *f*; **make a clean ~ of** cōnfitērī.
breastplate *n* lōrīca *f*.
breastwork *n* lōrīca *f*, pluteus *m*.
breath *n* spīritus *m*, anima *f*; (*bad*) hālitus *m*; (*quick*) anhēlitus *m*; (*of wind*) aura *f*, adflātus *m*; **below one's ~** mussitāns; **catch one's ~** obstipēscere; **hold one's ~** animam comprimere, continēre; **take a ~** spīritum dūcere; **take one's ~ away** exanimāre; **waste one's ~** operam perdere; **out of ~** exanimātus.
breathable *adj* spīrābilis.
breathe *vt, vi* spīrāre, respīrāre; (*quickly*) anhēlāre; ~ **again** respīrāre; ~ **in** *vt, vi* spīritum dūcere; ~ **out** *vt, vi* exspīrāre, exhālāre; ~ **upon** īnspīrāre (*dat*), adflāre (*dat*); ~ **one's last** animam agere, efflāre.
breathing *n* hālitus *m*, respīrātiō *f*.
breathing space *n* respīrātiō *f*.
breathless *adj* exanimātus.
breeches *n* brācae *fpl*.
breed *n* genus *nt* ♦ *vt* generāre, prōcreāre; (*raise*) ēducāre, alere; (*fig*) adferre, efficere; **well-bred** generōsus.
breeder *n* (*animal*) mātrix *f*; (*man*) generātor *m*; (*fig*) nūtrix *f*.
breeding *n* (*act*) fētūra *f*; (*manners*) mōrēs *mpl*; **good ~** hūmānitās *f*.
breeze *n* aura *f*, flātus *m*.
breezy *adj* ventōsus; (*manner*) hilaris.
brevity *n* brevitās *f*.
brew *vt* coquere ♦ *vi* (*fig*) parārī, imminēre.

bribe *vt* corrumpere ♦ *vi* largīrī ♦ *n* pecūnia *f*, mercēs *f*.
briber *n* corruptor *m*, largītor *m*.
bribery *n* ambitus *m*, largītiō *f*.
brick *n* later *m* ♦ *adj* latericius.
brickwork *n* latericium *nt*.
bridal *adj* nūptiālis; (*bed*) geniālis ♦ *n* nūptiae *fpl*.
bride *n* nūpta *f*.
bridegroom *m* marītus *m*.
bridge *n* pōns *m* ♦ *vt* pontem impōnere (*dat*).
bridle *n* frēnum *nt* ♦ *vt* frēnāre, īnfrēnāre.
brief *adj* brevis; **to be ~** nē longum sit, nē multa.
briefly *adv* breviter, paucīs verbīs.
briefness *n* brevitās *f*.
brier *n* veprēs *m*, sentis *m*.
brig *n* liburna *f*.
brigade *n* legiō *f*; (*cavalry*) turma *f*.
brigadier *n* lēgātus *m*.
brigand *n* latrō *m*, praedō *m*.
brigandage *n* latrōcinium *nt*.
bright *adj* clārus, lūculentus; (*sky*) serēnus; (*intellect*) ingeniōsus; (*manner*) hilaris, laetus; **be ~** lūcēre, splendēre.
brighten *vt* illūstrāre; laetificāre ♦ *vi* lūcēscere; (*person*) hilarem fierī.
brightly *adv* clārē.
brightness *n* fulgor, candor *m*; (*sky*) serēnitās *f*.
brilliance *n* splendor *m*, fulgor *m*; (*style*) nitor *m*, lūmen *nt*, īnsignia *ntpl*.
brilliant *adj* clārus, illūstris, splendidus; (*fig*) īnsignis, praeclārus, lūculentus.
brilliantly *adv* splendidē, praeclārē, lūculentē.
brim *n* lābrum *nt*, margō *f*; **fill to the ~** explēre.
brimstone *n* sulfur *nt*.
brindled *adj* varius.
brine *n* salsāmentum *nt*.
bring *vt* ferre; (*person*) dūcere; (*charge*) intendere; (*to a place*) adferre, addūcere, advehere, dēferre; (*to a destination*) perdūcere; (*to a worse state*) redigere; ~ **about** *vt* efficere; ~ **before** dēferre ad, referre ad; ~ **back** *vt* (*thing*) referre; (*person*) redūcere; ~ **down** *vt* dēdūcere, dēferre; ~ **forth** (*from store*) dēprōmere; (*child*) parere; (*crops*) ferre, ēdere; ~ **forward** *vt* (*for discussion*) iactāre, iacere; (*reason*) adferre; ~ **home** (*bride*) dēdūcere; (*in triumph*) dēportāre; ~ **home to** pervincere; ~ **in** *vt* invehere, indūcere, intrōdūcere; (*import*) importāre; (*revenue*) reddere; ~ **off** *vt* (*success*) reportāre; ~ **on** īnferre, importāre; (*stage*) indūcere; ~ **out** *vt* efferre; (*book*) ēdere; (*play*) dare; (*talent*) ēlicere; ~ **over** perdūcere, trādūcere; ~ **to bear** adferre; ~ **to light** nūdāre, dētegere; ~ **to pass** perficere, peragere; ~ **to shore** ad litus appellere; ~ **together** contrahere, cōgere; (*enemies*) conciliāre; ~ **up** *vt* (*child*) ēducāre, tollere; (*troops*) admovēre; (*topic*) prōferre; ~ **upon oneself** sibī cōnscīscere, sibī contrahere.

brink n ōra f, margō f.
briny adj salsus.
brisk adj alacer, vegetus, ācer.
briskly adv ācriter.
briskness n alacritās f.
bristle n sēta f ♦ vi horrēre, horrēscere.
bristly adj horridus, hirsūtus.
Britain n Brittania f.
Britons n Brittani mpl.
brittle adj fragilis.
broach vt (topic) in medium prōferre.
broad adj lātus; (accent) lātus; (joke)
  inurbānus; (daylight) multus.
broadcast vt dissēmināre.
broaden vt dīlātāre.
broadly adv lātē.
broadsword n gladius m.
brocade n Attalica ntpl.
brochure n libellus m.
brogue n pērō m.
broil n rixa f, iūrgium nt ♦ vt torrēre.
broiling adj torridus.
broken adj frāctus; (fig) cōnfectus; (speech)
  īnfrāctus.
broken-hearted adj dolōre cōnfectus.
broker n īnstitor m.
bronze n aes nt ♦ adj aēneus, aerātus.
brooch n fībula f.
brood n fētus m; (fig) gēns f ♦ vi incubāre (dat);
  (fig) incubāre (dat), fovēre; ~ over meditārī.
brook n rīvus m ♦ vt ferre, patī.
brooklet n rīvulus m.
broom n (plant) genista f; (brush) scōpae fpl.
broth n iūs nt.
brother n frāter m; (full) germānus m; ~ and
  sister marītus mpl.
brotherhood n frāternitās f.
brother-in-law n lēvir m, uxōris frāter m,
  sorōris marītus m.
brotherly adj frāternus.
brow n frōns f; (eye) supercilium nt; (hill)
  dorsum nt.
browbeat vt obiūrgāre, exagitāre.
brown adj fulvus, spādīx; (skin) adūstus.
browse vi pāscī, dēpāscī.
bruise vt atterere, frangere, contundere ♦ n
  vulnus nt.
bruit vt pervulgāre.
brunt n vīs f; bear the ~ of exhaurīre.
brush n pēniculus m; (artist's) pēnicillus m;
  (quarrel) rixa f ♦ vt verrere, dētergēre; (teeth)
  dēfricāre; ~ aside vt aspernārī, neglegere; ~
  up vt (fig) excolere.
brushwood n virgulta ntpl; (for cutting)
  sarmenta ntpl.
brusque adj parum cōmis.
brutal adj atrōx, saevus, inhūmānus.
brutality n atrōcitās f, saevitia f.
brutally adv atrōciter, inhūmānē.
brute n bēlua f, bestia f.
brutish adj stolidus.
bubble n bulla f ♦ vi bullāre; ~ over
  effervēscere; ~ up scatēre.

buccaneer n praedō m, pīrāta m.
buck n cervus m ♦ vi exsultāre.
bucket n situla f, fidēlia f.
buckle n fībula f ♦ vt fībulā nectere; ~ to
  accingī.
buckler n parma f.
buckram n carbasus m.
bucolic adj agrestis.
bucolics n būcolica ntpl.
bud n gemma f, flōsculus m ♦ vi gemmāre.
budge vi movērī, cēdere.
budget n pūblicae pecūniae ratiō f ♦ vi: ~ for
  prōvidēre (dat).
buff adj lūteus.
buffalo n ūrus m.
buffet n (blow) alapa f; (fig) plāga f; (sideboard)
  abacus m ♦ vt iactāre, tundere.
buffoon n scurra m, balatrō m.
buffoonery n scurrilitās f.
bug n cīmex m.
bugbear n terricula ntpl, terror m.
bugle n būcina f.
bugler n būcinātor m.
build vt aedificāre, struere; (bridge) facere;
  (road) mūnīre; ~ on vt (add) adstruere;
  (hopes) pōnere; ~ on sand in aquā
  fundāmenta pōnere; ~ up vt exstruere; (to
  block) inaedificāre; (knowledge) īnstruere; ~
  castles in the air spem inānem pāscere ♦ n
  statūra f.
builder n aedificātor m, structor m.
building n (act) aedificātiō f; (structure)
  aedificium nt.
bulb n bulbus m.
bulge vi tumēre, tumēscere, prōminēre ♦ vi
  tuberculum nt; (of land) locus prōminēns m.
bulk n māgnitūdō f, amplitūdō f; (mass) mōlēs
  f; (most) plērīque, māior pars.
bulky adj amplus, grandis.
bull n taurus m; ~'s taurīnus; take the ~ by the
  horns rem fortiter adgredī.
bulldog n Molossus m.
bullet n glāns f.
bulletin n libellus m.
bullion n aurum īnfectum nt, argentum
  īnfectum nt.
bullock n iuvencus m.
bully n obiūrgātor m, patruus m ♦ vt obiūrgāre,
  exagitāre.
bulrush n scirpus m.
bulwark n prōpugnāculum nt; (fig) arx f.
bump n (swelling) tuber nt, tuberculum nt;
  (knock) ictus m ♦ vi: ~ against offendere.
bumper n plēnum pōculum nt ♦ adj plēnus,
  māximus.
bumpkin n rūsticus m.
bumptious adj adrogāns.
bunch n fasciculus m; (of berries) racēmus m.
bundle n fascis m; (of hay) manipulus m ♦ vt
  obligāre.
bung n obtūrāmentum nt ♦ vt obtūrāre.
bungle vt male gerere.
bunk n lectus m, lectulus m.

buoy n cortex m ♦ vt sublevāre.
buoyancy n levitās f.
buoyant adj levis; (fig) hilaris.
bur n lappa f.
burden n onus nt; **beast of** ~ iūmentum nt ♦ vt onerāre; **be a** ~ oneri esse.
burdensome adj gravis, molestus.
bureau n scrīnium nt.
burgeon vi gemmāre.
burgess n mūniceps m.
burgh n mūnicipium nt.
burgher n mūniceps m.
burglar n fūr m.
burglary n fūrtum nt.
burial n fūnes nt, humātiō f, sepultūra f.
burin n caelum nt.
burlesque n imitātiō f ♦ vt per iocum imitārī.
burly adj crassus.
burn vt incendere, ūrere; (to ashes) cremāre ♦ vi ārdēre, flāgrāre; ~ **up** ambūrere, combūrere, exūrere; **be ~ed down** dēflāgrāre; ~ **out** vi exstinguī; ~ **the midnight oil** lūcubrāre ♦ n (MED) ambūstum nt.
burning adj igneus.
burnish vt polīre.
burrow n cuniculus m ♦ vi dēfodere.
burst vt rumpere, dīrumpere ♦ vi rumpī, dīrumpī; ~ **in** inrumpere; ~ **into tears** in lacrimās effundī; ~ **open** refringere; ~ **out** ērumpere, prōrumpere; ~ **out laughing** cachinnum tollere; ~ **through** perrumpere per (acc); ~ **upon** offerrī (dat), invādere ♦ n ēruptiō f; (noise) fragor m; ~ **of applause** clāmōrēs mpl; **with a ~ of speed** citātō gradū, citātō equō.
bury vt sepelīre, humāre; (ceremony) efferre; (hiding) condere; (things) dēfodere; (fig) obruere; ~ **the hatchet** amīcitiam reconciliāre.
bush n frutex m; dūmus m; **beat about the ~** circuitiōne ūtī.
bushel n medimnus m.
bushy adj fruticōsus; (thick) dēnsus; (hair) hirsūtus.
busily adv strēnuē, impigrē.
business n negōtium nt; (occupation) ars f, quaestus m; (public life) forum nt; (matter) rēs f, **it is your** ~ tuum est; **make it one's ~ to** id agere ut; **you have no** ~ **to** nōn tē decet (infin); **mind one's own** ~ suum negōtium agere; ~ **days** diēs fāstī mpl.
businessman negōtiātor m.
buskin n cothurnus m.
bust n imāgō f.
bustle vi trepidāre, festīnāre; ~ **about** discurrere.
busy adj negōtiōsus, occupātus; (active) operōsus, impiger, strēnuus; ~ **in** occupātus (abl); ~ **on** intentus (dat); **keep** ~ vt exercēre; ~ **oneself with** pertractāre, studēre (dat).
busybody n: **be a** ~ aliēnīs negōtīs sē immiscēre.
but conj sed, at; (2nd place) autem, tamen ♦ adv

modo ♦ prep praeter (acc); **nothing** ~ nihil nisī; ~ **that,** ~ **what** quīn; **not** ~ **what** nihilōminus.
butcher n lanius m ♦ vt trucīdāre.
butcher's shop n laniēna f.
butchery n strāgēs f, occīdiō f.
butler n prōmus m.
butt n (cask) cadus m; (of ridicule) lūdibrium nt ♦ vi arietāre; ~ **in** interpellāre.
butter n būtyrum nt.
butterfly n pāpiliō m.
buttock n clūnis m/f.
button n bulla f.
buttonhole vt (fig) dētinēre, prēnsāre.
buttress n antērides fpl ♦ vt fulcīre.
buxom adj nitidus.
buy vt emere; ~ **provisions** obsonāre; ~ **back** vt redimere; ~ **off** vt redimere; ~ **up** vt coemere.
buyer n emptor m; (at auctions) manceps m.
buzz n strīdor m, susurrus m ♦ vi strīdere, susurrāre.
buzzard n būteō m.
by prep (near) ad (acc), apud (acc); prope (acc); (along) secundum (acc); (past) praeter (acc); (agent) a, ab (abl); (instrument) abl; (time) ante (acc); (oath) per (acc) ♦ adv prope, iuxtā; ~ **and** ~ mox; **be** ~ adesse, adstāre; ~ **force of arms** vī et armās; ~ **land and sea** terrī marique.
bygone adj praeteritus.
bystander n arbiter m; pl circumstantēs mpl.
byway n dēverticulum nt, trāmes m, sēmita f.
byword n prōverbium nt.

C, c

cabal n factiō f.
cabbage n brassica f, caulis m.
cabin n casa f; (ship) cubiculum nt.
cabinet n armārium nt.
cable n fūnis m; (anchor) ancorāle nt.
cache n thēsaurus m.
cachet n nota f.
cackle vi strepere n ♦ strepitus m, clangor m.
cacophonous adj dissonus.
cacophony n vōcēs dissonae fpl.
cadaverous adj cadāverōsus.
cadence n clausula numerōsa f, numerus m.
cadet n (son) nātū minor; (MIL) contubernālis m.
cage n cavea f ♦ vt inclūdere.
caitiff n ignāvus m.
cajole vt blandīrī, dēlēnīre.
cake n placenta f.
calamitous adj exitiōsus, calamitōsus.

calamity n calamitās f, malum nt; (MIL) clādēs f.
calculate vt ratiōnem dūcere, inīre.
calculation n ratiō f.
calculator n ratiōcinātor m.
calendar n fāstī mpl.
calends n Kalendae fpl.
calf n (animal) vitulus m, vitula f; (leg) sūra f.
calibre n (fig) ingenium nt, auctōritās f.
call vt vocāre; (name) appellāre, nōmināre;
(aloud) clāmāre; (to a place) advocāre,
convocāre; ~ **aside** sēvocāre; ~ **down** (curse)
dētestārī; ~ **for** vt fus postulāre, requīrere; ~
forth ēvocāre, excīre, ēlicere; ~ **in** vt
advocāre; ~ **together** convocāre; ~ **on** vt fus
(for help) implōrāre; (visit) salūtāre; ~ **off** vt
āvocāre, revocāre; ~ **out** vi exclāmāre; ~ **up**
vt (dead) excitāre, ēlicere; (MIL) ēvocāre ♦ n
vōx f, clāmor m; (summons) invītātiō f; (visit)
salūtātiō f.
caller n salūtātor m.
calling n ars f, quaestus m.
callous adj dūrus; **become** ~ obdūrēscere.
callow adj rudis.
calm adj tranquillus, placidus; (mind) aequus
♦ vi: ~ **down** (fig) dēfervēscere ♦ vt sēdāre,
tranquillāre ♦ n tranquillitās f; **dead** ~ (at
sea) malacia f.
calmly adv tranquillē, placidē; aequō animō.
calumniate vt obtrectāre, crīminārī; (falsely)
calumniārī.
calumniator n obtrectātor m.
calumny n opprobria ntpl, obtrectātiō f.
calve vi parere.
cambric n linteum nt.
camel n camēlus m.
camouflage n dissimulātiō f ♦ vt dissimulāre.
camp n castra ntpl; **summer** ~ aestīva ntpl;
winter ~ hīberna ntpl; **in** ~ sub pellibus; **pitch**
~ castra pōnere; **strike** ~ castra movēre ♦ adj
castrēnsis ♦ vi tendere.
campaign n stīpendium nt, bellum nt; (rapid)
expedītiō f ♦ vi bellum gerere, stīpendium
merēre.
campaigner n mīles m; **old** ~ veterānus m; (fig)
veterātor m.
campbed n grabātus m.
camp followers n lixae mpl.
can n hirnea f.
can vi posse (+ infin); (know how) scīre.
canaille n vulgus nt, plebs f.
canal n fossa nāvigābilis f, eurīpus m.
cancel vt indūcere, abrogāre.
cancellation n (writing) litūra f; (law)
abrogātiō f.
cancer n cancer m; (fig) carcinōma nt, ulcus nt.
cancerous adj (fig) ulcerōsus.
candelabrum n candēlābrum nt.
candid adj ingenuus, apertus, līber, simplex.
candidate n petītor m; **be a** ~ **for** petere.
candidature n petītiō f.
candidly adv ingenuē.
candle n candēla f.
candlestick n candēlābrum nt.

candour n ingenuitās f, simplicitās f, lībertās
f.
cane n (reed) harundō f; (for walking, punishing)
virga f ♦ vt verberāre.
canine adj canīnus.
canister n capsula f.
canker n (plants) rōbigō f; (fig) aerūgō f,
carcinōma nt ♦ vt corrumpere.
Cannae n Cannae fpl.
cannibal n anthrōpophagus m.
cannon n tormentum nt.
cannot nōn posse, nequīre; **I** ~ **help but** ...
facere nōn possum quīn ... (subj), nōn
possum nōn ... (infin).
canny adj prūdens, prōvidus, cautus,
circumspectus.
canoe n linter f.
canon n nōrma f, rēgula f; (ECCL) canonicus m.
canopy n aulaeum nt.
cant n fūcus m, fūcāta verba ntpl ♦ vt
oblīquāre.
cantankerous adj importūnus.
cantankerousness n importūnitās f.
canter n lēnis cursus m ♦ vi lēniter currere.
canticle n canticum nt.
canto n carmen nt.
canton n pāgus m.
canvas n carbasus m, linteum nt ♦ adj
carbaseus; **under** ~ sub pellibus.
canvass vi ambīre ♦ vt prēnsāre, circumīre.
canvassing n ambitus m, ambitiō f.
cap n pilleus m; (priest's) galērus m, apex m.
capability n facultās f, potestās f.
capable adj capāx, doctus, perītus.
capably adv bene, doctē.
capacious adj capāx, amplus.
capacity n capācitās f, amplitūdō f; (mind)
ingenium nt.
caparison n ephippium nt.
cape n (GEOG) prōmunturium nt; (dress)
chlamys f.
caper vi saltāre; (animal) lascīvīre ♦ n saltus
m.
capering n lascivia f.
capital adj (chief) praecipuus, prīnceps;
(excellent) ēgregius; (law) capitālis; **convict
of a** ~ **offence** capitis damnāre ♦ n (town)
caput nt; (money) sors f; (class) negōtiātōrēs
mpl; **make** ~ **out of** ūtī (abl).
capitalist n faenerātor m.
capital punishment n capitis supplicum nt.
capitation tax n capitum exāctiō f.
Capitol n Capitolium nt.
capitulate vi sē dēdere; **troops who have** ~**d**
dēditīciī mpl.
capitulation n dēditiō f.
capon n capō m.
caprice n libīdō f, incōnstantia f.
capricious adj incōnstāns, levis.
capriciously adv incōnstanter, leviter.
capriciousness n incōnstantia f, libīdō f.
capsize vt ēvertere ♦ vi ēvertī.
captain m dux m, praefectus m, prīnceps m;

(*MIL*) centuriō *m*; (*naval*) nāvarchus *m*; (*of merchant ship*) magister *m* ♦ *vt* praeesse (*dat*), dūcere.
captaincy *n* centuriātus *m*.
caption *n* caput *nt*.
captious *adj* mōrōsus; (*question*) captiōsus.
captiously *adv* mōrōsē.
captiousness *n* mōrōsitās *f*.
captivate *vt* capere, dēlēnīre, adlicere.
captive *n* captīvus *m*.
captivity *n* captīvitās *f*, vincula *ntpl*.
captor *n* (*by storm*) expugnātor *m*; victor *m*.
capture *n* (*by storm*) expugnātiō *f* ♦ *vt* capere.
car *n* currus *m*.
caravan *n* commeātus *m*.
carbuncle *n* (*MED*) fūrunculus *m*; (*stone*) acaustus *m*.
carcass *n* cadāver *nt*.
card *n* charta *f*; (*ticket*) tessera *f*; (*wool*) pecten *nt* ♦ *vt* pectere.
cardamom *n* amōmum *nt*.
cardinal *adj* praecipuus; ~ **point** cardō *m* ♦ *n* (*ECCL*) cardinālis.
care *n* cūra *f*; (*anxiety*) sollicitūdō *f*; (*attention*) dīligentia *f*; (*charge*) custōdia *f*; **take ~** cavēre; **take ~ of** cūrāre ♦ *vi* cūrāre; **~ for** *vt fus* (*look after*) cūrāre; (*like*) amāre; **I don't ~** nīl moror; **I couldn't care less about** ... floccī nōn faciō ..., pendō; **I don't ~ about** mittō, nihil moror; **for all I ~** per mē.
career *n* curriculum *nt*; (*POL*) cursus honōrum; (*completed*) rēs gestae *fpl* ♦ *vi* ruere, volāre.
carefree *adj* sēcūrus.
careful *adj* (*cautious*) cautus; (*attentive*) dīligēns, attentus; (*work*) accūrātus.
carefully *adv* cautē; dīligenter, attentē; accūrātē.
careless *adj* incautus, neglegēns.
carelessly *adv* incautē, neglegenter.
carelessness *n* incūria *f*, neglegentia *f*.
caress *vt* fovēre, blandīrī ♦ *n* blandīmentum *nt*, amplexus *m*.
cargo *n* onus *nt*.
caricature *n* (*picture*) gryllus *m*; (*fig*) imāgō dētorta *f* ♦ *vt* dētorquēre.
carmine *n* coccum *nt* ♦ *adj* coccineus.
carnage *n* strāgēs *f*, caedēs *f*.
carnal *adj* corporeus; (*pleasure*) libīdinōsus.
carnival *n* fēriae *fpl*.
carol *n* carmen *nt* ♦ *vi* cantāre.
carouse *vi* perpōtāre, cōmissārī ♦ *n* cōmissātiō *f*.
carp *vi* obtrectāre; ~ **at** carpere, rōdere.
carpenter *n* faber *m*, lignārius *m*.
carpet *n* tapēte *nt*.
carriage *n* (*conveying*) vectūra *f*; (*vehicle*) vehiculum *nt*; (*for journeys*) raeda *f*, petorritum *nt*; (*for town*) carpentum *nt*, pīlentum *nt*; (*deportment*) gestus *m*, incessus *m*; ~ **and pair** bīgae *fpl*; ~ **and four** quadrīgae *fpl*.
carrier *n* vector *m*; (*porter*) bāiulus *m*; **letter ~** tabellārius *m*.

carrion *n* cadāver *nt*.
carrot *n* carōta *f*.
carry *vt* portāre, vehere, ferre, gerere; (*law*) perferre; (*by assault*) expugnāre; ~ **away** auferre, āvehere; (*by force*) rapere; (*with emotion*) efferre; ~ **all before one** ēvincere; ~ **along** (*building*) dūcere; ~ **back** reportāre; revehere, referre; ~ **down** dēportāre, dēvehere; ~ **in** invehere, intrōferre; ~ **off** auferre, asportāre, āvehere; (*by force*) abripere, ēripere; (*prize*) ferre, reportāre; (*success*) bene gerere; ~ **on** *vt* gerere; (*profession*) exercēre; ~ **out** *vi* efferre, ēgerere, ēvehere; (*task*) exsequī; ~ **out an undertaking** rem suscipere; ~ **over** trānsportāre, trānsferre; ~ **the day** vincere; ~ **one's point** pervincere; ~ **through** perferre; ~ **to** adferre, advehere; ~ **up** subvehere ♦ *vi* (*sound*) audīrī; ~ **on** *vi* pergere; (*flirt*) lascīvīre.
cart *n* plaustrum *nt*; carrus *nt*; **put the ~ before the horse** praeposterum dīcere ♦ *vt* plaustrō vehere.
Carthage *n* Carthāgō, Carthāginis *f*.
Carthaginian *adj* Carthāginiēnsis; Pūnicus; **the ~s** Poenī *mpl*.
carthorse *n* iūmentum *nt*.
carve *vt* sculpere; (*on surface*) caelāre; (*meat*) secāre; ~ **out** exsculpere.
carver *n* caelātor *m*.
carving *n* caelātūra *f*.
cascade *n* cataracta *m*.
case *n* (*instance*) exemplum *nt*, rēs *f*; (*legal*) āctiō *f*, līs *f*, causa *f*; (*plight*) tempus *nt*; (*GRAM*) cāsus *m*; (*receptacle*) thēca *f*, involucrum *nt*; **in ~** sī; (*to prevent*) nē; **in any ~** utut est rēs; **in that ~** ergō; **such is the ~** sic sē rēs habet; **civil ~** causa prīvāta; **criminal ~** causa pūblica; **win a ~** causam, lītem obtinēre; **lose a ~** causam, lītem āmittere.
casement *n* fenestra *f*.
cash *n* nummī *mpl*; (*ready*) numerātum *nt*, praesēns pecūnia *f*; **pay ~** ex arcā absolvere, repraesentāre.
cash box *n* arca *f*.
cashier *n* dispēnsātor *m* ♦ *vt* (*MIL*) exauctōrāre.
cash payment *n* repraesentātiō *f*.
cask *n* cūpa *f*.
casket *n* arcula *f*, pyxis *f*.
casque *n* galea *f*, cassis *f*.
cast *vt* iacere; (*account*) inīre; (*eyes*) conicere; (*lots*) conicere; (*covering*) exuere; (*metal*) fundere; ~ **ashore** ēicere; ~ **away** prōicere; ~ **down** dēicere; (*humble*) abicere; ~ **in one's teeth** exprobrāre; ~ **lots** sortīrī; ~ **off** *vi* abicere, exuere; ~ **out** prōicere, ēicere, pellere ♦ *n* iactus *m*; (*moulding*) typus *m*, fōrma *f*; **with a ~ in the eye** paetus.
castanet *n* crotalum *nt*.
castaway *n* ēiectus *m*.
caste *n* ōrdō *m*.
castigate *vt* animadvertere, castīgāre.
castigation *n* animadversiō *f*, castīgātiō *f*.

castle n arx f, castellum nt.
castrate vt castrāre.
casual adj fortuītus; (person) neglegēns.
casually adv temerē.
casualty n īnfortūnium nt; pl: **casualties** occīsī mpl.
casuist n sophistēs m.
cat n fēlēs f.
cataclysm n dīluvium nt, ruīna f.
catalogue n index m.
catapult n catapulta f, ballista f.
cataract n cataracta f.
catarrh n gravēdō f; **liable to ~** gravēdinōsus.
catastrophe n calamitās f, ruīna f.
catastrophic adj calamitōsus, exitiōsus.
catch vt capere, dēprehendere, excipere; (disease) contrahere, nancīscī; (fire) concipere, comprehendere; (meaning) intellegere; **~ at** captāre; **~ out** vi dēprehendere; **~ up with** adsequī; **~ birds** aucupārī; **~ fish** piscārī ♦ n bolus m.
categorical adj (statement) plānus.
categorically adv sine exceptiōne.
category n numerus m, genus nt.
cater vi obsōnāre.
cateran n praedātor m.
caterer n obsōnātor m.
caterpillar n ērūca f.
caterwaul vi ululāre.
catgut n chorda f.
catharsis n pūrgātiō f.
cathedral n aedēs f.
catholic adj generālis.
catkin n iūlus m.
cattle n (collectively) pecus nt; (singly) pecus f; (for plough) armenta ntpl.
cattle breeder n pecuārius m.
cattle market n forum boārium nt.
cattle thief n abāctor m.
cauldron n cortīna f.
cause n causa f; (person) auctor m; (law) causa f; (party) partēs fpl; **give ~ for** māteriam dare (gen); **make common ~ with** facere cum, stāre ab; **plead a ~** causam dīcere; **in the ~ of** prō (abl); **without ~** iniūriā ♦ vt efficere ut (+ subj), facere, facessere (with ut); cūrāre (with gerundive); (feelings) movēre, inicere, ciēre.
causeless adj vānus, sine causā.
causeway n agger m.
caustic adj (fig) mordāx.
cauterize vt adūrere.
caution n (wariness) cautiō f, prūdentia f; (warning) monitum nt ♦ vt monēre, admonēre.
cautious adj cautus, prōvidus, prūdens.
cautiously adv cautē, prūdenter.
cavalcade n pompa f.
cavalier n eques m ♦ adj adrogāns.
cavalierly adv adroganter.
cavalry n equitēs mpl, equitātus m ♦ adj equester; **troop of ~** turma f.
cavalryman n eques m.

cave n spēlunca f, caverna f; antrum nt; **~ in** vi concidere, conlābī.
cavern n spēlunca f, caverna f.
cavil vi cavillārī; **~ at** carpere, cavillārī ♦ n captiō f, cavillātiō f.
cavity n caverna f, cavum nt.
cavort vi saltāre.
caw vi cornīcārī.
cease vi dēsinere, dēsistere.
ceaseless adj adsiduus, perpetuus.
ceaselessly adv adsiduē, perpetuō.
cedar n cedrus f ♦ adj cedrinus.
cede vt cēdere, concēdere.
ceiling n tēctum nt; (panelled) lacūnar nt, laqueārium nt.
celebrate vt (rite) celebrāre, agitāre; (in crowds) frequentāre; (person, theme) laudāre, celebrāre, dīcere.
celebrated adj praeclārus, illūstris, nōtus; **the ~** ille.
celebration n celebrātiō f; (rite) sollemne nt.
celebrity n celebritās f, fāma f; (person) vir illūstris.
celerity n celeritās f, vēlōcitās f.
celery n apium nt.
celestial adj caelestis; dīvīnus.
celibacy n caelibātus m.
celibate n caelebs m.
cell n cella f.
cellar n cella f.
cement n ferrūmen nt ♦ vt coagmentāre.
cemetery n sepulchrētum nt.
cenotaph n tumulus honōrārius, tumulus inānis m.
censer n tūribulum nt, acerra f.
censor n cēnsor m ♦ vt cēnsēre.
censorious adj cēnsōrius, obtrectātor.
censorship n cēnsūra f.
censure n reprehēnsiō f, animadversiō f; (censor's) nota f ♦ vt reprehendere, animadvertere, increpāre; notāre.
census n cēnsus m.
cent n: **one per ~** centēsima f; **12 per ~ per annum** centēsima f (ie monthly).
centaur n centaurus m.
centaury n (plant) centaurēum nt.
centenarian n centum annōs nātus m, nāta f.
centenary n centēsimus annus m.
centesimal adj centēsimus.
central adj medius.
centralize vt in ūnum locum cōnferre; (power) ad ūnum dēferre.
centre n centrum nt, media pars f; **the ~ of** medius.
centuple adj centuplex.
centurion n centuriō m.
century n (MIL) centuria f; (time) saeculum nt.
ceramic adj fictilis.
cereal n frūmentum nt.
ceremonial adj sollemnis ♦ n rītus m.
ceremonious adj (rite) sollemnis; (person) officiōsus.
ceremoniously adv sollemniter; officiōsē.

ceremony n caerimōnia f, rītus m; (*politeness*) officium nt; (*pomp*) apparātus m; **master of ceremonies** dēsignātor m.

cerise n coccum nt ♦ adj coccineus.

certain adj (*sure*) certus; (*future*) explōrātus; **a ~** quīdam, quaedam, quoddam; **be ~** (*know*) prō certō scīre/habēre.

certainly adv certē, certō, sine dubiō; (*yes*) ita, māximē; (*concessive*) quidem.

certainty n (*thing*) certum nt; (*belief*) fidēs f; **for a ~** prō certō, explōrātē; **regard as a ~** prō explōrātō habēre.

certificate n testimōnium nt.

certify vt (*writing*) recognōscere; (*fact*) adfirmāre, testificārī.

cessation n fīnis m; (*from labour*) quiēs f; (*temporary*) intermissiō f; (*of hostilities*) indutiae fpl.

chafe vt ūrere; (*fig*) inrītāre ♦ vi stomachārī.

chaff n palea f ♦ vt lūdere.

chaffinch n fringilla f.

chagrin n dolor m, stomachus m ♦ vt stomachum facere (*dat*), sollicitāre.

chain n catēna f; (*for neck*) torquis m; (*sequence*) seriēs f; **~s** pl vincula ntpl ♦ vt vincīre.

chair n sella f; (*of office*) sella curūlis f; (*sedan*) sella gestātōria f, lectīca f; (*teacher's*) cathedra f.

chairman n (*at meeting*) magister m; (*of debate*) disceptātor m.

chalet n casa f.

chalice n calix m.

chalk n crēta f.

chalky adj crētōsus.

challenge n prōvocātiō f ♦ vt prōvocāre, lacessere; (*statement*) in dubium vocāre; (*fig*) invītāre, dēposcere.

challenger n prōvocātor m.

chamber n conclāve nt; (*bed*) cubiculum nt; (*bridal*) thalamus m; (*parliament*) cūria f.

chamberlain n cubiculārius m.

chambermaid n serva f, ancilla f.

chameleon n chamaeleōn f.

chamois n rūpicapra f.

champ vt mandere.

champion n prōpugnātor m, patrōnus m; (*winner*) victor m ♦ vt favēre (*dat*), adesse (*dat*).

chance n fors f, fortūna f, cāsus m; (*opportunity*) occāsiō f; potestās f, facultās f; (*prospect*) spēs f; **game of ~** ālea f; **by ~** cāsū, fortuītō; **have an eye to the main ~** forō ūtī; **on the ~ of** sī forte ♦ adj fortuītus ♦ vi accidere, ēvenīre; **it chanced that ...** accidit ut ... (+ *subj*); **~ upon** vt fus incidere in, invenīre ♦ vt periclitārī.

chancel n absis f.

chancellor n cancellārius m.

chancy adj dubius, perīculōsus.

chandelier n candēlābrum nt.

chandler n candēlārum propōla m.

change n mūtātiō f, commūtātiō f, permūtātiō f; (*POL*) rēs novae fpl; (*alternation*) vicēs fpl, vicissitūdō f; (*money*) nummī minōrēs mpl ♦ vt mūtāre, commūtāre, permūtāre ♦ vi mūtārī; **~ hands** abaliēnārī; **~ places** ōrdinem permūtāre, inter sē loca permūtāre.

changeable adj incōnstāns, mūtābilis.

changeableness n incōnstantia f, mūtābilitās f.

changeful adj varius.

changeless adj cōnstāns, immūtābilis.

changeling adj subditus m.

channel n canālis m; (*sea*) fretum nt; (*irrigation*) rīvus m; (*groove*) sulcus m.

chant vt cantāre, canere ♦ n cantus m.

chaos n chaos nt; (*fig*) perturbātiō f.

chaotic adj perturbātus.

chap n rīma f; (*man*) homō m.

chapel n sacellum nt, aedicula f.

chaplain n diāconus m.

chaplet n corōna f, sertum nt.

chaps n (*animal*) mālae fpl.

chapter n caput nt.

char vt ambūrere.

character n (*inborn*) indolēs f, ingenium nt, nātūra f; (*moral*) mōrēs mpl; (*reputation*) existimātiō f; (*kind*) genus nt; (*mark*) signum nt, littera f; (*THEAT*) persōna f, partēs fpl; **sustain a ~** persōnam gerere; **I know his ~** sciō quālis sit.

characteristic adj proprius ♦ n proprium nt.

characteristically adv suō mōre.

characterize vt dēscrībere; proprium esse (*gen*).

charcoal n carbō m.

charge n (*law*) accūsātiō f, crīmen nt; (*MIL*) impetus m, dēcursus m; (*cost*) impēnsa f; (*task*) mandātum nt, onus nt; (*trust*) cūra f, tūtēla f; **bring a ~ against** lītem intendere (*dat*); **entertain a ~ against** nōmen recipere (*gen*); **give in ~** in custōdiam trādere; **put in ~ of** praeficere (*acc, dat*); **be in ~ of** praeesse (*dat*) ♦ vt (*law*) accūsāre; (*falsely*) īnsimulāre; (*MIL*) incurrere in (*acc*), signa īnferre in (*acc*), impetum facere in (*acc*); (*duty*) mandāre; (*cost*) ferre, īnferre; (*empty space*) complēre; (*trust*) committere; (*speech*) hortārī; **~ to the account of** expēnsum ferre (*dat*).

chargeable adj obnoxius.

charger n (*dish*) lānx f; (*horse*) equus m.

charily adv cautē, parcē.

chariot n currus m; (*races*) quadrīgae fpl; (*war*) essedum nt.

charioteer n aurīga m; (*war*) essedārius m.

charitable adj benevolus, benignus.

charitably adv benevolē, benignē.

charity n amor m, benignitās f; līberālitās f.

charlatan n planus m.

charm n (*spell*) carmen nt; (*amulet*) bulla f; (*fig*) blanditiae fpl, dulcēdō f, illecebra f; (*beauty*) venus f, lepōs m ♦ vt (*magic*) fascināre; (*delight*) dēlectāre, dēlēnīre.

charming adj venustus, lepidus; (*speech*) blandus; (*scenery*) amoenus.

charmingly *adv* venustē, blandē.
chart *n* tabula *f*.
charter *n* diplōma *nt* ♦ *vt* condūcere.
chary *adj* (*cautious*) cautus; (*sparing*) parcus.
chase *vt* fugāre; (*hunt*) vēnārī; (*pursue*)
persequī, īnsequī; (*engrave*) caelāre; ~ **away**
pellere, abigere ♦ *n* vēnātus *m*, vēnātiō *f*;
(*pursuit*) īnsectātiō *f*.
chaser *n* (*in metal*) caelātor *m*.
chasm *n* hiātus *m*.
chaste *adj* castus, pudīcus; (*style*) pūrus.
chasten *vt* castīgāre, corrigere.
chastener *n* castīgātor *m*, corrēctor *m*.
chastise *vt* castīgāre, animadvertere.
chastisement *n* castīgātiō *f*, poena *f*.
chastity *n* castitās *f*, pudīcitia *f*.
chat *vi* colloquī, sermōcinārī ♦ *n* sermō *m*,
colloquium *nt*.
chatelaine *n* domina *f*.
chattels *n* bona *ntpl*, rēs mancipī.
chatter *vi* garrīre; (*teeth*) crepitāre ♦ *n*
garrulitās *f*, loquācitās *f*.
chatterbox *n* lingulāca *m/f*.
chatterer *n* garrulus *m*, loquāx *m*.
chattering *adj* garrulus, loquāx ♦ *n* garrulitās
f, loquācitās *f*; (*teeth*) crepitus *m*.
cheap *adj* vīlis; **hold** ~ parvī aestimāre; **buy** ~
bene emere.
cheapen *vt* pretium minuere (*gen*).
cheaply *adv* vīliter, parvō pretiō.
cheapness *n* vīlitās *f*.
cheat *vt* dēcipere, fraudāre, dēfraudāre,
frustrārī ♦ *n* fraudātor *m*.
check *vt* cohibēre, coercēre; (*movement*)
impedīre, inhibēre; (*rebuke*) reprehendere;
(*test*) probāre ♦ *n* impedīmentum *nt*, mora *f*,
(*MIL*) offēnsiō *f*; (*rebuke*) reprehēnsiō *f*; (*test*)
probātiō *f*; (*ticket*) tessera *f*.
checkmate *n* incitae calcēs *fpl* ♦ *vt* ad incitās
redigere.
cheek *n* gena *f*, (*impudence*) ōs *nt*; ~ **s** *pl* mālae
fpl; **how have you the ~ to say?** quō ōre dīcis?
cheekbone *n* maxilla *f*.
cheeky *adj* impudēns.
cheep *vi* pīpilāre.
cheer *vt* hilarāre, exhilarāre; hortārī; (*in
sorrow*) cōnsōlārī ♦ *vi* clāmāre, adclāmāre; ~
up! bonō animō es! ♦ *n* (*shout*) clāmor *m*,
plausus *m*; (*food*) hospitium *nt*; (*mind*) animus
m.
cheerful *adj* alacer, hilaris, laetus.
cheerfully *adv* hilare, laetē.
cheerfulness *n* hilaritās *f*.
cheerily *adv* hilare.
cheerless *adj* tristis, maestus.
cheerlessly *adv* triste.
cheery *adj* hilaris.
cheese *n* cāseus *m*.
chef *n* coquus *m*.
cheque *n* perscrīptiō *f*, syngrapha *f*.
chequer *vt* variāre.
chequered *adj* varius; (*mosaic*) tessellātus.
cherish *vt* fovēre, colere.

cherry *n* (*fruit*) cerasum *nt*; (*tree*) cerasus *f*.
chess *n* latrunculī *mpl*.
chessboard *n* abacus *m*.
chest *n* (*box*) arca *f*, arcula *f*; (*body*) pectus *nt*; ~
of drawers armārium *nt*.
chestnut *n* castanea *f* ♦ *adj* (*colour*) spādīx.
chevalier *n* eques *m*.
chevaux-de-frise *n* ēricius *m*.
chew *vt* mandere.
chic *adj* expolītus, concinnus.
chicanery *n* (*law*) calumnia *f*; (*fig*) dolus *m*.
chick *n* pullus *m*.
chicken *n* pullus *m*; **don't count your ~s before
they're hatched** adhūc tua messis in herbā
est.
chicken-hearted *adj* timidus, ignāvus.
chick-pea *n* cicer *nt*.
chide *vt* reprehendere, increpāre, obiūrgāre.
chief *n* prīnceps *m*, dux *m* ♦ *adj* praecipuus,
prīmus; ~ **point** caput *nt*.
chief command *n* summa imperī.
chiefly *adv* in prīmīs, praesertim, potissimum.
chieftain *n* prīnceps *m*, rēgulus *m*.
chilblain *n* perniō *m*.
child *n* īnfāns *m/f*; puer *m*, puerulus *m*, puella *f*;
fīlius *m*, fīlia *f*; ~'s **play** lūdus *m*.
childbed *n* puerperium *nt*.
childbirth *n* partus *m*.
childhood *n* pueritia *f*; **from** ~ ā puerō.
childish *adj* puerīlis.
childishly *adv* puerīliter.
childless *adj* orbus.
childlessness *n* orbitās *f*.
childlike *adj* puerīlis.
children *npl* līberī *mpl*.
chill *n* frīgus *nt* ♦ *adj* frīgidus ♦ *vt* refrīgerāre.
chilly *adj* frīgidus, frīgidior.
chime *vi* sonāre, canere; ~ **in** interpellāre; (*fig*)
cōnsonāre ♦ *n* sonus *m*.
chimera *n* chimaera *f*; (*fig*) somnium *nt*.
chimerical *adj* commentīcius.
chimney *n* camīnus *m*.
chin *n* mentum *nt*.
china *n* fictilia *ntpl*.
chink *n* rīma *f*, (*sound*) tinnītus *m* ♦ *vi* crepāre,
tinnīre.
chip *n* assula *f*, fragmentum *nt* ♦ *vt* dolāre.
chirp *vi* pīpilāre.
chirpy *adj* hilaris.
chisel *n* scalprum *nt*, scalpellum *nt* ♦ *vt*
sculpere.
chit *n* (*child*) pūsiō *m*, puerulus *m*.
chitchat *n* sermunculī *mpl*.
chitterlings *n* hillae *fpl*.
chivalrous *adj* generōsus.
chivalry *n* virtūs *f*; (*men*) iuventūs *f*; (*class*)
equitēs *mpl*.
chive *n* caepe *nt*.
chock *n* cuneus *m*.
chock-full *adj* refertus.
choice *n* dēlēctus *m*, ēlēctiō *f*; (*of alternatives*)
optiō *f* ♦ *adj* lēctus, eximius, exquīsītus.
choiceness *n* ēlegantia *f*, praestantia *f*.

choir n chorus m.
choke vt suffocāre; (emotion) reprimere; (passage) obstruere.
choler n bīlis f; (anger) īra f, stomachus m.
choleric adj īrācundus.
choose vt legere, ēligere, dēligere; (alternative) optāre; (for office) dēsignāre; (with infin) velle, mālle.
chop vt concīdere; ~ **off** praecīdere ♦ n (meat) offa f.
chopper n secūris f.
choppy adj (sea) asper.
choral adj symphōniacus.
chord n (string) nervus m, chorda f.
chortle vi cachinnāre.
chorus n (singers) chorus m; (song) concentus m, symphōnia f; **in ~** unā vōce.
christen vt baptizāre.
Christian adj Christiānus.
Christianity n Christiānismus m.
chronic adj inveterātus; **become ~** inveterāscere.
chronicle n annālēs mpl, ācta pūblica ntpl ♦ vt in annālēs referre.
chronicler n annālium scrīptor m.
chronological adj: **in ~ order** servātō temporum ōrdine; **make a ~ error** temporibus errāre.
chronology n temporum ratiō f, temporum ōrdō m.
chronometer n hōrologium nt.
chubby adj pinguis.
chuck vt conicere; **~ out** extrūdere.
chuckle vi rīdēre ♦ n rīsus m.
chum n sodālis m.
church n ecclēsia f.
churl n rūsticus m.
churlish adj difficilis, importūnus; avārus.
churlishly adv rūsticē, avārē.
churlishness n mōrōsitās f, avāritia f.
chute n (motion) lāpsus m; (place) dēclīve nt.
cicada n cicāda f.
cincture n cingulum nt.
cinder n cinis m.
cipher n numerus m, nihil nt; (code) notae fpl; **in ~** per notās.
circle n orbis m, circulus m, gȳrus m; **form a ~** in orbem cōnsistere ♦ vi sē circumagere, circumīre.
circlet n īnfula f.
circuit n ambitus m, circuitus m; (assizes) conventus m.
circuitous adj longus; **a ~ route** circuitus m; (speech) ambāgēs fpl.
circular adj rotundus.
circulate vt (news) pervulgāre ♦ vi circumagī; (news) circumferrī, percrēbrēscere.
circulation n ambitus m; **be in ~** in manibus esse; **go out of ~** obsolēscere.
circumcise vt circumcīdere.
circumference n ambitus m.
circumlocution n ambāgēs fpl, circuitiō f.
circumnavigate vt circumvehī.

circumscribe vt circumscrībere; (restrict) coercēre, fīnīre.
circumspect adj cautus, prūdēns.
circumspection n cautiō f, prūdentia f, circumspectiō f.
circumspectly adv cautē, prūdenter.
circumstance n rēs f; **~s** rērum status m; (wealth) rēs f; **as ~s arise** ē rē nātā; **under the ~s** cum haec ita sint, essent; **under no ~s** nēquāquam.
circumstantial adj adventīcius; (detailed) accūrātus; **~ evidence** coniectūra f.
circumstantially adv accūrātē, subtīliter.
circumvallation n circummūnītiō f.
circumvent vt circumvenīre, fallere.
circus n circus m.
cistern n lacus m, cisterna f.
citadel n arx f.
citation n (law) vocātiō f; (mention) commemorātiō f.
cite vt in iūs vocāre; (quote) commemorāre, prōferre.
citizen n cīvis m/f; (of provincial town) mūniceps m; **fellow ~** cīvis m/f; **Roman ~s** Quirītes mpl ♦ adj cīvīlis, cīvicus.
citizenship n cīvitās f; **deprived of ~** capite dēminūtus; **loss of ~** capitis dēminūtiō f.
citron n (fruit) citrum nt; (tree) citrus f.
city n urbs f, oppidum nt.
civic adj cīvīlis, cīvicus.
civil adj (of citizens) cīvīlis; (war) cīvilis, intestīnus, domesticus; (manners) urbānus, cōmis, officiōsus; (lawsuit) prīvātus.
civilian n togātus m.
civility n urbānitās f, cōmitās f; (act) officium nt.
civilization n exculta hominum vīta f, cultus atque hūmānitās.
civilize vt excolere, expolīre, ad hūmānum cultum dēdūcere.
civil war n bellum cīvīle, bellum domesticum, bellum intestīnum.
clad adj vestītus.
claim vt (for oneself) adrogāre, adserere; (something due) poscere, postulāre, vindicāre; (at law) petere; (statement) adfirmāre ♦ n postulātiō f, postulātum nt; (at law) petītiō f, vindiciae fpl.
claimant n petītor m.
clam n chāma f.
clamber vi scandere.
clammy adj ūmidus, lentus.
clamorous adj vōciferāns.
clamour n strepitus m, clāmōrēs mpl ♦ vi: **~ against** obstrepere (dat).
clamp n cōnfībula f.
clan n gēns f.
clandestine adj fūrtīvus.
clandestinely adv clam, fūrtim.
clang n clangor m, crepitus m ♦ vi increpāre.
clangour n clangor m.
clank n crepitus m ♦ vi crepitāre.
clansman n gentīlis m.

clap vi plaudere, applaudere; ~ **eyes on** cōnspicere; ~ **in prison** in vincula conicere ♦ n plausus m; (*thunder*) fragor m.

clapper n plausor m.

claptrap n iactātiō f.

claque n plausōrēs mpl, operae fpl.

clarify vt pūrgāre; (*knowledge*) illūstrāre ♦ vi liquēre.

clarinet n tībia f.

clarion n lituus m, cornū nt.

clarity n perspicuitās f.

clash n concursus m; (*sound*) strepitus m, crepitus m; (*fig*) discrepantia f ♦ vi concurrere; (*sound*) increpāre; (*fig*) discrepāre ♦ vt conflīgere.

clasp n fībula f; (*embrace*) amplexus m ♦ vt implicāre; amplectī, complectī; ~ **together** interiungere.

class n (POL) ōrdō m, classis f; (*kind*) genus nt; (*school*) classis f ♦ vt dēscrībere; ~ **as in** numerō (gen pl) referre, repōnere, habēre.

classic n scrīptor classicus m.

classical adj classicus; ~ **literature** litterae Graecae et Rōmānae.

classics npl scrīptōrēs Graecī et Rōmānī.

classify vt dēscrībere, in ōrdinem redigere.

class-mate n condiscipulus m.

clatter n crepitus m ♦ vi increpāre.

clause n (GRAM) incīsum nt, membrum nt; (*law*) caput nt; (*will*) ēlogium nt; **in short ~s** incīsim.

claw n unguis m, ungula f ♦ vt (unguibus) lacerāre.

clay n argilla f; **made of ~** fictilis.

clayey adj argillāceus.

claymore n gladius m.

clean adj mundus; (*fig*) pūrus, castus; ~ **slate** novae tabulae fpl; **make a ~ sweep of** omnia tollere; **show a ~ pair of heels** sē in pedēs conicere; **my hands are ~** innocēns sum ♦ adv prōrsus, tōtus ♦ vt pūrgāre.

cleanliness n munditia f.

cleanly adj mundus, nitidus ♦ adv mundē, pūrē.

cleanse vt pūrgāre, abluere, dētergēre.

clear adj clārus; (*liquid*) limpidus; (*space*) apertus, pūrus; (*sound*) clārus; (*weather*) serēnus; (*fact*) manifestus, perspicuus; (*language*) illūstris, dīlucidus; (*conscience*) rēctus, innocēns; **it is ~** liquet; ~ **of** līber (abl), expers (gen); **be ~ about** rēctē intellegere; **keep ~ of** ēvītāre; **the coast is ~** arbitrī absunt ♦ vt (*of obstacles*) expedīre, pūrgāre; (*of a charge*) absolvere; (*self*) pūrgāre; (*profit*) lucrārī; ~ **away** āmovēre, tollere; ~ **off** vt (*debt*) solvere, exsolvere ♦ vi facessere; ~ **out** ēluere, dētergēre; ~ **up** vt (*difficulty*) illūstrāre, ēnōdāre, explicāre ♦ vi (*weather*) disserēnāscere.

clearance n pūrgātiō f; (*space*) intervallum nt.

clearing n (*in forest*) lūcus m.

clearly adv clārē; manifestē, apertē, perspicuē; (*with clause*) vidēlicet.

clearness n clāritās f; (*weather*) serēnitās f;

(*mind*) acūmen nt; (*style*) perspicuitās f.

clear-sighted adj sagāx, perspicāx.

cleavage n discidium nt.

cleave vt (*out*) findere, discindere ♦ vi (*cling*): ~ **to** haerēre (dat), adhaerēre (dat).

cleaver n dolabra f.

cleft n rīma f, hiātus m ♦ adj fissus, discissus.

clemency n clēmentia f, indulgentia f; **with ~** clēmenter.

clement adj clēmēns, misericors.

clench vt (*nail*) retundere; (*hand*) comprimere.

clerk n scrība m; (*of court*) lēctor m.

clever adj callidus, ingeniōsus, doctus, astūtus.

cleverly adv doctē, callidē, ingeniōsē.

cleverness n calliditās f, sollertia f.

clew n glomus nt.

cliché n verbum trītum nt.

client n cliēns m/f; (*lawyer's*) cōnsultor m; **body of ~s** clientēla f.

clientele n clientēla f.

cliff n rūpēs f, scopulus m.

climate n caelum nt.

climax n (RHET) gradātiō f; (*fig*) culmen nt.

climb vt, vi scandere, ascendere; ~ **down** dēscendere ♦ n ascēnsus m.

climber n scandēns m.

clime n caelum nt, plāga f.

clinch vt cōnfirmāre.

cling vi adhaerēre; ~ **together** cohaerere.

clink vi tinnīre ♦ n tinnītus m.

clip vt tondēre; praecīdere.

clippers n forfex f.

clique n factiō f.

cloak n (*rain*) lacerna f; (*travel*) paenula f; (MIL) sagum nt; palūdāmentum nt; (*Greek*) pallium nt; (*fig*) involūcrum nt; (*pretext*) speciēs f ♦ vt tegere, dissimulāre.

clock n hōrologium nt; (*sun*) sōlārium nt; (*water*) clepsydra f; **ten o'~** quarta hōra.

clockwise adv dextrōvorsum, dextrōrsum.

clod n glaeba f.

clog n (*shoe*) sculpōnea f; (*fig*) impedīmentum nt ♦ vt impedīre.

cloister n porticus f.

cloistered adj (*fig*) umbrātilis.

close adj (*shut*) clausus; (*tight*) artus; (*narrow*) angustus; (*near*) propinquus; (*compact*) refertus, dēnsus; (*stingy*) parcus; (*secret*) obscūrus; (*weather*) crassus; ~ **together** dēnsus, refertus; **at ~ quarters** comminus; **be ~ at hand** īnstāre; **keep ~ to** adhaerēre; ~ **to** prope (acc), iuxtā (acc) ♦ adv prope, iuxtā ♦ n angiportus m.

close vt claudere, operīre; (*finish*) perficere, fīnīre, conclūdere, termināre; (*ranks*) dēnsāre ♦ vi claudī; conclūdī, terminārī; (*time*) exīre; (*wound*) coīre; (*speech*) perōrāre; ~ **with** (*fight*) manum cōnserere, signa cōnferre; (*deal*) pacīscī; (*offer*) accipere ♦ n fīnis m, terminus m; (*action*) exitus m; (*sentence*) conclūsiō f; **at the ~ of summer** aestāte exeunte.

closely adv prope; (*attending*) attentē;

(*associating*) coniūnctē; **follow** ~ īnstāre (*dat*).
closeness *n* propinquitās *f*; (*weather*) gravitās
f, crassitūdō *f*; (*with money*) parsimōnia *f*;
(*friends*) coniūnctiō *f*; (*manner*) cautiō *f*.
closet *n* cubiculum *nt*, cella *f* ♦ *vt* inclūdere.
clot *n* (*blood*) concrētus sanguis *m* ♦ *vi*
concrēscere.
cloth *n* textile *nt*; (*piece*) pannus *m*; (*linen*)
linteum *nt*; (*covering*) strāgulum *nt*.
clothe *vt* vestīre.
clothes *n* vestis *f*, vestītus *m*, vestīmenta *ntpl*.
clothier *n* vestiārius *m*.
clothing *n* vestis *f*, vestītus *m*, vestīmenta *ntpl*.
clotted *adj* concrētus.
cloud *n* nūbēs *f*; (*storm*) nimbus *m*; (*dust*)
globus *m*; (*disfavour*) invidia *f* ♦ *vt* nūbibus
obdūcere; (*fig*) obscūrāre.
clouded *adj* obnūbilus.
cloudiness *n* nūbilum *nt*.
cloudless *adj* pūrus, serēnus.
cloudy *adj* obnūbilus.
clout *n* pannus *m*.
clover *n* trifolium *nt*.
cloven *adj* (*hoof*) bifidus.
clown *n* (*boor*) rūsticus *m*; (*comic*) scurra *m*.
clownish *adj* rūsticus, inurbānus.
clownishness *n* rūsticitās *f*.
cloy *vt* satiāre.
cloying *adj* pūtidus.
club *n* (*stick*) fustis *m*, clāva *f*; (*society*)
sodālitās *f*; ~ **together** *vi* in commūne
cōnsulere, pecūniās cōnferre.
club-footed *adj* scaurus.
cluck *vi* singultīre ♦ *n* singultus *m*.
clue *n* indicium *nt*, vestīgium *nt*.
clump *n* massa *f*; (*earth*) glaeba *f*; (*trees*)
arbustum *nt*; (*willows*) salictum *nt*.
clumsily *adv* ineptē, inēleganter; incondītē,
īnfabrē.
clumsiness *n* īnscītia *f*.
clumsy *adj* (*person*) inconcinnus, ineptus;
(*thing*) inhabilis; (*work*) inconditus.
cluster *n* cumulus *m*; (*grapes*) racēmus *m*;
(*people*) corōna *f* ♦ *vi* congregārī.
clutch *vt* prehendere, adripere; ~ **at** captāre
nt, comprehēnsiō *f*; **from one's ~es** ē
manibus; **in one's ~es** in potestāte.
clutter *n* turba *f* ♦ *vt* impedīre, obstruere.
coach *n* currus *m*, raeda *f*, pīlentum *nt*; (*trainer*)
magister *m* ♦ *vt* ēdocēre, praecipere (*dat*).
coachman *n* aurīga *m*, raedārius *m*.
coagulate *vt* cōgere ♦ *vi* concrēscere.
coagulation *n* concrētiō *f*.
coal *n* carbō *m*; **carry ~s to Newcastle** in silvam
ligna ferre.
coalesce *vi* coīre, coalēscere.
coalition *n* coitiō *f*, cōnspīrātiō *f*.
coarse *adj* (*quality*) crassus; (*manners*)
rūsticus, inurbānus; (*speech*) īnfacētus.
coarsely *adv* inurbānē, inēleganter.
coarseness *n* crassitūdō *f*; rūsticitās *f*.
coast *n* lītus *nt*, ōra maritima *f* ♦ *vi*: ~ **along**
legere, praetervehī.

coastal *adj* lītorālis, maritimus.
coastline *n* lītus *nt*.
coat *n* pallium *nt*; (*animals*) pellis *f* ♦ *vt*
indūcere, inlinere.
coating *n* corium *nt*.
coax *vt* blandīrī, dēlēnīre.
coaxing *adj* blandus ♦ *n* blanditiae *fpl*.
cob *n* (*horse*) mannus *m*; (*swan*) cygnus *m*.
cobble *n* lapis *m* ♦ *vt* sarcīre.
cobbler *n* sūtor *m*.
cobweb *n* arāneum *nt*.
cock *n* gallus *m*, gallus gallīnāceus *m*; (*other
birds*) mās *m*; (*tap*) epitonium *nt*; (*hay*)
acervus *m*.
cockatrice *n* basiliscus *m*.
cockchafer *n* scarabaeus *m*.
cockcrow *n* gallī cantus *m* ♦ *vt* ērigere.
cockerel *n* pullus *m*.
cockroach *n* blatta *f*.
cocksure *adj* cōnfīdēns.
cod *n* callarias *m*.
coddle *vt* indulgēre (*dat*), permulcēre.
code *n* fōrmula *f*; (*secret*) notae *fpl*.
codicil *n* cōdicillī *mpl*.
codify *vt* in ōrdinem redigere.
coequal *adj* aequālis.
coerce *vt* cōgere.
coercion *n* vīs *f*.
coffer *n* arca *f*, cista *f*; (*public*) fiscus *m*.
coffin *n* arca *f*.
cog *n* dēns *m*.
cogency *n* vīs *f*, pondus *nt*.
cogent *adj* gravis, validus.
cogitate *vi* cōgitāre, meditārī.
cogitation *n* cōgitātiō *f*; meditātiō *f*.
cognate *adj* cognātus.
cognition *n* cognitiō *f*.
cognizance *n* cognitiō *f*; **take ~ of** cognōscere.
cognizant *adj* gnārus.
cohabit *vi* cōnsuēscere.
cohabitation *n* cōnsuētūdō *f*.
coheir *n* cohērēs *m/f*.
cohere *vi* cohaerēre; (*statement*) congruere.
coherence *n* coniūnctiō *f*; (*fig*) convenientia *f*.
coherent *adj* congruēns.
cohesion *n* coagmentātiō *f*.
cohesive *adj* tenāx.
cohort *n* cohors *f*.
coil *n* spīra *f* ♦ *vt* glomerāre.
coin *n* nummus *m* ♦ *vt* cūdere; (*fig*) fingere.
coinage *n* monēta *f*; (*fig*) fictum *nt*.
coincide *vi* concurrere; (*opinion*) cōnsentīre.
coincidence *n* concursus *m*; cōnsēnsus *m*; **by a
~** cāsū.
coincidental *adj* fortuītus.
coiner *n* (*of money*) signātor *m*.
col *n* iugum *nt*.
colander *n* cōlum *nt*.
cold *adj* frīgidus; (*icy*) gelidus; **very ~**
perfrīgidus; **be, feel ~** algēre, frīgēre; **get ~**
algēscere, frīgēscere ♦ *n* frīgus *nt*; (*felt*)
algor *m*; (*malady*) gravēdō *f*; **catch ~**
algēscere, frīgus colligere; **catch a ~**

gravēdinem contrahere; **have a** ~ gravēdine
labōrāre.
coldish *adj* frīgidulus, frīgidior.
coldly *adv* (*manner*) sine studiō.
coldness *n* frīgus *nt*, algor *m*.
cold water *n* frīgida *f*.
colic *n* tormina *ntpl*.
collar *n* collāre *nt*.
collarbone *n* iugulum *nt*.
collate *vt* cōnferre, comparāre.
collateral *adj* adiūnctus; (*evidence*)
cōnsentāneus.
collation *n* collātiō *f*; (*meal*) prandium *nt*,
merenda *f*.
colleague *n* collēga *m*.
collect *vt* colligere, cōgere, congerere;
(*persons*) congregāre, convocāre; (*taxes*)
exigere; (*something due*) recipere; ~ **oneself**
animum colligere; **cool and ~ed** aequō animō
♦ *vi* convenīre, congregārī.
collection *n* (*persons*) coetus *m*, conventus *m*;
(*things*) congeriēs *f*; (*money*) exāctiō *f*.
collective *adj* commūnis.
collectively *adv* commūniter.
collector *n* (*of taxes*) exāctor *m*.
college *n* collēgium *nt*.
collide *vi* concurrere, cōnflīctārī.
collier *n* carbōnārius *m*.
collision *n* concursus *m*.
collocation *n* collocātiō *f*.
collop *n* offa *f*.
colloquial *adj* cottīdiānus.
colloquy *n* sermō *m*, colloquium *nt*.
collude *vi* praevāricārī.
collusion *n* praevāricātiō *f*.
collusive *adj* praevāricātor.
colonel *n* lēgātus *m*.
colonial *adj* colōnicus ♦ *n* colōnus *m*.
colonist *n* colōnus *m*.
colonization *n* dēductiō *f*.
colonize *vt* colōniam dēdūcere, cōnstituere in
(*acc*).
colonnade *n* porticus *f*.
colony *n* colōnia *f*.
colossal *adj* ingēns, vastus.
colossus *n* colossus *m*.
colour *n* color *m*; (*paint*) pigmentum *nt*;
(*artificial*) fūcus *m*; (*complexion*) color *m*;
(*pretext*) speciēs *f*; **take on a** ~ colōrem
dūcere; **under** ~ **of** per speciem (*gen*); **local** ~
māteria dē regiōne sūmpta ♦ *vt* colōrāre;
(*dye*) īnficere, fūcāre; (*fig*) praetendere (*dat*)
♦ *vi* rubēre, ērubēscere.
colourable *adj* speciōsus.
coloured *adj* (*naturally*) colōrātus; (*artificially*)
fūcātus.
colourful *adj* fūcōsus, varius.
colouring *n* pigmentum *nt*; (*dye*) fūcus *m*.
colourless *adj* perlūcidus; (*person*) pallidus;
(*fig*) īnsulsus.
colours *n* (MIL) signum *nt*, vexillum *nt*; (POL)
partēs *fpl*; **sail under false** ~ aliēnō nōmine
ūtī; **with flying** ~ māximā cum gloriā.
colour sergeant *n* signifer *m*.

colt *n* equuleus *m*, equulus *m*.
coltsfoot *n* farfarus *m*.
column *n* columna *f*; (MIL) agmen *nt*.
coma *n* sopor *m*.
comb *n* pecten *m*; (*bird*) crista *f*; (*loom*) pecten
m; (*honey*) favus *m* ♦ *vt* pectere.
combat *n* pugna *f*, proelium *nt*, certāmen *nt* ♦
vi pugnāre, dīmicāre, certāre ♦ *vt* pugnāre
cum (*abl*), obsistere (*dat*).
combatant *n* pugnātor *m* ♦ *adj* pugnāns; **non** ~
imbellis.
combative *adj* ferōx, pugnāx.
combination *n* coniūnctiō *f*, cōnfūsiō *f*;
(*persons*) cōnspīrātiō *f*; (*illegal*) coniūrātiō *f*.
combine *vt* coniungere, iungere ♦ *vi* coīre,
coniungī ♦ *n* societās *f*.
combustible *adj* ignī obnoxius.
combustion *n* dēflāgrātiō *f*, incendium *nt*.
come *vi* venīre, advenīre; (*after a journey*)
dēvenīre; (*interj*) age!; **how ~s it that ...?**; quī
fit ut ...?; ~ **across** *vi* invenīre, offendere; ~
after sequī, excipere, succēdere (*dat*); ~
again revenīre, redīre; (*when pulled*) sequī; ~ **back** *vi* revenīre,
redīre; regredī; ~ **between** intervenīre,
intercēdere; (*from the past*) trādī, prōdī; ~
forward *vi* prōcēdere, prōdīre; ~ **from** *vi*
(*origin*) dēfluere; ~ **in** *vi* inīre, introīre;
ingredī; (*revenue*) redīre; ~ **near** accēdere ad
(*acc*), appropinquāre (*dat*); ~ **nearer and**
nearer adventāre; ~ **of** *vi* (*family*) ortum esse
ab, ex (*abl*); ~ **off** *vi* ēvādere, discēdere; ~ **on**
vi prōcēdere; (*progress*) prōficere; (*interj*)
age, agite; ~ **on the scene** intervenīre,
supervenīre, adesse; ~ **out** *vi* exīre, ēgredī;
(*hair, teeth*) cadere; (*flower*) flōrēscere; (*book*)
ēdī; ~ **over** *vi* trānsīre; (*feeling*) subīre,
occupāre; ~ **to** *vi* advenīre ad, in (*acc*);
(*person*) adīre; (*amount*) efficere; ~ **to the**
help of subvenīre (*dat*); succurrere (*dat*); ~ **to**
nought ad nihilum recidere; ~ **to pass**
ēvenīre, fierī; ~ **together** convenīre, coīre; ~
up *vi* subīre, succēdere; (*growth*) prōvenīre;
~ **upon** *vt fus* invenīre; **he is coming to** animus
eī redit.
comedian *n* (*actor*) cōmoedus *m*; (*writer*)
cōmicus *m*.
comedienne *n* mīma *f*.
comedy *n* cōmoedia *f*.
comeliness *n* decor *m*, decōrum *nt*.
comely *adj* decōrus, pulcher.
comestibles *n* vīctus *m*.
comet *n* comētēs *m*.
comfort *vt* sōlārī, cōnsōlārī, adlevāre ♦ *n*
sōlācium *nt*, cōnsōlātiō *f*.
comfortable *adj* commodus; **make oneself** ~
corpus cūrāre.
comfortably *adv* commodē.
comforter *n* cōnsōlātor *m*.
comfortless *adj* incommodus; **be** ~ sōlātiō
carēre.
comforts *npl* commoda *ntpl*.
comic *adj* cōmicus; facētus ♦ *n* scurra *m*.

comical *adj* facētus, rīdiculus.
coming *adj* futūrus ♦ *n* adventus *m*.
comity *n* cōmitās *f*.
command *vt* iubēre (+ *acc and infin*), imperāre (*dat and* **ut** *+subj*); dūcere; (*feelings*) regere; (*resources*) fruī (*abl*); (*view*) prōspectāre ♦ *n* (*MIL*) imperium *nt*; (*sphere*) prōvincia *f*; (*order*) imperium *nt*, iussum *nt*, mandātum *nt*; **be in ~ (of)** praeesse (*dat*); **put in ~ of** praeficere (*dat*); **~ of language** fācundia *f*.
commandant *n* praefectus *m*.
commandeer *vt* pūblicāre.
commander *n* dux *m*, praefectus *m*.
commander in chief *n* imperātor *m*.
commandment *n* mandātum *nt*.
commemorate *vt* celebrāre, memoriae trādere.
commemoration *n* celebrātiō *f*.
commence *vt* incipere, exōrdīrī, initium facere (*gen*).
commencement *n* initium *nt*, exōrdium *nt*, prīncipium *nt*.
commend *vt* laudāre; (*recommend*) commendāre; (*entrust*) mandāre; **~ oneself** sē probāre.
commendable *adj* laudābilis, probābilis.
commendation *n* laus *f*, commendātiō *f*.
commendatory *adj* commendātīcius.
commensurable *adj* pār.
commensurate *adj* congruēns, conveniēns.
comment *vi* dīcere, scrībere; **~ on** interpretārī; (*with notes*) adnotāre ♦ *n* dictum *nt*, sententia *f*.
commentary *n* commentāriī *mpl*.
commentator *n* interpres *m*.
commerce *n* mercātūra *f*, commercium *nt*; **engage in ~** mercātūrās facere, negōtiārī.
commercial dealings *n* commercium *nt*.
commercial traveller *n* īnstitor *m*.
commination *n* minae *fpl*.
comminatory *adj* mināx.
commingle *vt* intermiscēre.
commiserate *vt* miserērī (*gen*).
commiseration *n* misericordia *f*; (*RHET*) commiserātiō *f*.
commissariat *n* rēs frūmentāria *f*, commeātus *m*; (*staff*) frūmentāriī *mpl*.
commissary *n* lēgātus *m*; reī frūmentāriae praefectus *m*.
commission *n* (*charge*) mandātum *nt*; (*persons*) triumvirī *mpl*, decemvirī *mpl*, etc; (*abroad*) lēgātiō *f*; **get a ~** (*MIL*) tribūnum fierī; **standing ~** (*law*) quaestiō perpetua *f* ♦ *vt* mandāre, adlēgāre.
commissioner *n* lēgātus *m*; **three ~s** triumvirī *mpl*; **ten ~s** decemvirī *mpl*.
commit *vt* (*charge*) committere, mandāre; (*crime*) admittere; (*to prison*) conicere; (*to an undertaking*) obligāre, obstringere; **~ to memory** memoriae trādere; **~ to writing** litterīs mandāre; **~ an error** errāre; **~ a theft** fūrtum facere; *see also* **suicide.**
commitment *n* mūnus *nt*, officium *nt*.

committee *n* dēlēctī *mpl*.
commodious *adj* capāx.
commodity *n* merx *f*, rēs *f*.
commodore *n* praefectus classis *m*.
common *adj* (*for all*) commūnis; (*ordinary*) vulgāris, cottīdiānus; (*repeated*) frequēns, crēber; (*inferior*) nēquam ♦ *n* compāscuus ager *m*, prātum *nt*; **~ man** homō plēbēius *m*; **~ soldier** gregārius mīles *m*.
commonalty *n* plēbs *f*.
commoner *n* homō plēbēius *m*.
common law *n* mōs māiōrum *m*.
commonly *adv* ferē, vulgō.
common people *n* plēbs *f*, vulgus *nt*.
commonplace *n* trītum prōverbium *nt*; (*RHET*) locus commūnis *m* ♦ *adj* vulgāris, trītus.
commons *n* plēbs *f*; (*food*) diāria *ntpl*.
common sense *n* prūdentia *f*.
commonwealth *n* cīvitās *f*, rēs pūblica *f*.
commotion *n* perturbātiō *f*, tumultus *m*; **cause a ~** tumultuārī.
communal *adj* commūnis.
commune *n* pāgus *m* ♦ *vi* colloquī, sermōnēs cōnferre.
communicate *vt* commūnicāre; (*information*) nūntiāre, patefacere ♦ *vi*: **~ with** commūnicāre (*dat*), commercium habēre (*gen*), agere cum (*abl*).
communication *n* (*dealings*) commercium *nt*; (*information*) litterae *fpl*, nūntius *m*; (*passage*) commeātus *m*; **cut off the ~s of** interclūdere.
communicative *adj* loquāx.
communion *n* societās *f*.
communiqué *n* litterae *fpl*, praedicātiō *f*.
communism *n* bonōrum aequātiō *f*.
community *n* cīvitās *f*, commūne *nt*; (*participation*) commūniō *f*.
commutation *n* mūtātiō *f*.
commute *vt* mūtāre, commūtāre.
compact *n* foedus *nt*, conventum *nt* ♦ *adj* dēnsus ♦ *vt* dēnsāre.
companion *n* socius *m*, comes *m/f*; (*intimate*) sodālis *m*; (*at school*) condiscipulus *m*; (*in army*) commīlitō *m*, contubernālis *m*.
companionable *adj* facilis, commodus.
companionship *n* sodālitās *f*, cōnsuētūdō *f*; (*MIL*) contubernium *nt*.
company *n* societās *f*, cōnsuētūdō *f*; (*gathering*) coetus *m*, conventus *m*; (*guests*) cēnantēs *mpl*; (*commercial*) societās *f*; (*magistrates*) collēgium *nt*; (*MIL*) manipulus *m*; (*THEAT*) grex *m*, caterva *f*; **~ of ten** decuria *f*.
comparable *adj* comparābilis, similis.
comparative *adj* māgnus, sī cum aliīs cōnfertur.
comparatively *adv* ut in tālī tempore, ut in eā regiōne, ut est captus hominum; **~ few** perpaucī, nullus ferē.
compare *vt* comparāre, cōnferre; **~d with** ad (*acc*).
comparison *n* comparātiō *f*, collātiō *f*; (*RHET*) similitūdō *f*; **in ~ with** prō (*abl*).
compartment *n* cella *f*, pars *f*.

compass n ambitus m, spatium nt, modus m; **pair of ~es** circinus m ♦ vt circumdare, cingere; (attain) cōnsequī.
compassion n misericordia f.
compassionate adj misericors, clēmēns.
compassionately adv clēmenter.
compatibility n convenientia f.
compatible adj congruēns, conveniēns; **be ~** congruere.
compatibly adv congruenter, convenienter.
compatriot n cīvis m, populāris m.
compeer n pār m; aequālis m.
compel vt cōgere.
compendious adj brevis.
compendiously adv summātim.
compendium n epitomē f.
compensate vt compēnsāre, satisfacere (dat).
compensation n compēnsātiō f; pretium nt, poena f.
compete vi certāre, contendere.
competence n facultās f; (law) iūs nt; (money) quod sufficit.
competent adj perītus, satis doctus, capāx; (witness) locuplēs; **it is ~** licet.
competition n certāmen nt, contentiō f.
competitor n competītor m, aemulus m.
compilation n collectānea ntpl, liber m.
compile vt compōnere.
compiler n scrīptor m.
complacency n amor suī m.
complacent adj suī contentus.
complain vi querī, conquerī; **~ of** (person) nōmen dēferre (gen).
complainant n accūsātor m, petītor m.
complaint n questus m, querimōnia f; (law) crīmen nt; (MED) morbus m, valētūdō f.
complaisance n cōmitās f, obsequium nt, indulgentia f.
complaisant adj cōmis, officiōsus, facilis.
complement n complēmentum nt; numerus suus m; **make up the ~ of** complēre.
complete vt (amount, time) complēre, explēre; (work) cōnficere, perficere, absolvere, peragere ♦ adj perfectus, absolūtus, integer; (victory) iūstus; (amount) explētus.
completely adv funditus, omnīnō, absolūtē, plānē; penitus.
completeness n integritās f; (perfection) perfectiō f.
completion n (process) absolūtiō f, cōnfectiō f; (end) fīnis m; **bring to ~** absolvere.
complex adj implicātus, multiplex.
complexion n color m.
complexity n implicātiō f.
compliance n accommodātiō f, obsequium nt, obtemperātiō f.
compliant adj obsequēns, facilis.
complicate vt implicāre, impedīre.
complicated adj implicātus, involūtus, impedītus.
complication n implicātiō f.
complicity n cōnscientia f.

compliment n blandīmentum nt, honōs m ♦ vt blandīrī, laudāre; **~ on** grātulārī (dat) dē (abl).
complimentary adj honōrificus, blandus.
compliments npl (as greeting) salūs f.
comply vi obsequī (dat), obtemperāre (dat); mōrem gerere (dat), mōrigerārī (dat).
component n elementum nt, pars f.
comport vt gerere.
compose vt (art) compōnere, condere, pangere; (whole) efficere, cōnflāre; (quarrel) compōnere, dīrimere; (disturbance) sēdāre; **be ~d of** cōnsistere ex (abl), cōnstāre ex (abl).
composed adj tranquillus, placidus.
composer n auctor m, scrīptor m.
composite adj multiplex.
composition n (process) compositiō f, scrīptūra f; (product) opus nt, poēma nt, carmen nt; (quality) structūra f.
composure n sēcūritās f, aequus animus m; (face) tranquillitās f.
compound vt miscēre; (words) duplicāre, iungere ♦ vi (agree) pacīscī ♦ adj compositus ♦ n (word) iūnctum verbum nt; (area) saeptum nt.
compound interest n anatocismus m.
comprehend vt intellegere, comprehendere; (include) continēre, complectī.
comprehensible adj perspicuus.
comprehension n intellegentia f, comprehēnsiō f.
comprehensive adj capāx; **be ~** lātē patēre, multa complectī.
compress vt comprimere, coartāre ♦ n fōmentum nt.
compression n compressus m.
comprise vt continēre, complectī, comprehendere.
compromise n (by one side) accommodātiō f; (by both sides) comprōmissum nt ♦ vi comprōmittere ♦ vt implicāre, in suspiciōnem vocāre; **be ~d in suspiciōnem venīre.
comptroller n moderātor m.
compulsion n necessitās f, vīs f; **under ~** coāctus.
compulsory adj necesse, lēge imperātus; **use ~ measures** vim adhibēre.
compunction n paenitentia f.
computation n ratiō f.
compute vt computāre, ratiōnem dūcere.
comrade n socius m, contubernālis m.
comradeship n contubernium nt.
concatenation n seriēs f.
concave adj concavus.
conceal vt cēlāre, abdere, abscondere; (fact) dissimulāre.
concealment n occultātiō f; (place) latebrae fpl; (of facts) dissimulātiō f; **in ~** abditus, occultus; **be in ~** latēre, latitāre; **go into ~** dēlitēscere.
concede vt concēdere.
conceit n (idea) nōtiō f; (wit) facētiae fpl; (pride)

superbia *f*, adrogantia *f*, vānitās *f*.
conceited *adj* glōriōsus, adrogāns.
conceitedness *n* adrogantia *f*, vānitās *f*.
conceive *vt* concipere, comprehendere, intellegere.
concentrate *vt* (*in one place*) cōgere, congregāre; (*attention*) intendere, dēfīgere.
concentrated *adj* dēnsus.
concentration *n* animī intentiō *f*.
concept *n* nōtiō *f*.
conception *n* conceptus *m*; (*mind*) intellegentia *f*, īnfōrmātiō *f*; (*idea*) nōtiō *f*, cōgitātiō *f*, cōnsilium *nt*.
concern *vt* (*refer*) attinēre ad (*acc*), interesse (*gen*); (*worry*) sollicitāre; **it ~s me** meā rēfert, meā interest; **as far as I am ~ed** per mē ♦ *n* rēs *f*, negōtium *nt*; (*importance*) mōmentum *nt*; (*worry*) sollicitūdō *f*, cūra *f*; (*regret*) dolor *m*.
concerned *adj* sollicitus, anxius; **be ~** dolēre; **be ~ about** molestē ferre.
concerning *prep* dē (*abl*).
concernment *n* sollicitūdō *f*.
concert *n* (*music*) concentus *m*; (*agreement*) cōnsēnsus *m*; **in ~** ex compositō, ūnō animō ♦ *vt* compōnere; (*plan*) inīre.
concession *n* concessiō *f*; **by the ~ of** concessū (*gen*); **make a ~** concēdere, tribuere.
conciliate *vt* conciliāre.
conciliation *n* conciliātiō *f*.
conciliator *n* arbiter *m*.
conciliatory *adj* pācificus.
concise *adj* brevis; (*style*) dēnsus.
concisely *adv* breviter.
conciseness *n* brevitās *f*.
conclave *n* sēcrētus cōnsessus *m*.
conclude *vt* (*end*) termināre, fīnīre, cōnficere; (*settle*) facere, compōnere, pangere; (*infer*) īnferre, colligere.
conclusion *n* (*end*) fīnis *m*; (*of action*) exitus *m*; (*of speech*) perōrātiō *f*; (*inference*) coniectūra *f*; (*decision*) placitum *nt*, sententia *f*; **in ~** dēnique; **try ~s with** contendere cum.
conclusive *adj* certus, manifestus, gravis.
conclusively *adv* sine dubiō.
concoct *vt* coquere; (*fig*) cōnflāre.
concoction *n* (*fig*) māchinātiō *f*.
concomitant *adj* adiūnctus.
concord *n* concordia *f*; (*music*) harmonia *f*.
concordant *adj* concors.
concordat *n* pactum *nt*, foedus *nt*.
concourse *n* frequentia *f*, celebrātiō *f*; (*moving*) concursus *m*.
concrete *adj* concrētus; **in the ~** rē.
concretion *n* concrētiō *f*.
concubine *n* concubīna *f*.
concupiscence *n* libīdō *f*.
concur *vi* (*time*) concurrere; (*opinion*) cōnsentīre, adsentīre.
concurrence *n* (*time*) concursus *m*; (*opinion*) cōnsēnsus *m*.
concurrent *adj* (*time*) aequālis; (*opinion*) cōnsentāneus; **be ~** concurrere, cōnsentīre.

concurrently *adv* simul, ūnā.
concussion *n* ictus *m*.
condemn *vt* damnāre, condemnāre; (*disapprove*) improbāre; **~ to death** capitis damnāre; **~ for treason** dē māiestāte damnāre.
condemnation *n* damnātiō *f*; condemnātiō *f*.
condemnatory *adj* damnātōrius.
condense *vt* dēnsāre; (*words*) premere.
condescend *vi* dēscendere, sē submittere.
condescending *adj* cōmis.
condescension *n* cōmitās *f*.
condiment *n* condīmentum *nt*.
condition *n* (*of body*) habitus *m*; (*external*) status *m*, condiciō *f*, rēs *f*; (*in society*) locus *m*, fortūna *f*; (*of agreement*) condiciō *f*, lēx *f*; **~s of sale** mancipī lēx *f*; **on ~ that** eā condicione ut (*subj*); **in ~** (*animals*) nitidus ♦ *vt* fōrmāre, regere.
conditional *adj*: **the assistance is ~ on** eā condiciōne succurritur ut (*subj*).
conditionally *adv* sub condiciōne.
conditioned *adj* (*character*) mōrātus.
condole *vi*: **~ with** cōnsōlārī.
condolence *n* cōnsōlātiō *f*.
condonation *n* venia *f*.
condone *vt* condōnāre, ignōscere (*dat*).
conduce *vi* condūcere (ad), prōficere (ad).
conducive *adj* ūtilis, accommodātus.
conduct *vt* dūcere; (*escort*) dēdūcere; (*to a place*) addūcere, perdūcere; (*business*) gerere, administrāre; (*self*) gerere ♦ *n* mōrēs *mpl*; (*past*) vīta *f*, facta *ntpl*; (*business*) administrātiō *f*; **safe ~** praesidium *nt*.
conductor *m* dux *m*, ductor *m*.
conduit *n* canālis *m*, aquae ductus *m*.
cone *n* cōnus *m*.
coney *n* cunīculus *m*.
confabulate *vi* colloquī.
confection *n* cuppēdō *f*.
confectioner *n* cuppēdinārius *m*.
confectionery *n* dulcia *ntpl*.
confederacy *n* foederātae cīvitātēs *fpl*, societās *f*.
confederate *adj* foederātus ♦ *n* socius *m* ♦ *vi* coniūrāre, foedus facere.
confederation *n* societās *f*.
confer *vt* cōnferre, tribuere ♦ *vi* colloquī, sermōnem cōnferre; **~ about** agere dē (*abl*).
conference *n* colloquium *nt*, congressus *m*.
conferment *n* dōnātiō *f*.
confess *vt* fatērī, cōnfitērī.
confessedly *adv* manifestō.
confession *n* cōnfessiō *f*.
confidant *n* cōnscius *m*.
confide *vi* fīdere (*dat*), cōnfīdere (*dat*) ♦ *vt* crēdere, committere.
confidence *n* fidēs *f*, fīdūcia *f*; **have ~ in** fīdere (*dat*), cōnfīdere (*dat*); **inspire ~ in** fidem facere (*dat*); **tell in ~** tūtīs auribus dēpōnere.
confident *adj* fīdēns; **~ in** frētus (*abl*); **be ~ that** certō scīre, prō certō habēre.
confidential *adj* arcānus, intimus.

confidentially *adv* inter nōs.
confidently *adv* fīdenter.
confiding *adj* crēdulus.
configuration *n* figūra *f*, fōrma *f*.
confine *vt* (*prison*) inclūdere, in vincula conicere; (*limit*) termināre, circumscrībere; (*restrain*) coercēre, cohibēre; (*to bed*) dētinēre; **be ~d** (*women*) parturīre.
confinement *n* custōdia *f*, vincula *ntpl*, inclūsiō *f*; (*women*) puerperium *nt*.
confines *n* fīnēs *mpl*.
confirm *vt* (*strength*) corrōborāre, firmāre; (*decision*) sancīre, ratum facere; (*fact*) adfirmāre, comprobāre.
confirmation *n* cōnfirmātiō *f*, adfirmātiō *f*.
confirmed *adj* ratus.
confiscate *vt* pūblicāre.
confiscation *n* pūblicātiō *f*.
conflagration *n* incendium *nt*, dēflāgrātiō *f*.
conflict *n* (*physical*) concursus *m*; (*hostile*) certāmen *nt*, proelium *nt*; (*verbal*) contentiō *f*, contrōversia *f*; (*contradiction*) repugnantia *f*, discrepantia *f* ♦ *vi* inter sē repugnāre.
conflicting *adj* contrārius.
confluence *n* cōnfluēns *m*.
confluent *adj* cōnfluēns.
conform *vt* accommodāre ♦ *vi* sē cōnfōrmāre (ad), obsequī (*dat*), mōrem gerere (*dat*).
conformable *adj* accommodātus, conveniēns.
conformably *adv* convenienter.
conformation *n* structūra *f*, confōrmātiō *f*.
conformity *n* convenientia *f*, cōnsēnsus *m*.
confound *vt* (*mix*) cōnfundere, permiscēre; (*amaze*) obstupefacere; (*thwart*) frustrārī; (*suppress*) opprimere, obruere; **~ you!** dī tē perduint.
confounded *adj* miser, sacer, nefandus.
confoundedly *adv* mīrum quantum nefāriē.
confraternity *n* frāternitās *f*.
confront *vt* sē oppōnere (*dat*), obviam īre (*dat*), sē cōram offerre.
confuse *vt* permiscēre, perturbāre.
confused *adj* perturbātus.
confusedly *adv* perturbātē, prōmiscuē.
confusion *n* perturbātiō *f*; (*shame*) rubor *m*.
confutation *n* refūtātiō *f*.
confute *vt* refūtāre, redarguere, convincere.
congé *n* commeātus *m*.
congeal *vt* congelāre, dūrāre ♦ *vi* concrēscere.
congealed *adj* concrētus.
congenial *adj* concors, congruēns, iūcundus.
congeniality *n* concordia *f*, mōrum similitūdō *f*.
congenital *adj* nātīvus.
conger *n* conger *m*.
congested *adj* refertus, dēnsus; (*with people*) frequentissimus.
congestion *n* congeriēs *f*; frequentia *f*.
conglomerate *vt* glomerāre.
conglomeration *n* congeriēs *f*, cumulus *m*.
congratulate *vt* grātulārī (*dat*).
congratulation *n* grātulātiō *f*.

congratulatory *adj* grātulābundus.
congregate *vt* congregāre, cōgere ♦ *vi* convenīre, congregārī.
congregation *n* conventus *m*, coetus *m*.
congress *n* conventus *m*, cōnsessus *m*, concilium *nt*; senātus *m*.
congruence *n* convenientia *f*.
congruent *adj* conveniēns, congruēns.
congruently *adv* convenienter, congruenter.
congruous *adj* see **congruent**.
conical *adj* turbinātus.
coniferous *adj* cōnifer.
conjectural *adj* opīnābilis.
conjecturally *adv* coniectūrā.
conjecture *n* coniectūra *f* ♦ *vt* conicere, augurārī.
conjoin *vt* coniungere.
conjoint *adj* coniūnctus.
conjointly *adv* coniūnctē, ūnā.
conjugal *adj* coniugālis.
conjugate *vt* dēclīnāre.
conjugation *n* (*GRAM*) dēclīnātiō *f*.
conjunct *adj* coniūnctus.
conjunction *n* coniūnctiō *f*, concursus *m*.
conjure *vt* (*entreat*) obtestārī, obsecrāre; (*spirits*) ēlicere, ciēre ♦ *vi* praestigiīs ūtī.
conjurer *n* praestigiātor *m*.
conjuring *n* praestigiae *fpl*.
connate *adj* innātus, nātūrā īnsitus.
connect *vt* iungere, coniungere, cōpulāre, connectere.
connected *adj* coniūnctus; (*unbroken*) continēns; (*by marriage*) adfīnis; **be ~ed with** contingere; **be closely ~ed with** inhaerēre (*dat*), cohaerēre cum (*abl*).
connectedly *adv* coniūnctē, continenter.
connection *n* coniūnctiō *f*, contextus *m*, seriēs *f*; (*kin*) necessitūdō *f*; (*by marriage*) adfīnitās *f*; **~ between ... and ...** ratiō (*gen*) ... cum ... (*abl*); **I have no ~ with you** nīl mihī tēcum est.
connivance *n* venia *f*, dissimulātiō *f*.
connive *vi* conīvēre in (*abl*), dissimulāre.
connoisseur *n* intellegēns *m*.
connotation *n* vīs *f*, significātiō *f*.
connote *vt* significāre.
connubial *adj* coniugālis.
conquer *vt* vincere, superāre.
conquerable *adj* superābilis, expugnābilis.
conqueror *n* victor *m*.
conquest *n* victōria *f*; (*town*) expugnātiō *f*; (*prize*) praemium *nt*, praeda *f*; **the ~ of Greece** Graecia capta.
conscience *n* cōnscientia *f*; **guilty ~** mala cōnscientia; **have a clear ~** nullīus culpae sibi cōnscium esse; **have no ~** nullam rēligiōnem habēre.
conscientious *adj* probus, rēligiōsus.
conscientiously *adv* bonā fidē, rēligiōsē.
conscientiousness *n* fidēs *f*, rēligiō *f*.
conscious *adj* sibī cōnscius; (*aware*) gnārus; (*physically*) mentis compos; **be ~** sentīre.
consciously *adv* sciēns.
consciousness *n* animus *m*; (*of action*)

cōnscientia *f*; **he lost ~** animus eum relīquit.
conscript *n* tīrō *m* ♦ *vt* cōnscrībere.
conscription *n* dēlēctus *m*; (*of wealth*) pūblicātiō *f*.
consecrate *vt* dēdicāre, cōnsecrāre; (*self*) dēvovēre.
consecrated *adj* sacer.
consecration *n* dēdicātiō *f*, cōnsecrātiō *f*; (*self*) dēvōtiō *f*.
consecutive *adj* dēinceps, continuus.
consecutively *adv* dēinceps, ōrdine.
consensus *n* cōnsēnsus *m*.
consent *vi* adsentīre (*dat*), adnuere (*infin*); (*together*) cōnsentīre ♦ *n* (*one side*) adsēnsus *m*; (*all*) cōnsēnsus *m*; **by common ~** omnium cōnsēnsū.
consequence *n* ēventus *m*, exitus *m*; (*logic*) conclūsiō *f*; (*importance*) mōmentum *nt*, auctōritās *f*; **it is of ~** interest; **what will be the ~ of?** quō ēvādet?
consequent *adj* cōnsequēns.
consequential *adj* cōnsentāneus; (*person*) adrogāns.
consequently *adv* itaque, igitur, proptereā.
conservation *n* cōnservātiō *f*.
conservative *adj* reī pūblicae cōnservandae studiōsus; (*estimate*) mediōcris; **~ party** optimātēs *mpl*.
conservator *n* custōs *m*, cōnservātor *m*.
conserve *vt* cōnservāre, servāre.
consider *vt* cōnsīderāre, contemplārī; (*reflect*) sēcum volūtāre, meditari, dēlīberāre, cōgitāre; (*deem*) habēre, dūcere; (*respect*) respicere, observāre.
considerable *adj* aliquantus, nōnnullus; (*person*) illūstris.
considerably *adv* aliquantum; (*with compar*) aliquantō, multō.
considerate *adj* hūmānus, benignus.
considerately *adv* hūmānē, benignē.
consideration *n* cōnsīderātiō *f*, contemplātiō *f*, dēlīberātiō *f*; (*respect*) respectus *m*, ratiō *f*; (*importance*) mōmentum *nt*; (*reason*) ratiō *f*; (*pay*) pretium *nt*; **for a ~** mercēde, datā mercēde; **in ~ of** propter (*acc*), prō (*abl*); **on no ~** nēquāquam; **with ~** cōnsultō; **without ~** temerē; **take into ~** ad cōnsilium dēferre; **show ~ for** respectum habēre (*gen*).
considered *adj* (*reasons*) exquīsītus.
considering *prep* prō (*abl*), propter (*acc*) ♦ *conj* ut, quōniam.
consign *vt* mandāre, committere.
consist *vi* cōnstāre; **~ in** cōnstāre ex (*abl*), continērī (*abl*), positum esse in (*abl*); **~ with** congruere (*dat*), convenīre (*dat*).
consistence *n* firmitās *f*.
consistency *n* cōnstantia *f*.
consistent *adj* cōnstāns; (*with*) cōnsentāneus, congruens; (*of movement*) aequābilis; **be ~** cohaerēre.
consistently *adv* cōnstanter.
consolable *adj* cōnsōlābilis.
consolation *n* cōnsōlātiō *f*; (*thing*) sōlācium *nt*.

consolatory *adj* cōnsōlātōrius.
console *vt* cōnsōlārī.
consoler *n* cōnsōlātor *m*.
consolidate *vt* (*liquid*) cōgere; (*strength*) corrōborāre; (*gains*) obtinēre ♦ *vi* concrēscere.
consolidation *n* concrētiō *f*; cōnfirmātiō *f*.
consonance *n* concentus *m*.
consonant *adj* cōnsonus, haud absonus ♦ *n* cōnsonāns *f*.
consort *n* cōnsors *m/f*, socius *m*; (*married*) coniunx *m/f* ♦ *vi*: **~ with** familiāriter ūtī (*abl*), coniūnctissimē vīvere cum (*abl*).
conspectus *n* summārium *nt*.
conspicuous *adj* ēminēns, īnsignis, manifestus; **be ~** ēminēre.
conspicuously *adv* manifestō, palam, ante oculōs.
conspiracy *n* coniūrātiō *f*.
conspirator *n* coniūrātus *m*.
conspire *vi* coniūrāre; (*for good*) cōnspīrāre.
constable *n* lictor *m*.
constancy *n* cōnstantia *f*, firmitās *f*; **with ~** cōnstanter.
constant *adj* cōnstāns; (*faithful*) fīdus, fidēlis; (*continuous*) adsiduus.
constantly *adv* adsiduē, saepe, crēbrō.
constellation *n* sīdus *nt*.
consternation *n* trepidātiō *f*, pavor *m*; **throw into ~** perterrēre, cōnsternere.
constituency *n* suffrāgātōrēs *mpl*.
constituent *adj*: **~ part** elementum *nt* ♦ *n* (*voter*) suffrāgātor *m*.
constitute *vt* creāre, cōnstituere; esse.
constitution *n* nātūra *f*, status *m*; (*body*) habitus *m*; (*POL*) cīvitātis fōrma *f*, reī pūblicae status *m*, lēgēs *fpl*.
constitutional *adj* lēgitimus, iūstus.
constitutionally *adv* ē rē pūblicā.
constrain *vt* cōgere.
constraint *n* vīs *f*; **under ~** coāctus; **without ~** suā sponte.
constrict *vt* comprimere, cōnstringere.
constriction *n* contractiō *f*.
construct *vt* aedificāre, exstruere.
construction *n* aedificātiō *f*; (*method*) structūra *f*; (*meaning*) interpretātiō *f*; **put a wrong ~ on** in malam partem interpretārī.
construe *vt* interpretārī.
consul *n* cōnsul *m*; **~ elect** cōnsul dēsignātus; **ex ~** cōnsulāris *m*.
consular *adj* cōnsulāris.
consulship *n* cōnsulātus *m*; **stand for the ~** cōnsulātum petere; **hold the ~** cōnsulātum gerere; **in my ~** mē cōnsule.
consult *vt* cōnsulere; **~ the interests of** cōnsulere (*dat*) ♦ *vi* dēlīberāre, cōnsiliārī.
consultation *n* (*asking*) cōnsultātiō *f*; (*discussion*) dēlīberātiō *f*.
consume *vt* cōnsūmere, absūmere; (*food*) edere.
consumer *n* cōnsūmptor *m*.
consummate *adj* summus, perfectus ♦ *vt*

perficere, absolvere.
consummation *n* absolūtiō *f;* fīnis *m,* ēventus *m.*
consumption *n* cōnsūmptiō *f;* (*disease*) tābēs *f,* phthisis *f.*
consumptive *adj* pulmōnārius.
contact *n* tāctus *m,* contāgiō *f;* **come in ~ with** contingere.
contagion *n* contāgiō *f.*
contagious *adj* tābificus; **be ~** contāgiīs vulgārī.
contain *vt* capere, continēre; (*self*) cohibēre.
container *n* vās *nt.*
contaminate *vt* contāmināre, īnficere.
contamination *n* contāgiō *f,* lābēs *f.*
contemplate *vt* contemplārī, intuērī; (*action*) in animō habēre; (*prospect*) spectāre.
contemplation *n* contemplātiō *f;* (*thought*) cōgitātiō *f.*
contemplative *adj* cōgitāns, meditāns; **in a ~ mood** cōgitātiōnī dēditus.
contemporaneous *adj* aequālis.
contemporaneously *adv* simul.
contemporary *adj* aequālis.
contempt *n* contemptiō *f;* **be an object of ~** contemptuī esse; **treat with ~** contemptum habēre, conculcāre.
contemptible *adj* contemnendus, abiectus, vīlis.
contemptuous *adj* fastīdiōsus.
contemptuously *adv* contemptim, fastīdiōsē.
contend *vi* certāre, contendere; (*in battle*) dīmicāre, pugnāre; (*in words*) adfirmāre, adsevērāre.
contending *adj* contrārius.
content *adj* contentus ♦ *n* aequus animus *m* ♦ *vt* placēre (*dat*), satisfacere (*dat*); **be ~ed** satis habēre.
contentedly *adv* aequō animō.
contention *n* certāmen *nt;* contrōversia *f;* (*opinion*) sententia *f.*
contentious *adj* pugnāx, lītigiōsus.
contentiously *adv* pugnāciter.
contentiousness *n* contrōversiae studium *nt.*
contentment *n* aequus animus *m.*
contents *n* quod inest, quae insunt; (*of speech*) argūmentum *nt.*
conterminous *adj* adfīnis.
contest *n* certāmen *nt,* contentiō *f* ♦ *vt* (*law*) lēge agere dē (*abl*); (*office*) petere; (*dispute*) repugnāre (*dat*), resistere (*dat*).
contestable *adj* contrōversus.
contestant *n* petītor *m,* aemulus *m.*
context *n* contextus *m.*
contiguity *n* vīcīnia *f,* propinquitās *f.*
contiguous *adj* vīcīnus, adiacēns; **be ~ to** adiacēre (*dat*), contingere.
continence *n* continentia *f,* abstinentia *f.*
continent *adj* continēns, abstinēns ♦ *n* continēns *f.*
continently *adv* continenter, abstinenter.
contingency *n* cāsus *m,* rēs *f.*
contingent *adj* fortuītus ♦ *n* (*MIL*) numerus *m.*

continual *adj* adsiduus, perpetuus.
continually *adv* adsiduē, semper.
continuance *n* perpetuitās *f,* adsiduitās *f.*
continuation *n* continuātiō *f;* (*of a command*) prōrogātiō *f;* (*of a story*) reliqua pars *f.*
continue *vt* continuāre; (*time*) prōdūcere; (*command*) prōrogāre ♦ *vi* (*action*) pergere; (*time*) manēre; (*endurance*) perstāre, dūrāre; **~ to** *imperf indic.*
continuity *n* continuātiō *f;* (*of speech*) perpetuitās *f.*
continuous *adj* continuus, continēns, perpetuus.
continuously *adv* perpetuō, continenter.
contort *vt* contorquēre, dētorquēre.
contortion *n* distortiō *f.*
contour *n* fōrma *f.*
contraband *adj* interdictus, vetitus.
contract *n* pactum *nt,* mandātum *nt,* conventum *nt;* (*POL*) foedus *nt;* **trial for a breach of ~** mandātī iūdicium *nt* ♦ *vt* (*narrow*) contrahere, addūcere; (*short*) dēminuere; (*illness*) contrahere; (*agreement*) pacīscī; (*for work*) locāre; (*to do work*) condūcere ♦ *vi* pacīscī.
contraction *n* contractiō *f;* (*word*) compendium *nt.*
contractor *n* redemptor *m,* conductor *m.*
contradict *vt* (*person*) contrādīcere (*dat*), refrāgārī (*dat*); (*statement*) īnfitiās īre (*dat*); (*self*) repugnāre (*dat*).
contradiction *n* repugnantia *f,* īnfitiae *fpl.*
contradictory *adj* repugnāns, contrārius; **be ~** inter sē repugnāre.
contradistinction *n* oppositiō *f.*
contraption *n* māchina *f.*
contrariety *n* repugnantia *f.*
contrariwise *adv* ē contrāriō.
contrary *adj* contrārius, adversus; (*person*) difficilis, mōrōsus; **~ to** contrā (*acc*), praeter (*acc*); **~ to expectations** praeter opiniōnem ♦ *n* contrārium *nt;* **on the ~** ē contrāriō, contrā; (*retort*) immo.
contrast *n* discrepantia *f* ♦ *vt* comparāre, oppōnere ♦ *vi* discrepāre.
contravene *vt* (*law*) violāre; (*statement*) contrādīcere (*dat*).
contravention *n* violātiō *f.*
contribute *vt* cōnferre, adferre, contribuere. ♦ *vi:* **~ towards** cōnferre ad (*acc*), adiuvāre; **~ to the cost** impēnsās cōnferre.
contribution *n* conlātiō *f;* (*money*) stipem (*no nom*) *f.*
contributor *n* quī cōnfert.
contributory *adj* adiūnctus.
contrite *adj* paenitēns.
contrition *n* paenitentia *f.*
contrivance *n* māchinātiō *f,* excōgitātiō *f;* (*thing*) māchina *f;* (*idea*) cōnsilium *nt;* (*deceit*) dolus *m.*
contrive *vt* māchinārī, excōgitāre, struere; (*to do*) efficere ut.
contriver *n* māchinātor *m,* artifex *m,* auctor *m.*

control n (*restraint*) frēnum nt; (*power*) moderātiō f, potestās f, imperium nt; **have ~ of** praeesse (*dat*); **out of ~** impotēns ♦ vt moderārī (*dat*), imperāre (*dat*).

controller n moderātor m.

controversial adj concertātōrius.

controversy n contrōversia f, disceptātiō f.

controvert vt redarguere, impugnāre, in dubium vocāre.

contumacious adj contumāx, pervicāx.

contumaciously adv contumāciter, pervicāciter.

contumacy n contumācia f, pervicācia f.

contusion n sūgillātiō f.

conundrum n aenigma nt.

convalesce vi convalēscere.

convalescence n melior valētūdō f.

convalescent adj convalēscēns.

convene vt convocāre.

convenience n opportūnitās f, commoditās f; (*thing*) commodum nt; **at your ~** commodō tuō.

convenient adj idōneus, commodus, opportūnus; **be ~** convenīre; **very ~** percommodus.

conveniently adv opportūnē, commodē.

convention n (*meeting*) conventus m; (*agreement*) conventum nt; (*custom*) mōs m, iūsta ntpl.

conventional adj iūstus, solitus.

conventionality n mōs m, cōnsuētūdō f.

converge vi in medium vergere, in eundem locum tendere.

conversant adj perītus, doctus, exercitātus; **be ~ with** versārī in (*abl*).

conversation n sermō m, colloquium nt.

converse n sermō m, colloquium nt; (*opposite*) contrārium nt ♦ vi colloquī, sermōnem cōnferre ♦ adj contrārius.

conversely adv ē contrāriō, contrā.

conversion n mūtātiō f; (*moral*) mōrum ēmendātiō f.

convert vt mūtāre, convertere; (*to an opinion*) dēdūcere ♦ n discipulus m.

convertible adj commūtābilis.

convex adj convexus.

convexity n convexum nt.

convey vt vehere, portāre, convehere; (*property*) abaliēnāre; (*knowledge*) commūnicāre; (*meaning*) significāre; **~ across** trānsmittere, trādūcere, trānsvehere; **~ away** auferre, āvehere; **~ down** dēvehere, dēportāre; **~ into** importāre, invehere; **~ to** advehere, adferre; **~ up** subvehere.

conveyance n vehiculum nt; (*property*) abaliēnātiō f.

convict vt (*prove guilty*) convincere; (*sentence*) damnāre ♦ n reus m.

conviction n (*law*) damnātiō f; (*argument*) persuāsiō f; (*belief*) fidēs f; **carry ~** fidem facere; **have a ~** persuāsum habēre.

convince vt persuādēre (*dat*); **I am firmly ~d** mihi persuāsum habeō.

convincing adj (*argument*) gravis; (*evidence*) manifestus.

convincingly adv manifestō.

convivial adj convīvalis, festīvus.

conviviality n festīvitās f.

convocation n conventus m.

convoke vt convocāre.

convolution n spīra f.

convoy n praesidium nt ♦ vt prōsequī.

convulse vt agitāre; **be ~d with laughter** sē in cachinnōs effundere.

convulsion n (*MED*) convulsiō f; (*POL*) tumultus m.

convulsive adj spasticus.

coo vi gemere.

cook vt coquere ♦ n coquus m.

cookery n ars coquīnāria f.

cool adj frīgidus; (*conduct*) impudens; (*mind*) impavidus, lentus ♦ n frīgus nt ♦ vt refrīgerāre; (*passion*) restinguere, sēdāre ♦ vi refrīgēscere, refrīgerārī, dēfervēscere.

coolly adv aequō animō; impudenter.

coolness n frīgus nt; (*mind*) aequus animus m; impudentia f.

coop n hara f; (*barrel*) cūpa f ♦ vt inclūdere.

co-operate vi operam cōnferre; **~ with** adiuvāre, socius esse (*gen*).

co-operation n cōnsociātiō f; auxilium nt, opera f.

co-operative adj (*person*) officiōsus.

co-operator n socius m.

co-opt vt cooptāre.

coot n fulica f.

copartner n socius m.

copartnership n societās f.

cope vi: **~ with** contendere cum (*abl*); **able to ~ with** pār (*dat*); **unable to ~ with** impār (*dat*).

copier n librārius m.

coping n fastīgium nt.

copious adj cōpiōsus, largus, plēnus, abundāns.

copiously adv cōpiōsē, abundanter.

copiousness n cōpia f, ūbertās f.

copper n aes nt ♦ adj aēneus.

coppersmith n faber aerārius m.

coppice, copse n dūmētum nt, virgultum nt.

copy n exemplar nt ♦ vt imitārī; (*writing*) exscrībere, trānscrībere.

copyist n librārius m.

coracle n linter f.

coral n cūrālium nt.

cord n fūniculus m.

cordage n fūnēs mpl.

cordial adj cōmis, festīvus, amīcus; (*greetings*) multus.

cordiality n cōmitās f, studium nt.

cordially adv cōmiter, libenter, ex animō.

cordon n corōna f.

core n (*fig*) nucleus m.

cork n sūber nt; (*bark*) cortex m.

corn n frūmentum nt ♦ adj frūmentārius; (*on*

the foot) clāvus *m*; **price of** ~ annōna *f*.
corndealer *n* frūmentārius *m*.
cornfield *n* seges *f*.
cornel *n* (*tree*) cornus *f*.
corner *n* angulus *m*.
cornet *n* cornū *nt*.
cornice *n* corōna *f*.
coronet *n* diadēma *nt*.
corporal *adj* corporeus.
corporal punishment *n* verbera *ntpl*.
corporation *n* collēgium *nt*; (*civic*)
   magistrātūs *mpl*.
corporeal *adj* corporeus.
corps *n* manus *f*.
corpse *n* cadāver *nt*.
corpulence *n* obēsum corpus *nt*.
corpulent *adj* obēsus, pinguis.
corpuscle *n* corpusculum *nt*.
corral *n* praesēpe *nt*.
correct *vt* corrigere, ēmendāre; (*person*)
   castīgāre ♦ *adj* vērus; (*language*) integer;
   (*style*) ēmendātus.
correction *n* ēmendātiō *f*; (*moral*) corrēctiō *f*;
   (*punishment*) castīgātiō *f*.
correctly *adv* bene, vērē.
correctness *n* (*fact*) vēritās *f*; (*language*)
   integritās *f*; (*moral*) probitās *f*.
corrector *n* ēmendātor *m*, corrēctor *m*.
correspond *vi* (*agree*) respondēre (*dat*),
   congruere (*dat*); (*by letter*) inter sē scrībere.
correspondence *n* similitūdō *f*; epistulae *fpl*.
correspondent *n* epistulārum scrīptor *m*.
corresponding *adj* pār.
correspondingly *adv* pariter.
corridor *n* porticus *f*.
corrigible *adj* ēmendābilis.
corroborate *vt* cōnfīrmāre.
corroboration *n* cōnfīrmātiō *f*.
corrode *vt* ērōdere, edere.
corrosive *adj* edāx.
corrugate *vt* rūgāre.
corrugated *adj* rūgōsus.
corrupt *vt* corrumpere, dēprāvāre; (*text*)
   vitiāre ♦ *adj* corruptus, vitiātus; (*person*)
   prāvus, vēnālis; (*text*) vitiātus.
corrupter *n* corruptor *m*.
corruptible *adj* (*matter*) dissolūbilis; (*person*)
   vēnālis.
corruption *n* (*of matter*) corruptiō *f*; (*moral*)
   corruptēla *f*, dēprāvātiō *f*; (*bribery*) ambitus
   m.
corsair *n* pīrāta *m*.
cortège *n* pompa *f*.
coruscate *vi* fulgēre.
coruscation *n* fulgor *m*.
Corybant *n* Corybas *m*.
Corybantic *adj* Corybantius.
cosmetic *n* medicāmen *nt*.
cosmic *adj* mundānus.
cosmopolitan *adj* mundānus.
cosmos *n* mundus *m*.
cost *vt* emī, stāre (*dat*); **it** ~ **me dear** māgnō
   mihi stetit, male ēmī; **it** ~ **me a talent** talentō

mihi stetit, talentō ēmī; **it** ~ **me my freedom**
   lībertātem perdidi ♦ *n* pretium *nt*, impēnsa *f*;
   ~ **of living** annōna *f*; **to your** ~ incommodō tuō,
   dētrīmentō tuō; **at the** ~ **of one's reputation**
   violātā fāmā, nōn salvā existimātiōne; **I sell**
   at ~ **price** quantī ēmī vēndō.
costliness *n* sūmptus *m*; cāritās *f*.
costly *adj* cārus; (*furnishings*) lautus,
   sūmptuōsus.
costume *n* habitus *m*.
cosy *adj* commodus.
cot *n* lectulus *m*.
cote *n* columbārium *nt*.
cottage *n* casa *f*, tugurium *nt*.
cottager *n* rūsticus *m*.
cotton *n* (*tree*) gossympinus *f*; (*cloth*) xylinum
   nt.
couch *n* lectus *m* ♦ *vi* recumbere ♦ *vt* (*lance*)
   intendere; (*words*) exprimere, reddere.
cough *n* tussis *f* ♦ *vi* tussīre.
council *n* concilium *nt*; (*small*) cōnsilium *nt*.
councillor *n* (*town*) decuriō *m*.
counsel *n* (*debate*) cōnsultātiō *f*; (*advice*)
   cōnsilium *nt*; (*law*) advocātus *m*, patrōnus *m*;
   take ~ cōnsiliārī, dēlīberāre; **take** ~ **of**
   cōnsulere ♦ *vt* suādēre (*dat*), monēre.
counsellor *n* cōnsiliārius *m*.
count *vt* numerāre, computāre; ~ **as** dūcere,
   habēre; ~ **amongst** pōnere in (*abl*); ~ **up** *vt*
   ēnumerāre; ~ **upon** cōnfīdere (*dat*); **be** ~**ed**
   among in numerō esse (*gen*) ♦ *vi* aestimārī,
   habērī ♦ *n* ratiō *f*; (*in indictment*) caput *nt*;
   (*title*) comes *m*.
countenance *n* faciēs *f*, vultus *m*, ōs *nt*; (*fig*)
   favor *m*; **put out of** ~ conturbāre ♦ *vt* favēre
   (*dat*), indulgēre (*dat*).
counter *n* (*for counting*) calculus *m*; (*for play*)
   tessera *f*; (*shop*) mēnsa *f* ♦ *adj* contrārius ♦
   adv contrā, obviam ♦ *vt* obsistere (*dat*),
   respondēre (*dat*).
counteract *vt* obsistere (*dat*), adversārī (*dat*);
   (*malady*) medērī (*dat*).
counterattack *vt* in vicem oppugnāre,
   adgredī.
counterattraction *n* altera illecebra *f*.
counterbalance *vt* compēnsāre, exaequāre.
counterclockwise *adv* sinistrōrsus.
counterfeit *adj* falsus, fūcātus, adsimulātus,
   fictus ♦ *vt* fingere, simulāre, imitārī.
countermand *vt* renūntiāre.
counterpane *n* lōdīx *f*, strāgulum *nt*.
counterpart *n* pār *m/f/nt*.
counterpoise *n* aequum pondus *nt* ♦ *vt*
   compēnsāre, exaequāre.
countersign *n* (MIL) tessera *f*.
counting table *n* abacus *m*.
countless *adj* innumerābilis.
countrified *adj* agrestis, rūsticus.
country *n* (*region*) regiō *f*, terra *f*; (*territory*)
   fīnēs *mpl*; (*native*) patria *f*; (*not town*) rūs *nt*;
   (*open*) agrī *mpl*; **of our** ~ nostrās; **live in the** ~
   rūsticārī; **living in the** ~ rūsticātiō *f*.

country house n vīlla f.
countryman n agricola m; **fellow ~** populāris m, cīvis m.
countryside n agrī mpl, rus nt.
couple n pār nt; **a ~ of** duo ♦ vt cōpulare, coniungere.
couplet n distichon nt.
courage n fortitūdō f, animus m; (MIL) virtūs f; **have the ~ to** audēre; **lose ~** animōs dēmittere; **take ~** bonō animō esse.
courageous adj fortis, ācer; audāx.
courageously adv fortiter, ācriter.
courier n tabellārius m.
course n (movement) cursus m; (route) iter nt; (sequence) seriēs f; (career) dēcursus; (for races) stadium nt, circus m; (of dinner) ferculum nt; (of stones) ōrdō m; (of water) lāpsus m; **of ~** certē, sānē, scīlicet; **as a matter of ~** continuō; **in due ~** mox; **in the ~ of** inter (acc), in (abl); **keep on one's ~** cursum tenēre; **be driven off one's ~**dēicī; **second ~** secunda mēnsa.
court n (space) ārea f; (of house) ātrium nt; (of king) aula f; (suite) cohors f, comitēs mpl; (law) iūdicium nt, iūdicēs mpl; **pay ~ to** ambīre, īnservīre (dat); **hold a ~** forum agere; **bring into ~** in iūs vocāre ♦ vt colere, ambīre; (danger) sē offerre (dat); (woman) petere.
courteous adj cōmis, urbānus, hūmānus.
courteously adv cōmiter, urbānē.
courtesan n meretrīx f.
courtesy n (quality) cōmitās f, hūmānitās f; (act) officium nt.
courtier n aulicus m; **~s** pl aula f.
courtly adj officiōsus.
cousin n cōnsobrīnus m, cōnsobrīna f.
cove n sinus m.
covenant n foedus nt, pactum nt ♦ vi pacīscī.
cover vt tegere, operīre; (hide) vēlāre; (march) claudere; **~ over** obdūcere; **~ up** vi obtegere ♦ n integumentum nt, operculum nt; (shelter) latebrae fpl, suffugium nt; (pretence) speciēs f; **under ~ of** sub (abl), sub speciē (gen); **take ~** dēlitēscere.
covering n integumentum nt, involucrum nt, operculum nt; (of couch) strāgulum nt.
coverlet n lōdīx f.
covert adj occultus; (language) oblīquus ♦ n latebra f, perfugium nt; (thicket) dūmētum nt.
covertly adv occultē, sēcrētō.
covet vt concupīscere, expetere.
covetous adj avidus, cupidus.
covetously adv avidē, cupidē.
covetousness n avidītās f, cupidītās f.
covey n grex f.
cow n vacca f ♦ vt terrēre.
coward n ignāvus m.
cowardice n ignāvia f.
cowardly adj ignāvus.
cower vi subsīdere.
cowherd m bubulcus m.
cowl n cucullus m.
coxswain n rēctor m.

coy adj pudens, verēcundus.
coyly adv pudenter, modestē.
coyness n pudor m, verēcundia f.
cozen vt fallere, dēcipere.
crab n cancer m.
crabbed adj mōrōsus, difficilis.
crack n (chink) rīma f; (sound) crepitus m ♦ vt findere, frangere; (whip) crepitāre (abl) ♦ vi (open) fatīscere; (sound) crepāre, crepitāre.
crackle vi crepitāre.
crackling n crepitus m.
cradle n cūnae fpl; (fig) incūnābula ntpl.
craft n ars f; (deceit) dolus m; (boat) nāvigium nt.
craftily adv callidē, sollerter; dolōsē.
craftsman n artifex m, faber m.
craftsmanship n ars f, artificium nt.
crafty adj callidus, sollers; dolōsus.
crag n rūpēs f, scopulus m.
cram vt farcīre, refercīre; (with food) sagīnāre.
cramp n convulsiō f; (tool) cōnfībula f ♦ vt coercēre, coartāre.
crane n (bird) grus f; (machine) māchina f, trochlea f.
crank n uncus m; (person) ineptus m.
crannied adj rīmōsus.
cranny n rīma f.
crash n (fall) ruīna f; (noise) fragor m ♦ vi ruere; strepere.
crass adj crassus; **~ stupidity** mera stultitia.
crate n crātēs fpl.
crater n crātēr m.
cravat n fōcāle nt.
crave vt (desire) concupīscere, adpetere, exoptāre; (request) ōrāre, obsecrāre.
craven adj ignāvus.
craving n cupīdō f, dēsīderium nt, adpetītiō f.
crawl vi (animal) serpere; (person) rēpere.
crayfish n commarus m.
craze n libīdō f ♦ vt mentem aliēnāre.
craziness n dēmentia f.
crazy adj dēmēns, fatuus.
creak vi crepāre.
creaking n crepitus m.
cream n spūma lactis f; (fig) flōs m.
crease n rūga f ♦ vt rūgāre.
create vt creāre, facere, gignere.
creation n (process) fabricātiō f; (result) opus nt; (human) hominēs mpl.
creative adj (nature) creātrīx; (mind) inventor, inventrīx.
creator n creātor m, auctor m, opifex m.
creature n animal nt; (person) homō m/f.
credence n fidēs f.
credentials n litterae commendātīciae fpl; (fig) auctōritās f.
credibility n fidēs f; (source) auctōritās f.
credible adj crēdibilis; (witness) locuplēs.
credit n (belief) fidēs f; (repute) existimātiō f; (character) auctōritās f, grātia f; (COMM) fidēs f; **be a ~ to** decus esse (gen); **it is to your ~** tibī laudī est; **give ~ for** laudem tribuere (gen);

have ~ fidē stāre ♦ *vt* crēdere (*dat*); (*with money*) acceptum referre (*dat*).
creditable *adj* honestus, laudābilis.
creditably *adv* honestē, cum laude.
creditor *n* crēditor *m*.
credulity *n* crēdulitās *f*.
credulous *adj* crēdulus.
creed *n* dogma *nt*.
creek *n* sinus *m*.
creel *n* vīdulus *m*.
creep *vi* (*animal*) serpere; (*person*) rēpere; (*flesh*) horrēre.
cremate *vt* cremāre.
crescent *n* lūna *f*.
crescent-shaped *adj* lūnātus.
cress *n* nasturtium *nt*.
crest *n* crista *f*.
crested *adj* cristātus.
crestfallen *adj* dēmissus.
crevasse *n* hiātus *m*.
crevice *n* rīma *f*.
crew *n* nautae *mpl*, rēmigēs *mpl*, grex *f*, turba *f*.
crib *n* (*cot*) lectulus *m*; (*manger*) praesēpe *nt*.
cricket *n* gryllus *m*.
crier *n* praecō *m*.
crime *n* scelus *nt*, facinus *nt*, flāgitium *nt*.
criminal *adj* scelestus, facinorōsus, flāgitiōsus ♦ *n* reus *m*.
criminality *n* scelus *nt*.
criminally *adv* scelestē, flāgitiōsē.
crimson *n* coccum *nt* ♦ *adj* coccineus.
cringe *vi* adūlārī, adsentārī.
crinkle *n* rūga *f*.
cripple *vt* dēbilitāre, mūtilāre; (*fig*) frangere ♦ *adj* claudus.
crisis *n* discrīmen *nt*.
crisp *adj* fragilis; (*manner*) alacer; (*hair*) crispus.
crisscross *adj* in quīncūncem dispositus.
criterion *n* index *m*, indicium *nt*; **take as a ~** referre ad (*acc*).
critic *n* iūdex *m*; (*literary*) criticus, grammaticus *m*; (*adverse*) castīgātor *m*.
critical *adj* (*mind*) accūrātus, ēlegāns; (*blame*) cēnsōrius, sevērus; (*danger*) perīculōsus, dubius; **~ moment** discrīmen *nt*.
critically *adv* accūrātē, ēleganter; sevērē; cum perīculō.
criticism *n* iūdicium *nt*; (*adverse*) reprehēnsiō *f*.
criticize *vt* iūdicāre; reprehendere, castīgāre.
croak *vi* (*raven*) crōcīre; (*frog*) coaxāre.
croaking *n* cantus *m* ♦ *adj* raucus.
crock *n* olla *f*.
crockery *n* fictilia *ntpl*.
crocodile *n* crocodīlus *m*; **weep ~ tears** lacrimās cōnfingere.
crocus *n* crocus *m*.
croft *n* agellus *m*.
crone *n* anus *f*.
crony *n* sodālis *m*.
crook *n* pedum *nt* ♦ *vt* incurvāre.
crooked *adj* incurvus, aduncus; (*deformed*)

prāvus; (*winding*) flexuōsus; (*morally*) perversus.
crookedly *adv* perversē, prāvē.
crookedness *n* prāvitās *f*.
croon *vt*, *vi* cantāre.
crop *n* (*grain*) seges *f*, messis *f*; (*tree*) fructus *m*; (*bird*) ingluviēs *f* ♦ *vt* (*reap*) metere; (*graze*) carpere, tondēre; **~ up** *vi* intervenīre.
cross *n* (*mark*) decussis *m*; (*torture*) crux *f* ♦ *adj* trānsversus, oblīquus; (*person*) acerbus, īrātus ♦ *vt* trānsīre; (*water*) trāicere; (*mountain*) trānscendere; superāre; (*enemy*) obstāre (*dat*), frustrārī; **~ out** *vt* (*writing*) expungere ♦ *vi* trānsīre; **~ over** (*on foot*) trānsgredī; (*by sea*) trānsmittere.
crossbar *n* iugum *nt*.
crossbow *n* scorpiō *m*.
cross-examination *n* interrogātiō *f*.
cross-examine *vt* interrogāre, percontārī.
cross-grained *adj* (*fig*) mōrōsus.
crossing *n* trānsitus *m*; (*on water*) trāiectus *m*.
cross purpose *n*: **be at ~s** dīversa spectāre.
cross-question *vt* interrogāre.
crossroads *n* quadrivium *nt*.
crosswise *adv* ex trānsversō; **divide ~** decussāre.
crotchety *adj* mōrōsus, difficilis.
crouch *vi* subsīdere, sē submittere.
crow *n* cornīx *f*; **as the ~ flies** rēctā regiōne ♦ *vi* cantāre; (*fig*) exsultāre, gestīre.
crowbar *n* vectis *m*.
crowd *n* turba *f*, concursus *m*, frequentia *f*; (*small*) grex *m*; multitūdō *f*; **in ~s** gregātim ♦ *vi* frequentāre, celebrāre ♦ *vt* (*place*) complēre; (*person*) stīpāre.
crowded *adj* frequēns.
crown *n* corōna *f*; (*royal*) diadēma *nt*; (*of head*) vertex *m*; (*fig*) apex *m*, flōs *m*; **the ~ of** summus ♦ *vt* corōnāre; (*fig*) cumulāre, fastīgium impōnere (*dat*).
crucial *adj* gravissimus, māximī mōmentī; **~ moment** discrīmen *nt*.
crucifixion *n* crucis supplicium *nt*.
crucify *vt* crucī suffīgere.
crude *adj* crūdus; (*style*) dūrus, inconcinnus.
crudely *adv* dūrē, asperē.
crudity *n* asperitās *f*.
cruel *adj* crūdēlis, saevus, atrōx.
cruelly *adv* crūdēliter, atrōciter.
cruelty *n* crūdēlitās *f*, saevitia *f*, atrōcitās *f*.
cruise *n* nāvigātiō *f* ♦ *vi* nāvigāre.
cruiser *n* speculātōria nāvis *f*.
crumb *n* mīca *f*.
crumble *vi* corruere, putrem fierī ♦ *vt* putrefacere, friāre.
crumbling *adj* putris.
crumple *vt* rūgāre.
crunch *vt* dentibus frangere.
crupper *n* postilēna *f*.
crush *vt* frangere, contundere, obterere; (*fig*) adflīgere, opprimere, obruere ♦ *n* turba *f*, frequentia *f*.
crust *n* crusta *f*; (*bread*) frustum *nt*.

crusty *adj* (*fig*) stomachōsus.
crutch *n* baculum *nt*.
cry *vt, vi* clāmāre, clāmitāre; (*weep*) flēre; (*infant*) vāgīre; ~ **down** dētrectāre; ~ **out** exclāmāre, vōciferārī; ~ **out against** adclāmāre, reclāmāre; ~ **up** laudāre, vēnditāre ♦ *n* clāmor *m*, vōx *f*; (*child's*) vāgītus *m*; (*of grief*) plōrātus *m*.
cryptic *adj* arcānus.
crystal *n* crystallum *nt* ♦ *adj* crystallinus.
cub *n* catulus *m*.
cube *n* cubus *m*.
cubit *n* cubitum *nt*.
cuckoo *n* coccyx *m*.
cucumber *n* cucumis *m*.
cud *n*: **chew the** ~ rūminārī.
cudgel *n* fustis *m* ♦ *vt* verberāre.
cue *n* signum *nt*, indicium *nt*.
cuff *n* (*blow*) alapa *f*.
cuirass *n* lōrīca *f*.
culinary *adj* coquīnārius.
cull *vt* legere, carpere, dēlībāre.
culminate *vi* ad summum fastīgium venīre.
culmination *n* fastīgium *nt*.
culpability *n* culpa *f*, noxa *f*.
culpable *adj* nocēns.
culprit *n* reus *m*.
cultivate *vt* (*land*) colere, subigere; (*mind*) excolere; (*interest*) fovēre, studēre (*dat*).
cultivation *n* cultus *m*, cultūra *f*.
cultivator *n* cultor *m*, agricola *m*.
cultural *adj* hūmānior.
culture *n* hūmānitās *f*, bonae artēs *fpl*.
cultured *adj* doctus, litterātus.
culvert *n* cloāca *f*.
cumber *vt* impedīre, obesse (*dat*); (*load*) onerāre.
cumbersome *adj* molestus, gravis.
cumulative *adj* alius ex aliō; **be** ~ cumulārī.
cuneiform *adj* cuneātus.
cunning *adj* callidus, astūtus ♦ *n* ars *f*, astūtia *f*, calliditās *f*.
cunningly *adv* callidē, astūtē.
cup *n* pōculum *nt*; **drink the** ~ **of** (*fig*) exanclāre, exhaurīre; **in one's** ~**s** ēbrius, pōtus.
cupboard *n* armārium *nt*.
Cupid *n* Cupīdō *m*, Amor *m*.
cupidity *n* avāritia *f*.
cupola *n* tholus *m*.
cupping glass *n* cucurbita *f*.
cur *n* canis *m*.
curable *adj* sānābilis.
curative *adj* salūbris.
curator *n* custōs *m*.
curb *vt* frēnāre, īnfrēnāre; (*fig*) coercēre, cohibēre ♦ *n* frēnum *nt*.
curdle *vt* cōgere ♦ *vi* concrēscere.
curds *n* concrētum lac *nt*.
cure *vt* sānāre, medērī (*dat*) ♦ *n* remedium *nt*; (*process*) sānātiō *f*.
curio *n* dēliciae *fpl*.
curiosity *n* studium *nt*; (*thing*) mīrāculum *nt*.
curious *adj* (*inquisitive*) cūriōsus, cupidus;

(*artistic*) ēlābōrātus; (*strange*) mīrus, novus.
curiously *adv* cūriōsē; summā arte; mīrum in modum.
curl *n* (*natural*) cirrus *m*; (*artificial*) cincinnus *m* ♦ *vt* (*hair*) crispāre ♦ *vi* (*smoke*) volvī.
curling irons *n* calamistrī *mpl*.
curly *adj* crispus.
currency *n* (*coin*) monēta *f*; (*use*) ūsus *m*; **gain** ~ (*rumour*) percrēbrēscere.
current *adj* vulgātus, ūsitātus; (*time*) hīc ♦ *n* flūmen *nt*; **with the** ~ secundō flūmine; **against the** ~ adversō flūmine.
currently *adv* vulgō.
curriculum *n* īnstitūtiō *f*.
curry *vt* (*favour*) aucupārī.
curse *n* exsecrātiō *f*, maledictum *nt*; (*formula*) exsecrābile carmen *nt*; (*fig*) pestis *f*; ~**s** (*interj*) malum! ♦ *vt* exsecrārī, maledīcere (*dat*).
cursed *adj* exsecrātus, sacer; scelestus.
cursorily *adv* breviter, strictim.
cursory *adj* brevis.
curt *adj* brevis.
curtail *vt* minuere, contrahere.
curtailment *n* dēminūtiō *f*, contractiō *f*.
curtain *n* aulaeum *nt* ♦ *vt* vēlāre.
curule *adj* curūlis.
curve *n* flexus *m*, arcus *m* ♦ *vt* flectere, incurvāre, arcuāre.
cushion *n* pulvīnus *m*.
custodian *n* custōs *m*.
custody *n* custōdia *f*, tūtēla *f*; (*prison*) carcer *m*; **hold in** ~ custōdīre.
custom *n* mōs *m*, cōnsuētūdō *f*; (*national*) īnstitūtum *nt*; ~**s** *pl* portōria *ntpl*.
customarily *adv* plērumque, dē mōre, vulgō.
customary *adj* solitus, ūsitātus; (*rite*) sollemnis; **it is** ~ mōs est.
customer *n* emptor *m*.
customs officer *n* portitor *m*.
cut *vt* secāre, caedere, scindere; (*corn*) metere; (*branch*) amputāre; (*acquaintance*) āversārī; (*hair*) dētondēre; ~ **away** abscindere, resecāre; ~ **down** rescindere, caedere, succīdere; ~ **into** incīdere; ~ **off** *vt* abscīdere, praecīdere; (*exclude*) exclūdere; (*intercept*) interclūdere, intercipere; (*head*) abscindere; ~ **out** *vt* excīdere, exsecāre; (*omit*) ōmittere; ~ **out for** aptus ad, nātus ad (*acc*); ~ **round** circumcīdere; ~ **short** praecīdere; (*speech*) incīdere, interrumpere; ~ **through** intercīdere; ~ **up** *vt* concīdere ♦ *n* vulnus *nt*.
cutlass *n* gladius *m*.
cutlery *n* cultrī *mpl*.
cutter *n* sector *m*; (*boat*) lembus *m*.
cutthroat *n* sīcārius *m*.
cutting *n* (*plant*) propāgō *f* ♦ *adj* acūtus; (*fig*) acerbus, mordāx.
cuttlefish *n* sēpia *f*.
cyclamen *n* baccar *nt*.
cycle *n* orbis *m*.
cyclone *n* turbō *f*.

cylinder *n* cylindrus *m*.
cymbal *n* cymbalum *nt*.
cynic *n* (*PHILOS*) cynicus *m*.
cynical *adj* mordāx, acerbus.
cynically *adv* mordāciter, acerbē.
cynicism *n* acerbitās *f*.
cynosure *n* cynosūra *f*.
cypress *n* cypressus *f*.

D, d

dabble *vi*: ~ **in** gustāre, leviter attingere.
dactyl *n* dactylus *m*.
dactylic *adj* dactylicus.
dagger *n* sīca *f*, pugiō *f*.
daily *adj* diūrnus, cottīdiānus ♦ *adv* cottīdiē, in diēs.
daintily *adv* molliter, concinnē; fastīdiōsē.
daintiness *n* munditia *f*, concinnitās *f*; (*squeamish*) fastīdium *nt*.
dainty *adj* mundus, concinnus, mollis; fastīdiōsus ♦ *npl*: **dainties** cuppēdia *ntpl*.
dais *n* suggestus *m*.
daisy *n* bellis *f*.
dale *n* vallis *f*.
dalliance *n* lascīvia *f*.
dally *vi* lūdere; morārī.
dam *n* mōlēs *f*, agger *m*; (*animal*) māter *f* ♦ *vt* obstruere, exaggerāre.
damage *n* damnum *nt*, dētrīmentum *nt*, malum *nt*; (*inflicted*) iniūria *f*; (*law*) damnum *nt*; **assess ~s** lītem aestimāre ♦ *vt* laedere, nocēre (*dat*); (*by evidence*) laedere; (*reputation*) violāre.
damageable *adj* fragilis.
dame *n* mātrōna *f*, domina *f*.
damn *vt* damnāre, exsecrārī.
damnable *adj* dētestābilis, improbus.
damnably *adv* improbē.
damnation *n* malum *nt*.
damp *adj* ūmidus ♦ *n* ūmor *m* ♦ *vt* madefacere; (*enthusiasm*) restinguere, dēmittere.
damsel *n* puella *f*, virgō *f*.
damson *n* Damascēnum *nt*.
dance *vi* saltāre ♦ *n* saltātiō *f*; (*religious*) tripudium *nt*.
dancer *n* saltātor *m*, saltātrīx *f*.
dandruff *n* porrīgō *f*.
dandy *n* dēlicātus *m*.
danger *n* perīculum *nt*, discrīmen *nt*.
dangerous *adj* perīculōsus, dubius; (*in attack*) īnfestus.
dangerously *adv* perīculōsē.
dangle *vt* suspendere ♦ *vi* pendēre.

dank *adj* ūmidus.
dapper *adj* concinnus, nitidus.
dapple *vt* variāre, distinguere.
dappled *adj* maculōsus, distinctus.
dare *vt* audēre; (*challenge*) prōvocāre; **I ~ say** haud sciō an.
daring *n* audācia *f* ♦ *adj* audāx.
daringly *adv* audācter.
dark *adj* obscūrus, opācus; (*colour*) fuscus, āter; (*fig*) obscūrus; **it is getting ~** advesperāscit; **keep ~** silēre ♦ *n* tenebrae *fpl*; (*mist*) cālīgō *f*; **keep in the ~** cēlāre.
darken *vt* obscūrāre, occaecāre.
darkish *adj* subobscūrus.
darkling *adj* obscūrus.
darkness *n* tenebrae *fpl*; (*mist*) cālīgō *f*.
darksome *adj* obscūrus.
darling *adj* cārus, dīlēctus ♦ *n* dēliciae *fpl*, voluptās *f*.
darn *vt* resarcīre.
darnel *n* lolium *nt*.
dart *n* tēlum *nt*; iaculum *nt* ♦ *vi* ēmicāre, sē conicere ♦ *vt* iaculārī, iacere.
dash *vt* adflīgere; (*hope*) frangere; **~ against** illīdere, incutere; **~ down** dēturbāre; **~ out** ēlīdere; **~ to pieces** discutere; **~ to the ground** prōsternere ♦ *vi* currere, sē incitāre, ruere ♦ *n* impetus *m*; (*quality*) ferōcia *f*.
dashing *adj* ferōx, animōsus.
dastardly *adj* ignāvus.
date *n* (*fruit*) palmula *f*; (*time*) tempus *nt*, diēs *m*; **out of ~** obsolētus; **become out of ~** exolēscere; **to ~** adhūc; **be up to ~** praesentī mōre ūtī ♦ *vt* (*letter*) diem adscrībere; (*past event*) repetere ♦ *vi* initium capere.
dative *n* datīvus *m*.
daub *vt* inlinere.
daughter *n* fīlia *f*; (*little*) fīliola *f*.
daughter-in-law *n* nurus *f*.
daunt *vt* terrēre, perterrēre.
dauntless *adj* impavidus, intrepidus.
dauntlessly *adv* impavidē, intrepidē.
dawdle *vi* cessāre, cunctārī.
dawdler *n* cunctātor *m*.
dawn *n* aurōra *f*, dīlūculum *nt*; (*fig*) orīgō *f*; **prima lux** *f*; **at ~** prīmā lūce ♦ *vi* dīlūcēscere; **day ~s** diēs illūcēscit; **it ~s upon me** mente concipiō.
day *n* diēs *m/f*; (*period*) aetās *f*; **~ about** alternīs diēbus; **~ by ~** in diēs; cotīdiē; **by ~** *adj* diūrnus ♦ *adv* interdiū; **during the ~** interdiū; **every ~** cotīdiē; **from ~ to ~** in diēs, diem dē diē; **late in the ~** multō diē; **next ~** postrīdiē; **one ~/some ~** ōlim; **the ~ after** *adv* postrīdiē ♦ *conj* postrīdiē quam; **the ~ after tomorrow** perendiē; **the ~ before** *adv* prīdiē ♦ *conj* prīdiē quam; **the ~ before yesterday** nūdius tertius; **the present ~** haec aetās; **time of ~** hōra; **twice a ~** bis (in) diē; **~s of old** praeteritum tempus; **~s to come** posteritās; **better ~s** rēs prosperae; **evil ~s** rēs adversae; **three ~s** trīduum *nt*; **two ~s** biduum *nt*; **win**

the ~ vincere.
daybook n adversāria *ntpl*.
daybreak n aurōra *f*, prīma lūx *f*.
daylight n diēs *m*; **(become) ~** illūcēscere.
daystar n lūcifer *m*.
daytime n diēs *m*; **in the ~** interdiū.
daze *vt* obstupefacere ♦ n stupor *m*.
dazzle *vt* praestringere.
dazzling *adj* splendidus, nitēns.
deacon n diāconus *m*.
deaconess n diāconissa *f*.
dead *adj* mortuus; (*in battle*) occīsus; (*LIT*)
  frīgidus; (*place*) iners, sōlitarius; (*senses*)
  hebes; **~ of night** nox intempesta *f*; **be ~ to**
  nōn sentīre; **in ~ earnest** sēriō ac vērō; **rise**
  from the ~ revīvīscere ♦ *adv* prōrsus,
  omnīnō.
dead beat *adj* cōnfectus.
dead body n cadāver *m*.
dead calm n malacia *f*.
dead certainty n rēs certissima.
deaden *vt* (*senses*) hebetāre, obtundere; (*pain*)
  restinguere.
deadlock n incitae *fpl*; **reach a ~** ad incitās
  redigī.
dead loss n mera iactūra.
deadly *adj* fūnestus, exitiōsus, exitiābilis;
  (*enmity*) implācābilis; (*pain*) acerbissimus.
dead weight n mōlēs *f*.
deaf *adj* surdus; **become ~** obsurdēscere; **be ~**
  to nōn audīre, obdūrēscere contrā.
deafen *vt* (*with noise*) obtundere.
deafness n surditās *f*.
deal n (*amount*) cōpia *f*; **a good ~** aliquantum *nt*,
  bona pars *f*; (*wood*) abiēs *f* ♦ *adj* abiēgnus ♦ *vt*
  (*blow*) dare, īnflīgere; (*share*) dīvidere,
  partīrī ♦ *vi* agere, negōtiārī; **~ with** *vt fus*
  (*person*) agere cum (*abl*); (*matter*) tractāre.
dealer n (*wholesale*) negōtiātor *m*, mercātor *m*;
  (*retail*) caupō *m*.
dealings n commercium *nt*, negōtium *nt*, rēs *f*.
dean n decānus *m*.
dear *adj* (*love*) cārus, grātus; (*cost*) cārus,
  pretiōsus; **my ~ Quintus** mī Quīnte;
  (*beginning of letter from Marcus*) Marcus
  Quintō salūtem; **~ me!** (*sorrow*) hei!;
  (*surprise*) ehem!; **buy ~** male emere; **sell ~**
  bene vēndere.
dearly *adv* (*love*) valdē, ārdenter; (*value*)
  magnī.
dearness n cāritās *f*.
dearth n inopia *f*, pēnūria *f*.
death n mors *f*; (*natural*) obitus *m*; (*violent*) nex
  f, interitus *m*; **condemn to ~** capitis damnāre;
  put to ~ interficere; **give the ~ blow to**
  interimere.
deathbed n: **on one's ~** moriēns, moribundus.
deathless *adj* immortālis.
deathly *adj* pallidus.
debar *vt* prohibēre, exclūdere.
debase *vt* dēprāvāre, corrumpere; (*coin*)
  adulterāre; (*self*) prōsternere, dēmittere.
debasement n dēdecus *nt*; (*coin*) adulterium

nt.
debatable *adj* ambiguus, dubius.
debate *vt* disputāre, disceptāre ♦ n
  contrōversia *f*, disceptātiō *f*, altercātiō *f*.
debater n disputātor *m*.
debauch *vt* corrumpere, pellicere ♦ n
  cōmissātiō *f*.
debauched *adj* perditus, prāvus.
debauchee n cōmissātor *m*.
debaucher n corruptor *m*.
debauchery n luxuria *f*, stuprum *nt*.
debilitate *vt* dēbilitāre.
debility n īnfirmitās *f*.
debit n expēnsum *nt* ♦ *vt* in expēnsum referre.
debonair *adj* urbānus, cōmis.
debouch *vi* exīre.
debris n rūdus *nt*.
debt n aes aliēnum *nt*; (*booked*) nōmen *nt*; (*fig*)
  dēbitum *nt*; **be in ~** in aere aliēnō esse; **pay off**
  ~ aes aliēnum persolvere; **run up ~** aes
  aliēnum contrahere; **collect ~s** nōmina
  exigere; **abolition of ~s** novae tabulae *fpl*.
debtor n dēbitor *m*.
decade n decem annī *mpl*.
decadence n occāsus *m*.
decadent *adj* dēgener, dēterior.
decamp *vi* (*MIL*) castra movēre; (*fig*)
  discēdere, aufugere.
decant *vt* dēfundere, diffundere.
decanter n lagoena *f*.
decapitate *vt* dētruncāre.
decay *vi* dīlābī, perīre, putrēscere; (*fig*)
  tābēscere, senēscere ♦ n ruīna *f*, lāpsus *m*;
  (*fig*) occāsus *m*, dēfectiō *f*.
deceased *adj* mortuus.
deceit n fraus *f*, fallācia *f*, dolus *m*.
deceitful *adj* fallāx, fraudulentus, dolōsus.
deceitfully *adv* fallāciter, dolōsē.
deceive *vt* dēcipere, fallere, circumvenīre,
  fraudāre.
deceiver n fraudātor *m*.
December n mēnsis December *m*; **of ~**
  December.
decemvir n decemvir *m*; **of the ~s**
  decemvirālis.
decemvirate n decemvirātus *m*.
decency n honestum *nt*, decōrum *nt*, pudor *m*.
decent *adj* honestus, pudēns.
decently *adv* honestē, pudenter.
deception n fraus *f*, fallācia *f*.
deceptive *adj* fallāx, fraudulentus.
decide *vt*, *vi* (*dispute*) dīiūdicāre, dēcernere,
  dīrimere; **~ to do** statuere, cōnstituere
  (*infin*); **I have ~d** mihī certum est; **~ the issue**
  dēcernere.
decided *adj* certus, firmus.
decidedly *adv* certē, plānē.
deciduous *adj* cadūcus.
decimate *vt* decimum quemque occīdere.
decipher *vt* expedīre, ēnōdāre.
decision n (*of judge*) iūdicium *nt*; (*of council*)
  dēcrētum *nt*; (*of senate*) auctōritās *f*; (*of*
  referee) arbitrium *nt*; (*personal*) sententia *f*;

(_quality_) cōnstantia _f._
decisive _adj_ certus; ~ **moment** discrīmen _nt._
decisively _adv_ sine dubiō.
deck _vt_ ōrnāre, exōrnāre ♦ _n_
(_ship_) pōns _m_; **with a ~** cōnstrātus.
decked _adj_ ōrnātus; (_ship_) cōnstrātus.
declaim _vt, vi_ dēclāmāre, prōnūntiāre.
declamation _n_ dēclāmātiō _f._
declamatory _adj_ dēclāmātōrius.
declaration _n_ adfīrmātiō _f_, adsevērātiō _f_;
(_formal_) prōfessiō _f_; (_of war_) dēnūntiātiō _f._
declare _vt_ affīrmāre, adsevērāre; (_secret_)
aperīre, expōnere; (_proclamation_)
dēnūntiāre, ēdīcere; (_property in census_)
dēdicāre; (_war_) indīcere.
declension _n_ dēclīnātiō _f._
declination _n_ dēclīnātiō _f._
decline _n_ (_slope_) dēclīve _nt_, dēiectus _m_; (_of age_)
senium _nt_; (_of power_) dēfectiō _f_; (_of nation_)
occāsus _m_ ♦ _vi_ inclīnāre, occidere; (_fig_)
ruere, dēlābī, dēgenerāre ♦ _vt_ dētrectāre,
recūsare; (_GRAM_) dēclīnāre.
decode _vt_ expedīre, ēnōdāre.
decompose _vt_ dissolvere ♦ _vi_ putrēscere.
decomposed _adj_ putridus.
decomposition _n_ dissolūtiō _f._
decorate _vt_ ōrnāre, decorāre.
decoration _n_ ōrnāmentum _nt_; (_medal_) īnsigne
_nt._
decorous _adj_ pudēns, modestus, decōrus.
decorously _adv_ pudenter, modestē.
decorum _n_ pudor _m_, honestum _nt._
decoy _n_ illecebra _f_ ♦ _vt_ adlicere, inescāre.
decrease _n_ dēminūtiō _f_, dēcessiō _f_ ♦ _vt_
dēminuere, extenuāre ♦ _vi_ dēcrēscere.
decree _n_ (_of magistrate_) dēcrētum _nt_, ēdictum
_nt_; (_of senate_) cōnsultum _nt_, auctōritās _f_; (_of
people_) scītum _nt_ ♦ _vt_ ēdīcere, dēcernere;
(_people_) scīscere, iubēre; **the senate ~s**
placet senātuī.
decrepit _adj_ īnfirmus, dēbilis, dēcrepitus.
decrepitude _n_ īnfirmitās _f_, dēbilitās _f._
decry _vt_ obtrectāre, reprehendere.
decurion _n_ decuriō _m._
dedicate _vt_ dēdicāre, cōnsecrāre; (_life_)
dēvovēre.
dedication _n_ dēdicātiō _f_; dēvōtiō _f._
dedicatory _adj_ commendātīcius.
deduce _vt_ colligere, conclūdere.
deduct _vt_ dēmere, dētrahere.
deduction _n_ (_inference_) conclūsiō _f_,
cōnsequēns _nt_; (_subtraction_) dēductiō _f_,
dēminūtiō _f._
deed _n_, factum _nt_, facinus _nt_; gestum _nt_; (_legal_)
tabulae _fpl_; **~s** _pl_ rēs gestae _fpl._
deem _vt_ dūcere, cēnsēre, habēre.
deep _adj_ altus, profundus; (_discussion_)
abstrūsus; (_sleep_) artus; (_sound_) gravis;
(_width_) lātus; **three ~** (_MIL_) ternī in
lātitūdinem ♦ _n_ altum _nt._
deepen _vt_ dēfodere, altiōrem reddere; (_fig_)
augēre ♦ _vi_ altiōrem fierī; (_fig_) crēscere.
deepest _adj_ īmus.

deeply _adv_ altē, graviter; (_inside_) penitus; **very**
~ valdē, vehementer.
deep-seated _adj_ (_fig_) inveterātus.
deer _n_ cervus _m_, cerva _f_; (_fallow_) dāma _f._
deface _vt_ dēfōrmāre, foedāre.
defaced _adj_ dēfōrmis.
defacement _n_ dēfōrmitās _f._
defalcation _n_ peculātus _m._
defamation _n_ calumnia _f_, opprobrium _nt._
defamatory _adj_ contumēliōsus, probrōsus.
defame _vt_ īnfāmāre, obtrectāre, calumniārī.
default _vi_ dēesse; (_money_) nōn solvere ♦ _n_
dēfectiō _f_, culpa _f_; **let judgment go by ~**
vadimōnium dēserere, nōn respondēre.
defaulter _n_ reus _m._
defeat _vt_ vincere, superāre; (_completely_)
dēvincere; (_plan_) frustrārī, disicere ♦ _n_
clādēs _f_; (_at election_) repulsa _f_, offēnsiō _f_; (_of
plan_) frustrātiō _f._
defeatism _n_ patientia _f._
defeatist _n_ imbellis _m._
defect _n_ vitium _nt._
defection _n_ dēfectiō _f_, sēditiō _f._
defective _adj_ mancus, vitiōsus.
defence _n_ praesidium _nt_, tūtēla _f_; patrōcinium
_nt_; (_speech_) dēfēnsiō _f_; **speak in ~** dēfendere.
defenceless _adj_ inermis, indēfēnsus; **leave ~**
nūdāre.
defences _npl_ mūnīmenta _ntpl_, mūnītiōnēs _fpl._
defend _vt_ dēfendere, tuērī, custōdīre.
defendant _n_ reus _m._
defender _n_ dēfēnsor _m_, prōpugnātor _m_; (_law_)
patrōnus _m._
defensible _adj_ iūstus.
defensive _adj_ dēfēnsiōnis causā; **be on the ~**
sē dēfendere.
defensively _adv_ dēfendendō.
defer _vt_ differre, prōlātāre ♦ _vi_ mōrem gerere
(_dat_); **I ~ to you in this** hōc tibī tribuō.
deference _n_ obsequium _nt_, observantia _f_;
show ~ to observāre, īnservīre (_dat_).
deferential _adj_ observāns, officiōsus.
deferment _n_ dīlātiō _f_, prōlātiō _f._
defiance _n_ ferōcia _f_, minae _fpl._
defiant _adj_ ferōx, mināx.
defiantly _adv_ ferōciter, mināciter.
deficiency _n_ vitium _nt_; (_lack_) pēnūria _f_, inopia
_f._
deficient _adj_ vitiōsus, inops; **be ~** dēesse,
dēficere.
deficit _n_ lacūna _f._
defile _n_ faucēs _fpl_, angustiae _fpl_ ♦ _vt_ inquināre,
contāmināre.
defilement _n_ sordēs _f_, foeditās _f._
define _vt_ (_limits_) fīnīre, dēfīnīre, termināre;
(_meaning_) explicāre.
definite _adj_ certus, dēfīnītus.
definitely _adv_ dēfīnītē; prōrsus.
definition _n_ dēfīnītiō _f_, explicātiō _f._
definitive _adj_ dēfīnītīvus.
deflate _vt_ laxāre.
deflect _vt_ dēdūcere, dēclīnāre ♦ _vi_ dēflectere,
dēgredī.

deflection n dēclīnātiō f, flexus m.
deform vt dēfōrmāre.
deformed adj dēfōrmis, distortus.
deformity n dēfōrmitās f, prāvitās f.
defraud vt fraudāre, dēfraudāre.
defrauder n fraudātor m.
defray vt solvere, suppeditāre.
deft adj habilis.
deftly adv habiliter.
defunct adj mortuus.
defy vt contemnere, spernere, adversārī (dat); (challenge) prōvocāre, lacessere.
degeneracy n dēprāvātiō f.
degenerate adj dēgener ♦ vi dēgenerāre, dēscīscere.
degradation n īnfāmia f, ignōminia f, nota f.
degrade vt notāre, abicere; (from office) movēre.
degrading adj turpis, indignus.
degree n gradus; (social) locus m; **in some ~** aliquā ex parte; **by ~s** gradātim, sēnsim.
deification n apotheōsis f.
deified adj (emperor) dīvus.
deify vt cōnsecrāre, inter deōs referre.
deign vi dignārī.
deity n deus m.
dejected adj adflīctus, dēmissus.
dejectedly adv animō dēmissō.
dejection n maestitia f.
delay vt dēmorārī, dētinēre, retardāre ♦ vi cunctārī, cessāre ♦ n mora f, cunctātiō f.
delayer n morātor m, cunctātor m.
delectable adj iūcundus, amoenus.
delegate vt lēgāre, mandāre, committere ♦ n lēgātus m.
delegation n lēgātiō f, lēgātī mpl.
delete vt dēlēre.
deleterious adj perniciōsus, noxius.
deletion n (writing) litūra f.
deliberate vi dēlīberāre, cōnsulere ♦ adj (act) cōnsīderātus; (intention) certus; (manner) cōnsīderātus; (speech) lentus.
deliberately adv dē industriā.
deliberation n dēlīberātiō f.
deliberative adj dēlīberātīvus.
delicacy n (judgment) subtīlitās f, ēlegantia f; (manners) mollitia f, luxus m; (health) valētūdō f; (food) cuppēdia ntpl.
delicate adj mollis; (health) īnfirmus; (shape) gracilis; (feelings) hūmānus.
delicately adv molliter; hūmānē.
delicious adj suāvis, lautus.
delight n voluptās f, gaudium nt, dēlectātiō f ♦ vt dēlectāre, oblectāre, iuvāre ♦ vi gaudēre, dēlectārī.
delightful adj iūcundus, dulcis, fēstīvus; (scenery) amoenus.
delightfully adv iūcundē, suāviter.
delimitation n dēfīnītiō f.
delineate vt dēscrībere, dēpingere.
delineation n dēscrīptiō f.
delinquency n culpa f, dēlictum nt, noxa f.
delinquent n nocēns m/f, reus m.

delirious adj dēlīrus, āmēns, furiōsus; **be ~** furere, dēlīrāre.
delirium n furor m, āmentia f.
deliver vt (from) līberāre, exsolvere, ēripere; (blow) intendere; (message) referre; (speech) habēre; **~ to** dēferre, trādere, dare; **~ up** dēdere, trādere; **be ~ed of** parere.
deliverance n līberātiō f.
deliverer n līberātor m.
delivery n (of things due) trāditiō f; (of speech) āctiō f, prōnūntiātiō f; (of child) partus m.
dell n convallis f.
Delphi n Delphī mpl.
delude vt dēcipere, frustrārī, dēlūdere.
deluge n ēluviō f ♦ vt inundāre.
delusion n error m, fraus f.
delusive adj fallāx, inānis.
delve vt fodere.
demagogue n plēbicola m.
demand vt poscere, postulāre, imperāre; (urgently) flāgitāre, poscere; (thing due) exigere; (answer) quaerere; **~ back** repetere ♦ n postulātiō f, postulātum nt.
demarcation n līmes m.
demean vt (self) dēmittere.
demeanour n gestus m, mōs m, habitus m.
demented adj dēmēns, furiōsus.
demerit n culpa f, vitium nt.
demesne n fundus m.
demigod n hērōs m.
demise n obitus m ♦ vt lēgāre.
democracy n cīvitās populāris f.
democrat n homō populāris m/f.
democratic adj populāris.
demolish vt dēmōlīrī, dīruere, dēstruere; (argument) discutere.
demolition n ruīna f, ēversiō f.
demon n daemōn m.
demonstrate vt (show) mōnstrāre, ostendere, indicāre; (prove) dēmōnstrāre.
demonstration n exemplum nt; (proof) dēmōnstrātiō f.
demonstrative adj (manner) vehemēns; (RHET) dēmōnstrātīvus.
demoralization n corruptiō f, dēprāvātiō f.
demoralize vt corrumpere, dēprāvāre, labefactāre.
demote vt locō movēre.
demur vi gravārī, recūsāre ♦ n mora f, dubitātiō f.
demure adj modestus, verēcundus.
demurely adv modestē, verēcundē.
demureness n modestia f, verēcundia f, pudor m.
demurrer n (law) exceptiō f.
den n latibulum nt, latebra f; (of vice) lustrum nt.
denarius n dēnārius m.
denial n īnfitiātiō f, negātiō f.
denigrate vt obtrectāre, calumniārī.
denizen n incola m/f.
denominate vt nōmināre, appellāre.
denomination n nōmen nt; (religious) secta f.

denote *vt* notāre, significāre.
denouement *n* exitus *m*.
denounce *vt* dēferre, incūsāre.
denouncer *n* dēlātor *m*.
dense *adj* dēnsus; (*crowd*) frequēns; (*person*)
  stolidus.
density *n* crassitūdō *f*; (*crowd*) frequentia *f*.
dent *n* nota *f*.
dentate *adj* dentātus.
denture *n* dentēs *mpl*.
denudation *n* spoliātiō *f*.
denude *vt* spoliāre, nūdāre.
denunciation *n* (*report*) indicium *nt*, dēlātiō *f*;
  (*threat*) minae *fpl*.
deny *vt* īnfitiārī, īnfitiās īre, negāre, abnuere;
  (*on oath*) abiūrāre; ~ **oneself** genium
  dēfraudāre.
depart *vi* discēdere (*abl*), abīre, exīre, ēgredī.
department *n* (*district*) regiō *f*, pars *f*; (*duty*)
  prōvincia *f*, mūnus *nt*.
departure *n* discessus *m*, abitus *m*, dīgressus
  m, exitus *m*; (*change*) mūtātiō *f*; (*death*) obitus
  m.
depend *vi* pendēre; (*be dependent*) pendēre ex
  (*abl*), nītī (*abl*); (*rely*) fīdere, cōnfīdere; ~**ing**
  on frētus (*abl*).
dependable *adj* fīdus.
dependant *n* cliēns *m/f*.
dependence *n* clientēla *f*; (*reliance*) fīdūcia *f*.
dependency *n* prōvincia *f*.
dependent *adj* subiectus, obnoxius.
depict *vt* dēscrībere, dēpingere; (*to the life*)
  expingere.
deplete *vt* dēminuere.
depletion *n* dēminūtiō *f*.
deplorable *adj* turpis, nefandus, pessimus.
deplorably *adv* turpiter, pessimē, miserē.
deplore *vt* dēplōrāre, dēfiēre, conquerī.
deploy *vt* explicāre; instruere, dispōnere.
depopulate *vt* vastāre, nūdāre.
depopulation *n* vastātiō *f*, sōlitūdō *f*.
deport *vt* (*banish*) dēportāre; (*self*) gerere.
deportation *n* exsilium *nt*.
deportment *n* gestus *m*, habitus *m*.
depose *vt* dēmovēre, dēpellere; (*evidence*)
  testārī.
deposit *n* fīdūcia *f*, dēpositum *nt* ♦ *vt*
  dēpōnere, mandāre.
depositary *n* sequester *m*.
deposition *n* (*law*) testimōnium *nt*, indicium
  nt.
depository *n* apothēca *f*.
depot *n* (*for arms*) armāmentārium *nt*; (*for
  trade*) emporium *nt*.
deprave *vt* dēprāvāre, corrumpere.
depraved *adj* prāvus.
depravity *n* dēprāvātiō *f*, turpitūdō *f*.
deprecate *vt* abōminārī, dēprecārī.
deprecation *n* dēprecātiō *f*.
depreciate *vt* obtrectāre, dētrectāre.
depreciation *n* obtrectātiō *f*; (*price*) vīlitās *f*.
depredation *n* praedātiō *f*, dīreptiō *f*.
depress *vt* dēprimere; (*mind*) adflīgere,

frangere; **be ~ed** iacēre, animum
  dēspondēre.
depressing *adj* maestus, tristis.
depression *n* (*place*) cavum *nt*; (*mind*) tristitia
  f, sollicitūdō *f*.
deprivation *n* prīvātiō *f*, spoliātiō *f*.
deprive *vt* prīvāre, spoliāre.
depth *n* altitūdō *f*; (*place*) profundum *nt*,
  gurges *m*.
deputation *n* lēgātiō *f*, lēgātī *mpl*.
depute *vt* lēgāre, mandāre.
deputy *n* lēgātus *m*; (*substitute*) vicārius *m*.
derange *vt* conturbāre.
deranged *adj* īnsānus, mente captus.
derangement *n* perturbātiō *f*; (*mind*) īnsānia
  f, dēmentia *f*.
derelict *adj* dēsertus.
dereliction *n* (*of duty*) neglegentia *f*.
deride *vt* dērīdēre, inlūdere.
derision *n* rīsus *m*, irrīsiō *f*.
derisive *adj* mordāx.
derivation *n* orīgō *f*.
derive *vt* dūcere, trahere; (*advantage*) capere,
  parāre; (*pleasure*) dēcerpere, percipere; **be**
  ~d dēfluere.
derogate *vi* dērogāre, dētrahere; ~ **from**
  imminuere, obtrectāre.
derogation *n* imminūtiō *f*, obtrectātiō *f*.
derogatory *adj* indignus; ~ **remarks**
  obtrectātiō *f*.
derrick *n* trochlea *f*.
descant *vt* disserere ♦ *n* cantus *m*.
descend *vi* dēscendere; (*water*) dēlābī; (*from
  heaven*) dēlābī; (*by inheritance*) pervenīre,
  prōdī; (*morally*) dēlābī, sē dēmittere; **be ~ed**
  from orīrī ex (*abl*).
descendant *n* prōgeniēs *f*; ~**s** *pl* minōrēs *mpl*,
  posterī *mpl*.
descent *n* dēscensus *m*; (*slope*) clīvus *m*,
  dēiectus *m*; (*birth*) genus *nt*; (*hostile*) dēcursus
  m, incursiō *f*; **make a ~ upon** inrumpere in
  (*acc*), incursāre in (*acc*).
describe *vt* dēscrībere; (*tell*) nārrāre; (*portray*)
  dēpingere, exprimere.
description *n* dēscrīptiō *f*; (*tale*) nārrātiō *f*;
  (*kind*) genus *nt*.
descry *vt* cernere, cōnspicere, prōspectāre.
desecrate *vt* prōfānāre, exaugurāre.
desecration *n* exaugurātiō *f*, violātiō *f*.
desert *vt* dēserere, dērelinquere, dēstituere ♦
  vi dēscīscere, dēficere ♦ *adj* dēsertus,
  sōlitārius ♦ *n* (*place*) sōlitūdō *f*, loca dēserta
  ntpl; (*merit*) meritum *nt*.
deserted *adj* dēsertus.
deserter *n* dēsertor *m*; (*MIL*) trānsfuga *m*.
desertion *n* dēfectiō *f*, trānsfugium *nt*.
deserve *vt* merērī; dignus esse quī (+ *subj*); ~
  well of bene merērī dē (*abl*).
deserved *adj* meritus.
deservedly *adv* meritō.
deserving *adj* dignus.
desiccate *vt* siccāre.
design *n* (*drawing*) adumbrātiō *f*; (*plan*)

cōnsilium *nt*, prōpositum *nt*; **by ~** cōnsultō ♦ *vt* adumbrāre; **in animō habēre.**
designate *vt* dēsignāre, mōnstrāre; (*as heir*) scrībere; (*as official*) dēsignāre ♦ *adj* dēsignātus.
designation *n* nōmen *nt*, titulus *m*.
designedly *adv* dē industriā, cōnsultō.
designer *n* auctor *m*, inventor *m*.
designing *adj* vafer, dolōsus.
desirable *adj* optābilis, expetendus, grātus.
desire *n* cupīditās *f*; studium *nt*; (*uncontrolled*) libīdō *f*; (*natural*) adpetītiō *f* ♦ *vt* cupere; (*much*) exoptāre, expetere; (*command*) iubēre.
desirous *adj* cupidus, avidus, studiōsus.
desist *vi* dēsistere.
desk *n* scrīnium *nt*.
desolate *adj* dēsertus, sōlitārius; (*place*) vastus ♦ *vt* vastāre.
desolation *n* sōlitūdō *f*, vastitās *f*; (*process*) vastātiō *f*.
despair *vi* dēspērāre dē (*abl*), animum dēspondēre ♦ *n* dēspērātiō *f*.
despairingly *adv* dēspēranter.
despatch *see* dispatch.
desperado *n* homō dēspērātus *m*.
desperate *adj* (*hopeless*) dēspērātus; (*wicked*) perditus; (*dangerous*) perīculōsus.
desperately *adv* dēspēranter.
desperation *n* dēspērātiō *f*.
despicable *adj* dēspectus, abiectus, turpis.
despicably *adv* turpiter.
despise *vt* contemnere, dēspicere, spernere.
despiser *n* contemptor *m*.
despite *n* malevolentia *f*, odium *nt*.
despoil *vt* spoliāre, nūdāre.
despoiler *n* spoliātor *m*, praedātor *m*.
despond *vi* animum dēspondēre, dēspērāre.
despondency *n* dēspērātiō *f*.
despondent *adj* abiectus, adflīctus, dēmissus; **be ~** animum dēspondēre.
despondently *adv* animō dēmissō.
despot *n* dominus *m*, rēx *m*.
despotic *adj* imperiōsus, superbus.
despotically *adv* superbē.
despotism *n* dominātiō *f*, superbia *f*, rēgnum *nt*.
dessert *n* secunda mēnsa *f*.
destination *n* fīnis *m*.
destine *vt* dēstināre, dēsignāre; **~d to be** futūrus.
destiny *n* fātum *nt*; **of ~** fātālis.
destitute *adj* inops, pauper, prīvātus; **~ of** expers (*gen*).
destitution *n* inopia *f*, egestās *f*.
destroy *vt* dēlēre, ēvertere, dīrimere, perdere.
destroyer *n* ēversor *m*.
destructible *adj* fragilis.
destruction *n* exitium *nt*, ēversiō *f*, excidium *nt*.
destructive *adj* exitiābilis, perniciōsus.
destructively *adv* perniciōsē.

desuetude *n* dēsuētūdō *f*.
desultorily *adv* carptim.
desultory *adj* varius, incōnstāns.
detach *vt* abiungere, sēiungere, āmovēre, sēparāre.
detachment *n* (MIL) manus *f*, cohors *f*; (*mind*) integer animus *m*, līber animus.
detail *n*: **~s** *pl* singula *ntpl*; **in ~** singillātim ♦ *vt* exsequī.
detain *vt* dēmorārī, dētinēre, distinēre, morārī.
detect *vt* dēprehendere, patefacere.
detection *n* dēprehēnsiō *f*.
detective *n* inquīsītor *m*.
detention *n* retentiō *f*; (*prison*) vincula *ntpl*.
deter *vt* dēterrēre, absterrēre, impedīre.
deteriorate *vi* dēgenerāre.
deterioration *n* dēprāvātiō *f*, lāpsus *m*.
determinate *adj* certus, fīnītus.
determination *n* obstinātiō *f*, cōnstantia *f*; (*intention*) prōpositum *nt*, sententia *f*.
determine *vt* (*fix*) fīnīre; (*decide*) statuere, cōnstituere.
determined *adj* obstinātus; (*thing*) certus; **I am ~ to** mihī certum est (*infin*).
determinedly *adv* cōnstanter.
deterrent *n*: **act as a ~ to** dēterrēre.
detest *vt* ōdisse, dētestārī.
detestable *adj* dētestābilis, odiōsus.
detestation *n* odium *nt*, invidia *f*.
dethrone *vt* rēgnō dēpellere.
detour *n* circuitus *m*; **make a ~** iter flectere; (MIL) agmen circumdūcere.
detract *vi*: **~ from** dērogāre, dētrahere.
detraction *n* obtrectātiō *f*.
detractor *n* obtrectātor *m*, invidus *m*.
detriment *n* damnum *nt*, dētrīmentum *nt*.
detrimental *adj* damnōsus; **be ~ to** dētrīmentō esse (*dat*).
devastate *vt* vastāre, populārī.
devastation *n* vastātiō *f*, populātiō *f*; (*state*) vastitās *f*.
develop *vt* ēvolvere, explicāre; (*person*) ēducāre, alere ♦ *vi* crēscere; **~ into** ēvādere in (*acc*).
development *n* explicātiō *f*; (*of men*) ēducātiō *f*; (*of resources*) cultus *m*; (*of events*) exitus *m*.
deviate *vi* dēcēdere dē viā, aberrāre, dēclīnāre; (*speech*) dēgredī.
deviation *n* dēclīnātiō *f*; (*from truth*) error *m*; (*in speech*) dīgressus *m*.
device *n* (*plan*) cōnsilium *nt*; (*machine*) māchina *f*; (*emblem*) īnsigne *nt*.
devil *n* diabolus *m*; **go to the ~** abī in malam crucem!; **talk of the ~** lupus in fābulā!
devilish *adj* scelestus, impius.
devil-may-care *adj* praeceps, lascīvus.
devilment *n* malitia *f*.
devilry *n* magicae artēs *fpl*.
devious *adj* dēvius, errābundus.
devise *vt* excōgitāre, commentārī, fingere.
devoid *adj* vacuus, expers; **be ~ of** carēre (*abl*).
devolve *vi* obtingere, obvenīre ♦ *vt* dēferre,

committere.
devote *vt* dēdicāre; (*attention*) dēdere,
trādere; (*life*) dēvovēre.
devoted *adj* dēditus, studiōsus; (*victim*)
dēvōtus, sacer; **be ~ to** studēre (*dat*),
incumbere (*dat*).
devotee *n* cultor *m*.
devotion *n* amor *m*, studium *nt*; rēligiō *f*.
devour *vt* dēvorāre, cōnsūmere; (*fig*) haurīre.
devout *adj* pius, rēligiōsus.
devoutly *adv* piē, rēligiōsē.
dew *n* rōs *m*.
dewy *adj* rōscidus.
dexterity *n* ars *f*, sollertia *f*.
dexterous *adj* sollers, habilis.
dexterously *adv* sollerter, habiliter.
diabolical *adj* scelestus, nefārius.
diadem *n* diadēma *nt*.
diagnose *vt* discernere, diiūdicāre.
diagnosis *n* iūdicium *nt*.
diagonal *adj* oblīquus.
diagram *n* fōrma *f*.
dial *n* sōlārium *nt*.
dialect *n* dialectus *f*, sermō *m*.
dialectic *n* ars disserendī *f*, dialecticē *f* ♦ *adj*
dialecticus.
dialectician *n* dialecticus *m*.
dialogue *n* dialogus *m*, colloquium *nt*.
diameter *n* diametros *f*.
diamond *n* adamās *m*.
diaphanous *adj* perlūcidus.
diaphragm *n* praecordia *ntpl*.
diary *n* ephēmeris *f*.
diatribe *n* convīcium *nt*.
dice *n* tālus *m*, tessera *f*; **game of ~** ālea *f*.
dictate *vt* dictāre ♦ *n* praeceptum *nt*; **~s of**
nature nātūrae iūdicia *ntpl*.
dictation *n* dictāta *ntpl*; (*fig*) arbitrium *nt*.
dictator *n* dictātor *m*; **~'s** dictātōrius.
dictatorial *adj* imperiōsus, superbus.
dictatorship *n* dictātūra *f*.
diction *n* (*enunciation*) ēlocūtiō *f*; (*words*) ōrātiō
f.
dictionary *n* verbōrum thēsaurus *m*.
die *n* signum *nt*; **the ~ is cast** iacta ālea est ♦ *vi*
morī, perīre, obīre; (*in battle*) cadere,
occumbere; **~ off** dēmorī; **~ out** ēmorī; **be**
dying to exoptāre.
diet *n* (*food*) diaeta *f*; (*meeting*) conventus *m*.
differ *vi* differre, discrepāre, dissentīre.
difference *n* discrepantia *f*, dissimilitūdō *f*; (*of*
opinion) dissēnsiō *f*; **there is a ~** interest.
different *adj* dīversus, varius, dissimilis; **~**
from alius ... ac; **in ~ directions** dīversī; **they**
say ~ things alius aliud dīcit.
differentiate *vt* discernere.
differently *adv* dīversē, variē, alius aliter; **~**
from aliter ... ac.
difficult *adj* difficilis, arduus; **very ~**
perdifficilis, perarduus.
difficulty *n* difficultās *f*, labor *m*, negōtium *nt*;
with ~ difficulter, aegrē, vix; **be in ~**
labōrāre.

diffidence *n* diffīdentia *f*; (*shyness*) pudor *m*;
with ~ modestē.
diffident *adj* diffīdēns; (*shy*) modestus,
verēcundus.
diffidently *adv* modestē.
diffuse *vt* diffundere, dispergere; **be ~d**
diffluere ♦ *adj* fūsus, diffūsus, cōpiōsus.
diffusely *adv* diffūsē, cōpiōsē.
diffuseness *n* cōpia *f*.
dig *vt* fodere; dūcere; (*nudge*) fodicāre; **~ up** *vt*
effodere, ēruere.
digest *vt* coquere, concoquere ♦ *n*
summārium *nt*.
digestion *n* concoctiō *f*; **with a bad ~** crūdus.
digger *n* fossor *m*.
dignified *adj* gravis, augustus.
dignify *vt* honōrāre, honestāre.
dignity *n* gravitās *f*, māiestās *f*, amplitūdō *f*.
digress *vi* dēvertere, dīgredī, dēclīnāre.
digression *n* dēclīnātiō *f*, dīgressus *m*.
dike *n* (*ditch*) fossa *f*; (*mound*) agger *m*.
dilapidated *adj* ruīnōsus.
dilapidation *n* ruīna *f*.
dilate *vt* dīlātāre; (*speech*) plūra dīcere.
dilatorily *adv* tardē, cunctanter.
dilatoriness *n* mora *f*, cunctātiō *f*.
dilatory *adj* tardus, lentus, segnis.
dilemma *n* nōdus *m*, angustiae *fpl*; **be in a ~**
haerēre; **be on the horns of a ~** auribus
tenēre lupum.
diligence *n* dīligentia *f*, industria *f*, cūra *f*.
diligent *adj* dīligēns, industrius, sēdulus.
diligently *adv* dīligenter, sēdulō.
dill *n* anēthum *nt*.
dilly-dally *vi* cessāre.
dilute *vt* dīluere, temperāre.
dim *adj* obscūrus; (*fig*) hebes ♦ *vt* obscūrāre;
hebetāre.
dimension *n* modus *m*; **~s** *pl* amplitūdō *f*,
māgnitūdō *f*.
diminish *vt* minuere, imminuere, extenuāre,
īnfringere ♦ *vi* dēcrēscere.
diminution *n* imminūtiō *f*, dēminūtiō *f*.
diminutive *adj* parvulus, exiguus ♦ *n* (*word*)
dēminūtum *nt*.
diminutiveness *n* exiguitās *f*.
dimly *adv* obscūrē.
dimness *n* tenebrae *fpl*, cālīgō *f*.
dimple *n* gelasīnus *m*.
din *n* fragor *m*, strepitus *m*; **make a ~** strepere
♦ *vt* obtundere.
dine *vi* cēnāre.
diner *n* convīva *m*.
dinghy *n* scapha *f*.
dingy *adj* sordidus; (*colour*) fuscus.
dining room *n* cēnātiō *f*.
dinner *n* cēna *f*.
dinner party *n* convīvium *nt*.
dint *n* ictus *m*; **by ~ of** per (*acc*).
dip *vt* imbuere, mergere ♦ *vi* mergī; **~ into**
(*study*) perstringere.
diploma *n* diplōma *nt*.
diplomacy *n* (*embassy*) lēgātiō *f*; (*tact*)

iūdicium *nt*, sagācitās *f*.
diplomat *n* lēgātus *m*.
diplomatic *adj* sagāx, circumspectus.
diptych *n* tabellae *fpl*.
dire *adj* dīrus, horridus.
direct *vt* regere, dīrigere; (*attention*)
  attendere, admovēre, advertere; (*course*)
  tendere; (*business*) administrāre, moderārī;
  (*letter*) īnscrībere; (*order*) imperāre (*dat*),
  iubēre; (*to a place*) viam mōnstrāre (*dat*);
  (*weapon*) intendere ♦ *adj* rēctus, dīrēctus;
  (*person*) simplex; (*language*) apertus ♦ *adv*
  rēctā.
direction *n* (*of going*) cursus *m*, iter *nt*; (*of
  looking*) pars *f*, regiō *f*; (*control*) administrātiō
  f, regimen *nt*; (*order*) praeceptum *nt*, iussum
  nt; **in the ~ of Rome** Rōmam versus; **in all ~s**
  passim, undique; **in both ~s** utrōque.
directly *adv* (*place*) rēctā; (*time*) prōtinus,
  continuō, statim; (*language*) apertē ♦ *conj*
  simulac.
directness *n* (*fig*) simplicitās *f*.
director *n* dux *m*, gubernātor *m*, moderātor *m*.
dirge *n* nēnia *f*.
dirk *n* pūgiō *m*.
dirt *n* sordēs *f*; (*mud*) lūtum *nt*.
dirty *adj* sordidus, foedus; (*speech*) inquinātus
  ♦ *vt* foedāre, inquināre.
disability *n* vitium *nt*.
disable *vt* dēbilitāre, imminuere.
disabled *adj* mutilus, dēbilis.
disabuse *vt* errōrem dēmere (*dat*).
disaccustom *vt* dēsuēfacere.
disadvantage *n* incommodum *nt*,
  dētrīmentum *nt*; **it is a ~** dētrīmentō est.
disadvantageous *adj* incommodus, inīquus.
disadvantageously *adv* incommodē.
disaffected *adj* aliēnātus, sēditiōsus.
disaffection *n* aliēnātiō *f*, sēditiō *f*.
disagree *vi* discrepāre, dissentīre, dissidēre.
disagreeable *adj* molestus, incommodus,
  iniūcundus.
disagreeably *adv* molestē, incommodē.
disagreement *n* discordia *f*, dissēnsiō *f*,
  discrepantia *f*.
disallow *vt* improbāre, abnuere, vetāre.
disappear *vi* dēperīre, perīre, abīre,
  diffugere, ēvānēscere.
disappearance *n* dēcessiō *f*, fuga *f*.
disappoint *vt* dēcipere, spē dēicere, frustrārī;
  be ~ed in a hope ā spē dēcidere, dē spē dēicī.
disappointment *n* frustrātiō *f*, malum *nt*.
disapprobation *n* reprehēnsiō *f*, improbātiō *f*.
disapproval *n* improbātiō *f*.
disapprove *vt*, *vi* improbāre, reprehendere.
disarm *vt* exarmāre, dearmāre; (*fig*) mītigāre.
disarrange *vt* turbāre, cōnfundere.
disarranged *adj* incompositus.
disarrangement *n* turbātiō *f*.
disarray *n* perturbātiō *f* ♦ *vt* perturbāre.
disaster *n* calamitās *f*, cāsus *m*; (*MIL*) clādēs *f*.
disastrous *adj* īnfēlīx, exitiōsus, calamitōsus.
disavow *vt* diffitērī, īnfitiārī.

disavowal *n* īnfitiātiō *f*.
disband *vt* dīmittere.
disbelief *n* diffīdentia *f*, suspiciō *f*.
disbelieve *vt* diffīdere (*dat*).
disburden *vt* exonerāre.
disburse *vt* ērogāre, expendere.
disbursement *n* impēnsa *f*.
disc *n* orbis *m*.
discard *vt* mittere, pōnere, prōicere.
discern *vt* cōnspicere, dīspicere, cernere; (*fig*)
  intellegere.
discernment *n* iūdicium *nt*, intellegentia *f*,
  sagācitās *f*.
discharge *vt* (*load*) exonerāre; (*debt*)
  exsolvere; (*duty*) fungī (*abl*), exsequī;
  (*officer*) exauctōrāre; (*troops*) missōs facere,
  dīmittere; (*weapon*) iacere, iaculārī;
  (*prisoner*) absolvere; (*from body*) ēdere,
  reddere ♦ *vi* (*river*) effundī, īnfluere ♦ *n*
  (*bodily*) dēfluxiō *f*; (*MIL*) missiō *f*, dīmissiō *f*; (*of
  a duty*) perfūnctiō *f*.
disciple *n* discipulus *m*.
discipline *n* (*MIL*) modestia *f*; (*punishment*)
  castīgātiō *f*; (*study*) disciplīna *f* ♦ *vt* coercēre,
  castīgāre.
disciplined *adj* modestus.
disclaim *vt* renūntiāre, repudiāre, rēicere.
disclaimer *n* repudiātiō *f*.
disclose *vt* aperīre, patefacere, indicāre.
disclosure *n* indicium *nt*.
discoloration *n* dēcolōrātiō *f*.
discolour *vt* dēcolōrāre.
discoloured *adj* dēcolor.
discomfit *vt* vincere, conturbāre,
  dēprehendere.
discomfiture *n* clādēs *f*; (*POL*) repulsa *f*.
discomfort *n* molestia *f*, incommodum *nt*.
disconcert *vt* conturbāre, percellere.
disconcerting *adj* molestus.
disconnect *vt* abiungere, sēiungere.
disconnected *adj* dissolūtus, abruptus.
disconnectedly *adv* dissolūtē.
disconsolate *adj* maestus, dēmissus.
disconsolately *adv* animō dēmissō.
discontent *n* offēnsiō *f*, fastīdium *nt*, taedium
  nt.
discontented *adj* invidus, fastīdiōsus, parum
  contentus.
discontentedly *adv* invītus, inīquō animō.
discontinuance *n* intermissiō *f*.
discontinue *vt* intermittere ♦ *vi* dēsistere,
  dēsinere.
discord *n* discordia *f*; (*music*) dissonum *nt*.
discordance *n* discrepantia *f*, dissēnsiō *f*.
discordant *adj* discors, discrepāns; (*music*)
  dissonus, absonus.
discount *vt* dētrahere; (*fig*) praetermittere ♦
  n dēcessiō *f*; **be at a ~** iacēre.
discountenance *vt* improbāre.
discourage *vt* dēhortārī, dēterrēre; **be ~d**
  animum dēmittere, animō dēficere.
discouragement *n* animī abiectiō *f*; (*cause*)
  incommodum *nt*.

discourse n sermō m; (_lecture_) ōrātiō f ♦ vi conloquī, disserere, disputāre.
discourteous adj inurbānus, asper, inhūmānus.
discourteously adv inhūmānē, rūsticē.
discourtesy n inhūmānitās f, acerbitās f.
discover vt (_find_) invenīre, reperīre; (_detect_) dēprehendere; (_reveal_) aperīre, patefacere; (_learn_) cognōscere.
discoverer n inventor m.
discovery n inventum nt.
discredit vt notāre, fidem imminuere (_gen_) ♦ n invidia f, lābēs f; **be in ~** iacēre.
discreditable adj inhonestus, turpis.
discreditably adv inhonestē, turpiter.
discreet adj prūdēns, sagāx, cautus.
discreetly adv prūdenter, sagāciter, cautē.
discrepancy n discrepantia f, dissēnsiō f.
discretion n prūdentia f; (_tact_) iūdicium nt; (_power_) arbitrium nt, arbitrātus m; **at your ~** arbitrātū tuō; **surrender at ~** in dēditiōnem venīre, sine ullā pactiōne sē tradere; **years of ~** adulta aetās f.
discretionary adj līber.
discriminate vt, vi discernere, internōscere, distinguere.
discriminating adj perspicāx, sagāx.
discrimination n discrīmen nt, iūdicium nt.
discursive adj vagus, loquāx; **be ~** excurrere.
discuss vt agere, disputāre, disceptāre dē (_abl_); **~ terms of peace** dē pāce agere.
discussion n disceptātiō f, disputātiō f.
disdain vt contemnere, aspernārī, fastīdīre ♦ n contemptiō f, fastīdium nt.
disdainful adj fastīdiōsus, superbus.
disdainfully adv fastīdiōsē, superbē.
disease n morbus m; pestilentia f.
diseased adj aeger, aegrōtus.
disembark vi ē nave ēgredī ♦ vt mīlitēs ē nāve expōnere.
disembarkation n ēgressus m.
disembodied adj sine corpore.
disembowel vt exenterāre.
disencumber vt exonerāre.
disengage vt expedīre, līberāre; (_mind_) abstrahere, abdūcere.
disengaged adj vacuus, ōtiōsus.
disentangle vt expedīre, explicāre, exsolvere.
disfavour n invidia f.
disfigure vt dēfōrmāre, foedāre.
disfigured adj dēfōrmis.
disfigurement n dēfōrmātiō f.
disfranchise vt cīvitātem adimere (_dat_).
disfranchised adj capite dēminūtus.
disfranchisement n capitis dēminūtiō f.
disgorge vt ēvomere.
disgrace n dēdecus nt, ignōminia f, īnfāmia f ♦ vt dēdecorāre, dēdecorī esse (_dat_).
disgraceful adj ignōminiōsus, flāgitiōsus, turpis; **~ thing** flāgitium nt.
disgracefully adv turpiter, flāgitiōsē.
disgruntled adj mōrōsus, invidus.

disguise n integumentum nt; (_fig_) speciēs f, simulātiō f; **in ~** mūtātā veste ♦ vt obtegere, involvere; (_fact_) dissimulāre; **~ oneself** vestem mūtāre.
disgust vt displicēre (_dat_), fastīdium movēre (_dat_); **be ~ed** stomachārī; **I am ~ed** mē taedet, mē piget ♦ n fastīdium nt, taedium nt.
disgusting adj taeter, foedus, dēfōrmis.
disgustingly adv foedē.
dish n lanx f; (_course_) ferculum nt.
dishearten vt percellere; **be ~ed** animō dēficere, animum dēmittere.
dishevelled adj solūtus, passus.
dishonest adj perfidus, inīquus, improbus.
dishonestly adv improbē, dolō malō.
dishonesty n mala fidēs f, perfidia f, fraus f.
dishonour n dēdecus nt, ignōminia f, turpitūdō f ♦ vt dēdecorāre.
dishonourable adj ignōminiōsus, indecōrus, turpis.
dishonourably adv turpiter, inhonestē.
disillusion vt errōrem adimere (_dat_).
disinclination n odium nt.
disinclined adj invītus, āversus.
disinfect vt pūrgāre.
disingenuous adj dolōsus, fallāx.
disingenuously adv dolōsē.
disinherit vt abdicāre, exhērēdāre.
disinherited adj exhērēs.
disintegrate vt dissolvere ♦ vi dīlābī, dissolvī.
disinter vt effodere, ēruere.
disinterested adj grātuītus, favōris expers.
disinterestedly adv sine favōre.
disinterestedness n innocentia f, integritās f.
disjoin vt sēiungere.
disjointed adj parum cohaerēns.
disk n orbis m.
dislike n odium nt, offēnsiō f, invidia f ♦ vt ōdisse; **I ~** mihī displicet, mē piget (_gen_).
dislocate vt extorquēre.
dislocated adj luxus.
dislodge vt dēmovēre, dēicere, dēpellere, dētrūdere.
disloyal adj īnfīdus, īnfidēlis; (_to gods, kin, country_) impius.
disloyally adv īnfidēliter.
disloyalty n perfidia f, īnfidēlitās f; impietās f.
dismal adj fūnestus, maestus.
dismally adv miserē.
dismantle vt nūdāre; (_building_) dīruere.
dismay n pavor m, formīdō f ♦ vt terrēre, perturbāre.
dismember vt discerpere.
dismiss vt dīmittere; (_troops_) missōs facere; (_from service_) exauctōrāre; (_fear_) mittere, pōnere.
dismissal n missiō f, dīmissiō f.
dismount vi dēgredī, (ex equō) dēscendere.
disobedience n contumācia f.
disobedient adj contumāx.
disobediently adv contrā iūssa.
disobey vt nōn pārēre (_dat_), aspernārī.

disoblige vt displicēre (dat), offendere.
disobliging adj inofficiōsus, difficilis.
disobligingly adv contrā officium.
disorder n turba f, cōnfūsiō f; (MED) morbus m;
(POL) mōtus m, tumultus m ♦ vt turbāre,
miscēre, sollicitāre.
disorderly adj immodestus, inōrdinātus,
incompositus; (POL) turbulentus, sēditiōsus;
in a ~ manner nullō ōrdine, temerē.
disorganize vt dissolvere, perturbāre.
disown vt (statement) īnfitiārī; (thing) abnuere,
repudiāre; (heir) abdicāre.
disparage vt obtrectāre, dētrectāre.
disparagement n obtrectātiō f, probrum nt.
disparager n obtrectātor m, dētrectātor m.
disparate adj dispār.
disparity n discrepantia f, dissimilitūdō f.
dispassionate adj studiī expers.
dispassionately adv sine īrā et studiō.
dispatch vt mittere, dīmittere; (finish)
absolvere, perficere; (kill) interficere ♦ n
(letter) litterae fpl; (speed) celeritās f.
dispel vt dispellere, discutere.
dispensation n (distribution) partītiō f;
(exemption) venia f; (of heaven) sors f; **by
divine ~** dīvīnitus.
dispense vt dispertīrī, dīvidere ♦ vi: **~ with**
ōmittere, praetermittere, repudiāre.
dispersal n dīmissiō f, diffugium nt.
disperse vt dispergere, dissipāre, dīsicere ♦
vi diffugere, dīlābī.
dispirited adj dēmissō animō; **be ~** animō
dēficere, animum dēmittere.
displace vt locō movēre.
display n ostentātiō f, iactātiō f; **for ~** per
speciem ♦ vt exhibēre, ostendere, praestāre,
sē ferre.
displease vt displicēre (dat), offendere; **be ~d**
aegrē ferre, stomachārī, indignārī.
displeasing adj ingrātus, odiōsus.
displeasure n invidia f, offēnsiō f, odium nt.
disport vt: **~ oneself** lūdere.
disposal n (sale) vēnditiō f; (power) arbitrium
nt.
dispose vt (troops) dispōnere; (mind)
inclīnāre, addūcere ♦ vi: **~ of** abaliēnāre,
vēndere; (get rid) tollere; (argument)
refellere.
disposed adj adfectus, inclīnātus, prōnus;
well ~ benevolus, bonō animō.
disposition n animus m, adfectiō f, ingenium
nt, nātūra f; (of troops) dispositiō f.
dispossess vt dētrūdere, spoliāre.
disproportion n inconcinnitās f.
disproportionate adj impār, inconcinnus.
disproportionately adv inaequāliter.
disprove vt refūtāre, redarguere, refellere.
disputable adj dubius, ambiguus.
disputation n disputātiō f.
dispute n altercātiō f, contrōversia f; (violent)
iūrgium nt; **beyond ~** certissimus ♦ vi
altercārī, certāre, rixārī ♦ vt negāre, in

dubium vocāre.
disqualification n impedīmentum nt.
disqualify vt impedīre.
disquiet n sollicitūdō f ♦ vt sollicitāre.
disquisition n disputātiō f.
disregard n neglegentia f, contemptiō f ♦ vt
neglegere, contemnere, ōmittere.
disrepair n vitium nt; **in ~** male sartus.
disreputable adj inhonestus, īnfāmis.
disrepute n īnfāmia f.
disrespect n neglegentia f, contumācia f.
disrespectful adj contumāx, īnsolēns.
disrespectfully adv īnsolenter.
disrobe vt nūdāre, vestem exuere (dat) ♦ vi
vestem exuere.
disrupt vt dīrumpere, dīvellere.
disruption n discidium nt.
dissatisfaction n molestia f, aegritūdō f, dolor
m.
dissatisfied adj parum contentus; **I am ~ with**
... mē taedet (gen)....
dissect vt incīdere; (fig) investīgāre.
dissemble vt, vi dissimulāre; mentīrī.
dissembler n simulātor m.
disseminate vt dīvulgāre, dissēmināre.
dissension n discordia f, dissēnsiō f; (violent)
iūrgium nt.
dissent vi dissentīre, dissidēre ♦ n dissēnsiō f.
dissertation n disputātiō f.
disservice n iniūria f, incommodum nt.
dissimilar adj dispār, dissimilis.
dissimilarity n discrepantia f, dissimilitūdō f.
dissident adj discors.
dissimulation n dissimulātiō f.
dissipate vt dissipāre, diffundere,
disperdere.
dissipated adj dissolūtus, lascīvus,
luxuriōsus.
dissipation n dissipātiō f; (vice) luxuria f,
licentia f.
dissociate vt dissociāre, sēiungere.
dissociation n sēparātiō f, discidium nt.
dissoluble adj dissolūbilis.
dissolute adj dissolūtus, perditus, libīdinōsus.
dissolutely adv libīdinōsē, luxuriōsē.
dissoluteness n luxuria f.
dissolution n dissolūtiō f, discidium nt.
dissolve vt dissolvere; (ice) liquefacere;
(meeting) dīmittere; (contract) dīrimere ♦ vi
liquēscere; (fig) solvī.
dissonance n dissonum nt.
dissonant adj dissonus.
dissuade vt dissuādēre (dat), dēhortārī.
dissuasion n dissuāsiō f.
distaff n colus f.
distance n intervallum nt, spatium nt; (long
way) longinquitās f; **at a ~** (far) longē; (within
sight) procul; (fight) ēminus; **at a ~ of** ...
spatiō (gen) ...; **within striking ~** intrā iactum
tēlī.
distant adj longinquus; (measure) distāns;
(person) parum familiāris; **be ~** abesse (abl).

distaste *n* fastīdium *nt*.
distasteful *adj* molestus, iniūcundus.
distemper *n* morbus *m*.
distend *vt* distendere.
distil *vt, vi* stillāre.
distinct *adj* (*different*) dīversus; (*separate*) distinctus; (*clear*) clārus, argūtus; (*marked*) distinctus; (*sure*) certus; (*well-drawn*) expressus.
distinction *n* discrīmen *nt*; (*dissimilarity*) discrepantia *f*; (*public status*) amplitūdō *f*; (*honour*) honōs *m*, decus *nt*; (*mark*) īnsigne *nt*; **there is a ~** interest; **without ~** prōmiscuē.
distinctive *adj* proprius, īnsignītus.
distinctively *adv* propriē, īnsignītē.
distinctly *adv* clārē, distinctē, certē, expressē.
distinguish *vt* distinguere, internōscere, dīiūdicāre, discernere; (*honour*) decorāre, ōrnāre; **~ oneself** ēminēre.
distinguished *adj* īnsignis, praeclārus, ēgregius, amplissimus.
distort *vt* dētorquēre; (*fig*) dēprāvāre.
distorted *adj* distortus.
distortion *n* distortiō *f*; dēprāvātiō *f*.
distract *vt* distrahere, distinēre, āvocāre; (*mind*) aliēnāre.
distracted *adj* āmēns, īnsānus.
distraction *n* (*state*) indīligentia *f*; (*cause*) invītāmentum *nt*; (*madness*) furor *m*, dēmentia *f*; **to ~** efflīctim.
distraught *adj* āmēns, dēmēns.
distress *n* labor *m*, dolor *m*, aegrimōnia *f*, aerumna *f*; **be in ~** labōrāre ♦ *vt* adflīgere, sollicitāre.
distressed *adj* adflīctus, sollicitus; **be ~ at** rem aegrē ferre.
distressing *adj* tristis, miser, acerbus.
distribute *vt* distribuere, dīvidere, dispertīre.
distribution *n* partītiō *f*, distribūtiō *f*.
district *n* regiō *f*, pars *f*.
distrust *n* diffīdentia *f* ♦ *vt* diffīdere (*dat*), nōn crēdere (*dat*).
distrustful *adj* diffīdēns.
distrustfully *adv* diffīdenter.
disturb *vt* perturbāre, conturbāre; commovēre; (*mind*) sollicitāre.
disturbance *n* turba *f*, perturbātiō *f*; (*POL*) mōtus *m*, tumultus *m*.
disturber *n* turbātor *m*.
disunion *n* discordia *f*, discidium *nt*.
disunite *vt* dissociāre, sēiungere.
disuse *n* dēsuētūdō *f*; **fall into ~** obsolēscere.
disused *adj* dēsuētus, obsolētus.
disyllabic *adj* disyllabus.
ditch *n* fossa *f*, scrobis *m*.
dithyrambic *adj* dithyrambicus.
dittany *n* dictamnum *nt*.
ditty *n* carmen *nt*, cantilēna *f*.
diurnal *adj* diūrnus.
divan *n* lectus *m*, lectulus *m*.
dive *vi* dēmergī.
diver *n* ūrīnātor *m*.

diverge *vi* dēvertere, dīgredī; (*road*) sē scindere; (*opinions*) discrepāre.
divergence *n* dīgressiō *f*; discrepantia *f*.
divers *adj* complūrēs.
diverse *adj* varius, dīversus.
diversify *vt* variāre.
diversion *n* (*of water*) dērīvātiō *f*; (*of thought*) āvocātiō *f*; (*to amuse*) oblectāmentum *nt*; **create a ~** (*MIL*) hostēs dīstringere; **for a ~** animī causā.
diversity *n* varietās *f*, discrepantia *f*.
divert *vt* dēflectere, āvertere; (*attention*) āvocāre, abstrahere; (*water*) dērīvāre; (*to amuse*) oblectāre, placēre (*dat*).
diverting *adj* iūcundus; (*remark*) facētus.
divest *vt* exuere, nūdāre; **~ oneself of** (*fig*) pōnere, mittere.
divide *vt* dīvidere; (*troops*) dīdūcere; **~ among** partīrī, distribuere; **~ from** sēparāre ab, sēiungere ab; **~ out** dispertīrī, dīvidere ♦ *vi* discēdere, sē scindere; (*senate*) in sententiam īre; **be ~d** (*opinions*) discrepāre.
divination *n* dīvīnātiō *f*; (*from birds*) augurium *nt*; (*from entrails*) haruspicium *nt*.
divine *adj* dīvīnus ♦ *vt* dīvīnāre, augurārī, hariolārī; **by ~ intervention** dīvīnitus.
divinely *adv* dīvīnē.
diviner *n* dīvīnus *m*, augur *m*, haruspex *m*.
divinity *n* (*status*) dīvīnitās *f*; (*god*) deus *m*, dea *f*.
divisible *adj* dīviduus.
division *n* (*process*) dīvīsiō *f*, partītiō *f*; (*variance*) discordia *f*, dissēnsiō *f*; (*section*) pars *f*; (*grade*) classis *f*; (*of army*) legiō *f*; (*of time*) discrīmen *nt*; (*in senate*) discessiō *f*.
divorce *n* dīvortium *nt*, repudium *nt* ♦ *vt* (*wife*) nūntium mittere (*dat*); (*things*) dīvellere, sēparāre.
divulge *vt* aperīre, patefacere, ēvulgāre, ēdere.
dizziness *n* vertīgō *f*.
dizzy *adj* vertīginōsus; (*fig*) attonitus.
do *vt* facere, agere; (*duty*) fungī (*abl*); (*wrong*) admittere; **~ away with** *vt fus* tollere; (*kill*) interimere; **~ one's best to** id agere ut (*subj*); **~ without** repudiāre; **~ not ...** nolī/nolīte (+ *infin*); **how ~ you ~?** quid agis?; **I have nothing to ~ with you** mihī tēcum nihil est commercī; **it has nothing to ~ with me** nihil est ad mē; **that will ~** iam satis est; **be done** fierī; **have done with** dēfungī (*abl*).
docile *adj* docilis.
docility *n* docilitās *f*.
dock *n* (*ships*) nāvāle *nt*; (*law*) cancellī *mpl* ♦ *vt* praecīdere.
dockyard *n* nāvālia *ntpl*.
doctor *n* medicus *m*; (*UNIV*) doctor *m* ♦ *vt* cūrāre.
doctrine *n* dogma *nt*, dēcrētum *nt*; (*system*) ratiō *f*.
document *n* litterae *fpl*, tabula *f*.
dodge *vt* dēclīnāre, ēvādere ♦ *n* dolus *m*.
doe *n* cerva *f*.

doer n āctor m, auctor m.
doff vt exuere.
dog n canis m/f; **~ star** Canīcula f; **~'s** canīnus ♦ vt īnsequī, īnstāre (dat).
dogged adj pertināx.
doggedly adv pertināciter.
dogma n dogma nt, praeceptum nt.
dogmatic adj adrogāns.
dogmatically adv adroganter.
doing n factum nt.
dole n sportula f ♦ vt: **~ out** dispertīrī, dīvidere.
doleful adj lūgubris, flēbilis, maestus.
dolefully adv flēbiliter.
dolefulness n maestitia f, miseria f.
doll n pūpa f.
dolorous adj lūgubris, maestus.
dolour n maestitia f, dolor m.
dolphin n delphīnus m.
dolt n stīpes m, caudex m.
domain n ager m; (king's) rēgnum nt.
dome n tholus m, testūdō f.
domestic adj domesticus, familiāris; (animal) mānsuētus ♦ n famulus m, servus m, famula f, ancilla f; **~s** pl familia f.
domesticate vt mānsuēfacere.
domesticated adj mānsuētus.
domesticity n larēs suī mpl.
domicile n domicilium nt, domus f.
dominant adj superior, praepotēns.
dominate vt dominārī in (acc), imperāre (dat); (view) dēspectāre.
domination n dominātiō f, dominātus m.
domineer vi dominārī, rēgnāre.
dominion n imperium nt, rēgnum nt.
don vt induere ♦ n scholasticus m.
donate vt dōnāre.
donation n dōnum nt.
donkey n asellus m.
donor n dōnātor m.
doom n fātum nt ♦ vt damnāre.
door n (front) iānua f; (back) postīcum nt; (double) forēs fpl; **folding ~s** valvae fpl; **out of ~s** forīs; (to) forās; **next ~ to** iuxtā (acc).
doorkeeper n iānitor m.
doorpost n postis m.
doorway n ōstium nt.
dormant adj sōpītus; **lie ~** iacēre.
dormitory n cubiculum nt.
dormouse n glīs m.
dose n pōculum nt.
dot n pūnctum nt.
dotage n senium nt.
dotard n senex dēlīrus m.
dote vi dēsipere; **~ upon** dēamāre.
doting adj dēsipiēns, peramāns.
dotingly adv perditē.
double adj duplex; (amount) duplus; (meaning) ambiguus ♦ n duplum nt ♦ vt duplicāre; (promontory) superāre; (fold) complicāre ♦ vi duplicārī; (MIL) currere.
double-dealer n fraudātor m.
double-dealing adj fallāx, dolōsus ♦ n fraus f, dolus m.

doublet n tunica f.
doubly adv bis, dupliciter.
doubt n dubium nt; (hesitancy) dubitātiō f; (distrust) suspiciō f; **give one the benefit of the ~** innocentem habēre; **no ~** sānē; **I do not ~ that** ... non dubito quīn ... (+ subj); **there is no ~ that** nōn dubium est quīn (subj) ♦ vt dubitāre; (distrust) diffīdere (dat), suspicārī.
doubtful adj dubius, incertus; (result) anceps; (word) ambiguus.
doubtfully adv dubiē; (hesitation) dubitanter.
doubtless adv scīlicet, nīmīrum.
doughty adj fortis, strēnuus.
dove n columba f.
dovecote n columbārium nt.
dowdy adj inconcinnus.
dower n dōs f ♦ vt dōtāre.
dowerless adj indōtātus.
down n plūmae fpl, lānūgō f; (thistle) pappus m.
down adv deōrsum; **be ~** iacēre; **~ with!** perea(n)t; **up and ~** sūrsum deōrsum ♦ prep dē (abl); **~ from** dē (abl).
downcast adj dēmissus, maestus.
downfall n ruīna f; (fig) occāsus m.
downhearted adj dēmissus, frāctus animī.
downhill adj dēclīvis; (fig) prōclīvis ♦ adv in praeceps.
downpour n imber m.
downright adj dīrēctus; (intensive) merus.
downstream adv secundō flūmine.
downtrodden adj subiectus, oppressus.
downward adj dēclīvis, prōclīvis.
downwards adv deōrsum.
downy adj plūmeus.
dowry n dōs f.
doyen n pater m.
doze vi dormītāre.
dozen n duodecim.
drab adj sordidior.
drachma n drachma f.
draft n (writing) exemplum nt; (MIL) dīlēctus m; (money) syngrapha f; (literary) silva f ♦ vt scrībere; (MIL) mittere.
drag vt trahere ♦ vi (time) trahī; **~ on** vi (war) prōdūcere ♦ n harpagō m; (fig) impedīmentum nt.
dragnet n ēverriculum nt.
dragon n drācō m.
dragoon n eques m.
drain n cloāca f ♦ vt (water) dērīvāre; (land) siccāre; (drink) exhaurīre; (resources) exhaurīre.
drainage n dērīvātiō f.
drake n anas m.
drama n fābula f; **the ~** scaena f.
dramatic adj scaenicus.
dramatist n fābulārum scrīptor m.
dramatize vt ad scaenam compōnere.
drape vt vēlāre.
drapery n vestīmenta ntpl.
drastic adj vehemēns, efficāx.
draught n (air) aura f; (drink) haustus m; (net)

bolus _m_.
draughts _n_ latrunculī _mpl_.
draw _vt_ dūcere, trahere; (_bow_) addūcere;
(_inference_) colligere; (_picture_) scrībere,
pingere; (_sword_) stringere, dēstringere;
(_tooth_) eximere; (_water_) haurīre; **~ aside**
sēdūcere; **~ away** āvocāre; **~ back** _vt_
retrahere ♦ _vi_ recēdere; **~ near**
adpropinquāre; **~ off** dētrahere; (_water_)
dērīvāre; **~ out** _vi_ ēdūcere; (_lengthen_)
prōdūcere; **~ over** obdūcere; **~ taut**
addūcere; **~ together** contrahere; **~ up** _vt_ (_MIL_)
īnstruere; (_document_) scrībere.
drawback _n_ scrūpulus _m_; **this was the only ~**
hōc ūnum dēfuit.
drawing _n_ dēscrīptiō _f_; (_art_) graphicē _f_.
drawing room _n_ sellāria _f_.
drawings _npl_ līneāmenta _ntpl_.
drawl _vi_ lentē dīcere.
drawling _adj_ lentus in dīcendō.
dray _n_ plaustrum _nt_.
dread _n_ formīdō _f_, pavor _m_, horror _m_ ♦ _adj_
dīrus ♦ _vt_ expavēscere, extimēscere,
formīdāre.
dreadful _adj_ terribilis, horribilis,
formīdolōsus, dīrus.
dreadfully _adv_ vehementer, atrōciter.
dream _n_ somnium _nt_ ♦ _vt_, _vi_ somniāre.
dreamy _adj_ somniculōsus.
dreariness _n_ (_place_) vastitās _f_; (_mind_) tristitia
_f_.
dreary _adj_ (_place_) vastus; (_person_) tristis.
dregs _n_ faex _f_; (_of oil_) amurca _f_; **drain to the ~**
exhaurīre.
drench _vt_ perfundere.
dress _n_ vestis _f_, vestītus _m_, vestīmenta _ntpl_;
(_style_) habitus _m_ ♦ _vt_ vestīre; (_wound_) cūrāre;
(_tree_) amputāre ♦ _vi_ induī; **~ up** _vi_ vestum
induere.
dressing _n_ (_MED_) fōmentum _nt_.
drift _n_ (_motion_) mōtus _m_; (_snow_) agger _m_;
(_language_) vīs _f_; **I see the ~ of your speech**
videō quōrsum ōrātiō tua tendat ♦ _vi_ fluitāre;
(_fig_) lābī, ferrī.
drill _n_ terebra _f_; (_MIL_) exercitātiō _f_ ♦ _vt_ (_hole_)
terebrāre; (_MIL_) exercēre; (_pupil_) īnstruere.
drink _vt_, _vi_ bibere, pōtāre; **~ a health**
propīnāre, Graecō mōre bibere; **~ deep of**
exhaurīre; **~ in** haurīre; **~ up** ēpōtāre ♦ _n_
pōtiō _f_.
drinkable _adj_ pōtulentus.
drinker _n_ pōtor _m_.
drinking bout _n_ pōtātiō _f_.
drip _vi_ stillāre, dēstillāre.
drive _vt_ agere; (_force_) cōgere; **~ away** abigere;
(_fig_) pellere, prōpulsāre; **~ back** repellere; **~
home** dēfīgere; **~ in/into** īnfīgere in (_acc_);
(_flock_) cōgere in (_acc_); **~ off** dēpellere; **~ out**
exigere, expellere, exturbāre; **~ through**
trānsfīgere ♦ _vi_ vehī; **~ away** āvehī; **~ back**
revehī; **~ in** invehī; **~ on** _vt_ impellere; **~ round**
circumvehī; **~ past** praetervehī; **what are
you driving at?** quōrsum tua spectat ōrātiō?

♦ _n_ gestātiō _f_.
drivel _vi_ dēlīrāre.
drivelling _adj_ dēlīrus, ineptus ♦ _n_ ineptiae _fpl_.
driver _n_ aurīga _m_; rēctor _m_.
drizzle _vi_ rōrāre.
droll _adj_ facētus, ioculāris.
drollery _n_ facētiae _fpl_.
dromedary _n_ dromas _m_.
drone _n_ (_bee_) fūcus _m_; (_sound_) bombus _m_ ♦ _vi_
fremere.
droop _vi_ dēmittī; (_flower_) languēscere; (_mind_)
animum dēmittere.
drooping _adj_ languidus.
drop _n_ gutta _f_ ♦ _vi_ cadere; (_liquid_) stillāre ♦ _vt_
mittere; (_anchor_) iacere; (_hint_) ēmittere;
(_liquid_) īnstillāre; (_work_) dēsistere ab (_abl_) ♦
_vi_: **~ behind** cessāre; **~ in** _vi_ vīsere,
supervenīre; **~ out** excidere.
dross _n_ scōria _f_; (_fig_) faex _f_.
drought _n_ siccitās _f_.
drouth _n_ sitis _f_.
drove _n_ grex _f_.
drover _n_ bubulcus _m_.
drown _vt_ mergere, obruere; (_noise_) obscūrāre
♦ _vi_ aquā perīre.
drowse _vi_ dormītāre.
drowsily _adv_ somniculōsē.
drowsiness _n_ sopor _m_.
drowsy _adj_ sēmisomnus, somniculōsus.
drub _vt_ pulsāre, verberāre.
drudge _n_ mediastīnus _m_ ♦ _vi_ labōrāre.
drudgery _n_ labor _m_.
drug _n_ medicāmentum _nt_ ♦ _vt_ medicāre.
Druids _n_ Druidae, Druidēs _mpl_.
drum _n_ tympanum _nt_; (_container_) urna _f_.
drummer _n_ tympanista _m_.
drunk _adj_ pōtus, ēbrius, tēmulentus.
drunkard _n_ ēbriōsus _m_.
drunken _adj_ ēbriōsus, tēmulentus.
drunkenness _n_ ēbrietās _f_.
dry _adj_ siccus, āridus; (_thirst_) sitiēns; (_speech_)
āridus, frīgidus; (_joke_) facētus; **be ~** ārēre ♦
_vt_ siccāre ♦ _vi_ ārēscere; **~ up** exārēscere.
dryad _n_ dryas _f_.
dry rot _n_ rōbīgō _f_.
dual _adj_ duplex.
duality _n_ duplex nātūra _f_.
dubiety _n_ dubium _nt_.
dubious _adj_ dubius, incertus; (_meaning_)
ambiguus.
dubiously _adv_ dubiē; ambiguē.
duck _n_ anas _f_ ♦ _vt_ dēmergere ♦ _vi_ dēmergī, sē
dēmittere.
duckling _n_ anaticula _f_.
duct _n_ ductus _m_.
dudgeon _n_ dolor _m_, stomachus _m_.
due _adj_ dēbitus, meritus, iūstus; **be ~** dēbērī; **it
is ~ to me that ... not** per mē stat quōminus
(+ _subj_); **be ~ to** orīrī ex, fierī (_abl_) ♦ _n_ iūs _nt_,
dēbitum _nt_; (_tax_) vectīgal _nt_; (_harbour_)
portōrium _nt_; **give every man his ~** suum
cuīque tribuere ♦ _adv_ rēctā; **~ to** ob (+ _acc_);
propter (+ _acc_).

duel n certāmen nt.
dug n ūber nt.
duke n dux m.
dulcet adj dulcis.
dull adj hebes; (weather) subnūbilus; (language) frīgidus; (mind) tardus; **be ~** hebēre; **become ~** hebēscere ♦ vt hebetāre, obtundere, retundere.
dullard n stolidus m.
dulness n (mind) tarditās f, stultitia f.
duly adv rītē, ut pār est.
dumb adj mūtus; **be struck ~** obmūtēscere.
dun n flāgitātor m ♦ vt flāgitāre ♦ adj fuscus.
dunce n bārō m.
dune n tumulus m.
dung n fimus m.
dungeon n carcer m, rōbur nt.
dupe vt dēlūdere, fallere ♦ n crēdulus m.
duplicate n exemplar nt ♦ vt duplicāre.
duplicity n fraus f, perfidia f.
durability n firmitās f, firmitūdō f.
durable adj firmus, perpetuus.
durably adv firmē.
duration n spatium nt; (long) diūturnitās f.
duresse n vīs f.
during prep inter (acc), per (acc).
dusk n crepusculum nt, vesper m; **at ~** prīmā nocte, prīmīs tenebrīs.
dusky adj fuscus.
dust n pulvis m; **throw ~ in the eyes of** tenebrās offundere (dat) ♦ vt dētergēre.
dusty adj pulverulentus.
dutiful adj pius, officiōsus.
dutifully adv piē, officiōsē.
dutifulness n pietās f.
duty n (moral) officium nt; (task) mūnus nt; (tax) vectīgal nt; **be on ~** (MIL) statiōnem agere, excubāre; **do one's ~** officiō fungī; **do ~ for** (pers) in locum sufficī (gen); (thing) adhibērī prō (abl); **it is my ~** dēbeō, mē oportet, meum est; **it is the ~ of a commander** ducis est; **sense of ~** pietās f.
duty call n salūtātiō f.
duty-free adj immūnis.
dwarf n nānus m.
dwell vi habitāre; **~ in** incolere; **~ upon** (theme) commorārī in (abl).
dweller n incola m.
dwelling n domus f, domicilium nt; (place) sēdēs f.
dwindle vi dēcrēscere, extenuārī.
dye n fūcus m, color m ♦ vt īnficere, fūcāre.
dyer n īnfector m.
dying adj moribundus, moriēns.
dynasty n domus (rēgia) f.
dyspepsia n crūditās f.

E, e

each adj & pron quisque; (of two) uterque; **~ other** inter sē; **one ~** singulī; **~ year** quotannīs.
eager adj avidus, cupidus, alācer; **~ for** avidus (+ gen).
eagerly adv avidē, cupidē, ācriter.
eagerness n cupīdō f, ārdor m, studium nt; alacritās f.
eagle n aquila f.
ear n auris f; (of corn) spīca f; **give ~** aurem praebēre, auscultāre; **go in at one ~ and out at the other** surdīs auribus nārrārī; **prick up one's ~s** aurēs ērigere; **with long ~s** aurītus.
earl n comes m.
earlier adv ante; anteā.
early adj (in season) mātūrus; (in day) mātūtīnus; (at beginning) prīmus; (in history) antīquus ♦ adv (in day) māne; (before time) mātūrē, temperī; **~ in life** ab ineunte aetāte.
earn vt merērī, cōnsequī; **~ a living** vīctum quaerere, quaestum facere.
earnest adj (serious) sērius; (eager) ācer, sēdulus ♦ n pignus nt; (money) arrabō m; **in ~** sēdulō, ēnīxē.
earnestly adv sēriō, graviter, sēdulō.
earnestness n gravitās f, studium nt.
earnings n quaestus m.
earring n elenchus m.
earth n (planet) tellūs f; (inhabited) orbis terrārum m; (land) terra f; (soil) solum nt; humus f; (fox's) latibulum nt; **where on ~?** ubī gentium?; **of the ~** terrestris.
earthen adj (ware) fictilis; (mound) terrēnus.
earthenware n fictilia ntpl ♦ adj fictilis.
earthly adj terrestris.
earthquake n terrae mōtus m.
earthwork n agger m.
earthy adj terrēnus.
ease n facilitās f; (leisure) ōtium nt; **at ~** ōtiōsus; (in mind) sēcūrus; **ill at ~** sollicitus ♦ vt laxāre, relevāre; (pain) mītigāre.
easily adv facile; (gladly) libenter; (at leisure) ōtiōsē; **not ~** nōn temerē.
easiness n facilitās f.
east n Oriēns m, sōlis ortus m; **~ wind** eurus m.
Easter n Pascha f.
easterly, eastern adj orientālis.
eastward adv ad orientem.
easy adj facilis; (manner) adfābilis, facilis; (mind) sēcūrus; (speech) expedītus; (discipline) remissus; **~ circumstances** dīvitiae fpl, abundantia f.
eat vt edere; cōnsūmere; vescī (abl); **~ away** rōdere; **~ up** exedere.
eatable adj esculentus.
eating n cibus m.

eaves *n* suggrunda *f.*
eavesdropper *n* sermōnis auceps *m.*
ebb *n* dēcessus *m,* recessus *m;* **at ~tide**
minuente aestū; **be at a low ~** (*fig*) iacēre ♦ *vi*
recēdere.
ebony *n* ebenus *f.*
ebullient *adj* fervēns.
ebullition *n* fervor *m.*
eccentric *adj* īnsolēns.
eccentricity *n* īnsolentia *f.*
echo *n* imāgō *f* ♦ *vt, vi* resonāre.
eclipse *n* dēfectus *m,* dēfectiō *f* ♦ *vt* obscūrāre;
be ~d dēficere, labōrāre.
eclogue *n* ecloga *f.*
economic *adj* quaestuōsus, sine iactūrā.
economical *adj* (*person*) frūgī, parcus.
economically *adv* nullā iactūrā factā.
economics *n* reī familiāris dispēnsātiō *f.*
economize *vi* parcere.
economy *n* frūgālitās *f.*
ecstasy *n* alacritās *f,* furor *m.*
ecstatic *adj* gaudiō ēlātus.
eddy *n* vertex *m* ♦ *vi* volūtārī.
edge *n* ōra *f,* margō *f;* (*of dish*) labrum *nt;* (*of
blade*) aciēs *f;* **take the ~ off** obtundere; **on ~**
(*fig*) suspēnsō animō ♦ *vt* (*garment*)
praetexere; (*blade*) acuere ♦ *vi:* **~ in sē**
īnsinuāre.
edging *n* limbus *m.*
edible *adj* esculentus.
edict *n* ēdictum *nt,* dēcrētum *nt.*
edification *n* ērudītiō *f.*
edifice *n* aedificium *nt.*
edify *vt* ērudīre.
edit *vt* recognōscere, recēnsēre.
edition *n* ēditiō *f.*
educate *vt* ērudīre, īnfōrmāre; **~ in** īnstituere
ad (*acc*).
education *n* doctrīna *f,* (*process*) īnstitūtiō *f.*
eel *n* anguilla *f.*
eerie *adj* mōnstruōsus.
efface *vt* dēlēre, tollere.
effect *n* (*result*) ēventus *m;* (*impression*) vīs *f,*
effectus *m;* (*show*) iactātiō *f;* **~s** *pl* bona *ntpl;*
for ~ iactātiōnis causā; **in ~** rē vērā; **to this ~**
in hanc sententiam; **without ~** inritus ♦ *vt*
efficere, facere, patrāre.
effective *adj* valēns, validus; (*RHET*) gravis,
ōrnātus.
effectively *adv* validē, graviter, ōrnātē.
effectiveness *n* vīs *f.*
effectual *adj* efficāx, idōneus.
effectually *adv* efficāciter.
effectuate *vt* efficere, cōnsequī.
effeminacy *n* mollitiēs *f.*
effeminate *adj* mollis, effēminātus.
effeminately *adv* molliter, effēminātē.
effervesce *vi* effervēscere.
effete *adj* effētus.
efficacious *adj* efficāx.
efficaciously *adv* efficāciter.
efficacy *n* vīs *f.*
efficiency *n* virtūs *f,* perītia *f.*

efficient *adj* capāx, perītus; (*logic*) efficiēns.
efficiently *adv* perītē, bene.
effigy *n* simulācrum *nt,* effigiēs *f.*
effloresce *vi* flōrēscere.
efflorescence *n* (*fig*) flōs *m.*
effluvium *n* hālitus *m.*
effort *n* opera *f,* cōnātus *m;* (*of mind*) intentiō *f;*
make an ~ ēnītī.
effrontery *n* audācia *f,* impudentia *f.*
effusive *adj* officiōsus.
egg *n* ōvum *nt;* **lay an ~** ōvum parere ♦ *vt*
impellere, īnstīgāre.
egoism *n* amor suī *m.*
egoist *n* suī amāns *m.*
egotism *n* iactātiō *f.*
egotist *n* glōriōsus *m.*
egregious *adj* singulāris.
egress *n* exitus *m.*
eight *num* octō; **~ each** octōnī; **~ times** octiēns.
eighteen *num* duodēvīgintī.
eighteenth *adj* duodēvīcēsimus.
eighth *adj* octāvus.
eight hundred *num* octingentī.
eight hundredth *adj* octingentēsimus.
eightieth *adj* octōgēsimus.
eighty *num* octōgintā; **~ each** octōgēnī; **~ times**
octōgiēns.
either *pron* alteruter, uterlibet, utervīs ♦ *conj*
aut, vel; **~ . . . or** aut . . . aut; vel . . . vel.
ejaculation *n* clāmor *m.*
eject *vt* ēicere, expellere.
ejection *n* expulsiō *f.*
eke *vt:* **eke out** parcendō prōdūcere.
elaborate *vt* ēlabōrāre ♦ *adj* ēlabōrātus,
exquīsītus.
elaborately *adv* summō labōre, exquīsītē.
elan *n* ferōcia *f.*
elapse *vi* abīre, intercēdere; **allow to ~**
intermittere; **a year has ~d since** annus est
cum (*indic*).
elated *adj* ēlātus; **be ~** efferrī.
elation *n* laetitia *f.*
elbow *n* cubitum *nt.*
elder *adj* nātū māior, senior ♦ *n* (*tree*)
sambūcus *f.*
elderly *adj* aetāte prōvectus.
elders *npl* patrēs *mpl.*
eldest *adj* nātū māximus.
elecampane *n* inula *f.*
elect *vt* ēligere, dēligere; (*magistrate*) creāre;
(*colleague*) cooptāre ♦ *adj* dēsignātus;
(*special*) lēctus.
election *n* (*POL*) comitia *ntpl.*
electioneering *n* ambitiō *f.*
elector *n* suffrāgātor *m.*
elegance *n* ēlegantia *f,* lepōs *m,* munditia *f,*
concinnitās *f.*
elegant *adj* ēlegāns, concinnus, nitidus.
elegantly *adv* ēleganter, concinnē.
elegiac *adj:* **~ verse** elegī *mpl,* versūs alternī
mpl.
elegy *n* elegīa *f.*
element *n* elementum *nt;* **~s** *pl* initia *ntpl,*

prīncipia *ntpl*; **out of one's ~** peregrīnus.
elementary *adj* prīmus.
elephant *n* elephantus *m*, elephas *m*.
elevate *vt* efferre, ērigere.
elevated *adj* ēditus, altus.
elevation *n* altitūdō *f*; (*style*) ēlātiō *f*.
eleven *num* ūndecim; **~ each** ūndēnī; **~ times**
  ūndeciēns.
eleventh *adj* ūndecimus.
elf *n* deus *m*.
elicit *vt* ēlicere; (*with effort*) ēruere.
elide *vt* ēlīdere.
eligible *adj* idōneus, aptus.
eliminate *vt* tollere, āmovēre.
elite *n* flōs *m*, rōbur *nt*.
elk *n* alcēs *f*.
ell *n* ulna *f*.
ellipse *n* (*RHET*) dētractiō *f*; (*oval*) ōvum *nt*.
elm *n* ulmus *f* ♦ *adj* ulmeus.
elocution *n* prōnūntiātiō *f*.
elongate *vt* prōdūcere.
elope *vi* aufugere.
eloquence *n* ēloquentia *f*; (*natural*) fācundia *f*,
  dīcendī vīs *f*.
eloquent *adj* ēloquēns; (*natural*) fācundus;
  (*fluent*) disertus.
eloquently *adv* fācundē, disertē.
else *adv* aliōquī, aliter ♦ *adj* alius; **or ~** aliōquī;
  who ~ quis alius.
elsewhere *adv* alibī; **~ to** aliō.
elucidate *vt* ēnōdāre, illūstrāre.
elucidation *n* ēnōdātiō *f*, explicātiō *f*.
elude *vt* ēvītāre, frustrārī, fallere.
elusive *adj* fallāx.
emaciated *adj* macer.
emaciation *n* maciēs *f*.
emanate *vi* mānāre; (*fig*) ēmānāre, orīrī.
emanation *n* exhālātiō *f*.
emancipate *vt* ēmancipāre, manū mittere,
  līberāre.
emancipation *n* lībertās *f*.
emasculate *vt* ēnervāre, dēlumbāre.
embalm *vt* condīre.
embankment *n* agger *m*, mōlēs *f*.
embargo *n* interdictum *nt*.
embark *vi* cōnscendere, nāvem cōnscendere;
  ~ upon (*fig*) ingredī ♦ *vt* impōnere.
embarkation *n* cōnscēnsiō *f*.
embarrass *vt* (*by confusing*) perturbāre; (*by
  obstructing*) impedīre; (*by revealing*)
  dēprehendere; **be ~ed** haerēre.
embarrassing *adj* incommodus,
  intempestīvus.
embarrassment *n* (*in speech*) haesitātiō *f*; (*in
  mind*) sollicitūdō *f*; (*in business*) angustiae *fpl*,
  difficultās *f*; (*cause*) molestia *f*,
  impedīmentum *nt*.
embassy *n* lēgātiō *f*.
embedded *adj* dēfixus.
embellish *vt* adōrnāre, exōrnāre, decorāre.
embellishment *n* decus *nt*, exōrnātiō *f*,
  ōrnāmentum *nt*.
embers *n* cinis *m*, favilla *f*.

embezzle *vt* peculārī, dēpeculārī.
embezzlement *n* peculātus *m*.
embezzler *n* peculātor *m*.
embitter *vt* exacerbāre.
emblazon *vt* īnsignīre.
emblem *n* īnsigne *nt*.
embodiment *n* exemplar *nt*.
embody *vt* repraesentāre; (*MIL*) cōnscrībere.
embolden *vt* cōnfirmāre; **~ the hearts of**
  animōs cōnfirmāre.
emboss *vt* imprimere, caelāre.
embrace *vt* amplectī, complectī; (*items*)
  continēre, comprehendere; (*party*) sequī;
  (*opportunity*) adripere ♦ *nt* amplexus *m*,
  complexus *m*.
embroider *vt* acū pingere.
embroidery *n* vestis picta *f*.
embroil *vt* miscēre, implicāre.
emend *vt* ēmendāre, corrigere.
emendation *n* ēmendātiō *f*, corrēctiō *f*.
emerald *n* smaragdus *m*.
emerge *vi* ēmergere, exsistere; ēgredī.
emergency *n* tempus *nt*, discrīmen *nt* ♦ *adj*
  subitārius.
emigrate *vi* migrāre, ēmigrāre.
emigration *n* migrātiō *f*.
eminence *n* (*ground*) tumulus *m*, locus ēditus
  m; (*rank*) praestantia *f*, amplitūdō *f*.
eminent *adj* ēgregius, ēminēns, īnsignis,
  amplus.
eminently *adv* ēgregiē, prae cēterīs, in
  prīmīs.
emissary *n* lēgātus *m*.
emit *vt* ēmittere.
emolument *n* lucrum *nt*, ēmolumentum *nt*.
emotion *n* animī mōtus *m*, commōtiō *f*,
  adfectus *m*.
emotional *adj* (*person*) mōbilis; (*speech*)
  flexanimus.
emperor *n* prīnceps *m*, imperātor *m*.
emphasis *n* pondus *nt*; (*words*) impressiō *f*.
emphasize *vt* exprimere.
emphatic *adj* gravis.
emphatically *adv* adsevēranter, vehementer.
empire *n* imperium *nt*.
employ *vt* ūtī (*abl*); (*for purpose*) adhibēre;
  (*person*) exercēre.
employed *adj* occupātus.
employees *npl* operae *fpl*.
employer *n* redemptor *m*.
employment *n* (*act*) ūsus *m*; (*work*) quaestus
  m.
empower *vt* permittere (*dat*), potestātem
  facere (*dat*).
emptiness *n* inānitās *f*.
empty *adj* inānis, vacuus; (*fig*) vānus, inritus ♦
  vt exhaurīre, exinānīre ♦ *vi* (*river*) īnfluere.
emulate *vt* aemulārī.
emulation *n* aemulātiō *f*.
emulous *adj* aemulus.
emulously *adv* certātim.
enable *vt* potestātem facere (*dat*); efficere
  ut (*subj*).

enact _vt_ dēcernere, ēdīcere, scīscere; (_part_) agere.

enactment _n_ dēcrētum _nt_, lēx _f_.

enamoured _adj_ amāns; **be ~ of** dēamāre.

encamp _vi_ castra pōnere, tendere.

encampment _n_ castra _ntpl_.

encase _vt_ inclūdere.

enchant _vt_ fascināre; (_fig_) dēlectāre.

enchantment _n_ fascinātiō _f_; blandīmentum _nt_.

enchantress _n_ sāga _f_.

encircle _vt_ cingere, circumdare, amplectī.

enclose _vt_ inclūdere, saepīre.

enclosure _n_ saeptum _nt_, māceria _f_.

encompass _vt_ cingere, circumdare, amplectī.

encounter _vt_ obviam īre (_dat_), occurrere (_dat_); (_in battle_) concurrere cum (_abl_), congredī cum ♦ _n_ occursus _m_, concursus _m_.

encourage _vt_ cōnfirmāre, (co)hortārī, sublevāre, favēre (_dat_).

encouragement _n_ hortātiō _f_, favor _m_, auxilium _nt_.

encroach _vi_ invādere; **~ upon** occupāre; (_fig_) imminuere.

encrust _vt_ incrustāre.

encumber _vt_ impedīre, onerāre.

encumbrance _n_ impedīmentum _nt_, onus _nt_.

end _n_ fīnis _m_; (_aim_) prōpositum _nt_; (_of action_) ēventus _m_, exitus _m_; (_of speech_) perōrātiō _f_; **~ to ~** continuī; **at a loose ~** vacuus, ōtiōsus; **for two days on ~** biduum continenter; **in the ~** dēnique; **the ~ of** extrēmus; (_time_) exāctus; **put an ~ to** fīnem facere (_dat_), fīnem impōnere (_dat_); **to the ~ that** eō cōnsiliō ut (_subj_); **to what ~?** quō?, quōrsum? ♦ _vt_ fīnīre, cōnficere; (_mutual dealings_) dīrimere ♦ _vi_ dēsinere; (_event_) ēvādere; (_sentence_) cadere; (_speech_) perōrāre; (_time_) exīre; **~ up as** ēvādere; **~ with** dēsinere in (_acc_).

endanger _vt_ perīclitārī, in discrīmen addūcere.

endear _vt_ dēvincīre.

endearing _adj_ blandus.

endearment _n_ blanditiae _fpl_.

endeavour _vt_ cōnārī, ēnītī ♦ _n_ cōnātus _m_.

ending _n_ fīnis _m_, exitus _m_.

endive _n_ intubum _nt_.

endless _adj_ īnfīnītus; (_time_) aeternus, perpetuus.

endlessly _adv_ sine fīne, īnfīnītē.

endorse _vt_ ratum facere.

endow _vt_ dōnāre, īnstruere.

endowed _adj_ praeditus (+ _abl_).

endowment _n_ dōnum _nt_.

endurance _n_ patientia _f_.

endure _vi_ dūrāre, permanēre ♦ _vt_ ferre, tolerāre, patī.

enemy _n_ (_public_) hostis _m_, hostēs _mpl_; (_private_) inimīcus _m_; **greatest ~** inimīcissimus _m_; **~ territory** hosticum _nt_.

energetic _adj_ impiger, nāvus, strēnuus; (_style_) nervōsus.

energetically _adv_ impigrē, nāviter, strēnuē.

energy _n_ impigritās _f_, vigor _m_, incitātiō _f_; (_mind_) contentiō _f_; (_style_) nervī _mpl_.

enervate _vt_ ēnervāre, ēmollīre.

enervation _n_ languor _m_.

enfeeble _vt_ īnfirmāre, dēbilitāre.

enfold _vt_ involvere, complectī.

enforce _vt_ (_law_) exsequī; (_argument_) cōnfirmāre.

enfranchise _vt_ cīvitāte dōnāre; (_slave_) manū mittere.

engage _vt_ (_affection_) dēvincīre; (_attention_) distinēre, occupāre; (_enemy_) manum cōnserere cum (_abl_); (_hire_) condūcere; (_promise_) spondēre, recipere; **~ the enemy** proelium cum hostibus committere; **be ~d in** versārī in (_abl_) ♦ _vi_: **~ in** ingredī, suscipere.

engagement _n_ (_COMM_) occupātiō _f_; (_MIL_) pugna _f_, certāmen _nt_; (_agreement_) spōnsiō _f_; **keep an ~** fidem praestāre; **break an ~** fidem fallere; **I have an ~ at your house** prōmīsī ad tē.

engaging _adj_ blandus.

engender _vt_ ingenerāre, ingignere.

engine _n_ māchina _f_.

engineer _n_ māchinātor _m_ ♦ _vt_ mōlīrī.

engraft _vt_ īnserere.

engrave _vt_ īnsculpere, incīdere, caelāre.

engraver _n_ sculptor _m_, caelātor _m_.

engraving _n_ sculptūra _f_, caelātūra _f_.

engross _vt_ dīstringere, occupāre; **~ed in** tōtus in (_abl_).

engulf _vt_ dēvorāre, obruere.

enhance _vt_ amplificāre, augēre, exaggerāre.

enigma _n_ aenigma _nt_, ambāgēs _fpl_.

enigmatic _adj_ ambiguus, obscūrus.

enigmatically _adv_ per ambāgēs, ambiguē.

enjoin _vt_ imperāre (_dat_), iniungere (_dat_).

enjoy _vt_ fruī (_abl_); (_advantage_) ūtī (_abl_); (_pleasure_) percipere, dēcerpere; **~ oneself** dēlectārī, geniō indulgēre.

enjoyable _adj_ iūcundus.

enjoyment _n_ fructus _m_; dēlectātiō _f_, voluptās _f_.

enlarge _vt_ augēre, amplificāre, dīlātāre; (_territory_) prōpāgāre; **~ upon** amplificāre.

enlargement _n_ amplificātiō _f_, prōlātiō _f_.

enlighten _vt_ inlūstrāre; docēre, ērudīre.

enlightenment _n_ ērudītiō _f_, hūmānitās _f_.

enlist _vt_ scrībere, cōnscrībere; (_sympathy_) conciliāre ♦ _vi_ nōmen dare.

enliven _vt_ excitāre.

enmesh _vt_ impedīre, implicāre.

enmity _n_ inimīcitia _f_, simultās _f_.

ennoble _vt_ honestāre, excolere.

ennui _n_ taedium _nt_.

enormity _n_ immānitās _f_; (_deed_) scelus _nt_, nefās _nt_.

enormous _adj_ immānis, ingēns.

enormously _adv_ immēnsum.

enough _adj_ satis (_indecl gen_) ♦ _adv_ satis; **more than ~** satis superque; **I have had ~ of ...** mē taedet (_gen_) ....

enquire _vi_ quaerere, percontārī; **~ into**

cognōscere, inquīrere in (acc).
enquiry n percontātiō f; (legal) quaestiō f.
enrage vt inrītāre, incendere.
enrapture vt dēlectāre.
enrich vt dītāre, locuplētāre; ~ **with** augēre (abl).
enrol vt adscrībere, conscrībere ♦ vi nōmen dare.
enshrine vt dēdicāre; (fig) sacrāre.
enshroud vt involvere.
ensign n signum nt, īnsigne nt; (officer) signifer m.
enslave vt in servitūtem redigere.
enslavement n servitūs f.
ensnare vt dēcipere, inlaqueāre, inrētīre.
ensue vi īnsequī.
ensure vt praestāre; ~ **that** efficere ut (subj).
entail vt adferre.
entangle vt impedīre, implicāre, inrētīre.
entanglement n implicātiō f.
enter vi inīre, ingredī, intrāre; (riding) invehī; ~ **into** introīre in (acc); ~ **upon** inīre, ingredī ♦ vt (place) intrare; (account) ferre, indūcere; (mind) subīre.
enterprise n inceptum nt; (character) prōmptus animus m.
enterprising adj prōmptus, strēnuus.
entertain vt (guest) invītāre, excipere; (state of mind) habēre, concipere; (to amuse) oblectāre.
entertainer n acroāma nt.
entertainment n hospitium nt; oblectāmentum nt; acroāma nt.
enthral vt capere.
enthusiasm n studium nt, fervor m; ~ **for** studium nt (+ gen).
enthusiastic adj studiōsus, fervidus.
enthusiastically adv summō studiō.
entice vt inlicere, ēlicere, invītāre.
enticement n illecebra f, lēnōcinium nt.
entire adj integer, tōtus, ūniversus.
entirely adv omnīnō, funditus, penitus.
entitle vt (book) īnscrībere; **be ~d to** merērī, dignum esse quī (subj), iūs habēre (gen).
entity n rēs f.
entomb vt humāre, sepelīre.
entrails n intestīna ntpl, exta ntpl.
entrance n aditus m, introitus m; (act) ingressiō f; (of house) vestibulum nt; (of harbour) ōstium nt.
entrance vt fascināre, cōnsōpīre, capere.
entreat vt implōrāre, obsecrāre; (successfully) exōrāre.
entreaty n precēs fpl.
entrenchment n mūnītiō f.
entrust vt committere, crēdere, mandāre; (for keeping) dēpōnere.
entry n introitus m, aditus m; **make an ~** (book) in tabulās referre.
entwine vt implicāre, involvere.
enumerate vt numerāre, dīnumerāre.
enunciate vt ēdīcere; (word) exprimere.
envelop vt implicāre, involvere.

envelope n involucrum nt.
enviable adj beātus.
envious adj invidus, invidiōsus.
enviously adv invidiōsē.
environment n vīcīnia f; **our ~** ea in quibus versāmur.
envoy n lēgātus m.
envy n invidia f ♦ vt invidēre (dat).
enwrap vt involvere.
ephemeral adj brevis.
ephor n ephorus m.
epic adj epicus ♦ n epos nt.
epicure n dēlicātus m.
epigram n sententia f; (poem) epigramma nt.
epilepsy n morbus comitiālis m.
epilogue n epilogus m.
episode n ēventum nt.
epistle n epistula f, litterae fpl.
epitaph n epigramma nt, titulus m.
epithet n adsūmptum nt.
epitome n epitomē f.
epoch n saeculum nt.
equable adj aequālis; (temper) aequus.
equal adj aequus, pār; **be ~ to** aequāre; (task) sufficere (dat) ♦ n pār m/f ♦ vt aequāre, adaequāre.
equality n aequālitās f.
equalize vt adaequāre, exaequāre.
equally adv aequē, pariter.
equanimity n aequus animus m.
equate vt aequāre.
equator n aequinoctiālis circulus m.
equestrian adj equester.
equidistant adj: **be ~** aequō spatiō abesse, idem distāre.
equilibrium n lībrāmentum nt.
equine adj equīnus.
equinoctial adj aequinoctiālis.
equinox n aequinoctium nt.
equip vt armāre, īnstruere, ōrnāre.
equipment n arma ntpl, īnstrūmenta ntpl, adparātus m.
equipoise n lībrāmentum nt.
equitable adj aequus, iūstus.
equitably adv iūstē, aequē.
equity n aequum nt, aequitās f.
equivalent adj pār, īdem īnstar (gen).
equivocal adj anceps, ambiguus.
equivocally adv ambiguē.
equivocate vi tergiversārī.
era n saeculum nt.
eradicate vt ēvellere, exstirpāre.
erase vt dēlēre, indūcere.
erasure n litūra f.
ere conj priusquam.
erect vt ērigere; (building) exstruere; (statute) pōnere ♦ adj ērēctus.
erection n (process) exstructiō f; (product) aedificium nt.
erode vt rōdere.
erotic adj amātōrius.
err vi errāre, peccāre.
errand n mandātum nt.

errant *adj* vagus.
erratic *adj* incōnstāns.
erroneous *adj* falsus.
erroneously *adv* falsō, perperam.
error *n* error *m*; (*moral*) peccātum *nt*; (*writing*) mendum *nt*.
erudite *adj* doctus.
erudition *n* doctrīna *f*, ērudītiō *f*.
erupt *vi* ērumpere.
eruption *n* ēruptiō *f*.
escapade *n* ausum *nt*.
escape *vi* effugere, ēvādere ♦ *vt* fugere, ēvītāre; (*memory*) excidere ex (*abl*); ~ **the notice of** fallere, praeterīre ♦ *n* effugium *nt*, fuga *f*; **way of** ~ effugium *nt*.
eschew *vt* vītāre.
escort *n* praesidium *nt*; (*private*) dēductor *m* ♦ *vt* comitārī, prōsequī; (*out of respect*) dēdūcere.
especial *adj* praecipuus.
especially *adv* praecipuē, praesertim, māximē, in prīmīs.
espionage *n* inquīsītiō *f*.
espouse *vt* (*wife*) dūcere; (*cause*) fovēre.
espy *vt* cōnspicere, cōnspicārī.
essay *n* cōnātus *m*; (*test*) perīculum *nt*; (*literary*) libellus *m* ♦ *vt* cōnārī, incipere.
essence *n* vīs *f*, nātūra *f*.
essential *adj* necesse, necessārius.
essentially *adv* necessāriō.
establish *vt* īnstituere, condere; (*firmly*) stabilīre.
established *adj* firmus, certus; **be** ~ cōnstāre; **become** ~ (*custom*) inveterāscere.
establishment *n* (*act*) cōnstitūtiō *f*; (*domestic*) familia *f*.
estate *n* fundus *m*, rūs *nt*; (*in money*) rēs *f*; (*rank*) ōrdō *m*.
esteem *vt* aestimāre, respicere ♦ *n* grātia *f*, opīniō *f*.
estimable *adj* optimus.
estimate *vt* aestimāre, ratiōnem inīre (*gen*) ♦ *n* aestimātiō *f*, iūdicium *nt*.
estimation *n* opīniō *f*, sententia *f*.
estrange *vt* aliēnāre, abaliēnāre.
estrangement *n* aliēnātiō *f*, discidium *nt*.
estuary *n* aestuārium *nt*.
eternal *adj* aeternus, perennis.
eternally *adv* semper, aeternum.
eternity *n* aeternitās *f*.
etesian winds *n* etēsiae *fpl*.
ether *n* (*sky*) aethēr *m*.
ethereal *adj* aetherius, caelestis.
ethic, ethical *adj* mōrālis.
ethics *n* mōrēs *mpl*, officia *ntpl*.
Etruscan *n* Etruscus *m* ♦ *adj like* **bonus**.
etymology *n* verbōrum notātiō *f*.
eulogist *n* laudātor *m*.
eulogize *vt* laudāre, conlaudāre.
eulogy *n* laudātiō *f*.
eunuch *n* eunūchus *m*.
euphony *n* sonus *m*.
evacuate *vt* (*place*) exinānīre; (*people*)

dēdūcere.
evacuation *n* discessiō *f*.
evade *vt* dēclīnāre, dēvītāre, ēlūdere.
evaporate *vt* exhālāre ♦ *vi* exhālārī.
evaporation *n* exhālātiō *f*.
evasion *n* tergiversātiō *f*.
evasive *adj* ambiguus.
eve *n* vesper *m*; (*before festival*) pervigilium *nt*; **on the** ~ **of** prīdiē (*gen*).
even *adj* aequus, aequālis; (*number*) pār ♦ *adv* et, etiam; (*tentative*) vel; ~ **if** etsī, etiamsī; tametsī; ~ **more** etiam magis; ~ **so** nihilōminus; ~ **yet** etiamnum; **not** ~ ... nē quidem ♦ *vt* aequāre.
evening *n* vesper *m* ♦ *adj* vespertīnus; ~ **is drawing on** invesperāscit; **in the** ~ vesperī.
evening star *n* Vesper *m*, Hesperus *m*.
evenly *adv* aequāliter, aequābiliter.
evenness *n* aequālitās *f*, aequābilitās *f*.
event *n* ēventum *nt*; (*outcome*) ēventus *m*.
eventide *n* vespertīnum tempus *nt*.
eventuality *n* cāsus *m*.
eventually *adv* mox, aliquandō, tandem.
ever *adv* unquam; (*after* sī, nisī, num, nē) quandō; (*always*) semper; (*after interrog*) -nam, tandem; ~ **so** nimium, nimium quantum; **best** ~ omnium optimus; **for** ~ in aeternum.
everlasting *adj* aeternus, perpetuus, immortālis.
evermore *adv* semper, in aeternum.
every *adj* quisque, omnis; ~ **four years** quintō quōque annō; ~ **now and then** interdum; **in** ~ **direction** passim; undique; ~ **other day** alternis diebus; ~ **day** cottīdiē ♦ *adj* cottīdiānus.
everybody *pron* quisque, omnēs *mpl*; ~ **agrees** inter omnēs constat; ~ **knows** nēmō est quīn sciat.
everyday *adj* cottīdiānus.
everyone *pron see* **everybody**.
everything omnia *ntpl*; **your health is** ~ **to me** meā māximē interest tē valēre.
everywhere *adv* ubīque, passim.
evict *vt* dēicere, dētrūdere.
eviction *n* dēiectiō *f*.
evidence *n* testimōnium *nt*, indicium *nt*; (*person*) testis *m/f*; (*proof*) argūmentum *nt*; **on the** ~ **of** fidē (*gen*); **collect** ~ **against** inquīrere in (*acc*); **turn King's** ~ indicium profitērī.
evident *adj* manifestus, ēvidēns, clārus; **it is** ~ appāret.
evidently *adv* manifestō, clārē.
evil *adj* malus, improbus, scelerātus.
evildoer *n* scelerātus *m*, maleficus *m*.
evil eye *n* fascinum *nt*, malum *nt*, improbitās *f*.
evil-minded *adj* malevolus.
evince *vt* praestāre.
evoke *vt* ēvocāre, ēlicere.
evolution *n* seriēs *f*, prōgressus *m*; (*MIL*) dēcursus *m*, dēcursiō *f*.
evolve *vt* explicāre, ēvolvere ♦ *vi* crēscere.
ewe *n* ovis *f*.
ewer *n* hydria *f*.
exacerbate *vt* exacerbāre, exasperāre.

exact *vt* exigere ♦ *adj* accūrātus; (*person*) dīligēns; (*number*) exāctus.
exaction *n* exāctiō *f*.
exactly *adv* accūrātē; (*reply*) ita prōrsus; ~ **as** perinde que.
exactness *n* cūra *f*, dīligentia *f*.
exaggerate *vt* augēre, in māius extollere.
exalt *vt* efferre, extollere; laudāre.
exaltation *n* ēlātiō *f*.
examination *n* inquīsītiō *f*, scrūtātiō *f*; (*of witness*) interrogātiō *f*; (*test*) probātiō *f*.
examine *vt* investīgāre, scrūtārī; īnspicere; (*witness*) interrogāre; (*case*) quaerere dē (*abl*); (*candidate*) probāre.
examiner *n* scrūtātor *m*.
example *n* exemplum *nt*, documentum *nt*; **for ~** exemplī grātiā; **make an ~ of** animadvertere in (*acc*); **I am an ~** exemplō sum.
exasperate *vt* exacerbāre, inrītāre.
exasperation *n* inrītātiō *f*.
excavate *vt* fodere.
excavation *n* fossiō *f*.
excavator *n* fossor *m*.
exceed *vt* excēdere, superāre.
exceedingly *adv* nimis, valdē, nimium quantum.
excel *vt* praestāre (*dat*), exsuperāre ♦ *vi* excellere.
excellence *n* praestantia *f*, virtūs *f*.
excellent *adj* ēgregius, praestāns, optimus.
excellently *adv* ēgregiē, praeclārē.
except *vt* excipere ♦ *prep* praeter (*acc*) ♦ *adv* nisī ♦ *conj* praeterquam, nisī quod.
exception *n* exceptiō *f*; **make an ~ of** excipere; **take ~ to** gravārī quod; **with the ~ of** praeter (*acc*).
exceptional *adj* ēgregius, eximius.
exceptionally *adv* ēgregiē, eximiē.
excerpt *vt* excerpere ♦ *n* excerptum *nt*.
excess *n* immoderātiō *f*, intemperantia *f* ♦ *adj* supervacāneus; **be in ~** superesse.
excessive *adj* immoderātus, immodestus, nimius.
excessively *adv* immodicē, nimis.
exchange *vt* mūtāre, permūtāre ♦ *n* permūtātiō *f*; (*of currencies*) collybus *m*.
exchequer *n* aerārium *nt*; (*emperor's*) fiscus *m*.
excise *n* vectīgālia *ntpl* ♦ *vt* excīdere.
excision *n* excīsiō *f*.
excitable *adj* mōbilis.
excite *vt* excitāre, concitāre; (*to action*) incitāre, incendere; (*to hope*) ērigere, exacuere; (*emotion*) movēre, commovēre.
excitement *n* commōtiō *f*.
exclaim *vt* exclāmāre; ~ **against** adclāmāre (*dat*).
exclamation *n* clāmor *m*, exclāmātiō *f*.
exclude *vt* exclūdere.
exclusion *n* exclūsiō *f*.
exclusive *adj* proprius.
exclusively *adv* sōlum.
excogitate *vt* excōgitāre.
excrescence *n* tūber *nt*.

excruciating *adj* acerbissimus.
exculpate *vt* pūrgāre, absolvere.
excursion *n* iter *nt*; (MIL) excursiō *f*.
excuse *n* excūsātiō *f*; (*false*) speciēs *f* ♦ *vt* excūsāre, ignōscere (*dat*); (*something due*) remittere; **plead in ~** excūsāre; **put forward as an ~** praetendere.
execrable *adj* dētēstābilis, sacer, nefārius.
execrate *vt* dētestārī, exsecrārī.
execration *n* dētestātiō *f*, exsecrātiō *f*.
execute *vt* efficere, patrāre, exsequī; suppliciō afficere; (*behead*) secūrī percutere.
execution *n* effectus *m*; (*penalty*) supplicium *nt*, mors *f*.
executioner *n* carnifex *m*.
exemplar *n* exemplum *nt*.
exempt *adj* immūnis, līber ♦ *vt* līberāre.
exemption *n* (*from tax*) immūnitās *f*; (*from service*) vacātiō *f*.
exercise *n* exercitātiō *f*, ūsus *m*; (*school*) dictāta *ntpl* ♦ *vt* exercēre, ūtī (*abl*); (*mind*) acuere.
exert *vt* extendere, intendere, ūtī (*abl*); ~ **oneself** mōlīrī, ēnītī, sē intendere.
exertion *n* mōlīmentum *nt*; (*mind*) intentiō *f*.
exhalation *n* exhālātiō *f*, vapor *m*.
exhale *vt* exhālāre, exspīrāre.
exhaust *vt* exhaurīre; (*tire*) dēfatīgāre, cōnficere.
exhaustion *n* dēfatīgātiō *f*.
exhaustive *adj* plēnus.
exhibit *vt* exhibēre, ostendere, expōnere; (*on stage*) ēdere.
exhibition *n* expositiō *f*, ostentātiō *f*.
exhilarate *vt* exhilarāre.
exhort *vt* hortārī, cohortārī.
exhortation *n* hortātiō *f*, hortāmen *nt*.
exhume *vt* ēruere.
exigency *n* necessitās *f*.
exile *n* exsilium *nt*, fuga *f*; (*temporary*) relēgātiō *f*; (*person*) exsul *m*; **live in ~** exsulāre ♦ *vt* in exsilium pellere, dēportāre; (*temporarily*) relēgāre.
exist *vi* esse.
existence *n* vīta *f*.
exit *n* exitus *m*, ēgressus *m*.
exodus *n* discessus *m*.
exonerate *vt* absolvere.
exorbitant *adj* nimius, immoderātus.
exotic *adj* peregrīnus.
expand *vt* extendere, dīlātāre.
expanse *n* spatium *nt*, lātitūdō *f*.
expatiate *vi*: ~ **upon** amplificāre.
expatriate *vt* extermināre ♦ *n* extorris *m*.
expect *vt* exspectāre, spērāre.
expectancy, expectation *n* spēs *f*, exspectātiō *f*; opīniō *f*.
expediency *n* ūtile *nt*, ūtilitās *f*.
expedient *adj* ūtilis, commodus; **it is ~** expedit ♦ *n* modus *m*, ratiō *f*.
expediently *adv* commodē.
expedite *vt* mātūrāre.

expedition n (MIL) expedītiō f.
expeditious adj prōmptus, celer.
expeditiously adv celeriter.
expel vt pellere, expellere, ēicere.
expend vt impendere, expendere.
expenditure n impēnsae fpl, sūmptus m.
expense n impēnsae fpl, impendia ntpl; **at my ~**
meō sūmptū; **at the public ~** dē pūblicō.
expensive adj cārus, pretiōsus; (furnishings)
lautus.
expensively adv sūmptuōsē, māgnō pretiō.
experience n ūsus m, experientia f ♦ vt
experīrī, patī.
experienced adj perītus, expertus (+ gen).
experiment n experīmentum nt ♦ vi: ~ **with**
experīrī.
expert adj perītus, sciēns.
expertly adv perītē, scienter.
expertness n perītia f.
expiate vt expiāre, lūere.
expiation n (act) expiātiō f; (penalty) piāculum
nt.
expiatory adj piāculāris.
expiration n (breath) exspīrātiō f; (time) exitus
m.
expire vi exspīrāre; (die) animam agere,
animam efflāre; (time) exīre.
expiry n exitus m, fīnis m.
explain vt explicāre, expōnere, explānāre,
interpretārī; (lucidly) ēnōdāre; (in detail)
ēdisserere.
explanation n explicātiō f, ēnōdātiō f,
interpretātiō f.
explicit adj expressus, apertus.
explicitly adv apertē.
explode vt discutere ♦ vi dīrumpī.
exploit n factum nt, ausum nt; ~**s** pl rēs gestae
fpl ♦ vt ūtī (abl), fruī (abl).
explore vt, vi explōrāre, scrūtārī.
explorer n explōrātor m.
explosion n fragor m.
exponent n interpres m, auctor m.
export vt exportāre ♦ n exportātiō f.
exportation n exportātiō f.
expose vt dētegere, dēnūdāre, patefacere;
(child) expōnere; (to danger) obicere; (MIL)
nūdāre; (for sale) prōpōnere; ~ **o.s.** se
obicere.
exposed adj apertus, obnoxius.
exposition n explicātiō f, interpretātiō f.
expostulate vi expostulāre, conquerī.
expostulation n expostulātiō f.
exposure n (of child) expositiō f; (of guilt)
dēprehēnsiō f; (to hardship) patientia f.
expound vt expōnere, interpretārī.
expounder n interpres m.
express vt (in words) exprimere, dēclārāre,
ēloquī; (in art) effingere ♦ adj expressus;
(speed) celerrimus.
expression n significātiō f; (word) vōx f,
verbum nt; (face) vultus m.
expressive adj significāns; ~ **of** index (gen); **be**
very ~ māximam vim habēre.

expressively adv significanter.
expressiveness n vīs f.
expressly adv plānē.
expulsion n expulsiō f, ēiectiō f.
expurgate vt pūrgāre.
exquisite adj ēlegāns, exquīsītus, eximius;
(judgment) subtīlis.
exquisitely adv ēleganter, exquīsītē.
ex-service adj ēmeritus.
extant adj superstes; **be ~** exstāre.
extempore adv ex tempore, subitō ♦ adj
extemporālis.
extemporize vi subita dīcere.
extend vt extendere, dīlātāre; (hand)
porrigere; (line) dūcere; (office) prōrogāre;
(territory) propāgāre ♦ vi patēre, porrigī; ~
into incurrere in (acc).
extension n prōductiō f, prōlātiō f; (of office)
prōrogātiō f; (of territory) propāgātiō f; (extra)
incrēmentum nt.
extensive adj effūsus, amplus, lātus.
extensively adv lātē.
extent n spatium nt, amplitūdō f; **to a large ~**
māgnā ex parte; **to some ~** aliquā ex parte;
to this ~ hāctenus; **to such an ~** adeō.
extenuate vt levāre, mītigāre.
exterior adj externus, exterior ♦ n speciēs f.
exterminate vt occīdiōne occīdere,
interimere.
extermination n occīdiō f, interneciō f.
external adj externus.
externally adv extrīnsecus.
extinct adj mortuus; (custom) obsolētus.
extinction n exstinctiō f, interitus m.
extinguish vt exstinguere, restinguere.
extinguisher n exstinctor m.
extirpate vt exstirpāre, excīdere.
extol vt laudāre, laudibus efferre.
extort vt extorquēre, exprimere.
extortion n (offence) rēs repetundae fpl.
extortionate adj inīquus, rapāx.
extra adv īnsuper, praetereā ♦ adj additus.
extract vt excerpere, extrahere ♦ n: **make ~s**
excerpere.
extraction n ēvulsiō f; (descent) genus nt.
extraneous adj adventīcius, aliēnus.
extraordinarily adv mīrificē, eximiē.
extraordinary adj extraōrdinārius; (strange)
mīrus, novus; (outstanding) eximius,
īnsignis.
extravagance n intemperantia f; (language)
immoderātiō f, luxuria f; (spending) sūmptus
m.
extravagant adj immoderātus, immodestus;
(spending) sūmptuōsus, prōdigus.
extreme adj extrēmus, ultimus.
extremely adv valdē, vehementer.
extremity n extrēmum nt, fīnis m; (distress)
angustiae fpl; **the ~ of** extrēmus.
extricate vt expedīre, absolvere; ~ **oneself**
ēmergere.
exuberance n ūbertās f, luxuria f.
exuberant adj ūber, laetus, luxuriōsus.

exuberantly adv ūbertim.
exude vt exsūdāre ♦ vi mānāre.
exult vi exsultārī, laetārī, gestīre.
exultant adj laetus.
exultantly adv laetē.
exultation n laetitia f.
eye n oculus m; (needle) forāmen nt; **cast ~s on**
oculōs conicere in (acc); **have an ~ to**
spectāre; **in your ~s** iūdice tē; **keep one's ~s**
on oculōs dēfigere in (abl); **lose an ~** alterō
oculō capī; **see ~ to ~** cōnsentīre; **set ~s on**
cōnspicere; **shut one's ~s to** cōnīvēre in
(abl); **take one's ~s off** oculōs dēicere ab
(abl); **up to the ~s in** tōtus in (abl); **with a cast**
in the ~ paetus; **with sore ~s** lippus; **sore ~s**
lippitūdō f; **with one's own ~s** cōram; **with**
one's ~s open sciēns ♦ vt intuērī, aspicere.
eyeball n pūpula f.
eyebrow n supercilium nt.
eyelash n palpebrae pilus m.
eyelid n palpebra f.
eyeshot n oculōrum coniectus m.
eyesight n aciēs f, oculī mpl.
eyesore n turpe nt; **it is an ~ to me** oculī meī
dolent.
eye tooth n dēns canīnus m.
eyewash n sycophantia f.
eyewitness n arbiter m; **be an ~ of** interesse
(dat).

F, f

fable n fābula f, apologus m.
fabled adj fābulōsus.
fabric n (built) structūra f; (woven) textile nt.
fabricate vt fabricārī; (fig) comminīscī,
fingere.
fabricated adj commentīcius.
fabrication n (process) fabricātiō f; (thing)
commentum nt.
fabricator n auctor m.
fabulous adj commentīcius, fictus.
fabulously adv incrēdibiliter.
facade n frōns f.
face n faciēs f, ōs nt; (aspect) aspectus m;
(impudence) ōs nt; **~ to ~** cōram; **how shall**
I have the ~ to go back? quō ōre redībō?; **on**
the ~ of it ad speciem, prīmō aspectū; **put**
a bold ~ on fortem sē praebēre; **save ~**
factum pūrgāre; **set one's ~ against**
adversārī (dat) ♦ vt spectāre ad (acc);
(danger) obviam īre (dat), sē oppōnere
(dat) ♦ vi (place) spectāre, vergere; **~**
about (MIL) signa convertere.
facetious adj facētus, salsus.

facetiously adv facētē, salsē.
facetiousness n facētiae fpl, salēs mpl.
facile adj facilis.
facilitate vt expedīre.
facilities npl opportūnitās f.
facility n facilitās f.
facing adj adversus ♦ prep exadversus (acc).
facsimile n exemplār nt.
fact n rēs f, vērum nt; **as a matter of ~**
enimvērō; **the ~ that** quod; **in ~** rē vērā ♦ conj
etenim; (climax) dēnique.
faction n factiō f.
factious adj factiōsus, sēditiōsus.
factiously adv sēditiōsē.
factor n prōcūrātor m.
factory n officīna f.
faculty n facultās f, vīs f.
fad n libīdō f.
fade vi dēflōrēscere, marcēscere.
faded adj marcidus.
faggot n sarmentum nt.
fail vi dēficere, dēesse; (fig) cadere, dēcidere;
(in business) forō cēdere; **~ to** nōn posse; **~ to**
come nōn venīre ♦ vt dēficere, dēstituere.
failing n culpa f, vitium nt.
failure n (of supply) dēfectiō f; (in action)
offēnsiō f; (at election) repulsa f.
fain adv libenter.
faint adj (body) languidus, dēfessus;
(impression) hebes, levis; (courage) timidus;
(colour) pallidus; **be ~** languēre; hebēre ♦ vi
intermorī, animō linquī; **I feel ~** animō male
est.
faint-hearted adj animo dēmissus; timidus.
faintly adv languidē; leviter.
faintness n dēfectiō f, languor m; levitās f.
fair adj (appearance) pulcher, fōrmōsus; (hair)
flāvus; (skin) candidus; (weather) serēnus;
(wind) secundus; (copy) pūrus; (dealings)
aequus; (speech) speciōsus, blandus; (ability)
mediocris; (reputation) bonus ♦ n nūndinae
fpl; **~ and square** sine fūcō ac fallāciīs.
fairly adv iūre, iūstē; mediocriter.
fairness n aequitās f.
fair play n aequum et bonum nt.
fairy n nympha f.
faith n fidēs f; **in good ~** bonā fidē.
faithful adj fidēlis, fīdus.
faithfully adv fidēliter.
faithfulness n fidēlitās f.
faithless adj īnfidēlis, īnfīdus, perfidus.
faithlessly adv īnfidēliter.
faithlessness n īnfidēlitās f.
fake vt simulāre.
falchion n falx f.
falcon n falcō m.
fall vi cadere; (gently) lābī; (morally) prōlābī;
(dead) concidere, occidere; (fortress)
expugnārī, capī; **~ at** accidere; **~ away**
dēficere, dēscīscere; **~ back** recidere; (MIL)
pedem referre; **~ between** intercidere; **~**
behind cessāre; **~ by the way** intercidere; **~**
down dēcidere, dēlābī; (building) ruere,

corruere; ~ **due** cadere; ~ **flat** sē prōsternere; (*speech*) frīgēre; ~ **forward** prōlābī; ~ **foul of** incurrere in (*acc*); ~ **headlong** sē praecipitāre; ~ **in, into** incidere; ~ **in with** occurrere (*dat*); ~ **off** dēcidere; (*fig*) dēscīscere; ~ **on** incumbere in (*acc*), incidere in (*acc*); ~ **out** excidere; (*event*) ēvenīre; (*hair*) dēfluere; ~ **short of** deesse ad; ~ **to** (*by lot*) obtingere, obvenīre (*dat*); ~ **to the ground** (*case*) iacēre; ~ **upon** invādere, ingruere in (*acc*); (*one's neck*) in collum invādere ♦ *n* cāsus *m*; (*building*) ruīna *f*; (*moral*) lāpsus *m*; (*season*) autumnus *m*; **the ~ of Capua** Capua capta.

fallacious *adj* captiōsus, fallāx.

fallaciously *adv* fallāciter.

fallacy *n* captiō *f*.

fallible *adj*: **be ~** errāre solēre.

fallow *adj* (*land*) novālis ♦ *n* novāle *nt*; **lie ~** cessāre.

false *adj* falsus, fictus.

falsehood *n* falsum *nt*, mendācium *nt*; **tell a ~** mentīrī.

falsely *adv* falsō.

falsify *vt* vitiāre, interlinere.

falter *vi* (*speech*) haesitāre; (*gait*) titubāre.

faltering *adj* (*speech*) īnfrāctus; (*gait*) titubāns ♦ *n* haesitātiō *f*.

fame *n* fāma *f*, glōria *f*, nōmen *nt*.

famed *adj* illūstris, praeclārus.

familiar *adj* (*friend*) intimus; (*fact*) nōtus; (*manner*) cōmis; ~ **spirit** genius *m*; **be ~ with** nōvisse; **be on ~ terms with** familiāriter ūtī (*abl*).

familiarity *n* ūsus *m*, cōnsuētūdō *f*.

familiarize *vt* adsuēfacere.

familiarly *adv* familiāriter.

family *n* domus *f*, gēns *f* ♦ *adj* domesticus, familiāris; ~ **property** rēs familiāris *f*.

famine *n* famēs *f*.

famished *adj* famēlicus.

famous *adj* illūstris, praeclārus, nōbilis; **make ~** nōbilitāre; **the ~** ille.

fan *n* flābellum *nt*; (*winnowing*) vannus *f* ♦ *vt* ventilāre; ~ **the flames of** (*fig*) īnflammāre.

fanatic *n* (*religious*) fānāticus *m*.

fanciful *adj* (*person*) incōnstāns; (*idea*) commentīcius.

fancy *n* (*faculty*) mēns *f*; (*idea*) opīnātiō *f*; (*caprice*) libīdō *f*; **take a ~ to** amāre incipere; ~ **oneself** se amāre ♦ *vt* animō fingere, imāginārī, sibi prōpōnere; ~ **you thinking ... !** tē crēdere ... ! ♦ *adj* dēlicātus.

fancy-free *adj* sēcūrus, vacuus.

fang *n* dēns *m*.

fantastic *adj* commentīcius, mōnstruōsus.

fantasy *n* imāginātiō *f*; (*contemptuous*) somnium *nt*.

far *adj* longinquus ♦ *adv* longē, procul; (*with compar*) multō; **be ~ from** longē abesse ab; **be not ~ from doing** haud multum abest quin (+*subj*); **by ~** longē; **how ~?** quātenus?, quoūsque?; **so ~** hāctenus, eātenus; (*limited*) quādam tenus; **thus ~** hāctenus; ~ **and wide** lātē; ~ **be it from me to say** equidem dīcere nōlim; ~ **from thinking ... I** adeō nōn crēdō ... ut; **as ~ as** *prep* tenus (*abl*) ♦ *adv* ūsque ♦ *conj* quātenus; (*know*) quod.

farce *n* mīmus *m*.

farcical *adj* rīdiculus.

fare *vi* sē habēre, agere ♦ *n* vectūra *f*; (*boat*) naulum *nt*; (*food*) cibus *m*.

farewell *interj* valē, valēte; **say ~ to** valēre iubēre.

far-fetched *adj* quaesītus, arcessītus, altē repetītus.

farm *n* fundus *m*, praedium *nt* ♦ *vt* (*soil*) colere; (*taxes*) redimere; ~ **out** locāre.

farmer *n* agricola *m*; (*of taxes*) pūblicānus *m*.

farming *n* agrīcultūra *f*.

farrow *vt* parere ♦ *n* fētus *m*.

far-sighted *adj* prōvidus, prūdēns.

farther *adv* longius, ultrā ♦ *adj* ulterior.

farthest *adj* ultimus, extrēmus ♦ *adv* longissimē.

fasces *n* fascēs *mpl*.

fascinate *vt* dēlēnīre, capere.

fascination *n* dulcēdō *f*, dēlēnīmenta *ntpl*, lēnōcinia *ntpl*.

fashion *n* mōs *m*, ūsus *m*; (*manner*) modus *m*, ratiō *f*; (*shape*) fōrma *f* ♦ *vt* fingere, fōrmāre; **after the ~ of** rītū (*gen*); **come into ~** in mōrem venīre; **go out of ~** obsolēscere.

fashionable *adj* ēlegāns; **it is ~** mōris est.

fashionably *adv* ēleganter.

fast *adj* (*firm*) firmus; (*quick*) celer; **make ~** dēligāre ♦ *adv* firmē; celeriter; **be ~ asleep** artē dormīre ♦ *vi* iēiūnus esse, cibō abstinēre ♦ *n* iēiūnium *nt*.

fasten *vt* fīgere, ligāre; ~ **down** dēfīgere; ~ **on** inligāre; ~ **to** adligāre; ~ **together** conligāre, cōnfīgere.

fastening *n* iūnctūra *f*.

fastidious *adj* dēlicātus, ēlegāns.

fastidiously *adv* fastīdiōsē.

fastidiousness *n* fastīdium *nt*.

fasting *n* iēiūnium *nt*, inedia *f* ♦ *adj* iēiūnus.

fastness *n* arx *f*, castellum *nt*.

fat *adj* pinguis, opīmus, obēsus; **grow ~** pinguēscere ♦ *n* adeps *m/f*.

fatal *adj* (*deadly*) fūnestus, exitiābilis; (*fated*) fātālis.

fatality *n* fātum *nt*, cāsus *m*.

fatally *adv*: **be ~ wounded** vulnere perīre.

fate *n* fātum *nt*, fortūna *f*, sors *f*.

fated *adj* fātālis.

fateful *adj* fātālis; fūnestus.

Fates *npl* (*goddesses*) Parcae *fpl*.

father *n* pater *m*; (*fig*) auctor *m* ♦ *vt* gignere; ~ **upon** addīcere, tribuere.

father-in-law *n* socer *m*.

fatherland *n* patria *f*.

fatherless *adj* orbus.

fatherly *adj* paternus.

fathom *n* sex pedēs *mpl* ♦ *vt* (*fig*) expūtāre.

fathomless *adj* profundus.

fatigue n fatīgātiō f, dēfatīgātiō f ♦ vt fatīgāre, dēfatīgāre.
fatness n pinguitūdō f.
fatten vt sagīnāre.
fatty adj pinguis.
fatuity n īnsulsitās f, ineptiae fpl.
fatuous adj fatuus, īnsulsus, ineptus.
fault n culpa f, vitium nt; (written) mendum nt; **count as a ~** vitiō vertere; **find ~ with** incūsāre; **it is not your ~ that** ... nōn per tē stat quōminus (subj).
faultily adv vitiōsē, mendōsē.
faultiness n vitium nt.
faultless adj ēmendātus, integer.
faultlessly adv ēmendātē.
faulty adj vitiōsus, mendōsus.
faun n faunus m.
fauna n animālia ntpl.
favour n grātia f, favor m; (done) beneficium nt; **win ~ with** grātiam inīre apud; **by your ~** bonā veniā tuā ♦ vt favēre (dat), indulgēre (dat).
favourable adj faustus, prosperus, secundus.
favourably adv faustē, fēlīciter, benignē.
favourite adj dīlectus, grātissimus ♦ n dēliciae fpl.
favouritism n indulgentia f, studium nt.
fawn n hinnuleus m ♦ adj (colour) gilvus ♦ vi: **~ upon** adūlārī.
fawning adj blandus ♦ n adūlātiō f.
fear n timor m, metus m, formīdō f ♦ vt timēre, metuere, formīdāre, verērī; **fearing that** veritus ne (+ imperf subj).
fearful adj timidus; horrendus, terribilis, formīdolōsus.
fearfully adv timidē; formīdolōsē.
fearless adj impavidus, intrepidus.
fearlessly adv impavidē, intrepidē.
fearlessness n fīdentia f, audācia f.
fearsome adj formīdolōsus.
feasible adj: **it is ~** fierī potest.
feast n epulae fpl; (private) convīvium nt; (public) epulum nt; (religious) daps f; (festival) festus diēs m ♦ vi epulārī, convīvārī; (fig) pāscī ♦ vt: **~ one's eyes on** oculōs pāscere (abl).
feat n factum nt, facinus nt.
feather n penna f; (downy) plūma f; **birds of a ~ flock together** parēs cum paribus facillimē congregantur.
feathered adj pennātus.
feathery adj plūmeus.
feature n līneāmentum nt; (fig) proprium nt.
February n mēnsis Februārius m; **of ~** Februārius.
federal adj sociālis, foederātus.
federate vi societātem facere.
federated adj foederātus.
federation n societās f, foederātae cīvitātēs fpl.
fee n honōs m, mercēs f.
feeble adj imbēcillus, īnfirmus, dēbilis.
feebleness n imbēcillitās f, īnfirmitās f.
feebly adv īnfirmē.

feed vt alere, pāscere ♦ vi pāscī; **~ on** vescī (abl) ♦ n pābulum nt.
feel vt sentīre; (with hand) tractāre, tangere; (emotion) capere, adficī (abl); (opinion) cēnsēre, sentīre; **~ one's way** pedetemptim prōgredī ♦ vi sentīre; **I ~ glad** gaudeō; **~ sure** prō certō habēre.
feeling n sēnsus m, tāctus m; (mind) animus m, adfectus m; (pity) misericordia f; **good ~** voluntās f; **bad ~** invidia f.
feign vt simulāre, fingere.
feignedly adv simulātē, fictē.
feint n simulātiō f.
felicitate vt grātulārī (dat).
felicitation n grātulātiō f.
felicitous adj fēlīx, aptus.
felicity n fēlīcitās f.
feline adj fēlīnus.
fell vt (tree) succīdere; (enemy) sternere, caedere ♦ adj dīrus, crūdēlis, atrōx ♦ n mōns m; (skin) pellis f.
fellow n socius m, aequālis m; (contemptuous) homō m.
fellow citizen n cīvis m/f.
fellow countryman n cīvis m/f, populāris m/f.
fellow feeling n misericordia f.
fellowship n societās f, sodālitās f.
fellow slave n cōnservus m;
fellow soldier n commīlitō m.
fellow student n condiscipulus m.
felon n nocēns m.
felonious adj scelestus, scelerātus.
felony n scelus nt, noxa f.
felt n coāctum nt.
female adj muliebris ♦ n fēmina f.
feminine adj muliebris.
fen n palūs f.
fence n saepēs f; **sit on the ~** quiēscere, medium sē gerere ♦ vt saepīre; **~ off** intersaepīre ♦ vi bātuere, rudibus lūdere.
fencing n rudium lūdus m; **~ master** lānista m.
fend vt arcēre ♦ vi prōvidēre.
fennel n ferula f.
fenny adj palūster.
ferment n fermentum nt; (fig) aestus m ♦ vt fermentāre; (fig) excitāre, accendere ♦ vi fervēre.
fermentation n fervor m.
fern n filix f.
ferocious adj ferōx, saevus, truculentus.
ferociously adv truculentē.
ferocity n ferōcitās f, saevitia f.
ferret n viverra f ♦ vt: **~ out** rīmārī, ēruere.
ferry n trāiectus m; (boat) cymba f, pontō m ♦ vt trānsvehere.
ferryman n portitor m.
fertile adj fertīlis, fēcundus.
fertility n fertīlitās f, fēcunditās f.
fertilize vt fēcundāre, laetificāre.
fervent adj fervidus, ārdēns.
fervently adv ārdenter.
fervid adj fervidus.
fervour n ārdor m, fervor m.

festal *adj* festus.
fester *vi* exulcerārī.
festival *n* diēs festus *m*, sollemne *nt*.
festive *adj* (*time*) festus; (*person*) festīvus.
festivity *n* hilaritās *f*; (*event*) sollemne *nt*.
festoon *n* sertum *nt* ♦ *vt* corōnāre.
fetch *vt* arcessere, addūcere; (*price*) vēnīre (*gen*); ~ **out** dēprōmere; ~ **water** aquārī.
fetching *adj* lepidus, blandus.
fetid *adj* foetidus, pūtidus.
fetter *n* compēs *f*, vinculum *nt* ♦ *vt* compedēs inicere (*dat*), vincīre; (*fig*) impedīre.
fettle *n* habitus *m*, animus *m*.
feud *n* simultās *f*, inimīcitia *f*.
fever *n* febris *f*.
feverish *adj* febrīculōsus; (*fig*) sollicitus.
few *adj* paucī; **very** ~ perpaucī; **how** ~? quotus quisque?
fewness *n* paucitās *f*.
fiancé *n* spōnsus *m*.
fiasco *n* calamitās *f*; **be a** ~ frīgēre.
fiat *n* ēdictum *nt*.
fibre *n* fibra *f*.
fickle *adj* incōnstāns, levis, mōbilis.
fickleness *n* incōnstantia *f*, levitās *f*, mōbilitās *f*.
fiction *n* fābula *f*, commentum *nt*.
fictitious *adj* fictus, falsus, commentīcius; (*character*) persōnātus.
fictitiously *adv* fictē.
fidelity *n* fidēlitās *f*, fidēs *f*.
fidget *vi* sollicitārī.
field *n* ager *m*; (*ploughed*) arvum *nt*; (*of grain*) seges *f*; (MIL) campus *m*, aciēs *f*; (*scope*) campus *m*, locus *m*; **in the** ~ (MIL) mīlitiae; **hold the** ~ vincere, praevalēre; ~ **of vision** cōnspectus *m*.
fiend *n* diabolus *m*.
fiendish *adj* nefārius, improbus.
fierce *adj* saevus, ācer, atrōx; (*look*) torvus.
fiercely *adv* ācriter, atrōciter, saevē.
fierceness *n* saevitia *f*, atrōcitās *f*.
fieriness *n* ārdor *m*, fervor *m*.
fiery *adj* igneus, flammeus; (*fig*) ārdēns, fervidus.
fife *n* tībia *f*.
fifteen *num* quīndecim; ~ **each** quīndēnī; ~ **times** quīndeciēns.
fifteenth *adj* quīntus decimus.
fifth *adj* quīntus ♦ *n* quīnta pars *f*.
fiftieth *adj* quīnquāgēsimus.
fifty *num* quīnquāgintā.
fig *n* fīcus *f*; (*tree*) fīcus *f*; **of** ~ fīculnus; **not care a** ~ **for** floccī nōn facere.
fight *n* pugna *f*, proelium *nt* ♦ *vi* pugnāre, dīmicāre; ~ **it out** dēcernere, dēcertāre; ~ **to the end** dēpugnāre ♦ *vt* (*battle*) committere; (*enemy*) pugnāre cum (*abl*).
fighter *n* pugnātor *m*.
fighting *n* dīmicātiō *f*.
figment *n* commentum *nt*.
figurative *adj* trānslātus; **in** ~ **language** trānslātīs per similitūdinem verbīs; **use** ~**ly** trānsferre.
figure *n* figūra *f*, fōrma *f*; (*in art*) signum *nt*; (*of speech*) figūra *f*, trānslātiō *f*; (*pl, on pottery*) sigilla *ntpl* ♦ *vt* figūrāre, fōrmāre; (*art*) fingere, effingere; ~ **to oneself** sibi prōpōnere.
figured *adj* sigillātus.
figurehead *n* (*of ship*) īnsigne *nt*.
filament *n* fibra *f*.
filch *vt* fūrārī, surripere.
file *n* (*tool*) līma *f*; (*line*) ōrdō *m*, agmen *nt*; (*of papers*) fasciculus *m*; ~**s** *pl* tabulae *fpl*; **in single** ~ simplicī ōrdine; **the rank and** ~ gregāriī mīlitēs ♦ *vt* līmāre.
filial *adj* pius.
filigree *n* diatrēta *ntpl*.
fill *vt* implēre, explēre, complēre; (*office*) fungī (*abl*); ~ **up** supplēre.
fillet *n* īnfula *f*, vitta *f* ♦ *vt* (*fish*) exossāre.
fillip *n* stimulus *m*.
filly *n* equula *f*.
film *n* membrāna *f*.
filter *n* cōlum *nt* ♦ *vt* dēliquāre ♦ *vi* percōlārī.
filth *n* sordēs *f*, caenum *nt*.
filthily *adv* foedē, inquinātē.
filthiness *n* foeditās *f*, impūritās *f*.
filthy *adj* foedus, impūrus; (*speech*) inquinātus.
fin *n* pinna *f*.
final *adj* ultimus, postrēmus, extrēmus.
finally *adv* dēnique, tandem, postrēmō.
finance *n* rēs nummāria *f*; (*state*) vectīgālia *ntpl*.
financial *adj* aerārius.
financier *n* faenerātor *m*.
finch *n* fringilla *f*.
find *vt* invenīre, reperīre; (*supplies*) parāre; (*verdict*) iūdicāre; (*pleasure*) capere; ~ **fault with** incūsāre; ~ **guilty** damnāre; ~ **out** comperīre, cognōscere.
finder *n* inventor *m*.
finding *n* iūdicium *nt*, sententia *f*.
fine *n* (*law*) multa *f*, damnum *nt*; **in** ~ dēnique ♦ *vt* multāre ♦ *adj* (*thin*) tenuis, subtīlis; (*refined*) ēlegāns, mundus, decōrus; (*beautiful*) pulcher, venustus; (*showy*) speciōsus; (*of weather*) serēnus.
finely *adv* pulchrē, ēleganter, subtīliter.
fineness *n* tenuitās *f*; ēlegantia *f*; pulchritūdō *f*; speciēs *f*; serēnitās *f*.
finery *n* ōrnātus *m*, munditiae *fpl*.
finesse *n* astūtia *f*, ars *f*, argūtiae *fpl*.
finger *n* digitus *m*; **a** ~'**s breadth** trānsversus digitus; **not lift a** ~ (*in effort*) nē manum quidem vertere ♦ *vt* pertractāre.
fingertips *npl* extrēmī digitī.
finish *n* fīnis *m*; (*art*) perfectiō *f* ♦ *vt* fīnīre, perficere; cōnficere; (*with art*) perficere, expolīre ♦ *vi* dēsinere; ~ **off** transigere, peragere, absolvere.
finishing post *n* mēta *f*.
finishing touch *n* manus extrēma.
finite *adj* circumscrīptus.

fir n abiēs f; **of ~** abiēgnus.

fire n ignis m; (conflagration) incendium nt; (in hearth) focus m; (fig) ārdor m, calor m, impetus m; **be on ~** ārdēre, flagrāre; **catch ~** flammam concipere, ignem comprehendere; **set on ~** accendere, incendere ♦ vt incendere; (fig) īnflammāre; (missile) iaculārī.

firebrand n fax f.

fire brigade n vigilēs mpl.

fireplace n focus m.

fireside n focus m.

firewood n lignum nt.

firm n societās f ♦ adj firmus, stabilis; (mind) cōnstāns; **stand ~** perstāre.

firmament n caelum nt.

firmly adv firmē, cōnstanter.

firmness n firmitās f, firmitūdō f; cōnstantia f.

first adj prīmus, prīnceps; (of two) prior ♦ adv prīmum; **at ~** prīmō, prīncipiō; **at ~ hand** ipse, ab ipsō; **come in ~** vincere; **give ~ aid to** ad tempus medērī (dat); **I was the ~ to see** prīmus vīdī.

first-class adj classicus.

first fruits npl prīmitiae fpl.

firstly adv prīmum.

first-rate adj eximius, lūculentus.

firth n aestuārium nt, fretum nt.

fiscal adj vectīgālis, aerārius.

fish n piscis m ♦ vi piscārī; (fig) expiscārī.

fisher, fisherman n piscātor m.

fishing n piscātus m ♦ adj piscātōrius.

fishing-rod n harundō f.

fish market n forum piscārium nt.

fishmonger n piscārius m.

fish pond n piscīna f.

fissile adj fissilis.

fissure n rīma f.

fist n pugnus m.

fit n (MED) convulsiō f; (of anger, illness) impetus m; **by ~s and starts** temerē, carptim ♦ vt aptāre, accommodāre; (dress) sedēre (dat); **~ out** armāre, īnstruere ♦ adj aptus, idōneus, dignus; **I see ~ to** mihi vidētur; **~ for** aptus ad (+ acc).

fitful adj dubius, incōnstāns.

fitfully adv incōnstanter.

fitly adv dignē, aptē.

fitness n convenientia f.

fitting n adparātus m, īnstrūmentum nt ♦ adj idōneus, dignus; **it is ~** convenit, decet.

fittingly adv dignē, convenienter.

five num quīnque; **~ each** quīnī; **~ times** quīnquiēns; **~ years** quīnquennium nt, lūstrum nt; **~ sixths** quīnque partēs.

five hundred num quīngentī; **~ each** quīngēnī; **~ times** quīngentiēns.

five hundredth adj quīngentēsimus.

fix vt fīgere; (time) dīcere, cōnstituere; (decision) statuere ♦ n angustiae fpl; **put in a ~** dēprehendere.

fixed adj fixus; (attention) intentus; (decision) certus; (star) inerrāns; **be firmly ~ in** īnsidēre

(dat).

fixedly adv intentē.

fixity n stabilitās f; (of purpose) cōnstantia f.

fixtures npl adfīxa ntpl.

flabbergast vt obstupefacere.

flabbiness n mollitia f.

flabby adj flaccidus, mollis.

flag n vexillum nt; **~ officer** praefectus classis m ♦ vi flaccēre, flaccēscere, languēscere.

flagellate vt verberāre.

flagon n lagoena f.

flagrant adj manifestus; flāgitiōsus.

flagrantly adv flāgitiōsē.

flagship n nāvis imperātōria f.

flail n fūstis m.

flair n iūdicium nt.

flake n squāma f; **~s** pl (snow) nix f.

flame n flamma f ♦ vi flagrāre, exārdēscere.

flaming adj flammeus.

flamingo n phoenīcopterus m.

flank n latus nt; cornū m; **on the ~** ab latere, ad latus ♦ vt latus tegere (gen).

flap n flābellum nt; (dress) lacinia f ♦ vt plaudere (abl).

flare n flamma f, fulgor m ♦ vi exārdēscere, flagrāre.

flash n fulgor m; (lightning) fulgur nt; (time) mōmentum nt ♦ vi fulgēre; (motion) micāre.

flashy adj speciōsus.

flask n ampulla f.

flat adj plānus; (ground) aequus; (on back) supīnus; (on face) prōnus; (music) gravis; (style) āridus, frīgidus; **fall ~** (fig) frīgēre ♦ n (land) plānitiēs f; (sea) vadum nt; (house) tabulātum nt.

flatly adv prōrsus.

flatness n plānitiēs f.

flatten vt aequāre, complānāre.

flatter vt adūlārī (dat), adsentārī (dat), blandīrī (dat).

flatterer n adsentātor m.

flattering adj blandus.

flatteringly adv blandē.

flattery n adūlātiō f, adsentātiō f, blanditiae fpl.

flatulence n īnflātiō f.

flatulent adj īnflātus.

flaunt vt iactāre ♦ vi iactāre, glōriārī.

flaunting n iactātiō f ♦ adj glōriōsus.

flauntingly adv glōriōsē.

flautist n tībīcen m.

flavour n gustātus m, sapor m ♦ vt imbuere, condīre.

flavouring n condītiō f.

flavourless adj īnsulsus.

flaw n vitium nt.

flawless adj ēmendātus.

flax n līnum nt.

flaxen adj flāvus.

flay vt dēglūbere.

flea n pūlex m.

fleck n macula f ♦ vt variāre.

fledged adj pennātus.

flee vi fugere, effugere; (for refuge) cōnfugere.

fleece n vellus nt ♦ vt tondēre; (_fig_) spoliāre.
fleecy adj lāneus.
fleet n classis f ♦ adj vēlōx, celer.
fleeting adj fugāx.
fleetness n vēlōcitās f, celeritās f.
flesh n cārō f; (_fig_) corpus nt; **in the ~** vīvus; **one's own ~ and blood** cōnsanguineus; **put on ~** pinguēscere.
fleshiness n corpus nt.
fleshliness n libīdō f.
fleshly adj libīdinōsus.
fleshy adj pinguis.
flexibility n lentitia f.
flexible adj flexibilis, lentus.
flicker vi coruscāre.
flickering adj tremulus.
flight n (_flying_) volātus m; (_fleeing_) fuga f; (_steps_) scāla f; **put to ~** fugāre, in fugam conicere; **take to ~** sē in fugam dare, terga vertere.
flightiness n mōbilitās f.
flighty adj mōbilis, incōnstāns.
flimsy adj tenuis, pertenuis.
flinch vi recēdere.
fling vt iacere, conicere; (_missile_) intorquēre; **~ away** abicere, prōicere; **~ open** patefacere; **~ in one's teeth** obicere (_dat_); **~ to the ground** prōsternere ♦ vi sē incitāre ♦ n iactus m.
flint n silex m.
flinty adj siliceus.
flippancy n lascīvia f.
flippant adj lascīvus, protervus.
flippantly adv petulanter.
flirt vi lūdere, lascīvīre ♦ n lascīvus m, lascīva f.
flit vi volitāre.
flitch n succīdia f.
float vi innāre, fluitāre; (_in air_) volitāre; **~ down** dēfluere.
flock n grex m; (_wool_) floccus m ♦ vi concurrere, congregārī, cōnfluere; **~ in** adfluere.
flog vt verberāre, virgīs caedere.
flogging n verbera ntpl.
flood n (_deluge_) ēluviō f; (_river_) torrēns m; (_tide_) accessus m; (_fig_) flūmen nt ♦ vt inundāre.
floodgate n cataracta f.
floor n solum nt; (_paved_) pavīmentum nt; (_storey_) tabulātum nt; (_threshing_) ārea f ♦ vt contabulāre; **be ~ed** (_in argument_) iacēre.
flora n herbae fpl.
floral adj flōreus.
florid adj flōridus.
flotilla n classicula f.
flounce vi sē concitāre ♦ n īnstita f.
flounder vi volutāre; (_in speech_) haesitāre.
flour n fārīna f.
flourish vi flōrēre, vigēre ♦ vt vibrāre, iactāre ♦ n (_RHET_) calamistrī mpl; (_music_) clangor m.
flout vt aspernārī, inlūdere (_dat_).
flow vi fluere, mānāre; (_tide_) accēdere; **~ back** recēdere; **~ between** interfluere; **~ down**

dēfluere; **~ into** īnfluere in (_acc_); **~ out** prōfluere, ēmānāre; **~ past** praeterfluere; **~ through** permānāre; **~ together** cōnfluere; **~ towards** adfluere ♦ n flūmen nt, cursus m; (_tide_) accessus m; (_words_) flūmen nt.
flower n flōs m, flōsculus m ♦ vi flōrēre, flōrēscere.
floweret n flōsculus m.
flowery adj flōridus.
flowing adj prōfluēns; **~ with** abundāns (_abl_).
flowingly adv prōfluenter.
flown adj īnflātus.
fluctuate vi aestuāre, fluctuāre.
fluctuating adj incōnstāns, incertus.
fluctuation n aestus m, dubitātiō f.
fluency n fācundia f, verbōrum cōpia f.
fluent adj disertus, prōfluēns.
fluently adv disertē, prōfluenter.
fluid adj liquidus ♦ n liquor m.
fluidity n liquor m.
fluke n (_anchor_) dēns m; (_luck_) fortuītum nt.
flurry n trepidātiō f ♦ vt sollicitāre, turbāre.
flush n rubor m; **in the first ~ of victory** victōriā ēlātus ♦ vi ērubēscere ♦ adj (_full_) abundāns; (_level_) aequus.
fluster n trepidātiō f ♦ vt turbāre, sollicitāre.
flute n tībia f; **play the ~** tībiā canere.
fluted adj striātus.
flutter n tremor m; (_fig_) trepidātiō f ♦ vi (_heart_) palpitāre; (_mind_) trepidāre; (_bird_) volitāre.
fluvial adj fluviātilis.
flux n fluxus m; **be in a state of ~** fluere.
fly n musca f ♦ vi volāre; (_flee_) fugere; **~ apart** dissilīre; **~ at** involāre in (_acc_); **~ away** āvolāre; **~ from** fugere; **~ in the face of** obviam īre (_dat_); **~ out** ēvolāre; **~ to** advolāre ad (_acc_); **~ up** ēvolāre, subvolāre; **let ~ at** immittere in (_acc_).
flying adj volucer, volātilis; (_time_) fugāx.
foal n equuleus m, equulus m ♦ vt parere.
foam n spūma f ♦ vi spūmāre; (_with rage_) saevīre.
foaming adj spūmeus.
focus vt (_mind_) intendere.
fodder n pābulum nt.
foe n hostis m; (_private_) inimīcus m.
fog n cālīgō f, nebula f.
foggy adj cālīginōsus, nebulōsus.
foible n vitium nt.
foil n (_metal_) lāmina f; (_sword_) rudis f ♦ vt ēlūdere, ad inritum redigere.
foist vt inculcāre, interpōnere.
fold n sinus m; (_sheep_) ovīle nt ♦ vt plicāre, complicāre; (_hands_) comprimere; (_sheep_) inclūdere; **~ back** replicāre; **~ over** plicāre; **~ together** complicāre; **~ up** in involvere in (_abl_).
folding doors npl valvae fpl.
foliage n frondēs fpl.
folk n hominēs mpl ♦ adj patrius.
follow vt sequī; (_calling_) facere; (_candidate_) adsectārī; (_enemy_) īnsequī; (_example_) imitārī; (_instructions_) pārēre (_dat_);

(*predecessor*) succēdere (*dat*); (*road*)
pergere; (*speaker*) intellegere; ~ **closely**
īnsequī; ~ **hard on the heels of** īnsequī,
īnsistere (*dat*), īnstāre (*dat*); ~ **out** exsequī; ~
to the grave exsequī; ~ **up** subsequī,
īnsistere (*dat*) ♦ *vi* (*time*) īnsequī; (*inference*)
sequī; **as ~s** ita, in hunc modum.

follower *n* comes *m*; (*of candidate*) adsectātor
m; (*of model*) imitātor *m*; (*of teacher*) audītor
m.

following *adj* tālis; īnsequēns, proximus,
posterus; **on the ~ day** postrīdiē, postero diē,
proximo diē ♦ *n* adsectātōrēs *mpl*.

folly *n* stultitia *f*, dēmentia *f*, īnsipientia *f*.

foment *vt* fovēre; (*fig*) augēre.

fond *adj* amāns, studiōsus; ineptus; **be ~ of**
amāre.

fondle *vt* fovēre, mulcēre.

fondly *adv* amanter; ineptē.

food *n* cibus *m*; (*fig*) pābulum *nt*.

fool *n* stultus *m*, ineptus *m*; (*jester*) scurra *m*;
make a ~ of ludibriō habēre; **play the ~**
dēsipere ♦ *vt* dēcipere, lūdere; ~ **away**
disperdere ♦ *vi* dēsipere.

foolery *n* ineptiae *fpl*, nūgae *fpl*.

foolhardy *adj* temerārius.

foolish *adj* stultus, ineptus, īnsipiēns.

foolishly *adv* stultē, ineptē.

foolishness *n* stultitia *f*, īnsipientia *f*.

foot *n* pēs *m*; (*MIL*) peditātus *m*; **a ~ long** pedālis;
on ~ pedes; **set ~ on** īnsistere (*dat*); **set on ~**
īnstituere; **the ~ of** īmus ♦ *vt* (*bill*) solvere.

football *n* follis *m*.

footing *n* locus *m*, status *m*; **keep one's ~**
īnsistere; **on an equal ~** ex aequō.

footman *n* pedisequus *m*.

footpad *n* grassātor *m*.

footpath *n* sēmita *f*, trāmes *m*.

footprint *n* vestīgium *nt*.

foot soldier *n* pedes *m*.

footstep *n* vestīgium *nt*; **follow in the ~s of**
vestīgiīs ingredī (*gen*).

foppish *adj* dēlicātus.

for *prep* (*advantage*) *dat*; (*duration*) *acc*; (*after
noun*) *gen*; (*price*) *abl*; (*behalf*) prō (*abl*); (*cause*)
propter (*acc*), causā (*gen*); (*after neg*) prae
(*abl*); (*feelings*) erga (*acc*); (*lieu*) prō (*abl*);
(*purpose*) ad, in (*acc*); (*time fixed*) in (*acc*) ♦
conj namque; nam (*1st word*), enim (*2nd
word*); (*with pron*) quippe quī; ~ **a long time**
diū; ~ **some time** aliquamdiū.

forage *n* pābulum *nt* ♦ *vi* pābulārī, frūmentārī.

forager *n* pābulātor *m*, frūmentātor *m*.

foraging *n* pābulātiō *f*, frūmentātiō *f*.

forasmuch as *conj* quōniam.

foray *n* incursiō *f*.

forbear *vi* parcere (*dat*), supersedēre (*infin*).

forbearance *n* venia *f*, indulgentia *f*.

forbears *n* māiōrēs *mpl*.

forbid *vt* vetāre (+ *acc* and *infin*), interdīcere
(*dat and quominus and subj*); **Heaven ~!** dī
meliōra!

forbidding *adj* tristis.

force *n* vīs *f*; (*band of men*) manus *m*; **by ~ of
arms** vī et armis ♦ *vt* cōgere, impellere;
(*way*) rumpere, mōlīrī; (*growth*) festīnāre; ~
an engagement hostes proeliārī cogere; ~
down dētrūdere; ~ **out** extrūdere, expellere,
exturbāre; ~ **upon** inculcāre; ~ **a way in**
intrōrumpere, inrumpere.

forced *adj* (*march*) māgnus; (*style*) quaesītus; ~
march māgnum iter.

forceful *adj* validus.

forceps *n* forceps *m/f*.

forces *npl* (*MIL*) cōpiae *fpl*.

forcible *adj* validus; (*fig*) gravis.

forcibly *adv* vī, violenter; (*fig*) graviter.

ford *n* vadum *nt* ♦ *vt* vadō trānsīre.

fore *adj* prior; **to the ~** praestō ♦ *adv*: ~ **and aft**
in longitūdinem.

forearm *n* bracchium *nt* ♦ *vt*: **be ~ed**
praecavēre.

forebode *vt* ōminārī, portendere; prasentīre.

foreboding *n* praesēnsiō *f*; ōmen *nt*.

forecast *n* praedictiō *f* ♦ *vt* praedīcere,
prōvidēre.

forecourt *n* vestibulum *nt*.

forefathers *n* māiōrēs *mpl*.

forefinger *n* index *m*.

foreground *n* ēminentia *ntpl*.

forehead *n* frōns *f*.

foreign *adj* peregrīnus, externus; (*goods*)
adventīcius; ~ **to** aliēnus ab; ~ **ways**
peregrīnitās *f*.

foreigner *n* peregrīnus *m*, advena *m*.

foreknow *vt* praenōscere.

foreknowledge *n* prōvidentia *f*.

foreland *n* prōmunturium *nt*.

foremost *adj* prīmus, prīnceps.

forenoon *n* antemerīdiānum tempus *nt*.

forensic *adj* forēnsis.

forerunner *n* praenūntius *m*.

foresee *vt* praevidēre.

foreshadow *vt* praemonēre.

foresight *n* prōvidentia *f*.

forest *n* silva *f*.

forestall *vt* occupāre, antevenīre.

forester *n* silvicola *m*.

foretaste *vt* praegustāre.

foretell *vt* praedīcere, vāticinārī.

forethought *n* prōvidentia *f*.

forewarn *vt* praemonēre.

foreword *n* praefātiō *f*.

forfeit *n* multa *f*, damnum *nt* ♦ *vt* āmittere,
perdere, multārī (*abl*); (*bail*) dēserere.

forfeiture *n* damnum *nt*.

forgather *vi* congregārī, convenīre.

forge *n* fornāx *f* ♦ *vt* fabricārī, excūdere;
(*document*) subicere; (*will*) suppōnere;
(*signature*) imitārī; (*money*) adulterīnōs
nummōs percutere.

forged *adj* falsus, adulterīnus, commentīcius.

forger *n* (*of will*) subiector *m*.

forgery *n* falsum *nt*, commentum *nt*.

forget *vt* oblīvīscī (*gen*); (*thing learnt*)
dēdiscere; **be forgotten** memoriā cadere, ex

animō effluere.
forgetful *adj* immemor; (*by habit*) oblīviōsus.
forgetfulness *n* oblīviō *f*.
forgive *vt* ignōscere (*dat*), veniam dare (*dat*).
forgiveness *n* venia *f*.
forgo *vt* dīmittere, renūntiāre; (*rights*) dēcēdere dē iūre.
fork *n* furca *f*; (*small*) furcula *f*; (*road*) trivium *nt*.
forlorn *adj* inops, dēstitūtus, exspēs.
form *n* fōrma *f*, figūra *f*; (*of procedure*) fōrmula *f*; (*condition*) vigor *m*; (*etiquette*) mōs *m*; (*seat*) scamnum *nt*; (*school*) schola *f*; (*hare's*) latibulum *nt* ♦ *vt* fōrmāre, fingere, efficere; (*MIL*) īnstruere; (*plan*) inīre, capere.
formal *adj* iūstus; (*rite*) sollemnis.
formality *n* iūsta *ntpl*, rītus *m*; **as a ~** dicis causā; **with due ~** rītē.
formally *adv* rītē.
formation *n* fōrma *f*, figūra *f*; (*process*) cōnfōrmātiō *f*; **in ~** (*MIL*) īnstructus.
former *adj* prior, prīstinus, vetus; **the ~** ille.
formerly *adv* anteā, ōlim, quondam.
formidable *adj* formīdolōsus.
formidably *adv* formīdolōsē.
formula *n* fōrmula *f*; (*dictated*) praefātiō *f*.
formulate *vt* compōnere.
forsake *vt* dērelinquere, dēstituere, dēserere.
forswear *vt* pēierāre, abiūrāre.
fort *n* castellum *nt*.
forth *adv* forās; (*time*) posthāc.
forthwith *adv* extemplō, statim, prōtinus.
fortieth *adj* quadragēsimus.
fortification *n* (*process*) mūnītiō *f*; (*place*) mūnīmentum *nt*, arx *f*.
fortify *vt* mūnīre, ēmūnīre, commūnīre; (*fig*) cōnfirmāre.
fortitude *n* fortitūdō *f*.
fortnight *n* quīndecim diēs *mpl*.
fortnightly *adv* quīntō decimō quōque diē.
fortress *n* arx *f*, castellum *nt*.
fortuitous *adj* fortuītus.
fortuitously *adv* fortuītō, cāsū.
fortunate *adj* fēlīx, fortūnātus.
fortunately *adv* fēlīciter, bene.
fortune *n* fortūna *f*, fors *f*; (*wealth*) rēs *f*, dīvitiae *fpl*; **good ~** fēlīcitās *f*, secundae rēs *fpl*; **bad ~** adversae rēs *fpl*; **make one's ~** rem facere, rem quaerere; **tell ~s** hariolārī.
fortune-hunter *n* captātor *m*.
fortune-teller *n* hariolus *m*, sāga *f*.
forty *num* quadrāgintā; **~ each** quadrāgēnī; **~ times** quadrāgiēns.
forum *n* forum *nt*.
forward *adj* (*person*) protervus, audāx; (*fruit*) praecox ♦ *adv* porrō, ante; **bring ~** prōferre; **come ~** prōdīre ♦ *vt* (*letter*) perferre; (*cause*) adiuvāre, favēre (*dat*).
forwardness *n* audācia *f*, alacritās *f*.
forwards *adv* porrō, prōrsus; **backwards and ~** rursum prōrsum, hūc illūc.
fosse *n* fossa *f*.
foster *vt* alere, nūtrīre; (*fig*) fovēre.

foster child *n* alumnus *m*, alumna *f*.
foster father *n* altor *m*, ēducātor *m*.
foster mother *n* altrīx *f*, nūtrīx *f*.
foul *adj* foedus; (*speech*) inquinātus; **fall ~ of** inruere in (*acc*).
foully *adv* foedē, inquinātē.
foul-mouthed *adj* maledicus.
foulness *n* foedītās *f*.
found *vt* condere, fundāre, īnstituere; (*metal*) fundere.
foundation *n* fundāmenta *ntpl*.
founder *n* fundātor *m*, conditor *m* ♦ *vi* submergī, naufragium facere.
foundling *n* expositīcia *f*.
fount *n* fōns *m*.
fountain *n* fōns *m*.
fountainhead *n* fōns *m*, orīgō *f*.
four *num* quattuor (*indecl*); **~ each** quaternī; **~ times** quater; **~ days** quadriduum *nt*; **~ years** quadriennium *nt*.
fourfold *adj* quadruplex ♦ *adv* quadrifāriam.
four hundred *num* quadringentī; **~ each** quadringēnī; **~ times** quadringentiēns.
four hundredth *adj* quadringentēsimus.
fourteen *num* quattuordecim; **~ each** quaternī dēnī; **~ times** quater deciēns.
fourteenth *adj* quartus decimus.
fourth *adj* quartus ♦ *n* quadrāns *m*; **three ~s** dōdrāns *m*, trēs partēs *fpl*.
fowl *n* avis *f*; gallīna *f*.
fowler *n* auceps *m*.
fox *n* vulpēs *f*; **~'s** vulpīnus.
foxy *adj* astūtus, vafer.
fracas *n* rīxa *f*.
fraction *n* pars *f*.
fractious *adj* difficilis.
fracture *n* frāctum os *nt* ♦ *vt* frangere.
fragile *adj* fragilis.
fragility *n* fragilitās *f*.
fragment *n* fragmentum *nt*.
fragrance *n* odor *m*.
fragrant *adj* suāvis.
fragrantly *adv* suāviter.
frail *adj* fragilis, īnfirmus, dēbilis.
frailty *n* dēbilitās *f*; (*moral*) error *m*.
frame *vt* fabricārī, fingere, effingere; (*document*) compōnere ♦ *n* fōrma *f*; (*of mind*) adfectiō *f*, habitus *m*; **in a ~ of mind** animātus.
framer *n* fabricātor *m*, opifex *m*; (*of law*) lātor *m*.
framework *n* compāgēs *f*.
franchise *n* suffrāgium *nt*, cīvitās *f*.
frank *adj* ingenuus, apertus; (*speech*) līber.
frankincense *n* tūs *nt*.
frankly *adv* ingenuē, apertē; līberē.
frankness *n* ingenuitās *f*; (*speech*) lībertās *f*.
frantic *adj* furēns, furiōsus, dēlīrus.
frantically *adv* furenter.
fraternal *adj* frāternus.
fraternally *adv* frāternē.
fraternity *n* frāternitās *f*; (*society*) sodālitās *f*; (*guild*) collēgium *nt*.
fraternize *vi* amīcitiam iungere.
fratricide *n* frātricīda *m*; (*act*) frātris

parricīdium nt.
fraud n fraus f, dolus m, falsum nt; (criminal) dolus malus m.
fraudulence n fraus f.
fraudulent adj fraudulentus, dolōsus.
fraudulently adv dolōsē, dolō malō.
fraught adj plēnus.
fray n pugna f, rīxa f ♦ vt terere.
freak n mōnstrum nt; (caprice) libīdō f.
freckle n lentīgō f.
freckly adj lentīginōsus.
free adj līber; (disengaged) vacuus; (generous) līberālis; (from cost) grātuītus; (from duty) immūnis; (from encumbrance) expedītus; **be ~ from** vacāre (abl); **I am still ~ to** integrum est mihī (infin); **set ~** absolvere, līberāre; (slave) manū mittere ♦ adv grātīs, grātuītō ♦ vt līberāre, expedīre, exsolvere.
freebooter n praedō m.
freeborn adj ingenuus.
freedman n lībertus m.
freedom n lībertās f; (from duty) immūnitās f.
freehold n praedium līberum nt ♦ adj immūnis.
freely adv līberē; (lavishly) cōpiōsē, largē; (frankly) apertē; (voluntarily) ultrō, suā sponte.
freeman n cīvis m.
free will n voluntās f; **of one's own ~** suā sponte.
freeze vt gelāre, glaciāre ♦ vi concrēscere.
freezing adj gelidus; **it is ~** gelat.
freight n vectūra f; (cargo) onus nt ♦ vt onerāre.
freighter n nāvis onerāria f.
frenzied adj furēns, furiōsus, fānāticus.
frenzy n furor m, īnsānia f.
frequency n adsiduitās f.
frequent adj frequēns, crēber ♦ vt frequentāre, commeāre in (acc).
frequently adv saepe, saepenumerō, frequenter.
fresh adj (new) recēns, novus; (vigorous) integer; (water) dulcis; (wind) ācer.
freshen vt renovāre ♦ vi (wind) incrēbrēscere.
freshly adv recenter.
freshman n tīrō m.
freshness n novitās f, viriditās f.
fret vi maerēre, angī ♦ vt sollicitāre.
fretful adj mōrōsus, querulus.
fretfulness n mōrōsitās f.
fretted adj laqueātus.
friable adj puter.
friction n trītus m.
friend n amīcus m, familiāris m/f; hospes m, sodālis m; **make ~s with** sē cōnferre ad amīcitiam (gen).
friendless adj sine amīcīs.
friendliness n cōmitās f, officium nt.
friendly adj cōmis, facilis, benīgnus; **on ~ terms** familiāriter.
friendship n amīcitia f, familiāritās f.

frigate n liburna f.
fright n horror m, pavor m, terror m; **take ~** extimēscere, expavēscere.
frighten vt terrēre, exterrēre, perterrēre; **~ away** absterrēre; **~ off** dēterrēre; **~ the life out of** exanimāre.
frightful adj horribilis, immānis; (look) taeter.
frightfully adv foedē.
frigid adj frīgidus.
frigidity n frīgus nt.
frill n fimbriae fpl; (RHET) calamistrī mpl.
fringe n fimbriae fpl.
frisk vi lascīvīre, exsultāre.
frisky adj lascīvus.
fritter vt: **~ away** dissipāre; (time) extrahere.
frivolity n levitās f.
frivolous adj levis, inānis.
frivolously adv ināniter.
fro adv: **to and ~** hūc illūc.
frock n stola f.
frog n rāna f.
frolic n lūdus m ♦ vi lūdere, lascīvīre.
frolicsome adj lascīvus, hilaris.
from prep ab (abl), ā (before consonants); (out) ē, ex (abl); (cause) propter (acc); (prevention) quōminus, quīn; **~ all directions** undique.
front n frōns f; **in ~** ā fronte, adversus; **in ~ of** prō (+ abl).
frontier n līmes m, cōnfīnia ntpl; **~s** fīnēs mpl.
front line n prima aciēs.
frost n gelū nt.
frostbitten adj: **be ~** vī frīgoris ambūrī.
frosty adj gelidus, glaciālis.
froth n spūma f ♦ vi spūmās agere.
frothy adj spūmeus.
froward adj contumāx.
frown n frontis contractiō f ♦ vi frontem contrahere.
frozen adj glaciālis.
fructify vt fēcundāre.
frugal adj parcus, frūgī.
frugality n frūgālitās f, parsimōnia f.
frugally adv parcē, frūgāliter.
fruit n fructus m; (tree) māla ntpl; (berry) bāca f; (fig) fructus m; **~s** pl (of earth) frūgēs fpl.
fruiterer n pōmārius m.
fruitful adj fēcundus, fructuōsus.
fruitfully adv ferāciter.
fruitfulness n fēcunditās f, ūbertās f.
fruition n fructus m.
fruitless adj inūtilis, vānus.
fruitlessly adv nēquīquam, frustrā.
fruit tree n pōmum nt.
frustrate vt frustrārī, ad inritum redigere.
frustration n frustrātiō f.
fry vt frīgere.
frying pan n sartāgō f; **out of the ~ into the fire** incidit in Scyllam quī vult vītāre Charybdim.
fuel n fōmes m.
fugitive adj fugitīvus ♦ n fugitīvus m, trānsfuga m; (from abroad) extorris m.
fulfil vt (duty) explēre, implēre; (promise)

praestāre; (*order*) exsequī, perficere.
fulfilment *n* absolūtiō *f*.
full *adj* plēnus (+ *abl*), refertus, explētus;
(*entire*) integer; (*amount*) solidus; (*brother*)
germānus; (*measure*) iūstus; (*meeting*)
frequēns; (*style*) cōpiōsus; **at ~ length**
porrēctus; **at ~ speed** citātō gradū, citātō
equō.
fuller *n* fullō *m*.
full-grown *adj* adultus.
full moon *n* lūna plēna.
fullness *n* (*style*) cōpia *f*; (*time*) mātūritās *f*.
fully *adv* plēnē, penitus, funditus.
fulminate *vi* intonāre.
fulsome *adj* fastīdiōsus, pūtidus.
fumble *vi* haesitāre.
fume *n* fūmus *m*, hālitus *m* ♦ *vi* stomachārī.
fumigate *vt* suffīre.
fun *n* iocus *m*, lūdus *m*; **for ~** animī causā; **make
~ of** inlūdere, dēlūdere, lūdibriō habēre.
function *n* officium *nt*, mūnus *nt*.
fund *n* cōpia *f*.
fundamental *adj* prīmus ♦ *n* prīncipium *nt*,
elementum *nt*.
funds *npl* sors *f*, pecūniae *fpl*.
funeral *n* fūnus *nt*, exsequiae *fpl* ♦ *adj* fūnebris.
funeral pile *n* rogus *m*.
funeral pyre *n* rogus *m*.
funeral rites *npl* exsequiae *fpl*, Īnferiae *fpl*.
funereal *adj* fūnebria, lūgubris.
funnel *n* īnfundibulum *nt*.
funny *adj* ioculāris, rīdiculus.
fur *n* pellis *m*.
furbelow *n* Īnstita *f*.
furbish *vt* expolīre; **~ up** interpolāre.
Furies *npl* Furiae *fpl*.
furious *adj* saevus, vehemēns, perīrātus.
furiously *adv* furenter, saevē, vehementer.
furl *vt* (*sail*) legere.
furlong *n* stadium *nt*.
furlough *n* commeātus *m*.
furnace *n* fornāx *f*.
furnish *vt* praebēre, suppeditāre; (*equip*)
īnstruere, ōrnāre.
furniture *n* supellex *f*.
furrow *n* sulcus *m* ♦ *vt* sulcāre.
furry *adj* villōsus.
further *adj* ulterior ♦ *adv* ultrā, porrō; amplius
♦ *vt* adiuvāre, cōnsulere (*dat*).
furtherance *n* prōgressus *m*; (*means*)
īnstrūmentum *nt*.
furthermore *adv* praetereā, porrō.
furthest *adj* ultimus ♦ *adv* longissimē.
furtive *adj* fūrtīvus, clandestīnus.
furtively *adv* clam, fūrtim.
fury *n* furor *m*, saevitia *f*; īra *f*.
fuse *vt* fundere; (*together*) coniungere.
fusion *n* coniūnctiō *f*.
fuss *n* importūnitās *f*, querimōnia *f* ♦ *vi*
conquerī, sollicitārī.
fussy *adj* importūnus, incommodus.
fusty *adj* mūcidus.
futile *adj* inānis, inūtilis, futtilis.

futility *n* vānitās *f*, futtilitās *f*.
future *adj* futūrus, posterus ♦ *n* posterum *nt*,
reliquum *nt*; **in ~** posthāc; **for the ~** in
posterum.
futurity *n* posterum tempus *nt*, posteritās *f*.

G, g

gabble *vi* garrīre.
gable *n* fastīgium *nt*.
gadfly *n* tabānus *m*.
gag *vt* ōs praeligāre (*dat*), ōs obvolvere (*dat*).
gage *n* pignus *nt*.
gaiety *n* laetitia *f*, hilaritās *f*, festīvitās *f*.
gaily *adv* hilare, festīve.
gain *n* lucrum *nt*, quaestus *m* ♦ *vt* comparāre;
adipīscī; (*profit*) lucrārī; (*thing*) parāre,
cōnsequī, capere; (*case*) vincere; (*place*)
pervenīre ad; (*possession of*) potīrī (*gen*);
(*victory*) reportāre; **~ over** conciliāre; **~
ground** incrēbrēscere; **~ possession of**
potior (+ *abl*); **~ the upper hand** rem obtinēre.
gainful *adj* quaestuōsus.
gainsay *vt* contrādīcere (*dat*).
gait *n* incessus *m*, ingressiō *f*.
gaiters *n* ocreae *fpl*.
gala *n* diēs festus *m*.
galaxy *n* circulus lacteus *m*.
gale *n* ventus *m*.
gall *n* fel *nt*, bīlis *m* ♦ *vt* ūrere.
gallant *adj* fortis, audāx; (*courteous*)
officiōsus.
gallantly *adv* fortiter; officiōsē.
gallantry *n* virtūs *f*; urbānitās *f*.
gall bladder *n* fel *nt*.
gallery *n* porticus *f*.
galley *n* nāvis āctuāria *f*; (*cook's*) culīna *f*.
galling *adj* amārus, mordāx.
gallon *n* congius *m*.
gallop *n* cursus *m*; **at the ~** citātō equō,
admissō equō ♦ *vi* admissō equō currere.
gallows *n* Īnfēlīx arbor *m*, furca *f*.
gallows bird *n* furcifer *m*.
galore *adv* adfatim.
gamble *n* ālea *f* ♦ *vi* āleā lūdere.
gambler *n* āleātor *m*.
gambling *n* ālea *f*.
gambol *n* lūsus *m* ♦ *vi* lūdere, lascīvīre,
exsultāre.
game *n* lūdus *m*; (*with dice*) ālea *f*; (*hunt*)
praeda *f*; **play the ~** rēctē facere; **public ~s**
lūdī *mpl*; **Olympic ~s** Olympia *npl*; **the ~'s up**
āctum est ♦ *adj* animōsus.
gamester *n* āleātor *m*.
gammon *n* perna *f*.
gander *n* ānser *m*.

gang n grex m, caterva f.
gangster n grassātor m.
gangway n forus m.
gaol n carcer m.
gaoler n custōs m.
gap n hiātus m, lacūna f.
gape vi hiāre, inhiāre; (opening) dēhiscere.
garb n habitus m, amictus m ♦ vt amicīre.
garbage n quisquiliae fpl.
garden n hortus m; (public) hortī mpl.
gardener n hortulānus m; (ornamental)
  topiārius m.
gardening n hortī cultūra f; (ornamental)
  topiāria f.
gargle vi gargarissāre.
garish adj speciōsus, fūcātus.
garland n sertum nt, corōna f ♦ vt corōnāre.
garlic n ālium nt.
garment n vestis f, vestīmentum nt.
garnish vt ōrnāre, decorāre.
garret n cēnāculum nt.
garrison n praesidium nt, dēfēnsōrēs mpl ♦ vt
  praesidiō mūnīre, praesidium collocāre in
  (abl).
garrotte vt laqueō gulam frangere (dat).
garrulity n garrulitās f.
garrulous adj garrulus, loquāx.
gas n vapor m.
gash n vulnus nt ♦ vt caedere, lacerāre.
gasp n anhēlitus m, singultus m ♦ vi anhēlāre.
gastronomy n gula f.
gate n porta f.
gather vt colligere, cōgere; (fruit) legere;
  (inference) colligere, conicere ♦ vi
  congregārī.
gathering n conventus m, coetus m.
gauche adj inconcinnus, illepidus.
gaudily adv splendidē, speciōsē.
gaudy adj speciōsus, fūcātus, lautus.
gauge n modulus m ♦ vt mētīrī.
Gaul n Gallia f; (person) Gallus m.
gaunt adj macer.
gauntlet n manica f.
gauze n Coa ntpl.
gay adj hilaris, festīvus, laetus.
gaze vi intuērī; ~ **at** intuērī, adspectāre,
  contemplārī.
gazelle n oryx m.
gazette n ācta diūrna ntpl, ācta pūblica ntpl.
gear n īnstrūmenta ntpl; (ship's) armāmenta
  ntpl.
gelding n cantērius m.
gelid adj gelidus.
gem n gemma f.
gender n genus nt.
genealogical adj dē stirpe.
genealogical table n stemma nt.
genealogist n geneālogus m.
genealogy n geneālogia f.
general adj generālis, ūniversus; (usual)
  vulgāris, commūnis; **in** ~ omnīnō ♦ n dux m,
  imperātor m; **~'s tent** praetōrium nt.
generalissimo n imperātor m.

generality n vulgus nt, plērīque mpl.
generalize vi ūnīversē loquī.
generally adv ferē, plērumque; (discuss)
  īnfīnītē.
generalship n ductus m.
generate vt gignere, generāre.
generation n aetās f, saeculum nt.
generic adj generālis.
generically adv genere.
generosity n līberālitās f, largitās f.
generous adj līberālis, largus, benīgnus.
generously adv līberāliter, largē, benīgnē.
genesis n orīgō f, prīncipium nt.
genial adj cōmis, hilaris.
geniality n cōmitās f, hilaritās f.
genially adv cōmiter, hilare.
genitive n genitīvus m.
genius n (deity) genius m; (talent) ingenium nt,
  indolēs f; **of** ~ ingeniōsus.
genre n genus nt.
genteel adj urbānus, polītus.
gentility n urbānitās f, ēlegantia f.
gentle adj (birth) ingenuus; (manner) hūmānus,
  indulgēns, mītis; (slope) lēnis, mollis; (thing)
  placidus, lēnis.
gentleman n vir m, ingenuus m, vir honestus
  m.
gentlemanly adj ingenuus, līberālis,
  honestus.
gentleness n hūmānitās f, indulgentia f,
  lēnitās f.
gentlewoman n ingenua f, mulier honesta f.
gently adv lēniter, molliter, placidē.
gentry n ingenuī mpl, optimātēs mpl;
  (contempt) hominēs mpl.
genuine adj vērus, germānus, sincērus.
genuinely adv germānē, sincērē.
genuineness n fidēs f.
geographical adj geōgraphicus; ~ **position**
  situs m.
geography n geōgraphia f.
geometrical adj geōmetricus.
geometry n geōmetria f.
Georgics n Geōrgica ntpl.
germ n germen nt, sēmen nt.
germane adj adfīnis.
germinate vi gemmāre.
gesticulate vi sē iactāre, gestū ūtī.
gesticulation n gestus m.
gesture n gestus m, mōtus m.
get vt adipīscī, nancīscī, parāre; (malady)
  contrahere; (request) impetrāre; (return)
  capere; (reward) ferre; ~ **sth done** cūrāre
  (with gerundive); ~ **sb to do** persuādēre (dat),
  addūcere; ~ **by heart** ēdiscere; ~ **in** repōnere;
  ~ **the better of** superāre; **go and** ~ arcessere
  ♦ vi fierī; ~ **about** (rumour) palam fierī,
  percrēbrēscere; ~ **away** effugere; ~ **at**
  (intent) spectāre; ~ **behind** cessāre; ~ **off**
  absolvī; ~ **on** prōficere; ~ **out** effugere,
  ēvādere; ~ **out of hand** lascīvīre; ~ **out of the**
  way dē viā dēcēdere; ~ **ready** parāre; ~ **rid of**
  abicere, tollere; ~ **to** pervenīre ad;

~ **to know** cognōscere; ~ **together** congregārī; ~ **up** exsurgere.
get-up n ōrnātus m.
ghastliness n pallor m.
ghastly adj pallidus; (sight) taeter.
ghost n larva f, īdōlon nt; ~**s** pl mānēs mpl; **give up the** ~ animam agere, efflāre.
giant n Gigas m.
gibberish n barbaricus sermō m.
gibbet n furca f.
gibe vi inrīdēre.
giddiness n vertīgō f.
giddy adj vertīginōsus; (fig) levis.
gift n dōnum nt; (small) mūnusculum nt; ~**s** pl (mind) ingenium nt.
gifted adj ingeniōsus.
gig n cisium nt.
gigantic adj ingēns, immānis.
gild vt inaurāre.
gill n (measure) quartārius m; (fish) branchia f.
gilt adj aurātus.
gimlet n terebra f.
gin n pedica f, laqueus m.
ginger n zingiberī nt.
gingerly adv pedetemptim.
giraffe n camēlopardālis f.
gird vt circumdāre; ~ **on** accingere; ~ **oneself** cingī; ~ **up** succingere.
girder n tignum nt.
girdle n cingulus m ♦ vt cingere.
girl n puella f, virgō f.
girlhood n aetās puellāris f.
girlish adj puellāris.
girth n ambitus m, amplitūdō f.
gist n firmāmentum nt.
give vt dare, dōnāre, tribuere; (thing due) reddere; ~ **away** largīrī; (bride) in matrimōnium collocāre; (secret) prōdere; ~ **back** reddere, restituere; ~ **birth (to)** pārēre; ~ **in** (name) profiterī; ~ **off** ēmittere; ~ **out** (orders) ēdere; (sound) ēmittere; ~ **thanks** gratias agere; ~ **up** dēdere, trādere; (hope of) dēspērāre; (rights) dēcēdere dē, renūntiāre; ~ **way** cēdere; (MIL) inclīnāre ♦ vi labāre; ~ **in** sē victum fatērī; (MIL) manūs dare; ~ **out** (fail) dēficere; (pretend) ferre; ~ **up** dēsistere; ~ **way** cēdere.
giver n dator m.
glacial adj glaciālis.
glad adj laetus, alacer, hilaris; **be** ~ gaudēre.
gladden vt exhilarāre, oblectāre.
glade n saltus m.
gladiator n gladiātor m.
gladiatorial adj gladiātōrius; **present a** ~ **show** gladiātōrēs dare.
gladly adv laetē, libenter.
gladness n laetitia f, alacritās f, gaudium nt.
glamorous adj venustus.
glamour n venustās f.
glance n aspectus m ♦ vi oculōs conicere; ~ **at** aspicere; (fig) attingere, perstringere; ~ **off** stringere.

glare n fulgor m ♦ vi fulgēre; ~ **at** torvīs oculīs intuērī.
glaring adj (look) torvus; (fault) manifestus; **be** ~ ante pedēs positum esse.
glass n vitrum nt; (mirror) speculum nt.
glassy adj vitreus.
glaze vt vitrō obdūcere.
gleam n fulgor m, lūx f ♦ vi fulgēre, lūcēre.
gleaming adj splendidus, nitidus.
glean vi spīcās legere.
gleaning n spīcilegium nt.
glebe n fundus m.
glee n hilaritās f, gaudium nt.
gleeful adj hilaris, festīvus, laetus.
gleefully adv hilare, laetē.
glen n vallis f.
glib adj prōfluēns, fācundus.
glibly adv prōfluenter.
glide n lāpsus m ♦ vi labī; ~ **away** ēlābī.
glimmer vi sublūcēre ♦ n: **a** ~ **of hope** spēcula f.
glimpse n aspectus m ♦ vt cōnspicārī.
glint vi renīdēre.
glisten vi fulgēre, nitēre.
glitter vi micāre.
gloaming n crepusculum nt.
gloat vi: ~ **over** inhiāre, animō haurīre, oculōs pāscere (abl).
globe n globus m, sphaera f; (inhabited) orbis terrārum m.
globular adj globōsus.
globule n globulus m, pilula f.
gloom n tenebrae fpl; tristitia f.
gloomy adj tenebricōsus; tristis, dēmissus.
glorify vt illūstrāre, extollere, laudāre.
glorious adj illūstris, praeclārus, splendidus.
gloriously adv praeclārē, splendidē.
glory n laus f, glōria f, decus nt ♦ vi glōriārī, sē iactāre.
gloss n nitor m ♦ vt: ~ **over** (fig) dissimulāre.
glossy adj nitidus.
glove n manica f.
glow n (light) lūmen nt; (heat) ārdor m; (passion) calor m ♦ vi lūcēre, ārdēre, calēre, candēre.
glowing adj candēns, ārdēns, calidus.
glue n glūten nt ♦ vt glūtināre.
glum adj tristis, maestus.
glut vt explēre, saturāre ♦ n satietās f, abundantia f.
glutton n gāneō m, helluō m.
gluttonous adj edāx, vorāx, avidus.
gluttony n gula f, edācitās f.
gnarled adj nōdōsus.
gnash vt, vi frendere; ~ **one's teeth** dentibus frendere.
gnat n culex m.
gnaw vt rōdere; ~ **away** ērōdere.
gnawing adj mordāx.
go vi īre, vādere; (depart) abīre, discēdere; (event) ēvādere; (mechanism) movērī; ~ **about** incipere, adgredī; ~ **after** īnsequī; ~ **away** abīre, discēdere; ~ **back** redīre,

regredī; **~ before** anteīre, praeīre; **~ by**
praeterīre; (*rule*) sequī, ūtī (*abl*); **~ down**
dēscendere; (*storm*) cadere; (*star*) occidere;
~ for petere; **~ forward** prōgredī; **~ in** intrāre,
ingredī; **~ in for** (*profession*) facere,
exercēre; **~ off** abīre; **~ on** pergere; (*event*)
agī; **~ out** exīre, ēgredī; (*fire*) extinguī; **~ over**
trānsīre; (*to enemy*) dēscīscere; (*preparation*)
meditārī; (*reading*) legere; (*work done*)
retractāre; **~ round** circumīre, ambīre; **~
through** percurrere; penetrāre; (*suffer*)
perferre; **~ to** adīre, petere; **~ up** ascendere;
~ to the help of subvenīre (+ *dat*); **~ to meet**
obviam īre; **~ with** comitārī; **~ without**
carēre (*abl*), sē abstinēre (*abl*) ♦ *n* vīs *f*,
ācrimōnia *f*.
goad *n* stimulus *m* ♦ *vt* irrītāre; pungere; (*fig*)
stimulāre.
go-ahead *adj* impiger.
goal *n* fīnis *m*, mēta *f*.
goat *n* caper *m*, capra *f*.
gobble *vt* dēvorāre.
go-between *n* internūntius *m*, internūntia *f*;
(*bribery*) sequester *m*.
goblet *n* pōculum *nt*, scyphus *m*.
god *n* deus *m*.
goddess *n* dea *f*.
godhead *n* dīvīnitās *f*, nūmen *nt*.
godless *adj* impius.
godlike *adj* dīvīnus.
godliness *n* pietās *f*, rēligiō *f*.
godly *adj* pius.
godsend *n* quasi caelō dēmissus.
going *n* itiō *f*; (*way*) iter *nt*; (*departure*)
profectiō *f*, discessus *m*.
goitre *n* strūma *nt*.
gold *n* aurum *nt* ♦ *adj* aureus.
golden *adj* aureus; (*hair*) flāvus.
gold leaf *n* bractea *f*.
goldmine *n* aurāria *f*.
goldsmith *n* aurārius *m*, aurifex *m*.
good *adj* bonus, probus; (*fit*) idōneus, aptus;
(*considerable*) magnus; **~ day!** salvē, salvēte!;
~ looks fōrma *f*, pulchritūdō *f*; **~ nature**
facilitās *f*, cōmitās *f* ♦ *n* bonum *nt*,
commodum *nt*; **do ~ to** prōdesse (*dat*); **make ~**
supplēre, praestāre; **seem ~** vidērī; ♦ *interj*
bene.
goodbye *interj* valē, valēte; **say ~ to** valēre
iubēre.
good-for-nothing *adj* nēquam.
good-humoured *adj* cōmis.
good-looking *adj* pulcher.
goodly *adj* pulcher; (*size*) amplus.
good nature *n* facilitās *f*, cōmitās *f*.
good-natured *adj* facilis, benīgnus,
benevolus.
goodness *n* bonitās *f*, (*character*) virtūs *f*,
probitās *f*, pietās *f*.
goods *npl* bona *ntpl*, rēs *f*; (*for sale*) merx *f*.
good-tempered *adj* mītis, lēnis.
goodwill *n* benevolentia *f*, favor *m*, grātia *f*.
goose *n* ānser *m/f*.

goose flesh *n* horror *m*.
gore *n* cruor *m* ♦ *vt* cornibus cōnfodere.
gorge *n* faucēs *fpl*, gula *f*; (GEOG) angustiae *fpl* ♦
vt: **~ oneself** sē ingurgitāre.
gorgeous *adj* lautus, splendidus.
gorgeously *adv* lautē, splendidē.
gorgeousness *n* lautitia *f*.
gormandize *vi* helluārī.
gory *adj* cruentus.
gospel *n* ēvangelium *nt*.
gossip *n* (*talk*) sermunculus *m*, rūmusculus *m*,
fāma *f*; (*person*) lingulāca *f* ♦ *vi* garrīre.
gouge *vt* ēruere.
gourd *n* cucurbita *f*.
gourmand *n* helluō *m*, gāneō *m*.
gout *n* podagra *f*, articulāris morbus *m*.
gouty *adj* arthrīticus.
govern *vt* (*subjects*) regere; (*state*)
administrāre, gubernāre; (*emotion*)
moderārī (*dat*), cohibēre.
governess *n* ēducātrīx *f*.
government *n* gubernātiō *f*, administrātiō *f*;
(*men*) magistrātūs *mpl*.
governor *n* gubernātor *m*, moderātor *m*;
(*province*) prōcōnsul *m*, prōcūrātor *m*.
gown *n* (*men*) toga *f*; (*women*) stola *f*.
grab *vt* adripere, corripere.
grace *n* grātia *f*, lepōs *m*, decor *m*; (*favour*)
grātia *f*, venia *f*; (*of gods*) pāx *f*; **be in the good
~s of** in grātiā esse apud (*acc*); **with a bad ~**
invītus ♦ *vt* decorāre, ōrnāre.
graceful *adj* decōrus, venustus, lepidus.
gracefully *adv* venustē, lepidē.
graceless *adj* illepidus, impudēns.
gracious *adj* benīgnus, prōpitius, misericors.
graciously *adv* benīgnē, līberāliter.
graciousness *n* benīgnitās *f*, līberālitās *f*.
gradation *n* gradus *m*.
grade *n* gradus *m*.
gradient *n* clīvus *m*.
gradual *adj* lēnis.
gradually *adv* gradātim, sēnsim, paulātim.
graft *n* surculus *m*; (POL) ambitus *m* ♦ *vt*
īnserere.
grafting *n* īnsitiō *f*.
grain *n* frūmentum *nt*; (*seed*) grānum *nt*;
against the ~ invītā Minervā.
grammar *n* grammatica *f*.
grammarian *n* grammaticus *m*.
granary *n* horreum *nt*.
grand *adj* (*person*) amplus, illūstris, ēgregius;
(*way of life*) lautus, māgnificus; (*language*)
grandis, sublīmis.
granddaughter *n* neptis *f*; **great ~** prōneptis *f*.
grandeur *n* māiestās *f*, māgnificentia *f*; (*style*)
granditās *f*.
grandfather *n* avus *m*; **great ~** proavus *m*;
great-great-~ abavus *m*; **of a ~** avītus.
grandiloquence *n* māgniloquentia *f*.
grandiloquent *adj* grandiloquus, tumidus.
grandiose *adj* māgnificus.
grandmother *n* avia *f*; **great ~** proavia *f*.
grandson *n* nepōs *m*; **great ~** prōnepōs *m*.

grant vt dare, concēdere, tribuere; (admit) fatērī ♦ n concessiō f.
grape n ūva f.
graphic adj expressus; **give a ~ account of** ante oculōs ponere, oculīs subicere.
grapnel n manus ferrea f, harpagō f.
grapple vi luctārī. 7
grappling iron n manus ferrea f.
grasp vt prēnsāre, comprehendere; (with mind) complectī, adsequī, percipere, intellegere; **~ at** captāre, adpetere ♦ n manus f, comprehēnsiō f; (mind) captus m.
grasping adj avārus, rapāx.
grass n herba f.
grasshopper n gryllus m.
grassy adj herbōsus; herbidus.
grate n focus m ♦ vt atterere; **~ upon** offendere.
grateful adj grātus; **feel ~** grātiam habēre.
gratefully adv grātē.
gratification n voluptās f.
gratify vt mōrem gerere (dat), mōrigerārī (dat), grātificārī (dat).
gratifying adj iūcundus.
gratis adv grātuītō, grātīs.
gratitude n grātia f; **show ~** grātiam referre.
gratuitous adj grātuītus.
gratuitously adv grātuītō.
gratuity n stips f; (MIL) dōnātīvum nt.
grave n sepulchrum nt ♦ adj gravis, austērus ♦ vt scalpere.
gravel n glārea f.
gravely adv graviter, sevērē.
gravitate vi vergere.
gravity n (person) sevēritās f, tristitia f; (CIRCS) gravitās f, mōmentum nt; (physics) nūtus m; **by force of ~** nūtū suō.
gray adj rāvus; (hair) cānus.
graze vi pāscī ♦ vt (cattle) pāscere; (by touch) stringere.
grazing n pāstus m.
grease n arvīna f ♦ vt ungere.
greasy adj pinguis, ūnctus.
great adj māgnus, grandis, ingēns, amplus; (fame) īnsignis, praeclārus; **as ~ as ... tantus ... quantus; ~ deal** plūrimum; **~ many** plūrimī; **how ~** quantus; **very ~** permāgnus.
greatcoat n lacerna f.
greatest adj māximus.
greatly adv multum, māgnopere.
greave n ocrea f.
greed n avāritia f.
greedily adv avārē, cupidē.
greedy adj avārus, cupidus; avidus.
Greek adj Graecus.
green adj viridis; (unripe) crūdus; **be ~** virēre.
greenness n viriditās f.
greens n olus nt.
greet vt salūtāre.
greeting n salūs f, salūtātiō f.
grey adj rāvus; (hair) cānus.
greyhound n vertagus m.
grief n dolor m, maeror m, lūctus m; **come to ~**

perīre.
grievance n querimōnia f; iniūria f.
grieve vi dolēre, maerēre, lūgēre.
grievous adj tristis, lūctuōsus; molestus, gravis, acerbus.
grievously adv graviter, valdē.
grim adj trux, truculentus; atrōx.
grimace n ōris dēprāvātiō f; **make a ~** ōs dūcere.
grime n sordēs f, lutum nt.
grimy adj sordidus, lutulentus.
grin n rīsus m ♦ vi adrīdēre.
grind vt contundere; (corn) molere; (blade) acuere; **~ down** (fig) opprimere.
grindstone n cōs f.
grip vt comprehendere, arripere ♦ n comprehēnsiō f; **come to ~s with** in complexum venīre (gen).
gripe n tormina ntpl.
grisly adj horridus, dīrus.
grist n (fig) ēmolumentum nt.
grit n harēna f.
groan n gemitus m ♦ vi gemere, ingemere.
groin n inguen nt.
groom n agāsō m.
groove n canālis m, stria f.
grope vi praetentāre.
gross adj crassus, pinguis; (morally) turpis, foedus.
grossly adv foedē, turpiter; (very) valdē.
grossness n crassitūdō f; turpitūdō f.
grotto n spēlunca f, antrum nt.
ground n (bottom) solum nt; (earth) terra f, humus f; (cause) ratiō f, causa f; (sediment) faex f; **on the ~** humī; **on the ~s that** quod (+ subj); **to the ~** humum; **gain ~** prōficere; (rumour) incrēbrēscere; **lose ~** cēdere; (MIL) inclīnāre ♦ vt īnstituere ♦ vi (ship) sīdere.
grounding n īnstitūtiō f.
groundless adj vānus, inānis.
groundlessly adv frustrā, temerē.
grounds n faex f; (property) praedium nt; (reason) causa f; **I have good ~ for doing** nōn sine causā faciō, iūstīs dē causīs faciō.
groundwork n fundāmentum nt.
group n globus m, circulus m ♦ vt dispōnere.
grouse n (bird) tetraō m; (complaint) querēla f ♦ vi querī.
grove n nemus nt, lūcus m.
grovel vi serpere, sē prōsternere, sē advolvere.
grovelling adj humilis, abiectus.
grow vi crēscere, glīscere; (spread) percrēbrēscere; (become) fierī; **~ old** (con)senēscere; **~ up** adolēscere, pūbēscere; **let ~** (hair) prōmittere ♦ vt (crops) colere; (beard) dēmittere.
growl n fremitus m ♦ vi fremere.
grown-up adj adultus, grandis.
growth n incrēmentum nt, auctus m.
grub n vermiculus m.
grudge n invidia f ♦ vt invidēre (dat); (thing) gravārī.
grudgingly adv invītus, gravātē.

gruesome *adj* taeter.
gruff *adj* acerbus, asper.
grumble *vi* querī, mussāre ♦ *n* querēla *f*.
grumpy *adj* mōrōsus, querulus.
grunt *n* grunnītus *m* ♦ *vi* grunnīre.
guarantee *n* (*money*) spōnsiō *f*; (*promise*) fidēs
f; (*person*) praes *m* ♦ *vt* spondēre, praestāre.
guarantor *n* spōnsor *m*.
guard *n* custōdia *f*, praesidium *nt*; (*person*)
custōs *m*; **on ~ in statiōne; be on one's ~**
cavēre; **keep ~ statiōnem agere; off one's ~**
imprūdēns, inopīnāns; **be taken off one's ~**
dē gradū dēicī ♦ *vt* custōdīre, dēfendere;
(*keep*) cōnservāre; **~ against** cavēre.
guarded *adj* cautus.
guardedly *adv* cautē.
guardhouse *n* custōdia *f*.
guardian *n* custōs *m*; (*of minors*) tūtor *m*.
guardianship *n* custōdia *f*, tūtēla *f*.
guardian spirit *n* genius *m*.
gudgeon *n* gōbius *m*.
guerdon *n* praemium *nt*, mercēs *f*.
guess *n* coniectūra *f* ♦ *vt* dīvīnāre, conicere.
guest *n* hospes *m*, hospita *f*; (*at dinner*) convīva
m; **uninvited ~** umbra *f*; **~'s** hospitālis.
guffaw *n* cachinnus *m* ♦ *vi* cachinnāre.
guidance *n* moderātiō *f*; **under the ~ of God**
dūcente deō.
guide *n* dux *m*, ductor *m*; (*in policy*) auctor *m* ♦
vt dūcere; (*steer*) regere; (*control*) moderārī.
guild *n* collēgium *nt*.
guile *n* dolus *m*, fraus *f*.
guileful *adj* dolōsus, fraudulentus.
guilefully *adv* dolosē.
guileless *adj* simplex, innocēns.
guilelessly *adv* sine fraude.
guilt *n* culpa *f*, scelus *nt*.
guiltless *adj* innocēns, īnsōns.
guiltlessly *adv* integrē.
guilty *adj* nocēns, sōns; **find ~** damnāre.
guise *n* speciēs *f*.
guitar *n* fidēs *fpl*; **play the ~** fidibus canere.
gulf *n* sinus *m*; (*chasm*) hiātus *m*.
gull *n* mergus *m* ♦ *vt* dēcipere.
gullet *n* gula *f*, guttur *nt*.
gullible *adj* crēdulus.
gulp *vt* dēvorāre, haurīre.
gum *n* gummī *nt*; (*mouth*) gingīva *f*.
gumption *n* prūdentia *f*.
gurgle *vi* singultāre.
gush *vi* sē prōfundere, ēmicāre ♦ *n*
scatūrīginēs *fpl*.
gust *n* flāmen *nt*, impetus *m*.
gusto *n* studium *nt*.
gusty *adj* ventōsus.
gut *n* intestīnum *nt* ♦ *vt* exenterāre; (*fig*)
extergēre.
gutter *n* canālis *m*.
guzzle *vi* sē ingurgitāre.
gymnasium *n* gymnasium *nt*, palaestra *f*;
head of a ~ gymnasiarchus *m*.
gymnastic *adj* gymnicus; **~s** *pl* palaestra *f*.
gyrate *vi* volvī.

H, h

habit *n* mōs *m*, cōnsuētūdō *f*; (*dress*) habitus *m*,
vestītus *m*; **be in the ~ of** solēre.
habitable *adj* habitābilis.
habitation *n* domus *f*, domicilium *nt*; (*place*)
sēdēs *f*.
habitual *adj* ūsitātus.
habitually *adv* ex mōre, persaepe.
habituate *vt* adsuēfacere, īnsuēscere.
hack *vt* caedere, concīdere ♦ *n* (*horse*)
caballus *m*.
hackneyed *adj* trītus.
Hades *n* īnferī *mpl*.
haft *n* manubrium *nt*.
hag *n* anus *f*.
haggard *adj* ferus.
haggle *vi* altercārī.
hail *n* grandō *f* ♦ *vi*: **it ~s** grandinat ♦ *vt*
salūtāre, adclāmāre ♦ *interj* avē, avēte; salvē,
salvēte; **I ~ from Rome** Rōma mihi patria est.
hair *n* capillus *m*; crīnis *m*; (*single*) pīlus *m*;
(*animals*) sēta *f*, villus *nt*; **deviate a ~'s**
breadth from trānsversum digitum
discēdere ab; **split ~s** cavillārī.
hairdresser *n* tōnsor *m*.
hairless *adj* (*head*) calvus; (*body*) glaber.
hairpin *n* crīnāle *nt*.
hairsplitting *adj* captiōsus ♦ *n* cavillātiō *f*.
hairy *adj* pīlōsus.
halberd *n* bipennis *f*.
halcyon *n* alcēdō *f*; **~ days** alcēdōnia *ntpl*.
hale *adj* validus, rōbustus ♦ *vt* trahere, rapere.
half *n* dīmidium *nt*, dīmidia pars *f* ♦ *adj*
dīmidius, dīmidiātus; **~ as much again**
sesquī; **well begun is ~ done** dīmidium factī
quī coepit habet.
half-asleep *adj* sēmisomnus.
half-baked *adj* (*fig*) rudis.
half-dead *adj* sēmianimis, sēmivīvus.
half-full *adj* sēmiplēnus.
half-hearted *adj* incūriōsus, sōcors.
half-heartedly *adv* sine studiō.
half-hour *n* sēmihōra *f*.
half-moon *n* lūna dīmidiāta *f*.
half-open *adj* sēmiapertus.
half pound *n* sēlībra *f*.
half-way *adj* medius; **~ up the hill** in mediō
colle.
half-yearly *adj* sēmestris.
hall *n* ātrium *nt*; (*public*) exedra *f*.
hallo *interj* heus.

hallow vt sacrāre.
hallucination n error m, somnium nt.
halo n corōna f.
halt vi īnsistere, cōnsistere ♦ vt sistere ♦ n:
come to a ~ cōnsistere, agmen cōnstituere ♦
adj claudus.
halter n capistrum nt; (fig) laqueus m.
halve vt bipartīre.
ham n perna f.
hamlet n vīcus m.
hammer n malleus m ♦ vt tundere; ~ out
excūdere.
hamper n corbis f ♦ vt impedīre; (with debt)
obstringere.
hamstring vt poplitem succīdere (dat).
hand n manus f; left ~ laeva f, sinistra f; right ~
dextra f; an old ~ veterātor m; at ~ praestō,
ad manum; be at ~ adesse; at first ~ ipse; at
second ~ ab aliō; on the one ~ ... on the other
et ... et, quidem ... at; near at ~ in expedītō,
inibī; the matter in ~ quod nunc īnstat, quae
in manibus sunt; get out of ~ lascīvīre; have
a ~ in interesse (dat); have one's ~s full satis
agere; lay ~s on manum adferre, inicere
(dat); live from ~ to mouth ad hōram vīvere;
pass from ~ to ~ per manūs trādere; take in ~
suscipere; ~s pl (workmen) operae fpl ♦ vt
trādere, porrigere; ~ down trādere,
prōdere; ~ over dēferre, reddere.
handbill n libellus m.
handbook n ars f.
handcuffs n manicae fpl.
handful n manipulus m.
handicap n impedīmentum nt.
handicraft n artificium nt, ars operōsa f.
handily adv habiliter.
handiness n habilitās f, commoditās f.
handiwork n opus nt, manus f.
handkerchief n sūdārium nt.
handle n (cup) ānsa f; (knife) manubrium nt;
(fig) ānsa f, occāsiō f ♦ vt tractāre.
handling n tractātiō f.
handmaid n famula f.
handsome adj fōrmōsus, pulcher; (gift)
līberālis.
handsomely adv pulchrē; līberāliter.
handsomeness n pulchritūdō f, fōrma f.
hand-to-hand adv: fight ~ manum cōnserere,
comminus pugnāre.
handwriting n manus f.
handy adj (to use) habilis; (near) praestō.
hang vt suspendere; (head) dēmittere; (wall)
vestīre ♦ vi pendēre; ~ back gravārī,
dubitāre; ~ down dēpendēre; ~ on to haerēre
(dat); ~ over imminēre (dat), impendēre (dat);
go and be ~ed abī in malam crucem!
hanger-on n cliēns m/f, assecla m/f.
hanging n (death) suspendium nt; ~s pl aulaea
ntpl ♦ adj pendulus.
hangman n carnifex m.
hanker vi: ~ after appetere, exoptāre.
hap n fors f.
haphazard adj fortuītus.

hapless adj miser, īnfēlīx.
haply adv fortasse.
happen vi accidere, ēvenīre, contingere;
(become) fierī; as usually ~s ut fit; ~ upon
incidere in (acc); it ~s that accidit ut
(+subj).
happily adv fēlīciter, beātē, bene.
happiness n fēlīcitās f.
happy adj fēlīx, beātus; laetus; (in some
respect) fortūnātus.
harangue n cōntiō f ♦ vt cōntiōnārī apud (+
acc), hortārī.
harass vt vexāre, lacessere, exagitāre,
sollicitāre.
harassing adj molestus.
harbinger n praenūntius m.
harbour n portus m ♦ vt recipere.
harbour dues n portōria ntpl.
hard adj dūrus; (circs) asper, inīquus; (task)
difficilis, arduus; ~ of hearing surdaster;
grow ~ dūrēscere ♦ adv sēdulō, valdē; ~ by
prope, iuxtā; I am ~ put to it to do aegerrimē
faciō.
hard cash n praesēns pecūnia f.
harden vt dūrāre ♦ vi dūrēscere; (fig)
obdūrēscere; become ~ed obdūrēscere.
hard-fought adj atrōx.
hard-hearted adj crūdēlis, dūrus, inhūmānus.
hardihood n audācia f.
hardily adv sevērē.
hardiness n rōbur nt; dūritia f.
hardly adv vix, aegrē; (severely) dūriter,
acerbē; ~ any nullus ferē.
hardness n dūritia f; (fig) asperitās f, inīquitās
f; (difficulty) difficultās f; ~ of hearing surditās
f.
hard-pressed adj: be ~ labōrāre.
hardship n labor m, malum nt, iniūria f.
hard-working adj industrius, nāvus, sēdulus.
hardy adj dūrus, rōbustus, sevērus.
hare n lepus m.
hark interj auscultā, auscultāte ♦ vi: ~ back to
repetere.
harm n iniūria f, damnum nt, malum nt,
dētrīmentum nt; come to ~ dētrīmentum
capere, accipere ♦ vt laedere, nocēre (dat).
harmful adj damnōsus, noxius.
harmfully adv male.
harmless adj innocēns.
harmlessly adv innocenter; (escape) salvus,
incolumis, inviolātus.
harmonious adj cōnsonus, canōrus; (fig)
concors; (things) congruēns.
harmoniously adv modulātē; concorditer;
convenienter.
harmonize vi concinere, cōnsentīre,
congruere.
harmony n concentus m; (fig) concordia f,
cōnsēnsus m.
harness n arma ntpl ♦ vt īnfrēnāre, iungere.
harp n fidēs fpl; play the ~ fidibus canere ♦ vi: ~
on (fig) cantāre, dictitāre; be always ~ing on
the same thing cantilēnam eandem canere.

harpist n fidicen m, fidicina f.
harpoon n iaculum nt.
harpy n Harpyia f.
harrow n rāstrum nt ♦ vt occāre.
harrower n occātor m.
harrowing adj horrendus.
harry vt vexāre, dīripere.
harsh adj dūrus, acerbus, asper; (person) inclēmēns, sevērus.
harshly adv acerbē, asperē; sevērē.
harshness n acerbitās f, asperitās f; crūdēlitās f.
hart n cervus m.
harvest n messis f ♦ vt metere, dēmetere.
harvester n messor m.
hash n farrāgō f ♦ vt comminuere.
haste n festīnātiō f, properātiō f; in ~ festīnanter; in hot ~ incitātus; make ~ festīnāre.
hasten vt mātūrāre, adcelerāre ♦ vi festīnāre, properāre, mātūrāre.
hastily adv properē, raptim; temerē, incōnsultē; īrācundē.
hastiness n temeritās f; (temper) īrācundia f.
hasty adj properus, celer; (action) incōnsultus, temerārius; (temper) īrācundus, ācer; over ~ praeproperus.
hat n petasus m.
hatch vt exclūdere, parere.
hatchet n dolābra f.
hate n odium nt, invidia f ♦ vt ōdisse.
hated adj: to be ~ (by sb) odiō esse (+ dat).
hateful adj odiōsus, invīsus.
hatefully adv odiōsē.
hatred n odium nt.
haughtily adv adroganter, superbē, insolenter.
haughtiness n fastus m, adrogantia f, superbia f.
haughty adj adrogāns, superbus, īnsolēns.
haul vt trahere ♦ n bolus m.
haulage n vectūra f.
haulm n culmus m.
haunch n femur nt.
haunt vt frequentāre ♦ n locus m; (animals) lustrum nt.
have vt habēre, tenēre; (get done) cūrāre (gerundive); I ~ a house est mihī domus; I ~ to go mihī abeundum est; ~ it out with rem dēcernere cum; ~ on gerere, gestāre, indui; I had better go melius est īre, praestat īre; I had rather mālim, māllem.
haven n portus m; (fig) perfugium nt.
havoc n exitium nt, vastātiō f, ruīna f.
hawk n accipiter m ♦ vt (wares) circumferre.
hawker n īnstitor m.
hay n faenum nt; make ~ while the sun shines forō ūtī.
hazard n perīculum nt, discrīmen nt, ālea f ♦ vt perīclitārī, in āleam dare.
hazardous adj perīculōsus.
haze n nebula f.
hazel n corylus f.
hazy adj nebulōsus; (fig) incertus.

he pron hic, ille, is.
head n caput nt; (person) dux m, prīnceps m; (composition) caput nt; (mind) animus m, ingenium nt; ~ over heels cernuus; off one's ~ dēmēns; be at the ~ of dūcere, praeesse (dat); come to a ~ caput facere; (fig) in discrīmen addūcī; give one his ~ indulgēre (dat), habēnās immittere (dat); keep one's ~ praesentī animō ūtī; lose one's ~ suī compotem nōn esse; shake one's ~ abnuere ♦ vt dūcere, praeesse (dat); ~ off intercipere ♦ vi (in a direction) tendere.
headache n capitis dolor m.
headfirst adj praeceps.
heading n caput nt.
headland n prōmunturium nt.
headlong adj praeceps ♦ adv in praeceps; rush ~ sē praecipitāre.
headquarters n (MIL) praetōrium nt.
headship n prīncipātus m.
headsman n carnifex m.
headstrong adj impotēns, pervicāx.
headway n prōfectus m.
heady adj incōnsultus; (wine) vehemēns.
heal vt sānāre, medērī (dat) ♦ vi sānēscere; ~ over obdūcī.
healer n medicus m.
healing adj salūbris.
health n valētūdō f, salūs f; state of ~ valētūdō f; ill ~ valētūdō f; be in good ~ valēre; drink the ~ of propīnāre (dat).
healthful adj salūbris.
healthiness n sānitās f.
healthy adj sānus, integer; (conditions) salūber.
heap n acervus m, cumulus m; in ~s acervātim ♦ vt acervāre; ~ together congerere; ~ up adcumulāre, coacervāre, congerere.
hear vt audīre; (case) cognōscere; ~ clearly exaudīre; ~ in secret inaudīre.
hearer n audītor m.
hearing n (sense) audītus m; (act) audītiō f; (of case) cognitiō f; get a ~ sibī audientiam facere; hard of ~ surdaster; without a ~ indictā causā.
hearken vi auscultāre.
hearsay n fāma f, rūmor m.
heart n cor nt; (emotion) animus m, pectus nt; (courage) animus m; (interior) viscera ntpl; by ~ memoriā, memoriter; learn by ~ ēdiscere; the ~ of the matter rēs ipsa; lose ~ animum dēspondēre; take to ~ graviter ferre.
heartache n dolor m, angor m.
heartbroken adj animī frāctus, aeger; be ~ animō labōrāre.
heartburning n invidia f.
heartfelt adj sincērus.
hearth n focus m; ~ and home ārae et focī.
heartily adv vehementer, valdē.
heartiness n studium nt, vigor m.
heartless adj dūrus, inhūmānus, crūdēlis.
heartlessly adv inhūmānē.
heartlessness n inhūmānitās f, crūdēlitās f.
hearty adj studiōsus, vehemēns; (health)

rōbustus; (*feeling*) sincērus.

heat *n* ārdor *m*, calor *m*; (*emotion*) ārdor *m*, aestus *m*; (*race*) missus *m* ♦ *vt* calefacere, fervefacere; (*fig*) accendere; **become ~ed** incalēscere.

heatedly *adv* ferventer, ārdenter.

heath *n* inculta loca *ntpl*.

heathcock *n* attagēn *m*.

heathen *n* pāgānus *m*.

heather *n* erīcē *f*.

heave *vt* tollere; (*missile*) conicere; (*sigh*) dūcere ♦ *vi* tumēre, fluctuāre.

heaven *n* caelum *nt*, dī *mpl*; (*fig*) meliōra; **from ~** dīvīnitus; **in ~'s name** prō deum fidem!; **be in seventh ~** digitō caelum attingere.

heavenly *adj* caelestis, dīvīnus.

heavily *adv* graviter.

heaviness *n* gravitās *f*, pondus *nt*; (*of spirit*) maestitia *f*.

heavy *adj* gravis; (*air*) crassus; (*spirit*) maestus; (*shower*) māgnus, dēnsus.

heckle *vt* interpellāre.

heckler *n* interpellātor *m*.

hectic *adj* violēns, ācer, fervidus.

hector *vt* obstrepere (*dat*).

hedge *n* saepēs *f* ♦ *vt* saepīre; **~ off** intersaepīre ♦ *vi* tergiversārī.

hedgehog *n* echīnus *m*, ēricius *m*.

heed *vt* cūrāre, respicere ♦ *n* cūra *f*, opera *f*; **pay ~** animum attendere; **take ~** cavēre.

heedful *adj* attentus, cautus, dīligēns.

heedfully *adv* attentē, cautē.

heedfulness *n* cūra *f*, dīligentia *f*.

heedless *adj* incautus, immemor, neglegēns.

heedlessly *adv* incautē, neglegenter, temerē.

heedlessness *n* neglegentia *f*.

heel *n* calx *f*; **take to one's ~s** sē in pedēs conicere ♦ *vi* sē inclīnāre.

hegemony *n* prīncipātus *m*.

heifer *n* būcula *f*.

height *n* altitūdō *f*; (*person*) prōcēritās *f*; (*hill*) collis *m*, iugum *nt*; (*fig*) fastīgium *nt*; **the ~ of** summus.

heighten *vt* augēre, exaggerāre.

heinous *adj* atrōx, nefārius.

heinously *adv* atrōciter, nefāriē.

heinousness *n* atrōcitās *f*.

heir *n* hērēs *m*; **sole ~** hērēs ex asse.

heiress *n* hērēs *f*.

heirship *n* hērēditās *f*.

hell *n* Tartarus *m*, Īnfernī *mpl*.

hellish *adj* Īnfernus, scelestus.

helm *n* gubernāculum *nt*, clāvus *m*.

helmet *n* galea *f*.

helmsman *n* gubernātor *m*.

helots *n* Hīlōtae *mpl*.

help *n* auxilium *nt*, subsidium *nt*; **I am a ~** auxiliō sum ♦ *vt* iuvāre (+ *acc*), auxiliārī, subvenīre (*dat*), succurrere (*dat*) ♦ *vi* prōdesse; **I cannot ~** facere nōn possum quīn (*subj*); **it can't be ~ed** fierī nōn potest aliter; **so ~ me God** ita me dī ament.

helper *n* adiūtor *m*, adiūtrix *f*.

helpful *adj* ūtilis; **be ~ to** auxiliō esse (*dat*).

helpless *adj* inops.

helplessness *n* inopia *f*.

hem *n* ōra *f*, limbus *m* ♦ *vt*: **~ in** interclūdere, circumsedēre.

hemlock *n* cicūta *f*.

hemp *n* cannabis *f*.

hen *n* gallīna *f*.

hence *adv* hinc; (*consequence*) igitur, ideō.

henceforth, henceforward *adv* dehinc, posthāc, ex hōc tempore.

her *adj* suus, ēius.

herald *n* praecō *m*; (*POL*) fētiālis *m* ♦ *vt* praenūntiāre.

herb *n* herba *f*, olus *nt*.

herbage *n* herbae *fpl*.

herd *n* pecus *nt*; grex *f*, armentum *nt* ♦ *vi* congregārī.

herdsman *n* pāstor *m*.

here *adv* hīc; **be ~** adesse; **~ and there** passim; **here ... there** alibī ... alibī; **from ~** hinc; **~ is ... ecce** (*acc*) ....

hereabouts *adv* hīc ferē.

hereafter *adv* posthāc, posteā.

hereat *adv* hīc.

hereby *adv* ex hōc, hinc.

hereditary *adj* hērēditārius, patrius.

heredity *n* genus *nt*.

herein *adv* hīc.

hereinafter *adv* īnfrā.

hereof *adv* ēius reī.

hereupon *adv* hīc, quō factō.

herewith *adv* cum hōc, ūnā.

heritable *adj* hērēditārius.

heritage *n* hērēditās *f*.

hermaphrodite *n* androgynus *m*.

hermit *n* homō sōlitārius *m*.

hero *n* vir fortissimus *m*; (*demigod*) hērōs *m*.

heroic *adj* fortissimus, māgnanimus; (*epic*) hērōicus; (*verse*) hērōus.

heroically *adv* fortissimē, audācissimē.

heroism *n* virtūs *f*, fortitūdō *f*.

heron *n* ardea *f*.

hers *pron* suus, ēius.

herself *pron* ipsa *f*; (*reflexive*) sē.

hesitancy *n* dubitātiō *f*.

hesitant *adj* incertus, dubius.

hesitate *vi* dubitāre, haesitāre.

hesitating *adj* dubius.

hesitatingly *adv* cunctanter.

hesitation *n* dubitātiō *f*; **with ~** dubitanter.

heterogeneous *adj* dīversus, aliēnigenus.

hew *vt* dolāre, caedere; **~ down** excīdere, interscindere.

hexameter *n* hexameter *m*.

heyday *n* flōs *m*.

hiatus *n* hiātus *m*.

hiccup *n* singultus *m* ♦ *vi* singultīre.

hide *vt* cēlāre, abdere, abscondere, occultāre; **~ away** abstrūdere; **~ from** cēlāre (*acc*) ♦ *vi* sē abdere, latēre; **~ away** dēlitēscere ♦ *n* pellis *f*, corium *nt*.

hideous adj foedus, dēfōrmis, turpis.
hideously adv foedē.
hideousness n foeditās f, dēfōrmitās f.
hiding n (place) latebra f.
hierarchy n ōrdinēs mpl.
high adj altus, excelsus; (ground) ēditus; (pitch) acūtus; (rank) amplus; (price) cārus; (tide) māximus; (wind) māgnus; ~ **living** luxuria f; ~ **treason** māiestās f; ~ **and mighty** superbus; **on** ~ sublīmis ♦ adv altē.
highborn adj nōbilis, generōsus.
high-class adj (goods) lautus.
high-flown adj īnflātus, tumidus.
high-handed adj superbus, īnsolēns.
high-handedly adv superbē, licenter.
high-handedness n licentia f, superbia f.
highland adj montānus.
highlander n montānus m.
highlands npl montāna ntpl.
highly adv (value) māgnī; (intensity) valdē.
highly-strung adj trepidus.
high-minded adj generōsus.
high-spirited adj ferōx, animōsus.
highway n via f.
highwayman n grassātor m, latrō m.
hilarious adj festīvus, hilaris.
hilariously adv festīvē, hilare.
hilarity n festīvitās f, hilaritās f.
hill n collis m, mōns m; (slope) clīvus m.
hillock n tumulus m.
hilly adj montuōsus, clīvōsus.
hilt n manubrium nt, capulus m.
himself pron ipse; (reflexive) sē.
hind n cerva f.
hinder vt impedīre, obstāre (dat), morārī.
hindmost adj postrēmus; (in column) novissimus.
hindrance n impedīmentum nt, mora f.
hinge n cardō f.
hint n indicium nt, suspiciō f; **throw out a** ~ inicere ♦ vt subicere, significāre.
hip n coxendīx f.
hippodrome n spatium nt.
hire vt condūcere; ~ **out** locāre ♦ n conductiō f, locātiō f; (wages) mercēs f.
hired adj mercennārius, conductus.
hireling n mercennārius m.
hirsute adj hirsūtus.
his adj suus, ēius.
hiss vi sībilāre ♦ vt: ~ **off stage** explōdere, exsībilāre ♦ n sībilus m.
historian n historicus m, rērum scrīptor m.
historical adj historicus.
history n historia f; **the** ~ **of Rome** rēs Rōmānae fpl; **since the beginning of** ~ post hominum memoriam; **ancient** ~ antīquitās f.
histrionic adj scaenicus.
hit n ictus m, plāga f; **a** ~! (in duel) habet! ♦ vt ferīre, icere, percutere; ~ **against** offendere; ~ **upon** invenīre.
hitch n mora f ♦ vt implicāre; ~ **up** succingere.
hither adv hūc; ~ **and thither** hūc illūc ♦ adj citerior.

hitherto adv adhūc, hāctenus, hūcusque.
hive n alveārium nt.
hoar adj cānus ♦ n pruīna f.
hoard n thēsaurus m, acervus m ♦ vt condere, recondere.
hoarfrost n pruīna f.
hoarse adj raucus, fuscus.
hoarsely adv raucā vōce.
hoary adj cānus.
hoax n fraus f, fallācia f, lūdus m ♦ vt dēcipere, fallere.
hobble vi claudicāre.
hobby n studium nt.
hob-nob vi familiāriter ūtī (abl).
hocus-pocus n trīcae fpl.
hoe n sarculum nt ♦ vt sarrīre.
hog n sūs m, porcus m; ~'s porcīnus.
hogshead n dōlium nt.
hoist vt tollere; (sail) vēla dare.
hold n (grasp) comprehēnsiō f; (power) potestās f; (ship) alveus m; **gain a** ~ **over** obstringere, sibi dēvincīre; **get** ~ **of** potīrī (abl); **keep** ~ **of** retinēre; **lose** ~ **of** ōmittere; **take** ~ **of** prehendere, comprehendere ♦ vt tenēre, habēre; (possession) obtinēre, possidēre; (office) gerere, fungī (abl); (capacity) capere; (meeting) habēre; ~ **a meeting** concilium habēre; ~ **one's own with** parem esse (dat); ~ **over** differre, prōlātāre; ~ **water** (fig) stāre ♦ vi manēre, dūrāre; (opinion) dūcere, existimāre, affirmāre; ~ **back** vt retinēre, inhibēre ♦ vi gravārī, dubitāre; ~ **cheap** parvī facere; ~ **fast** vt retinere, amplectī ♦ vi haerēre; ~ **good** valēre; ~ **out** vt porrigere, extendere; (hope) ostendere ♦ vi dūrāre, perstāre; ~ **together** cohaerēre; ~ **up** tollere; (falling) sustinēre; (movement) obstāre (dat), morārī; ~ **with** adsentīre (dat).
holdfast n fībula f.
holding n (land) agellus m.
hole n forāmen nt, cavum nt; **make a** ~ **in** pertundere, perforāre.
holiday n ōtium nt; festus diēs m; **on** ~ fēriātus; ~**s** pl fēriae fpl.
holily adv sanctē.
holiness n sanctitās f.
hollow adj cavus, concavus; (fig) inānis, vānus ♦ n cavum nt, caverna f ♦ vt excavāre.
hollowness n (fig) vānitās f.
holly n aquifolium nt.
holy adj sanctus.
homage n observantia f, venerātiō f; **pay** ~ **to** venerārī, colere.
home n domus f; (town, country) patria f; **at** ~ domī; **from** ~ domō ♦ adj domesticus ♦ adv domum.
homeless adj profugus.
homely adj simplex, rūsticus; (speech) plēbēius.
homestead n fundus m.
homewards adv domum.
homicide n (act) homicīdium nt, caedēs f;

(_person_) homicīda _m_.
homily _n_ sermō _m_.
homogeneous _adj_ aequābilis.
homologous _adj_ cōnsimilis.
hone _n_ cōs _f_ ♦ _vt_ acuere.
honest _adj_ probus, frūgī, integer.
honestly _adv_ probē, integrē.
honesty _n_ probitās _f_, fidēs _f_.
honey _n_ mel _nt_.
honeycomb _n_ favus _m_.
honeyed _adj_ mellītus, mulsus.
honorarium _n_ stips _f_.
honorary _adj_ honōrārius.
honour _n_ honōs _m_; (_repute_) honestās _f_;
existimātiō _f_; (_chastity_) pudor _m_; (_trust_) fidēs _f_;
(_rank_) dignitās _f_; (_award_) decus _nt_, īnsigne _nt_;
(_respect_) observantia _f_ ♦ _vt_ honōrāre,
decorāre; (_respect_) observāre, colere; **do ~ to**
honestāre.
honourable _adj_ honestus, probus; (_rank_)
illūstris, praeclārus.
honourably _adv_ honestē.
hood _n_ cucullus _m_.
hoodwink _vt_ verba dare (_dat_).
hoof _n_ ungula _f_.
hook _n_ uncus _m_, hāmus _m_ ♦ _vt_ hāmō capere.
hooked _adj_ aduncus, hāmātus.
hoop _n_ circulus _m_; (_toy_) trochus _m_.
hoot _vi_ obstrepere; **~ off** (_stage_) explōdere.
hop _n_ saltus _m_; **catch on the ~** in ipsō articulō
opprimere ♦ _vi_ salīre.
hope _n_ spēs _f_; **in the ~ that** sī forte; **give up ~**
spem dēpōnere, dēspērāre; **past ~**
dēspērātus; **entertain ~s** spem habēre ♦ _vt_
spērāre.
hopeful _adj_ bonae speī; **be ~** aliquam spem
habēre.
hopefully _adv_ nōn sine spē.
hopeless _adj_ dēspērātus.
hopelessly _adv_ dēspēranter.
hopelessness _n_ dēspērātiō _f_.
horde _n_ multitūdō _f_.
horizon _n_ fīniēns _m_.
horizontal _adj_ aequus, lībrātus.
horizontally _adv_ ad lībram.
horn _n_ cornū _nt_; (_shepherd's_) būcina _f_.
horned _adj_ corniger.
hornet _n_ crabrō _m_; **stir up a ~'s nest** crabrōnēs
inrītāre.
horny _adj_ corneus.
horoscope _n_ sīdus nātālicium _nt_.
horrible _adj_ horrendus, horribilis, dīrus,
foedus.
horribly _adv_ foedē.
horrid _adj_ horribilis.
horrify _vt_ terrēre, perterrēre.
horror _n_ horror _m_, terror _m_; odium _nt_.
horse _n_ equus _m_; (_cavalry_) equitēs _mpl_; **flog a
dead ~** asellum currere docēre; **spur a
willing ~** currentem incitāre; **~'s** equīnus.
horseback _n_: **ride on ~back** in equō vehī; **fight
on ~back** ex equō pugnāre.
horseman _n_ eques _m_.

horseradish _n_ armoracia _f_.
horse soldier _n_ eques _m_.
horticulture _n_ hortōrum cultus _m_.
hospitable _adj_ hospitālis.
hospitably _adv_ hospitāliter.
hospital _n_ valētūdinārium _nt_.
hospitality _n_ hospitālitās _f_, hospitium _nt_.
host _n_ hospes _m_; (_inn_) caupō _m_; (_number_)
multitūdō _f_; (_MIL_) exercitus _m_.
hostage _n_ obses _m/f_.
hostelry _n_ taberna _f_, dēversōrium _nt_.
hostile _adj_ hostīlis, īnfēnsus, inimīcus;
īnfestus; **in a ~ manner** īnfēnsē, hostīliter,
inimīcē.
hostility _n_ inimīcitia _f_; **hostilities** _pl_ bellum _nt_.
hot _adj_ calidus, fervidus, aestuōsus; (_boiling_)
fervēns; (_fig_) ārdēns; **be ~** calēre, fervēre,
ārdēre; **get ~** calēscere.
hotch-potch _n_ farrāgō _f_.
hotel _n_ dēversōrium _nt_.
hot-headed _adj_ ārdēns, temerārius, praeceps.
hotly _adv_ ārdenter, ācriter.
hot-tempered _adj_ īrācundus.
hot water _n_ calida _f_.
hound _n_ canis _m_ ♦ _vt_ īnstāre (_dat_).
hour _n_ hōra _f_.
hourly _adv_ in hōrās.
house _n_ domus _f_, aedēs _fpl_; (_country_) vīlla _f_;
(_family_) domus _f_, gēns _f_; **at the ~ of** apud (_acc_);
full ~ frequēns senātus, frequēns theātrum
♦ _vt_ hospitiō accipere, recipere; (_things_)
condere.
household _n_ familia _f_, domus _f_ ♦ _adj_
familiāris, domesticus.
householder _n_ paterfamiliās _m_, dominus _m_.
housekeeping _n_ reī familiāris cūra _f_.
housemaid _n_ ancilla _f_.
housetop _n_ fastīgium _nt_.
housewife _n_ māterfamiliās _f_, domina _f_.
housing _n_ hospitium _nt_; (_horse_) ōrnāmenta
ntpl.
hovel _n_ gurgustium _nt_.
hover _vi_ pendēre; (_fig_) impendēre.
how _adv_ (_interrog_) quemadmodum; quōmodō;
quō pactō; (_excl_) quam; **~ great/big/large**
quantus; **~ long** (_time_) quamdiū; **~ many** quot;
~ much quantum; **~ often** quotiēns.
howbeit _adv_ tamen.
however _adv_ tamen; autem, nihilōminus;
utcumque, quōquō modō; **~ much** quamvīs,
quantumvīs; **~ great** quantuscumque.
howl _n_ ululātus _m_ ♦ _vi_ ululāre; (_wind_) fremere.
howsoever _adv_ utcumque.
hub _n_ axis _m_.
hubbub _n_ tumūltus _m_.
huckster _n_ īnstitor _m_, propōla _m_.
huddle _n_ turba _f_ ♦ _vi_ congregārī.
hue _n_ color _m_; **~ and cry** clāmor _m_.
huff _n_ offēnsiō _f_ ♦ _vt_ offendere.
hug _n_ complexus _m_ ♦ _vt_ complectī.
huge _adj_ ingēns, immānis, immēnsus, vastus.
hugely _adv_ vehementer.
hugeness _n_ immānitās _f_.

hulk n alveus m.
hull n alveus m.
hum n murmur nt, fremitus m ♦ vi
murmurāre, fremere.
human adj hūmānus.
human being n homō m/f.
humane adj hūmānus, misericors.
humanely adv hūmānē, hūmāniter.
humanism n litterae fpl.
humanist n homō litterātus m.
humanity n hūmānitās f; misericordia f.
humanize vt excolere.
humanly adv hūmānitus.
human nature n hūmānitās f.
humble adj humilis, modestus ♦ vt dēprimere;
(oneself) summittere.
humbleness n humilitās f.
humbly adv summissē, modestē.
humbug n trīcae fpl.
humdrum adj vulgāris; (style) pedester.
humid adj ūmidus, madidus; **be ~** madēre.
humidity n ūmor m.
humiliate vt dēprimere, dēdecorāre.
humiliation n dēdecus nt.
humility n modestia f, animus summissus m.
humorist n homō facētus m.
humorous adj facētus, ioculāris, rīdiculus.
humorously adv facētē.
humour n facētiae fpl; (disposition) ingenium
nt; (mood) libīdō f; **be in a bad ~** sibī
displicēre ♦ vt indulgēre (dat), mōrem
gerere (dat), mōrigerārī (dat).
hump n gibbus m.
hunchback n gibber m.
hundred num centum; **~ each** centēnī; **~ times**
centiēns.
hundredth adj centēsimus.
hundredweight n centumpondium nt.
hunger n famēs f ♦ vi ēsurīre.
hungrily adv avidē.
hungry adj ēsuriēns, iēiūnus, avidus; **be ~**
ēsurīre.
hunt n vēnātiō f, vēnātus m ♦ vt vēnārī,
indāgāre, exagitāre.
hunter n vēnātor m.
hunting n vēnātiō f; (fig) aucupium nt.
hunting spear n vēnābulum nt.
huntress n vēnātrix f.
huntsman n vēnātor m.
hurdle n crātēs f; (obstacle) obex m/f.
hurl vt conicere, ingerere, iaculārī, iācere.
hurly-burly n turba f, tumultus m.
hurrah interj euax, iō.
hurricane n procella f.
hurried adj praeproperus, praeceps, trepidus.
hurriedly adv properātō, cursim, festīnanter.
hurry vt adcelerāre, mātūrāre ♦ vi festīnāre,
properāre; **~ along** vt rapere; **~ away** vi
discēdere, properāre; **~ about** vi discurrere;
~ on vt mātūrāre; **~ up** vi properāre ♦ n
festīnātiō f; **in a ~** festīnanter, raptim.
hurt n iniūria f, damnum nt; vulnus nt ♦ vt
laedere, nocēre (dat); **it ~s** dolet.

hurtful adj nocēns, damnōsus.
hurtfully adv nocenter, damnōsē.
hurtle vi volāre; sē praecipitāre.
husband n vir m, marītus m ♦ vt parcere (dat).
husbandry n agrī cultūra f; (economy)
parsimōnia f.
hush n silentium nt ♦ vt silentium facere (dat),
lēnīre ♦ vi tacēre, silēre; **~ up** comprimere,
cēlāre ♦ interj st!
hushed adj tacitus.
husk n folliculus m, siliqua f ♦ vt dēglūbāre.
husky adj fuscus, raucus.
hustle vt trūdere, īnstāre (dat).
hut n casa f, tugurium nt.
hutch n cavea f.
hyacinth n hyacinthus m.
hybrid n hibrida m/f.
hydra n hydra f.
hyena n hyaena f.
hygiene n salūbritās f.
hygienic adj salūbris.
hymeneal adj nūptiālis.
hymn n carmen nt ♦ vt canere.
hyperbole n superlātiō f.
hypercritical adj Aristarchus m.
hypocaust n hypocaustum nt.
hypocrisy n simulātiō f, dissimulātiō f.
hypocrite n simulātor m, dissimulātor m.
hypocritical adj simulātus, fictus.
hypothesis n positum nt, sūmptiō f,
coniectūra f.
hypothetical adj sūmptus.

I, i

I pron ego.
iambic adj iambēus.
iambus n iambus m.
ice n glaciēs f.
icicle n stīria f.
icon n simulacrum nt.
icy adj glaciālis, gelidus.
idea n nōtiō f, nōtitia f, imāgō f; (Platonic) fōrma
f; (expressed) sententia f; **conceive the ~ of**
īnfōrmāre; **with the ~ that** eō cōnsiliō ut (+
subj).
ideal adj animō comprehēnsus; (perfect)
perfectus, optimus ♦ n specimen nt, speciēs
f, exemplar nt.
identical adj īdem, cōnsimilis.
identify vt agnōscere.
identity n: **establish the ~ of** cognōscere quis
sit.
Ides n Idūs fpl.
idiocy n animī imbēcillitās f.

idiom n proprium nt, sermō m.
idiomatic adj proprius.
idiomatically adv sermōne suō, sermōne
 propriō.
idiosyncrasy n proprium nt, libīdō f.
idiot n excors m.
idiotic adj fatuus, stultus.
idiotically adv stultē, ineptē.
idle adj ignāvus, dēses, iners; (*unoccupied*)
 ōtiōsus, vacuus; (*useless*) inānis, vānus; **be ~**
 cessāre, dēsidēre; **lie ~** (*money*) iacēre ♦ vi
 cessāre.
idleness n ignāvia f, dēsidia f, inertia f; ōtium
 nt.
idler n cessātor m.
idly adv ignāvē; ōtiōsē; frustrā, nēquīquam.
idol n simulacrum nt; (*person*) dēliciae fpl.
idolater n falsōrum deōrum cultor m.
idolatry n falsōrum deōrum cultus m.
idolize vt venerārī.
idyll n carmen Theocritēum nt.
if conj sī; (*interrog*) num, utrum; **~ anyone** sī
 quis; **~ ever** sī quandō; **~ not** nisī; **~ only** dum,
 dummodo; **~ ... or** sīve ... sīve; **as ~** quasi,
 velut; **but ~** sīn, quodsī; **even ~** etiamsī.
igneous adj igneus.
ignite vt accendere, incendere ♦ vi ignem
 concipere.
ignoble adj (*birth*) ignōbilis; (*repute*)
 illīberālis, turpis.
ignominious adj ignōminiōsus, īnfāmis,
 turpis.
ignominiously adv turpiter.
ignominy n ignōminia f, īnfāmia f, dēdecus nt.
ignoramus n idiōta m, indoctus m.
ignorance n īnscītia f, ignōrātiō f.
ignorant adj ignārus, indoctus; (*of something*)
 īnscītus, rudis; (*unaware*) īnscius; **be ~ of**
 nescīre, ignōrāre.
ignorantly adv īnscienter, īnscītē, indoctē.
ignore vt praetermittere.
ilex n īlex f.
Iliad n Ilias f.
ill adj aeger, aegrōtus, invalidus; (*evil*) malus;
 be ~ aegrōtāre; **fall ~ in** morbum incidere; **~**
 at ease sollicitus ♦ adv male, improbē ♦ n
 malum nt, incommodum nt, aerumna f,
 damnum nt.
ill-advised adj incōnsultus.
ill-bred adj agrestis, inurbānus.
ill-disposed adj malevolus, invidus.
illegal adj illicitus, vetitus.
illegally adv contrā lēgēs.
ill-fated adj īnfēlīx.
ill-favoured adj turpis.
ill-gotten adj male partus.
ill-health n valētūdō f.
illicit adj vetitus.
illimitable adj īnfīnītus.
illiteracy n litterārum īnscītia f.
illiterate adj illitterātus, inērudītus.
ill-natured adj malevolus, malignus.
illness n morbus m, valētūdō f.

illogical adj absurdus.
ill-omened adj dīrus, īnfaustus.
ill-starred adj īnfēlīx.
ill-tempered adj īrācundus, amārus,
 stomachōsus.
ill-timed adj immātūrus, intempestīvus.
ill-treat vt malefacere (*dat*).
illuminate vt illūmināre, illūstrāre.
illumination n lūmina ntpl.
illusion n error m, somnium nt.
illusive, illusory adj fallāx.
illustrate vt illūstrāre; (*with instances*)
 exemplō cōnfīrmāre.
illustration n exemplum nt.
illustrious adj illūstris, īnsignis, praeclārus.
illustriously adv praeclārē.
ill will n invidia f.
image n imāgō f, effigiēs f; (*idol*) simulacrum
 nt; (*verbal*) figūra f, similitūdō f.
imagery n figūrae fpl.
imaginary adj commentīcius, fictus.
imagination n cōgitātiō f, opīnātiō f.
imaginative adj ingeniōsus.
imagine vt animō fingere, animum indūcere,
 ante oculōs pōnere; (*think*) opīnārī, arbitrārī.
imbecile adj animō imbēcillus, fatuus, mente
 captus.
imbecility n animī imbēcillitās f.
imbibe vt adbibere; (*fig*) imbuī (*abl*).
imbrue vt īnficere.
imbue vt imbuere, īnficere, tingere.
imitable adj imitābilis.
imitate vt imitārī.
imitation n imitātiō f; (*copy*) imāgō f.
imitator n imitātor m, imitātrix f, aemulātor
 m.
immaculate adj integer, ēmendātus.
immaculately adv integrē, sine vitiō.
immaterial adj indifferēns.
immature adj immātūrus.
immeasurable adj immēnsus, īnfīnītus.
immediate adj īnstāns, praesēns; (*neighbour*)
 proximus.
immediately adv statim, extemplō,
 cōnfestim.
immemorial adj antīquissimus; **from time ~**
 post hominum memoriam.
immense adj immēnsus, immānis, ingēns,
 vastus.
immensely adv vehementer.
immensity n immēnsum nt, māgnitūdō f.
immerse vt immergere, mergere.
immigrant n advena m.
immigrate vi migrāre.
imminent adj īnstāns, praesēns; **be ~**
 imminēre, impendēre.
immobile adj fīxus, immōbilis.
immoderate adj immoderātus, immodestus.
immoderately adv immoderātē, immodestē.
immodest adj impudīcus, inverēcundus.
immolate vt immolāre.
immoral adj prāvus, corruptus, turpis.
immorality n corruptī mōrēs mpl, turpitūdō f.

immorally *adv* prāvē, turpiter.
immortal *adj* immortālis, aeternus.
immortality *n* immortālitās *f*.
immortalize *vt* in astra tollere.
immortally *adv* aeternum.
immovable *adj* fīxus, immōbilis.
immune *adj* immūnis, vacuus.
immunity *n* immūnitās *f*, vacātiō *f*.
immure *vt* inclūdere.
immutability *n* immūtābilitās *f*.
immutable *adj* immūtābilis.
imp *n* puer improbus *m*.
impact *n* ictus *m*, incussus *m*.
impair *vt* imminuere, corrumpere.
impale *vt* induere, īnfīgere.
impalpable *adj* tenuissimus.
impart *vt* impertīre, commūnicāre; (*courage*) addere.
impartial *adj* aequus, medius.
impartiality *n* aequābilitās *f*.
impartially *adv* sine favōre.
impassable *adj* invius; (*mountains*) inexsuperābilis; (*fig*) inexplicābilis.
impasse *n* mora *f*, incitae *fpl*.
impassioned *adj* ārdēns, fervidus.
impassive *adj* rigidus, sēnsū carēns.
impatience *n* aviditās *f*; (*of anything*) impatientia *f*.
impatient *adj* trepidus, avidus; impatiēns.
impatiently *adv* aegrē.
impeach *vt* diem dīcere (*dat*), accūsāre.
impeachment *n* accūsātiō *f*, crīmen *nt*.
impeccable *adj* ēmendātus.
impecunious *adj* pauper.
impede *vt* impedīre, obstāre (*dat*).
impediment *n* impedīmentum *nt*.
impel *vt* impellere, incitāre.
impend *vi* impendēre, imminēre, īnstāre.
impenetrable *adj* impenetrābilis; (*country*) invius, impervius.
impenitent *adj*: **I am ~** nīl mē paenitet.
imperative *adj* necessārius.
imperceptible *adj* tenuissimus, obscurus.
imperceptibly *adv* sēnsim.
imperfect *adj* imperfectus, vitiōsus.
imperfection *n* vitium *nt*.
imperfectly *adv* vitiōsē.
imperial *adj* imperātōrius, rēgius.
imperil *vt* in discrīmen addūcere, labefactāre.
imperious *adj* imperiōsus, superbus.
imperiously *adv* superbē.
imperishable *adj* immortālis, aeternus.
impersonate *vt* partēs agere (*gen*).
impertinence *n* importūnitās *f*, protervitās *f*.
impertinent *adj* importūnus, protervus, ineptus.
impertinently *adv* importūnē, ineptē, protervē.
imperturbable *adj* immōtus, gravis.
impervious *adj* impervius, impenetrābilis.
impetuosity *n* ārdor *m*, violentia *f*, vīs *f*.
impetuous *adj* violēns, fervidus, effrēnātus.
impetuously *adv* effrēnātē.

impetus *n* impetus *m*.
impiety *n* impietās *f*.
impinge *vi* incidere.
impious *adj* impius, profānus; **it is ~** nefas est.
impiously *adv* impiē.
impish *adj* improbus.
implacable *adj* implācābilis, inexōrābilis, dūrus.
implacably *adv* dūrē.
implant *vt* īnserere, ingignere.
implement *n* īnstrūmentum *nt* ♦ *vt* implēre, exsequī.
implicate *vt* implicāre, impedīre.
implication *n* indicium *nt*.
implicit *adj* tacitus; absolūtus.
implicitly *adv* absconditē; (*trust*) omnīnō, summā fidē.
implore *vt* implōrāre, obsecrāre.
imply *vt* significāre, continēre; **be ~ied** inesse.
impolite *adj* inurbānus, illepidus.
impolitely *adv* inurbānē.
impolitic *adj* incōnsultus, imprūdēns.
imponderable *adj* levissimus.
import *vt* importāre, invehere; (*mean*) velle ♦ *n* significātiō *f*.
importance *n* gravitās *f*, mōmentum *nt*; (*rank*) dignitās *f*, amplitūdō *f*, auctōritās *f*; **it is of great ~ to me** meā māgnī rēfert.
important *adj* gravis, māgnī mōmentī; **it is ~** interest (+ *gen*) rēfert; **more ~, most ~** antīquior, antīquissimus.
importation *n* invectiō *f*.
imports *npl* importātīcia *ntpl*.
importunate *adj* molestus.
importune *vt* flāgitāre, īnstāre (*dat*).
impose *vt* impōnere; (*by order*) indīcere, iniungere; **~ upon** illūdere, fraudāre, abūtī (*abl*).
imposing *adj* māgnificus, lautus.
imposition *n* fraus *f*; (*tax*) tribūtum *nt*.
impossible *adj*: **it is ~** fierī nōn potest.
impost *n* tribūtum *nt*, vectīgal *nt*.
impostor *n* planus *m*, fraudātor *m*.
imposture *n* fraus *f*, fallācia *f*.
impotence *n* īnfirmitās *f*.
impotent *adj* īnfirmus, dēbilis; (*with rage*) impotēns.
impotently *adv* frustrā; (*rage*) impotenter.
impound *vt* inclūdere; (*confiscate*) pūblicāre.
impoverish *vt* in inopiam redigere.
impracticable *adj*: **be ~** fierī nōn posse.
imprecate *vt* exsecrārī.
imprecation *n* exsecrātiō *f*.
impregnable *adj* inexpugnābilis.
impregnate *vt* imbuere, īnficere.
impress *vt* imprimere; (*on mind*) īnfīgere; (*person*) permovēre; (*MIL*) invītum scrībere.
impression *n* (*copy*) exemplar *nt*; (*mark*) signum *nt*; (*feeling*) impulsiō *f*; (*belief*) opīnātiō *f*; **make an ~ of** exprimere; **make an ~ on** commovēre; **have the ~** opīnārī.
impressionable *adj* crēdulus.
impressive *adj* gravis.

impressively *adv* graviter.
impressiveness *n* gravitās *f.*
imprint *n* impressiō *f*, signum *nt* ♦ *vt* imprimere; (*on mind*) īnfīgere, inūrere.
imprison *vt* inclūdere, in vincula conicere.
imprisonment *n* custōdia *f*, vincula *ntpl.*
improbable *adj* incrēdibilis, haud vērīsimilis.
impromptu *adv* ex tempore.
improper *adj* indecōrus, ineptus.
improperly *adv* prāvē, perperam.
impropriety *n* culpa *f*, offēnsa *f.*
improve *vt* ēmendāre, corrigere; (*mind*) excolere ♦ *vi* prōficere, meliōrem fierī.
improvement *n* ēmendātiō *f*, prōfectus *m.*
improvident *adj* imprōvidus; (*with money*) prōdigus.
improvidently *adv* imprōvidē; prōdigē.
improvise *vt* ex tempore compōnere, excōgitāre.
imprudence *n* imprūdentia *f.*
imprudent *adj* imprūdēns.
imprudently *adv* imprūdenter.
impudence *n* impudentia *f*, audācia *f.*
impudent *adj* impudēns, audāx.
impudently *adv* impudenter, protervē.
impugn *vt* impugnāre, in dubium vocāre.
impulse *n* impetus *m*, impulsus *m.*
impulsive *adj* praeceps, violentus.
impulsively *adv* impetū quōdam animī.
impulsiveness *n* impetus *m*, violentia *f.*
impunity *n* impūnitās *f*; **with ~** impūne.
impure *adj* impūrus, incestus, inquinātus.
impurely *adv* impūrē, incestē, inquinātē.
impurity *n* impūritās *f*, sordēs *fpl.*
imputation *n* crīmen *nt.*
impute *vt* attribuere, adsignāre; **~ as a fault** vitiō vertere.
in *prep* in (*abl*); (*with motion*) in (*acc*); (*authors*) apud (*acc*); (*time*) *abl*; **~ doing this** dum hoc faciō; **~ my youth** adulēscēns; **~ that** quod ♦ *adv* (*rest*) intrā; (*motion*) intrō.
inaccessible *adj* inaccessus.
inaccuracy *n* neglegentia *f*, incūria *f*; (*error*) mendum *nt.*
inaccurate *adj* parum dīligēns, neglegēns.
inaccurately *adv* neglegenter.
inaction *n* inertia *f.*
inactive *adj* iners, quiētus; **be ~** cessāre.
inactivity *n* inertia *f*, ōtium *nt.*
inadequate *adj* impār, parum idōneus.
inadequately *adv* parum.
inadvertency *n* imprūdentia *f.*
inadvertent *adj* imprūdēns.
inadvertently *adv* imprūdenter.
inane *adj* inānis, vānus; ineptus, stultus.
inanely *adv* ineptē.
inanimate *adj* inanimus.
inanity *n* ineptiae *fpl*, stultitia *f.*
inapplicable *adj*: **be ~** nōn valēre.
inappropriate *adj* aliēnus, parum aptus.
inarticulate *adj* īnfāns.
inartistic *adj* sine arte, dūrus, inēlegāns.
inasmuch as *conj* quōniam, cum (*subj*).

inattention *n* incūria *f*, neglegentia *f.*
inattentive *adj* neglegēns.
inattentively *adv* neglegenter.
inaudible *adj*: **be ~** audīrī nōn posse.
inaugurate *vt* inaugurāre, cōnsecrāre.
inauguration *n* cōnsecrātiō *f.*
inauspicious *adj* īnfaustus, īnfēlix.
inauspiciously *adv* malīs ōminibus.
inborn *adj* innātus.
incalculable *adj* inaestimābilis.
incantation *n* carmen *nt.*
incapable *adj* inhabilis, indocilis; **be ~** nōn posse.
incapacitate *vt* dēbilitāre.
incapacity *n* inertia *f*, īnscītia *f.*
incarcerate *vt* inclūdere, in vincula conicere.
incarnate *adj* hūmānā speciē indūtus.
incautious *adj* incautus, temerārius.
incautiously *adv* incautē.
incendiary *adj* incendiārius.
incense *n* tūs *nt* ♦ *vt* inrītāre, stomachum movēre (*dat*); **be ~d** stomachārī.
incentive *n* incitāmentum *nt*, stimulus *m.*
inception *n* initium *nt*, exōrdium *nt.*
incessant *adj* adsiduus.
incessantly *adv* adsiduē.
incest *n* incestus *m.*
inch *n* digitus *m*, ūncia *f.*
incident *n* ēventum *nt*, cāsus *m*, rēs *f.*
incidental *adj* fortuītus.
incidentally *adv* cāsū.
incipient *adj* prīmus.
incisive *adj* ācer.
incite *vt* īnstīgāre, impellere, hortārī, incitāre.
incitement *n* invītāmentum *nt*, stimulus *m.*
inciter *n* īnstimulātor *m.*
incivility *n* importūnitās *f*, inhūmānitās *f.*
inclemency *n* (*weather*) intemperiēs *f.*
inclement *adj* asper, tristis.
inclination *n* inclīnātiō *f*, animus *m*, libīdō *f*; (*slope*) clīvus *m.*
incline *vt* inclīnāre; (*person*) indūcere ♦ *vi* inclīnāre, incumbere; **~ towards** sē adclīnāre ♦ *n* adclīvitās *f*, clīvus *m.*
inclined *adj* inclīnātus, prōpēnsus; **I am ~ to think** haud sciō an.
include *vt* inclūdere, continēre, complectī.
incognito *adv* clam.
incoherent *adj* interruptus; **be ~** nōn cohaerēre.
income *n* fructus *m*, mercēs *f.*
incommensurate *adj* dispār.
incommode *vt* molestiam adferre (*dat*).
incomparable *adj* singulāris, eximius.
incompatibility *n* discrepantia *f*, repugnantia *f.*
incompatible *adj* īnsociābilis, repugnāns; **be ~ with** dissidēre ab, repugnāre (*dat*).
incompetence *n* inertia *f*, īnscītia *f.*
incompetent *adj* iners, īnscītus.
incomplete *adj* imperfectus.
incomprehensible *adj* incrēdibilis.

inconceivable *adj* incrēdibilis.
inconclusive *adj* inānis.
incongruous *adj* absonus, aliēnus.
inconsiderable *adj* exiguus.
inconsiderate *adj* imprōvidus, incōnsultus.
inconsistency *n* discrepantia *f*, incōnstantia *f*.
inconsistent *adj* incōnstāns; **be ~** discrepāre;
  be ~ with abhorrēre ab, repugnāre (*dat*).
inconsistently *adv* incōnstanter.
inconsolable *adj* nōn cōnsōlābilis.
inconspicuous *adj* obscūrus; **be ~** latēre.
inconstancy *n* incōnstantia *f*, levitās *f*.
inconstant *adj* incōnstāns, levis, mōbilis.
inconstantly *adv* incōnstanter.
incontestable *adj* certus.
incontinence *n* incontinentia *f*.
incontinent *adj* intemperāns.
inconvenience *n* incommodum *nt* ♦ *vt*
  incommodāre.
inconvenient *adj* incommodus.
inconveniently *adv* incommodē.
incorporate *vt* īnserere, adiungere.
incorrect *adj* falsus; **be ~** nōn cōnstāre.
incorrectly *adv* falsō, perperam.
incorrigible *adj* improbus, perditus.
incorruptibility *n* integritās *f*.
incorruptible *adj* incorruptus.
increase *n* incrēmentum *nt*, additāmentum *nt*,
  auctus *m* ♦ *vt* augēre, amplificāre ♦ *vi*
  crēscere, incrēscere.
increasingly *adv* magis magisque.
incredible *adj* incrēdibilis.
incredibly *adv* incrēdibiliter.
incredulous *adj* incrēdulus.
increment *n* incrēmentum *nt*.
incriminate *vt* crīminārī.
inculcate *vt* inculcāre, īnfīgere.
incumbent *adj*: **it is ~ on** oportet.
incur *vt* subīre; (*guilt*) admittere.
incurable *adj* īnsānābilis.
incursion *n* incursiō *f*.
indebted *adj* obnoxius; **be ~** dēbēre.
indecency *n* obscēnitās *f*.
indecent *adj* obscēnus, impudīcus.
indecently *adv* obscēnē.
indecision *n* dubitātiō *f*.
indecisive *adj* anceps, dubius; **the battle is ~**
  ancipitī Marte pugnātur.
indecisively *adv* incertō ēventū.
indecorous *adj* indecōrus.
indeed *adv* profectō, sānē; (*concessive*)
  quidem; (*interrog*) itane vērō?; (*reply*) certē,
  vērō; (*with pron*) dēmum; (*with adj, adv, conj*)
  adeō.
indefatigable *adj* impiger.
indefensible *adj*: **be ~** dēfendī nōn posse;
  (*belief*) tenērī nōn posse; (*offence*) excūsārī
  nōn posse.
indefinite *adj* incertus, ambiguus, īnfīnītus.
indefinitely *adv* ambiguē; (*time*) in incertum.
indelicate *adj* pūtidus, indecōrus.
independence *n* lībertās *f*.
independent *adj* līber, suī iūris.

indescribable *adj* inēnārrābilis.
indestructible *adj* perennis.
indeterminate *adj* incertus.
index *n* index *m*.
indicate *vt* indicāre, significāre.
indication *n* indicium *nt*, signum *nt*.
indict *vt* diem dīcere (*dat*), accūsāre, nōmen
  dēferre (*gen*).
indictment *n* accūsātiō *f*.
indifference *n* neglegentia *f*, languor *m*.
indifferent *adj* (*manner*) neglegēns, frīgidus,
  sēcūrus; (*quality*) mediocris.
indifferently *adv* neglegenter; mediocriter;
  (*without distinction*) promiscuē, sine
  discrīmine.
indigence *n* indigentia *f*, egestās *f*.
indigenous *adj* indigena.
indigent *adj* indigēns, egēnus.
indigestible *adj* crūdus.
indigestion *n* crūditās *f*.
indignant *adj* indignābundus, īrātus; **be ~**
  indignārī.
indignantly *adv* īrātē.
indignation *n* indignātiō *f*, dolor *m*.
indignity *n* contumēlia *f*, indignitās *f*.
indigo *n* Indicum *nt*.
indirect *adj* oblīquus.
indirectly *adv* oblīquē, per ambāgēs.
indirectness *n* ambāgēs *fpl*.
indiscipline *n* lascīvia *f*, licentia *f*.
indiscreet *adj* incōnsultus, imprūdēns.
indiscreetly *adv* incōnsultē, imprūdenter.
indiscretion *n* imprūdentia *f*; (*act*) culpa *f*.
indiscriminate *adj* prōmiscuus.
indiscriminately *adv* prōmiscuē, sine
  discrīmine.
indispensable *adj* necesse, necessārius.
indisposed *adj* īnfīrmus, aegrōtus, (*will*)
  āversus, aliēnātus; **be ~** aegrōtāre;
  abhorrēre, aliēnārī.
indisposition *n* īnfīrmitās *f*, valētūdō *f*.
indisputable *adj* certus, manifestus.
indisputably *adv* certē, sine dubiō.
indissoluble *adj* indissolūbilis.
indistinct *adj* obscūrus, obtūsus; (*speaker*)
  balbus.
indistinctly *adv* obscūrē; **pronounce ~**
  opprimere; **speak ~** balbutīre.
individual *adj* proprius ♦ *n* homō *m/f*, prīvātus
  m; **~s** *pl* singulī *mpl*.
individuality *n* proprium *nt*.
individually *adv* singulātim, prīvātim.
indivisible *adj* indīviduus.
indolence *n* dēsidia *f*, ignāvia *f*, inertia *f*.
indolent *adj* dēses, ignāvus, iners.
indolently *adv* ignāvē.
indomitable *adj* indomitus.
indoor *adj* umbrātilis.
indoors *adv* intus; (*motion*) intrā.
indubitable *adj* certus.
indubitably *adv* sine dubiō.
induce *vt* indūcere, addūcere, persuādēre
  (*dat*).

inducement n illecebra f, praemium nt.
induction n (*logic*) inductiō f.
indulge vt indulgēre (*dat*).
indulgence n indulgentia f, venia f; (*favour*) grātia f.
indulgent adj indulgēns, lēnis.
indulgently adv indulgenter.
industrious adj industrius, impiger, dīligēns.
industriously adv industriē.
industry n industria f, dīligentia f, labor m.
inebriated adj ēbrius.
inebriation n ēbrietās f.
ineffable adj eximius.
ineffective adj inūtilis, invalidus.
ineffectively adv ināniter.
ineffectual adj inritus.
inefficient adj īnscītus, parum strēnuus.
inelegant adj inēlegāns, inconcinnus.
inelegantly adv inēleganter.
inept adj ineptus.
ineptly adv ineptē.
inequality n dissimilitūdō f, inīquitās f.
inert adj iners, sōcors, immōbilis.
inertia n inertia f.
inertly adv tardē, lentē.
inestimable adj inaestimābilis.
inevitable adj necessārius.
inevitably adv necessāriō.
inexact adj parum subtīlis.
inexhaustible adj perennis.
inexorable adj inexōrābilis.
inexpediency n inūtilitās f, incommodum nt.
inexpedient adj inūtilis; **it is ~** nōn expedit.
inexpensive adj vīlis.
inexperience n imperītia f, īnscītia f.
inexperienced adj imperītus, rudis, īnscītus.
inexpert adj imperītus.
inexpiable adj inexpiābilis.
inexplicable adj inexplicābilis, inēnōdābilis.
inexpressible adj inēnārrābilis.
inextricable adj inexplicābilis.
infallible adj certus, errōris expers.
infamous adj īnfāmis, flāgitiōsus.
infamously adv flāgitiōsē.
infamy n īnfāmia f, flāgitium nt, dēdecus nt.
infancy n īnfantia f; (*fig*) incūnābula ntpl.
infant n īnfāns m/f.
infantile adj puerīlis.
infantry n peditēs mpl, peditātus m.
infantryman n pedes m.
infatuate vt īnfatuāre.
infatuated adj dēmēns.
infatuation n dēmentia f.
infect vt īnficere.
infection n contāgiō f.
infer vt īnferre, colligere.
inference n conclūsiō f.
inferior adj (*position*) īnferior; (*quality*) dēterior.
infernal adj īnfernus.
infest vt frequentāre.
infidel adj impius.
infidelity n perfidia f, īnfidēlitās f.

infiltrate vi sē īnsinuāre.
infinite adj īnfīnītus, immēnsus.
infinitely adv longē, immēnsum.
infinitesimal adj minimus.
infinity n īnfīnitās f.
infirm adj īnfirmus, invalidus.
infirmary n valētūdinārium nt.
infirmity n morbus m.
inflame vt accendere, incendere, īnflammāre.
be ~d exārdēscere.
inflammation n (*MED*) īnflātiō f.
inflate vt īnflāre.
inflated adj (*fig*) īnflātus, tumidus.
inflexible adj rigidus.
inflexion n (*GRAM*) flexūra f; (*voice*) flexiō f.
inflict vt īnflīgere, incutere; (*burden*) impōnere; (*penalty*) sūmere; **be ~ed with** labōrāre ex.
infliction n poena f; malum nt.
influence n (*physical*) impulsiō f, mōmentum nt; (*moral*) auctōritās f; (*partial*) grātia f; **have ~** valēre; **have great ~ with** plūrimum posse apud; **under the ~ of** īnstinctus (*abl*) ♦ vt impellere, movēre, addūcere.
influential adj gravis, potēns; grātiōsus.
influenza n gravēdō f.
inform vt docēre, certiōrem facere; **~ against** nōmen dēferre (*gen*).
informant n index m, auctor m.
information n indicium nt, nūntius m.
informer n index m, dēlātor m; **turn ~** indicium profitērī.
infrequent adj rārus.
infrequently adv rārō.
infringe vt violāre, imminuere.
infringement n violātiō f.
infuriate vt efferāre.
infuriated adj furibundus.
infuse vt īnfundere; (*fig*) inicere.
ingenious adj ingeniōsus, callidus; (*thing*) artificiōsus.
ingeniously adv callidē, summā arte.
ingenuity n ars f, artificium nt, acūmen nt.
ingenuous adj ingenuus, simplex.
ingenuously adv ingenuē, simpliciter.
ingenuousness n ingenuitās f.
ingle n focus m.
inglorious adj inglōrius, ignōbilis, inhonestus.
ingloriously adv sine glōriā, inhonestē.
ingot n later m.
ingrained adj īnsitus.
ingratiate vt: **~ oneself with** grātiam inīre ab, sē īnsinuāre in familiāritātem (*gen*); **~ oneself into** sē īnsinuāre in (*acc*).
ingratitude n ingrātus animus m.
ingredient n pars f.
inhabit vt incolere, habitāre in (*abl*).
inhabitable adj habitābilis.
inhabitant n incola m/f.
inhale vt haurīre.
inharmonious adj dissonus.
inherent adj īnsitus; **be ~ in** inhaerēre (*dat*), inesse (*dat*).

inherently *adv* nātūrā.
inherit *vt* excipere.
inheritance *n* hērēditās *f*, patrimōnium *nt*;
divide an ~ herctum ciēre; **come into an ~**
hērēditātem adīre.
inheritor *n* hērēs *m/f*.
inhibit *vt* prohibēre, inhibēre.
inhospitable *adj* inhospitālis.
inhuman *adj* inhūmānus, immānis, crūdēlis.
inhumanity *n* inhūmānitās *f*, crūdēlitās *f*.
inhumanly *adv* inhūmānē, crūdēliter.
inimical *adj* inimīcus.
inimitable *adj* singulāris, eximius.
iniquitous *adj* inīquus, improbus, nefārius.
iniquity *n* scelus *nt*, flāgitium *nt*.
initial *adj* prīmus.
initiate *vt* initiāre; (*with knowledge*) imbuere.
initiative *n* initium *nt*; **take the ~** initium
capere, facere; occupāre (*inf*).
inject *vt* inicere.
injudicious *adj* incōnsultus, imprūdēns.
injunction *n* iussum *nt*, praeceptum *nt*.
injure *vt* laedere, nocēre (*dat*).
injurious *adj* damnōsus, nocēns.
injury *n* iniūria *f*, damnum *nt*; (*bodily*) vulnus
nt.
injustice *n* iniūria *f*, inīquitās *f*.
ink *n* ātrāmentum *nt*.
inkling *n* audītiō *f*, suspiciō *f*.
inland *adj* mediterrāneus; **further ~** interior.
inlay *vt* īnserere.
inlet *n* sinus *m*, aestuārium *nt*.
inly *adv* penitus.
inmate *n* inquilīnus *m*.
inmost *adj* intimus.
inn *n* dēversōrium *nt*; caupōna *f*, taberna *f*.
innate *adj* innātus, īnsitus.
inner *adj* interior.
innermost *adj* intimus.
innkeeper *n* caupō *m*.
innocence *n* innocentia *f*.
innocent *adj* innocēns, īnsōns; (*character*)
integer, castus.
innocently *adv* innocenter, integrē, castē.
innocuous *adj* innoxius.
innovate *vt* novāre.
innovation *n* novum *nt*, nova rēs *f*.
innovator *n* novārum rērum auctor *m*.
innuendo *n* verbum inversum *nt*.
innumerable *adj* innumerābilis.
inoffensive *adj* innocēns.
inoffensively *adv* innocenter.
inopportune *adj* intempestīvus.
inopportunely *adv* intempestīvē.
inordinate *adj* immodicus, immoderātus.
inordinately *adv* immoderātē.
inquest *n* quaestiō *f*; **hold an ~ on** quaerere dē.
inquire *vi* exquīrere, rogāre; **~ into** inquīrere
in (*acc*), investigāre.
inquiry *n* quaestiō *f*, investīgātiō *f*; (*asking*)
interrogātiō *f*; **make ~** exquīrere; **make ~ies**
about inquīrere in (*acc*); **hold an ~ on**
quaerere dē, quaestiōnem īnstituere dē.

inquisition *n* inquīsītiō *f*.
inquisitive *adj* cūriōsus.
inquisitiveness *n* cūriōsitās *f*.
inquisitor *n* inquīsītor *m*.
inroad *n* incursiō *f*, impressiō *f*; **make an ~**
incursāre.
insane *adj* īnsānus, mente captus; **be ~**
īnsānīre.
insanity *n* īnsānia *f*, dēmentia *f*.
insatiable *adj* īnsatiābilis, inexplēbilis,
īnsaturābilis.
insatiably *adv* īnsaturābiliter.
inscribe *vt* īnscrībere.
inscription *n* epigramma *nt*; (*written*)
īnscrīptiō *f*.
inscrutable *adj* obscūrus.
insect *n* bestiola *f*.
insecure *adj* īnstabilis, intūtus.
insecurity *n* perīcula *ntpl*.
insensate *adj* ineptus, stultus.
insensible *adj* torpidus; (*fig*) dūrus.
insensitive *adj* dūrus.
inseparable *adj* coniūnctus; **be the ~**
companion of ab latere esse (*gen*).
inseparably *adv* coniūnctē.
insert *vt* īnserere, immittere, interpōnere.
insertion *n* interpositiō *f*.
inshore *adv* prope lītus.
inside *adv* intus; (*motion*) intrō ♦ *adj* interior ♦
n pars *f* interior ♦ *prep* intrā (*acc*); **get right ~**
sē īnsinuāre in (*acc*); **turn ~ out** excutere; **on**
the ~ interior.
insidious *adj* īnsidiōsus, subdolus.
insidiously *adv* īnsidiōsē.
insight *n* intellegentia *f*, cognitiō *f*.
insignia *n* īnsignia *ntpl*.
insignificance *n* levitās *f*.
insignificant *adj* levis, exiguus, nullīus
mōmentī; (*position*) humilis.
insincere *adj* simulātus, fūcōsus.
insincerely *adv* simulātē.
insincerity *n* simulātiō *f*, fraus *f*.
insinuate *vt* īnsinuāre; (*hint*) significāre ♦ *vi*
sē īnsinuāre.
insinuating *adj* blandus.
insinuation *n* ambigua verba *ntpl*.
insipid *adj* īnsulsus, frīgidus.
insipidity *n* īnsulsitās *f*.
insist *vi* īnstāre; **~ on** postulāre.
insistence *n* pertinācia *f*.
insistent *adj* pertināx.
insolence *n* īnsolentia *f*, contumācia *f*,
superbia *f*.
insolent *adj* īnsolēns, contumāx, superbus.
insolently *adv* īnsolenter.
insoluble *adj* inexplicābilis.
insolvency *n* reī familiāris naufragium *nt*.
insolvent *adj*: **be ~** solvendō nōn esse.
inspect *vt* īnspicere; (*MIL*) recēnsēre.
inspection *n* cognitiō *f*; (*MIL*) recēnsiō *f*.
inspector *n* cūrātor *m*.
inspiration *n* adflātus *m*, īnstinctus *m*.
inspire *vt* īnstinguere, incendere.

instability *n* mōbilitās *f*.
install *vt* inaugurāre.
instalment *n* pēnsiō *f*.
instance *n* exemplum *nt*; **for ~** exemplī causā, grātiā; **at the ~** admonitū; **at my ~** mē auctōre ♦ *vt* memorāre.
instant *adj* īnstāns, praesēns ♦ *n* temporis pūnctum *nt*, mōmentum *nt*.
instantaneous *adj* praesēns.
instantaneously *adv* continuō, īlicō.
instantly *adv* īlicō, extemplō.
instead of *prep* prō (*abl*), locō (*gen*); (*with verb*) nōn . . . sed.
instigate *vt* īnstigāre, impellere.
instigation *n* impulsus *m*, stimulus *m*; auctōritās *f*; **at my ~** mē auctōre.
instigator *n* īnstimulātor *m*, auctor *m*.
instil *vt* imbuere, adspīrāre, inicere.
instinct *n* nātūra *f*, ingenium *nt*, sēnsus *m*.
instinctive *adj* nātūrālis.
instinctively *adv* nātūrā, ingeniō suō.
institute *vt* īnstituere, inaugurāre.
institution *n* īnstitūtum *nt*; societās *f*.
instruct *vt* docēre, īnstituere, īnstruere; ērudīre; (*order*) praecipere (*dat*).
instruction *n* doctrīna *f*, disciplīna *f*; praeceptum *nt*; **give ~s** dēnūntiāre, praecipere.
instructor *n* doctor *m*, praeceptor *m*.
instructress *n* magistra *f*.
instrument *n* īnstrūmentum *nt*; (*music*) fidēs *fpl*; (*legal*) tabulae *fpl*.
instrumental *adj* ūtilis.
instrumentalist *n* fidicen *m*, fidicina *f*.
instrumentality *n* opera *f*.
insubordinate *adj* turbulentus, sēditiōsus.
insubordination *n* intemperantia *f*, licentia *f*.
insufferable *adj* intolerandus, intolerābilis.
insufficiency *n* inopia *f*.
insufficient *adj* minor; **be ~** nōn sufficere.
insufficiently *adv* parum.
insulate *vt* sēgregāre.
insult *n* iniūria *f*, contumēlia *f*, probrum *nt* ♦ *vt* maledīcere (*dat*), contumēliam impōnere (*dat*).
insulting *adj* contumēliōsus.
insultingly *adv* contumēliōsē.
insuperable *adj* inexsuperābilis.
insupportable *adj* intolerandus, intolerābilis.
insurance *n* cautiō *f*.
insure *vi* cavēre.
insurgent *n* rebellis *m*.
insurmountable *adj* inexsuperābilis.
insurrection *n* mōtus *m*, sēditiō *f*.
intact *adj* integer, intāctus, incolumis.
integrity *n* integritās *f*, innocentia *f*, fidēs *f*.
intellect *n* ingenium *nt*, mēns *f*, animus *m*.
intellectual *adj* ingeniōsus.
intelligence *n* intellegentia *f*, acūmen *nt*; (*MIL*) nūntius *m*.
intelligent *adj* ingeniōsus, sapiēns, argūtus.
intelligently *adv* ingeniōsē, sapienter, satis acutē.

intelligible *adj* perspicuus, apertus.
intemperance *n* intemperantia *f*, licentia *f*.
intemperate *adj* intemperāns, intemperātus.
intemperately *adv* intemperanter.
intend *vt* (*with inf*) in animō habēre, velle; (*with object*) dēstināre.
intense *adj* ācer, nimius.
intensely *adv* valdē, nimium.
intensify *vt* augēre, amplificāre; **be ~ied** ingravēscere.
intensity *n* vīs *f*.
intensive *adj* ācer, multus, adsiduus.
intensively *adv* summō studiō.
intent *adj* ērēctus, intentus; **be ~ on** animum intendere in (*acc*) ♦ *n* cōnsilium *nt*; **with ~** cōnsultō.
intention *n* cōnsilium *nt*, prōpositum *nt*; **it is my ~** mihī in animō est; **with the ~ of** eā mente, eō cōnsiliō ut (*subj*).
intentionally *adv* cōnsultō, dē industriā.
inter *vt* humāre.
intercalary *adj* intercalāris.
intercalate *vt* intercalāre.
intercede *vi* intercēdere, dēprecārī.
intercept *vt* excipere, intercipere; (*cut off*) interclūdere.
intercession *n* dēprecātiō *f*; (*tribune's*) intercessiō *f*.
intercessor *n* dēprecātor *m*.
interchange *vt* permūtāre ♦ *n* permūtātiō *f*, vicissitūdō *f*.
intercourse *n* commercium *nt*, ūsus *m*, cōnsuētūdō *f*.
interdict *n* interdictum *nt* ♦ *vt* interdīcere (*dat*), vetāre.
interest *n* (*advantage*) commodum *nt*; (*study*) studium *nt*; (*money*) faenus *nt*, ūsūra *f*; **compound ~** anatocismus *m*; **rate of ~** faenus *nt*; **~ at 12 per cent (per annum)** centēsimae *fpl*; **it is of ~** interest; **it is in my ~s** meā interest; **consult the ~s of** cōnsulere (*dat*); **take an ~ in** animum intendere (*dat*) ♦ *vt* dēlectāre, capere; (*audience*) tenēre; **~ oneself in** studēre (*dat*).
interested *adj* attentus; (*for gain*) ambitiōsūs.
interesting *adj* iūcundus, novus.
interfere *vi* intervenīre; (*with*) sē interpōnere (*dat*), sē admiscēre ad; (*hinder*) officere (*dat*).
interference *n* interventus *m*, intercessiō *f*.
interim *n*: **in the ~** interim, intereā.
interior *adj* interior ♦ *n* pars interior *f*; (*country*) interiōra *ntpl*.
interject *vt* exclāmāre.
interjection *n* interiectiō *f*.
interlace *vt* intexere.
interlard *vt* variāre.
interlock *vt* implicāre.
interloper *n* interpellātor *m*.
interlude *n* embolium *nt*.
intermarriage *n* cōnūbium *nt*.
intermediary *adj* medius ♦ *n* internūntius *m*.
intermediate *adj* medius.
interment *n* humātiō *f*.

interminable *adj* sempiternus, longus.
intermingle *vt* intermiscēre ♦ *vi* sē
   immiscēre.
intermission *n* intercapēdō *f*, intermissiō *f*.
intermittent *adj* interruptus.
intermittently *adv* interdum.
intern *vt* inclūdere.
internal *adj* internus; (*POL*) domesticus.
internally *adv* intus, domī.
international *adj*: ~ **law** iūs gentium.
internecine *adj* internecīvus.
interplay *n* vicēs *fpl*.
interpolate *vt* interpolāre.
interpose *vt* interpōnere ♦ *vi* intercēdere.
interposition *n* intercessiō *f*.
interpret *vt* interpretārī.
interpretation *n* interpretātiō *f*.
interpreter *n* interpres *m/f*.
interrogate *vt* interrogāre, percontārī.
interrogation *n* interrogātiō *f*, percontātiō *f*.
interrupt *vt* (*action*) intercipere; (*speaker*)
   interpellāre; (*talk*) dirimere; (*continuity*)
   intermittere.
interrupter *n* interpellātor *m*.
interruption *n* interpellātiō *f*; intermissiō *f*.
intersect *vt* dīvidere, secāre.
intersperse *vt* distinguere.
interstice *n* rīma *f*.
intertwine *vt* intexere, implicāre.
interval *n* intervallum *nt*, spatium *nt*; **after an ~**
   spatiō interpositō; **after an ~ of a year** annō
   interiectō; **at ~s** interdum; **at frequent ~s**
   identidem; **leave an ~** intermittere.
intervene *vt* intercēdere, intervenīre.
intervention *n* intercessiō *f*, interventus *m*; **by**
   the ~ of intercursū (*gen*).
interview *n* colloquium *nt*, aditus *m* ♦ *vt*
   convenīre.
interweave *vt* implicāre, intexere.
intestate *adj* intestātus ♦ *adv* intestātō.
intestine *adj* intestīnus; (*POL*) domesticus ♦ *npl*
   intestīna *ntpl*; (*victim's*) exta *ntpl*.
intimacy *n* familiāritās *f*.
intimate *adj* familiāris; **be an ~ friend of** ab
   latere esse (*gen*); **a very ~ friend**
   perfamiliāris *m/f* ♦ *vt* dēnūntiāre.
intimately *adv* familiāriter.
intimation *n* dēnūntiātiō *f*; (*hint*) indicium *nt*.
intimidate *vt* minārī (*dat*), terrōrem inicere
   (*dat*).
intimidation *n* metus *m*, minae *fpl*.
into *prep* in (*acc*), intrā (*acc*).
intolerable *adj* intolerandus, intolerābilis.
intolerably *adv* intoleranter.
intolerance *n* impatientia *f*.
intolerant *adj* impatiēns, intolerāns.
intonation *n* sonus *m*, flexiō *f*.
intone *vt* cantāre.
intoxicate *vt* ēbrium reddere.
intoxicated *adj* ēbrius.
intoxication *n* ēbrietās *f*.
intractable *adj* indocilis, difficilis.
intransigent *adj* obstinātus.

intrepid *adj* intrepidus, impavidus.
intrepidity *n* audācia *f*, fortitūdō *f*.
intricacy *n* implicātiō *f*.
intricate *adj* implicātus, involūtus.
intricately *adv* implicitē.
intrigue *n* factiō *f*, artēs *fpl*, fallācia *f* ♦ *vi*
   māchinārī, fallāciīs ūtī.
intriguing *adj* factiōsus; blandus.
intrinsic *adj* vērus, innātus.
intrinsically *adv* per sē.
introduce *vt* indūcere, īnferre, importāre;
   (*acquaintance*) commendāre; (*custom*)
   īnstituere.
introduction *n* exōrdium *nt*, prooemium *nt*; (*of*
   person) commendātiō *f*; **letter of ~** litterae
   commendātīciae *fpl*.
intrude *vi* sē interpōnere, intervenīre.
intruder *n* interpellātor *m*, advena *m*; (*fig*)
   aliēnus *m*.
intrusion *n* interpellātiō *f*.
intuition *n* sēnsus *m*, cognitiō *f*.
inundate *vt* inundāre.
inundation *n* ēluviō *f*.
inure *vt* dūrāre, adsuēfacere.
invade *vt* invādere.
invalid *adj* aeger, dēbilis; (*null*) inritus.
invalidate *vt* īnfīrmāre.
invaluable *adj* inaestimābilis.
invariable *adj* cōnstāns, immūtābilis.
invariably *adv* semper.
invasion *n* incursiō *f*.
invective *n* convīcium *nt*.
inveigh *vi*: ~ **against** invehī in (*acc*), īnsectārī.
inveigle *vt* illicere, pellicere.
invent *vt* fingere, comminīscī, invenīre.
invention *n* inventum *nt*; (*faculty*) inventiō *f*.
inventor *n* inventor *m*, auctor *m*.
inverse *adj* inversus.
inversely *adv* inversō ōrdine.
invert *vt* invertere.
invest *vt* (*in office*) inaugurāre; (*MIL*) obsidēre,
   circumsedēre; (*money*) locāre.
investigate *vt* investīgāre, indāgāre; (*case*)
   cognōscere.
investigation *n* investīgātiō *f*, indāgātiō *f*;
   (*case*) cognitiō *f*.
investment *n* (*MIL*) obsessiō *f*; (*money*) locāta
   pecūnia *f*.
inveterate *adj* inveterātus, vetus; **become ~**
   inveterāscere.
invidious *adj* invidiōsus.
invidiously *adv* invidiōsē.
invigorate *vt* recreāre, reficere.
invincible *adj* invictus.
inviolable *adj* inviolātus; (*person*)
   sacrōsanctus.
inviolably *adv* inviolātē.
inviolate *adj* integer.
invisible *adj* caecus; **be ~** vidērī nōn posse.
invitation *n* invītātiō *f*; **at the ~ of** invītātū
   (*gen*).
invite *vt* invītāre, vocāre.
inviting *adj* suāvis, blandus.

invitingly *adv* blandē, suāviter.
invocation *n* testātiō *f*.
invoke *vt* invocāre, testārī.
involuntarily *adv* īnscienter, invītus.
involuntary *adj* coāctus.
involve *vt* implicāre, involvere; **be ~d in** inligārī (*abl*).
invulnerable *adj* inviolābilis; **be ~** vulnerārī nōn posse.
inward *adj* interior.
inwardly *adv* intus.
inwards *adv* intrōrsus.
inweave *vt* intexere.
inwrought *adj* intextus.
irascibility *n* īrācundia *f*.
irascible *adj* īrācundus.
irate *adj* īrātus.
ire *n* īra *f*.
iris *n* hyacinthus *m*.
irk *vt* incommodāre; **I am ~ed** mē piget.
irksome *adj* molestus.
irksomeness *n* molestia *f*.
iron *n* ferrum *nt*; **of ~** ferreus ♦ *adj* ferreus.
ironical *adj* inversus.
ironically *adv* inversīs verbīs.
iron mine *n* ferrāria *f*.
ironmonger *n* negōtiātor ferrārius *m*.
ironmongery *n* ferrāmenta *ntpl*.
iron ore *n* ferrum īnfectum *nt*.
iron-tipped *adj* ferrātus.
irony *n* illūsiō *f*, verbōrum inversiō *f*, dissimulātiō *f*.
irradiate *vt* illūstrāre.
irrational *adj* absurdus, ratiōnis expers; (*animal*) brūtus.
irrationally *adv* absurdē, sine ratiōne.
irreconcilable *adj* repugnāns, īnsociābilis.
irrefutable *adj* certus, invictus.
irregular *adj* incompositus; (*ground*) inaequālis; (*meeting*) extraōrdinārius; (*troops*) tumultuārius.
irregularity *n* inaequālitās *f*, (*conduct*) prāvitās *f*, licentia *f*; (*election*) vitium *nt*.
irregularly *adv* nullō ōrdine; (*elected*) vitiō.
irrelevant *adj* aliēnus.
irreligion *n* impietās *f*.
irreligious *adj* impius.
irremediable *adj* īnsānābilis.
irreparable *adj* inrevocābilis.
irreproachable *adj* integer, innocēns.
irresistible *adj* invictus.
irresolute *adj* dubius, anceps.
irresolutely *adv* dubitanter.
irresolution *n* dubitātiō *f*.
irresponsibility *n* licentia *f*.
irresponsible *adj* lascīvus, levis.
irretrievable *adj* inrevocābilis.
irreverence *n* impietās *f*.
irreverent *adj* impius.
irreverently *adv* impiē.
irrevocable *adj* inrevocābilis.
irrigate *vt* inrigāre.
irrigation *n* inrigātiō *f*.

irritability *n* īrācundia *f*.
irritable *adj* īrācundus.
irritate *vt* inrītāre, stomachum movēre (*dat*).
irritation *n* īrācundia *f*, stomachus *m*.
island *n* īnsula *f*.
islander *n* īnsulānus *m*.
isle *n* īnsula *f*.
isolate *vt* sēgregāre, sēparāre.
isolation *n* sōlitūdō *f*.
issue *n* (*result*) ēventus *m*, exitus *m*; (*children*) prōlēs *f*; (*question*) rēs *f*; (*book*) ēditiō *f*; **decide the ~** dēcernere, dēcertāre; **the point at ~** quā dē rē agitur ♦ *vt* distribuere; (*book*) ēdere; (*announcement*) prōmulgāre; (*coin*) ērogāre ♦ *vi* ēgredī, ēmānāre; (*result*) ēvādere, ēvenīre.
isthmus *n* isthmus *m*.
it *pron* hōc, id.
itch *n* (*disease*) scabiēs *f*; (*fig*) cacoēthes *nt* ♦ *vi* prūrīre.
item *n* nōmen *nt*, rēs *f*.
iterate *vt* iterāre.
itinerant *adj* vāgus, circumforāneus.
itinerary *n* iter *nt*.
its *adj* suus, ēius.
itself *pron* ipse, ipsa, ipsum.
ivory *n* ebur *nt* ♦ *adj* eburneus.
ivy *n* hedera *f*.

J, j

jabber *vi* blaterāre.
jackdaw *n* grāculus *m*.
jaded *adj* dēfessus, fatīgātus.
jagged *adj* serrātus.
jail *n* carcer *m*.
jailer *n* custōs *m*, carcerārius *m*.
jam *vt* comprimere; (*way*) obstruere.
jamb *n* postis *m*.
jangle *vi* crepitāre; rixārī.
janitor *n* iānitor *m*.
January *n* mēnsis Iānuārius *m*; **of ~** Iānuārius.
jar *n* urna *f*, (*for wine*) amphora *f*; (*for water*) hydria *f*; (*sound*) offēnsa *f*; (*quarrel*) rixa *f* ♦ *vi* offendere.
jasper *n* iaspis *f*.
jaundice *n* morbus arquātus.
jaundiced *adj* ictericus.
jaunt *n*: **take a ~** excurrere.
jauntily *adv* hilare, festīvē.
jauntiness *n* hilaritās *f*.
jaunty *adj* hilaris, festīvus.
javelin *n* iaculum *nt*, pīlum *nt*; **throw the ~** iaculārī.
jaw *n* māla *f*; **~s** *pl* faucēs *fpl*.

jay n grāculus m.
jealous adj invidus; **be ~ of** invidēre (dat).
jealousy n invidia f.
jeer n irrīsiō f ♦ vi irrīdēre; **~ at** illūdere.
jejune adj iēiūnus, exīlis.
jeopardize vt in perīculum addūcere.
jeopardy n perīculum nt.
jerk n subitus mōtus m.
jest n iocus m.
jester n scurra m.
jet n (mineral) gagātēs m; (of water) saltus m ♦ vi salīre.
jetsam n ēiectāmenta ntpl.
jettison vt ēicere.
jetty n mōlēs f.
Jew n Iūdaeus.
jewel n gemma f.
Jewish adj Iūdaicus.
jig n tripudium nt.
jilt vt repudiāre.
jingle n nēnia f ♦ vi crepitāre, tinnīre.
job n opus nt.
jocose adj see **jocular.**
jocular adj facētus, ioculāris.
jocularity n facētiae fpl.
jocularly adv facētē, per iocum.
jocund adj hilaris, festīvus.
jog vt fodicāre; (fig) stimulāre ♦ vi ambulāre.
join vt iungere, coniungere, cōpulāre ♦ vi coniungī, sē coniungere; **~ in** interesse (dat), sē immiscēre (dat); **~ battle with** proelium committere (+ abl).
joiner n faber m.
joint adj commūnis ♦ n commissūra f; (of body) articulus m, nōdus m; **~ by ~** articulātim.
jointed adj geniculātus.
joint-heir n cohērēs m/f.
jointly adv ūnā, coniūnctē.
joist n tignum nt.
joke n iocus m ♦ vi iocārī, lūdere.
joking n iocus m; **~ apart** remōtō iocō.
jokingly adv per iocum.
jollity n hilaritās f, festīvitās f.
jolly adj hilaris, festīvus.
jolt vt iactāre.
jolting n iactātiō f.
jostle vt agitāre, offendere.
jot n minimum nt; **not a ~** nihil; **not care a ~** nōn floccī facere.
journal n ācta diūrna ntpl.
journey n iter nt.
journeyman n opifex m.
Jove n Iuppiter m.
jovial adj hilaris.
joviality n hilaritās f.
jovially adv hilare.
jowl n māla f; **cheek by ~** iuxtā.
joy n gaudium nt, laetitia f, alacritās f.
joyful adj laetus, hilaris.
joyfully adv laetē, hilare.
joyfulness n gaudium nt, laetitia f.
joyless adj tristis, maestus.

joyous adj see **joyful.**
joyously adv see **joyfully.**
jubilant adj laetus, gaudiō exsultāns.
judge n iūdex m, arbiter m ♦ vt iūdicāre; (think) exīstimāre, cēnsēre; **~ between** diiūdicāre.
judgeship n iūdicātus m.
judgment n iūdicium nt, arbitrium nt; (opinion) sententia f; (punishment) poena f; (wisdom) iūdicium nt; **in my ~** meō animō, meō arbitrātū; **pass ~ on** statuere dē; **sit in ~** iūdicium exercēre.
judgment seat n tribūnal nt.
judicature n iūrisdictiō f; (men) iūdicēs mpl.
judicial adj iūdiciālis; (law) iūdiciārius.
judiciary n iūdicēs mpl.
judicious adj prūdēns, cōnsīderātus.
judiciously adv prūdenter.
jug n hydria f, urceus m.
juggler n praestīgiātor m.
juggling n praestīgiae fpl.
juice n liquor m, sūcus m.
juicy adj sūcī plēnus.
July n mēnsis Quīnctīlis, Iūlius m; **of ~** Quīnctīlis, Iūlius.
jumble n congeriēs f ♦ vt cōnfundere.
jump n saltus m ♦ vi salīre; **~ across** transilīre; **~ at** (opportunity) captāre, adripere, amplectī; **~ down** dēsilīre; **~ on to** īnsilīre in (acc).
junction n coniūnctiō f.
juncture n tempus nt.
June n mēnsis Iūnius; **of ~** Iūnius.
junior adj iūnior, nātū minor.
juniper n iūniperus f.
Juno n Iūnō, Iūnōnis f.
Jupiter n Iuppiter, Iovis m.
juridical adj iūdiciārius.
jurisconsult n iūriscōnsultus m.
jurisdiction n iūrisdictiō f, diciō f; **exercise ~** iūs dīcere.
jurisprudence n iūrisprūdentia f.
jurist n iūriscōnsultus m.
juror n iūdex m.
jury n iūdicēs mpl.
just adj iūstus, aequus ♦ adv (exactly) prōrsus; (only) modo; (time) commodum, modo; (with adv) dēmum, dēnique; (with pron) adeō dēmum, ipse; **~ as** (comparison) aequē ac, perinde ac, quemadmodum; sīcut; **~ before** (time) cum māximē, sub (acc); **~ now** modo, nunc; **~ so** ita prōrsus, sānē; **only ~** vix.
justice n iūstitia f, aequitās f, iūs nt; (person) praetor m; **administer ~** iūs reddere.
justiciary n praetor m.
justifiable adj iūstus.
justifiably adv iūre.
justification n pūrgātiō f, excūsātiō f.
justify vt excūsāre, pūrgāre.
justly adv iūstē, aequē; iūre, meritō.
jut vi prōminēre, excurrere.
jutting adj prōiectus.
juvenile adj iuvenīlis, puerīlis.

K, k

keel n carīna f.

keen adj ācer; (mind) acūtus, argūtus; (sense) sagāx; (pain) acerbus; **I am ~ on** studeō.

keenly adv ācriter, sagāciter, acūtē, acerbē.

keenness n (scent) sagācitās f; (sight) aciēs f; (pain) acerbitās f; (eagerness) studium nt, ārdor m.

keep vt servāre, tenēre, habēre; (celebrate) agere, celebrāre; (guard) custōdīre; (obey) observāre; (preserve) cōnservāre; (rear) alere, pāscere; (store) condere; **~ apart** distinēre; **~ away** arcēre; **~ back** dētinēre, reservāre; **~ down** comprimere; (exuberance) dēpāscere; **~ in** cohibēre, claudere; **~ in with** grātiam sequī (gen); **~ off** arcēre, dēfendere; **~ one's word** fidem praestāre; **~ one's hands off** manūs abstinēre; **~ house** domī sē retinēre; **~ secret** cēlāre; **~ together** continēre; **~ up** sustinēre, cōnservāre; **~ up with** subsequī; **~ waiting** dēmorārī ♦ vi dūrāre, manēre ♦ n arx f.

keeper n custōs m.

keeping n custōdia f; **in ~ with** prō (abl); **be in ~ with** convenīre (dat).

keg n cadus m.

ken n cōnspectus m.

kennel n stabulum nt.

kerb n crepīdō f.

kernel n grānum nt, nucleus m.

kettle n lebēs f.

key n clāvis f; (fig) claustra ntpl, iānua f; **~ position** cardō m.

kick vi calcitrāre ♦ vt calce ferīre.

kid n haedus m.

kidnap vt surripere.

kidnapper n plagiārius m.

kidney n rēn m.

kidney bean n phasēlus m.

kid's adj haedīnus.

kill vt interficere, interimere; (in battle) occīdere; (murder) necāre, iugulāre; (time) perdere.

killer n interfector m.

kiln n fornāx f.

kin n cognātī mpl, propinqui mpl; **next of ~** proximī mpl.

kind adj bonus, benīgnus, benevolus ♦ n genus nt; **of such a ~** tālis; **what ~ of** quālis ♦ adj cōmis.

kindle vt incendere, succendere, īnflammāre.

kindliness n cōmitās f, hūmānitās f.

kindling n (fuel) fōmes m.

kindly adv benīgnē.

kindness n benīgnitās f, benevolentia f; (act) beneficium nt, officium nt, grātia f.

kindred n necessitūdō f, cognātiō f; propinquī mpl, cognātī mpl ♦ adj cognātus, adfīnis.

king n rēx m.

kingdom n rēgnum nt.

kingfisher n alcēdō f.

kingly adj rēgius, rēgālis.

kingship n rēgnum nt.

kink n vitium nt.

kinsfolk n cognātī mpl, necessāriī mpl.

kinsman n cognātus m, propinquus m, necessārius m.

kinswoman n cognāta f, propinqua f, necessāria f.

kismet n fātum nt.

kiss n ōsculum nt ♦ vt ōsculārī.

kit n (MIL) sarcina f.

kitchen n culīna f.

kitchen garden n hortus m.

kite n mīluus m.

kite's adj mīluīnus.

knack n calliditās f, artificium nt; **have the ~ of** callēre.

knapsack n sarcina f.

knave n veterātor m.

knavish adj improbus.

knavishly adv improbē.

knead vt depsere, subigere.

knee n genū nt.

kneel vi genibus nītī.

knife n culter m; (surgeon's) scalprum nt.

knight n eques m ♦ vt in ōrdinem equestrem recipere.

knighthood n ōrdō equester m.

knightly adj equester.

knit vt texere; (brow) contrahere.

knob n bulla f.

knock vt ferīre, percutere; **~ at** pulsāre; **~ against** offendere; **~ down** dēicere, adflīgere; (at auction) addīcere; **~ off** dēcutere; (work) dēsistere ab; **~ out** ēlīdere, excutere; (unconscious) exanimāre; (fig) dēvincere; **~ up** suscitāre ♦ n pulsus m, ictus m.

knock-kneed adj vārus.

knoll n tumulus m.

knot n nōdus m ♦ vt nectere.

knotty adj nōdōsus; **~ point** nōdus m.

know vt scīre; (person) nōvisse; **~ all about** explōrātum habēre; **~ again** agnōscere; **~ how to** scīre; **not ~** ignōrāre, nescīre; **let me ~** fac sciam, fac mē certiōrem; **get to ~** cognōscere ♦ n **in the ~** cōnscius.

knowing adj prūdēns, callidus.

knowingly adv cōnsultō, sciēns.

knowledge n scientia f, doctrīna f; (practical) experientia f; (of something) cognitiō f.

knowledgeable adj gnārus, doctus.

known adj nōtus; **make ~** dēclārāre.

knuckle n articulus m.

knuckle bone n tālus m.

kotow vi adulārī.

kudos n glōria f, laus f.

L, l

label *n* titulus *m* ♦ *vt* titulō īnscrībere.
laboratory *n* officīna *f*.
laborious *adj* labōriōsus, operōsus.
laboriously *adv* operōsē.
laboriousness *n* labor *m*.
labour *n* labor *m*, opera *f*; (*work done*) opus *nt*; (*work allotted*) pēnsum *nt*; (*workmen*) operae *fpl*; **be in ~** parturīre ♦ *vi* labōrāre, ēnītī; **~ at** ēlabōrāre; **~ under a delusion** errōre fallī.
laboured *adj* adfectātus.
labourer *n* operārius *m*; **~s** *pl* operae *fpl*.
labyrinth *n* labyrinthus *m*.
lace *n* texta rēticulāta *ntpl*; (*shoe*) ligula *f* ♦ *vt* nectere.
lacerate *vt* lacerāre.
laceration *n* lacerātiō *f*.
lack *n* inopia *f*, dēfectiō *f* ♦ *vt* egēre (*abl*), carēre (*abl*).
lackey *n* pedisequus *m*.
laconic *adj* brevis.
laconically *adv* ūnō verbō, paucīs verbīs.
lacuna *n* lacūna *f*.
lad *n* puer *m*.
ladder *n* scāla *f*.
lade *vt* onerāre.
laden *adj* onustus, onerātus.
lading *n* onus *nt*.
ladle *n* trulla *f*.
lady *n* domina *f*, mātrōna *f*, mulier *f*.
ladylike *adj* līberālis, honestus.
lag *vi* cessāre.
lagoon *n* stagnum *nt*.
lair *n* latibulum *nt*.
lake *n* lacus *m*.
lamb *n* agnus *m*; (*flesh*) agnīna *f*; **ewe ~** agna *f*.
lame *adj* claudus; (*argument*) inānis; **be ~** claudicāre.
lameness *n* claudicātiō *f*.
lament *n* lāmentātiō *f*, lāmentum *nt* ♦ *vt* lūgēre, lāmentārī; (*regret*) dēplōrāre.
lamentable *adj* lāmentābilis, miserābilis.
lamentably *adv* miserābiliter.
lamentation *n* lāmentātiō *f*.
lamp *n* lucerna *f*, lychnus *m*.
lampoon *n* satura *f* ♦ *vt* carmine dēstringere.
lance *n* hasta *f*, lancea *f*.
lancer *n* hastātus *m*.
lancet *n* scalpellum *nt*.
land *n* terra *f*; (*country*) terra *f*, regiō *f*; (*territory*) fīnēs *mpl*; (*native*) patria *f*; (*property*) praedium *nt*, ager *m*; (*soil*) solum *nt* ♦ *vt* expōnere ♦ *vi* ē nāve ēgredī ♦ *adj* terrēnus, terrestris.
landfall *n* adpulsus *m*.
landing place *n* ēgressus *m*.

landlady *n* caupōna *f*.
landlord *n* dominus *m*; (*inn*) caupō *m*.
landmark *n* lapis *m*; **be a ~** ēminēre.
landscape *n* agrōrum prōspectus *m*.
landslide *n* terrae lābēs *f*, lāpsus *m*.
landwards *adv* terram versus.
lane *n* (*country*) sēmita *f*; (*town*) angiportus *m*.
language *n* lingua *f*; (*style*) ōrātiō *f*, sermō *m*; (*diction*) verba *ntpl*; **bad ~** maledicta *ntpl*.
languid *adj* languidus, remissus.
languidly *adv* languidē.
languish *vi* languēre, languēscere; (*with disease*) tābēscere.
languor *n* languor *m*.
lank, lanky *adj* exīlis, gracilis.
lantern *n* lanterna *f*, lucerna *f*.
lap *n* gremium *nt*, sinus *m* ♦ *vt* lambere; (*cover*) involvere.
lapse *n* (*time*) lāpsus *m*; (*mistake*) errātum *nt*; **after the ~ of a year** interiectō annō ♦ *vi* lābī; (*agreement*) inritum fierī; (*property*) revertī.
larceny *n* fūrtum *nt*.
larch *n* larix *f* ♦ *adj* larignus.
lard *n* adeps *m/f*.
larder *n* cella penāria *f*.
large *adj* māgnus, grandis, amplus; **at ~** solūtus; **very ~** permāgnus; **as ~ as ...** tantus ... quantus.
largely *adv* plērumque.
largesse *n* largitiō *f*; (MIL) dōnātīvum *nt*; (*civil*) congiārium *nt*; **give ~** largīrī.
lark *n* alauda *f*.
lascivious *adj* libīdinōsus.
lasciviously *adv* libīdinōsē.
lasciviousness *n* libīdō *f*.
lash *n* flagellum *nt*, lōrum *nt*; (*eye*) cilium *nt* ♦ *vt* verberāre; (*tie*) adligāre; (*with words*) castīgāre.
lashing *n* verbera *ntpl*.
lass *n* puella *f*.
lassitude *n* languor *m*.
last *adj* ultimus, postrēmus, suprēmus; (*in line*) novissimus; (*preceding*) proximus; **at ~** tandem, dēmum, dēnique; **for the ~ time** postrēmum ♦ *n* fōrma *f*; **let the cobbler stick to his ~** nē sūtor suprā crepidam ♦ *vi* dūrāre, permanēre.
lasting *adj* diūtinus, diūturnus.
lastly *adv* postrēmō, dēnique.
latch *n* pessulus *m*.
latchet *n* corrigia *f*.
late *adj* sērus; (*date*) recēns; (*dead*) dēmortuus; (*emperor*) dīvus; **~ at night** multā nocte; **till ~ in the day** ad multum diem ♦ *adv* sērō; **too ~** sērō; **too ~ to** sērius quam quī (*subj*); **of ~** nūper.
lately *adv* nūper.
latent *adj* occultus, latitāns.
later *adj* posterior ♦ *adv* posteā, posthāc, mox.
latest *adj* novissimus.
lath *n* tigillum *nt*.
lathe *n* tornus *m*.
lather *n* spūma *f*.

Latin adj Latīnus; **speak** ~ Latīnē loquī;
  understand ~ Latīnē scīre; **translate into** ~
  Latīnē reddere; **in Latin** latinē.
Latinity n Latīnitās f.
latitude n (GEOG) caelum nt; (scope) lībertās f.
latter adj posterior; **the** ~ hīc.
latterly adv nūper.
lattice n trānsenna f.
laud n laus f ♦ vt laudāre.
laudable adj laudābilis, laude dignus.
laudatory adj honōrificus.
laugh n rīsus m; (loud) cachinnus m ♦ vi rīdēre,
  cachinnāre; ~ **at** (joke) rīdēre; (person)
  dērīdēre; ~ **up one's sleeve** in sinū gaudēre.
laughable adj rīdiculus.
laughing stock n lūdibrium nt.
laughter n rīsus m.
launch vt (missile) contorquēre; (ship)
  dēdūcere; ~ **an attack** impetum dare ♦ vi: ~
  out into ingredī in (acc) ♦ n celōx f, lembus
  m.
laureate adj laureātus.
laurel n laurus m ♦ adj laureus.
lave vt lavāre.
lavish adj prōdigus, largus ♦ vt largīrī,
  profundere.
lavishly adv prōdigē, effūsē.
lavishness n largitās f.
law n lēx f; (system) iūs nt; (divine) fās nt; **civil** ~
  iūs cīvīle; **constitutional** ~ iūs pūblicum;
  international ~ iūs gentium; **go to** ~ lēge
  agere, lītigāre; **break the** ~ lēges violāre;
  pass a ~ (magistrate) lēgem perferre; (people)
  lēgem iubēre.
law-abiding adj bene mōrātus.
law court n iūdicium nt; (building) basilica f.
lawful adj lēgitimus; (morally) fās.
lawfully adv lēgitimē, lēge.
lawgiver n lēgum scrīptor m.
lawless adj exlēx.
lawlessly adv licenter.
lawlessness n licentia f.
lawn n prātulum nt.
law-suit n līs f, āctiō f.
lawyer n iūriscōnsultus m, causidicus m.
lax adj dissolūtus, remissus.
laxity n dissolūtiō f.
lay vt pōnere, locāre; (ambush) collocāre,
  tendere; (disorder) sēdāre; (egg) parere;
  (foundation) iacere; (hands) inicere; (plan)
  capere, inīre; (trap) tendere; (wager) facere;
  ~ **aside** pōnere; (in store) repōnere; ~ **by**
  repōnere; ~ **down** dēpōnere; (rule) statuere;
  ~ **hold of** prehendere, adripere; ~ **in** condere;
  ~ **a motion before** referre ad; ~ **on** impōnere;
  ~ **open** patefacere; (to attack) nūdāre; ~ **out**
  (money) impendere, ērogāre; (camp) mētārī;
  ~ **siege to** obsidēre; ~ **to heart** in pectus
  dēmittere; ~ **up** recondere; ~ **upon**
  iniungere, impōnere; ~ **violent hands on** vim
  adferre, adhibēre (dat); **whatever they could**
  ~ **hands on** quod cuīque in manum vēnisset;
  ~ **waste** vastāre ♦ n carmen nt, melos nt.

lay adj (ECCL) lāicus.
layer n corium nt; (stones) ōrdō m; (plant)
  propāgō f.
layout n dēsignātiō f.
laze vi ōtiārī.
lazily adv ignāvē, ōtiōsē.
laziness n ignāvia f, dēsidia f, pigritia f.
lazy adj ignāvus, dēsidiōsus, piger.
lea n prātum nt.
lead vt dūcere; (life) agere; (wall) perdūcere;
  (water) dērīvāre; ~ **across** trādūcere; ~
  around circumdūcere; ~ **astray** in errōrem
  indūcere; ~ **away** abdūcere; ~ **back**
  redūcere; ~ **down** dēdūcere; ~ **in**
  intrōdūcere; ~ **on** addūcere; ~ **out** ēdūcere; ~
  over trādūcere; ~ **the way** dūcere, praeīre; ~
  up to tendere ad, spectare ad; **the road** ~**s** . . .
  via fert . . . .
lead n plumbum nt ♦ adj plumbeus.
leaden adj (colour) līvidus.
leader n dux m, ductor m.
leadership n ductus m.
leading adj prīmus, prīnceps, praecipuus.
leaf, pl **leaves** n folium nt, frōns f; (paper)
  scheda f; **put forth leaves** frondēscere.
leaflet n libellus m.
leafy adj frondōsus.
league n foedus nt, societās f; (distance) tria
  mīlia passuum ♦ vi coniūrāre, foedus
  facere.
leagued adj foederātus.
leak n rīma f ♦ vi mānāre, rimās agere.
leaky adj rīmōsus.
lean adj macer, exīlis, gracilis ♦ vi nītī; ~ **back**
  sē reclīnāre; ~ **on** innītī in (abl), incumbere
  (dat); ~ **over** inclīnāre.
leaning n prōpēnsiō f ♦ adj inclīnātus.
leanness n gracilitās f, maciēs f.
leap n saltus m ♦ vi salīre; (for joy) exsultāre; ~
  down dēsilīre; ~ **on to** īnsilīre in (acc).
leap year n annus bissextilis m.
learn vt discere; (news) accipere, audīre; (by
  heart) ēdiscere; (discover) cognoscēre.
learned adj doctus, ērudītus, litterātus.
learnedly adv doctē.
learner n tīrō m, discipulus m.
learning n doctrīna f, ērudītiō f, litterae fpl.
lease n (taken) conductiō f; (given) locātiō f ♦ vt
  condūcere; locāre.
leash n cōpula f.
least adj minimus ♦ adv minimē; **at** ~ saltem; **to
  say the** ~ ut levissimē dīcam; **not in the** ~
  haudquāquam.
leather n corium nt, alūta f.
leathery adj lentus.
leave n (of absence) commeātus m; (permission)
  potestās f, venia f; **ask** ~ veniam petere; **give**
  ~ potestātem facere; **obtain** ~ impetrāre; **by**
  your ~ pace tuā, bonā tuā veniā ♦ vt
  relinquere, dēserere; (legacy) lēgāre; ~ **alone**
  nōn tangere, manum abstinēre ab; ~ **behind**
  relinquere; ~ **in the lurch** dēstituere,
  dērelinquere; ~ **off** dēsinere, dēsistere ab;

(*temporarily*) intermittere; (*garment*) pōnere;
~ **out** praetermittere, ōmittere ♦ *vi*
discēdere ab (*+ abl*), abīre.
leaven *n* fermentum *nt*.
leavings *n* rēliquiae *fpl*.
lecherous *adj* salāx.
lecture *n* acroāsis *f*, audītiō *f* ♦ *vi* docēre,
scholam habēre.
lecturer *n* doctor *m*.
lecture room *n* audītōrium *nt*.
ledge *n* līmen *nt*.
ledger *n* cōdex acceptī et expēnsī.
lee *n* pars ā ventō tūta.
leech *n* hirūdō *f*.
leek *n* porrum *nt*.
leer *vi* līmīs oculīs intuērī.
lees *n* faex *f*; (*of oil*) amurca *f*.
left *adj* sinister, laevus ♦ *n* sinistra *f*, laeva *f*; **on
the** ~ ā laevā, ad laevam, ā sinistrā.
leg *n* crūs *nt*; (*of table*) pēs *m*.
legacy *n* lēgātum *nt*; ~ **hunter** captātor *m*.
legal *adj* lēgitimus.
legalize *vt* sancīre.
legally *adv* secundum lēgēs, lēge.
legate *n* lēgātus *m*.
legation *n* lēgātiō *f*.
legend *n* fābula *f*; (*inscription*) titulus *m*.
legendary *adj* fābulōsus.
legerdemain *n* praestīgiae *fpl*.
legging *n* ocrea *f*.
legible *adj* clārus.
legion *n* legiō *f*; **men of the 10th** ~ decumānī
mpl.
legionary *n* legiōnārius *m*.
legislate *vi* lēgēs scrībere, lēgēs facere.
legislation *n* lēgēs *fpl*, lēgēs scrībendae.
legislator *n* lēgum scrīptor *m*.
legitimate *adj* lēgitimus.
legitimately *adv* lēgitimē.
leisure *n* ōtium *nt*; **at** ~ ōtiōsus, vacuus; **have** ~
for vacāre (*dat*).
leisured *adj* ōtiōsus.
leisurely *adj* lentus.
lend *vt* commodāre, mūtuum dare; (*at interest*)
faenerārī; (*ear*) aures praebēre, admovēre; ~
a ready ear aurēs patefacere; ~ **assistance**
opem ferre.
length *n* longitūdō *f*; (*time*) diūturnitās *f*; **at** ~
tandem, dēmum, dēnique; (*speech*) cōpiōsē.
lengthen *vt* extendere; (*time*) prōtrahere;
(*sound*) prōdūcere.
lengthwise *adv* in longitūdinem.
lengthy *adj* longus, prōlixus.
leniency *n* clēmentia *f*.
lenient *adj* clēmēns, mītis.
leniently *adv* clēmenter.
lentil *n* lēns *f*.
leonine *adj* leōnīnus.
leopard *n* pardus *m*.
less *adj* minor ♦ *adv* minus; ~ **than** (*num*) intrā
(*acc*); **much** ~, **still** ~ nēdum.
lessee *n* conductor *m*.
lessen *vt* minuere, imminuere, dēminuere ♦

vi dēcrēscere.
lesson *n* documentum *nt*; **be a** ~ **to** documento
esse (*dat*); ~**s** *pl* dictāta *ntpl*; **give** ~**s** scholās
habēre; **give** ~**s in** docēre.
lessor *n* locātor *m*.
lest *conj* nē (*+ subj*).
let *vt* (*allow*) sinere; (*lease*) locāre; (*imper*) fac;
~ **alone** ōmittere; (*mention*) nē dīcam; ~
blood sanguinem mittere; ~ **down**
dēmittere; ~ **fall** ā manibus mittere; (*word*)
ēmittere; ~ **fly** ēmittere; ~ **go** mittere,
āmittere; (*ship*) solvere; ~ **in** admittere; ~
loose solvere; ~ **off** absolvere, ignōscere
(*dat*); ~ **oneself go** geniō indulgēre; ~ **out**
ēmittere; ~ **slip** āmittere, ōmittere.
lethal *adj* mortifer.
lethargic *adj* veternōsus.
lethargy *n* veternus *m*.
letter *n* epistula *f*, litterae *fpl*; (*of alphabet*)
littera *f*; **the** ~ **of the law** scrīptum *nt*; **to the** ~
ad praescrīptum; **by** ~ per litterās; ~**s**
(*learning*) litterae *fpl*; **man of** ~**s** scrīptor *m*.
lettered *adj* litterātus.
lettuce *n* lactūca *f*.
levee *n* salūtātiō *f*.
level *adj* aequus, plānus ♦ *n* plānitiēs *f*;
(*instrument*) lībra *f*; **do one's** ~ **best** prō virīlī
parte agere; **put on a** ~ **with** exaequāre cum
♦ *vt* aequāre, adaequāre, inaequāre; (*to the
ground*) solō aequāre, sternere; (*weapon*)
intendere.
level-headed *adj* prūdēns.
levelled *adj* (*weapon*) īnfestus.
lever *n* vectis *m*.
levity *n* levitās *f*; (*fun*) iocī *mpl*, facētiae *fpl*.
levy *vt* (*troops*) scrībere; (*tax*) exigere ♦ *n*
dīlectus *m*.
lewd *adj* impudīcus.
lewdness *n* impudīcitia *f*.
liable *adj* obnoxius; **render** ~ obligāre.
liaison *n* cōnsuētūdō *f*.
liar *n* mendāx *m*.
libel *n* probrum *nt*, calumnia *f* ♦ *vt* calumniārī.
libellous *adj* probrōsus, fāmōsus.
liberal *adj* līberālis; (*in giving*) largus,
benīgnus; ~ **education** bonae artēs *fpl*.
liberality *n* līberālitās *f*, largitās *f*.
liberally *adv* līberāliter, largē, benīgnē.
liberate *vt* līberāre; (*slave*) manū mittere.
liberation *n* līberātiō *f*.
liberator *n* līberātor *m*.
libertine *n* libīdinōsus *m*.
liberty *n* lībertās *f*; (*excess*) licentia *f*; **I am at** ~
to mihī licet (*inf*); **I am still at** ~ **to** integrum
est mihī (*inf*); **take a** ~ **with** licentius ūtī (*abl*),
familiārius sē gerere in (*acc*).
libidinous *adj* libīdinōsus.
librarian *n* librārius *m*.
library *n* bibliothēca *f*.
licence *n* (*permission*) potestās *f*; (*excess*)
licentia *f*.
license *vt* potestātem dare (*dat*).
licentious *adj* dissolūtus.

licentiousness n libīdō f, licentia f.
lick vt lambere; mulcēre.
lictor n lictor m.
lid n operculum nt.
lie n mendācium nt; **give the ~ to** redarguere;
tell a ~ mentīrī ♦ vi mentīrī; (*lie down*) iacēre;
(*place*) situm esse; (*consist*) continērī; **as far
as in me ~s** quantum in mē est; **~ at anchor**
stāre; **~ between** interiacēre; **~ down**
cubāre, discumbere; **~ heavy on** premere; **~
hid** latēre; **~ in wait** īnsidiārī; **~ low**
dissimulāre; **~ on** incumbere (*dat*); **~ open**
patēre; hiāre.
lien n nexus m.
lieu n: **in ~ of** locō (*gen*).
lieutenant n decuriō m; legātus m.
life n vīta f; (*in danger*) salūs f, caput nt;
(*biography*) vīta f; (*breath*) anima f; (*RHET*)
sanguis m; (*time*) aetās f; **come to ~ again**
revīvīscere; **draw to the ~** exprimere; **for ~**
aetātem; **matter of ~ and death** capitāle nt;
prime of ~ flōs aetātis; **way of ~** mōrēs mpl.
lifeblood n sanguis m.
life-giving adj almus, vītalis.
lifeguard n custōs m; (*emperor's*) praetōriānus
m.
lifeless adj exanimis; (*style*) exsanguis.
lifelike adj expressus.
lifelong adj perpetuus.
lifetime n aetās f.
lift vt tollere, sublevāre; **~ up** efferre,
attollere.
light n lūx f, lūmen nt; (*painting*) lūmen nt; **bring
to ~** in lūcem prōferre; **see in a favourable ~**
in meliōrem partem interpretārī; **throw ~ on**
lūmen adhibēre (*dat*) ♦ vt accendere,
incendere; (*illuminate*) illūstrāre, illūmināre;
be lit up collūcēre ♦ vi: **~ upon** invenīre,
offendere ♦ adj illūstris; (*movement*) agilis;
(*weight*) levis; **grow ~** illūcēscere,
dīlūcēscere; **make ~ of** parvī pendere.
light-armed adj expedītus.
lighten vi fulgurāre ♦ vt levāre.
lighter n linter f.
light-fingered adj tagāx.
light-footed adj celer, pernīx.
light-headed adj levis, volāticus.
light-hearted adj hilaris, laetus.
lightly adv leviter; pernīciter.
lightness n levitās f.
lightning n fulgur nt; (*striking*) fulmen nt; **be
hit by ~** dē caelō percutī; **of ~** fulgurālis.
like adj similis, pār; **~ this** ad hunc modum ♦
adv similiter, sīcut, rītū (*gen*) ♦ vt amāre; **I ~**
mihī placet, mē iuvat; **I ~ to** libet (*inf*); **I don't
~** nīl moror, mihī displicet; **look ~** similem
esse, referre.
likelihood n vērī similitūdō f.
likely adj vērī similis ♦ adv sānē.
liken vt comparāre, aequiperāre.
likeness n īmāgō f, īnstar nt, similitūdō f.
likewise adv item; (*also*) etiam.
liking n libīdō f, grātia f; **to one's ~** ex

sententiā.
lily n līlium nt.
limb n membrum nt, artus m.
lime n calx f; (*tree*) tilia f.
limelight n celebritās f; **enjoy the ~** mōnstrārī
digitō.
limestone n calx f.
limit n fīnis m, terminus m, modus m; **mark the
~s of** dētermināre ♦ vt fīnīre, dēfīnīre,
termināre; (*restrict*) circumscrībere.
limitation n modus m.
limp adj mollis, flaccidus ♦ vi claudicāre.
limpid adj limpidus.
linden n tilia f.
line n līnea f; (*battle*) aciēs f; (*limit*) modus m;
(*outline*) līneāmentum nt; (*writing*) versus m;
in a straight ~ ē regiōne; **~ of march** agmen nt;
read between the ~s dissimulātā dispicere;
ship of the ~ nāvis longa; **write a ~** pauca
scrībere ♦ vt (*street*) saepīre.
lineage n genus nt, stirps f.
lineal adj (*descent*) gentīlis.
lineaments n līneāmenta ntpl, ōris ductūs mpl.
linen n linteum nt ♦ adj linteus.
liner n nāvis f.
linger vi cunctārī, cessāre, dēmorārī.
lingering adj tardus ♦ n cunctātiō f.
linguist n: **be a ~** complūrēs linguās callēre.
link n ānulus m; (*fig*) nexus m, vinculum nt ♦ vt
coniungere.
lintel n līmen superum nt.
lion n leō m; **~'s** leōnīnus; **~'s share** māior pars.
lioness n leaena f.
lip n lābrum nt; **be on everyone's ~s** in ōre
omnium hominum esse, per omnium ōra
ferrī.
lip service n: **pay ~ to** verbō tenus obsequī
(*dat*).
liquefy vt liquefacere.
liquid adj liquidus ♦ n liquor m.
liquidate vt persolvere.
liquor n liquor m; vīnum nt.
lisp vi balbūtīre.
lisping adj blaesus.
lissom adj agilis.
list n index m, tabula f; (*ship*) inclīnātiō f ♦ vt
scrībere ♦ vi (*lean*) sē inclīnāre; (*listen*)
auscultāre; (*wish*) cupere.
listen vi auscultāre; **~ to** auscultāre, audīre.
listener n audītor m, auscultātor m.
listless adj languidus.
listlessness n languor m.
literally adv ad verbum.
literary adj (*man*) litterātus; **~ pursuits** litterae
fpl, studia ntpl.
literature n litterae fpl.
lithe adj mollis, agilis.
litigant n lītigātor m.
litigate vi lītigāre.
litigation n līs f.
litigious adj lītigiōsus.
litter n (*carriage*) lectīca f; (*brood*) fētus m;
(*straw*) strāmentum nt; (*mess*) strāgēs f ♦ vt

sternere; (*young*) parere.

little *adj* parvus, exiguus; (*time*) brevis; **very ~** perexiguus, minimus; **~ boy** puerulus *m* ♦ *n* paulum *nt*, aliquantulum *nt*; **for a ~** paulisper, parumper; **~ or nothing** vix quicquam ♦ *adv* paulum, nōnnihil; (*with comp*) paulō; **~ by ~** paulātim, sēnsim, gradātim; **think ~ of** parvī aestimāre; **too ~** parum (+ *gen*).

littleness *n* exiguitās *f*.

littoral *n* lītus *nt*.

live *vi* vīvere, vītam agere; (*dwell*) habitāre; **~ down** (*reproach*) ēluere; **~ on** (*food*) vescī (*abl*) ♦ *adj* vīvus.

livelihood *n* vīctus *m*.

liveliness *n* alacritās *f*, hilaritās *f*.

livelong *adj* tōtus.

lively *adj* alacer, hilaris.

liven *vt* exhilarāre.

liver *n* iecur *nt*.

livery *n* vestis famulāris *f*.

livid *adj* līvidus; **be ~** līvēre.

living *adj* vīvus ♦ *n* vīctus *m*; (*earning*) quaestus *m*.

lizard *n* lacerta *f*.

lo *interj* ecce.

load *n* onus *nt* ♦ *vt* onerāre.

loaf *n* pānis *m* ♦ *vi* grassārī.

loafer *n* grassātor *m*.

loam *n* lutum *nt*.

loan *n* mūtuum *nt*, mūtua pecūnia *f*.

loathe *vt* fastīdīre, ōdisse.

loathing *n* fastīdium *nt*.

loathsome *adj* odiōsus, taeter.

lobby *n* vestibulum *nt*.

lobe *n* fibra *f*.

lobster *n* astacus *m*.

local *adj* indigena, locī.

locality *n* locus *m*.

locate *vt* reperīre; **be ~d** situm esse.

location *n* situs *m*.

loch *n* lacus *m*.

lock *n* (*door*) sera *f*; (*hair*) coma *f* ♦ *vt* obserāre.

locomotion *n* mōtus *m*.

locust *n* locusta *f*.

lodge *n* casa *f* ♦ *vi* dēversārī ♦ *vt* īnfīgere; (*complaint*) dēferre.

lodger *n* inquilīnus *m*.

lodging *n* hospitium *nt*, dēversōrium *nt*.

loft *n* cēnāculum *nt*.

loftiness *n* altitūdō *f*, sublīmitās *f*.

lofty *adj* excelsus, sublīmis.

log *n* stīpes *m*; (*fuel*) lignum *nt*.

loggerhead *n*: **be at ~s** rixārī.

logic *n* dialecticē *f*.

logical *adj* dialecticus, ratiōne frētus.

logically *adv* ex ratiōne.

logician *n* dialecticus *m*.

loin *n* lumbus *m*.

loiter *vi* grassārī, cessāre.

loiterer *n* grassātor *m*, cessātor *m*.

loll *vi* recumbere.

lone *adj* sōlus, sōlitārius.

loneliness *n* sōlitūdō *f*.

lonely, lonesome *adj* sōlitārius.

long *adj* longus; (*hair*) prōmissus; (*syllable*) prōductus; (*time*) longus, diūturnus; **in the ~ run** aliquandō; **for a ~ time** diū; **to make a ~ story short** nē longum sit, nē longum faciam ♦ *adv* diū; **~ ago** iamprīdem, iamdūdum; **as ~ as** *conj* dum; **before ~** mox; **for ~** diū; **how ~** quamdiū, quōusque; **I have ~ been wishing** iam prīdem cupiō; **not ~ after** haud multō post; **any ~er** (*time*) diūtius; (*distance*) longius; **no ~er nōn** iam ♦ *vi*: **~ for** dēsīderāre, exoptāre, expetere; **~ to** gestīre.

longevity *n* vīvācitās *f*.

longing *n* dēsīderium *nt*, cupīdō *f* ♦ *adj* avidus.

longingly *adv* avidē.

longitudinally *adv* in longitūdinem.

long-lived *adj* vīvāx.

long-suffering *adj* patiēns.

long-winded *adj* verbōsus, longus.

longwise *adv* in longitūdinem.

look *n* aspectus *m*; (*expression*) vultus *m* ♦ *vi* aspicere; (*seem*) vidērī, speciem praebēre; **~ about** circumspicere; **~ after** prōvidēre (*dat*) cūrāre; **~ at** spectāre ad (+ *acc*), aspicere, intuērī; (*with mind*) contemplārī; **~ back** respicere; **~ down** on dēspectāre; (*fig*) dēspicere; **~ for** quaerere, petere; **~ forward to** exspectāre; **~ here** heus tu, ehodum; **~ into** īnspicere, intrōspicere; **~ out** prōspicere; (*beware*) cavēre; **~ round** circumspicere; **~ through** perspicere; **~ to** ratiōnem habēre (*gen*); (*leader*) spem pōnere in (*abl*); **~ towards** spectāre ad; **~ up** suspicere; **~ up to** suspicere; **~ upon** habēre.

looker-on *n* arbiter *m*.

lookout *n* (*place*) specula *f*; (*man*) vigil *m*, excubiae *fpl*.

looks *npl* speciēs *f*; **good ~** fōrma *f*, pulchritūdō *f*.

loom *n* tēla *f* ♦ *vi* in cōnspectum sē dare.

loop *n* orbis *m*, sinus *m*.

loophole *n* fenestra *f*.

loose *adj* laxus, solūtus, remissus; (*morally*) dissolūtus; **let ~ on** immittere in (*acc*) ♦ *vt* (*undo*) solvere; (*slacken*) laxāre.

loosely *adv* solūtē, remissē.

loosen *vt* (re)solvere; (*structure*) labefacere.

looseness *n* dissolūtiō *f*, dissolūtī mōrēs *mpl*.

loot *n* praeda *f*, rapīna *f*.

lop *vt* amputāre.

lopsided *adj* inaequālis.

loquacious *adj* loquāx.

loquacity *n* loquācitās *f*.

lord *n* dominus *m* ♦ *vi*: **~ it** dominārī.

lordliness *n* superbia *f*.

lordly *adj* superbus; (*rank*) nōbilis.

lordship *n* dominātiō *f*, imperium *nt*.

lore *n* litterae *fpl*, doctrīna *f*.

lose *vt* āmittere, perdere; **~ an eye** alterō oculō capī; **~ heart** animum dēspondēre; **~ one's way** deerrāre ♦ *vi* (*in contest*) vincī.

loss *n* damnum *nt*, dētrīmentum *nt*; **be at a ~** haerēre, haesitāre; **suffer ~** damnum

accipere, facere; **~es** (*in battle*) caesī *mpl.*
lost *adj* āmissus, absēns; **be ~** perīre, interīre;
give up for **~** dēplōrāre.
lot *n* sors *f;* **be assigned by ~** sorte obvenīre;
draw a ~ sortem dūcere; **draw ~s for** sortīrī;
a ~ of multus, plūrimus.
loth *adj* invītus.
lottery *n* sortēs *fpl;* (*fig*) ālea *f.*
lotus *n* lōtos *f.*
loud *adj* clārus, māgnus.
loudly *adv* māgnā vōce.
loudness *n* māgna vōx *f.*
lounge *vi* ōtiārī.
louse *n* pedis *m/f.*
lout *n* agrestis *m.*
lovable *adj* amābilis.
love *n* amor *m;* **be hopelessly in ~** dēperīre; **fall
in ~ with** adamāre ♦ *vt* amāre, dīligere; **I ~ to**
mē iuvat (*inf*).
love affair *n* amor *m.*
loveless *adj* amōre carēns.
loveliness *n* grātia *f,* venustās *f.*
lovely *adj* pulcher, amābilis, venustus.
love poem *n* carmen amātōrium *nt.*
lover *n* amāns *m,* amātor *m.*
lovesick *adj* amōre aeger.
loving *adj* amāns.
lovingly *adv* amanter.
low *adj* humilis; (*birth*) ignōbilis; (*price*) vīlis;
(*sound*) gravis; (*spirits*) dēmissus; (*voice*)
dēmissus; **at ~ water** aestūs dēcessū; **be ~**
iacēre; **lay ~** interficere ♦ *vi* mūgīre.
lower *adj* īnferior; **the ~ world** īnferī *mpl;* **of
the ~ world** īnfernus ♦ *adv* īnferius ♦ *vt*
dēmittere, dēprimere ♦ *vi* (*cloud*) obscūrārī,
minārī.
lowering *adj* mināx.
lowest *adj* īnfimus, īmus.
lowing *n* mūgītus *m.*
lowland *adj* campestris.
lowlands *n* campī *mpl.*
lowliness *n* humilitās *f.*
lowly *adj* humilis, obscūrus.
low-lying *adj* dēmisssus; **be ~** sedēre.
lowness *n* humilitās *f;* (*spirit*) tristitia *f.*
loyal *adj* fidēlis, fīdus; (*citizen*) bonus.
loyally *adv* fidēliter.
loyalty *n* fidēs *f,* fidēlitās *f.*
lubricate *vt* ungere.
lucid *adj* clārus, perspicuus.
lucidity *n* perspicuitās *f.*
lucidly *adv* clārē, perspicuē.
luck *n* fortūna *f,* fors *f;* **good ~** fēlicitās *f;* **bad ~**
īnfortūnium *nt.*
luckily *adv* fēlīciter, faustē, prosperē.
luckless *adj* īnfēlīx.
lucky *adj* fēlīx, fortūnātus; (*omen*) faustus.
lucrative *adj* quaestuōsus.
lucre *n* lucrum *nt,* quaestus *m.*
lucubration *n* lūcubrātiō *f.*
ludicrous *adj* rīdiculus.
ludicrously *adv* rīdiculē.
lug *vt* trahere.

luggage *n* impedīmenta *ntpl,* sarcina *f.*
lugubrious *adj* lūgubris, maestus.
lukewarm *adj* tepidus; (*fig*) segnis, neglegēns;
be ~ tepēre.
lukewarmly *adv* segniter, neglegenter.
lukewarmness *n* tepor *m;* (*fig*) neglegentia *f,*
incūria *f.*
lull *vt* sōpīre; (*storm*) sēdāre ♦ *n* intermissiō *f.*
lumber *n* scrūta *ntpl.*
luminary *n* lūmen *nt,* astrum *nt.*
luminous *adj* lūcidus, illūstris.
lump *n* massa *f;* (*on body*) tuber *nt.*
lumpish *adj* hebes, crassus, stolidus.
lunacy *n* īnsānia *f.*
lunar *adj* lūnāris.
lunatic *n* īnsānus *m.*
lunch *n* prandium *nt* ♦ *vi* prandēre.
lung *n* pulmō *m;* *pl* (*RHET*) latera *ntpl.*
lunge *n* ictus *m* ♦ *vi* prōsilīre.
lurch *n:* **leave in the ~** dērelinquere, dēstituere
♦ *vi* titubāre.
lure *n* esca *f* ♦ *vt* allicere, illicere, ēlicere.
lurid *adj* lūridus.
lurk *vi* latēre, latitāre, dēlitēscere.
luscious *adj* praedulcis.
lush *adj* luxuriōsus.
lust *n* libīdō *f* ♦ *vi* libīdine flagrāre,
concupīscere.
lustful *adj* libīdinōsus.
lustily *adv* validē, strēnuē.
lustiness *n* vigor *m,* nervī *mpl.*
lustration *n* lūstrum *nt.*
lustre *n* fulgor *m,* splendor *m.*
lustrous *adj* illūstris.
lusty *adj* validus, lacertōsus.
lute *n* cithara *f,* fidēs *fpl.*
lute player *n* citharista *m,* citharistria *f,*
fidicen *m,* fidicina *f.*
luxuriance *n* luxuria *f.*
luxuriant *adj* luxuriōsus.
luxuriate *vi* luxuriārī.
luxuries *pl* lautitiae *fpl.*
luxurious *adj* luxuriōsus, sūmptuōsus, lautus.
luxuriously *adv* sūmptuōsē, lautē.
luxury *n* luxuria *f,* luxus *m.*
lynx *n* lynx *m/f;* **~-eyed** lyncēus.
lyre *n* lyra *f,* fidēs *fpl;* **play the ~** fidibus canere.
lyric *adj* lyricus ♦ *n* carmen *nt.*
lyrist *n* fidicen *m,* fidicina *f.*

M, m

mace *n* scīpiō *m.*
machination *n* dolus *m.*
machine *n* māchina *f.*

mackerel n scomber m.
mad adj īnsānus, furiōsus, vēcors, dēmēns; **be ~** īnsānīre, furere.
madam n domina f.
madden vt furiāre, mentem aliēnāre (dat).
madly adv insānē, furiōsē, dēmenter.
madness n īnsānia f, furor m, dēmentia f; (animals) rabiēs f.
maelstrom n vertex m.
magazine n horreum nt, apothēca f.
maggot n vermiculus m.
magic adj magicus ♦ n magicae artēs fpl.
magician n magus m, veneficus m.
magistracy n magistrātus m.
magistrate n magistrātus m.
magnanimity n māgnanimitās f, līberalitās f.
magnanimous adj generōsus, līberālis, māgnanimus.
magnet n magnēs m.
magnificence n māgnificentia f, adparātus m.
magnificent adj māgnificus, amplus, splendidus.
magnificently adv māgnificē, amplē, splendidē.
magnify vt amplificāre, exaggerāre.
magnitude n māgnitūdō f.
magpie n pīca f.
maid n virgō f; (servant) ancilla f.
maiden n virgō f.
maidenhood n virginitās f.
maidenly adj virginālis.
mail n (armour) lōrīca f; (letters) epistulae fpl.
maim vt mutilāre.
maimed adj mancus.
main adj prīnceps, prīmus; **~ point** caput nt ♦ n (sea) altum nt, pelagus nt; **with might and ~** manibus pedibusque, omnibus nervīs.
mainland n continēns f.
mainly adv praecipuē, plērumque.
maintain vt (keep) tenēre, servāre; (keep up) sustinēre; (keep alive) alere, sustentāre; (argue) adfīrmāre, dēfendere.
maintenance n (food) alimentum nt.
majestic adj augustus, māgnificus.
majestically adv augustē.
majesty n māiestās f.
major adj māior.
majority n māior pars f, plērīque; **have attained one's ~** suī iūris esse.
make vt facere, fingere; (appointment) creāre; (bed) sternere; (cope) superāre; (compulsion) cōgere; (consequence) efficere; (craft) fabricārī; (harbour) capere; (living) quaerere; (sum) efficere; (with adj) reddere; (with verb) cōgere; **~ away with** tollere, interimere; **~ good** supplēre, resarcīre; **~ light of** parvī facere; **~ one's way** iter facere; **~ much of** māgnī aestimāre, multum tribuere (dat); **~ for** petere; **~ out** arguere; **~ over** dēlēgāre, trānsferre; **~ ready** parāre; **~ a speech** oratiōnem habēre; **~ a truce** indutias compōnere; **~ war on** bellum inferre; **~ up** (loss) supplēre; (total) efficere; (story)

fingere; **be made** fierī.
make-believe n simulātiō f.
maker n fabricātor m, auctor m.
make-up n medicāmina ntpl.
maladministration n (charge) repetundae fpl.
malady n morbus m.
malcontent adj novārum rērum cupidus.
male adj mās, māsculus.
malefactor n nocēns m, reus m.
malevolence n malevolentia f.
malevolent adj malevolus, malignus.
malevolently adv malignē.
malformation n dēprāvātiō f.
malice n invidia f, malevolentia f; **bear ~ towards** invidēre (dat).
malicious adj invidiōsus, malevolus, malignus.
maliciously adv malignē.
malign adj malignus, invidiōsus ♦ vt obtrectāre.
malignant adj malevolus.
maligner n obtrectātor m.
malignity n malevolentia f.
malleable adj ductilis.
mallet n malleus m.
mallow n malva f.
malpractices n dēlicta ntpl.
maltreat vt laedere, vexāre.
malversation n pecūlātus m.
man n (human being) homō m/f; (male) vir m; (MIL) mīles m; (chess) latrunculus m; **to a ~** omnēs ad ūnum; **~ who** is qui; **old ~** senex m; **young ~** adulēscēns m; **~ of war** nāvis longa f ♦ vt (ship) complēre; (walls) praesidiō firmāre.
manacle n manicae fpl ♦ vt manicās inicere (dat).
manage vt efficere, gerere, gubernāre, administrāre; (horse) moderārī; (with verb) posse.
manageable adj tractābilis, habilis.
management n administrātiō f, cūra f; (finance) dispēnsātiō f.
manager n administrātor m, moderātor m; dispēnsātor m.
mandate n mandātum nt.
mane n iuba f.
manful adj virīlis, fortis.
manfully adv virīliter, fortiter.
manger n praesēpe nt.
mangle vt dīlaniāre, lacerāre.
mangy adj scaber.
manhood n pūbertās f, toga virīlis f.
mania n īnsānia f.
maniac n furiōsus m.
manifest adj manifestus, apertus, clārus ♦ vt dēclārāre, aperīre.
manifestation n speciēs f.
manifestly adv manifestō, apertē.
manifesto n ēdictum nt.
manifold adj multiplex, varius.
manikin n homunciō m, homunculus m.
manipulate vt tractāre.

manipulation n tractātiō f.
mankind n hominēs mpl, genus hūmānum nt.
manliness n virtūs f.
manly adj fortis, virīlis.
manner n modus m, ratiō f; (custom) mōs m,
　ūsus m; ~s pl mōrēs mpl; **after the ~ of** rītū,
　mōre (gen); **good ~s** hūmānitās f, modestia f.
mannered adj mōrātus.
mannerism n mōs m.
mannerly adj bene mōrātus, urbānus.
manoeuvre n (MIL) dēcursus m, dēcursiō f; (fig)
　dolus m ♦ vi dēcurrere; (fig) māchinārī.
manor n praedium nt.
mansion n domus f.
manslaughter n homicīdium nt.
mantle n pallium nt; (women's) palla f.
manual adj: ~ **labour** opera f ♦ n libellus m, ars
　f.
manufacture n fabrica f ♦ vt fabricārī.
manumission n manūmissiō f.
manumit vt manū mittere, ēmancipāre.
manure n fimus m, stercus nt ♦ vt stercorāre.
manuscript n liber m, cōdex m.
many adj multī; **as ~ as** tot . . . quot; **how ~?**
　quot?; **so ~** tot; **in ~ places** multifāriam; **a**
　good ~ complūrēs; **too ~** nimis multī; **the ~**
　vulgus nt; **very ~** permultī, plūrimī.
map n tabula f ♦ vt: ~ **out** dēscrībere,
　dēsignāre.
maple n acer nt ♦ adj acernus.
mar vt corrumpere, dēfōrmāre.
marauder n praedātor m, dēpopulātor m.
marble n marmor nt ♦ adj marmoreus.
March n mēnsis Martius m; **of ~** Martius.
march n iter nt; **line of ~** agmen nt; **by forced**
　~es māgnīs itineribus; **on the ~** ex itinere, in
　itinere; **quick ~** plēnō gradū; **a regular day's ~**
　iter iūstum nt ♦ vi contendere, iter facere,
　incēdere, īre; ~ **out** exīre; ~ **on** signa
　prōferre, prōgredī ♦ vt dūcere; ~ **out**
　ēdūcere; ~ **in** intrōdūcere.
mare n equa f.
margin n margō f; (fig) discrīmen nt.
marigold n caltha f.
marine adj marīnus ♦ n mīles classicus m.
mariner n nauta m.
marital adj marītus.
maritime adj maritimus.
marjoram n amāracus m.
mark n nota f; (of distinction) īnsigne nt; (target)
　scopos m; (trace) vestīgium nt; **beside the ~**
　nihil ad rem; **it is the ~ of a wise man to**
　sapientis est (inf); **be wide of the ~** errāre ♦
　vt notāre, dēsignāre; (observe)
　animadvertere, animum attendere; ~ **out**
　(site) mētārī, dēsignāre; (for purpose)
　dēnotāre.
marked adj īnsignis, manifestus.
markedly adv manifestō.
marker n index m.
market n macellum nt; ~ **day** nūndinae fpl; ~
　town emporium nt; **cattle ~** forum boārium
　nt; **fish ~** forum piscārium nt.

marketable adj vēndibilis.
marketplace n forum nt.
market prices npl annōna f.
market town n emporium nt.
marking n macula f.
maroon vt dērelinquere.
marriage n mātrimōnium nt, coniugium nt;
　(ceremony) nūptiae fpl; **give in ~** collocāre; ~
　bed lectus geniālis m.
marriageable adj nūbilis.
marrow n medulla f.
marry vt (a wife) dūcere, in mātrimōnium
　dūcere; (a husband) nūbere (dat).
marsh n palūs f.
marshal n imperātor m ♦ vt īnstruere.
marshy adj palūster.
mart n forum nt.
marten n mēlēs f.
martial adj bellicōsus, ferōx.
martyr n dēvōtus m; (ECCL) martyr m/f.
marvel n mīrāculum nt, portentum nt ♦ vi
　mīrārī; ~ **at** admīrārī.
marvellous adj mīrus, mīrificus, mīrābilis.
marvellously adv mīrē, mīrum quantum.
masculine adj mās, virīlis.
mash n farrāgō f ♦ vt commiscēre,
　contundere.
mask n persōna f ♦ vt persōnam induere (dat);
　(fig) dissimulāre.
mason n structor m.
masonry n lapidēs mpl, caementum nt.
masquerade n simulātiō f ♦ vi vestem
　mūtāre; ~ **as** speciem sibi induere (gen),
　persōnam ferre (gen).
mass n mōlēs f; (of small things) congeriēs f; (of
　people) multitūdō f; (ECCL) missa f; **the ~**
　vulgus nt, plēbs f ♦ vt congerere, coacervāre.
massacre n strāgēs f, caedēs f, interneciō f ♦
　vt trucīdāre.
massive adj ingēns, solidus.
massiveness n mōlēs f, soliditās f.
mast n mālus m.
master n dominus m; (school) magister m; **be ~**
　of dominārī in (abl); (skill) perītum esse
　(gen); **become ~ of** potīrī (abl); **be one's own**
　~ suī iūris esse; **not ~ of** impotēns (gen); **a**
　past ~ veterātor m ♦ vt dēvincere; (skill)
　ēdiscere; (passion) continēre.
masterful adj imperiōsus.
masterly adj doctus, perītus.
masterpiece n praeclārum opus nt.
mastery n dominātiō f, imperium nt,
　arbitrium nt.
masticate vt mandere.
mastiff n Molossus m.
mat n storea f.
match n (person) pār m/f; (marriage) nūptiae fpl;
　(contest) certāmen nt; **a ~ for** pār (dat); **no ~**
　for impār (dat) ♦ vt exaequāre, adaequāre ♦
　vi congruere.
matchless adj singulāris, ūnicus.
mate n socius m; (married) coniunx m/f ♦ vi
　coniungī.

material–menace

material *adj* corporeus; (*significant*) haud levis
♦ *n* māteriēs *f*; (*literary*) silva *f*.
materialize *vi* ēvenīre.
materially *adv* māgnopere.
maternal *adj* māternus.
mathematical *adj* mathēmaticus.
mathematician *n* mathēmaticus *m*,
geōmetrēs *m*.
mathematics *n* ars mathēmatica *f*, numerī
mpl.
matin *adj* mātūtīnus.
matricide *n* (*act*) mātricīdium *nt*; (*person*)
mātricīda *m*.
matrimony *n* mātrimōnium *nt*.
matrix *n* fōrma *f*.
matron *n* mātrōna *f*.
matter *n* māteria *f*, corpus *nt*; (*affair*) rēs *f*; (*MED*)
pūs *nt*; **what is the ~ with you?** quid tibī est?
vi: **it ~s** interest, rēfert.
matting *n* storea *f*.
mattock *n* dolābra *f*.
mattress *n* culcita *f*.
mature *adj* mātūrus; (*age*) adultus ♦ *vi*
mātūrēscere.
maturity *n* mātūritās *f*; (*age*) adulta aetās *f*.
maul *n* fistūca *f* ♦ *vt* contundere, dīlaniāre.
maw *n* ingluviēs *f*.
mawkish *adj* pūtidus.
mawkishly *adv* pūtidē.
maxim *n* dictum *nt*, praeceptum *nt*, sententia *f*.
maximum *adj* quam māximus, quam
plūrimus.
May *n* mēnsis Māius *m*; **of ~** Māius.
may *vi* posse; **I ~** licet mihī.
mayor *n* praefectus *m*.
maze *n* labyrinthus *m*.
mead *n* (*drink*) mulsum *nt*; (*land*) prātum *nt*.
meagre *adj* exīlis, iēiūnus.
meagrely *adv* exīliter, iēiūnē.
meagreness *n* exīlitās *f*.
meal *n* (*flour*) farīna *f*; (*repast*) cibus *m*.
mealy-mouthed *adj* blandiloquus.
mean *adj* humilis, abiectus; (*birth*) ignōbilis;
(*average*) medius, mediocris ♦ *n* modus *m*,
mediocritās *f* ♦ *vt* dīcere, significāre; (*word*)
valēre; (*intent*) velle, in animō habēre.
meander *vi* sinuōsō cursū fluere.
meaning *n* significātiō *f*, vīs *f*, sententia *f*;
what is the ~ of? quid sibī vult?, quōrsum
spectat?.
meanly *adv* abiectē, humiliter.
meanness *n* humilitās *f*; (*conduct*) illīberālitās
f, avāritia *f*.
means *n* īnstrūmentum *nt*; (*of doing*) facultās
f; (*wealth*) opēs *fpl*; **by ~ of** per (*acc*); **by all ~**
māximē; **by no ~** nūllō modō, haudquāquam;
of small ~ pauper.
meantime, meanwhile *adv* intereā, interim.
measles *n* boa *f*.
measure *n* modus *m*, mēnsūra *f*; (*rhythm*)
numerī *mpl*; (*plan*) cōnsilium *nt*; (*law*) rogātiō
f, lēx *f*; **beyond ~** nimium; **in some ~** aliquā ex
parte; **take ~s** cōnsulere; **take the ~ of** quālis

sit cognōscere; **without ~** immoderātē ♦ *vt*
mētīrī; **~ out** dīmētīrī; (*land*) mētārī.
measured *adj* moderātus.
measureless *adj* īnfīnītus, immēnsus.
measurement *n* mēnsūra *f*.
meat *n* carō *f*.
mechanic *n* opifex *m*, faber *m*.
mechanical *adj* mēchanicus.
mechanical device māchinātiō *f*.
mechanics *n* māchinālis scientia *f*.
mechanism *n* māchinātiō *f*.
medal *n* īnsigne *nt*.
meddle *vi* sē interpōnere.
meddlesome *adj* cūriōsus.
Medes *n* Mīdi *mpl*.
mediate *vi* intercēdere; **~ between**
compōnere, conciliāre.
mediator *n* intercessor *m*, dēprecātor *m*.
medical *adj* medicus.
medicate *vt* medicāre.
medicinal *adj* medicus, salūbris.
medicine *n* (*art*) medicīna *f*; (*drug*)
medicāmentum *nt*.
medicine chest *n* narthēcium *nt*.
mediocre *adj* mediocris.
mediocrity *n* mediocritās *f*.
meditate *vi* meditārī, cōgitāre, sēcum
volūtāre.
meditation *n* cōgitātiō *f*, meditātiō *f*.
medium *n* internūntius *m*; (*means*) modus *m* ♦
adj mediocris.
medley *n* farrāgō *f*.
meek *adj* mītis, placidus.
meekly *adv* summissō animō.
meet *adj* idōneus, aptus ♦ *n* conventus *m* ♦ *vi*
convenīre ♦ *vt* obviam īre (*dat*), occurrere
(*dat*); (*fig*) obīre; **~ with** invenīre, excipere.
meeting *n* cōnsilium *nt*, conventus *m*.
melancholic *adj* melancholicus.
melancholy *n* ātra bīlis *f*; tristitia *f*, maestitia *f*
♦ *adj* tristis, maestus.
mêlée *n* turba *f*, concursus *m*.
mellow *adj* mītis; (*wine*) lēnis; **become ~**
mītēscere; **make ~** mītigāre.
mellowness *n* mātūritās *f*.
melodious *adj* canōrus, numerōsus.
melodiously *adv* numerōsē.
melody *n* melos *nt*, modī *mpl*.
melt *vt* liquefacere, dissolvere; (*fig*) movēre ♦
vi liquēscere, dissolvī; (*fig*) commovērī; **~**
away dēliquēscere.
member *n* membrum *nt*; (*person*) socius *m*.
membrane *n* membrāna *f*.
memento *n* monumentum *nt*.
memoir *n* commentārius *m*.
memorable *adj* memorābilis,
commemorābilis.
memorandum *n* hypomnēma *nt*.
memorial *n* monumentum *nt*.
memorize *vt* ēdiscere.
memory *n* memoria *f*; **from ~** memoriter.
menace *n* minae *fpl* ♦ *vt* minārī, minitārī;
(*things*) imminēre (*dat*).

menacing *adj* mināx.
menacingly *adv* mināciter.
menage *n* familia *f*.
mend *vt* sarcīre, reficere ♦ *vi* meliōrem fierī; (*health*) convalēscere.
mendacious *adj* mendāx.
mendacity *n* mendācium *nt*.
mendicant *n* mendīcus *m*.
mendicity *n* mendīcitās *f*.
menial *adj* servīlis, famulāris ♦ *n* servus *m*, famulus *m*.
menstrual *adj* mēnstruus.
mensuration *n* mētiendī ratiō *f*.
mental *adj* cōgitātiōnis, mentis.
mentality *n* animī adfectus *m*, mēns *f*.
mentally *adv* cōgitātiōne, mente.
mention *n* mentiō *f* ♦ *vt* memorāre, mentiōnem facere (*gen*); (*casually*) inicere; (*briefly*) attingere; **omit to ~** praetermittere.
mentor *n* auctor *m*, praeceptor *m*.
mercantile *adj* mercātōrius.
mercenary *adj* mercennārius, vēnālis ♦ *n* mercennārius mīles *m*.
merchandise *n* mercēs *fpl*.
merchant *n* mercātor *m*.
merchantman *n* nāvis onerāria *f*.
merchant ship *n* nāvis onerāria *f*.
merciful *adj* misericors, clēmens.
mercifully *adv* clēmenter.
merciless *adj* immisericors, inclēmens, inhūmānus.
mercilessly *adv* inhūmānē.
mercurial *adj* hilaris.
mercy *n* misericordia *f*, clēmentia *f*, venia *f*; **at the ~ of** obnoxius (*dat*), in manū (*gen*).
mere *n* lacus *m* ♦ *adj* merus, ipse.
merely *adv* sōlum, tantum, dumtaxat.
meretricious *adj* meretricius; **~ attractions** lēnōcinia *ntpl*.
merge *vt* cōnfundere ♦ *vi* cōnfundī.
meridian *n* merīdiēs *m* ♦ *adj* merīdiānus.
merit *n* meritum *nt*, virtūs *f* ♦ *vt* merērī.
meritorious *adj* laudābilis.
meritoriously *adv* optimē.
mermaid *n* nympha *f*.
merrily *adv* hilare, festīvē.
merriment *n* hilaritās *f*, festīvitās *f*.
merry *adj* hilaris, festīvus; **make ~** lūdere.
merrymaking *n* lūdus *m*, festīvitās *f*.
mesh *n* macula *f*.
mess *n* (*dirt*) sordēs *f*, squālor *m*; (*trouble*) turba *f*; (*food*) cibus *m*; (*MIL*) contubernālēs *mpl*.
message *n* nūntius *m*.
messenger *n* nūntius *m*.
messmate *n* contubernālis *m*.
metal *n* metallum *nt* ♦ *adj* ferreus, aereus.
metamorphose *vt* mūtāre, trānsfōrmāre.
metamorphosis *n* mūtātiō *f*.
metaphor *n* trānslātiō *f*.
metaphorical *adj* trānslātus.
metaphorically *adv* per trānslātiōnem.
metaphysics *n* dialectica *ntpl*.

mete *vt* mētīrī.
meteor *n* fax caelestis *f*.
meteorology *n* prognōstica *ntpl*.
methinks *vi*: **~ I am** mihī videor esse.
method *n* ratiō *f*, modus *m*.
methodical *adj* dispositus; (*person*) dīligēns.
methodically *adv* dispositē.
meticulous *adj* accūrātus.
meticulously *adv* accūrātē.
meticulousness *n* cūra *f*.
metonymy *n* immūtātiō *f*.
metre *n* numerī *mpl*, modī *mpl*.
metropolis *n* urbs *f*.
mettle *n* ferōcitās *f*, virtūs *f*.
mettlesome *adj* ferōx, animōsus.
mew *n* (*bird*) larus *m*; **~s** *pl* stabula *ntpl* ♦ *vi* vāgīre.
miasma *n* hālitus *m*.
mid *adj* medius ♦ *prep* inter (*acc*).
midday *n* merīdiēs *m* ♦ *adj* merīdiānus.
middle *adj* medius ♦ *n* medium *nt*; **in the ~** medius, in mediō; **~ of** medius.
middling *adj* mediocris.
midge *n* culex *m*.
midget *n* pūmiliō *m/f*.
midland *adj* mediterrāneus.
midnight *n* media nox *f*.
midriff *n* praecordia *ntpl*.
midst *n* medium *nt*; **in the ~** medius; **in the ~ of** inter (*acc*); **through the ~ of** per medium.
midsummer *n* sōlstitium *nt* ♦ *adj* sōlstitiālis.
midway *adv* medius.
midwife *n* obstetrix *f*.
midwinter *n* brūma *f* ♦ *adj* brūmālis.
mien *n* aspectus *m*, vultus *m*.
might *n* vīs *f*, potentia *f*; **with ~ and main** omnibus nervīs, manibus pedibusque.
mightily *adv* valdē, magnopere.
mighty *adj* ingēns, validus.
migrate *vi* abīre, migrāre.
migration *n* peregrīnātiō *f*.
migratory *adj* advena.
mild *adj* mītis, lēnis, clēmēns.
mildew *n* rōbīgō *f*.
mildly *adv* lēniter, clēmenter.
mildness *n* clēmentia *f*, mānsuētūdō *f*; (*weather*) caelī indulgentia *f*.
mile *n* mīlle passūs *mpl*; **~s** *pl* mīlia passuum.
milestone *n* lapis *m*, mīliārium *nt*.
militant *adj* ferōx.
military *adj* mīlitāris ♦ *n* mīlitēs *mpl*.
military service *n* mīlitia *f*.
militate *vi*: **~ against** repugnāre (*dat*), facere contrā (*acc*).
militia *n* mīlitēs *mpl*.
milk *n* lac *nt* ♦ *vt* mulgēre.
milk pail *n* mulctra *f*.
milky *adj* lacteus.
mill *n* pistrīnum *nt*.
milled *adj* (*coin*) serrātus.
millennium *n* mīlle annī *mpl*.
miller *n* pistor *m*.
millet *n* mīlium *nt*.

million *num* deciēs centēna mīlia *ntpl*.
millionaire *n* rēx *m*.
millstone *n* mola *f*, molāris *m*.
mime *n* mīmus *m*.
mimic *n* imitātor *m*, imitātrīx *f* ♦ *vt* imitārī.
mimicry *n* imitātiō *f*.
minatory *adj* mināx.
mince *vt* concīdere; **not ~ words** plānē
apertēque dīcere ♦ *n* minūtal *nt*.
mind *n* mēns *f*, animus *m*, ingenium *nt*;
(*opinion*) sententia *f*; (*memory*) memoria *f*; **be
in one's right ~** mentis suae esse; **be of the
same ~** eadem sentīre; **be out of one's ~**
īnsānīre; **bear in ~** meminisse (*gen*),
memorem esse (*gen*); **call to ~** memoriā
repetere, recordārī; **have a ~ to** libet; **have in
~** in animō habēre; **put one's ~ to** animum
applicāre ad (+ *acc*); **make up one's ~**
animum indūcere, animō obstināre,
statuere; **put in ~ of** admonēre (*gen*); **speak
one's ~** sententiam suam aperīre; **to one's ~**
ex sententiā ♦ *vt* cūrāre, attendere; **~ one's
own business** suum negōtium agere ♦ *vi*
gravārī; **I don't ~** nīl moror; **never ~** mitte.
minded *adj* animātus.
mindful *adj* memor.
mine *n* metallum *nt*; (*MIL*) cuniculus *m*; (*fig*)
thēsaurus *m* ♦ *vi* fodere; (*MIL*) cuniculum
agere ♦ *pron* meus.
miner *n* fossor *m*.
mineral *n* metallum *nt*.
mingle *vt* miscēre, commiscēre ♦ *vi* sē
immiscēre.
miniature *n* minima pictūra *f*.
minimize *vt* dētrectāre.
minimum *n* minimum *nt* ♦ *adj* quam minimus.
minion *n* cliēns *m/f*; dēlicātus *m*.
minister *n* administer *m* ♦ *vi* ministrāre,
servīre.
ministry *n* mūnus *nt*, officium *nt*.
minor *adj* minor ♦ *n* pupillus *m*, pupilla *f*.
minority *n* minor pars *f*; **in one's ~** nōndum suī
iūris.
Minotaur *n* Mīnōtaurus *m*.
minstrel *n* fidicen *m*.
minstrelsy *n* cantus *m*.
mint *n* (*plant*) menta *f*; (*money*) Monēta *f* ♦ *vt*
cūdere.
minute *n* temporis mōmentum *nt*.
minute *adj* minūtus, exiguus, subtīlis.
minutely *adv* subtīliter.
minuteness *n* exiguitās *f*, subtīlitas *f*.
minutiae *n* singula *ntpl*.
minx *n* lascīva *f*.
miracle *n* mīrāculum *nt*, mōnstrum *nt*.
miraculous *adj* mīrus, mīrābilis.
miraculously *adv* dīvīnitus.
mirage *n* falsa speciēs *f*.
mire *n* lutum *nt*.
mirror *n* speculum *nt* ♦ *vt* reddere.
mirth *n* hilaritās *f*, laetitia *f*.
mirthful *adj* hilaris, laetus.
mirthfully *adv* hilare, laetē.

miry *adj* lutulentus.
misadventure *n* īnfortūnium *nt*, cāsus *m*.
misapply *vt* abūtī (*abl*); (*words*) invertere.
misapprehend *vt* male intellegere.
misapprehension *n* error *m*.
misappropriate *vt* intervertere.
misbegotten *adj* nothus.
misbehave *vi* male sē gerere.
miscalculate *vi* errāre, fallī.
miscalculation *n* error *m*.
miscall *vt* maledīcere (*dat*).
miscarriage *n* abortus *m*; (*fig*) error *m*.
miscarry *vi* aborīrī; (*fig*) cadere, inritum esse.
miscellaneous *adj* prōmiscuus, varius.
miscellany *n* farrāgō *f*.
mischance *n* īnfortūnium *nt*.
mischief *n* malum *nt*, facinus *nt*, maleficium *nt*;
(*children*) lascīvia *f*.
mischievous *adj* improbus, maleficus;
lascīvus.
misconceive *vt* male intellegere.
misconception *n* error *m*.
misconduct *n* dēlictum *nt*, culpa *f*.
misconstruction *n* prāva interpretātiō *f*.
misconstrue *vt* male interpretārī.
miscreant *n* scelerātus *m*.
misdeed *n* maleficium *nt*, dēlictum *nt*.
misdemeanour *n* peccātum *nt*, culpa *f*.
miser *n* avārus *m*.
miserable *adj* miser, īnfēlīx; **make oneself ~**
sē cruciāre.
miserably *adv* miserē.
miserliness *n* avāritia *f*.
miserly *adj* avārus.
misery *n* miseria *f*, aerumna *f*.
misfortune *n* malum *nt*, īnfortūnium *nt*,
incommodum *nt*, rēs adversae *fpl*.
misgiving *n* suspiciō *f*, cūra *f*; **have ~s** parum
cōnfīdere.
misgovern *vt* male regere.
misgovernment *n* prāva administrātiō *f*.
misguide *vt* fallere, dēcipere.
misguided *adj* dēmēns.
mishap *n* īnfortūnium *nt*.
misinform *vt* falsa docēre.
misinterpret *vt* male interpretārī.
misinterpretation *n* prāva interpretātiō *f*.
misjudge *vt* male iūdicāre.
mislay *vt* āmittere.
mislead *vt* dēcipere, indūcere, auferre.
mismanage *vt* male gerere.
misnomer *n* falsum nōmen *nt*.
misogyny *n* mulierum odium *nt*.
misplace *vt* in aliēnō locō collocāre.
misplaced *adj* (*fig*) vānus.
misprint *n* mendum *nt*.
mispronounce *vt* prāvē appellāre.
misquote *vt* perperam prōferre.
misrepresent *vt* dētorquēre, invertere;
(*person*) calumniārī.
misrepresentation *n* calumnia *f*.
misrule *n* prāva administrātiō *f*.
miss *vt* (*aim*) aberrāre (*abl*); (*loss*) requīrere,

dēsīderāre; (_notice_) praetermittere ♦ _n_ error _m_; (_girl_) virgō _f_.
misshapen _adj_ distortus, dēfōrmis.
missile _n_ tēlum _nt_.
missing _adj_ absēns; **be ~** dēesse, dēsīderārī.
mission _n_ lēgātiō _f_.
missive _n_ litterae _fpl_.
misspend _vt_ perdere, dissipāre.
misstatement _n_ falsum _nt_, mendācium _nt_.
mist _n_ nebula _f_, cālīgō _f_.
mistake _n_ error _m_; (_writing_) mendum _nt_; **full of ~s** mendōsus ♦ _vt_: **~ for** habēre prō (_abl_); **be ~n** errāre, fallī.
mistletoe _n_ viscum _nt_.
mistranslate _vt_ prāvē reddere.
mistress _n_ domina _f_; (_school_) magistra _f_; (_lover_) amīca _f_.
mistrust _n_ diffīdentia _f_, suspiciō _f_ ♦ _vt_ diffīdere (_dat_).
mistrustful _adj_ diffīdēns.
mistrustfully _adv_ diffīdenter.
misty _adj_ nebulōsus.
misunderstand _vt_ male intellegere ♦ _vi_ errāre.
misunderstanding _n_ error _m_; (_quarrel_) discidium _nt_.
misuse _n_ malus ūsus _m_ ♦ _vt_ abūtī (_abl_).
mite _n_ parvulus _m_; (_insect_) vermiculus _m_.
mitigate _vt_ mītigāre, lēnīre.
mitigation _n_ mītigātiō _f_.
mix _vt_ miscēre; **~ in** admiscēre; **~ together** commiscēre; **get ~ed up with** admiscērī cum, sē interpōnere (_dat_).
mixed _adj_ prōmiscuus.
mixture _n_ (_act_) temperātiō _f_; (_state_) dīversitās _f_.
mnemonic _n_ artificium memoriae _nt_.
moan _n_ gemitus _m_ ♦ _vi_ gemere.
moat _n_ fossa _f_.
mob _n_ vulgus _nt_, turba _f_ ♦ _vt_ circumfundī in (_acc_).
mobile _adj_ mōbilis, agilis.
mobility _n_ mōbilitās _f_, agilitās _f_.
mobilize _vt_ (_MIL_) ēvocāre.
mock _vt_ irrīdēre, lūdibriō habēre, lūdificārī; (_ape_) imitārī; **~ at** inlūdere ♦ _n_ lūdibrium _nt_ ♦ _adj_ simulātus, fictus.
mocker _n_ dērīsor _m_.
mockery _n_ lūdibrium _nt_, irrīsus _m_.
mode _n_ modus _m_, ratiō _f_.
model _n_ exemplar _nt_, exemplum _nt_ ♦ _vt_ fingere.
modeller _n_ fictor _m_.
moderate _adj_ (_size_) modicus; (_conduct_) moderātus ♦ _vt_ temperāre; (_emotion_) temperāre (_dat_) ♦ _vi_ mītigārī.
moderately _adv_ modicē, moderātē, mediocriter.
moderation _n_ moderātiō _f_, modus _m_; (_mean_) mediocritās _f_.
moderator _n_ praefectus _m_.
modern _adj_ recēns.
modernity _n_ haec aetās _f_.

modest _adj_ pudīcus, verēcundus.
modestly _adv_ verēcundē, pudenter.
modesty _n_ pudor _m_, verēcundia _f_.
modicum _n_ paullulum _nt_, aliquantulum _nt_.
modification _n_ mūtātiō _f_.
modify _vt_ immūtāre; (_law_) derogāre aliquid dē.
modulate _vt_ (_voice_) īnflectere.
modulation _n_ flexiō _f_, inclīnātiō _f_.
moiety _n_ dīmidia pars _f_.
moist _adj_ ūmidus.
moisten _vt_ ūmectāre, rigāre.
moisture _n_ ūmor _m_.
molar _n_ genuīnus _m_.
mole _n_ (_animal_) talpa _f_; (_on skin_) naevus _m_; (_pier_) mōlēs _f_.
molecule _n_ corpusculum _nt_.
molehill _n_: **make a mountain out of a ~** ē rīvō flūmina māgna facere, arcem facere ē cloācā.
molest _vt_ sollicitāre, vexāre.
molestation _n_ vexātiō _f_.
mollify _vt_ mollīre, lēnīre.
molten _adj_ liquefactus.
moment _n_ temporis mōmentum _nt_, temporis pūnctum _nt_; **for a ~** parumper; **in a ~** iam; **without a ~'s delay** nullā interpositā morā; **be of great ~** māgnō mōmentō esse; **it is of ~** interest.
momentary _adj_ brevis.
momentous _adj_ gravis, māgnī mōmentī.
momentum _n_ impetus _m_.
monarch _n_ rēx _m_, tyrannus _m_.
monarchical _adj_ rēgius.
monarchy _n_ rēgnum _nt_.
monastery _n_ monastērium _nt_.
monetary _adj_ pecūniārius.
money _n_ pecūnia _f_; (_cash_) nummī _mpl_; **for ~** mercēde; **ready ~** nummī, praesēns pecūnia; **make ~** rem facere, quaestum facere.
moneybag _n_ fiscus _m_.
moneyed _adj_ nummātus, pecūniōsus.
moneylender _n_ faenerātor _m_.
moneymaking _n_ quaestus _m_.
mongoose _n_ ichneumōn _m_.
mongrel _n_ hibrida _m_.
monitor _n_ admonitor _m_.
monk _n_ monachus _m_.
monkey _n_ sīmia _f_.
monograph _n_ libellus _m_.
monologue _n_ ōrātiō _f_.
monopolize _vt_ absorbēre, sibī vindicāre.
monopoly _n_ arbitrium _nt_.
monosyllabic _adj_ monosyllabus.
monosyllable _n_ monosyllabum _nt_.
monotonous _adj_ aequābilis.
monotony _n_ taedium _nt_.
monster _n_ mōnstrum _nt_, portentum _nt_, bēlua _f_.
monstrosity _n_ mōnstrum _nt_.
monstrous _adj_ immānis, mōnstruōsus; improbus.
month _n_ mēnsis _m_.
monthly _adj_ mēnstruus.

monument n monumentum nt.
monumental adj ingēns.
mood n adfectiō f, adfectus m, animus m; (GRAM) modus m; **I am in the ~ for** libet (inf).
moody adj mōrōsus, tristis.
moon n lūna f; **new ~** interlūnium nt.
moonlight n: **by ~** ad lūnam.
moonshine n somnia ntpl.
moonstruck adj lūnāticus.
moor vt religāre ♦ n tesqua ntpl.
moorings n ancorae fpl.
moot n conventus m; **it is a ~ point** discrepat ♦ vt iactāre.
mop n pēniculus m ♦ vt dētergēre.
mope vi maerēre.
moral adj honestus, probus; (opposed to physical) animī; (PHILOS) mōrālis ♦ n documentum nt.
morale n animus m; **~ is low** iacet animus.
morality n bonī mōrēs mpl, virtūs f.
moralize vi dē officiīs disserere.
morally adv honestē.
morals npl mōrēs mpl.
morass n palūs f.
moratorium n mora f.
morbid adj aeger.
mordant adj mordāx.
more adj plūs, pluris (in sg + gen, in pl + adj) ♦ adv plūs, magis, amplius; (extra) ultrā; **~ than** amplius quam; **~ than three feet** amplius trēs pedēs; **~ and ~** magis magisque; **never ~** immo; **~ or less** ferē; **no ~** (time) nōn diūtius, nunquam posteā.
moreover adv tamen, autem, praetereā.
moribund adj moribundus.
morning n māne nt; **early in the ~** bene māne; **this ~** hodiē māne; **good ~** salvē ♦ adj mātūtīnus.
morning call n salūtātiō f.
morning watch n (NAUT) tertia vigilia f.
moron n sōcors m.
morose adj acerbus, tristis.
moroseness n acerbitās f, tristitia f.
morrow n posterus diēs m; **on the ~** posterō diē, postrīdiē.
morsel n offa f.
mortal adj mortālis, hūmānus; (wound) mortifer ♦ n mortālis m/f, homō m/f; **poor ~** homunculus m.
mortality n mortālitās f; (death) mors f; **the ~ was high** plūrimī periērunt.
mortally adv: **be ~ wounded** mortiferum vulnus accipere.
mortar n mortārium nt.
mortgage n pignus nt, fīdūcia f ♦ vt obligāre.
mortification n dolor m, angor m.
mortified adj: **be ~ at** aegrē ferre.
mortify vt mordēre, vexāre; (lust) coercēre ♦ vi putrēscere.
mortise vt immittere.
mosaic n emblēma nt, lapillī mpl ♦ adj tessellātus.
mosquito n culex m.

mosquito net n cōnōpēum nt.
moss n muscus m.
mossy adj muscōsus.
most adj plūrimus, plērusque; **for the ~ part** māximam partem ♦ adv māximē, plūrimum.
mostly adv plērumque, ferē.
mote n corpusculum nt.
moth n tinea f.
mother n māter f; **of a ~** māternus.
mother-in-law n socrus f.
motherless adj mātre orbus.
motherly adj māternus.
mother tongue n patrius sermō m.
mother wit n Minerva f.
motif n argūmentum nt.
motion n mōtus m; (for law) rogātiō f; (in debate) sententia f; **propose a ~** ferre; **set in ~** movēre ♦ vt innuere.
motionless adj immōbilis.
motive n causa f, ratiō f; **I know your ~ in asking** sciō cūr rogēs.
motley adj versicolor, varius.
mottled adj maculōsus.
motto n sententia f.
mould n fōrma f; (soil) humus f; (fungus) mūcor m ♦ vt fingere, fōrmāre.
moulder vi putrēscere ♦ n fictor m.
mouldering adj puter.
mouldiness n situs m.
mouldy adj mūcidus.
moult vi pennas exuere.
mound n agger m, tumulus m.
mount n mōns m; (horse) equus m ♦ vt scandere, cōnscendere, ascendere ♦ vi ascendere; **~ up** ēscendere.
mountain n mōns m.
mountaineer n montānus m.
mountainous adj montuōsus.
mourn vi maerēre, lūgēre ♦ vt dēflēre, lūgēre.
mourner n plōrātor m; (hired) praefica f.
mournful adj (cause) lūctuōsus, acerbus; (sound) lūgubris, maestus.
mournfully adv maestē.
mourning n maeror m, lūctus m; (dress) sordēs fpl; **in ~** fūnestus; **be in ~** lūgere; **put on ~** vestem mūtāre, sordēs suscipere; **wearing ~** ātrātus.
mouse n mūs m.
mousetrap n mūscipulum nt.
mouth n ōs nt; (river) ōstium nt.
mouthful n bucca f.
mouthpiece n interpres m.
movable adj mōbilis ♦ npl: **~s rēs** fpl, supellex f.
move vt movēre; (emotion) commovēre; **~ backwards and forwards** reciprocāre; **~ out of the way** dēmovēre; **~ up** admovēre ♦ vi movērī; (residence) dēmigrāre; (proposal) ferre, cēnsēre; **~ into** immigrāre in (acc); **~ on** prōgredī.
movement n mōtus m; (process) cursus m; (society) societās f.

mover n auctor m.
moving adj flēbilis, flexanimus.
mow vt secāre, dēmetere.
mower n faenisex m.
much adj multus ♦ adv multum; (with compar) multō; **as ~ as** tantum quantum; **so ~** tantum; (with verbs) adeo; **~ less** nēdum; **too ~** nimis ♦ n multum nt.
muck n stercus nt.
mud n lutum nt.
muddle n turba f ♦ vt turbāre.
muffle vt involvere; **~ up** obvolvere.
muffled adj surdus.
mug n pōculum nt.
mulberry n mōrum nt; (tree) mōrus f.
mule n mūlus m.
muleteer n mūliō m.
mulish adj obstinātus.
mullet n mullus m.
multifarious adj multiplex, varius.
multiform adj multifōrmis.
multiply vt multiplicāre ♦ vi crēscere.
multitude n multitūdō f.
multitudinous adj crēberrimus.
mumble vt (words) opprimere ♦ vi murmurāre.
munch vt mandūcāre.
mundane adj terrestris.
municipal adj mūnicipālis.
municipality n mūnicipium nt.
munificence n largitās f.
munificent adj largus, mūnificus.
munificently adv mūnificē.
munitions n bellī adparātus m.
mural adj mūrālis.
murder n parricīdium nt, caedēs f; **charge with ~** inter sīcāriōs accūsāre; **trial for ~** quaestiō inter sīcāriōs ♦ vt interficere, iūgulāre, necāre.
murderer n sīcārius m, homicīda m, parricīda m, percussor m.
murderess n interfectrīx f.
murderous adj cruentus.
murky adj tenebrōsus.
murmur n murmur nt; (angry) fremitus m ♦ vi murmurāre; fremere.
murmuring n admurmurātiō f.
muscle n torus m.
muscular adj lacertōsus.
muse vi meditārī ♦ n Mūsa f.
mushroom n fungus m, bōlētus m.
music n (art) mūsica f; (sound) cantus m, modī mpl.
musical adj (person) mūsicus; (sound) canōrus.
musician n mūsicus m; (strings) fidicen m; (wind) tībīcen m.
muslin n sindōn f.
must n (wine) mustum nt ♦ vi dēbēre; **I ~ go** mē oportet īre, mihī eundum est.
mustard n sināpi nt.
muster vt convocāre, cōgere; (review) recēnsēre ♦ vi convenīre, coīre ♦ n conventus m; (review) recēnsiō f.
muster roll n album nt.
mustiness n situs m.
musty adj mūcidus.
mutability n incōnstantia f.
mutable adj incōnstāns, mūtābilis.
mute adj mūtus.
mutilate vt mūtilāre, truncāre.
mutilated adj mūtilus, truncus.
mutilation n lacerātiō f.
mutineer n sēditiōsus m.
mutinous adj sēditiōsus.
mutiny n sēditiō f ♦ vi sēditiōnem facere.
mutter vi mussitāre.
mutton n carō ovilla f.
mutual adj mūtuus.
mutually adv mūtuō, inter sē.
muzzle n ōs nt, rōstrum nt; (guard) fiscella f ♦ vt fiscellā capistrāre.
my adj meus.
myriad n decem mīlia; (any large no.) sēscentī.
myrmidon n satelles m.
myrrh n murra f.
myrtle n myrtus f ♦ adj myrteus.
myrtle grove n myrtētum nt.
myself pron ipse, egomet; (reflexive) mē.
mysterious adj arcānus, occultus.
mysteriously adv occultē.
mystery n arcānum nt; (rites) mystēria ntpl; (fig) latebra f.
mystic adj mysticus.
mystical adj mysticus.
mystification n fraus f, ambāgēs fpl.
mystify vt fraudāre, cōnfundere.
myth n fābula f.
mythical adj fābulōsus.
mythology n fābulae fpl.

N, n

nabob n rēx m.
nadir n fundus m.
nag n caballus m ♦ vt obiūrgitāre.
naiad n nāias f.
nail n clāvus m; (finger) unguis m; **hit the ~ on the head** rem acū tangere ♦ vt clāvīs adfīgere.
naive adj simplex.
naively adv simpliciter.
naiveté n simplicitās f.
naked adj nūdus.
nakedly adv apertē.
name n nōmen nt; (repute) existimātiō f; (term) vocābulum nt; **by ~** nōmine; **have a bad ~** male audīre; **have a good ~** bene audīre; **in**

the ~ of verbīs (gen); (oath) per ♦ vt
appellāre, vocāre, nōmināre; (appoint)
dīcere.
nameless adj nōminis expers, sine nōmine.
namely adv nempe, dīcō.
namesake n gentīlis m/f.
nanny goat n capra f.
nap n brevis somnus m; (cloth) villus nt.
napkin n linteum nt.
narcissus n narcissus m.
narcotic adj somnifer.
nard n nardus f.
narrate vt nārrāre, ēnārrāre.
narration n nārrātiō f.
narrative n fābula f.
narrator n nārrātor m.
narrow adj angustus ♦ vt coartāre ♦ vi
coartārī.
narrowly adv aegrē, vix.
narrowness n angustiae fpl.
narrows n angustiae fpl.
nasal adj nārium.
nascent adj nāscēns.
nastily adv foedē.
nastiness n foeditās f.
nasty adj foedus, taeter, impūrus.
natal adj nātālis.
nation n populus m; (foreign) gēns f.
national adj pūblicus, cīvīlis; (affairs)
domesticus.
nationality n cīvitās f.
native adj indigena; (speech) patrius ♦ n incola
m, indigena m/f.
native land n patria f.
nativity n ortus m.
natural adj nātūrālis; (innate) nātīvus,
genuīnus, īnsitus.
naturalization n cīvitās f.
naturalize vt cīvitāte dōnāre.
naturalized adj (person) cīvitāte dōnātus;
(thing) īnsitus.
naturally adv nātūrāliter, secundum nātūram;
(of course) scīlicet, certē.
nature n nātūra f; rērum nātūra f; (character)
indolēs f, ingenium nt; (species) genus nt;
course of ~ nātūra f; **I know the ~ of** sciō
quālis sit.
naught n nihil nt; **set at ~** parvī facere.
naughty adj improbus.
nausea n nausea f; (fig) fastīdium nt.
nauseate vt fastīdium movēre (dat); **be ~d**
with fastīdīre.
nauseous adj taeter.
nautical adj nauticus, maritimus.
naval adj nāvālis.
navel n umbilīcus m.
navigable adj nāvigābilis.
navigate vt, vi nāvigāre.
navigation n rēs nautica f; (sailing) nāvigātiō f.
navigator n nauta m, gubernātor m.
navy n classis f, cōpiae nāvālēs fpl.
nay adv nōn; **~ more** immo.
near adv prope ♦ adj propinquus ♦ prep prope

(acc), ad (acc); **lie ~** adiacēre (dat) ♦ vt
adpropinquāre (dat).
nearby adj iuxtā.
nearer adj propior.
nearest adj proximus.
nearly adv paene, prope, fermē.
neat adj nitidus, mundus, concinnus; (wine)
pūrus.
neatly adv mundē, concinnē.
neatness n munditia f.
nebulous adj nebulōsus; (fig) incertus.
necessaries n rēs ad vīvendum necessāriae
fpl.
necessarily adv necessāriō, necesse.
necessary adj necessārius, necesse; **it is ~**
oportet (+ acc and infin or gerundive of vt).
necessitate vt cōgere (inf), efficere ut (subj).
necessitous adj egēnus, pauper.
necessity n necessitās f; (thing) rēs necessāria
f; (want) paupertās f, egestās f.
neck n collum nt.
neckcloth n fōcāle nt.
necklace n monīle nt, torquis m.
nectar n nectar nt.
need n (necessity) necessitās f; (want) egestās f,
inopia f, indigentia f; **there is ~ of** opus est
(abl); **there is no ~ to** nihil est quod, cūr (subj)
♦ vt egēre (abl), carēre, indigēre (abl); **I ~**
opus est mihī (abl).
needful adj necessārius.
needle n acus f.
needless adj vānus, inūtilis.
needlessly adv frustrā, sine causā.
needs adv necesse ♦ npl necessitātēs fpl.
needy adj egēns, inops, pauper.
nefarious adj nefārius, scelestus.
negation n negātiō f, īnfitiātiō f.
negative adj negāns ♦ n negātiō f; **answer in**
the ~ negāre ♦ vt vetāre, contrādīcere (dat).
neglect n neglegentia f, incūria f; (of duty)
dērelictiō f ♦ vt neglegere, ōmittere.
neglectful adj neglegēns, immemor.
negligence n neglegentia f, incūria f.
negligent adj neglegēns, indīligēns.
negligently adv neglegenter, indīligenter.
negligible adj levissimus, minimī mōmentī.
negotiate vi agere dē ♦ vt (deal) peragere;
(difficulty) superāre.
negotiation n āctiō f, pactum nt.
negotiator n lēgātus m, conciliātor m.
negro n Aethiops m.
neigh vi hinnīre.
neighbour n vīcīnus m, fīnitimus m.
neighbourhood n vīcīnia f, vīcīnitās f.
neighbouring adj vīcīnus, fīnitimus,
propinquus.
neighbourly adj hūmānus, amīcus.
neighing n hinnītus m.
neither adv neque, nec; nēve, neu ♦ pron
neuter ♦ adj neuter, neutra, neutrum (like
alter); **~ ... nor** nec/neque ... nec/neque.
neophyte n tīrō m.
nephew n frātris fīlius m, sorōris fīlius m.

Nereid n Nērēis f.
nerve n nervus m; (_fig_) audācia f; **~s** pl pavor m, trepidātiō f; **have the ~ to** audēre ♦ vt cōnfirmāre.
nervous adj diffīdēns, sollicitus, trepidus.
nervously adv trepidē.
nervousness n sollicitūdō f, diffīdentia f.
nest vt nīdus m ♦ vi nīdificāre.
nestle vi recubāre.
nestling n pullus m.
net n rēte nt ♦ vt inrētīre.
nether adj īnferior.
nethermost adj īnfimus, īmus.
netting n rēticulum nt.
nettle n urtīca f ♦ vt inrītāre, ūrere.
neuter adj neuter.
neutral adj medius; **be ~** neutrī partī sē adiungere, medium sē gerere.
neutralize vt compēnsāre.
never adv nunquam.
nevertheless adv nihilōminus, at tamen.
new adj novus, integer, recēns.
newcomer n advena m/f.
newfangled adj novus, inaudītus.
newly adv nūper, modo.
newness n novitās f.
news n nūntius m; **what ~?** quid novī?; **~ was brought that** nūntiātum est (+ acc and infin).
newspaper n ācta diūrna/pūblica ntpl.
newt n lacerta f.
next adj proximus; (_time_) īnsequēns ♦ adv deīnde, deīnceps; **~ day** postrīdiē; **~ to** iuxtā; **come ~** to excipere.
nibble vi rōdere.
nice adj bellus, dulcis; (_exact_) accūrātus; (_particular_) fastīdiōsus.
nicely adv bellē, probē.
nicety n subtīlitās f.
niche n aedicula f.
nick n: **in the ~ of time** in ipsō articulō temporis.
nickname n cognōmen nt.
niece n frātris fīlia f, sorōris fīlia f.
niggardliness n illīberālitās f, avāritia f.
niggardly adj illīberālis, parcus, avārus.
nigh adv prope.
night n nox f; **by ~** noctū; **all ~** pernox; **spend the ~** pernoctāre; **be awake all ~** pervigilāre ♦ adj nocturnus.
night bird n noctua f.
nightfall n prīmae tenebrae fpl; **at ~** sub noctem.
nightingale n luscinia f.
nightly adj nocturnus ♦ adv noctū.
nightmare n incubus m.
night work n lūcubrātiō f.
nimble adj agilis, pernīx.
nimbleness n agilitās f, pernīcitās f; (_mind_) argūtiae fpl.
nimbly adv pernīciter.
nine num novem; **~ each** novēnī; **~ times** noviēns; **~ days'** novendiālis.
nine hundred num nōngentī.
nine hundredth adj nōngentēsimus.

nineteen num ūndēvigintī; **~ each** ūndēvīcēnī; **~ times** deciēns et noviēns.
nineteenth adj ūndēvīcēsimus.
ninetieth adj nōnāgēsimus.
ninety num nōnāgintā; **~ each** nōnāgēnī; **~ times** nōnāgiēns.
ninth adj nōnus.
nip vt vellicāre; (_frost_) ūrere.
nippers n forceps m.
nipple n papilla f.
no adv nōn; (_correcting_) immo; **say ~** negāre ♦ adj nullus.
nobility n nōbilitās f; (_persons_) optimātēs mpl, nōbilēs mpl.
noble adj nōbilis; (_birth_) generōsus; (_appearance_) decōrus.
nobleman n prīnceps m, optimās m.
nobly adv nōbiliter, praeclārē.
nobody n nēmō m.
nocturnal adj nocturnus.
nod n nūtus m ♦ vi nūtāre; (_sign_) adnuere; (_sleep_) dormītāre.
noddle n caput nt.
node n nōdus m.
noise n strepitus m, sonitus m; (_loud_) fragor m; **make a ~** increpāre, strepere ♦ vt: **~ abroad** ēvulgāre; **be ~d abroad** percrēbrēscere.
noiseless adj tacitus.
noiselessly adv tacitē.
noisily adv cum strepitū.
noisome adj taeter, gravis.
noisy adj clāmōsus.
nomadic adj vagus.
nomenclature n vocābula ntpl.
nominally adv nōmine, verbō.
nominate vt nōmināre, dīcere; (_in writing_) scrībere.
nomination n nōminātiō f.
nominative adj nōminātīvus.
nominee n nōminātus m.
nonappearance n absentia f.
nonce n: **for the ~** semel.
nonchalance n aequus animus m.
nonchalantly adv aequō animō.
noncombatant adj imbellis.
noncommittal adj circumspectus.
nondescript adj īnsolitus.
none adj nullus ♦ pron nēmō m.
nonentity n nihil nt, nullus m.
nones n Nōnae fpl.
nonexistent adj quī nōn est.
nonplus vt ad incitās redigere.
nonresistance n patientia f.
nonsense n nūgae fpl, ineptiae fpl.
nonsensical adj ineptus, absurdus.
nook n angulus m.
noon n merīdiēs m ♦ adj merīdiānus.
no one pron nēmō m (_for gen/abl use_ **nullus**).
noose n laqueus m.
nor adv neque, nec; nēve, neu.
norm n nōrma f.
normal adj solitus.
normally adv plērumque.

north n septentriōnēs mpl ♦ adj septentriōnālis.
northeast adv inter septentriōnēs et orientem.
northerly adj septentriōnālis.
northern adj septentriōnālis.
North Pole n arctos f.
northwards adv ad septentriōnēs versus.
northwest adv inter septentriōnēs et occidentem ♦ adj: ~ **wind** Cōrus m.
north wind n aquilō m.
nose n nāsus m, nārēs fpl; **blow the ~** ēmungere; **lead by the ~** labiīs ductāre ♦ vi scrūtārī.
nostril n nāris f.
not adv nōn, haud; ~ **at all** haudquāquam; ~ **as if** nōn quod, nōn quō; ~ **but what** nōn quīn; ~ **even** nē ... quidem; ~ **so very** nōn ita; ~ **that** nōn quō; **and** ~ neque; **does** ~, **did** ~ (interrog) nonne; **if** ... ~ nisi; **that** ~ (purpose) nē; (fear) nē nōn; ~ **long after** haud multō post; ~ **only** ... **but also** non modo/solum ... sed etiam; ~ **yet** nōndum.
notability n vir praeclārus m.
notable adj īnsignis, īnsignītus, memorābilis.
notably adv īnsignītē.
notary n scrība m.
notation n notae fpl.
notch n incīsūra f ♦ vt incīdere.
note n (mark) nota f; (comment) adnotātiō f; (letter) litterulae fpl; (sound) vōx f; **make a ~ of** in commentāriōs referre ♦ vt notāre; (observe) animadvertere.
notebook n pugillārēs mpl.
noted adj īnsignis, praeclārus, nōtus.
noteworthy adj memorābilis.
nothing n nihil, nīl nt; ~ **but** merus, nīl nisi; **come to ~** in inritum cadere; **for ~** frustrā; (gift) grātīs, grātuītō; **good for ~** nēquam; **think ~ of** nihilī facere.
notice n (official) prōscrīptiō f; (private) libellus m; **attract ~** cōnspicī; **escape ~** latēre; **escape the ~ of** fallere; **give ~ of** dēnūntiāre; **take ~ of** animadvertere ♦ vt animadvertere, cōnspicere.
noticeable adj cōnspicuus, īnsignis.
noticeably adv īnsignītē.
notification n dēnūntiātiō f.
notify vt (event) dēnūntiāre, indicāre; (person) renūntiāre (dat), certiōrem facere.
notion n nōtiō f, īnfōrmātiō f; suspiciō f.
notoriety n īnfāmia f.
notorious adj fāmōsus, īnfāmis; (thing) manifestus.
notoriously adv manifestō.
notwithstanding adv nihilōminus, tamen ♦ prep: ~ **the danger** in tantō discrīmine.
nought n nihil, nīl nt.
noun n nōmen nt.
nourish vt alere, nūtrīre.
nourisher n altor m, altrīx f.
nourishment n cibus m, alimenta ntpl.
novel adj novus, inaudītus ♦ n fābella f.
novelty n rēs nova f; novitās f, īnsolentia f.

November n mēnsis November m; **of ~** November.
novice n tīrō m.
now adv nunc; (past) iam; ~ **and then** interdum; **just ~** nunc; (lately) dūdum, modo; ~ ... ~ modo ... modo ♦ conj at, autem.
nowadays adv nunc, hodiē.
nowhere adv nusquam.
nowise adv nullō modō, haudquāquam.
noxious adj nocēns, noxius.
nuance n color m.
nucleus n sēmen nt.
nude adj nūdus.
nudge vt fodicāre.
nudity n nūdātum corpus nt.
nugget n massa f.
nuisance n malum nt, incommodum nt.
null adj inritus.
nullify vt inritum facere; (law) abrogāre.
numb adj torpēns, torpidus; **be ~** torpēre; **become ~** torpēscere.
number n numerus m; **a ~ of** complūrēs, aliquot; **a great ~** multitūdō f, frequentia f; **a small ~** īnfrequentia f; **in large ~s** frequentēs ♦ vt numerāre, ēnumerāre.
numberless adj innumerābilis.
numbness n torpor m.
numerous adj frequēns, crēber, plūrimī.
nun n monacha f.
nuptial adj nūptiālis.
nuptials n nūptiae fpl.
nurse n nūtrīx f ♦ vt (child) nūtrīre; (sick) cūrāre; (fig) fovēre.
nursery n (children) cubiculum nt; (plants) sēminārium nt.
nursling n alumnus m, alumna f.
nurture n ēducātiō f.
nut n nux f.
nutrition n alimenta ntpl.
nutritious adj salūbris.
nutshell n putāmen nt.
nut tree n nux f.
nymph n nympha f.

O, o

O interj ō!
oaf n agrestis m.
oak n quercus f; (evergreen) īlex f; (timber) rōbur nt ♦ adj quernus, īlignus, rōboreus; ~ **forest** quercētum nt.
oakum n stuppa f.
oar n rēmus m.
oarsman n rēmex m.
oaten adj avēnāceus.
oath n iūsiūrandum nt; (MIL) sacrāmentum nt;

(*imprecation*) exsecrātiō *f*; **false ~** periūrium *nt*; **take an ~** iūrāre; **take an ~ of allegiance to** in verba iūrāre (*gen*).

oats *n* avēna *f*.

obduracy *n* obstinātus animus *m*.

obdurate *adj* obstinātus, pervicāx.

obdurately *adv* obstinātē.

obedience *n* oboedientia *f*, obsequium *nt*.

obedient *adj* oboediēns, obsequēns; **be ~ to** pārēre (*dat*), obtemperāre (*dat*), obsequī (*dat*).

obediently *adv* oboedienter.

obeisance *n* obsequium *nt*; **make ~ to** adōrāre.

obelisk *n* obeliscus *m*.

obese *adj* obēsus, pinguis.

obesity *n* obēsitās *f*, pinguitūdō *f*.

obey *vt* pārēre (*dat*), obtemperāre (*dat*), oboedīre (*dat*); **~ orders** dictō pārēre.

obituary *n* mortēs *fpl*.

object *n* rēs *f*; (*aim*) fīnis *m*, prōpositum *nt*; **be an ~ of hate** odiō esse; **with what ~** quō cōnsiliō ♦ *vi* recūsāre, gravārī; **but, it is ~ed** at enim; **~ to** improbāre.

objection *n* recūsātiō *f*, mora *f*; **I have no ~** nīl moror.

objectionable *adj* invīsus, iniūcundus.

objective *adj* externus ♦ *n* prōpositum *nt*, fīnis *m*.

objurgate *vt* obiūrgāre, culpāre.

oblation *n* dōnum *nt*.

obligation *n* (*legal*) dēbitum *nt*; (*moral*) officium *nt*; **lay under an ~** obligāre, obstringere.

obligatory *adj* dēbitus, necessārius.

oblige *vt* (*force*) cōgere; (*contract*) obligāre, obstringere; (*compliance*) mōrem gerere (*dat*), mōrigerārī (*dat*); **I am ~d to** (*action*) dēbeō (*inf*); (*person*) amāre, grātiam habēre (*dat*).

obliging *adj* cōmis, officiōsus.

obligingly *adv* cōmiter, officiōsē.

oblique *adj* oblīquus.

obliquely *adv* oblīquē.

obliquity *n* (*moral*) prāvitās *f*.

obliterate *vt* dēlēre, oblitterāre.

obliteration *n* litūra *f*.

oblivion *n* oblīviō *f*.

oblivious *adj* oblīviōsus, immemor.

oblong *adj* oblongus.

obloquy *n* vītuperātiō *f*, opprobrium *nt*.

obnoxious *adj* invīsus.

obscene *adj* obscaenus, impūrus.

obscenity *n* obscaenitās *f*, impūritās *f*.

obscure *adj* obscūrus, caecus ♦ *vt* obscūrāre, officere (*dat*).

obscurely *adv* obscūrē; (*speech*) per ambāgēs.

obscurity *n* obscūritās *f*; (*speech*) ambāgēs *fpl*.

obsequies *n* exsequiae *fpl*.

obsequious *adj* officiōsus, ambitiōsus.

obsequiously *adv* officiōsē.

obsequiousness *n* adsentātiō *f*.

observance *n* observantia *f*; (*rite*) rītus *m*.

observant *adj* attentus, dīligēns.

observation *n* observātiō *f*, animadversiō *f*; (*remark*) dictum *nt*.

observe *vt* animadvertere, contemplārī; (*see*) cernere, cōnspicere; (*remark*) dīcere; (*adhere to*) cōnservāre, observāre.

observer *n* spectātor *m*, contemplātor *m*.

obsess *vt* occupāre; **I am ~ed by** tōtus sum in (*abl*).

obsession *n* studium *nt*.

obsolescent *adj*: **be ~** obsolēscere.

obsolete *adj* obsolētus; **become ~** exolēscere.

obstacle *n* impedīmentum *nt*, mora *f*.

obstinacy *n* pertinācia *f*, obstinātus animus *m*.

obstinate *adj* pertināx, obstinātus.

obstinately *adv* obstinātō animō.

obstreperous *adj* clāmōsus, ferus.

obstruct *vt* impedīre, obstruere, obstāre (*dat*); (*POL*) intercēdere (*dat*); (*fig*) officere (*dat*).

obstruction *n* impedīmentum *nt*; (*POL*) intercessiō *f*

obstructionist *n* intercessor *m*.

obtain *vt* adipīscī, nancīscī, cōnsequī; comparāre; (*by request*) impetrāre ♦ *vi* tenēre, obtinēre.

obtrude *vi* sē inculcāre ♦ *vt* ingerere.

obtrusive *adj* importūnus, molestus.

obtuse *adj* hebes, stolidus.

obtusely *adv* stolidē.

obtuseness *n* stupor *m*.

obverse *adj* obversus.

obviate *vt* tollere, praevertere.

obvious *adj* ēvidēns, manifestus, apertus; **it is ~** appāret.

obviously *adv* ēvidenter, apertē, manifestō.

occasion *n* occāsiō *f*, locus *m*; (*reason*) causa *f* ♦ *vt* movēre, facessere, auctōrem esse (*gen*).

occasional *adj* fortuītus.

occasionally *adv* interdum, nōnnunquam.

occidental *adj* occidentālis.

occult *adj* arcānus.

occupancy *n* possessiō *f*.

occupant *n* habitātor *m*, possessor *m*.

occupation *n* quaestus *m*, occupātiō *f*.

occupier *n* possessor *m*.

occupy *vt* possidēre; (*MIL*) occupāre; (*space*) complēre; (*attention*) distinēre, occupāre.

occur *vi* ēvenīre, accidere; (*to mind*) occurrere, in mentem venīre.

occurrence *n* ēventum *nt*; rēs *f*.

ocean *n* mare *nt*, ōceanus *m*.

October *n* mēnsis Octōber *m*; **of ~** Octōber.

ocular *adj* oculōrum; **give ~ proof of** ante oculōs pōnere, videntī dēmōnstrāre.

odd *adj* (*number*) impār; (*moment*) subsecīvus; (*appearance*) novus, īnsolitus.

oddity *n* novitās *f*; (*person*) homō rīdiculus *m*.

oddly *adv* mīrum in modum.

odds *n* praestantia *f*; **be at ~ with** dissidēre cum; **the ~ are against us** imparēs sumus; **the ~ are in our favour** superiōrēs sumus.

ode *n* carmen *nt*.

odious *adj* invīsus, odiōsus.

odium *n* invidia *f*.

odorous *adj* odōrātus.
odour *n* odor *m*.
of *prep gen*; (*origin*) ex, dē; (*cause*) *abl*; **all ~ us** nōs omnēs; **the city ~ Rome** urbs Rōma.
off *adv* procul; (*prefix*) ab-; **~ and on** interdum; **~ with you** aufer tē; **come ~** ēvādere; **well ~** beātus; **well ~ for** abundāns (*abl*).
offal *n* quisquiliae *fpl*.
offence *n* offēnsiō *f*; (*legal*) dēlictum *nt*; **commit an ~** dēlinquere.
offend *vt* laedere, offendere; **be ~ed** aegrē ferre ♦ *vi* dēlinquere; **~ against** peccāre in (*acc*), violāre.
offender *n* reus *m*.
offensive *adj* odiōsus; (*smell*) gravis; (*language*) contumēliōsus; **take the ~** bellum īnferre.
offensively *adv* odiōsē; graviter.
offer *vt* offerre, dare, praebēre; (*hand*) porrigere; (*violence*) adferre; (*honour*) dēferre; (*with verb*) profitērī, pollicērī ♦ *n* condiciō *f*; **~ for sale** venditāre.
offering *n* dōnum *nt*; (*to the dead*) īnferiae *fpl*.
off-hand *adj* neglegēns, incūriōsus.
office *n* (*POL*) magistrātus *m*, mūnus *nt*, honōs *m*; (*kindness*) officium *nt*; (*place*) mēnsa *f*.
officer *n* praefectus *m*; lēgātus *m*.
official *adj* pūblicus ♦ *n* adiūtor *m*, minister *m*.
officially *adv* pūblicē.
officiate *vi* operārī, officiō fungī.
officious *adj* molestus.
officiously *adv* molestē.
officiousness *n* occursātiō *f*.
offing *n*: **in the ~** procul.
offset *vt* compēnsāre.
offspring *n* prōgeniēs *f*, līberī *mpl*; (*animal*) fētus *m*.
often *adv* saepe, saepenumerō; **as ~ as** quotiēns; totiēs . . . quotiēs; **how ~?** quotiēns?; **so ~** totiēns; **very ~** persaepe.
ogle *vi*: **~ at** līmīs oculīs intuērī.
ogre *n* mōnstrum *nt*.
oh *interj* (*joy, surprise*) ōh!; (*sorrow*) prō!
oil *n* oleum *nt* ♦ *vt* ungere.
oily *adj* oleōsus.
ointment *n* unguentum *nt*.
old *adj* (*person*) senex; (*thing*) vetus; (*ancient*) antīquus, prīscus; **~ age** senectūs *f*; **be ten years ~** decem annōs habēre; **ten years ~** decem annōs nātus; **two years ~** bīmus; **good ~** antīquus; **good ~ days** antīquitās *f*; **grow ~** senēscere; **of ~** quondam.
olden *adj* prīscus, prīstinus.
older *adj* nātū māior, senior.
oldest *adj* nātū māximus.
old-fashioned *adj* antīquus, obsolētus.
old man *n* senex *m*.
oldness *n* vetustās *f*.
old woman *n* anus *f*.
oligarchy *n* paucōrum dominātiō *f*, optimātium factiō *f*.
olive *n* olea *f*; **~ orchard** olīvētum *nt*.

Olympiad *n* Olympias *f*.
Olympic *adj* Olympicus; **win an ~ victory** Olympia vincere.
Olympic Games *n* Olympia *ntpl*.
omen *n* ōmen *nt*, auspicium *nt*; **announce a bad ~** obnūntiāre; **obtain favourable ~s** litāre.
ominous *adj* īnfaustus, mināx.
omission *n* praetermissiō *f*, neglegentia *f*.
omit *vt* ōmittere, praetermittere.
omnipotence *n* īnfīnīta potestās *f*.
omnipotent *adj* omnipotēns.
on *prep* (*place*) in (*abl*), in- (*prefix*); (*time*) *abl*; (*coast of*) ad (*acc*); (*subject*) dē (*abl*); (*side*) ab (*abl*) ♦ *adv* porrō, usque; **and so ~** ac deinceps; **~ hearing the news** nūntiō acceptō; **~ equal terms** (*in battle*) aequō Marte; **~ the following day** posterō/proximō diē; postrīdiē; **~ this side of** citrā (+ *acc*).
once *adv* semel; (*past*) ōlim, quondam; **at ~** extemplō, statim; (*together*) simul; **for ~** aliquandō; **~ and for all** semel; **~ more** dēnuō, iterum; **~ upon a time** ōlim, quondam.
one *num* ūnus ♦ *pron* quīdam; (*of two*) alter, altera, alterum; **~ and the same** ūnus; **~ another** inter sē, alius alium; **~ or the other** alteruter; **~ day** ōlim; **~ each** singulī; **~ would have thought** crēderēs; **be ~ of** in numerō esse (*gen*); **be at ~** idem sentīre; **it is all ~** nihil interest; **the ~ . . . the other** alter, hic; **this is the ~** hōc illud est.
one-eyed *adj* luscus.
oneness *n* ūnitās *f*.
onerous *adj* gravis.
oneself *pron* ipse; (*reflexive*) sē.
one-sided *adj* inaequālis, inīquus.
onion *n* caepe *nt*.
onlooker *n* spectātor *m*.
only *adj* ūnus, sōlus; (*son*) ūnicus ♦ *adv* sōlum, tantum, modo; (*with clause*) nōn nisi, nīl nisi, nihil aliud quam; (*time*) dēmum; **if ~** sī modo; (*wish*) utinam.
onrush *n* incursus *m*.
onset *n* impetus *m*.
onslaught *n* incursus *m*; **make an ~ on** (*words*) invehī in (*acc*).
onto *prep* in (+ *acc*).
onus *n* officium *nt*.
onward, onwards *adv* porrō.
onyx *n* onyx *m*.
ooze *vi* mānāre, stillāre.
opaque *adj* haud perlūcidus.
open *adj* apertus; (*wide*) patēns, hiāns; (*ground*) pūrus, apertus; (*question*) integer; **lie ~** patēre; **stand ~** hiāre; **throw ~** adaperīre, patefacere; **it is ~ to me to** mihī integrum est (*inf*); **while the question is still ~** rē integrā ♦ *vt* aperīre, patefacere; (*book*) ēvolvere; (*letter*) resolvere; (*speech*) exōrdīrī; (*with ceremony*) inaugurāre; (*will*) resignāre ♦ *vi* aperīrī, hiscere; (*sore*) recrūdēscere; **~ out** extendere, pandere; **~ up** (*country*) aperīre.
open air *n*: **in the ~** sub dīvō.

open-handed *adj* largus, mūnificus.
open-handedness *n* largitās *f*.
open-hearted *adj* ingenuus.
opening *n* forāmen *nt*, hiātus *m*; (*ceremony*) cōnsecrātiō *f*; (*opportunity*) occāsiō *f*, ānsa *f* ♦ *adj* prīmus.
openly *adv* palam, apertē.
open-mouthed *adj*: **stand ~ at** inhiāre.
operate *vi* rem gerere ♦ *vt* movēre.
operation *n* opus *nt*, āctiō *f*; (*MED*) sectiō *f*.
operative *adj* efficāx.
ophthalmia *n* lippitūdō *f*.
opiate *adj* somnifer.
opine *vi* opīnārī, existimāre.
opinion *n* sententia *f*; (*of person*) existimātiō *f*; **public ~** fāma *f*; **in my ~** meō iūdiciō, meō animō.
opponent *n* adversārius *m*, hostis *m*.
opportune *adj* opportūnus, tempestīvus.
opportunely *adv* opportūnē.
opportunity *n* occāsiō *f*; (*to act*) facultās *f*; potestās *f*.
oppose *vt* (*barrier*) obicere; (*contrast*) oppōnere ♦ *vi* adversārī (*dat*), resistere (*dat*), obstāre (*dat*); **be ~d to** adversārī (*dat*); (*opinion*) dīversum esse ab.
opposite *adj* (*facing*) adversus; (*contrary*) contrārius, dīversus ♦ *prep* contrā (*acc*), adversus (*acc*); **directly ~** ē regiōne (*gen*) ♦ *adv* ex adversō.
opposition *n* repugnantia *f*; (*party*) factiō adversa *f*.
oppress *vt* opprimere, adflīgere; (*burden*) premere, onerāre.
oppression *n* iniūria *f*, servitūs *f*.
oppressive *adj* gravis, inīquus; **become more ~** ingravēscere.
oppressor *n* tyrannus *m*.
opprobrious *adj* turpis.
opprobriously *adv* turpiter.
opprobrium *n* dēdecus *nt*, ignōminia *f*.
optical *adj* oculōrum.
optical illusion *n* oculōrum lūdibrium *nt*.
optimism *n* spēs *f*.
option *n* optiō *f*, arbitrium *nt*; **I have no ~** nōn est arbitriī meī.
optional *adj*: **it is ~ for you** optiō tua est.
opulence *n* opēs *fpl*, cōpia *f*.
opulent *adj* dīves, cōpiōsus.
or *conj* aut, vel, -ve; (*after* **utrum**) an; **~ else** aliōquīn; **~ not** (*direct*) annōn; (*indirect*) necne.
oracle *n* ōrāculum *nt*.
oracular *adj* fātidicus; (*fig*) obscūrus.
oral *adj*: **give an ~ message** vōce nūntiāre.
orally *adv* vōce, verbīs.
oration *n* ōrātiō *f*.
orator *n* ōrātor *m*.
oratorical *adj* ōrātōrius.
oratory *n* ēloquentia *f*, rhētoricē *f*; (*for prayer*) sacellum *nt*; **of ~** dīcendī, ōrātōrius.
orb *n* orbis *m*.
orbit *n* orbis *m*, ambitus *m*.
orchard *n* pōmārium *nt*.

ordain *vt* ēdīcere, sancīre.
ordeal *n* labor *m*.
order *n* (*arrangement*) ōrdō *m*; (*class*) ōrdō *m*; (*battle*) aciēs *f*; (*command*) iussum *nt*, imperium *nt*; (*money*) perscrīptiō *f*; **in ~** dispositus; (*succession*) deinceps; **in ~ that/to** ut (*+ subj*); **in ~ that not** nē (*+ subj*); **put in ~** dispōnere, ōrdināre; **by ~ of** iussū (*gen*); **out of ~** incompositus; **without ~s from** iniussū (*gen*) ♦ *vt* (*arrange*) dispōnere, ōrdināre; (*command*) iubēre (*+ acc and infin*), imperāre (*dat and ut/nē +subj*).
orderly *adj* ōrdinātus; (*conduct*) modestus ♦ *n* accēnsus *m*.
ordinance *n* ēdictum *nt*, institūtum *nt*.
ordinarily *adv* plērumque, ferē.
ordinary *adj* ūsitātus, solitus, cottīdiānus.
ordnance *n* tormenta *ntpl*.
ordure *n* stercus *m*.
ore *n* aes *nt*; **iron ~** ferrum īnfectum *nt*.
Oread *n* (*MYTH*) Oreas *f*.
organ *n* (*bodily*) membrum *nt*; (*musical*) organum *nt*, hydraulus *m*.
organic *adj* nātūrālis.
organically *adv* nātūrā.
organization *n* ōrdinātiō *f*, structūra *f*.
organize *vt* ōrdināre, īnstituere, adparāre.
orgies *n* orgia *ntpl*.
orgy *n* cōmissātiō *f*.
orient *n* oriēns *m*.
oriental *adj* Asiāticus.
orifice *n* ōstium *nt*.
origin *n* orīgō *f*, prīncipium *nt*; (*source*) fōns *m*; (*birth*) genus *nt*.
original *adj* prīmus, prīstinus; (*LIT*) proprius ♦ *n* exemplar *nt*.
originally *adv* prīncipiō, antīquitus.
originate *vt* īnstituere, auctōrem esse (*gen*) ♦ *vi* exorīrī; **~ in** innāscī in (*abl*), initium dūcere ab.
originator *n* auctor *m*.
orisons *n* precēs *fpl*.
ornament *n* ōrnāmentum *nt*; (*fig*) decus *nt* ♦ *vt* ōrnāre, decorāre; **I am ~** ornamentō sum.
ornamental *adj* decōrus; **be ~** decorī esse.
ornamentally *adv* ōrnātē.
ornate *adj* ōrnātus.
ornately *adv* ōrnātē.
orphan *n* orbus *m*, orba *f*.
orphaned *adj* orbātus.
orthodox *adj* antīquus.
orthography *n* orthographia *f*.
oscillate *vi* reciprocāre.
osculate *vt* ōsculārī.
osier *n* vīmen *nt* ♦ *adj* vīmineus.
osprey *n* haliaeetos *m*.
ostensible *adj* speciōsus.
ostensibly *adv* per speciem.
ostentation *n* iactātiō *f*, ostentātiō *f*.
ostentatious *adj* glōriōsus, ambitiōsus.
ostentatiously *adv* glōriōsē.
ostler *n* agāsō *m*.
ostrich *n* strūthiocamēlus *m*.

other–overlay

other adj alius; (of two) alter; **one or the ~** alteruter; **every ~ year** tertiō quōque annō; **on the ~ side of** ultrā (+ acc); **of ~s** aliēnus.
otherwise adv aliter; (if not) aliōquī.
otter n lutra f.
ought vi dēbēre (+ infin or gerundive of vt); **I ~ mē** oportet; **I ~ to have said** dēbuī dīcere.
ounce n ūncia f; **two ~s** sextāns m; **three ~s** quadrāns m; **four ~s** triēns m; **five ~s** quīncūnx m; **six ~s** sēmis m; **seven ~s** septūnx m; **eight ~s** bēs m; **nine ~s** dōdrāns m; **ten ~s** dextāns m; **eleven ~s** deūnx m.
our adj noster.
ourselves pron ipsī; (reflexive) nōs.
oust vt extrūdere, ēicere.
out adv (rest) forīs; (motion) forās; **~ of** dē, ē/ex (abl); (cause) propter (acc); (beyond) extrā, ultrā (acc); **be ~** (book) in manibus esse; (calculation) errāre; (fire) exstinctum esse; (secret) palam esse.
outbreak n initium nt, ēruptiō f.
outburst n ēruptiō f.
outcast n profugus m.
outcome n ēventus m, exitus m.
outcry n clāmor m, adclāmātiō f; **raise an ~ against** obstrepere (dat).
outdistance vt praevertere.
outdo vt superāre.
outdoor adj sub dīvō.
outer adj exterior.
outermost adj extrēmus.
outfit n īnstrūmenta ntpl; vestīmenta ntpl.
outflank vt circumīre.
outgrow vt excēdere ex.
outing n excursiō f.
outlandish adj barbarus.
outlaw n prōscrīptus m ♦ vt prōscrībere, aquā et ignī interdīcere (dat).
outlawry n aquae et ignis interdictiō f.
outlay n impēnsa f, sūmptus m.
outlet n ēmissārium nt, exitus m.
outline n ductus m, adumbrātiō f ♦ vt adumbrāre.
outlive vt superesse (dat).
outlook n prōspectus m.
outlying adj longinquus, exterior.
outnumber vt numerō superiōrēs esse, multitūdine superāre.
out-of-doors adv forīs.
outpost n statiō f.
outpouring n effūsiō f.
output n frūctus m.
outrage n flāgitium nt, iniūria f ♦ vt laedere, violāre.
outrageous adj flāgitiōsus, indignus.
outrageously adv flāgitiōsē.
outrider n praecursor m.
outright adv penitus, prōrsus; semel.
outrun vt praevertere.
outset n initium nt.
outshine vt praelūcēre (dat).
outside adj externus ♦ adv extrā, forīs; (motion to) forās; **~ in** inversus; **from ~**

extrīnsecus ♦ n exterior pars f; (show) speciēs f; **at the ~** summum, ad summum; **on the ~** extrīnsecus ♦ prep extrā (acc).
outsider n aliēnus m; (POL) novus homō m.
outskirts n suburbānus ager m; **on the ~** suburbānus.
outspoken adj līber.
outspokenness n lībertās f.
outspread adj patulus.
outstanding adj ēgregius, īnsignis, singulāris; (debt) residuus.
outstep vt excēdere.
outstretched adj passus, porrēctus, extentus.
outstrip vt praevertere.
outvote vt suffrāgiīs superāre.
outward adj externus; **~ form** speciēs f ♦ adv domō, forās.
outweigh vt praeponderāre.
outwit vt dēcipere, circumvenīre.
outwork n prōpugnāculum nt, bracchium nt.
outworn adj exolētus.
oval adj ōvātus ♦ n ōvum nt.
ovation n (triumph) ovātiō f; **receive an ~** cum laudibus excipī.
oven n furnus m, fornāx f.
over prep (above) super (abl), suprā (acc); (across) super (acc); (extent) per (acc); (time) inter (acc); **~ and above** super (acc), praeter (acc); **all ~** per; **~ against** adversus (acc) ♦ adv suprā; (excess) nimis; (done) cōnfectus; **~ again** dēnuō; **~ and above** īnsuper; **~ and ~ identidem; be left ~** superesse, restāre; **it is all ~ with** āctum est dē.
overall adj tōtus ♦ adv ubīque, passim.
overawe vt formīdinem inicere (dat).
overbalance vi titubāre.
overbearing adj superbus.
overboard adv ē nāvī, in mare; **throw ~** excutere, iactāre.
overbold adj importūnus.
overburden vt praegravāre.
overcast adj nūbilus.
overcoat n paenula f, lacerna f.
overcome vt superāre, vincere.
overconfidence n cōnfīdentia f.
overconfident adj cōnfīdēns.
overdo vt modum excēdere in (abl).
overdone adj (style) pūtidus.
overdraw vt (style) exaggerāre.
overdue adj (money) residuus.
overestimate vt māiōris aestimāre.
overflow n ēluviō f ♦ vi abundāre, redundāre ♦ vt inundāre.
overgrown adj obsitus; **be ~** luxuriāre.
overhang vt, vi impendēre, imminēre (dat).
overhaul vt reficere.
overhead adv īnsuper.
overhear vt excipere, auscultāre.
overjoyed adj nimiō gaudiō ēlātus.
overladen adj praegravātus.
overland adv terrā.
overlap vt implicāre.
overlay vt indūcere.

overload *vt* (*fig*) obruere.
overlook *vt* (*place*) dēspectāre, imminēre (*dat*); (*knowledge*) ignōrāre; (*notice*) neglegere, praetermittere; (*fault*) ignōscere (*dat*).
overlord *n* dominus *m*.
overmaster *vt* dēvincere.
overmuch *adv* nimis, plūs aequō.
overnight *adj* nocturnus ♦ *adv* noctū.
overpower *vt* superāre, domāre, obruere, opprimere.
overpraise *vt* in māius extollere.
overrate *vt* māiōris aestimāre.
overreach *vt* circumvenīre.
overriding *adj* praecipuus.
overrule *vt* rescindere.
overrun *vt* pervagārī; (*fig*) obsidēre.
oversea *adj* trānsmarīnus.
oversee *vt* praeesse (*dat*).
overseer *n* cūrātor *m*, custōs *m*.
overset *vt* ēvertere.
overshadow *vt* officere (*dat*).
overshoot *vt* excēdere.
oversight *n* neglegentia *f*.
overspread *vt* offendere (*dat*), obdūcere.
overstep *vt* excēdere.
overt *adj* apertus.
overtake *vt* cōnsequī; (*surprise*) opprimere, dēprehendere.
overtax *vt* (*fig*) abūtī (*abl*).
overthrow *vt* ēvertere; (*destroy*) prōflīgāre, dēbellāre ♦ *n* ēversiō *f*, ruīna *f*.
overtly *adv* palam.
overtop *vt* superāre.
overture *n* exōrdium *nt*; **make ~s to** temptāre, agere cum, lēgātōs mittere ad.
overturn *vt* ēvertere.
overweening *adj* superbus, adrogāns, īnsolēns.
overwhelm *vt* obruere, dēmergere, opprimere.
overwhelming *adj* īnsignis, vehementissimus.
overwhelmingly *adv* mīrum quantum.
overwork *vi* plūs aequō labōrāre ♦ *vt* cōnficere ♦ *n* immodicus labor *m*.
overwrought *adj* (*emotion*) ēlātus; (*style*) ēlabōrātus.
owe *vt* dēbēre.
owing *adj*: **be ~** dēbērī; **~ to** (*person*) per; (*cause*) ob/propter (*acc*).
owl *n* būbō *m*; ulula *f*.
own *adj* proprius; **my ~** meus; **have of one's ~** domī habēre; **hold one's ~** parem esse ♦ *vt* possidēre, habēre; (*admit*) fatērī, cōnfitērī.
owner *n* dominus *m*, possessor *m*.
ownership *n* possessiō *f*, mancipium *nt*.
ox *n* bōs *m*.
ox herd *n* bubulcus *m*.
oyster *n* ostrea *f*.

P, p

pace *n* passus *m*; (*speed*) gradus *m*; **keep ~** gradum cōnferre ♦ *vi* incēdere; **~ up and down** spatiārī, inambulāre.
pacific *adj* pācificus; (*quiet*) placidus.
pacification *n* pācificātiō *f*.
pacifist *n* imbellis *m*.
pacify *vt* (*anger*) plācāre; (*rising*) sēdāre.
pack *n* (*MIL*) sarcina *f*; (*animals*) grex *m*; (*people*) turba *f* ♦ *vt* (*kit*) colligere; (*crowd*) stīpāre; **~ together** coartāre; **~ up** colligere, compōnere ♦ *vi* vāsa colligere; **send ~ing** missum facere ♦ *adj* (*animal*) clītellārius.
package *n* fasciculus *m*, sarcina *f*.
packet *n* fasciculus *m*; (*ship*) nāvis āctuāria *f*.
packhorse *n* iūmentum *nt*.
packsaddle *n* clītellae *fpl*.
pact *n* foedus *nt*, pactum *nt*.
pad *n* pulvillus *m*.
padding *n* tōmentum *nt*.
paddle *n* rēmus *m* ♦ *vi* rēmigāre.
paddock *n* saeptum *nt*.
paean *n* paeān *m*.
pagan *adj* pāgānus.
page *n* (*book*) pāgina *f*; (*boy*) puer *m*.
pageant *n* pompa *f*, spectāculum *nt*.
pageantry *n* adparātus *m*.
pail *n* situla *f*.
pain *n* dolor *m*; **be in ~** dolēre ♦ *vt* dolōre adficere.
painful *adj* acerbus; (*work*) labōriōsus.
painfully *adv* acerbē, labōriōsē.
painless *adj* dolōris expers.
painlessly *adv* sine dolōre.
painlessness *n* indolentia *f*.
pains *npl* opera *f*; **take ~** operam dare; **take ~ with** (*art*) ēlabōrāre.
painstaking *adj* dīligēns, operōsus.
painstakingly *adv* dīligenter, summā cūrā.
paint *n* pigmentum *nt*; (*cosmetic*) fūcus *m* ♦ *vt* pingere; (*red*) fūcāre; (*in words*) dēpingere; (*portrait*) dēpingere.
paintbrush *n* pēnicillus *m*.
painter *n* pictor *m*.
painting *n* pictūra *f*.
pair *n* pār *nt* ♦ *vt* coniungere, compōnere.
palace *n* rēgia *f*.
palatable *adj* suāvis, iūcundus.
palate *n* palātum *nt*.
palatial *adj* rēgius.
palaver *n* colloquium *nt*, sermunculī *mpl*.
pale *n* pālus *m*, vallus *m*; **beyond the ~** extrāneus ♦ *adj* pallidus; **look ~** pallēre; **grow ~** pallēscere; **~ brown** subfuscus; **~ green** subviridis ♦ *vi* pallēscere.
paleness *n* pallor *m*.

palimpsest n palimpsēstus m.
paling n saepēs f.
palisade n (MIL) vallum nt.
palish adj pallidulus.
pall n (funeral) pallium nt ♦ vi taedēre.
pallet n grabātus m.
palliasse n strāmentum nt.
palliate vt extenuāre, excūsāre.
palliation n excūsātiō f.
palliative n lēnīmentum nt.
pallid adj pallidus.
pallor n pallor m.
palm n (hand) palma f; (tree) palma f ♦ vt: ~ off impōnere.
palmy adj flōrēns.
palpable adj tractābilis; (fig) manifestus.
palpably adv manifestō, propalam.
palpitate vi palpitāre, micāre.
palpitation n palpitātiō f.
palsied adj membrīs captus.
palsy n paralysis f.
paltry adj vīlis, frīvolus.
pamper vt indulgēre (dat).
pampered adj dēlicātus.
pamphlet n libellus m.
pan n patina f, patella f; (frying) sartāgō f; (of balance) lanx f.
pancake n laganum nt.
pander n lēnō m ♦ vi: ~ to lēnōcinārī (dat).
panegyric n laudātiō f.
panegyrist n laudātor m.
panel n (wall) abacus m; (ceiling) lacūnār nt; (judges) decuria f.
panelled adj laqueātus.
pang n dolor m.
panic n pavor m ♦ vi trepidāre.
panic-stricken adj pavidus.
panniers n clītellae fpl.
panoply n arma ntpl.
panorama n prōspectus m.
panpipe n fistula f.
pant vi anhēlāre.
panther n panthēra f.
panting n anhēlitus m.
pantomime n mīmus m.
pantry n cella penāria f.
pap n mamma f.
paper n charta f.
papyrus n papyrus f.
par n: on a ~ with pār (dat).
parable n parabolē f.
parade n pompa f; (show) adparātus m ♦ vt trādūcere, iactāre ♦ vi pompam dūcere, incēdere.
paradox n verba sēcum repugnantia; ~es pl paradoxa ntpl.
paragon n exemplar nt, specimen nt.
paragraph n caput nt.
parallel adj parallēlus; (fig) cōnsimilis.
paralyse vt dēbilitāre; (with fear) percellere; be ~d torpēre.
paralysis n dēbilitās f; (fig) torpēdō f.
paramount adj prīnceps, summus.

paramour n adulter m.
parapet n lōrīca f.
paraphernalia n adparātus m.
paraphrase vt vertere.
parasite n parasītus m.
parasol n umbella f.
parboiled adj subcrūdus.
parcel n fasciculus m ♦ vt: ~ out distribuere, dispertīre.
parch vt torrēre.
parched adj torridus, āridus; be ~ ārēre.
parchment n membrāna f.
pardon n venia f ♦ vt ignōscere (dat); (offence) condōnāre.
pardonable adj ignōscendus.
pare vt dēglūbere; (nails) resecāre.
parent n parēns m/f, genitor m, genetrīx f.
parentage n stirps f, genus nt.
parental adj patrius.
parenthesis n interclūsiō f.
parings n praesegmina ntpl.
parish n (ECCL) paroecia f.
parity n aequālitās f.
park n hortī mpl.
parlance n sermō m.
parley n colloquium nt ♦ vi colloquī, agere.
parliament n senātus m; house of ~ cūria f.
parliamentary adj senātōrius.
parlour n exedrium nt.
parlous adj difficilis, perīculōsus.
parochial adj mūnicipālis.
parody n carmen ioculāre nt ♦ vt calumniārī.
parole n fidēs f.
paronomasia n agnōminātiō f.
paroxysm n accessus m.
parricide n (doer) parricīda m; (deed) parricīdium nt.
parrot n psittacus m.
parry vt ēlūdere, prōpulsāre.
parsimonious adj parcus.
parsimoniously adv parcē.
parsimony n parsimōnia f, frūgālitās f.
part n pars f; (play) partēs fpl, persōna f; (duty) officium nt; ~s loca ntpl; (ability) ingenium nt; for my ~ equidem; for the most ~ māximam partem; on the ~ of ab; act the ~ of persōnam sustinēre, partēs agere; have no ~ in expers esse (gen); in ~ partim; it is the ~ of a wise man sapientis est; play one's ~ officiō satisfacere; take ~ in interesse (dat), particeps esse (gen); take in good ~ in bonam partem accipere; take someone's ~ adesse alicuī, dēfendere aliquem; from all ~s undique; in foreign ~s peregrē; in two ~s bifāriam; (MIL) bipartītō; in three ~s trifāriam; (MIL) tripartītō; of ~s ingeniōsus ♦ vt dīvidere, sēparāre, dirimere; ~ company dīversōs discēdere ♦ vi dīgredī, discēdere; (things) dissilīre; ~ with renūntiāre.
partake vi interesse, particeps esse; ~ of gustāre.
partial adj (biased) inīquus, studiōsus; (incomplete) mancus; be ~ to favēre (dat),

studēre (*dat*); **win a ~ victory** aliquā ex parte
vincere.
partiality *n* favor *m*, studium *nt*.
partially *adv* partim, aliquā ex parte.
participant *n* particeps *m/f*.
participate *vi* interesse, particeps esse.
participation *n* societās *f*.
particle *n* particula *f*.
parti-coloured *adj* versicolor, varius.
particular *adj* (*own*) proprius; (*special*)
praecipuus; (*exact*) dīligēns, accūrātus;
(*fastidious*) fastīdiōsus; **a ~ person** quīdam ♦
n rēs *f*; **with full ~s** subtīliter; **give all the ~s**
omnia exsequī; **in ~** praesertim.
particularity *n* subtīlitās *f*.
particularize *vt* singula exsequī.
particularly *adv* praecipuē, praesertim, in
prīmīs, māximē.
parting *n* dīgressus *m*, discessus *m* ♦ *adj*
ultimus.
partisan *n* fautor *m*, studiōsus *m*.
partisanship *n* studium *nt*.
partition *n* (*act*) partītiō *f*; (*wall*) pariēs *m*;
(*compartment*) loculāmentum *nt* ♦ *vt*
dīvidere.
partly *adv* partim, ex parte.
partner *n* socius *m*; (*in office*) collēga *f*.
partnership *n* societās *f*; **form a ~** societātem
inīre.
partridge *n* perdīx *m/f*.
parturition *n* partus *m*.
party *n* (*POL*) factiō *f*, partēs *fpl*; (*entertainment*)
convīvium *nt*; (*MIL*) manus *f*; (*individual*) homō
m/f; (*associate*) socius *m*, cōnscius *m*.
party spirit *n* studium *nt*.
parvenu *n* novus homō *m*.
pass *n* (*hill*) saltus *m*; (*narrow*) angustiae *fpl*,
faucēs *fpl*; (*crisis*) discrīmen *nt*; (*document*)
diplōma *nt*; (*fighting*) petītiō *f*; **things have
come to such a ~** in eum locum ventum est,
adeō rēs rediit ♦ *vi* īre, praeterīre; (*time*)
trānsīre; (*property*) pervenīre; **~ away** abīre;
(*die*) morī, perīre; (*fig*) dēfluere; **~ by**
praeterīre; **~ for** habērī prō (*abl*); **~ off** abīre;
~ on pergere; **~ over** trānsīre; **come to ~** fierī,
ēvenīre; **let ~** intermittere, praetermittere ♦
vt praeterīre; (*riding*) praetervehī; (*by hand*)
trādere; (*law*) iubēre; (*limit*) excēdere;
(*sentence*) interpōnere, dīcere; (*test*)
satisfacere (*dat*); (*time*) dēgere, agere; **~
accounts** ratiōnēs ratās habēre; **~ the day**
diem cōnsūmere; **~ a law** lēgem ferre; **~ a
decree** dēcernere; **~ off** ferre; **~ over**
praeterīre, mittere; (*fault*) ignōscere (*dat*); **~
round** trādere; **~ through** trānsīre.
passable *adj* (*place*) pervius; (*standard*)
mediocris.
passably *adv* mediocriter.
passage *n* iter *nt*, cursus *m*; (*land*) trānsitus *m*;
(*sea*) trānsmissiō *f*; (*book*) locus *m*; **of ~** (*bird*)
advena.
passenger *n* vector *m*.
passer-by *n* praeteriēns *m*.

passing *n* obitus *m* ♦ *adj* admodum.
passion *n* animī mōtus *m*, permōtiō *f*, ārdor *m*;
(*anger*) īra *f*; (*lust*) libīdō *f*.
passionate *adj* ārdēns, impotēns, ācer;
īrācundus.
passionately *adv* vehementer, ārdenter;
īrācundē; **be ~ in love** amōre ārdēre.
passive *adj* iners.
passiveness *n* inertia *f*, patientia *f*.
passport *n* diplōma *nt*.
password *n* tessera *f*.
past *adj* praeteritus; (*recent*) proximus ♦ *n*
praeterita *ntpl* ♦ *prep* praeter (*acc*); (*beyond*)
ultrā (*acc*).
paste *n* glūten *nt* ♦ *vt* glūtināre.
pastime *n* lūdus *m*, oblectāmentum *nt*.
pastoral *adj* pastōrālis; (*poem*) būcolicus.
pastry *n* crustum *nt*.
pasture *n* pāstus *m*, pāscuum *nt* ♦ *vt* pāscere.
pat *vt* dēmulcēre ♦ *adj* opportūnus.
patch *n* pannus *m* ♦ *vt* resarcīre.
patchwork *n* centō *m*.
pate *n* caput *nt*.
patent *adj* apertus, manifestus ♦ *n*
prīvilēgium *nt*.
patently *adv* manifestō.
paternal *adj* paternus.
path *n* sēmita *f*, trāmes *m*.
pathetic *adj* miserābilis.
pathetically *adv* miserābiliter.
pathfinder *n* explorātor *m*.
pathless *adj* āvius.
pathos *n* misericordia *f*; (*RHET*) dolor *m*.
pathway *n* sēmita *f*.
patience *n* patientia *f*.
patient *adj* patiēns ♦ *n* aeger *m*.
patiently *adv* patienter, aequō animō.
patois *n* sermō *m*.
patrician *adj* patricius ♦ *n* patricius *m*.
patrimony *n* patrimōnium *nt*.
patriot *n* amāns patriae *m*.
patriotic *adj* pius, amāns patriae.
patriotically *adv* prō patriā.
patriotism *n* amor patriae *m*.
patrol *n* excubiae *fpl* ♦ *vi* circumīre.
patron *n* patrōnus *m*, fautor *m*.
patronage *n* patrōcinium *nt*.
patroness *n* patrōna *f*, fautrīx *f*.
patronize *vt* favēre (*dat*), fovēre.
patronymic *n* nōmen *nt*.
patter *vi* crepitāre ♦ *n* crepitus *m*.
pattern *n* exemplar *nt*, exemplum *nt*, nōrma *f*;
(*ideal*) specimen *nt*; (*design*) figūra *f*.
paucity *n* paucitās *f*.
paunch *n* abdōmen *nt*, venter *m*.
pauper *n* pauper *m*.
pause *n* mora *f*, intervallum *nt* ♦ *vi* īnsistere,
intermittere.
pave *vt* sternere; **~ the way** (*fig*) viam mūnīre.
pavement *n* pavīmentum *nt*.
pavilion *n* tentōrium *nt*.
paw *n* pēs *m* ♦ *vt* pede pulsāre.
pawn *n* (*chess*) latrunculus *m*; (*COMM*) pignus *nt*,

fīdūcia *f* ♦ *vt* oppignerāre.
pawnbroker *n* pignerātor *m.*
pay *n* mercēs *f*; (*MIL*) stīpendium *nt*; (*workman*) manupretium *nt* ♦ *vt* solvere, pendere; (*debt*) exsolvere; (*in full*) persolvere; (*honour*) persolvere; (*MIL*) stīpendium numerāre (*dat*); (*penalty*) dare, luere; **~ down** numerāre; **~ for** condūcere; **~ off** dissolvere, exsolvere; **~ out** expendere; (*publicly*) ērogāre; **~ up** dēpendere; **~ a compliment to** laudāre; **~ respects to** salūtāre ♦ *vi* respondēre; **it ~s** expedit.
payable *adj* solvendus.
paymaster *n* (*MIL*) tribūnus aerārius *m.*
payment *n* solūtiō *f*; (*money*) pēnsiō *f.*
pea *n* pīsum *n*; **like as two ~s** tam similis quam lac lactī est.
peace *n* pāx *f*; **~ and quiet** ōtium *nt*; **breach of the ~** vīs *f*; **establish ~** pācem conciliāre; **hold one's ~** reticēre; **sue for ~** pācem petere.
peaceable *adj* imbellis, placidus.
peaceably *adv* placidē.
peaceful *adj* tranquillus, placidus, pācātus.
peacefully *adv* tranquillē.
peacemaker *n* pācificus *m.*
peace-offering *n* piāculum *nt.*
peach *n* Persicum *nt.*
peacock *n* pāvō *m.*
peak *n* apex *m*, vertex *m.*
peal *n* (*bell*) sonitus *m*; (*thunder*) fragor *m* ♦ *vi* sonāre.
pear *n* pirum *nt*; (*tree*) pirus *f.*
pearl *n* margarīta *f.*
pearly *adj* gemmeus; (*colour*) candidus.
peasant *n* agricola *m*, colōnus *m.*
peasantry *n* agricolae *mpl.*
pebble *n* calculus *m.*
pebbly *adj* lapidōsus.
peccadillo *n* culpa *f.*
peck *n* (*measure*) modius *m* ♦ *vt* vellicāre.
peculate *vi* pecūlārī.
peculation *n* pecūlātus *m.*
peculiar *adj* (*to one*) proprius; (*strange*) singulāris.
peculiarity *n* proprietās *f*, nota *f.*
peculiarly *adv* praecipuē, praesertim.
pecuniary *adj* pecūniārius.
pedagogue *n* magister *m.*
pedant *n* scholasticus *m.*
pedantic *adj* nimis dīligenter.
pedantically *adv* dīligentior.
pedantry *n* nimia dīligentia *f.*
peddle *vt* circumferre.
pedestal *n* basis *f.*
pedestrian *adj* pedester ♦ *n* pedes *m.*
pedigree *n* stirps *f*, stemma *nt* ♦ *adj* generōsus.
pediment *n* fastīgium *nt.*
pedlar *n* īnstitor *m*, circumforāneus *m.*
peel *n* cortex *m* ♦ *vt* glūbere.
peep *vi* dīspicere ♦ *n* aspectus *m*; **at ~ of day** prīmā lūce.
peer *vi*: **~ at** intuērī ♦ *n* pār *m*; (*rank*) patricius *m.*

peerless *adj* ūnicus, ēgregius.
peevish *adj* stomachōsus, mōrōsus.
peevishly *adv* stomachōsē, mōrōsē.
peevishness *n* stomachus *m*, mōrōsitās *f.*
peg *n* clāvus *m*; **put a round ~ in a square hole** bovī clītellās impōnere ♦ *vt* clāvīs dēfīgere.
pelf *n* lucrum *nt.*
pellet *n* globulus *m.*
pell-mell *adv* prōmiscuē, turbātē.
pellucid *adj* perlūcidus.
pelt *n* pellis *f* ♦ *vt* petere ♦ *vi* violenter cadere.
pen *n* calamus *m*, stilus *m*; (*cattle*) saeptum *nt* ♦ *vt* scrībere.
penal *adj* poenālis.
penalize *vt* poenā adficere, multāre.
penalty *n* poena *f*, damnum *nt*; (*fine*) multa *f*; **pay the ~** poenās dare.
penance *n* supplicium *nt.*
pencil *n* graphis *f.*
pending *adj* sub iūdice ♦ *prep* inter (*acc*).
penetrable *adj* pervius.
penetrate *vt* penetrāre.
penetrating *adj* ācer, acūtus; (*mind*) perspicāx.
penetration *n* (*mind*) acūmen *nt.*
peninsula *n* paenīnsula *f.*
penitence *n* paenitentia *f.*
penitent *adj*: **I am ~** mē paenitet.
penknife *n* scalpellum *nt.*
penmanship *n* scrīptiō *f*, manus *f.*
pennant *n* vexillum *nt.*
penny *n* dēnārius *m.*
pension *n* annua *ntpl.*
pensioner *n* ēmeritus *m.*
pensive *adj* attentus.
pensiveness *n* cōgitātiō *f.*
pent *adj* inclūsus.
penthouse *n* (*MIL*) vīnea *f.*
penurious *adj* parcus, avārus, tenāx.
penuriousness *n* parsimōnia *f*, tenācitās *f.*
penury *n* egestās *f*, inopia *f.*
people *n* hominēs *mpl*; (*nation*) populus *m*, gēns *f*; **common ~** plēbs *f* ♦ *vt* frequentāre.
peopled *adj* frequēns.
pepper *n* piper *nt.*
peradventure *adv* fortasse.
perambulate *vi* spatiārī, inambulāre.
perceive *vt* sentīre, percipere, intellegere.
perceptible *adj*: **be ~** sentīrī posse, audīrī posse.
perception *n* sēnsus *m.*
perch *n* (*bird's*) pertica *f*; (*fish*) perca *f* ♦ *vi* īnsīdēre.
perchance *adv* fortasse, forsitan (*subj*).
percolate *vi* permānāre.
percussion *n* ictus *m.*
perdition *n* exitium *nt.*
peregrinate *vi* peregrīnārī.
peregrination *n* peregrīnātiō *f.*
peremptorily *adv* praecīsē, prō imperiō.
peremptory *adj* imperiōsus.
perennial *adj* perennis.
perfect *adj* perfectus, absolūtus; (*entire*)

integer; (*faultless*) ēmendātus ♦ *vt* perficere, absolvere.
perfection *n* perfectiō *f*, absolūtiō *f*.
perfectly *adv* perfectē, ēmendātē; (*quite*) plānē.
perfidious *adj* perfidus, perfidiōsus.
perfidiously *adv* perfidiōsē.
perfidy *n* perfidia *f*.
perforate *vt* perforāre, terebrāre.
perforation *n* forāmen *nt*.
perforce *adv* per vim, necessāriō.
perform *vt* perficere, peragere; (*duty*) exsequī, fungī (*abl*); (*play*) agere.
performance *n* (*process*) exsecūtiō *f*, fūnctiō *f*; (*deed*) factum *nt*; (*stage*) fābula *f*.
performer *n* āctor *m*; (*music*) tībīcen *m*, fidicen *m*; (*stage*) histriō *m*.
perfume *n* odor *m*, unguentum *nt* ♦ *vt* odōrāre.
perfumer *n* unguentārius *m*.
perfumery *n* unguenta *ntpl*.
perfunctorily *adv* neglegenter.
perfunctory *adj* neglegēns.
perhaps *adv* fortasse, forsitan (*subj*), nesciō an (*subj*); (*tentative*) vel; (*interrog*) an.
peril *n* perīculum *m*, discrīmen *nt*.
perilous *adj* perīculōsus.
perilously *adv* perīculōsē.
perimeter *n* ambitus *m*.
period *n* tempus *nt*, spatium *nt*; (*history*) aetās *f*; (*end*) terminus *m*; (*sentence*) complexiō *f*, ambitus *m*.
periodic *adj* (*style*) circumscrīptus.
periodical *adj* status.
periodically *adv* certīs temporibus, identidem.
peripatetic *adj* vagus; (*sect*) peripatēticus.
periphery *n* ambitus *m*.
periphrasis *n* circuitus *m*.
perish *vi* perīre, interīre.
perishable *adj* cadūcus, fragilis, mortālis.
peristyle *n* peristȳlium *nt*.
perjure *vi*: ~ o.s. pēierāre.
perjured *adj* periūrus.
perjurer *n* periūrus *m*.
perjury *n* periūrium *nt*; **commit** ~ pēierāre.
permanence *n* cōnstantia *f*, stabilitās *f*.
permanent *adj* stabilis, diūturnus, perpetuus.
permanently *adv* perpetuō.
permeable *adj* penetrābilis.
permeate *vt* penetrāre ♦ *vi* permānāre.
permissible *adj* licitus, concessus; **it is** ~ licet.
permission *n* potestās *f*; **ask** ~ veniam petere; **give** ~ veniam dare, potestātem facere; **by** ~ **of** permissū (*gen*); **with your kind** ~ bonā tuā veniā; **without your** ~ tē invītō.
permit *vt* sinere, permittere (*dat*); **I am ~ted** licet mihī.
pernicious *adj* perniciōsus, exitiōsus.
perorate *vi* perōrāre.
peroration *n* perōrātiō *f*, epilogus *m*.
perpendicular *adj* dīrēctus.
perpendicularly *adv* ad perpendiculum, ad līneam.

perpetrate *vt* facere, admittere.
perpetual *adj* perpetuus, perennis, sempiternus.
perpetually *adv* perpetuō.
perpetuate *vt* continuāre, perpetuāre.
perpetuity *n* perpetuitās *f*.
perplex *vt* sollicitāre, cōnfundere.
perplexing *adj* ambiguus, perplexus.
perplexity *n* haesitātiō *f*.
perquisite *n* pecūlium *nt*.
persecute *vt* īnsectārī, exagitāre; persequi.
persecution *n* īnsectātiō *f*.
persecutor *n* īnsectātor *m*.
perseverance *n* peseveērantia *f*, cōnstantia *f*.
persevere *vi* perseverāre, perstāre; **~ in** tenēre.
Persian *n* Persa *m*.
persist *vt* īnstāre, perstāre, perseverāre.
persistence, persistency *n* pertinācia *f*, perseverāntia *f*.
persistent *adj* pertināx.
persistently *adv* pertināciter, perseveranter.
person *n* homō *m/f*; (*counted*) caput *nt*; (*character*) persōna *f*; (*body*) corpus *nt*; **in ~** ipse praesēns.
personage *n* vir *m*.
personal *adj* prīvātus, suus.
personality *n* nātūra *f*; (*person*) vir ēgregius *m*.
personally *adv* ipse, cōram.
personal property *n* pecūlium *nt*.
personate *vt* persōnam gerere (*gen*).
personification *n* prosōpopoeia *f*.
personify *vt* hūmānam nātūram tribuere (*dat*).
personnel *n* membra *ntpl*, sociī *mpl*.
perspective *n* scaenographia *f*.
perspicacious *adj* perspicāx, acūtus.
perspicacity *n* perspicācitās *f*, acūmen *nt*.
perspicuity *n* perspicuitās *f*.
perspicuous *adj* perspicuus.
perspiration *n* sūdor *m*.
perspire *vi* sūdāre.
persuade *vt* persuādēre (*dat*); (*by entreaty*) exōrāre.
persuasion *n* persuāsiō *f*.
persuasive *adj* blandus.
persuasively *adv* blandē.
pert *adj* procāx, protervus.
pertain *vi* pertinēre, attinēre.
pertinacious *adj* pertināx.
pertinaciously *adv* pertināciter.
pertinacity *n* pertinācia *f*.
pertinent *adj* appositus; **be ~** ad rem pertinēre.
pertinently *adv* appositē.
pertly *adv* procāciter, protervē.
perturb *vt* perturbāre.
perturbation *n* animī perturbātiō *f*, trepidātiō *f*.
peruke *n* capillāmentum *nt*.
perusal *n* perlēctiō *f*.
peruse *vt* perlegere; (*book*) ēvolvere.

pervade vt permānāre per, complēre; (emotion) perfundere.
pervasive adj crēber.
perverse adj perversus, prāvus.
perversely adv perversē.
perversion n dēprāvātiō f.
perversity n perversitās f.
pervert vt dēprāvāre; (words) dētorquēre; (person) corrumpere.
perverter n corruptor m.
pessimism n dēspērātiō f.
pest n pestis f.
pester vt sollicitāre.
pestilence n pestilentia f, pestis f.
pestilential adj pestilēns, nocēns.
pestle n pistillum nt.
pet n dēliciae fpl ♦ vt in dēliciīs habēre, dēlēnīre.
petard n: be hoist with his own ~ suō sibī gladiō iugulārī.
petition n precēs fpl; (POL) libellus m ♦ vt ōrāre.
petrify vt (fig) dēfīgere; **be petrified** stupēre, obstupēscere.
pettifogger n lēgulēius m.
pettiness n levitās f.
pettish adj stomachōsus.
petty adj levis, minūtus.
petulance n protervitās f.
petulant adj protervus, petulāns.
petulantly adv petulanter.
pew n subsellium nt.
phalanx n phalanx f.
phantasy n commentīcia ntpl.
phantom n simulacrum nt, īdōlon nt.
phases npl vicēs fpl.
pheasant n phāsiānus m.
phenomenal adj eximius, singulāris.
phenomenon n rēs f, novum nt, spectāculum nt.
philander vi lascīvīre.
philanthropic adj hūmānus, beneficus.
philanthropically adv hūmānē.
philanthropy n hūmānitās f, beneficia ntpl.
Philippic n Philippica f.
philologist n grammaticus m.
philology n grammatica ntpl.
philosopher n philosophus m, sapiēns m.
philosophical adj philosophus; (temperament) aequābilis.
philosophize vi philosophārī.
philosophy n philosophia f, sapientia f.
philtre n philtrum nt.
phlegm n pituīta f; (temper) lentitūdō f.
phlegmatic adj lentus.
phoenix n phoenīx m.
phrase n locūtiō f; (GRAM) incīsum nt.
phraseology n verba ntpl, ōrātiō f.
physic n medicāmentum nt; ~s pl physica ntpl.
physical adj physicus; (of body) corporis.
physician n medicus m.
physicist n physicus m.
physique n corpus nt, vīrēs fpl.

piazza n forum nt.
pick n (tool) dolabra f; (best part) lēctī mpl, flōs m ♦ vt (choose) legere, dēligere; (pluck) carpere; ~ **out** ēligere, excerpere; ~ **up** colligere.
pickaxe n dolabra f.
picked adj ēlēctus, dēlēctus.
picket n (MIL) statiō f.
pickle n muria f ♦ vt condīre.
picture n pictūra f, tabula f ♦ vt dēpingere; (to oneself) ante oculōs pōnere.
picturesque adj (scenery) amoenus.
pie n crustum nt.
piebald adj bicolor, varius.
piece n pars f; (broken off) fragmentum nt; (food) frustum nt; (coin) nummus m; (play) fābula f; **break in ~s** comminuere; **fall to ~s** dīlābī; **take to ~s** dissolvere; **tear in ~s** dīlaniāre.
piecemeal adv membrātim, minūtātim.
pied adj maculōsus.
pier n mōlēs f.
pierce vt perfodere, trānsfīgere; (bore) perforāre; (fig) pungere.
piercing adj acūtus.
piety n pietās f, religiō f.
pig n porcus m, sūs m/f; **buy a ~ in a poke** spem pretiō emere; ~'**s** suillus.
pigeon n columba f; **wood ~** palumbēs f.
pig-headed adj pervicāx.
pigment n pigmentum nt.
pigsty n hara f.
pike n dolō m, hasta f.
pikeman n hastātus m.
pile n acervus m, cumulus m; (funeral) rogus m; (building) mōlēs f; (post) sublica f ♦ vt cumulāre, congerere; ~ **up** exstruere, adcumulāre, coacervāre.
pile-driver n fistūca f.
pilfer vt fūrārī, surripere.
pilferer n fūr m, fūrunculus m.
pilgrim n peregrīnātor m.
pilgrimage n peregrīnātiō f.
pill n pilula f.
pillage n rapīna f, dēpopulātiō f, expīlātiō f ♦ vt dīripere, dēpopulārī, expīlāre.
pillager n expīlātor m, praedātor m.
pillar n columen nt, columna f.
pillory n furca f.
pillow n pulvīnus nt, culcita f.
pilot n gubernātor m, ductor m ♦ vt regere, gubernāre.
pimp n lēnō m.
pimple n pustula f.
pin n acus f ♦ vt adfīgere.
pincers n forceps m/f.
pinch vt pervellere, vellicāre; (shoe) ūrere; (for room) coartāre.
pine n pīnus f ♦ vi tābēscere; ~ **away** intābēscere; ~ **for** dēsīderāre.
pinion n penna f.
pink adj rubicundus.
pinnace n lembus m.

pinnacle n fastīgium nt.
pint n sextārius m.
pioneer n antecursor m.
pious adj pius, religiōsus.
piously adv piē, religiōsē.
pip n grānum nt.
pipe n (*music*) fistula f, tībia f; (*water*) canālis m
♦ vi fistulā canere.
piper n tībīcen m.
pipkin n olla f.
piquancy n sāl m, vīs f.
piquant adj salsus, argūtus.
pique n offēnsio f, dolor m ♦ vt offendere.
piracy n latrōcinium nt.
pirate n pīrāta m praedō m.
piratical adj pīrāticus.
piscatorial adj piscātōrius.
piston n embolus m.
pit n fovea f, fossa f; (THEAT) cavea f.
pitch n pix f; (*sound*) sonus m ♦ vt (*camp*)
pōnere; (*tent*) tendere; (*missile*) conicere.
pitch-black adj piceus.
pitched battle n proelium iustum nt.
pitcher n hydria f.
pitchfork n furca f.
pitch pine n picea f.
piteous adj miserābilis, flēbilis.
piteously adv miserābiliter.
pitfall n fovea f.
pith n medulla f.
pithy adj (*style*) dēnsus; ~ **saying** sententia f.
pitiable adj miserandus.
pitiful adj miser, miserābilis; misericors.
pitifully adv miserē, miserābiliter.
pitiless adj immisericors, immītis.
pitilessly adv crūdēliter.
pittance n (*food*) dēmēnsum nt; (*money*) stips
f.
pity n misericordia f; **take ~ on** miserērī (+acc
of person, gen of things); **it is a ~ that** male
accidit quod ♦ vt miserērī (gen); **I ~ me**
miseret (gen).
pivot n cardō m.
placability n plācābilitās f.
placable adj plācābilis.
placard n libellus m.
placate vt plācāre.
place n locus m; **in another ~** alibī; **in the first ~**
prīmum; **in ~ of** locō (gen), prō (+ abl); **to this
~** hūc; **out of ~** intempestīvus; **give ~ to**
cēdere (dat); **take ~** fierī, accidere; **take the ~**
of in locum (gen) succēdere ♦ vt pōnere,
locāre, collocāre; **~ beside** adpōnere; **~ over**
(*in charge*) praepōnere; **~ round** circumdare;
~ upon impōnere.
placid adj placidus, tranquillus, quiētus.
placidity n tranquillitās f, sedātus animus m.
placidly adv placidē, quiētē.
plagiarism n fūrtum nt.
plagiarize vt fūrārī.
plague n pestilentia f, pestis f.
plain adj (*lucid*) clārus, perspicuus;
(*unadorned*) subtīlis, simplex; (*frank*)
sincērus; (*ugly*) invenustus ♦ n campus m,

plānitiēs f; **of the ~** campester.
plainly adv perspicuē; simpliciter, sincērē.
plainness n perspicuitās f; simplicitās f.
plaint n querella f.
plaintiff n petītor m.
plaintive adj flēbilis, queribundus.
plaintively adv flēbiliter.
plait vt implicāre, nectere.
plan n cōnsilium nt; (*of a work*) fōrma f,
dēsignātiō f; (*of living*) ratiō f; (*intent*)
prōpositum nt; (*drawing*) dēscrīptiō f ♦ vt (*a*
work) dēsignāre, dēscrībere; (*intent*)
cōgitāre, meditārī; cōnsilium capere or
inīre; (*with verb*) in animō habēre (inf).
plane n (*surface*) plānitiēs f; (*tree*) platanus f;
(*tool*) runcīna f ♦ adj aequus, plānus ♦ vt
runcīnāre.
planet n stēlla errāns f.
plank n tabula f.
plant n herba f, planta f ♦ vt (*tree*) serere; (*field*)
cōnserere; (*colony*) dēdūcere; (*feet*) pōnere;
~ firmly īnfīgere.
plantation n arbustum nt.
planter n sator m, colōnus m.
plaque n tabula f.
plaster n albārium nt, tectōrium nt; (MED)
emplastrum nt; **~ of Paris** gypsum nt ♦ vt
dealbāre.
plasterer n albārius m.
plastic adj ductilis, fūsilis.
plate n (*dish*) catillus m; (*silver*) argentum nt;
(*layer*) lāmina f ♦ vt indūcere.
platform n suggestus m; rōstrum nt, tribūnal
nt.
platitude n trīta sententia f.
platter n patella f, lanx f.
plaudit n plausus m.
plausibility n vērīsimilitūdō f.
plausible adj speciōsus, vērī similis.
play n lūdus m; (THEAT) fābula f; (*voice*)
inclīnātiō f; (*scope*) campus m; (*hands*) gestus
m; **~ on words** agnōminātiō f; **fair ~** aequum et
bonum ♦ vi lūdere; (*fountain*) scatēre ♦ vt
(*music*) canere; (*instrument*) canere (abl);
(*game*) lūdere (abl); (*part*) agere; **~ the part of**
agere; **~ a trick on** lūdificārī, impōnere (dat).
playbill n ēdictum nt.
player n lūsor m; (*at dice*) āleātor m; (*on flute*)
tībīcen m; (*on lyre*) fidicen m; (*on stage*)
histriō m.
playful adj lascīvus; (*words*) facētus.
playfully adv per lūdum, per iocum.
playfulness n lascīvia f; facētiae fpl.
playground n ārea f.
playmate n collūsor m.
playwright n fābulārum scrīptor m.
plea n causa f; (*in defence*) dēfēnsiō f, excūsātiō
f.
plead vi causam agere, causam ōrāre, causam
dīcere; (*in excuse*) dēprecārī, excūsāre; **~**
with obsecrāre.
pleader n āctor m, causidicus m.
pleasant adj iūcundus, dulcis, grātus; (*place*)

amoenus.
pleasantly *adv* iūcundē, suāviter.
pleasantry *n* facētiae *fpl*, iocus *m*.
please *vt* placēre (*dat*), dēlectāre; **try to ~** īnservīre (*dat*); **just as you ~** quod commodum est; **if you ~** sīs; **~d with** contentus (*abl*); **be ~d with oneself** sibī placēre ♦ *adv* amābō.
pleasing *adj* grātus, iūcundus, amoenus; **be ~ to** cordī esse (*dat*).
pleasurable *adj* iūcundus.
pleasure *n* voluptās *f*; (*decision*) arbitrium *nt*; **it is my ~** libet; **derive ~** voluptātem capere ♦ *vt* grātificārī (*dat*).
pleasure grounds *n* hortī *mpl*.
pleasure-loving *adj* dēlicātus.
plebeian *adj* plēbēius ♦ *n*: **the ~s** plēbs *f*.
plebiscite *n* suffrāgium *nt*.
plectrum *n* plēctrum *nt*.
pledge *n* pignus *nt* ♦ *vt* obligāre; **~ oneself** prōmittere, spondēre; **~ one's word** fidem obligāre, fidem interpōnere.
Pleiads *n* Plēiadēs *fpl*.
plenary *adj* īnfīnītus.
plenipotentiary *n* lēgātus *m*.
plenitude *n* cōpia *f*, mātūritās *f*.
plentiful *adj* cōpiōsus, largus.
plentifully *adv* cōpiōsē, largē.
plenty *n* cōpia *f*, abundantia *f*; (*enough*) satis.
pleonasm *n* redundantia *f*.
pleurisy *n* lateris dolor *m*.
pliable *adj* flexibilis, mollis, lentus.
pliant *adj* flexibilis, mollis, lentus.
pliers *n* forceps *m/f*.
plight *n* habitus *m*, discrīmen *nt* ♦ *vt* spondēre.
plod *vi* labōrāre, operam īnsūmere.
plot *n* coniūrātiō *f*, īnsidiae *fpl*; (*land*) agellus *m*; (*play*) argūmentum *nt* ♦ *vi* coniūrāre, mōlīrī.
plotter *n* coniūrātus *m*.
plough *n* arātrum *nt* ♦ *vt* arāre; (*sea*) sulcāre; **~ up** exarāre.
ploughing *n* arātiō *f*.
ploughman *n* arātor *m*.
ploughshare *n* vōmer *m*.
pluck *n* fortitūdō *f* ♦ *vt* carpere, legere; **~ out** ēvellere; **~ up courage** animum recipere, animō adesse.
plucky *adj* fortis.
plug *n* obtūrāmentum *nt* ♦ *vt* obtūrāre.
plum *n* prūnum *nt*; (*tree*) prūnus *f*.
plumage *n* plūmae *fpl*.
plumb *n* perpendiculum *nt* ♦ *adj* dīrēctus ♦ *adv* ad perpendiculum ♦ *vt* (*building*) ad perpendiculum exigere; (*depth*) scrūtārī.
plumber *n* artifex plumbārius *m*.
plumb line *n* līnea *f*, perpendiculum *nt*.
plume *n* crista *f* ♦ *vt*: **~ oneself on** iactāre, prae sē ferre.
plummet *n* perpendiculum *nt*.
plump *adj* pinguis.
plumpness *n* nitor *m*.
plunder *n* (*act*) rapīna *f*; (*booty*) praeda *f* ♦ *vi* praedārī ♦ *vt* dīripere, expīlāre.

plunderer *n* praedātor *m*, spoliātor *m*.
plundering *n* rapīna *f* ♦ *adj* praedābundus.
plunge *vt* mergere, dēmergere; (*weapon*) dēmittere ♦ *vi* mergī, sē dēmergere.
plural *adj* plūrālis.
plurality *n* multitūdō *f*, plūrēs *pl*.
ply *vt* exercēre.
poach *vt* surripere.
pocket *n* sinus *m*.
pocket money *n* pecūlium *nt*.
pod *n* siliqua *f*.
poem *n* poēma *nt*, carmen *nt*.
poesy *n* poēsis *f*.
poet *n* poēta *m*.
poetess *n* poētria *f*.
poetic *adj* poēticus.
poetical *adj* = **poetic**.
poetically *adv* poēticē.
poetry *n* (*art*) poētica *f*; (*poems*) poēmata *ntpl*, carmina *ntpl*.
poignancy *n* acerbitās *f*.
poignant *adj* acerbus, acūtus.
poignantly *adv* acerbē, acūtē.
point *n* (*dot*) pūnctum *nt*; (*place*) locus *m*; (*item*) caput *nt*; (*sharp end*) aciēs *f*; (*of sword*) mucrō *m*; (*of epigram*) acūleī *mpl*; **~ of honour** officium *nt*; **beside the ~** ab rē; **to the ~** ad rem; **from this ~** hinc; **to that ~** eō; **up to this ~** hāctenus, adhūc; **without ~** īnsulsus; **in ~ of fact** nempe; **make a ~ of doing** consultō facere; **on the ~ of death** moritūrus; **on the ~ of happening** inibī; **I was on the ~ of saying** in eō erat ut dīcerem; **matters have reached such a ~** eō rēs recidit; **come to the ~** ad rem redīre; **the ~ at issue is** illud quaeritur; **the main ~** cardō *m*, caput *nt*; **turning ~** articulus temporis *m* ♦ *vt* acuere, exacuere; (*aim*) intendere; (*punctuate*) distinguere; **~ out** indicāre, dēmōnstrāre; ostendere.
point-blank *adj* simplex ♦ *adv* praecīsē.
pointed *adj* acūtus; (*criticism*) acūleātus; (*wit*) salsus.
pointedly *adv* apertē, dīlūcidē.
pointer *n* index *m*.
pointless *adj* īnsulsus, frīgidus.
pointlessly *adv* īnsulsē.
point of view *n* iūdicium *nt*, sententia *f*.
poise *n* lībrāmen *nt*; (*fig*) urbānitās *f* ♦ *vt* lībrāre.
poison *n* venēnum *nt* ♦ *vt* venēnō necāre; (*fig*) īnficere.
poisoned *adj* venēnātus.
poisoner *n* venēficus *m*.
poisoning *n* venēficium *nt*.
poisonous *adj* noxius.
poke *vt* trūdere, fodicāre.
polar *adj* septentriōnālis.
pole *n* asser *m*, contus *m*; (*ASTRO*) polus *m*.
poleaxe *n* bipennis *f*.
polemic *n* contrōversia *f*.
police *n* lictōrēs *mpl*; (*night*) vigilēs *mpl*.
policy *n* ratiō *f*, cōnsilium *nt*; **honesty is the**

best ~ ea māximē condūcunt quae sunt rēctissima.
polish n (*appearance*) nitor m; (*character*) urbānitās f; (*LIT*) līma f ♦ vt polīre; (*fig*) expolīre.
polished adj polītus, mundus; (*person*) excultus, urbānus; (*style*) līmātus.
polite adj urbānus, hūmānus, cōmis.
politely adv urbānē, cōmiter.
politeness n urbānitās f, hūmānitās f, cōmitās f.
politic adj prūdēns, circumspectus.
political adj cīvīlis, pūblicus; ~ **life** rēs pūblica f.
politician n magistrātus m.
politics n rēs pūblica f; **take up** ~ ad rem pūblicam accēdere.
polity n reī pūblicae fōrma f.
poll n caput nt; (*voting*) comitia ntpl ♦ vi suffrāgia inīre.
poll tax n tribūtum nt in singula capita impositum.
pollute vt inquināre, contāmināre.
pollution n corruptēla f.
poltroon n ignāvus m.
pomegranate n mālum Pūnicum nt.
pomp n adparātus m.
pomposity n māgnificentia f, glōria f.
pompous adj māgnificus, glōriōsus.
pompously adv māgnificē, glōriōsē.
pompousness n māgnificentia f.
pond n stagnum nt, lacūna f.
ponder vi sēcum reputāre ♦ vt animō volūtāre, in mente agitāre.
ponderous adj gravis, ponderōsus.
ponderously adv graviter.
poniard n pugiō m.
pontiff n pontifex m.
pontifical adj pontificālis, pontificius.
pontoon n pontō m.
pony n mannus m.
pooh-pooh vt dērīdēre.
pool n lacūna f, stagnum nt ♦ vt cōnferre.
poop n puppis f.
poor adj pauper, inops; (*meagre*) exīlis; (*inferior*) improbus; (*pitiable*) miser; ~ **little** misellus.
poorly adj aeger, aegrōtus ♦ adv parum, tenuiter.
pop n crepitus m ♦ vi ēmicāre.
pope n pāpa m.
poplar n pōpulus f.
poppy n papāver nt.
populace n vulgus nt, plēbs f.
popular adj grātus, grātiōsus; (*party*) populāris.
popularity n populī favor m, studium nt.
popularly adv vulgō.
populate vt frequentāre.
population n populus m, cīvēs mpl.
populous adj frequēns.
porcelain n fictilia ntpl.
porch n vestibulum nt.

porcupine n hystrīx f.
pore n forāmen nt ♦ vi: ~ **over** scrūtārī, incumbere in (*acc*).
pork n porcīna f.
porous adj rārus.
porridge n puls f.
port n portus m ♦ adj (*side*) laevus, sinister.
portage n vectūra f.
portal n porta f.
portcullis n cataracta f.
portend vt portendere.
portent n mōnstrum nt, portentum nt.
portentous adj mōnstruōsus.
porter n iānitor m; (*carrier*) bāiulus m.
portico n porticus f.
portion n pars f; (*marriage*) dōs f; (*lot*) sors f.
portliness n amplitūdō f.
portly adj amplus, opīmus.
portrait n imāgō f, effigiēs f.
portray vt dēpingere, exprimere, effingere.
pose n status m, habitus m ♦ vt pōnere ♦ vi habitum sūmere.
poser n nōdus m.
posit vt pōnere.
position n (*GEOG*) situs m (*body*) status m, gestus m; (*rank*) dignitās f; (*office*) honōs m; (*MIL*) locus m; **be in a** ~ **to** habēre (*inf*); **take up a** ~ (*MIL*) locum capere.
positive adj certus; **be** ~ **about** adfirmāre.
positively adv certō, adfirmātē, rē vērā.
posse n manus f.
possess vt possidēre, habēre; (*take*) occupāre, potīrī (*abl*).
possession n possessiō f; ~**s** pl bona ntpl, fortūnae fpl; **take** ~ **of** potīrī (*abl*), occupāre, manum inicere (*dat*); (*inheritance*) obīre; (*emotion*) invādere, incēdere (*dat*); **gain** ~ **of** potior (+ *abl*).
possessor n possessor m, dominus m.
possibility n facultās f; **there is a** ~ fierī potest.
possible adj: **it is** ~ fierī potest; **as big as** ~ quam māximus.
possibly adv fortasse.
post n pālus m; (*MIL*) statiō f; (*office*) mūnus nt; (*courier*) tabellārius m; **leave one's** ~ locō cēdere, signa relinquere ♦ vt (*troops*) locāre, collocāre; (*at intervals*) dispōnere; (*letter*) dare, tabellāriō dare; (*entry*) in cōdicem referre; **be** ~**ed** (*MIL*) in statiōne esse.
postage n vectūra f.
poster n libellus m.
posterior adj posterior.
posterity n posterī mpl; (*time*) posteritās f.
postern n postīcum nt.
posthaste adv summā celeritāte.
posthumous adj postumus.
posthumously adv (*born*) patre mortuō; (*published*) auctōre mortuō.
postpone vt differre, prōferre.
postponement n dīlātiō f.
postscript n: **add a** ~ adscrībere, subicere.
postulate vt sūmere ♦ n sūmptiō f.
posture n gestus m, status m.

pot n olla f, matella f.
pot-bellied adj ventriōsus.
potency n vīs f.
potent adj efficāx, valēns.
potentate n dynastēs m, tyrannus m.
potential adj futūrus.
potentiality n facultās f.
potentially adv ut fierī posse vidētur; ~ **an emperor** capāx imperiī.
potently adv efficienter.
potion n pōtiō f.
pot-pourri n farrāgō f.
potsherd n testa f.
pottage n iūs nt.
potter n figulus m; **~'s** figulāris.
pottery n fictilia ntpl.
pouch n pēra f, sacculus m.
poultice n fōmentum nt, emplastrum nt.
poultry n gallīnae fpl.
pounce vi involāre, īnsilīre.
pound n lībra f; **five ~s** (weight) **of gold** aurī quīnque pondo ♦ vt conterere; pulsāre.
pour vt fundere; **~ forth** effundere; **~ in** īnfundere; **~ on** superfundere; **~ out** effundere ♦ vi fundī, fluere; **~ down** ruere, sē praecipitāre.
pouring adj (rain) effūsus.
poverty n paupertās f, egestās f, inopia f; (style) iēiūnitās f.
powder n pulvis m.
powdery adj pulvereus.
power n potestās f; (strength) vīrēs fpl; (excessive) potentia f; (supreme) imperium nt; (divine) nūmen nt; (legal) auctōritās f; (of father) manus f; **as far as is in my ~** quantum in mē est; **have great ~** multum valēre, posse; **have of ~ attorney** cognitōrem esse; **it is still in my ~ to** integrum est mihī (inf).
powerful adj validus, potēns.
powerfully adv valdē.
powerless adj impotēns, imbēcillus; **be ~** nihil valēre.
powerlessness n imbēcillitas f.
practicable adj in apertō; **be ~** fierī posse.
practical adj (person) habilis.
practical joke n lūdus m.
practical knowledge n ūsus m.
practically adv ferē, paene.
practice n ūsus m, exercitātiō f; (RHET) meditātiō f; (habit) cōnsuētūdō f, mōs m; **corrupt ~s** malae artēs.
practise vt (occupation) exercēre, facere; (custom) factitāre; (RHET) meditārī ♦ vi (MED) medicīnam exercēre; (law) causās agere.
practised adj exercitātus, perītus.
practitioner n (MED) medicus m.
praetor n praetor nt; **~'s** praetōrius.
praetorian adj praetōrius.
praetorian guards npl praetōriānī mpl.
praetorship n praetūra f.
praise n laus f ♦ vt laudāre.
praiser n laudātor m.
praiseworthy adj laudābilis, laude dignus.

prance vi exsultāre.
prank n lūdus m.
prate vi garrīre.
prating adj garrulus.
pray vi deōs precārī, deōs venerārī ♦ vt precārī, ōrāre; **~ for** petere, precārī; **~ to** adōrāre.
prayer(s) n precēs fpl.
prayerful adj supplex.
preach vt, vi docēre, praedicāre.
preacher n ōrātor m.
preamble n exōrdium nt.
prearranged adj cōnstitūtus.
precarious adj dubius, perīculōsus.
precariousness n discrīmen nt.
precaution n cautiō f, prōvidentia f; **take ~s** cavēre, praecavēre.
precede vt praeīre (dat), anteīre (dat), antecēdere.
precedence n prīmārius locus m; **give ~ to** cēdere (dat); **take ~** (thing) antīquius esse; (person) prīmās agere.
precedent n exemplum nt; (law) praeiūdicium nt; **breach of ~** īnsolentia f; **in defiance of ~** īnsolenter.
preceding adj prior, superior.
precept n praeceptum nt.
preceptor n doctor m, magister m.
precinct n terminus m, templum nt.
precious adj cārus; pretiōsus; (style) pūtidus.
precious stone n gemma f.
precipice n locus praeceps m, rūpēs f.
precipitancy n festīnātiō f.
precipitate vt praecipitāre ♦ adj praeceps; praeproperus.
precipitation n festīnātiō f.
precipitous adj dēruptus, praeceps, praeruptus.
precise adj certus, subtīlis; (person) accūrātus.
precisely adv dēmum.
precision n cūra f.
preclude vt exclūdere, prohibēre.
precocious adj praecox.
precocity n festīnāta mātūritās f.
preconceive vt praecipere; **~d idea** praeiūdicāta opīniō f.
preconception n praeceptiō f.
preconcerted adj ex compositō factus.
precursor n praenūntius m.
predatory adj praedātōrius.
predecessor n dēcessor m; **my ~** cui succēdō.
predestination n fātum nt, necessitās f.
predestine vt dēvovēre.
predetermine vt praefīnīre.
predicament n angustiae fpl, discrīmen nt.
predicate n attribūtum nt.
predict vt praedīcere, augurārī.
prediction n praedictiō f.
predilection n amor m, studium nt.
predispose vt inclīnāre, praeparāre.
predisposition n inclīnātiō f.
predominance n potentia f, praestantia f.

predominant *adj* praepotēns, praecipuus.
predominantly *adv* plērumque.
predominate *vi* pollēre, dominārī.
pre-eminence *n* praestantia *f*.
pre-eminent *adj* ēgregius, praecipuus, excellēns.
pre-eminently *adv* ēgregiē, praecipuē, excellenter.
preface *n* prooemium *nt*, praefātiō *f* ♦ *vi* praefārī.
prefect *n* praefectus *m*.
prefecture *n* praefectūra *f*.
prefer *vt* (*charge*) dēferre; (*to office*) anteferre; (*choice*) antepōnere (*acc and dat*), posthabēre (*dat and acc*); (*with verb*) mālle.
preferable *adj* potior.
preferably *adv* potius.
preference *n* favor *m*; **give ~ to** antepōnere, praeoptāre; **in ~ to** potius quam.
preferment *n* honōs *m*, dignitās *f*.
prefix *vt* praetendere ♦ *n* praepositiō *f*.
pregnancy *n* graviditās *f*.
pregnant *adj* gravida.
prejudge *vt* praeiūdicāre.
prejudice *n* praeiūdicāta opīniō *f*; (*harmful*) invidia *f*, incommodum *nt*; **without ~** cum bonā veniā ♦ *vt* obesse (*dat*); **be ~d against** invidēre (*dat*), male opīnārī dē (*abl*).
prejudicial *adj* damnōsus; **be ~ to** obesse (*dat*), nocēre (*dat*), officere (*dat*), dētrīmentō esse (*dat*).
preliminaries *npl* praecurrentia *ntpl*.
preliminary *adj* prīmus ♦ *n* prōlūsiō *f*.
prelude *n* prooemium *nt*.
premature *adj* immātūrus; (*birth*) abortīvus.
prematurely *adv* ante tempus.
premeditate *vt* praecōgitāre, praemeditārī.
premeditated *adj* praemeditātus.
premier *adj* prīnceps, praecipuus.
premise *n* (*major*) prōpositiō *f*; (*minor*) adsūmptiō *f*; **~s** *pl* aedēs *fpl*, domus *f*.
premium *n* praemium *nt*; **be at a ~** male emī.
premonition *n* monitus *m*.
preoccupation *n* sollicitūdō *f*.
preoccupied *adj* sollicitus, districtus.
preordain *vt* praefīnīre.
preparation *n* (*process*) adparātiō *f*, comparātiō *f*; (*product*) adparātus *m*; (*of speech*) meditātiō *f*; **make ~s for** īnstruere, exōrnāre, comparāre.
prepare *vt* parāre, adparāre, comparāre; (*speech*) meditārī; (*with verb*) parāre; **~d for** parātus ad (*+ acc*).
preponderance *n* praestantia *f*.
preponderate *vi* praepollēre, vincere.
preposition *n* praepositiō *f*.
prepossess *vt* commendāre (*dat and acc*), praeoccupāre.
prepossessing *adj* suāvis, iūcundus.
prepossession *n* favor *m*.
preposterous *adj* absurdus.
prerogative *n* iūs *nt*.
presage *n* ōmen *nt* ♦ *vt* ōminārī,

portendere.
prescience *n* prōvidentia *f*.
prescient *adj* prōvidus.
prescribe *vt* imperāre; (*MED*) praescrībere; (*limit*) fīnīre.
prescription *n* (*MED*) compositiō *f*; (*right*) ūsus *m*.
presence *n* praesentia *f*; (*appearance*) aspectus *m*; **~ of mind** praesēns animus *m*; **in the ~ of** cōram (*abl*); apud (*abl*); **in my ~** mē praesente.
present *adj* praesēns, īnstāns; **be ~** adesse; **be ~ at** interesse (*dat*) ♦ *n* praesēns tempus *nt*; (*gift*) dōnum *nt*; **at ~** in praesentī, nunc; **for the ~** in praesēns ♦ *vt* dōnāre, offerre; (*on stage*) indūcere; (*in court*) sistere; **~ itself** occurrere.
presentable *adj* spectābilis.
presentation *n* dōnātiō *f*.
presentiment *n* augurium *nt*.
presently *adv* mox.
preservation *n* cōnservātiō *f*.
preserve *vt* cōnservāre, tuērī; (*food*) condīre.
preside *vi* praesidēre (*dat*).
presidency *n* praefectūra *f*.
president *n* praefectus *m*.
press *n* prēlum *nt* ♦ *vt* premere; (*crowd*) stīpāre; (*urge*) īnstāre (*dat*); **~ for** flāgitāre; **~ hard** (*pursuit*) īnsequī, īnstāre (*dat*), īnsistere (*dat*); **~ out** exprimere; **~ together** comprimere.
pressing *adj* īnstāns, gravis.
pressure *n* pressiō *f*, nīsus *m*.
prestige *n* auctōritās *f*, opīniō *f*.
presumably *adv* sānē.
presume *vt* sūmere, conicere ♦ *vi* audēre, cōnfīdere; **I ~** opīnor, crēdō.
presuming *adj* adrogāns.
presumption *n* coniectūra *f*; (*arrogance*) adrogantia *f*, licentia *f*.
presumptuous *adj* adrogāns, audāx.
presumptuously *adv* adroganter, audacter.
presuppose *vt* praesūmere.
pretence *n* simulātiō *f*, speciēs *f*; **under ~ of** per speciem (*gen*); **under false ~s** dolō malō.
pretend *vt* simulāre, fingere; **~ that ... not** dissimulāre.
pretender *n* captātor *m*.
pretension *n* postulātum *nt*; **make ~s to** adfectāre, sibī adrogāre.
pretentious *adj* adrogāns, glōriōsus.
pretext *n* speciēs *f*; **under ~ of** per speciem (*gen*); **on the ~ that** quod *+ subj*.
prettily *adv* pulchrē, bellē.
prettiness *n* pulchritūdō *f*, lepōs *m*.
pretty *adj* formōsus, pulcher, bellus ♦ *adv* admodum, satis.
prevail *vi* vincere; (*custom*) tenēre, obtinēre; **~ upon** persuādēre (*dat*); (*by entreaty*) exōrāre.
prevailing *adj* vulgātus.
prevalent *adj* vulgātus; **be ~** obtinēre; **become ~** incrēbrēscere.
prevaricate *vi* tergiversārī.

prevarication n tergiversātiō f.
prevaricator n veterātor m.
prevent vt impedīre (+ **quōminus/quīn** and subj), prohibēre (+ acc and infin).
prevention n impedītiō f.
previous adj prior, superior.
previously adv anteā, antehāc.
prevision n prōvidentia f.
prey n praeda f ♦ vi: ~ **upon** īnsectārī; (fig) vexāre, carpere.
price n pretium nt; (of corn) annōna f; **at a high** ~ māgnī; **at a low** ~ parvī ♦ vt pretium cōnstituere (gen).
priceless adj inaestimābilis.
prick vt pungere; (goad) stimulāre; ~ **up the ears** aurēs adrigere.
prickle n acūleus m.
prickly adj aculeātus, horridus.
pride n superbia f, fastus m; (boasting) glōria f; (object) decus nt; (best part) flōs m ♦ vt: ~ **oneself on** iactāre, prae sē ferre.
priest n sacerdōs m; (especial) flāmen m; **high** ~ pontifex m, antistēs m.
priestess n sacerdōs f; **high** ~ antistita f.
priesthood n sacerdōtium nt, flāminium nt.
prig n homō fastīdiōsus m.
priggish adj fastīdiōsus.
prim adj modestior.
primarily adv prīncipiō, praecipuē.
primary adj prīmus, praecipuus.
prime adj prīmus, ēgregius; ~ **mover** auctor m ♦ n flōs m; **in one's** ~ flōrēns ♦ vt īnstruere, ērudīre.
primeval adj prīscus.
primitive adj prīstinus, incultus.
primordial adj prīscus.
prince n rēgulus m; rēgis fīlius m; prīnceps m.
princely adj rēgālis.
princess n rēgis fīlia f.
principal adj praecipuus, prīnceps, māximus ♦ n (person) prīnceps m/f; (money) sors f.
principally adv in prīmīs, māximē, māximam partem.
principle n prīncipium nt; (rule) fōrmula f, ratiō f; (character) fidēs f; ~**s** pl īnstitūta ntpl, disciplīna f; **first** ~**s** elementa ntpl, initia ntpl.
print n nota f, signum nt; (foot) vestīgium nt ♦ vt imprimere.
prior adj prior, potior.
priority n: **give** ~ **to** praevertere (dat).
prise vt sublevāre; ~ **open** vectī refringere.
prison n carcer m, vincula ntpl; **put in** ~ **in** vincula conicere.
prisoner n reus m; (for debt) nexus m; (of war) captīvus m; ~ **at the bar** reus m, rea f; **take** ~ capere.
pristine adj prīscus, prīstinus, vetus.
privacy n sēcrētum nt.
private adj (individual) prīvātus; (home) domesticus; (secluded) sēcrētus ♦ n (MIL) gregārius mīles m.
privately adv clam, sēcrētō.
private property n res familiāris f.
privation n inopia f, egestās f.

privet n ligustrum nt.
privilege n iūs nt, immūnitās f.
privileged adj immūnis.
privy adj sēcrētus; ~ **to** cōnscius (gen).
prize n praemium nt; (captured) praeda f; ~ **money** manubiae fpl ♦ vt māgnī aestimāre.
pro-Athenian adj rērum Athēniēnsium studiōsus.
probability n vērī similitūdō f.
probable adj vērī similis; **more** ~ vērō propior.
probably adv fortasse.
probation n probātiō f.
probationer n tīrō m.
probe vt īnspicere, scrūtārī.
probity n honestās f, integritās f.
problem n quaestiō f; **the** ~ **is** illud quaeritur.
problematical adj dubius, anceps.
procedure n ratiō f, modus m; (law) fōrmula f.
proceed vi pergere, prōcēdere, prōgredī; (narrative) īnsequī; ~ **against** persequī, lītem intendere (dat); ~ **from** orīrī, proficīscī ex.
proceedings n ācta ntpl.
proceeds n fructus m, reditus m.
process n ratiō f; (law) āctiō f; **in the** ~ **of time** post aliquod tempus.
procession n pompa f; (fig) agmen nt.
proclaim vt ēdīcere, prōnūntiāre, praedicāre, dēclārāre; ~ **war upon** bellum indīcere + dat.
proclamation n ēdictum nt.
proclivity n prōpēnsiō f.
proconsul n prōcōnsul m.
proconsular adj prōcōnsulāris.
proconsulship n prōcōnsulātus m.
procrastinate vt differre, prōferre ♦ vi cunctārī.
procrastination n prōcrāstinātiō f, mora f.
procreate vt generāre, prōcreāre.
procreation n prōcreātiō f.
procreator n generātor m.
procumbent adj prōnus.
procurator n prōcūrātor m.
procure vt parāre, adipīscī, adquīrere; (by request) impetrāre.
procurer n lēnō m.
prod vt stimulāre.
prodigal adj prōdigus ♦ n nepōs m.
prodigality n effūsiō f.
prodigally adv effūsē.
prodigious adj ingēns, immānis.
prodigy n prōdigium nt, portentum nt; (fig) mīrāculum nt.
produce vt ēdere; (young) parere; (crops) ferre; (play) dare, docēre; (line) prōdūcere; (in court) sistere; (into view) prōferre; (from store) prōmere, dēprōmere ♦ n fructus m; (of earth) frūgēs fpl; (in money) reditus m.
product n opus nt; ~ **of** fructus (gen).
production n opus nt.
productive adj fēcundus, ferāx, fructuōsus.
productivity n fēcunditās f, ūbertās f.
profanation n violātiō f.
profane adj profānus, impius ♦ vt violāre, polluere.

profanely _adv_ impiē.
profanity _n_ impietās _f_.
profess _vt_ profitērī, prae sē ferre; ~ **to be**
profitērī sē.
profession _n_ professiō _f_; (_occupation_) ars _f_,
haeresis _f_.
professor _n_ doctor _m_.
proffer _vt_ offerre, pollicērī.
proficiency _n_ prōgressus _m_, perītia _f_; **attain** ~
prōficere.
proficient _adj_ perītus.
profile _n_ ōris līneāmenta _ntpl_; (_portrait_) oblīqua
imāgō _f_.
profit _n_ lucrum _nt_, ēmolumentum _nt_, fructus
_m_; **make a ~ out of** quaestuī habēre ♦ _vt_
prōdesse (_dat_) ♦ _vi_: ~ **by** fruī (_abl_), ūtī (_abl_);
(_opportunity_) arripere.
profitable _adj_ fructuōsus, ūtilis.
profitably _adv_ ūtiliter.
profligacy _n_ flāgitium _nt_, perditī mōrēs _mpl_.
profligate _adj_ perditus, dissolūtus ♦ _n_ nepōs
_m_.
profound _adj_ altus; (_discussion_) abstrūsus.
profoundly _adv_ penitus.
profundity _n_ altitūdō _f_.
profuse _adj_ prōdigus, effūsus.
profusely _adv_ effūsē.
profusion _n_ abundantia _f_, adfluentia _f_; **in ~**
abundē.
progenitor _n_ auctor _m_.
progeny _n_ prōgeniēs _f_, prōlēs _f_.
prognostic _n_ signum _nt_.
prognosticate _vt_ ōminārī, augurārī,
praedīcere.
prognostication _n_ ōmen _nt_, praedictiō _f_.
programme _n_ libellus _m_.
progress _n_ prōgressus _m_; **make ~** prōficere ♦
_vi_ prōgredī.
progression _n_ prōgressus _m_.
progressively _adv_ gradātim.
prohibit _vt_ vetāre, interdīcere (_dat_).
prohibition _n_ interdictum _nt_.
project _n_ prōpositum _nt_ ♦ _vi_ ēminēre, exstāre;
(_land_) excurrere ♦ _vt_ prōicere.
projectile _n_ tēlum _nt_.
projecting _adj_ ēminēns.
projection _n_ ēminentia _f_.
proletarian _adj_ plēbēius.
proletariat _n_ plēbs _f_.
prolific _adj_ fēcundus.
prolix _adj_ verbōsus, longus.
prolixity _n_ redundantia _f_.
prologue _n_ prologus _m_.
prolong _vt_ dūcere, prōdūcere; (_office_)
prōrogāre.
prolongation _n_ (_time_) propāgātiō _f_; (_office_)
prōrogātiō _f_.
promenade _n_ ambulātiō _f_ ♦ _vi_ inambulāre,
spatiārī.
prominence _n_ ēminentia _f_.
prominent _adj_ ēminēns, īnsignis; **be ~**
ēminēre.
promiscuous _adj_ prōmiscuus.

promiscuously _adv_ prōmiscuē.
promise _n_ prōmissum _nt_; **break a ~** fidem
fallere; **keep a ~** fidem praestāre; **make a ~**
fidem dare; **a youth of great ~** summae speī
adulēscēns ♦ _vt_ prōmittere, pollicērī; (_in_
marriage) dēspondēre; ~ **in return**
reprōmittere ♦ _vi_: ~ **well** bonam spem
ostendere.
promising _adj_ bonae speī.
promissory note _n_ syngrapha _f_.
promontory _n_ prōmunturium _nt_.
promote _vt_ favēre (_dat_); (_growth_) alere; (_in_
rank) prōdūcere.
promoter _n_ auctor _m_, fautor _m_.
promotion _n_ dignitās _f_.
prompt _adj_ alacer, prōmptus ♦ _vt_ incitāre,
commovēre; (_speaker_) subicere.
prompter _n_ monitor _m_.
promptitude _n_ alacritās _f_, celeritās _f_.
promptly _adv_ extemplō, citō.
promulgate _vt_ prōmulgāre, palam facere.
promulgation _n_ prōmulgātiō _f_.
prone _adj_ prōnus; (_mind_) inclīnātus.
prong _n_ dēns _m_.
pronounce _vt_ ēloquī, appellāre; (_oath_)
interpōnere; (_sentence_) dīcere,
prōnūntiāre.
pronounced _adj_ manifestus, īnsignis.
pronouncement _n_ ōrātiō _f_, adfirmātiō _f_.
pronunciation _n_ appellātiō _f_.
proof _n_ documentum _nt_, argūmentum _nt_; (_test_)
probātiō _f_ ♦ _adj_ immōtus, impenetrābilis.
prop _n_ adminiculum _f_, firmāmentum _nt_ ♦ _vt_
fulcīre.
propaganda _n_ documenta _ntpl_.
propagate _vt_ propāgāre.
propagation _n_ propāgātiō _f_.
propel _vt_ incitāre, prōpellere.
propensity _n_ inclīnātiō _f_.
proper _adj_ idōneus, decēns, decōrus; rēctus; **it**
is ~ decet.
properly _adv_ decōrē; rēctē.
property _n_ rēs _f_, rēs mancipī, bona _ntpl_;
(_estate_) praedium _nt_; (_attribute_) proprium _nt_;
(_slave's_) pecūlium _nt_.
prophecy _n_ vāticinium _nt_, praedictiō _f_.
prophesy _n_ vāticinārī, praedīcere.
prophet _n_ vātēs _m_, fātidicus _m_.
prophetess _n_ vātēs _f_.
prophetic _adj_ dīvīnus, fātidicus.
prophetically _adv_ dīvīnitus.
propinquity _n_ (_place_) vīcīnitās _f_; (_kin_)
propinquitās _f_.
propitiate _vt_ plācāre.
propitiation _n_ plācātiō _f_, litātiō _f_.
propitious _adj_ fēlīx, faustus; (_god_) praesēns.
proportion _n_ mēnsūra _f_; **in ~** prō portiōne, prō
ratā parte; **in ~ to** prō (_abl_).
proportionately _adv_ prō portiōne, prō ratā
parte.
proposal _n_ condiciō _f_.
propose _vt_ prōpōnere; (_motion_) ferre, rogāre;
(_penalty_) inrogāre; (_candidate_) rogāre

magistrātum.
proposer n auctor m, lātor m.
proposition n (*offer*) condiciō f; (*plan*)
cōnsilium nt, prōpositum nt; (*logic*)
prōnūntiātum nt.
propound vt expōnere, in medium prōferre.
propraetor n prōpraetor m.
proprietor n dominus m.
propriety n decōrum nt; (*conduct*) modestia f;
with ~ decenter.
propulsion n impulsus m.
prorogation n prōrogātiō f.
prorogue vt prōrogāre.
prosaic adj pedester.
proscribe vt prōscrībere.
proscription n prōscrīptiō f.
prose n ōrātiō f, ōrātiō solūta f.
prosecute vt (*task*) exsequī, gerere; (*at law*)
accūsāre, lītem intendere (*dat*).
prosecution n exsecūtiō f; (*at law*) accūsātiō f;
(*party*) accūsātor m.
prosecutor n accūsātor m.
prosody n numerī mpl.
prospect n prōspectus m; (*fig*) spēs f ♦ vi
explōrāre.
prospective adj futūrus, spērātus.
prosper vi flōrēre, bonā fortūnā ūtī ♦ vt
fortūnāre.
prosperity n fortūna f, rēs secundae fpl,
fēlīcitās f.
prosperous adj fēlīx, fortūnātus, secundus.
prosperously adv prosperē.
prostrate adj prōstrātus, adflīctus; **lie** ~ iacēre
♦ vt prōsternere, dēicere; ~ **oneself**
prōcumbere, sē prōicere.
prostration n frāctus animus m.
prosy adj longus.
protagonist n prīmārum partium āctor m.
protect vt tuērī, dēfendere, custōdīre,
prōtegere.
protection n tūtēla f, praesidium nt; (*law*)
patrōcinium nt; (*POL*) fidēs f; **put oneself under
the ~ of** in fidem venīre (*gen*); **take under
one's ~** in fidem recipere.
protector n patrōnus m, dēfēnsor m, custōs m.
protectress n patrōna f.
protégé n cliēns m.
protest n obtestātiō f; (*POL*) intercessiō f ♦ vi
obtestārī, reclāmāre; (*POL*) intercēdere.
protestation n adsevērātiō f.
prototype n archetypum nt.
protract vt dūcere, prōdūcere.
protrude vi prōminēre.
protruding adj exsertus.
protuberance n ēminentia f, tūber nt.
protuberant adj ēminēns, turgidus.
proud adj superbus, adrogāns, īnsolēns; **be ~**
superbīre; **be ~ of** iactāre.
proudly adv superbē.
prove vt dēmōnstrāre, arguere, probāre; (*test*)
experīrī ♦ vi (*person*) se praebēre; (*event*)
ēvādere; ~ **oneself** sē praebēre, sē praestāre;
not ~n nōn liquet.

proved adj expertus.
provenance n orīgō f.
provender n pābulum nt.
proverb n prōverbium nt.
proverbial adj trītus; **become ~** in prōverbium
venīre.
provide vt parāre, praebēre; ~ **for** prōvidēre
(*dat*); **the law ~s** lēx iubet; ~ **against**
praecavēre.
provided that conj dum, dummodo (+ subj).
providence n prōvidentia f; Deus m.
provident adj prōvidus, cautus.
providential adj dīvīnus; secundus.
providentially adv dīvīnitus.
providently adv cautē.
providing conj dum, dummodo.
province n prōvincia f.
provincial adj prōvinciālis; (*contemptuous*)
oppidānus, mūnicipālis.
provision n parātus m; **make ~ for** prōvidēre
(*dat*); **make ~** cavēre.
provisionally adv ad tempus.
provisions n cibus m, commeātus m, rēs
frūmentāria f.
proviso n condiciō f; **with this ~** hāc lēge.
provocation n inrītāmentum nt, offēnsiō f.
provocative adj (*language*) molestus,
invidiōsus.
provoke vt inrītāre, lacessere; (*to action*)
excitāre.
provoking adj odiōsus, molestus.
provost n praefectus m.
prow n prōra f.
prowess n virtūs f.
prowl vi grassārī, vagārī.
proximate adj proximus.
proximity n propinquitās f, vīcīnia f.
proxy n vicārius m.
prude n fastīdiōsa f.
prudence n prūdentia f.
prudent adj prūdēns, cautus, sagāx.
prudently adv prūdenter, cautē.
prudery n fastīdiōsa quaedam pudīcitia f.
prudish adj fastīdiōsus.
prune vt amputāre.
pruner n putātor m.
pruning hook n falx f.
pry vi inquīrere; ~ **into** scrūtārī.
pseudonym n falsum nōmen nt.
psychology n animī ratiō f.
Ptolemy n Ptolemaeus m.
puberty n pūbertās f.
public adj pūblicus; (*speech*) forēnsis; ~ **life** rēs
pūblica f, forum nt; **in ~** forīs; **appear in ~** in
medium prōdīre; **make ~** in mediō pōnere,
forās perferre; **make a ~ case of** in medium
vocāre; **act for the ~ good** in medium
cōnsulere; **be a ~ figure** in lūce versārī,
digitō mōnstrārī ♦ n vulgus nt, hominēs mpl.
publican n (*taxes*) pūblicānus m; (*inn*) caupō m.
publication n ēditiō f, prōmulgātiō f; (*book*)
liber m.
publicity n lūx f, celebritās f.

publicly *adv* palam; (*by the state*) pūblicē.
public opinion *n* fāma *f*.
publish *vt* vulgāre, dīvulgāre; (*book*) ēdere.
pucker *vt* corrūgāre.
puerile *adj* puerīlis.
puerility *n* ineptiae *fpl*.
puff *n* aura *f* ♦ *vt* īnflāre ♦ *vi* anhēlāre.
puffed up *adj* īnflātus, tumidus.
pugilism *n* pugilātus *m*.
pugilist *n* pugil *m*.
pugnacious *adj* pugnāx.
pugnacity *n* ferōcitās *f*.
puissance *n* potentia *f*, vīrēs *fpl*.
puissant *adj* potēns.
pull *n* tractus *m*; (*of gravity*) contentiō *f* ♦ *vt*
   trahere, tractāre; ~ **apart** distrahere; ~ **at**
   vellicāre; ~ **away** āvellere; ~ **back** retrahere;
   ~ **down** dēripere, dētrahere; (*building*)
   dēmōlīrī; ~ **off** āvellere; ~ **out** ēvellere,
   extrahere; ~ **through** *vi* pervincere; (*illness*)
   convalēscere; ~ **up** (*plant*) ēruere;
   (*movement*) coercēre; ~ **to pieces** dīlaniāre.
pullet *n* pullus gallīnāceus *m*.
pulley *n* trochlea *f*.
pulmonary *adj* pulmōneus.
pulp *n* carō *f*.
pulpit *n* suggestus *m*.
pulsate *vi* palpitāre, micāre.
pulse *n* (*plant*) legūmen *nt*; (*of blood*) vēnae *fpl*;
   feel the ~ vēnās temptāre.
pulverize *vt* contundere.
pumice stone *n* pūmex *m*.
pummel *vt* verberāre.
pump *n* antlia *f* ♦ *vt* haurīre; ~ **out** exhaurīre.
pumpkin *n* cucurbita *f*.
pun *n* agnōminātiō *f*.
punch *n* ictus *m* ♦ *vt* pertundere, percutere.
punctilious *adj* rīligiōsus.
punctiliousness *n* rīligiō *f*.
punctual *adj* accūrātus, dīligēns.
punctuality *n* dīligentia *f*.
punctually *adv* ad hōram, ad tempus.
punctuate *vt* distinguere.
punctuation *n* interpūnctiō *f*.
puncture *n* pūnctiō *f* ♦ *vt* pungere.
pundit *n* scholasticus *m*.
pungency *n* ācrimōnia *f*; (*in debate*) acūleī *mpl*.
pungent *adj* ācer, mordāx.
punish *vt* pūnīre, animadvertere in (*acc*);
   poenam sūmere dē (+ *abl*); **be ~ed** poenās
   dare.
punishable *adj* poenā dignus.
punisher *n* vindex *m*, ultor *m*.
punishment *n* poena *f*, supplicium *nt*;
   (*censors'*) animadversiō *f*; **capital ~** capitis
   supplicium *nt*; **corporal ~** verbera *ntpl*; **inflict**
   ~ **on** poenā adficere, poenam capere dē (*abl*),
   supplicium sūmere dē (*abl*); **submit to ~**
   poenam subīre; **undergo ~** poenās dare,
   pendere, solvere.
punitive *adj* ulcīscendī causā.
punt *n* pontō *m*.
puny *adj* pusillus.

pup *n* catulus *m* ♦ *vi* parere.
pupil *n* discipulus *m*, discipula *f*; (*eye*) aciēs *f*,
   pūpula *f*.
pupillage *n* tūtēla *f*.
puppet *n* pūpa *f*.
puppy *n* catulus *m*.
purblind *adj* luscus.
purchase *n* emptiō *f*; (*formal*) mancipium *nt* ♦
   vt emere.
purchaser *n* emptor *m*; (*at auction*) manceps *m*.
pure *adj* pūrus, integer; (*morally*) castus;
   (*mere*) merus.
purely *adv* pūrē, integrē; (*solely*) sōlum, nīl
   nisi; (*quite*) omnīnō, plānē.
purgation *n* pūrgātiō *f*.
purge *vt* pūrgāre, expūrgāre.
purification *n* lūstrātiō *f*, pūrgātiō *f*.
purify *vt* pūrgāre, expūrgāre.
purist *n* fastīdiōsus *m*.
purity *n* integritās *f*, castitās *f*.
purloin *vt* surripere, fūrārī.
purple *n* purpura *f* ♦ *adj* purpureus.
purport *n* sententia *f*; (*of words*) vīs *f*; **what is**
   the ~ of? quō spectat?, quid vult? ♦ *vt* velle
   spectāre ad.
purpose *n* prōpositum *nt*, cōnsilium *nt*, mēns *f*;
   for that ~ eō; **for the ~ of** ad (*acc*), ut (*subj*), eā
   mente ut, eō cōnsiliō ut (*subj*); **on ~** cōnsultō,
   dē industriā; **to the ~** ad rem; **to what ~?**
   quō?, quōrsum?; **to no ~** frustrā, nēquīquam;
   without achieving one's ~ rē īnfectā ♦ *vt* in
   animō habēre, velle.
purposeful *adj* intentus.
purposeless *adj* inānis.
purposely *adv* cōnsultō, dē industriā.
purr *n* murmur *nt* ♦ *vi* murmurāre.
purse *n* marsupium *nt*, crumēna *f*; **privy ~**
   fiscus *m* ♦ *vt* adstringere.
pursuance *n* exsecūtiō *f*; **in ~ of** secundum
   (*acc*).
pursue *vt* īnsequī, īnsectārī, persequī;
   (*closely*) īnstāre (*dat*), īnsistere (*dat*); (*aim*)
   petere; (*course*) īnsistere.
pursuer *n* īnsequēns *m*; (*law*) accūsātor *m*.
pursuit *n* īnsectātiō *f*; (*hunt*) vēnātiō *f*;
   (*ambition*) studium *nt*.
purvey *vt* parāre; (*food*) obsōnāre.
purveyance *n* prōcūrātiō *f*.
purveyor *n* obsōnātor *m*.
purview *n* prōvincia *f*.
pus *n* pūs *nt*.
push *n* pulsus *m*, impetus *m* ♦ *vt* impellere,
   trūdere, urgēre; ~ **away** āmovēre; ~ **back**
   repellere; ~ **down** dēprimere, dētrūdere; ~
   forward prōpellere; ~ **in** intrūdere; ~ **on**
   incitāre; ~ **through** perrumpere.
pushing *adj* cōnfīdēns.
pusillanimity *n* ignāvia *f*, timor *m*.
pusillanimous *adj* ignāvus, timidus.
pustule *n* pustula *f*.
put *vt* (*in a state*) dare; (*in a position*) pōnere; (*in*
   words) reddere; (*argument*) pōnere; (*spur*)
   subdere; (*to some use*) adhibēre; ~ **an end to**

fīnem facere (*dat*); **~ a question to** interrogāre; **~ against** adpōnere; **~ among** intericere; **~ aside** sēpōnere; **~ away** pōnere, dēmovēre; (*store*) repōnere; **~ back** repōnere; repellere; **~ beside** adpōnere; **~ between** interpōnere; (*revolt*) opprimere; **~ forth** extendere; (*growth*) mittere; **~ forward** ostentāre; (*plea*) adferre; **~ in** immittere, īnserere; (*ship*) adpellere; **~ off** differre; **~ on** impōnere; (*clothes*) induere; (*play*) dare; **~ out** ēicere; (*eye*) effodere; (*fire*) exstinguere; (*money*) pōnere; (*tongue*) exserere; **~ out of the way** dēmovēre; **~ out to sea** in altum ēvehi, solvere; **~ over** superimpōnere; **~ to** adpōnere; (*flight*) dare in (*acc*), fugāre, prōflīgāre; in fugam conicere; (*sea*) solvere; **~ together** cōnferre; **~ under** subicere; **~ up** (*for sale*) prōpōnere; (*lodge*) dēvertere, dēversārī apud; **~ up with** ferre, patī; **~ upon** impōnere.

putrefaction *n* pūtor *m*.
putrefy *vi* putrēscere.
putrid *adj* putridus.
puzzle *n* nōdus *m* ♦ *vt* impedīre, sollicitāre; **be ~d** haerēre.
puzzling *adj* ambiguus, perplexus.
pygmy *n* pygmaeus *m*.
pyramid *n* pȳramis *f*.
pyramidal *adj* pȳramidātus.
pyre *n* rogus *m*.
Pyrenees *npl* Pyrenaeī (montēs) *mpl*.
python *n* pȳthōn *m*.

Q, q

quack *n* (*doctor*) circulātor *m* ♦ *vi* tetrinnīre.
quadrangle *n* ārea *f*.
quadruped *n* quadrupēs *m/f*.
quadruple *adj* quadruplex.
quaestor *n* quaestor *m*; **~'s** quaestōrius.
quaestorship *n* quaestūra *f*.
quaff *vt* ēpōtāre, haurīre.
quagmire *n* palūs *f*.
quail *n* (*bird*) coturnīx *f* ♦ *vi* pāvēscere, trepidāre.
quaint *adj* novus, īnsolitus.
quaintness *n* īnsolentia *f*.
quake *vi* horrēre, horrēscere ♦ *n* (*earth*) mōtus *m*.
quaking *n* horror *m*, tremor *m* ♦ *adj* tremulus.
qualification *n* condiciō *f*; (*limitation*) exceptiō *f*.
qualified *adj* (*for*) aptus, idōneus, dignus; (*in*) perītus, doctus.

qualify *vi* prōficere ♦ *vt* temperāre, mītigāre.
qualities *npl* ingenium *nt*.
quality *n* nātūra *f*, vīs *f*; indolēs *f*; (*rank*) locus *m*, genus *nt*; **I know the ~ of** sciō quālis sit.
qualm *n* rīligiō *f*, scrūpulus *m*.
quandary *n* angustiae *fpl*; **be in a ~** haerēre.
quantity *n* cōpia *f*, numerus *m*; (*metre*) vōcum mēnsiō *f*; **a large ~** multum *nt*, plūrimum *nt*; **a small ~** aliquantulum *nt*.
quarrel *n* dissēnsiō *f*, contrōversia *f*; (*violent*) rixa *f*, iūrgium *nt* ♦ *vi* rixārī, altercārī.
quarrelsome *adj* pugnāx, lītigiōsus.
quarry *n* lapicīdinae *fpl*, metallum *nt*; (*prey*) praeda *f* ♦ *vt* excīdere.
quart *n* duō sextāriī *mpl*.
quartan *n* (*fever*) quartāna *f*.
quarter *n* quarta pars *f*, quadrāns *m*; (*sector*) regiō *f*; (*direction*) pars *f*, regiō *f*; (*respite*) missiō *f*; **~s** castra *ntpl*; (*billet*) hospitium *nt*; **come to close ~s** manum cōnserere; (*armies*) signa cōnferre; **winter ~s** hīberna *ntpl* ♦ *vt* quadrifidam dīvidere; (*troops*) in hospitia dīvidere.
quarterdeck *n* puppis *f*.
quarterly *adj* trimestris ♦ *adv* quartō quōque mēnse.
quartermaster *n* (*navy*) gubernātor *m*; (*army*) castrōrum praefectus *m*.
quarterstaff *n* rudis *f*.
quash *vt* comprimere; (*decision*) rescindere.
quatrain *n* tetrastichon *nt*.
quaver *n* tremor *m* ♦ *vi* tremere.
quavering *adj* tremebundus.
quay *n* crepīdō *f*.
queasy *adj* fastīdiōsus.
queen *n* rēgīna *f*; (*bee*) rēx *m*.
queer *adj* īnsolēns, rīdiculus.
quell *vt* opprimere, domāre, dēbellāre.
quench *vt* exstinguere, restinguere; (*thirst*) sēdāre, explēre.
querulous *adj* querulus, queribundus.
query *n* interrogātiō *f* ♦ *vt* in dubium vocāre ♦ *vi* rogāre.
quest *n* investīgātiō *f*; **go in ~ of** investīgāre, anquīrere.
question *n* interrogātiō *f*; (*at issue*) quaestiō *f*, rēs *f*; (*in doubt*) dubium *nt*; **ask a ~** rogāre, quaerere, scīscitārī, percontārī; **call in ~** in dubium vocāre, addubitāre; **out of the ~** indignus; **be out of the ~** improbārī, fierī nōn posse; **the ~ is** illud quaeritur; **there is no ~ that** nōn dubium est quīn (*subj*); **without ~** sine dubiō ♦ *vt* interrogāre; (*closely*) percontārī; (*doubt*) in dubium vocāre ♦ *vi* dubitāre.
questionable *adj* incertus, dubius.
questioner *n* percontātor *m*.
questioning *n* interrogātiō *f*.
queue *n* agmen *nt*.
quibble *n* captiō *f* ♦ *vi* cavillārī.
quibbler *n* cavillātor *m*.
quibbling *adj* captiōsus.
quick *adj* (*speed*) celer, vēlōx, citus; (*to act*)

alacer, impiger; (*to perceive*) sagāx; (*with hands*) facilis; (*living*) vīvus; **be ~** properāre, festīnāre; **cut to the ~** ad vīvum resecāre; (*fig*) mordēre.
quicken *vt* adcelerāre; (*with life*) animāre.
quickening *adj* vītālis.
quickly *adv* celeriter, citō; (*haste*) properē; (*mind*) acūtē; **as ~ as possible** quam celerrimē.
quickness *n* celeritās *f*, vēlōcitās *f*; (*to act*) alacritās *f*; (*to perceive*) sagācitās *f*, sollertia *f*.
quicksand *n* syrtis *f*.
quick-tempered *adj* īrācundus.
quick-witted *adj* acūtus, sagāx, perspicāx.
quiescence *n* inertia *f*, ōtium *nt*.
quiescent *adj* iners, ōtiōsus.
quiet *adj* tranquillus, quiētus, placidus; (*silent*) tacitus; **be ~** quiēscere; silēre ♦ *n* quiēs *f*, tranquillitās *f*; silentium *nt*; (*peace*) pāx *f* ♦ *vt* pācāre, compōnere.
quietly *adv* tranquillē, quiētē; tacitē, per silentium; aequō animō.
quietness *n* tranquillitās *f*; silentium *nt*.
quill *n* penna *f*.
quince *n* cydōnium *nt*.
quinquennial *adj* quinquennālis.
quinquereme *n* quinquerēmis *f*.
quintessence *n* flōs *m*, vīs *f*.
quip *n* sāl *m*, facētiae *fpl*.
quirk *n* captiuncula *f*; **~s** *pl* trīcae *fpl*.
quit *vt* relinquere ♦ *adj* līber, solūtus.
quite *adv* admodum, plānē, prōrsus; **not ~** minus, parum; (*time*) nōndum.
quits *n* parēs *mpl*.
quiver *n* pharetra *f* ♦ *vi* tremere, contremere.
quivering *adj* tremebundus, tremulus.
quoit *n* discus *m*.
quota *n* pars *f*, rata pars *f*.
quotation *n* (*act*) commemorātiō *f*; (*passage*) locus *m*.
quote *vt* prōferre, commemorāre.
quoth *vt* inquit.

R, r

rabbit *n* cunīculus *m*.
rabble *n* turba *f*; (*class*) vulgus *nt*, plēbēcula *f*.
rabid *adj* rabidus.
rabidly *adv* rabidē.
race *n* (*descent*) genus *nt*, stirps *f*; (*people*) gēns *f*, nōmen *nt*; (*contest*) certāmen *nt*; (*fig*) cursus *m*, curriculum *nt*; (*water*) flūmen *nt*; **run a ~** cursū certāre; **run the ~** (*fig*) spatium dēcurrere ♦ *vi* certāre, contendere.
racecourse *n* (*foot*) stadium *nt*; (*horse*)

spatium *nt*.
racer *n* cursor *m*.
racial *adj* gentīlis.
rack *n* (*torture*) tormentum *nt*; (*shelf*) pluteus *m*; **be on the ~** (*fig*) cruciārī ♦ *vt* torquēre, cruciāre; **~ off** (*wine*) diffundere.
racket *n* (*noise*) strepitus *m*.
racy *adj* (*style*) salsus.
radiance *n* splendor *m*, fulgor *m*.
radiant *adj* splendidus, nitidus.
radiantly *adv* splendidē.
radiate *vi* fulgēre; (*direction*) dīversōs tendere ♦ *vt* ēmittere.
radical *adj* īnsitus, innātus; (*thorough*) tōtus ♦ *n* novārum rērum cupidus *m*.
radically *adv* omnīnō, penitus, funditus.
radish *n* rādīx *f*.
radius *n* radius *m*.
raffish *adj* dissolūtus.
raffle *n* ālea *f* ♦ *vt* āleā vēndere.
raft *n* ratis *f*.
rafter *n* trabs *f*, tignum *nt*.
rag *n* pannus *m*.
rage *n* īra *f*, furor *m*; **be all the ~** in ōre omnium esse; **spend one's ~** exsaevīre ♦ *vi* furere, saevīre; (*furiously*) dēbacchārī.
ragged *adj* pannōsus.
raid *n* excursiō *f*, incursiō *f*, impressiō *f*; **make a ~** excurrere ♦ *vt* incursiōnem facere in (*acc*).
rail *n* longurius *m* ♦ *vt* saepīre ♦ *vi*: **~ at** maledīcere (*dat*), convīcia facere (*dat*).
railing *n* saepēs *f*, cancellī *mpl*.
raillery *n* cavillātiō *f*.
raiment *n* vestis *f*.
rain *n* pluvia *f*, imber *m* ♦ *vi* pluere; **it is raining** pluit.
rainbow *n* arcus *m*.
rainstorm *n* imber *m*.
rainy *adj* pluvius.
raise *vt* tollere, ēlevāre; (*army*) cōgere, cōnscrībere; (*children*) ēducāre; (*cry*) tollere; (*from dead*) excitāre; (*laugh*) movēre; (*money*) cōnflāre; (*price*) augēre; (*siege*) exsolvere; (*structure*) exstruere; (*to higher rank*) ēvehere; **~ up** ērigere, sublevāre.
raisin *n* astaphis *f*.
rajah *n* dynastēs *m*.
rake *n* rastrum *nt*; (*person*) nepōs *m* ♦ *vt* rādere; **~ in** conrādere; **~ up** (*fig*) ēruere.
rakish *adj* dissolūtus.
rally *n* conventus *m* ♦ *vt* (*troops*) in ōrdinem revocāre; (*with words*) hortārī; (*banter*) cavillārī ♦ *vi* sē colligere.
ram *n* ariēs *m*; (*battering*) ariēs *m* ♦ *vt*: **~ down** fistūcāre; **~ home** (*fact*) inculcāre.
ramble *n* errātiō *f* ♦ *vi* vagārī, errāre.
rambling *adj* vagus; (*plant*) errāticus; (*speech*) fluēns.
ramification *n* rāmus *m*.
rammer *n* fistūca *f*.
rampage *vi* saevīre.
rampant *adj* ferōx.

rampart n agger m, vallum nt.
ranch n lātifundium nt.
rancid adj pūtidus.
rancour n odium nt, acerbitās f, invidia f.
random adj fortuītus; **at ~** temerē.
range n ōrdō m, seriēs f; (mountain) iugum nt;
(of weapon) iactus m; **within ~** intrā tēlī
iactum; **come within ~** sub ictum venīre ♦ vt
ōrdināre ♦ vi ēvagārī, pervagārī; (in speech)
excurrere.
rank n (line) ōrdō m; (class) ōrdō m; (position)
locus m, dignitās f; **~ and file** gregāriī mīlitēs
mpl; **keep the ~s** ōrdinēs observāre; **the ~s**
(MIL) aciēs, acieī f; **leave the ~s** ōrdine ēgredī,
ab signīs discēdere; **reduce to the ~s** in
ōrdinem redigere ♦ vt numerāre ♦ vi in
numerō habērī.
rank adj luxuriōsus; (smell) gravis, foetidus.
rankle vi exulcerāre.
rankness n luxuriēs f.
ransack vt dīripere, spoliāre.
ransom n redemptiō f, pretium nt ♦ vt
redimere.
rant vi latrāre.
ranter n rabula m, latrātor m.
rap n ictus m ♦ vt ferīre.
rapacious adj rapāx, avidus.
rapaciously adv avidē.
rapacity n rapācitās f, aviditās f.
rape n raptus m.
rapid adj rapidus, vēlōx, citus, incitātus.
rapidity n celeritās f, vēlōcitās f, incitātiō f.
rapidly adv rapidē, vēlōciter, citō.
rapine n rapīna f.
rapt adj intentus.
rapture n laetitia f, alacritās f.
rare adj rārus; (occurrence) īnfrequēns;
(quality) singulāris.
rarefy vt extenuāre.
rarely adv rārō.
rarity n rāritās f; (thing) rēs īnsolita f.
rascal n furcifer m, scelestus m.
rascally adj improbus.
rash adj temerārius, audāx, incōnsultus;
praeceps.
rashly adv temerē, incōnsultē.
rashness n temeritās f, audācia f.
rat n mūs m/f.
rate n (cost) pretium nt; (standard) nōrma f;
(tax) vectīgal nt; (speed) celeritās f; **at any ~**
(concessive) utique, saltem; (adversative)
quamquam, tamen ♦ vt (value) aestimāre;
(scold) increpāre, obiūrgāre.
rather adv potius, satius; (somewhat)
aliquantum; (with comp) aliquantō; (with
verbs) mālō; (correcting) immo; **~ sad** tristior;
I would ~ mālō; **I ~ think** haud sciō an; **~ than**
magis quam, potius quam.
ratification n (formal) sanctiō f.
ratify vt ratum facere, sancīre; (law) iubēre.
rating n taxātiō f, aestimātiō f; (navy) nauta m;
(scolding) obiūrgātiō f.
ratiocinate vi ratiōcinārī.

ratiocination n ratiōcinātiō f.
ration n dēmēnsum nt.
rational adj animō praeditus; **be ~** sapere.
rationality n ratiō f.
rationally adv ratiōne.
rations npl cibāria ntpl, diāria ntpl.
rattle n crepitus m; (toy) crotalum nt ♦ vi
crepitāre, increpāre.
raucous adj raucus.
ravage vt dēpopulārī, vastāre, dīripere.
rave vi furere, īnsānīre; (fig) bacchārī,
saevīre.
raven n cornīx f.
ravenous adj rapāx, vorāx.
ravenously adv avidē.
ravine n faucēs fpl, hiātus m.
raving adj furiōsus, īnsānus ♦ n furor m.
ravish vt rapere; (joy) efferre.
raw adj crūdus; (person) rudis, agrestis.
ray n radius m; **the first ~ of hope appeared**
prīma spēs adfulsit.
raze vt excīdere, solō aequāre.
razor n novācula f.
reach n (space) spatium nt; (mind) captus m;
(weapon) ictus m; **out of ~** of extrā (acc);
within ~ ad manum ♦ vt advenīre ad (+ acc);
attingere; (space) pertinēre ad; (journey)
pervenīre ad.
react vi adficī; **~ to** ferre.
reaction n: **what was his ~ to?** quō animō
tulit?
read vt legere; (a book) ēvolvere; (aloud)
recitāre; **~ over** perlegere.
reader n lēctor m.
readily adv facile, libenter, ultrō.
readiness n facilitās f; **in ~** ad manum, in
prōmptū, in expedītō.
reading n lēctiō f.
readjust vt dēnuō accommodāre.
ready adj parātus, prōmptus; (manner) facilis;
(money) praesēns; **get, make ~** parāre,
expedīre, adōrnāre.
reaffirm vt iterum adfirmāre.
real adj vērus, germānus.
real estate n fundus m, solum nt.
realism n vēritās f.
realistic adj vērī similis.
reality n rēs f, rēs ipsa f, vērum nt; **in ~** rēvērā.
realize vt intellegere, animadvertere; (aim)
efficere, peragere; (money) redigere.
really adv vērē, rēvērā, profectō; **~?** itane
vērō?
realm n rēgnum nt.
reap vt metere; **~ the reward of** fructum
percipere ex.
reaper n messor m.
reappear vi revenīre.
rear vt alere, ēducāre; (structure) exstruere ♦
vi sē ērigere ♦ n tergum nt; (MIL) novissima
aciēs f, novissimum agmen nt; **in the ~** ā
tergō; **bring up the ~** agmen claudere, agmen
cōgere ♦ adj postrēmus, novissimus.
rearguard n novissimum agmen nt,

novissimī *mpl.*

rearrange *vt* ōrdinem mūtāre (*gen*).

reason *n* (*faculty*) mēns *f*, animus *m*, ratiō *f*; (*sanity*) sānitās *f*; (*argument*) ratiō *f*; (*cause*) causa *f*; (*moderation*) modus *m*; **by ~ of** propter (*acc*); **for this ~** idcircō, ideō, proptereā; **in ~** aequus, modicus; **with good ~** iūre; **without ~** temerē, sine causā; **without good ~** frustrā, iniūriā; **give a ~ for** ratiōnem adferre (*gen*); **I know the ~ for** sciō cūr, quamobrem (*subj*); **there is no ~ for** nōn est cūr, nihil est quod (*subj*); **lose one's ~** īnsānīre ♦ *vi* ratiōcinārī, disserere.

reasonable *adj* aequus, iūstus; (*person*) modestus; (*amount*) modicus.

reasonably *adv* ratiōne, iūstē; modicē.

reasoning *n* ratiō *f*, ratiōcinātiō *f*.

reassemble *vt* colligere, cōgere.

reassert *vt* iterāre.

reassume *vt* recipere.

reassure *vt* firmāre, cōnfirmāre.

rebate *vt* dēdūcere.

rebel *n* rebellis *m* ♦ *adj* sēditiōsus ♦ *vi* rebelliōnem facere, rebellāre, dēscīscere.

rebellion *n* sēditiō *f*, mōtus *m*.

rebellious *adj* sēditiōsus.

rebound *vi* resilīre.

rebuff *n* repulsa *f* ♦ *vt* repellere, āversārī.

rebuild *vt* renovāre, restaurāre.

rebuke *n* reprehēnsiō *f*, obiūrgātiō *f* ♦ *vt* reprehendere, obiūrgāre, increpāre.

rebut *vt* refūtāre, redarguere.

recalcitrant *adj* invītus.

recall *n* revocātiō *f*, reditus *m* ♦ *vt* revocāre; (*from exile*) redūcere; (*to mind*) reminīscī (*gen*), recordārī (*gen*).

recant *vt* retractāre.

recantation *n* receptus *m*.

recapitulate *vt* repetere, summātim dīcere.

recapitulation *n* ēnumerātiō *f*.

recapture *vt* recipere.

recast *vt* reficere, retractāre.

recede *vi* recēdere.

receipt *n* (*act*) acceptiō *f*; (*money*) acceptum *nt*; (*written*) apocha *f*.

receive *vt* accipere, capere; (*in turn*) excipere.

receiver *n* receptor *m*.

recent *adj* recēns.

recently *adv* nūper, recēns.

receptacle *n* receptāculum *nt*.

reception *n* aditus *m*, hospitium *nt*.

receptive *adj* docilis.

recess *n* recessus *m*, angulus *m*; (*holiday*) fēriae *fpl*.

recharge *vt* replēre.

recipe *n* compositiō *f*.

recipient *n* quī accipit.

reciprocal *adj* mūtuus.

reciprocally *adv* mūtuō, inter sē.

reciprocate *vt* referre, reddere.

reciprocity *n* mūtuum *nt*.

recital *n* nārrātiō *f*, ēnumerātiō *f*; (*LIT*) recitātiō *f*.

recitation *n* recitātiō *f*.

recite *vt* recitāre; (*details*) ēnumerāre.

reciter *n* recitātor *m*.

reck *vt* ratiōnem habēre (*gen*).

reckless *adj* temerārius, incautus, praeceps.

recklessly *adv* incautē, temerē.

recklessness *n* temeritās *f*, neglegentia *f*.

reckon *vt* (*count*) computāre, numerāre; (*think*) cēnsēre, dūcere; (*estimate*) aestimāre; **~ on** cōnfīdere (*dat*); **~ up** dīnumerāre; (*cost*) aestimāre; **~ with** contendere cum.

reckoning *n* ratiō *f*.

reclaim *vt* repetere; (*from error*) revocāre.

recline *vi* recumbere; (*at table*) accumbere; (*plur*) discumbere.

recluse *n* homō sōlitārius *m*.

recognition *n* cognitiō *f*.

recognizance *n* vadimōnium *nt*.

recognize *vt* agnōscere; (*approve*) accipere; (*admit*) fatērī.

recoil *vi* resilīre; **~ from** refugere; **~ upon** recidere in (*acc*).

recollect *vt* reminīscī (*gen*).

recollection *n* memoria *f*, recordātiō *f*.

recommence *vt* renovāre, redintegrāre.

recommend *vt* commendāre; (*advise*) suādēre (*dat*).

recommendation *n* commendātiō *f*; (*advice*) cōnsilium *nt*; **letter of ~** litterae commendātīciae.

recompense *vt* remūnerārī, grātiam referre (*dat*) ♦ *n* praemium *nt*, remūnerātiō *f*.

reconcile *vt* compōnere, reconciliāre; **be ~d in** grātiam redīre.

reconciliation *n* reconciliātiō *f*, grātia *f*.

recondite *adj* reconditus, abstrūsus.

recondition *vt* reficere.

reconnaissance *n* explōrātiō *f*.

reconnoitre *vt*, *vi* explōrāre; **without reconnoitring** inexplōrātō.

reconquer *vt* recipere.

reconsider *vt* reputāre, retractāre.

reconstruct *vt* restituere, renovāre.

reconstruction *n* renovātiō *f*.

record *n* monumentum *nt*; (*LIT*) commentārius *m*; **~s** *pl* tabulae *fpl*, fāstī *mpl*, ācta *ntpl*; **break the ~** priōrēs omnēs superāre ♦ *vt* in commentārium referre; (*history*) perscrībere, nārrāre.

recount *vt* nārrāre, commemorāre.

recourse *n*: **have ~ to** (*for safety*) cōnfugere ad; (*as expedient*) dēcurrere ad.

recover *vt* recipere, recuperāre; (*loss*) reparāre; **~ oneself** sē colligere; **~ one's senses** ad sānitātem revertī ♦ *vi* convalēscere.

recovery *n* recuperātiō *f*; (*from illness*) salūs *f*.

recreate *vt* recreāre.

recreation *n* requiēs *f*, remissiō *f*, lūdus *m*.

recriminate *vi* in vicem accūsāre.

recrimination *n* mūtua accūsātiō *f*.

recruit *n* tīrō *m* ♦ *vt* (*MIL*) cōnscrībere; (*strength*) reficere.

recruiting officer n conquīsītor m.
rectify vt corrigere, ēmendāre.
rectitude n probitās f.
recumbent adj supīnus.
recuperate vi convalēscere.
recur vi recurrere, redīre.
recurrence n reditus m, reversiō f.
recurrent adj adsiduus.
red adj ruber.
redden vi ērubēscere ♦ vt rutilāre.
reddish adj subrūfus.
redeem vt redimere, līberāre.
redeemer n līberātor m.
redemption n redemptiō f.
red-haired adj rūfus.
red-handed adj: **catch ~ in** manifestō scelere dēprehendere.
red-hot adj fervēns.
red lead n minium nt.
redness n rubor m.
redolent adj: **be ~ of** redolēre.
redouble vt ingemināre.
redoubt n prōpugnāculum nt.
redoubtable adj īnfestus, formīdolōsus.
redound vi redundāre; **it ~s to my credit** mihī honōrī est.
redress n remedium nt; **demand ~** rēs repetere ♦ vt restituere.
reduce vt minuere, attenuāre; (to a condition) redigere, dēdūcere; (MIL) expugnāre; **~ to the ranks** in ōrdinem cōgere.
reduction n imminūtiō f; (MIL) expugnātiō f.
redundancy n redundantia f.
redundant adj redundāns; **be ~** redundāre.
reduplication n gemīnātiō f.
re-echo vt reddere, referre ♦ vi resonāre.
reed n harundō f.
reedy adj harundineus.
reef n saxa ntpl ♦ vt (sail) subnectere.
reek n fūmus m ♦ vi fūmāre.
reel vi vacillāre, titubāre.
re-enlist vt rescrībere.
re-establish vt restituere.
refashion vt reficere.
refer vt (person) dēlēgāre; (matter) rēicere, remittere ♦ vi: **~ to** spectāre ad; (in speech) attingere, perstringere.
referee n arbiter m.
reference n ratiō f; (in book) locus m.
refine vt excolere, expolīre; (metal) excoquere.
refined adj hūmānus, urbānus, polītus.
refinement n hūmānitās f, cultus m, ēlegantia f.
refit vt reficere.
reflect vt reddere, repercutere ♦ vi meditārī; **~ upon** cōnsīderāre, sēcum reputāre; (blame) reprehendere.
reflection n (of light) repercussus m; (image) imāgō f; (thought) meditātiō f, cōgitātiō f; (blame) reprehēnsiō f; **cast ~s on** maculīs aspergere, vitiō vertere; **with due ~** cōnsīderātē; **without ~** incōnsultē.

reflux n recessus m.
reform n ēmendātiō f ♦ vt (lines) restituere; (error) corrigere, ēmendāre, meliōrem facere ♦ vi sē corrigere.
reformation n corrēctiō f.
reformer n corrēctor m, ēmendātor m.
refract vt īnfringere.
refractory adj contumāx.
refrain vi temperāre, abstinēre (dat), supersedēre (inf).
refresh vt recreāre, renovāre, reficere; (mind) integrāre.
refreshed adj requiētus.
refreshing adj dulcis, iūcundus.
refreshment n cibus m.
refuge n perfugium nt; (secret) latebra f; **take ~ with** perfugere ad (acc); **take ~ in** confugere.
refugee n profugus m.
refulgence n splendor m.
refulgent adj splendidus.
refund vt reddere.
refusal n recūsātiō f, dētrectātiō f.
refuse n pūrgāmenta ntpl; (fig) faex f ♦ vt (request) dēnegāre; (offer) dētrectāre, recūsāre; (with verb) nōlle.
refutation n refūtātiō f, reprehēnsiō f.
refute vt refellere, redarguere, revincere.
regain vt recipere.
regal adj rēgius, rēgālis.
regale vt excipere, dēlectāre; **~ oneself** epulārī.
regalia n īnsignia ntpl.
regally adv rēgāliter.
regard n respectus m, ratiō f; (esteem) grātia f; **with ~ to** ad (acc), quod attinet ad ♦ vt (look) intuērī, spectāre; (deem) habēre, dūcere; **send ~s to** salūtem dīcere (dat).
regarding prep dē (abl).
regardless adj neglegēns, immemor.
regency n interrēgnum nt.
regent n interrēx m.
regicide n (person) rēgis interfector m; (act) rēgis caedēs f.
regime n administrātiō f.
regimen n vīctus m.
regiment n legiō f.
region n regiō f, tractus m.
register n tabulae fpl, album nt ♦ vt in tabulās referre, perscrībere; (emotion) ostendere, sūmere.
registrar n tabulārius m.
registry n tabulārium nt.
regret n dolor m; (for past) dēsīderium nt; (for fault) paenitentia f ♦ vt dolēre; **I ~** mē paenitet, mē piget (gen).
regretful adj maestus.
regretfully adv dolenter.
regrettable adj īnfēlīx, īnfortūnātus.
regular adj (consistent) cōnstāns; (orderly) ōrdinātus; (habitual) solitus, adsiduus; (proper) iūstus, rēctus.
regularity n moderātiō f, ōrdō m; (consistency) cōnstantia f.

regularly *adv* ōrdine; cōnstanter; iūstē, rēctē.
regulate *vt* ōrdināre, dīrigere; (*control*) moderārī.
regulation *n* lēx *f*, dēcrētum *nt*.
rehabilitate *vt* restituere.
rehearsal *n* meditātiō *f*.
rehearse *vt* meditārī.
reign *n* rēgnum *nt*; (*emperor's*) prīncipātus *m*; **in the ~ of Numa** rēgnante Numā ♦ *vi* rēgnāre; (*fig*) domonārī.
reimburse *vt* rependere.
rein *n* habēna *f*; **give full ~ to** habēnās immittere ♦ *vt* īnfrēnāre.
reindeer *n* rēnō *m*.
reinforce *vt* firmāre, cōnfirmāre.
reinforcement *n* subsidium *nt*; **~s** *pl* novae cōpiae *fpl*.
reinstate *vt* restituere, redūcere.
reinstatement *n* restitūtiō *f*, reductiō *f*; (*to legal privileges*) postlīminium *nt*.
reinvigorate *vt* recreāre.
reiterate *vt* dictitāre, iterāre.
reiteration *n* iterātiō *f*.
reject *vt* rēicere; (*with scorn*) respuere, aspernārī, repudiāre.
rejection *n* rēiectiō *f*, repulsa *f*.
rejoice *vi* gaudēre, laetārī ♦ *vt* dēlectāre.
rejoicing *n* gaudium *nt*.
rejoin *vt* redīre ad ♦ *vi* respondēre.
rejoinder *n* respōnsum *nt*.
rejuvenate *vt*: **be ~d** repuerāscere.
rekindle *vt* suscitāre.
relapse *vi* recidere.
relate *vt* (*tell*) nārrāre, commemorāre, expōnere; (*compare*) cōnferre ♦ *vi* pertinēre.
related *adj* propinquus; (*by birth*) cognātus; (*by marriage*) adfīnis; (*fig*) fīnitimus.
relation *n* (*tale*) nārrātiō *f*; (*connection*) ratiō *f*; (*kin*) necessārius *m*, cognātus *m*, adfīnis *m*.
relationship *n* necessitūdō *f*; (*by birth*) cognātiō *f*; (*by marriage*) adfīnitās *f*; (*connection*) vīcīnitās *f*.
relative *adj* cum cēterīs comparātus ♦ *n* propinquus *m*, cognātus *m*, adfīnis *m*, necessārius *m*.
relatively *adv* ex comparātiōne.
relax *vt* laxāre, remittere ♦ *vi* languēscere.
relaxation *n* remissiō *f*, requiēs *f*, lūdus *m*.
relay *n*: **~s of horses** dispositī equī *mpl*.
release *vt* solvere, exsolvere, līberāre, expedīre; (*law*) absolvere ♦ *n* missiō *f*, līberātiō *f*.
relegate *vt* relēgāre.
relent *vi* concēdere, plācārī, flectī.
relentless *adj* immisericors, inexōrābilis; (*things*) improbus.
relevant *adj* ad rem.
reliability *n* fīdūcia *f*.
reliable *adj* fīdus.
reliance *n* fīdūcia *f*, fidēs *f*.
reliant *adj* frētus.
relic *n* rēliquiae *fpl*.

relief *n* levātiō *f*, levāmen *nt*, adlevāmentum *nt*; (*aid*) subsidium *nt*; (*turn of duty*) vicēs *fpl*; (*art*) ēminentia *f*; (*sculpture*) toreuma *nt*; **bas ~** anaglypta *ntpl*; **in ~** ēminēns, expressus; **throw into ~** exprimere, distinguere.
relieve *vt* levāre, sublevāre; (*aid*) subvenīre (*dat*); (*duty*) succēdere (*dat*), excipere; (*art*) distinguere.
religion *n* religiō *f*, deōrum cultus *m*.
religious *adj* religiōsus, pius; **~ feeling** religiō *f*.
religiously *adv* religiōsē.
relinquish *vt* relinquere; (*office*) sē abdicāre (*abl*).
relish *n* sapor *m*; (*sauce*) condīmentum *nt*; (*zest*) studium *nt* ♦ *vt* dēlectārī (*abl*).
reluctance *n*: **with ~** invītus.
reluctant *adj* invītus.
reluctantly *adv* invītus, gravātē.
rely *vi* fīdere (*dat*), cōnfīdere (*dat*).
relying *adj* frētus (*abl*).
remain *vi* manēre, morārī; (*left over*) restāre, superesse.
remainder *n* reliquum *nt*.
remaining *adj* reliquus; **the ~** cēterī *pl*.
remains *n* rēliquiae *fpl*.
remand *vt* (*law*) ampliāre.
remark *n* dictum *nt* ♦ *vt* dīcere; (*note*) observāre.
remarkable *adj* īnsignis, ēgregius, memorābilis.
remarkably *adv* īnsignītē, ēgregiē.
remediable *adj* sānābilis.
remedy *n* remedium *nt* ♦ *vt* medērī (*dat*), sānāre.
remember *vt* meminisse (*gen*); (*recall*) recordārī (*gen*), reminīscī (*gen*).
remembrance *n* memoria *f*, recordātiō *f*.
remind *vt* admonēre, commonefacere.
reminder *n* admonitiō *f*, admonitum *nt*.
reminiscence *n* recordātiō *f*.
remiss *adj* dissolūtus, neglegēns.
remission *n* venia *f*.
remissness *n* neglegentia *f*.
remit *vt* remittere; (*fault*) ignōscere (*dat*); (*debt*) dōnāre; (*punishment*) condōnāre; (*question*) referre.
remittance *n* pecūnia *f*.
remnant *n* fragmentum *nt*; **~s** *pl* rēliquiae *fpl*.
remonstrance *n* obtestātiō *f*, obiūrgātiō *f*.
remonstrate *vi* reclāmāre; **~ with** obiūrgāre; **~ about** expostulāre.
remorse *n* paenitentia *f*, cōnscientia *f*.
remorseless *adj* immisericors.
remote *adj* remōtus, reconditus.
remotely *adv* procul.
remoteness *n* longinquitās *f*.
removal *n* āmōtiō *f*; (*going*) migrātiō *f*.
remove *vt* āmovēre, dēmere, eximere, removēre; (*out of the way*) dēmovēre ♦ *vi* migrāre, dēmigrāre.
remunerate *vt* remūnerārī.
remuneration *n* mercēs *f*, praemium *nt*.

rend vt scindere, dīvellere.

render vt reddere; (*music*) interpretārī; (*translation*) vertere; (*thanks*) referre.

rendering n interpretātiō f.

rendez-vous n cōnstitūtum nt.

renegade n dēsertor m.

renew vt renovāre, integrāre, īnstaurāre, redintegrāre.

renewal n renovātiō f; (*ceremony*) īnstaurātiō f.

renounce vt renūntiāre, mittere, repudiāre.

renovate vt renovāre, reficere.

renown n fāma f, glōria f.

renowned adj praeclārus, īnsignis, nōtus.

rent n (*tear*) fissum nt; (*pay*) mercēs f ♦ vt (*hire*) condūcere; (*lease*) locāre.

renunciation n cessiō f, repudiātiō f.

repair vt reficere, sarcīre ♦ vi sē recipere ♦ n: **keep in good ~** tuērī; **in bad ~** ruīnōsus.

reparable adj ēmendābilis.

reparation n satisfactiō f.

repartee n facētiae fpl, salēs mpl.

repast n cēna f, cibus m.

repay vt remūnerārī, grātiam referre (*dat*); (*money*) repōnere.

repayment n solūtiō f.

repeal vt abrogāre ♦ n abrogātiō f.

repeat vt iterāre; (*lesson*) reddere; (*ceremony*) īnstaurāre; (*performance*) referre.

repeatedly adv identidem, etiam atque etiam.

repel vt repellere, dēfendere.

repellent adj iniūcundus.

repent vi: **I ~** mē paenitet (+ *gen of thing*).

repentance n paenitentia f.

repentant adj paenitēns.

repercussion n ēventus m.

repertory n thēsaurus m.

repetition n iterātiō f.

repine vi conquerī.

replace vt repōnere, restituere; **~ by** substituere.

replacement n supplēmentum nt.

replenish vt replēre, supplēre.

replete adj plēnus.

repletion n satietās f.

replica n apographon nt.

reply vi respondēre ♦ n respōnsum nt.

report n (*talk*) fāma f, rūmor m; (*repute*) opīniō f; (*account*) renūntiātiō f, litterae fpl; (*noise*) fragor m; **make a ~** renūntiāre ♦ vt referre, dēferre, renūntiāre.

repose n quiēs f, requiēs f ♦ vt repōnere, pōnere ♦ vi quiēscere.

repository n horreum nt.

reprehend vt reprehendere, culpāre.

reprehensible adj accūsābilis, improbus.

reprehension n reprehēnsiō f, culpa f.

represent vt dēscrībere, effingere, exprimere, imitārī; (*character*) partēs agere (*gen*), persōnam gerere (*gen*); (*case*) prōpōnere; (*substitute for*) vicārium esse (*gen*).

representation n imāgō f, imitātiō f; **make ~s to** admonēre.

representative n lēgātus m.

repress vt reprimere, cohibēre.

repression n coercitiō f.

reprieve n mora f, venia f ♦ vt veniam dare (*dat*).

reprimand vt reprehendere, increpāre ♦ n reprehēnsiō f.

reprisals n ultiō f.

reproach vt exprobāre, obicere (*dat*) ♦ n exprobrātiō f, probrum nt; (*cause*) opprobrium nt.

reproachful adj contumēliōsus.

reprobate adj perditus.

reproduce vt propāgāre; (*likeness*) referre.

reproduction n prōcreātiō f; (*likeness*) imāgō f.

reproductive adj genitālis.

reproof n reprehēnsiō f, obiūrgātiō f.

reprove vt reprehendere, increpāre, obiūrgāre.

reptile n serpēns f.

republic n lībera rēspūblica f, cīvitās populāris f.

republican adj populāris.

repudiate vt repudiāre.

repudiation n repudiātiō f.

repugnance n fastīdium nt, odium nt.

repugnant adj invīsus, adversus.

repulse n dēpulsiō f; (*at election*) repulsa f ♦ vt repellere, āversārī, prōpulsāre.

repulsion n repugnantia f.

repulsive adj odiōsus, foedus.

reputable adj honestus.

reputation n fāma f, existimātiō f; (*for something*) opīniō f (*gen*); **have a ~** nōmen habēre.

repute n fāma f, existimātiō f; **bad ~** īnfāmia f.

reputed adj: **I am ~ to be** dīcor esse.

request n rogātiō f, postulātum nt; **obtain a ~** impetrāre ♦ vt rogāre, petere; (*urgently*) dēposcere.

require vt (*demand*) imperāre, postulāre; (*need*) egēre (*abl*); (*call for*) requīrere.

requirement n postulātum nt, necessārium nt.

requisite adj necessārius.

requisition n postulātiō f ♦ vt imperāre.

requital n grātia f, vicēs fpl.

requite vt grātiam referre (*dat*), remūnerārī.

rescind vt rescindere, abrogāre.

rescript n rescrīptum nt.

rescue vt ēripere, expedīre, servāre ♦ n salūs f; **come to the ~ of** subvenīre (*dat*).

research n investīgātiō f.

resemblance n similitūdō f, imāgō f, īnstar nt.

resemble vt similem esse (*dat*), referre.

resent vt aegrē ferre, indignārī.

resentful adj īrācundus.

resentment n dolor m, indignātiō f.

reservation n (*proviso*) exceptiō f.

reserve vt servāre; (*store*) recondere; (*in a deal*) excipere ♦ nt (*MIL*) subsidium nt; (*disposition*) pudor m, reticentia f; (*caution*) cautiō f; **in ~** in succenturiātus; **without ~**

palam.
reserved *adj* (*place*) adsignātus; (*disposition*) taciturnus, tēctus.
reservedly *adv* circumspectē.
reserves *npl* subsidia *ntpl*.
reservoir *n* lacus *m*.
reside *vi* habitāre; ~ **in** incolere.
residence *n* domicilium *nt*, domus *f*.
resident *n* incola *m/f*.
residual *adj* reliquus.
residue, residuum *n* reliqua pars *f*.
resign *vt* cēdere; (*office*) abdicāre mē, tē *etc* dē (+ *abl*); ~ **oneself** acquiēscere ♦ *vi* sē abdicāre.
resignation *n* abdicātiō *f*; (*state of mind*) patientia *f*, aequus animus *m*.
resigned *adj* patiēns; **be ~ to** aequō animō ferre.
resilience *n* mollitia *f*.
resilient *adj* mollis.
resist *vt* resistere (*dat*), adversārī (*dat*), repugnāre (*dat*).
resistance *n* repugnantia *f*; **offer ~** obsistere (*dat*).
resistless *adj* invictus.
resolute *adj* fortis, cōnstāns.
resolutely *adv* fortiter, cōnstanter.
resolution *n* (*conduct*) fortitūdō *f*, cōnstantia *f*; (*decision*) dēcrētum *nt*, sententia *f*; (*into parts*) sēcrētiō *f*.
resolve *n* fortitūdō *f*, cōnstantia *f* ♦ *vt* dēcernere, cōnstituere; (*into parts*) dissolvere; **the senate ~s** placet senātuī.
resonance *n* sonus *m*.
resonant *adj* canōrus.
resort *n* locus celeber *m*; **last ~** ultimum auxilium *nt* ♦ *vi* frequentāre, ventitāre; (*have recourse*) dēcurrere, dēscendere, cōnfugere.
resound *vi* resonāre, personāre.
resource *n* subsidium *nt*; (*means*) modus *m*; **~s** *pl* opēs *fpl*, cōpiae *fpl*.
resourceful *adj* versūtus, callidus.
resourcefulness *n* calliditās *f*, versūtus animus *m*.
respect *n* (*esteem*) honōs *m*, observantia *f*; (*reference*) ratiō *f*; **out of ~** honōris causā; **pay one's ~s to** salūtāre; **show ~ for** observāre; **in every ~** ex omnī parte, in omnī genere; **in ~ of** ad (*acc*), ab (*abl*) ♦ *vt* honōrāre, observāre, verērī.
respectability *n* honestās *f*.
respectable *adj* honestus, līberālis, frūgī.
respectably *adv* honestē.
respectful *adj* observāns.
respectfully *adv* reverenter.
respectfulness *n* observantia *f*.
respective *adj* suus (*with* quisque).
respectively *adv* alius ... alius.
respiration *n* respīrātiō *f*, spīritus *m*.
respire *vi* respīrāre.
respite *n* requiēs *f*, intercapēdō *f*, intermissiō *f*.
resplendence *n* splendor *m*.

resplendent *adj* splendidus, illūstris.
resplendently *adv* splendidē.
respond *vi* respondēre.
response *n* respōnsum *nt*.
responsibility *n* auctōritās *f*, cūra *f*.
responsible *adj* reus; (*witness*) locuplēs; **be ~ for** praestāre.
responsive *adj* (*pupil*) docilis; (*character*) facilis.
rest *n* quiēs *f*, ōtium *nt*; (*after toil*) requiēs *f*; (*remainder*) reliqua pars *f*; **be at ~** requiēscere; **set at ~** tranquillāre; **the ~ of** reliquī ♦ *vi* requiēscere, acquiēscere; **~ on** nītī (*abl*), innītī in (*abl*) ♦ *vt* (*hope*) pōnere in (*abl*).
rest *n* cēterī *mpl*.
resting place *n* cubīle *nt*, sēdēs *f*.
restitution *n* satisfactiō *f*; **make ~** restituere; **demand ~** rēs repetere.
restive *adj* contumāx.
restless *adj* inquiētus, sollicitus; **be ~** fluctuārī.
restlessness *n* sollicitūdō *f*.
restoration *n* renovātiō *f*; (*of king*) reductiō *f*.
restore *vt* reddere, restituere; (*to health*) recreāre; (*to power*) redūcere; (*damage*) reficere, redintegrāre.
restorer *n* restitūtor *m*.
restrain *vt* coercēre, comprimere, cohibēre.
restraint *n* moderātiō *f*, temperantia *f*, frēnī *mpl*; **with ~** abstinenter.
restrict *vt* continēre, circumscrībere.
restricted *adj* artus; **~ to** proprius (*gen*).
restriction *n* modus *m*, fīnis *m*; (*limitation*) exceptiō *f*.
result *n* ēventus *m*, ēventum *nt*, exitus *m*; **the ~ is that** quō fit ut ♦ *vi* ēvenīre, ēvādere.
resultant *adj* cōnsequēns.
resume *vt* repetere.
resuscitate *vt* excitāre, suscitāre.
retail *vt* dīvēndere, vēndere.
retailer *n* caupō *m*.
retain *vt* retinēre, tenēre, cōnservāre.
retainer *n* satelles *m*.
retake *vt* recipere.
retaliate *vi* ulcīscī.
retaliation *n* ultiō *f*.
retard *vt* retardāre, remorārī.
retention *n* cōnservātiō *f*.
retentive *adj* tenāx.
reticence *n* taciturnitās *f*.
reticent *adj* taciturnus.
reticulated *adj* rēticulātus.
retinue *n* satellitēs *mpl*, comitātus *m*.
retire *vi* recēdere, abscēdere; (*from office*) abīre; (*from province*) dēcēdere; (*MIL*) pedem referre, sē recipere.
retired *adj* ēmeritus; (*place*) remōtus.
retirement *n* (*act*) recessus *m*, dēcessus *m*; (*state*) sōlitūdō *f*, ōtium *nt*; **life of ~** vīta prīvāta.
retiring *adj* modestus, verēcundus.
retort *vt* respondēre, referre ♦ *n*

respōnsum *nt.*
retouch *vt* retractāre.
retrace *vt* repetere, iterāre.
retract *vt* revocāre, renūntiāre.
retreat *n* (MIL) receptus *m;* (*place*) recessus *m,*
sēcessus *m;* **sound the ~** receptuī canere ♦ *vi*
sē recipere, pedem referre; regredī.
retrench *vt* minuere, recīdere.
retrenchment *n* parsimōnia *f.*
retribution *n* poena *f.*
retributive *adj* ultor, ultrīx.
retrieve *vt* reparāre, recipere.
retrograde *adj* (*fig*) dēterior.
retrogression *n* regressus *m.*
retrospect *n:* **in ~** respicientī.
retrospective *adj:* **be ~** retrōrsum sē referre.
retrospectively *adv* retrō.
return *n* reditus *m;* (*pay*) remūnerātiō *f;* (*profit*)
fructus *m,* pretium *nt;* (*statement*) professiō *f;*
make a ~ of profitērī; **in ~ for** prō (+ *abl*); **in ~**
in vicem, vicissim ♦ *vt* reddere, restituere,
referre ♦ *vi* redīre, revenīre, revertī; (*from*
province) dēcēdere.
reunion *n* convīvium *nt.*
reunite *vt* reconciliāre.
reveal *vt* aperīre, patefacere.
revel *n* cōmissātiō *f,* bacchātiō *f;* **~s** *pl* orgia *ntpl*
♦ *vi* cōmissārī, bacchārī; **~ in** luxuriārī.
revelation *n* patefactiō *f.*
reveller *n* cōmissātor *m.*
revelry *n* cōmissātiō *f.*
revenge *n* ultiō *f;* **take ~ on** vindicāre in (*acc*) ♦
vt ulcīscī.
revengeful *adj* ulcīscendī cupidus.
revenue *n* fructus *m,* reditus *m,* vectīgālia *ntpl.*
reverberate *vi* resonāre.
reverberation *n* repercussus *m.*
revere *vt* venerārī, colere.
reverence *n* venerātiō *f;* (*feeling*) religiō *f;*
reverentia *f.*
reverent *adj* religiōsus, pius.
reverently *adv* religiōsē.
reverie *n* meditātiō *f,* somnium *nt.*
reversal *n* abrogātiō *f.*
reverse *adj* contrārius ♦ *n* contrārium *nt;* (MIL)
clādēs *f* ♦ *vt* invertere; (*decision*) rescindere.
reversion *n* reditus *m.*
revert *vi* redīre, revertī.
review *n* recognitiō *f,* recēnsiō *f* ♦ *vt* (MIL)
recēnsēre.
revile *vt* maledīcere (*dat*).
revise *vt* recognōscere, corrigere; (LIT) līmāre.
revision *n* ēmendātiō *f;* (LIT) līma *f.*
revisit *vt* revīsere.
revival *n* renovātiō *f.*
revive *vt* recreāre, excitāre ♦ *vi* revīvīscere,
renāscī.
revocation *n* revocātiō *f.*
revoke *vt* renūntiāre, īnfectum reddere.
revolt *n* sēditiō *f,* dēfectiō *f* ♦ *vi* dēficere,
rebellāre.
revolting *adj* taeter, obscēnus.
revolution *n* (*movement*) conversiō *f;* (*change*)

rēs novae *fpl;* (*revolt*) mōtus *m;* **effect a ~** rēs
novāre.
revolutionary *adj* sēditiōsus, novārum rērum
cupidus.
revolve *vi* volvī, versārī, convertī ♦ *vt* (*in*
mind) volūtāre.
revulsion *n* mūtātiō *f.*
reward *n* praemium *nt,* mercēs *f* ♦ *vt*
remūnerārī, compēnsāre.
rhapsody *n* carmen *nt;* (*epic*) rhapsōdia *f.*
rhetoric *n* rhētorica *f;* **of ~** rhētoricus; **exercise**
in ~ dēclāmātiō *f;* **practise ~** dēclāmāre;
teacher of ~ rhētōr *m.*
rhetorical *adj* rhētoricus, dēclāmātōrius.
rhetorically *adv* rhētoricē.
rhetorician *n* rhētōr *m,* dēclāmātor *m.*
rhinoceros *n* rhīnocerōs *m.*
rhyme *n* homoeoteleuton *nt;* **without ~ or**
reason temerē.
rhythm *n* numerus *m,* modus *m.*
rhythmical *adj* numerōsus.
rib *n* costa *f.*
ribald *adj* obscēnus.
ribaldry *n* obscēnitās *f.*
ribbon *n* īnfula *f.*
rice *n* oryza *f.*
rich *adj* dīves, locuplēs; opulentus; (*fertile*)
ūber, opīmus; (*food*) pinguis.
riches *n* dīvitiae *fpl,* opēs *fpl.*
richly *adv* opulentē, largē, lautē.
richness *n* ūbertās *f,* cōpia *f.*
rid *vt* līberāre; **get ~ of** dēpōnere, dēmovēre,
exuere.
riddle *n* aenigma *nt;* (*sieve*) cribrum *nt* ♦ *vt*
(*with wounds*) cōnfodere.
ride *vi* equitāre, vehī; **~ a horse** in equō vehī; **~**
at anchor stāre; **~ away** abequitāre, āvehī; **~**
back revehī; **~ between** interequitāre; **~**
down dēvehī; **~ into** invehī; **~ off** āvehī; **~ out**
ēvehī; **~ past** praetervehī; **~ round**
circumvehī (*dat*), circumequitāre; **~ up and**
down perequitāre; **~ up to** adequitāre ad,
advehī ad.
rider *n* eques *m.*
ridge *n* iugum *nt.*
ridicule *n* lūdibrium *nt,* irrīsus *m* ♦ *vt* irrīdēre,
illūdere, lūdibriō habēre.
ridiculous *adj* rīdiculus, dērīdiculus.
ridiculously *adv* rīdiculē.
riding *n* equitātiō *f.*
rife *adj* frequēns.
riff-raff *n* faex populī *f.*
rifle *vt* expīlāre, spoliāre.
rift *n* rīma *f.*
rig *vt* (*ship*) armāre, ōrnāre ♦ *n* habitus *m.*
rigging *n* rudentēs *mpl.*
right *adj* rēctus; (*just*) aequus, iūstus; (*true*)
rēctus, vērus; (*proper*) lēgitimus, fās; (*hand*)
dexter; **it is ~** decet (+ *acc and infin*); **it is not ~**
dēdecet (+ *acc and infin*); **you are ~** vēra dīcis;
if I am ~ nisi fallor; **in the ~ place** in locō; **at**
the ~ time ad tempus; **at ~ angles** ad parēs
angulōs; **on the ~** ā dextrā ♦ *adv* rēctē, bene,

probē; (_justifiably_) iūre; ~ **up to** usque ad
(+ _acc_); ~ **on** rēctā ♦ _n_ (_legal_) iūs _nt_; (_moral_) fās
_nt_ ♦ _vt_ (_replace_) restituere; (_correct_)
corrigere; (_avenge_) ulcīscī.
righteous _adj_ iūstus, sanctus, pius.
righteously _adv_ iūstē, sanctē, piē.
righteousness _n_ sanctitās _f_, pietās _f_.
rightful _adj_ iūstus, lēgitimus.
rightfully _adv_ iūstē, lēgitimē.
right hand _n_ dextra _f_.
right-hand _adj_ dexter; ~ **man** comes _m_.
rightly _adv_ rēctē, bene; iūre.
right-minded _adj_ sānus.
rigid _adj_ rigidus.
rigidity _n_ rigor _m_; (_strictness_) sevēritās _f_.
rigidly _adv_ rigidē, sevērē.
rigmarole _n_ ambāgēs _fpl_.
rigorous _adj_ dūrus; (_strict_) sevērus.
rigorously _adv_ dūriter, sevērē.
rigour _n_ dūritia _f_; sevēritās _f_.
rile _vt_ inrītāre, stomachum movēre (_dat_).
rill _n_ rīvulus _m_.
rim _n_ labrum _nt_.
rime _n_ pruīna _f_.
rind _n_ cortex _m_.
ring _n_ ānulus _m_; (_circle_) orbis _m_; (_of people_)
corōna _f_; (_motion_) gȳrus _m_ ♦ _vt_ circumdare;
(_bell_) movēre ♦ _vi_ tinnīre, sonāre.
ringing _n_ tinnītus _m_ ♦ _adj_ canōrus.
ringleader _n_ caput _nt_, dux _m_.
ringlet _n_ cincinnus _m_.
rinse _vt_ colluere.
riot _n_ tumultus _m_, rixa _f_; **run** ~ exsultāre,
luxuriārī, tumultuārī, turbās efficere; (_revel_)
bacchārī.
rioter _n_ cōmissātor _m_.
riotous _adj_ tumultuōsus, sēditiōsus;
(_debauched_) dissolūtus; ~ **living** cōmissātiō _f_,
luxuria _f_.
riotously _adv_ tumultuōsē; luxuriōsē.
rip _vt_ scindere.
ripe _adj_ mātūrus; **of** ~ **judgment** animī
mātūrus.
ripen _vt_ mātūrāre ♦ _vi_ mātūrēscere.
ripeness _n_ mātūritās _f_.
ripple _n_ unda _f_ ♦ _vi_ trepidāre.
rise _vi_ orīrī, surgere; (_hill_) ascendere; (_wind_)
cōnsurgere; (_passion_) tumēscere; (_voice_)
tollī; (_in size_) crēscere; (_in rank_) ascendere;
(_in revolt_) coorīrī, arma capere; ~ **and fall**
(_tide_) reciprocāre; ~ **above** superāre; ~ **again**
resurgere; ~ **in** (_river_) orīrī ex (_abl_); ~ **out**
ēmergere; ~ **up** exsurgere ♦ _n_ ascēnsus _m_;
(_slope_) clīvus _m_; (_increase_) incrēmentum _nt_;
(_start_) ortus _m_; **give** ~ **to** parere.
rising _n_ (_sun_) ortus _m_; (_revolt_) mōtus _m_ ♦ _adj_
(_ground_) ēditus.
risk _n_ perīculum _nt_; **run a** ~ perīculum subīre,
ingredī ♦ _vt_ perīclitārī, in āleam dare.
risky _adj_ perīculōsus.
rite _n_ rītus _m_.
ritual _n_ caerimōnia _f_.
rival _adj_ aemulus ♦ _n_ aemulus _m_, rīvālis _m_ ♦ _vt_

aemulārī.
rivalry _n_ aemulātiō _f_.
river _n_ flūmen _nt_, fluvius _m_ ♦ _adj_ fluviātilis.
riverbed _n_ alveus _m_.
riverside _n_ rīpa _f_.
rivet _n_ clāvus _m_ ♦ _vt_ (_attention_) dēfīgere.
rivulet _n_ rīvulus _m_, rīvus _m_.
road _n_ via _f_, iter _nt_; **on the** ~ in itinere, ex
itinere; **off the** ~ dēvius; **make a** ~ viam
mūnīre.
roadstead _n_ statiō _f_.
roam _vi_ errāre, vagārī; ~ **at large** ēvagārī.
roar _n_ fremitus _m_ ♦ _vi_ fremere.
roast _vt_ torrēre ♦ _adj_ assus ♦ _n_ assum _nt_.
rob _vt_ spoliāre, exspoliāre, expīlāre; (_of hope_)
dēicere dē.
robber _n_ latrō _m_, fūr _m_; (_highway_) grassātor _m_.
robbery _n_ latrōcinium _nt_.
robe _n_ vestis _f_; (_woman's_) stola _f_; (_of state_)
trabea _f_ ♦ _vt_ vestīre.
robust _adj_ rōbustus, fortis.
robustness _n_ rōbur _nt_, firmitās _f_.
rock _n_ saxum _nt_; (_steep_) rūpēs _f_, scopulus _m_ ♦ _vt_
agitāre ♦ _vi_ agitārī, vacillāre.
rocky _adj_ saxōsus, scopulōsus.
rod _n_ virga _f_; (_fishing_) harundō _f_.
roe _n_ (_deer_) capreolus _m_, caprea _f_; (_fish_) ōva _ntpl_.
rogue _n_ veterātor _m_.
roguery _n_ nēquitia _f_, scelus _nt_.
roguish _adj_ improbus, malus.
role _n_ partēs _fpl_.
roll _n_ (_book_) volūmen _nt_; (_movement_) gȳrus _m_;
(_register_) album _nt_; **call the** ~ **of** legere;
answer the ~ **call** ad nōmen respondēre ♦ _vt_
volvere ♦ _vi_ volvī, volūtārī; ~ **down** _vt_
dēvolvere ♦ _vi_ dēfluere; ~ **over** _vt_ prōvolvere
♦ _vi_ prōlābī; ~ **up** _vt_ convolvere.
roller _n_ (_AGR_) cylindrus _m_; (_for moving_)
phalangae _fpl_; (_in book_) umbilīcus _m_.
rollicking _adj_ hilaris.
rolling _adj_ volūbilis.
Roman _adj_ Rōmānus ♦ _n_: **the** ~**s** Rōmānī _mpl_.
romance _n_ fābula _f_; amor _m_.
romantic _adj_ fābulōsus; amātōrius.
Rome _n_ Rōma _f_; **at** ~ Rōmae; **from** ~ Rōmā; **to** ~
Rōmam.
romp _vi_ lūdere.
roof _n_ tēctum _nt_; (_of mouth_) palātum _nt_ ♦ _vt_
tegere, integere.
rook _n_ corvus _m_.
room _n_ conclāve _nt_; camera _f_; (_small_) cella _f_;
(_bed_) cubiculum _nt_; (_dining_) cēnāculum _nt_;
(_dressing_) apodytērium _nt_; (_space_) locus _m_;
make ~ **for** locum dare (_dat_), cēdere (_dat_).
roominess _n_ laxitās _f_.
roomy _adj_ capāx.
roost _vi_ stabulārī.
rooster _n_ gallus gallīnāceus _m_.
root _n_ rādīx _f_; **take** ~ coalēscere ♦ _vt_: ~ **out**
ērādīcāre.
rooted _adj_ (_fig_) dēfixus; **deeply** ~ (_custom_)
inveterātus; **be** ~ **in** īnsidēre (_dat_); **become**
deeply ~ inveterāscere.

rope n fūnis m; (thin) restis f; (ship's) rudēns m; **know the ~s** perītum esse.
rose n rosa f.
rosemary n rōs marīnus m.
rostrum n rōstra ntpl, suggestus m.
rosy adj roseus, purpureus.
rot n tābēs f ♦ vi putrēscere, pūtēscere ♦ vt putrefacere.
rotate vi volvī, sē convertere.
rotation n conversiō f; (succession) ōrdō m, vicissitūdō f; **in ~** ōrdine; **move in ~** in orbem īre.
rote n: **by ~** memoriter.
rotten adj putridus.
rotund adj rotundus.
rotundity n rotunditās f.
rouge n fūcus m ♦ vt fūcāre.
rough adj asper; (art) incultus, rudis; (manners) agrestis, inurbānus; (stone) impolītus; (treatment) dūrus, sevērus; (weather) atrōx, procellōsus ♦ vi: **~ it** dūram vītam vīvere.
rough-and-ready adj fortuītus.
rough draft n (LIT) silva f.
roughen vt asperāre, exasperāre.
rough-hew vt dolāre.
roughly adv asperē, dūriter; (with numbers) circiter.
roughness n asperitās f.
round adj rotundus; (spherical) globōsus; (cylindrical) teres ♦ n (circle) orbis m; (motion) gȳrus m; (series) ambitus m; **go the ~s** (MIL) vigiliās circumīre ♦ vt (cape) superāre; **~ off** rotundāre; (sentence) concludere; **~ up** compellere ♦ adv circum, circā; **go ~** ambīre ♦ prep circum (acc), circā (acc).
roundabout adj: **~ story** ambāgēs fpl; **~ route** circuitus m, ānfrāctus m.
roundly adv (speak) apertē, līberē.
rouse vt excīre, excitāre; (courage) adrigere.
rousing adj vehemēns.
rout n fuga f; (crowd) turba f ♦ vt fugāre, fundere; **in fugam conicere**; prōflīgāre.
route n cursus m, iter nt.
routine n ūsus m, ōrdō m.
rove vi errāre, vagārī.
rover n vagus m; (sea) pīrāta m.
row n (line) ōrdō m; (noise) turba f, rixa f ♦ vi (boat) rēmigāre ♦ vt rēmīs incitāre.
rowdy adj turbulentus.
rower n rēmex m.
rowing n rēmigium nt.
royal adj rēgius, rēgālis.
royally adv rēgiē, rēgāliter.
royalty n (power) rēgnum nt; (persons) rēgēs mpl, domus rēgia f.
rub vt fricāre, terere; **~ away** conterere; **~ hard** dēfricāre; **~ off** dētergēre; **~ out** dēlēre; **~ up** expolīre.
rubbing n trītus m.
rubbish n quisquiliae fpl; (talk) nūgae fpl.
rubble n rūdus nt.
rubicund adj rubicundus.

rudder n gubernāculum nt, clāvus m.
ruddy adj rubicundus, rutilus.
rude adj (uncivilized) barbarus, dūrus, inurbānus; (insolent) asper, importūnus.
rudely adv horridē, rusticē; petulanter.
rudeness n barbariēs f, petulantia f, importūnitās f.
rudiment n elementum nt, initium nt.
rudimentary adj prīmus, incohātus.
rue n (herb) rūta f ♦ vt: **I ~ mē** paenitet (gen).
rueful adj maestus.
ruffian n grassātor m.
ruffle vt agitāre; (temper) sollicitāre, commovēre.
rug n strāgulum nt.
rugged adj horridus, asper.
ruggedness n asperitās f.
ruin n ruīna f; (fig) exitium nt, perniciēs f; **go to ~** pessum īre, dīlābī ♦ vt perdere, dēperdere, pessum dare; (moral) corrumpere, dēprāvāre; **be ~ed** perīre.
ruined adj ruīnōsus.
ruinous adj exitiōsus, damnōsus.
rule n (instrument) rēgula f, amussis f; (principle) nōrma f, lēx f, praeceptum nt; (government) dominātiō f, imperium nt; **ten-foot ~** decempeda f; **as a ~** ferē; **lay down ~s** praecipere; **make it a ~ to** īnstituere (inf); **~ of thumb** ūsus m ♦ vt regere, moderārī ♦ vi rēgnāre, dominārī; (judge) ēdīcere; (custom) obtinēre; **~ over** imperāre (dat).
ruler n (instrument) rēgula f; (person) dominus m, rēctor m.
ruling n ēdictum nt.
rumble vi mūgīre.
rumbling n mūgītus m.
ruminate vi rūminārī.
rummage vi: **~ through** rīmārī.
rumour n fāma f, rūmor m.
rump n clūnis f.
run vi currere; (fluid) fluere, mānāre; (road) ferre; (time) lābī ♦ n cursus m; **~ about** discurrere, cursāre; **~ across** incidere in (acc); **~ after** sectārī; **~ aground** offendere; **~ away** aufugere, terga vertere; (from) fugere, dēfugere; **~ down** dēcurrere, dēfluere ♦ vt (in words) obtrectāre; **~ high** (fig) glīscere; **~ into** incurrere in (acc), īnfluere in (acc); **~ off with** abripere, abdūcere; **~ on** pergere; **~ out** (land) excurrere; (time) exīre; (supplies) dēficere; **~ over** vt (with car) obterere; (details) percurrere; **~ riot** luxuriārī; **~ through** (course) dēcurrere; (money) disperdere; **~ short** dēficere; **~ up to** adcurrere ad; **~ up against** incurrere in (acc); **~ wild** lascīvīre ♦ vt gerere, administrāre.
runaway adj fugitīvus.
rung n gradus m.
runner n cursor m.
running n cursus m ♦ adj (water) vīvus.
rupture n (fig) dissidium nt ♦ vt dīrumpere.
rural adj rūsticus, agrestis.

ruse n fraus f, dolus m.
rush n (plant) cārex f, iuncus m; (movement)
impetus m ♦ vi currere, sē incitāre, ruere; ~
forward sē prōripere; prōruere; ~ **in** inruere,
incurrere; ~ **out** ēvolāre, sē effundere ♦ adj
iunceus.
russet adj flāvus.
rust n (iron) ferrūgō f; (copper) aerūgō f ♦ vi
rōbīginem trahere.
rustic adj rūsticus, agrestis.
rusticate vi rūsticārī ♦ vt relēgāre.
rusticity n mōrēs rūsticī mpl.
rustle vi increpāre, crepitāre ♦ n crepitus m.
rusty adj rōbīginōsus.
rut n orbita f.
ruthless adj inexōrābilis, crūdēlis.
ruthlessly adv crūdēliter.
rye n secāle nt.

S, s

sabbath n sabbata ntpl.
sable adj āter, niger.
sabre n acīnacēs m.
sacerdotal adj sacerdōtālis.
sack n saccus m; (MIL) dīreptiō f ♦ vt dīripere,
expīlāre; spoliāre.
sackcloth n cilicium nt.
sacred adj sacer, sanctus.
sacredly adv sanctē.
sacredness n sanctitās f.
sacrifice n sacrificium nt, sacrum nt; (act)
immolātiō f; (victim) hostia f; (fig) iactūra f ♦
vt immolāre, sacrificāre, mactāre; (fig)
dēvovēre, addīcere ♦ vi sacra facere; (give
up) prōicere.
sacrificer n immolātor m.
sacrilege n sacrilegium nt.
sacrilegious adj sacrilegus.
sacristan n aedituus m.
sacrosanct adj sacrōsanctus.
sad adj maestus, tristis; (thing) tristis.
sadden vt dolōre adficere.
saddle n strātum nt ♦ vt sternere; (fig)
impōnere.
saddlebags n clītellae fpl.
sadly adv maestē.
sadness n tristitia f, maestitia f.
safe adj tūtus; (out of danger) incolumis,
salvus; (to trust) fīdus. ~ **and sound** salvus ♦
n armārium nt.
safe-conduct n fidēs pūblica f.
safeguard n cautiō f, prōpugnāculum nt ♦ vt
dēfendere.
safely adv tūtō, impūne.
safety n salūs f, incolumitās f;

seek ~ **in flight** salutem fugā petere.
saffron n crocus m ♦ adj croceus.
sag vi dēmittī.
sagacious adj prūdēns, sagāx, acūtus.
sagaciously adv prūdenter, sagāciter.
sagacity n prūdentia f, sagācitās f.
sage n sapiēns m; (herb) salvia f ♦ adj sapiēns.
sagely adv sapienter.
sail n vēlum nt; **set** ~ vēla dare, nāvem solvere;
shorten ~ vēla contrahere ♦ vi nāvigāre; ~
past legere, praetervehī.
sailing n nāvigātiō f.
sailor n nauta m.
sail yard n antenna f.
saint n vir sanctus m.
sainted adj beātus.
saintly adj sanctus.
sake n: **for the** ~ **of** grātiā (gen), causā (gen),
propter (acc); (behalf) prō (abl).
salacious adj salāx.
salad n morētum nt.
salamander n salamandra f.
salary n mercēs f.
sale n vēnditiō f; (formal) mancipium nt;
(auction) hasta f; **for** ~ vēnālis; **be for** ~
prōstāre; **offer for** ~ vēnum dare.
saleable adj vēndibilis.
salient adj ēminēns; ~ **points** capita ntpl.
saline adj salsus.
saliva n salīva f.
sallow adj pallidus.
sally n ēruptiō f; (wit) facētiae fpl ♦ vi
ērumpere, excurrere.
salmon n salmō m.
salon n ātrium nt.
salt n sal m ♦ adj salsus.
saltcellar n salīnum nt.
saltpetre n nitrum nt.
salt-pits n salīnae fpl.
salty adj salsus.
salubrious adj salūbris.
salubriously adv salūbriter.
salubriousness n salūbritās f.
salutary adj salūtāris, ūtilis.
salutation n salūs f.
salute vt salūtāre.
salvage vt servāre, ēripere.
salvation n salūs f.
salve n unguentum nt.
salver n scutella f.
same adj īdem; ~ **as** īdem ac; **all the** ~
nihilōminus; **one and the** ~ūnus et īdem;
from the ~ **place** indidem; **in the** ~ **place**
ibīdem; **to the** ~ **place** eōdem; **at the** ~ **time**
simul, eōdem tempore; (adversative) tamen;
it is all the ~ **to me** meā nōn interest.
Samnites n Samnītēs, Samnītium mpl.
sample n exemplum nt, specimen nt ♦ vt
gustāre.
sanctify vt cōnsecrāre.
sanctimony n falsa rēligiō f.
sanction n comprobātiō f, auctōritās f ♦ vt
ratum facere.

sanctity n sanctitās f.
sanctuary n fānum nt, dēlubrum nt; (for men) asylum nt.
sand n harēna f.
sandal n (outdoors) crepida f; (indoors) solea f.
sandalled adj crepidātus, soleātus.
sandpit n harēnāria f.
sandstone n tōfus m.
sandy adj harēnōsus; (colour) flāvus.
sane adj sānus.
sangfroid n aequus animus m.
sanguinary adj cruentus.
sanguine adj laetus.
sanitary adj salūbris.
sanity n mēns sāna f.
sap n sūcus m ♦ vt subruere.
sapience n sapientia f.
sapient adj sapiēns.
sapling n surculus m.
sapper n cunīculārius m.
sapphire n sapphīrus f.
sarcasm n aculeī mpl, dicācitās f.
sarcastic adj dicāx, acūleātus.
sardonic adj amārus.
sash n cingulum nt.
satchel n loculus m.
sate vt explēre, satiāre.
satellite n satelles m.
satiate vt explēre, satiāre, saturāre.
satiety n satietās f.
satire n satura f; (pl, of Horace) sermōnēs mpl.
satirical adj acerbus.
satirist n saturārum scrīptor m.
satirize vt perstringere, notāre.
satisfaction n (act) explētiō f; (feeling) voluptās f; (penalty) poena f; **demand ~** rēs repetere.
satisfactorily adv ex sententiā.
satisfactory adj idōneus, grātus.
satisfied adj: **be ~** satis habēre, contentum esse.
satisfy vt satisfacere (dat); (desire) explēre.
satrap n satrapēs m.
saturate vt imbuere.
satyr n satyrus m.
sauce n condīmentum nt; (fish) garum nt.
saucer n patella f.
saucily adv petulanter.
saucy adj petulāns.
saunter vi ambulāre.
sausage n tomāculum nt, hīllae fpl.
savage adj ferus, efferātus; (cruel) atrōx, inhūmānus; saevus.
savagely adv ferōciter, inhūmānē.
savagery n ferōcitās f, inhūmānitās f.
savant n vir doctus m.
save vt servāre; **~ up** reservāre ♦ prep praeter (acc).
saving adj parcus; **~ clause** exceptiō f ♦ n compendium nt; **~s** pl peculium nt.
saviour n līberātor m.
savory n thymbra f.
savour n sapor m; (of cooking) nīdor m ♦ vi

sapere; **~ of** olēre, redolēre.
savoury adj condītus.
saw n (tool) serra f; (saying) prōverbium nt ♦ vt serrā secāre.
sawdust n scobis f.
say vt dīcere; **~ that ... not** negāre; **~ no** negāre; **he ~s** (quoting) inquit; **he ~s yes** āit; **they ~** ferunt (+ acc and infin).
saying n dictum nt.
scab n (disease) scabiēs f; (over wound) crusta f.
scabbard n vāgīna f.
scabby adj scaber.
scaffold, scaffolding n fala f.
scald vt ūrere.
scale n (balance) lanx f; (fish, etc) squāma f; (gradation) gradūs mpl; (music) diagramma nt ♦ vt scālīs ascendere.
scallop n pecten m.
scalp n capitis cutis f.
scalpel n scalpellum nt.
scamp n verberō m.
scamper vi currere.
scan vt contemplārī; (verse) mētīrī.
scandal n īnfāmia f, opprobrium nt; (talk) calumnia f.
scandalize vt offendere.
scandalous adj flāgitiōsus, turpis.
scansion n syllabārum ēnārrātiō f.
scant adj exiguus, parvus.
scantily adv exiguē, tenuiter.
scantiness n exiguitās f.
scanty adj exiguus, tenuis, exīlis; (number) paucus.
scapegoat n piāculum nt.
scar n cicātrīx f.
scarce adj rārus; **make oneself ~** sē āmovēre, dē mediō recēdere ♦ adv vix, aegrē.
scarcely adv vix, aegrē; **~ anyone** nēmō ferē.
scarcity n inopia f, angustiae fpl.
scare n formīdō f ♦ vt terrēre; **~ away** absterrēre.
scarecrow n formīdō f.
scarf n fōcāle nt.
scarlet n coccum nt ♦ adj coccinus.
scarp n rūpēs f.
scathe n damnum nt.
scatter vt spargere; dispergere, dissipāre; (violently) disicere ♦ vi diffugere.
scatterbrained adj dēsipiēns.
scattered adj rārus.
scene n spectāculum nt; (place) theātrum nt.
scenery n locī faciēs f, speciēs f; (beautiful) amoenitās f.
scent n odor m; (sense) odōrātus m; **keen ~** sagācitās f ♦ vt odōrārī; (perfume) odōribus perfundere.
scented adj odōrātus.
sceptic n Pyrrhōnēus m.
sceptical adj incrēdulus.
sceptre n scēptrum nt.
schedule n tabulae fpl, ratiō f.
scheme n cōnsilium nt, ratiō f ♦ vt māchinārī,

mōlīrī.
schemer *n* māchinātor *m*.
schism *n* discidium *nt*, sēcessiō *f*.
scholar *n* vir doctus *m*; litterātus *m*; (*pupil*) discipulus *m*.
scholarly *adj* doctus, litterātus.
scholarship *n* litterae *fpl*, doctrīna *f*.
scholastic *adj* umbrātilis.
school *n* (*elementary*) lūdus *m*; (*advanced*) schola *f*; (*high*) gymnasium *nt*; (*sect*) secta *f*, domus *f* ♦ *vt* īnstituere.
schoolboy *n* discipulus *m*.
schoolmaster *n* magister *m*.
schoolmistress *n* magistra *f*.
science *n* doctrīna *f*, disciplīna *f*, ars *f*.
scimitar *n* acīnacēs *m*.
scintillate *vi* scintillāre.
scion *n* prōgeniēs *f*.
Scipio *n* Scīpiō, Scipiōnis *m*.
scissors *n* forfex *f*.
scoff *vi* irrīdēre; **~ at** dērīdēre.
scoffer *n* irrīsor *m*.
scold *vt* increpāre, obiūrgāre.
scolding *n* obiūrgātiō *f*.
scoop *n* trulla *f* ♦ *vt*: **~ out** excavāre.
scope *n* (*aim*) fīnis *m*; (*room*) locus *m*, campus *m*; **ample ~** laxus locus.
scorch *vt* exūrere, torrēre.
scorched *adj* torridus.
score *n* (*mark*) nota *f*; (*total*) summa *f*; (*reckoning*) ratiō *f*; (*number*) vīgintī ♦ *vt* notāre ♦ *vi* vincere.
scorn *n* contemptiō *f* ♦ *vt* contemnere, spernere.
scorner *n* contemptor *m*.
scornful *adj* fastīdiōsus.
scornfully *adv* contemptim.
scorpion *n* scorpiō *m*, nepa *f*.
scot-free *adj* immūnis, impūnītus.
scoundrel *n* furcifer *m*.
scour *vt* (*clean*) tergēre; (*range*) percurrere.
scourge *n* flagellum *nt*; (*fig*) pestis *f* ♦ *vt* verberāre, virgīs caedere.
scout *n* explōrātor *m*, speculātor *m* ♦ *vi* explōrāre, speculārī ♦ *vt* spernere, repudiāre.
scowl *n* frontis contractiō *f* ♦ *vi* frontem contrahere.
scraggy *adj* strigōsus.
scramble *vi*: **~ for** certātim captāre; **~ up** scandere.
scrap *n* frūstum *nt*.
scrape *vt* rādere, scabere; **~ off** abrādere.
scraper *n* strigilis *f*.
scratch *vt* rādere; (*head*) perfricāre; **~ out** exsculpere, ērādere.
scream *n* clāmor *m*, ululātus *m* ♦ *vi* clāmāre, ululāre.
screech *n* ululātus *m* ♦ *vi* ululāre.
screen *n* obex *m/f*; (*from sun*) umbra *f*; (*fig*) vēlāmentum *nt* ♦ *vt* tegere.
screw *n* clāvus *m*; (*of winepress*) cochlea *f*.
scribble *vt* properē scrībere.

scribe *n* scrība *m*.
script *n* scrīptum *nt*; (*handwriting*) manus *f*.
scroll *n* volūmen *nt*.
scrub *vt* dētergēre, dēfricāre.
scruple *n* rēligiō *f*, scrūpulus *m*.
scrupulous *adj* rēligiōsus; (*careful*) dīligēns.
scrupulously *adv* rēligiōsē, dīligenter.
scrupulousness *n* rēligiō *f*; dīligentia *f*.
scrutinize *vt* scrūtārī, intrōspicere in (*acc*), excutere.
scrutiny *n* scrūtātiō *f*.
scud *vi* volāre.
scuffle *n* rixa *f*.
scull *n* calvāria *f*; (*oar*) rēmus *m*.
scullery *n* culīna *f*.
sculptor *n* fictor *m*, sculptor *m*.
sculpture *n* ars fingendī *f*; (*product*) statuae *fpl* ♦ *vt* sculpere.
scum *n* spūma *f*.
scurf *n* porrīgō *f*.
scurrility *n* maledicta *ntpl*.
scurrilous *adj* maledicus.
scurvy *adj* (*fig*) turpis, improbus.
scythe *n* falx *f*.
sea *n* mare *nt*; aequor *nt*; **open ~** altum *nt*; **put to ~** solvere; **be at ~** nāvigāre; (*fig*) in errōre versārī ♦ *adj* marīnus; (*coast*) maritimus.
seaboard *n* lītus *nt*.
seafaring *adj* maritimus, nauticus.
seafight *n* nāvāle proelium *nt*.
seagull *n* larus *m*.
seal *n* (*animal*) phōca *f*; (*stamp*) signum *nt* ♦ *vt* signāre; **~ up** obsignāre.
seam *n* sūtūra *f*.
seaman *n* nauta *m*.
seamanship *n* scientia et ūsus nauticārum rērum.
seaport *n* portus *m*.
sear *vt* adūrere, torrēre.
search *n* investigātiō *f* ♦ *vi* investīgāre, explōrāre ♦ *vt* excutere, scrūtārī; **in ~ of** causa (+ *gen*); **for** quaerere, exquīrere, investīgāre; **~ into** inquīrere, anquīrere; **~ out** explōrāre, indāgāre.
searcher *n* inquīsītor *m*.
searching *adj* acūtus, dīligēns.
seashore *n* lītus *nt*.
seasick *adj*: **be ~** nauseāre.
seasickness *n* nausea *f*.
seaside *n* mare *nt*.
season *n* annī tempus *nt*, tempestās *f*; (*right time*) tempus *nt*, opportūnitās *f*; **in ~** tempestīvē ♦ *vt* condīre.
seasonable *adj* tempestīvus.
seasonably *adv* tempestīvē.
seasoned *adj* (*food*) condītus; (*wood*) dūrātus.
seasoning *n* condīmentum *nt*.
seat *n* sēdēs *f*; (*chair*) sedīle *nt*; (*home*) domus *f*, domicilium *nt*; **keep one's ~** (*riding*) in equō haerēre ♦ *vt* collocāre; **~ oneself** īnsidēre.
seated *adj*: **be ~** sedēre.
seaweed *n* alga *f*.
seaworthy *adj* ad nāvigandum ūtilis.

secede *vi* sēcēdere.
secession *n* sēcessiō *f*.
seclude *vt* sēclūdere, abstrūdere.
secluded *adj* sēcrētus, remōtus.
seclusion *n* sōlitūdō *f*, sēcrētum *nt*.
second *adj* secundus, alter; **a ~ time** iterum ♦
n temporis pūnctum *nt*; (*person*) fautor *m*; **~
sight** hariolātiō *f* ♦ *vt* favēre (*dat*), adesse
(*dat*).
secondary *adj* īnferior, dēterior.
seconder *n* fautor *m*.
second-hand *adj* aliēnus, trītus.
secondly *adv* deinde.
secrecy *n* sēcrētum *nt*, silentium *nt*.
secret *adj* secretus; occultus, arcānus;
(*stealth*) fūrtīvus ♦ *n* arcānum *nt*; **keep ~**
dissimulāre, cēlāre; **in ~** clam; **be ~** latēre.
secretary *n* scrība *m*, ab epistolīs, ā manū.
secrete *vt* cēlāre, abdere.
secretive *adj* tēctus.
secretly *adv* clam, occultē, sēcrētō.
sect *n* secta *f*, schola *f*, domus *f*.
section *n* pars *f*.
sector *n* regiō *f*.
secular *adj* profānus.
secure *adj* tūtus ♦ *vt* (*MIL*) firmāre, ēmūnīre;
(*fasten*) religāre; (*obtain*) parāre, nancīscī.
securely *adj* tūtō.
security *n* salūs *f*, impūnitās *f*; (*money*) cautiō
f, pignus *nt*, spōnsiō *f*; **sense of ~** sēcūritās *f*;
give good ~ satis dare; **on good ~** (*loan*)
nōminibus rēctis cautus; **stand ~ for**
praedem esse prō (*abl*).
sedan *n* lectīca *f*.
sedate *adj* placidus, temperātus, gravis.
sedately *adv* placidē.
sedateness *n* gravitās *f*.
sedge *n* ulva *f*.
sediment *n* faex *f*.
sedition *n* sēditiō *f*, mōtus *m*.
seditious *adj* sēditiōsus.
seditiously *adv* sēditiōsē.
seduce *vt* illicere, pellicere.
seducer *n* corruptor *m*.
seduction *n* corruptēla *f*.
seductive *adj* blandus.
seductively *adv* blandē.
sedulity *n* dīligentia *f*.
sedulous *adj* dīligēns, sēdulus.
sedulously *adv* dīligenter, sēdulō.
see *vt* vidēre, cernere; (*suddenly*) cōnspicārī;
(*performance*) spectāre; (*with mind*)
intellegere; **go and ~** vīsere, invīsere; **~ to**
vidēre, cōnsulere (*dat*); curare (+ *acc and
gerundive*); **~ through** dīspicere; **~ that you
are** vidē ut sīs, fac sīs; **~ that you are not** vidē
nē sīs, cavē sīs.
seed *n* sēmen *nt*; (*in a plant*) grānum *nt*; (*in fruit*)
acinum *nt*; (*fig*) stirps *f*, prōgeniēs *f*.
seedling *n* surculus *m*.
seed-time *n* sēmentis *f*.
seeing that *conj* quōniam, siquidem.
seek *vt* petere, quaerere.

seeker *n* indāgātor *m*.
seem *vi* vidērī.
seeming *adj* speciōsus ♦ *n* speciēs *f*.
seemingly *adv* ut vidētur.
seemly *adj* decēns, decōrus; **it is ~** decet.
seep *vi* mānāre, percōlārī.
seer *n* vātēs *m/f*.
seethe *vi* fervēre.
segregate *vt* sēcernere, sēgregāre.
segregation *n* sēparātiō *f*.
seize *vt* rapere, corripere, adripere,
prehendere; (*MIL*) occupāre; (*illness*) adficere;
(*emotion*) invādere, occupāre.
seizure *n* ēreptiō *f*, occupātiō *f*.
seldom *adv* rārō.
select *vt* ēligere, excerpere, dēligere ♦ *adj*
lēctus, ēlēctus.
selection *n* ēlēctiō *f*, dēlēctus *m*; (*LIT*) ecloga *f*.
self *n* ipse; (*reflexive*) sē; **a second ~** alter īdem.
self-centred *adj* glōriōsus.
self-confidence *n* cōnfīdentia *f*, fidūcia *f*.
self-confident *adj* cōnfīdēns.
self-conscious *adj* pudibundus.
self-control *n* temperantia *f*.
self-denial *n* abstinentia *f*.
self-evident *adj* manifestus; **it is ~** ante pedēs
positum est.
self-governing *adj* līber.
self-government *n* lībertās *f*.
self-important *adj* adrogāns.
self-interest *n* ambitiō *f*.
selfish *adj* inhūmānus, avārus; **be ~** suā causā
facere.
selfishly *adv* inhūmānē, avārē.
selfishness *n* inhūmānitās *f*, incontinentia *f*,
avāritia *f*.
self-made *adj* (*man*) novus.
self-possessed *adj* aequō animō.
self-possession *n* aequus animus *m*.
self-reliant *adj* cōnfīdēns.
self-respect *n* pudor *m*.
self-restraint *n* modestia *f*.
self-sacrifice *n* dēvōtiō *f*.
selfsame *adj* ūnus et īdem.
sell *vt* vēndere; (*in lots*) dīvēndere; **be sold**
vēnīre.
seller *n* vēnditor *m*.
selvage *n* limbus *m*.
semblance *n* speciēs *f*, imāgō *f*.
semicircle *n* hēmicyclium *nt*.
senate *n* senātus *m*; **hold a meeting of the ~**
senātum habēre; **decree of the ~** senātus
cōnsultum *nt*.
senate house *n* cūria *f*.
senator *n* senātor *m*; (*provincial*) decuriō *m*; **~s**
pl patrēs *mpl*.
senatorial *adj* senātōrius.
send *vt* mittere; **~ across** trānsmittere;
~ ahead praemittere; **~ away** dīmittere; **~
back** remittere; **~ for** arcessere; (*doctor*)
adhibēre; **~ forth** ēmittere; **~ forward**
praemittere; **~ in** immittere, intrōmittere; **~
out** ēmittere; (*in different directions*)

dīmittere; ~ **out of the way** ablēgāre; ~ **up** submittere.
senile _adj_ senīlis.
senility _n_ senium _nt._
senior _adj_ nātū māior; (_thing_) prior.
sensation _n_ sēnsus _m_; (_event_) rēs nova _f_; **lose ~** obtorpēscere; **create a ~** hominēs obstupefacere.
sensational _adj_ novus, prōdigiōsus.
sense _n_ (_faculty_) sēnsus _m_; (_wisdom_) prūdentia _f_; (_meaning_) vis _f_, sententia _f_; **common ~** prūdentia _f_; **be in one's ~s** apud sē esse, mentis suae esse; **out of one's ~s** dēmēns; **recover one's ~s** resipīscere; **what is the ~ of** quid sibī vult? ♦ _vt_ sentīre.
senseless _adj_ absurdus, ineptus, īnsipiēns.
senselessly _adv_ īnsipienter.
senselessness _n_ īnsipientia _f_.
sensibility _n_ sēnsus _m_.
sensible _adj_ prūdēns, sapiēns.
sensibly _adv_ prūdenter, sapienter.
sensitive _adj_ mollis, inrītābilis, patibilis.
sensitiveness _n_ mollitia _f_.
sensual _adj_ libīdinōsus.
sensuality _n_ libīdō _f_, voluptās _f_.
sensually _adv_ libīdinōsē.
sentence _n_ (_judge_) iūdicium _nt_, sententia _f_; (_GRAM_) sententia _f_; **pass ~** iūdicāre; **execute ~** lēge agere ♦ _vt_ damnāre; **~ to death** capitis damnāre.
sententious _adj_ sententiōsus.
sententiously _adv_ sententiōsē.
sentient _adj_ patibilis.
sentiment _n_ (_feeling_) sēnsus _m_; (_opinion_) sententia _f_; (_emotion_) mollitia _f_.
sentimental _adj_ mollis, flēbilis.
sentimentality _n_ mollitia _f_.
sentimentally _adv_ molliter.
sentries _npl_ statiōnēs _fpl_, excubiae _fpl_.
sentry _n_ custōs _m_, vigil _m_; **be on ~ duty** in statiōne esse.
separable _adj_ dīviduus, sēparābilis.
separate _vt_ sēparāre, dīvidere, disiungere; (_forcibly_) dīrimere, dīvellere ♦ _vi_ dīgredī ♦ _adj_ sēparātus, sēcrētus.
separately _adv_ sēparātim, seōrsum.
separation _n_ sēparātiō _f_; (_violent_) discidium _nt._
September _n_ mēnsis September _m_; **of ~** September.
sepulchral _adj_ fūnebris.
sepulchre _n_ sepulcrum _nt._
sepulture _n_ sepultūra _f._
sequel _n_ exitus _m_, quae sequuntur.
sequence _n_ seriēs _f_, ōrdō _m._
sequestered _adj_ sēcrētus.
serenade _vt_ occentāre.
serene _adj_ tranquillus, sēcūrus.
serenely _adv_ tranquillē.
serenity _n_ sēcūritās _f._
serf _n_ servus _m._
serfdom _n_ servitūs _f._
sergeant _n_ signifer _m._

series _n_ seriēs _f_, ōrdō _m._
serious _adj_ gravis, sērius, sevērus.
seriously _adv_ graviter, sēriō, sevērē.
seriousness _n_ gravitās _f._
sermon _n_ ōrātiō _f._
serpent _n_ serpēns _f._
serpentine _adj_ tortuōsus.
serrated _adj_ serrātus.
serried _adj_ cōnfertus.
servant _n_ (_domestic_) famulus _m_, famula _f_; (_public_) minister _m_, ministra _f_; **family ~s** familia _f._
servant maid _n_ ancilla _f._
serve _vt_ servīre (_dat_); (_food_) ministrāre, adpōnere; (_interest_) condūcere (_dat_) ♦ _vi_ (_MIL_) stīpendia merēre, mīlitāre; (_suffice_) sufficere; **~ as** esse prō (_abl_); **~ in the cavalry** equō merēre; **~ in the infantry** pedibus merēre; **having ~d one's time** ēmeritus; **~ a sentence** poenam subīre; **~ well** bene merērī dē (_abl_).
service _n_ (_status_) servitium _nt_, famulātus _m_; (_work_) ministerium _nt_; (_help_) opera _f_; (_by an equal_) meritum _nt_, beneficium _nt_; (_MIL_) mīlitia _f_, stīpendia _ntpl_; **be of ~ to** prōdesse (_dat_), bene merērī dē; **I am at your ~** adsum tibī; **complete one's ~** stīpendia ēmerērī.
serviceable _adj_ ūtilis.
servile _adj_ servīlis; (_fig_) abiectus, humilis.
servility _n_ adūlātiō _f._
servitude _n_ servitūs _f._
session _n_ conventus _m_; **be in ~** sedēre.
sesterce _n_ sēstertius _m_; **10 ~s** decem sēstertiī; **10,000 ~s** dēna sēstertia _ntpl_; **1,000,000 ~s** deciēs sēstertium.
set _vt_ pōnere, locāre, statuere, sistere; (_bone_) condere; (_course_) dīrigere; (_example_) dare; (_limit_) impōnere; (_mind_) intendere; (_music_) modulārī; (_sail_) dare; (_sentries_) dispōnere; (_table_) īnstruere; (_trap_) parāre ♦ _vi_ (_ASTRO_) occidere; **~ about** incipere; **~ against** oppōnere; **~ apart** sēpōnere; **~ aside** sēpōnere; **~ down** (_writing_) perscrībere; **~ eyes on** cōnspicere; **~ foot on** ingredī; **~ forth** expōnere, ēdere; **~ free** līberāre; **~ in motion** movēre; **~ in order** compōnere, dispōnere; **~ off** (_decoration_) distinguere; (_art_) illūmināre; **~ on** (_to attack_) immittere; **~ on foot** īnstituere; **~ on fire** incendere; **~ one's heart on** exoptāre; **~ out** _vi_ proficīscī; **~ over** praeficere, impōnere; **~ up** statuere; (_fig_) cōnstituere.
set _adj_ (_arrangement_) status; (_purpose_) certus; (_rule_) praescrīptus; (_speech_) compositus; **of ~ purpose** cōnsultō ♦ _n_ (_persons_) numerus _m_; (_things_) congeriēs _f_; (_current_) cursus _m._
setback _n_ repulsa _f._
settee _n_ lectulus _m._
setting _n_ (_ASTRO_) occāsus _m_; (_event_) locus _m._
settle _n_ sella _f_ ♦ _vt_ statuere; (_annuity_) praestāre; (_business_) trānsigere; (_colony_) dēdūcere; (_debt_) exsolvere; (_decision_) cōnstituere; (_dispute_) dēcīdere, compōnere

♦ vi (*abode*) cōnsīdere; (*agreement*)
cōnstituere, convenīre; (*sediment*) dēsīdere;
~ **in** īnsidēre (*dat*).
settled *adj* certus, explōrātus.
settlement n (*of a colony*) dēductiō f; (*colony*)
colōnia f; (*of dispute*) dēcīsiō f, compositiō f;
(*to wife*) dōs f.
settler n colōnus m.
set to n pugna f.
seven *num* septem; ~ **each** septēnī; ~ **times**
septiēns.
seven hundred *num* septingentī.
seven hundredth *adj* septingentēsimus.
seventeen *num* septendecim.
seventeenth *adj* septimus decimus.
seventh *adj* septimus; **for the** ~ **time**
septimum.
seventieth *adj* septuāgēsimus.
seventy *num* septuāgintā; ~ **each** septuāgēnī; ~
times septuāgiēns.
sever *vt* incīdere, sēparāre, dīvidere.
several *adj* complūrēs, aliquot.
severally *adv* singulī.
severe *adj* gravis, sevērus, dūrus; (*style*)
austērus; (*weather*) asper; (*pain*) ācer,
gravis.
severely *adv* graviter, sevērē.
severity n gravitās f, asperitās f, sevēritās f.
sew *vt* suere; ~ **up** cōnsuere; ~ **up in** īnsuere in
(*acc*).
sewer n cloāca f.
sex n sexus m.
shabbily *adv* sordidē.
shabbiness n sordēs fpl.
shabby *adj* sordidus.
shackle n compēs f, vinculum nt ♦ vt impedīre,
vincīre.
shade n umbra f; (*colour*) color m; ~**s** pl mānēs
mpl; **put in the** ~ officere (*dat*) ♦ vt opācāre,
umbram adferre (*dat*).
shadow n umbra f.
shadowy *adj* obscūrus; (*fig*) inānis.
shady *adj* umbrōsus, opācus.
shaft n (*missile*) tēlum nt, sagitta f; (*of spear*)
hastīle nt; (*of cart*) tēmō m; (*of light*) radius m;
(*excavation*) puteus m.
shaggy *adj* hirsūtus.
shake *vt* quatere, agitāre; (*structure*)
labefacere, labefactāre; (*belief*) īnfīrmāre;
(*resolution*) labefactāre, commovēre; ~
hands with dextram dare (*dat*) ♦ vi quatī,
agitārī, tremere, horrēscere; ~ **off** dēcutere,
excutere; ~ **out** excutere.
shaking n tremor m.
shaky *adj* īnstābilis, tremebundus.
shall *aux vb* = *fut indic*.
shallot n caepa Ascalōnia f.
shallow *adj* brevis, vadōsus; (*fig*) levis.
shallowness n vada ntpl; (*fig*) levitās f.
shallows n brevia ntpl, vada ntpl.
sham *adj* fictus, falsus, fūcōsus ♦ n simulātiō f,
speciēs f ♦ vt simulāre.
shambles n laniēna f.

shame n (*feeling*) pudor m; (*cause*) dēdecus nt,
ignōminia f; **it** ~**s** pudet (+ *acc of person, gen of
thing*); **it is a** ~ flāgitium est ♦ vt rubōrem
incutere (*dat*) ♦ *interj* prō pudor!
shamefaced *adj* verēcundus.
shameful *adj* ignōminiōsus, turpis.
shamefully *adv* turpiter.
shameless *adj* impudēns.
shamelessly *adv* impudenter.
shamelessness n impudentia f.
shank n crūs nt.
shape n fōrma f, figūra f ♦ vt fōrmāre, fingere;
(*fig*) īnfōrmāre ♦ vi: ~ **well** prōficere.
shapeless *adj* īnfōrmis, dēfōrmis.
shapelessness n dēfōrmitās f.
shapeliness n fōrma f.
shapely *adj* fōrmōsus.
shard n testa f.
share n pars f; (*plough*) vōmer m; **go** ~**s with**
inter sē partīrī ♦ vt (*give*) partīrī, impertīre;
(*have*) commūnicāre, participem esse (*gen*).
sharer n particeps m/f, socius m.
shark n volpēs marīna f.
sharp *adj* acūtus; (*fig*) ācer, acūtus; (*bitter*)
amarus.
sharpen *vt* acuere; (*fig*) exacuere.
sharply *adv* ācriter, acūtē.
sharpness n aciēs f; (*mind*) acūmen nt,
argūtiae fpl; (*temper*) acerbitās f.
shatter *vt* quassāre, perfringere, adflīgere;
(*fig*) frangere.
shave *vt* rādere; ~ **off** abrādere.
shavings n rāmenta ntpl.
she *pron* haec, ea, illa.
sheaf n manipulus m.
shear *vt* tondēre, dētondēre.
shears n forficēs fpl.
sheath n vāgīna f.
sheathe *vt* recondere.
shed *vt* fundere; (*blood*) effundere; (*one's
own*) profundere; (*tears*) effundere;
(*covering*) exuere; ~ **light on** (*fig*) lūmen
adhibēre (*dat*).
sheen n nitor m.
sheep n ovis f; (*flock*) pecus nt.
sheepfold n ovīle nt.
sheepish *adj* pudibundus.
sheepishly *adv* pudenter.
sheer *adj* (*absolute*) merus; (*steep*) praeruptus.
sheet n (*cloth*) linteum nt; (*metal*) lāmina f;
(*paper*) carta f, scheda f; (*sail*) pēs m; (*water*)
aequor nt.
shelf n pluteus m, pēgma nt.
shell n concha f; (*egg*) putāmen nt; (*tortoise*)
testa f.
shellfish n conchȳlium nt.
shelter n suffugium nt, tegmen nt; (*refuge*)
perfugium nt, asȳlum nt; (*lodging*) hospitium
nt; (*fig*) umbra f ♦ vt tegere, dēfendere;
(*refugee*) excipere ♦ vi latēre; ~ **behind** (*fig*)
dēlitēscere in (*abl*).
sheltered *adj* (*life*) umbrātilis.
shelve *vt* differre ♦ vi sē dēmittere.

shelving *adj* dēclīvis.
shepherd *n* pastor *m*.
shield *n* scūtum *nt*; clipeus *m*; (*small*) parma *f*;
(*fig*) praesidium *nt* ♦ *vt* prōtegere,
dēfendere.
shift *n* (*change*) mūtātiō *f*; (*expedient*) ars *f*,
dolus *m*; **make ~ to** efficere ut; **in ~s** per vicēs
♦ *vt* mūtāre; (*move*) movēre ♦ *vi* mūtārī;
discēdere.
shiftless *adj* iners, inops.
shifty *adj* vafer, versūtus.
shilling *n* solidus *m*.
shimmer *vi* micāre ♦ *n* tremulum lūmen *nt*.
shin *n* tībia *f*.
shine *vi* lūcēre, fulgēre; (*reflecting*) nitēre; (*fig*)
ēminēre; **~ forth** ēlūcēre, ēnitēre; effulgēre;
~ upon adfulgēre (*dat*) ♦ *n* nitor *m*.
shingle *n* lapillī *mpl*, glārea *f*.
shining *adj* lūcidus, splendidus; (*fig*) illūstris.
shiny *adj* nitidus.
ship *n* nāvis *f*; **admiral's ~** nāvis praetōria;
decked ~ nāvis tēcta, nāvis cōnstrāta ♦ *vt*
(*cargo*) impōnere; (*to a place*) nāvī invehere.
shipowner *n* nāviculārius *m*.
shipping *n* nāvēs *fpl*.
shipwreck *n* naufragium *nt*; **suffer ~**
naufragium facere.
shipwrecked *adj* naufragus.
shirk *vt* dēfugere, dētrectāre.
shirt *n* subūcula *f*.
shiver *n* horror *m* ♦ *vi* horrēre, tremere ♦ *vt*
perfringere, comminuere.
shivering *n* horror *m*.
shoal *n* (*fish*) exāmen *nt*; (*water*) vadum *nt*; **~s** *pl*
brevia *ntpl*.
shock *n* impulsus *m*; (*battle*) concursus *m*,
cōnflīctus *m*; (*hair*) caesariēs *f*; (*mind*)
offēnsiō *f* ♦ *vt* percutere, offendere.
shocking *adj* atrōx, dētestābilis, flāgitiōsus.
shoddy *adj* vīlis.
shoe *n* calceus *m*.
shoemaker *n* sūtor *m*.
shoot *n* surculus *m*; (*vine*) pampinus *m* ♦ *vi*
frondēscere; (*movement*) volāre; **~ up**
ēmicāre ♦ *vt* (*missile*) conicere, iaculārī;
(*person*) iaculārī, trānsfīgere.
shop *n* taberna *f*.
shore *n* lītus *nt*, ōra *f* ♦ *vt* fulcīre.
short *adj* brevis; (*broken*) curtus; (*amount*)
exiguus; **for a ~ time** parumper, paulisper; **~
of** (*number*) intrā (*acc*); **be ~ of** indigēre (*abl*);
cut ~ interpellāre; **in ~** ad summam, dēnique;
very ~ perbrevis; **fall ~ of** nōn pervenīre ad,
abesse ab; **run ~** dēficere; **to cut a long story
~** nē multīs morer, nē multa.
shortage *n* inopia *f*.
shortcoming *n* dēlictum *nt*, culpa *f*.
short cut *n* via compendiāria *f*.
shorten *vt* curtāre, imminuere, contrahere;
(*sail*) legere.
shorthand *n* notae *fpl*.
shorthand writer *n* āctuārius *m*.
short-lived *adj* brevis.

shortly *adv* (*time*) brevī; (*speak*) breviter; **~
after** paulō post, nec multō post.
shortness *n* brevitās *f*, exiguitās *f*; (*difficulty*)
angustiae *fpl*.
short-sighted *adj* (*fig*) imprōvidus,
imprūdēns.
short-sightedness *n* imprūdentia *f*.
short-tempered *adj* īrācundus.
shot *n* ictus *m*; (*range*) iactus *m*.
should *vi* (*duty*) dēbēre.
shoulder *n* umerus *m*; (*animal*) armus *m* ♦ *vt*
(*burden*) suscipere.
shout *n* clāmor *m*, adclāmātiō *f* ♦ *vt*, *vi*
clāmāre, vōciferārī; **~ down** obstrepere
(*dat*); **~ out** exclāmāre.
shove *vt* trūdere, impellere.
shovel *n* rutrum *nt*.
show *n* speciēs *f*; (*entertainment*) lūdī *mpl*,
spectāculum *nt*; (*stage*) lūdicrum *nt*; **for ~** in
speciem; **put on a ~** spectācula dare ♦ *vt*
mōnstrāre, indicāre, ostendere, ostentāre;
(*point out*) dēmōnstrāre; (*qualities*) praestāre;
~ off *vi* sē iactāre ♦ *vt* ostentāre.
shower *n* imber *m* ♦ *vt* fundere, conicere.
showery *adj* pluvius.
showiness *n* ostentātiō *f*.
showing off *n* iactātiō *f*.
showy *adj* speciōsus.
shred *n* fragmentum *nt*; **in ~s** minūtātim; **tear
to ~s** dīlaniāre ♦ *vt* concīdere.
shrew *n* virāgō *f*.
shrewd *adj* acūtus, ācer, sagāx.
shrewdly *adv* acūtē, sagāciter.
shrewdness *n* acūmen *nt*, sagācitās *f*.
shriek *n* ululātus *m* ♦ *vi* ululāre.
shrill *adj* acūtus, argūtus.
shrine *n* fānum *nt*, dēlubrum *nt*.
shrink *vt* contrahere ♦ *vi* contrahī; **~ from**
abhorrēre ab, refugere ab, dētrectāre.
shrivel *vt* corrūgāre ♦ *vi* exārēscere.
shroud *n* integumentum *nt*; **~s** *pl* rudentēs *mpl*
♦ *vt* involvere.
shrub *n* frutex *m*.
shrubbery *n* fruticētum *nt*.
shudder *n* horror *m* ♦ *vi* exhorrēscere; **~ at**
horrēre.
shuffle *vt* miscēre ♦ *vi* claudicāre; (*fig*)
tergiversārī.
shun *vt* vītāre, ēvītāre, dēfugere.
shut *vt* claudere; (*with cover*) operīre; (*hand*)
comprimere; **~ in** inclūdere; **~ off**
interclūdere; **~ out** exclūdere; **~ up**
inclūdere.
shutter *n* foricula *f*, lūmināre *nt*.
shuttle *n* radius *m*.
shy *adj* timidus, pudibundus, verēcundus.
shyly *adv* timidē, verēcundē.
shyness *n* verēcundia *f*.
sibyl *n* sibylla *f*.
sick *adj* aeger, aegrōtus; **be ~** aegrōtāre; **feel ~**
nauseāre; **I am ~ of** mē taedet (*gen*).
sicken *vt* fastīdium movēre (*dat*) ♦ *vi*
nauseāre, aegrōtāre.

sickle n falx f.
sickly adj invalidus.
sickness n nausea f; (*illness*) morbus m, aegritūdō f.
side n latus nt; (*direction*) pars f; (*faction*) partēs fpl; (*kin*) genus nt; **on all ~s** undique; **on both ~s** utrimque; **on one ~** unā ex parte; **on our ~** ā nōbīs; **be on the ~ of** stāre ab, sentīre cum; **on the far ~ of** ultrā (*acc*); **on this ~** hīnc; **on this ~ of** cis (*acc*), citrā (*acc*) ♦ vi: **~ with** stāre ab, facere cum.
sideboard n abacus m.
sidelong adj oblīquus.
sideways adv oblīquē, in oblīquum.
sidle vi oblīquō corpore incēdere.
siege n obsidiō f, oppugnātiō f; **lay ~ to** obsidēre.
siege works n opera ntpl.
siesta n merīdiātiō f; **take a ~** merīdiāre.
sieve n crībrum nt.
sigh n suspīrium nt; (*loud*) gemitus m ♦ vi suspīrāre, gemere.
sight n (*sense*) vīsus m; (*process*) aspectus m; (*range*) cōnspectus m; (*thing seen*) spectāculum nt, speciēs f; **at ~** ex tempore; **at first ~** prīmō aspectū; **in ~** in cōnspectū; **come into ~** in cōnspectum sē dare; **in the ~ of** in oculīs (*gen*); **catch ~ of** cōnspicere; **lose ~ of** ē cōnspectū āmittere; (*fig*) oblīvīscī (*gen*) ♦ vt cōnspicārī.
sightless adj caecus.
sightly adj decōrus.
sign n signum nt, indicium nt; (*distinction*) īnsigne nt; (*mark*) nota f; (*trace*) vestīgium nt; (*proof*) documentum nt; (*portent*) ōmen nt; (*Zodiac*) signum nt; **give a ~** innuere ♦ vi signum dare, innuere ♦ vt subscrībere (*dat*); (*as witness*) obsignāre.
signal n signum nt; **give the ~ for retreat** receptuī canere ♦ vi signum dare ♦ adj īnsignis, ēgregius.
signalize vt nōbilitāre.
signally adv ēgregiē.
signature n nōmen nt, manus f, chīrographum nt.
signet n signum nt.
signet ring n anulus m.
significance n interpretātiō f, significātiō f, vīs f; (*importance*) pondus nt.
significant adj gravis, clārus.
signification n significātiō f.
signify vt significāre, velle; (*omen*) portendere; **it does not ~** nōn interest.
silence n silentium nt; **in ~** per silentium ♦ vt comprimere; (*argument*) refūtāre.
silent adj tacitus; (*habit*) taciturnus; **be ~** silēre, tacēre; **be ~ about** silēre, tacēre; **become ~** conticēscere.
silently adv tacitē.
silhouette n adumbrātiō f.
silk n bombȳx m; (*clothes*) sērica ntpl ♦ adj bombȳcinus, sēricus.
silken adj bombȳcinus.

sill n līmen nt.
silliness n stultitia f, ineptiae fpl.
silly adj fatuus, ineptus; stultus; **be ~** dēsipere.
silt n līmus m.
silver n argentum nt ♦ adj argenteus.
silver mine n argentāria f.
silver plate n argentum nt.
silver-plated adj argentātus.
silvery adj argenteus.
similar adj similis.
similarity n similitūdō f.
similarly adv similiter.
simile n similitūdō f.
simmer vi lēniter fervēre.
simper vi molliter subrīdēre.
simple adj simplex; (*mind*) fatuus; (*task*) facilis.
simpleton n homō ineptus m.
simplicity n simplicitās f; (*mind*) stultitia f.
simplify vt faciliōrem reddere.
simply adv simpliciter; (*merely*) sōlum, tantum.
simulate vt simulāre.
simulation n simulātiō f.
simultaneously adv simul, ūnā, eōdem tempore.
sin n peccātum nt, nefās nt, dēlictum nt ♦ vi peccāre.
since adv abhinc; **long ~** iamdūdum ♦ conj (*time*) ex quō tempore, postquam; (*reason*) cum (+ *subj*), quōniam; **~ he** quippe quī ♦ prep ab (*abl*), ex (*abl*), post (*acc*); **ever ~** usque ab.
sincere adj sincērus, simplex, apertus.
sincerely adv sincērē, ex animō.
sincerity n fidēs f, simplicitās f.
sinew n nervus m.
sinewy adj nervōsus.
sinful adj improbus, impius, incestus.
sinfully adv improbē, impiē.
sing vt canere, cantāre; **~ of** canere.
singe vt adūrere.
singer n cantor m.
singing n cantus m ♦ adj canōrus.
single adj ūnus, sōlus, ūnicus; (*unmarried*) caelebs ♦ vt: **~ out** ēligere, excerpere.
single-handed adj ūnus.
singly adv singillātim, singulī.
singular adj singulāris; (*strange*) novus.
singularly adv singulāriter, praecipuē.
sinister adj īnfaustus, malevolus.
sink vi dēsīdere; (*in water*) dēmergī; **~ in** inlābī, īnsīdere ♦ vt dēprimere, mergere; (*well*) fodere; (*fig*) dēmergere.
sinless adj integer, innocēns, castus.
sinner n peccātor m.
sinuous adj sinuōsus.
sip vt gustāre, lībāre.
siphon n siphō m.
sir n (*to master*) ere; (*to equal*) vir optime; (*title*) eques m.
sire n pater m.
siren n sīrēn f.

sirocco n Auster m.
sister n soror f; ~'s sorōrius.
sisterhood n germānitās f; (*society*) sorōrum societās f.
sister-in-law n glōs f.
sisterly adj sorōrius.
sit vi sedēre; ~ **beside** adsidēre (*dat*); ~ **down** cōnsīdere; ~ **on** īnsidēre (*dat*); (*eggs*) incubāre; ~ **at table** accumbere; ~ **up** (*at night*) vigilāre.
site n situs m, locus m; (*for building*) ārea f.
sitting n sessiō f.
situated adj situs.
situation n situs m; (*CIRCS*) status m, condiciō f.
six num sex; ~ **each** sēnī; ~ **or seven** sex septem; ~ **times** sexiēns.
six hundred num sēscentī; ~ **each** sēscēnī; ~ **times** sēscentiēns.
six hundredth adj sēscentēsimus.
sixteen num sēdecim; ~ **each** sēnī dēnī; ~ **times** sēdeciēns.
sixteenth adj sextus decimus.
sixth adj sextus; **for the** ~ **time** sextum.
sixtieth adj sexagēsimus.
sixty num sexāgintā; ~ **each** sexāgēnī; ~ **times** sexāgiēns.
size n māgnitūdō f, amplitūdō f; (*measure*) mēnsūra f, fōrma f.
skate vi per glaciem lābī; ~ **on thin ice** (*fig*) incēdere per ignēs suppositōs cinerī dolōsō.
skein n glomus nt.
skeleton n ossa ntpl.
sketch n adumbrātiō f, dēscrīptiō f ♦ vt adumbrāre, īnfōrmāre.
skewer n verū nt.
skiff n scapha f, lēnunculus m.
skilful adj perītus, doctus, scītus; (*with hands*) habilis.
skilfully adv perītē, doctē; habiliter.
skill n ars f, perītia f, sollertia f.
skilled adj perītus, doctus; ~ **in** perītus (+ *gen*).
skim vt dēspūmāre; ~ **over** (*fig*) legere, perstringere.
skin n cutis f; (*animal*) pellis f ♦ vt pellem dētrahere (*dat*).
skinflint n avārus m.
skinny adj macer.
skip vi exsultāre ♦ vt praeterīre.
skipper n magister m.
skirmish n leve proelium nt ♦ vi vēlitārī.
skirmisher n vēles m, excursor m.
skirt n īnstita f; (*border*) limbus m ♦ vt contingere (*dat*); (*motion*) legere.
skittish adj lascīvus.
skulk vi latēre, dēlitēscere.
skull n caput nt.
sky n caelum nt; **of the** ~ caelestis.
skylark n alauda f.
slab n tabula f.
slack adj remissus, laxus; (*work*) piger, neglegēns.
slacken vt remittere, dētendere ♦ vi laxārī.
slackness n remissiō f; pigritia f.

slag n scōria f.
slake vt restinguere, sēdāre.
slam vt adflīgere.
slander n maledicta ntpl, obtrectātiō f; (*law*) calumnia f ♦ vt maledīcere (*dat*), īnfāmāre, obtrectāre (*dat*).
slanderer n obtrectātor m.
slanderous adj maledicus.
slang n vulgāria verba ntpl.
slant vi in trānsversum īre.
slanting adj oblīquus, trānsversus.
slantingly adv oblīquē, ex trānsversō.
slap n alapa f ♦ vt palmā ferīre.
slapdash adj praeceps, temerārius.
slash vt caedere ♦ n ictus m.
slate n (*roof*) tēgula f; (*writing*) tabula f ♦ vt increpāre.
slatternly adj sordidus, incōmptus.
slaughter n caedēs f, strāgēs f ♦ vt trucīdāre.
slaughterhouse n laniēna f.
slave n servus m; (*domestic*) famulus m; (*home-born*) verna m; **be a** ~ **to** īnservīre (*dat*); **household** ~s familia f.
slave girl n ancilla f.
slavery n servitūs f.
slavish adj servīlis.
slavishly adv servīliter.
slay vt interficere, occīdere.
slayer n interfector m.
sleek adj nitidus, pinguis.
sleep n somnus m; **go to** ~ obdormīscere ♦ vi dormīre; ~ **off** vt ēdormīre.
sleeper n dormītor m.
sleepiness n sopor m.
sleepless adj īnsomnis, vigil.
sleeplessness n īnsomnia f.
sleepy adj somniculōsus; **be** ~ dormītāre.
sleeve n manica f.
sleight of hand n praestīgiae fpl.
slender adj gracilis, exīlis.
slenderness n gracilitās f.
slice n frūstum nt ♦ vt secāre.
slide n lāpsus m ♦ vi lābī.
slight adj levis, exiguus, parvus ♦ n neglegentia f ♦ vt neglegere, offendere.
slightingly adv contemptim.
slightly adv leviter, paululum.
slightness n levitās f.
slim adj gracilis.
slime n līmus m.
slimness n gracilitās f.
slimy adj līmōsus, mūcōsus.
sling n funda f ♦ vt mittere, iaculārī.
slinger n funditor m.
slink vi sē subdūcere.
slip n lāpsus m; (*mistake*) offēnsiuncula f; (*plant*) surculus m ♦ vi lābī; ~ **away** ēlābī, dīlābī; ~ **out** ēlābī; (*word*) excidere; **give the** ~ **to** ēlūdere; **let** ~ āmittere, ēmittere; (*opportunity*) ōmittere; **there's many a** ~ **twixt the cup and the lip** inter ōs et offam multa interveniunt.
slipper n solea f.

slippery *adj* lūbricus.

slipshod *adj* neglegēns.

slit *n* rīma *f* ♦ *vt* findere, incīdere.

sloe *n* spīnus *m*.

slope *n* dēclīve *nt*, clīvus *m*; (*steep*) dēiectus *m* ♦ *vi* sē dēmittere, vergere.

sloping *adj* dēclīvis, dēvexus; (*up*) adclīvis.

slot *n* rīma *f*.

sloth *n* inertia *f*, segnitia *f*, dēsidia *f*, ignāvia *f*.

slothful *adj* ignāvus, iners, segnis.

slothfully *adv* ignāvē, segniter.

slouch *vi* languidē incēdere.

slough *n* (*skin*) exuviae *fpl*; (*bog*) palūs *f*.

slovenliness *n* ignāvia *f*, sordēs *fpl*.

slovenly *adj* ignāvus, sordidus.

slow *adj* tardus, lentus; (*mind*) hebes.

slowly *adv* tardē, lentē.

slowness *n* tarditās *f*.

sludge *n* līmus *m*.

slug *n* līmāx *f*.

sluggard *n* homō ignāvus *m*.

sluggish *adj* piger, segnis; (*mind*) hebes.

sluggishly *adv* pigrē, segniter.

sluggishness *n* pigritia *f*, inertia *f*.

sluice *n* cataracta *f*.

slumber *n* somnus *m*, sopor *m* ♦ *vi* dormīre.

slump *n* vīlis annōna *f*.

slur *n* nota *f*; **cast ~ on** dētrectāre ♦ *vt*: **~ words** balbūtīre.

sly *adj* astūtus, vafer, callidus; **on the ~** ex opīnātō.

slyly *adv* astūtē, callidē.

slyness *n* astūtia *f*.

smack *n* (*blow*) ictus *m*; (*with hand*) alapa *f*; (*boat*) lēnunculus *m*; (*taste*) sapor *m* ♦ *vt* ferīre ♦ *vi*: **~ of** olēre, redolēre.

small *adj* parvus, exiguus; **how ~** quantulus, quantillus; **so ~** tantulus; **very ~** perexiguus, minimus; **a ~ meeting of** īnfrequēns.

smaller *adj* minor.

smallest *adj* minimus.

smallness *n* exiguitās *f*, brevitās *f*.

small talk *n* sermunculus *m*.

smart *adj* (*action*) ācer, alacer; (*dress*) concinnus, nitidus; (*pace*) vēlōx; (*wit*) facētus, salsus ♦ *n* dolor *m* ♦ *vi* dolēre; (*fig*) ūrī, mordērī.

smartly *adv* ācriter; nitidē; vēlōciter; facētē.

smartness *n* alacritās *f*; (*dress*) nitor *m*; (*wit*) facētiae *fpl*, sollertia *f*.

smash *n* ruīna *f* ♦ *vt* frangere, comminuere.

smattering *n*: **get a ~ of** odōrārī, prīmīs labrīs attingere; **with a ~ of** imbūtus (*abl*).

smear *vt* oblinere, ungere.

smell *n* (*sense*) odōrātus *m*; (*odour*) odor *m*; (*of cooking*) nīdor *m* ♦ *vt* olfacere, odōrārī ♦ *vi* olēre.

smelly *adj* olidus.

smelt *vt* fundere.

smile *n* rīsus *m* ♦ *vi* subrīdēre; **~ at** adrīdēre (*dat*); **~ upon** rīdēre ad; (*fig*) secundum esse (*dat*).

smiling *adj* laetus.

smirk *vi* subrīdēre.

smith *n* faber *m*.

smithy *n* fabrica *f*.

smock *n* tunica *f*.

smoke *n* fūmus *m* ♦ *vi* fūmāre.

smoky *adj* fūmōsus.

smooth *adj* lēvis; (*skin*) glaber; (*talk*) blandus; (*sea*) placidus; (*temper*) aequus; (*voice*) lēvis, teres ♦ *vt* sternere, līmāre.

smoothly *adv* lēviter, lēniter.

smoothness *n* lēvitās *f*, lēnitās *f*.

smother *vt* opprimere, suffocāre.

smoulder *vi* fūmāre.

smudge *n* macula *f*.

smug *adj* suī contentus.

smuggle *vt* fūrtim importāre.

smugness *n* amor suī *m*.

smut *n* fūlīgō *f*.

snack *n* cēnula *f*; **take a ~** gustāre.

snag *n* impedīmentum *nt*, scrūpulus *m*.

snail *n* cochlea *f*.

snake *n* anguis *m*, serpēns *f*.

snaky *adj* vīpereus.

snap *vt* rumpere, praerumpere; **~ the fingers** digitīs concrepāre ♦ *vi* rumpī, dissilīre; **~ at** mordēre; **~ up** corripere.

snare *n* laqueus *m*, plaga *f*, pedica *f* ♦ *vt* inrētīre.

snarl *n* gannītus *m* ♦ *vi* gannīre.

snatch *vt* rapere, ēripere, adripere, corripere; **~ at** captāre.

sneak *n* perfidus *m* ♦ *vi* conrēpere; **~ in** sē īnsinuāre; **~ out** ēlābī.

sneaking *adj* humilis, fūrtīvus.

sneer *n* irrīsiō *f* ♦ *vi* irrīdēre, dērīdēre.

sneeze *n* sternūtāmentum *nt* ♦ *vi* sternuere.

sniff *vt* odōrārī.

snip *vt* praecīdere, secāre.

snob *n* homō ambitiōsus *m*.

snood *n* mitra *f*.

snooze *vi* dormītāre.

snore *vi* stertere.

snoring *n* rhoncus *m*.

snort *n* fremitus *m* ♦ *vi* fremere.

snout *n* rōstrum *nt*.

snow *n* nix *f* ♦ *vi* ningere; **~ed under** nive obrutus; **it is ~ing** ningit.

snowy *adj* nivālis; (*colour*) niveus.

snub *vt* neglegere, praeterīre.

snub-nosed *adj* sīmus.

snuff *n* (*candle*) fungus *m*.

snug *adj* commodus.

snugly *adv* commodē.

so *adv* (*referring back*) sīc; (*referring forward*) ita; (*with adj and adv*) tam; (*with verb*) adeō; (*consequence*) ergō, itaque, igitur; **and ~** itaque; **~ great** tantus; **so-so** sīc; **~ as to** ut; **~ be it** estō; **~ big** tantus; **~ far** usque adeō, adhūc; **~ far as** quod; **~ far from** adeō nōn; **~ little** tantillus; **~ long as** dum; **~ many** tot; **~ much** *adj* tantus ♦ *adv* tantum; (*with compar*) tantō; **~ often** totiēns; **~ that** ut (+ *subj*); **~ that ... not** (*purpose*) nē; (*result*) ut nōn; **and ~ on** deinceps; **not ~ very** haud ita; **say ~** id dīcere.

soak vt imbuere, madefacere.
soaking adj madidus.
soap n sapō m.
soar vi in sublīme ferrī, subvolāre; ~ **above** superāre.
sob n singultus m ♦ vi singultāre.
sober adj sobrius; (*conduct*) modestus; (*mind*) sānus.
soberly adv sobriē, modestē.
sobriety n modestia f, continentia f.
so-called adj quī dīcitur.
sociability n facilitās f.
sociable adj facilis, cōmis.
sociably adv faciliter, cōmiter.
social adj sociālis, commūnis.
socialism n populāris ratiō f.
socialist n homō populāris m/f.
society n societās f; (*class*) optimātēs mpl; (*being with*) convīctus m; **cultivate the ~ of** adsectārī; **secret ~** sodālitās f.
sod n caespes m, glaeba f.
soda n nitrum nt.
sodden adj madidus.
soever adv -cumque.
sofa n lectus m.
soft adj mollis; (*fruit*) mītis; (*voice*) submissus; (*character*) dēlicātus; (*words*) blandus.
soften vt mollīre; (*body*) ēnervāre; (*emotion*) lēnīre, mītigāre ♦ vi mollēscere, mītēscere.
soft-hearted adj misericors.
softly adv molliter, lēniter; blandē.
softness n mollitia f, mollitiēs f.
soil n sōlum nt, humus f ♦ vt inquināre, foedāre.
sojourn n commorātiō f, mānsiō f ♦ vi commorārī.
sojourner n hospes m, hospita f.
solace n sōlātium nt, levātiō f ♦ vt sōlārī, cōnsōlārī.
solar adj sōlis.
solder n ferrūmen nt ♦ vt ferrūmināre.
soldier n mīles m; **be a ~** mīlitāre; **common ~** manipulāris m, gregārius mīles m; **fellow ~** commīlitō m; **foot ~** pedes m; **old ~** veterānus m ♦ vi mīlitāre.
soldierly adj mīlitāris.
soldiery n mīles m.
sole adj sōlus, ūnus, ūnicus ♦ n (*foot*) planta f; (*fish*) solea f.
solecism n soloecismus m.
solely adv sōlum, tantum, modō.
solemn adj gravis; (*religion*) sanctus.
solemnity n gravitās f; sanctitās f.
solemnize vt agere.
solemnly adv graviter; rītē.
solicit vt flāgitāre, obsecrāre.
solicitation n flāgitātiō f.
solicitor n advocātus m.
solicitous adj anxius, trepidus.
solicitously adv anxiē, trepidē.
solicitude n cūra f, anxietās f.
solid adj solidus; (*metal*) pūrus; (*food*) firmus; (*argument*) firmus; (*character*) cōnstāns,

spectātus; **become ~** concrēscere; **make ~** cōgere.
solidarity n societās f.
solidify vt cōgere ♦ vi concrēscere.
solidity n soliditās f.
solidly adv firmē, cōnstanter.
soliloquize vi sēcum loquī.
soliloquy n ūnīus ōrātiō f.
solitary adj sōlus, sōlitārius; (*instance*) ūnicus; (*place*) dēsertus.
solitude n sōlitūdō f.
solo n canticum nt.
solstice n (*summer*) sōlstitium nt; (*winter*) brūma f.
solstitial adj sōlstitiālis, brūmālis.
soluble adj dissolūbilis.
solution n (*of puzzle*) ēnōdātiō f.
solve vt ēnōdāre, explicāre.
solvency n solvendī facultās f.
solvent adj: **be ~** solvendō esse.
sombre adj obscūrus; (*fig*) tristis.
some adj aliquī; (*pl*) nonnullī, aliquot; ~ **people** sunt quī (+ *subj*); ~ ... **other** alius ... alius; **for ~ time** aliquamdiū; **with ~ reason** nōn sine causā ♦ pron aliquis; (*pl*) nonnullī, sunt quī (*subj*), erant quī (*subj*).
somebody pron aliquis; ~ **or other** nescioquis.
somehow adv quōdammodō, nescio quōmodō.
someone pron aliquis; (*negative*) quisquam; ~ **or other** nescioquis; ~ **else** alius.
something pron aliquid; ~ **or other** nescioquid; ~ **else** aliud.
sometime adv aliquandō; (*past*) quondam.
sometimes adv interdum, nonnumquam; ~ ... ~ **modo** ... **modo**.
somewhat adv aliquantum, nōnnihil, paulum; (*with compar*) paulō, aliquantō.
somewhere adv alicubi; (*to*) aliquō; ~ **else** alibī; (*to*) aliō; **from ~** alicunde; **from ~ else** aliunde.
somnolence n somnus m.
somnolent adj sēmisomnus.
son n filius m; **small ~** fīliolus m.
song n carmen nt, cantus m.
son-in-law n gener m.
sonorous adj sonōrus, canōrus.
soon adv mox, brevi, citō; **as ~ as** ut prīmum, cum prīmum (+ *fut perf*), simul āc/atque (+ *perf indic*); **as ~ as possible** quam prīmum; **too ~** praemātūrē, ante tempus.
sooner adv prius, mātūrius; (*preference*) libentius, potius; ~ **or later** sērius ōcius; **no ~ said than done** dictum factum.
soonest adv mātūrissimē.
soot n fūlīgō f.
soothe vt dēlēnīre, permulcēre.
soothing adj lēnis, blandus.
soothingly adv blandē.
soothsayer n hariolus m, vātēs m/f, haruspex m.
sooty adj fūmōsus.
sop n offa f; (*fig*) dēlēnīmentum nt.

sophism n captiō f.
sophist n sophistēs m.
sophistical adj acūleātus, captiōsus.
sophisticated adj lepidus, urbānus.
sophistry n captiō f.
soporific adj sopōrifer, somnifer.
soprano adj acūtus.
sorcerer n veneficus m.
sorceress n venefica f, saga f.
sorcery n venēficium nt; (means) venēna ntpl, carmina ntpl.
sordid adj sordidus; (conduct) illīberālis.
sordidly adv sordidē.
sordidness n sordēs fpl; illīberālitās f.
sore adj molestus, gravis, acerbus; **feel** ~ dolēre ♦ n ulcus nt.
sorely adv graviter, vehementer.
sorrel n lapathus f, lapathum nt.
sorrow n dolor m, aegritūdō f; (outward) maeror m; (for death) lūctus m ♦ vi dolēre, maerere, lūgēre.
sorrowful adj maestus, tristis.
sorrowfully adv maestē.
sorry adj paenitēns; (poor) miser; **I am ~ for** (remorse) mē paenitet, mē piget (gen); (pity) mē miseret (gen).
sort n genus nt; **a ~ of** quīdam; **all ~s of** omnēs; **the ~ of** tālis; **this ~ of** huiusmodī; **the common ~** plēbs f; **I am not the ~ of man to** nōn is sum quī (+ subj); **I am out of ~s** mihī displiceō ♦ vt dīgerere, compōnere; (votes) diribēre.
sortie n excursiō f, excursus m, ēruptiō f; **make a ~** ērumpere, excurrere.
sot n ēbriōsus m.
sottish adj ēbriōsus, tēmulentus.
sottishness n vīnolentia f.
soul n anima f, animus m; (essence) vīs f; (person) caput nt; **not a ~** nēmō ūnus; **the ~ of** (fig) medulla f.
soulless adj caecus, dūrus.
sound n sonitus m, sonus m; (articulate) vōx f; (confused) strepitus m; (loud) fragor m; (strait) fretum nt ♦ vt (signal) canere; (instrument) īnflāre; (depth) scrūtārī, temptāre; (person) animum temptāre (gen) ♦ vi canere, sonāre; (seem) vidērī; ~ **a retreat** receptuī canere ♦ adj sānus, salūbris; (health) firmus; (sleep) artus; (judgment) exquīsītus; (argument) vērus; **safe and ~** salvus, incolumis.
soundly adv (beat) vehementer; (sleep) artē; (study) penitus, dīligenter.
soundness n sānitās f, integritās f.
soup n iūs nt.
sour adj acerbus, amārus, acidus; **turn ~** acēscere; (fig) coacēscere ♦ vt (fig) exacerbāre.
source n fōns m; (river) caput nt; (fig) fōns m, orīgō f; **have its ~ in** orīrī ex; (fig) proficīscī ex.
sourness n acerbitās f; (temper) mōrōsitās f.
souse vt immergere.

south n merīdiēs f ♦ adj austrālis ♦ adv ad merīdiem.
south-east adv inter sōlis ortum et merīdiem.
southerly adj ad merīdiem versus.
southern adj austrālis.
south-west adv inter occāsum sōlis et merīdiem.
south wind n auster m.
souvenir n monumentum nt.
sovereign n rēx m, rēgīna f ♦ adj prīnceps, summus.
sovereignty n rēgnum nt, imperium nt, prīncipātus m; (of the people) māiestās f.
sow n scrōfa f, sūs f.
sow vt serere; (field) cōnserere ♦ vi sementem facere.
sower n sator m.
sowing n sēmentis f.
spa n aquae fpl.
space n (extension) spatium nt; (not matter) ināne nt; (room) locus m; (distance) intervallum nt; (time) spatium nt; **open ~** ārea f; **leave a ~ of** intermittere ♦ vt: ~ **out** dispōnere.
spacious adj amplus, capāx.
spaciousness n amplitūdō f.
spade n pāla f, rūtrum nt.
span n (measure) palmus m; (extent) spatium nt ♦ vt iungere.
spangle n bractea f.
spangled adj distinctus.
spar n tignum nt.
spare vt parcere (dat); (to give) suppeditāre; ~ **time for** vacāre (dat) ♦ adj exīlis; (extra) subsecīvus.
sparing adj parcus.
sparingly adv parcē.
spark n scintilla f; (fig) igniculus m.
sparkle vi scintillāre, nitēre, micāre.
sparrow n passer m.
sparse adj rārus.
spasm n convulsiō f.
spasmodically adv interdum.
spatter vt aspergere.
spawn n ōva ntpl.
speak vt, vi loquī; (make speech) dīcere, contiōnārī, ōrātiōnem habēre; ~ **out** ēloquī; ~ **to** adloquī; (converse) colloquī cum; ~ **well of** bene dīcere (dat); **it ~s for itself** rēs ipsa loquitur.
speaker n ōrātor m.
speaking n: **art of ~** dīcendī ars f; **practise public ~** dēclāmāre ♦ adj: **likeness ~** vīvida imāgō.
spear n hasta f.
spearman n hastātus m.
special adj praecipuus, proprius.
speciality n proprium nt.
specially adv praecipuē, praesertim.
species n genus nt.
specific adj certus.
specification n dēsignātiō f.
specify vt dēnotāre, dēsignāre.

specimen n exemplar nt, exemplum nt.
specious adj speciōsus.
speciously adv speciōsē.
speciousness n speciēs f.
speck n macula f.
speckled adj maculīs distinctus.
spectacle n spectāculum nt.
spectacular adj spectābilis.
spectator n spectātor m.
spectral adj larvālis.
spectre n larva f.
speculate vi cōgitāre, coniectūrās facere; (COMM) forō ūtī.
speculation n cōgitātiō f, coniectūra f; (COMM) āleā f.
speculator n contemplātor m; (COMM) āleātor m.
speech n ōrātiō f; (language) sermō m, lingua f; (to people or troops) cōntiō f; **make a ~** ōrātiōnem/cōntiōnem habēre.
speechless adj ēlinguis, mūtus.
speed n celeritās f, cursus m, vēlōcitās f; **with all ~** summa celeritate; **at full ~** māgnō cursū, incitātus; (riding) citātō equō ♦ vt adcelerāre, mātūrāre ♦ vi properāre, festīnāre.
speedily adv celeriter, citō.
speedy adj celer, vēlōx, citus.
spell n carmen nt.
spellbound adj: **be ~** obstipēscere.
spelt n far nt.
spend vt impendere, īnsūmere; (public money) ērogāre; (time) agere, cōnsūmere, terere; (strength) effundere; **~ itself** (storm) dēsaevīre; **~ on** īnsūmere (acc & dat).
spendthrift n nepōs m, prōdigus m.
sphere n globus m; (of action) prōvincia f.
spherical adj globōsus.
sphinx n sphinx f.
spice n condīmentum nt; **~s** pl odōrēs mpl ♦ vt condīre.
spicy adj odōrātus; (wit) salsus.
spider n arānea f; **~'s web** arāneum nt.
spike n dēns m, clāvus m.
spikenard n nardus m.
spill vt fundere, profundere ♦ vi redundāre.
spin vt (thread) nēre, dēdūcere; (top) versāre; **~ out** (story) prōdūcere ♦ vi circumagī, versārī.
spindle n fūsus m.
spine n spīna f.
spineless adj ēnervātus.
spinster n virgō f.
spiral adj intortus ♦ n spīra f.
spire n cōnus m.
spirit n (life) anima f; (intelligence) mēns f; (soul) animus m; (vivacity) spīritus m, vigor m, vīs f; (character) ingenium nt; (intention) voluntās f; (of an age) mōrēs mpl; (ghost) anima f; **~s** pl mānēs mpl; **full of ~** alacer, animōsus.
spirited adj animōsus, ācer.
spiritless adj iners, frāctus, timidus.
spiritual adj animī.

spit n verū nt ♦ vi spuere, spūtāre; **~ on** cōnspūtāre; **~ out** exspuere.
spite n invidia f, malevolentia f, līvor m; **in ~ of me** mē invītō; **in ~ of the difficulties** in his angustiīs ♦ vt incommodāre, offendere.
spiteful adj malevolus, malignus, invidus.
spitefully adv malevolē, malignē.
spitefulness n malevolentia f.
spittle n spūtum nt.
splash n fragor m ♦ vt aspergere.
spleen n splēn m; (fig) stomachus m.
splendid adj splendidus, lūculentus; īnsignis; (person) amplus.
splendidly adv splendidē, optimē.
splendour n splendor m, fulgor m; (fig) lautitia f, adparātus m.
splenetic adj stomachōsus.
splice vt iungere.
splint n ferula f.
splinter n fragmentum nt, assula f ♦ vt findere.
split vt findere ♦ vi dissilīre ♦ adj fissus ♦ n fissum nt; (fig) dissidium nt.
splutter vi balbūtīre.
spoil n praeda f ♦ vt (rob) spoliāre; (mar) corrumpere ♦ vi corrumpī.
spoiler n spoliātor m; corruptor m.
spoils npl spolia ntpl, exuviae fpl.
spoke n radius m; **put a ~ in one's wheel** inicere scrūpulum (dat).
spokesman n interpres m, ōrātor m.
spoliation n spoliātiō f, dīreptiō f.
spondee n spondēus m.
sponge n spongia f.
sponsor n spōnsor m; (fig) auctor m.
spontaneity n impulsus m, voluntās f.
spontaneous adj voluntārius.
spontaneously adv suā sponte, ultrō.
spoon n cochlear nt.
sporadic adj rārus.
sporadically adv passim.
sport n lūdus m; (in Rome) campus m; (fun) iocus m; (ridicule) lūdibrium nt; **make ~ of** illūdere (dat) ♦ vi lūdere.
sportive adj lascīvus.
sportiveness n lascīvia f.
sportsman n vēnātor m.
sportsmanlike adj honestus, generōsus.
spot n macula f; (place) locus m; (dice) pūnctum nt; **on the ~** īlicō ♦ vt maculāre; (see) animadvertere.
spotless adj integer, pūrus; (character) castus.
spotted adj maculōsus.
spouse n coniunx m/f.
spout n (of jug) ōs nt; (pipe) canālis m ♦ vi ēmicāre.
sprain vt intorquēre.
sprawl vi sē fundere.
sprawling adj fūsus.
spray n aspergō f ♦ vt aspergere.
spread vt pandere, extendere; (news) dīvulgāre; (infection) vulgāre ♦ vi patēre; (rumour) mānāre, incrēbrēscere; (feeling) glīscere.

spreadeagle *vt* dispandere.
spreading *adj* (*tree*) patulus.
spree *n* cōmissātiō *f*.
sprig *n* virga *f*.
sprightliness *n* alacritās *f*.
sprightly *adj* alacer, hilaris.
spring *n* (*season*) vēr *nt*; (*water*) fōns *m*; (*leap*) saltus *m* ♦ *vi* (*grow*) crēscere, ēnāscī; (*leap*) salīre; ~ **from** orirī ex, proficīscī ex; ~ **on to** īnsilīre in (*acc*); ~ **up** exorīrī, exsilīre ♦ *vt*: ~ **a leak** rīmās agere; ~ **a surprise on** admīrātiōnem movēre (*dat*) ♦ *adj* vērnus.
springe *n* laqueus *m*.
sprinkle *vt* aspergere; ~ **on** īnspergere (*dat*).
sprint *vi* currere.
sprout *n* surculus *m* ♦ *vi* fruticārī.
spruce *adj* nitidus, concinnus.
sprung *adj* ortus, oriundus.
spume *n* spūma *f*.
spur *n* calcar *nt*; ~ **of a hill** prōminēns collis; **on the ~ of the moment** ex tempore ♦ *vt* incitāre; ~ **the willing horse** currentem incitāre; ~ **on** concitāre.
spurious *adj* falsus, fūcōsus, fictus.
spurn *vt* spernere, aspernārī, respuere.
spurt *vi* ēmicāre; (*run*) sē incitāre ♦ *n* impetus *m*.
spy *n* speculātor *m*, explōrātor *m* ♦ *vi* speculārī ♦ *vt* cōnspicere; ~ **out** explōrāre.
squabble *n* iūrgium *nt* ♦ *vi* rixārī.
squad *n* (*MIL*) decuria.
squadron *n* (*cavalry*) āla *f*, turma *f*; (*ships*) classis *f*.
squalid *adj* sordidus, dēfōrmis.
squall *n* procella *f*.
squally *adj* procellōsus.
squalor *n* sordēs *fpl*, squālor *m*.
squander *vt* dissipāre, disperdere, effundere.
squanderer *n* prōdigus *m*.
square *n* quadrātum *nt*; (*town*) ārea *f* ♦ *vt* quadrāre; (*account*) subdūcere ♦ *vi* cōnstāre, congruere ♦ *adj* quadrātus.
squash *vt* conterere, contundere.
squat *vi* subsīdere ♦ *adj* brevis atque obēsus.
squatter *n* (*on land*) agripeta *m*.
squawk *vi* crōcīre.
squeak *n* strīdor *m* ♦ *vi* strīdēre.
squeal *n* vāgītus *m* ♦ *vi* vāgīre.
squeamish *adj* fastīdiōsus; **feel ~** nauseāre, fastīdīre.
squeamishness *n* fastīdium *nt*, nausea *f*.
squeeze *vt* premere, comprimere; ~ **out** exprimere.
squint *adj* perversus ♦ *n*: **person with a ~** strabō *m* ♦ *vi* strabō esse.
squinter *n* strabō *m*.
squinting *adj* paetus.
squire *n* armiger *m*; (*landed*) dominus *m*.
squirm *vi* volūtārī.
squirrel *n* sciūrus *m*.
squirt *vt* ēicere, effundere ♦ *vi* ēmicāre.
stab *n* ictus *m*, vulnus *nt* ♦ *vt* fodere, ferīre, percutere.

stability *n* stabilitās *f*, firmitās *f*, cōnstantia *f*.
stabilize *vt* stabilīre, firmāre.
stable *adj* firmus, stabilis ♦ *n* stabulum *nt*, equīle *nt*; **shut the ~ door after the horse is stolen** clipeum post vulnera sūmere.
stack *n* acervus *m* ♦ *vt* congerere, cumulāre.
stadium *n* spatium *nt*.
staff *n* scīpiō *m*, virga *f*; (*augur's*) lituus *m*; (*officers*) contubernālēs *mpl*.
stag *n* cervus *m*.
stage *n* pulpitum *nt*, proscēnium *nt*; (*theatre*) scēna *f*, theātrum *nt*; (*scene of action*) campus *m*; (*of journey*) iter *nt*; (*of progress*) gradus *m* ♦ *adj* scēnicus ♦ *vt* (*play*) dare, docēre.
stage fright *n* horror *m*.
stagger *vi* titubāre ♦ *vt* obstupefacere.
stagnant *adj* iners.
stagnate *vi* (*fig*) cessāre, refrīgēscere.
stagnation *n* cessātiō *f*, torpor *m*.
stagy *adj* scēnicus.
staid *adj* sevērus, gravis.
stain *n* macula *f*, lābēs *f*; (*fig*) dēdecus *nt*, ignōminia *f* ♦ *vt* maculāre, foedāre, contāmināre; ~ **with** īnficere (*abl*).
stainless *adj* pūrus, integer.
stair *n* scālae *fpl*, gradus *mpl*.
staircase *n* scālae *fpl*.
stake *n* pālus *m*, stīpes *m*; (*pledge*) pignus *nt*; **be at ~** agī, in discrīmine esse ♦ *vt* (*wager*) dēpōnere.
stale *adj* obsolētus, effētus; (*wine*) vapidus.
stalemate *n*: **reach a ~** ad incitās redigī.
stalk *n* (*corn*) calamus *m*; (*plant*) stīpes *m* ♦ *vi* incēdere ♦ *vt* vēnārī, īnsidiārī (*dat*).
stall *n* (*animal*) stabulum *nt*; (*seat*) subsellium *nt*; (*shop*) taberna *f* ♦ *vt* stabulāre.
stallion *n* equus *m*.
stalwart *adj* ingēns, rōbustus, fortis.
stamina *n* patientia *f*.
stammer *n* haesitātiō *f* ♦ *vi* balbūtīre.
stammering *adj* balbus.
stamp *n* fōrma *f*; (*mark*) nota *f*, signum *nt*; (*of feet*) supplōsiō *f* ♦ *vt* imprimere; (*coin*) ferīre, signāre; (*fig*) inūrere; ~ **one's feet** pedem supplōdere; ~ **out** exstinguere.
stampede *n* discursus *m*; (*fig*) pavor *m* ♦ *vi* discurrere; (*fig*) expavēscere.
stance *n* status *m*.
stanchion *n* columna *f*.
stand *n* (*position*) statiō *f*; (*platform*) suggestus *m*; **make a ~** resistere, restāre ♦ *vi* stāre; (*remain*) manēre; (*matters*) sē habēre ♦ *vt* statuere; (*tolerate*) ferre, tolerāre; ~ **against** resistere (*dat*); ~ **aloof** abstāre; ~ **by** adsistere (*dat*); (*friend*) adesse (*dat*); (*promise*) praestāre; ~ **convicted** manifestum tenērī; ~ **down** concēdere; ~ **fast** cōnsistere; ~ **one's ground** in locō perstāre; ~ **for** (*office*) petere; (*meaning*) significāre; (*policy*) postulāre; ~ **in awe of** in metū habēre; ~ **in need of** indigēre (*abl*); ~ **on** īnsistere in (*abl*); ~ **on end** horrēre; ~ **on one's dignity** gravitātem suam tuērī; ~ **out** ēminēre, exstāre; (*against*)

resistere (*dat*); (*to sea*) in altum prōvehī; ~
out of the way of dēcēdere (*dat*); ~ **over**
(*case*) ampliāre; ~ **still** cōnsistere, īnsistere;
~ **to reason** sequī; ~ **trial** reum fierī; ~ **up**
surgere, cōnsurgere; ~ **up for** dēfendere,
adesse (*dat*); ~ **up to** respōnsāre (*dat*).
standard *n* (*MIL*) signum *nt*; (*measure*) nōrma *f*;
~ **author** scrīptor classicus *m*; **up to** ~ iūstus;
judge by the ~ **of** referre ad.
standard-bearer *n* signifer *m*.
standing *adj* perpetuus ♦ *n* status *m*; (*social*)
locus *m*, ōrdō *m*; **of long** ~ inveterātus; **be of**
long ~ inveterāscere.
stand-offish *adj* tēctus.
standstill *n*: **be at a** ~ haerēre, frīgēre; **bring**
to a ~ ad incitās redigere; **come to a** ~
īnsistere.
stanza *n* tetrastichon *nt*.
staple *n* uncus *m* ♦ *adj* praecipuus.
star *n* stēlla *f*, astrum *nt*; sīdus *nt*; **shooting ~s**
acontiae *fpl*.
starboard *adj* dexter.
starch *n* amylum *nt*.
stare *n* obtūtus *m* ♦ *vi* intentīs oculīs intuērī,
stupēre; ~ **at** contemplārī.
stark *adj* rigidus; simplex ♦ *adv* plānē, omnīnō.
starling *n* sturnus *m*.
starry *adj* stēllātus.
start *n* initium *nt*; (*movement*) saltus *m*;
(*journey*) profectiō *f*; **by fits and ~s** carptim;
have a day's ~ **on** diē antecēdere ♦ *vt*
incipere, īnstituere; (*game*) excitāre;
(*process*) movēre ♦ *vi* (*with fright*) resilīre;
(*journey*) proficīscī; ~ **up** exsilīre.
starting place *n* carcerēs *mpl*.
startle *vt* excitāre, terrēre.
starvation *n* fāmēs *f*.
starve *vi* fāme cōnficī; (*cold*) frīgēre ♦ *vt* fāme
ēnecāre.
starveling *n* fāmēlicus *m*.
state *n* (*condition*) status *m*, condiciō *f*; (*pomp*)
adparātus *m*; (*POL*) cīvitās *f*, rēs pūblica *f*; **the**
~ **of affairs is** ita sē rēs habet; **I know the** ~ **of**
affairs quō in locō rēs sit sciō; **of the** ~
pūblicus ♦ *adj* pūblicus ♦ *vt* adfirmāre,
expōnere, profitērī; ~ **one's case** causam
dīcere.
stateliness *n* māiestās *f*, gravitās *f*.
stately *adj* gravis, grandis, nōbilis.
statement *n* adfirmātiō *f*, dictum *nt*; (*witness*)
testimōnium *nt*.
state of health *n* valētūdō *f*.
state of mind *n* adfectiō *f*.
statesman *n* vir reī pūblicae gerendae
perītus *m*, cōnsilī pūblicī auctor *m*.
statesmanlike *adj* prūdēns.
statesmanship *n* cīvīlis prūdentia *f*.
static *adj* stabilis.
station *n* locus *m*; (*MIL*) statiō *f*; (*social*) locus *m*,
ōrdō *m* ♦ *vt* collocāre, pōnere; (*in different*
places) dispōnere.
stationary *adj* immōtus, statārius, stabilis.
statistics *n* cēnsus *m*.

statuary *n* fictor *m*.
statute *n* statua *f*, signum *nt*, imāgō *f*.
statuette *n* sigillum *nt*.
stature *n* fōrma *f*, statūra *f*.
status *n* locus *m*.
status quo *n*: **restore the** ~ ad integrum
restituere.
statutable *adj* lēgitimus.
statute *n* lēx *f*.
staunch *vt* (*blood*) sistere ♦ *adj* fīdus,
cōnstāns.
stave *vt* perrumpere, perfringere; ~ **off**
arcēre.
stay *n* firmāmentum *nt*; (*fig*) columen *nt*;
(*sojourn*) mānsiō *f*, commorātiō *f* ♦ *vt* (*prop*)
fulcīre; (*stop*) dētinēre, dēmorārī ♦ *vi*
manēre, commorārī.
stead *n* locus *m*; **stand one in good** ~ prōdesse
(*dat*).
steadfast *adj* firmus, stabilis, cōnstāns; ~ **at**
home tenēre sē domī.
steadfastly *adv* cōnstanter.
steadfastness *n* firmitās *f*, cōnstantia *f*.
steadily *adv* firmē, cōnstanter.
steadiness *n* stabilitās *f*; (*fig*) cōnstantia *f*.
steady *adj* stabilis, firmus; (*fig*) gravis,
cōnstāns.
steak *n* offa *f*.
steal *vt* surripere, fūrārī ♦ *vi*: ~ **away** sē
subdūcere; ~ **over** subrēpere (*dat*); ~ **into** sē
īnsinuāre in (*acc*); ~ **a march on** occupāre.
stealing *n* fūrtum *nt*.
stealth *n* fūrtum *nt*; **by** ~ fūrtim, clam.
stealthily *adv* fūrtim, clam.
stealthy *adj* fūrtīvus, clandestīnus.
steam *n* aquae vapor *m*, fūmus *m* ♦ *vi* fūmāre.
steed *n* equus *m*.
steel *n* ferrum *nt*, chalybs *m* ♦ *adj* ferreus ♦ *vt*
dūrāre; ~ **oneself** obdūrēscere.
steely *adj* ferreus.
steelyard *n* statēra *f*.
steep *adj* arduus, praeceps, praeruptus;
(*slope*) dēclīvis ♦ *vt* imbuere.
steeple *n* turris *f*.
steepness *n* arduum *nt*.
steer *vt* gubernāre, regere, dīrigere ♦ *n*
iuvencus *m*.
steering *n* gubernātiō *f*.
steersman *n* gubernātor *m*; rector *m*.
stellar *adj* stēllārum.
stem *n* stīpes *m*, truncus *m*; (*ship*) prōra *f* ♦ *vt*
adversārī (*dat*); ~ **the tide of** (*fig*) obsistere
(*dat*).
stench *n* foetor *m*.
stenographer *n* exceptor *m*, āctuārius *m*.
stenography *n* notae *fpl*.
stentorian *adj* (*voice*) ingēns.
step *n* gradus *m*; (*track*) vestīgium *nt*; (*of stair*)
gradus *m*; ~ **by** ~ gradātim; **flight of ~s**
gradus *mpl*; **take a** ~ gradum facere; **take ~s**
to ratiōnem inīre ut, vidēre ut; **march in** ~ in
numerum īre; **out of** ~ extrā numerum ♦ *vi*
gradī, incēdere; ~ **aside** dēcēdere; ~ **back**

regredī; ~ **forward** prōdīre; ~ **on** insistere (*dat*).

stepdaughter *n* prīvīgna *f*.

stepfather *n* vītricus *m*.

stepmother *n* noverca *f*.

stepson *n* prīvīgnus *m*.

stereotyped *adj* trītus.

sterile *adj* sterilis.

sterility *n* sterilitās *f*.

sterling *adj* integer, probus, gravis.

stern *adj* dūrus, sevērus; (*look*) torvus ♦ *n* puppis *f*.

sternly *adv* sevērē, dūriter.

sternness *n* sevēritās *f*.

stew *vt* coquere.

steward *n* prōcūrātor *m*; (*of estate*) vīlicus *m*.

stewardship *n* prōcūrātiō *f*.

stick *n* (*for beating*) fūstis *m*; (*for walking*) baculum *nt* ♦ *vi* haerēre; ~ **at nothing** ad omnia dēscendere; ~ **fast in** inhaerēre (*dat*), inhaerēscere in (*abl*); ~ **out** ēminēre; ~ **to** adhaerēre (*dat*); ~ **up** ēminēre; ~ **up for** dēfendere ♦ *vt* (*with glue*) conglūtināre; (*with point*) fīgere; ~ **into** īnfīgere; ~ **top on** praefīgere.

stickler *n* dīligēns (*gen*).

sticky *adj* lentus, tenāx.

stiff *adj* rigidus; (*difficult*) difficilis; **be** ~ rigēre.

stiffen *vt* rigidum facere ♦ *vi* rigēre.

stiffly *adv* rigidē.

stiff-necked *adj* obstinātus.

stiffness *n* rigor *m*.

stifle *vt* suffocāre; (*fig*) opprimere, restinguere.

stigma *n* nota *f*.

stigmatize *vt* notāre.

stile *n* saepēs *f*.

still *adj* immōtus, tranquillus, quiētus; tacitus ♦ *vt* lēnīre, sēdāre ♦ *adv* etiam, adhūc, etiamnum; (*past*) etiam tum; (*with compar*) etiam; (*adversative*) tamen, nihilōminus.

stillness *n* quiēs *f*; silentium *nt*.

stilly *adj* tacitus.

stilted *adj* (*language*) īnflātus.

stilts *n* grallae *fpl*.

stimulant *n* stimulus *m*.

stimulate *vt* stimulāre, acuere, exacuere, excitāre.

stimulus *n* stimulus *m*.

sting *n* aculeus *m*; (*wound*) ictus *m*; (*fig*) aculeus *m*, morsus *m* ♦ *vt* pungere, mordēre.

stingily *adv* sordidē.

stinginess *n* avāritia *f*, sordēs *fpl*, tenācitās *f*.

stinging *adj* (*words*) aculeātus, mordāx.

stingy *adj* sordidus, tenāx.

stink *n* foetor *m* ♦ *vi* foetere; ~ **of** olēre.

stinking *adj* foetidus.

stint *n* modus *m*; **without** ~ abundē ♦ *vt* circumscrībere.

stipend *n* mercēs *f*.

stipulate *vt* pacīscī, stipulārī.

stipulation *n* condiciō *f*, pactum *nt*.

stir *n* tumultus *m* ♦ *vt* movēre, agitāre; (*fig*)

commovēre; ~ **up** excitāre, incitāre ♦ *vi* movērī.

stirring *adj* impiger, tumultuōsus; (*speech*) ārdēns.

stitch *vt* suere ♦ *n* sūtūra *f*; (*in side*) dolor *m*.

stock *n* stirps *f*, genus *nt*, gēns *f*; (*equipment*) īnstrūmenta *ntpl*; (*supply*) cōpia *f*; (*investment*) pecūniae *fpl*; **live**~ rēs pecuāria *f* ♦ *vt* īnstruere ♦ *adj* commūnis, trītus.

stockade *n* vallum *nt*.

stock dove *n* palumbēs *m/f*.

stock in trade *n* īnstrūmenta *ntpl*.

stocks *n* (*ship*) nāvālia *ntpl*; (*torture*) compedēs *fpl*.

stock-still *adj* plānē immōtus.

stocky *adj* brevis atque obēsus.

stodgy *adj* crūdus, īnsulsus.

stoic *n* Stōicus *m* ♦ *adj* Stōicus.

stoical *adj* dūrus, patiēns.

stoically *adv* patienter.

stoicism *n* Stōicōrum ratiō *f*, Stōicōrum disciplīna *f*.

stoke *vt* agitāre.

stole *n* stola *f*.

stolid *adj* stolidus.

stolidity *n* īnsulsitās *f*.

stolidly *adv* stolidē.

stomach *n* stomachus *m*; venter *m* ♦ *vt* patī, tolerāre.

stone *n* lapis *m*, saxum *nt*; (*precious*) gemma *f*, lapillus *m*; (*of fruit*) acinum *nt*; **leave no** ~ **unturned** omnia experīrī; **kill two birds with one** ~ ūnō saltū duōs aprōs capere; **hewn** ~ saxum quadrātum; **unhewn** ~ caementum *nt* ♦ *vt* lapidibus percutere ♦ *adj* lapideus; ~ **blind** plānē caecus; ~ **deaf** plānē surdus.

stonecutter *n* lapicīda *m*.

stony *adj* (*soil*) lapidōsus; (*path*) scrūpōsus; (*feeling*) dūrus, ferreus.

stool *n* sēdēcula *f*.

stoop *vi* sē dēmittere; ~ **to** dēscendere in (*acc*).

stop *n* mora *f*; (*punctuation*) pūnctum *nt*; **come to a** ~ īnsistere; **put a** ~ **to** comprimere, dirimere ♦ *vt* sistere, inhibēre, fīnīre; (*restrain*) cohibēre; (*hole*) obtūrāre; ~ **up** occlūdere, interclūdere ♦ *vi* dēsinere, dēsistere; (*motion*) īnsistere.

stopgap *n* tībīcen *m*.

stoppage *n* interclūsiō *f*, impedīmentum *nt*.

stopper *n* obtūrāmentum *nt*.

store *n* cōpia *f*; (*place*) horreum *nt*; (*for wine*) apothēca *f*; **be in** ~ **for** manēre; **set great** ~ **by** magnī aestimāre ♦ *vt* condere, repōnere; ~ **away** recondere; ~ **up** repōnere, congerere.

storehouse *n* (*fig*) thēsaurus *m*.

storekeeper *n* cellārius *m*.

storeship *n* nāvis frūmentāria *f*.

storey *n* tabulātum *nt*.

stork *n* cicōnia *f*.

storm *n* tempestās *f*, procella *f*; **take by** ~ expugnāre ♦ *vt* (MIL) expugnāre ♦ *vi* saevīre; ~ **at** īnsectārī, invehī in (*acc*).

stormbound *adj* tempestāte dētentus.
stormer *n* expugnātor *m*.
storming *n* expugnātiō *f*.
stormy *adj* turbidus, procellōsus; (*fig*)
turbulentus.
story *n* fābula *f*, nārrātiō *f*; (*short*) fābella *f*;
(*untrue*) mendācium *nt*.
storyteller *n* nārrātor *m*; (*liar*) mendāx *m*.
stout *adj* pinguis; (*brave*) fortis; (*strong*)
validus, rōbustus; (*material*) firmus.
stouthearted *adj* māgnanimus.
stoutly *adv* fortiter.
stove *n* camīnus *m*, fornāx *f*.
stow *vt* repōnere, condere; ~ **away** *vi* in nāvī
dēlitēscere.
straddle *vi* vāricāre.
straggle *vi* deerrāre, pālārī.
straggler *n* pālāns *m*.
straggling *adj* dispersus, rārus.
straight *adj* rēctus, dīrēctus; (*fig*) apertus,
vērāx; **in a ~ line** rēctā, ē regiōne; **set ~**
dīrigere ♦ *adv* dīrēctō, rēctā.
straighten *vt* corrigere, extendere.
straightforward *adj* simplex, dīrēctus; (*easy*)
facilis.
straightforwardness *n* simplicitās *f*.
straightness *n* (*fig*) integritās *f*.
straightway *adv* statim, extemplō.
strain *n* contentiō *f*; (*effort*) labor *m*; (*music*)
modī *mpl*; (*breed*) genus *nt* ♦ *vt* intendere,
contendere; (*injure*) nimiā contentiōne
dēbilitāre; (*liquid*) dēliquāre, percōlāre ♦ *vi*
ēnītī, vīrēs contendere.
strained *adj* (*language*) arcessītus.
strainer *n* cōlum *nt*.
strait *adj* angustus ♦ *n* fretum *nt*; **~s** *pl*
angustiae *fpl*.
straiten *vt* coartāre, contrahere; **~ed**
circumstances angustiae *fpl*.
strait-laced *adj* tristis, sevērus.
strand *n* lītus *nt*; (*of rope*) fīlum *nt* ♦ *vt* (*ship*)
ēicere.
strange *adj* novus, īnsolitus; (*foreign*)
peregrīnus; (*another's*) aliēnus; (*ignorant*)
rudis, expers.
strangely *adv* mīrē, mīrum in modum.
strangeness *n* novitās *f*, īnsolentia *f*.
stranger *n* (*from abroad*) advena *f*; peregrīnus
m; (*visiting*) hospes *m*, hospita *f*; (*not of the
family*) externus *m*; (*unknown*) ignōtus *m*.
strangle *vt* strangulāre, laqueō gulam
frangere.
strap *n* lōrum *nt*, habēna *f*.
strapping *adj* grandis.
stratagem *n* cōnsilium *nt*, fallācia *f*.
strategic *adj* (*action*) prūdēns; (*position*)
idōneus.
strategist *n* artis bellicae perītus *m*.
strategy *n* ars imperātōria *f*, cōnsilia *ntpl*.
straw *n* (*stalk*) culmus *m*; (*collective*)
strāmentum *nt*; **not care a ~ for** floccī nōn
facere ♦ *adj* strāmenticius.
strawberry *n* frāgum *nt*.

strawberry tree *n* arbutus *m*.
stray *vt* aberrāre, deerrāre; vagārī ♦ *adj*
errābundus.
streak *n* līnea *f*, macula *f*; (*light*) radius *m*;
(*character*) vēna *f* ♦ *vt* maculāre.
stream *n* flūmen *nt*, fluvius *m*; **down** ~ secundō
flūmine; **up** ~ adversō flūmine ♦ *vi* fluere, sē
effundere; ~ **into** īnfluere in (*acc*).
streamlet *n* rīvus *m*, rīvulus *m*.
street *n* via *f*, platea *f*.
strength *n* vīrēs *fpl*; (*of material*) firmitās *f*; (*fig*)
rōbur *nt*, nervī *mpl*; (MIL) numerus *m*; **know**
the enemy's ~ quot sint hostēs scīre; **on the ~**
of frētus (*abl*).
strengthen *vt* firmāre, corrōborāre; (*position*)
mūnīre.
strenuous *adj* impiger, strēnuus, sēdulus.
strenuously *adv* impigrē, strēnuē.
strenuousness *n* industria *f*.
stress *n* (*words*) ictus *m*; (*meaning*) vīs *f*;
(*importance*) mōmentum *nt*; (*difficulty*) labor
m; **lay great ~ on** in māgnō discrīmine pōnere
♦ *vt* exprimere.
stretch *n* spatium *nt*, tractus *m*; **at a ~** sine ullā
intermissiōne ♦ *vt* tendere, intendere;
(*length*) prōdūcere, extendere; (*facts*) in
māius crēdere; ~ **a point** indulgēre; ~ **before**
obtendere; ~ **forth** porrigere; ~ **oneself** (*on
ground*) sternī; ~ **out** porrigere, extendere ♦
vi extendī, patēscere.
strew *vt* (*things*) sternere; (*place*) cōnsternere.
stricken *adj* saucius.
strict *adj* (*defined*) ipse, certus; (*severe*)
sevērus, rigidus; (*accurate*) dīligēns.
strictly *adv* sevērē; dīligenter; ~ **speaking**
scīlicet, immo.
strictness *n* sevēritās *f*; dīligentia *f*.
stricture *n* vītuperātiō *f*.
stride *n* passus *m*; **make great ~s** (*fig*) multum
prōficere ♦ *vi* incēdere, ingentēs gradūs
ferre.
strident *adj* asper.
strife *n* discordia *f*, pugna *f*.
strike *vt* ferīre, percutere; (*instrument*)
pellere, pulsāre; (*sail*) subdūcere; (*tent*)
dētendere; (*mind*) venīre in (*acc*); (*camp*)
movēre; (*fear into*) incutere in (*acc*); ~ **against**
offendere; ~ **out** dēlēre; ~ **up** (*music*)
incipere; ~ **a bargain** pacīscī; **be struck**
vāpulāre ♦ *vi* (*work*) cessāre.
striking *adj* īnsignis, īnsignītus, ēgregius.
strikingly *adv* īnsignītē.
string *n* (*cord*) resticula *f*; (*succession*) seriēs *f*;
(*instrument*) nervus *m*; (*bow*) nervus *m*; **have**
two ~s to one's bow duplicī spē ūtī ♦ *vt* (*bow*)
intendere; (*together*) coniungere.
stringency *n* sevēritās *f*.
stringent *adj* sevērus.
strip *vt* nūdāre, spoliāre, dēnūdāre; ~ **off**
exuere; (*leaves*) stringere, dēstringere ♦ *n*
lacinia *f*.
stripe *n* virga *f*; (*on tunic*) clāvus *m*; **~s** *pl*
verbera *ntpl*.

striped adj virgātus.
stripling n adulescentulus m.
strive vi nītī, ēnītī, contendere; (contend) certāre.
stroke n ictus m; (lightning) fulmen nt; (oar) pulsus m; (pen) līnea f; ~ **of luck** fortūna secunda f ♦ vt mulcēre, dēmulcēre.
stroll vi deambulāre, spatiārī.
strong adj fortis, validus; (health) rōbustus, firmus; (material) firmus; (smell) gravis; (resources) pollēns, potēns; (feeling) ācer, māgnus; (language) vehemēns, probrōsus; **be** ~ valēre; **be twenty** ~ vīgintī esse numerō.
strongbox n arca f.
stronghold n arx f.
strongly adv validē, vehementer, fortiter, ācriter, graviter.
strong-minded adj pertināx, cōnstans.
strophe n stropha f.
structure n aedificium nt; (form) structūra f; (arrangement) compositiō f.
struggle n (effort) cōnātus m; (fight) pugna f, certāmen nt ♦ vi nītī; certāre, contendere; (fight) luctārī; ~ **upwards** ēnītī.
strut vi māgnificē incēdere.
stubble n stipula f.
stubborn adj pertināx, pervicāx.
stubbornly adv pertināciter, pervicāciter.
stubbornness n pertinācia f, pervicācia f.
stucco n gypsum nt.
stud n clāvus m; (horses) equī mpl.
studded adj distinctus.
student n discipulus m; **be a** ~ **of** studēre (dat).
studied adj meditātus, accūrātus; (language) exquīsītus.
studio n officīna f.
studious adj litterīs dēditus, litterārum studiōsus; (careful) attentus.
studiously adv dē industriā.
study vt studēre (dat); (prepare) meditārī; ~ **under** audīre ♦ n studium nt; (room) bibliothēca f.
stuff n māteria f; (cloth) textile nt ♦ vt farcīre, refercīre; (with food) sagināre.
stuffing n sagina f; (of cushion) tōmentum nt.
stultify vt ad irritum redigere.
stumble vi offendere; ~ **upon** incidere in (acc), offendere.
stumbling block n offēnsiō f.
stump n stīpes m.
stun vt stupefacere; (fig) obstupefacere, cōnfundere.
stunned adj attonitus.
stunt vt corporis auctum inhibēre.
stunted adj curtus.
stupefaction n stupor m.
stupefied adj: **be** ~ stupēre, obstupefacere.
stupefy vt obstupefacere.
stupendous adj mīrus, mīrificus.
stupid adj stultus, hebes, ineptus.
stupidity n stultitia f.
stupidly adv stultē, ineptē.
stupor n stupor m.

sturdily adv fortiter.
sturdiness n rōbur nt, firmitās f.
sturdy adj fortis, rōbustus.
sturgeon n acipēnser m.
stutter vi balbūtire.
stuttering adj balbus.
sty n hara f.
style n (kind) genus nt, ratiō f; (of dress) habitus m; (of prose) ēlocūtiō f, ōrātiō f; (pen) stilus m ♦ vt appellāre.
stylish adj ēlegāns, lautus, expolītus.
stylishly adv ēleganter.
suasion n suāsiō f.
suave adj blandus, urbānus.
suavity n urbānitās f.
subaltern n succenturiō m.
subdivide vt dīvidere.
subdivision n pars f, mōmentum nt.
subdue vt subigere, dēvincere, redigere, domāre; (fig) cohibēre.
subdued adj dēmissus, summissus.
subject n (person) cīvis m/f; (matter) rēs f; (theme) locus m, argūmentum nt ♦ adj subiectus; ~ **to** obnoxius (dat) ♦ vt subicere; obnoxium reddere.
subjection n servitūs f.
subjective adj proprius.
subject matter n māteria f.
subjoin vt subicere, subiungere.
subjugate vt subigere, dēbellāre, domāre.
sublime adj sublīmis, ēlātus, excelsus.
sublimely adv excelsē.
sublimity n altitūdō f, ēlātiō f.
submarine adj submersus.
submerge vt dēmergere; (flood) inundāre ♦ vi sē dēmergere.
submersed adj submersus.
submission n obsequium nt, servitium nt; (fig) patientia f.
submissive adj submissus, docilis, obtemperāns.
submissively adv submissē, oboedienter, patienter.
submit vi sē dēdere; ~ **to** pārēre (dat), obtemperāre (dat), patī, subīre ♦ vt (proposal) referre.
subordinate adj subiectus, secundus ♦ vt subiungere, subicere.
suborn vt subicere, subōrnāre.
subpoena vt testimōnium dēnūntiāre (dat).
subscribe vt (name) subscrībere; (money) cōnferre.
subscription n collātiō f.
subsequent adj sequēns, posterior.
subsequently adv posteā, mox.
subserve vt subvenīre (dat), commodāre.
subservience n obsequium nt.
subservient adj obsequēns; (thing) ūtilis, commodus.
subside vi dēsīdere, resīdere; (fever) dēcēdere; (wind) cadere; (passion) dēfervēscere.
subsidence n lābēs f.

subsidiary *adj* subiectus, secundus.
subsidize *vt* pecūniās suppeditāre (*dat*).
subsidy *n* pecūniae *fpl*, vectīgal *nt*.
subsist *vi* cōnstāre, sustentārī.
subsistence *n* vīctus *m*.
substance *n* (*matter*) rēs *f*, corpus *nt*; (*essence*) nātūra *f*; (*gist*) summa *f*; (*reality*) rēs *f*; (*wealth*) opēs *fpl*.
substantial *adj* solidus; (*real*) vērus; (*important*) gravis; (*rich*) opulentus, dīves.
substantially *adv* rē; māgnā ex parte.
substantiate *vt* cōnfirmāre.
substitute *vt* subicere, repōnere, substituere ♦ *n* vicārius *m*.
substratum *n* fundāmentum *nt*.
subterfuge *n* latebra *f*, perfugium *nt*.
subterranean *adj* subterrāneus.
subtle *adj* (*fine*) subtīlis; (*shrewd*) acūtus, astūtus.
subtlety *n* subtīlitās *f*; acūmen *nt*, astūtia *f*.
subtly *adv* subtīliter; acūtē, astūtē.
subtract *vt* dētrahere, dēmere; (*money*) dēdūcere.
subtraction *n* dētractiō *f*, dēductiō *f*.
suburb *n* suburbium *nt*.
suburban *adj* suburbānus.
subvention *n* pecūniae *fpl*.
subversion *n* ēversiō *f*, ruīna *f*.
subversive *adj* sēditiōsus.
subvert *vt* ēvertere, subruere.
subverter *n* ēversor *m*.
succeed *vi* (*person*) rem bene gerere; (*activity*) prosperē ēvenīre; ~ **in obtaining** impetrāre ♦ *vt* īnsequī, excipere, succēdere (*dat*).
success *n* bonus ēventus *m*, rēs bene gesta *f*.
successful *adj* fēlīx; (*thing*) secundus; **be** ~ rem bene gerere; (*play*) stāre.
successfully *adv* fēlīciter, prosperē, bene.
succession *n* (*coming next*) successiō *f*; (*line*) seriēs *f*, ōrdō *m*; **alternate** ~ vicissitūdō *f*; **in** ~ deinceps, ex ōrdine.
successive *adj* continuus, perpetuus.
successively *adv* deinceps, ex ōrdine; (*alternately*) vicissim.
successor *n* successor *m*.
succinct *adj* brevis, pressus.
succinctly *adv* breviter, pressē.
succour *n* auxilium *nt*, subsidium *nt* ♦ *vt* subvenīre (*dat*), succurrere (*dat*), opem ferre (*dat*).
succulence *n* sūcus *m*.
succulent *adj* sūcidus.
succumb *vi* succumbere, dēficere.
such *adj* tālis, ēiusmodī, hūiusmodī; (*size*) tantus; **at** ~ **a time** id temporis; ~ **great** tantus.
suchlike *adj* hūiusmodī, ēiusdem generis.
suck *vt* sūgere; ~ **in** sorbēre; ~ **up** exsorbēre, ēbibere.
sucker *n* surculus *m*.
sucking *adj* (*child*) lactēns.
suckle *vt* nūtrīcārī, mammam dare (*dat*).
suckling *n* lactēns *m/f*.

sudden *adj* subitus, repentīnus.
suddenly *adv* subitō, repente.
sue *vt* in iūs vocāre, lītem intendere (*dat*); ~ **for** rogāre, petere, ōrāre.
suffer *vt* patī, ferre, tolerāre; (*injury*) accipere; (*loss*) facere; (*permit*) patī, sinere ♦ *vi* dolōre adficī; ~ **defeat** cladem accipere; ~ **from** labōrāre ex, adficī (*abl*); ~ **for** poenās dare (*gen*).
sufferable *adj* tolerābilis.
sufferance *n* patientia *f*, tolerantia *f*.
suffering *n* dolor *m*.
suffice *vi* sufficere, suppetere.
sufficiency *n* satis.
sufficient *adj* idōneus, satis (*gen*).
sufficiently *adv* satis.
suffocate *vt* suffocāre.
suffrage *n* suffrāgium *nt*.
suffuse *vt* suffundere.
sugar *n* saccharon *nt*.
suggest *vt* admonēre, inicere, subicere; ~ **itself** occurrere.
suggestion *n* admonitiō *f*; **at the** ~ **of** admonitū (*gen*); **at my** ~ mē auctōre.
suicidal *adj* fūnestus.
suicide *n* mors voluntāria *f*; **commit** ~ mortem sibī cōnscīscere.
suit *n* (*law*) līs *f*, āctiō *f*; (*clothes*) vestītus *m* ♦ *vt* convenīre (*dat*), congruere (*dat*); (*dress*) sedēre (*dat*), decēre; **it ~s** decet; **to** ~ **me** dē meā sententiā.
suitability *n* convenientia *f*.
suitable *adj* aptus (+ *acc*), idōneus (+ *acc*).
suitably *adv* aptē, decenter.
suite *n* comitēs *mpl*, comitātus *m*.
suitor *n* procus *m*, amāns *m*.
sulk *vi* aegrē ferre, mōrōsus esse.
sulky *adj* mōrōsus, tristis.
sullen *adj* tristis, mōrōsus.
sullenness *n* mōrōsitās *f*.
sully *vt* īnfuscāre, contāmināre.
sulphur *n* sulfur *nt*.
sultriness *n* aestus *m*.
sultry *adj* aestuōsus.
sum *n* summa *f*; ~ **of money** pecūnia *f* ♦ *vt* subdūcere, computāre; ~ **up** summātim dēscrībere; **to** ~ **up** ūnō verbō, quid plūra?
summarily *adv* strictim, summātim; sine mōrā.
summarize *vt* summātim dēscrībere.
summary *n* summārium *nt*, epitomē *f* ♦ *adj* subitus, praesēns.
summer *n* aestās *f* ♦ *adj* aestīvus; **of** ~ aestīvus.
summit *n* vertex *m*, culmen *nt*; (*fig*) fastīgium *nt*; **the** ~ **of** summus.
summon *vt* arcessere; (*meeting*) convocāre; (*witness*) citāre; ~ **up courage** animum sūmere.
summons *n* (*law*) vocātiō *f* ♦ *vt* in iūs vocāre, diem dīcere (*dat*).
sumptuary *adj* sūmptuārius.
sumptuous *adj* sūmptuōsus, adparātus,

mágnificus, lautus.
sumptuously *adv* sūmptuōsē, mágnificē.
sun *n* sōl *m* ♦ *vt*: ~ **oneself** aprīcārī.
sunbeam *n* radius *m*.
sunburnt *adj* adūstus.
sunder *vt* sēparāre, dīvidere.
sundial *n* sōlārium *nt*.
sundry *adj* dīversī, complūrēs.
sunlight *n* sōl *m*.
sunlit *adj* aprīcus.
sunny *adj* aprīcus, serēnus.
sunrise *n* sōlis ortus *m*.
sunset *n* sōlis occāsus *m*.
sunshade *n* umbella *f*.
sunshine *n* sōl *m*.
sup *vi* cēnāre.
superabundance *n* abundantia *f*.
superabundant *adj* nimius.
superabundantly *adv* satis superque.
superannuated *adj* ēmeritus.
superb *adj* mágnificus.
superbly *adv* mágnificē.
supercilious *adj* adrogāns, superbus.
superciliously *adv* adroganter, superbē.
superciliousness *n* adrogantia *f*, fastus *m*.
supererogation *n*: **of** ~ ultrō factus.
superficial *adj* levis; **acquire a ~ knowledge of**
 prīmīs labrīs gustāre.
superficiality *n* levitās *f*.
superficially *adv* leviter, strictim.
superfluity *n* abundantia *f*.
superfluous *adj* supervacāneus, nimius; **be ~**
 redundāre.
superhuman *adj* dīvīnus, hūmānō māior.
superimpose *vt* superimpōnere.
superintend *vt* prōcūrāre, praeesse (*dat*).
superintendence *n* cūra *f*.
superintendent *n* cūrātor *m*, praefectus *m*.
superior *adj* melior, amplior; **be ~** praestāre,
 superāre ♦ *n* prīnceps *m*, praefectus *m*.
superiority *n* praestantia *f*; **have the ~**
 superāre; (*in numbers*) plūrēs esse.
superlative *adj* ēgregius, optimus.
supernatural *adj* dīvīnus.
supernaturally *adv* dīvīnitus.
supernumerary *adj* adscrīptīcius; **~ soldiers**
 accēnsī *mpl*.
superscription *n* titulus *m*.
supersede *vt* succēdere (*dat*), in locum
 succēdere (*gen*); **~ gold with silver** prō aurō
 argentum suppōnere.
superstition *n* rēligiō *f*, superstitiō *f*.
superstitious *adj* rēligiōsus, superstitiōsus.
supervene *vi* īnsequī, succēdere.
supervise *vt* prōcūrāre.
supervision *n* cūra *f*.
supervisor *n* cūrātor *m*.
supine *adj* supīnus; (*fig*) neglegēns, segnis.
supinely *adv* segniter.
supper *n* cēna *f*; **after ~** cēnātus.
supperless *adj* iēiūnus.
supplant *vt* praevertere.
supple *adj* flexibilis, mollis.

supplement *n* appendix *f* ♦ *vt* amplificāre.
supplementary *adj* additus.
suppleness *n* mollitia *f*.
suppliant *n* supplex *m/f*.
supplicate *vt* supplicāre, obsecrāre.
supplication *n* precēs *fpl*.
supplies *npl* commeātus *m*.
supply *n* cōpia *f* ♦ *vt* suppeditāre, praebēre;
 (*loss*) supplēre.
support *n* firmāmentum *nt*; (*help*) subsidium *nt*,
 adiūmentum *nt*; (*food*) alimenta *ntpl*; (*of party*)
 favor *m*; (*of needy*) patrōcinium *nt*; **I ~** subsidiō
 sum (*dat*); **lend ~ to rumours** alimenta
 rūmōribus addere ♦ *vt* fulcīre; (*living*)
 sustinēre, sustentāre; (*with help*) adiuvāre,
 opem ferre (*dat*); (*at law*) adesse (*dat*).
supportable *adj* tolerābilis.
supporter *n* fautor *m*; (*at trial*) advocātus *m*; (*of
 proposal*) auctor *m*.
supporting cast *n* adiūtōrēs *mpl*.
suppose *vi* (*assume*) pōnere; (*think*)
 existimāre, opīnārī, crēdere; **~ it is true** fac
 vērum esse.
supposedly *adv* ut fāma est.
supposing *conj* sī; (*for the sake of argument*) sī
 iam.
supposition *n* opīniō *f*; **on this ~** hōc positō.
supposititious *adj* subditus, subditīvus.
suppress *vt* opprimere, comprimere;
 (*knowledge*) cēlāre, reticēre; (*feelings*)
 coercēre, reprimere.
suppression *n* (*of fact*) reticentia *f*.
supremacy *n* imperium *nt*, dominātus *m*,
 prīncipātus *m*.
supreme *adj* summus; **be ~** dominārī; **~
 command** imperium *nt*.
supremely *adv* ūnicē, plānē.
sure *adj* certus; (*fact*) explōrātus; (*friend*) fīdus;
 be ~ of compertum habēre; **feel ~** persuāsum
 habēre, haud scīre an; pro certō habēre;
 make ~ of (*fact*) comperīre; (*action*) efficere
 ut; **to be ~** quidem; **~ enough** rē vērā.
surely *adv* certō, certē, nonne; (*tentative*)
 scīlicet, sānē; **~ you do not think?** num
 putās?; **~ not** num.
surety *n* (*person*) vās *m*, praes *m*, spōnsor *m*;
 (*deposit*) fīdūcia *f*; **be ~ for** spondēre prō.
surf *n* fluctus *m*.
surface *n* superficiēs *f*; **~ of the water** summa
 aqua.
surfeit *n* satietās *f* ♦ *vt* satiāre, explēre.
surge *n* aestus *m*, fluctus *m* ♦ *vi* tumēscere.
surgeon *n* chīrūrgus *m*.
surgery *n* chīrūrgia *f*.
surlily *adv* mōrōsē.
surliness *n* mōrōsitās *f*.
surly *adj* mōrōsus, difficilis.
surmise *n* coniectūra *f* ♦ *vi* suspicārī,
 conicere, augurārī.
surmount *vt* superāre.
surmountable *adj* superābilis.
surname *n* cognōmen *nt*.
surpass *vt* excellere, exsuperāre, antecēdere.

surpassing *adj* excellēns.
surplus *n* reliquum *nt*; (*money*) pecūniae residuae *fpl*.
surprise *n* admīrātiō *f*; (*cause*) rēs inopīnāta *f*; **take by ~** dēprehendere ♦ *adj* subitus ♦ *vt* dēprehendere; (*MIL*) opprimere; **be ~d** dēmīrārī; **be ~d at** admīrārī.
surprising *adj* mīrus, mīrābilis.
surprisingly *adv* mīrē, mīrābiliter.
surrender *vt* dēdere, trādere, concēdere ♦ *vi* sē dēdere; **~ unconditionally to** sē suaque omnia potestātī permittere (*gen*) ♦ *n* dēditiō *f*; (*legal*) cessiō *f*; **unconditional ~** permissiō *f*.
surreptitious *adj* fūrtīvus.
surreptitiously *adv* fūrtim, clam; **get in ~** inrēpere in (*acc*).
surround *vt* circumdare, cingere, circumvenīre, circumfundere.
surrounding *adj* circumiectus; **~s** *n* vīcīnia *f*.
survey *vt* contemplārī, cōnsīderāre; (*land*) mētārī ♦ *n* contemplātiō *f*; (*land*) mēnsūra *f*.
surveyor *n* fīnītor *m*, agrīmēnsor *m*, mētātor *m*.
survival *n* salūs *f*.
survive *vt* superāre ♦ *vt* superesse (*dat*).
survivor *n* superstes *m/f*.
susceptibility *n* mollitia *f*.
susceptible *adj* mollis.
suspect *vt* suspicārī; **be ~ed** in suspiciōnem venīre.
suspend *vt* suspendere; (*activity*) differre; (*person*) locō movēre; **be ~ed** pendēre.
suspense *n* dubitātiō *f*; **be in ~** animī pendēre, haerēre.
suspicion *n* suspiciō *f*; **direct ~ to** suspiciōnem adiungere ad.
suspicious *adj* (*suspecting*) suspiciōsus; (*suspected*) dubius, anceps.
sustain *vt* (*weight*) sustinēre; (*life*) alere, sustentāre; (*hardship*) ferre, sustinēre; (*the part of*) agere.
sustenance *n* alimentum *nt*, vīctus *m*.
sutler *n* lixa *m*.
suzerain *n* dominus *m*.
swaddling clothes *n* incūnābula *ntpl*.
swagger *vi* sē iactāre.
swaggerer *n* homō glōriōsus *m*.
swallow *n* hirundō *f* ♦ *vt* dēvorāre; **~ up** absorbēre.
swamp *n* palūs *f* ♦ *vt* opprimere.
swampy *adj* ūlīginōsus.
swan *n* cycnus *m*; **~'s** cycnēus.
swank *vi* sē iactāre.
sward *n* caespes *m*.
swarm *n* exāmen *nt*; (*fig*) nūbēs *f* ♦ *vi*: **~ round** circumfundī.
swarthy *adj* fuscus, aquilus.
swathe *vt* conligāre.
sway *n* dīciō *f*, imperium *nt*; **bring under one's ~** suae dīciōnis facere ♦ *vt* regere ♦ *vi* vacillāre.
swear *vi* iūrāre; **~ allegiance to** iūrāre in verba (*gen*).

sweat *n* sūdor *m* ♦ *vi* sūdāre.
sweep *vt* verrere; **~ away** rapere; **~ out** ēverrere.
sweet *adj* dulcis, suāvis.
sweeten *vt* dulcem reddere.
sweetheart *n* dēliciae *fpl*.
sweetly *adv* dulciter, suāviter.
sweetness *n* dulcitūdō *f*, suāvitās *f*.
sweet-tempered *adj* suāvis, cōmis.
swell *n* tumor *m* ♦ *vi* tumēre, tumēscere; (*fig*) glīscere ♦ *vt* inflāre.
swelling *adj* tumidus ♦ *n* tumor *m*.
swelter *vi* aestū labōrāre.
swerve *vi* dēclīnāre, dēvertere ♦ *n* dēclīnātiō *f*.
swift *adj* celer, vēlōx, incitātus.
swiftly *adv* celeriter, vēlōciter.
swiftness *n* celeritās *f*, vēlōcitās *f*.
swill *vt* (*rinse*) colluere; (*drink*) ēpōtāre.
swim *vi* nāre, innāre; (*place*) natāre; **~ across** trānāre; **~ ashore** ēnāre; **~ to** adnāre.
swimming *n* natātiō *f*.
swindle *vt* circumvenīre, verba dare (*dat*) ♦ *n* fraus *f*.
swine *n* sūs *m/f*.
swineherd *n* subulcus *m*.
swing *n* (*motion*) oscillātiō *f* ♦ *vi* oscillāre ♦ *vt* lībrāre.
swinish *adj* obscēnus.
swirl *n* vertex *m* ♦ *vi* volūtārī.
switch *n* virga *f* ♦ *vt* flectere, torquēre.
swivel *n* cardō *f*.
swollen *adj* tumidus, turgidus, īnflātus.
swoon *n* dēfectiō *f* ♦ *vi* intermorī.
swoop *n* impetus *m* ♦ *vi* lābī; **~ down on** involāre in (*acc*).
sword *n* gladius *m*; **put to the ~** occīdere; **with fire and ~** ferrō ignīque.
swordsman *n* gladiātor *m*.
sworn *adj* iūrātus.
sybarite *n* dēlicātus *m*.
sycophancy *n* adsentātiō *f*, adūlātiō *f*.
sycophant *n* adsentātor *m*, adūlātor *m*.
syllable *n* syllaba *f*.
syllogism *n* ratiōcinātiō *f*.
sylvan *adj* silvestris.
symbol *n* signum *nt*, īnsigne *nt*.
symmetrical *adj* concinnus, aequus.
symmetry *n* concinnitās *f*, aequitās *f*.
sympathetic *adj* concors, misericors.
sympathetically *adv* misericorditer.
sympathize *vi* cōnsentīre; **~ with** miserērī (*gen*).
sympathy *n* concordia *f*, cōnsēnsus *m*; misericordia *f*.
symphony *n* concentus *m*.
symptom *n* signum *nt*, indicium *nt*.
syndicate *n* societās *f*.
synonym *n* verbum idem dēclārāns *nt*.
synonymous *adj* idem dēclārāns.
synopsis *n* summārium *nt*.
syringe *n* clystēr *m*.
system *n* ratiō *f*, fōrmula *f*; (*PHILOS*) disciplīna *f*.

systematic *adj* ōrdinātus, cōnstāns.
systematically *adv* ratiōne, ōrdine.
systematize *vt* in ōrdinem redigere.

T, t

tabernacle *n* tabernāculum *nt.*
table *n* mēnsa *f;* (*inscribed*) tabula *f;* (*list*) index *m;* **at ~** inter cēnam; **turn the ~s on** pār parī referre.
tablet *n* tabula *f,* tabella *f.*
taboo *n* rēligiō *f.*
tabulate *vt* in ōrdinem redigere.
tacit *adj* tacitus.
tacitly *adv* tacitē.
taciturn *adj* taciturnus.
taciturnity *n* taciturnitās *f.*
tack *n* clāvulus *m;* (*of sail*) pēs *m* ♦ *vt:* **~ on** adsuere ♦ *vi* (*ship*) reciprocārī, nāvem flectere.
tackle *n* armāmenta *ntpl* ♦ *vt* adgredī.
tact *n* iūdicium *nt,* commūnis sēnsus *m,* hūmānitās *f.*
tactful *adj* prūdēns, hūmānus.
tactfully *adv* prūdenter, hūmāniter.
tactician *n* reī mīlitāris perītus *m.*
tactics *n* rēs mīlitāris *f,* bellī ratiō *f.*
tactless *adj* ineptus.
tactlessly *adv* ineptē.
tadpole *n* rānunculus *m.*
tag *n* appendicula *f.*
tail *n* cauda *f;* **turn ~** terga vertere.
tailor *n* vestītor *m.*
taint *n* lābēs *f,* vitium *nt* ♦ *vt* inquināre, contāmināre, īnficere.
take *vt* capere, sūmere; (*auspices*) habēre; (*disease*) contrahere; (*experience*) ferre; (*fire*) concipere; (*meaning*) accipere, interpretārī; (*in the act*) dēprehendere; (*person*) dūcere; **~ after** similem esse (*dat, gen*); **~ across** trānsportāre; **~ arms** arma sūmere; **~ away** dēmere, auferre, adimere, abdūcere; **~ back** recipere; **~ by storm** expugnāre; **~ care that** curāre ut/ne (+ *subj*); **~ down** dētrahere; (*in writing*) exscrībere; **~ for** habēre prō; **~ hold of** prehendere; **~ in** (*as guest*) recipere; (*information*) percipere, comprehendere; (*with deceit*) dēcipere; **~ in hand** incipere, suscipere; **~ off** dēmere; (*clothes*) exuere; **~ on** suscipere; **~ out** eximere, extrahere; (*from store*) prōmere; **~ over** excipere; **~ place** fierī, accidere; **~ prisoner** capere; **~ refuge in** cōnfugere ad (+ *infin*); **~ the field** in aciem dēscendere; **~ to** sē dēdere (*dat*), amāre; **~ to oneself** suscipere; **~ up** sūmere,

tollere; (*task*) incipere, adgredī ad; (*in turn*) excipere; (*room*) occupāre; **~ upon oneself** recipere, sibī sūmere.
taking *adj* grātus ♦ *n* (*MIL*) expugnātiō *f.*
tale *n* fābula *f,* fābella *f.*
talent *n* (*money*) talentum *nt;* (*ability*) ingenium *nt,* indolēs *f.*
talented *adj* ingeniōsus.
talk *n* sermō *m;* (*with another*) colloquium *nt;* **common ~** fāma *f;* **be the ~ of the town** in ōre omnium esse ♦ *vi* loquī; (*to one*) colloquī cum; **~ down to** ad intellectum audientis dēscendere; **~ over** cōnferre, disserere dē.
talkative *adj* loquāx.
talkativeness *n* loquācitās *f.*
tall *adj* prōcērus, grandis.
tallness *n* prōcēritās *f.*
tallow *n* sēbum *nt.*
tally *n* tessera *f* ♦ *vi* congruere.
talon *n* unguis *m.*
tamarisk *n* myrīca *f.*
tambourine *n* tympanum *nt.*
tame *vt* domāre, mānsuēfacere ♦ *adj* mānsuētus; (*character*) ignāvus; (*language*) īnsulsus, frīgidus.
tamely *adv* ignāvē, lentē.
tameness *n* mānsuētūdō *f;* (*fig*) lentitūdō *f.*
tamer *n* domitor *m.*
tamper *vi:* **~ with** (*person*) sollicitāre; (*writing*) interpolāre.
tan *vt* imbuere.
tang *n* sapor *m.*
tangible *adj* tāctilis.
tangle *n* nōdus *m* ♦ *vt* implicāre.
tank *n* lacus *m.*
tanned *adj* (*by sun*) adūstus.
tanner *n* coriārius *m.*
tantalize *vt* lūdere.
tantamount *adj* pār, īdem.
tantrum *n* īra *f.*
tap *n* epitonium *nt;* (*touch*) plāga *f* ♦ *vt* (*cask*) relinere; (*hit*) ferīre.
tape *n* taenia *f.*
taper *n* cēreus *m* ♦ *vi* fastīgārī.
tapestry *n* aulaea *ntpl.*
tar *n* pix *f.*
tardily *adv* tardē, lentē.
tardiness *n* tarditās *f,* segnitia *f.*
tardy *adj* tardus, lentus.
tare *n* lolium *nt.*
targe *n* parma *f.*
target *n* scopus *m.*
tariff *n* portōrium *nt.*
tarn *n* lacus *m.*
tarnish *vt* īnfuscāre, inquināre ♦ *vi* īnfuscārī.
tarry *vi* morārī, commorārī, cunctārī.
tart *adj* acidus, asper ♦ *n* scriblīta *f.*
tartly *adv* acerbē.
tartness *n* asperitās *f.*
task *n* pēnsum *nt,* opus *nt,* negōtium *nt;* **take to ~** obiūrgāre.
taskmaster *n* dominus *m.*
tassel *n* fimbriae *fpl.*

taste n (*sense*) gustātus m; (*flavour*) sapor m; (*artistic*) iūdicium nt, ēlegantia f; (*for rhetoric*) aurēs fpl; **of ~** doctus; **in good ~** ēlegāns ◆ vt gustāre, dēgustāre ◆ vi sapere; **~ of** resipere.
tasteful adj ēlegāns.
tastefully adv ēleganter.
tastefulness n ēlegantia f.
tasteless adj īnsulsus, inēlegāns.
tastelessly adv īnsulsē, inēleganter.
tastelessness n īnsulsitās f.
taster n praegustātor m.
tasty adj dulcis.
tattered adj pannōsus.
tatters n pannī mpl.
tattoo vt compungere.
taunt n convīcium nt, probrum nt ◆ vt exprobrāre, obicere (*dat of pers, acc of charge*).
taunting adj contumēliōsus.
tauntingly adv contumēliōsē.
taut adj intentus; **draw ~** addūcere.
tavern n taberna f, hospitium nt.
tawdry adj vīlis.
tawny adj fulvus.
tax n vectīgal nt, tribūtum nt; **a 5 per cent ~** vīcēsima f; **free from ~** immūnis ◆ vt vectīgal impōnere (*dat*); (*strength*) contendere; **~ with** (*charge*) obicere (*acc & dat*), īnsimulāre.
taxable adj vectīgālis.
taxation n vectīgālia ntpl.
tax collector n exāctor m.
tax farmer n pūblicānus m.
taxpayer n assiduus m.
teach vt docēre, ērudīre, īnstituere; (*thoroughly*) ēdocēre; (*pass*) discere; **~ your grandmother** sūs Minervam.
teachable adj docilis.
teacher n magister m, magistra f, doctor m; (*PHILOS*) praeceptor m; (*of literature*) grammaticus m; (*of rhetoric*) rhētor m.
teaching n doctrīna f, disciplīna f.
team n (*animals*) iugum nt.
tear n lacrima f; **shed ~s** lacrimās effundere ◆ vt scindere; **~ down** revellere; **~ in pieces** dīlaniāre, discerpere, lacerāre; **~ off** abscindere, dēripere; **~ open** rescindere; **~ out** ēvellere; **~ up** convellere.
tearful adj flēbilis.
tease vt lūdere, inrītāre.
teat n mamma f.
technical adj (*term*) proprius.
technique n ars f.
tedious adj longus, lentus, odiōsus.
tediously adv molestē.
tedium n taedium nt, molestia f.
teem vi abundāre.
teeming adj fēcundus, refertus.
teens n: **in one's ~** adulescentulus.
teethe vi dentīre.
tell vt (*story*) nārrāre; (*person*) dīcere (*dat*); (*number*) ēnumerāre; (*inform*) certiorem facere; (*difference*) intellegere; (*order*) iubēre (+ *acc and infin*), imperare (+ **ut/ne** and subj);

~ the truth vēra dīcere; **~ lies** mentior ◆ vi valēre; **~ the difference between** discernere; **I cannot ~** nesciō.
telling adj validus.
temerity n temeritās f.
temper n animus m, ingenium nt; (*bad*) īra f, īrācundia f; (*of metal*) temperātiō f ◆ vt temperāre; (*fig*) moderārī (*dat*).
temperament n animī habitus m, animus m.
temperamental adj incōnstāns.
temperance n temperantia f, continentia f.
temperate adj temperātus, moderātus, sobrius.
temperately adv moderātē.
temperature n calor m, frīgus nt; **mild ~** temperiēs f.
tempest n tempestās f, procella f.
tempestuous adj procellōsus.
temple n templum nt, aedēs f; (*head*) tempus nt.
temporal adj hūmānus, profānus.
temporarily adv ad tempus.
temporary adj brevis.
temporize vi temporis causā facere, tergiversārī.
tempt vt sollicitāre, pellicere, invītāre.
temptation n illecebra f.
tempter n impulsor m.
ten num decem; **~ each** dēnī; **~ times** deciēns.
tenable adj inexpugnābilis, stabilis, certus.
tenacious adj tenāx, firmus.
tenaciously adv tenāciter.
tenacity n tenācitās f.
tenant n inquilīnus m, habitātor m; (*on land*) colōnus m.
tenantry n colōnī mpl.
tend vi spectāre, pertinēre ◆ vt cūrāre, colere.
tendency n inclīnātiō f, voluntās f.
tender adj tener, mollis ◆ vt dēferre, offerre.
tenderhearted adj misericors.
tenderly adv indulgenter.
tenderness n indulgentia f, mollitia f.
tendon n nervus m.
tendril n clāviculus m.
tenement n habitātiō f; **block of ~s** īnsula f.
tenet n dogma nt, dēcrētum nt.
tennis court n sphaeristērium nt.
tenor n (*course*) tenor m; (*purport*) sententia f.
tense adj intentus ◆ n tempus nt.
tension n intentiō f.
tent n tabernāculum nt; (*general's*) praetōrium nt.
tentacle n bracchium nt.
tentatively adv experiendō.
tenterhooks n: **on ~** animī suspēnsus.
tenth adj decimus; **for the ~ time** decimum; **men of the ~ legion** decumānī mpl.
tenuous adj rārus.
tenure n possessiō f.
tepid adj tepidus; **be ~** tepēre.
tergiversation n tergiversātiō f.
term n (*limit*) terminus m; (*period*) spatium nt; (*word*) verbum nt ◆ vt appellāre, nuncupāre.

terminate *vt* termināre, fīnīre ♦ *vi* dēsinere; (*words*) cadere.

termination *n* fīnis *m*, terminus *m*.

terminology *n* vocābula *ntpl*.

terms *npl* condiciō *f*, lēx *f*; **propose ~** condiciōnem ferre; **be on good ~** in grātiā esse; **we come to ~** inter nōs convenit.

terrain *n* ager *m*.

terrestrial *adj* terrestris.

terrible *adj* terribilis, horribilis, horrendus.

terribly *adv* horrendum in modum.

terrific *adj* formīdolōsus; vehemēns.

terrify *vt* terrēre, perterrēre, exterrēre.

terrifying *adj* formīdolōsus.

territory *n* ager *m*, fīnēs *mpl*.

terror *n* terror *m*, formīdō *f*, pavor *m*; **object of ~** terror *m*; **be a ~ to** terrōrī esse (*dat*).

terrorize *vt* metum inicere (*dat*).

terse *adj* pressus, brevis.

tersely *adv* pressē.

terseness *n* brevitās *f*.

tessellated *adj* tessellātus.

test *n* experīmentum *nt*, probātiō *f*, (*standard*) obrussa *f*; **put to the ~** experīrī, perīclitārī; **stand the ~** spectārī ♦ *vt* experīrī, probāre, spectāre.

testament *n* testāmentum *nt*.

testamentary *adj* testāmentārius.

testator *n* testātor *m*.

testify *vt* testificārī.

testifying *n* testificātiō *f*.

testily *adv* stomachōsē.

testimonial *n* laudātiō *f*.

testimony *n* testimōnium *nt*.

testy *adj* difficilis, stomachōsus.

tether *n* retināculum *nt*, vinculum *nt* ♦ *vt* religāre.

tetrarch *n* tetrarchēs *m*.

tetrarchy *n* tetrarchia *f*.

text *n* verba *ntpl*.

textbook *n* ars *f*.

textile *adj* textilis.

textual *adj* verbōrum.

texture *n* textus *m*.

than *conj* quam *abl*; **other ~** alius ac.

thank *vt* grātiās agere (*dat*); **~ you** bene facis; **no, ~ you** benīgnē.

thankful *adj* grātus.

thankfully *adv* grātē.

thankfulness *n* grātia *f*.

thankless *adj* ingrātus.

thanklessly *adv* ingrātē.

thanks *n* grātiae *fpl*, grātēs *fpl*; **return ~** grātiās agere, grātēs persolvere; **~ to you** operā tuā, beneficiō tuō; **it is ~ to sb that ... not** per aliquem stat quōminus (+ *subj*).

thanksgiving *n* grātulātiō *f*, (*public*) supplicātiō *f*.

that *pron* (*demonstrative*) ille; (*relat*) quī ♦ *conj* (*statement*) *acc* & *infin*; (*command, purpose, result*) ut; (*fearing*) nē; (*emotion*) quod; **oh ~** utinam.

thatch *n* culmus *m*, strāmenta *ntpl* ♦ *vt* tegere, integere.

thaw *vt* dissolvere ♦ *vi* liquēscere, tābēscere.

the *art not expressed*; (*emphatic*) ille; (*with compar*) quō ... eō.

theatre *n* theātrum *nt*.

theatrical *adj* scēnicus.

theft *n* fūrtum *nt*.

their *adj* eōrum; (*ref to subject*) suus.

theme *n* māteria *f*, argūmentum *nt*.

themselves *pron* ipsī; (*reflexive*) sē.

then *adv* (*time*) tum, tunc; (*succession*) deinde, tum, posteā; (*consequence*) igitur, ergō; **now and ~** interdum; **only ~** tum dēmum.

thence *adv* inde.

thenceforth *adv* inde, posteā, ex eō tempore.

theologian *n* theologus *m*.

theology *n* theologia *f*.

theorem *n* prōpositum *nt*.

theoretical *adj* contemplātīvus.

theory *n* ratiō *f*; **~ and practice** ratiō atque ūsus.

there *adv* ibī, illīc; (*thither*) eō, illūc; **from ~** inde, illinc; **here and ~** passim; **~ is** est; (*interj*) ecce.

thereabout(s) *adv* circā, circiter, prope.

thereafter *adv* deinde, posteā.

thereby *adv* eā rē, hōc factō.

therefore *adv* itaque, igitur, ergō, idcircō.

therein *adv* inibī, in eō.

thereof *adv* ēius, ēius reī.

thereon *adv* īnsuper, in eō.

thereupon *adv* deinde, statim, inde, quo facto.

therewith *adv* cum eō.

thesis *n* prōpositum *nt*.

thews *n* nervī *mpl*.

they *pron* iī, hī, illī.

thick *adj* dēnsus; (*air*) crassus.

thicken *vt* dēnsāre ♦ *vi* concrēscere.

thickening *n* concrētiō *f*.

thicket *n* dūmētum *nt*.

thickheaded *adj* stupidus, hebes.

thickly *adv* dēnsē; **~ populated** frequēns.

thickness *n* crassitūdō *f*.

thickset *adj* brevis atque obēsus.

thick-skinned *adj*: **be ~** callēre; **become ~** occallēscere.

thief *n* fūr *m*.

thieve *vt* fūrārī, surripere.

thievery *n* fūrtum *nt*.

thievish *adj* fūrāx.

thigh *n* femur *nt*.

thin *adj* exīlis, gracilis, tenuis; (*attendance*) īnfrequēns ♦ *vt* attenuāre, extenuāre; **~ out** rārefacere; **~ down** dīluere.

thine *adj* tuus.

thing *n* rēs *f*; **as ~s are** nunc, cum haec ita sint.

think *vi* cōgitāre; (*opinion*) putāre, existimāre, arbitrārī, rērī, crēdere; **as I ~** meā sententiā; **~ about** cōgitāre dē; **~ highly of** māgnī aestimāre; **~ nothing of** nihilī facere; **~ out** excōgitāre; **~ over** reputāre, in mente agitāre.

thinker *n* philosophus *m*.

thinking *adj* sapiēns ♦ *n* cōgitātiō *f*; ~ **that** ratus, arbitratus.

thinly *adv* exīliter, tenuiter; rārē.

thinness *n* exīlitās *f*, gracilitās *f*; (*person*) maciēs *f*; (*number*) exiguitās *f*, īnfrequentia *f*; (*air*) tenuitās *f*.

thin-skinned *adj* inrītābilis.

third *adj* tertius; **for the ~ time** tertium ♦ *n* tertia pars *f*, triēns *m*; **two ~s** duae partēs, bēs *m*.

thirdly *adv* tertiō.

thirst *n* sitis *f* ♦ *vi* sitīre; ~ **for** sitīre.

thirstily *adv* sitienter.

thirsty *adj* sitiēns.

thirteen *num* tredecim; ~ **each** ternī dēnī; ~ **times** terdeciēns.

thirteenth *adj* tertius decimus.

thirtieth *adj* trīcēsimus.

thirty *num* trīgintā; ~ **each** trīcēnī; ~ **times** trīciēns.

this *pron* hīc.

thistle *n* carduus *m*.

thither *adv* eō, illūc.

thole *n* scalmus *nt*.

thong *n* lōrum *nt*, habēna *f*.

thorn *n* spīna *f*, sentis *m*.

thorny *adj* spīnōsus.

thorough *adj* absolūtus, germānus; (*work*) accūrātus.

thoroughbred *adj* generōsus.

thoroughfare *n* via *f*.

thoroughly *adv* penitus, omnīnō, funditus.

thoroughness *n* cūra *f*, diligentia *f*.

thou *pron* tū.

though *conj* etsī, etiamsī, quamvīs (+ *subj*), quamquam all (+ *indic*).

thought *n* (*faculty*) cōgitātiō *f*, mēns *f*, animus *m*; (*an idea*) cōgitātum *nt*, nōtiō *f*; (*design*) cōnsilium *nt*, prōpositum *nt*; (*expressed*) sententia *f*; (*heed*) cautiō *f*, prōvidentia *f*; (*RHET*) inventiō *f*; **second ~s** posteriōrēs cōgitātiōnēs.

thoughtful *adj* cōgitābundus; prōvidus.

thoughtfully *adv* prōvidē.

thoughtless *adj* incōnsīderātus, incōnsultus, imprōvidus, immemor.

thoughtlessly *adv* temerē, incōnsultē.

thoughtlessness *n* incōnsīderantia *f*, imprūdentia *f*.

thousand *num* mīlle; **~s** *pl* mīlia (+ *gen*) *ntpl*; ~ **each** mīllēnī; ~ **times** mīlliēns; **three ~** tria mīlia.

thousandth *adj* mīllēsimus.

thrall *n* servus *m*.

thraldom *n* servitūs *f*.

thrash *vt* verberāre.

thrashing *n* verbera *ntpl*.

thread *n* fīlum *nt*; **hang by a ~** (*fig*) fīlō pendēre ♦ *vt*: ~ **one's way** sē īnsinuāre.

threadbare *adj* trītus, obsolētus.

threat *n* minae *fpl*, minātiō *f*.

threaten *vt* minārī (*dat of pers*), dēnūntiāre ♦ *vi* imminēre, impendēre.

threatening *adj* mināx, imminēns.

threateningly *adv* mināciter.

three *num* trēs; ~ **each** ternī; ~ **times** ter; ~ **days** triduum *nt*; ~ **years** triennium *nt*; ~ **quarters** trēs partēs *fpl*, dōdrāns *m*.

three-cornered *adj* triangulus, triquetrus.

threefold *adj* triplex.

three hundred *num* trecentī; ~ **each** trecēnī; ~ **times** trecentiēns.

three hundredth *adj* trecentēsimus.

three-legged *adj* tripēs.

three-quarters *n* dōdrāns *m*, trēs partēs *fpl*.

thresh *vt* terere, exterere.

threshing floor *n* ārea *f*.

threshold *n* līmen *nt*.

thrice *adv* ter.

thrift *n* frūgālitās *f*, parsimōnia *f*.

thriftily *adv* frūgāliter.

thrifty *adj* parcus, frūgī.

thrill *n* horror *m* ♦ *vt* percellere, percutere ♦ *vi* trepidāre.

thrilling *adj* mīrābilis.

thrive *vi* vigēre, valēre, crēscere.

thriving *adj* valēns, vegetus; (*crops*) laetus.

throat *n* faucēs *fpl*, guttur *nt*; **cut the ~ of** iugulāre.

throaty *adj* gravis, raucus.

throb *vi* palpitāre, micāre ♦ *n* pulsus *m*.

throe *n* dolor *m*; **be in the ~s of** labōrāre ex.

throne *n* solium *nt*; (*power*) rēgnum *nt*.

throng *n* multitūdō *f*, frequentia *f* ♦ *vt* celebrāre; ~ **round** stīpāre, circumfundī (*dat*).

throttle *vt* strangulāre.

through *prep* per (*acc*); (*cause*) propter (*acc*), *abl* ♦ *adv*: ~ **and** ~ penitus; **carry** ~ exsequī, peragere; **go** ~ trānsīre; **run** ~ percurrere; **be** ~ **with** perfūnctum esse (*abl*).

throughout *adv* penitus, omnīnō ♦ *prep* per (*acc*).

throw *n* iactus *m*, coniectus *m* ♦ *vt* iacere, conicere; ~ **about** iactāre; ~ **across** trāicere; ~ **away** abicere; (*something precious*) prōicere; ~ **back** rēicere; ~ **down** dēturbāre, dēicere; ~ **into** inicere; ~ **into confusion** perturbāre; ~ **off** excutere, exsolvere; ~ **open** patefacere; ~ **out** ēicere, prōicere; ~ **over** inicere; (*fig*) dēstituere; ~ **overboard** iactūram facere (*gen*); ~ **to** (*danger*) obicere; ~ **up** ēicere; (*building*) exstruere; ~ **a bridge over** pontem inicere (*dat*), pontem faciendum cūrāre in (*abl*); ~ **light on** (*fig*) lūmen adhibēre (*dat*); ~ **a rider** equitem excutere.

throwing *n* coniectiō *f*, iactus *m*.

thrum *n* līcium *nt*.

thrush *n* turdus *m*.

thrust *vt* trūdere, pellere, impingere; ~ **at** petere; ~ **away** dētrūdere; ~ **forward** prōtrūdere; ~ **home** dēfīgere; ~ **into** īnfīgere, impingere; ~ **out** extrūdere.

thud *n* gravis sonitus *m*.

thug *n* percussor *m*, sīcārius *m*.

thumb–titled

thumb n pollex m; **have under one's ~** in potestāte suā habēre.
thump n plāga f ♦ vt tundere, pulsāre.
thunder n tonitrus m ♦ vi tonāre, intonāre; **it ~s** tonāt.
thunderbolt n fulmen nt.
thunderer n tonāns m.
thunderstruck adj attonitus.
thus adv (referring back) sīc; (referring forward) ita; **~ far** hāctenus.
thwack vt verberāre.
thwart vt obstāre (dat), officere (dat), remorārī, frustrārī ♦ n (boat's) trānstrum nt.
thy adj tuus.
thyme n thymum nt; (wild) serpyllum nt.
tiara n diadēma nt.
ticket n tessera f.
tickle vt titillāre.
tickling n titillātiō f.
ticklish adj lūbricus.
tidal adj: **~ waters** aestuārium nt.
tide n aestus m; (time) tempus nt; **ebb ~** aestūs recessus m; **flood ~** aestūs accessus m; **turn of the ~** commūtātiō aestūs; **the ~ will turn** (fig) circumagētur hīc orbis.
tidily adv concinnē, mundē.
tidiness n concinnitās f, munditia f.
tidings n nūntius m.
tidy adj concinnus, mundus.
tie n (bond) vinculum nt, cōpula f; (kin) necessitūdō f ♦ vt ligāre; (knot) nectere; **~ fast** dēvincīre, cōnstringere; **~ on** illigāre; **~ to** adligāre; **~ together** colligāre; **~ up** adligāre; (wound) obligāre.
tier n ōrdō m.
tiff n dissēnsiō f.
tiger n tigris m, more usu f.
tight adj strictus, astrictus, intentus; (close) artus; **draw ~** intendere, addūcere.
tighten vt adstringere, contendere.
tightly adv artē, angustē.
tightrope n extentus fūnis; **~ walker** n fūnambulus m.
tigress n tigris f.
tile n tegula f, imbrex f, later nt.
till conj dum, dōnec ♦ prep usque ad (acc), in (acc); **not ~** dēmum ♦ n arca f ♦ vt colere.
tillage n cultus m.
tiller n (AGR) cultor m; (ship) clāvus m, gubernāculum nt.
tilt vt inclīnāre.
tilth n cultus m, arvum nt.
timber n (for building) māteria f; (firewood) lignum nt.
timbrel n tympanum nt.
time n tempus nt; (lifetime) aetās f; (interval) intervallum nt, spatium nt; (of day) hōra f; (leisure) ōtium nt; (rhythm) numerus m; **another ~** aliās; **at ~s** aliquandō, interdum; **at all ~s** semper; **at any ~** umquam; **at one ~ ...** **at another** aliās ... aliās; **at that ~** tunc, id temporis; **at the right ~** ad tempus, mātūrē, tempestīvē; **at the same ~** simul; tamen; **at the wrong ~** intempestīvē; **beating ~** percussiō f; **convenient ~** opportūnitās f; **for a ~** aliquantisper, parumper; **for a long ~** diū; **for some ~** aliquamdiū; **for the ~ being** ad tempus; **from ~ to ~** interdum, identidem; **have a good ~** geniō indulgēre; **have ~ for** vacāre (dat); **in ~** ad tempus, tempore; **in a short ~** brevī; **in good ~** tempestīvus; **in the ~ of** apud (acc); **keep ~** (marching) gradum cōnferre; (music) modulārī; **many ~s** saepe, saepenumerō; **pass, spend ~** tempus sūmere, dēgere; **several ~s** aliquotiēns; **some ~** aliquandō; **waste ~** tempus terere; **what is the ~?** quota hōra est?; **~ expired** ēmeritus.
time-honoured adj antīquus.
timeliness n opportūnitās f.
timely adj opportūnus, tempestīvus, mātūrus.
timid adj timidus.
timidity n timiditās f.
timidly adv timidē.
timorous adj timidus.
timorously adv timidē.
tin n stannum nt, plumbum album nt ♦ adj stanneus.
tincture n color m, sapor m ♦ vt īnficere.
tinder n fōmes m.
tinge vt imbuere, īnficere, tingere.
tingle vi horrēre.
tingling n horror m.
tinkle vi tinnīre ♦ n tinnītus m.
tinsel n bractea f; (fig) speciēs f, fūcus m.
tint n color m ♦ vt colōrāre.
tiny adj minūtus, pusillus, perexiguus.
tip n apex m, cacūmen nt, extrēmum nt; **the ~ of** prīmus, extrēmus ♦ vt praefīgere; **~ over** invertere.
tipple vi pōtāre.
tippler n pōtor m, ēbrius m.
tipsy adj tēmulentus.
tiptoes n: **on ~** suspēnsō gradū.
tirade n obiūrgātiō f, dēclāmātiō f.
tire vt fatīgāre; **~ out** dēfatīgāre ♦ vi dēfetīscī, fatīgārī; **I ~ of** mē taedet (gen); **it ~s** taedet (+ acc of person, gen of thing).
tired adj (dē)fessus, lassus; **~ out** dēfessus; **I am ~ of** mē taedet.
tiresome adj molestus, difficilis.
tiring adj labōriōsus, operōsus.
tiro n tīrō m, rudis m.
tissue n textus m.
tit n: **give ~ for tat** pār parī respondēre.
Titan n Tītān m.
titanic adj immānis.
titbit n cuppēdium nt.
tithe n decuma f.
tithe gatherer n decumānus m.
titillate vt titillāre.
titillation n titillātiō f.
title n (book) īnscrīptiō f, index m; (inscription) titulus m; (person) nōmen nt, appellātiō f; (claim) iūs nt, vindiciae fpl; **assert one's ~ to** vindicāre; **give a ~ to** īnscrībere.
titled adj nōbilis.

title deed n auctōritās f.
titter n rīsus m ♦ vi rīdēre.
tittle-tattle n sermunculus m.
titular adj nōmine.
to prep ad (acc), in (acc); (attitude) ergā (acc); (giving) dat; (towns, small islands, domus, rūs) acc ♦ conj (purpose) ut ♦ adv: **come ~** animum recipere; **~ and fro** hūc illūc.
toad n būfō m.
toady n adsentātor m, parasītus m ♦ vt adsentārī (dat).
toadyism n adsentātiō f.
toast n: **drink a ~** propīnāre ♦ vt torrēre; (drink) propīnāre (dat).
today adv hodiē; **~'s** hodiernus.
toe n digitus m; **big ~** pollex m.
toga n toga f.
together adv ūnā, simul; **bring ~** cōgere, congerere; **come ~** convenīre, congregārī; **put ~** cōnferre, compōnere.
toil n labor m; (snare) rēte nt ♦ vi labōrāre; **~ at** ēlabōrāre in (abl).
toilet n (lady's) cultus m.
toilsome adj labōriōsus, operōsus.
toil-worn adj labōre cōnfectus.
token n īnsigne nt, signum nt, indicium nt.
tolerable adj tolerābilis, patibilis; (quality) mediocris; (size) modicus.
tolerably adv satis, mediocriter.
tolerance n patientia f, tolerantia f.
tolerant adj indulgēns, tolerāns.
tolerantly adv indulgenter.
tolerate vt tolerāre, ferre, indulgēre (dat).
toleration n patientia f; (freedom) lībertās f.
toll n vectīgal nt; (harbour) portōrium nt.
toll collector n exāctor m; portitor m.
tomb n sepulcrum nt.
tombstone n lapis m.
tome n liber m.
tomorrow adv crās; **~'s** crāstinus; **the day after ~** perendiē; **put off till ~** in crāstinum differre.
tone n sonus m, vōx f; (painting) color m.
tongs n forceps m/f.
tongue n lingua f; (shoe) ligula f; **on the tip of one's ~** in prīmōribus labrīs.
tongue-tied adj ēlinguis, īnfāns.
tonnage n amphorae fpl.
tonsils n tōnsillae fpl.
tonsure n rāsūra f.
too adv (also) etiam, īnsuper, quoque; (excess) nimis ♦ compar adj: **~ far** extrā modum; **~ much** nimium; **~ long** nimium diū; **~ great to** māior quam quī (subj); **~ late** sērius; **~ little** parum (+ gen).
tool n īnstrūmentum nt; (AGR) ferrāmentum nt; (person) minister m.
tooth n dēns m; **~ and nail** tōtō corpore atque omnibus ungulīs; **cast in one's teeth** exprobrāre, obicere; **cut teeth** dentīre; **in the teeth of** obviam (dat), adversus (acc); **with the teeth** mordicus.
toothache n dentium dolor m.

toothed adj dentātus.
toothless adj ēdentulus.
toothpick n dentiscalpium nt.
toothsome adj suāvis, dulcis.
top n vertex m, fastīgium nt; (tree) cacūmen nt; (toy) turbō m; **from ~ to toe** ab īmīs unguibus usque ad verticem summum; **the ~ of** summus ♦ vt exsuperāre; **~ up** supplēre ♦ adj superior, summus.
tope vi pōtāre.
toper n pōtor m.
topiary adj topiārius. ♦ n topiārium opus nt.
topic n rēs f; (RHET) locus m; **~ of conversation** sermō m.
topical adj hodiernus.
topmost adj summus.
topography n dēscrīptiō f.
topple vi titubāre; **~ over** prōlābī.
topsail n dolō m.
topsyturvy adv praeposterē; **turn ~** sūrsum deōrsum versāre, permiscēre.
tor n mōns m.
torch n fax f, lampas f.
torment n cruciātus m; (mind) angor m ♦ vt cruciāre; (mind) discruciāre, excruciāre, angere.
tormentor n tortor m.
tornado n turbō m.
torpid adj torpēns; **be ~** torpēre; **grow ~** obtorpēscere.
torpor n torpor m, inertia f.
torrent n torrēns m.
torrid adj torridus.
torsion n tortus m.
torso n truncus m.
tortoise n testūdō f.
tortoiseshell n testūdō f.
tortuous adj flexuōsus.
torture n cruciātus m, supplicium nt; **instrument of ~** tormentum nt ♦ vt torquēre, cruciāre, excruciāre.
torturer n tortor m, carnifex m.
toss n iactus m ♦ vt iactāre, excutere; **~ about** agitāre; **be ~ed** (at sea) fluitāre.
total adj tōtus, ūniversus ♦ n summa f.
totality n ūniversitās f.
totally adv omnīnō, plānē.
totter vi lābāre, titubāre; **make ~** labefactāre.
tottering n titubātiō f.
touch n tāctus m; **a ~ of** aliquantulum (gen); **finishing ~** manus extrēma f ♦ vt tangere, attingere; (feelings) movēre, tangere ♦ vi inter sē contingere; **~ at** nāvem appellere ad; **~ on** (topic) attingere, perstringere; **~ up** expolīre.
touch-and-go adj anceps ♦ n discrīmen nt.
touching adj (place) contiguus; (emotion) flexanimus ♦ prep quod attinet ad (acc).
touchstone n (fig) obrussa f.
touchy adj inrītābilis, stomachōsus.
tough adj dūrus.
toughen vt dūrāre.
toughness n dūritia f.

tour n iter nt; (abroad) peregrīnātiō f.
tourist n viātor m, peregrīnātor m.
tournament n certāmen nt.
tow n stuppa f; of ~ stuppeus ♦ vt adnexum trahere, remulcō trahere.
toward(s) prep ad (acc), versus (after noun, acc); (feelings) in (acc), ergā (acc); (time) sub (acc).
towel n mantēle nt.
tower n turris f ♦ vi ēminēre.
towered adj turrītus.
town n urbs f, oppidum nt; **country ~** mūnicipium nt ♦ adj urbānus.
town councillor n decuriō m.
townsman n oppidānus m.
townspeople npl oppidānī mpl.
towrope n remulcum nt.
toy n crepundia ntpl ♦ vi lūdere.
trace n vestīgium nt, indicium nt ♦ vt investīgāre; (draw) dēscrībere; **~ out** dēsignāre.
track n (mark) vestīgium nt; (path) callis m, sēmita f; (of wheel) orbita f; (of ship) cursus m ♦ vt investīgāre, indāgāre.
trackless adj invius.
tract n (country) tractus m, regiō f; (book) libellus m.
tractable adj tractābilis, facilis, docilis.
trade n mercātūra f, mercātus m; (a business) ars f, quaestus m; **freedom of ~** commercium nt ♦ vi mercātūrās facere, negōtiārī; **~ in** vēndere, vēnditāre.
trader n mercātor m, negōtiātor m.
tradesman n opifex m.
tradition n fāma f, mōs māiōrum m, memoria f.
traditional adj ā māiōribus trāditus, patrius.
traditionally adv mōre māiōrum.
traduce vt calumniārī, obtrectāre (dat).
traducer n calumniātor m, obtrectātor m.
traffic n commercium nt; (on road) vehicula ntpl ♦ vi mercātūrās facere; **~ in** vēndere, vēnditāre.
tragedian n (author) tragoedus m; (actor) āctor tragicus m.
tragedy n tragoedia f; (fig) calamitās f, malum nt.
tragic adj tragicus; (fig) tristis.
tragically adv tragicē; male.
tragicomedy n tragicōcōmoedia f.
trail n vestīgia ntpl ♦ vt trahere ♦ vi trahī.
train n (line) agmen nt, ōrdō m; (of dress) īnstita f; (army) impedīmenta ntpl; (followers) comitēs mpl, satellitēs mpl, cohors f ♦ vt īnstituere, īnstruere, docēre, adsuēfacere; exercēre; (weapon) dīrigere.
trainer n (sport) lanista m, aliptēs m.
training n disciplīna f, īnstitūtiō f; (practice) exercitātiō f.
trait n līneāmentum nt.
traitor n prōditor m.
traitorous adj perfidus, perfidiōsus.
traitorously adv perfidiōsē.

trammel vt impedīre.
tramp n (man) planus m; (of feet) pulsus m ♦ vi gradī.
trample vi: **~ on** obterere, prōterere, prōculcāre.
trance n stupor m; (prophetic) furor m.
tranquil adj tranquillus, placidus, quiētus, sēdātus.
tranquility n tranquillitās f, quiēs f, pāx f.
tranquillize vt pācāre, sēdāre.
tranquilly adv tranquillē, placidē, tranquillō animō.
transact vt agere, gerere, trānsigere.
transaction n rēs f, negōtium nt.
transactor n āctor m.
transalpine adj trānsalpīnus.
transcend vt superāre, excēdere.
transcendence n praestantia f.
transcendent adj eximius, ēgregius, excellēns.
transcendental adj dīvīnus.
transcendentally adv eximiē, ēgregiē, ūnicē.
transcribe vt dēscrībere, trānscrībere.
transcriber n librārius m.
transcript n exemplar nt, exemplum nt.
transfer n trānslātiō f; (of property) aliēnātiō f ♦ vt trānsferre; (troops) trādūcere; (property) abaliēnāre; (duty) dēlēgāre.
transference n trānslātiō f.
transfigure vt trānsfōrmāre.
transfix vt trānsfīgere, trāicere, trānsfodere; (mind) obstupefacere; **be ~ed** stupēre, stupēscere.
transform vt commūtāre, vertere.
transformation n commūtātiō f.
transgress vt violāre, perfringere ♦ vi dēlinquere.
transgression n dēlictum nt.
transgressor n violātor m.
transience n brevitās f.
transient adj fluxus, cadūcus, brevis.
transit n trānsitus m.
transition n mūtātiō f; (speech) trānsitus m.
transitory adj brevis, fluxus.
translate vt vertere, reddere; **~ into Latin** Latīnē reddere.
translation n: **a Latin ~ of Homer** Latīnē redditus Homērus.
translator n interpres m.
translucent adj perlūcidus.
transmarine adj trānsmarīnus.
transmission n missiō f.
transmit vt mittere; (legacy) trādere, prōdere.
transmutable adj mūtābilis.
transmutation n mūtātiō f.
transmute vt mūtāre, commūtāre.
transom n trabs f.
transparency n perlūcida nātūra f.
transparent adj perlūcidus; (fig) perspicuus.
transparently adv perspicuē.
transpire vi (get known) ēmānāre, dīvulgārī; (happen) ēvenīre.
transplant vt trānsferre.

transport n vectūra f; (ship) nāvis onerāria f;
(emotion) ēlātiō f, summa laetitia f ♦ vt
trānsportāre, trānsvehere, trānsmittere; **be
~ed** (fig) efferrī, gestīre.
transportation n vectūra f.
transpose vt invertere; (words) trāicere.
transposition n (words) trāiectiō f.
transverse adj trānsversus, oblīquus.
transversely adv in trānsversum, oblīquē.
trap n laqueus m; (fig) īnsidiae fpl ♦ vt dēcipere,
excipere; (fig) inlaqueāre.
trappings n ōrnāmenta ntpl, īnsignia ntpl;
(horse's) phalerae fpl.
trash n nūgae fpl.
trashy adj vīlis.
Trasimene n Trasimēnus m.
travail n labor m, sūdor m; (woman's)
puerperium nt ♦ vi labōrāre, sūdāre;
parturīre.
travel n itinera ntpl; (foreign) peregrīnātiō f ♦ vi
iter facere; (abroad) peregrīnārī; ~ **through**
peragrāre; ~ **to** contendere ad, in (acc),
proficīscī in (acc).
traveller n viātor m; (abroad) peregrīnātor m.
traverse vt peragrāre, lūstrāre; ~ **a great
distance** multa mīlia passuum iter facere.
travesty n perversa imitātiō f ♦ vt perversē
imitārī.
tray n ferculum nt.
treacherous adj perfidus, perfidiōsus;
(ground) lūbricus.
treacherously adv perfidiōsē.
treachery n perfidia f.
tread vi incēdere, ingredī; ~ **on** īnsistere (dat)
♦ n gradus m, incessus m.
treadle n (loom) īnsilia ntpl.
treadmill n pistrīnum nt.
treason n māiestās f, perduelliō f; **be charged
with** ~ māiestātis accūsārī; **be guilty of high
~ against** māiestātem minuere, laedere
(gen).
treasonable adj perfidus, perfidiōsus.
treasure n gāza f, thēsaurus m; (person)
dēliciae fpl ♦ vt māximī aestimāre, dīligere,
fovēre; ~ **up** condere, congerere.
treasure house n thēsaurus m.
treasurer n aerārī praefectus m; (royal)
dioecētēs m.
treasury n aerārium nt; (emperor's) fiscus m.
treat n convīvium nt; dēlectātiō f ♦ vt (in any
way) ūtī (abl), habēre, tractāre, accipere;
(patient) cūrāre; (topic) tractāre; (with
hospitality) invītāre; ~ **with** agere cum; ~ **as a
friend** amīcī locō habēre.
treatise n liber m.
treatment n tractātiō f; (MED) cūrātiō f.
treaty n foedus nt; **make a** ~ foedus ferīre.
treble adj triplus; (voice) acūtus ♦ n acūtus
sonus m ♦ vt triplicāre.
tree n arbor f.
trek vi migrāre ♦ n migrātiō f.
trellis n cancellī mpl.
tremble vi tremere, horrēre.

trembling n tremor m, horror m ♦ adj
tremulus.
tremendous adj immānis, ingēns, vastus.
tremendously adv immāne quantum.
tremor n tremor m.
tremulous adj tremulus.
trench n fossa f.
trenchant adj ācer.
trenchantly adv ācriter.
trend n inclīnātiō f ♦ vi vergere.
trepidation n trepidātiō f.
trespass n dēlictum nt ♦ vi dēlinquere; ~ **on**
(property) invādere in (acc); (patience, time,
etc) abūtī (abl).
trespasser n quī iniussū dominī ingreditur.
tress n crīnis m.
trial n (essay) experientia f; (test) probātiō f;
(law) iūdicium nt, quaestiō f; (trouble) labor m,
aerumna f; **make** ~ **of** experīrī, perīculum
facere (gen); **be brought to** ~ in iūdicium
venīre; **put on** ~ in iūdicium vocāre; **hold a** ~
on quaestiōnem habēre dē (abl).
triangle n triangulum nt.
triangular adj triangulus, triquetrus.
tribe n tribus m; gēns f; (barbarian) nātiō f.
tribulation n aerumna f.
tribunal n iūdicium nt.
tribune n tribūnus m; (platform) rōstra ntpl.
tribuneship, tribunate n tribūnātus m.
tribunician adj tribūnicius.
tributary adj vectīgālis ♦ n: **be a** ~ **of** (river)
īnfluere in (acc).
tribute n tribūtum nt, vectīgal nt; (verbal)
laudātiō f; **pay a** ~ **to** laudāre.
trice n: **in a** ~ mōmentō temporis.
trick n dolus m, fallācia f, fraus f, īnsidiae fpl,
ars f; (conjurer's) praestīgiae fpl; (habit) mōs m
♦ vt fallere, dēcipere, ēlūdere; (with words)
verba dare (dat); ~ **out** ōrnāre, distinguere.
trickery n dolus m, fraus f, fallāciae fpl.
trickle n guttae fpl ♦ vi mānāre, dēstillāre.
trickster n fraudātor m, veterātor m.
tricky adj lūbricus, difficilis.
trident n tridēns m, fuscina f.
tried adj probātus, spectātus.
triennial adj trietēricus.
triennially adv quartō quōque annō.
trifle n nūgae fpl, paululum nt ♦ vi lūdere,
nūgārī; ~ **with** lūdere.
trifling adj levis, exiguus.
triflingly adv leviter.
trig adj lepidus, concinnus.
trigger n manulea f.
trim adj nitidus, concinnus ♦ vt putāre,
tondēre; (lamp) oleum īnstillāre (dat) ♦ vi
temporibus servīre.
trimly adv concinnē.
trimness n nitor, munditia f.
trinket n crepundia ntpl.
trip n iter nt ♦ vt supplantāre ♦ vi lābī, titubāre;
~ **along** currere; ~ **over** incurrere in (acc).
tripartite adj tripartītus.

tripe n omāsum nt.
triple adj triplex, triplus ♦ vt triplicāre.
triply adv trifāriam.
tripod n tripus m.
trireme n trirēmis f.
trite adj trītus.
triumph n triumphus m; (victory) victōria f ♦ vi triumphāre; vincere; ~ **over** dēvincere.
triumphal adj triumphālis.
triumphant adj victor; laetus.
triumvir n triumvir m.
triumvirate n triumvirātus m.
trivial adj levis, tenuis.
triviality n nūgae fpl.
trochaic adj trochaicus.
trochee n trochaeus m.
Trojan n Trōiānus m.
troop n grex f, caterva f; (cavalry) turma f ♦ vi cōnfluere, congregārī.
trooper n eques m.
troops npl cōpiae fpl.
trope n figūra f, trānslātiō f.
trophy n tropaeum nt; **set up a ~** tropaeum pōnere.
tropic n sōlstitiālis orbis m; ~**s** pl loca fervida ntpl.
tropical adj tropicus.
trot vi tolūtim īre.
troth n fidēs f.
trouble n incommodum nt, malum nt, molestia f, labor m; (effort) opera f, negōtium nt; (disturbance) turba f, tumultus m; **take the ~ to** operam dare ut; **be worth the ~** operae pretium esse ♦ vt (disturb) turbāre; (make uneasy) sollicitāre, exagitāre; (annoy) incommodāre, molestiam exhibēre (dat); ~ **oneself about** cūrāre, respicere; **be ~d with** labōrāre ex.
troubler n turbātor m.
troublesome adj molestus, incommodus, difficilis.
troublesomeness n molestia f.
troublous adj turbidus, turbulentus.
trough n alveus m.
trounce vt castīgāre.
troupe n grex f, caterva f.
trousered adj brācātus.
trousers n brācae fpl.
trow vi opīnārī.
truant adj tardus ♦ n cessātor m; **play ~** cessāre, nōn compārēre.
truce n indutiae fpl.
truck n carrus m; **have no ~ with** nihil commercī habēre cum.
truckle vi adsentārī.
truculence n ferōcia f, asperitās f.
truculent adj truculentus, ferōx.
truculently adv ferōciter.
trudge vi rēpere, pedibus incēdere.
true adj vērus; (genuine) germānus, vērus; (loyal) fīdus, fidēlis; (exact) rēctus, iūstus.
truism n verbum trītum nt.
truly adv rēvērā, profectō, vērē.

trumpery n nūgae fpl ♦ adj vīlis.
trumpet n tuba f, būcina f.
trumpeter n būcinātor m, tubicen m.
trump up vt ēmentīrī, cōnfingere.
truncate vt praecīdere.
truncheon n fustis m, scīpiō m.
trundle vt volvere.
trunk n truncus m; (elephant's) manus f; (box) cista f.
truss n fascia f ♦ vt colligāre.
trust n fidēs f, fīdūcia f; **breach of ~** mala fidēs; **held in ~** fīdūciārius; **put ~ in** fidem habēre (dat) ♦ vt cōnfīdere (dat), crēdere (dat); (entrust) committere, concrēdere.
trustee n tūtor m.
trusteeship n tūtēla f.
trustful adj crēdulus, fīdēns.
trustfully adv fīdenter.
trustily adv fidēliter.
trustiness n fidēs f, fidēlitās f.
trusting adj fīdēns.
trustingly adv fīdenter.
trustworthily adv fidēliter.
trustworthiness n fidēs f, integritās f.
trustworthy adj fīdus, certus; (witness) locuplēs; (authority) certus, bonus.
trusty adj fīdus, fidēlis.
truth n vēritās f, vērum nt; **in ~** rē vērā.
truthful adj vērāx.
truthfully adv vērē.
truthfulness n fidēs f.
try vt (attempt) cōnārī; (test) experīrī, temptāre; (harass) exercēre; (judge) iūdicāre, cognōscere; ~ **for** petere, quaerere.
trying adj molestus.
tub n alveus m, cūpa f.
tubby adj obēsus.
tube n fistula f.
tufa n tōfus m.
tuft n crista f.
tug vt trahere, tractāre.
tuition n īnstitūtiō f.
tumble vi concidere, corruere, prōlābī ♦ n cāsus m.
tumbledown adj ruīnōsus.
tumbler n pōculum nt.
tumid adj tumidus, īnflātus.
tumour n tūber nt.
tumult n tumultus m, turba f; (fig) perturbātiō f.
tumultuous adj tumultuōsus, turbidus.
tumultuously adv tumultuōsē.
tumulus n tumulus m.
tun n dolium nt.
tune n modī mpl, carmen nt; **keep in ~** concentum servāre; **out of ~** absonus, dissonus; (strings) incontentus ♦ vt (strings) intendere.
tuneful adj canōrus.
tunefully adv numerōsē.
tunic n tunica f; **wearing a ~** tunicātus.
tunnel n cunīculus m.
tunny n thunnus m.

turban *n* mitra *f*, mitella *f*.
turbid *adj* turbidus.
turbot *n* rhombus *m*.
turbulence *n* tumultus *m*.
turbulent *adj* turbulentus, turbidus.
turbulently *adv* turbulentē, turbidē.
turf *n* caespes *m*.
turgid *adj* turgidus, īnflātus.
turgidity *n* (*RHET*) ampullae *fpl*.
turgidly *adv* īnflātē.
turmoil *n* turba *f*, tumultus *m*; (*mind*)
  perturbātiō *f*.
turn *n* (*motion*) conversiō *f*; (*bend*) flexus *m*,
  ānfrāctus *m*; (*change*) commūtātiō *f*,
  vicissitūdō *f*; (*walk*) spatium *nt*; (*of mind*)
  adfectus *m*; (*of language*) sententia *f*,
  cōnfōrmātiō *f*; ~ **of events** mūtātiō rērum *f*;
  bad ~ iniūria *f*; **good** ~ beneficium *nt*; ~ **of the
  scale** mōmentum *nt*; **take a** ~ **for the worse** in
  pēiōrem partem vertī; **in ~s** invicem,
  vicissim, alternī; **in one's** ~ locō ōrdine ♦ *vt*
  vertere, convertere, flectere; (*change*)
  vertere, mūtāre; (*direct*) intendere, dīrigere;
  (*translate*) vertere, reddere; (*on a lathe*)
  tornāre; ~ **the edge of** retundere; ~ **the head**
  mentem exturbāre; ~ **the laugh against**
  rīsum convertere in (*acc*); ~ **the scale** (*fig*)
  mōmentum habēre; ~ **the stomach** nauseam
  facere; ~ **to account** ūtī (*abl*), in rem suam
  convertere ♦ *vi* versārī, circumagī; (*change*)
  vertere, mūtārī; (*crisis*) pendēre; (*direction*)
  convertī; (*scale*) prōpendēre; ~ **king's/
  queen's evidence** indicium profitērī; ~
  against *vt* aliēnāre ab ♦ *vi* dēscīscere ab; ~
  around (se) circumvertere; ~ **aside** *vt*
  dēflectere, dēclīnāre ♦ *vi* dēvertere, sē
  dēclīnāre; ~ **away** *vt* āvertere, dēpellere ♦ *vi*
  āversārī, discēdere; ~ **back** *vi* revertī; ~
  down *vt* invertere; (*proposal*) rēicere; ~ **into**
  vi vertere in (*acc*), mūtārī in (*acc*); ~ **out** *vt*
  ēicere, expellere ♦ *vi* cadere, ēvenīre,
  ēvādere; ~ **outside in** excutere; ~ **over** *vt*
  ēvertere; (*book*) ēvolvere; (*in mind*) volūtāre,
  agitāre; ~ **round** *vt* circumagere ♦ *vi*
  convertī; ~ **up** *vt* retorquēre; (*earth*) versāre;
  (*nose*) corrūgāre ♦ *vi* adesse, intervenire; ~
  upside down invertere.
turncoat *n* trānsfuga *m*.
turning *n* flexus *m*, ānfrāctus *m*.
turning point *n* discrīmen *nt*, mēta *f*.
turnip *n* rāpum *nt*.
turpitude *n* turpitūdō *f*.
turquoise *n* callais *f* ♦ *adj* callainus.
turret *n* turris *f*.
turreted *adj* turrītus.
turtle *n* testūdō *f*; **turn** ~ invertī.
turtle dove *n* turtur *m*.
tusk *n* dēns *m*.
tussle *n* luctātiō *f* ♦ *vi* luctārī.
tutelage *n* tūtēla *f*.
tutelary *adj* praeses.
tutor *n* praeceptor *m*, magister *m* ♦ *vt* docēre,
  praecipere (*dat*).

tutorship *n* tūtēla *f*.
twaddle *n* nūgae *fpl*.
twang *n* sonus *m* ♦ *vi* increpāre.
tweak *vi* vellicāre.
tweezers *n* forceps *m/f*, volsella *f*.
twelfth *adj* duodecimus ♦ *n* duodecima pars *f*,
  ūncia *f*; **eleven ~s** deūnx *m*; **five ~s** quīncūnx
  m; **seven ~s** septūnx *m*.
twelve *num* duodecim; ~ **each** duodēnī; ~ **times**
  duodeciēns.
twelvemonth *n* annus *m*.
twentieth *adj* vīcēsimus ♦ *n* vīcēsima pars *f*;
  (*tax*) vīcēsima *f*.
twenty *num* vīgintī; ~ **each** vīcēnī; ~ **times**
  vīciēns.
twice *adv* bis; ~ **as much** duplus, bis tantō; ~ **a
  day** bis diē, bis in diē.
twig *n* virga *f*, rāmulus *m*.
twilight *n* (*morning*) dīlūculum *nt*; (*evening*)
  crepusculum *nt*.
twin *adj* geminus ♦ *n* geminus *m*, gemina *f*.
twine *n* resticula *f* ♦ *vt* nectere, implicāre,
  contexere ♦ *vi* sē implicāre; ~ **round**
  complectī.
twinge *n* dolor *m*.
twinkle *vi* micāre.
twirl *vt* intorquēre, contorquēre ♦ *vi*
  circumagī.
twist *vt* torquēre, intorquēre ♦ *vi* torquērī.
twit *vt* obicere (*dat*).
twitch *vt* vellicāre ♦ *vi* micāre.
twitter *vi* pīpilāre.
two *num* duo; ~ **each** bīnī; ~ **days** biduum *nt*; ~
  years biennium *nt*; ~ **years old** bīmus; ~ **by**
  bīnī; ~ **feet long** bipedālis; **in ~ parts**
  bifāriam, bipartītō.
two-coloured *adj* bicolor.
two-edged *adj* anceps.
twofold *adj* duplex, anceps.
two-footed *adj* bipēs.
two-headed *adj* biceps.
two-horned *adj* bicornis.
two hundred *num* ducentī; ~ **each** ducēnī; ~
  times ducentiēns.
two hundredth *adj* ducentēsimus.
two-oared *adj* birēmis.
two-pronged *adj* bidēns, bifurcus.
two-way *adj* bivius.
type *n* (*pattern*) exemplar *nt*; (*kind*) genus
  nt.
typhoon *n* turbō *m*.
typical *adj* proprius, solitus.
typically *adv* dē mōre, ut mōs est.
typify *vt* exprimere.
tyrannical *adj* superbus, crūdēlis.
tyrannically *adv* superbē, crūdēliter.
tyrannize *vi* dominārī, rēgnāre.
tyrannous *adj see* **tyrannical**
tyrannously *adv see* **tyrannically**.
tyranny *n* dominātiō *f*, rēgnum *nt*.
tyrant *n* rēx *m*, crūdēlis dominus *m*; (*Greek*)
  tyrannus *m*.
tyro *n* tīrō *m*, rudis *m*.

U, u

ubiquitous *adj* omnibus locīs praesēns.
ubiquity *n* ūniversa praesentia *f*.
udder *n* ūber *nt*.
ugliness *n* foedītās *f*, dēfōrmitās *f*, turpitūdō *f*.
ugly *adj* foedus, dēfōrmis, turpis.
ulcer *n* ulcus *nt*, vomica *f*.
ulcerate *vi* ulcerārī.
ulcerous *adj* ulcerōsus.
ulterior *adj* ulterior.
ultimate *adj* ultimus, extrēmus.
ultimately *adv* tandem, ad ultimum.
umbrage *n* offēnsiō *f*; **take ~ at** indignē ferre, patī.
umbrageous *adj* umbrōsus.
umbrella *n* umbella *f*.
umpire *n* arbiter *m*, disceptātor *m*.
unabashed *adj* intrepidus, impudēns.
unabated *adj* integer.
unable *adj* impotēns; **be ~** nōn posse, nequīre.
unacceptable *adj* ingrātus.
unaccompanied *adj* sōlus.
unaccomplished *adj* īnfectus, imperfectus; (*person*) indoctus.
unaccountable *adj* inexplicābilis.
unaccountably *adv* sine causā, repente.
unaccustomed *adj* īnsuētus, īnsolitus.
unacquainted *adj* ignārus (*gen*), imperītus (*gen*).
unadorned *adj* inōrnātus, incōmptus; (*speech*) nūdus, ēnucleātus.
unadulterated *adj* sincērus, integer.
unadvisedly *adv* imprūdenter, incōnsultē.
unaffected *adj* simplex, candidus.
unaffectedly *adv* simpliciter.
unaided *adj* sine auxiliō, nūdus.
unalienable *adj* proprius.
unalloyed *adj* pūrus.
unalterable *adj* immūtābilis.
unaltered *adj* immūtātus.
unambiguous *adj* apertus, certus.
unambitious *adj* humilis, modestus.
unanimity *n* cōnsēnsiō *f*, ūnanimitās *f*.
unanimous *adj* concors, ūnanimus; **be ~** idem omnēs sentīre.
unanimously *adv* ūnā vōce, omnium cōnsēnsū.
unanswerable *adj* necessārius.
unanswerably *adv* sine contrōversiā.
unappreciative *adj* ingrātus.
unapproachable *adj* inaccessus; (*person*) difficilis.
unarmed *adj* inermis.
unasked *adj* ultrō, suā sponte.
unassailable *adj* inexpugnābilis.
unassailed *adj* intāctus, incolumis.

unassuming *adj* modestus, dēmissus; **~ manners** modestia *f*.
unassumingly *adv* modestē.
unattached *adj* līber.
unattempted *adj* intentātus; **leave ~** praetermittere.
unattended *adj* sōlus, sine comitibus.
unattractive *adj* invenustus.
unauthentic *adj* incertō auctōre.
unavailing *adj* inūtilis, inānis.
unavenged *adj* inultus.
unavoidable *adj* necessārius.
unavoidably *adv* necessāriō.
unaware *adj* īnscius, ignārus.
unawares *adv* inopīnātō, dē imprōvīsō; incautus.
unbalanced *adj* turbātus.
unbar *vt* reserāre.
unbearable *adj* intolerābilis, intolerandus.
unbearably *adv* intoleranter.
unbeaten *adj* invictus.
unbecoming *adj* indecōrus, inhonestus; **it is ~** dēdecet.
unbeknown *adj* ignōtus.
unbelief *n* diffīdentia *f*.
unbelievable *adj* incrēdibilis.
unbelievably *adv* incrēdibiliter.
unbelieving *adj* incrēdulus.
unbend *vt* remittere, laxāre ♦ *vi* animum remittere, aliquid dē sevēritāte remittere.
unbending *adj* inexōrābilis, sevērus.
unbiassed *adj* integer, incorruptus, aequus.
unbidden *adj* ultrō, sponte.
unbind *vt* solvere, resolvere.
unblemished *adj* pūrus, integer.
unblushing *adj* impudēns.
unblushingly *adv* impudenter.
unbolt *vt* reserāre.
unborn *adj* nōndum nātus.
unbosom *vt* patefacere, effundere.
unbound *adj* solūtus.
unbounded *adj* īnfīnītus, immēnsus.
unbridled *adj* īnfrēnātus; (*fig*) effrēnātus, indomitus, impotēns.
unbroken *adj* integer; (*animal*) intractātus; (*friendship*) inviolātus; (*series*) perpetuus, continuus.
unburden *vt* exonerāre; **~ oneself of** aperīre, patefacere.
unburied *adj* inhumātus, īnsepultus.
unbusinesslike *adj* iners.
uncalled-for *adj* supervacāneus.
uncanny *adj* mīrus, mōnstruōsus.
uncared-for *adj* neglectus.
unceasing *adj* perpetuus, adsiduus.
unceasingly *adv* perpetuō, adsiduē.
unceremonious *adj* agrestis, inurbānus.
unceremoniously *adv* inurbānē.
uncertain *adj* incertus, dubius, anceps; **be ~** dubitāre, pendēre.
uncertainly *adv* incertē, dubitanter.
uncertainty *n* incertum *nt*; (*state*) dubitātiō *f*.
unchangeable *adj* immūtābilis; (*person*)

cōnstāns.
unchanged adj immūtātus, īdem; **remain ~**
permanēre.
uncharitable adj inhūmānus, malignus.
uncharitableness n inhūmānitās f.
uncharitably adv inhūmānē, malignē.
unchaste adj impudīcus, libīdinōsus.
unchastely adv impudīcē.
unchastity n incestus m, libīdō f.
unchecked adj līber, indomitus.
uncivil adj inurbānus, importūnus,
inhūmānus.
uncivilized adj barbarus, incultus, ferus.
uncivilly adv inurbānē.
uncle n (_paternal_) patruus m; (_maternal_)
avunculus m.
unclean adj immundus; (_fig_) impūrus,
obscēnus.
uncleanly adv impūrē.
uncleanness n sordēs fpl; (_fig_) impūritās f,
obscēnitās f.
unclose vt aperīre.
unclothe vt nūdāre, vestem dētrahere (_dat_).
unclothed adj nūdus.
unclouded adj serēnus.
uncoil vt explicāre, ēvolvere.
uncomely adj dēfōrmis, turpis.
uncomfortable adj incommodus, molestus.
uncomfortably adv incommodē.
uncommitted adj vacuus.
uncommon adj rārus, īnsolitus, inūsitātus;
(_eminent_) ēgregius, singulāris, eximius.
uncommonly adv rārō; ēgregiē, ūnicē.
uncommonness n īnsolentia f.
uncommunicative adj tēctus, taciturnus.
uncomplaining adj patiēns.
uncompleted adj imperfectus.
uncompromising adj dūrus, rigidus.
unconcern n sēcūritās f.
unconcerned adj sēcūrus, ōtiōsus.
unconcernedly adv lentē.
uncondemned adj indemnātus.
unconditional adj absolūtus.
unconditionally adv nullā condiciōne.
uncongenial adj ingrātus.
unconnected adj sēparātus, disiūnctus;
(_style_) dissolūtus.
unconquerable adj invictus.
unconquered adj invictus.
unconscionable adj improbus.
unconscionably adv improbē.
unconscious adj: **~ of** īnscius (_gen_), ignārus
(_gen_); **become ~** sōpīrī, animō linquī.
unconsciousness n sopor m.
unconsecrated adj profānus.
unconsidered adj neglectus.
unconstitutional adj illicitus.
unconstitutionally adv contrā lēgēs, contrā
rem pūblicam.
uncontaminated adj pūrus, incorruptus,
integer.
uncontrollable adj impotēns, effrēnātus.
uncontrollably adv effrēnātē.

uncontrolled adj līber, solūtus.
unconventional adj īnsolitus, solūtus.
unconvicted adj indemnātus.
unconvincing adj incrēdibilis, nōn vērī
similis.
uncooked adj crūdus.
uncorrupted adj incorruptus, integer.
uncouple vt disiungere.
uncouth adj horridus, agrestis, inurbānus.
uncouthly adv inurbānē.
uncouthness n inhūmānitās f, rūsticitās f.
uncover vt dētegere, aperīre, nūdāre.
uncritical adj indoctus, crēdulus.
uncultivated adj incultus; (_fig_) agrestis,
rūsticus, impolītus.
uncultured adj agrestis, rudis.
uncut adj intōnsus.
undamaged adj integer, inviolātus.
undaunted adj intrepidus, fortis.
undecayed adj incorruptus.
undeceive vt errōrem tollere (_dat_), errōrem
ēripere (_dat_).
undecided adj dubius, anceps; (_case_) integer.
undecked adj (_ship_) apertus.
undefended adj indēfēnsus, nūdus.
undefiled adj integer, incontāminātus.
undemonstrative adj taciturnus.
undeniable adj certus.
undeniably adv sine dubiō.
undependable adj inconstāns, mōbilis.
under adv īnfrā, subter ◆ prep sub (_abl_), īnfrā
(_acc_); (_number_) intrā (_acc_); (_motion_) sub (_acc_);
~ arms in armīs; **~ colour** (pretext of) speciē
(_gen_), per speciem (_gen_); **~ my leadership** mē
duce; **~ the circumstances** cum haec ita sint;
labour ~ labōrāre ex; **~ the eyes of** in
cōnspectū (+ _gen_); **~ the leadership of** abl +
duce.
underage adj impūbēs.
undercurrent n: **an ~ of** lātens.
underestimate vt minōris aestimāre.
undergarment n subūcula f.
undergo vt subīre, patī, ferre.
underground adj subterrāneus ◆ adv sub
terrā.
undergrowth n virgulta ntpl.
underhand adj clandestīnus, fūrtīvus ◆ adv
clam, fūrtim.
underline vt subscrībere.
underling n minister m, satelles m/f.
undermine vt subruere; (_fig_) labefacere,
labefactāre.
undermost adj īnfimus.
underneath adv īnfrā ◆ prep sub (_abl_), īnfrā
(_acc_); (_motion_) sub (_acc_).
underprop vt fulcīre.
underrate vt obtrectāre, extenuāre, minōris
aestimāre.
understand vt intellegere, comprehendere;
(_be told_) accipere, comperīre; (_in a sense_)
interpretārī; **~ Latin** Latīnē scīre.
understandable adj crēdibilis.
understanding adj sapiēns, perītus ◆ n

intellegentia *f*; (*faculty*) mēns *f*, intellectus *m*; (*agreement*) cōnsēnsus *m*; (*condition*) condiciō *f*.

undertake *vt* suscipere, sūmere, adīre ad; (*business*) condūcere; (*case*) agere, dēfendere; (*promise*) recipere, spondēre.

undertaker *n* dissignātor *m*.

undertaking *n* inceptum *nt*, inceptiō *f*.

undervalue *vt* minōris aestimāre.

underwood *n* virgulta *ntpl*.

underworld *n* Īnferī *mpl*.

undeserved *adj* immeritus, iniūstus.

undeservedly *adv* immeritō, indignē.

undeserving *adj* indignus.

undesigned *adj* fortuītus.

undesignedly *adv* fortuītō, temerē.

undesirable *adj* odiōsus, ingrātus.

undeterred *adj* immōtus.

undeveloped *adj* immātūrus.

undeviating *adj* dīrēctus.

undigested *adj* crūdus.

undignified *adj* levis, inhonestus.

undiminished *adj* integer.

undiscernible *adj* invīsus, obscūrus.

undisciplined *adj* lascīvus, immoderātus; (*MIL*) inexercitātus.

undiscovered *adj* ignōtus.

undisguised *adj* apertus.

undisguisedly *adv* palam, apertē.

undismayed *adj* impavidus, intrepidus.

undisputed *adj* certus.

undistinguished *adj* ignōbilis, inglōrius.

undisturbed *adj* tranquillus, placidus.

undo *vt* (*knot*) expedīre, resolvere; (*sewing*) dissuere; (*fig*) Īnfectum reddere.

undoing *n* ruīna *f*.

undone *adj* infectus; (*ruined*) perditus; **be ~** perīre, disperīre; **hopelessly ~** dēperditus.

undoubted *adj* certus.

undoubtedly *adv* sine dubiō, plānē.

undress *vt* exuere, vestem dētrahere (*dat*).

undressed *adj* nūdus.

undue *adj* nimius, immoderātus, inīquus.

undulate *vi* fluctuāre.

undulation *n* spīra *f*.

unduly *adv* nimis, plūs aequō.

undutiful *adj* impius.

undutifully *adv* impiē.

undutifulness *n* impietās *f*.

undying *adj* immortālis, aeternus.

unearth *vt* ēruere, dētegere.

unearthly *adj* mōnstruōsus, dīvīnus, hūmānō māior.

uneasily *adv* aegrē.

uneasiness *n* sollicitūdō *f*, perturbātiō *f*.

uneasy *adj* sollicitus, anxius, inquiētus.

uneducated *adj* illitterātus, indoctus, rudis; **be ~** litterās nescīre.

unemployed *adj* ōtiōsus.

unemployment *n* cessātiō *f*.

unencumbered *adj* expedītus, līber.

unending *adj* perpetuus, sempiternus.

unendowed *adj* indōtātus.

unendurable *adj* intolerandus, intolerābilis.

unenjoyable *adj* iniūcundus, molestus.

unenlightened *adj* rudis, inērudītus.

unenterprising *adj* iners.

unenviable *adj* nōn invidendus.

unequal *adj* impār, dispār.

unequalled *adj* ūnicus, singulāris.

unequally *adv* inaequāliter, inīquē.

unequivocal *adj* apertus, plānus.

unerring *adj* certus.

unerringly *adv* certē.

unessential *adj* adventīcius, supervacāneus.

uneven *adj* impār; (*surface*) asper, inīquus, inaequābilis.

unevenly *adv* inīquē, inaequāliter.

unevenness *n* inīquitās *f*, asperitās *f*.

unexamined *adj* (*case*) incognitus.

unexampled *adj* inaudītus, ūnicus, singulāris.

unexceptionable *adj* ēmendātus; (*authority*) certissimus.

unexpected *adj* imprōvīsus, inopīnātus, Īnsperātus.

unexpectedly *adv* dē imprōvīsō, ex Īnspērātō, inopīnātō, necopīnātō.

unexplored *adj* inexplōrātus.

unfading *adj* perennis, vīvus.

unfailing *adj* perennis, certus, perpetuus.

unfailingly *adv* semper.

unfair *adj* inīquus, iniūstus.

unfairly *adv* inīquē, iniūstē.

unfairness *n* inīquitās *f*, iniūstitia *f*.

unfaithful *adj* Īnfidēlis, Īnfīdus, perfidus.

unfaithfully *adv* Īnfidēliter.

unfaithfulness *n* Īnfidēlitās *f*.

unfamiliar *adj* novus, ignōtus, Īnsolēns; (*sight*) invīsitātus.

unfamiliarity *n* Īnsolentia *f*.

unfashionable *adj* obsolētus.

unfasten *vt* solvere, refīgere.

unfathomable *adj* Īnfīnītus, profundus.

unfavourable *adj* inīquus, adversus, importūnus.

unfavourably *adv* inīquē, male; **be ~ disposed** āversō animō esse.

unfed *adj* iēiūnus.

unfeeling *adj* dūrus, crūdēlis, ferreus.

unfeelingly *adv* crūdēliter.

unfeigned *adj* sincērus, vērus, simplex.

unfeignedly *adv* sincērē, vērē.

unfilial *adj* impius.

unfinished *adj* Īnfectus, imperfectus.

unfit *adj* inūtilis, incommodus, aliēnus.

unfix *vt* refīgere.

unflinching *adj* impavidus, firmus.

unfold *vt* explicāre, ēvolvere; (*story*) expōnere, ēnārrāre.

unfolding *n* explicātiō *f*.

unforeseen *adj* imprōvīsus.

unforgettable *adj* memorābilis.

unforgiving *adj* implācābilis.

unformed *adj* Īnfōrmis.

unfortified *adj* immūnītus, nūdus.

unfortunate adj īnfēlīx, īnfortūnātus.
unfortunately adv īnfēlīciter, male; **~ you did
not come** male accidit quod nōn vēnistī.
unfounded adj inānis, vānus.
unfrequented adj dēsertus.
unfriendliness n inimīcitia f.
unfriendly adj inimīcus, malevolus; **in an ~
manner** inimīcē.
unfruitful adj sterilis; (fig) inānis, vānus.
unfruitfulness n sterilitās f.
unfulfilled adj īnfectus, inritus.
unfurl vt explicāre, pandere.
unfurnished adj nūdus.
ungainly adj agrestis, rūsticus.
ungallant adj inurbānus, parum cōmis.
ungenerous adj illīberālis; **~ conduct**
illīberālitās f.
ungentlemanly adj illīberālis.
ungirt adj discinctus.
ungodliness n impietās f.
ungodly adj impius.
ungovernable adj impotēns, indomitus.
ungovernableness n impotentia f.
ungraceful adj inconcinnus, inēlegāns.
ungracefully adv inēleganter.
ungracious adj inhūmānus, petulāns,
importūnus.
ungraciously adv acerbē.
ungrammatical adj barbarus; **be ~**
soloecismum facere.
ungrateful adj ingrātus.
ungrudging adj largus, nōn invītus.
ungrudgingly adv sine invidiā.
unguarded adj intūtus; (word) incautus,
incōnsultus.
unguardedly adv temerē, incōnsultē.
unguent n unguentum nt.
unhallowed adj profānus, impius.
unhand vt mittere.
unhandy adj inhabilis.
unhappily adv īnfēlīciter, miserē.
unhappiness n miseria f, tristitia f, maestitia
f.
unhappy adj īnfēlix, miser, tristis.
unharmed adj incolumis, integer, salvus.
unharness vt disiungere.
unhealthiness n valētūdō f; (climate) gravitās
f.
unhealthy adj invalidus, aeger; (climate)
gravis, pestilens.
unheard adj inaudītus; (law) indictā causā.
unheard-of adj inaudītus.
unheeded adj neglectus.
unheeding adj immemor, sēcūrus.
unhelpful adj difficilis, invītus.
unhesitating adj audāx, prōmptus.
unhesitatingly adv sine dubitātiōne.
unhewn adj rudis.
unhindered adj expedītus.
unhinged adj mente captus.
unhistorical adj fictus, commentīcius.
unholiness n impietās f.
unholy adj impius.

unhonoured adj inhonōrātus.
unhoped-for adj īnspērātus.
unhorse vt excutere, equō dēicere.
unhurt adj integer, incolumis.
unicorn n monocerōs m.
uniform adj aequābilis, aequālis ♦ n īnsignia
ntpl; (MIL) sagum nt; **in ~** sagātus; **put on ~** saga
sūmere.
uniformity n aequābilitās f, cōnstantia f.
uniformly adv aequābiliter, ūnō tenōre.
unify vt coniungere.
unimaginative adj hebes, stolidus.
unimpaired adj integer, incolumis, illībātus.
unimpeachable adj (character) integer; (style)
ēmendātus.
unimportant adj levis, nullīus mōmentī.
uninformed adj indoctus, ignārus.
uninhabitable adj inhabitābilis.
uninhabited adj dēsertus.
uninitiated adj profānus; (fig) rudis.
uninjured adj integer, incolumis.
unintelligent adj īnsipiēns, tardus, excors.
unintelligible adj obscūrus.
unintelligibly adv obscūrē.
unintentionally adv imprūdēns, temerē.
uninteresting adj frīgidus, āridus.
uninterrupted adj continuus, perpetuus.
uninterruptedly adv continenter, sine ullā
intermissiōne.
uninvited adj invocātus; **~ guest** umbra f.
uninviting adj iniūcundus, invenustus.
union n coniūnctiō f; (social) cōnsociātiō f,
societās f; (POL) foederātae cīvitātēs fpl;
(agreement) concordia f, cōnsēnsus m;
(marriage) coniugium nt.
unique adj ūnicus, ēgregius, singulāris.
unison n concentus m; (fig) concordia f,
cōnsēnsus m.
unit n ūniō f.
unite vt coniungere, cōnsociāre, cōpulāre ♦ vi
coīre; cōnsentīre, cōnspīrāre; (rivers)
cōnfluere.
unity n (concord) concordia f, cōnsēnsus m.
universal adj ūniversus, commūnis.
universally adv ūniversus, omnis; (place)
ubīque.
universe n mundus m, rērum nātūra f.
university n acadēmia f.
unjust adj iniūstus, inīquus.
unjustifiable adj indignus, inexcūsābilis.
unjustly adv iniūstē, iniūriā.
unkempt adj horridus.
unkind adj inhūmānus, inīquus.
unkindly adv inhūmānē, asperē.
unkindness n inhūmānitās f.
unknowingly adv imprūdēns, īnscius.
unknown adj ignōtus, incognitus; (fame)
obscūrus.
unlawful adj vetitus, iniūriōsus.
unlawfully adv iniūriōsē, iniūriā.
unlearn vt dēdiscere.
unlearned adj indoctus, inērudītus.
unless conj nisī.

unlettered adj illitterātus.
unlike adj dissimilis (+ gen or dat), dispār.
unlikely adj nōn vērīsimilis.
unlimited adj īnfīnītus, immēnsus.
unload vt exonerāre, deonerāre; (from ship) expōnere.
unlock vt reserāre, reclūdere.
unlooked-for adj īnspērātus, inexpectātus.
unloose vt solvere, exsolvere.
unlovely adj invenustus.
unluckily adv īnfēlīciter.
unlucky adj īnfēlīx, īnfortūnātus; (day) āter.
unmake vt īnfectum reddere.
unman vt mollīre, frangere, dēbilitāre.
unmanageable adj inhabilis.
unmanly adj mollis, ēnervātus, muliebris.
unmannerliness n importūnitās f, inhūmānitās f.
unmannerly adj importūnus, inhūmānus.
unmarried adj (man) caelebs; (woman) vidua.
unmask vt nūdāre, dētegere.
unmatched adj ūnicus, singulāris.
unmeaning adj inānis.
unmeasured adj īnfīnītus, immoderātus.
unmeet adj parum idōneus.
unmelodious adj absonus, absurdus.
unmentionable adj īnfandus.
unmentioned adj indictus; **leave ~** ōmittere.
unmerciful adj immisericors, inclēmēns.
unmercifully adv inclēmenter.
unmerited adj immeritus, indignus.
unmindful adj immemor.
unmistakable adj certus, manifestus.
unmistakably adv sine dubiō, certē.
unmitigated adj merus.
unmixed adj pūrus.
unmolested adj intāctus.
unmoor vt solvere.
unmoved adj immōtus.
unmusical adj absonus, absurdus.
unmutilated adj integer.
unnatural adj (event) mōnstruōsus; (feelings) impius, inhūmānus; (style) arcessītus, pūtidus.
unnaturally adv contrā nātūram; impiē, inhūmānē; pūtidē.
unnavigable adj innāvigābilis.
unnecessarily adv nimis.
unnecessary adj inūtilis, supervacāneus.
unnerve vt dēbilitāre, frangere.
unnoticed adj: **be ~** latēre, fallere.
unnumbered adj innumerus.
unobjectionable adj honestus, culpae expers.
unobservant adj tardus.
unobserved adj: **be ~** latēre, fallere.
unobstructed adj apertus, pūrus.
unobtrusive adj verēcundus; **be ~** fallere.
unobtrusiveness n verēcundia f.
unoccupied adj vacuus, ōtiōsus.
unoffending adj innocēns.
unofficial adj prīvātus.
unorthodox adj abnōrmis.
unostentatious adj modestus, verēcundus.

unostentatiously adv nullā iactātiōne.
unpaid adj (services) grātuītus; (money) dēbitus.
unpalatable adj amārus; (fig) iniūcundus, īnsuāvis.
unparalleled adj ūnicus, inaudītus.
unpardonable adj inexcūsābilis.
unpatriotic adj impius.
unpitying adj immisericors, ferreus.
unpleasant adj iniūcundus, ingrātus, īnsuāvis, gravis, molestus.
unpleasantly adv iniūcundē, ingrātē, graviter.
unpleasantness n iniūcunditās f, molestia f.
unpleasing adj ingrātus, invenustus.
unploughed adj inarātus.
unpoetical adj pedester.
unpolished adj impolītus; (person) incultus, agrestis, inurbānus; (style) inconditus, rudis.
unpopular adj invidiōsus, invīsus.
unpopularity n invidia f, odium nt.
unpractised adj inexercitātus, imperītus.
unprecedented adj īnsolēns, novus, inaudītus.
unprejudiced adj integer, aequus.
unpremeditated adj repentīnus, subitus.
unprepared adj imparātus.
unprepossessing adj invenustus, illepidus.
unpretentious adj modestus, verēcundus.
unprincipled adj improbus, levis, prāvus.
unproductive adj infēcundus, sterilis.
unprofitable adj inūtilis, vānus.
unprofitably adv frustrā, ab rē.
unpropitious adj īnfēlīx, adversus.
unpropitiously adv malīs ōminibus.
unprotected adj indēfēnsus, intūtus, nūdus.
unprovoked adj ultrō (adv).
unpunished adj impūnītus ♦ adv impūne.
unqualified adj nōn idōneus; (unrestricted) absolūtus.
unquestionable adj certus.
unquestionably adv facile, certē.
unquestioning adj crēdulus.
unravel vt retexere; (fig) ēnōdāre, explicāre.
unready adj imparātus.
unreal adj falsus, vānus.
unreality n vānitās f.
unreasonable adj inīquus, importūnus.
unreasonableness n inīquitās f.
unreasonably adv inīquē.
unreasoning adj stolidus, temerārius.
unreclaimed adj (land) incultus.
unrefined adj impolītus, inurbānus, rudis.
unregistered adj incēnsus.
unrelated adj aliēnus.
unrelenting adj implācābilis, inexōrābilis.
unreliable adj incertus, levis.
unreliably adv leviter.
unrelieved adj perpetuus, adsiduus.
unremitting adj adsiduus.
unrequited adj inultus, inānis.
unreservedly adv apertē, sine ullā exceptiōne.

unresponsive *adj* hebes.
unrest *n* inquiēs *f*, sollicitūdō *f*.
unrestrained *adj* līber, impotēns, effrēnātus, immoderātus.
unrestricted *adj* līber, absolūtus.
unrevenged *adj* inultus.
unrewarded *adj* inhonōrātus.
unrewarding *adj* ingrātus, vānus.
unrighteous *adj* iniūstus, impius.
unrighteously *adv* iniūstē, impiē.
unrighteousness *n* impietās *f*.
unripe *adj* immātūrus, crūdus.
unrivalled *adj* ēgregius, singulāris, ūnicus.
unroll *vt* ēvolvere, explicāre.
unromantic *adj* pedester.
unruffled *adj* immōtus, tranquillus.
unruliness *n* licentia *f*, impotentia *f*.
unruly *adj* effrēnātus, impotēns, immoderātus.
unsafe *adj* perīculōsus, dubius; (*structure*) īnstābilis.
unsaid *adj* indictus.
unsatisfactorily *adv* nōn ex sententiā, male.
unsatisfactory *adj* parum idōneus, malus.
unsatisfied *adj* parum contenus.
unsavoury *adj* īnsuāvis, taeter.
unscathed *adj* incolumis, integer.
unschooled *adj* indoctus, inērudītus.
unscrupulous *adj* improbus, impudēns.
unscrupulously *adv* improbē, impudenter.
unscrupulousness *n* improbitās *f*, impudentia *f*.
unseal *vt* resignāre, solvere.
unseasonable *adj* intempestīvus, importūnus.
unseasonableness *n* incommoditās *f*.
unseasonably *adv* intempestīvē, importūnē.
unseasoned *adj* (*food*) nōn condītus; (*wood*) viridis.
unseat *vt* (*rider*) excutere.
unseaworthy *adj* īnfirmus.
unseeing *adj* caecus.
unseemly *adj* indecōrus.
unseen *adj* invīsus; (*ever before*) invīsitātus.
unselfish *adj* innocēns, probus, līberālis.
unselfishly *adv* līberāliter.
unselfishness *n* innocentia *f*, līberālitās *f*.
unsettle *vt* ad incertum revocāre, turbāre, sollicitāre.
unsettled *adj* incertus, dubius; (*mind*) sollicitus, suspēnsus; (*times*) turbidus.
unsew *vt* dissuere.
unshackle *vt* expedīre, solvere.
unshaken *adj* immōtus, firmus, stabilis.
unshapely *adj* dēfōrmis.
unshaven *adj* intōnsus.
unsheathe *vt* dēstringere, stringere.
unshod *adj* nūdis pedibus.
unshorn *adj* intōnsus.
unsightliness *n* dēfōrmitās *f*, turpitūdō *f*.
unsightly *adj* foedus, dēfōrmis.
unskilful *adj* indoctus, īnscītus, incallidus.

unskilfully *adv* indoctē, īnscītē, incallide.
unskilfulness *n* īnscītia *f*, imperītia *f*.
unskilled *adj* imperītus, indoctus; ~ **in** imperitus (+ *gen*).
unslaked *adj* (*lime*) vīvus; (*thirst*) inexplētus.
unsociable *adj* īnsociābilis, difficilis.
unsoiled *adj* integer, pūrus.
unsolicited *adj* voluntārius ♦ *adv* ultrō.
unsophisticated *adj* simplex, ingenuus.
unsound *adj* īnfirmus; (*mind*) īnsānus; (*opinion*) falsus, perversus.
unsoundness *n* īnfirmitās *f*, īnsānitās *f*; prāvitās *f*.
unsparing *adj* inclēmēns, immisericors; (*lavish*) prōdigus.
unsparingly *adv* inclēmenter; prōdigē.
unspeakable *adj* īnfandus, incrēdibilis.
unspeakably *adv* incrēdibiliter.
unspoilt *adj* integer.
unspoken *adj* indictus, tacitus.
unspotted *adj* integer, pūrus.
unstable *adj* īnstabilis; (*fig*) incōnstāns, levis.
unstained *adj* pūrus, incorruptus, integer.
unstatesmanlike *adj* illīberālis.
unsteadily *adv* incōnstanter; **walk** ~ titubāre.
unsteadiness *n* (*fig*) incōnstantia *f*.
unsteady *adj* īnstabilis; (*fig*) incōnstāns.
unstitch *vt* dissuere.
unstring *vt* retendere.
unstudied *adj* simplex.
unsubdued *adj* invictus.
unsubstantial *adj* levis, inānis.
unsuccessful *adj* īnfēlīx; (*effort*) inritus; **be** ~ offendere; **I am** ~ mihī nōn succēdit.
unsuccessfully *adv* īnfēlīciter, rē īnfectā.
unsuitable *adj* incommodus, aliēnus, importūnus; **it is** ~ dēdecet.
unsuitableness *n* incommoditās *f*.
unsuitably *adv* incommodē, ineptē.
unsuited *adj* parum idōneus.
unsullied *adj* pūrus, incorruptus.
unsure *adj* incertus, dubius.
unsurpassable *adj* inexsuperābilis.
unsurpassed *adj* ūnicus, singulāris.
unsuspected *adj* latēns, nōn suspectus; **be** ~ latēre, in suspiciōnem nōn venīre.
unsuspecting *adj* imprōvidus, imprūdēns.
unsuspicious *adj* nōn suspicāx, crēdulus.
unswerving *adj* cōnstāns.
unsworn *adj* iniūrātus.
unsymmetrical *adj* inaequālis.
untainted *adj* incorruptus, integer.
untamable *adj* indomitus.
untamed *adj* indomitus, ferus.
untaught *adj* indoctus, rudis.
unteach *vt* dēdocēre.
unteachable *adj* indocilis.
untenable *adj* inānis, īnfirmus.
unthankful *adj* ingrātus.
unthankfully *adv* ingrātē.
unthankfulness *n* ingrātus animus *m*.
unthinkable *adj* incrēdibilis.
unthinking *adj* incōnsīderātus, imprōvidus.

unthriftily *adv* prōdigē.
unthrifty *adj* prōdigus, profūsus.
untidily *adv* neglegenter.
untidiness *n* neglegentia *f*.
untidy *adj* neglegēns, inconcinnus, squālidus.
untie *vt* solvere.
until *conj* dum, dōnec ♦ *prep* usque ad (*acc*), in (*acc*); ~ **now** adhūc.
untilled *adj* incultus.
untimely *adj* intempestīvus, immātūrus, importūnus.
untiring *adj* impiger; (*effort*) adsiduus.
unto *prep* ad (*acc*), in (*acc*).
untold *adj* innumerus.
untouched *adj* intāctus, integer.
untoward *adj* adversus, malus.
untrained *adj* inexercitātus, imperītus, rudis.
untried *adj* intemptātus, inexpertus; (*trial*) incognitus.
untrodden *adj* āvius.
untroubled *adj* tranquillus, placidus, quiētus; (*mind*) sēcūrus.
untrue *adj* falsus, fictus; (*disloyal*) īnfīdus, īnfidēlis.
untrustworthy *adj* īnfīdus, mōbilis.
untruth *n* mendācium *nt*, falsum *nt*.
untruthful *adj* mendāx, falsus.
untruthfully *adv* falsō, falsē.
untuneful *adj* absonus.
unturned *adj*: **leave no stone** ~ nihil intemptātum relinquere, omnia experīrī.
untutored *adj* indoctus, incultus.
unused *adj* (*person*) īnsuētus, īnsolitus; (*thing*) integer.
unusual *adj* īnsolitus, inūsitātus, īnsolēns, novus.
unusually *adv* īnsolenter, praeter cōnsuētūdinem.
unusualness *n* īnsolentia *f*, novitās *f*.
unutterable *adj* īnfandus, inēnārrābilis.
unvarnished *adj* (*fig*) simplex, nūdus.
unveil *vt* (*fig*) aperīre, patefacere.
unversed *adj* ignārus (*gen*), imperītus (*gen*).
unwanted *adj* supervacāneus.
unwarily *adv* imprudenter, incautē, incōnsultē.
unwariness *n* imprūdentia *f*.
unwarlike *adj* imbellis.
unwarrantable *adj* inīquus, iniūstus.
unwarrantably *adv* iniūriā.
unwary *adj* imprūdēns, incautus, incōnsultus.
unwavering *adj* stabilis, immōtus.
unwearied, unwearying *adj* indēfessus, adsiduus.
unweave *vt* retexere.
unwedded *adj* (*man*) caelebs; (*woman*) vidua.
unwelcome *adj* ingrātus.
unwell *adj* aeger, aegrōtus.
unwept *adj* indēflētus.
unwholesome *adj* pestilēns, gravis.
unwieldy *adj* inhabilis.
unwilling *adj* invītus; **be** ~ nolle.
unwillingly *adv* invītus.

unwind *vt* ēvolvere, retexere.
unwise *adj* stultus, īnsipiēns, imprūdēns.
unwisely *adv* īnsipienter, imprūdenter.
unwittingly *adv* imprūdēns, īnsciēns.
unwonted *adj* īnsolitus, inūsitātus.
unworthily *adv* indignē.
unworthiness *n* indignitās *f*.
unworthy *adj* indignus (+ *abl*).
unwounded *adj* intāctus, integer.
unwrap *vt* ēvolvere, explicāre.
unwritten *adj* nōn scrīptus; ~ **law** mōs *m*.
unwrought *adj* īnfectus, rudis.
unyielding *adj* dūrus, firmus, inexōrābilis.
unyoke *vt* disiungere.
up *adv* sūrsum; ~ **and down** sūrsum deōrsum; ~ **to** usque ad (*acc*), tenus (*abl, after noun*); **bring** ~ subvehere; (*child*) ēducāre; **climb** ~ ēscendere; **come** ~ **to** aequāre; **lift** ~ ērigere, sublevāre; **from childhood** ~ ā puerō; **it is all** ~ **with** āctum est dē; **well** ~ **in** gnārus (*gen*), perītus (*gen*); **what is he** ~ **to?** quid struit? ♦ *prep* (*motion*) in (*acc*) ♦ *n*: ~**s and downs** (*fig*) vicissitūdinēs *fpl*.
upbraid *vt* exprobrāre (*dat pers, acc charge*); obicere (*dat and acc*), increpāre, castīgāre.
upbringing *n* ēducātiō *f*.
upheaval *n* ēversiō *f*.
upheave *vt* ēvertere.
uphill *adj* acclīvis ♦ *adv* adversō colle, in adversum collem.
uphold *vt* sustinēre, tuērī, servāre.
upholstery *n* supellex *f*.
upkeep *n* impēnsa *f*.
upland *adj* montānus.
uplift *vt* extollere, sublevāre.
upon *prep* in (*abl*), super (*abl*); (*motion*) in (*acc*), super (*acc*); (*dependence*) ex (*abl*); ~ **this** quō factō.
upper *adj* superior; **gain the** ~ **hand** superāre, vincere.
uppermost *adj* suprēmus, summus.
uppish *adj* superbus.
upright *adj* rēctus, ērēctus; (*character*) integer, probus, honestus.
uprightly *adv* rēctē; integrē.
uprightness *n* integritās *f*.
upriver *adj, adv* adversō flūmine.
uproar *n* tumultus *m*; clāmor *m*.
uproarious *adj* tumultuōsus.
uproariously *adv* tumultuōsē.
uproot *vt* ērādīcāre, exstirpāre, ēruere.
upset *vt* ēvertere, invertere, subvertere; ~ **the apple cart** plaustrum percellere ♦ *adj* (*fig*) perturbātus.
upshot *n* ēventus *m*.
upside-down *adv*: **turn** ~ ēvertere, invertere; (*fig*) miscēre.
upstart *n* novus homō *m* ♦ *adj* repentīnus.
upstream *adj, adv* adversō flūmine.
upward(s) *adv* sūrsum; ~ **of** (*number*) amplius.
urban *adj* urbānus, oppidānus.
urbane *adj* urbānus, cōmis.
urbanely *adv* urbānē, cōmiter.

V, v

urbanity *n* urbānitās *f.*
urchin *n* (*boy*) puerulus *m*; (*animal*) echīnus *m.*
urge *vt* urgēre, impellere; (*speech*) hortārī,
  incitāre; (*advice*) suādēre; (*request*)
  sollicitāre; ~ **on** incitāre ♦ *n* impulsus *m*;
  dēsīderium *nt.*
urgency *n* necessitās *f.*
urgent *adj* praesēns, gravis; **be** ~ instāre.
urgently *adv* graviter.
urn *n* urna *f.*
usage *n* mōs *m*, īnstitūtum *nt*, ūsus *m.*
use *n* ūsus *m*; (*custom*) mōs *m*, cōnsuētūdō *f*; **be**
  of ~ ūsuī esse, prōdesse, condūcere; **out of** ~
  desuētus; **go out of** ~ exolēscere; **in common**
  ~ ūsitātus; **it's no** ~ nīl agis, nīl agimus ♦ *vt*
  ūtī (*abl*); (*improperly*) abūtī; (*for a purpose*)
  adhibēre; (*word*) ūsurpāre; ~ **up** cōnsūmere,
  exhaurīre; ~**d to** adsuētus (*dat*); solēre (+
  infin); **I** ~**d to do** faciēbam.
useful *adj* ūtilis; **be** ~ ūsuī esse.
usefully *adv* ūtiliter.
usefulness *n* ūtilitās *f.*
useless *adj* inūtilis; (*thing*) inānis, inritus; **be** ~
  nihil valēre.
uselessly *adv* inūtiliter, frustrā.
uselessness *n* inānitās *f.*
usher *n* (*court*) apparitor *m*; (*theatre*)
  dēsignātor *m* ♦ *vt*: ~ **in** indūcere,
  intrōdūcere.
usual *adj* ūsitātus, solitus; **as** ~ ut adsolet, ut
  fert cōnsuētūdō, ex cōnsuētūdine; **out of the**
  ~ īnsolitus, extrā ōrdinem.
usually *adv* ferē, plērumque; **he** ~ **comes**
  venīre solet.
usufruct *n* ūsus et fructus *m.*
usurer *n* faenerātor *m.*
usurp *vt* occupāre, invādere in (*acc*),
  ūsurpāre.
usurpation *n* occupātiō *f.*
usury *n* faenerātiō *f*, ūsūra *f*; **practise** ~
  faenerārī.
utensil *n* īnstrūmentum *nt*, vās *nt.*
utility *n* ūtilitās *f*, commodum *nt.*
utilize *vt* ūtī (*abl*); (*for a purpose*) adhibēre.
utmost *adj* extrēmus, summus; **at the** ~
  summum; **do one's** ~ omnibus vīribus
  contendere.
utter *adj* tōtus, extrēmus, summus ♦ *vt*
  ēmittere, ēdere, ēloquī, prōnūntiāre.
utterance *n* dictum *nt*; (*process*) prōnūntiātiō *f.*
utterly *adv* funditus, omnīnō, penitus.
uttermost *adj* extrēmus, ultimus.

vacancy *n* inānitās *f*; (*office*) vacuitās *f*; **there is**
  a ~ locus vacat; **elect to fill a** ~ sufficere.
vacant *adj* inānis, vacuus; **be** ~ vacāre.
vacate *vt* vacuum facere.
vacation *n* fēriae *fpl.*
vacillate *vi* vacillāre, dubitāre.
vacillation *n* dubitātiō *f.*
vacuity *n* inānitās *f.*
vacuous *adj* vacuus.
vacuum *n* ināne *nt.*
vagabond *n* grassātor *m* ♦ *adj* vagus.
vagary *n* libīdō *f.*
vagrancy *n* errātiō *f.*
vagrant *n* grassātor *m*, vagus *m.*
vague *adj* incertus, dubius.
vaguely *adv* incertē.
vain *n* vānus, inānis, inritus; (*person*)
  glōriōsus; **in** ~ frustrā.
vainglorious *adj* glōriōsus.
vainglory *n* glōria *f*, iactantia *f.*
vainly *adv* frustrā, nēquīquam.
vale *n* vallis *f.*
valet *n* cubiculārius *m.*
valiant *adj* fortis, ācer.
valiantly *adv* fortiter, ācriter.
valid *adj* ratus; (*argument*) gravis, firmus.
validity *n* vīs *f*, auctōritās *f.*
valley *n* vallis *f.*
valorous *adj* fortis.
valour *n* virtūs *f.*
valuable *adj* pretiōsus.
valuation *n* aestimātiō *f.*
value *n* pretium *nt*; (*fig*) vīs *f*, honor *m* ♦ *vt*
  aestimāre; (*esteem*) dīligere; ~ **highly** māgnī
  aestimāre; ~ **little** parvī aestimāre, parvī
  facere.
valueless *adj* vīlis, minimī pretī.
valuer *n* aestimātor *m.*
van *n* (*in battle*) prīma aciēs *f*; (*on march*)
  prīmum agmen *nt.*
vanguard *n* prīmum agmen *nt.*
vanish *vi* diffugere, ēvānēscere, dīlābī.
vanity *n* (*unreality*) vānitās *f*; (*conceit*) glōria *f.*
vanquish *vt* vincere, superāre, dēvincere.
vanquisher *n* victor *m.*
vantage *n* (*ground*) locus superior *m.*
vapid *adj* vapidus, īnsulsus.
vapidly *adv* īnsulsē.
vaporous *adj* nebulōsus.
vapour *n* vapor *m*, nebula *f*; (*from earth*)
  exhālātiō *f.*
variable *adj* varius, mūtābilis.
variableness *n* mūtābilitās *f*, incōnstantia *f.*
variance *n* discordia *f*, dissēnsiō *f*,
  discrepantia *f*; **at** ~ discors; **be at** ~ dissidēre,

inter sē discrepāre; **set at** ~ aliēnāre.
variant *adj* varius.
variation *n* varietās *f*, vicissitūdō *f*.
variegate *vt* variāre.
variegated *adj* varius.
variety *n* varietās *f*; (*number*) multitūdō *f*;
    (*kind*) genus *nt*; **a** ~ **of** dīversī.
various *adj* varius, dīversus.
variously *adv* variē.
varlet *n* verberō *m*.
varnish *n* pigmentum *nt*; (*fig*) fūcus *m*.
varnished *adj* (*fig*) fūcātus.
vary *vt* variāre, mūtāre; (*decorate*) distinguere
    ♦ *vi* mūtārī.
vase *n* vās *nt*.
vassal *n* ambāctus *m*; (*fig*) cliēns *m*.
vast *adj* vastus, immānis, ingēns, immēnsus.
vastly *adv* valdē.
vastness *n* māgnitūdō *f*, immēnsitās *f*.
vat *n* cūpa *f*.
vault *n* (ARCH) fornix *f*; (*jump*) saltus *m* ♦ *vi*
    salīre.
vaulted *adj* fornicātus.
vaunt *vt* iactāre, ostentāre ♦ *vi* sē iactāre,
    glōriārī.
vaunting *n* ostentātiō *f*, glōria *f* ♦ *adj*
    glōriōsus.
veal *n* vitulīna *f*.
vedette *n* excursor *m*.
veer *vi* sē vertere, flectī.
vegetable *n* holus *nt*.
vehemence *n* vīs *f*, violentia *f*; (*passion*) ārdor
    m, impetus *m*.
vehement *adj* vehemēns, violentus, ācer.
vehemently *adv* vehementer, ācriter.
vehicle *n* vehiculum *nt*.
Veii *n* Veiī, Vēiorum *mpl*.
veil *n* rīca *f*; (*bridal*) flammeum *nt*; (*fig*)
    integumentum *nt* ♦ *vt* vēlāre, tegere.
vein *n* vēna *f*.
vellum *n* membrāna *f*.
velocity *n* celeritās *f*, vēlōcitās *f*.
venal *adj* vēnālis.
vend *vt* vēndere.
vendetta *n* simultās *f*.
vendor *n* caupō *m*.
veneer *n* (*fig*) speciēs *f*, fūcus *m*.
venerable *adj* gravis, augustus.
venerate *vt* colere, venerārī.
veneration *n* venerātiō *f*, cultus *m*.
venerator *n* cultor *m*.
vengeance *n* ultiō *f*, poena *f*; **take** ~ **on** ulcīscī,
    vindicāre in (*acc*); **take** ~ **for** ulcīscī,
    vindicāre.
vengeful *adj* ultor.
venial *adj* ignōscendus.
venison *n* dāma *f*, ferīna *f*.
venom *n* venēnum *nt*; (*fig*) vīrus *nt*.
venomous *adj* venēnātus.
vent *n* spīrāculum *nt*; (*outlet*) exitus *m*; **give** ~
    to profundere, ēmittere ♦ *vt* ēmittere;
    (*feelings on*) profundere in (*acc*), ērumpere
    in (*acc*).

ventilate *vt* perflāre; (*opinion*) in medium
    prōferre, vulgāre.
ventilation *n* perflāre.
venture *n* perīculum *nt*; (*gamble*) ālea *f*; **at a** ~
    temerē ♦ *vi* audēre ♦ *vt* perīclitārī, in āleam
    dare.
venturesome *adj* audāx, temerārius.
venturesomeness *n* audācia *f*, temeritās *f*.
veracious *adj* vērāx, vēridicus.
veracity *n* vēritās *f*, fidēs *f*.
verb *n* verbum *nt*.
verbally *adv* per colloquia; (*translate*) ad
    verbum, verbum prō verbō.
verbatim *adv* ad verbum, totidem verbīs.
verbiage *n* verba *ntpl*.
verbose *adj* verbōsus.
verbosity *n* loquendī prōfluentia *f*.
verdant *adj* viridis.
verdict *n* sententia *f*, iūdicium *nt*; **deliver a** ~
    sententiam prōnūntiāre; **give a** ~ **in favour of**
    causam adiūdicāre (*dat*).
verdigris *n* aerūgō *f*.
verdure *n* viriditās *f*.
verge *n* ōra *f*; **the** ~ **of** extrēmus; **on the** ~ **of**
    (*fig*) prope (*acc*) ♦ *vi* vergere.
verification *n* cōnfirmātiō *f*.
verify *vt* cōnfirmāre, comprobāre.
verily *adv* profectō, certē.
verisimilitude *n* vērī similitūdō *f*.
veritable *adj* vērus.
veritably *adv* vērē.
verity *n* vēritās *f*.
vermilion *n* sandīx *f*.
vermin *n* bestiolae *fpl*.
vernacular *adj* patrius ♦ *n* patrius sermō *m*.
vernal *adj* vērnus.
versatile *adj* versūtus, varius.
versatility *n* versātile ingenium *nt*.
verse *n* (*line*) versus *m*; (*poetry*) versus *mpl*,
    carmina *ntpl*.
versed *adj* īnstructus, perītus, exercitātus.
versification *n* ars versūs faciendī.
versify *vt* versū inclūdere ♦ *vi* versūs facere.
version *n* (*of story*) fōrma *f*; **give a Latin** ~ **of**
    Latīnē reddere.
vertex *n* vertex *m*, fastīgium *nt*.
vertical *adj* rēctus, dīrēctus.
vertically *adv* ad līneam, rēctā līneā, ad
    perpendiculum.
vertigo *n* vertīgō *f*.
vervain *n* verbēna *f*.
verve *n* ācrimōnia *f*.
very *adj* ipse ♦ *adv* admodum, valdē,
    vehementer ♦ *superl*: **at that** ~ **moment** tum
    māximē; **not** ~ nōn ita.
vessel *n* (*receptacle*) vās *nt*; (*ship*) nāvigium *nt*.
vest *n* subūcula *f* ♦ *vt*: ~ **power in** imperium
    dēferre (*dat*); ~**ed interests** nummī locātī *mpl*.
vestal *adj* vestālis ♦ *n* virgō vestālis *f*.
vestibule *n* vestibulum *nt*.
vestige *n* vestīgium *nt*, indicium *nt*.
vestment *n* vestīmentum *nt*.
vesture *n* vestis *f*.

vetch n vicia f.
veteran adj veterānus ♦ n (MIL) veterānus m; (fig) veterātor m.
veto n interdictum nt; (tribune's) intercessiō f ♦ vt interdīcere (dat); (tribune) intercēdere (dat).
vex vt vexāre, sollicitāre, stomachum movēre (dat); **be ~ed** aegrē ferre, stomachārī.
vexation n (caused) molestia f; (felt) dolor m, stomachus m.
vexatious adj odiōsus, molestus.
vexatiously adv molestē.
vexed adj īrātus; (question) anceps.
via prep per (acc).
viaduct n pōns m.
viands n cibus m.
vibrate vi vībrāre, tremere.
vibration n tremor m.
vicarious adj vicārius.
vice n (general) prāvitās f, perditī mōrēs mpl; (particular) vitium nt, flāgitium nt; (clamp) fībula f.
viceroy n prōcūrātor m.
vicinity n vīcīnia f, vīcīnitās f.
vicious adj prāvus, vitiōsus, flāgitiōsus; (temper) contumāx.
viciously adv flāgitiōsē; contumāciter.
vicissitude n vicissitūdō f; **~s** pl vicēs fpl.
victim n victima f, hostia f; (fig) piāculum nt; (exploited) praeda f; **be the ~ of** labōrāre ex; **fall a ~ to** morī (abl); (trickery) circumvenīrī (abl).
victimize vt nocēre (dat), circumvenīre.
victor n victor m.
victorious adj victor m, victrīx f; **be ~** vincere.
victory n victōria f; **win a ~** victōriam reportāre; **win a ~ over** vincere, superāre.
victory message n laureātae litterae fpl.
victory parade n triumphus m.
victual vt rem frūmentāriam suppeditāre (dat).
victualler n caupō m; (MIL) frūmentārius m.
victuals n cibus m; (MIL) frūmentum nt, commeātus m.
vie vi certāre, contendere; **~ with** aemulārī.
view n cōnspectus m; (from far) prōspectus m; (from high) dēspectus m; (opinion) sententia f; **exposed to ~** in mediō; **entertain a ~** sentīre; **in ~ of** propter (acc); **in my ~** meā sententiā, meō iūdiciō; **end in ~** prōpositum nt; **have in ~** spectāre; **point of ~** iūdicium nt; **with a ~ to** eō cōnsiliō ut ♦ vt īnspicere, spectāre, intuērī.
vigil n pervigilium nt; **keep a ~** vigilāre.
vigilance n vigilantia f, dīligentia f.
vigilant adj vigilāns, dīligēns.
vigilantly adv vigilanter, dīligenter.
vigorous adj ācer, vegetus, integer; (style) nervōsus.
vigorously adv ācriter, strēnuē.
vigour n vīs f, nervī mpl, integritās f.
vile adj turpis, impūrus, abiectus.
vilely adv turpiter, impūrē.

vileness n turpitūdō f, impūritās f.
vilification n obtrectātiō f, calumnia f.
vilify vt obtrectāre, calumniārī, maledīcere (dat).
villa n vīlla f.
village n pāgus m, vīcus m; **in every ~** pāgātim.
villager n pāgānus m, vīcānus m.
villain n furcifer m, scelerātus m.
villainous adj scelestus, scelerātus, nēquam.
villainously adv scelestē.
villainy n scelus nt, nēquitia f.
vindicate vt (right) vindicāre; (action) pūrgāre; (belief) arguere; (person) dēfendere, prōpugnāre prō (abl).
vindication n dēfēnsiō f, pūrgātiō f.
vindicator n dēfēnsor m, prōpugnātor m.
vindictive adj ultor, ulcīscendī cupidus.
vine n vītis f; **wild ~** labrusca f.
vinedresser n vīnitor m.
vinegar n acētum nt.
vineyard n vīnea f, vīnētum nt.
vintage n vindēmia f.
vintner n vīnārius m.
violate vt violāre.
violation n violātiō f.
violator n violātor m.
violence n violentia f, vīs f, iniūria f; **do ~ to** violāre; **offer ~ to** vim īnferre (dat).
violent adj violentus, vehemēns; (passion) ācer, impotēns; **~ death** nex f.
violently adv vehementer, per vim.
violet n viola f.
viper n vīpera f.
viperous adj (fig) malignus.
virgin n virgō f ♦ adj virginālis.
virginity n virginitās f.
virile adj virīlis.
virility n virtūs f.
virtually adv rē vērā, ferē.
virtue n virtūs f, honestum nt; (woman's) pudīcitia f; (power) vis f, potestās f; **by ~ of** ex (abl).
virtuous adj honestus, probus, integer.
virtuously adv honestē.
virulence n vīs f, vīrus nt.
virulent adj acerbus.
virus n vīrus nt.
visage n ōs n, faciēs f.
vis-à-vis prep exadversus (acc).
viscosity n lentor m.
viscous adj lentus, tenāx.
visible adj ēvidēns, cōnspicuus, manifestus; **be ~** appārēre.
visibly adv manifestō.
vision n (sense) vīsus m; (power) aspectus m; (apparition) vīsum nt, vīsiō f; (whim) somnium nt.
visionary adj vānus ♦ n somniāns m.
visit n adventus m; (formal) salūtātiō f; (long) commorātiō f; **pay a ~ to** invīsere ♦ vt vīsere; **~ occasionally** intervīsere; **go to ~** invīsere.
visitation n (to inspect) recēnsiō f; (to punish) animadversiō f.

visitor n hospes m, hospita f; (*formal*) salūtātor m.
visor n buccula f.
vista n prōspectus m.
visual adj oculōrum.
visualize vt animō cernere, ante oculōs pōnere.
visually adv oculīs.
vital adj (*of life*) vītālis; (*essential*) necessārius, māximī mōmentī.
vitality n vīs f; (*style*) sanguis m.
vitally adv praecipuē, imprīmīs.
vitals n viscera ntpl.
vitiate vt corrumpere, vitiāre.
vitreous adj vitreus.
vitrify vt in vitrum excoquere.
vituperate vt vituperāre, obiūrgāre.
vituperation n vituperātiō f, maledicta ntpl.
vituperative adj maledicus.
vivacious adj alacer, vegetus, hilaris.
vivaciously adv hilare.
vivacity n alacritās f, hilaritās f.
vivid adj vīvidus, ācer.
vividly adv ācriter.
vivify vt animāre.
vixen n vulpēs f.
vocabulary n verbōrum cōpia f.
vocal adj: ~ **music** vōcis cantus m.
vocation n officium nt, mūnus nt.
vociferate vt, vi vōciferārī, clāmāre.
vociferation n vōciferātiō f, clāmor m.
vociferous adj vōciferāns.
vociferously adv māgnīs clāmōribus.
vogue n mōs m; **be in** ~ flōrēre, in honōre esse.
voice n vōx f ♦ vt exprimere, ēloquī.
void adj inānis, vacuus; ~ **of** expers (*gen*); **null and** ~ inritus ♦ n ināne nt ♦ vt ēvomere, ēmittere.
volatile adj levis, mōbilis.
volatility n levitās f.
volition n voluntās f.
volley n imber m.
volubility n volūbilitās f.
voluble adj volūbilis.
volume n (*book*) liber m; (*mass*) mōlēs f; (*of sound*) māgnitūdō f.
voluminous adj cōpiōsus.
voluntarily adv ultrō, suā sponte.
voluntary adj voluntārius; (*unpaid*) grātuītus.
volunteer n (MIL) ēvocātus m ♦ vt ultrō offerre ♦ vi (MIL) nōmen dare.
voluptuary n dēlicātus m, homō voluptārius m.
voluptuous adj voluptārius, mollis, dēlicātus, luxuriōsus.
voluptuously adv molliter, dēlicātē, luxuriōsē.
voluptuousness n luxuria f, libīdō f.
vomit vt vomere, ēvomere; ~ **up** ēvomere.
voracious adj vorāx, edāx.
voraciously adv avidē.
voracity n edācitās f, gula f.
vortex n vertex m, turbō m.

votary n cultor m.
vote n suffrāgium nt; (*opinion*) sententia f; ~ **for** (*candidate*) suffrāgārī (*dat*); (*senator's motion*) discēdere in sententiam (*gen*) ♦ vi (*election*) suffrāgium ferre; (*judge*) sententiam ferre; (*senator*) cēnsēre; **take a** ~ (*senate*) discessiōnem facere ♦ vt (*senate*) dēcernere; ~ **against** (*bill*) antīquāre.
voter n suffrāgātor m.
votive adj vōtīvus.
vouch vi spondēre; ~ **for** praestāre, testificārī.
voucher n (*person*) auctor m; (*document*) auctōritās f.
vouchsafe vt concēdere.
vow n vōtum nt; (*promise*) fidēs f ♦ vt vovēre; (*promise*) spondēre.
vowel n vōcālis f.
voyage n nāvigātiō f, cursus m ♦ vi nāvigāre.
vulgar adj (*common*) vulgāris; (*low*) plēbēius, sordidus, īnsulsus.
vulgarity n sordēs fpl, īnsulsitās f.
vulgarly adv vulgō; īnsulsē.
vulnerable adj nūdus; (*fig*) obnoxius; **be** ~ vulnerārī posse.
vulture n vultur m; (*fig*) vulturius m.

W, w

wad n massa f.
wade vi per vada īre; ~ **across** vadō trānsīre.
waft vt ferre, vehere.
wag n facētus homō m, ioculātor m ♦ vt movēre, mōtāre, agitāre ♦ vi movērī, agitārī.
wage n mercēs f; (*pl*) mercēs f, manupretium nt; (*fig*) pretium nt, praemium nt ♦ vt gerere; ~ **war on** bellum īnferre (*dat*)/gerere.
wager n spōnsiō f ♦ vi spōnsiōnem facere ♦ vt dēpōnere, oppōnere.
waggery n facētiae fpl.
waggish adj facētus, rīdiculus.
waggle vt agitāre, mōtāre.
wagon n plaustrum nt, carrus m.
waif n inops m/f.
wail n ēiulātus m ♦ vi ēiulāre, dēplōrāre, lāmentārī.
wailing n plōrātus m, lāmentātiō f.
waist n medium corpus nt; **hold by the** ~ medium tenēre.
wait n: **have a long** ~ diū exspectāre; **lie in** ~ īnsidiārī ♦ vi manēre, opperīrī, exspectāre; ~ **for** exspectāre; ~ **upon** (*accompany*) adsectārī, dēdūcere; (*serve*) famulārī (*dat*); (*visit*) salūtāre.
waiter n famulus m, minister m.

waive vt dēpōnere, remittere.
wake vt excitāre, suscitāre ♦ vi expergīscī.
wake n vestīgia ntpl; **in the ~** pōne, ā tergō;
follow in the ~ of vestīgiīs instāre (gen).
wakeful adj vigil.
wakefulness n vigilantia f.
waken vt excitāre ♦ vi expergīscī.
walk n (act) ambulātiō f, deambulātiō f; (gait)
incessus m; (place) ambulātiō f, xystus m; **~ of**
life status m; **go for a ~** spatiārī, deambulāre
♦ vi ambulāre, īre, gradī; (with dignity)
incēdere; **~ about** inambulāre; **~ out** ēgredī.
wall n mūrus m; (indoors) pariēs m; (afield)
māceria f; **~s** pl (of town) moenia ntpl ♦ vt
mūnīre, saepīre; **~ up** inaedificāre.
wallet n pēra f.
wallow vi volūtārī.
walnut n iūglāns f.
wan adj pallidus.
wand n virga f.
wander vi errāre, vagārī; (in mind) ālūcinārī;
~ over pervagārī.
wanderer n errō m, vagus m.
wandering adj errābundus, vagus ♦ n errātiō
f, error m.
wane vi dēcrēscere, senēscere.
want n inopia f, indigentia f, egestās f, pēnūria
f; (craving) dēsīderium nt; **in ~** inops; **be in ~**
egēre ♦ vt (lack) carēre (abl), egēre (abl),
indigēre (abl); (miss) dēsīderāre; (wish)
velle.
wanting adj (missing) absēns; (defective)
vitiōsus, parum idōneus; **be ~** deesse,
dēficere ♦ prep sine (abl).
wanton adj lascīvus, libīdinōsus ♦ vi
lascīvīre.
wantonly adv lascīvē, libīdinōsē.
war n bellum nt; **regular ~** iūstum bellum;
fortunes of ~ fortūna bellī; **outbreak of ~**
exortum bellum; **be at ~ with** bellum gerere
cum; **declare ~** bellum indīcere; **discontinue**
~ bellum dēpōnere; **end ~** (by agreement)
compōnere; (by victory) cōnficere; **enter ~**
bellum suscipere; **give the command of a ~**
bellum mandāre; **make ~** bellum īnferre;
prolong a ~ bellum trahere; **provoke ~**
bellum movēre; **wage ~** bellum gerere;
wage ~ on bellum īnferre (dat) ♦ vi bellāre.
warble vi canere, cantāre.
warbling adj garrulus, canōrus ♦ n cantus m.
war cry n clāmor m.
ward n custōdia f; (person) pupillus m, pupilla
f; (of town) regiō f ♦ vt: **~ off** arcēre,
dēfendere, prōpulsāre.
warden n praefectus m.
warder n custōs m.
wardrobe n vestiārium nt.
wardship n tūtēla f.
warehouse n apothēca f.
wares n merx f, mercēs fpl.
warfare n bellum nt.
warily adv prōvidenter, cautē.
wariness n circumspectiō f, cautiō f.

warlike adj ferōx, bellicōsus.
warm adj calidus; (fig) ācer, studiōsus; **be ~**
calēre; **become ~** calefierī, incalēscere; **keep**
~ fovēre; **~ baths** thermae fpl ♦ vt calefacere,
tepefacere, fovēre ♦ vi calefierī.
warmly adv (fig) ferventer, studiōsē.
warmth n calor m.
warn vt monēre, admonēre.
warning n (act) monitiō f; (particular) monitum
nt; (lesson) documentum nt, exemplum nt.
warp n stāmina ntpl ♦ vt dēprāvāre, īnflectere.
warped adj (fig) prāvus.
warrant n auctōritās f ♦ vt praestāre.
warranty n cautiō f.
warrior n bellātor m, bellatrīx f, mīles m.
warship n nāvis longa f.
wart n verrūca f.
wary adj prōvidus, cautus, prūdēns.
wash vt lavāre; (of rivers, sea) adluere; **~ away**
dīluere; **~ clean** abluere; **~ out** (fig) ēluere ♦
vi lavārī.
washbasin n aquālis m.
washing n lavātiō f.
wasp n vespa f.
waspish adj acerbus, stomachōsus.
waste n dētrīmentum nt, intertrīmentum nt;
(extravagance) effūsiō f; (of time) iactūra f;
(land) sōlitūdō f, vastitās f ♦ adj dēsertus,
vastus; **lay ~** vastāre, populārī ♦ vt
cōnsūmere, perdere, dissipāre; (time)
terere, absūmere; (with disease) absūmere ♦
vi: **~ away** tābēscere, intābēscere.
wasteful adj prōdigus, profūsus; (destructive)
damnōsus, perniciōsus.
wastefully adv prōdigē.
wasting n tābēs f.
wastrel n nebulō m.
watch n (being awake) vigilia f; (sentry) statiō f,
excubiae fpl; **keep ~** excubāre; **keep ~ on,**
over custōdīre, invigilāre (dat); **set ~** vigiliās
dispōnere; **at the third ~** ad tertiam būcinam
♦ vt (guard) custōdīre; (observe) intuērī,
observāre, spectāre ad (+ acc); **~ for**
observāre, exspectāre; (enemy) īnsidiārī
(dat); **~ closely** adservāre.
watcher n custōs m.
watchful adj vigilāns.
watchfully adv vigilanter.
watchfulness n vigilantia f.
watchman n custōs m, vigil m.
watchtower n specula f.
watchword n tessera f, signum nt.
water n aqua f; **deep ~** gurges m; **fresh ~** aqua
dulcis; **high ~** māximus aestus; **running ~**
aqua prōfluēns; **still ~** stagnum nt; **fetch ~**
aquārī; **fetching ~** aquātiō f; **cold ~** frīgida f;
hot ~ calida f; **troubled ~s** (fig) turbidae rēs ♦
vt (land) irrigāre; (animal) adaquāre.
water carrier n aquātor m; (Zodiac) Aquārius
m.
water clock n clepsydra f.
waterfall n cataracta f.
watering n aquātiō f; **~ place** n (spa) aquae fpl.

water pipe n fistula f.
watershed n aquārum dīvortium nt.
water snake n hydrus m.
water spout n prēstēr m.
watery adj aquōsus, ūmidus.
wattle n crātēs f.
wave n unda f, fluctus m ♦ vt agitāre, iactāre ♦
vi fluctuāre.
waver vi dubitāre, fluctuārī, nūtāre, vacillāre,
labāre, inclināre.
wavering adj dubius, incōnstāns ♦ n dubitātiō
f, fluctuātiō f.
wavy adj undātus; (hair) crispus.
wax n cēra f ♦ vt cērāre ♦ vi crēscere.
waxen adj cēreus.
waxy adj cērōsus.
way n via f; (route) iter nt; (method) modus m,
ratiō f; (habit) mōs m; (ship's) impetus m; **all
the ~ to, from** usque ad, ab; **by the ~**
(parenthesis) etenim; **get in the ~ of**
intervenīre (dat), impedīre; **get under ~**
nāvem solvere; **give ~** (structure) labāre; (MIL)
cēdere; **give ~ to** indulgēre (dat); **go out of
one's ~ to do** ultrō facere; **have one's ~**
imperāre; **in a ~** quōdam modō; **in this ~** ad
hunc modum; **it is not my ~ to** nōn meum est
(infin); **lose one's ~** deerrare; **make ~** dē viā
dēcēdere; **make ~ for** cēdere (dat); **make
one's ~ into** sē īnsinuāre in (acc); **on the ~**
inter viam, in itinere; **out of the ~** āvius,
dēvius; (fig) reconditus; **pave the ~ for**
praeparāre; **put out of the ~** tollere; **right of ~**
iter; **stand in the ~ of** obstāre (dat); **that ~**
illāc; **this ~** hāc; **~s and means** opēs fpl,
reditūs mpl.
wayfarer n viātor m.
waylay vt īnsidiārī (dat).
wayward adj protervus, incōnstāns, levis.
waywardness n libīdō f, levitās f.
we pron nōs.
weak adj dēbilis, īnfirmus, imbēcillus; (health)
invalidus; (argument) levis, tenuis; (senses)
hebes.
weaken vt dēbilitāre, īnfirmāre; (resistance)
frangere, labefactāre ♦ vi imminuī, labāre.
weakling n imbēcillus m.
weakly adj invalidus, aeger ♦ adv īnfirmē.
weak-minded adj mollis.
weakness n dēbilitās f, īnfirmitās f; (of
argument) levitās f; (of mind) mollitia f,
imbēcillitās f; (flaw) vitium nt; **have a ~ for**
delectārī (abl).
weal n salūs f, rēs f; (mark of blow) vībex f; **the
common ~** rēs pūblica f.
wealth n dīvitiae fpl, opēs fpl; **a ~ of** cōpia f,
abundantia f.
wealthy adj dīves, opulentus, locuplēs,
beātus; **make ~** locuplētāre, dītāre; **very ~**
praedīves.
wean vt lacte dēpellere; (fig) dēdocēre.
weapon n tēlum nt.
wear n (dress) habitus m; **~ and tear**
intertrīmentum nt ♦ vt gerere, gestāre; (rub)

terere, conterere; **~ out** cōnficere ♦ vi
dūrāre; **~ off** minuī.
wearily adv cum lassitūdine, languidē.
weariness n fatīgātiō f, lassitūdō f; (of)
taedium nt.
wearisome adj molestus, operōsus,
labōriōsus.
weary adj lassus, fessus, dēfessus, fatīgātus ♦
vt fatīgāre; **I am weary of** me taedet (+ gen).
weasel n mustēla f.
weather n tempestās f, caelum nt; **fine ~**
serēnitās f ♦ vt superāre.
weather-beaten adj tempestāte dūrātus.
weave vt texere.
weaver n textor m, textrix f.
web n (on loom) tēla f; (spider's) arāneum nt.
wed vt (a wife) dūcere; (a husband) nūbere
(dat).
wedding n nūptiae fpl.
wedge n cuneus m ♦ vt cuneāre.
wedlock n mātrimōnium nt.
weed n inūtilis herba f ♦ vt runcāre.
weedy adj exīlis.
week n hebdomas f.
ween vt arbitrārī, putāre.
weep vi flēre, lacrimārī; **~ for** dēflēre,
dēplōrāre.
weeping n flētus m, lacrimae fpl.
weevil n curculiō m.
weft n subtēmen nt; (web) tēla f.
weigh vt pendere, exāmināre; (anchor) tollere;
(thought) ponderāre; **~ down** dēgravāre,
opprimere; **~ out** expendere ♦ vi pendere.
weight n pondus nt; (influence) auctōritās f,
mōmentum nt; (burden) onus nt; **have great ~**
(fig) multum valēre; **he is worth his ~ in gold**
aurō contrā cōnstat.
weightily adv graviter.
weightiness n gravitās f.
weighty adj gravis.
weir n mōlēs f.
weird adj mōnstruōsus ♦ n fātum nt.
welcome adj grātus, exspectātus, acceptus ♦
n salūtātiō f ♦ vt excipere, salvēre iubēre ♦
interj salvē, salvēte.
welfare n salūs f.
well n puteus m; (spring) fōns m ♦ vi scatēre ♦
adj salvus, sānus, valēns; **be ~** valēre ♦ adv
bene, probē; (transition) age ♦ interj
(concession) estō; (surprise) heia; **~ and good**
estō; **~ begun is half done** dīmidium factī quī
coepit habet; **~ done!** probē!; **~ met**
opportūnē venis; **~ on in years** aetāte
prōvectus; **all is ~** bene habet; **as ~** etiam; **as
~ as** cum ... tum, et ... et; **let ~ alone** quiēta
nōn movēre; **take ~** in bonam partem
accipere; **wish ~** favēre (dat); **you may ~ say**
iūre dīcis; **you might as ~ say** illud potius
dīcās.
well-advised adj prudēns.
well-behaved adj modestus.
wellbeing n salūs f.
well-bred adj generōsus, līberālis.

well-disposed *adj* benevolus, amīcus.
well-informed *adj* ērudītus.
well-judged *adj* ēlegāns.
well-knit *adj* dēnsus.
well-known *adj* nōtus, nōbilis; (*saying*) trītus.
well-nigh *adv* paene.
well-off *adj* beātus, fortūnātus; **you are ~** bene est tibī.
well-read *adj* litterātus.
well-timed *adj* opportūnus.
well-to-do *adj* beātus, dīves.
well-tried *adj* probātus.
well-turned *adj* rotundus.
well-versed *adj* perītus, expertus.
well-wisher *n* amīcus *m*, benevolēns *m*.
well-worn *adj* trītus.
welter *n* turba *f* ♦ *vi* miscērī, turbārī; (*wallow*) volūtārī.
wench *n* muliercula *f*.
wend *vt*: **~ one's way** īre, sē ferre.
west *n* occidēns *m*, sōlis occāsus *m* ♦ *adj* occidentālis.
westerly, western *adj* occidentālis.
westwards *adv* ad occidentem.
west wind *n* Favōnius *m*.
wet *adj* ūmidus, madidus; **be ~** madēre; **~ weather** pluvia *f* ♦ *vt* madefacere.
wether *n* vervēx *m*.
wet nurse *n* nūtrīx *f*.
whack *n* ictus *m*, plāga *f* ♦ *vt* pulsāre, verberāre.
whale *n* bālaena *f*.
wharf *n* crepīdō *f*.
what *pron* (*interrog*) quid; (*adj*) quī; (*relat*) id quod, ea quae; **~ kind of?** quālis.
whatever, whatsoever *pron* quidquid, quodcumque; (*adj*) quīcumque.
wheat *n* trīticum *nt*.
wheaten *adj* trīticeus.
wheedle *vt* blandīrī, pellicere.
wheedling *adj* blandus ♦ *n* blanditiae *fpl*.
wheel *n* rota *f* ♦ *vt* flectere, circumagere ♦ *vi* sē flectere, circumagī.
wheelbarrow *n* pabō *m*.
wheeze *vi* anhēlāre.
whelm *vt* obruere.
whelp *n* catulus *m*.
when *adv* (*interrog*) quandō, quō tempore ♦ *conj* (*time*) cum (+ *subj*), ubī (+ *indic*).
whence *adv* unde.
whenever *conj* quotiēns, utcumque, quandocumque, cum (+ *perf/pluperf indic*); (*as soon as*) simul āc.
where *adv* ubī; (*to*) quō; **~ ... from** unde; **~ to** quo (*interrog and relat*).
whereabouts *n* locus *m*; **your ~** quō in locō sīs.
whereas *conj* quōniam; (*contrast*) **not** expressed.
whereby *adv* quō pāctō, quō.
wherefore *adv* (*interrog*) quārē, cūr; (*relat*) quamobrem, quāpropter.
wherein *adv* in quō, in quā.
whereof *adv* cūius, cūius reī.

whereon *adv* in quō, in quā.
whereupon *adv* quō factō.
wherever *conj* ubiubī, quācumque.
wherewith *adv* quī, cum quō.
wherry *n* linter *f*.
whet *vt* acuere; (*fig*) exacuere.
whether *conj* (*interrog*) utrum; (*single question*) num; (*condition*) sīve, seu; **~ ... or** utrum ... an (*in indir question*); (*in cond clauses*) seu (sive) ... seu (sive); **~ ... not** utrum ... necne (*in indir question*).
whetstone *n* cōs *f*.
whey *n* serum *nt*.
which *pron* (*interrog*) quis; (*of two*) uter; (*relat*) quī ♦ *adj* quī; (*of two*) uter.
whichever *pron* quisquis, quīcumque; (*of two*) utercumque.
whiff *n* odor *m*.
while *n* spatium *nt*, tempus *nt*; **for a ~** parumper; **a little ~** paulisper; **a long ~** diū; **it is worth ~** expedit, operae pretium est; **once in a ~** interdum ♦ *conj* dum + *pres indic* (= *during the time that*); + *imperf indic* (= *all the time that*) ♦ *vt*: **~ away** dēgere, fallere.
whilst *conj* dum.
whim *n* libīdō *f*, arbitrium *nt*.
whimper *n* vāgītus *m* ♦ *vi* vāgīre.
whimsical *adj* facētus, īnsolēns.
whimsically *adv* facētē.
whimsy *n* dēliciae *fpl*, facētiae *fpl*.
whine *n* quīritātiō *f* ♦ *vi* quīritāre.
whinny *n* hinnītus *m* ♦ *vi* hinnīre.
whip *n* flagellum *nt*, flagrum *nt* ♦ *vt* flagellāre, verberare.
whirl *n* turbō *m* ♦ *vt* intorquēre contorquēre ♦ *vi* contorquērī.
whirlpool *n* vertex *m*, vōragō *f*.
whirlwind *n* turbō *m*.
whisper *n* susurrus *m* ♦ *vt*, *vi* susurrāre, īnsusurrāre; **~ to** ad aurem admonēre, in aurem dīcere.
whistle *n* (*instrument*) fistula *f*; (*sound*) sībilus *m* ♦ *vi* sībilāre.
white *adj* albus; (*shining*) candidus; (*complexion*) pallidus; (*hair*) cānus; **turn ~** exalbēscere ♦ *n* album *nt*; (*egg*) albūmen *nt*.
white-hot *adj*: **to be ~** excandēscere.
whiten *vt* dealbāre ♦ *vi* albēscere.
whiteness *n* candor *m*.
whitewash *n* albārium *nt* ♦ *vt* dealbāre.
whither *adv* quō; **~soever** quōcumque.
whitish *adj* albulus.
whizz *n* strīdor *m* ♦ *vi* strīdere, increpāre.
who *pron* quis; (*relat*) quī.
whoever *pron* quisquis, quīcumque.
whole *adj* tōtus, cūnctus; (*unhurt*) integer, incolumis; (*healthy*) sānus ♦ *n* tōtum *nt*, summa *f*, ūniversitās *f*; **on the ~** plērumque.
wholehearted *adj* studiōsissimus.
wholeheartedly *adv* ex animō.
wholesale *adj* māgnus, cōpiōsus; **~ business** negōtiātiō *f*; **~ dealer** mercātor *m*, negōtiātor *m*.

wholesome *adj* salūtāris, salūbris.
wholesomeness *n* salūbritās *f.*
wholly *adv* omnīnō, tōtus.
whoop *n* ululātus *m* ♦ *vi* ululāre.
whose *pron* cūius.
why *adv* cūr, quārē, quamobrem, qua de causa.
wick *n* mergulus *m.*
wicked *adj* improbus, scelestus; (*to gods, kin, country*) impius.
wickedly *adv* improbē, scelestē, impiē.
wickedness *n* improbitās *f,* scelus *nt,* impietās *f.*
wicker *adj* vīmineus ♦ *n* vīmen *nt.*
wide *adj* lātus, amplus; **be ~ of** aberrāre ab ♦ *adv* lātē; **far and ~** longē lātēque.
widely *adv* lātē; (*among people*) vulgō.
widen *vt* laxāre, dilātāre.
widespread *adj* effūsus, vulgātus.
widow *n* vidua *f.*
widowed *adj* viduus, orbus.
widower *n* viduus *m.*
widowhood *n* viduitās *f.*
width *n* lātitūdō *f,* amplitūdō *f.*
wield *vt* tractāre, gestāre, ūtī (*abl*).
wife *n* uxor *f.*
wifely *adj* uxōrius.
wig *n* capillāmentum *nt.*
wild *adj* ferus, indomitus, saevus; (*plant*) agrestis; (*land*) incultus; (*temper*) furibundus, impotens, āmēns; (*shot*) temerārius; **~ state** feritās *f.*
wild beast *n* fera *f.*
wilderness *n* sōlitūdō *f,* loca dēserta *ntpl.*
wildly *adv* saevē.
wildness *n* feritās *f.*
wile *n* dolus *m,* ars *f,* fraus *f.*
wilful *adj* pervicāx, contumāx; (*action*) cōnsultus.
wilfully *adv* contumāciter; cōnsultō.
wilfulness *n* pervicācia *f,* libīdō *f.*
wilily *adv* astūtē, vafrē.
wiliness *n* astūtia *f.*
will *n* (*faculty*) voluntās *f,* animus *m;* (*intent*) cōnsilium *nt;* (*decision*) arbitrium *nt;* (*of gods*) nūtus *m;* (*document*) testāmentum *nt;* **~ and pleasure** libīdō *f;* **against one's ~** invītus; **at ~** ad libīdinem suam; **good ~** studium *nt;* **ill ~** invidia *f;* **with a ~** summō studiō; **without making a ~** intestātus, intestātō ♦ *vt* velle, *fut;* (*legacy*) lēgāre; **as you ~** ut libet.
willing *adj* libēns, parātus; **be ~** velle; **not be ~** nōlle.
willingly *adv* libenter.
willingness *n* voluntās *f.*
willow *n* salix *f* ♦ *adj* salignus.
willowy *adj* gracilis.
wilt *vi* flaccēscere.
wily *adj* astūtus, vafer, callidus.
wimple *n* mitra *f.*
win *vt* ferre, obtinēre, adipisci; (*after effort*) auferre; (*victory*) reportāre; (*fame*) cōnsequī, adsequī; (*friends*) sibī conciliāre; **~ the day**

vincere; **~ over** dēlēnire, conciliāre ♦ *vi* vincere.
wince *vi* resilīre.
winch *n* māchina *f,* sucula *f.*
wind *n* ventus *m;* (*north*) aquilō *m;* (*south*) auster *m;* (*east*) eurus *m;* (*west*) favōnius *m;* **I get ~ of** subolet mihī; **run before the ~** vento sē dare; **take the ~ out of one's sails** suō sibī gladiō iugulāre; **there is something in the ~** nescioquid olet; **which way the ~ blows** quōmodo sē rēs habeat.
wind *vt* torquēre; **~ round** intorquēre ♦ *vi* flectī, sinuāre; **~ up** (*speech*) perōrāre.
windbag *n* verbōsus *m.*
winded *adj* anhēlāns.
windfall *n* repentīnum bonum *nt.*
winding *adj* flexuōsus, tortuōsus ♦ *n* flexiō *f,* flexus *m;* **~s** *pl* (*speech*) ambāgēs *fpl.*
windlass *n* māchina *f,* sucula *f.*
window *n* fenestra *f.*
windpipe *n* aspera artēria *f.*
windward *adj* ad ventum conversus ♦ *adv:* **to ~** ventum versus.
windy *adj* ventōsus.
wine *n* vīnum *nt;* (*new*) mustum *nt;* (*undiluted*) merum *nt.*
winebibber *n* vīnōsus *m.*
wine cellar *n* apothēca *f.*
wine merchant *n* vīnārius *m.*
wine press *n* prēlum *nt.*
wing *n* āla *f;* (*MIL*) cornū *nt,* āla *f;* (*of bird*) penna *f;* **take ~** ēvolāre; **take under one's ~** patrōnus fierī (*gen*), clientem habēre, in custōdiam recipere.
winged *adj* ālātus, pennātus, volucer.
wink *n* nictus *m* ♦ *vi* nictāre; **~ at** cōnīvēre (*dat*).
winner *n* victor *m.*
winning *adj* blandus, iūcundus.
winningly *adv* blandē, iūcundē.
winning post *n* mēta *f.*
winnings *n* lucra *ntpl.*
winnow *vt* ventilāre; (*fig*) excutere.
winnowing-fan *n* vannus *f.*
winsome *adj* blandus, suāvis.
winter *n* hiems *f;* (*mid*) brūma *f* ♦ *adj* hiemālis, hībernus ♦ *vi* hībernāre.
winter quarters *n* hīberna *ntpl.*
wintry *adj* hiemālis, hībernus.
wipe *vt* dētergēre; **~ away** abstergēre; **~ dry** siccāre; **~ off** dētergēre; **~ out** dēlēre; **~ the nose** ēmungere.
wire *n* fīlum aēneum *nt.*
wiry *adj* nervōsus.
wisdom *n* sapientia *f;* (*in action*) prūdentia *f;* (*in judgment*) cōnsilium *nt.*
wise *adj* sapiēns, prūdēns.
wisely *adv* sapienter, prūdenter.
wish *n* optātum *nt,* vōtum *nt;* (*for something missing*) dēsīderium *nt;* **~es** *pl* (*greeting*) salūs *f* ♦ *vt* optāre, cupere, velle; **~ for** exoptāre, expetere, dēsīderāre; **~ good-day** salvēre iubēre; **as you ~** ut libet; **I ~ I could** utinam

possim.
wishful *adj* cupidus.
wishing *n* optātiō *f*.
wisp *n* manipulus *m*.
wistful *adj* dēsīderī plenus.
wistfully *adv* cum dēsīderiō.
wistfulness *n* dēsīderium *nt*.
wit *n* (*humour*) facētiae *fpl*, salēs *mpl*; (*intellect*) argūtiae *fpl*, ingenium *nt*; **caustic ~** dicācitās *f*; **be at one's wits' end** valdē haerēre; **be out of one's ~s** dēlīrāre; **have one's ~s about one** prūdens esse; **to ~** nempe, dīcō.
witch *n* sāga *f*, strīga *f*.
witchcraft *n* veneficium *nt*, magicae artēs *fpl*.
with *prep* (*person*) cum (*abl*); (*thing*) abl; (*in company*) apud (*acc*); (*fight*) cum (*abl*), contrā (*acc*); **be angry ~** īrāscī (*dat*); **begin ~** incipere ab; **rest ~** esse penes (*acc*); **end ~** dēsinere in (*acc*); **what do you want ~ me?** quid mē vis?
withdraw *vt* dēdūcere, dētrahere; (*fig*) āvocāre; (*words*) retractāre ♦ *vi* discēdere, abscēdere, sē recipere, sē subdūcere.
withdrawal *n* (*MIL*) receptus *m*.
wither *vt* torrēre ♦ *vi* dēflōrēscere.
withered *adj* marcidus.
withhold *vt* abstinēre, retinēre, supprimere.
within *adv* intus, intrā; (*motion*) intrō ♦ *prep* intrā (*acc*), in (*abl*).
without *adv* extrā, forīs; **from ~** extrīnsecus; **be ~** vacāre (*abl*), carēre (*abl*) ♦ *prep* sine (*abl*), expers (*gen*); **I admire ~ fearing** ita laudō ut nōn timeam; **~ breaking the law** salvīs lēgibus; **you cannot see ~ admiring** vidēre nōn potes quīn laudēs; **you cannot appreciate ~ seeing for yourself** aestimāre nōn potes nisī ipse vīderis; **~ doubt** sine dubio; **~ the order of** iniūssū (*gen*); **~ striking a blow** rē integrā.
withstand *vt* resistere (*dat*), obsistere (*dat*); (*attack*) ferre, sustinēre.
withy *n* vīmen *nt*.
witless *adj* excors, ineptus, stultus.
witness *n* (*person*) testis *m/f*; (*to a document*) obsignātor *m*; (*spectator*) arbiter *m*; (*evidence*) testimōnium *nt*; **call as ~** antestārī; **bear ~** testificārī; **call to ~** testārī ♦ *vt* testificārī; (*see*) vidēre, intuērī.
witnessing *n* testificātiō *f*.
witticism *n* dictum *nt*; **~s** *pl* facētiae *fpl*.
wittily *adv* facētē, salsē.
wittingly *adv* sciēns.
witty *adj* facētus, argūtus, salsus; (*caustic*) dicāx.
wizard *n* magus *m*, veneficus *m*.
wizardry *n* magicae artēs *fpl*.
wizened *adj* marcidus.
woad *n* vitrum *nt*.
wobble *vi* titubāre; (*structure*) labāre.
woe *n* luctus *m*, dolor *m*, aerumna *f*; **~s** *pl* mala *ntpl*, calamitātēs *fpl*; **~ to** vae (*dat*).
woeful *adj* tristis, maestus, aerumnōsus.
woefully *adv* triste, miserē.
wolf *n* lupus *m*, lupa *f*; **~'s** lupīnus.

woman *n* fēmina *f*, mulier *f*; **old ~** anus *f*; **married ~** mātrōna *f*; **~'s** muliebris.
womanish *adj* muliebris, effēminātus.
womanly *adj* muliebris.
womb *n* uterus *m*.
wonder *n* admīrātiō *f*; (*of a thing*) admīrābilitās *f*; (*thing*) mīrāculum *nt*, mīrum *nt*, portentum *nt* ♦ *vi* mīrārī; **~ at** admīrārī, dēmīrārī.
wonderful *adj* mīrus, mīrābilis, admīrābilis; **~ to relate** mīrābile dictu.
wonderfully *adv* mīrē, mīrābiliter, mīrum quantum.
wonderfulness *n* admīrābilitās *f*.
wondering *adj* mīrābundus.
wonderment *n* admīrātiō *f*.
wondrous *adj* mīrus, mīrābilis.
wont *n* mōs *m*, cōnsuētūdō *f*.
wonted *adj* solitus.
woo *vt* petere.
wood *n* silva *f*, nemus *nt*; (*material*) lignum *nt*; **gather ~** lignārī; **touch ~!** absit verbō invidia ♦ *adj* ligneus.
woodcutter *n* lignātor *m*.
wooded *adj* silvestris, saltuōsus.
wooden *adj* ligneus.
woodland *n* silvae *fpl* ♦ *adj* silvestris.
woodman *n* lignātor *m*.
wood nymph *n* dryas *f*.
woodpecker *n* pīcus *m*.
wood pigeon *n* palumbēs *m/f*.
woodwork *n* tigna *ntpl*.
woodworker *n* faber tignārius *m*.
woody *adj* silvestris, silvōsus.
wooer *n* procus *m*.
woof *n* subtēmen *nt*.
wool *n* lāna *f*.
woollen *adj* lāneus.
woolly *adj* lānātus.
word *n* verbum *nt*; (*spoken*) vōx *f*; (*message*) nūntius *m*; (*promise*) fidēs *f*; (*term*) vocābulum *nt*; **~ for ~** ad verbum, verbum ē verbō; **a ~ with you!** paucīs tē volō!; **break one's ~** fidem fallere; **bring back ~** renūntiāre; **by ~ of mouth** ōre; **fair ~s** blanditiae *fpl*; **give one's ~** fidem dare; **have a ~ with** colloquī cum; **have ~s with** iūrgāre cum; **have a good ~ for** laudāre; **in a ~** ūnō verbō, dēnique; **keep one's ~** fidem praestāre; **of few ~s** taciturnus; **take at one's ~** crēdere (*dat*).
wording *n* verba *ntpl*.
wordy *adj* verbōsus.
work *n* (*energy*) labor *m*, opera *f*; (*task*) opus *nt*; (*thing done*) opus *nt*; (*book*) liber *m*; (*trouble*) negōtium *nt*; **~s** (*MIL*) opera *ntpl*; (*mechanism*) māchinātiō *f*; (*place*) officīna *f* ♦ *vi* labōrāre ♦ *vt* (*men*) exercēre; (*metal*) fabricārī; (*soil*) subigere; (*results*) efficere; **~ at** ēlabōrāre; **~ in** admiscēre; **~ off** exhaurīre; **~ out** ēlabōrāre; **~ up** (*emotion*) efferre; **~ one's way up** prōficere ♦ *vi* gerī.
workaday *adj* cottīdiānus.

workhouse n ergastulum nt.
working n (mechanism) māchinātiō f; (soil) cultus m.
workman n (unskilled) operārius m; (skilled) opifex m, faber m; **workmen** operae fpl.
workmanship n ars f, artificium nt.
workshop n fabrica f, officīna f.
world n (universe) mundus m; (earth) orbis terrārum m; (nature) rērum nātūra f; (mankind) hominēs mpl; (masses) vulgus nt; **of the ~** mundānus; **man of the ~** homō urbānus m; **best in the ~** rērum optimus, omnium optimus; **where in the ~** ubī gentium.
worldliness n quaestūs studium nt.
worldly adj quaestuī dēditus.
worm n vermis m ♦ vi: **~ one's way** sē īnsinuāre.
worm-eaten adj vermiculōsus.
wormwood n absinthium nt.
worn adj trītus.
worried adj sollicitus, anxius.
worry n cūra f, sollicitūdō f ♦ vi sollicitārī ♦ vt vexāre, sollicitāre; (of dogs) lacerāre.
worse adj pēior, dēterior; **grow ~** ingravēscere; **make matters ~** rem exasperāre ♦ adv pēius, dēterius.
worsen vi ingravēscere, dēteriōr fierī.
worship n venerātiō f, deōrum cultus m; (rite) sacra ntpl, rēs dīvīnae fpl ♦ vt adōrāre, venerārī, colere.
worst adj pessimus, dēterrimus; **~ enemy** inimīcissimus m; **endure the ~** ultima patī; vincere.
worsted n lāna f.
worth n (value) pretium nt; (moral) dignitās f, frūgālitās f, virtūs f; (prestige) auctōritās f ♦ adj dignus; **for all one's ~** prō virīlī parte; **how much is it ~?** quanti vēnit?; **it is ~ a lot** multum valet; **it is ~ doing** operae pretium est.
worthily adv dignē, meritō.
worthiness n dignitās f.
worthless adj (person) nēquam; (thing) vīlis, inānis.
worthlessness n levitās f, nēquitia f; vīlitās f.
worthy adj dignus; (person) frūgī, honestus; **~ of** dignus (abl).
wound n vulnus nt ♦ vt vulnerāre; (feelings) offendere.
wounded adj saucius.
wrangle n iūrgium nt, rixa f ♦ vi iūrgāre, rixārī, altercārī.
wrap vt involvere, obvolvere; **~ round** intorquēre; **~ up** involvere.
wrapper n involucrum nt.
wrapping n integumentum nt.
wrath n īra f, īrācundia f.
wrathful adj īrātus.
wrathfully adv īrācundē.
wreak vt: **~ vengeance on** saevīre in (acc), ulcīscī.
wreath n corōna f, sertum nt.
wreathe vt (garland) torquēre; (object)

corōnāre.
wreck n naufragium nt ♦ vt frangere; (fig) perdere; **be ~ed** naufragium facere.
wreckage n fragmenta ntpl.
wrecked adj (person) naufragus; (ship) frāctus.
wrecker n perditor m.
wren n rēgulus m.
wrench vt intorquēre, extorquēre; **~ away** ēripere; **~ open** effringere.
wrest vt extorquēre.
wrestle vi luctārī.
wrestler n luctātor m, athlēta m.
wrestling n luctātiō f.
wretch n scelerātus m, nēquam homō m; **poor ~** miser homō m.
wretched adj īnfēlīx, miser; (pitiful) flēbilis.
wretchedly adv miserē.
wretchedness n miseria f; maestitia f.
wriggle vi sē torquēre.
wriggling adj sinuōsus.
wright n faber m.
wring vt torquēre; **~ from** extorquēre.
wrinkle n rūga f ♦ vt corrūgāre.
wrinkled adj rūgōsus.
wrist n prīma palmae pars f.
writ n (legal) auctōritās f.
write vt scrībere; (book) cōnscrībere; **~ off** indūcere; **~ on** īnscrībere (dat); **~ out** exscrībere, dēscrībere; **~ out in full** perscrībere.
writer n (LIT) scrīptor m, auctor m; (clerk) scrība m.
writhe vi torquērī.
writing n (act) scrīptiō f; (result) scrīptum nt.
wrong adj falsus, perversus, prāvus; (unjust) iniūstus, inīquus; **be ~**, **go ~** errāre ♦ n iniūria f, culpa f, noxa f, malum nt; **do ~** peccāre, dēlinquere; **right and ~** (moral) honesta ac turpia ntpl ♦ vt laedere, nocēre (dat); (by deceit) fraudāre.
wrongdoer n, maleficus m, scelerātus m.
wrongdoing n scelus nt.
wrongful adj iniūstus, iniūriosus, inīquus.
wrongfully adv iniūriā, iniūstē, inīquē.
wrong-headed adj perversus.
wrong-headedness n perversitās f.
wrongly adv falsō, dēprāvātē, male, perperam.
wroth adj īrātus.
wrought adj factus.
wry adj dētortus; **make a ~ face** ōs dūcere.
wryness n prāvitās f.

Y, y

yacht n phasēlus m.
yard n (*court*) ārea f; (*measure*) trēs pedēs.
yardarm n antenna f.
yarn n fīlum nt; (*story*) fābula f.
yawn n hiātus m ♦ vi hiāre, ōscitāre; (*chasm*) dehiscere.
ye pron vōs.
yean vt parere.
year n annus m; **every ~** quotannīs; **for a ~** in annum; **half ~** sēmēstre spatium nt; **this ~'s** hōrnus; **twice a ~** bis annō; **two ~s** biennium nt; **three ~s** triennium nt; **four ~s** quadriennium nt; **five ~s** quinquennium nt.
yearly adj annuus, anniversārius ♦ adv quotannīs.
yearn vi: **~ for** dēsīderāre, exoptāre.
yearning n dēsīderium nt.
yeast n fermentum nt.
yell n clāmor m; (*of pain*) ēiulātiō f ♦ vi clāmāre, eiulāre.
yellow adj flāvus; (*pale*) gilvus; (*deep*) fulvus; (*gold*) luteus; (*saffron*) croceus.
yelp n gannītus m ♦ vi gannīre.
yeoman n colōnus m.
yes adv ita vērō (est), māximē; (*correcting*) immo.
yesterday adv herī ♦ n hesternus diēs m; **~'s** hesternus; **the day before ~** nudius tertius.
yet adv (*contrast*) tamen, nihilōminus, attamen; (*time*) adhūc, etiam; (*with compar*) etiam; **and ~** atquī, quamquam; **as ~** adhūc; **not ~** nōndum.
yew n taxus f.
yield n fructus m ♦ vt (*crops*) ferre, efferre; (*pleasure*) adferre; (*concession*) dare, concēdere; (*surrender*) dēdere ♦ vi cēdere; (*surrender*) sē dēdere, sē trādere; **~ to the**

wishes of mōrem gerere (*dat*), obsequī (*dat*).
yielding adj (*person*) facilis, obsequēns; (*thing*) mollis ♦ n cessiō f; dēditiō f.
yoke n iugum nt ♦ vt iungere, coniungere.
yokel n agrestis m.
yolk n vitellus m.
yonder adv illīc ♦ adj ille, iste.
yore n: **of ~** quondam, ōlim.
you pron tū, vōs.
young adj iuvenis, adulēscēns; (*child*) parvus; **~er** iūnior, nātū minor; **~est** nātū minimus ♦ n fētus m, pullus m, catulus m.
young man n iuvenis m; adulēscēns m.
youngster n puer m.
your adj tuus, vester.
yourself pron ipse.
youth n (*age*) iuventūs f, adulescentia f; (*person*) iuvenis m, adulēscēns m; (*collective*) iuventūs f.
youthful adj iuvenīlis, puerīlis.
youthfully adv iuvenīliter.

Z, z

zeal n studium nt, ārdor m.
zealot n studiōsus m, fautor m.
zealous adj studiōsus, ārdēns.
zealously adv studiōsē, ārdenter.
zenith n vertex m.
zephyr n Favōnius m.
zero n nihil nt.
zest n (*taste*) sapor m; (*fig*) gustātus m, impetus m.
zigzag n ānfrāctus m ♦ adj tortuōsus.
zither n cithara f.
zodiac n signifer orbis m.
zone n cingulus m.

Grammar and Verb Tables

This book is designed to help pupils and students of Latin to understand the grammar of the language. For beginners, the book provides an introduction to and explanation of the basic forms. More advanced students will find it an invaluable guide for reference and revision.

All parts of speech (nouns, pronouns, adjectives etc) are treated separately and clearly explained for the benefit of learners. Differences in usages are illustrated by extensive examples from many Latin authors. *American students and teachers, please note: this book is designed for use by students around the world, many of whom use British case ordering (Nom, Voc, Acc, Gen, Dat, Abl).*

A special section on word order in Latin, one of the greatest problems for students and pupils, has been included to guide the learner through both simple and compound sentences.

For ease of reference, all necessary structures, such as Indirect Statement, Conditional Sentences etc, have been listed under Contents. Each is then explained, for both English and Latin usage, to show the learner how to recognize the structure and translate it into English. Further examples of all structures are provided, for practice.

Handy, practical hints are given in the section on Translation Guidelines, to highlight the more common problems that confront students, and to assist in translation.

The final part of the grammar section lists the many "false friends" or confusable words that often lead students and pupils astray when translating from Latin. This section is of particular importance for examination candidates.

Tables of regular verbs provide information on verb formation and usage, while unique verbs are given in full with their meanings. A special feature of the grammar is a list of the 400 most common verbs, both regular and irregular. Irregular parts of verbs are highlighted and the conjugation number of each listed, so that by referring to the table indicated by this number, any part of the verb may be deduced.

Abbreviations used

abl	ablative	m, masc	masculine
acc	accusative	nt, neut	neuter
adv	adverb	nom	nominative
conj	conjunction	pl	plural
dat	dative	plup	pluperfect
dep	deponent	p(p)	page(s)
f, fem	feminine	prep	preposition
gen	genitive	pron	pronoun
indic	indicative	sing	singular
intrans	intransitive	voc	vocative

Nouns

A noun is the name of a person, thing or quality.

Gender

- In Latin, as in English, the gender of nouns, representing persons or living creatures, is decided by meaning. Nouns denoting male people and animals are masculine

vir	a man
Gaius	Gaius
cervus	stag

- Nouns denoting female people and animals are feminine

femina	a woman
Cornelia	Cornelia
cerva	doe/hind

- However, the gender of things or qualities in Latin is decided by the ending of the noun.

anulus (ring)	*masc*
sapientia (wisdom)	*fem*
barba (beard)	*fem*
gaudium (joy)	*nt*

Number

• Nouns may be singular, denoting one, or plural, denoting two or more. This is shown by change of ending

sing	pl
terra (land)	terrae
modus (way)	modi
opus (work)	opera

Cases

• There are six cases in Latin, expressing the relationship of the noun to the other words in the sentence.

Nominative
the subject of the verb: **Caesar** died

Vocative
addressing someone/thing: Welcome, **Alexander**

Accusative
the object of the verb: The cat ate **the mouse**

Genitive
belonging to someone/thing: The home **of my friend**

Dative
the indirect object of the verb: I gave the book **to my son**

Ablative
says by, with or from whom/what: This was agreed **by the Senate**

Declensions

• Latin nouns are divided into five groups or declensions by the ending of their stems. Each declension has six cases, both singular and plural, denoted by different endings. The endings of the genitive singular case help to distinguish the different declensions.

	STEMS	GENITIVE SINGULAR
1st Declension	-a	-ae
2nd Declension	-ŏ or u	-ī
3rd Declension	-i, u, consonant	-is
4th Declension	-ŭ	-ūs
5th Declension	-ē	-ēī

First Declension

• All nouns end in **-a** in the nominative case and all are feminine except when the noun indicates a male, *eg* **poēta** (a poet), **agricola** (a farmer), *etc.*

	SINGULAR		PLURAL	
	fēmina	*the woman*	fēminae	*women*
Nom	fēmina	*the woman*	fēminae	*women*
Voc	fēmina	*o woman*	fēminae	*o women*
Acc	fēminam	*the woman*	fēminās	*women*
Gen	fēminae	*of the woman*	fēminārum	*of the women*
Dat	fēminae	*to/for the woman*	fēminīs	*to/for the women*
Abl	fēminā	*by/with/ from the woman*	fēminīs	*by/with/ from the women*

• Note that **dea** (goddess) and **filia** (daughter), have their dative and ablative plurals **deābus** and **filiābus**

Declensions (contd)

Second Declension

- Nouns of the second declension end in **-us**, or a few in **-er** or **-r**. All are masculine. Those few which end in **-um** are neuter.

	SINGULAR		PLURAL	
Nom	servus	slave	servī	slaves
Voc	serve		servī	
Acc	servum		servōs	
Gen	servī		servōrum	
Dat	servō		servīs	
Abl	servō		servīs	

	SINGULAR		PLURAL	
Nom	puer	boy	puerī	boys
Voc	puer		puerī	
Acc	puerum		puerōs	
Gen	puerī		puerōrum	
Dat	puerō		puerīs	
Abl	puerō		puerīs	

	SINGULAR		PLURAL	
Nom	bellum	war	bella	wars
Voc	bellum		bella	
Acc	bellum		bella	
Gen	bellī		bellōrum	
Dat	bellō		bellīs	
Abl	bellō		bellīs	

- Note that proper names ending in **-ius** have vocative in **-ī**, o Vergilī – o Virgil!

- **deus** (god), has an alternative vocative **deus**, and plural forms **dī** in nominative and **dīs** in dative and ablative.

Third Declension

This is the largest group of nouns and may be divided into two broad categories, stems ending in a consonant and those ending in **-i**. All genders in this declension must be learnt.

Consonant Stems

- ending in **-l**

consul, -is *m* (consul)

	SINGULAR	PLURAL
Nom	cōnsul	cōnsulēs
Voc	cōnsul	cōnsulēs
Acc	cōnsulem	cōnsulēs
Gen	cōnsulis	cōnsulum
Dat	cōnsulī	cōnsulibus
Abl	cōnsule	cōnsulibus

- ending in **-n**

legio, -onis *f* (legion)

	SINGULAR	PLURAL
Nom	legiō	legiōnēs
Voc	legiō	legiōnēs
Acc	legiōnem	legiōnēs
Gen	legiōnis	legiōnum
Dat	legiōnī	legiōnibus
Abl	legiōne	legiōnibus

Continued

Declensions (contd)

flumen, -inis *nt* (river)

	SINGULAR	PLURAL
Nom	flumen	flumina
Voc	flumen	flumina
Acc	flumen	flumina
Gen	fluminis	fluminum
Dat	flumini	fluminibus
Abl	flumine	fluminibus

- Note that the genitive plural of these nouns ends in **-um.**

- Stems ending in **-i**

civis, -is *m/f* (citizen)

	SINGULAR	PLURAL
Nom	civis	cives
Voc	civis	cives
Acc	civem	cives
Gen	civis	civium
Dat	civi	civibus
Abl	cive	civibus

- Note that these nouns have genitive plural in **-ium.**

Neuter Nouns

mare, -is *nt* (sea)

	SINGULAR	PLURAL
Nom	mare	maria
Voc	mare	maria
Acc	mare	maria
Gen	maris	marium
Dat	mari	maribus
Abl	mari	maribus

animal, -is *nt* (animal)

	SINGULAR	PLURAL
Nom	animal	animalia
Voc	animal	animalia
Acc	animal	animalia
Gen	animalis	animalium
Dat	animali	animalibus
Abl	animali	animalibus

- Note that the ablative singular of these neuter nouns ends in **-i.**

- Nominative, vocative and accusative singular endings of neuter nouns are identical.

- Nominative, vocative and accusative plural endings of neuter nouns in **all declensions** end in **-a.**

Continued

Declensions (contd)

Monosyllabic Consonant Stems

The following have their genitive plural in -ium:

arx, arcis f (citadel) — arcium (of citadels)
gēns, gentis f (race) — gentium (of races)
mōns, montis m (mountain) — montium (of mountains)
nox, noctis f (night) — noctium (of nights)
pōns, pontis m (bridge) — pontium (of bridges)
urbs, urbis f (city) — urbium (of cities)

Fourth Declension

Nouns in this declension end in -us in the nominative singular and are mainly masculine. A few end in -u and are neuter.

exercitus, -ūs m (army)

	SINGULAR	PLURAL
Nom	exercitus	exercitūs
Voc	exercitus	exercitūs
Acc	exercitum	exercitūs
Gen	exercitūs	exercituum
Dat	exercituī	exercitibus
Abl	exercitū	exercitibus

genū, -ūs nt (knee)

	SINGULAR	PLURAL
Nom	genū	genua
Voc	genū	genua
Acc	genū	genua
Gen	genūs	genuum
Dat	genū	genibus
Abl	genū	genibus

- Note that a few common nouns are feminine, eg **domus** (house), **manus** (hand), **Idus** (Ides or 15th of the month).

- The form **domi** (at home) is an old form called locative. **domō** (from home) abl sing, **domōs** acc pl and **domōrum** gen pl are also used besides the fourth declension forms of **domus** (house).

Fifth Declension

There are only a few nouns in this declension. All end in -ēs in the nominative case. Most are feminine, but **diēs** (day) and **meridiēs** (midday) are masculine.

diēs, -diēī m (day)

	SINGULAR	PLURAL
Nom	diēs	diēs
Voc	diēs	diēs
Acc	diem	diēs
Gen	diēī	diērum
Dat	diēī	diēbus
Abl	diē	diēbus

Cases

Use Of Cases

Nominative Case

The nominative case is used where:

- the noun is the **subject** of the verb (→**1**)
- the noun is a **complement** (→**2**)
- the noun is in **apposition** to the subject (→**3**)

Accusative Case

The accusative case is used:

- for the **direct object** of the verb (→**4**)
- with verbs of teaching and asking which take accusative of person and thing (→**5**)
- Verbs of naming, making *etc* take two accusatives for the same person or thing (→**6**)
- in exclamations (→**7**)
- to show extent of space (→**8**)
- to show extent of time (→**9**)
- to show motion to a place or country usually with a preposition (→**10**)
- to show motion towards, without a preposition, before names of towns and small islands (→**11**)

  Note also: **domum** (home), **rus** (to the country), **foras** (outside)

- for an object with similar meaning to the verb (*cognate*) (→**12**)

Continued

1 **Sextus** ridet
Sextus laughs

2 Romulus **rex** factus est
Romulus was made king

3 Marcus Annius, **eques Romanus,** hoc dicit
Marcus Annius, a Roman businessman, says this

4 canis **baculum** petit
the dog fetches the stick

5 **puerum litteras** docebo
I shall teach the boy literature

6 **Ancum Martium regem** populus creavit
The people made Ancus Martius king

7 o **tempora,** o **mores**
what times, what conduct!

8 murus decem **pedes** altus est
the wall is 10 foot high

9 Troia decem **annos** obsessa est
Troy was under siege for 10 years

10 **ad Hispaniam** effugerunt
they escaped to Spain

11 **Athenas** legati missi sunt
Ambassadors were sent to Athens

12 **vitam** bonam **vixit**
he lived a good life

Cases (contd)

Dative Case

- Indirect object (*ie* to or for whom an action is performed) (→**1**)

- used with verbs of obeying (**parēre**), resisting (**resistere**), pleasing (**placēre**), ordering (**imperāre**) *etc* (→**2**)

- verb compounds (beginning **ad-**, **ob-**, **prae-**, **sub-**) denoting helping or hindering take dative (→**3**)

  adesse – come to help
  subvenire – help

- indicates possession (→**4**)

- is used with adjectives meaning "like" (**similis**), "fit" (**aptus**), "near" (**proximus**) (→**5**)

- indicates a purpose (known as *predicative dative*) (→**6**)

- shows the agent of gerund/gerundive (→**7**)

Continued

1 pecuniam **domino** dedit
he gave the money to his master

2 maria terraeque **Deo** parent
land and sea obey God

3 Pompeius **hostibus** obstitit
Pompey opposed the enemy

4 Poppaea amica est **Marciae**
Poppaea is Marcia's friend

5 feles **tigri similis** est
the cat is like a tiger

6 nemo mihi **auxilio** est
there is no-one to help me

7 omnia erant agenda **nobis**
everything had to be done by us

Cases (contd)

Genitive Case

- Indicates possession (→**1**)
- Denotes part of a whole (→**2**)
- Indicates a quality, always with an adjective (→**3**)
- Is used as a predicate, where a person represents a quality (→**4**)
- Is used with superlatives (→**5**)
- Precedes **causa** and **gratia** (for the sake of) (→**6**)
- Is used after certain adjectives (→**7**)

sciens	(knowing)
inscius	(ignorant of)
cupidus	(desiring)
particeps	(sharing) *etc*

- Is used with verbs of remembering (**memini**) and forgetting (**obliviscor**) (→**8**)
- Follows verbs of accusing, convicting *etc* (→**9**)
- Represents value or worth (→**10**)

Examples

1 domus **regis**
the king's house
uxor **Augusti**
the wife of Augustus

2 quid **novi**
what news?
plus **cibi**
more food

3 magnae **auctoritatis** es
your reputation is great

4 **stulti est** hoc facere
it is the mark of a fool to do this

5 Indus est **omnium fluminum** maximum
the Indus is the greatest of all rivers

6 tu me **amoris causa** servavisti
you saved me for love's sake

7 Verres, **cupidus pecuniae**, ex hereditate praedatus est
Verres, greedy for money, robbed the estate

8 **mortis** memento
remember death

9 ante **actarum rerum** Antonius accusatus est
Antony was accused of previous offences

10 frumentum **minimi** vendidit
he sold corn at the lowest price
flocci non facio
I don't care at all

Continued

Cases (contd)

Ablative Case

- Indicates place, usually with the preposition "in" (→1)
  Note, however: **totā Asiā** – throughout Asia
  terrā marīque – by land and sea

- Indicates motion from, or down from a place, usually with prepositions **ex, de, a(b)** (→2)

- Note prepositions are omitted before names of towns, small islands and **domo** (from home), **rure** (from the country), **foris** (from outside) (→3)

- Represents time when or within which something happens (→4)

- Indicates origin, sometimes with prepositions **in, ex, a(b)** (→5)

- Is used to show material from which something is made (→6)

- Indicates manner (how something is done), usually with **cum** when there is no adjective, and without **cum** when there is an adjective (→7)

- Is used with verbs of depriving, filling, needing and with **opus est** (→8)

- Is used with deponent verbs **utor** (use), **abutor** (abuse), **fungor** (accomplish), **potior** (gain possession of) (→9)

- States cause (→10)

- To form **ablative absolute**, where a noun in the ablative is combined with a participle or another noun or adjective in the same case, to form an idea independent of the rest of the sentence. This is equivalent to an adverbial clause (→11)

Examples

1 Milo **in urbe** mansit
  Milo remained in the city

2 **de equo** cecidit
  He fell down from his horse
  praedam **ex urbe ornatissima** sustulit
  He stole booty from the rich city

3 **domo** cucurrerunt servi
  The slaves ran from the house

4 **hac nocte** Agricola obiit
  Agricola died on this night
  decem annis Lacedaimonii non haec confecerunt
  The Spartans did not complete this task within 10 years

5 Romulus et Remus, **Marte nati**
  Romulus and Remus, sons of Mars
  flumina **in Caucaso monte** orta
  Rivers rising in the Caucasus mountains

6 statua **ex auro** facta est
  The statue was made of gold

7 mulieres **cum virtute** vixerunt
  The women lived virtuously
  summa celeritate Poeni regressi sunt
  The Carthaginians retreated at top speed

8 aliquem **vita** privare   opus est mihi **divitiis**
  to deprive someone of life   I need wealth

9 **vi et armis** usus est
  He used force of arms

10 leo **fame** decessit
  The lion died of hunger

11 **exigua parte aestatis reliqua**, Caesar in Britanniam proficisci contendit
  Although only a little of the summer remained, Caesar hurried to set out for Britain

Adjectives

An adjective adds a quality to the noun. It usually follows the noun but sometimes comes before it for emphasis. The adjective agrees with its noun in number, case and gender.

Gender
vir bonus (*masc*)   a good man
fēmina pulchra (*fem*)   a beautiful woman
bellum longum (*neut*)   a long war

Number
virī bonī (*pl*)   good men
fēminae pulchrae (*pl*)   beautiful women
bella longa (*pl*)   long wars

Case
virō bonō (*dat sing*)   for a good man
fēminās pulchrās (*acc pl*)   beautiful women
bellī longī (*gen sing*)   of a long war

- Adjectives are declined like nouns and usually arranged in two groups:

1 those with endings of the first and second declensions
2 those with endings of the third declension

First and Second Declensions

bonus, bona, bonum (good)

SINGULAR

	Masc	Fem	Neut
Nom	bonus	bona	bonum
Voc	bone	bona	bonum
Acc	bonum	bonam	bonum
Gen	bonī	bonae	bonī
Dat	bonō	bonae	bonō
Abl	bonō	bonā	bonō

PLURAL

	Masc	Fem	Neut
Nom	bonī	bonae	bona
Voc	bonī	bonae	bona
Acc	bonōs	bonās	bona
Gen	bonōrum	bonārum	bonōrum
Dat	bonīs	bonīs	bonīs
Abl	bonīs	bonīs	bonīs

Declensions (contd)

miser, misera, miserum (unhappy)

SINGULAR

	Masc	Fem	Neut
Nom	miser	misera	miserum
Voc	miser	misera	miserum
Acc	miserum	miseram	miserum
Gen	miserī	miserae	miserī
Dat	miserō	miserae	miserō
Abl	miserō	miserā	miserō

PLURAL

	Masc	Fem	Neut
Nom	miserī	miserae	misera
Voc	miserī	miserae	misera
Acc	miserōs	miserās	misera
Gen	miserōrum	miserārum	miserōrum
Dat	miserīs	miserīs	miserīs
Abl	miserīs	miserīs	miserīs

- **liber** (free) and **tener** (tender) are declined like **miser**

pulcher, pulchra, pulchrum (beautiful)

SINGULAR

	Masc	Fem	Neut
Nom	pulcher	pulchra	pulchrum
Voc	pulcher	pulchra	pulchrum
Acc	pulchrum	pulchram	pulchrum
Gen	pulchrī	pulchrae	pulchrī
Dat	pulchrō	pulchrae	pulchrō
Abl	pulchrō	pulchrā	pulchrō

PLURAL

	Masc	Fem	Neut
Nom	pulchrī	pulchrae	pulchra
Voc	pulchrī	pulchrae	pulchra
Acc	pulchrōs	pulchrās	pulchra
Gen	pulchrōrum	pulchrārum	pulchrōrum
Dat	pulchrīs	pulchrīs	pulchrīs
Abl	pulchrīs	pulchrīs	pulchrīs

- **aeger** (sick), **crēber** (frequent), **integer** (whole), **niger** (black), **piger** (slow) and **sacer** (sacred) are declined like **pulcher**

Declensions (contd)

- The following group of adjectives form their genitive singular in **-ius** and dative singular in **-i**:

alius, -a, -ud	another
alter, altera, alterum	one of two
neuter, neutra, neutrum	neither
nūllus, -a, -um	none
sōlus, -a, -um	alone
tōtus, -a, -um	whole
ūllus, -a, -um	any
ūnus, -a, -um	one
uter, utra, utrum	which of two?

solus (alone)

SINGULAR

	Masc	Fem	Neut
Nom	solus	sola	solum
Acc	solum	solam	solum
Gen	solius	solius	solius
Dat	soli	soli	soli
Abl	solo	sola	solo

PLURAL

	Masc	Fem	Neut
Nom	soli	solae	sola
Acc	solos	solas	sola
Gen	solorum	solarum	solorum
Dat	solis	solis	solis
Abl	solis	solis	solis

Third Declension

Adjectives of the third declension, like nouns, may be divided into two broad types, those with consonant stems and those with vowel stems in **-i**.

Consonant Stems

These have **one** ending in nominative singular.

prūdēns (wise)

SINGULAR

	Masc	Fem	Neut
Nom	prūdēns	prūdēns	prūdēns
Voc	prūdēns	prūdēns	prūdēns
Acc	prūdentem	prūdentem	prūdēns
Gen	prūdentis	prūdentis	prūdentis
Dat	prūdentī	prūdentī	prūdentī
Abl	prūdentī	prūdentī	prūdentī

PLURAL

	Masc	Fem	Neut
Nom	prūdentēs	prūdentēs	prūdentia
Voc	prūdentēs	prūdentēs	prūdentia
Acc	prūdentēs	prūdentēs	prūdentia
Gen	prūdentium	prūdentium	prūdentium
Dat	prūdentibus	prūdentibus	prūdentibus
Abl	prūdentibus	prūdentibus	prūdentibus

- **dīligēns** (careful), **innocēns** (innocent), **potēns** (powerful), **frequēns** (frequent), **ingēns** (huge) are declined like **prūdēns**

Declensions (contd)

amāns (loving)

SINGULAR

	Masc	Fem	Neut
Nom	amāns	amāns	amāns
Voc	amāns	amāns	amāns
Acc	amantem	amantem	amāns
Gen	amantis	amantis	amantis
Dat	amantī	amantī	amantī
Abl	amante	amante	amante

PLURAL

	Masc	Fem	Neut
Nom	amantēs	amantēs	amantia
Voc	amantēs	amantēs	amantia
Acc	amantēs	amantēs	amantia
Gen	amantium	amantium	amantium
Dat	amantibus	amantibus	amantibus
Abl	amantibus	amantibus	amantibus

- All Present participles are declined like **amāns**, although Present participles of the other conjugations end in **-ēns**

- When participles are used as adjectives **-ī** is used instead of **-e** in ablative singular case

fēlix (lucky)

SINGULAR

	Masc	Fem	Neut
Nom	fēlix	fēlix	fēlix
Voc	fēlix	fēlix	fēlix
Acc	fēlicem	fēlicem	fēlix
Gen	fēlicis	fēlicis	fēlicis
Dat	fēlicī	fēlicī	fēlicī
Abl	fēlicī	fēlicī	fēlicī

PLURAL

	Masc	Fem	Neut
Nom	fēlicēs	fēlicēs	fēlicia
Voc	fēlicēs	fēlicēs	fēlicia
Acc	fēlicēs	fēlicēs	fēlicia
Gen	fēlicium	fēlicium	fēlicium
Dat	fēlicibus	fēlicibus	fēlicibus
Abl	fēlicibus	fēlicibus	fēlicibus

audāx (bold) and **ferōx** (fierce) are declined like **fēlix**

- Note that all the above adjectives have the same case endings in all genders except for the neuter accusative singular and the neuter nominative, vocative and accusative plural.

Declensions (contd)

Vowel Stems

The following adjectives have **two** endings in nominative singular, one for masculine and feminine, one for neuter.

fortis, forte (brave)

	Masc	Fem	Neut
		SINGULAR	
Nom	fortis	fortis	forte
Voc	fortis	fortis	forte
Acc	fortem	fortem	forte
Gen	fortis	fortis	fortis
Dat	fortī	fortī	fortī
Abl	fortī	fortī	fortī
		PLURAL	
Nom	fortēs	fortēs	fortia
Voc	fortēs	fortēs	fortia
Acc	fortēs	fortēs	fortia
Gen	fortium	fortium	fortium
Dat	fortibus	fortibus	fortibus
Abl	fortibus	fortibus	fortibus

- **brevis** (short), **facilis** (easy), **gravis** (heavy), **levis** (light), **omnis** (all), **tristis** (sad), **turpis** (disgraceful), **talis** (of such a kind), and **qualis** (of which kind), are declined like **fortis**.

The following adjectives have **three** endings in nominative singular.

ācer, ācris, ācre (sharp)

	Masc	Fem	Neut
		SINGULAR	
Nom	ācer	ācris	ācre
Voc	ācer	ācris	ācre
Acc	ācrem	ācrem	ācre
Gen	ācris	ācris	ācris
Dat	ācrī	ācrī	ācrī
Abl	ācrī	ācrī	ācrī
		PLURAL	
Nom	ācrēs	ācrēs	ācria
Voc	ācrēs	ācrēs	ācria
Acc	ācrēs	ācrēs	ācria
Gen	ācrium	ācrium	ācrium
Dat	ācribus	ācribus	ācribus
Abl	ācribus	ācribus	ācribus

- **alacer** (lively), **equester** (of cavalry), and **volucer** (winged), are declined like **acer**, and **celer** (swift), declines similarly, but keeps **-e-** throughout (eg **celer, celeris, celere**)

Use of Adjectives

There are two ways of using adjectives.

- They can be used **attributively**, where the adjective in English comes before the noun: the new car

- An attributive adjective in Latin usually follows its noun but may sometimes come before it with a change of meaning (→**1**)

- They can be used **predicatively**, where the adjective comes after the verb: the car is new (→**2**)

- If an adjective describes two nouns, it agrees in gender with the nearer (→**3**)

- When an adjective describes two subjects of different sex it is often masculine plural (→**4**)

- When an adjective describes two subjects representing things without life it is often neuter plural (→**5**)

Examples

1 res **parvae**
small things

in parvis rebus
in unimportant matters

civis **Romanus** sum
I am a Roman citizen

2 Servi erant **fideles**
The slaves were faithful

3 Antonius, vir consilii **magni** et prudentiae
Antony, a man of great wisdom and prudence

4 frater et soror sunt **timidi**
Brother and sister are frightened

5 Calor et ventus per artus **praesentia** erant
Warmth and wind were present in the limbs

Comparative and Superlative

Adjectives also have comparative forms *eg* I am **luckier** than you, and superlative forms *eg* the **noblest** Roman of them all.

Formation

● The comparative is formed by adding **-ior** (*masc* and *fem*) and **-ius** (*neut*) to the consonant stem of the adjective and the superlative by adding **-issimus, -a, -um** to the stem:

POSITIVE		
altus	high	
audāx	bold	
brevis	short	
prūdēns	wise	

COMPARATIVE		
altior	higher	
audācior	bolder	
brevior	shorter	
prūdentior	wiser	

SUPERLATIVE		
altissimus	highest	
audācissimus	boldest	
brevissimus	shortest	
prūdentissimus	wisest	

Continued

● If the adjective ends in **-er** (*in masc nom sing*) add **-rimus** to form the superlative.

POSITIVE		
ācer	sharp	
celer	swift	
miser	unhappy	
pulcher	beautiful	

COMPARATIVE		
ācrior	sharper	
celerior	swifter	
miserior	more unhappy	
pulchrior	more beautiful	

SUPERLATIVE		
ācerrimus	sharpest	
celerrimus	swiftest	
miserrimus	most unhappy	
pulcherrimus	most beautiful	

● Six adjectives ending in **-ilis** (*in masc nom sing*) add **-limus** to the stem to form the superlative.

POSITIVE		
facilis	easy	
difficilis	difficult	
similis	like	
dissimilis	unlike	
gracilis	slight	
humilis	low	

COMPARATIVE		
facilior	easier	
difficilior	more difficult	
similior	more like	
dissimilior	more unlike	
gracilior	more slight	
humilior	lower	

SUPERLATIVE		
facillimus	easiest	
difficillimus	most difficult	
simillimus	most like	
dissimillimus	most unlike	
gracillimus	most slight	
humillimus	lowest	

Comparative and Superlative (contd)

Irregular comparison

● Some adjectives have irregular comparative and superlative forms:

POSITIVE

bonus	good
malus	bad
parvus	small
magnus	big
multus	much
multi	many

COMPARATIVE

melior	better
pēior	worse
minor	smaller
māior	bigger
plūs	more
plūrēs	more

SUPERLATIVE

optimus	best
pessimus	worst
minimus	smallest, least
māximus	biggest
plūrimus	most
plūrimī	most

Continued

● Note that all adjectives ending in **-us** preceded by a vowel (except those ending in **-quus**) form comparative and superlative thus:

idōneus	suitable
magis idōneus	more suitable
māximē idōneus	most suitable

but

antiquus	old
antiquior	older
antiquissimus	oldest

● Note the following comparatives and superlatives where there is no positive form:

exterior	outer	**extrēmus**	furthest
inferior	lower	**infimus** *or* **īmus**	lowest
superior	upper, higher	**suprēmus** *or* **summus**	highest
posterior	later	**postrēmus**	latest

Comparative and Superlative (contd)

Declension of Comparative and Superlative

- All comparatives decline like adjectives of the third declension.

	SINGULAR			PLURAL	
	Masc/Fem	Neut		Masc/Fem	Neut
Nom	altior	altius		altiōrēs	altiōra
Voc	altior	altius		altiōrēs	altiōra
Acc	altiōrem	altius		altiōrēs	altiōra
Gen	altiōris	altiōris		altiōrum	altiōrum
Dat	altiōrī	altiōrī		altiōribus	altiōribus
Abl	altiōre	altiōre		altiōribus	altiōribus

- Note ablative singular in **-e**.

- All superlatives decline like adjectives of first and second declensions (*eg* **bonus, bona, bonum**).

Use

- The comparative is often followed by **quam** (than), or the thing or person compared is given in the ablative case (→**1**)

- Sometimes the comparative can be translated by "rather" or "quite" (→**2**)

- The comparative is often strengthened by "**multo**" (→**3**)

- Sometimes the superlative can be translated by "very", or even as a positive adjective in English (→**4**)

- "**quam**" with the superlative means "as ... as possible" (→**5**)

ADJECTIVES **41**

Examples

1 Marcus est **altior quam soror**
Marcus est **altior sorore**
Marcus is taller than his sister

2 Gallus erat **fortior**
the Gaul was rather brave

3 **multo carior**
much dearer

4 **vir sapientissimus**
a very wise man
integerrima vita
of virtuous life

5 **quam paucissimi**
as few people as possible

42 ADVERBS

Adverbs

An adverb modifies a verb, adjective, another adverb or a noun. It answers questions such as "how?", "when?", "why?", "where?", "to what extent?".

Formation

- Some are formed from nouns *eg* **furtim** (stealthily) or pronouns **aliās** (at other times) but most are formed from adjectives.

- Accusative singular neuter of adjectives of extent:

multum	much	**nimium**	too much
paulum	a little	**aliquantum**	somewhat
prīmum	first	**cēterum**	for the rest

- Adjectives in -**us** and -**er** change to -**ē**:

altē	highly	**miserē**	wretchedly

- Ablative forms of these adjectives in -**o** or -**a**:

certē *or* **certō**	certainly	**vērē**	in truth
dextrā	on the right	**vērō**	certainly

- Adjectives of the third declension add -**ter**/-**iter**:

audacter	boldly	**celeriter**	quickly
prudenter	wisely		

Position

- An adverb comes before the verb, adjective, adverb or noun that it modifies (→**1**)

- However adverbs of time often come at the beginning of the sentence (→**2**)

Continued

Examples   ADVERBS 43

1 **vehementer** errabas, Verres
you were making a big mistake, Verres

   nimium libera respublica
   too free a state

   bis consul
   twice consul

2 **cras mane** putat se venturum esse
He thinks he will come tomorrow morning

   saepe hoc mecum cogitavi
   I often thought this over by myself

44 ADVERBS

Common Adverbs

● **Manner** – "how?"

ita	thus	crudeliter	cruelly
sic	thus	iustē	justly
aliter	otherwise	liberē	freely
fortē	by chance	repentē	suddenly
magnoperē	greatly		

● **Time** – "when?"

iam, nunc	now	(n)umquam	(n)ever
simul	at the same time	iterum	again
anteā	before	saepe	often
posteā	afterwards	hodiē	today
cōtīdiē	every day	herī	yesterday
diū	for a long time	crās	tomorrow
mox	soon	postrīdiē	next day
interim *or* -ea	meanwhile	statim	immediately
tum	then		

ADVERBS 45

● **Place** – "where?"

ubi?	where?	unde?	where from	quō?	where to?
ibi	there	inde	from there	eō	to there
hīc	here	hinc	from here	hūc	to here
usquam	any-where	nusquam	nowhere		

Others

etiam	also	fortasse	perhaps
quoque	also	consultō	on purpose
quidem	indeed	scīlicet	no doubt

Comparison of Adverbs

The comparative form of the adverb is the nominative singular neuter of the comparative adjective. The superlative of the adverb is formed by changing -us of the superlative adjective to -ē.

POSITIVE		COMPARATIVE		SUPERLATIVE	
altē	highly	altius	more highly	altissimē	most highly
audācter	boldly	audācius	more boldly	audācissimē	most boldly
bene	well	melius	better	optimē	best
breviter	briefly	brevius	more briefly	brevissimē	most briefly
diū	for a long time	diūtius	longer	diūtissimē	longest
facile	easily	facilius	more easily	facillimē	most easily
magnoperē	greatly	magis	more	maximē	most
male	badly	peius	worse	pessimē	worst
miserē	wretchedly	miserius	more wretchedly	miserrimē	most wretchedly
multum	much	plūs	more	plūrimum	most
paulum	a little	minus	less	minimē	least
prope	near	propius	nearer	proximē	nearest
saepe	often	saepius	more often	saepissimē	most often

- Notes on use of the comparative adjective may be applied also to the comparative adverb (*see p 40*).

rem tōtam brevius cognōscite
Find out about the whole matter more briefly

magis cōnsiliō quam virtūte vīcit
He won more because of his strategy than his courage

legiōnēs diūtius sine cōnsule fuērunt
The legions were too long without a consul

multō plūs
much more

optimē
very well

mihi placēbat Pompōnius maximē vel minimē
I liked Pomponius the most or disliked him the least

optimus quisque id optimē facit
All the best people do it best

quam celerrimē   as quickly as possible

Pronouns

Personal Pronouns

The pronouns **ego** (I), **nōs** (we), **tū** (you, *sing*), **vōs** (you, *pl*) decline as follows:

SINGULAR

Nom	ego	I	tū	you
Acc	mē	me	tē	you
Gen	meī	of me	tuī	of you
Dat	mihi	to/for me	tibi	to/for you
Abl	mē	by/with/from me	tē	by/with/from you

PLURAL

Nom	nōs	we	vōs	you
Acc	nōs	us	vōs	you
Gen	nostrum	of us	vestrum	of you
Dat	nōbis	to/for us	vōbis	to/for you
Abl	nōbis	by/with/from us	vōbis	by/with/from you

Possessive

meus, -a, -um my   tuus, -a, -um your
noster, -ra, -rum our   vester, -ra, -rum your

- **nostri** and **vestri** are alternative forms of genitive plural.
- Possessives are sometimes used instead of the genitive of personal pronouns:

odium tuum
hatred of you

- For the third person pronoun, he/she/it, Latin uses **is, ea, id**:

SINGULAR

	Masc		Fem		Neut	
Nom	is	he	ea	she	id	it
Acc	eum	him	eam	her	id	it
Gen	eius	of him	eius	of her	eius	of it
Dat	ei	to him	ei	to her	ei	to it
Abl	eō	by him	eā	by her	eō	by it

PLURAL

	Masc		Fem		Neut	
Nom	ei	they	eae	they	ea	they
Acc	eōs	them	eās	them	ea	them
Gen	eōrum	of them	eārum	of them	eōrum	of them
Dat	eis	to them	eis	to them	eis	to them
Abl	eis	by them	eis	by them	eis	by them

Use

- Pronouns as subjects (I, you) are not usually used in Latin. The person of the verb is indicated by the ending (*eg* **misimus** – we sent). **ego**, **nos** *etc* are used only for emphasis:

ego vulgus odi, **tū** amas
I hate crowds, you love them

- The genitive forms **nostrum** and **vestrum** are used partitively:

multi nostrum
many of us

pauci vestrum
a few of you

Reflexive Pronouns

		myself			yourself
Acc	mē		tē		
Gen	meī		tuī		
Dat	mihi		tibi		
Abl	mē		tē		
Acc	nōs	ourselves	vōs		yourselves
Gen	nostrum		vestrum		
Dat	nōbis		vōbis		
Abl	nōbis		vōbis		

● These are identical in form to personal pronouns.

		himself/herself/itself/themselves
Acc	sē	
Gen	suī	
Dat	sibi	
Abl	sē	

● Reflexive pronouns are used to refer to the subject of
the sentence:

quisque **se** amat
everybody loves themselves

me lavo
I wash myself

Determinative Pronouns

● **is** – he/that, **ea** – she, **id** – it: as above
● **idem** (the same)

SINGULAR

	Masc	Fem	Neut
Nom	idem	eadem	idem
Acc	eundem	eandem	idem
Gen	eiusdem	eiusdem	eiusdem
Dat	eidem	eidem	eidem
Abl	eōdem	eadem	eōdem

PLURAL

	Masc	Fem	Neut
Nom	eidem	eaedem	eadem
Acc	eōsdem	eāsdem	eadem
Gen	eōrundem	eārundem	eōrundem
Dat	eisdem	eisdem	eisdem
Abl	eisdem	eisdem	eisdem

● **ipse** (himself/herself/itself/themselves)

SINGULAR

	Masc	Fem	Neut
Nom	ipse	ipsa	ipsum
Acc	ipsum	ipsam	ipsum
Gen	ipsīus	ipsīus	ipsīus
Dat	ipsī	ipsī	ipsī
Abl	ipsō	ipsā	ipsō

PLURAL

	Masc	Fem	Neut
Nom	ipsī	ipsae	ipsa
Acc	ipsōs	ipsās	ipsa
Gen	ipsōrum	ipsārum	ipsōrum
Dat	ipsīs	ipsīs	ipsīs
Abl	ipsīs	ipsīs	ipsīs

Demonstrative Pronouns

- **hic** (this/these)

	SINGULAR		
	Masc	Fem	Neut
Nom	hic	haec	hōc
Acc	hunc	hanc	hōc
Gen	hūius	hūius	hūius
Dat	huīc	huīc	huīc
Abl	hōc	hāc	hōc

	PLURAL		
Nom	hī	hae	haec
Acc	hōs	hās	haec
Gen	hōrum	hārum	hōrum
Dat	hīs	hīs	hīs
Abl	hīs	hīs	hīs

- **ille** (that/those)

	SINGULAR		
	Masc	Fem	Neut
Nom	ille	illa	illud
Acc	illum	illam	illud
Gen	illīus	illīus	illīus
Dat	illī	illī	illī
Abl	illō	illā	illō

	PLURAL		
Nom	illī	illae	illa
Acc	illōs	illās	illa
Gen	illōrum	illārum	illōrum
Dat	illīs	illīs	illīs
Abl	illīs	illīs	illīs

- Note that **īdem**, **hic**, **ille** and all their parts may be adjectives as well as pronouns

Examples

1. **eadem** femina
   the same woman

   hic puer
   this boy

2. **tu** autem **eadem** ages?
   Are you going to do the same things?

   patria est carior quam **nos ipsi**
   Our native land is dearer than ourselves

3. **hac** remota, quomodo **illum** aestimemus?
   When she is removed, how are we to judge him?

4. **nos** oportet opus conficere
   We must complete the task

5. accusatores dicunt **te ipsam** testem **eius** criminis esse
   The prosecutors claim that you yourself are the witness of that crime

6. sed **haec** omitto; ad **illa** quae **me** magis moverunt respondeo
   But I pass over these matters; I reply to those which have affected me more deeply

7. pax **vobiscum**
   Peace be with you!

8. puella intravit; **ea mihi** litteras dedit
   The girl came in; she gave me a letter

Relative Pronouns

SINGULAR

	Masc	Fem	
Nom	quī	quae	who
Acc	quem	quam	whom
Gen	cūius	cūius	whose
Dat	cui	cui	to whom
Abl	quō	quā	by whom

	Neut		
Nom	quod		which/that
Acc	quod		which/that
Gen	cūius		of which
Dat	cui		to which
Abl	quō		by which

PLURAL

	Masc	Fem	
Nom	quī	quae	who
Acc	quōs	quās	whom
Gen	quōrum	quārum	whose
Dat	quibus	quibus	to whom
Abl	quibus	quibus	by whom

	Neut		
Nom	quae		which
Acc	quae		which
Gen	quōrum		of which
Dat	quibus		to which
Abl	quibus		by which

● A relative pronoun attaches a subordinate clause to a word preceding it (its antecedent). It agrees with this word in number and gender but takes its case from its own clause (→**1**)

● **quīdam, quaedam, quoddam** (a certain, somebody) **quīcumque, quaecumque, quodcumque** (whoever/whatever), decline in the same way as the relative above (→**2**)

Examples

1 **iuvenis cuius librum Sextus legit laetus erat**
The young man, whose book Sextus read, was happy

Fortunata, quae erat uxor Trimalchionis, saltāre coeperat
Fortunata, who was Trimalchio's wife, had begun to dance

tum duo crotalia protulit quae Fortunātae consideranda dedit
Then she brought out a pair of earrings which she gave to Fortunata to look at

2 **quidam ex legatis**
a certain ambassador

tu, quicumque es
you, whoever you are

Interrogative Pronouns

SINGULAR

	Masc	Fem	Neut	
Nom	quis	quis/quae	quid	who? what?
Acc	quem	quam	quid	whom? what?
Gen	cūius	cūius	cūius	whose? of what?
Dat	cui	cui		to whom? to what?
Abl	quō	quā		by whom? by what?

PLURAL

	Masc	Fem	Neut	
Nom	quī	quae	quae	who? what?
Acc	quōs	quās	quae	whom? what?
Gen	quōrum	quārum	quōrum	whose? of what?
Dat	quibus	quibus	quibus	to whom? to what?
Abl	quibus	quibus	quibus	by whom? by what?

- The interrogative pronoun is used to ask questions and usually is the first word in the sentence (→1)

- quisquis, quisquid, quidquid (whoever, whatever)
  quisque, quisque, quidque (each)
  quisquam, quisquam, quicquam (anyone, anything)
  aliquis, aliquam, aliquid (someone, something)
  These pronouns decline in the same way as **quis** above
  (→2)

Examples

1 quae fuit enim causa quamobrem isti mulieri venenum dare vellet Caelius?
What was the reason why Caelius wanted to give that woman poison?

quid agam, iudices?
What am I to do, men of the jury?

quos ad cenam invitavisti?
Whom did you invite for dinner?

quorum agros Galli incenderunt?
Whose fields did the Gauls burn?

2 quisque is est
whoever he is

si **quemquam** video
if I see anyone

liber **alicuius**
someone's book

Prepositions

A preposition expresses the relationship of one word to another. Each Latin preposition governs a noun or pronoun in the accusative or ablative case. Some prepositions govern both cases. Some may also be used as adverbs *eg* **prope** (near).

Position

● Prepositions generally come before the noun, or an adjective or equivalent qualifying the noun *eg*

ad villam
to the house

ad Ciceronis villam
to Cicero's house

● **cum** follows a personal pronoun *eg*

mēcum
with me

Prepositions governing the Accusative

On the following pages you will find some of the most frequent uses of prepositions in Latin. In the list below, the broad meaning is given on the left, with examples of usage following. Prepositions are given in alphabetical order.

ad

to/towards (*a place or person*)

oculos ad caelum sustulit
he raised his eyes to heaven

at, in the direction of, with regard to

ad Capuam profectus sum
I set out in the direction of Capua

ad portas
at the gates

ad duo milia occisi
about 2000 were killed

nil ad me attinet
it means nothing to me

adversum (-us)

opposite

sedens adversus te
sitting opposite you

towards

adversus Italiam
towards (*ie* facing) Italy

against

adversum flumen
against the stream

Continued

Prepositions governing the Accusative (contd)

ante

before (*of place and time*), used with ordinal number in dates	**ante meridiem** before midday
	ante limen before the doorway
	ante diem quintum Kalendas Ianuarias 28th December (*ie* 5th before Kalends of January)

apud

at/near (*usually with persons*)	**Crassus apud eum sedet** Crassus is sitting near him
in the writing of	**apud Platonem** in Plato's writings
before (*authorities*)	**apud pontifices** before the high priests

circum (circa)

around, about (*of place, people*)	**circum forum** around the forum
	circum Hectorem around Hector
	circa montes around the mountains
	circa decem milia Gallorum about ten thousand Gauls

contra

against	**contra hostes** against the enemy
	contra ventos against the wind
opposite	**contra Britanniam** facing Britain

extra

outside of	**extra muros** outside the walls
beyond (*of place and time*)	**extra iocum** beyond a joke

inter

between	**inter oppositos exercitus** between the opposing armies
	amans inter se loving each other
among	**inter saucios** among the wounded
	inter manus within reach
during	**inter hos annos** during these years

Continued

Prepositions governing the Accusative (contd)

intra

within (of place and time)

intra parietes
within the walls

intra quattuor annos
within four years

ob

on account of

quam ob rem
therefore

ob stultitiam
on account of your foolishness

per

through

per noctem
through the night

by means of

per vos
by means of you

per aetatem periit
he died of old age

per deos iuro
I swear by the gods

post

after (of time and place)

post urbem conditam
after the foundation of the city

post tergum
behind your back

praeter

beyond

praeter naturam
beyond nature

besides

praeter se tres alios adduxit
he brought three others besides himself

except for

praeter paucos
except for a few

prope

near

prope me habitavit
he lived near me

propter

on account of

propter metum mortis
on account of fear of death

Continued

Prepositions governing the Accusative (contd)

secundum

along (*of place*)	**secundum flumen** along the river
immediately after (*time*)	**secundum quietem** on waking from sleep
according to	**secundum naturam** according to nature

trans

across	**vexillum trans vallum traicere** to take the standard across the rampart
	trans Rhenum across the Rhine

ultra

beyond (*of time, degree etc*)	**ultra vires** beyond one's power

Prepositions governing the Ablative

Those which are spatial represent the idea of rest in a place or motion from a place.

a(b)

from (*of place, people, direction, time*)	**ab arce hostes deiecti sunt** the enemy were driven from the citadel
	a nobis abesse to be distant from us
	a dextrā from the right
	a tertiā horā from the third hour
by (*agent*)	**ab amicis desertus** abandoned by friends

cum

with	**vade mecum** go with me!
	cum curā loqui to speak with care
	cum Augusto coniurare to conspire with Augustus
	summa cum laude with distinction

Continued

Prepositions governing the Ablative (contd)

dē

down from	**dē caelō dēmittere** to send down from heaven
away from	**dē triclīniō exīre** to go away from the dining room
about	**cōgitāre dē hāc rē** to think about this matter
	dē industriā on purpose
during *or* at *(of time)*	**dē nocte** at night, during the night

ē(x)

out of *(from)*	**ē carcere effūgērunt.** they escaped from prison
	ex equīs dēsilīre to jump from their horses
	quīdam ex Hispāniā someone from Spain
	statua ex argentō facta a statue made of silver
immediately after	**ex cōnsulātu** immediately after his consulship
from	**ex hōc diē** from that day
	ex aequō equally

pro

for/on behalf of	**pro sē quisque** each one for himself/herself
	pro patriā morī to die for one's country
according to	**pro vīribus agere** to act according to one's ability
in front of	**pro rostrīs** in front of the rostrum

sine

without	**sine spē** without hope
	sine pecūniā without money

Prepositions governing Accusative and Ablative

in

with accusative

into   **in hanc urbem venire**
to come into the city

till   **in primam lucem dormivit**
he slept till dawn

against   **in rem publicam aggredi**
to attack the state

with ablative

in   **puella in illā domō laetē vivebat**
the girl lived happily in that house

on   **in capite coronam gerebat**
he wore a crown on his head

   in animo habere
to intend (to have in one's mind)

within (*of time*)   **in omni aetate**
within every age

in (*of condition*)   **in parte facilis, in parte difficilis**
easy in parts, difficult in others

---

sub

with accusative

beneath   **sub iugum mittere**
to send beneath the yoke
(*ie* into slavery)

below (*with verb of motion*)   **sub ipsum murum**
just below the wall

before (*of time*)   **sub vesperum**
just before nightfall

with ablative

under (*of place and power*)   **sub montibus constituere**
to station under the mountains

   sub Nerone
under the power of Nero

super

with accusative

over, above (*of place*), in addition   **super capita hostium**
over the heads of the enemy

   alii, super alios, advenerunt
they arrived one after the other

with ablative

concerning/about   **super his rebus scribam**
I shall write about these matters

Numerals

Cardinal and Ordinal Numbers

		CARDINAL	ORDINAL
1	I	ūnus, -a, -um	prīmus, -a, -um
2	II	duo, -ae, -o	secundus, -a, -um
3	III	trēs, tria	tertius, -a, -um
4	IV	quattuor	quartus, -a, -um
5	V	quīnque	quīntus, -a, -um
6	VI	sex	sextus, -a, -um
7	VII	septem	septimus, -a, -um
8	VIII	octō	octāvus, -a, -um
9	IX	novem	nōnus, -a, -um
10	X	decem	decimus, -a, -um
11	XI	ūndecim	ūndecimus, -a, -um
12	XII	duodecim	duodecimus, -a, -um
13	XIII	tredecim	tredecimus, -a, -um
14	XIV	quattuordecim	quartus decimus, -a, -um
15	XV	quīndecim	quīntus decimus, -a, -um
16	XVI	sēdecim	sextus decimus, -a, -um
17	XVII	septendecim	septimus decimus, -a, -um
18	XVIII	duodēvigintī	duodēvicēsimus, -a, -um
19	XIX	ūndēvigintī	ūndēvicēsimus, -a, -um
20	XX	vigintī	vicēsimus, -a, -um
21	XXI	vigintī ūnus	vicēsimus prīmus
30	XXX	trigintā	tricēsimus
40	XL	quadrāgintā	quadrāgēsimus
50	L	quīnquāgintā	quīnquāgēsimus
60	Lx	sexāgintā	sexāgēsimus
70	LXX	septuāgintā	septuāgēsimus
80	LXXX	octōgintā	octōgēsimus
90	XC	nōnāgintā	nōnāgēsimus
100	C	centum	centēsimus

		CARDINAL	ORDINAL
200	CC	ducentī, -ae, -a	ducentēsimus
300	CCC	trecentī, -ae, -a	trecentēsimus
400	CCCC	quadringentī, -ae, -a	quadringentēsimus
500	D (IↃ)	quīngentī, -ae, -a	quīngentēsimus
600	DC	sescentī, -ae, -a	sescentēsimus
700	DCC	septingentī, -ae, -a	septingentēsimus
800	DCCC	octingentī, -ae, -a	octingentēsimus
900	DCCCC	nōngentī, -ae, -a	nōngentēsimus
1000	M (CIↃ)	mīlle	mīllēsimus
2000	MM	duo mīlia	bis mīllēsimus
1,000,000		deciēs centēna (centum)	mīlia

- Fractions are expressed as follows:
  dimidia pars 1/2
  tertia pars 1/3
  quārta pars 1/4

Continued

Cardinal and Ordinal Numbers (contd)

- Ordinal numbers (→1) decline like 1st and 2nd declension adjectives

- Cardinal numbers (→2) do not decline except for ūnus, duo, trēs and hundreds (ducentī etc)

- ūnus declines as 1st and 2nd declension adjectives except that the genitive singular ends in -īus and the dative in -ī

- duo (two) declines as follows:

	Masc	Fem	Neut
Nom	duo	duae	duo
Acc	duōs	duās	duo
Gen	duōrum	duārum	duōrum
Dat	duōbus	duābus	duōbus
Abl	duōbus	duābus	duōbus

ambō, -ae, -a (both) declines in the same way

- trēs (three) declines as follows:

	Masc	Fem	Neut
Nom	trēs	trēs	tria
Acc	trēs	trēs	tria
Gen	trium	trium	trium
Dat	tribus	tribus	tribus
Abl	tribus	tribus	tribus

- Genitive of hundreds, eg trecentī ends -um (→3)

- mīlia (thousands) declines as follows:

Nom	mīlia	
Acc	mīlia	Dat mīlibus
Gen	mīlium	Abl mīlibus

- mīlle (thousand) does not decline.

1   coquus **secundam** mensam paraverat
    The cook had prepared the second course
    legionis **nonae** milites magnam partem hostium interfecerunt
    Soldiers of the ninth legion killed a large number of the enemy

2   **decem milia** passuum exercitus progressus est
    The army advanced 10 miles
    Cerberus, qui **tria** capita habebat, in antro recubuit
    Cerberus, who had three heads, crouched in the cave
    Stellae **novem** orbes confecerunt
    The stars completed nine orbits
    duodeviginti onerariae naves huc accedebant
    Eighteen cargo ships were approaching
    Caesar **trecentos** milites trans Padanum traiecit
    Caesar transported three hundred soldiers across the River Po

    da mi basia **mille**
    Give me a thousand kisses

3   **trecentum militum**
    of three hundred soldiers

4   **duo milia passuum** (gen)
    2000 paces or 2 miles

Distributive Numerals

These are used when repetition is involved as when multi-plying (→**1**)

1	singulī, -ae, -a	one each
2	bīnī, -ae, -a	two each
3	ternī (trinī)	
4	quaternī	
5	quīnī	
6	sēnī	
7	septēnī	
8	octōnī	
9	novēnī	
10	dēnī	

Numeral Adverbs

1	semel	once
2	bis	twice
3	ter	
4	quater	
5	quīnquiēs	
6	sexiēs	
7	septiēs	
8	octiēs	
9	noviēs	
10	deciēs	

(→**2**)

1 **bīnī gladiātōrēs**
(*describing pairs of gladiators*)

bīna castra
two camps

quaternōs dēnariōs in singulās vīnī amphorās
4 denarii each for a bottle of wine

2 nōn plus quam **semel**
not more than once

deciēs centēna mīlia sestertium *or* **deciēs** sestertium
1,000,000 sesterces

ter quattuor
twelve (*three times four*)

Dates

- Events of the year were usually recorded by using the names of the consuls holding office that year (→**1**)

- From the late republic the date of the foundation of Rome was established – 753 BC and time was calculated from this date (→**2**)

- The four seasons were: (→**3**)

ver, veris (*nt*)   spring
aestās, -ātis (*f*)   summer
autumnus, -i (*m*) autumn
hiems, -is (*f*)   winter

- The months were reformed by Julius Caesar (7 of 31 days, 4 of 30, 1 of 28, and an extra day each leap year). Each month (mensis, -is, *m*) was identified by the following adjectives:

Iānuārius	January
Februārius	February
Mārtius	March
Aprīlis	April
Māius	May
Iūnius	June
Iūlius (Quintīlis)	July
Augustus (Sextīlis)	August
September	September
Octōber	October
November	November
December	December

- Three important days each month were:

Kalendae, -ārum (*fpl*) Kalends *or* 1st
Nōnae, -ārum (*fpl*)   Nones *or* 5th/7th
Īdus, -uum (*fpl*)   Ides *or* 13th/15th

Continued

Examples

1 **Nerone iterum L. Pisone consulibus** pauca memoria digna evenerunt
Few incidents worth recording took place during the year when Nero and Lucius Piso were consuls (AD 57)

Lentulo Gaetulico C. Calvisio consulibus decreta sunt triumphi insignia Poppaeo Sabino
A triumph was voted to Poppaeus Sabinus during the consulship of Lentulus Gaetulicius and Gaius Calvisius

2 **ab urbe condita**
since the foundation of Rome

ante urbem conditam
before the foundation of the city

post urbem conditam
after the foundation of the city

3 **ineunte aestate**
in the beginning of summer

media aestate
midsummer

iam hieme confecta
when winter was already over

vere ineunte Antonius Tarentum navigavit
At the beginning of spring, Antony sailed to Tarentum

Dates (contd)

- In March, July, October and May, Nones fall on the 7th and Ides on the 15th day (5th and 13th in all other months).

- To refer to these dates, the ablative is used (→1)

- To refer to the day before these dates, use **pridiē** (→2)

- All other days were reckoned by counting (inclusively) the days before the next main date. "ante diem" + accusative of ordinal numbers and the next main date were used:
9th of February is 5 days before the 13th of February (counting inclusively). 28th April is 4 days before 1st May (→3)

- An easy way to work out such dates is to add one to Nones and Ides and subtract the Latin number. Add two to the number of days in the month before the Kalends, again subtracting the given Latin number. You will then have the date in English.

- The day was divided into twelve hours **horae, -arum** (*fpl*). The hours of darkness were divided into four watches of three hours each, **vigiliae, -arum** (*fpl*), from 6–9 pm, 9–12 pm, 12–3 am, 3–6 am

- Other ways of expressing time:

primā luce	at dawn
sōlo orto	at sunrise
sōlis occāsu	at sunset
mediā nocte	at midnight
noctū, nocte	at night
māne	in the morning
merīdiē	at midday
sub vesperum	towards evening
vespere	in the evening (→4)

Examples

1 **Kalendīs Martiīs**
on the 1st of March

Īdibus Decembribus
on the 13th of December

Īdibus Martiīs Caesar ā Brūtō interfectus est
Caesar was killed by Brutus on the 15th of March

2 **prīdiē Nōnas Iānuāriās (Nōn. Iān.)**
4th January

3 **ante diem quintum Īdūs Februāriās**
9th February

ante diem quartum Kalendās Maiās
28th April

4 **prīma hōra**
at the first hour (6–7 am)

tertiā vigiliā
during the third watch (midnight–3 am)

tertiā ferē vigiliā nāvem solvit (during the third watch)
He set sail after midnight

ipse **hōrā circiter quartā diēī** cum primīs nāvibus
Britanniam attigit
He himself reached Britain with the first ships around
10 o'clock in the morning

vespere vīnum optimum convīvae bibunt
In the evening, the guests drink vintage wine

Word Order

Simple Sentences

Word order in English is stricter than in Latin. The usual English order – subject + verb + object – differentiates the meaning of sentences such as, "The cat caught the mouse" and "The mouse caught the cat". Latin order is more flexible since the endings of words clearly show their function, whatever their position in the sentence.

Compare the following:

feles murem cepit   the cat caught the mouse
murem cepit feles   it was the cat that caught the mouse

The sentences are identical in meaning, although the emphasis in word order often makes it difficult for English translators to unravel long Latin sentences. However there are certain principles to help:

- The normal *grammatical* word order in Latin is:

  Subject first, Predicate after (by Predicate understand "verb")

- Expressions qualifying the subject (*ie* adjectives) must be near the subject

- Expressions qualifying the predicate (*eg* objects, adverbs, prepositional phrases) must be near the verb

  Thus the usual word order of a simple sentence is:

  (Connecting Word)
  Subject
  (Adjective)
  Object
  Adverbs *or* Prepositional Phrases
  Predicate (verb) (→**1**)

Continued

1 at **hostes** magnam virtutem in extrema spe salutis **praestiterunt**
  But the enemy showed great courage, finally hoping to save themselves

  Ariovistus ad postulata Caesaris pauca **respondit**
  Ariovistus briefly replied to Caesar's demands

  iste **Hannibal** sic hanc Tertiam **dilexit**
  Thus that Hannibal loved this Tertia

Simple Sentences (contd)

- Another principle is *emphasis*, where the words are in an unusual order, eg subject last, predicate first (→**1**)

- Questions usually begin with interrogatives (→**2**)

- Adjectives may precede or follow nouns. Check agreement of endings (→**3**)

- Genitives usually follow the governing word (→**4**)

- Words in apposition usually follow one another, although "rex" often comes first (→**5**)

- Adverbs usually come before their verb, adjective or adverb (→**6**)

- Prepositions usually come before their nouns (→**7**) but note, magna **cum** cura (with great care).

- Finally, watch out for the omission of words, particularly parts of **esse** (to be) (→**8**)

1 horum adventu **redintegratur** | **seditio** (subject last)
On their arrival trouble broke out once more

confecerunt me | **infirmitates** meorum (verb first)
I have been upset by the illnesses of my slaves

2 **quid** hoc loco potes dicere, homo amentissime?
What can you say at this point, you madman?

quis clarior in Graecia Themistocle?
Who (is) more famous in Greece than Themistocles?

3 **bello magno** victus   **magna domus**
conquered in a great war   a large house

4 multi **nostrum**   filius **Augusti**
many of us   Augustus' son

5 Cicero, **consul**
Cicero, the consul

rex Tarquinius
King Tarquinius

6 **vix** cuiquam persuadebatur
hardly anyone could be persuaded

multo carius
much dearer

7 **in** villam
into the house

sub monte
under the mountain

8 **pudor inde et miseratio et patris Agrippae, Augusti avi memoria (est)**
A feeling of pity and shame came over them and they remembered her father Agrippa and her grandfather Augustus

Compound Sentences

A compound sentence is one with a main clause and one or more subordinate clauses. In Latin this is called a **period**, where the most important idea is kept to the end.

● conservate parenti filium, parentem filio, (1) ne aut senectutem plenam desperatam contempsisse aut adulescentiam plenam spei|maximae non modo non aluisse vos verum etiam perculisse atque adflixisse videamini (2). (Cic. – Pro Caelio 32.80)

1. Main clause
   save a son for his father, a father for his son.

2. Negative purpose clause
   lest you appear either to have cast aside an old man near despair or that you have failed to sustain a young man full of the highest hopes, but have even struck him down and ruined him.

Note that this sentence builds towards a climax at the end. The most important verbs here are **perculisse** and **adflixisse** rather than **videamini** (you may seem). Notice also the rhythm of the last two words. Repetition of similar phrases is common – **parenti filium, parentem filio**. This sentence is a good illustration of an orator's style.

● Historical style is much simpler, often a subordinate clause followed by a main clause:

cum equites nostri funditoribus sagittariisque flumen transgressi essent (1), cum equitatu proelium commiserunt

1. Subordinate adverbial clause of time
   when our cavalry had crossed the river with slingers and archers

2. Main clause
   they joined battle with the cavalry

● Participle phrase followed by the **main clause** and **subordinate** clause:

nec patrum cognitionibus satiatus iudiciis (1) adsidebat in cornu tribunalis (2), ne praetorem curuli depelleret (Tac Ann I 75)

1. Participle phrase
   nor was he (the emperor) satisfied with taking part in Senate trials

2. Main clause
   he used to sit in the ordinary lawcourts

3. Subordinate clause of purpose
   in case he pushed the praetor from his curule chair

Many other combinations of clauses are possible. It is important to relate the sentence to its context and to the passage as a whole as Latin sentences are linked logically. It is often helpful when translating a long sentence to pick out subjects and verbs in order to recognize the structure of the clauses and grasp the overall meaning of the sentence.

Simple Sentences

Direct Statement

The basic patterns involved in direct statement have been illustrated under **Word Order** (*see* p 80).

Direct Questions

In Latin a direct question can be expressed as follows by:

- an interrogative pronoun (→**1**)

  quis? (who?), **quid?** (what?), **cur?** (why?)

- adding **-ne** to the first word, where no definite answer is indicated (→**2**)

- **nonne**, when the expected answer is YES (→**3**)

- **num**, when the expected answer is NO (→**4**)

- **utrum ... am(non)**
  -ne ...an(non) } (whether) ... or (not)
  ... an(non)
  in double questions (→**5**)

Examples

1   **quis** est
Who is it?

  quid dicit?
What is he saying?

  cur lacrimas?
Why are you crying?

  timesne Verrem?
Are you scared of Verres?

2

3   **nonne** cladem audivisti?
Surely you heard of the defeat?
or You heard of the defeat, didn't you?

4   **num** heri venisti?
Surely you didn't come yesterday?
or You didn't come yesterday, did you?

5   utrum has condiciones accepistis **annon**?
Have you accepted these conditions or not?

Continued

Simple Sentences (contd)

Direct Command

- A direct command in Latin is expressed in the second person by the imperative if positive, by **nōlī(te)** with the present infinitive if negative (→**1**)

- A direct command in the first or third persons is expressed by the present subjunctive, with **nē** if negative (→**2**)

Wishes

- Wishes are expressed in Latin by **utinam** with the subjunctive, **utinam nē** when negative (→**3**)

- **vellem** may also be used with imperfect or pluperfect subjunctive to express wishes (→**4**)

Examples

1 **venite** mecum
come with me

nōlī me tangere
don't touch me

2 **vivamus** atque **amemus**
let us live and let us love

ne **fiat** lux
let there not be light

3 **utinam** frater redeat
I wish my brother would return (*future*)

utinam nē vere scriberem
I wish I were not writing the truth (*present*)

utinam brevi moratus esses
I wish you had stayed a little (*past*)

4 **vellem** me ad cenam **invitavisses**
I wish you had invited me to dinner

Compound Sentences

Indirect Statement

"You are making a mistake" is a *direct statement.* "I think that you are making a mistake" is an *indirect statement.*

- The indirect statement is the object clause of "I think". In indirect statement in Latin, the subject of the clause (*eg* te) goes into the accusative case, the verb is an infinitive (errare):

Puto **te errare**
I think that you are making a mistake

- This pattern is used after verbs of saying, thinking, perceiving, knowing (→**1**)

Examples

1			
audire	hear	**negare**	say … not
cognoscere	discover	**nescire**	not to know
credere	believe	**putare**	think
dicere	say	**scire**	know
intellegere	understand	**sentire**	perceive
meminisse	remember	**videre**	see
narrare	tell		

Continued

Indirect Statement (contd)

Translation

- The *present infinitive* refers to actions happening at the same time and may be translated – is, are, was, were.

- The *perfect infinitive* refers to prior action and may be translated – has, have, had.

- The *future infinitive* refers to future action and may be translated – will, would.

putamus	**te errāre** **te errāvisse** **te errātūrum esse**	
We think		that you are making a mistake that you have made a mistake that you will make a mistake

putabamus	**te errāre** **te errāvisse** **te errātūrum esse**	
We thought		that you were making a mistake that you had made a mistake that you would make a mistake

- Notice that when the main verb is *past* tense, translate the present infinitive – "was, were", the past infinitive – "had", the future infinitive – "would". (→**1**)

- The reflexive pronoun **sē** is used to refer to the subject of the main verb (→**2**)

- Translate **negō** – I say that ... not (→**2**)

- Verbs of promising, hoping, threatening or swearing (*eg* **promittō, pollicēor, spērō, minor, iuro**) are followed by an accusative and future infinitive (→**3**)

Examples

1 senex dixit **se** thesaurum invenisse
The old man said that he had found treasure

2 **negavit** servum domum venturum esse
He said that the slave would not come home

3 **promisi me festinaturum esse**
I promised that I would hurry

sperabat se hoc confecturum esse
He hoped that he could complete this
or He hoped to complete this

Further Examples

creditores existimabant **eum** totam pecuniam per-
didisse
His creditors thought that he had lost all his money

memini **simulacra** deorum de caelo **percussa esse**
I remember that the gods' statues were struck down
from the heavens

vidistine **Catonem** in bibliotheca **sedere**?
Did you see Cato sitting in the library?

iuro **me** pro patria fortiter **pugnaturum esse**
I swear that I shall fight bravely for my country

iam ego credo **vos** verum **dixisse**
I now believe that you spoke the truth

negavit **nihil** umquam pulchrius statua **fuisse**
He said that nothing had ever been more beautiful
than that statue

Indirect Question

"Where did he come from?" is a *direct question*. "I asked where he had come from" is an *indirect question*. Latin uses the same interrogative words (quis – who, quid – what *etc*) and the verb in indirect questions is always subjunctive

rogavi unde venisset
I asked where he had come from

• Latin uses six different forms of the subjunctive in this construction in a precise sequence depending on the main verb (→1)

Examples

1 rogo

I ask

unde veniat	(present)
unde venerit	(perfect)
unde venturus sit	(future)

where he comes from	(present)
where he has come from	(perfect)
where he will come from	(future)

rogavi

I asked

unde veniret	(imperfect)
unde venisset	(pluperfect)
unde venturus esset	(future perfect)

where he was coming from	(imperfect)
where he had come from	(pluperfect)
where he would come from	(future perfect)

Continued

Indirect Question (contd)

Translation

Translation of tenses in indirect question is *easy*, because English uses the same tenses as Latin, as can be seen on page 94.

- The reflexive pronoun **se** is used to refer to the subject of the main verb (→**1**)

- **utrum ... an** (if ... or), **utrum ... necne** (whether ... or not) are also used in indirect questions (→**2**)

- **num** is used to mean "if" in indirect questions (→**3**)

Examples

1 rogavit **quando se visuri essemus**
He asked when we would see him

2 roga **utrum** iverit **an** manserit
Ask whether he went or stayed

roga **utrum** manserit **necne**
Ask whether he stayed or not

rogavit **utrum** Scylla infestior **esset** Charybdis **necne**
He asked whether Charybdis was more dangerous than Scylla or not

3 nescio **num** venturi sint
I don't know if they will come

Further Examples

nescimus **quid facturi simus**
We don't know what we shall do

mirum est **quanta sit Roma**
It is amazing how big Rome is
or The size of Rome is amazing

exploratores cognoverunt **quanti essent** Poeni
Scouts discovered what the numbers of the Carthaginians were

incredibile est **quomodo** talia facere **potuerit**
It is incredible how he was able to do such things

nemo audivit **quid rex constituisset**
No one heard what the king had decided
or No one heard the king's decision

Indirect Command

"Come here" is a *direct command.* "I ordered you to come here" is an *indirect command.* Indirect commands in Latin are expressed by **ut** (when positive) or **nē** (when negative) and have their verbs in the subjunctive (→**1**)

- Latin uses two tenses of the subjunctive, present or imperfect, in this construction. It uses the present subjunctive if the main verb is present or future tense and imperfect subjunctive if the main verb is in the past tense. (→**2**)

Translation

- The English translation of the indirect command is the same, whichever tense is used in Latin – the infinitive (*eg* to come)

- The reflexive **se** is used to refer to the subject of the main verb (→**3**)

- Common verbs introducing indirect command are:

hortor	encourage
moneo	warn
oro	beg
persuadeo	persuade
rogo	ask

- *Only* **iubeo** (to order), **veto** (to tell ... not), are usually used with the infinitive in Latin (→**4**)

1   tibi imperavi **ut** venīrēs
I ordered you to come
tibi imperavi **ne** venires
I forbade you to come

milites oravit **ne** in castris diutius **manerent**
He begged his soldiers not to stay in camp any longer

hoc rogo, mi Tiro, **ne** temere **naviges**
I beg you, my dear Tiro, not to sail carelessly

2   tibi **impero ut** venias   (*present*)
I order you to come
tibi **imperavi ut** venires   (*imperfect*)
I ordered you to come

deos precor **ut** nobis **parcant**
I beg the gods to spare us

amicos roga **ut veniant**, operamque **dent**, et messim hanc nobis **adiuvent**
Ask your friends to come and lend a hand and help us with this harvest

3   nos oravit ut **sibi** cibum daremus
He begged us to give him food

4   **iubeo** eos navigare
I order them to sail

veto eos navigare
I tell them not to sail

mater me **vetuit** in murum ascendere
Mother forbade me to climb on the wall

Antonius eos **iussit** adventum **suum** exspectare
Antony told them to await his arrival

Purpose or Final Clauses

There are two ways of expressing purpose in English:

I am hurrying to the city to see the games

or I am hurrying to the city so that I may see the games

- In Latin **ut** is used with the present or imperfect subjunctive, to express purpose. The present subjunctive is used if the main verb is in the present or future tense and the imperfect subjunctive if the main verb is in the past tense (→**1**)

- Negative purpose clauses are introduced by **ne** which can be translated "so that … not", "in case", "to avoid", "lest" etc (→**2**)

- If there is a comparative adjective or adverb in the Latin sentence **quō** is used instead of **ut** (→**3**)

- The relative **qui, quae, quod** may be used instead of **ut**, if it refers to an object in the main clause (→**4**)

- After negative **ne**, **quis** is used instead of **aliquis** to mean "anyone"

Note that **se** is used to refer to the subject of the main verb (→**5**)

- **ad** is used with the gerundive to express purpose (→**6**)

- The supine **-um** is used after verbs of motion to express purpose (→**7**)

1 ad urbem festino **ut** ludos **videam**
I am hurrying to the city to see the games
ad urbem festinavi **ut** ludos **viderem**
I hurried to the city to see the games
filium multo cum fletu complexus, pepulit **ut abiret**
Embracing his son tearfully, he drove him to leave

2 Tiberius hoc recusavit **ne** Germanicus imperium hab-
eret
Tiberius refused this lest Germanicus had power
pontem resciderunt **ne** hostes flumen **transirent**
They broke down the bridge in case the enemy crossed
the river

3 puellae cantabant **quo** laetiores essent **hospites**
The girls sang to make their guests happier

4 rex sex milites delegit **qui** ad Graeciam **proficiscerentur**
The king chose six soldiers to set off for Greece

5 in silvis se abdidit **ne quis** se **videret**
He hid in the woods lest anyone should see him
sed **ut** venenum manifesto comprehendi **posset**, con-
stituit locum iussit, **ut** eo **mitteret** amicos, **qui laterent**,
cum venisset Licinius, venenumque traderet, com-
prehenderent
*But so that the poison could be seized openly, he
ordered that a place be appointed, to send friends
there, to hide.* When Licinius came to hand over the
poison they could arrest him.

6 Verres ad Siciliam venit **ad urbes diripiendas**
Verres came to Sicily to plunder its cities

7 veniunt **spectatum**
They come to see

Result or Consecutive Clauses

The road is so long that I am tired
It was so hot that we could not work

In both these sentences, a result or consequence is expressed in English by using words such as

so … that (positive)
so that … not (negative)

- In Latin the following words are frequently used in the main clause

adeo	to such an extent
ita	thus, so
talis	of such a kind
tam	so
tantus	so great
tot	so many

- In the result clause, **ut** (so that) and **ut … non** (so that … not) are used with the present or imperfect subjunctive. Present subjunctive is used where the main verb is in the present and the imperfect subjunctive is used where the main verb is past (→**1**)

- **Note** that **eum** is used to refer to "him" instead of **se** when referring to the subject of the main clause as in the first example (→**1**)

Examples

1   Gallus **tam** ferox est **ut** omnes Romani eum **timeant**
The Gaul is so fierce that all the Romans are scared of him

tanta erat tempestas **ut** nautae navem **non solverent**
So great was the storm that the sailors could not set sail

nemo est **adeo** stultus **ut** non discere **possit**
No one is so stupid that he can't learn

tot sententiae erant **ut** nemo consentiret
There were so many opinions that no one could agree

tales nos esse putamus **ut** ab omnibus **laudemur**
We think that we are the sort of people to be praised by everyone

Verbs of Fearing

In Latin, verbs of fearing (**timeo, metuo, paveo, vereor**) are followed by **nē, nē non** or **ut** with the present and perfect, imperfect and pluperfect subjunctive according to sequence of tenses:

- The present subjunctive represents present and future tenses in English

  I am afraid he is coming
  I am afraid he will come

- The perfect subjunctive represents the past tense in English

  I am afraid that he has come

- When the verb of fearing is in the past tense, imperfect and pluperfect subjunctive are used in Latin instead (→**1**)

- **nē** is used if the fear is expressed in a positive sentence (*ie* I am afraid he will come). **nē nōn, ut** is used if the fear is expressed negatively (*ie* I am afraid that he won't come) (→**2**)

- As in English, the infinitive can follow a verb of fearing, provided that the subjects of both are the same (→**3**)

Examples

1   veritus sum **ne veniret**
I was afraid he was coming

veritus sum **ne venisset**
I was afraid that he had come

2   **vereor ne** amicus **veniat**
I am afraid lest my friend comes

or lest my friend will come

vereor ne amicus **non veniat**
I am afraid that my friend won't come

vereor ut amicus **venerit**
I am afraid that my friend has not come

verebar ne amicus **non venisset**
I was afraid that my friend had not come

metuo ne virtutis maiorum nostrum **obliviscamur**
I am afraid that we shall forget the courage of our ancestors

paves ne ducas tu illam
You are afraid to marry her

veritus, veritus ne servi bellum in Sicilia **facerent,**
multos in vincula coniecit
Verres, fearing that slaves might revolt in Sicily, threw many into prison

Romani **verebantur ne** fortiter **non pugnavissent**
The Romans were afraid that they had not fought bravely

3   timeo **abire**
I am afraid to go away

mulier **timebat manere** sola
The woman was scared to remain alone

106 SENTENCES

Conditional Sentences

Compare the following two sentences in English:

(a) If I tell you a lie, you will be angry
(b) If I were to tell you a lie, you would be angry

The first is a *logical statement of fact*, stating what *will* happen, the second is a *hypothesis*, stating what *would* happen.

For the first type of sentence, Latin uses the indicative mood in both main and conditional clauses. For the second type, Latin uses the subjunctive mood in both main and conditional clauses.

Translate type (a) as follows:

si hoc dicis, sapiens es
if you say this, you are wise

si hoc dicebas, sapiens eras
if you were saying this, you were wise

si hoc dixisti, erravisti
if you said this, then you made a mistake

si hoc dixeris, errabis
if you say this, you will make a mistake

Notice that the same tenses in English are used as in Latin except in the last sentence. Latin is more precise - you *will have said* this, before you make a mistake, therefore Latin uses the *future perfect* tense.

Continued

SENTENCES 107

• Consider also the following sentence:

si me amabis, mecum manebis
If you love me, you will stay with me

Latin uses the *future* tense in both clauses. English uses the *present* tense in the "if" clause. Both actions, "loving" and "remaining" *logically* refer to the *future*.

Translate type (b) as follows:

(*present*)
si hoc dicas, erres
if you were to say this, you would be making a mistake

(*imperfect*)
si hoc diceres, errares
if you said (*or* were saying) that, you would be making a mistake

(*pluperfect*)
si hoc dixisses, erravisses
if you had said that, you would have made a mistake

Notice that both tenses of the subjunctive are the same in the above examples. Sometimes an imperfect may be used in one clause and the pluperfect in the other:

si pudorem haberes, Romā abiisses
if you had any sense of shame, you would have left Rome

Conditional Sentences (contd)

Negative Conditional Sentences

- **nisi** (unless) is the negative of **si** (if). (→**1**)

- **si non** (if not), is less common and negates *one* word, or is used when the same verb is repeated (→**2**)

Examples

1 **nisi** id statim **feceris**, ego te **tradam** magistratui
Unless you do this immediately, I shall hand you over
to the magistrate

nisi utilem **crederem**, non pacem **peterem**
Unless I thought it useful, I would not be seeking
peace

2 **si** me **adiuveris**, laeta **ero**; **si** me **non adiuveris**, tristis
ero
If you help me, I shall be happy; if you don't help me,
I shall be sad

si navigatio **non morabitur**, mox te **videbo**
If my sailing is not delayed, I shall see you soon

Further Examples

(b) quis illum sceleratum fuisse **putavisset**, **si tacuisset**?
Who would have thought he was a rascal, if he had
kept quiet?

(b) multi **agerent** et **pugnarent si** rei publicae **videretur**
Many would act and fight, if the state decided

(a) **gaudemus si** liberi in horto **ludunt**
We are happy if the children play in the garden

(b) **si quis** in caelum **ascendisset**, pulchritudinem side-
rum **conspexisset**
If anyone had gone up to heaven, he would have seen
the beauty of the stars

Concessive Clauses

In English, Concessive clauses usually begin with "although":

Although he is rich, he is not happy
I shall succeed although it is difficult

- **quamquam** (although) is followed by the indicative (→**1**)

  Note that **tamen** (however) is often used in the main clause in concessive sentences

- **quamvis** (although) is always followed by the subjunctive (→**2**)

- **cum** in the sense "although" is always followed by the subjunctive (→**3**)

- **etsi** (although) takes the indicative or subjunctive according to the same rules as **si** (*see p 106*). The indicative is more common (→**4**)

1 medici **quamquam intellegunt,** numquam **tamen** aegris de morbo dicunt
Although doctors know, they never tell their patients about their illness

quamquam Aeneas dicere **volebat,** Dido solo fixos oculos aversa tenebat
Although Aeneas wished to speak, Dido turned away and kept her eyes fixed on the ground

2 **quamvis** frater **esset** molestus, Marcus eum amavit
Although his brother was a nuisance, Marcus loved him

feminae, **quamvis** in periculo **essent,** tamen liberos servaverunt
Although the women were in danger, yet they saved their children

3 **cum non didicissem** geometrias, litteras sciebam
Although I had not learnt geometry, I knew my letters

non poterant, **cum vellent,** Lucium liberare
They were not able, although they wished, to free Lucius

4 **etsi** servus **est,** certe persona est
Although he is a slave, he is a person

etsi victoriam non **reportavissetis,** tamen vos contentos esse oportebat
Although you had not won a victory, yet you should have been content

etsi domi **esset filius iuvenis,** agros ipse colebat
Although he had a young son at home, he cultivated the fields by himself

112 SENTENCES

Causal Clauses

Clauses which begin with the words "because" or "since" and give a reason for something are often called causal clauses in English.

- Causal clauses have their verbs in the indicative when the *actual* cause is stated. They are introduced by **quod** and **quia** (because), and **quoniam** (since) (→**1**)

- **quod** is used with the subjunctive when the cause is only *suggested* (→**2**)

- **non quod** (+ *subj*) ... **sed quia** (+ *indic*) not because ... but because ..., is used when the first reason is discarded. The true reason is expressed in the indicative (→**3**)

- **cum** (since, as) is always followed by the subjunctive (→**4**)

- **qui** with the subjunctive can be used to mean "since" (→**5**)

1 non iratus sum **quod** in me **fuisti** asperior
I am not angry because you were too harsh towards me

in crypta Neapolitana vecti, timebamus **quia** longior et obscurior carcere **erat**
Travelling in the Naples tunnel, we were afraid because it was longer and darker than a prison

quoniam ita tu **vis**, ego Puteolos tecum proficiscar
Since you wish this, I shall set off with you to Pozzuoli

2 templa spoliare non poterant **quod** religione im-pedirentur
They could not plunder the temples because (they said) they were prevented by religious feelings

3 mater semper maxime laboravit **non quod** necessarium **esset sed quia** honestum esse **videbatur**
Mother always worked very hard, not because it was necessary but because it seemed proper

4 quae **cum** ita **sint**, Catilina, egredere ex urbe!
Since this is so, Catilina, leave the city!

Caesar, **cum** in continente hiemare **constituisset**, ad Galliam rediit
Since Caesar had decided to spend the winter on the mainland, he returned to Gaul

5 sapiens erat **qui** studiis totos annos **dedisset**
He was wise since he had devoted all his years to study

Temporal Clauses

Clauses denoting time are introduced by conjunctions, *eg* **ubi** (when) followed by verbs in the indicative. Some conjunctions, *eg* **cum** (when) may also take the subjunctive. (→**1**)

Conjunctions followed by the indicative:

ut **ubi**	when, as when
cum primum **ubi primum** **ut primum**	as soon as
simul ac **simul atque**	as soon as
quotiens **quamdiu** **ex quo (tempore)**	as often as, whenever as long as, while ever since
postquam **posteaquam**	after (**post** or **postea** may be separated from **quam**)

---

1 **ut** valetudo Germanici Romae **nuntiata est,** magna ira erat
When Germanicus' state of health was announced in Rome, there was great anger

ubi primum classis visa est, **complentur** non modo portus sed moenia ac tecta
As soon as the fleet was seen, not only the harbour but the walls and rooftops were filled (with people)

quod **ubi cognitum est** hostibus, universi nonam legionem nocte aggressi sunt
When this was discovered by the enemy, all of them attacked the ninth legion at night

quotiens proficiscor, pluit
Every time I set out, it rains

manebat **quamdiu poterat**
He stayed as long as he could

septimus annus est, milites, **ex quo** Britanniam **vicistis**
It is seven years, soldiers, since you conquered Britain

postquam vallum **intravit,** portas stationibus confirmavit
After entering the fortification, he strengthened the gates with guards

post tertium diem quam **redierat,** mortuus est
He died three days after his return

Continued

Temporal Clauses (contd)

Conjunctions which take the indicative or subjunctive:

cum

- **when**   with indicative and often **tum** in the main clause (→**1**)

- **whenever**   with the following pattern of tenses in the indicative: (→**2**)

     + **perfect** followed by **present** tense
     + **future perfect** followed by **future** tense
     + **pluperfect** followed by **imperfect** tense

- **when, as**   with the imperfect or pluperfect subjunctive narrative (→**3**)

dum

- **while**   with indicative

  the present tense is used when **dum** means "during the time that" (→**4**)

- Note that where the same tense (here, the future) is used in both clauses, **dum** means "all the time that". Latin uses future **vivam** more accurately than English "live" (→**5**)

Continued

Examples

1 **cum** tu Romae **eras, tum** ego domi eram
When you were in Rome, I was then at home

2 **cum surrexerat, cadebat**
Whenever he got up, he fell down

   cum domum **veni,** amicum **visito**
Whenever I come home, I visit my friend

3 Socrates, **cum** triginta tyranni **essent,** non exibat
Socrates didn't go out when there were 30 tyrants

   cum id Caesari **nuntiatum esset** ab urbe profectus est
When that message had been given to Caesar, he set out from the city

4 **dum** haec **geruntur** sex milia hominum ad Rhenum contenderunt
While this was going on, 6000 men marched to the Rhine

5 **dum vivam,** laeta **ero**
While I live, I shall be happy

118 SENTENCES

Temporal Clauses (contd)

Clauses which take Indicative or Subjunctive (contd)

dum, donec

- **until**   with subjunctive, often with the sense of purpose or suspense (→**1**)

antequam, priusquam

- **before**   with indicative (→**2**)

- **ante and prius**   may be separated from **quam** especially in negative sentences (→**3**)

- **before**   with subjunctive, usually with a sense of purpose or limit (→**4**)

Examples   SENTENCES 119

1   multa Antonio concessit **dum** interfectores patris **ulcisceretur**
He made many concessions to Antony until he could avenge his father's killers

    Haterius in periculo erat **donec** Augustam auxilium **oraret**
Haterius was in danger until he begged for Augusta's help

2   **antequam finiam**, hoc dicam
Before I finish, I shall say this

    priusquam gallus **cantabit**, ter me negabis
Before the cock crows, you will deny me three times

3   neque **prius** fugere destiterunt **quam** ad castra **pervenerunt**
They didn't stop running away before reaching their camp

4   consul Romam festinavit **antequam** Hannibal eo **perveniret**
The consul hurried to Rome before Hannibal could reach it

    ita cassita nidum migravit **priusquam** agricola frumentum **meteret**
And so the lark abandoned her nest before the farmer could reap the corn

Comparative Clauses

- These are adverbial clauses which express likeness, agreement (or the opposite) with what is stated in the main clause. (→**1**)

- When the comparative clause states a fact (as above) the verb is in the **indicative**. The commonest words of comparison are (→**2**)

  ut (as), **sicut** (just as), **aliter ac, aliter ut** (different from), **idem ac, idem atque, qui** *etc* (the same as)

- When the comparative clause is purely **imaginary**, the verb is **subjunctive**. The commonest words used with this type of clause are (→**3**)

  velut(si), quasi, tamquam (si) (as if)

Examples

1   eadem dixi ac prius dixeram
I said the same as I had said before

2   **ego ita ero, ut me esse oportet**
I shall be as I should be

sicut lupus agnos rapit, ita mater liberos servat
Just as the wolf snatches the lamb, so the mother saves her children

haud aliter se gerebat ac solebat
He behaved as he usually did
or He behaved no differently from usual

idem abierunt qui venerant
The same men vanished as came

3   **velutsi haec res nihil ad se pertinuisset, tacebat**
He remained silent, as if this thing had nothing to do with him

hic flammae Aetnae minantur quasi ad caelum sublatae sint
Here Aetna's flames threaten, as if raised to the heavens

Cleopatram salutaverunt tamquam si esset regina
They greeted Cleopatra as if she were queen

122 SENTENCES

Relative Clauses

- Relative clauses are more common in Latin than in English. They are introduced by the following:

qui, quae, quod	which, who, that
ubi	where, in which
unde	from where, from which

- These relatives come at the beginning of the clause but after prepositions.

- The relative agrees with a word which precedes it – its *antecedent* – in gender and number, but takes its case from its own clause (→**1**)

  qui is masculine plural agreeing with antecedent **Romani**, nominative because it is the subject of **incenderunt**

- **quā** is feminine singular agreeing with **regio**, ablative after preposition **in** (→**2**)

- **quos** is masculine plural agreeing with **servos**, accusative because it is the object of **iudicavit** (→**3**)

- The relative **quod** refers to a sentence, and **id** is omitted (**id quod** – that which). This is often used in parenthesis, and not attached grammatically to the rest of the sentence

- After **cuius** (of, concerning which) the noun **laudationis** is repeated (→**4**)

- The relative sometimes agrees with the following word, especially with the verb **esse** (→**5**)

Continued

Examples   SENTENCES   123

1 hi sunt Romani **qui** libros incenderunt
       These are the Romans who burnt the books

2 haec est regio **in qua** ego sum natus
       This is the region in which I was born

3 servos **quos** ipse iudicavit, eos sua sponte liberavit
       He willingly freed those slaves whom he himself had
       judged

4 deinde, **quod** alio loco antea dixi, quae est ista tandem
       laudatio, **cuius laudationis** legati et principes et publice
       tibi navem aedificatam, et privatim se ipsos abs te
       spoliatos esse dixerunt? (**Cicero**, Verres V 58)
       Well then, as I said earlier elsewhere, what does that
       praise consist of, namely that publicly the ambassadors
       and chief citizens said a ship had been built for you,
       but privately that they themselves had been robbed by
       you?

5 iusta gloria **qui** fructus virtutis est, bello quaeritur
       True glory, which is the reward of courage, is looked
       for in war

124 SENTENCES

Relative Clauses (contd)

Use Of Subjunctive In Relative Clauses

- The subjunctive is used in relative clauses dependent on infinitives or subjunctives (→**1**)

- When **qui** is used with the subjunctive, it may express cause (→**2**)

  quippe is sometimes used with **qui** in this sense

- When **qui** *etc* is used with the present or imperfect subjunctive, it may express purpose (→**3**)

- **qui** with the subjunctive is used with the following (→**4**)

dignus est **qui**	he is worthy of
idoneus est **qui**	he is fit to
sunt **qui**	there are people who
nemo est **qui**	there is no one who

- At the beginning of a sentence, any part of **qui, quae, quod** may be used as a connective (instead of the demonstrative) with the previous sentence. Translate it in English by "this" or "that" (→**5**)

Examples   SENTENCES 125

1 quis sit **cui** vita talis **placeat?**
Who is there that likes such a life?

2 multa de mea sententia questus est Caesar (**quippe**) **qui** Ravennae Crassum ante **vidisset**
Caesar complained a lot about my decision since he had seen Crassus at Ravenna previously

3 legatos misit **qui** pacem **peterent**
He sent ambassadors to ask for peace

4 **Sunt qui dicere timeant**
There are some who are afraid to speak

  nemo **idoneus** aderat **qui responderet**
There was nobody there capable of replying

5 **quod** cum **audivisset**, soror lacrimas fudit
When she heard this, my sister shed tears

  quae cum ita **sint,** Vatinium defendam
Since this is so, I shall defend Vatinius

Negatives

There are several ways of forming a negative in Latin.

non

- This is the common negative in the indicative and usually stands before the verb, although it may be put in front of any word for emphasis (→**1**)

- Two negatives in the same sentence make an affirmative (→**2**)

haud

- This makes a single word negative, usually an adjective or an adverb (→**3**)

- It is also used in expressions such as **haud scio an** (I don't know whether), and **haud dubito** (I don't doubt) (→**4**)

- **haudquaquam** means not at all (→**5**)

Continued

---

1 ante horam tertiam noctis de foro **non discedit**
He didn't leave the forum before nine o'clock at night

Ambarri Caesarem certiorem faciunt se, vastatis agris, **non facile** vim hostium ab oppidis prohibere
The Ambarri informed Caesar that it was **not easy** for them, since their territory was destroyed, to keep the enemy force away from their towns

Caesar **non exspectandum** sibi statuit dum Helvetii pervenirent
Caesar decided **not to wait** till the Swiss arrived

2 non possum **non facere**
I must do

non sumus **ignari**
We are well aware

3 **haud** magnus
not great

haud procul
not far away

4 **haud scio an** ire mihi liceat
I don't know whether I am allowed to go

5 homo bonus, **haudquaquam** eloquens
A good man but not at all a good speaker

Negatives (contd)

ne

- This is the negative of the imperative and subjunctive.
  It is also used in many subordinate clauses where the
  verb is in the subjunctive (→1)

- Wishes (→2)

- Purpose (→3)

- Indirect command (→4)

- Fearing (→5)

1 **ne** diutius **vivamus**
   Let us **not live** any longer

2 utinam **ne** id **accidisset**
   I wish that it **had not happened**

3 agnus celeriter fugit **ne** lupi se **caperent**
   The lamb ran away quickly in **case** the wolves caught
   it

4 pater mihi imperavit **ne abirem**
   Father told me **not to go away**

5 cives metuebant **ne** Tiberius libertatem sibi **non**
   redderet
   The citizens were afraid that Tiberius **would not give**
   them **back** their freedom

   veritus sum **ne** id quod accidit **adveniret**
   I was afraid that what did in fact happen **might take**
   place

Continued

Negatives (contd)

Other Negatives

- **neque ... neque**   neither ... nor (→**1**)
- **neque ... quisquam**   neither anyone *or* and no one
- **neque ... quidquam**   neither anything *or* and nothing
- **neque ... umquam**   neither ever *or* and never
- **nemo ... umquam**   no one ever *or* never anyone
- **nihil ... umquam**   nothing ever *or* never anything (→**2**)

- Notice the following combinations:

  nonnulli some   *but* **nulli ... non** all
  nonnihil somewhat   *but* **nihil ... non** everything (→**3**)

- **non solum ... sed etiam** } not only ... but also
  non solum ... sed quoque } (→**4**)

- Roman authors repeat negatives for effect (→**5**)

1   **neque** illo adit **quisquam neque** eis ipsis **quidquam** praeter oram maritimam notum est
Neither did anyone approach that place, nor did they themselves know anything except the coast

2   **neque** post id tempus **umquam** summis nobiscum copiis hostes contenderunt
And after that the enemy never engaged in battle with us at full strength

ego **nihil umquam** feci solus
I never did anything alone

3   **nonnulli** amici
some friends

nulli amici **non** venerunt
all my friends came

4   Herennius Pontius, iam gravis annis, **non solum** militaribus **sed quoque** civilibus muneribus abscesserat
Herennius Pontius, now old, had withdrawn not only from military but also from civic duties

5   **nihil** audio quod audisse, **nihil** dico quod dixisse paeniteat; **nemo** apud me quemquam sinistris sermonibus carpit, **neminem** ipse reprehendo, **nisi** tamen me cum parum commode scribo; **nulla** spe, **nullo** timore sollicitor, **nullis** rumoribus inquietor; mecum tantum et cum libellis loquor (**Pliny** Ep 1, 9)
I hear nothing that I would regret having heard, I say nothing that I would regret having said; at home nobody nags me with vicious remarks, I don't blame anyone except myself when I write badly; no hope or fear worries me, no idle talk disturbs me; I speak only to myself and to my books

Translation Guidelines

Translating from Latin into English can be both a challenge and a pleasure. The word order of both languages is different: word order shows the relationship of words in English, in Latin it is shown by word endings. Sentences are generally shorter in English, structures simpler. Latin sentences often contain more subordinate clauses, sometimes embedded in other clauses, and often build up to form a long periodic sentence. Subject matter is two thousand years distant in time, although many ideas are still familiar to us today. The following guidelines are suggested to help in translation.

Guidelines

- *Establish the context* of the passage to be translated. Read the introduction in English carefully, find out *who* or *what* is being discussed, *when* and *where* the action took place.

- *Read through the whole passage* fairly quickly to gain some general understanding of the passage, however incomplete.

- *Focus on each sentence*, either taking each word as it comes, or establishing subject/verb/object according to your normal approach. Many find it helpful to pick out the verbs and work out the structure of the clauses. Watch for agreement of adjectives with nouns and how prepositional phrases fit in.

- *Watch conjunctions et, sed etc* and connectives such as **tamen** (however), and **igitur** (therefore). These help explain the logic of the passage as a whole.

- *Note punctuation.* It can be helpful in isolating clauses within the sentences, or marking off an ablative absolute.

- *Be open-minded.* Does **cum**, for example, mean "when", "since", or "although"? Don't decide till the whole sentence is worked out.

- *Use dictionaries carefully.* Check words of similar spelling, check endings. Once you have found the right Latin word, check all of its meanings before deciding on the correct translation.

- *Watch out for features of style eg* use of two adjectives with same meaning etc.

- Finally, *check your translation.* Does the narrative or logic of the passage seem consistent? Does your English sound natural? Does it represent the tone or style of the Latin passage? At this stage, fill in any blanks or make corrections.

Translation Problems

Finding the subject

- Look for a noun with a nominative ending. Check with verb ending for agreement. If there is no nominative, the subject will be indicated by the verb ending. Remember that, in Latin, the subject is continued from the previous sentence unless there is clear indication otherwise (→**1**)

Adjective agreement

- Check which adjective agrees with which noun in number, case and gender. Remember that it may be separated from its noun.

  a   b   b   a

  te **flagrantis atrox hora Caniculae** nescit tangere
  The blazing Dog Star's fierce daytime heat can't touch you

Passive

- Often it is better to turn a Latin passive verb into an active verb in English (→**2**)

Tense

- English is not so precise as Latin in its use of tenses. Use the tense that seems most natural in English, for example, English past tense for historic present in Latin, or English present tense for Latin future perfect in a conditional clause (→**3**)

Continued

1 **consules** et armare plebem et inermem pati timebant. sedabant tumultum, sedando interdum movebant.
    The consuls were afraid both to arm the people and to leave them unarmed. **They quelled** the riot, but sometimes, in quelling it, **they stirred it up again.**

2 hoc a tu **demonstrari** et **probari** volo
    I wish you to demonstrate and prove this
    or I wish this to be demonstrated and proved by you

3 hoc faciam si **potuero** (*future perfect*)
    I shall do this if I can (*present*)

136 TRANSLATION

Translation Problems (contd)

Ablative absolute

hostibus victis can be translated:

when the enemy had been beaten
after beating the enemy
they beat the enemy and …
although the enemy were beaten

Choose the version that makes most sense within the context of the passage.

Omission of esse

- Parts of esse (to be) are often omitted and have to be supplied in English (→1)

Omission of small words (ut, id, eo, hic etc)

- Check that you do not omit to translate these words – they are often very important (→2)

Neuter plurals

- **omnia** (everything) and **multa** (many things) are often mistranslated.

Impersonal passives

- It is worthwhile learning these (→3)

Continued

TRANSLATION 137

Examples

1 sed Germanicus quanto (**erat**) summae spei propior, tanto impensius pro Tiberio niti
But the nearer Germanicus **was** to succeeding, the more strenuously he exerted himself on behalf of Tiberius

2 eo   to there (*adv*), by, with *or* from him (*abl of pronoun*)
id … quod   that which
hic   this (*pron*), here (*adv*)
fit … ut   it happens … that

3 allatum est   it was announced
cognitum est   it was discovered
pugnatum est   a battle was fought
traditum est   it was recorded
visum est   it seemed

Translation Problems (contd)

Similarity of English/Latin Words

A higher percentage of English words are derived from Latin than from any other source. This can be helpful when trying to deduce the meaning of a Latin word, *eg* **portus** (port). But **porta** (gate) may cause confusion. The following examples taken from actual examination scripts provide a cautionary note. The correct translation follows in brackets:

Examples

prima luce nuntius hic **Ameriam** venit
At dawn the messenger came to America
(*At dawn the messenger came to Ameria*)

sex et quinquaginta **milia passuum** in cisio pervolavit
56 thousand flew past in a chariot
(*He quickly travelled fifty-six miles in a chariot*)

ut mori **mallet**
He would rather be killed by a mallet
(*To prefer to die*)

legati **crediderunt**
The embassy got credit
(*The ambassadors believed*)

False Friends/Confusables

ad (+ acc)	to, towards
ab (+ abl)	from, by, with
adeo	to such an extent
adeō	I approach
aestās	summer
aestus	heat, tide
aetas	age
aura	breeze
aurēs (pl)	ears
aurum	gold
avis	bird
avus	grandfather
cadō	I fall
caedō	I cut, kill
cēdō	I go, yield
campus	plain
castra (pl)	camp
cēterum	but
cēterī (pl)	the rest
coepī	I began
coēgī	I forced
constituō	I decide
consistō	I stop

Continued

crīmen	charge
scelus	crime
cum (prep)	with
cum (conj)	when, since, although
dominus	master
domus	house
equitēs (pl)	horsemen
equus	horse
fama	fame, report
fames	hunger
forte	by chance
fortis	brave (not strong)
fugāre	to put to flight
fugere	to flee, escape
hōra	hour
hōrum (gen pl)	of these
iaceō	I lie
iaciō	I throw
imperātor	general (not emperor)
imperātus	ordered (past participle)
inveniō	I find (not come in)
invītō	I invite
invītus	unwilling
iter, -ineris	journey
iterum	again
lātus, -a, -um	broad
lātus, -a, -um	brought
lātus, -eris	side

False Friends/Confusables (contd)

liber, -rī	book
līber, -a, -um	free
līberī, -ōrum (pl)	children
lībertus, -ī	freedman
magister, -rī	master
magistrātus	magistrate
malus, -a, -um	bad
mālum, -ī	apple
mālō, mālle	I prefer
manus, -ūs	hand, band
mānēs, -ium	spirits of dead
miser, -a, -um	unhappy
mīseram	I had sent (plup of mitto)
morior, -ī	I die
moror, -ārī	I delay
nauta	sailor
nāvis	ship
nēmō	no one
nimium	too much
occāsio	opportunity
occāsus (solis)	setting (of sun)
occidere	to fall, set
occīdere	to kill
opem	help
opera, -ae	work
opus, -eris	task
opus est	it is necessary

Continued

ōra, -ae	coast
ōrō, -āre	I pray, beg
ōs, ōris	face
ŏs, ŏssis	bone
parcō, -ere	I spare
pareō, -ēre	I obey
pariō, -ere	I give birth to
parō, -āre	I prepare
passus, -ūs	a pace
passus, -a, -um	suffered (past participle of patior)
porta, -ae	gate
portus, -ūs	port
portō, -āre	I carry
quaerō, -ere	I seek
queror, -ī	I complain
quīdam	a certain (person)
quīdem	indeed
reddō, -ere	I give back
redeō, -īre	I go back
serviō, -īre	I serve
servō, -āre	I save
sōl, -is	sun
soleō, -ēre	I am accustomed
solitus sum	
solum, -ī	soil
sōlus, -a, -um	alone

False Friends/Confusables (contd)

tamen	however
tandem	at last
ut(ī)	in order that, as, when
utī (*dep*)	to use
vallis, -is	valley
vallum, -i	wall, rampart
victor	winner
victus (*past part*)	beaten
vinctus (*past part*)	bound
vīs	force
vīres, -ium	strength
vir, -ī	man
virga, -ae	stick
virgō, -inis	girl
vīta, -ae	life
vītō, -āre	I avoid

VERB TABLES

146 VERBS

Conjugations

There are four patterns of regular Latin verbs called conjugations. Each can be identified by the ending of the **present infinitive**:

- First conjugation verbs end in -**āre** (eg amāre – to love)

- Second conjugation verbs end in -**ēre** (eg habēre – to have)

- Third conjugation verbs end in -**ere** (eg mittere – to send)

- Fourth conjugation verbs end in -**īre** (eg audīre – to hear)

VERBS 147

Each regular verb has three **stems**:

- A **present stem** which is found by cutting off -**re** from the present infinitive (eg amāre, habēre, mittere, audīre).

- A **perfect stem** which is formed by adding -**v** to the present stem in the first and fourth conjugations (eg amāvī, audīvī), and by adding -**u** to the present stem in the second conjugation (eg habuī).

  In the third conjugation there are several possible endings (eg scrīpsī, dīxī).

  Some short verbs lengthen the stem vowel (eg lēgī), others double the first consonant and vowel (eg cucurrī).

- A **supine stem** which is formed by cutting off -**um** from the supine forms (eg amātum, habitum, missum, audītum).

Tenses

These forms of the verb show when an action takes place, in the present, in the past or in the future.

In Latin there are six tenses:

1 Present ⎫
2 Imperfect ⎬ formed from the **present** stem
3 Future   ⎭

4 Perfect   ⎫
5 Pluperfect ⎬ formed from the **perfect** stem
6 Future   ⎭
  Perfect

Tenses Formed from the Present Stem

The following endings are added to the stem:

	PRESENT	IMPERFECT	FUTURE Conj 1&2	FUTURE Conj 3&4
sing				
1st person	-ō	-bam	-bō	-am
2nd person	-s	-bas	-bis	-ēs
3rd person	-t	-bat	-bit	-et
pl				
1st person	-mus	-bāmus	-bimus	-ēmus
2nd person	-tis	-bātis	-bitis	-ētis
3rd person	-nt	-bant	-bunt	-ent

Note that the above endings show the number and person of the subject of the verb. Subject pronouns are therefore not normally necessary in Latin.

Continued

Conjugations

	1	2	3	4
INFINITIVE	amāre	habēre	mittere	audīre
PRESENT STEM	amā-	habē-	mitte-	audī-
PRESENT				
	amō	habeō	mittō	audiō
	amās	habēs	mittis	audīs
	amat	habet	mittit	audit
	amāmus	habēmus	mittimus	audīmus
	amātis	habētis	mittitis	audītis
	amant	habent	mittunt	audiunt
IMPERFECT				
	amābam	habēbam	mittēbam	audiēbam
	amābās	habēbās	mittēbās	audiēbās
	amābat	habēbat	mittēbat	audiēbat
	amābāmus	habēbāmus	mittēbāmus	audiēbāmus
	amābātis	habēbātis	mittēbātis	audiēbātis
	amābant	habēbant	mittēbant	audiēbant
FUTURE				
	amābō	habēbō	mittam	audiam
	amābis	habēbis	mittēs	audiēs
	amābit	habēbit	mittet	audiet
	amābimus	habēbimus	mittēmus	audiēmus
	amābitis	habēbitis	mittētis	audiētis
	amābunt	habēbunt	mittent	audient

Tenses (contd)

Use:

The Present

In Latin, the present tense expresses what is going on now and can be translated into English in two ways (*eg laborat* – he works, he is working)

- The present is often used in Latin instead of a past tense to make the action more exciting (→**1**)

- Sometimes the Latin present tense is used to describe an action begun in the past and and still continuing (→**2**)

The Imperfect

- Describes what went on or continued for a time (→**3**)
- Denotes an action repeated in the past (→**4**)
- Is used when an action is intended or interrupted (→**5**)
- Is sometimes translated "had" when used with **iam** (→**6**)

The Future

- Is used in Latin as in English to denote what will or is going to be or to happen (→**7**)
- Is occasionally used as a command (→**8**)
- After "**si**" (if) in conditional sentences, it is sometimes translated as present tense in English (→**9**)

Examples

1 **prima luce Caesar Gallos oppugnat**
Caesar attacked the Gauls at dawn

2 **Alexander iam tres annos regit**
Alexander has been ruling for three years now

3 **pluebat** – it was raining

4 **fortiter pugnabant**
They used to fight bravely
or They kept fighting bravely

5 **Romam intrabam**
I was about to enter Rome

6 **multos iam dies villam habitabat**
He had already lived in the house for many days

7 **hoc faciemus**
We shall do this
or We are going to do this

   erit gloria
There will be glory

8 **non me vocabis**
Don't call me

9 **si id credes, errabis**
If you believe this, you will be making a mistake

Tenses (contd)

Tenses Formed from the Perfect Stem

To the appropriate perfect stem add the following endings:

sing	PERFECT	PLUPERFECT	FUTURE PERFECT
1st person	-ī	-eram	-erō
2nd person	-istī	-erās	-eris
3rd person	-it	-erat	-erit
pl			
1st person	-imus	-erāmus	-erimus
2nd person	-istis	-erātis	-eritis
3rd person	-ērunt	-erant	-erint

Conjugations

	1	2	3	4
PERFECT STEM	amāv-	habu-	mīs-	audī-
PERFECT				
	amāvī	habuī	mīsī	audīvī
	amāvistī	habuistī	mīsistī	audīvistī
	amāvit	habuit	mīsit	audīvit
	amāvimus	habuimus	mīsimus	audīvimus
	amāvistis	habuistis	mīsistis	audīvistis
	amāvērunt	habuērunt	mīsērunt	audīvērunt
PLUPERFECT				
	amāveram	habueram	mīseram	audīveram
	amāverās	habuerās	mīserās	audīverās
	amāverat	habuerat	mīserat	audīverat
	amāverāmus	habuerāmus	mīserāmus	audīverāmus
	amāverātis	habuerātis	mīserātis	audīverātis
	amāverant	habuerant	mīserant	audīverant
FUTURE PERFECT				
	amāverō	habuerō	mīserō	audīverō
	amāveris	habueris	mīseris	audīveris
	amāverit	habuerit	mīserit	audīverit
	amāverimus	habuerimus	mīserimus	audīverimus
	amāveritis	habueritis	mīseritis	audīveritis
	amāverint	habuerint	mīserint	audīverint

Continued

Tenses (contd)

Use:

The Perfect

- In Latin, the perfect tense is equivalent to the simple past tense (*eg* **vīdī** – I saw) and the perfect tense (*eg* **vīdī** – I have seen) in English.

- It states past action particularly in narrative (→**1**)

- Expresses an action completed in the past which still has effect in the present (→**2**)

The Pluperfect

- Denotes an action completed in the past before another past action (→**3**)

The Future Perfect

- Denotes completing something in the future (→**4**)

- Is often used with **volō, possum, nolō** *etc* (→**5**)

- Denotes an action which precedes another action in the future, often in a subordinate clause (→**6**)

Examples

1 **veni, vidi, vici**
I came, I saw, I conquered

2 **spem in fide alicuius habuerunt**
They place their hope in someone's good faith

3 **Mithridates urbem Asiae clarissimam obsederat quam L. Lucullus virtute liberavit**
Mithridates had besieged the most famous city in Asia that Lucius Lucullus freed by his courage

4 **id fecero**
I shall have done it

5 **si potuero, faciam**
If I can, I shall do it

6 **qui prior venerit, prior discedet**
First to come will be first to go

The Passive

Verbs may be active or passive. In **active** forms of the verb, the subject carries out the action (*eg* Brutus **killed** Caesar). In **passive** forms of the verb, the subject receives the action (*eg* Caesar **was killed** by Brutus).

Conjugation

To form the passive tenses of regular verbs, substitute the following endings for those of the present, imperfect and future active tenses (conjugated on page 148):

- In the present 1st person sing the ending is -**or**.
- In the imperfect, the endings are added to -**ba**.
- In the future (conjugations 1 and 2), the endings are added to -**bo** (*1st person sing*), -**be** (*2nd person sing*), and -**bi** for other persons. In conjugations 3 and 4, the 1st person *sing* ending is -**ar**.

Continued

sing	1st person	-r
	2nd person	-ris
	3rd person	-tur
pl	1st person	-mur
	2nd person	-mini
	3rd person	-ntur

Conjugations

	1	2	3	4
PRESENT PASSIVE				
	amor	habēor	mittor	audior
	amāris	habēris	mitteris	audīris
	amātur	habētur	mittitur	audītur
	amāmur	habēmur	mittimur	audīmur
	amāminī	habēminī	mittiminī	audīminī
	amantur	habēntur	mittuntur	audiuntur
IMPERFECT PASSIVE				
	amābar	habēbar	mittēbar	audiēbar
	amābāris	habēbāris	mittēbāris	audiēbāris
	amābātur	habēbātur	mittēbātur	audiēbātur
	amābāmur	habēbāmur	mittēbāmur	audiēbāmur
	amābāminī	habēbāminī	mittēbāminī	audiēbāminī
	amābantur	habēbantur	mittēbantur	audiēbantur
FUTURE PASSIVE				
	amābor	habēbor	mittar	audiar
	amāberis	habēberis	mitteris	audiēris
	amābitur	habēbitur	mittētur	audiētur
	amābimur	habēbimur	mittēmur	audiēmur
	amābiminī	habēbiminī	mittēminī	audiēminī
	amābuntur	habēbuntur	mittentur	audientur

The Passive (contd)

Translation

Present Passive

1	I am loved	we are loved
	you (*sing*) are loved	you (*pl*) are loved
	he/she/it is loved	they are loved
2	I am held *etc*	
3	I am sent *etc*	
4	I am heard *etc*	

Imperfect Passive

1	I was loved	we were loved
	you (*sing*) were loved	you (*pl*) were loved
	he/she/it was loved	they were loved
2	I was held *etc*	
3	I was sent *etc*	
4	I was heard *etc*	

Future Passive

1	I shall be loved	we shall be loved
	you (*sing*) will be loved	you (*pl*) will be loved
	he/she/it will be loved	they will be loved
2	I shall be held *etc*	
3	I shall be sent *etc*	
4	I shall be heard *etc*	

● "going to be" may also be used to translate the future.
Continued

The Passive (contd)

Perfect, Pluperfect and Future Perfect Passive

These tenses consist of the past participle (formed from the supine stem) and tenses of the verb **sum** (to be). The past participle endings agree in number and gender with the subject of the verb.

Conjugations

	1	2	3	4	
PERFECT PASSIVE	amātus -a, -um	habitus -a, -um	missus -a, -um	audītus -a, -um	sum es est
	amātī -ae, -a	habitī -ae, -a	missī -ae, -a	audītī -ae, -a	sumus estis sunt
PLUPERFECT PASSIVE	amātus	habitus	missus	audītus	eram erās erat
	amātī	habitī	missī	audītī	erāmus erātis erant
FUTURE PERFECT PASSIVE	amātus	habitus	missus	audītus	erō eris erit
	amātī	habitī	missī	audītī	erimus eritis erunt

The Passive (contd)

Translation

Perfect Passive

1. I have been loved   we have been loved
   you (*sing*) have been loved   you (*pl*) have been loved
   he/she/it has been loved   they have been loved

2. I have been held *etc*
3. I have been sent *etc*
4. I have been heard *etc*

Pluperfect Passive

1. I had been loved   we had been loved
   you (*sing*) had been loved   you (*pl*) had been loved
   he/she/it had been loved   they had been loved

2. I had been held *etc*
3. I had been sent *etc*
4. I had been heard *etc*

Future Perfect Passive

1. I shall have been loved   we shall have been loved
   you (*sing*) will have been loved   you (*pl*) will have been loved
   he/she/it will have been loved   they will have been loved

2. I shall have been held *etc*
3. I shall have been sent *etc*
4. I shall have been heard *etc*

Examples

1. **milites a populo occisi sunt**
   The soldiers were killed by the people

2. **populus milites occidit**
   The people killed the soldiers

- Note that the subject of the passive verb in (1) becomes the object of the active verb in (2).

- Often in English it is better to translate the meaning actively as in (2).

- The **agent** of the action is translated by **a(b)** with the ablative case as in **a populo** (1) – by the people.

- The **thing** causing the action is translated by the ablative case alone

   saxo percussus erat
   He had been struck by a rock

162 VERBS

The Subjunctive

So far all verbs described have belonged to the indicative mood, which states facts. The subjunctive mood represents ideas, possibilities or necessities and is often translated by auxiliary verbs such as **may, might, could, would, should** or **must**. There are four tenses active and passive – present, imperfect, perfect and pluperfect.

Formation of Active

The present subjunctive active is formed from the present stem, the imperfect from the infinitive. To these add the endings

-m, -s, -t, -mus, -tis, -nt.

- Note that in first conjugation present the preceding vowel is **-e**, and in all others **-a**.

- The present subjunctive active is sometimes translated by using "**may**" (→**1**)

- The imperfect subjunctive active is sometimes translated by using "**might**" (→**2**)

Continued

Conjugations

	1	2	3	4
PRESENT SUBJUNCTIVE ACTIVE				
	amem	habeam	mittam	audiam
	amēs	habeās	mittās	audiās
	amet	habeat	mittat	audiat
	amēmus	habeāmus	mittāmus	audiāmus
	amētis	habeātis	mittātis	audiātis
	ament	habeant	mittant	audiant
IMPERFECT SUBJUNCTIVE ACTIVE				
	amārem	habērem	mitterem	audīrem
	amārēs	habērēs	mitterēs	audīrēs
	amāret	habēret	mitteret	audīret
	amārēmus	habērēmus	mitterēmus	audīrēmus
	amārētis	habērētis	mitterētis	audīrētis
	amārent	habērent	mitterent	audīrent

1 **amem** – I may love
   mittas – you (*sing*) may send
   habeat – he may have
   audiant – they may hear

2 **mitteretis** – you (*pl*) might send
   haberem – I might have
   amaret – she might love
   audirent – they might hear

The Subjunctive (contd)

Formation of Passive

The passive of the present and imperfect subjunctive is easily formed by substituting the normal passive endings (-r, -ris, -tur, -mur, -mini, -ntur) for the active ones.

Conjugation

	1	2	3	4
PRESENT SUBJUNCTIVE PASSIVE				
	amer	habear	mittar	audiar
	amēris	habeāris	mittāris	audiāris
	amētur	habeātur	mittātur	audiātur
	amēmur	habeāmur	mittāmur	audiāmur
	amēminī	habeāminī	mittāminī	audiāminī
	amentur	habeantur	mittantur	audiantur
IMPERFECT SUBJUNCTIVE PASSIVE				
	amārer	habērer	mitterer	audīrer
	amārēris	habērēris	mitterēris	audīrēris
	amārētur	habērētur	mitterētur	audīrētur
	amārēmur	habērēmur	mitterēmur	audīrēmur
	amārēminī	habērēminī	mitterēminī	audīrēminī
	amārentur	habērentur	mitterentur	audīrentur

- The present subjunctive passive is sometimes translated by using "may be" (→**1**)

- The imperfect subjunctive passive is sometimes translated by using "might be" (→**2**)

Continued

Examples

1 habeāmur – we may be held
amer – I may be loved
mittāminī – you (*pl*) may be sent
audiantur – they may be heard

2 audīrēminī – you (*pl*) might be heard
amārētur – he might be loved
haberentur – they might be held
mitterer – I might be sent

The Subjunctive (contd)

Perfect and Pluperfect Subjunctive Active

Both perfect and pluperfect subjunctive active are formed from the perfect stem as follows:

Conjugation

1	2	3	4
PERFECT SUBJUNCTIVE ACTIVE			
amāverim	habuerim	mīserim	audīverim
amāveris	habueris	mīseris	audīveris
amāverit	habuerit	mīserit	audīverit
amāverimus	habuerimus	mīserimus	audīverimus
amāveritis	habueritis	mīseritis	audīveritis
amāverint	habuerint	mīserint	audīverint
PLUPERFECT SUBJUNCTIVE ACTIVE			
amāvissem	habuissem	mīsissem	audīvissem
amāvissēs	habuissēs	mīsissēs	audīvissēs
amāvisset	habuisset	mīsisset	audīvisset
amāvissēmus	habuissēmus	mīsissēmus	audīvissēmus
amāvissētis	habuissētis	mīsissētis	audīvissētis
amāvissent	habuissent	mīsissent	audīvissent

- The Perfect subjunctive active is sometimes translated by using **"may have"** with the past participle in English (→**1**)

- The Pluperfect subjunctive active is sometimes translated by using **"might have"** with the past participle in English (→**2**)

Continued

1 **miserit** – he may have sent
habuerint – they may have had
audīveris – you (*sing*) may have heard
amāveritis – you (*pl*) may have loved

2 **amāvissēmus** – we might have loved
habuisset – he might have had
audīvissent – they might have heard
misissem – I might have sent

The Subjunctive (contd)

Perfect and Pluperfect Subjunctive Passive

Both perfect and pluperfect subjunctive passive are formed from the supine stem and the present and imperfect subjunctive of **sum** respectively:

Conjugation

1

PERFECT SUBJUNCTIVE PASSIVE

amātus	habitus	sim
		sīs
		sit

pl

amātī	habitī	sīmus
		sītis
		sint

PLUPERFECT SUBJUNCTIVE PASSIVE

amātus	habitus	essem
		essēs
		esset

pl

amātī	habitī	essēmus
		essētis
		essent

2

Conjugation

3

PERFECT SUBJUNCTIVE PASSIVE

missus	auditus	sim
		sīs
		sit

pl

missī	audītī	sīmus
		sītis
		sint

PLUPERFECT SUBJUNCTIVE PASSIVE

missus	auditus	essem
		essēs
		esset

pl

missī	audītī	essēmus
		essētis
		essent

4

Continued

The Subjunctive (contd)

- The perfect subjunctive passive is sometimes translated by using **"may have been"** with the past participle in English (→**1**)

- The pluperfect subjunctive passive is sometimes translated by using **"might have been"** with the past participle in English (→**2**)

Examples

1 **habitus sis** – you (*sing*) may have been held
missi simus – we may have been sent
auditus sim – I may have been heard
amati sint – they may have been loved

2 **amati essemus** – we might have been loved
habiti essent – they might have been held
missus esses – you (*sing*) might have been sent
auditus essem – I might have been heard

The Imperative

This is the mood of command. It has two forms, 2nd person *sing* and *pl*, active (→1) and passive: (→2)

Conjugations

	1	2	3	4
IMPERATIVE ACTIVE				
sing	amā	habē	mitte	audī
pl	amāte	habēte	mittite	audīte
IMPERATIVE PASSIVE				
sing	amāre	habēre	mittere	audīre
pl	amāminī	habēminī	mittīminī	audīminī

1 pecuniam mittite, o cives
Citizens, send money! (active)

spem habe
Have hope! (active)

2 in curia audimini
Be heard in the senate! (passive)

ab omnibus semper amare, Romule
Always be loved by everyone, Romulus (passive)

The Infinitive

The infinitive was originally a noun and can be used in this way in Latin (eg **amāre** – to love or loving). There are three types, present, future and perfect, both active and passive, formed as follows:

Active

	1	**2**
PRESENT	amāre	habēre
FUTURE	amātūrus esse	habitūrus esse
PERFECT	amāvisse	habuisse

	3	**4**
PRESENT	mittere	audīre
FUTURE	missūrus esse	auditūrus esse
PERFECT	mīsisse	audivisse

Translation

to love
to be going to love
to have loved

to have
to be going to have
to have had

to send
to be going to send
to have sent

to hear
to be going to hear
to have heard

Continued

Passive

	1	**2**
PRESENT	amārī	habērī
FUTURE	amātum īrī	habitum īrī
PERFECT	amātus esse	habitus esse

	3	**4**
PRESENT	mittī	audīrī
FUTURE	missum īrī	audītum īrī
PERFECT	missus esse	audītus esse

Translation

to be loved
to be going to be loved
to have been loved

to be had
to be going to be had
to have been had

to be sent
to be going to be sent
to have been sent

to be heard
to be going to be heard
to have been heard

- In the future active **-ūrus**, **-a**, **-um** and in the perfect passive **-us**, **-a**, **-um** agree in number and gender with the noun or pronoun in indirect speech.

The Infinitive (contd)

Uses of the Infinitive

- It can be used as a neuter noun
- As the subject of the sentence (→1)
- With certain nouns such as **fas** (right), **nefas** (wrong) (→2)
- As the object of the following verbs: (→3)

volō	I wish	**cupiō**	I desire
nolō	I do not wish	**sinō**	I allow
possum	I am able to, can	**cogō**	I force
sciō	I know (how)	**audeō**	I dare
nesciō	I do not know	**conor**	I try
debeō	I ought	**desinō**	I stop
soleō	I am accustomed	**dubitō**	I hesitate
incipiō	I begin	**coepi**	I begin

- It can be used to describe a rapid series of events instead of using the perfect tense (→4)

1 **errare est humanum**
To err is human

2 **nefas est templa destruere**
It is wrong to destroy temples

3 **volo domum redire**
I wish to return home

desine mortuos commemorare
Stop remembering the dead

Romam exstinctam esse cupit
He wishes Rome blotted out

4 **ille non tollere oculos, non remittere stilum, tum fragor adventare et intra limen audiri**
He did not raise his eyes nor put down his pen, then the noise came closer and could be heard inside the door.

178 VERBS

Participles

There are three participles (or verbal adjectives) in Latin: the present active, the perfect passive and the future active.

The Present Participle

This is formed from the present stem by adding **-ns** and lengthening the previous vowel. The genitive ending is **-ntis**.

Conjugation

1	2	3	4
amāns	habēns	mittēns	audiēns
loving	having	sending	hearing

- Note that these decline like group 3 adjectives ending in **-ns** with ablative singular, in **-ī** when used as an adjective and in **-e** when used as a verb. They agree in number, case and gender with nouns or pronouns in the sentence.

Use

- It denotes an action going on at the same time as the main verb (→**1**)

- It can be used as a noun (→**2**)

Continued

Examples

1 **pro patria pugnantes iuvenes mortui sunt**
The young men died *while fighting* for their country

Romulo regnante, Roma urbs parva erat
While Romulus was ruling, Rome was a small city

2 **lacrimae adstantium**
the tears of *people standing by*

Participles (contd)

The Perfect Participle

This is formed from the supine stem by adding the endings
-us, -a, -m. It declines like first and second declension
adjectives (*see pages 25–28*)

Conjugation

1	2	3	4
amātus (having been) loved	habitus (having been) held	missus (having been) sent	audītus (having been) heard

Use

- It denotes an action that is completed before that of
  the main verb (→**1**)

- English is less precise in the use of tenses and frequently
  uses a present to translate a Latin past participle.

The Future Participle

This is formed by adding -ūrus, -a, -um to the supine stem.
It declines like first and second declension adjectives.

Conjugation

1	2	3	4
amātūrus going to love	habitūrus going to have	missūrus going to send	audītūrus going to hear

Use

- It denotes an action that is going to take place (→**2**)

- The forms **futūrus** (going to be) and **ventūrus** (going
  to come) are often used as adjectives.

Examples

1 **equites Romani auditi ad senatum adducti sunt**
The Roman businessmen *were heard* and then were
brought before the Senate

castra capta incendimus
We *captured* the camp and burnt it
or Capturing the camp, we burnt it

2 **nos morituri te salutamus**
We who are about to die salute you

Gerunds and Gerundives

The **gerund** is a **verbal noun** and is active.

The **gerundive** is a **verbal adjective** and is passive.

The gerund is formed by adding **-ndum** to the present stem. It declines like a neuter noun **-ndum**, **-ndī**, **-ndō**.

The gerundive declines like first and second declension adjectives **-us**, **-a**, **-um** (A)

Conjugation

	1	2	3	4
GERUND	amandum loving	habendum having	mittendum sending	audiendum hearing
GERUNDIVE	amandus requiring to be loved	habendus requiring to be held	mittendus requiring to be sent	audiendus requiring to be heard

Gerunds and Gerundives (contd)

Use of Gerund and Gerundive

- The gerund is often used with the accusative case to express **purpose** (→**1**)

- If the verb has a direct object, the gerundive is used instead (→**2**)

- The gerund is used in the genitive case with nouns and adjectives (→**3**) such as

  ars (art), **spes** (hope), **cupidus** (eager), **peritus** (skilled)

- Both the gerund and the gerundive can be used in the genitive with **causa** to express **purpose** (→**4**)

- The gerundive can be used to imply **obligation** and the person is expressed by the dative case (→**5**)

- If the verb cannot take a direct object, the impersonal form is used (→**6**)

- Both the gerund and the gerundive can be used in the ablative case (→**7**)

Examples

1   **venit ad regnandum**
      He came to rule

2   **venit ad pacem petendam**
      He came to make peace

3   **spes videndi**
      Hope of seeing
      peritus equitandi
      Skilled in riding

4   **dicendi causa**
      to speak
      pacis petendae causa
      For the sake of making peace

5   **poenae nobis timendae sunt**
      Punishment must be feared by us
      or We must fear punishment

6   **mihi parendum est**
      You must obey me

7   **docendo discimus**
      We learn by teaching
      me puniendo effugit
      By punishing me he escaped

Impersonal Verbs

Impersonal verbs are used in the third person singular only

- To describe the weather (→**1**)

- To express feeling. The person affected appears in the accusative case and the cause in the genitive case (→**2**)

- To express permission or pleasure. The person affected appears in the dative case. The verb is often followed by a present infinitive (→**3**)

- To express happening, following *etc.* These are followed by **ut** with the subjunctive mood (→**4**)

   fit ut   it happens that
   accidit ut   it happens that
   sequitur ut   it follows that

- Certain intransitive verbs are used impersonally in the passive (→**5**)

- Verbs of saying, believing *etc* are used impersonally in the perfect passive tense (→**6**)

- The verbs, **interest** (it is of importance), and **refert** (it is of concern), are followed usually by **meā, tuā, nostrā, vestrā** (→**7**)

- Sometimes **interest** is followed by genitive of the person (→**8**)

- The following verbs are followed by a present infinitive. The person involved appears in the accusative case (→**9**)

   me decet   it is fitting for me
   me oportet I must/ought

1
pluit   **fulgurat**
it is raining   there is lightning
tonat   **ningit**
there is thunder   it is snowing

2
me miseret   **me miseret sociorum**
I am sorry for   I am sorry for my
me paenitet   comrades
I repent of

3
mihi licet   **nobis placet**
I am allowed to   it is pleasing to us
tibi videtur   *or* we like
it seems good to you
or you decide

4
fit ut   **fit ut fallar**
it happens that   it happens that I am
accidit ut   mistaken
it happens that

5
pugnatum est in mari
the battle was fought at sea
vivitur in oculis omnium
life is lived in the sight of everyone

6
nuntiatum est
it has been announced
mihi dictum est Germanos transiisse Rhenum
I was told that the Germans had crossed the Rhine

7
nihil mea refert
it is of no interest to me

8
Caesaris interest
it is important to Caesar

9
nos morari oportuit
we ought to have waited

Deponent Verbs

Deponent verbs are passive in form but active in meaning. They also have present and future participles and future infinitive which are active. The perfect participle is also active in meaning. Otherwise the conjugation is similar to that of regular verbs.

1st Conjugation

cōnārī (to try)

INDICATIVE		SUBJUNCTIVE	
PRESENT			
cōnor	I try etc	cōner	I may try etc
cōnāris		cōnēris	
cōnātur		cōnētur	
cōnāmur		cōnēmur	
cōnāminī		cōnēminī	
cōnantur		cōnentur	
IMPERFECT			
cōnābar	I was trying etc	cōnārer	I might try etc
cōnābāris		cōnārēris	
cōnābātur		cōnārētur	
cōnābāmur		cōnārēmur	
cōnābāminī		cōnārēminī	
cōnābantur		cōnārentur	
FUTURE			
cōnābor	I shall try etc		
cōnāberis			
cōnābitur			
cōnābimur			
cōnābiminī			
cōnābuntur			

Continued

PERFECT				
cōnātus sum	I tried	cōnātus sim	I may have tried
-a, -um es	you tried etc	-a, -um sis	you may have tried etc
PLUPERFECT				
cōnātus eram	I had tried	cōnātus essem	I might have tried
-a, -um eras	you had tried etc	-a, -um esses	you might have tried etc
FUTURE PERFECT			
cōnātus ero	I shall have tried		
-a, -um eris	you will have tried etc		

IMPERATIVE		
cōnāre	sing	try
cōnāminī	pl	try

INFINITIVES	
present	cōnārī	to try
future	cōnātūrus esse	to be going to try
perfect	cōnātus esse	to have tried

PARTICIPLES	
present	cōnāns	trying
future	cōnātūrus	going to try
perfect	cōnātus	having tried

GERUND	cōnandum	trying
GERUNDIVE	cōnandus	requiring to be tried

Second, Third, Fourth Conjugations

These are conjugated like the passive form of verbs of the corresponding conjugations. A summary is provided as follows:

Second Conjugation

verērī (to fear, be afraid)

INDICATIVE		
Present	vereor	I am afraid
Imperfect	verēbar	I was afraid
Future	verēbor	I shall be afraid
Perfect	veritus sum	I was afraid
Pluperfect	veritus eram	I had been afraid
Future Perfect	veritus erō	I shall have been afraid

SUBJUNCTIVE		
Present	verear	I may be afraid
Imperfect	verērer	I might be afraid
Perfect	veritus sim	I may have been afraid
Pluperfect	veritus essem	I might have been afraid

IMPERATIVE		
Singular	verēre	be afraid
Plural	verēminī	be afraid

Continued

INFINITIVES		
Present	verērī	to be afraid
Future	veritūrus esse	to be going to be afraid
Perfect	veritus esse	to have been afraid

PARTICIPLES		
Present	verēns	fearing, being afraid
Future	veritūrus	going to fear or be afraid
Perfect	veritus	having feared or been afraid (active)

| GERUND | verendum | fearing |
| GERUNDIVE | verendus | requiring to be feared |

Second, Third, Fourth Conjugations (contd)

Third Conjugation

sequī (to follow)

INDICATIVE		
Present	sequor	I follow
Imperfect	sequēbar	I was following
Future	sequar	I shall follow
Perfect	secūtus sum	I followed
Pluperfect	secūtus eram	I had followed
Future Perfect	secūtus erō	I shall have followed
SUBJUNCTIVE		
Present	sequar	I may follow
Imperfect	sequerer	I might follow
Perfect	secūtus sim	I may have followed
Pluperfect	secūtus essem	I might have followed
IMPERATIVE		
Singular	sequere	follow
Plural	sequiminī	follow
INFINITIVES		
Present	sequī	to follow
Future	secūtūrus esse	to be going to follow
Perfect	secūtus esse	to have followed
PARTICIPLES		
Present	sequēns	following
Future	secūtūrus	going to follow
Perfect	secūtus	having followed
GERUND	sequendum	following
GERUNDIVE	sequendus	requiring to be followed

Fourth Conjugation

mentīrī (to lie)

INDICATIVE		
Present	mentior	I lie
Imperfect	mentiēbar	I was lying
Future	mentiar	I shall lie
Perfect	mentītus sum	I lied
Pluperfect	mentītus eram	I had lied
Future Perfect	mentītus erō	I shall have lied
SUBJUNCTIVE		
Present	mentiar	I may lie
Imperfect	mentīrer	I might lie
Perfect	mentītus sim	I may have lied
Pluperfect	mentītus essem	I might have lied
IMPERATIVE		
Singular	mentīre	lie
Plural	mentiminī	lie
INFINITIVES		
Present	mentīrī	to lie
Future	mentītūrus esse	to be going to lie
Perfect	mentītus esse	to have lied
PARTICIPLES		
Present	mentiēns	lying
Future	mentītūrus	going to lie
Perfect	mentītus	having lied
GERUND	mentiendum	lying
GERUNDIVE	mentiendus	requiring to be lied to

Semi-deponent Verbs

A few verbs are passive in meaning in and active in form in only the perfect tenses. All other tenses are active in form and meaning. These are:

audēre	to dare
gaudēre	to be glad
solēre	to be accustomed
confidere	to trust

INDICATIVE

Present	audeō	I dare
Imperfect	audēbam	I was daring
Future	audēbo	I shall dare

SUBJUNCTIVE

Present	audeam	I may dare
Imperfect	audērem	I might dare

IMPERATIVE

Singular	audē	dare
Plural	audētē	dare

INFINITIVE

Present	audēre	to dare

PRES PARTICIPLE	audēns	daring
GERUND	audendum	daring
GERUNDIVE	audendus	requiring to be dared

All other parts are **passive** in form:

INDICATIVE

Perfect	**ausus sum**	I dared
Pluperfect	**ausus eram**	I had dared
Future Perfect	**ausus erō**	I shall have dared

SUBJUNCTIVE

Perfect	**ausus sim**	I may have dared
Pluperfect	**ausus essem**	I might have dared

PARTICIPLES

Perfect	**ausus**	having dared
Future	**ausūrus**	going to dare

INFINITIVES

Perfect	**ausus esse**	to have dared
Future	**ausūrus esse**	to be going to dare

Unique Verbs

The following verbs are different from the conjugations described so far:

esse (to be)

Indicative

PRESENT
sum	I am
es	you (*sing*) are
est	he/she/it is
sumus	we are
estis	you (*pl*) are
sunt	they are

IMPERFECT
eram	I was
erās	you (*sing*) were
erat	he/she/it was
erāmus	we were
erātis	you (*pl*) were
erant	they were

FUTURE
erō	I shall be
eris	you (*sing*) will be
erit	he/she/it will be
erimus	we shall be
eritis	you (*pl*) will be
erunt	they will be

Subjunctive

PRESENT
sim	I may be
sīs	you (*sing*) may be
sit	he/she/it may be
sīmus	we may be
sītis	you (*pl*) may be
sint	they may be

IMPERFECT
essem	I might be
essēs	you (*sing*) might be
esset	he/she/it might be
essēmus	we might be
essētis	you (*pl*) might be
essent	they might be

Continued

esse (to be) (contd)

Indicative

PERFECT

fuī	I have been, was
fuistī	you (*sing*) have been/were
fuit	he/she/it has been/was
fuimus	we have been/were
fuistis	you (*pl*) have been/were
fuērunt	they have been/were

PLUPERFECT

fueram	I had been
fuerās	you (*sing*) had been
fuerat	he/she/it had been
fuerāmus	we had been
fuerātis	you (*pl*) had been
fuerant	they had been

FUTURE PERFECT

fuerō	I shall have been
fueris	you (*sing*) will have been
fuerit	he/she/it will have been
fuerīmus	we shall have been
fuerītis	you (*pl*) will have been
fuerint	they will have been

Subjunctive

PERFECT

fuerim	I may have been
fueris	you (*sing*) may have been
fuerit	he/she/it may have been
fuerīmus	we may have been
fuerītis	you (*pl*) may have been
fuerint	they may have been

PLUPERFECT

fuissem	I might have been
fuissēs	you (*sing*) might have been
fuisset	he/she/it might have been
fuissēmus	we might have been
fuissētis	you (*pl*) might have been
fuissent	they might have been

Imperative

Singular	es	be
Plural	este	be

Infinitives

Present	esse	to be
Future	futūrus esse / fore	to be going to be
Perfect	fuisse	to have been

Participle futūrus going to be

● Compounds of **esse** are listed in the principal parts
  page 220.

posse (to be able)

• This verb is formed from **pot-** and **-esse**. Note that **t** becomes **s** before another **s**.

Indicative

PRESENT

possum	I am able
potes	you (*sing*) are able
potest	he/she/it is able
possumus	we are able
potestis	you (*pl*) are able
possunt	they are able

IMPERFECT

poteram	I was able *etc*
poterās	
poterat	
poterāmus	
poterātis	
poterant	

FUTURE

poterō	I shall be able *etc*
poteris	
poterit	
poterimus	
poteritis	
poterunt	

Subjunctive

PRESENT

possim	I may be able *etc*
possis	
possit	
possīmus	
possītis	
possint	

IMPERFECT

possem	I might be able *etc*
possēs	
posset	
possēmus	
possētis	
possent	

Continued

posse (to be able) (contd)

Indicative

PERFECT
potuī I have been able *etc*
potuistī
potuit
potuimus
potuistis
potuērunt

PLUPERFECT
potueram I had been able *etc*
potuerās
potuerat
potuerāmus
potuerātis
potuerant

FUTURE PERFECT
potuerō I shall have been able *etc*
potueris
potuerit
potuerimus
potueritis
potuerint

Subjunctive

PERFECT
potuerim I may have been able *etc*
potueris
potuerit
potuerimus
potueritis
potuerint

PLUPERFECT
potuissem I might have been able *etc*
potuissēs
potuisset
potuissēmus
potuissētis
potuissent

Infinitives
posse to be able
potuisse to have been able

ferre (to bear)

Active

Indicative

PRESENT
ferō I bear *etc*
fers
fert
ferimus
fertis
ferunt

IMPERFECT
ferēbam I was bearing

FUTURE
feram I shall bear

PERFECT
tuli I bore

PLUPERFECT
tuleram I had borne

FUTURE PERFECT
tulerō I shall have borne

Subjunctive

PRESENT
feram I may bear *etc*
ferās
ferat
ferāmus
ferātis
ferant

IMPERFECT
ferrem I might bear

PERFECT
tulerim I may have borne

PLUPERFECT
tulissem I might have borne

Infinitives
Present **ferre** to bear
Future **lātūrus esse** to be going to bear
Perfect **tulisse** to have borne

Imperatives
Singular **fer** bear
Plural **ferte** bear

Supine **lātum**

Continued

ferre (to bear) (contd)

Passive

Indicative

PRESENT
feror	I am borne *etc*
ferris	
fertur	
ferimur	
feriminī	
feruntur	

IMPERFECT
| ferēbar | I was being borne |

FUTURE
| ferar | I shall be borne |

PERFECT
| lātus sum | I was borne |

PLUPERFECT
| lātus eram | I had been borne |

FUTURE PERFECT
| lātus erō | I shall have been borne |

Subjunctive

PRESENT
ferar	I may be borne *etc*
ferāris	
ferātur	
ferāmur	
ferāminī	
ferantur	

IMPERFECT
| ferrer | I might be borne |

PERFECT
| lātus sim | I may have been borne |

PLUPERFECT
| lātus essem | I might have been borne |

Infinitives
Present	ferri	to be borne
Future	lātum īrī	to be going to be borne
Perfect	lātus esse	to have been borne

Imperatives
| Singular | ferre | be borne |
| Plural | feriminī | be borne |

Participles
Present	ferēns	bearing
Future	lātūrus	going to bear
Perfect	lātus	having been borne/carried

| Gerund | ferendum | bearing |
| Gerundive | ferendus | requiring to be borne |

Continued

fieri (to become, be made)

- This verb is the passive form of **facere** – to make.

Indicative

PRESENT
fīō — I become
fīs — you (*sing*) become
fit — he/she/it becomes
(fīmus)
(fītis)
fīunt

IMPERFECT
fiēbam — I was becoming

FUTURE
fīam — I shall become

PERFECT
factus sum — I became

PLUPERFECT
factus eram — I had become

FUTURE PERFECT
factus erō — I shall have become

Subjunctive

PRESENT
fīam — I may become *etc*
fīās
fīat
fīāmus
fīātis
fīant

IMPERFECT
fierem — I might become

PERFECT
factus sim — I may have become

PLUPERFECT
factus essem — I might have become

Infinitives
Present **fierī** — to become
Future **factum īrī** — to be going to become
Perfect **factus esse** — to have become

Participle
Perfect **factus** — having become

Gerundive **faciendus** — becoming

īre (to go)

- The stem is **i-**. Before a, o, u, it changes to **e-**.

Indicative

PRESENT
eo I go *etc*
īs
it
īmus
ītis
eunt

IMPERFECT
ībam I was going

FUTURE
ībō I shall go

PERFECT
īvī or iī I went/have gone

PLUPERFECT
īveram I had gone

FUTURE PERFECT
īverō I shall have gone

Subjunctive

PRESENT
eam I may go *etc*
eās
eat
eāmus
eātis
eant

IMPERFECT
īrem I might go

PERFECT
īverim I may have gone

PLUPERFECT
īvissem I might have gone

Infinitives
Present   **īre**   to go
Future   **ītūrus esse**   to be going to go
Perfect   **īvisse** *or* **īsse**   to have gone

Imperative
Singular   **ī**   go
Plural   **īte**   go

Participles
Present   **iēns** (*gen* **euntis**)   going
Future   **ītūrus**   going to go

Gerund   **eundum**   going

velle (to wish)

Indicative

PRESENT
volō — I wish/am willing *etc*
vīs
vult
volumus
vultis
volunt

IMPERFECT
volēbam — I was wishing
volēbās
volēbat
volēbāmus
volēbātis
volēbant

FUTURE
volam — I shall wish

PERFECT
voluī — I wished/have wished

PLUPERFECT
volueram — I had wished

FUTURE PERFECT
voluerō — I shall have wished

Subjunctive

PRESENT
velim — I may wish
velis
velit
velīmus
velītis
velint

IMPERFECT
vellem — I might wish
vellēs
vellet
vellēmus
vellētis
vellent

PERFECT
voluerim — I may have wished

PLUPERFECT
voluissem — I might have wished

Infinitives
Present   velle — to wish
Perfect   voluisse — to have wished

Participle   volēns, -entis — wishing

Continued

nōlle (not to wish, to be unwilling)

- This verb was originally **nōn volo**.

Indicative

PRESENT

nōlō — I do not wish *etc*
nōn vīs
nōn vult
nōlumus
nōn vultis
nōlunt

IMPERFECT

nōlēbam — I was not wishing
nōlēbās
nōlēbat
nōlēbāmus
nōlēbātis
nōlēbant

FUTURE

nōlam — I shall not wish

PERFECT

nōluī — I have not wished

PLUPERFECT

nōlueram — I had not wished

FUTURE PERFECT

nōluerō — I shall not have wished

Continued

Subjunctive

PRESENT

nōlim — I may not wish
nōlīs
nōlit
nōlīmus
nōlītis
nōlint

IMPERFECT

nōllem — I might not wish
nōllēs
nōllet
nōllēmus
nōllētis
nōllent

PERFECT

nōluerim — I may not have wished

PLUPERFECT

nōluissem — I might not have wished

Infinitives
Present   **nōlle** — not to wish
Perfect   **nōluisse** — not to have wished

Participle   **nōlēns, -entis** — not wishing

mālle (to prefer)

- This verb is formed from **ma volō** or **magis volō** (I wish more).

Indicative

PRESENT
mālō	I prefer
māvis	
māvult	
mālumus	
māvultis	
mālunt	

IMPERFECT
mālēbam	I was preferring
mālēbās	
mālēbat	
malebamus	
mālēbātis	
mālēbant	

FUTURE
mālam	I shall prefer

PERFECT
mālui	I preferred

PLUPERFECT
mālueram	I had preferred

FUTURE PERFECT
māluerō	I shall have preferred

Subjunctive

PRESENT
mālim	I may prefer
mālīs	
mālit	
mālīmus	
mālītis	
mālint	

IMPERFECT
māllem	I might prefer
māllēs	
māllet	
māllēmus	
māllētis	
māllent	

PERFECT
māluerim	I may have preferred

PLUPERFECT
māluissem	I might have preferred

Infinitives

Present	mālle	to prefer
Perfect	māluisse	to have preferred

Defective Verbs

The following verbs have only a few forms which are used. These are shown below.

inquam (I say)

PRESENT

inquam	
inquis	
inquit	
inquimus	
inquitis	
inquiunt	

This verb is mainly used in the third person singular

inquiēbat	he said
inquiet	he will say
inquit	he said

avēre	to hail, say "hello"
salvēre	to hail
valēre	to say goodbye

- These verbs are found mainly in infinitives as above or imperatives:

avē, salvē	
avēte, salvēte	hello (*sing*)
valē (*sing*), **valēte** (*pl*)	hello (*pl*)
	goodbye

- Four verbs, **ōdī**, **meminī**, **coepī**, **nōvī** are found only in the perfect stem but are translated as follows:

ōdī	I hate
ōderam	I hated
ōderō	I shall hate
ōdisse	to hate
meminī	I remember
memineram	I remembered
meminerō	I shall remember
meminisse	to remember
coepī	I begin
coeperam	I began
coeperō	I shall begin
coepisse	to begin
nōvī	I know
nōveram	I knew
nōverō	I shall know
nōvisse	to know

Likewise subjunctive:

ōderim	I may hate
ōdissem	I might hate
meminerim	I may remember
meminissem	I might remember
coeperim	I may begin
coepissem	I might begin
nōverim	I may know
nōvissem	I might know

Principal Parts of Common Verbs

Latin verbs are most usefully listed under four principal parts, from which all other tenses *etc* may be formed or recognized

	1ST PERSON PRESENT ACTIVE	PRESENT INFINITIVE	1ST PERSON PERFECT ACTIVE	SUPINE
1st Conjugation	amō	amāre	amāvī	amātum
2nd Conjugation	habeō	habēre	habuī	habitum
3rd Conjugation	mittō	mittere	mīsī	missum
4th Conjugation	audiō	audīre	audīvī	audītum

400 of the most common verbs in Latin are listed below. Included are the following:

● 120 regular verbs. Their conjugations are indicated by numbers 1–4. All parts of these verbs can be deduced from the model conjugations on pp 148–185.

● Nearly 300 verbs which are irregular in parts (highlighted in bold), mainly in the perfect and supine. Again their conjugation is indicated by the number of the group to which they belong. Regular parts of these verbs and person endings etc may be deduced from the models of conjugations 1–4. Many compound verbs are included (*eg* afficio from ad-facio).

● Eight unique verbs and their compounds. These are marked bold throughout and a page reference is given *in italics* for these.

● Defective verbs which are shown in full in the main text. Again a page reference *in italics* is provided.

		Conj Page
		3
abdō, abdere, **abdidī, abditum**	hide	3
abeō, abīre, abiī, abitum	go away	3
abicio, abicere, **abiēcī, abiectum**	throw away	3
absum, abesse, āfuī	be present	1
accēdō, accēdere, **accessī, accessum**	approach	3
accidō, accidere, **accidī**	happen	3
accipiō, accipere, **accēpī, acceptum**	receive	1
accūsō, accūsāre, accūsāvī, accūsātum	accuse	3
addō, addere, **addidī, additum**	add	3
adeō, adīre, adiī, aditum	approach	1
adimō, adimere, **adēmī, ademptum**	take away	1
adiuvō, adiuvāre, **adiūvī, adiūtum**	help	1
administrō, administrāvī, administrātum	administer	4
adsum, adesse, adfuī	be present	1
adveniō, advenīre, **advēnī, adventum**	reach	4
aedificō, aedificāre, aedificāvī, aedificātum	build	1
afferō, afferre, attulī, allātum	bring to	3
afficiō, afficere, **affēcī, affectum**	affect	3
aggredior, aggredī, **aggressus sum**	attack	3
agnōscō, agnōscere, **agnōvī, agnitum**	recognize	3
agō, agere, ēgī, āctum	do/drive	3
alō, alere, **aluī, altum**	feed	3
ambulō, ambulāre, ambulāvī, ambulātum	walk	1
āmittō, āmittere, **āmīsī, āmissum**	lose	3
amō, amāre, amāvī, amātum	love	1

		Conj Page
animadvertō, animadvertere, **animadvertī, animadversum**	notice	3
aperiō, aperīre, **aperuī, apertum**	open	4
appāreō, appārēre, appāruī, appāritum	appear	2
appellō, appellāre, appellāvī, appellātum	call	1
appropinquō, appropinquāre, appropinquāvī, appropinquātum	approach	1
arbitror, arbitrārī, arbitrātus sum	think	1
arcessō, arcessere, **arcessīvī, arcessītum**	send for	3
ardeō, ārdēre, **ārsī, ārsum**	burn	2
armō, armāre, armāvī, armātum	arm	1
ascendō, ascendere, **ascendī, ascēnsum**	climb up	3
aspiciō, aspicere, **aspexī, aspectum**	look at	3
attingō, attingere, **attigī, attāctum**	touch	3
audeō, audēre, **ausus sum**	dare	2
audiō, audīre, audīvī, audītum	hear	4
auferō, auferre, **abstulī, ablātum**	take away	2
augeō, augēre, **auxī, auctum**	increase	2
bibō, bibere, **bibī**	drink	3
cadō, cadere, **cecidī, cāsum**	fall	3
caedō, caedere, **cecīdī, caesum**	cut/kill	3
canō, canere, **cecinī, cantum**	sing	3
capiō, capere, **cēpī, captum**	take	3
careō, carēre	lack	2
carpō, carpere, **carpsī, carptum**	pick	3
caveō, cavēre, **cāvī, cautum**	beware	2
cedō, cedere, **cessī, cessum**	go/give way	3

		Conj Page
celō, celāre, celāvī, celātum	hide	1
cernō, cernere, **crēvī, crētum**	perceive	3
cieō, ciēre, **cīvī, citum**	rouse	2
cingō, cingere, **cinxī, cinctum**	surround	3
circumdō, circumdāre, **circumdedī, circumdātum**	place round	1
clāmō, clāmāre, clāmāvī, clāmātum	shout	1
claudō, claudere, **clausī, clausum**	close	3
coepī, coeptus	begin	219
cōgitō, cōgitāre, cōgitāvī, cōgitātum	think	1
cognōscō, cognōscere, **cōgnōvī, cōgnitum**	find out	3
cōgō, cōgere, **coēgī, coāctum**	collect/compel	3
colō, colere, **coluī, cultum**	look after/worship	3
collocō, collocāre, collocāvī, collocātum	place	1
commoveō, commovēre, **commōvī, commōtum**	upset	2
comparō, comparāre, comparāvī, comparātum	get ready	1
comperiō, comperīre, **comperī, compertum**	discover	4
compleō, complēre, **complēvī, complētum**	fill	2
comprehendō, comprehendere, **comprehendī, comprehēnsum**	grasp	3
concurrō, concurrere, **concurrī, concursum**	run together	3
condō, condere, **condidī, conditum**	found	3
conficiō, conficere, **confēcī, confectum**	finish	3
confīdō, confīdere, **confīsus sum**	trust	3

		Conj	Page
confirmō, confirmāre, confirmāvī, confirmātum	strengthen	1	
confiteor, confitērī, confessus sum	confess	2	
congredior, congredī, congressus sum	meet	3	
coniciō, conicere, coniēcī, coniectum	throw	3	
coniungō, coniungere, coniūnxī, coniūnctum	join	3	
coniūrō, coniūrāre, coniūrāvī, coniūrātum	conspire	1	
cōnor, cōnārī, cōnātus sum	try	1	
cōnsentiō, cōnsentīre, cōnsēnsī, cōnsēnsum	agree	4	
cōnsistō, cōnsistere, cōnstitī,	stop	3	
cōnspiciō, cōnspicere, cōnspexī, cōnspectum	catch sight of	3	
cōnstō, cōnstāre, cōnstitī,	agree	1	
cōnstituō, cōnstituere, cōnstituī, cōnstitūtum	decide	3	
cōnstruō, cōnstruere, cōnstrūxī, cōnstructum	construct	3	
cōnsulō, cōnsulere, cōnsuluī, cōnsultum	consult	3	
cōnsūmō, cōnsūmere, cōnsūmpsī, cōnsūmptum	use up	3	
contemnō, contemnere, contempsī, contemptum	despise	3	
contendō, contendere, contendī, contentum	strive/hurry	3	
contingō, contingere, contigī, contāctum	touch	3	

		Conj	Page
convenio, convenīre, convēnī, conventum	meet	4	
corripio, corripere, corripuī, correptum	seize	3	
crēdō, crēdere, crēdidī, crēditum	believe	3	
crēscō, crēscere, crēvī, crētum	grow	3	
culpō, culpāre, culpāvī, culpātum	blame	1	
cunctor, cunctārī, cunctātus sum	delay	1	
cupiō, cupere, cupīvī, cupītum	desire	3	
cūrō, cūrāre, cūrāvī, cūrātum	look after	1	
currō, currere, cucurrī, cursum	run	3	
custōdiō, custōdīre, custōdīvī, custōdītum	guard	4	
damnō, damnāre, damnāvī, damnātum	condemn	1	
dēbeō, dēbēre, dēbuī, dēbitum	have to/owe	2	
dēdō, dēdere, dēdidī, dēditum	hand over/yield	3	
dēdūcō, dēdūcere, dēdūxī, dēductum	bring/escort	3	
dēfendō, dēfendere, dēfendī, dēfēnsum	defend	3	
dēficiō, dēficere, dēfēcī, dēfectum	revolt/fail	3	
dēiciō, dēicere, dēiēcī, dēiectum	throw down	3	
dēlectō, dēlectāre, dēlectāvī, dēlectātum	delight	1	
dēleō, dēlere, dēlēvī, dēlētum	destroy	2	
dēligō, dēligere, dēlēgī, dēlēctum	choose	3	
dēmōnstrō, dēmōnstrāre, dēmōnstrāvī, dēmōnstrātum	show	1	
dēpōnō, dēpōnere, dēposuī, dēpositum	lay down	3	

		Conj	Page
dēscendō, dēscendere, dēscendī, dēscensum	go down	3	
dēserō, dēsere, dēseruī, dēsertum	desert	3	
dēsīderō, dēsīderāre, dēsīderāvī, dēsīderātum	long for	1	
dēsiliō, dēsilīre, dēsiluī, dēsultum	jump down	3	
dēsinō, dēsinere, dēsiī, dēsitum	stop/leave off	3	
dēsistō, dēsistere, dēstitī	stop/leave off	3	
dēspērō, dēspērāre, dēspērāvī, dēspērātum	despair	1	
dēstruō, dēstruere, dēstruxī, dēstructum	destroy	3	
dīcō, dīcere, dīxī, dictum	tell/say	3	
dīligō, dīligere, dīlexī, dīlēctum	love	3	
dīmittō, dīmittere, dīmīsī, dīmissum	send away	3	
discēdō, discēdere, discessī, discessum	go away	3	
discō, discere, didicī	learn	3	
dīvidō, dīvidere, dīvīsī, dīvīsum	divide	3	
dō, dāre, dedī, datum	give	1	
doceō, docēre, docuī, doctum	teach	2	
doleō, dolēre, doluī, dolitum	grieve	2	
dormiō, dormīre, dormīvī, dormītum	sleep	4	
dubitō, dubitāre, dubitāvī, dubitātum	doubt	1	
dūcō, dūcere, dūxī, ductum	lead	3	
ēdō, ēdere, ēdī, ēsum	eat	3	
efficiō, efficere, effēcī, effectum	complete	3	
effugiō, effugere, effūgī	escape	3	
ēgredior, ēgredī, ēgressus sum	go out	3	
emō, emere, ēmī, ēmptum	buy	3	
eō, īre, īvī, ītum	go		210

		Conj	Page
errō, errāre, errāvī, errātum	wander/be wrong	1	
ērumpō, ērumpere, ērūpī, ēruptum	burst out	3	
excitō, excitāre, excitāvī, excitātum	arouse	1	
exeō, exīre, exiī, exitum	go out	2	
exerceō, exercēre, exercuī, exercitum	exercise/train	2	
existimō, existimāre, existimāvī, existimātum	think	1	
expellō, expellere, expulī, expulsum	drive out	3	
experior, experīrī, expertus sum	try/test	4	
exspectō, exspectāre, exspectāvī, exspectātum	wait for	1	
exuō, exuere, exuī, exūtum	take off	3	
faciō, facere, fēcī, factum	do/make	3	
fallō, fallere, fefellī, falsum	deceive	3	
faveō, favēre, fāvī, fautum	favour	2	
ferō, ferre, tulī, lātum	bring/bear		204
festīnō, festīnāre, festīnāvī, festīnātum	hurry	1	
fīgō, fīgere, fīxī, fīxum	fix	3	
fingō, fingere, finxī, fictum	invent	3	
fīō, fierī, factus sum	become/happen		208
flectō, flectere, flexī, flexum	bend	3	
fleō, flēre, flēvī, flētum	weep	2	
fluō, fluere, flūxī, flūxum	flow	3	
frangō, frangere, frēgī, frāctum	break	3	
fruor, fruī, frūctus or fruitus sum	enjoy	3	
fugiō, fugere, fūgī, fugitum	flee/escape	3	
fugō, fugāre, fugāvī, fugātum	put to flight	1	
fundō, fundere, fūdī, fūsum	pour	3	
fungor, fungī, fūnctus sum	perform	3	

		Conj Page
gaudeō, gaudēre, **gāvīsus sum**	be glad	2
gemō, gemere, **gemuī, gemitum**	groan	3
gerō, gerere, **gessī, gestum**	carry on/wear	3
gignō, gignere, **genuī, genitum**	produce	3
habeō, habēre, habuī, habitum	have/keep	2
habitō, habitāre, habitāvī, habitātum	live (in)	1
haereō, haerēre, **haesī, haesum**	stick	2
hauriō, haurīre, **hausī, haustum**	drain away	4
horreō, horrēre, horruī	stand on end	2
hortor, hortārī, hortātus sum	encourage	1
iaceō, iacēre, iacuī	lie down	2
iaciō, iacere, **iēcī, iactum**	throw	3
ignōscō, ignōscere, **ignōvī, ignōtum**	forgive	3
immineō, imminēre	threaten	2
impediō, impedīre, impedīvī, impedītum	hinder	4
impellō, impellere, **impulī, impulsum**	drive on	3
imperō, imperāre, imperāvī, imperātum	order	1
incendō, incendere, **incendī, incēnsum**	burn	3
incipiō, incipere, **coepī, coeptum**	begin	3
incitō, incitāre, incitāvī, incitātum	drive on	1
inclūdō, inclūdere, **inclūsī, inclūsum**	include	3
incolō, incolere, incoluī	live (in)	3
inferō, inferre, intulī, illātum	bring against	3
ingredior, ingredī, **ingressus sum**	enter	3

		Conj Page
instituō, Instituere, **Instituī,** **Institūtum**	set up	3
instruō, Instruere, **Instruxī,** **Instrūctum**	set/draw up	3
intellegō, intellegere, **intellēxī,** **intellēctum**	realize	3
interficiō, interficere, **interfēcī,** **interfectum**	kill	3
intersum, interesse	be among/be important	(impers)
intrō, intrāre, intrāvī, intrātum	enter	1
inveniō, invenīre, **invēnī, inventum**	come upon/ find	4
invītō, invītāre, invītāvī, invītātum	invite	1
irrumpō, irrumpere, **irrūpī, irruptum**	rush into	3
iubeō, iubēre, **iussī, iussum**	order	2
iūdicō, iūdicāre, iūdicāvī, iūdicātum	judge	1
iungō, iungere, **iūnxī, iūnctum**	join	3
iūrō, iūrāre, iūrāvī, iūrātum	swear	1
iuvō, iuvāre, **iūvī, iūtum**	help	1
labor, lābī, **lāpsus sum**	slip	3
labōrō, labōrāre, labōrāvī, labōrātum	work	1
lacessō, lacessere, **lacessīvī,** **lacessītum**	harass	3
lacrimō, lacrimāre, lacrimāvī, lacrimātum	weep	1
laedō, laedere, **laesī, laesum**	hurt	3
lateō, latēre, latuī	lie hidden	2
laudō, laudāre, laudāvī, laudātum	praise	1
lavō, lavāre, **lāvī, lautum/lavātum/** **lōtum**	wash	1
legō, legere, **lēgī, lēctum**	read/choose	3

Latin	English	Conj/Page
levō, levāre, levāvī, levātum	lighten	1
liberō, liberāre, liberāvī, liberātum	free	1
licet, licēre, licuit	it is allowed	2
locō, locāre, locāvī, locātum	place	1
loquor, loquī, locūtus sum	speak	3
lūdō, lūdere, lūsī, lūsum	play	3
lustrō, lustrāre, lustrāvī, lustrātum	purify/scan	1
mālō, mālle, māluī	prefer	*216*
mandō, mandāre, mandāvī, mandātum	command/trust	1
maneō, manēre, mānsī, mānsum	remain/stay	2
meminī, meminisse	remember	*219*
mentior, mentīrī, mentītus sum	tell lies	4
metuō, metuere, **metuī**	fear	3
minor, minārī, minātus sum	threaten	1
minuō, minuere, **minuī, minūtum**	lessen	3
miror, mirārī, mirātus sum	wonder (at)	1
misceō, miscēre, miscuī, mixtum	mix	2
misereor, miserērī, miseritus sum / miseret, miserēre, miseruit (eg me miseret tuī – I am sorry for you)	pity	2
mittō, mittere, **mīsī, missum**	send	3
mōlior, mōlīrī, mōlītus sum	strive/toil	4
moneō, monēre, monuī, monitum	advise/warn	2
morior, morī, **mortuus sum**	die	3
moror, morārī, morātus sum	delay/loiter	1
moveō, movēre, mōvī, mōtum	move	2
mūniō, mūnīre, mūnīvī/mūniī, mūnītum	fortify	4
mūtō, mūtāre, mūtāvī, mūtātum	change	1
nanciscor, nanciscī, **na(n)ctus sum**	obtain	3
narrō, narrāre, narrāvī, narrātum	tell	1

Latin	English	Conj/Page
nāscor, nāscī, **nātus sum**	be born	3
nāvigō, nāvigāre, nāvigāvī, nāvigātum	sail	1
necō, necāre, necāvī, necātum	kill	1
negō, negāre, negāvī, negātum	refuse/deny	1
neglegō, neglegere, **neglēxī, neglēctum**	neglect	3
nesciō, nescīre, nescīvī or iī, nescītum	not to know	4
noceō, nocēre, nocuī, nocitum	harm	2
nōlō, nōlle, nōluī	not to wish/be unwilling	*214*
nōscō, nōscere, **nōvī, nōtum** (in perfect tenses translate as "know")	get to know	3 *219*
nūntiō, nūntiāre, nūntiāvī, nūntiātum	announce	1
obeō, obīre, obīvī or iī, obitum	die	
obiciō, obicere, **obiēcī, obiectum**	throw to/oppose	3
oblīvīscor, oblīvīscī, **oblītus sum**	forget	3
obsideō, obsidēre, **obsēdī, obsessum**	besiege	2
obtineō, obtinēre, obtinuī, **obtentum**	hold/obtain	2
occidō, occidere, **occidī, occāsum**	fall	3
occīdō, occīdere, **occīdī, occīsum**	kill	3
occupō, occupāre, occupāvī, occupātum	seize	1
occurrō, occurrere, **occurrī, occursum**	meet	3
ōdī, ōdisse	hate	*219*
offerō, offerre, obtulī, oblātum	present	3

		Conj/Page
oportet, oportēre, oportuit	be proper/ought	2
opprimō, opprimere, **oppressī, oppressum**	crush	3
oppugnō, oppugnāre, oppugnāvī, oppugnātum	attack	1
optō, optāre, optāvī, optātum	wish	1
orior, orīrī, **ortus sum**	arise	4
orō, orāre, orāvī, orātum	beg/plead	1
ornō, ornāre, ornāvī, ornātum	decorate/equip	1
ostendō, ostendere, **ostendī, ostentum**	show	3
pācō, pācāre, pācāvī, pācātum	pacify	1
paenitet, paenitēre, paenituit	repent of	2
pandō, pandere, **pandī, passum**	spread out	3
parcō, parcere, **pepercī, parsum**	spare	3
pāreō, pārēre, pāruī	obey	2
pariō, parere, **peperī, partum**	give birth to	3
parō, parāre, parāvī, parātum	prepare	1
pāscō, pāscere, **pāvī, pāstum**	feed	3
patefaciō, patefacere, **patefēcī, patefactum**	open	3
pateō, patēre, patuī	be open	2
patior, patī, **passus sum**	suffer/allow	3
paveō, pavēre, **pavī**	fear	2
pellō, pellere, **pepulī, pulsum**	drive	3
pendeō, pendēre, **pependī, pēnsum** (*intrans*)	hang	2
pendō, pendere, **pependī, pēnsum**	weigh/pay	3
perdō, perdere, **perdidī, perditum**	lose/destroy	3
pereō, **perīre, periī, peritum**	perish	1
perficiō, perficere, **perfēcī, perfectum**	complete	3

		Conj/Page
pergō, pergere, **perrēxī, perrēctum**	proceed	3
permittō, permittere, **permīsī, permissum**	allow	3
persuadeō, persuadēre, **persuāsī, persuāsum**	persuade	2
pertineō, pertinēre, pertinuī, **pertentum**	concern	2
perturbō, perturbāre, perturbāvī, perturbātum	confuse	1
perveniō, pervenīre, **pervēnī, perventum**	arrive at	4
petō, petere, **petīvī, petītum**	seek/ask	3
placeō, placēre, placuī, placitum	please	2
placet, placēre, placuit	it seems good	2
polliceor, pollicērī, **pollicitus sum**	promise	2
pōnō, pōnere, **posuī, positum**	place/put	3
portō, portāre, portāvī, portātum	carry	1
poscō, poscere, **poposcī**	ask for/demand	3
possum, posse, potuī	to be able	200
postulō, postulāre, postulāvī, postulātum	demand	1
potior, potīrī, potītus sum	gain possession of	4
praebeō, praebēre, praebuī, praebitum	show	2
praeficiō, praeficere, **praefēcī, praefectum**	put in command of	3
praestō, praestāre, **praestitī, praestatum**	stand out	1
premō, premere, **pressī, pressum**	press	3
prōcēdō, prōcēdere, **prōcessī, prōcessum**	advance	3

	Conj/Page	
pródó, pródere, **pródidí, próditum**	3	betray
proficíscor, proficíscí, **profectus sum**	3	set out
prógredior, prógredí, **progressus sum**	3	advance
prohibeó, prohibére, prohibuí, prohibitum	2	prevent
prómittó, prómittere, **prómísí, prómissum**	3	promise
próvideó, próvidére, **próvidí, próvisum**	2	take precautions
pugnó, pugnáre, pugnávi, pugnátum	1	fight
púnió, púníre, púnívi or íi, púnítum	4	punish
putó, putáre, putávi, putátum	1	think
quaeró, quaerere, **quaesívi, quaesítum**	3	ask/seek
queror, querí, **questus sum**	3	complain
quiescó, quiescere, **quiévi, quiétum**	3	keep quiet
rapió, rapere, **rapuí, raptum**	3	snatch/seize
recipió, recipere, **recépi, receptum**	3	receive/recover
recúsó, recúsáre, recúsáví, recúsátum	1	refuse
reddó, reddere, **reddidí, redditum**	3	give back/return
redeó, redíre, redií, reditum		come back/return
redúcó, redúcere, **redúxí, reductum**	3	bring back
regó, regere, **réxí, réctum**	3	rule
regredior, regredí, **regressus sum**	3	retreat
relinquó, relinquere, **relíquí, relictum**	3	leave

	Conj/Page	
remittó, remittere, **remísí, remissum**	3	send back
reor, rérí, **ratus sum**	2	think
repelló, repellere, **reppulí, repulsum**	3	drive back
reperió, reperíre, **repperí, repertum**	4	find
resistó, resistere, **restití**	3	resist
respició, respicere, respexí, **respectum**	3	look back
respondeó, respondére, **respondí, respónsum**	2	answer
restó, restáre, **restití**	1	remain
restituó, restituere, restituí, **restitútum**	3	restore
retineó, retinére, retinuí, retentum	2	hold back
rídeó, rídére, **rísí, rísum**	2	laugh
rogó, rogáre, rogáví, rogátum	1	ask
rumpó, rumpere, **rúpí, ruptum**	3	burst
ruó, ruere, **ruí, rutum (ruitúrus – fut part)**	3	rush/fall
sció, scíre, **scíví/íí, scítum**	4	know
scríbó, scríbere, **scrípsí, scríptum**	3	write
sécernó, sécernere, **sécréví, sécrétum**	3	set apart
secó, secáre, **secuí, sectum**	1	cut
sedeó, sedére, **sédí, sessum**	2	sit
sentió, sentíre, **sénsí, sénsum**	4	feel/perceive
sepelió, sepelíre, sepelíví, **sepultum**	4	bury
sequor, sequí, **secútus sum**	3	follow
seró, serere, **séví, satum**	3	sow
servió, servíre, servíví, servítum	4	serve/be a slave
servó, serváre, serváví, servátum	1	save

		Conj Page
simulō, simulāre, simulāvī, simulātum	pretend	1
sinō, sinere, **sīvī, situm**	allow	3
sistō, sistere, **stitī, statum**	set up	3
soleō, solēre, **solitus sum**	be used to	2
sollicitō, sollicitāre, sollicitāvī, sollicitātum	worry	1
solvō, solvere, **solvī, solūtum**	loosen	3
sonō, sonāre, **sonuī, sonitum**	sound	1
spargō, spargere, **sparsī, sparsum**	scatter/sprinkle	3
spectō, spectāre, spectāvī, spectātum	look at	1
spērō, spērāre, spērāvī, spērātum	hope	1
spoliō, spoliāre, spoliāvī, spoliātum	rob/plunder	1
statuō, statuere, **statuī, statūtum**	set up	3
sternō, sternere, **strāvī, strātum**	cover/overthrow	3
stō, stāre, **stetī, statum**	stand	1
struō, struere, **strūxī, strūctum**	build	3
studeō, studēre, **studuī**	study	2
suādeō, suādēre, **suāsī, suāsum**	advise	2
subeō, subīre, **subiī, subitum**	undergo	3
succēdō, succēdere, **successī, successum**	go up/relieve	3
succurrō, succurrere, **succurrī, succursum**	help	3
sum, esse, fuī, futūrus	take	196
sūmō, sūmere, **sūmpsī, sūmptum**	take	3
superō, superāre, superāvī, superātum	overcome	1
supersum, superesse, superfuī	survive	3
surgō, surgere, **surrēxī, surrēctum**	rise/get up	3
suscipiō, suscipere, **suscēpī, susceptum**	undertake	3

		Conj Page
suspicor, suspicārī, suspicātus sum	suspect	1
sustineō, sustinēre, sustinuī, **sustentum**	sustain	2
taceō, tacēre, tacuī, tacitum	be silent	2
taedet, taedēre, taeduit, **taesum est**	be tired of	2
tangō, tangere, **tetigī, tactum**	touch	3
tegō, tegere, **tēxī, tēctum**	cover	3
tendō, tendere, **tetendī, tentum** or **tēnsum**	stretch	3
teneō, tenēre, tenuī, **tentum**	hold	2
terreō, terrēre, terruī, territum	terrify	2
timeō, timēre, timuī	fear	2
tollō, tollere, **sustulī, sublātum**	raise/remove	3
tonō, tonāre, **tonuī**	thunder	1
torqueō, torquēre, **torsī, tortum**	twist	2
trādō, trādere, **trādidī, trāditum**	hand over	3
trahō, trahere, **trāxī, tractum**	drag	3
trāiciō, trāicere, **trāiēcī, trāiectum**	take across	3
trānseō, trānsīre, trānsiī, trānsitum	cross over	2
tueor, tuērī, tuitus sum	look at	2
ulcīscor, ulcīscī, **ultus sum**	punish/avenge	3
urgeō, urgēre, **ursī**	press/urge	2
ūrō, ūrere, **ussī, ustum**	burn	3
ūtor, ūtī, **ūsus sum**	use	2
valeō, valēre, valuī, valitum	be strong	2
vastō, vastāre, vastāvī, vastātum	destroy	1
vehō, vehere, **vēxī, vectum**	carry	3
vendō, vendere, **vendidī, venditum**	sell	3
veniō, venīre, **vēnī, ventum**	come	4
vereor, verērī, veritus sum	fear	2

		Conj *Page*
vertō, vertere, vertī, versum	turn	3
vescor, vescī	feed on	3
vetō, vetāre, vetuī, vetitum	forbid	1
videō, vidēre, vīdī, vīsum	see	2
vigilō, vigilāre, vigilāvī, vigilātum	stay awake	1
vinciō, vincīre, vīnxī, vīnctum	bind	4
vincō, vincere, vīcī, victum	defeat/conquer	3
vitō, vitāre, vitāvī, vitātum	avoid	1
vīvō, vīvere, vīxī, victum	live	3
vocō, vocāre, vocāvī, vocātum	call/invite	1
volō, velle, voluī	wish/want	*212*
volvō, volvere, volvī, volūtum	roll	3
voveō, vovēre, vōvī, vōtum	vow	2

The following index lists comprehensively both grammatical terms and key words in English and Latin.